GLENCOE

LITERATURE

The Reader's Choice

GLENCOE
LITERATURE
The Reader's Choice

Program Consultants

Beverly Ann Chin

Denny Wolfe

Jeffrey Copeland

Mary Ann Dudzinski

William Ray

Jacqueline Jones Royster

Jeffrey Wilhelm

Course 2

Mc Graw Hill
Glencoe
McGraw-Hill

New York, New York   Columbus, Ohio   Woodland Hills, California   Peoria, Illinois

Acknowledgments

Grateful acknowledgment is given authors, publishers, photographers, museums, and agents for permission to reprint the following copyrighted material. Every effort has been made to determine copyright owners. In case of any omissions, the Publisher will be pleased to make suitable acknowledgments in future editions.

Acknowledgments continued on page R152.

The Standardized Test Practice pages in this book were written by The Princeton Review, the nation's leader in test preparation. Through its association with McGraw-Hill, The Princeton Review offers the best way to help students excel on standardized assessments.

The Princeton Review is not affiliated with Princeton University or Educational Testing Service.

Glencoe/McGraw-Hill

A Division of The McGraw·Hill Companies

Copyright © 2002 by The McGraw-Hill Companies, Inc. All rights reserved. Except as permitted under the United States Copyright Act of 1976, no part of this publication may be reproduced or distributed in any form or means, or stored in a database or retrieval system, without the prior written permission of the publisher.

Printed in the United States of America

Send all inquiries to:
Glencoe/McGraw-Hill
8787 Orion Place
Columbus, OH 43240

ISBN 0-07-825106-0
(Student Edition)

ISBN 0-07-825137-0
(Teacher's Wraparound Edition)

6 7 8 9 10   027/055   08 07 06 05

Senior Program Consultants

Beverly Ann Chin is Professor of English, Director of the English Teaching Program, Director of the Montana Writing Project, and former Director of Composition at the University of Montana in Missoula. In 1995–1996, Dr. Chin served as President of the National Council of Teachers of English. She currently serves as a Member of the Board of Directors of the National Board for Professional Teaching Standards. Dr. Chin is a nationally recognized leader in English language arts standards, curriculum, and assessment. Formerly a high school English teacher and adult education reading teacher, Dr. Chin has taught in English language arts education at several universities and has received awards for her teaching and service.

Denny Wolfe, a former high school English teacher and department chair, is Professor of English Education, Director of the Tidewater Virginia Writing Project, and Director of the Center for Urban Education at Old Dominion University in Norfolk, Virginia. For the National Council of Teachers of English, he has served as Chairperson of the Standing Committee on Teacher Preparation, President of the International Assembly, member of the Executive Committee of the Council on English Education, and editor of the SLATE Newsletter. Author of more than seventy-five articles and books on teaching English, Dr. Wolfe is a frequent consultant to schools and colleges on the teaching of English language arts.

Program Consultants

Jeffrey S. Copeland is Professor and Head of the Department of English Language and Literature at the University of Northern Iowa, where he teaches children's and young adult literature courses and a variety of courses in English education. A former public school teacher, he has published many articles in the professional journals in the language arts. The twelve books he has written or edited include *Speaking of Poets: Interviews with Poets Who Write for Children and Young Adults* and *Young Adult Literature: A Contemporary Reader.*

Mary Ann Dudzinski is a former high school English teacher and recipient of the Ross Perot Award for Teaching Excellence. She also has served as a member of the core faculty for the National Endowment for the Humanities Summer Institute for Teachers of Secondary School English and History at the University of North Texas. After fifteen years of classroom experience in grades 9–12, she currently is a language arts consultant.

William Ray has taught English in the Boston Public Schools; at Lowell University; University of Wroclaw, Poland; and, for the last fourteen years, at Lincoln-Sudbury Regional High School in Sudbury,

Massachusetts. He specializes in world literature. He has worked on a variety of educational texts, as editor, consultant, and contributing writer.

Jacqueline Jones Royster is Professor of English and Associate Dean of the College of Humanities at The Ohio State University. She is also on the faculty of the Bread Loaf School of English at Middlebury College in Middlebury, Vermont. In addition to the teaching of writing, Dr. Royster's professional interests include the rhetorical history of African American women and the social and cultural implications of literate practices.

Jeffrey Wilhelm, a former English and reading teacher, is currently an assistant professor at the University of Maine where he teaches courses in middle and secondary level literacy. He is the author or co-author of several books on the teaching of reading and literacy, including *You Gotta BE the Book* and *Boys and Books.* He also works with local schools as part of the fledgling Adolescent Literacy Project and is the director of two annual summer institutes: the Maine Writing Project and Technology as a Learning Tool.

Teacher Reviewers

Bill Beyer
General Wayne Middle School
Malvern, Pennsylvania

Sister Marian Christi
St. Matthew School
Philadelphia, Pennsylvania

Christine Ferguson
North Buncombe Middle School
Asheville, North Carolina

Elizabeth Fischer
Tower Heights Middle School
Centerville, Ohio

Diane Gerrety
Bridgetown Junior High
Cincinnati, Ohio

Susan Giddings
Marble Falls Middle School
Marble Falls, Texas

Denise Goeckel
Magsig Middle School
Centerville, Ohio

Debbie Hampton
Central Davidson Middle School
Lexington, North Carolina

Tammy Harris
Walnut Springs Middle School
Columbus, Ohio

Marlene Henry
Northwood Elementary
Troy, Ohio

Brian Hinders
Tower Heights Middle School
Centerville, Ohio

Cheryl Keffer
Fayette County Schools Gifted
Program
Oak Hill, West Virginia

Sheryl Kelso
Oldtown School
Oldtown, Maryland

Gail Kidd
Center Middle School
Azusa, California

Karen Mantia
Northmont City Schools
Clayton, Ohio

Nancy Mast
Hobart Middle School
Hobart, Indiana

Chiyo Masuda
Albany Middle School
Albany, California

Kim Mistler
Delhi Junior High School
Cincinnati, Ohio

Wilma Jean Nix
Baldwin Junior High School
Montgomery, Alabama

Joe Olague
Alder Junior High
Fontana, California

Bonita Rephann
Musselman Middle School
Bunker Hill, West Virginia

Marie Rinaudo
St. John Berchman's Cathedral
School
Shreveport, Louisiana

Carol Schowalter
El Roble Intermediate School
Claremont, California

Karen Shannon
Davis Drive Middle School
Apex, North Carolina

Joan Slater
Strack Intermediate
Klein, Texas

Joyce Stakem
St. Catherine of Siena School
Wilmington, Delaware

Elizabeth Struckman
Bridgetown Junior High School
Centerville, Ohio

Debbie Trepanier
Jenkins Middle School
Chewelah, Washington

Sarah Vick
Central Davidson Middle School
Lexington, North Carolina

Erin Watts
Albright Middle School
Houston, Texas

Anne Welch
Huntsville Middle School
Huntsville, Alabama

James Zartler
Centennial Middle School
Portland, Oregon

Book Overview

Contents

THEME ❦ ONE

What I Am, What I Want to Be......1

THEME ❧ TWO

Winds of Change

CONTENTS

THEME ✣ THREE

Facing Challenge

CONTENTS

THEME ❧ FOUR

Where the Heart Is

CONTENTS

CONTENTS

THEME ❦ FIVE

At the Crossroads

CONTENTS

THEME ✿ SIX

Twists and Turns

THEME ❧ SEVEN

A Different Dimension

CONTENTS

THEME ❧ EIGHT

A Delicate Balance

CONTENTS

Reference Section

Features

Active Reading Strategies

Interdisciplinary Connection

Writing WORKSHOP

Skills

Grammar Link

Listening, Speaking, and Viewing

Reading and Thinking Skills

Technology Skills

Vocabulary Skills

Writing Skills

FEATURES

Skill Minilessons

Selections by Genre

What I Am, What I Want to Be

Girl at Mirror, 1954. Norman Rockwell. Printed by permission of the Norman Rockwell Family Trust. ©1954 the Norman Rockwell Family Trust.

THEME 1

> **❝** *Only one of me and nobody can get a second one from a photocopy machine.* **❞**
>
> –James Berry, "One"

THEME CONTENTS

GENRE FOCUS *AUTOBIOGRAPHY*

Exploring the Theme

What I Am, What I Want to Be

How do other people see you? More importantly, how do you see yourself? In this theme, you will explore what makes you who you are and what it will take to become who you want to be. To begin, try one of the options below.

Starting Points

ONE AMONG MANY

What do you think makes each of these penguins stand out in a crowd?

- Write a short conversation between two of the penguins. Imagine they are introducing themselves.

YOU ARE THE ONLY YOU

You are the only you. Think about yourself for a minute, and get ready to sketch yourself in words.

- Draw a name tag. Write your name in the center of it. What are the first words that come to mind when you read your name? Around the name tag, list several words that describe what makes you unique. You may also wish to include photos or drawings on your name tag.

Drawing by Chas. Addams. Courtesy of Tee and Charles Addams Foundation.

Theme Projects

As you read the selections in this theme, choose one of the projects below. Work on your own, with a partner, or in a group.

LEARNING FOR LIFE
Writing a Job Description

What do you dream of doing when you grow up? Do you think about being a dancer, or a veterinarian, or a designer of video games? Think about your dream job. Then write a description of your job.

1. When you have made your choice, do some library research to find out more about it. Talk to people in your community who have similar jobs. Take notes about their job descriptions.

2. Write your job description, and contribute it to a classroom Career Notebook. As you learn about other interesting careers, add new descriptions to the notebook.

MULTIMEDIA PROJECT
A Self-Portrait

Create a multimedia self-portrait.

1. Gather information about yourself. Create a summary of interesting facts about your life, perhaps using a visual format such as a timeline or a graph to chart these highlights.

2. Gather photos or drawings of you and your family or friends. Try to include music, videos, and taped interviews to showcase your life.

3. Present your self-portrait to your class.

*inter*NET CONNECTION

Check out the Web for more project ideas. Use your favorite search engine to find other job-related ideas or other topics related to the "What I Am, What I Want to Be" theme. Key words such as *jobs, employment,* and career fields like *medicine* and *aviation* can get you started.

CRITICAL LISTENING
Musical Notes

Your taste in music reflects who you are, as well as your interests.

1. Do you enjoy popular music, oldies, jazz, reggae, rap, or some other type of music? Bring in examples of different kinds of music you enjoy.

2. Talk to older family members about the kinds of music they listened to when they were your age. Research their favorite kinds of music, and bring examples, photographs, or articles about that music to class. You might even create a musical timeline showing the kinds of music young people have enjoyed over time.

3. Plan a musical tour through history. Display your research and photographs. Using tapes or CDs, play examples of a wide variety of music. Invite another class or family members to your classroom to participate in your musical tour.

Before You Read

Names/Nombres

MEET JULIA ALVAREZ

Asked where she finds the ideas for her richly detailed stories, Julia Alvarez says, "I think when I write, I write out of who I am and the questions I need to figure out. A lot of what I have worked through has to do with coming to this country and losing a homeland and a culture, as a way of making sense." Alvarez has written several novels, including *How the Garcia Girls Lost Their Accents*, *Yo!*, and *In the Time of the Butterflies*.

Julia Alvarez was born in 1950. This selection was published in 1985.

READING FOCUS

Have you ever stopped to think about your name? What does your name tell others about you?

Sharing Ideas
In small groups, talk about what names mean to you. Does your own name seem to capture any of the real you?

Setting a Purpose
Read the selection to find out what names mean to Julia Alvarez.

BUILDING BACKGROUND

The Time and Place
This selection is set in the early 1960s in New York City. Julia Alvarez was born in New York, but she lived in the Dominican Republic until the age of ten.

VOCABULARY PREVIEW

ironically (ī ron′ i kəl ē) *adv.* in a way that is different from what would be expected; p. 6

initial (i nish′ əl) *adj.* at the beginning; first; p. 7

merge (murj) *v.* to join together so as to become one; unite; p. 7

inevitably (i nev′ ə tə blē) *adv.* in a way that cannot be avoided or prevented; p. 7

vaguely (vāg′ lē) *adv.* in a way that is not clear, exact, or definite; p. 7

specify (spes′ ə fī′) *v.* to state or describe in detail; p. 7

exotic (ig zot′ ik) *adj.* strangely attractive; foreign; p. 8

chaotic (kā ot′ ik) *adj.* confused and disorganized; in great disorder; p. 8

commencement (kə mens′ mənt) *n.* a beginning; start; graduation ceremonies; p. 9

Judith   Hoo-lee-ah

Julia   juLiet

Names/Nombres

Julia Alvarez ❧

When we arrived in New York City, our names changed almost immediately. At Immigration, the officer asked my father, *Mister Elbures*, if he had anything to declare. My father shook his head, "No," and we were waved through. I was too afraid we wouldn't be let in if I corrected the man's pronunciation, but I said our name to myself, opening my mouth wide for the organ blast of the *a*, trilling my tongue for the drumroll of the *r*, *All-vah-rrr-es!* How could anyone get *Elbures* out of that orchestra of sound?

Nombres is a Spanish word for "names."

Portrait of Virginia, 1929. Frida Kahlo. Fundacion Dolores Olmedo, Mexico City, D.F., Mexico.

Judy   Jules

Names/Nombres

At the hotel my mother was *Missus Alburest*, and I was *little girl*, as in, "Hey, little girl, stop riding the elevator up and down. It's *not* a toy!"

When we moved into our new apartment building, the super called my father *Mister Alberase*, and the neighbors who became mother's friends pronounced her name *Jew-lee-ah* instead of *Hoo-lee-ah*. I, her namesake, was known as *Hoo-lee-tah* at home. But at school, I was *Judy* or *Judith*, and once an English teacher mistook me for *Juliet*.

It took awhile to get used to my new names. I wondered if I shouldn't correct my teachers and new friends. But my mother argued that it didn't matter. "You know what your friend Shakespeare said, '*A rose by any other name would smell as sweet.*'"[1] My family had gotten into the habit of calling any literary figure "my friend" because I had begun to write poems and stories in English class.

By the time I was in high school, I was a popular kid, and it showed in my name. Friends called me *Jules* or *Hey Jude*, and once a group of troublemaking friends my mother forbid me to hang out with called me *Alcatraz*.[2] I was *Hoo-lee-tah* only to Mami and Papi and uncles and aunts who came over to eat *sancocho*[3] on Sunday afternoons—old world folk whom I just as soon would go back to where they came from and leave me to pursue whatever mischief I wanted to in America. *JUDY*

ALCATRAZ: the name on the Wanted Poster would read. Who would ever trace her to me?

My older sister had the hardest time getting an American name for herself because Mauricia did not translate into English. <u>Ironically</u>, although she had the most foreign-sounding name, she and I were the Americans in the family. We had been born in New York City when our parents had first tried immigration and then gone back "home," too homesick to stay. My mother often told the story of how she had almost changed my sister's name in the hospital.

After the delivery, Mami and some other new mothers were cooing over their new baby sons and daughters and exchanging names and weights and delivery stories. My mother was embarrassed among the Sallys and Janes and Georges and Johns to reveal the rich, noisy name of *Mauricia*, so when her turn came to brag, she gave her baby's name as *Maureen*.

"Why'd ya give her an Irish name with so many pretty Spanish names to choose from?" one of the women asked her.

My mother blushed and admitted her baby's real name to the group. Her mother-in-law had recently died, she apologized,

---

1. This line is from William Shakespeare's play *Romeo and Juliet*.
2. *Alcatraz* is an island in San Francisco Bay that once was the home of a very tough federal prison.
3. *Sancocho* (sän kō′ chō) is a meat stew.

Vocabulary
ironically (ī ron′ i kəl ē) *adv.* in a way that is different from what would be expected

and her husband had insisted that the first daughter be named after his mother, *Mauran*. My mother thought it the ugliest name she had ever heard, and she talked my father into what she believed was an improvement, a combination of *Mauran* and her own mother's name *Felicia*.

"Her name is *Mao-ree-chee-ah*," my mother said to the group.

"Why that's a beautiful name," the new mothers cried. *"Moor-ee-sha, Moor-ee-sha,"* they cooed into the pink blanket.

Moor-ee-sha it was when we returned to the States eleven years later. Sometimes, American tongues found even that mispronunciation tough to say and called her *Maria* or *Marsha* or *Maudy* from her nickname *Maury*. I pitied her. What an awful name to have to transport across borders!

My little sister, Ana, had the easiest time of all. She was plain *Anne*—that is, only her name was plain, for she turned out to be the pale, blond "American beauty" in the family. The only Hispanic-seeming thing about her was the affectionate nickname her boyfriends sometimes gave her, *Anita*, or as one goofy guy used to sing to her to the tune of the Chiquita Banana advertisement, *Anita Banana*.

Later, during her college years in the late '60s, there was a push to pronounce Third World[4] names correctly. I remember calling her long distance at her group house and a roommate answering.

"Can I speak to Ana?" I asked, pronouncing her name the American way.

"Ana?" The man's voice hesitated. "Oh! you mean *Ah-nah!*"

Our first few years in the States, though, ethnicity[5] was not yet "in." Those were the blond, blue-eyed, bobby socks years of junior high and high school before the '60s ushered in peasant blouses, hoop earrings, serapes. My initial desire to be known by my correct Dominican name faded. I just wanted to be Judy and merge with the Sallys and Janes in my class. But inevitably, my accent and coloring gave me away. "So where are you from, Judy?"

Did You Know?
A *serape* (sə rä′ pā) is a blanketlike outer garment similar to a shawl. It is often woven with bright colors and patterns and is worn chiefly by men in Latin American countries.

"New York," I told my classmates. After all, I had been born blocks away at Columbia Presbyterian Hospital.

"I mean, *originally*."

"From the Caribbean," I answered vaguely, for if I specified, no one was quite sure what continent our island was on.

---

4. *Third World* refers to poorer, less developed countries, mainly in Latin America, Africa, and Asia.

5. *Ethnicity* is a word for certain things that a group of people share, such as language, culture, history, race, and national origin. U.S. citizens come from many different ethnic backgrounds.

Vocabulary
initial (i nish′ əl) *adj.* at the beginning; first
merge (murj) *v.* to join together so as to become one; unite
inevitably (i nev′ ə tə blē) *adv.* in a way that cannot be avoided or prevented
vaguely (vāg′ lē) *adv.* in a way that is not clear, exact, or definite
specify (spes′ ə fī′) *v.* to state or describe in detail

The Musicians, 1979. Fernando Botero. Oil on canvas, 85¾ x 74¾ in. Private collection.

Viewing the painting: Which scene from the story would you like to see painted in the style of Botero?

"Say your name in Spanish, oh please say it!" I had made mouths drop one day by rattling off my full name, which according to Dominican custom, included my middle names, mother's and father's surnames for four generations back.

"Julia Altagracia Maria Teresa Alvarez Tavares Perello Espaillat Julia Pérez Rochet González," I pronounced it slowly, a name as chaotic with sounds as a Middle Eastern bazaar or market day in a South American village.

I suffered most whenever my extended family attended school occasions. For my graduation, they all came, the whole noisy, foreign-looking lot of old, fat aunts in their dark mourning dresses and hair nets, uncles with full, droopy mustaches and baby-blue or salmon-colored suits and white pointy shoes and fedora[6] hats, the many little cousins who

"Really? I've been to Bermuda. We went last April for spring vacation. I got the worst sunburn! So, are you from Portoriko?"

"No," I shook my head. "From the Dominican Republic."

"Where's that?"

"South of Bermuda."

They were just being curious, I knew, but I burned with shame whenever they singled me out as a "foreigner," a rare, exotic friend.

---

6. A *fedora* is a soft felt hat with a curved brim and a crease along the top.

Vocabulary
exotic (ig zot′ ik) *adj.* strangely attractive; foreign
chaotic (kā ot′ ik) *adj.* confused and disorganized; in great disorder

snuck in without tickets. They sat in the first row in order to better understand the Americans' fast-spoken English. But how could they listen when they were constantly speaking among themselves in florid-sounding phrases, rococo[7] consonants, rich, rhyming vowels. Their loud voices carried . . .

How could I introduce them to my friends? These relatives had such complicated names and there were so many of them, and their relationships to myself were so convoluted. There was my Tía Josefina, who was not really an aunt but a much older cousin. And her daughter, Aída Margarita, who was adopted, *una hija de crianza*. My uncle of affection, Tío José, brought my *madrina* Tía Amelia and her *comadre* Tía Pilar.[8] My friends rarely had more than their nuclear family[9] to introduce.

After the commencement ceremony my family waited outside in the parking lot while my friends and I signed yearbooks with nicknames which recalled our high school good times: "Beans" and "Pepperoni" and "Alcatraz." We hugged and cried and promised to keep in touch.

Our good-byes went on too long. I heard my father's voice calling out across the parking lot, *"Hoo-lee-tah! Vámonos!"*[10]

Back home, my *tíos* and *tías* and *primas*, Mami and Papi, and *mis hermanas* had a party for me with *sancocho* and a storebought *pudín*,[11] inscribed with *Happy Graduation, Julie*. There were many gifts—that was a plus to a large family! I got several wallets and a suitcase with my initials and a graduation charm from my godmother and money from my uncles. The biggest gift was a portable typewriter from my parents for writing my stories and poems.

Someday, the family predicted, my name would be well-known throughout the United States. I laughed to myself, wondering which one I would go by.

---

7. *Florid* and *rococo* both mean "very showy, highly decorated, or flowery."
8. Something that is *convoluted* is all twisted, coiled, and wound around. The rest of this paragraph identifies some of the writer's convoluted family relationships. *Tía* (tē′ ə) and *Tío* (tē′ ō) mean "Aunt" and "Uncle." *Una hija de crianza* (ōō′ nə ē′ hə dā krē än′ zə) is an adopted daughter. *Madrina* (mə drē′ nə) and *comadre* (kō mä′ drä) both mean "godmother." Later, the writer mentions *primas* (prē′ məs) and *hermanas* (är män′ əs), her female cousins and sisters.
9. Parents and their children make up what is called a *nuclear family*. An *extended family* includes other close relatives, such as grandparents, aunts, uncles, and cousins.

---

10. *"Vámonos!"* (vä′ mə nōs) means "Let's go!"
11. A *pudín* (pōō dēn′) is a pudding.

❖

Vocabulary
commencement (kə mens′ mənt) *n.* a beginning; start; graduation ceremonies

Responding to Literature

PERSONAL RESPONSE

◆ Describe your impressions as you read about the writer's problems and triumphs living in two very different cultures.

Analyzing Literature

RECALL

1. How is the Alvarez family name changed when they go through immigration?

2. Why does the teenage Alvarez just want to be called Judy?

3. Which occasions make Alvarez suffer the most? Find a **description** from the story to help explain your answer.

4. What does the Alvarez family predict about Julia's future career?

INTERPRET

5. How do you think Julia Alvarez feels about the change made to her family's name at the immigration office? Support your opinion with evidence from the selection.

6. Find a passage showing Alvarez's wish to be just like her classmates. How do you think her attitude changes as she grows up?

7. Why does Alvarez feel the way she does when her relatives appear at school functions? How would you feel?

8. Which of Alvarez's many names does she choose to use as a professional writer? In your opinion, why does she choose that one?

EVALUATE AND CONNECT

9. In your opinion, why does Alvarez give this story the title of "Names/Nombres"?

10. Theme Connection   What different cultures or groups do you belong to? When do you choose to identify with one group versus another?

LITERARY ELEMENTS

Theme

The main idea of a written work is usually expressed as a general statement called a **theme.** Sometimes a piece of writing has a **stated theme**—one that is expressed directly. More often, a piece of writing has an **implied theme,** which is not stated directly but is revealed gradually as the piece unfolds.

1. What do you think is the theme of "Names/Nombres"? Is the theme stated directly, or is it implied? Support your opinion with examples and quotations from the story.

2. How does the title of the story relate to its theme?

● See **Literary Terms Handbook,** p. R11.

Extending Your Response

Writing About Literature

Sensory Imagery Julia Alvarez uses imagery that appeals to the senses. You can hear "the drumroll of the *r*," taste *sancocho,* and see "uncles with full, droopy mustaches." Find other sensory imagery in the selection. Name the senses they appeal to.

Literature Groups

Debating Shakespeare Julia's mother quotes Shakespeare—"a rose by any other name would smell as sweet." Do names affect how people are treated in this story? In your life? Is this fair? Share your ideas with your group.

Performing

Readers Theater Work with two or three other students to prepare a readers theater presentation of a scene from "Names/Nombres." Choose a scene that relates to the theme of the selection.

Personal Writing

What's in a Name? Use the ideas in the **Reading Focus** on page 4 to write a journal entry about what names, including your own, mean to you and what names tell others.

Listening and Speaking

Conducting an Interview Pick three people to interview about their names. Be sure to ask people to explain how they got these names. Record their answers and share your results.

Reading Further

For more about living in two cultures, try these:

In the Year of the Boar and Jackie Robinson by Bette Bao Lord

Going Home by Nicholasa Mohr

Child of the Owl by Laurence Yep

📔 **Save your work for your portfolio.**

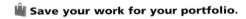

Skill Minilesson

VOCABULARY • ANTONYMS

Many words have antonyms—words that mean the opposite. For example, antonyms for *happy* include *sad, miserable, gloomy,* and *unhappy.* Choosing among antonyms helps you think about the exact meaning of a word.

PRACTICE Match each word with its antonym.

1. ironically
2. chaotic
3. merge
4. initial
5. vaguely

a. final
b. clearly
c. separate
d. predictably
e. orderly

Avoiding Sentence Fragments

A complete sentence contains both a subject and a predicate. The **subject** tells who or what the sentence is about. The **predicate** tells what is happening or being done. The predicate always includes a **verb.**

Morris sniffed.

In this complete sentence, *Morris* is the subject, and *sniffed* is the verb.
A **sentence fragment** is incomplete. It leaves out the subject or the verb or both.

Problem 1 The subject is missing.

Wrote stories and poems.

Solution Add a subject.

Julia Alvarez wrote stories and poems.

Problem 2 The verb is missing.

Julia's obvious talent as a writer.

Solution Add a verb to the fragment.

Julia's obvious talent as a writer soon became apparent to her parents.

Problem 3 The subject and verb are missing.

Her parents bought her a portable typewriter. As a graduation gift.

Solution Combine the fragment with another sentence.

Her parents bought her a portable typewriter as a graduation gift.

● For more about sentence fragments, see **Language Handbook,** p. R12.

ACTIVITY

Rewrite the following paragraph, correcting any sentence fragments you find. You may be able to combine a fragment with another sentence, or you may need to add a subject or a verb.

At school, Julia's friends called her Judy. Or sometimes Judith or Jules or Jude. Some troublemaking friends. They called her Alcatraz. These nicknames didn't bother her. Just showed her popularity with other kids.

Before You Read

One and *I'm Nobody! Who are you?*

MEET JAMES BERRY

When James Berry looked around the British classroom where he was teaching and saw no books about African and Caribbean children, he began to write about his Caribbean homeland. He describes his poems as "scooped bits of the times I've lived in."

James Berry was born in Jamaica in 1925. "One" is from When I Dance: Poems, *published in 1988.*

MEET EMILY DICKINSON

Emily Dickinson has been called a private poetic genius. Of the 1,775 poems she wrote, only seven were published during her lifetime, and none with her consent.

Emily Dickinson was born in 1830 and died in 1886. "I'm Nobody! Who are you?" was first published in 1891.

READING FOCUS

What is it that makes you unique, or special, in this world?

QuickWrite
Reflect on your unique qualities. Then jot down these qualities, and tell how they set you apart from all others.

Setting a Purpose
Read to find out what these two poems have in common.

BUILDING BACKGROUND

James Berry and Emily Dickinson lived in different centuries and on different continents. Although their paths never crossed, these two poets shared a sense of "otherness," of what it is like to be a unique individual. In his writing, James Berry often explores what it means to be part of a racial minority, something he experienced firsthand when he immigrated to Great Britain from Jamaica in 1948 at the age of 23.

A shy woman, Emily Dickinson seldom left her home in Amherst, Massachusetts. On the surface, her life seemed uneventful. She lived a quiet life, seeing few people outside of her own family. Dickinson's poetry, however, reveals a lively, sensitive, and original human being, committed to writing about the world from her own unique perspective.

Emily Dickinson's home in Amherst.

One

James Berry :~

Only one of me
and nobody can get a second one
from a photocopy machine.

Nobody has the fingerprints I have.
5   Nobody can cry my tears, or laugh my laugh
or have my expectancy° when I wait.

But anybody can mimic° my dance with my dog.
Anybody can howl how I sing out of tune.
And mirrors can show me multiplied
10   many times, say, dressed up in red
or dressed up in grey.

Nobody can get into my clothes for me
or feel my fall for me, or do my running.
Nobody hears my music for me, either.

15   I am just this one.
Nobody else makes the words
I shape with sound, when I talk.

But anybody can act how I stutter in a rage.
Anybody can copy echoes I make.
20   And mirrors can show me multiplied
many times, say, dressed up in green
or dressed up in blue.

---

6 An *expectancy* is the feeling one has while expecting
something.
7 To *mimic* is to copy, or imitate.

I'm Nobody! Who are you?

Emily Dickinson

I'm Nobody! Who are you?
Are you—Nobody—Too?
Then there's a pair of us!
Don't tell! they'd advertise—you know!

5   How dreary°—to be—Somebody!
How public—like a Frog—
To tell one's name—the livelong June°—
To an admiring Bog!°

---

5 *Dreary* means "sad; depressing; dull; uninteresting."
7 The *livelong June* would be the whole month.
8 A *bog* is the swampy sort of ground where frogs live.

"Sun Shower," 1995. Diana Ong. Computer graphic, 5 x 4 in. Chrome.

Responding to Literature

PERSONAL RESPONSE

- ◆ What did you realize about yourself while reading these poems?
- ◆ What do the poems say about promoting yourself?

Analyzing Literature

RECALL

1. In what ways does the speaker in James Berry's poem feel unique? In what ways is he not unique?
2. Into what two categories does the speaker in Emily Dickinson's poem divide people, including herself? Describe each category.

INTERPRET

3. How does "One" celebrate the uniqueness of individuals?
4. Why does the speaker in Emily Dickinson's poem feel that being "Nobody" is preferable to being "Somebody"?

EVALUATE AND CONNECT

5. Which aspects of being human do you think the speaker in "One" values most? Which aspects are less valuable?
6. If you had to decide to be Dickinson's Nobody or Somebody, which would you choose? Explain.
7. What lasting impression do you imagine the speaker in "One" would want to leave on people he has known?
8. Theme Connection   Which of these poems better expresses how you feel about yourself? Explain.
9. How would the world change if everyone decided to be a "Nobody"?
10. What is it about Emily Dickinson's writing **style** that makes you feel as if she is actually talking to you?

LITERARY ELEMENTS

Visual Imagery

Visual imagery is the collection of details that writers use to help readers visualize scenes. Visual imagery makes writing come to life. In "One," James Berry repeats, "And mirrors can show me multiplied / many times. . . ." These lines help readers "see" a young man preening as he looks at himself in a mirror in different-colored clothes.

1. Reread "I'm Nobody! Who are you?" and "One." Find an example of visual imagery that helps you "see" what the speaker is describing in each poem.

2. How does Berry's use of the image of a photocopy machine reflect his thoughts about individuality?

● See **Literary Terms Handbook,** p. R11.

Extending Your Response

Writing About Literature

Theme The **theme** of a poem is its central idea or message. Write a paragraph identifying the message of each of these two poems.

Personal Writing

New Thoughts About Myself Return to the notes you wrote in the **Reading Focus** on page 13. Would you change the qualities you listed after reading these two poems? Write a short self-portrait that shows who you are. Explore your unique character traits and personality more than your appearance.

Interdisciplinary Activity

Music In his poem, Berry writes "Nobody hears my music for me." What does that mean? Put together a listening brochure that reflects the real you. Illustrate your brochure, keeping it "in tune" with your musical tastes.

Literature Groups

Present Yourself! Read each poem line by line. Identify the line that is the most thought provoking. How does the line challenge or confirm your own thoughts about yourself? Does it make you reconsider what makes a person unique? Does it give you a strong visual image? With your group, choose the line that provokes the most interest. Write the line on a banner to present to the class. Be ready to defend your choice in a larger group discussion.

Reading Further

If you enjoyed the work of these poets, you might like to check out these other works:

Short Stories: *A Thief in the Village and Other Stories* by James Berry

Biography: *Emily Dickinson* by Victoria Olsen

📖 **Save your work for your portfolio.**

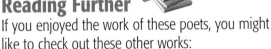

Skill Minilesson

READING AND THINKING • COMPARING AND CONTRASTING

In the poems "One" and "I'm Nobody! Who are you?" the speakers share private thoughts and feelings about their own identities with you, the reader. In some ways the poems are similar. In other ways they are very different.

PRACTICE Try your hand at comparing and contrasting.

1. Write one paragraph that compares the poems, describing how they are alike.

2. Write a second paragraph that contrasts the poems, showing how they are different. Think about the structure, rhyme, rhythm, and punctuation in each poem. Pay special attention to imagery, meaning, and word choice. You might begin by examining how each poet uses the word *nobody*. They both use the word several times, but the intended meaning is quite different.

● For more about comparing and contrasting, see **Reading Handbook,** p. R93.

Before You Read

Face It and *Almost Ready*

READING FOCUS

What is the real *you* like? Do you have your father's chin or your grandmother's sense of humor? Think about your physical characteristics and your personality traits. Do you know which ones are family traits?

Chart It!

Make a chart showing some of your personality traits and physical characteristics. Label the ones you think are family traits and those that are unique to you.

Setting a Purpose

Read to find out what the speakers in these poems think about how they look.

BUILDING BACKGROUND

Our cultural and ethnic heritage is also part of what makes each of us unique. Janet S. Wong writes: "Sometimes the first question a stranger will ask me, even before learning my name, is 'What are you?' or 'Where are you from?' These kinds of people usually stare hard at my face, as if they are testing themselves on how well they can tell the difference between Chinese and Korean and Japanese."

PEANUTS reprinted by permission of United Feature Syndicate, Inc.

FACE IT

Janet S. Wong

My nose belongs
to Guangdong, China—
short and round, a Jang family nose.

My eyes belong
to Alsace, France—
wide like Grandmother Hemmerling's.

But my mouth, my big-talking mouth, belongs
to me, alone.

ALMOST READY

Arnold Adoff

I   as
am   this
going   cool
to   and
her   in-
birth-   control
day   young
party   dude:

as   as   as   as
soon   soon   soon   soon
as   as   as   as
I   I   I   I
find   find   find   find
my   my   my   my
new   hip   deep   right
shirt, shoes, voice, mask.

Responding to Literature

PERSONAL RESPONSE

- ◆ What is your response to these two poems?
- ◆ Which lines from each poem did you find most memorable? Why?

Analyzing Literature

RECALL

1. What images does the poem "Face It" focus on?
2. Summarize what happens in "Almost Ready."

INTERPRET

3. How do you think the images and the title of the poem "Face It" relate to the poem's **theme?**
4. What inner **conflict** is the speaker of "Almost Ready" feeling? How does the conflict relate to the poem's title? Explain.

EVALUATE AND CONNECT

5. Do you agree with the speaker of "Face It" that people are a combination of their ancestors' characteristics and their own unique traits? Why or why not?
6. Do you agree that young people often show an exterior that is "cool and in-control," while their inner feelings are quite different? Explain.
7. How does the arrangement of the lines of "Almost Ready" relate to the meaning of the poem? How does this special structure affect the actual reading of the poem?
8. How do *you* prepare to go to a birthday party? In what ways are you like the speaker in "Almost Ready"? In what ways are you different?
9. Theme Connection   What did you discover or realize about yourself as you read these poems? Explain.
10. Did you find these poems humorous, serious, or both? Explain.

LITERARY ELEMENTS

Irony

When something awful happens and you say "Oh, great!" you are being ironic. In literature, **verbal irony** exists when the writer, or a character the writer creates, says the opposite of what he or she really means. Similarly, **situational irony** exists when what actually happens in a situation is the opposite of what we expect.

Irony may be used for humorous purposes, as when someone says "Nice weather" during a blizzard. It also can be used in a serious, or even bitter, way. For example, you might mutter "Nice guy" after someone has done something rude.

Watch for irony in literature. If you don't see when a writer is using irony, you may misunderstand what that author is trying to say.

1. Find and explain an example of irony in either poem.

2. Is the title of one of these poems an example of irony? Why or why not?

● See **Literary Terms Handbook,** p. R6.

Extending Your Response

Writing About Literature

Character The speakers in both poems reveal a great deal about themselves in very few words. Write a paragraph describing the speaker from either poem as you picture that person.

Literature Groups

Poet's Corner Both of these poems offer surprise endings. In "Almost Ready," the speaker says "as soon as I find my right mask." What does this line mean? Do you agree or disagree that clothing and "put-on" airs such as a "deep voice" can be a mask? The poem "Face It" also ends with a surprise. When the speaker refers to her "big-talking mouth," what is she revealing about herself?

Girl with a Red Hat, 1940. Raphael Soyer. Oil on canvas, 76.8 x 43.2 cm. Fundacion Coleccion Thyssen-Bornemisza, Madrid.

Creative Writing

Who Am I? Write a short poem that describes you or a person you know, such as a friend or a relative. Try to include as much information as possible, using exact words. If you are writing about yourself, review your chart from the **Reading Focus** on page 18 before you begin.

Listening and Speaking

Listening to Poetry To be fully enjoyed, a poem is best read aloud. Listeners can close their eyes and picture the images as they hear the rhythm of the lines. With a partner, take turns reading these poems to each other.

Reading Further

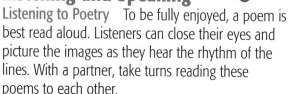

If you would like to read more by these poets, try these books:
All the Colors of the Race by Arnold Adoff
Good Luck Gold and Other Poems by Janet S. Wong

💼 **Save your work for your portfolio.**

Skill Minilesson

READING AND THINKING • VISUALIZING

Visualizing a story or a poem is a skill that can help you enjoy and understand that piece of writing better. As you read or listen, try to re-create images or scenes in your mind. Pay close attention to the details the writer chooses. Ask yourself: what does this image or scene look like, smell like, feel like? What is going on here?

PRACTICE Reread each of the poems. As you do, try to visualize the images in each poem.

Write a paragraph describing some of the images that come to mind as you read or listen to each poem. You might want to sketch some of the images to accompany your paragraph.

● For more about visualizing, see **Reading Handbook,** p. R87.

Writing Skills

Using Dialogue in a Narrative

Dialogue, or conversation quoting the exact words of characters, is an effective narrative technique. It can rivet the reader's attention. And no wonder. Dialogue can bring characters to life and dramatically show them reacting to one another.

When you use dialogue in your writing, try to weave it in smoothly. Dialogue may be introduced in several ways—at the beginning, middle, or end of a sentence. Sometimes a block of conversation can continue for several lines. Following are some examples of how dialogue can be used. As you read, notice how the writer has used capitalization and punctuation marks.

How Dialogue Can Be Used in Writing	

At the beginning of a sentence:
"It's a polite Chinese custom to show you are satisfied," explained my father to our astonished guests.
–Amy Tan, "Fish Cheeks"
 	
In the middle of a sentence:
He said, "Let me have those front seats," because they were the front seats of the black section.
–Rosa Parks, from *Rosa Parks: My Story*
 	
At the end of a sentence:
Ernie groaned and said, "Ah, man."
–Gary Soto, "Broken Chain"
	As a block of conversation:
	. . . inevitably, my accent and coloring gave me away. "So where are you from, Judy?"
	   "New York," I told my classmates. After all, I had been born blocks away at Columbia Presbyterian Hospital.
	   "I mean, *originally.*"
	   "From the Caribbean," I answered vaguely, for if I specified, no one was quite sure what continent our island was on.
	–Julia Alvarez, "Names/Nombres"
	Mechanics Tip: Indent each time the speaker changes.
	
	An interrupted quotation:
	   "Children," Miss Ryan called for attention. "Ernesto has learned how to pronounce butterfly!"
	–Ernesto Galarza, from *Barrio Boy*

ACTIVITIES

1. Write at least three sentences of dialogue about a childhood memory. Use dialogue to begin one sentence, to form the middle of another, and to end a third.

2. Write a paragraph in which one friend tells a joke to another. Include a block of dialogue and indent correctly.

NEWSPAPER COLUMN

This column was written in 1981, after John McEnroe won the tennis championship at Wimbledon, England. The young McEnroe had a reputation for behaving badly on the tennis court. Do you think Erma Bombeck's comments are relevant today?

Heroes

by Erma Bombeck—Syndicated Newspaper Column, August 2, 1981

On the first Saturday of last month, a 22-year-old U.S. tennis player hoisted a silver bowl over his head at Centre Court at Wimbledon.

The day before, five blind mountain climbers, a man with an artificial leg, an epileptic, and two deaf adventurers stood atop the snowcapped summit of Mount Rainier.

It was a noisy victory for the tennis player, who shared it with thousands of fans, some of whom had slept on the sidewalks outside the club for six nights waiting for tickets.

It was a quiet victory for the climbers, who led their own cheering, punctuated by a shout from one of them that echoed on the winds: "There's one for the epileptics!"

There was a lot of rhetoric exchanged at Wimbledon regarding "bad calls."

At Mount Rainier they learned to live with life's bad calls a long time ago. The first man to reach the mountaintop tore up his artificial leg to get there.

Somehow, I see a parallel here that all Americans are going to have to come to grips with. In our search for heroes and heroines, we often lose our perspective.

We applaud beauty pageant winners; we ignore the woman without arms who paints pictures with a brush in her teeth. We extol the courage of a man who will sail over 10 cars on a motorcycle; we give no thought (or parking place) to the man who threads his way though life in a world of darkness or silence.

The care and feeding of heroes is solely in the hands of the public. Not all winners are heroes. Not all people with disabilities are heroes. "Hero" is a term that should be awarded to those who, given a set of circumstances, will react with courage, dignity,

decency, and compassion—people who make us feel better for having seen or touched them.

I think the crowds went to the wrong summit and cheered the wrong champion.

Analyzing Media

1. The author writes mostly very short paragraphs. Why do you suppose she does so?

2. Do you agree that we cheer the wrong heroes? Give examples to support your opinion.

Before You Read
Strong Men Weep

MEET BENEDICT COSGROVE

A lifetime sports fan, journalist, and writer, Benedict Cosgrove is also the co-editor of *Gluttony*, an anthology of short stories and essays. Cosgrove's most recent book, *Covering the Bases*, from which this selection is taken, is a collection of sports writing, radio transcripts, and photographs of the most unforgettable moments in baseball, as recorded by the writers and broadcasters who were there.

Benedict Cosgrove lives in San Francisco, California. This work was published in 1996.

READING FOCUS

Do you have a hero? Why do you consider this person a hero?

Sharing Ideas

In small groups, discuss the qualities you think heroes share. Then make a list of people you think are heroes, and explain why each person is on the list. Do heroes have to be famous?

Setting a Purpose

Read to find out why Lou Gehrig is considered a hero.

BUILDING BACKGROUND

This essay is about an event that took place at Yankee Stadium, New York City, in 1939. The author sets the scene for Shirley Povich's account.

Shirley Povich (1905–1998) was, at age twenty, the youngest sports reporter in the U.S. Considered the *Washington Post*'s "most revered sports columnist," he wrote for that paper for 75 years. His approach to writing was simply stated: "I write what I like to read."

Shirley Povich

VOCABULARY PREVIEW

consecutive (kən sek′ yə tiv) *adj.* following one after another in order without interruption; p. 26

discrepancy (dis krep′ ən sē) *n.* a lack of agreement, as between facts; p. 27

eloquent (el′ ə kwənt) *adj.* expressive, effective, and stirring in speech or writing; p. 29

esteem (es tēm′) *n.* favorable opinion; high regard; p. 29

elicit (i lis′ it) *v.* to draw forth or bring out; p. 29

hindrance (hin′ drəns) *n.* something that holds back progress or movement; obstacle; p. 30

Strong Men Weep

Lou Gehrig's Famous Farewell
July 4, 1939

Benedict Cosgrove

Cal Ripken breaking Lou Gehrig's streak

of 2,130 <u>consecutive</u> games might have been the best thing that could have happened to the old Yankee captain's reputation.

For months and weeks leading up to that great night in September 1995, when Ripken finally passed Gehrig, a disturbing thread began to weave through the endless discussions surrounding The Streak.

Vocabulary
consecutive (kən sek′ yə tiv) *adj.* following one after another in order without interruption

Among all the factions[1] that had formed as it became clear that Ripken was going to just keep on going (factions that seemed to dissolve—along with everyone else who cared at all about the record—into a mass, warm embrace of the man the moment he began his spontaneous, lump-in-the-throat jog around the field at Camden Yards),[2] there was, it seemed, a small but nonetheless significant group of voices that appeared bent on pointing out the questionable <u>discrepancies</u> in Gehrig's original record.

Gehrig played first base, as opposed to Cal, who played a far more demanding shortstop. Gehrig often played only an inning or two when he wasn't feeling 100 percent—or when he was on the road, in order to keep the streak going—while Ripken played in something insane, like eight and two-thirds of every nine innings during his streak. Gehrig never had to deal with coast-to-coast airplane travel or Astroturf or blah blah blah. The point, it seemed, was that Gehrig's legendary streak, while kind of impressive, was really nothing compared to Ripken's *more genuine* streak.

And I'll buy that. Ripken's is the more amazing streak. By far. Hands down. No question.

With his streak broken, though, perhaps Gehrig can be fully appreciated as the great, great ballplayer that he was, the ballplayer whose career was cut short when he still had some good years left in him, rather than as the guy whose tainted consecutive-game streak Cal Ripken finally obliterated.[3]

But no matter how Gehrig is remembered as a player, no matter how fine or fearsome a hitter the man was (a .340 lifetime average; a .632 slugging percentage; the career mark for grand slams; 1,990 RBIs), or how loyal a teammate, or how worthy a leader as the captain of the awesome Yankee teams of the 1920s, he

---

3. *Tainted* means "spoiled or made inferior." To *obliterate* something is to destroy it completely.

Lou Gehrig poses with another baseball legend, his teammate Babe Ruth.

---

1. *Factions* are small groups of people, within a larger group, who disagree on an issue or set of issues.
2. The home field of Ripken's team, the Baltimore Orioles, is named *Camden Yards*.

Vocabulary
discrepancy (dis krep′ ən sē) *n.* a lack of agreement, as between facts

Viewing the poster: Can you fairly compare athletes who lived more than fifty years apart? Why or why not?

will always be most-readily associated with July 4, 1939, when 60,000 fans, old teammates, and Gehrig's own words filled Yankee Stadium for the game's most famous farewell: "Today I consider myself the luckiest man on the face of the earth."

Gehrig didn't speak for long, but not too many baseball fans are unfamiliar with what he said. No words ever uttered by another athlete have resonated[4] for so many years in the hearts and minds of so many fans, most of whom weren't even born at the time the words themselves were echoing around the far reaches of the park.

Gesturing to the "grand men," his teammates and friends, standing beside him, Gehrig asked: "Which of you wouldn't consider it the highlight of his career just to associate with them for even one day?" He went on to thank the fans, his managers, the groundskeepers, his father and mother, and his wife, in an eloquent and tremendously moving few minutes that ended with Gehrig breaking down and Babe Ruth stepping forward to lend his old teammate support.

Gehrig's words that day might not have been recorded verbatim[5] by Shirley Povich in his memorable *Washington Post* piece on the tribute, but no writer present when Gehrig walked to the mike better captured the esteem and affection Gehrig seemed to elicit from all who knew him—esteem and affection which, on that Tuesday afternoon, was finally given full voice.

---

4. Here, *resonated* means "echoed."
5. *Verbatim* (vər bā′ tim) means "word for word; in exactly the same words."

SHIRLEY POVICH

WASHINGTON POST, JULY 4, 1939
I saw strong men weep this afternoon, expressionless umpires swallow hard, and emotion pump the hearts and glaze the eyes of 61,000 baseball fans in Yankee Stadium. Yes, and hard-boiled news photographers clicked their shutters with fingers that trembled a bit.

It was Lou Gehrig Day at the stadium, and the first 100 years of baseball saw nothing quite like it. It was Lou Gehrig, tributes, honors, gifts heaped upon him, getting an overabundance of the thing he wanted least—sympathy. But it wasn't maudlin.[6] His friends were just letting their hair down in their earnestness to pay him honor. And they stopped just short of a good, mass cry.

They had Lou out there at home plate between games of a double-header, with the 60,000 massed in the triple tiers that rimmed the field, microphones and cameras trained on him, and he couldn't take it that way. Tears streamed down his face, circuiting the most famous pair of dimples in baseball, and he looked chiefly at the ground.

Seventy-year-old Ed Barrow, president of the Yankees, who had said to newspapermen, "Boys, I have bad news for you," when Gehrig's ailment was diagnosed as infantile paralysis[7] two weeks

---

6. If something is *maudlin*, it is overly or tearfully sentimental.
7. *Infantile paralysis* is a name for polio, a highly contagious disease that occurs mainly in children and can cause total paralysis. Gehrig's actual illness was not polio but a similar disease called amyotrophic lateral sclerosis, or ALS. It causes weakness, paralysis, and, in the end, death.

Vocabulary
eloquent (el′ ə kwənt) *adj.* expressive, effective, and stirring in speech or writing
esteem (es tēm′) *n.* favorable opinion; high regard
elicit (i lis′ it) *v.* to draw forth or bring out

ago, stepped out of the background halfway through the presentation ceremonies, and draped his arm across Gehrig's shoulder. But he was doing more than that. He was holding Gehrig up, for Big Lou needed support.

As he leaned on Barrow, Gehrig said, "Thanks, Ed." He bit his lip hard, was grateful for the supporting arm, as the Yankees of 1927 stepped to the microphone after being introduced. Babe Ruth, Bob Meusel, Waite Hoyt, Herb Pennock, Benny Bengough, Bob Shawkey, Mark Koenig, Tony Lazzeri, all of the class of '27 were there. And Gehrig had been one of them, too. He had been the only one among them to bestride both eras.

Still leaning on Barrow, Gehrig acknowledged gifts from his Yankee mates, from the Yankee Stadium ground crew, and the hot dog butchers, from fans as far as Denver, and from his New York rivals, the Giants. There was a smile through his tears, but he wasn't up to words. He could only shake the hands of the small army of officials who made the presentations.

He stood there twisting his doffed baseball cap into a braid in his fingers as Manager Joe McCarthy followed Mayor La Guardia and Postmaster General Farley in tribute to "the finest example of ball player, sportsman, and citizen that baseball has ever known," but Joe McCarthy couldn't take it that way, either. The man who has driven the highest-salaried prima donnas[8] of baseball into action, who has baited a thousand umpires, broke down.

McCarthy openly sobbed as he stood in front of the microphone and said, "Lou, what else can I say except that it was a sad day in the life of everybody who knew you when you came to my hotel room that day in Detroit and told me you were quitting as a ball player because you felt yourself a hindrance to the team. My God, man, you were never that."

And as if to emphasize the esteem in which he held Gehrig though his usefulness to the Yankees as a player was ended, McCarthy, too, stepped out of the fringe full into the circle where Gehrig stood and half embraced the big fellow.

Now it was Gehrig's turn to talk into the microphone, to acknowledge his gifts. The 60,000 at intervals had set up the shout, "We want Lou!" even as they used to shout "We want Ruth"—yells that they reserved for the only two men at Yankee Stadium for which the crowd ever organized a cheering section.

But Master of Ceremonies Sid Mercer was anticipating Gehrig. He saw the big fellow choked up. Infinitesimally[9] Gehrig shook his head, and Mercer announced: "I shall not ask Lou Gehrig to make a speech. I do not believe that I should."

They started to haul away the microphones. Gehrig half turned toward the dugout, with the ceremonies apparently at an end. And then he wheeled suddenly, strode back to the loud-speaking apparatus, held up his hand for attention, gulped, managed a smile, and then spoke.

---

8. Originally, a *prima donna* was the leading female singer of an opera company. Now, the term is applied to any "star" who is overly proud or demanding.

---

9. *Infinitesimally* means "in such a small way as to be almost unnoticeable."

Vocabulary
hindrance (hin′ drəns) *n.* something that holds back progress or movement; obstacle

Gehrig is overcome with emotion at his final appearance in Yankee Stadium.

DONT QUIT

"For weeks," said Gehrig, "I have been reading in the newspapers that I am a lucky fellow who got a tough break. I don't believe it. I have been a lucky guy. For 16 years, into every ballpark in which I have ever walked, I received nothing but kindness and encouragement. Mine has been a full life."

He went on, fidgeting with his cap, pawing the ground with his spikes as he spoke, choking back emotions that threatened to silence him, summoning courage from somewhere. He thanked everybody. He didn't forget the ballpark help; he told of his gratitude to newspapermen who had publicized him. He didn't forget the late Miller Huggins, or his six years with him; or Manager Joe McCarthy, or the late Col. Ruppert,[10] or Babe Ruth, or "my roommate, Bill Dickey."

And he thanked the Giants— "The fellows from across the river, who we would give our right arm to beat"—he was more at ease in front of the mike now, and he had a word for Mrs. Gehrig and for the immigrant father and mother who had made his education, his career, possible. And he denied again that he had been the victim of a bad break in life. He said, "I've lots to live for, honest."

And thousands cheered.

---

10. When Gehrig first joined the Yankees, *Huggins* managed the team and helped Gehrig develop his baseball skills. *McCarthy* became manager after Huggins. Jacob *Ruppert* was the owner or co-owner of the Yankees from 1914 to 1939.

Responding to Literature

PERSONAL RESPONSE

- ◆ What thoughts and feelings did you have at the end of this selection?
- ◆ Think back to the discussion in the **Reading Focus** on page 25. Do you think that Lou Gehrig was a hero? Why or why not?

Analyzing Literature

RECALL

1. What player broke Lou Gehrig's streak of 2,130 consecutive games? What was the focus of the "endless discussions surrounding The Streak"?
2. With what event does Cosgrove believe Gehrig will always be most associated?
3. To whom was the journalist Shirley Povich referring when he wrote, "I saw strong men weep this afternoon"?
4. What did Gehrig say that July day that made people cheer?

INTERPRET

5. According to Cosgrove, what were the main points of discussion concerning the differences between the streaks of Cal Ripken and Lou Gehrig? Support your ideas with quotations from the selection.
6. "Today I consider myself the luckiest man on the face of the earth." Explain the significance of this statement.
7. The opening image in Povich's piece is emotional and powerful. Why do you think Povich chose this image? Explain.
8. What did you learn about Lou Gehrig's character from reading some of his farewell words?

EVALUATE AND CONNECT

9. "Strong Men Weep" is an example of **nonfiction.** It is about real events and a real person. Does knowing that this is a true story affect your experience of this man's character? Explain.
10. In your opinion, was Gehrig "the luckiest man on the face of the earth"? Explain.

LITERARY ELEMENTS

Author's Purpose

All writers have a purpose or goal they want to achieve in their writing. To **entertain** is one purpose for writing. To **describe** something is another purpose. Sometimes writers want to **inform** the reader or to **explain** something. Sometimes writers want to **persuade** their readers to believe something. A strong piece of writing often combines purposes: A persuasive essay, for example, may include description and information.

1. What was Shirley Povich's purpose in writing his memorable piece in the *Washington Post*? Support your opinion with examples from the account.

2. How would Povich's piece have been different if his purpose had been to describe Gehrig's batting statistics?

● See **Literary Terms Handbook,** p. R2.

Extending Your Response

Writing About Literature

Critical Review Write a paragraph reviewing "Strong Men Weep." Consider these questions: What did you learn from this selection? What kinds of details did Cosgrove and Povich include? How did these details affect your opinion of Gehrig?

Personal Writing

My Hero "Strong Men Weep" recounts the famous farewell of a legendary sports hero. Who is one of your heroes? Think about the people you listed in the **Reading Focus** on page 25. Write a paragraph using effective details to convince your reader that the person you chose is a true hero.

Literature Groups

A Sporting Debate Benedict Cosgrove and Shirley Povich wrote about a good and courageous man who happened to be a great baseball player. Does a reader have to love the game of baseball to be affected by this account of Lou Gehrig? Why or why not? Support your opinion with examples from the selection and other stories about heroes.

Reading Further

For more about sports, try these:

Dreams into Deeds: Nine Women Who Dared by Linda Peavy and Ursula Smith

The Random House Book of Sports Stories by L. M. Schulman

📎 **Save your work for your portfolio.**

Skill Minilesson

VOCABULARY • OWNING A WORD

Reading the definition of a word doesn't make the word yours, but it's a first step. Words become truly part of your vocabulary when you understand how they're used and you start using them yourself.

PRACTICE Use what you know about the meanings of the underlined words to complete the sentences.

1. Tainted meat is likely to contain
   a. fat   c. germs
   b. ice crystals

2. The response to an eloquent speech would be
   a. applause   c. yawns
   b. boos

3. You would obliterate an answer by
   a. choosing it   c. erasing it
   b. repeating it

4. A _____ could be a hindrance to a driver.
   a. seat belt   c. store
   b. traffic jam

5. Two consecutive days are Saturday and
   a. Sunday   c. the next Saturday
   b. Monday

Before You Read

from *Wait Till Next Year*

MEET DORIS KEARNS GOODWIN

Doris Kearns Goodwin became a baseball fan at the age of six, when her father taught her to keep score as she listened to the Brooklyn Dodgers games. This early training in summarizing baseball games for her father helped her develop the storytelling skills she continues to use as an adult. In addition to *No Ordinary Time*, her Pulitzer Prize–winning book about Franklin and Eleanor Roosevelt, she has written books about other American presidents, taught at Harvard University, and appears frequently on TV news programs.

Wait Till Next Year, Doris Kearns Goodwin's memories of growing up in the 1950s, was published in 1997.

READING FOCUS

Sports heroes need not always be a single person. They can be an entire team. You can also find a hero closer to home, as young Doris Kearns Goodwin did.

Sharing Ideas

Have you ever become very enthusiastic about a group, such as a sports team or a musical group? What effect did that enthusiasm have on you? How do you feel about it now?

Setting a Purpose

As you read, think about why the young Doris became such a loyal fan of the Dodgers.

BUILDING BACKGROUND

The Time and Place   This selection is set in a Long Island, New York, suburb in 1949. This was ten years after Lou Gehrig said his farewell to the New York Yankees.

Did You Know?   The period 1949–1956 was a glorious period for New York baseball fans. Each year, one or two of the city's three baseball teams–the Yankees, the Giants, and the Brooklyn Dodgers–competed in the World Series. The Yankees won the championship in six of those years.

VOCABULARY PREVIEW

juncture (jungk′ chər) *n.* a critical point of time; p. 36
agitated (aj′ ə tāt′ ed) *adj.* upset; disturbed; p. 36
narrative (nar′ ə tiv) *n.* story; storytelling; p. 37
ritual (rich′ o͞o əl) *n.* an established form of doing something; ceremony; p. 37
naive (nä ēv′) *adj.* simple in nature; childlike; p. 37
divulge (di vulj′) *v.* to make known; give away; p. 38
staple (stā′ pəl) *adj.* important; main; p. 38

from
Wait Till Next Year

Doris Kearns Goodwin ~

WHEN I WAS SIX, my father gave me a bright-red scorebook that opened my heart to the game of baseball. After dinner on long summer nights, he would sit beside me in our small enclosed porch to hear my account of that day's Brooklyn Dodger[1] game.

---

1. Until 1958, when they moved to Los Angeles, the *Dodgers* were based in Brooklyn, a part of New York City.

Night after night he taught me the odd collection of symbols, numbers, and letters that enable a baseball lover to record every action of the game. Our score sheets had blank boxes in which we could draw our own slanted lines in the form of a diamond as we followed players around the bases. Wherever the baserunner's progress stopped, the line stopped. He instructed me to fill in the unused boxes at the end of each

Duke Snider

inning with an elaborate checkerboard design which made it absolutely clear who had been the last to bat and who would lead off the next inning. By the time I had mastered the art of scorekeeping, a lasting bond had been forged among my father, baseball, and me.

All through the summer of 1949, my first summer as a fan,

I spent my afternoons sitting cross-legged before the squat Philco radio which stood as a permanent fixture on our porch in Rockville Centre, on the South Shore of Long Island, New York. With my scorebook spread before me, I attended Dodger games through the courtly voice of Dodger announcer Red Barber. As he announced the lineup, I carefully printed each player's name in a column on the left side of my sheet. Then, using the standard system my father had taught me, . . . I recorded every play. I found it difficult at times to sit still. As the Dodgers came to bat, I would walk around the room, talking to the players as if they were standing in front of me. At critical junctures, I tried to make a bargain, whispering and cajoling while Pee Wee Reese or Duke Snider[2] stepped into the batter's box: "Please, please, get a hit. If you get a hit now, I'll make my bed every day for a week." Sometimes, when the score was close and the opposing team at bat with men on base, I was too agitated to listen. Asking my mother to keep notes, I left the house for a walk around the block, hoping that when I returned the enemy threat would be over, and once again we'd be up at bat. Mostly, however, I stayed at my post, diligently recording each inning so that, when my father returned from his

2. *Pee Wee Reese* and *Duke Snider* were two of the star players on the Dodgers team during the 1950s.

Vocabulary
juncture (jungk′ chər) *n.* a critical point of time
agitated (aj′ ə tāt′ ed) *adj.* upset; disturbed

job as bank examiner for the State of New York, I could re-create for him the game he had missed.

When my father came home from the city, he would change from his three-piece suit into long pants and a short-sleeved sport shirt. . . . Then my parents would summon me for dinner from my play on the street outside our house. All through dinner I had to restrain myself from telling him about the day's game, waiting for the special time to come when we would sit together on the couch, my scorebook on my lap.

"Well, did anything interesting happen today?" he would begin. And even before the daily question was completed I had eagerly launched into my narrative

Pee Wee Reese

of every play, and almost every pitch, of that afternoon's contest. It never crossed my mind to wonder if, at the close of a day's work, he might find my lengthy account the least bit tedious. For there was mastery as well as pleasure in our nightly ritual. Through my knowledge, I commanded my father's undivided attention, the sign of his love. It would instill in me an early awareness of the power of narrative, which would introduce a lifetime of storytelling, fueled by the naive confidence that others would find me as entertaining as my father did. . . .

These nightly recountings of the Dodgers' progress provided my first lessons in the narrative art. From the scorebook, with its tight squares of neatly arranged symbols, I could unfold the tale of an entire game and tell a story that seemed to last almost as long as the game itself. At first, I was unable to resist the temptation to skip ahead to an important play in later innings. At times, I grew so excited about a Dodger victory that I blurted out the final score before I had hardly begun. But as I became more experienced in my storytelling, I learned to build a dramatic story with a beginning, middle, and end. Slowly, I learned that if I could recount the game, one batter at a time, inning by inning, without

Vocabulary
narrative (nar′ ə tiv) *n.* story; storytelling
ritual (rich′ o͞o əl) *n.* an established form of doing something; ceremony
naive (nä ēv′) *adj.* simple in nature; childlike

Jackie Robinson

divulging the outcome, I could keep the suspense and my father's interest alive until the very last pitch. . . .

All through that summer, my father kept from me the knowledge that running box scores appeared in the daily newspapers. He never mentioned that these abbreviated histories had been a <u>staple</u> feature of the sports pages since the nineteenth century and were generally the first thing he and his fellow commuters turned to when they opened the *Daily News* and the *Herald Tribune* in the morning. I believed that, if I did not recount the games he had missed, my father would never have been able to follow our Dodgers the proper way, day by day, play by play, inning by inning. In other words, without me, his love of baseball would be forever unfulfilled.

Vocabulary
divulge (di vulj′) *v.* to make known; give away
staple (stā′ pəl) *adj.* important; main

Responding to Literature

PERSONAL RESPONSE

◆ Think back to the group discussion in the **Reading Focus** on page 34. Do you think the kind of devoted team loyalty the author describes is a good thing? Why or why not?

Analyzing Literature

RECALL

1. What triggers Doris Kearns Goodwin's interest in baseball?
2. How does Doris learn about the games she describes to her father?
3. What does Doris learn from her experience in re-creating games for her father?
4. From what other source could Doris's father have gotten the information?

INTERPRET

5. Why do you think Doris's father never tells her that he could have read about the games in the daily newspaper?
6. Why do you suppose her father never complains about her lengthy accounts of the games? Use details from the story to support your opinion.
7. In what ways did her experience in describing baseball games help Doris develop her writing skills? Explain.
8. What did you learn about the relationship between Doris and her father from the selection? Use references to the selection to back up your answer.

EVALUATE AND CONNECT

9. Considering this selection, who do you think was Doris's greatest childhood hero? Explain why you think so.
10. Doris Kearns Goodwin writes, "I learned to build a dramatic story with a beginning, middle, and end." Do you think that's a good idea for a young writer? Is it the only way to tell a story? Is it the best way? Explain.

LITERARY ELEMENTS

Memoir

Goodwin's *Wait Till Next Year* is a personal **memoir**—a record of her own experiences, related from her own memories. In a memoir, the author describes events for us as he or she recalls them. It usually expresses the author's opinions about events and people. In this selection, Goodwin writes from the point of view of an adult author looking back at herself as a child.

1. How do you think Doris Kearns Goodwin feels about her younger self? Use examples from the selection to support your answer.

2. How would this selection differ if it had been written in the late 1950s by a teenaged Doris rather than in the 1990s by the adult author? How would it differ if it had been written by Doris's father? Explain your answers with examples from the selection.

● See **Literary Terms Handbook**, p. R6.

COMPARING SELECTIONS

Strong Men Weep **and** *from* Wait Till Next Year

COMPARE **RESPONSES**

Both "Strong Men Weep" and the selection from *Wait Till Next Year* deal with the topic of baseball.

- How are the selections alike? How are they different? Support your responses with examples from the selections.
- Which selection did you prefer? Why?
- Which piece did you learn more from, and which challenged you more as a reader? Explain.

COMPARE **EXPERIENCES**

Think about your own experiences with sports and games. Do you prefer participating, like Lou Gehrig, or are you happy to be just an observer, like the young Doris Kearns Goodwin? Do you like solitary sports such as running, or do you prefer team sports? Do you prefer to be a spectator or to read about the events?

- Consider your feelings about sports and games. What is it that you really enjoy about different games? Is it the team effort of soccer or the individual positions in baseball or softball? Do you like a challenge on your own, as in chess, or do you prefer close interaction, as in volleyball? Try to figure out exactly what it is you enjoy most about your favorite sports and games.
- In small groups, take turns discussing your favorite sports and games. Respond to questions and comments from your group members.
- In your group, take a poll of favorite sporting events. Share a graph of the results of your polls in a class discussion.

COMPARE **CREATIONS**

Write a radio, television, or newspaper advertisement for a school or local baseball or softball team. The team may be an imaginary one or an actual team you know about. Use language and sensory details in your ad that will excite the public about the team's upcoming season.

MEDIA *Connection*

TELEVISION SCRIPT

These scenes from the first episode of the TV series *The Wonder Years* first aired January 31, 1988. In this episode, it is fall 1968 and the first day of junior high for Kevin, his best friend Paul, and Winnie. Wayne is Kevin's older brother, who likes to torment Kevin. The Narrator is the adult Kevin, looking back on his "wonder years."

from *The Wonder Years*
Episode 1: "The Wonder Years"
—by Neal Marlens and Carol Black

[Exterior. Day. Bus stop.
Kevin and Paul stand beside one another at the bus stop. Wayne and others are there.]

KEVIN
[To Paul.] Don't worry about it, you look fine.

PAUL
Let me see our class schedule one more time.

KEVIN
No.

NARRATOR
He was gonna have to get a grip on himself. This was the junior high bus stop and if we were gonna hold our own with the older kids we were gonna have to act mature. We seemed to have something of a height disadvantage, but we did our best to fit in. *[Kevin and Paul stick their tongues out, mimicking the older kids. They spot Winnie who is walking toward the bus stop.]*

NARRATOR
What an incredible stroke of luck, a new kid. A helpless waif would be even more lost than we were, a helpless waif in fishnet tights and gogo boots.

WINNIE
Hi Kevin. Hi Paul.

PAUL
[Amazed.] Winnie Cooper?

WINNIE
Gwendolyn. I don't want to be called Winnie anymore, my real name is Gwendolyn.

NARRATOR
Well, there was no question now, we were entering uncharted territory. Even the familiar was cloaked in the vestments of the devil. Junior high school was a whole new ball of wax.

[Later that day.
Interior. Day. Cafeteria.
Kevin and Paul carry their trays and look for a table to sit at in the cafeteria.]

NARRATOR
Lunch, at last, something I figured even I couldn't screw up.

PAUL
Where do you want to sit?

KEVIN
Anywhere. Let's just sit here.
[Kevin and Paul sit down at a table.]

NARRATOR
A suburban junior high school cafeteria is like a microcosm of the world. The goal is to protect yourself, and safety comes in groups. You have your cool kids, you have your smart kids, you have your greasers, and in those days, of course, you had your hippies. In fact, in junior high school, who you are is defined less by who you are than by who's the person sitting next to you—a sobering thought.

KEVIN
[To Paul.] Try to look like you're having fun.
[Winnie approaches the table at which Kevin and Paul are sitting.]

WINNIE
Hi. Do you guys mind if I sit with you?

KEVIN
Sure, Winnie.

NARRATOR
We were on our way. Our group was forming. And Winnie, I mean, Gwendolyn, was not chopped liver. Who knows, maybe we even had an outside chance to become the cool seventh grade group, if we could just remain inconspicuous until we picked up a few more members.

[Wayne, at another table with friend Steve, spots Kevin, Paul and Winnie and approaches them.]

WAYNE
Hey Steve, it looks like my baby brother and his girlfriend have found each other.

KEVIN
She's not my girlfriend.

WAYNE
[To Winnie.] He thinks you are so cute.

KEVIN
I don't think she's cute.

WAYNE
He wants to give you a big wet kiss.
[Wayne makes a sucking noise.]

WAYNE
He told me.

KEVIN
You liar, I never said that! I don't want to kiss her, I don't even like her!
[Kevin picks up his apple and walks briskly to exit the cafeteria.]

Analyzing Media

1. Why do you think Kevin exits the cafeteria so quickly?

2. Did you ever have a nervous first day at a new school or in a new grade? What do you think about it now?

Before You Read

Broken Chain

MEET GARY SOTO

Gary Soto's experiences growing up in a Spanish-speaking neighborhood inspire much of his work. Like his parents and grandparents, Soto labored for a time as a migrant farm worker picking fruit. His love of literature came later, when he went to college. "Writing is my one talent," he says. "There are a lot of people who never discover what their talent is. . . . I am very lucky to have found mine." His writing includes award-winning poetry, novels, memoirs, essays, and films for both young people and adults.

Gary Soto was born in 1952. This story was published in 1990.

READING FOCUS

Why are some people so concerned about their appearance?

Discuss
Discuss with the class why teenagers are often so concerned about how they look, how they dress, and what others think of them.

Setting a Purpose
Read to find out what concerns the main character has about his appearance.

BUILDING BACKGROUND

The Time and Place   A Mexican American neighborhood in Fresno, California, in the 1980s is the setting for this selection.

Did You Know?   "Broken Chain" takes place in a Spanish-speaking neighborhood in Fresno, California, a neighborhood where Mexican American families have made their homes for many decades.

VOCABULARY PREVIEW

sullen (sul′ ən) *adj.* stubbornly withdrawn or gloomy; sulky; p. 45

swagger (swag′ ər) *v.* to walk or behave in a bold, rude, or overly proud way; p. 45

wince (wins) *v.* to draw back slightly, as in pain; p. 48

impulse (im′ puls) *n.* an internal force that causes one to act without thinking; p. 50

retrieve (ri trēv′) *v.* to locate and bring back; recover; fetch; p. 50

desperation (des′ pə rā′ shən) *n.* distress caused by great need or loss of hope; p. 50

emerge (i murj′) *v.* to come out; p. 52

Broken Chain

Gary Soto

Alfonso sat on the porch trying to push his crooked teeth to where he thought they belonged. He hated the way he looked. Last week he did fifty sit-ups a day, thinking that he would burn those already apparent ripples on his stomach to even deeper ripples, dark ones, so when he went swimming at the canal next summer, girls in cut-offs would notice. And the guys would think he was tough, someone who could take a punch and give it back. He wanted "cuts"[1] like those he had seen on a calendar of an Aztec warrior standing on a pyramid with a woman in his arms. (Even she had cuts he could see beneath her thin dress.) The calendar hung above the cash register at La Plaza. Orsua, the owner, said Alfonso could have the calendar at the end of the year if the waitress, Yolanda, didn't take it first.

---

1. Here, *cuts* is slang for "good, solid abdominal muscles."

Alfonso studied the magazine pictures of rock stars for a hairstyle. He liked the way Prince looked—and the bass player from Los Lobos.[2] Alfonso thought he would look cool with his hair razored into a V in the back and streaked purple. But he knew his mother wouldn't go for it. And his father, who was *puro Mexicano*,[3] would sit in his chair after work, <u>sullen</u> as a toad, and call him "sissy."

Alfonso didn't dare color his hair. But one day he had had it butched on the top, like in the magazines. His father had come home that evening from a softball game, happy that his team had drilled four homers in a thirteen-to-five bashing of Color Tile. He'd <u>swaggered</u> into the living room, but had stopped cold when he saw Alfonso and asked, not joking but with real concern, "Did you hurt your head at school? *Qué pasó?*"[4]

Alfonso had pretended not to hear his father and had gone to his room, where he studied his hair from all angles in the mirror. He liked what he saw until he smiled and realized for the first time that his teeth were crooked, like a pile of wrecked cars. He grew depressed and turned away

from the mirror. He sat on his bed and leafed through the rock magazine until he came to the rock star with the butched top. His mouth was closed, but Alfonso was sure his teeth weren't crooked.

Alfonso didn't want to be the handsomest kid at school, but he was determined to be better-looking than average. The next day he spent his lawn-mowing money on a new shirt, and, with a pocket-knife, scooped the moons of dirt from under his fingernails.

He spent hours in front of the mirror trying to herd his teeth into place with his thumb. He asked his mother if he could have braces, like Frankie Molina, her godson, but he asked at the wrong time. She was at the kitchen table licking the envelope to the house payment. She glared up at him. "Do you think money grows on trees?"

His mother clipped coupons from magazines and newspapers, kept a vegetable garden in the summer, and shopped at Penney's and K-Mart. Their family ate a lot of *frijoles*, which was OK because nothing else tasted so good, though one time Alfonso had had Chinese pot stickers[5] and thought they were the next best food in the world.

---

2. *Prince* is the former name of a rock star. *Los Lobos* (lōs lō′ bōs), "The Wolves," is a Mexican American band.
3. *Puro Mexicano* (pōō′ rō   me′ hē kä′ nō) means "pure Mexican."
4. *"Qué pasó?"* (kā   pä sō′) translates as "What happened?"

5. *Frijoles* (frē hō′ les) are beans—pinto bean, kidney beans, or black beans—that are cooked until very tender, mashed, and fried. A *pot sticker* is a kind of Chinese dumpling.

Vocabulary
sullen (sul′ ən) *adj.* stubbornly withdrawn or gloomy; sulky
swagger (swag′ ər) *v.* to walk or behave in a bold, rude, or overly proud way

Viewing the photograph: What might a bike like this one symbolize, or stand for?

He didn't ask his mother for braces again, even when she was in a better mood. He decided to fix his teeth by pushing on them with his thumbs. After breakfast that Saturday he went to his room, closed the door quietly, turned the radio on, and pushed for three hours straight.

He pushed for ten minutes, rested for five, and every half hour, during a radio commercial, checked to see if his smile had improved. It hadn't.

Eventually he grew bored and went outside with an old gym sock to wipe down his bike, a ten-speed from Montgomery Ward. His thumbs were tired and wrinkled and pink, the way they got when he stayed in the bathtub too long.

Alfonso's older brother, Ernie, rode up on *his* Montgomery Ward bicycle looking depressed. He parked his bike against the peach tree and sat on the back steps, keeping his head down and stepping on ants that came too close.

Alfonso knew better than to say anything when Ernie looked mad. He turned his bike over, balancing it on the handlebars and seat, and flossed the spokes with the sock. When he was finished, he pressed a knuckle to his teeth until they tingled.

Ernie groaned and said, "Ah, man."

Alfonso waited a few minutes before asking, "What's the matter?" He pretended not to be too interested. He picked up a wad of steel wool and continued cleaning the spokes.

Ernie hesitated, not sure if Alfonso would laugh. But it came out. "Those girls didn't show up. And you better not laugh."

"What girls?"

Then Alfonso remembered his brother bragging about how he and Frostie met two girls from Kings Canyon Junior High last week on Halloween night. They were dressed as gypsies, the costume for all poor Chicanas—they just had to borrow scarves and gaudy red lipstick from their *abuelitas*.[6]

Alfonso walked over to his brother. He compared their two bikes: his gleamed like a handful of dimes, while Ernie's looked dirty.

"They said we were supposed to wait at the corner. But they didn't show up. Me

and Frostie waited and waited like fools. They were playing games with us."

Alfonso thought that was a pretty dirty trick but sort of funny too. He would have to try that some day.

"Were they cute?" Alfonso asked.

"I guess so."

"Do you think you could recognize them?"

"If they were wearing red lipstick, maybe."

Alfonso sat with his brother in silence, both of them smearing ants with their floppy high tops. Girls could sure act weird, especially the ones you meet on Halloween.

Later that day, Alfonso sat on the porch pressing on his teeth. Press, relax; press, relax. His portable radio was on, but not loud enough to make Mr. Rojas come down the steps and wave his cane at him.

Alfonso's father drove up. Alfonso could tell by the way he sat in his truck, a Datsun with a different-colored front fender, that his team had lost their softball game. Alfonso got off the porch in a hurry because he knew his father would be in a bad mood. He went to the backyard, where he unlocked his bike, sat on it with the kickstand down, and pressed on his teeth. He punched himself in the stomach, and growled, "Cuts." Then he patted his butch and whispered, "Fresh."

After a while Alfonso pedaled up the street, hands in his pockets, toward Foster's Freeze, where he was chased by a ratlike Chihuahua. At his old school, John Burroughs

Did You Know?

The *Chihuahua*, the world's smallest breed of dog, grows to about five inches tall at the shoulder. It was originally native to Mexico and is named for a city there.

---

6. Young Mexican American women are called *Chicanas* (chi kä′ nəs); *abuelitas* (ä′ bwə lē′ təs) are old women, or "grannies."

Broken Chain

Elementary, he found a kid hanging upside down on the top of a barbed-wire fence with a girl looking up at him. Alfonso skidded to a stop and helped the kid untangle his pants from the barbed wire. The kid was grateful. He had been afraid he would have to stay up there all night. His sister, who was Alfonso's age, was also grateful. If she had to go home and tell her mother that Frankie was stuck on a fence and couldn't get down, she would get scolded.

"Thanks," she said. "What's your name?"

Alfonso remembered her from his school and noticed that she was kind of cute, with ponytails and straight teeth. "Alfonso. You go to my school, huh?"

"Yeah. I've seen you around. You live nearby?"

"Over on Madison."

"My uncle used to live on that street, but he moved to Stockton."

"Stockton's near Sacramento, isn't it?"

"You been there?"

"No." Alfonso looked down at his shoes. He wanted to say something clever the way people do on TV. But the only thing he could think to say was that the governor lived in Sacramento. As soon as he shared this observation, he <u>winced</u> inside.

Alfonso walked with the girl and the boy as they started for home. They didn't talk much. Every few steps, the girl, whose name was Sandra, would look at him out of the corner of her eye, and Alfonso would look away. He learned that she was in seventh grade, just like him, and that she had a pet terrier named Queenie. Her father was a mechanic at Rudy's Speedy

Repair, and her mother was a teacher's aide at Jefferson Elementary.

When they came to the street, Alfonso and Sandra stopped at her corner, but her brother ran home. Alfonso watched him stop in the front yard to talk to a lady he guessed was their mother. She was raking leaves into a pile.

"I live over there," she said, pointing.

Alfonso looked over her shoulder for a long time, trying to muster enough nerve to ask her if she'd like to go bike riding tomorrow.

Shyly, he asked, "You wanna go bike riding?"

"Maybe." She played with a ponytail and crossed one leg in front of the other. "But my bike has a flat."

"I can get my brother's bike. He won't mind."

She thought for a moment before she said, "OK. But not tomorrow. I have to go to my aunt's."

"How about after school on Monday?"

"I have to take care of my brother until my mom comes home from work. How 'bout four-thirty?"

"OK," he said. "Four-thirty." Instead of parting immediately, they talked for a while, asking questions like, "Who's your favorite group?" "Have you ever been on the Big Dipper at Santa Cruz?" and "Have you ever tasted pot stickers?" But the question-and-answer period ended when Sandra's mother called her home.

Alfonso took off as fast as he could on his bike, jumped the curb, and, cool as he could be, raced away with his hands stuffed in his pockets. But when he looked back

---

Vocabulary

wince (wins) *v.* to draw back slightly, as in pain

over his shoulder, the wind raking through his butch, Sandra wasn't even looking. She was already on her lawn, heading for the porch.

> *Alfonso felt his stomach knot up. "She's going to be my girlfriend, not yours!"*

That night he took a bath, pampered his hair into place, and did more than his usual set of exercises. In bed, in between the push-and-rest on his teeth, he pestered his brother to let him borrow his bike.

"Come on, Ernie," he whined. "Just for an hour."

"*Chale,*[7] I might want to use it."

"Come on, man, I'll let you have my trick-or-treat candy."

"What you got?"

"Three baby Milky Ways and some Skittles."

"Who's going to use it?"

Alfonso hesitated, then risked the truth. "I met this girl. She doesn't live too far."

Ernie rolled over on his stomach and stared at the outline of his brother, whose head was resting on his elbow. "*You* got a girlfriend?"

"She ain't my girlfriend, just a girl."

"What does she look like?"

"Like a girl."

"Come on, what does she look like?"

"She's got ponytails and a little brother."

"Ponytails! Those girls who messed with Frostie and me had ponytails. Is she cool?"

"I think so."

Ernie sat up in bed. "I bet you that's her."

Alfonso felt his stomach knot up. "She's going to be my girlfriend, not yours!"

"I'm going to get even with her!"

"You better not touch her," Alfonso snarled, throwing a wadded Kleenex at him. "I'll run you over with my bike."

For the next hour, until their mother threatened them from the living room to be quiet or else, they argued whether it was the same girl who had stood Ernie up. Alfonso said over and over that she was too nice to pull a stunt like that. But Ernie argued that she lived only two blocks from where those girls had told them to wait, that she was in the same grade, and, the clincher, that she had ponytails. Secretly, however, Ernie was jealous that his brother, two years younger than himself, might have found a girlfriend.

Sunday morning, Ernie and Alfonso stayed away from each other, though over breakfast they fought over the last tortilla.[8] Their mother, sewing at the kitchen table, warned them to knock it off. At church they made faces at one another when the priest, Father Jerry,

---

7. If you want someone to "cool it" or "knock it off," say *"Chale"* (chä′ lä).

8. A *tortilla* (tôr tē′ yə) is made from cornmeal or flour and baked on a griddle so that it resembles a thin pancake.

Broken Chain

wasn't looking. Ernie punched Alfonso in the arm, and Alfonso, his eyes wide with anger, punched back.

Monday morning they hurried to school on their bikes, neither saying a word, though they rode side by side. In first period, Alfonso worried himself sick. How would he borrow a bike for her? He considered asking his best friend, Raul, for his bike. But Alfonso knew Raul, a paper boy with dollar signs in his eyes, would charge him, and he had less than sixty cents, counting the soda bottles he could cash.

Between history and math, Alfonso saw Sandra and her girlfriend huddling at their lockers. He hurried by without being seen.

During lunch Alfonso hid in metal shop[9] so he wouldn't run into Sandra. What would he say to her? If he weren't mad at his brother, he could ask Ernie what girls and guys talk about. But he *was* mad, and anyway, Ernie was pitching nickels with his friends.

Alfonso hurried home after school. He did the morning dishes as his mother had asked and raked the leaves. After finishing his chores, he did a hundred sit-ups, pushed on his teeth until they hurt, showered, and combed his hair into a perfect butch. He then stepped out to the patio to clean his bike. On an impulse, he removed the chain to wipe off the gritty oil. But while he was unhooking it from the back

sprocket, it snapped. The chain lay in his hand like a dead snake.

Did You Know?

A *sprocket* is a wheel that has teeth around its edge to grab the links of a chain. A bicycle has a small sprocket on the rear wheel and a larger one between the two wheels.

Alfonso couldn't believe his luck. Now, not only did he not have an extra bike for Sandra, he had no bike for himself. Frustrated, and on the verge of tears, he flung the chain as far as he could. It landed with a hard slap against the back fence and spooked his sleeping cat, Benny. Benny looked around, blinking his soft gray eyes, and went back to sleep.

Alfonso retrieved the chain, which was hopelessly broken. He cursed himself for being stupid, yelled at his bike for being cheap, and slammed the chain onto the cement. The chain snapped in another place and hit him when it popped up, slicing his hand like a snake's fang.

"Ow!" he cried, his mouth immediately going to his hand to suck on the wound.

After a dab of iodine, which only made his cut hurt more, and a lot of thought, he went to the bedroom to plead with Ernie, who was changing to his after-school clothes.

"Come on, man, let me use it," Alfonso pleaded. "Please, Ernie, I'll do anything."

Although Ernie could see Alfonso's desperation, he had plans with his friend Raymundo. They were going to catch frogs at the Mayfair canal. He felt sorry for

---

9. The *metal shop* is a room where students learn the skills of working with metals. Schools often also have wood shops and car shops to teach similar skills.

Vocabulary

impulse (im′ puls) *n.* an internal force that causes one to act without thinking
retrieve (ri trēv′) *v.* to locate and bring back; recover; fetch
desperation (des′ pə rā′ shən) *n.* distress caused by great need or loss of hope

his brother, and gave him a stick of gum to make him feel better, but there was nothing he could do. The canal was three miles away, and the frogs were waiting.

Alfonso took the stick of gum, placed it in his shirt pocket, and left the bedroom with his head down. He went outside, slamming the screen door behind him, and sat in the alley behind his house. A sparrow landed in the weeds, and when it tried to come close, Alfonso screamed for it to scram. The sparrow responded with a squeaky chirp and flew away.

At four he decided to get it over with and started walking to Sandra's house, trudging slowly, as if he were waist-deep in water. Shame colored his face. How could he disappoint his first date? She would probably laugh. She might even call him *menso*.[10]

He stopped at the corner where they were supposed to meet and watched her house. But there was no one outside, only a rake leaning against the steps.

_____

10. *Menso* (men′ sō) means "ignorant or foolish."

Sibling Rivals, 1989. Phoebe Beasley. Collage, 32 x 41 in. Stella Jones Gallery, New Orleans.

Viewing the collage: What does this collage say to you about rivalry? Could these figures be Alfonso and Ernie? Why or why not?

Broken Chain

Why did he have to take the chain off? he scolded himself. He always messed things up when he tried to take them apart, like the time he tried to repad his baseball mitt. He had unlaced the mitt and filled the pocket with cotton balls. But when he tried to put it back together, he had forgotten how it laced up. Everything became tangled like kite string. When he showed the mess to his mother, who was at the stove cooking dinner, she scolded him but put it back together and didn't tell his father what a dumb thing he had done.

Now he had to face Sandra and say, "I broke my bike, and my stingy brother took off on his."

He waited at the corner for a few minutes, hiding behind a hedge for what seemed like forever. Just as he was starting to think about going home, he heard footsteps and knew it was too late. His hands, moist from worry, hung at his sides, and a thread of sweat raced down his armpit.

He peeked through the hedge. She was wearing a sweater with a checkerboard pattern. A red purse was slung over her shoulder. He could see her looking for him, standing on tiptoe to see if he was coming around the corner.

What have I done? Alfonso thought. He bit his lip, called himself *menso*, and pounded his palm against his forehead. Someone slapped the back of his head. He turned around and saw Ernie.

"We got the frogs, Alfonso," he said, holding up a wiggling plastic bag. "I'll show you later."

Ernie looked through the hedge, with one eye closed, at the girl. "She's not the one who messed with Frostie and me," he said finally. "You still wanna borrow my bike?"

Alfonso couldn't believe his luck. What a brother! What a pal! He promised to take Ernie's turn next time it was his turn to do the dishes. Ernie hopped on Raymundo's handlebars and said he would remember that promise. Then he was gone as they took off without looking back.

Free of worry now that his brother had come through, Alfonso emerged from behind the hedge with Ernie's bike, which was mud-splashed but better than nothing. Sandra waved.

"Hi," she said.

"Hi," he said back.

She looked cheerful. Alfonso told her his bike was broken and asked if she wanted to ride with him.

"Sounds good," she said, and jumped on the crossbar.

It took all of Alfonso's strength to steady the bike. He started off slowly, gritting his teeth, because she was heavier than he thought. But once he got going, it got easier. He pedaled smoothly, sometimes with only one hand on the handlebars, as they sped up one street and down another. Whenever he ran over a pothole, which was often, she screamed with delight, and once, when it looked like they were going to crash, she placed her hand over his, and it felt like love.

Vocabulary
emerge (i murj′) *v.* to come out

Responding to Literature

PERSONAL RESPONSE

- ◆ What thoughts and feelings did you have at the end of the story? Describe your reactions in your journal.
- ◆ In what ways did you identify with Alfonso? Explain in detail.

Analyzing Literature

RECALL

1. What aspects of his appearance would Alfonso like to change?
2. Describe the difference between Alfonso's and Ernie's bikes.
3. How does Alfonso break his bicycle chain?
4. What is Sandra's reaction to Alfonso's appearing with just one beat-up bike?

INTERPRET

5. Why is Alfonso unhappy with the way he looks?
6. How does the author show that Alfonso cares very much about the appearance of his bike?
7. Why is Alfonso so upset when he breaks his bicycle chain? Do you think he is overreacting? Why or why not?
8. At the end of the story, Alfonso is different. How has he changed? What caused the change? Use examples to support your answers.

EVALUATE AND CONNECT

9. Alfonso is always trying to straighten his teeth. What does the **repetition** of this image show you about his state of mind throughout the story?

10. **Theme Connection** Does reading a story about someone your own age make you feel more connected to the character? Why or why not?

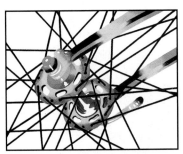

LITERARY ELEMENTS

Conflict

The struggle between two opposing forces that lie at the center of a plot in a story is called the **conflict.** An **external conflict** exists when a character struggles against an outside force—another person, nature, society, or fate. An **internal conflict** exists within the mind of the character who is torn between opposing feelings or goals. In "Broken Chain" Alfonso struggles with both kinds of conflicts.

1. What are the external conflicts that seem to prevent Alfonso from reaching his goal of meeting Sandra for a "date"? Find two or more examples.

2. Alfonso is desperately searching for his own style. Describe how his lack of confidence about his looks could be interpreted as an internal conflict.

● See **Literary Terms Handbook,** p. R3.

Spokes, 1983. John D. Wibberley. Acrylic on canvas, 16 x 24 in. Artist's collection.

Literature and Writing

Writing About Literature

Details In "Broken Chain," Gary Soto includes many details about Alfonso's family and neighborhood. Write a paragraph or two about how Soto's use of details helps you understand what his life at home and at school must have been like. Choose details from the story to prove your point.

Creative Writing

Dear Advice Columnist Recall your discussion in the **Reading Focus** on page 43 about peoples' concern with their appearance. Alfonso is self-conscious about his appearance. Imagine that he has written to an advice column. What questions might Alfonso ask? What advice might a helpful person give him? Write the letter and the response.

Extending Your Response

Literature Groups

Comparing Alfonso with Himself Together, read the first and last paragraphs in the story. Then have a discussion comparing how Alfonso feels at the beginning of the story with how he feels at the end. Make a comparison chart that shows the results of your discussion.

	AT THE BEGINNING	AT THE END
ALFONSO'S FEELINGS ABOUT HIMSELF		

Performing

Improvisation Work with a partner to improvise a scene between Alfonso and Sandra after their bike ride at the end of the story. What would the two say to each other? Would they be nervous or shy? What would their body language look like? Perform your improvised scene in front of the class.

Reading Further

Check out these books by Gary Soto:

Poetry: *Neighborhood Odes*

Novel: *Taking Sides*

Short Stories: *Baseball in April and Other Stories*

 **Save your work for your portfolio.**

Interdisciplinary Activity

Science Why does a bicycle need a chain? Can a bike work without one? With a partner, examine a bike scientifically. Write your own explanation of how a bicycle works. Use diagrams to illustrate your ideas. Check with a reference book or your science teacher to see whether your explanation is correct and revise it as needed.

Skill Minilessons

GRAMMAR AND LANGUAGE • SUBJECT-VERB AGREEMENT

A subject and a verb are basic parts of a sentence. The subject and its verb must agree in number. A singular noun used as a subject of a sentence calls for a singular form of the verb:

Alfonso rides his bike after school.

A plural noun used as the subject calls for a plural form of the verb:

Alfonso and Ernie ride their bikes after school.

PRACTICE For each sentence, write the subject and the correct form of the verb.

1. Gary Soto (writes, write) stories about teens.
2. The book *Baseball in April and Other Stories* (is, are) an award winner.
3. There (is, are) eleven short stories, most about Latino young people.
4. The stories, like "Broken Chain," (focuses, focus) on the difficulties of growing up.
5. The end of the book (contains, contain) a list of Spanish words and their English translations.

● For more about subject-verb agreement, see **Language Handbook,** pp. R14–R15.

READING AND THINKING • ACTIVATING PRIOR KNOWLEDGE

Things you already know can help you understand what you read. Even if you read about an adventure in another galaxy, you will understand some parts easily because of knowledge you acquired previously. All the life experiences you have had contribute to your prior knowledge.

PRACTICE What have you read or experienced that helped you better understand the characters' thoughts and feelings in "Broken Chain"? Write a paragraph describing how this prior knowledge helped you understand the story.

● For more about this and related reading strategies, see **Reading Handbook,** p. R86.

VOCABULARY • SYNONYMS

Synonyms are words that mean nearly the same thing. When you know synonyms for a word, you can decide which one best expresses the exact meaning you want. For example, *desperation* expresses a more frantic feeling than *hopelessness*. A hopeless person might just sit and do nothing. But a desperate person would try something– anything! Still, *desperation* and *hopelessness* are synonyms, because they are close in meaning. A **thesaurus,** a book that lists and defines synonyms,

can help you understand how synonyms differ in meaning.

PRACTICE Write a synonym for each word below. Then write one sentence using each word and another sentence using its synonym.

1. sullen
2. retrieve
3. swagger
4. wince
5. impulse

Technology Skills

Word Processing: Desktop Publishing

With a small group, examine several books, magazines, and newspapers. Notice how text and illustrations are arranged on the page. Can you tell who the intended readers are just by the way a page is designed? How do book, magazine, and newspaper pages differ? Summarize what your examination tells you about page design.

Menu bar —

Toolbars —

Ruler —

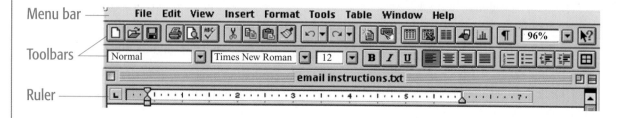

Getting Oriented

Get to know some important features of your word processing software. Start with a document that has some text in it. Experiment with each feature by selecting a portion of text before choosing a menu command or clicking an icon.

1. Pull down the **View** menu, and select **Page Layout.** Use this view for the remaining items in this list.

2. Pull down the **Format** menu, and select **Columns.** Locate the columns icon in the toolbar.

3. Find the **Font Box** in the toolbar. Locate the **Font** feature in the **Format** menu. Experiment with some fonts. (See the **TYPOGRAPHY** chart on the next page for more information about fonts, or typefaces.)

4. Find the **Font Size** box in the toolbar. Select **Font** in the **Format** menu.

5. On the toolbar, find the buttons for align left, align right, center, and align left and right (also called justification).

6. Look under **Tools** to find the feature **Hyphenation.** (It may be in a Tools submenu under **Language.**)

7. Find the buttons that automatically create numbered and bulleted lists.

8. Locate the buttons that will decrease or increase indentations.

9. On the ruler, find the button that controls tab stops, or locate its feature in the **Format** menu.

10. Experiment with the margin markers on the ruler.

Sample Typefaces
(all in 12 pt. size)

Serif Faces
Bookman Old Style
Courier New
Garamond
Times New Roman

Sans-Serif Faces
Ariel
Avant Garde Book
Helvetica Condensed Light

TYPOGRAPHY

Typeface	Type size
Many different typefaces—each with unique roman, *italic,* and **bold** styles—are available on computers. A few are illustrated on page 56.	Type size is measured in points. One point equals about $1/72$ inch. The main text in most publications is between ten and twelve points.
Serif type	**Sans-serif type**
On serif type, the main strokes of letters are embellished with little strokes, or "feet," that are thought to make words more readable.	Sans-serif type lacks "feet." Traditionally used only for headings, sans-serif type is also used for the main text in many contemporary designs.
Headings	**Display typefaces**
Headings are often bold and usually larger than the main text. Different levels of heading may have different "weights," or sizes.	Display typefaces are typically large and eye-catching and often quite unusual. This book uses display type for its selection and feature titles.

Creating an Autobiographical Sketch

1. In the selection from *Wait Till Next Year,* Doris Kearns Goodwin tells how her relationship with her father led to a lifelong fascination with baseball. Think about the major events in your own life. Was there a particular person or incident that had a strong or lasting effect on you? Focus on a particular experience that you can describe. Try to recall the experience and the feelings you had at the time. Ask yourself: What other people were involved? What writing elements will I use—humor? irony? suspense?

2. Use your computer and word processing software to plan, draft, revise, and edit a brief autobiographical sketch relating that experience.

3. Before presenting your sketch, prepare a design for it that will be appropriate to your subject. Share your designed sketch with a partner, and ask for suggestions for improvement.

4. Prepare a final version, and print your document.

ACTIVITIES

1. Use the word processing features you learned about to complete the **Writing Workshop** in this theme.

2. In a group, interview your school's newspaper sponsor (if there is one) to determine how word processing is used in the production of the school newspaper.

Before You Read
Without Commercials

MEET ALICE WALKER

From the time she was eight, Alice Walker kept a notebook of poetry. Today her writings include novels, poems, short stories, and essays. As the youngest of eight children in a Georgia sharecropping family, Walker says, "I always seemed to need more peace and quiet than anybody else. . . . Books became my world, because the world I was in was very hard." Walker is the first African American woman to win the Pulitzer Prize for a novel. Much of her writing focuses on the difficult lives of poor, heroic, African American women.

Alice Walker was born in 1944. This poem was published in 1984.

READING FOCUS

How many different kinds of people are there in the world? Think about the variety of faces you see in a large crowd at a parade or a sports event.

Sharing Ideas
With a small group, discuss the variety of people you see in advertisements. Do ads reflect the broad diversity of human beings in the world?

Setting a Purpose
Read the poem to find out what the speaker thinks about ads.

BUILDING BACKGROUND

Alice Walker grew up attending all-black schools that "gave us a feeling that they really belonged to us. There was a lot of self-help and community." Even in this supportive environment, however, Walker felt like an outcast after an older brother accidentally shot her in the eye with a BB gun. Her blinded eye was covered with scar tissue. "I used to pray every night that I would wake up and somehow it would be gone. I couldn't look people in the eye because I thought I was ugly." It was this experience that first inspired Walker to record her observations and feelings. Later, surgery repaired much of the scar tissue. This change helped improve her self-image considerably.

Walker is considered one of the major American writers of this century. She is active in both the Civil Rights and women's rights movements. She helped reintroduce readers to the author Zora Neale Hurston, another important African American writer.

Without Commercials

Alice Walker ❧

Listen,
stop tanning yourself
and talking about
fishbelly
5   white.
The color white
is not bad at all.
There are white mornings
that bring us days.
10   Or, if you must,
tan only because
it makes you happy
to be brown,
to be able to see
15   for a summer
the whole world's
darker
face
reflected
20   in your own.

❋

Stop unfolding
your eyes.
Your eyes are
beautiful.
25   Sometimes
seeing you in the street
the fold zany°

and unexpected
I want to kiss
30   them
and usually
it is only
old
gorgeous
35   black people's eyes
I want
to kiss.

❋   ❋

Stop trimming
your nose.
40   When you
diminish°
your nose
your songs
become little
45   tinny, muted°
and snub.
Better you should
have a nose
impertinent°
50   as a flower,
sensitive

---

27 A thing that's *zany* is odd or crazy in a comical way.

41 To *diminish* means "to make smaller in size."

45 In this context, *muted* means "muffled, softened, or less strong."

49 Something *impertinent* is improperly bold or rude.

as a root;
wise, elegant,
serious and deep.
55 A nose that
sniffs
the essence°
of Earth. And knows
the message
60 of every
leaf.

* * *

Stop bleaching
your skin
and talking
65 about
so much black
is not beautiful
The color black
is not bad
70 at all.
There are black nights
that rock
us
in dreams.
75 Or, if you must,
bleach only
because it pleases you
to be brown,
to be able to see
80 for as long
as you can bear it
the whole world's

lighter face
reflected
85 in your own.

* * * *

As for me,
I have learned
to worship
the sun
90 again.
To affirm°
the adventures
of hair.

For we are all
95 *splendid*
descendants
of Wilderness,
Eden:
needing only
100 to see
each other
without
commercials
to believe.

105 Copied skillfully
as Adam.

Original

as Eve.

---

57 Here, *essence* means "perfume."

91 To *affirm* is to state firmly and positively.

Responding to Literature

PERSONAL RESPONSE

◆ Do you recognize yourself or anyone you know in any of the descriptions in "Without Commercials"? Explain.

Analyzing Literature

RECALL

1. Whom does the speaker address in the first stanza of the poem?

2. What message is expressed about people's differences?

INTERPRET

3. According to the poem, what effect do commercials have on people? Why is the poem called "Without Commercials"?

4. What does the speaker suggest that people of every race have in common?

EVALUATE AND CONNECT

5. Does this poem make you think twice about how you or people you know feel about their physical features? Explain.

6. Choose your favorite example of **visual imagery** in the poem, and explain why it appeals to you.

7. In your opinion, why does the poem end with a reference to Adam and Eve?

8. Think about the diversity of people you discussed in the **Reading Focus** on page 58. Choose a few lines from the poem that talk about diverse groups of people.

9. Why might people feel they should look like the people in commercials? If there were no commercials, do you think that people would change their attitudes about how they look? Give reasons to support your opinion.

10. Knowing what you do about the poet Alice Walker, what do you think she would say about her own features?

LITERARY ELEMENTS

Speaker

In talking about "Without Commercials," you might be tempted to say something like "According to her poem, Alice Walker believes that . . ." You identify the thoughts, ideas, or events in the poem with the person who wrote it. This may be true in many cases. Poets *do* use their poems to express their ideas. However, poets do so through a **speaker** that they create to express these ideas. The ideas expressed by a speaker could be the opposite of what the poet really believes. When you discuss or write about a poem, don't confuse the speaker with the poet.

1. In your opinion, are the ideas expressed in "Without Commercials" Alice Walker's ideas? Why or why not?

2. Read another poem anywhere in this book. Tell why you think the speaker can or cannot be closely identified with the poet.

● See **Literary Terms Handbook,** p. R10.

AUTOBIOGRAPHY

Are you a fan of autobiography? An **autobiography** is a person's story of his or her own life. This form of nonfiction has been popular since the days of the ancient Egyptians. More than any other form of writing, autobiography offers readers a direct, personal connection with the author.

Most autobiographies are book-length. However, there are many shorter kinds of autobiographical writing. Here are some of them:

- **diary entries**
- **travel journals**
- **memoirs**—stories of important people or periods in the author's life
- **eyewitness accounts**—stories of memorable events, written by people who were there
- **anecdotes**—brief stories of small, simple incidents

Although autobiography is a form of **nonfiction,** its structure often follows that of fiction. For example, autobiography is usually written as a story—with characters and action or events. The main difference between autobiographical writing and fiction is that autobiography is a factual account of real events of a person's life, written by that person.

Autobiographies often share the literary elements below.

CHARACTERS In autobiography, the author is almost always the main character. To make themselves believable as characters, authors of autobiography reveal their weaknesses as well as their strengths. They also show the feelings and reasons behind the things they do.

EVENTS As in fiction, events in autobiographies unfold in chronological (time) order. Authors may use **flashback** to show what led up to events or **flash-forward** to show outcomes or offer views of events still to come.

TIME AND PLACE, OR SETTING In autobiography, the author draws on real places, times, and political or social situations. The setting is portrayed in accurate detail, with enough background to let readers "put themselves there," but not so much background that it slows the story.

POINT OF VIEW Point of view is the viewpoint from which a story is told. In an autobiography, the point of view is almost always the author's, who describes his or her life, using pronouns such as *I* and *me*.

	Ask Yourself	**Model**
CHARACTER	How does the author help readers identify with a character?	Rosa Parks, in *Rosa Parks: My Story,* recalls her feelings during her historic refusal to give up her bus seat. Readers can identify with her sense of being pushed too far.
SETTING	How does the author help readers understand the time and/or place?	In *Barrio Boy,* Ernesto Galarza specifies the exact place and name of his school. He describes the furniture and layout of the principal's office, so that readers can picture it in their minds.
EVENTS	How does the author make the order of events clear to readers?	In "Fish Cheeks," Amy Tan describes, in chronological order, the preparation, celebration, and aftermath of a Christmas Eve dinner. She uses flash-forward to show readers what she later realizes about that night.
POINT OF VIEW	How does the author help readers see things through his or her eyes?	In *Barrio Boy,* Ernesto Galarza describes his feelings as a child. He shows how tall and foreign his teacher and principal looked to him and how strange the English language seemed.
THEME	What main message(s) about life or human nature might the author's experiences illustrate?	"Names/Nombres" is about more than names. When Julia Alvarez moves to the United States, the changes in her name illustrate the culture clashes that she faces.

THEME A **theme** is a message that readers can take from the story. A theme can be stated directly, or it can be implied. Authors of autobiographies don't tell everything that's happened in their lives. They choose events and details that add up to the theme or themes they want to convey.

When you read autobiographical writing, look for the elements discussed on these pages. Ask yourself what the author does with each element. The chart above shows questions you might use. It also shows how you might analyze the elements of autobiographical writings that you read.

Active Reading Strategies

Tips for Reading Autobiographical Writing

How do you get the most out of your reading? One way to become an effective reader is to become an active reader. Active readers use strategies to better understand a selection. They ask themselves questions as they read. Use the strategies below to help you read autobiographical writing.

● For more about reading strategies, see **Reading Handbook,** pp. R73–R102.

PREVIEW

Previewing a selection will help prepare you before you actually read. Look at the title and pictures, and skim through the pages to find hints about the author.

Ask Yourself . . .

● How can I tell that this selection is autobiographical?

● Has this author written anything that I've previously read?

● What do the photographs or illustrations tell me?

PREDICT

Combine clues in the text with what you already know to make predictions about what will come next.

Ask Yourself . . .

● Based on my preview, what do I expect this selection to be about?

● How will the author be affected by this event?

● From my reading so far, I'd adjust my prediction to _.

QUESTION

Questioning helps you clarify your understanding of the text as you go along.

Ask Yourself . . .

● Why did the author choose to write about this particular event?

● Do I understand this passage? What strategies can I use to make it clearer?

● Why does the author reveal this detail?

● I wonder why _____ .

VISUALIZE

Form pictures in your mind. Pay attention to the autobiographical details writers share about their lives.

Ask Yourself . . .

- How does this scene look?

- Can I picture the author and the people he describes?

RESPOND

Respond while you are reading. Think about what events strike you as most interesting.

Ask Yourself . . .

- What I admire most about this person is _ .

- I'd like to ask the writer why _____ .

- If I wrote an autobiography like this, I would include _____ .

APPLYING THE STRATEGIES

Read the following selection from the book *Barrio Boy*. Use the Active Reading Model in the margins as you read. Write your responses on a separate piece of paper or use stick-on notes.

Before You Read

from *Barrio Boy*

MEET ERNESTO GALARZA

Ernesto Galarza (ār nes′ tō gä lär′ zä), a Mexican American union leader and writer, spent most of his life fighting for the rights of farm workers. He used his writing to expose the abuses they suffered. According to Galarza, "*Barrio Boy* is the story of a Mexican family, uprooted from its home in a mountain village. . . . The episodes of the journey were typical of those of hundreds of thousands of refugees. They settled permanently in California and other border states. The barrio of this tale is that of Sacramento, California."

Ernesto Galarza was born in 1905. He died in 1984. This selection is from Barrio Boy, *published in 1971.*

READING FOCUS

How did you feel the first time you walked into your school as a new student? What were your first impressions of the building, the teachers, and your new classmates?

Sharing Ideas

Take a moment to jot down your responses to these questions. Then share your thoughts and feelings with a partner.

Setting a Purpose

Read the selection to learn how the author, as a young boy, faced starting at a new school.

BUILDING BACKGROUND

The Time and Place The setting is the Lincoln School, an elementary school in Sacramento, California, in the early 1900s. The author has moved from Mazatlán, Mexico, to California.

VOCABULARY PREVIEW

wholeheartedly (hōl′ här′ tid lē) *adv.* completely; sincerely; enthusiastically; p. 68

maneuver (mə nōō′ vər) *v.* to move or handle skillfully, as into a position or toward a goal; p. 68

menace (men′ əs) *n.* a threat or danger; p. 68

formidable (for′ mi də bəl) *adj.* causing fear or dread by reason of size, strength, or power; p. 69

obnoxious (ob nok′ shəs) *adj.* annoying and disagreeable; p. 69

persistently (pər sis′ tənt lē) *adv.* repeatedly; p. 70

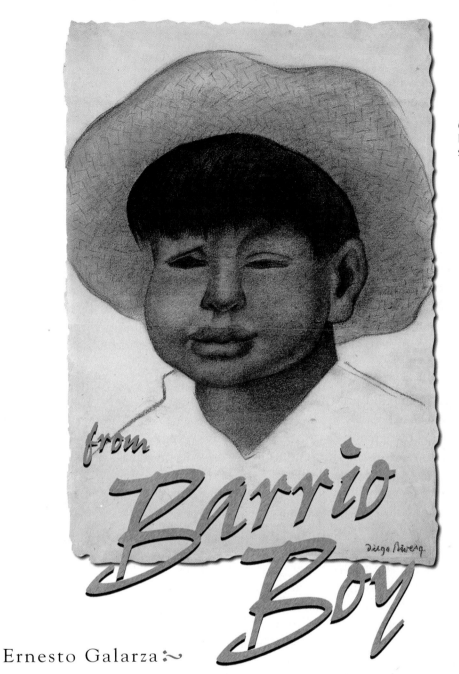

Cabeza de Nino, 1921–1929.
Diego Rivera. Dibujo a la
sanguina, 38 x 27.5 cm.

from Barrio Boy

Ernesto Galarza ~

The two of us walked south on Fifth Street one morning to the corner of Q Street and turned right. Half of the block was occupied by the Lincoln School. It was a three-story wooden building, with two wings that gave it the shape of a double-T connected by a central hall. It was a new building, painted yellow, with a shingled roof that was not like the red tile of the school in Mazatlán.[1] I noticed other differences, none of them very reassuring.

---

1. *Mazatlán* (mäz′ ət län′) is a city on Mexico's central Pacific coast.

from *Barrio Boy*

ACTIVE READING MODEL

RESPOND

Would you be anxious if you were entering a new school for the first time? Why or why not?

We walked up the wide staircase hand in hand and through the door, which closed by itself. A mechanical contraption screwed to the top shut it behind us quietly.

Up to this point the adventure of enrolling me in the school had been carefully rehearsed. Mrs. Dodson had told us how to find it and we had circled it several times on our walks. Friends in the *barrio*[2] explained that the director was called a principal, and that it was a lady and not a man. They assured us that there was always a person at the school who could speak Spanish.

Exactly as we had been told, there was a sign on the door in both Spanish and English: "Principal." We crossed the hall and entered the office of Miss Nettie Hopley.

Miss Hopley was at a roll-top desk[3] to one side, sitting in a swivel chair that moved on wheels. There was a sofa against the opposite wall, flanked by two windows and a door that opened on a small balcony. Chairs were set around a table and framed pictures hung on the walls of a man with long white hair and another with a sad face and a black beard.

The principal half turned in the swivel chair to look at us over the pinch glasses crossed on the ridge of her nose. To do this she had to duck her head slightly as if she were about to step through a low doorway.

What Miss Hopley said to us we did not know but we saw in her eyes a warm welcome and when she took off her glasses and straightened up she smiled <u>wholeheartedly</u>, like Mrs. Dodson. We were, of course, saying nothing, only catching the friendliness of her voice and the sparkle in her eyes while she said words we

Did You Know?
Pinch glasses are eyeglasses clipped to the nose. Often, they're called by their French name, *pince-nez* (paNs′ nā′).

did not understand. She signaled us to the table. Almost tiptoeing across the office, I <u>maneuvered</u> myself to keep my mother between me and the gringo[4] lady. In a matter of seconds I had to decide whether she was a possible friend or a <u>menace</u>. We sat down.

PREDICT

Do you think the narrator will like Miss Hopley? Why do you think so?

---

2. In the United States, *barrio* (bä′ rē ō) refers to a Hispanic neighborhood.
3. A *roll-top desk* is a writing desk with a slatted, movable top.
4. *Gringo* is a sometimes scornful term for a non-Hispanic, white, North American male.

Vocabulary
wholeheartedly (hōl′ här′ tid lē) *adv.* completely; sincerely; enthusiastically
maneuver (mə no͞o′ vər) *v.* to move or handle skillfully, as toward a goal
menace (men′ əs) *n.* a threat or danger

Then Miss Hopley did a <u>formidable</u> thing. She stood up. Had she been standing when we entered she would have seemed tall. But rising from her chair she soared. And what she carried up and up with her was a buxom superstructure, firm shoulders, a straight sharp nose, full cheeks slightly molded by a curved line along the nostrils, thin lips that moved like steel springs, and a high forehead topped by hair gathered in a bun. Miss Hopley was not a giant in body but when she mobilized it to a standing position she seemed a match for giants. I decided I liked her.

She strode to a door in the far corner of the office, opened it and called a name. A boy of about ten years appeared in the doorway. He sat down at one end of the table. He was brown like us, a plump kid with shiny black hair combed straight back, neat, cool, and faintly <u>obnoxious</u>.

Viewing the photograph: This class photo was taken in the early 1900s, around the time Ernesto Galarza attended the Lincoln School. What can you learn about the school and the students from studying the photo?

Vocabulary
formidable (for′ mi də bəl) *adj.* causing fear or dread by reason of size, strength, or power
obnoxious (ob nok′ shəs) *adj.* annoying and disagreeable

from *Barrio Boy*

ACTIVE READING MODEL

Miss Hopley joined us with a large book and some papers in her hand. She, too, sat down and the questions and answers began by way of our interpreter. My name was Ernesto. My mother's name was Henriqueta. My birth certificate was in San Blas. Here was my last report card from the Escuela Municipal Numero 3 para Varones[5] of Mazatlán, and so forth. Miss Hopley put things down in the book and my mother signed a card.

As long as the questions continued, Doña[6] Henriqueta could stay and I was secure. Now that they were over, Miss Hopley saw her to the door, dismissed our interpreter and without further ado took me by the hand and strode down the hall to Miss Ryan's first grade.

Miss Ryan took me to a seat at the front of the room, into which I shrank—the better to survey her. She was, to skinny, somewhat runty me, of a withering height when she patrolled the class. And when I least expected it, there she was, crouching by my desk, her blond radiant face level with mine, her voice patiently maneuvering me over the awful idiocies of the English language.

During the next few weeks Miss Ryan overcame my fears of tall, energetic teachers as she bent over my desk to help me with a word in the pre-primer. Step by step, she loosened me and my classmates from the safe anchorage of the desks for recitations at the blackboard and consultations at her desk. Frequently she burst into happy announcements to the whole class. "Ito can read a sentence," and small Japanese Ito, squint-eyed and shy, slowly read aloud while the class listened in wonder: "Come, Skipper, come. Come and run." The Korean, Portuguese, Italian, and Polish first graders had similar moments of glory, no less shining than mine the day I conquered "butterfly," which I had been <u>persistently</u>

RESPOND

If you were the narrator, how would you feel walking into Miss Ryan's class?

PREDICT

How will Miss Ryan help Ernesto overcome his fears?

---

5. That is, her first name is *Henriqueta* (en´ ri kā´ tə). *San Blas* is a small city down the coast from Mazatlán but in a different state. In Mazatlán, the writer attended a public school for boys, *Escuela Municipal para Varones* (es kwā´ lə mōō ni´ si päl´ pär´ ə vä rō´ nās).

6. *Doña* (dōn´ yə) is a form of respectful address for a married woman, like the English words *lady* and *madam*. For a man, one says *Don* (dōn), meaning "sir."

Vocabulary
persistently (pər sis´ tənt lē) *adv.* repeatedly

pronouncing in standard Spanish as boo-ter-flee. "Children," Miss Ryan called for attention. "Ernesto has learned how to pronounce *butterfly!*" And I proved it with a perfect imitation of Miss Ryan. From that celebrated success, I was soon able to match Ito's progress as a sentence reader with "Come, butterfly, come fly with me."

Like Ito and several other first graders who did not know English, I received private lessons from Miss Ryan in the closet, a narrow hall off the classroom with a door at each end. Next to one of these doors Miss Ryan placed a large chair for herself and a small one for me. Keeping an eye on the class through the open door she read with me about sheep in the meadow and a frightened chicken going to see the king, coaching me out of my phonetic[7] ruts in words like *pasture, bow-wow-wow, hay,* and *pretty,* which to my Mexican ear and eye had so many unnecessary sounds and letters. She made me watch her lips and then close my eyes as she repeated words I found hard to read. When we came to know each other better, I tried interrupting to tell Miss Ryan how we said it in Spanish. It didn't work. She only said "oh" and went on with *pasture, bow-wow-wow,* and *pretty.* It was as if in that closet we were both discovering together the secrets of the English language and grieving together over the tragedies of Bo-Peep. The main reason I was graduated with honors from the first grade was that I had fallen in love with Miss Ryan. Her radiant, no-nonsense character made us either afraid not to love her or love her so we would not be afraid, I am not sure which. It was not only that we sensed she was with it, but also that she was with us.

> *The Korean, Portuguese, Italian, and Polish first graders had similar moments of glory, no less shining than mine the day I conquered "butterfly"* . . .

Like the first grade, the rest of the Lincoln School was a sampling of the lower part of town where many races made their home. My pals in the second grade were Kazushi, whose parents spoke only Japanese; Matti, a skinny Italian boy; and Manuel, a fat Portuguese who would never get into a fight but wrestled you to the ground and just sat on you. Our assortment of nationalities included Koreans, Yugoslavs, Poles, Irish, and home-grown Americans.

---

7. *Phonetic* (fə net′ ik) means "having to do with speech sounds."

ACTIVE READING MODEL

VISUALIZE

Take a moment to picture the private lessons in the closet.

RESPOND

Why do you think Ernesto falls in love with Miss Ryan?

ACTIVE READING MODEL

QUESTION

What does the narrator mean when he calls the school a "griddle"?

RESPOND

What do you like about this concluding paragraph? Why?

Miss Hopley and her teachers never let us forget why we were at Lincoln: for those who were alien,[8] to become good Americans; for those who were so born, to accept the rest of us. Off the school grounds we traded the same insults we heard from our elders. On the playground we were sure to be marched up to the principal's office for calling someone a wop, a chink, a dago, or a greaser. The school was not so much a melting pot[9] as a griddle where Miss Hopley and her helpers warmed knowledge into us and roasted racial hatreds out of us.

At Lincoln, making us into Americans did not mean scrubbing away what made us originally foreign. The teachers called us as our parents did, or as close as they could pronounce our names in Spanish or Japanese. No one was ever scolded or punished for speaking in his native tongue on the playground. Matti told the class about his mother's down quilt, which she had made in Italy with the fine feathers of a thousand geese. Encarnación[10] acted out how boys learned to fish in the Philippines. I astounded the third grade with the story of my travels on a stagecoach, which nobody else in the class had seen except in the museum at Sutter's Fort. After a visit to the Crocker Art Gallery and its collection of heroic paintings of the golden age of California, someone showed a silk scroll with a Chinese painting. Miss Hopley herself had a way of expressing wonder over these matters before a class, her eyes wide open until they popped slightly. It was easy for me to feel that becoming a proud American, as she said we should, did not mean feeling ashamed of being a Mexican.

---

8. Here, *alien* refers to those who are foreign born.
9. [*wop . . . greaser*] These are all offensive names for people of various nationalities or lifestyles. Here, *melting pot* refers to the idea of a place where people of all races and cultures blend smoothly into a single society.
10. *Encarnación* (en kär nä sē ōn′)

Responding to Literature

PERSONAL RESPONSE

◆ Describe your thoughts as you followed the writer from his first day at school to his success in mastering English.

Active Reading Response

Look back at the strategies described in the **Active Reading Strategies** on pages 64–65. Choose one of the strategies, and find two places in the selection where you could apply it.

Analyzing Literature

RECALL

1. Where were Ernesto and his mother going as they walked down Fifth Street?
2. What was Ernesto's first impression of Miss Hopley?
3. What did Ernesto think of Miss Ryan as he surveyed her from his seat in the class?
4. What happened to students at the school when they traded insults on the playground?

INTERPRET

5. How do you think Ernesto felt as he walked into the Lincoln School for the first time? Support your opinion.
6. How do details from the selection show Ernesto's attitude toward the "gringo lady"?
7. How did Ernesto's feelings about Miss Ryan change over the course of the year? Support your opinions with examples.
8. What helped make it easier for Ernesto to feel that "becoming a proud American . . . did not mean feeling ashamed of being Mexican"?

EVALUATE AND CONNECT

9. From whose **point of view** is this selection told? How would it be different if it were told from Miss Ryan's point of view?
10. What lessons, beyond the academic ones, did Ernesto learn at the Lincoln School? Why were those lessons important?

LITERARY ELEMENTS

Description

A detailed portrayal of a person, a place, a thing, or an event is called a **description**. While description is the writer's primary purpose in descriptive writing, description is used widely in all kinds of fiction and nonfiction writing. Strong writers select details carefully so their readers can see, hear, smell, taste, and feel what is being described. The excerpt from *Barrio Boy* is filled with colorful descriptions of life in the Lincoln School that enable readers to feel as if they are attending school with Ernesto.

1. Pick out a description of a person or a place in the selection that helps you picture it clearly. Explain which details help you "see" the person as the writer did.

2. Choose your favorite description in this work, and explain why you chose it.

● See **Literary Terms Handbook**, p. R3.

Extending Your Response

Writing About Literature

Setting   Write a paragraph or two explaining how the time and place of the excerpt from *Barrio Boy* contribute to the story. Think about how time and place affect events in the story. What details help you visualize the place?

Creative Writing

A Letter Home   Imagine that you are Ernesto. Write a letter to a relative in Mexico, describing the Lincoln School and your feelings about your experiences there. Before you write, review your notes from the **Reading Focus** on page 66.

Art Activity

Create a School   Draw pictures of the Lincoln School based on Ernesto's point of view. Use details from the selection as well as your imagination to help you sketch the school, both inside and out.

Reading Further

To read more stories about the challenges of adapting to a new culture, try these books:

Kim/Kimi by Hadley Irwin

Homesick: My Own Story by Jean Fritz

📖 **Save your work for your portfolio.**

Skill Minilesson

VOCABULARY • COMPOUND WORDS

Compound words are formed by putting two words together. The meaning of the new word combines the meanings of the words in some way. If you see an unfamiliar word that is made from words you know, think about the meanings of the individual words. There is a good chance you can figure out the meaning of the new word.

Let your imagination help. For example, a *spitfire* is a hot-tempered person, and *hogwash* is nonsense. If *heart* can mean "the center of emotion," then it's easy to see why saying that Miss Hopley smiled *wholeheartedly* indicates her sincere enthusiasm.

PRACTICE   Think about the words that form the compounds in the left column. Then match each one with its definition.

1. broadcast
2. blockhead
3. aftereffect
4. heartfelt
5. overstate

a. to exaggerate
b. sincere
c. a later result
d. to scatter widely
e. a foolish person

Vo·cab·u·lar·y Skills

Base Words

The words *trusting, trusty, mistrust,* and *distrustful* are formed by attaching prefixes or suffixes (or both) to *trust.* A **base word** serves as the "base" for any number of other words. Base words are whole words, not just parts of words, as roots can be.

Adding a prefix or suffix to a base word changes the meaning of the word. Sometimes the change is small. A *trusty* friend is one you can *trust.* Other times the change is major. To *distrust* someone means that you have no *trust* in that person.

Base Words	Words Formed from Base Words
happy	**happi**ness, un**happy**, **happi**ly
change	**change**s, un**chang**ing, **change**able
forget	**forget**ful, **forget**ting, un**forget**table

As you can see, small spelling changes may occur at the ends of base words when suffixes are added.

When you come across a word you don't know, check to see whether it has a base word that you *do* know. If it does, you can often figure out the meaning of the unfamiliar word, especially if the prefix or suffix is familiar to you.

EXERCISES

- Write the base word contained in the following words:
  1. laughter
  2. unrecognizable
  3. capitalize
  4. joylessness
  5. previewing

- Use your knowledge of the base word in the underlined word to complete the statement that follows.
  6. The immigration officer's pronunciation was <u>indicative</u> of future problems. This means it
     a. created them.   **b.** stopped them.   **c.** pointed to them.
  7. It was <u>habitual</u> for Julia's mother to call any writer Julia's "friend." This means she did it
     a. rarely.   **b.** often.   **c.** never.
  8. When Julia's friends <u>sportively</u> called her "Alcatraz," they were being
     a. foolish.   **b.** mean.   **c.** playful.
  9. Julia thought that having the name Ana was <u>advantageous</u> to her sister, because it did **not** cause
     a. help.   **b.** problems.   **c.** admiration.
  10. Once Julia had <u>familiarized</u> herself with her new names, she was
     a. used to them.   **b.** annoyed by them.   **c.** confused by them.

Before You Read

Fish Cheeks

Amy Tan did not always embrace her Chinese heritage. "When I was a teenager, I rejected everything Chinese. . . . I once felt ashamed to eat 'horrible' Chinese meals. I thought I'd grow up to look more American if I ate more 'American' foods." Only after her mother shared stories about the family's life in China did Tan become determined to learn all she could about her culture. Her novel *The Joy Luck Club* focuses on relationships between Chinese mothers and their American-born daughters.

Amy Tan was born in 1952. This piece was first published in a magazine in 1987.

READING FOCUS

Think about a situation in your life that was extremely embarrassing for you. Why did you feel the way you did?

Journal Writing

Write in your journal about an embarrassing situation and your feelings about it. Would you be willing to tell a classmate about the experience? Why or why not?

Setting a Purpose

Read to find out about an embarrassing event in the life of the author, Amy Tan.

BUILDING BACKGROUND

The Time and Place   It is 1966 in Oakland, California, when Amy Tan was fourteen years old.

Did You Know?
Chinese food is known the world over as one of the most sophisticated, complex, and delicious of cuisines. Meals served in Chinese homes and restaurants are most often eaten family style. Large bowls containing rice and a wide variety of dishes are placed in the middle of the table. Using chopsticks and spoons, diners share the food.

VOCABULARY PREVIEW

appalling (ə pô′ ling) *adj.* shocking; horrifying; p. 79
clamor (klam′ ər) *n.* a loud, continuous noise; uproar; p. 79
grimace (grim′ əs) *v.* to twist the face, as in pain or displeasure; p. 79

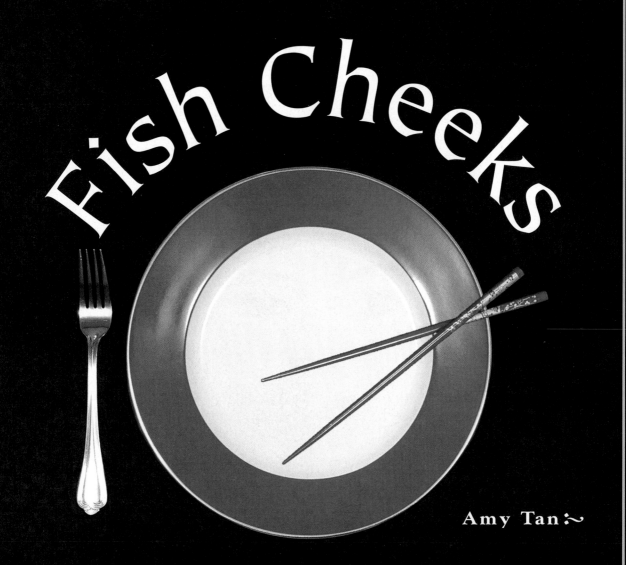

Fish Cheeks

Amy Tan

I fell in love with the minister's son the winter I turned fourteen. He was not Chinese, but as white as Mary in the manger. For Christmas I prayed for this blond-haired boy, Robert, and a slim new American nose.

When I found out that my parents had invited the minister's family over for Christmas Eve dinner, I cried. What would Robert think of our shabby *Chinese* Christmas? What would he think of our noisy *Chinese* relatives who

Portrait of Pang Tao, 1944. Qui Ti. Oil. Collection of Dr. Michael Sullivan. St. Catherine's College, Oxford, England.

Viewing the painting: Choose three words to describe the mood of the girl in this painting. Would the same words describe the story's narrator? Explain.

lacked proper American manners? What terrible disappointment would he feel upon seeing not a roasted turkey and sweet potatoes but *Chinese* food?

On Christmas Eve I saw that my mother had outdone herself in creating a strange menu. She was pulling black veins out of the backs of fleshy prawns. The kitchen was littered with appalling mounds of raw food: A slimy rock cod with bulging fish eyes that pleaded not to be thrown into a pan of hot oil. Tofu,[1] which looked like stacked wedges of rubbery white sponges. A bowl soaking dried fungus back to life. A plate of squid, their backs crisscrossed with knife markings so they resembled bicycle tires.

And then they arrived—the minister's family and all my relatives in a clamor of doorbells and rumpled Christmas packages. Robert grunted hello, and I pretended he was not worthy of existence.

Dinner threw me deeper into despair. My relatives licked the ends of their chopsticks and reached across the table, dipping them into the dozen or so plates of food. Robert and his family waited patiently for platters to be passed to them. My relatives murmured with pleasure when my mother

---

1. *Tofu* (tō′ fōō) is a protein-rich food made from soybeans and used in soups, salads, and stir fries.

brought out the whole steamed fish. Robert grimaced. Then my father poked his chopsticks just below the fish eye and plucked out the soft meat. "Amy, your favorite," he said, offering me the tender fish cheek. I wanted to disappear.

At the end of the meal my father leaned back and belched loudly, thanking my mother for her fine cooking. "It's a polite Chinese custom to show you are satisfied," explained my father to our astonished guests. Robert was looking down at his plate with a reddened face. The minister managed to muster up a quiet burp. I was stunned into silence for the rest of the night.

After everyone had gone, my mother said to me, "You want to be the same as American girls on the outside." She handed me an early gift. It was a miniskirt in beige tweed. "But inside you must always be Chinese. You must be proud you are different. Your only shame is to have shame."

And even though I didn't agree with her then, I knew that she understood how much I had suffered during the evening's dinner. It wasn't until many years later—long after I had gotten over my crush on Robert—that I was able to fully appreciate her lesson and the true purpose behind our particular menu. For Christmas Eve that year, she had chosen all my favorite foods.

Vocabulary
appalling (ə pô′ ling) *adj.* shocking; horrifying
clamor (klam′ ər) *n.* a loud, continuous noise; uproar
grimace (grim′ əs) *v.* to twist the face, as in pain or displeasure

Responding to Literature

PERSONAL RESPONSE

- ◆ What images from this story linger in your mind? Do they cause you to recall similar experiences from your own life?

Analyzing Literature

RECALL

1. What guests are invited to the Tans' Christmas Eve dinner?
2. Why does Amy assume that Robert will be disappointed by the food served at the meal?
3. What are some of the cultural differences Robert and his family notice in how food is eaten in a Chinese meal?
4. What does Amy's mother give her for an early Christmas present?

INTERPRET

5. Why is Amy so upset by the thought of entertaining the minister's family?
6. How does Amy's **description** of food preparation in the kitchen show how she feels about the food?
7. In what ways does the author make clear that the minister and his family are not used to eating in a traditional Chinese style?
8. Do you think Mrs. Tan's gift for Amy is a wise choice? Why or why not?

EVALUATE AND CONNECT

9. What do you think is the purpose of the final paragraph of this story?
10. Theme Connection   Amy Tan, as narrator and author, is able to stand back from this early experience and learn something about her mother and about herself. What have you learned from a similarly difficult experience in your own life?

LITERARY ELEMENTS

Sensory Imagery

Sensory imagery is language that appeals to a reader's five senses: hearing, sight, touch, taste, and smell. Imagery is used not only in poetry, but also in prose. Even if you have never seen or tasted tofu, you can picture it after reading Tan's description: "Tofu, which looked like stacked wedges of rubbery white sponges." "Fish Cheeks" is full of vivid images of a Chinese dinner being prepared and served.

1. Which two senses does the phrase "a slimy rock cod with bulging fish eyes" appeal to? Find another phrase that appeals to more than one sense.

2. Reread the paragraph about belching. How does Tan bring the scene to life for readers? Support your opinion with examples of sensory imagery from this scene.

● See **Literary Terms Handbook**, p. R10.

Extending Your Response

Writing About Literature

Point of View The dinner in "Fish Cheeks" is described from young Amy's point of view. What do you think might be Robert's opinion about the foods served? Write a brief summary of the meal from Robert's point of view.

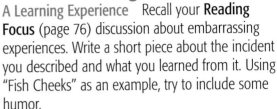

Use the Internet to find out more about traditional Chinese cooking. Look up the names and menu offerings of Chinese restaurants. You can also find recipes for Chinese food at various cooking Web sites.

Personal Writing

A Learning Experience Recall your **Reading Focus** (page 76) discussion about embarrassing experiences. Write a short piece about the incident you described and what you learned from it. Using "Fish Cheeks" as an example, try to include some humor.

Literature Groups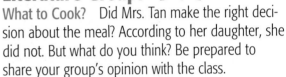

What to Cook? Did Mrs. Tan make the right decision about the meal? According to her daughter, she did not. But what do you think? Be prepared to share your group's opinion with the class.

Reading Further

If you enjoyed reading "Fish Cheeks," check out these books by Amy Tan:

The Moon Lady
The Chinese Siamese Cat

🛍 **Save your work for your portfolio.**

Skill Minilesson

VOCABULARY • ANALOGIES

Analogies are used in informational texts to explain something unfamiliar in terms of something familiar. They are also used in tests to compare the relationships between things or ideas. For example, *big : small :: happy : sad.* You can read this analogy as "*big* is to *small* as *happy* is to *sad.*" (In each set, the words have opposite meanings.)

PRACTICE Choose the pair of words that best completes each analogy.

1. appalling : pleasing ::
   a. cheerful : lucky
   b. lazy : sleepy
   c. interesting : boring
   d. furry : cold

2. silence : clamor ::
   a. roar : zoo
   b. year : month
   c. breakfast : lunch
   d. frown : smile

● For more about analogies, see **Literary Terms Handbook,** p. R1 and **Communications Skills Handbook,** p. R67.

Food with Attitude

The young Amy Tan had a tense Christmas Eve dinner. Her mother had prepared all of her favorite foods—tofu, squid, dried mushrooms, and fish cheeks—but Amy was too embarrassed to enjoy them. She worried that these foods and her family's meal customs would be strange and unappetizing to her non-Chinese guests.

Today, a young Amy Tan might not have to worry as much. Americans have become much more sophisticated in their dining habits. You'll probably find tofu, squid, and many other once-exotic items in almost any large super-market. Still, some dishes popular elsewhere have not yet made it into the American mainstream, and maybe never will. Here are a few of them.

Insects (including termites, ants, and grasshoppers) have been, and still are, eaten by people all over the world. They are an excellent source of protein—even better than beef. Depending on the insect and the location, insects may be eaten raw, cooked, or ground up and used as a spice or a medicine.

Headcheese is not really a cheese, but it is made from a head—a calf's head, including the brain. You can find the recipe in many cookbooks.

Haggis is a Scottish dish containing the chopped heart, liver, and lungs of a sheep mixed with suet (hard fat), oatmeal, onions, and spices. All this is stuffed into a cleaned sheep's stomach and boiled.

Fugu is a dish of puffer fish, or blowfish, so-called because the fish pumps itself full of air or water to appear larger when in danger. Highly prized in Japan, fugu must be cleaned and prepared by specially trained chefs because the fish's internal organs contain a very powerful poison. The danger seems to add to its popularity.

ACTIVITY

Pretend you are a social scientist trying to understand your family's eating customs. Interview family members, especially older ones, about foods. Ask questions such as:

- What food or meal traditions do we have in our family?
- Where did these traditions come from?
- What dishes from other countries or from other parts of our country do you enjoy?
- What foods did you enjoy as a child?
- How have your food likes and dislikes changed over the years?

Write a report summarizing the results of your survey.

Reading and Thinking Skills

Sequencing

Sequencing is organizing things into some kind of order, or sequence. Writers often use chronological order, or time order, to sequence their stories. Events take place one after another in time order. A skillful reader looks for clues that tell the order in which events actually occurred. Consider these passages from "Fish Cheeks."

> On Christmas Eve I found out that my mother had outdone herself in creating a strange menu. . . .
>
> And then they arrived—the minister's family and all my relatives in a clamor of doorbells and rumpled Christmas packages. . . .
>
> Dinner threw me deeper into despair. . . .
>
> At the end of the meal my father leaned back and belched loudly, thanking my mother for her fine cooking. . . .
>
> After everyone had gone, my mother said to me, "You want to be the same as American girls on the outside."

As you can see, each new paragraph moves the story a little further along in time. Author Amy Tan lets you know when each event happened. She makes use of words and phrases such as *on Christmas Eve, at the end of the meal, then,* and *after.* Not all stories contain clues as specific as these. Sometimes a story moves backward as well as forward in time. Still, you can usually figure out the order in which events occur. Watch especially for words and phrases such as *meanwhile, before, after, first, second, last, eventually, then, next, earlier,* and *later.*

● For more about sequencing, see **Reading Handbook,** p. R91.

ACTIVITY

Look through a short story of your choice. List all the words you find that provide clues to the time order of the events in the story. Then make a chart sequencing at least five events from the story in their correct time order.

Before You Read

from *Rosa Parks: My Story*

MEET
ROSA PARKS

Rosa Parks experienced the injustice of segregation on a daily basis growing up in Alabama. In the 1930s, she became active in Civil Rights, focusing on voter registration. Despite much effort, little had changed for African Americans in the South. Then one day in the 1950s, Rosa Parks refused to give up her bus seat. Without planning it, she became "the mother of the Civil Rights movement."

Rosa Parks was born in 1913. This story is part of her autobiography, first published in 1992.

READING FOCUS

When something in the world seems unjust, what can an ordinary person do about it?

List Ideas
Work with a partner and think of a situation that seems to affect people unfairly. Then make a list of actions that ordinary people might take to improve the situation.

Setting a Purpose
Find out what Rosa Parks did to improve a situation.

BUILDING BACKGROUND

The Time and Place This selection begins on December 1, 1955, in racially segregated Montgomery, Alabama.

Did You Know? Until the 1960s, Southern states had laws to separate the races. African Americans fought in the courts and through organized protests to end such discrimination.

VOCABULARY PREVIEW

comply (kəm plī′) *v.* to go along with a request; p. 86
resigned (ri zīnd′) *adj.* giving in without resistance; p. 88
boycott (boi′ kot) *n.* an organized protest in which the participants refuse to buy, sell, or use a product or service; p. 90
mobilize (mō′ bə līz′) *v.* to become prepared, as for war or an emergency; p. 91
inconvenience (in′ kən vēn′ yəns) *v.* to cause someone difficulty, bother, or hassle; p. 93
indignity (in dig′ nə tē) *n.* an offense against one's pride or dignity; humiliation; p. 94
oppression (ə presh′ ən) *n.* the act of controlling or governing by the cruel and unjust use of force or authority; p. 95
negotiate (ni gō′ shē āt′) *v.* to discuss in order to bring about an agreement; p. 97
impose (im pōz′) *v.* to apply legally; enforce; p. 100

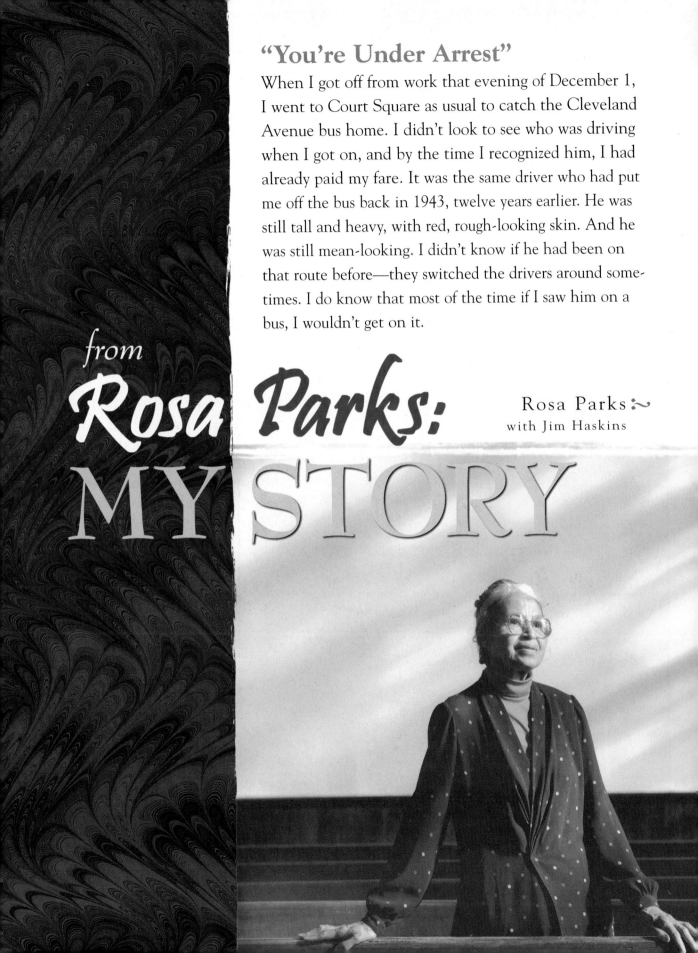

"You're Under Arrest"

When I got off from work that evening of December 1, I went to Court Square as usual to catch the Cleveland Avenue bus home. I didn't look to see who was driving when I got on, and by the time I recognized him, I had already paid my fare. It was the same driver who had put me off the bus back in 1943, twelve years earlier. He was still tall and heavy, with red, rough-looking skin. And he was still mean-looking. I didn't know if he had been on that route before—they switched the drivers around sometimes. I do know that most of the time if I saw him on a bus, I wouldn't get on it.

from

Rosa Parks: MY STORY

Rosa Parks
with Jim Haskins

I saw a vacant seat in the middle section of the bus and took it. I didn't even question why there was a vacant seat even though there were quite a few people standing in the back. If I had thought about it at all, I would probably have figured maybe someone saw me get on and did not take the seat but left it vacant for me. There was a man sitting next to the window and two women across the aisle.

The next stop was the Empire Theater, and some whites got on. They filled up the white seats, and one man was left standing. The driver looked back and noticed the man standing. Then he looked back at us. He said, "Let me have those front seats," because they were the front seats of the black section. Didn't anybody move. We just sat right where we were, the four of us. Then he spoke a second time: "Y'all better make it light on yourselves and let me have those seats."

The man in the window seat next to me stood up, and I moved to let him pass by me, and then I looked across the aisle and saw that the two women were also standing. I moved over to the window seat. I could not see how standing up was going to "make it light" for me. The more we gave in and complied, the worse they treated us.

I thought back to the time when I used to sit up all night and

THIS PART OF THE BUS FOR THE COLORED RACE

African Americans usually had to sit in the back of the bus in the segregated South.

Vocabulary
comply (kəm plī′) *v.* to go along with a request

didn't sleep, and my grandfather would have his gun right by the fireplace, or if he had his one-horse wagon going anywhere, he always had his gun in the back of the wagon. People always say that I didn't give up my seat because I was tired, but that isn't true. I was not tired physically, or no more tired than I usually was at the end of a working day. I was not old, although some people have an image of me as being old then. I was forty-two. No, the only tired I was, was tired of giving in.

The driver of the bus saw me still sitting there, and he asked was I going to stand up. I said, "No." He said, "Well, I'm going to have you arrested." Then I said, "You may do that." These were the only words we said to each other. I didn't even know his name, which was James Blake, until we were in court together. He got out of the bus and stayed outside for a few minutes, waiting for the police.

As I sat there, I tried not to think about what might happen. I knew that anything was possible. I could be manhandled or beaten. I could be arrested. People have asked me if it occurred to me then that I could be the test case the NAACP[1] had been looking for. I did not think about that at all. In fact if I had let myself think too deeply about what might happen to me, I might have gotten off the bus. But I chose to remain.

Meanwhile there were people getting off the bus and asking for transfers, so that began to loosen up the crowd, especially in the back of the bus. Not everyone got off,

but everybody was very quiet. What conversation there was, was in low tones; no one was talking out loud. It would have been quite interesting to have seen the whole bus empty out. Or if the other three had stayed where they were, because if they'd had to arrest four of us instead of one, then that would have given me a little support. But it didn't matter. I never thought hard of them at all and never even bothered to criticize them.

Eventually two policemen came. They got on the bus, and one of them asked me why I didn't stand up. I asked him, "Why do you all push us around?" He said to me, and I quote him exactly, "I don't know, but the law is the law and you're under arrest." One policeman picked up my purse, and the second one picked up my shopping bag and escorted me to the squad car. In the squad car they returned my personal belongings to me. They did not put their hands on me or force me into the car. After I was seated in the car, they went back to the driver and asked him if he wanted to swear out a warrant. He answered that he would finish his route and then come straight back to swear out the warrant. I was only in custody, not legally arrested, until the warrant was signed.

As they were driving me to the city desk, at City Hall, near Court Street, one of them asked me again, "Why didn't you stand up when the driver spoke to you?" I did not answer. I remained silent all the way to City Hall.

As we entered the building, I asked if I could have a drink of water, because my throat was real dry. There was a fountain, and I was standing right next to it. One of the policemen said yes, but by the time

---

1. *NAACP* stands for National Association for the Advancement of Colored People. It wanted an opportunity to test *segregation* laws in federal court. Such laws required *discrimination* against, or unfair treatment of, African Americans.

Rosa Parks, civil rights leader Edgar Daniel Nixon (center), and her attorney, Fred Gray (right), photographed after Parks was fined $10 for breaking Montgomery's segregation laws.

as what my name was and where I lived. I asked if I could make a telephone call and they said, "No." Since that was my first arrest, I didn't know if that was more discrimination because I was black or if it was standard practice. But it seemed to me to be more discrimination. Then they escorted me back to the squad car, and we went to the city jail on North Ripley Street.

I wasn't frightened at the jail. I was more resigned than anything else. I don't recall being real angry, not enough to have an argument. I was just prepared to accept whatever I had to face. I asked again if I could make a telephone call. I was ignored.

I bent down to drink, another policeman said, "No, you can't drink no water. You have to wait until you get to the jail." So I was denied the chance to drink a sip of water. I was not going to do anything but wet my throat. I wasn't going to drink a whole lot of water, even though I was quite thirsty. That made me angry, but I did not respond.

At the city desk they filled out the necessary forms as I answered questions such

They told me to put my purse on the counter and to empty my pockets of personal items. The only thing I had in my pocket was a tissue. I took that out. They didn't search me or handcuff me.

I was then taken to an area where I was fingerprinted and where mug shots were taken. A white matron[2] came to escort me to my jail cell, and I asked again if I might

_____
2. A *matron* is a female guard who supervises female prisoners.

Vocabulary
resigned (ri zīnd′) *adj.* giving in without resistance

use the telephone. She told me that she would find out.

She took me up a flight of stairs (the cells were on the second level), through a door covered with iron mesh, and along a dimly lighted corridor. She placed me in an empty dark cell and slammed the door closed. She walked a few steps away, but then she turned around and came back. She said, "There are two girls around the other side, and if you want to go over there with them instead of being in a cell by yourself, I will take you over there." I told her that it didn't matter, but she said, "Let's go around there, and then you won't have to be in a cell alone." It was her way of being nice. It didn't make me feel any better.

As we walked to the other cell, I asked her again, "May I use the telephone?" She answered that she would check.

There were two black women in the cell that the matron took me to, as she had said. One of them spoke to me and the other didn't. One just acted as if I wasn't there. The one who spoke to me asked me what had happened to me. I told her that I was arrested on the bus.

She said, "Some of those bus drivers sure are mean. You married?"

I said, "Yes," and she said, "Your husband ain't going to let you stay in here."

She wanted to know if there was anything she could do, and I said, "If you have a cup, I could drink a little water." She had a dark metal mug hanging above the toilet, and she caught a little water from the tap, and I took two swallows of that. She then started telling me about her problems. I became interested in her story and wondered how I could assist her. . . .

When the matron returned she told me to come out of the cell. I did not know where I was going until we reached the telephone booth. She gave me a card and told me to write down who I was calling and the telephone number. She placed a dime in the slot, dialed the number, and stayed close by to hear what I was saying.

I called home. My husband and mother were both there. She answered the telephone. I said, "I'm in jail. See if Parks will come down here and get me out."

She wanted to know, "Did they beat you?"

I said, "No, I wasn't beaten, but I am in jail."

She handed him the telephone, and I said, "Parks, will you come get me out of jail?"

He said, "I'll be there in a few minutes." He didn't have a car, so I knew it would be longer. But while we were still on the phone, a friend came by in his car. He'd heard about my being in jail and had driven to our place on Cleveland Court to see if he could help. He said he'd drive Parks to the jail.

The matron then took me back to the cell.

As Parks' friend had indicated, the word was already out about my arrest. Mr. [E. D.] Nixon [of the Montgomery NAACP] had been notified by his wife, who was told by a neighbor, Bertha Butler, who had seen me escorted off the bus. Mr. Nixon called the jail to find out what the charge was, but they wouldn't tell him. Then he had tried to reach Fred Gray, one of the two black lawyers in Montgomery, but he wasn't home. So finally Mr. Nixon called Clifford Durr, the white lawyer who was Mrs. Virginia Durr's husband. Mr. Durr called the jail and found out that I'd been arrested under the segregation laws. He also found out what the bail was.

Meanwhile Parks had called a white man he knew who could raise the bail. His friend took him over to the man's house to pick him up. I don't remember how much the bail was. . . .

The matron came to let me know that I was being released. Mrs. Durr was the first person I saw as I came through the iron mesh door with matrons on either side of me. There were tears in her eyes, and she seemed shaken, probably wondering what they had done to me. As soon as they released me, she put her arms around me, and hugged and kissed me as if we were sisters.

I was real glad to see Mr. Nixon and Attorney Durr too. We went to the desk, where I picked up my personal belongings and was given a trial date. Mr. Nixon asked that the date be the following Monday, December 5, 1955, explaining that he was a Pullman[3] porter and would be out of Montgomery until then. We left without very much conversation, but it was an emotional moment. I didn't realize how much being in jail had upset me until I got out.

As we were going down the stairs, Parks and his friends were driving up, so I got in the car with them, and Mr. Nixon followed us home.

By the time I got home, it was about nine-thirty or ten at night. My mother was glad to have me home and wanted to know what she could do to make me comfortable.

I told her I was hungry (for some reason I had missed lunch that day), and she prepared some food for me. Mrs. Durr and my friend Bertha Butler were there, and they helped my mother. I was thinking about having to go to work the next day, but I knew I would not get to bed anytime soon.

Everyone was angry about what had happened to me and talking about how it should never happen again. I knew that I would never, never ride another segregated bus, even if I had to walk to work. But it still had not occurred to me that mine could be a test case against the segregated buses.

Then Mr. Nixon asked if I would be willing to make my case a test case against segregation. I told him I'd have to talk with my mother and husband. Parks was pretty angry. He thought it would be difficult to get people to support me as a test case. We discussed and debated the question for a while. In the end Parks and my mother supported the idea. They were against segregation and were willing to fight it. And I had worked on enough cases to know that a ruling could not be made without a plaintiff.[4] So I agreed to be the plaintiff.

"They've Messed with the Wrong One Now"

Meanwhile Fred Gray, the black attorney, had called Jo Ann Robinson and told her about my arrest. She got in touch with other leaders of the Women's Political Council, and they agreed to call for a boycott of the

---

3. Mr. Nixon was an attendant on a passenger train. The *Pullman* Company was a major manufacturer of railroad cars.

4. The *plaintiff* is the "injured party" who brings a case to court. If no one claims to have been harmed by a *defendant's* actions, a judge is not likely to allow a trial.

Vocabulary
boycott (boi′ kot) *n.* an organized protest in which the participants refuse to buy, sell, or use a product or service

buses starting Monday, December 5, the day of my trial. So on the Thursday night I was arrested, they met at midnight at Alabama State, cut a mimeograph stencil,[5] and ran off 35,000 handbills. The next morning she and some of her students loaded the handbills into her car, and she drove to all the local black elementary and junior high and high schools to drop them off so the students could take them home to their parents.

This is what the handbill said:

This is for Monday, December 5, 1955.

Another Negro woman has been arrested and thrown into jail because she refused to get up out of her seat on the bus and give it to a white person.

It is the second time since the Claudette Colvin case that a Negro woman has been arrested for the same thing. This has to be stopped.

Negroes have rights, too, for if Negroes did not ride the buses, they could not operate. Three-fourths of the riders are Negroes, yet we are arrested, or have to stand over empty seats. If we do not do something to stop these arrests, they will continue. The next time it may be you, or your daughter, or mother.

This woman's case will come up on Monday. We are, therefore, asking every Negro to stay off the buses Monday in protest of the arrest and trial. Don't ride the buses to work, to town, to school, or anywhere on Monday.

You can afford to stay out of school for one day. If you work, take a cab, or walk. But please, children and grown-ups, don't ride the bus at all on Monday. Please stay off all buses Monday.

Early that Friday morning, Mr. Nixon called the Reverend Ralph David Abernathy, minister of the First Baptist Church. Mr. Nixon had decided that black ministers could do more to mobilize support in the community than anyone else. He also called eighteen other ministers and arranged a meeting for that evening. Mr. Nixon had to work as a porter on the Montgomery–Atlanta–New York route, so he would be unable to attend, but he talked to them all about what he wanted them to do.

Then he called a white reporter for the *Montgomery Advertiser* named Joe Azbell and arranged a meeting down at Union Station to show him one of the handbills. Mr. Nixon wanted the story on the front page. Joe Azbell said he would see what he could do. Meanwhile, the story of my arrest was reported in a small article in that day's paper.

On the morning of Friday, December 2, I called Felix Thomas, who operated a cab company, and took a cab to work. I was not going to ride the bus anymore. Mr. John Ball, who was in charge of men's alterations[6] at Montgomery Fair, was surprised to see me. He said, "I didn't think you would be here. I thought you would be a nervous wreck." I said, "Why should going to jail make a nervous wreck out of

---

5. Before the photocopier, a *mimeograph* machine could be used to print copies from an original called a *stencil.*

6. Mr. Ball supervises the *alterations,* or changes necessary for proper fit, of men's clothes at a local store.

Vocabulary
mobilize (mō′ bə līz′) *v.* to become prepared, as for war or an emergency

me?" And then as soon as I got off for lunch, I went to Fred Gray's office.

Ever since Fred had opened his law practice in Montgomery, I had often done that. I'd pick up something from the store for my lunch. He usually brought his lunch. We would eat lunch together, and then sometimes I would answer the telephone while he ran out and did an errand or something, and then it was time for me to go back to work. Fred didn't have a secretary, and I often helped him out. The day after I was arrested, Fred Gray's office was like a beehive. People were calling and dropping by to ask about the boycott and the meeting the ministers had called for that night.

After work, I went to that meeting at the Dexter Avenue Baptist Church. I explained how I had been arrested, and then there were long discussions about what to do. Some of the ministers wanted to talk about how to support the protest, but others wanted to talk about whether or not to have a protest. Many of them left the meeting before any decisions were made. But most of those who stayed agreed to talk about the protest in their Sunday sermons and to hold another meeting on Monday evening to decide if the protest should continue.

On Sunday the *Montgomery Advertiser* ran a copy of Jo Ann Robinson's handbill on the front page, and that helped spread the word to people who might have missed the leaflets or didn't go to church. But no one could be sure if the protest would be successful. Just because they read a leaflet or heard about it in church, it didn't mean that people would stay away from the buses. All eighteen black-owned cab companies in Montgomery had agreed to make stops at all the bus stops and charge only ten cents, the same fare as on the buses.

But people would have to wait for a cab that had room for them. To make matters worse, it looked like rain for Monday.

The sky was dark on Monday morning, but that didn't make any difference. Most black people had finally had enough of segregation on the buses. They stayed off those buses. They waited at the bus stops for the black-owned cabs to come along. Or they

Bus boycotters wait at one of the volunteer cab stops.

walked or got a ride. As a result, the Montgomery city buses were practically empty. Oh, a few black people took the buses, but they were mostly people who had not heard about the protest. Some of them were scared away from the buses. The city police had vowed to protect anyone who wanted to ride, and each bus had two motorcycle escorts. But some of the people who didn't know what was going on thought the police were there to arrest them for riding the buses, not to protect them. And then there were those few who didn't want to be inconvenienced. When the bus they were on passed a bus stop full of black people waiting for cabs, they ducked down low so nobody would see them.

That day I had no idea what the result was going to be, but I think everybody was quite amazed at that demonstration of people staying off the buses. It was a surprise to everybody, I think. As Mr. Nixon said, "We surprised ourselves." Never before had black people demonstrated so clearly how much those city buses depended on their business. More important, never before had the black community of Montgomery united in protest against segregation on the buses.

I didn't go to work that Monday. Instead that morning I went down to the courthouse for my trial. Parks went with me. I did not spend a lot of time planning what to wear, but I remember very clearly that I wore a straight, long-sleeved black dress with a white collar and cuffs, a small black velvet hat with pearls across the top, and a charcoal-gray coat. I carried a black purse and wore white gloves. I was not especially nervous. I knew what I had to do.

A lot of folks were down at the courthouse. Some people couldn't get in. Parks was almost prohibited from entering the courthouse. But when he said he was my husband, he was permitted to enter. You could hardly see the street for the crowds. Many members of the NAACP Youth Council were there, and they were all shouting their support.

There was a girl in the crowd named Mary Frances. She had a high-pitched voice, and it just came through the air: "Oh, she's so sweet. They've messed with the wrong one now." She said it like a little chant, "They've messed with the wrong one now."

It wasn't a long trial. The bus driver [James Blake] was the main prosecution witness.

I was not called to testify in my own behalf. Although my lawyers, Charles Langford and Fred Gray, entered a plea of "Not Guilty" for me, they did not intend to try to defend me against the charges. The point of making mine a test case was to allow me to be found guilty and then to appeal the conviction to a higher court. Only in higher courts could the segregation laws actually be changed, because the judges in the local courts were not going to do anything to change the way things were. So I was found guilty of violating the segregation laws and given a suspended sentence.[7] I was fined $10.00, plus $4.00 in court costs. The

---

7. In giving a *suspended sentence,* the judge has ordered Mrs. Parks to serve time in jail but, at least temporarily, will not actually require her to do so.

Vocabulary
inconvenience (in′ kən vēn′ yəns) *v.* to cause someone difficulty, bother, or hassle

crowd reacted angrily, but there was no organized protest.

I didn't go home after my trial was over. Instead I stayed downtown. I wanted to know what I could do. Fred Gray said he would appreciate it if I would stay in his office and answer the telephone, so I did. As soon as I got there, the telephone started ringing, because people had heard the news. I never did tell anybody who called that I was the one they were calling about. I just answered the phone and took messages. When Fred came back, Mr. Nixon took me home. It was getting pretty close to night, and I had to go home to get ready for the meeting at the Holt Street Baptist Church that evening.

Earlier that day Reverend Abernathy, who was about twenty-nine years old at the time, and some other ministers had met and decided to form the Montgomery Improvement Association (MIA). Mr. Nixon was there, and so was Fred Gray. The reason they wanted to form a brand-new organization was that they thought it would be better than just leaving the organizing to an established group like the NAACP. The NAACP was a relatively weak organization in Alabama; it was not a mass organization. Membership was kind of small, and you could hardly get people to join. They also wanted to rule out the NAACP so that the powers that be could not charge that this demonstration, this show of strength, was being led by outside agitators.

So they met that afternoon, and then they decided they should elect a president, and they elected the Reverend Martin Luther King, Jr., pastor of the Dexter Avenue Baptist Church. . . .

That night they had the meeting at the Holt Street Baptist Church, which was right in the black community so people wouldn't be afraid to attend. They didn't know how many people to expect, and they were not prepared for how many showed up. People filled that church, and hundreds more stood outside, so they set up a loudspeaker system so those people outside could hear what was going on inside. The meeting was already on when I got there, and I had a hard time getting into the church because there were so many people, inside and outside. I made it to the platform, and they gave me a seat.

The main thing they wanted to decide at that meeting was whether to continue the boycott. Some people thought we should quit while we were still ahead. And hardly anybody thought the boycott could go longer than the end of the week, which was four more days. If it did, it could be very dangerous, because everyone knew the whites wouldn't stand for it.

Mr. Nixon spoke first, as I recall. He was probably worried that people wouldn't really support a long boycott. He remembered all those years when it had been impossible to get black people to stand together. He said, "You who are afraid, you better get your hat and coat and go home. This is going to be a long-drawn-out affair. I want to tell you something: For years and years I've been talking about how I didn't want the children who came along behind me to have to suffer the indignities that I've suffered all these years. Well, I've

---

Vocabulary

indignity (in dig′ nə tē) *n.* an offense against one's pride or dignity; humiliation

The Reverend Martin Luther King Jr. addresses supporters of the bus boycott at the Holt Street Baptist Church, December 5, 1955.

changed my mind—I want to enjoy some of that freedom myself."

Dr. King was introduced to the audience as the president of the new Montgomery Improvement Association. He was a fine speaker, and he gave a speech that really got the crowd excited. This is part of what he said:

There comes a time that people get tired. We are here this evening to say to those who have mistreated us so long that we are tired—tired of being segregated and humiliated; tired of being kicked about by the brutal feet of <u>oppression</u>. . . . For many years we have shown amazing patience. We have sometimes given our white brothers the feeling that we like the way we are being treated. But we come here tonight to be saved from that patience that makes us patient with anything less than freedom and justice. One of the great glories of democracy is the right to protest for right. . . . [I]f you will protest courageously and yet with dignity and Christian love, when the history books are written in future generations the historians will pause and say, "There lived a great people—a black people—who injected new meaning and dignity into the veins of civilization." That is our challenge and our overwhelming responsibility.
(*Eyes on the Prize: America's Civil Rights Years 1954–1965*, page 76)

He received loud cheers and applause and *Amens*. . . .

After that the Reverend Ralph Abernathy read the list of demands that the Montgomery Improvement Association was going to present to the bus company and the city's white leaders. There were three demands: 1) Courteous treatment on the buses; 2) First-come, first-served seating, with whites in front and blacks in back; 3) Hiring of black drivers for the black bus routes. Then he asked the audience to vote on these demands by standing

Vocabulary

oppression (ə presh′ ən) *n.* the act of controlling or governing by the cruel and unjust use of force or authority

if they wanted to continue the boycott and make the demands. People started getting up, one or two at a time at first, and then more and more, until every single person in that church was standing, and outside the crowd was cheering "Yes!"

Stride Toward Freedom

The following Thursday, December 8, Dr. King and Attorney Fred Gray and others met with the three Montgomery city commissioners and representatives of the bus company. They presented the three demands. The bus company people denied that the drivers were discourteous to black riders and would not hear of hiring any black drivers on the predominantly[8] black routes. They also said the first-come, first-served seating arrangement was in violation of the city's segregation laws. Fred Gray said that wasn't true and that the same bus company allowed that type of arrangement in the city of Mobile, Alabama. But they wouldn't change their minds.

The city commissioners wouldn't go along with any of the demands either. They didn't want to give an inch, not even to reasonable demands. They were afraid of compromising in any way with black people.

The boycott lasted through that week, and then through the next. No one had any idea how long it would last. Some people said it couldn't last, but it seemed like those who said that were the white people and not us. The whites did everything they could do to stop it.

The police started getting after the groups of blacks who were waiting at the bus stops for the black-owned cabs to pick them up. Then they threatened to arrest the cab drivers if they did not charge their regular fare, which I think was forty-five cents, to go downtown instead of ten cents like the buses charged. White private citizens resisted the boycott too.

A lot of people lost their jobs because they supported the boycott. Both Parks and I lost our jobs. . . .

After that I worked at home, taking in sewing. I started traveling quite a bit, making appearances because of my arrest and the boycott. And then I did work for the MIA.

I was on the executive board of directors of the MIA and I did whatever was needed. I dispensed clothing and shoes to people who needed them. We had an abundance of clothing and shoes sent to us from all parts of the country. Many people needed those things because they were out of work and unable to buy clothing. Those who had jobs wore out many pairs of shoes walking to and from work. I also worked for a short while as a dispatcher for the MIA Transportation Committee.

When the police started arresting cab drivers for not charging full fare, the MIA asked for volunteer drivers. Jo Ann Robinson was one. The churches collected money and bought several station wagons. Ordinary black people contributed, and so did some important white people in Montgomery, like the Durrs. As a dispatcher, I was responsible for taking calls from people who needed rides and then making calls to the drivers of private cars and the church station wagons to see that the people were picked up wherever they were.

8. Here, *predominantly* means "chiefly; for the most part."

After a while quite a sophisticated[9] system was developed. There were twenty private cars and fourteen station wagons. There were thirty-two pickup and transfer sites, and scheduled service from five-thirty in the morning until twelve-thirty at night. About 30,000 people were transported to and from work every day. . . .

The Montgomery Improvement Association held regular meetings, every Monday and Thursday night, to keep the people inspired and to talk about the latest problems and what to do about them. January came. The white people were getting angrier and angrier. . . .

Now Mayor Gayle announced that he would no longer negotiate with the boycotters, although we didn't see that he'd been doing much negotiating anyhow. He called the leaders of the boycott a bunch of Negro radicals.[10] There was real violence against the people by this time. Dr. King's home was bombed at the end of January. Two days later Mr. Nixon's home was bombed. Nobody tried to bomb my home, but I did get a lot of threatening telephone calls. They'd say things like, "You're the cause of all this. You should be killed." It was frightening to get those calls, and it really bothered me when Mama answered the telephone and it was one of those calls.

In early February Fred Gray filed suit in U.S. District Court saying that bus segregation was unconstitutional. By that time the appeal of my case had been thrown out on a technicality,[11] meaning my conviction was upheld. The new suit was our way of getting tough. The City Commission and the bus company and the mayor wouldn't even agree that bus drivers were not polite. Fred Gray wanted to challenge the whole bus-segregation system and go all the way to the Supreme Court. Clifford Durr offered to assist him. The suit was filed on behalf of five women who had been mistreated on the buses.

Meanwhile, the boycott was costing the bus company money. Every day bus after bus would go by with only one or two white riders. Then they stopped running the buses altogether. The boycott was also hurting downtown businesses, and so a group of white businessmen calling themselves Men of Montgomery decided to try to negotiate with the MIA themselves. But nothing came of those meetings.

Around the middle of February a group of white attorneys came up with an old law that prohibited boycotts, and on February 21 a grand jury handed down eighty-nine indictments[12] against Dr. King, more than twenty other ministers, leaders of the MIA, and other citizens. I was reindicted.

We were all fingerprinted. News photographers had heard about the indictments and were there to photograph us being fingerprinted. The picture of me

---

9. A *sophisticated* system is one that is developed to a high degree.
10. A *radical* is someone who supports or demands extreme change.

11. In legal terms, a *technicality* is a very small detail.
12. A *grand jury* is a special jury that hears accusations in criminal cases. If its members decide that there is enough evidence for a trial, they issue an *indictment,* which is the formal legal charge against the accused.

Vocabulary
negotiate (ni gō′ shē āt′) *v.* to discuss in order to bring about an agreement

being fingerprinted was carried on the front page of *The New York Times*. In later years people would use that picture thinking it was from my first arrest. The MIA paid everybody's bail, and we were released and went home until the trials started.

The trials began in March, and Dr. King was the first to be tried. It was March 19 and I went down to the courthouse. People crowded around and tried to get inside, but they weren't letting in anyone unless they had a seat. They wouldn't let anyone sit on the floor or stand in the aisle. There were a lot of witnesses in his defense, testifying about conditions on the buses. . . . People were not reluctant to speak out.

They found Dr. King guilty. He was sentenced to pay a $500 fine or serve a year at hard labor. He never did either, because the conviction was appealed successfully. He was the only one they actually tried. But of course he was more determined than ever to continue the boycott, because of the way the city of Montgomery had treated us. The people were willing. All through the spring we walked and carpooled.

Rosa Parks is fingerprinted after she and eighty-eight others were indicted on February 21, 1956 for boycotting the Montgomery buses.

There was a lot of interest in the boycott from outside Montgomery now, because of all the attention from the press. I was invited to tell about what had happened to me at various churches, schools, and organizations. I did whatever I could—accepting expense money but no speaking fees—and this helped raise money for station wagons and other expenses. I spent most of the spring making appearances and speeches. Parks was concerned for my safety, but I had no unpleasant experiences.

In June a special three-judge federal District Court ruled two to one in favor of our suit against segregation on the buses. But the city commissioners appealed the decision to the U.S. Supreme Court. We knew it would take several months for the Supreme Court to decide.

Summer came and I was back in Montgomery. We still stayed off the buses. The white people tried to break the boycott by not giving the church cars any insurance. All the churches operated the station wagons, and had their names on the sides. Without insurance, the cars could not operate legally. Every time they got insurance from a new company, the policy would suddenly be canceled. But Dr. King got in touch with a black insurance agent in Atlanta named T. M. Alexander, and T. M. Alexander got Lloyd's of London, the big insurance company in England, to write a policy for the church-operated cars.

E. D. Nixon escorts Parks up the courtroom steps for the boycott trial in March 1956.

Next, Mayor Gayle went to court to try to get an order preventing black people from gathering on street corners while waiting for the church cars. Mayor Gayle said they were a "public nuisance" because they sang loudly and bothered other people. He got a court to issue such an order, but that order came on the very same day that the U.S. Supreme Court ruled in our favor, that segregation on the Montgomery buses was unconstitutional.

That was on November 13, 1956. Dr. King called a mass meeting to tell us the news, and everybody was overjoyed. But the MIA did not tell the people to go back on the buses. The written order from the

Supreme Court would not arrive for another month or so. We stayed off the buses until it was official.

The written order from the U.S. Supreme Court arrived on December 20, and the following day we returned to the buses. The boycott had lasted more than a year. Dr. King, the Reverend Abernathy, Mr. Nixon, and Glen Smiley, one of the few white people in Montgomery who had supported the boycott, made a great show of riding the first integrated bus in Montgomery. . . . Three reporters from *Look* magazine . . . had me get on and off buses so they could take pictures.

James Blake, the driver who'd had me arrested, was the driver of one of the buses I got on. He didn't want to take any honors, and I wasn't too happy about being there myself. I really could have done without that. I got on two different buses, I guess, and each time they took pictures until they were satisfied. The reporter sat behind me each time while the photographer took pictures. . . .

Integrating the Montgomery buses did not go smoothly. Snipers[13] fired at buses, and the city imposed curfews on the buses, not letting them run after five P.M., which meant that people who worked from nine to five couldn't ride the buses home. A group of

whites tried to form a whites-only bus line, but that didn't work. The homes and churches of some ministers were bombed, as I mentioned. But eventually most of the violence died down. Black people were not going to be scared off the buses any more than they were going to be scared onto them when they refused to ride.

African Americans in other cities, like Birmingham, Alabama, and Tallahassee, Florida, started their own boycotts of the segregated buses.

The direct-action civil-rights movement had begun.

Civil Rights Activist, 1983. Marshall D. Rumbaugh. Painted limewood, height: 33 in. National Portrait Gallery, Washington, D.C. Gift of Barry Bingham.

Viewing the sculpture: How do you think the artist feels about what the sculpture shows? How can you tell?

---

13. *Snipers* are people who shoot at others from concealed places.

Vocabulary
impose (im pōz′) *v.* to apply legally; enforce

Responding to Literature

PERSONAL RESPONSE

- ◆ What questions would you like to ask Rosa Parks about the courage she showed? Record your questions in your journal.
- ◆ Which part of Rosa Parks's experience affected you more as a reader? What details about historic events did you find most surprising? Write your response in your journal.

Analyzing Literature

RECALL

1. Why did Rosa Parks decide not to give up her seat on the bus?
2. Who did Rosa Parks consult before deciding to become a test case for desegregation of buses?
3. How did Dr. Martin Luther King Jr. contribute to the success of the bus boycott?
4. How did the bus boycott make life difficult for local African Americans?

INTERPRET

5. Why do you think Rosa Parks chose to include so many details about the incident on the bus?
6. Why did Parks agree to become a test case and support the boycott? Was she right to be concerned about the results? Explain your answer.
7. Why was Dr. King a good leader for the boycott?
8. In what ways did the African American community show its courage during the boycott?

EVALUATE AND CONNECT

9. Rosa Parks does not reveal very much about her emotions during the difficult year that began with her arrest. Why do you think she chose to use this factual **tone** in her autobiography?
10. If you were living in Alabama during the time of segregation, what do you imagine you would have thought about segregated buses?

LITERARY ELEMENTS

Sequence of Events

In nonfiction, when the writer is describing actual events, **sequence** is extremely important. If the article or book is about important moments in history, having the correct sequence is essential. Rosa Parks helps the reader keep track of sequence by using dates and words that indicate time, such as *then, earlier, eventually, meanwhile,* and *after.*

1. How well does Rosa Parks help the reader keep track of the events during the Montgomery bus boycott? Support your opinion with examples.

2. Find three examples of the use of sequence words in the selection.

● See **Literary Terms Handbook,** p. R10.

Extending Your Response

Writing About Literature

Summarizing A **summary** briefly tells the main ideas, important events, or key points in a piece of writing. Only the most essential details should be included. Summarize the main events that took place in the excerpt from *Rosa Parks: My Story,* beginning with Rosa Parks's arrest. Write your summary so that someone who has not read the selection will clearly appreciate the importance of the events Parks describes.

Creative Writing

Writing the Story of Rosa Parks Using what you know about Rosa Parks's role in the bus boycott, write the text for a children's picture book about this Civil Rights movement heroine. You might want to illustrate your story and present it in a book format.

Literature Groups

Picture It! Imagine that your group has been asked to design a poster to celebrate the anniversary of the Montgomery bus boycott. Discuss a memorable scene from the selection. As a group, assign roles to plan and create a sketch that best represents the boycott. Label the poster and present it to the other groups.

Interdisciplinary Activity

Social Studies—Time line Study the selection, and take notes on every important date mentioned. Plot out the dates on a time line, and label the major events of the bus boycott. If you can't tell the exact date on which an event occurred, try to figure out which dates the event would fit between and note it in that place on the line. Use your time line to retell the story of the bus boycott to a classmate.

Performing

Create a Skit Rosa Parks has given the reader a minute-by-minute description of the bus ride that led to her arrest. Use her words to write a script to be performed as a short skit. Choose actors for the speaking and nonspeaking parts. Line up desk chairs with an aisle between them to represent the bus.

Reading Further

If you would like to read more about the Civil Rights movement, try these books:

Martin Luther King, Jr. by Jacqueline L. Harris
They Had a Dream by Jules Archer
We Shall Overcome by Fred Powledge

📖 **Save your work for your portfolio.**

Skill Minilessons

GRAMMAR AND LANGUAGE • NOUNS

A *common noun* names any person, place, thing, or idea. A *proper noun* names a specific person, place, thing, or idea. Proper nouns are capitalized.

PRACTICE Write each noun in the sentences below in one of two lists: proper nouns and common nouns. Capitalize any proper nouns.
1. The story of rosa parks is inspiring.
2. Rosa parks showed courage in a simple act.
3. The results of her arrest in montgomery, alabama, still affect life in the united states.
4. No state can make a law that discriminates against individuals.
5. The rights of all people are guaranteed under the federal law of the united states.

● For more about nouns, see **Language Handbook,** p. R30.

READING AND THINKING • CAUSE AND EFFECT

When historians study historic events, they often think in terms of **cause and effect.** Each event was caused by other events. For example, during the Montgomery bus boycott, Rosa Parks refused to give up her seat. The effect was that she was arrested. Her arrest caused people in the Civil Rights movement to start the bus boycott.

PRACTICE Answer these questions about other causes and effects in *Rosa Parks: My Story.*
1. What caused African American cab drivers to stop at all the bus stops?
2. What effect did the availability of inexpensive cab rides have on the African Americans trying to get to work?
3. What effect did Dr. King's speech about the boycott have on the people listening?
4. What action did the city commissioners take because the federal district court ruled against segregation on the buses?
5. What finally caused Montgomery city officials to integrate the city's buses?

● For more about cause and effect, see **Reading Handbook,** p. R89.

VOCABULARY • UNLOCKING MEANING

Sometimes a new word is just a word you know with a prefix or suffix attached. Sometimes it shares a root with a familiar word. Use what you know. For example, now that you know what the verb *mobilize* means, you can guess that the noun *mobilization* means an effort to organize or prepare people and resources for action.

PRACTICE Match each word with its meaning.
1. compliance
2. resignation
3. renegotiate
4. demobilize
5. oppressive

a. to try to reach a new, modified agreement
b. harsh; cruel and unfair
c. a patient, but not happy, acceptance
d. a yielding to authority
e. to return to a normal condition after preparing for an emergency

Writing WORKSHOP

Narrative Writing: Autobiographical Anecdote

A story of your own experiences—an **autobiographical anecdote**—can speak to readers and to you in a special way. When you write an autobiographical anecdote, you may see your experiences in a new light.

Assignment: Use the process shown in this Workshop to create a memorable autobiographical anecdote.

● As you write your autobiographical anecdote, see the **Writing Handbook,** pp. R48–R52.

> ### EVALUATION RUBRIC
> By the time you complete this Writing Workshop, you will have
> - written about a memorable personal experience
> - used the first-person point of view
> - written an action-oriented introduction and arranged events in time order
> - developed a setting and vivid characters, using dialogue and describing gestures and movements
> - created a meaningful conclusion
> - presented an anecdote free of errors in grammar, usage, and mechanics

The Writing Process

PREWRITING

PREWRITING TIP
A small experience that you recall clearly will work better than a big experience that you can only vaguely remember.

● Gather Ideas

Which experiences have meant the most to you? Rosa Parks wrote about her involvement in a historic event; Amy Tan and Ernesto Galarza selected more personal experiences to write about. Try the following to get your ideas flowing:

- Brainstorm to make a list of events in your life, big and small.

- List your experiences by category, such as *funniest, hardest, saddest, most mysterious, most surprising,* or *most rewarding.*

Choose one event as your topic. To gather the details you'll need, try filling in a chart like the one below.

Event: when my friend Ray fell into the canal				
Sight	**Sound**	**Touch**	**Smell**	**Taste**
brown, surging water	swoosh and churn of water	Ray's slippery hands	musty flood smell	
Ray's frightened eyes	big splash	pull of current		

● Know Your Audience and Purpose

Will you write to share an insight? Or will you write just to entertain? Decide on a purpose. Then consider your audience—probably this will be your classmates and teacher. What details can help them relive your experience? Think of specifics about the setting—time and place—and about the people involved—including you. You might jot notes on a story map, as shown below.

● Map It Out

Like a good short story, your anecdote will have a plot with a beginning, a middle, and an end. As you plan your anecdote, review the Stages in Plot Development chart on pages 144–145 of this book. Filling in a story map can help you organize the stages of your anecdote.

Setting	**Beginning**	**Middle**	**End**
by the canal after a storm	Ray fell in. The current caught him. I grabbed his hand.	_____ _____ _____ _____ _____ _____	_____ _____ _____ _____ _____
People my friend Ray, age 9, always joking; me, age 9, no confidence			

Writing WORKSHOP

DRAFTING

DRAFTING TIP

Remember that as the first-person narrator, you are telling what happened from your point of view. Transitions, such as *at first, then, soon, in a few hours, that night,* or *finally,* will help you keep the order of events clear for your readers.

● Start with Action and Dialogue

In your first sentence, describe a specific incident that will catch the attention of your readers. Then set the scene and describe the people involved. Add details from your prewriting notes. Use dialogue and describe gestures and movements to show more about personalities, actions, and feelings.

> **STUDENT MODEL • DRAFTING**
>
> Muddy water surged past our feet. A storm had turned our irrigation canal into a rushing river. Ray struck a goofy pose. "Look!" he laughed. "I'm a surfer!" Then there was a slip and a splash.

Complete Student Model on pp. R103–R104.

● Use Chronological Order

With your story map as a guide, write what happened first, next, and last. You might start a new paragraph whenever the scene or action shifts. At the end, don't just stop. Sum up what the experience means to you or how it has changed you.

REVISING

REVISING TIP

Be sure that your conclusion fits your purpose. To entertain, close with a striking comment or scene. To share an insight, state it clearly at the end.

● Consider Changes

Use the **Rubric for Revising** to find ways to strengthen your draft. Then, ask a classmate to read your anecdote and to retell it. If your reader is confused, you may need to work on your organization. Try rearranging paragraphs or adding transitions.

> **RUBRIC FOR REVISING**
>
> Your revised autobiographical anecdote should have
> - an introduction that describes an action and establishes the setting
> - a first-person point of view
> - a plot with a clear beginning, middle, and end
> - transitions that point out the order of events
> - vividly described narrative action and well-developed characters
> - lively dialogue and effective descriptions
> - a striking conclusion
> - no vaguely worded or irrelevant details
> - no errors in grammar, usage, and mechanics

EDITING/PROOFREADING

The **Proofreading Checklist** here and on the inside back cover can help you spot errors. To check your sentences for sentence fragments, use information from the **Grammar Link** on page 12.

Grammar Hint

When you review your sentences, check verb tenses. Avoid accidental shifts from past to present tense. Keep tenses consistent.

My hand ached so much, I just gave up. I relaxed my grip, and Ray was gone.

PROOFREADING CHECKLIST
- ☑ Each sentence has a subject and predicate.
- ☑ Verb tenses are consistent.
- ☑ Dialogue is punctuated correctly.
- ☑ End marks and commas are used correctly.
- ☑ Capital letters are used correctly.
- ☑ Spelling is correct.

STUDENT MODEL · EDITING/PROOFREADING

Ray crawled onto the bank, shivering. "Why did you let go?" he asks.^ed

Complete Student Model on pp. R103–R104.

Complete Student Model

For a complete version of the model developed in this Workshop, see **Writing Workshop Models**, pp. R103–R104.

PUBLISHING/PRESENTING

If possible, use word processing software to make a neat final copy of your anecdote. You might read it aloud to a small group. Ask group members to write you notes telling you which parts they found most memorable and why.

PRESENTING TIP
When reading aloud, don't rush. Pause for commas, periods, and paragraph breaks.

Reflecting

Write a page exploring your response to these questions:

- Which part of this Workshop did you enjoy most?

- Would you like to write more autobiographical anecdotes? Why or why not?

📖 **Save your work for your portfolio.**

Theme Assessment

 ## Responding to the Theme

1. Which selection in this theme most helped you think about who you are and what you want to be? Explain your answer.

2. What new thoughts and ideas do you have about the following after reading the selections in this theme?
   - people's feelings and thoughts about their own identities
   - the importance of setting life goals and working hard to achieve those goals

3. Present your theme project to the class.

 ## Analyzing Literature

COMPARE POEMS

Choose two selections from this theme to compare. You may compare the characters, the events, or the themes of the selections. Use quotations from the selections to support your comparison.

Evaluate and Set Goals

1. Which of the following tasks was most rewarding? Which was most difficult?
   - reading and thinking about the selections
   - doing independent writing
   - analyzing the selections in discussions
   - making presentations
   - performing dramatizations
   - doing research

2. Use the following scale to assess your work in this theme. Give at least two reasons for your assessment.

   4 = outstanding   2 = fair

   3 = good   1 = weak

3. Based on what you found difficult in this theme, choose a goal to work toward in the next theme.
   - Write down your goal and three steps you will take to help you reach it.
   - Meet with your teacher to review your goal and your plan for achieving it.

 # Build Your Portfolio

SELECT

Choose two pieces of work you did in this theme to include in your portfolio. Use these questions to help you choose.

- ✦ Which do you think is your best work?
- ✦ Which work "stretched" you the most?
- ✦ From which work did you learn the most?
- ✦ Which did you enjoy the most?

REFLECT

Write some notes to accompany the pieces you selected. Use these questions to guide you.

- ✦ What do you like best about the piece?
- ✦ What did you learn from creating it?
- ✦ What might you do differently if you were beginning this piece again?

Reading on Your Own

Have you enjoyed reading the stories and poems in this theme? If you have, you might try reading the following books.

The Witch of Blackbird Pond
by Elizabeth George Speare
In Puritan New England in 1687, a high-spirited teenager befriends an old woman known as the Witch of Blackbird Pond and finds herself accused of witchcraft.

Baseball in April and Other Stories
by Gary Soto Soto's own life while growing up poor in California's Central Valley inspired these stories about Mexican American teenagers facing the kinds of experiences most teens face.

No-No Boy
by John Okada Kenji and Ichiro, two young men sent to a "relocation camp" when the United States was fighting Japan in World War II, take different routes as they struggle with their identity as Japanese Americans.

Where You Belong
by Mary Ann McGuigan
Fiona, her mother, and three siblings are evicted from their home. After an abusive father seems to provide no refuge for her, the thirteen-year-old Fiona tries to discover where she belongs.

Standardized Test Practice

Read the following passage. Then read each question on page 111. Decide which is the best answer to each question. Mark the letter for that answer on your paper.

Taking Inventory

Mr. Krauzer seemed pleased with Randy's application for a job as stock boy. He gestured toward the aisles of groceries. "We need an accurate inventory," he said. "Are you up to it? Here's an instruction page. Look it over, and we'll talk about it."

Inventory Instructions

Fill out all parts of the inventory page. Accuracy is very important.

1 Fill in the appropriate information at the top of the inventory sheet.

2 List the items and the price per unit. Record the number of units on the shelf in the TALLY column.

3 If an item is on sale, put an X in the appropriate column.

4 Do not record more than one aisle's inventory on a single sheet. Do not use two sheets to record the inventory of a single aisle.

5 Double-check all information.

6 When you are satisfied that the report is accurate, sign your name and write your employee number at the bottom before <u>submitting</u> it to the manager on duty.

7 Bring your finished inventory sheets to the manager on duty.

INVENTORY SHEET

Date May 5, 1999
Aisle 3

Item	Tally	Price	Sale
Juicy O's 8 oz. Cans	25	$0.99	X
Jalapeño Rings	35	1.09	
Stewed Tomatoes in Water	15	0.89	
Miller's Premium Sardines	20	1.99	X

Joe Johnson
Employee Number 410

---

1   An inventory sheet is most like —
    A   a schedule.
    B   an article.
    C   a list.
    D   a brochure.

2   If all the numbers in the tally column were added up, the total wold show —
    J   the price of each item.
    K   the number of items in the store.
    L   the number of employees.
    M   the number of items in Aisle 3.

3   There is enough information in the passage to conclude that —
    A   Randy has never had a job before.
    B   Jalapeno rings cost more than stewed tomatoes.
    C   Mr. Krauzer is the owner of the grocery store.
    D   Juicy O's costs the same as stewed tomatoes when on sale.

4   Which is a FACT in this passage?
    J   The inventory system at Krauzer's is remarkably efficient.
    K   Double-checking your tallies is a sure-fire way to avoid making mistakes.
    L   It is necessary to note when items are on sale.
    M   More than one aisle's inventory is supposed to be recorded on a single regular Inventory Sheet.

5   In this passage, the word <u>submitting</u> means —
    A   giving.
    B   being defeated.
    C   hiding.
    D   recording.

6   All finished sheets should be —
    J   filed in the office at the end of each day.
    K   brought to the manager on duty.
    L   given to Mr. Krauzer.
    M   filled out in triplicate.

Winds of Change

66 **The need for change bulldozed a road down the center of my mind.** 99

—Maya Angelou, *I Know Why the Caged Bird Sings*

Hawthorne Dusk, 1996. Diane Griffiths. Watercolor and crayon, 60 x 75 cm.
The Grand Design Gallery, Leeds, England.

112

THEME CONTENTS

GENRE FOCUS *FICTION*

Exploring the Theme

Winds of Change

Life never stays the same. The world is constantly changing. In this theme, you will meet people who learn to deal with changes within themselves and in their lives. Try one of the options below to start thinking about the theme of change.

Starting Points

TIMES CHANGE
Think of several things Calvin's father may have done as a child on a nice day. Then think about an invention, a game, or another activity you enjoy that did not exist when your parents were your age.

- Work with a partner. Role-play a trip in a time machine. Introduce your invention, game, or activity to a teenager from the past.

CHANGE IS IN THE AIR
Think about the changes in your own life. Write a few notes to answer these questions.

- What has changed in your life in the last few years? What effect have these changes had?
- What would you like to change about your life? What would you like to always stay the same?

Calvin and Hobbes
by Bill Watterson

Theme Projects

As you read the selections in this theme, try out one of these projects. Work on your own, with a partner, or with a group.

LEARNING FOR LIFE
Writing a Proposal
How can your school be improved? Develop a proposal addressed to the board of education. Think about improvements that could be made without spending a huge amount of time or money. Suggest ideas for ways to accomplish your goals. Draft your proposal and share it with your class.

CRITICAL VIEWING
Picturing Myself in the Future
What will you be doing ten years from now? Where will you live? How will your life be different?

1. List changes you think might happen to you in the next ten years. Will you go to college? Have a job? Travel? Have a family?

2. Draw a picture or make a collage showing how your life may change in the future.

*inter*NET CONNECTION

Search the Web for more project ideas. Also, learn more about the authors and ideas featured in this theme by visiting lit.glencoe.com.

MULTIMEDIA PROJECT
Create a Visual History Exhibit
Use collected photographs and objects to create a history exhibit of your city, town, or neighborhood that shows how it has changed over the years.

1. Find and copy pictures that show the oldest buildings and the people who lived or worked in them. Gather objects from your local historical society, historians, neighbors, and your local government.

2. Design an exhibit that compares then and now. Include photographs, documents, and objects from the past and present.

Before You Read
Hollywood and the Pits

MEET CHERYLENE LEE

I t's hard to imagine a successful stage, movie, and TV performer becoming a paleontologist, but that's just what Cherylene Lee did. Like the narrator in "Hollywood and the Pits," Lee was a child performer in her hometown of Los Angeles. After earning degrees in paleontology and geology, she began writing stories, poetry, and plays.

"Hollywood and the Pits" appears in the collection American Dragons: Twenty-Five Asian American Voices, *edited by Laurence Yep and published in 1995.*

READING FOCUS

Are there parts of your childhood self that you have left behind in the past few years?

Journal

Describe how your interests and hobbies have—or have not—changed in the last year or two. Write about how becoming a teenager has affected your childhood interests.

Setting a Purpose

Read to discover one teen's view on change.

BUILDING BACKGROUND

The Time and Place   It is 1968 in Los Angeles, California. In the middle of the city, close to the glamour of Hollywood, is an archaeological site filled with the skeletons of prehistoric creatures.

VOCABULARY PREVIEW

obsessed (əb sesd′) *adj.* overly concentrated or focused on a single emotion or idea; p. 118

bewildered (bi wil′ dərd) *adj.* very confused; p. 118

barrage (bə räzh′) *n.* a heavy concentration or great outpouring, as of words; p. 119

excavated (eks′ kə vāt′ əd) *adj.* uncovered or removed by digging; unearthed; p. 119

immobilize (i mō′ bə līz′) *v.* to make unable to move; fix in place; p. 119

painstaking (pānz′ tā′ king) *adj.* requiring close, careful labor or attention; p. 123

predator (pred′ ə tər) *n.* an animal, such as a lion or hawk, that kills other animals for food; p. 125

deception (di sep′ shən) *n.* that which fools or misleads; p. 125

scavenger (skav′ in jər) *n.* an animal, such as a hyena or vulture, that feeds on dead, decaying animals; p. 125

HOLLYWOOD AND THE PITS

Cherylene Lee

In 1968 when I was fifteen, the pit opened its secret to me. I breathed, ate, slept, dreamed about the La Brea[1] Tar Pits. I spent summer days working the archaeological dig[2] and in dreams saw the bones glistening, the broken pelvises, the skulls, the vertebrae looped like a woman's pearls hanging on an invisible cord. I welcomed those dreams. I wanted to know where the next skeleton was, identify it, record its position, discover whether it was whole or not. I wanted to know where to dig in the coarse, black, gooey sand. I lost myself there and found something else.

---

1. *La Brea* (lə brā′ ə)
2. An *archaeological* (är′ kē ə loj′ i kəl) *dig* is a place where objects such as ancient bones are dug up for study.

Hollywood and the Pits

My mother thought something was wrong with me. Was it good for a teenager to be fascinated by death? Especially animal death in the Pleistocene?[3] Was it normal to be so obsessed by a sticky brown hole in the ground in the center of Los Angeles? I don't know if it was normal or not, but it seemed perfectly logical to me. After all, I grew up in Hollywood, a place where dreams and nightmares can often take the same shape. What else would a child actor do?

"Thank you very much, dear. We'll be letting you know."

I knew what that meant. It meant I would never hear from them again. I didn't get the job. I heard that phrase a lot that year.

I walked out of the plush office, leaving behind the casting director, producer, director, writer, and whoever else came to listen to my reading for a semiregular role on a family sit-com.[4] The carpet made no sound when I opened and shut the door.

I passed the other girls waiting in the reception room, each poring over her script. The mothers were waiting in a separate room, chattering about their daughters' latest commercials, interviews, callbacks, jobs. It sounded like every Oriental[5] kid in Hollywood was working except me.

My mother used to have a lot to say in those waiting rooms. Ever since I was three, when I started at the Meglin Kiddie Dance Studio, I was dubbed "The Chinese Shirley Temple"—always the one to be picked at auditions and interviews, always the one to get the speaking lines, always called "the one-shot kid," because I could do my scenes in one take—even tight close-ups. My mother would only talk about me behind my back because she didn't want me to hear her brag, but I knew that she was proud. In a way I was proud too, though I never dared admit it. I didn't want to be called a show-off. But I didn't exactly know what I did to be proud of either. I only knew that at fifteen I was now being passed over at all these interviews when before I would be chosen.

My mother looked at my face hopefully when I came into the room. I gave her a quick shake of the head. She looked bewildered. I felt bad for my mother then. How could I explain it to her? I didn't understand it myself. We left saying polite good-byes to all the other mothers.

We didn't say anything until the studio parking lot, where we had to search for our old blue Chevy among rows and rows of parked cars baking in the Hollywood heat.

"How did it go? Did you read clearly? Did you tell them you're available?"

"I don't think they care if I'm available or not, Ma."

"Didn't you read well? Did you remember to look up so they could see your eyes? Did they ask you if you could play the piano? Did you tell them you could learn?"

---

3. *Pleistocene* (plīs´ tə sēn´) is the name of the period that began about two million years ago, when glaciers covered much of North America and Europe.
4. *Sit-com* is short for "situation comedy," the most common type of TV comedy series.
5. People of eastern Asia and their descendants are sometimes referred to as being *Oriental*, which means "of the East."

Vocabulary

obsessed (əb sesd´) *adj.* overly concentrated or focused on a single emotion or idea
bewildered (bi wil´ dərd) *adj.* very confused

The barrage of questions stopped when we finally spotted our car. I didn't answer her. My mother asked about the piano because I lost out in an audition once to a Chinese girl who already knew how to play.

My mother took off the towel that shielded the steering wheel from the heat. "You're getting to be such a big girl," she said, starting the car in neutral. "But don't worry, there's always next time. You have what it takes. That's special." She put the car into forward and we drove through a parking lot that had an endless number of identical cars all facing the same direction. We drove back home in silence.

In the La Brea Tar Pits many of the excavated bones belong to juvenile mammals. Thousands of years ago thirsty young animals in the area were drawn to watering holes, not knowing they were traps. Those inviting pools had false bottoms made of sticky tar, which immobilized its victims and preserved their bones when they died. Innocence trapped by ignorance. The tar pits record that well.

I suppose a lot of my getting into show business in the first place was a matter of luck—being in the right place at the right time. My sister, seven years older than me, was a member of the Meglin Kiddie Dance Studio long before I started lessons. Once during the annual recital held at the Shrine Auditorium, she was spotted by a Hollywood agent who handled only Oriental performers. The agent sent my sister out for a role in the CBS *Playhouse 90* television show *The Family Nobody Wanted*. The producer said she was too tall for the part. But true to my mother's training of always having a positive reply, my sister said to the producer, "But I have a younger sister . . ." which started my show-biz career at the tender age of three.

My sister and I were lucky. We enjoyed singing and dancing, we were natural hams, and our parents never discouraged us. In fact they were our biggest fans. My mother chauffeured us to all our dance lessons, lessons we begged to take. She drove us to interviews, took us to studios, went on location with us, drilled us on our lines, made sure we kept up our schoolwork and didn't sass back the tutors hired by studios to teach us for three hours a day. She never complained about being a stage mother. She said that we made her proud.

My father must have felt pride too, because he paid for a choreographer[6] to put together our sister act: "The World Famous Lee Sisters," fifteen minutes of song and dance, real vaudeville stuff. We joked about that a

---

6. A *choreographer* creates or directs dance movements.

Vocabulary
barrage (bə räzh′) *n.* a heavy concentration or great outpouring, as of words
excavated (eks′ kə vāt′ əd) *adj.* uncovered or removed by digging; unearthed
immobilize (i mō′ bə līz′) *v.* to make unable to move; fix in place

As a child, Cherylene Lee performed with some of the great Hollywood entertainers. Here, she's seen with dancer Gene Kelly (above) and with singer and TV-show host Dinah Shore (right).

lot, "Yeah, the Lee Sisters—Ug-Lee and Home-Lee," but we definitely had a good time. So did our parents. Our father especially liked our getting booked into Las Vegas at the New Frontier Hotel on the Strip. He liked to gamble there, though he said the craps tables in that hotel were "cold," not like the casinos in downtown Las Vegas, where all the "hot" action took place.

In Las Vegas our sister act was part of a show called "Oriental Holiday." The show was about a Hollywood producer going to the Far East, finding undiscovered talent, and bringing it back to the U.S. We did two shows a night in the main showroom, one at eight and one at twelve, and on weekends a third show at two in the morning. It ran the entire summer often to standing-room-only audiences—a thousand people a show.

Our sister act worked because of the age and height difference. My sister then was fourteen and nearly five foot two; I was seven and very small for my age—people thought we were cute. We had song-and-dance routines to old tunes like

"Ma, He's Making Eyes at Me," "Together," and "I'm Following You," and my father hired a writer to adapt the lyrics to "I Enjoy Being a Girl," which came out "We Enjoy Being Chinese." We also told corny jokes, but the Las Vegas audience seemed to enjoy it. Here we were, two kids, staying up late and jumping around, and getting paid besides. To me the applause sometimes sounded like static, sometimes like distant waves. It always amazed me when people applauded. The owner of the hotel liked us so much, he invited us back to perform in shows for three summers in a row. That was before I grew too tall and the sister act didn't seem so cute anymore.

Many of the skeletons in the tar pits are found incomplete—particularly the skeletons of the young, which have only soft cartilage connecting the bones. In life the soft tissue allows for growth, but in death it dissolves quickly. Thus the skeletons of young animals are more apt to be scattered, especially the vertebrae protecting the spinal cord. In the tar pits, the central ends of many vertebrae are found unconnected to any skeleton. Such bone fragments are shaped like valentines, disks that are slightly lobed—heart-shaped shields that have lost their connection to what they were meant to protect.

I never felt my mother pushed me to do something I didn't want to do. But I always knew if something I did pleased her. She was generous with her praise, and I was sensitive when she withheld it. I didn't like to disappoint her.

I took to performing easily, and since I had started out so young, making movies or doing shows didn't feel like anything special. It was part of my childhood—like going to the dentist one morning or going to school the next. I didn't wonder if I wanted a particular role or wanted to be in a show or how I would feel if I didn't get in. Until I was fifteen, it never occurred to me that one day I wouldn't get parts or that I might not "have what it takes."

When I was younger, I got a lot of roles because I was so small for my age. When I was nine years old, I could pass for five or six. I was really short. I was always teased about it when I was in elementary school, but I didn't mind because my height got me movie jobs. I could read and memorize lines that actual five-year-olds couldn't. My mother told people she made me sleep in a drawer so I wouldn't grow any bigger.

But when I turned fifteen, it was as if my body, which hadn't grown for so many years, suddenly made up for lost time. I grew five inches in seven months. My mother was amazed. Even I couldn't get used to it. I kept knocking into things, my clothes didn't fit right, I felt awkward and clumsy when I moved. Dumb things that I had gotten away with, like paying children's prices at the movies instead of junior admission, I couldn't do anymore. I wasn't a shrimp or a small fry any longer. I was suddenly normal.

Before that summer my mother had always claimed she wanted me to be normal. She didn't want me to become spoiled by the attention I received when I was working at the studios. I still had chores to do at home, went to public school when I wasn't working, was punished severely when I behaved badly. She didn't want me to feel I was different just because I was in the movies. When I was eight, I was interviewed by a reporter who wanted to know if I thought I had a big head.

Hollywood and the Pits

"Sure," I said.

"No you don't," my mother interrupted, which was really unusual, because she generally never said anything. She wanted me to speak for myself.

I didn't understand the question. My sister had always made fun of my head. She said my body was too tiny for the weight—I looked like a walking Tootsie Pop. I thought the reporter was making the same observation.

"She better not get that way," my mother said fiercely. "She's not any different from anyone else. She's just lucky and small for her age."

The reporter turned to my mother, "Some parents push their children to act. The kids feel like they're used."

"I don't do that—I'm not that way," my mother told the reporter.

But when she was sitting silently in all those waiting rooms while I was being turned down for one job after another, I could almost feel her wanting to shout, "Use her. Use her. What is wrong with her? Doesn't she have it anymore?" I didn't know what I had had that I didn't seem to have anymore. My mother had told the reporter that I was like everyone else. But when my life was like everyone else's, why was she disappointed?

The churning action of the La Brea Tar Pits makes interpreting the record of past events extremely difficult. The usual order of deposition—the oldest on the bottom, the youngest on the top—loses all meaning when some of the oldest fossils can be brought to the surface by the movement of natural gas. One must look for an undisturbed spot, a place untouched by the action of underground springs or natural gas or human interference. Complete skeletons

become important, because they indicate areas of least disturbance. But such spots of calm are rare. Whole blocks of the tar pit can become displaced, making false sequences of the past, skewing the interpretation[7] for what is the true order of nature.

That year before my sixteenth birthday, my mother seemed to spend a lot of time looking through my old scrapbooks, staring at all the eight-by-ten glossies of the shows that I had done. In the summer we visited with my grandmother often, since I wasn't working and had lots of free time. I would go out to the garden to read or sunbathe, but I could hear my mother and grandmother talking.

"She was so cute back then. She worked with Gene Kelly when she was five years old. She was so smart for her age. I don't know what's wrong with her."

"She's fifteen."

"She's too young to be an ingenue[8] and too old to be cute. The studios forget so quickly. By the time she's old enough to play an ingenue, they won't remember her."

"Does she have to work in the movies? Hand me the scissors."

My grandmother was making false eyelashes using the hair from her hairbrush. When she was young she had incredible hair. I saw an old photograph of her when it flowed beyond her waist like a cascading black waterfall. At seventy, her hair was still black as night, which made her few strands of silver look like shooting stars. But her hair had thinned greatly with age. It sometimes fell out in clumps.

---

7. *Skewing* (skū′ ing) *the interpretation* is twisting it so that it is wrong or off the mark.
8. An *ingenue* (än′ jə nōō′) is an actress who plays innocent, inexperienced young women.

Oil seeping up through the earth's surface evaporated, leaving soft tar that trapped Ice Age animals in the area now called the La Brea Tar Pits.

She wore it brushed back in a bun with a hairpiece for added fullness. My grandmother had always been proud of her hair, but once she started making false eyelashes from it, she wasn't proud of the way it looked anymore. She said she was proud of it now because it made her useful.

It was painstaking work—tying knots into strands of hair, then tying them together to form feathery little crescents.

Vocabulary

painstaking (pānz′ tā′ king) *adj.* requiring close, careful labor or attention

Hollywood and the Pits

Her glamorous false eyelashes were much sought after. Theatrical make-up artists waited months for her work. But my grandmother said what she liked was that she was doing something, making a contribution, and besides it didn't cost her anything. No overhead. "Till I go bald," she often joked.

She tried to teach me her art that summer, but for some reason strands of my hair wouldn't stay tied in knots.

"Too springy," my grandmother said. "Your hair is still too young." And because I was frustrated[9] then, frustrated with everything about my life, she added,

"You have to wait until your hair falls out, like mine. Something to look forward to, eh?" She had laughed and patted my hand.

My mother was going on and on about my lack of work, what might be wrong, that something she couldn't quite put her finger on. I heard my grandmother reply, but I didn't catch it all: "Movies are just make-believe, not real life. Like what I make with my hair that falls out—false. False eyelashes. Not meant to last."

The remains in the La Brea Tar Pits are mostly of carnivorous animals. Very few herbivores are found—the

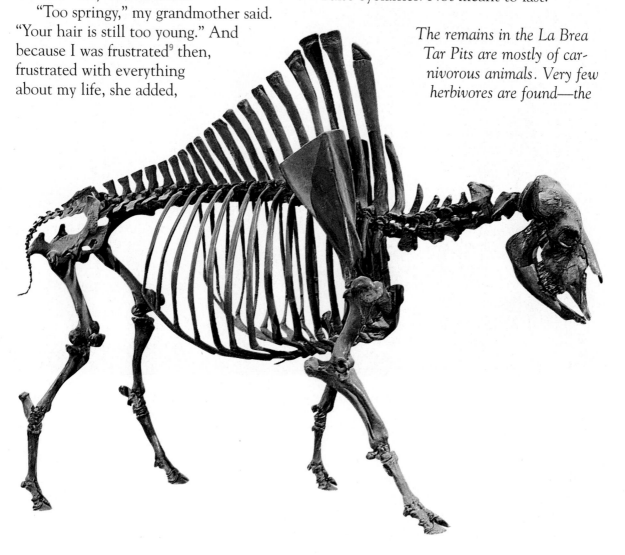

---

9. To be *frustrated* is to be kept from doing something or achieving some goal.

124 🦴 THEME 2

ratio is five to one, a perversion of the natural food chain. The ratio is easy to explain. Thousands of years ago a thirsty animal sought a drink from the pools of water only to find itself trapped by the bottom, gooey with subterranean[10] oil. A shriek of agony from the trapped victim drew flesh-eating <u>predators</u>, which were then trapped themselves by the very same ooze which provided the bait. The cycle repeated itself countless times. The number of victims grew, lured by the image of easy food, the <u>deception</u> of an easy kill. The animals piled on top of one another. For over ten thousand years the promise of the place drew animals of all sorts, mostly predators and <u>scavengers</u>—dire wolves, panthers, coyotes, vultures—all hungry for their chance. Most were sucked down against their will in those watering holes destined to be called the La Brea Tar Pits in a place to be named the City of Angels, home of Hollywood movie stars.

I spent a lot of time by myself that summer, wondering what it was that I didn't have anymore. Could I get it back? How could I if I didn't know what it was?

That's when I discovered the La Brea Tar Pits. Hidden behind the County Art Museum on trendy[11] Wilshire Boulevard, I found a job that didn't require me to be small or cute for my age. I didn't have to audition. No one said, "Thank you very much, we'll call you." Or if they did, they meant it. I volunteered my time one afternoon, and my fascination stuck—like tar on the bones of a saber-toothed tiger.

My mother didn't understand what had changed me. I didn't understand it myself. But I liked going to the La Brea Tar Pits. It meant I could get really messy and I was doing it with a purpose. I didn't feel awkward there. I could wear old stained pants. I could wear T-shirts with holes in them. I could wear disgustingly filthy sneakers and it was all perfectly justified. It wasn't a costume for a role in a film or a part in a TV sit-com. My mother didn't mind my dressing like that when she knew I was off to the pits. That was okay so long as I didn't track tar back into the house. I started going to the pits every day, and my mother wondered why. She couldn't believe I would rather be groveling[12] in tar than going on auditions or interviews.

While my mother wasn't proud of the La Brea Tar Pits (she didn't know or care what a fossil was), she didn't discourage me either. She drove me there, the same way she used to drive me to the studios.

"Wouldn't you rather be doing a show in Las Vegas than scrambling around in a pit?" she asked.

"I'm not in a show in Las Vegas, Ma. The Lee Sisters are retired." My older sister

10. *Carnivorous* (kär niv′ ər əs) animals eat meat; *herbivores* (hur′ bə vôrz′) eat mainly plants. So, the remains in the pits are a *perversion* because they give a false picture of reality. *Subterranean* means "underground."
11. *Trendy* describes what is currently popular, and Wilshire Boulevard is loaded with trendy shops, stores, and restaurants.

12. *Groveling* is lying or crawling facedown in a demeaning manner.

Vocabulary
predator (pred′ ə tər) *n.* an animal, such as a lion or hawk, that kills other animals for food
deception (di sep′ shən) *n.* that which fools or misleads
scavenger (skav′ in jər) *n.* an animal, such as a hyena or vulture, that feeds on dead, decaying animals

Hollywood and the Pits

had married and was starting a family of her own.

"But if you could choose between . . ."

"There isn't a choice."

"You really like this tar-pit stuff, or are you just waiting until you can get real work in the movies?"

I didn't answer.

My mother sighed. "You could do it if you wanted, if you really wanted. You still have what it takes."

I didn't know about that. But then, I couldn't explain what drew me to the tar pits either. Maybe it was the bones, finding out what they were, which animal they belonged to, imagining how they got there, how they fell into the trap. I wondered about that a lot.

At the La Brea Tar Pits, everything dug out of the pit is saved—including the sticky sand that covered the bones through the ages. Each bucket of sand is washed, sieved, and examined for pollen grains, insect remains, any evidence of past life. Even the grain size is recorded—the percentage of silt to sand to gravel that reveals the history of deposition, erosion, and disturbance. No single fossil, no one observation, is significant enough to tell the entire story. All the evidence must be weighed before a semblance[13] of truth emerges.

The tar pits had its lessons. I was learning I had to work slowly, become observant, to concentrate. I learned about time in a way that I would never experience—not in hours, days, and months, but in thousands

and thousands of years. I imagined what the past must have been like, envisioned Los Angeles as a sweeping basin, perhaps slightly colder and more humid, a time before people and studios arrived. The tar pits recorded a warming trend; the kinds of animals found there reflected the changing climate. The ones unadapted disappeared. No trace of their kind was found in the area. The ones adapted to warmer weather left a record of bones in the pit. Amid that collection of ancient skeletons, surrounded by evidence of death, I was finding a secret preserved over thousands and thousands of years. There was something cruel about natural selection and the survival of the fittest.[14] Even those successful individuals that "had what it took" for adaptation still wound up in the pits.

I never found out if I had what it took, not the way my mother meant. But I did adapt to the truth: I wasn't a Chinese Shirley Temple any longer, cute and short for my age. I had grown up. Maybe not on a Hollywood movie set, but in the La Brea Tar Pits.

---

13. A *semblance* of truth would be the slightest likeness of truth.

14. *[Natural . . . fittest]* refers to natural selection, the theory that the plants and animals best suited to their environment tend to survive and pass on their characteristics to their offspring.

Responding to Literature

PERSONAL RESPONSE

◆ If you were the main character, would you have continued to pursue your career as a performer? Discuss your opinions with a partner.

Analyzing Literature

RECALL

1. Describe the narrator's career as a successful child star.
2. What begins to happen to the narrator's success after she turns fifteen?
3. What does the narrator do in the tar pits?
4. How does the narrator's mother react to her daughter's lack of jobs as she becomes a teenager and her newfound interest in the tar pits?

INTERPRET

5. In your opinion, why was "The World Famous Lee Sisters" act so successful?
6. In your opinion, how does the narrator feel about the slump in her Hollywood career?
7. In your opinion, why does the narrator find working in the tar pits so rewarding?
8. How does the narrator's relationship with her mother change over the course of the story?

EVALUATE AND CONNECT

9. Why is the story of the narrator's life interrupted from time to time with factual material about the tar pits? What connection do you think the author is making between Hollywood and the La Brea Tar Pits?
10. Theme Connection   "Hollywood and the Pits" describes the changes in one person's life from childhood to adolescence. Does the story remind you about changes in your own life? Add these ideas to your journal entry from the **Reading Focus.**

LITERARY ELEMENTS

Symbol

A **symbol** is any object, person, place, or experience that stands for more than what it is. In "Hollywood and the Pits," the narrator uses the animals trapped in the La Brea Tar Pits to symbolize her experience as a child actor.

1. On page 119, find the statement "Innocence trapped by ignorance." How does this phrase help you understand Lee's use of symbolism in the story?

2. Find and explain another example of symbolism from a section of the selection printed in slanted, or italic, type.

● See **Literary Terms Handbook**, p. R11.

Extending Your Response

Writing About Literature

Point of View Most fiction is written from one of two points of view. The events are described from the point of view of either a character in the story or an unknown, all-seeing narrator. In "Hollywood and the Pits," Cherylene Lee uses the point of view of her main character. The reader sees the events as the main character saw them. Do you think this was the most effective point of view to use for this story? Explain your opinion.

Personal Writing

Moving On Look back at your journal entry for the **Reading Focus** on page 116. Write a letter to Cherylene Lee, comparing the narrator's experience of becoming a teenager and abandoning her childhood interests with your own experience.

*inter*NET
C O N N E C T I O N

You can find out more about prehistoric animals at many sites on the World Wide Web. Just type *"prehistoric animals"* in the subject window of your browser or search engine. Don't forget the quotation marks. They help to narrow the number of choices.

Literature Groups

Follow-up Interview The narrator tells about being interviewed when she was in the movies at age eight. Imagine that the reporter has come back ten years later to interview the narrator, again in the presence of her mother. What questions might the reporter ask, and how might the narrator's responses differ from her mother's? Devise questions and answers using details from the story.

Learning for Life

News Broadcast Imagine that you are a science news reporter, and a complete skeleton of a prehistoric animal has just been discovered at the La Brea Tar Pits. First, research animals that have been found at the pits during the last ninety years. Then choose one animal, research its characteristics, and write a news story about the finding of its skeleton. Add illustrations to your story.

Reading Further

If you would like to read more about life as a child actor or about the La Brea Tar Pits, try these books:

Shirley Temple Black by James Haskins

Death Trap: The Story of the La Brea Tar Pits by Sharon Elaine Thompson

📖 **Save your work for your portfolio.**

Skill Minilessons

GRAMMAR AND LANGUAGE • ITALICS

Italic type is a special *slanted* type used to set off titles of books, plays, movies, CDs, magazines, newspapers, and other long works. Italic type is also used to call out a foreign word or a word used as a word. In handwritten work, underline the words you want read as italic.

PRACTICE Write each sentence, underlining for italics where needed.

1. I read an article about fossils in National Geographic.

2. My teacher said that I overused terrifying in my review of the movie Jurassic Park.

3. Ed learned that the book Dinosaur Defeat was made into a play called The End of Their World.

4. I can't believe that the Times misspelled the word riot as rot in this morning's headline.

5. I learned from the local newspaper, Our Town, about the future filming of a movie in our city.

● For more about using italics, see **Language Handbook,** pp. R39–R40.

READING AND THINKING • CAUSE AND EFFECT

A **cause** is a condition or event that makes something happen. What happens as the result of a cause is an **effect**. Many events in stories are connected by cause-and-effect relationships. In "Hollywood and the Pits," when the narrator's older sister is too tall for a part in a TV show, the narrator gets the part. This begins her acting career.

Cause Older sister is too tall		**Effect** Younger sister gets part

PRACTICE Answer these questions about other causes and effects in "Hollywood and the Pits."

1. What causes the narrator's mother to worry that her daughter is fascinated by death?

2. What is a possible cause of the narrator's lack of acting work?

3. What led prehistoric mammals to become trapped in the tar pits?

4. What effect did the screaming of trapped animals in the pits have on predators in the area?

● For more about cause and effect, see **Reading Handbook,** p. R89.

VOCABULARY • RELATED FORMS OF WORDS

If you know the meaning of *happy* (an adjective), you probably also know the meaning of *happiness* (a noun) and *happily* (an adverb). If you know the meaning of one form of a word, you can usually figure out the meanings of its other forms. For example, if you know that a *predator* hunts its food, you can figure out what *predatory* behavior is.

PRACTICE Use what you know about the vocabulary words in "Hollywood and the Pits" to write definitions of the underlined words below.

1. to have an obsession
2. the child's bewilderment
3. the car's immobilization
4. to work painstakingly
5. a deceptive statement

Radiocarbon Dating

If you're a scientist who wants to know the age of a fossil you dug up, radiocarbon dating might help you. This type of dating tells us that the bone and plant fossils found in the La Brea Tar Pits range from 8,000 to 40,000 years old.

Only a small sample of a fossil, as little as a few grams, is needed for radiocarbon dating. Before dating the sample, a scientist cleans it by placing the sample in a jar filled with a chemical solution. Every tool the scientist uses to handle the fossil must also be clean and dry to prevent inaccurate results. Data about where the object was found can help confirm a dating.

Radiocarbon dating works by measuring the level of a radioactive form of carbon called carbon-14 inside a fossil. All living things contain carbon-14. Plants constantly absorb this element from the atmosphere. Human beings and other animals absorb it mainly through food provided by plants. Once an organism dies, however, it stops absorbing carbon-14. The carbon-14 remaining in its body begins to decay, or break down. Scientists know that carbon-14 decays at a particular rate, or speed. It takes 5,730 years for carbon-14 to reach what scientists call a half-life. By measuring the amount of carbon-14 left in an object, scientists can get an accurate idea of its age.

Radiocarbon dating doesn't work with every found object. Metal objects, such as ancient coins, tools, or weapons, were never alive, so scientists must use other methods to date them. Objects less than 50,000 years old qualify best for radiocarbon dating. That's pretty young for a fossil when you consider that scientists have uncovered the skeletal remains of sea animals that lived more than 500 million years ago!

ACTIVITY

Some states have an official state fossil or dinosaur. Find out which fossil or dinosaur, if any, represents your state. Locate a picture of the creature or its fossilized remains. During which time period was it alive? What do scientists know about it? Do research and share what you learned with your class.

If your state doesn't have an official state fossil, you might plan a campaign to have one adopted. Begin by finding out what fossils have been found in your state. Then choose the one you think would best represent the state.

MEDIA Connection

SONG

This song was written for the January 14, 1972, episode of the TV show *The Brady Bunch.* In the episode, the oldest brother, Greg, writes the song for the Brady Six to record after Peter's voice unexpectedly starts to change.

Time to Change

Words and Music by Raymond Bloodworth, Chris Welch, and Billy Meshel

Sha na na na na na na na na
Sha na na na na
Sha na na na na na na na na
Sha na na na na

Autumn turns to winter,
and then winter turns
to spring.
It's not just the seasons,
you know; it goes for
everything.
It's even true for voices as
boys begin to grow.
You gotta take a lesson
from Mother Nature,
and if you do you'll
know
When it's time to change,
then it's time to change.

Don't fight the tide, come
along for the ride.
Don't you see?
When it's time to change,
you've got to rearrange
Who you are into what
you're going to be.
Sha na na na . . . [repeat]

Day by day it's hard to see
the changes you've
been through.
A little bit of livin', a little
bit of growin' all adds
up to you.

Every boy's a man inside,
a girl's a woman too.
And if you want to reach
your destiny, here's
what you've got to do.
When it's time to change,
then it's time to change.
Don't fight the tide, come
along for the ride.
Don't you see?
When it's time to change,
you've got to rearrange
Who you are into what
you're going to be.

Sha na na na . . .
[repeat]

©1971 Famous Music Corporation

Analyzing Media

1. What does the song mean by "you've got to rearrange / Who you are into what you're going to be"? Explain in your own words.

2. Describe a time when you've had to rearrange yourself into "what you're going to be" or a time when you expect you'll need to.

Before You Read
Growing Pains

MEET
JEAN LITTLE

Jean Little was born with seriously impaired eyesight. As she grew, however, her sight improved enough so that she could learn to read on her own. "Reading," she says, "became my greatest joy." As Little went through school, she showed enthusiasm for writing. When she was eighteen, a magazine published two of her poems. She remembers her father reading them aloud. "I listened, and [when] his voice broke, I knew why I wanted to be a writer."

Jean Little was born in 1932 in Taiwan. "Growing Pains" was first published in 1986.

READING FOCUS

Think about how you feel when someone is angry with you. When you get angry with someone, do you keep your anger inside or do you express it? How do you feel after the person who expressed anger with you apologizes?

Think/Pair/Share
After you have jotted down your responses to these questions, share your thoughts with a partner.

Setting a Purpose
Read to discover one person's feelings about anger—and growing up.

BUILDING BACKGROUND

Writers and Blindness
Jean Little is one of a long line of distinguished writers who happened to be seriously sight impaired or totally blind. Many scholars believe that Homer, the ancient Greek who composed the epic poems the *Iliad* and the *Odyssey,* was blind. The seventeenth century English poet and essayist John Milton became blind before he wrote his greatest epic poem *Paradise Lost.* Closer to our own time, Helen Keller, who wrote a famous autobiography, was deaf as well as blind, and humorist James Thurber lost his sight late in life but continued to write.

Growing Pains

Jean Little

Mother got mad at me tonight and bawled me out.
She said I was lazy and self-centered.
She said my room was a pigsty.
She said she was sick and tired of forever nagging but I gave her no choice.
5   She went on and on until I began to cry.
I hate crying in front of people. It was horrible.

I got away, though, and went to bed and it was over.
I knew things would be okay in the morning;
Stiff with being sorry, too polite, but okay.
10   I was glad to be by myself.

Then she came to my room and apologized.
She explained, too.
Things had gone wrong all day at the store.
She hadn't had a letter from my sister and she was worried.
15   Dad had also done something to hurt her.
She even told me about that.
Then *she* cried.
I kept saying, "It's all right. Don't worry."
And wishing she'd stop.

20   I'm just a kid.
I can forgive her getting mad at me. That's easy.
But her sadness . . .
I don't know what to do with her sadness.
I yell at her often, "You don't understand me!"
25   But I don't want to have to understand her.
That's expecting too much.

Responding to Literature

PERSONAL RESPONSE

◆ What went through your mind as you read this poem? What, if anything, would you have done differently?

Analyzing Literature

RECALL

1. Who is the **speaker** in the poem, and what is she feeling?
2. What does the main character do that she wishes her mother would not do?

INTERPRET

3. Why do you think the author chose "Growing Pains" as the title for this poem?
4. How do you think the speaker's feelings about her own crying in front of people affect how she feels about her mother's crying?

EVALUATE AND CONNECT

5. Does the speaker think she deserved to be "bawled out"? How can you tell?
6. How do the main character's feelings about her mother's behavior seem true to life? Support your opinion with examples.
7. Do you think the poet showed both sides of the conflict between the mother and the daughter? Why or why not?
8. What does the poem tell you is one common reason that people often lose their tempers?
9. Theme Connection   About how old do you think the speaker might be? Why do you think her mother suddenly confides in her?
10. How does the poem express feelings about the new responsibilities that come with growing up?

LITERARY ELEMENTS

Mood

The emotional atmosphere, or feeling, of a story or poem is called the **mood**. Writers choose details to create a mood or feeling that brings a scene to life. Descriptive words, setting, dialogue, and characters' actions can all contribute to the mood of a piece of writing. In "Growing Pains," the poet uses such lines as, "It was horrible" and "I was glad to be by myself" to express the mood of the poem.

1. Reread "Growing Pains." How would you describe the mood of the poem?

2. Find two other examples of details that express the mood of the poem.

3. Compare the mood of the first two stanzas with the mood of the last stanza.

● See **Literary Terms Handbook,** p. R7.

Extending Your Response

Writing About Literature

Appreciating Rhythm   "Growing Pains" is an example of a poem that does not rhyme but that has a rhythm most easily grasped if you read the poem aloud. Working with a partner, read the poem aloud to each other, and then write about how the rhythm affects the listener or contributes to the effect of the poem.

Creative Writing

Expressing Yourself   Return to your notes from the **Reading Focus** on page 132. Write a short poem telling about a time when you were angry or confused because someone had hurt your feelings. Use details that describe why you were angry or confused.

Performing

Words Set to Music   Work with a small group to find instrumental music that evokes the mood of "Growing Pains." Then make a tape of the music to use as background during a group reading of the poem. Try various effects—for example, by grouping low and high voices or single and group voices.

Literature Groups

Problem Solving   The speaker in the poem is having trouble communicating with her mother. Find examples from the poem that describe how the two characters are not getting along. Then work together to come up with a list of recommendations to help them better understand each other. Write a plan with suggestions for both characters, and share it with the class.

Reading Further

If you enjoyed this poem, try these other books by Jean Little:
Mama's Going to Buy You a Mockingbird
Little by Little: A Writer's Education

📖 **Save your work for your portfolio.**

Skill Minilesson

READING AND THINKING • SEQUENCE OF EVENTS

Jean Little divided "Growing Pains" into four stanzas. The first three tell a story that is a sequence of events. The events appear in the order they happened. Paying attention to the sequence of events in a story or poem helps you better understand the piece of literature. How would "Growing Pains" be different if the poem began with the mother crying?

PRACTICE   Reread "Growing Pains," paying special attention to the events that happen in each stanza. Then write one paragraph that explains the sequence of events in the poem.

● For more about sequencing, see **Reading Handbook**, p. R91.

MEDIA Connection

MAGAZINE ARTICLE

This article comes from the business section of a weekly newsmagazine. In your opinion, why did it appear in the business section?

from "The N.B.A.'s Sister Act"

by Steve Wulf—*Time*, August 4, 1997

An hour and a half before the tip-off last Wednesday, the doors of the Charlotte Coliseum swung open, and America came pouring in. Charlotte was about to play New York, and the excitement was as palpable as it would be before any game between the Hornets and the Knicks.

Except this was July, the teams were called the Sting and the Liberty, and the players that the fans were beseeching for autographs were not Ewing and Rice but Lobo and Bullett. One of the hottest items at the souvenir stands was a T-shirt that read
INVENTED BY MAN,
PERFECTED BY WOMAN.

"This is phenomenal," said a woman who drove 65 miles from South Carolina to bring her daughter to the game. "My daughter thinks I'm the best mama in the world." Following the laser lights and loud music required of every N.B.A. pregame show, the announcer thundered, "O.K., Charlotte, We Got Next!"

Welcome to the W.N.B.A., the Women's National Basketball Association, or the N.B.A.'s baby sister. On the court, the sneakers squeak with the same urgency as they do in the N.B.A., the coaches yell, "Why isn't that a foul?" at the refs, and the players get fined for roughhousing—though

the $500 recently assessed Nancy Lieberman-Cline of the Phoenix Mercury for holding Jamila Wideman of the Los Angeles Sparks by the neck equals what Dennis Rodman spends in a year for eyeliner.

Backed by the N.B.A., the W.N.B.A. has exceeded all expectations midway through its two-month inaugural season, averaging 8,766 in attendance, and occasionally eclipsing Major League Soccer and P.G.A. golf in television ratings. W.N.B.A. games are televised nationally. Viewers watching the N.B.A. playoffs in June were besieged with the W.N.B.A. slogan, "We Got Next." The phrase is commonly used on playgrounds to reserve the next game, but in light of the early success of the league, it takes on a new meaning. "We are building a first-class operation that appeals to fans, players, television, corporate sponsors," says Val Ackerman, W.N.B.A.'s president. "Our dream is to become the fifth major league."

Analyzing Media

1. What do you think makes basketball such a popular sport?

2. How is the W.N.B.A. a sign of the "winds of change" during our time?

Before You Read
Slam, Dunk, & Hook

MEET YUSEF KOMUNYAKAA

READING FOCUS

What do you like about sports? Which games do you prefer, and why?

QuickWrite

Make a quick list of your feelings about sports. Tell which games you love and which games you hate. Then explain your own role in sports: do you prefer to play or to watch? Which do you value more—fierce competition between teams or intense loyalty among team members? Describe your feelings.

Setting a Purpose

Read this poem to appreciate the speaker's love of basketball.

The poet and educator Yusef Komunyakaa (ū′ sef   kō mun yä′ kä) uses his Louisiana childhood and his time in Vietnam as an Army correspondent as resources for the material in his poetry. A winner of the Pulitzer Prize for Poetry in 1994, Komunyakaa writes poems on a wide variety of subjects, including jazz, racial prejudice, and war.

Yusef Komunyakaa was born in 1947. "Slam, Dunk, & Hook" was published in 1992 in a collection of his poetry called Magic City.

BUILDING BACKGROUND

Did You Know?   Basketball was invented in 1891 by James Naismith, an instructor in physical education who lived in Springfield, Massachusetts. In need of an indoor game for the winter months, Naismith used a soccer ball and two peach baskets, one hung at each end of a gym. The rules Naismith made up for that game form the basis of today's game.

Slam, Dunk, & Hook

Yusef Komunyakaa

Fast breaks. Lay ups. With Mercury's°
Insignia on our sneakers,
We outmaneuvered the footwork
Of bad angels. Nothing but a hot
5 Swish of strings like silk
Ten feet out. In the roundhouse°
Labyrinth° our bodies
Created, we could almost
Last forever, poised in midair
10 Like storybook sea monsters.
A high note hung there
A long second. Off
The rim. We'd corkscrew
Up & dunk balls that exploded
15 The skullcap of hope & good
Intention. Bug-eyed, lanky,
All hands & feet . . . sprung rhythm.
We were metaphysical° when girls
Cheered on the sidelines.

20 Tangled up in a falling,
Muscles were a bright motor
Double-flashing to the metal hoop
Nailed to our oak.
When Sonny Boy's mama died
25 He played nonstop all day, so hard
Our backboard splintered.
Glistening with sweat, we jibed°
& rolled the ball off our
Fingertips. Trouble
30 Was there slapping a blackjack°
Against an open palm.
Dribble, drive to the inside, feint,°
& glide like a sparrow hawk.
Lay ups. Fast breaks.
35 We had moves we didn't know
We had. Our bodies spun
On swivels of bone & faith,
Through a lyric slipknot
Of joy, & we knew we were
40 Beautiful & dangerous.

---

1 In ancient Roman mythology, *Mercury* was the swift messenger of the gods. He was often portrayed wearing winged sandals.

6–7 *Roundhouse* is a slang term for a sweeping movement—in this case, wide, swinging arm movements. A *labyrinth* is any confusing, complicated arrangement.

18 Here, *metaphysical* means that the players seemed to go beyond the limits of the physical world.

---

27 To *jibe* is to be in harmony with one another.

30 A *blackjack* is a weighted, flexible, leather-covered weapon.

32 A *feint* is a movement intended to "fake out" an opponent.

Responding to Literature

PERSONAL RESPONSE

◆ What is your response to this poem? Which line from the poem did you find most memorable? Why?

Analyzing Literature

RECALL

1. What are some of the terms in "Slam, Dunk, & Hook" that are directly related to the game of basketball? Make a list of terms.
2. Summarize the action in "Slam, Dunk, & Hook."

INTERPRET

3. Why is "Slam, Dunk, & Hook" a good title for this poem?
4. What message about team sports does "Slam, Dunk, & Hook" express?

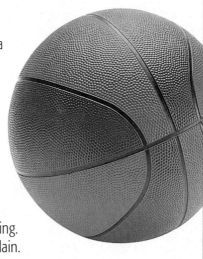

EVALUATE AND CONNECT

5. According to "Slam, Dunk, & Hook," team sports are dramatic, emotional, and exhilarating. Do you agree or disagree? Explain.
6. How do the structure and the rhythm of the poem help to create the feel of an actual game of basketball? Explain.
7. Does this poem remind you of an experience of your own? Explain.
8. What is Komunyakaa saying about the connection between participation in basketball and friendship? Do you agree or disagree? Explain.
9. What did you learn about basketball, or about the attitude of the players, from reading this poem? Explain.
10. **Theme Connection** How do you think playing basketball might have changed the speaker of the poem? Has participation in sports or other activities changed you? How?

LITERARY ELEMENTS

Alliteration

Alliteration is the repetition of sounds, most often consonant sounds, at the beginnings of words. Writers often use alliteration in their poetry to enhance the sounds of the lines as a poem is read aloud. Consider the example of alliteration in these lines from "Slam, Dunk, & Hook":

Our bodies spun

On swivels of bone & faith

The words *bodies* and *bone* both begin with *b;* the words *spun* and *swivels* both begin with *s.*

1. Find another example of alliteration in this poem or in another poem in this book. Read the example aloud and point out the alliteration.

2. Write your own short poem or paragraph about a real or imaginary sports event. Use images to help your readers see, hear, and feel what you describe in your writing. Try to use alliteration appropriate to your subject.

● See **Literary Terms Handbook**, p. R1.

Extending Your Response

Writing About Literature

Sensory Imagery "Slam, Dunk, & Hook" is filled with **sensory imagery,** or words that appeal to our senses. Pick out your favorite image, and write a paragraph explaining why it is memorable.

Creative Writing

Sports: Up Close and Personal What do you like best about sports in general? What specific sport do you like best? Do you prefer to play or to watch? Review your response to the **Reading Focus** on page 137. Then write a short poem or a paragraph or two that describes your feelings about sports.

Literature Groups

Hooray for Sports! "Slam, Dunk, & Hook" strongly endorses participation in team sports. What about the win-at-all-costs attitude that sometimes comes with competition? Should amateur teams feel and act differently than professional teams? Debate the issue. Support your opinions with examples from the poem and from your own experience.

Listening and Speaking

Appreciating Poetry In small groups, choose the most dramatic and exhilarating images from the poem. One group member should read the lines aloud while the remaining members dramatize the scene. Share your dramatization with your classmates.

Reading Further

If you would like to read more poems about basketball or other sports, try these books:

Slam Dunk: Basketball Poems, compiled by Lillian Morrison

American Sports Poems, edited by R. R. Knudson and May Swenson

Jump Ball: Basketball A Basketball Season in Poems by Mel Glenn

Save your work for your portfolio.

Skill Minilesson

GRAMMAR AND LANGUAGE • VIVID VERBS

"Slam, Dunk, & Hook" is filled with colorful, **vivid verbs** that help readers visualize the quick action taking place on the basketball court. For example, think about this description:

"We'd corkscrew
Up & dunk balls that exploded"

The vivid verbs help you visualize the scene. The image is much more effective than just saying, "We'd jump up and throw balls that went into the basket." A **thesaurus,** a book of synonyms, can help you find vivid verbs.

PRACTICE Reread the poem. As you do, pick out some of the vivid verbs that helped you visualize the images in the poem. Keep a list of vivid verbs in your journal, and add verbs to the list as you find them in your reading.

● For more about verbs, see **Language Handbook,** p. R33.

Identifying Main Idea and Supporting Details

Skillful readers know to look for the **main idea** in a paragraph. In many paragraphs, a topic sentence states the main idea. The other sentences add **supporting details.**

> In the La Brea Tar Pits many of the excavated bones belong to juvenile mammals. Thousands of years ago thirsty young animals in the area were drawn to watering holes, not knowing they were traps. Those inviting pools had false bottoms made of sticky tar, which immobilized its victims and preserved their bones when they died. Innocence trapped by ignorance. The tar pits record that well.

In this passage, the main idea is stated in a topic sentence. That sentence, the first one, tells us that many of the bones found in the tar pits are those of young animals. The other sentences further explain the main idea by adding supporting details.

Often, the main idea is implied, not stated directly. Without a topic sentence, the reader needs to figure out the main idea that connects the supporting details. If you can't find a topic sentence, try to state the implied main idea in your own words.

● For more about main idea and details, see **Reading Handbook,** pp. 90–91.

EXERCISE

Read the following excerpt from "Hollywood and the Pits." Then write a paragraph to answer the questions.

> My mother looked at my face hopefully when I came into the room. I gave her a quick shake of the head. She looked bewildered. I felt bad for my mother then. How could I explain it to her? I didn't understand it myself. We left saying polite good-byes to all the other mothers.

1. What is the implied main idea of the paragraph?

2. List three details that support the main idea.

Vo•cab•u•lar•y *Skills*

Context Clues

She gave me an *imperious* smile.   He makes *imperious* remarks.

These sentences are no help to you in figuring out what *imperious* means because they provide no useful **context clues.** Context is the sentence or group of sentences in which a word appears. The context often provides clues as to what an unfamiliar word means. Following are some kinds of context clues:

Definition: *She gave me an imperious—overbearing and arrogant—smile.*

The writer provides a definition: imperious means "overbearing and arrogant."

Example: *He makes imperious remarks, such as, "You will immediately do as I say."*

Here an example is provided. You can tell what an *imperious* person is like by the kind of remark such a person would make.

Restatement: *I don't know how to react to imperious people. I don't know what to say or do around those who are so bossy and sure of themselves.*

The writer has used other words to restate the idea.

Contrast: *She's humble and unassuming—not at all imperious like her brother.*

Here, the reader can tell that an *imperious* person must be the opposite of the type of person described.

EXERCISE

Use context clues to figure out what the underlined words mean. Write a synonym or a short definition for each.

1. Lee interrupts her story to interpose descriptions of the tar pits.
2. These pits were lethal to every animal that stepped into them, for death was certain.
3. The sticky mud precluded the animals' escape, trapping them forever.
4. Is Lee intimating that Hollywood is also a trap, suggesting without actually saying it?
5. She makes it clear that child actors are not at all safe. Instead, child actors are in peril of failure when they outgrow their childish cuteness.

FICTION

Stages in Plot Development

Fiction—writing about imaginary people and events—can be divided into three types, based on length. You can read a **short story** in a single session lasting between several minutes to an hour or two. A **novel** (usually well over a hundred pages) might take you several days or a few weeks to get through. A **novella** is longer than a short story but shorter than a novel. Some novellas and most novels feature more characters, plot developments, and settings than would be included in a short story.

Novels, novellas, and short stories all share the elements described below. The models demonstrate those elements in the short story "Hollywood and the Pits."

The main character is a teenage girl who has worked as a child actor but now is interested only in her work on an archaeological dig at the La Brea Tar Pits. Her mother doesn't understand her new interest.

1 EXPOSITION is background information about characters and setting. It sets the scene for the conflict.

ELEMENTS OF PROSE FICTION

SETTING is the time and place of the story's action. Setting also includes the customs, values, and beliefs of a place or a time. A short story or novella usually has a limited setting. A novel is likely to stretch across different locations and a long period of time.

CHARACTERS are the actors in the story. They can be people, animals, robots, or whatever the writer chooses. The main character is called the **protagonist.** A short story or novella usually has a single protagonist. A novel may include more than one.

MODEL: "Hollywood and the Pits"

"Hollywood and the Pits" opens in Los Angeles in 1968 and, in **flashbacks,** moves through the 1950s and 1960s.

The characters include the two Lee sisters, their mother, and various unnamed minor characters. The younger Lee sister is the protagonist.

3 CLIMAX is the point of highest interest, conflict, or suspense in the story.

4 FALLING ACTION shows what happens to the character after the climax.

As the main character grows up, demand for her at the Hollywood studios declines. No longer a novelty, she's become an average, awkward teenager. She grows discouraged, but her mother keeps taking her to auditions.

In the summer of 1968, she works on a dig at the La Brea Tar Pits and decides to give up show business.

The main character's mother is disappointed by her decision. Although she doesn't understand it, she accepts it and drives her daughter to the tar pits rather than to auditions.

Working in the tar pits, the main character realizes the cruelty of what happened there. She sees the pits as a symbol of what happens to many performers who are used and then discarded by the Hollywood studios.

As young children, the main character and her older sister develop a song-and-dance act and become successful. The main character gets roles in Hollywood films because she is cute and can do her scenes in one take. Her mother encourages her career.

2 RISING ACTION develops the conflict.

5 RESOLUTION gives the final outcome.

PLOT is the basic structure of the story. It is a series of related events in which a problem is explored and then solved. Plot is created through **conflict**—a struggle between people, ideas, or forces.

The conflict is between the younger Lee sister and her mother. The diagram on these pages shows how the plot develops.

POINT OF VIEW is the vantage point from which a story is told. The person telling the story is the **narrator.** In **first-person** point of view, the narrator is a character in the story. In **third-person** point of view, the narrator is someone outside the story. In some longer works of fiction, the author may use more than one narrator, telling a story from different points of view.

"Hollywood and the Pits" is told from the first-person point of view. The narrator is the younger Lee sister. She is probably an adult looking back at herself between the ages of three and fifteen.

THEME is the main message that the reader can take from the story. A theme may be stated directly in the story or in its title. However, most stories have **implied** themes, suggested by what the characters learn or by what their experiences illustrate. Readers' ideas about implied themes may vary.

The theme of "Hollywood and the Pits" is implied. A reader might state its theme this way: Hollywood can trap and destroy young performers just as the La Brea Tar Pits trapped many young animals.

Active Reading Strategies

Tips for Reading Fiction

How do you approach reading fiction? You can begin by sorting out the basic elements: the characters, setting, plot, point of view, and theme. A short story or novella will usually have fewer characters than a novel–in some cases as few as one or two. Often a story will have a single setting. Since a short story is usually meant to be read in one sitting, the plot and theme usually revolve around how the characters respond to a single event. Looking for these elements and using the strategies below can help you read works of fiction with greater understanding.

● For more about reading strategies, see **Reading Handbook,** pp. R73–R102.

PREDICT

At certain points in your reading, take time to wonder what will happen next.

Ask Yourself . . .

● Can I tell from the title if this story is going to be humorous or dramatic?

● How will these characters respond to this development?

● How will the story end?

VISUALIZE

Keep the characters and the setting in your mind's eye as you read.

Ask Yourself . . .

● What does this character look like? Has the author given me hints or specific details?

● Have I ever seen a setting like this? Can I picture it?

REVIEW

If you are reading a novel, a novella, or a long short story, it might help to stop from time to time to review what you have found out so far.

Ask Yourself . . .

● Who are the main characters?

● How would I summarize the plot up to this point?

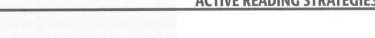

CONNECT

As you read, keep trying to make connections. How does the work of fiction connect to your current life or to your past or future?

Ask Yourself . . .

- Does this character remind me of someone I know or another character I have read about?

- Have I ever felt like this character?

- Would I have responded in this way if this event had happened to me?

EVALUATE

As you read, form opinions about how the work is written and how you feel about the characters and their actions. Don't wait until the end to decide if you like it. Make judgments from the very beginning, but feel free to change your opinions as you read.

Ask Yourself . . .

- Has the author made this character believable?

- Has this story grabbed me? Do I want to find out what happens?

- Are these characters people I care about?

APPLYING THE STRATEGIES

Practice applying the strategies to the following short story, "A Crush." Use the Active Reading Model notes in the margins as you read. Write your responses on a separate piece of paper or use stick-on notes.

Before You Read

A Crush

MEET CYNTHIA RYLANT

Cynthia Rylant (rī′ lənt) grew up poor in the Appalachian Mountains of West Virginia in a home without electricity or running water. In her early writings, she drew on this experience to describe ordinary characters in difficult situations. "I get a lot of personal gratification," says Rylant, "thinking of those people who don't get any attention in the world and making them really valuable in my fiction—making them absolutely shine with their beauty. . . . I want to deal with people who don't have what they want."

Cynthia Rylant was born in 1954. This story was first published in 1990.

READING FOCUS

Think about someone your age you wish you knew better. How could you let that person know you are interested?

List Ideas

List ways you might quietly let someone know you'd like to get to know him or her better.

Setting a Purpose

Read "A Crush" to discover how one person decides to show interest in another.

BUILDING BACKGROUND

The Time and Place   It is the late 1900s in a small town in the United States.

VOCABULARY PREVIEW

excess (ek′ ses) *adj.* more than usual or necessary; p. 149

speculation (spek′ yə lā′ shən) *n.* the act of forming an opinion or conclusion based on guesswork; p. 150

taut (tôt) *adj.* stretched tight; p. 150

improbable (im prob′ ə bəl) *adj.* not likely; p. 151

illuminated (i lōō′ mə nāt id) *adj.* lit up; p. 152

venture (ven′ chər) *v.* to do something in spite of possible risk or danger; p. 152

eventually (i ven′ chōō ə lē) *adv.* in the end; finally; p. 153

intently (in tent′ lē) *adv.* in a firmly focused way; with concentration; p. 154

discreetly (dis krēt′ lē) *adv.* in a manner showing good judgment; cautiously; p. 155

hardy (här′ dē) *adj.* able to endure hardship; strong and healthy; p. 155

A Crush

Cynthia Rylant ～

When the windows of Stan's

Hardware started filling up with flowers, everyone in town knew something had happened. Excess flowers usually mean death, but since these were all real flowers bearing the aroma of nature instead of floral preservative,[1] and since they stood bunched in clear mason jars instead of impaled on styrofoam crosses, everyone knew nobody had died. So they all figured somebody had a crush and kept quiet.

QUESTION

What is the author telling us about the size of the town?

---

1. *Floral preservative* is a chemical that helps cut flowers stay fresh looking.

Vocabulary

excess (ek′ ses) *adj.* more than usual or necessary

A Crush

ACTIVE READING MODEL

There wasn't really a Stan of Stan's Hardware. Dick Wilcox was the owner, and since he'd never liked his own name, he gave his store half the name of his childhood hero, Stan Laurel in the movies. Dick had been married for twenty-seven years. Once, his wife Helen had dropped a German chocolate cake on his head at a Lion's Club dance, so Dick and Helen were not likely candidates for the honest expression of the flowers in those clear mason jars lining the windows of Stan's Hardware, and speculation had to move on to Dolores.

Dolores was the assistant manager at Stan's and had worked there for twenty years, since high school. She knew the store like a mother knows her baby, so Dick—who had trouble keeping up with things like prices and new brands of drywall compound[2]—tried to keep himself busy in the back and give Dolores the run of the floor. This worked fine because the carpenters and plumbers and painters in town trusted Dolores and took her advice to heart. They also liked her tattoo.

Dolores was the only woman in town with a tattoo. On the days she went sleeveless, one could see it on the taut brown skin of her upper arm: "Howl at the Moon." The picture was of a baying coyote which must have been a dark gray in its early days but which had faded to the color of the spackling paste Dolores stocked in the third aisle. Nobody had gotten out of Dolores the true story behind the tattoo. Some of the men who came in liked to show off their own, and they'd roll up their sleeves or pull open their shirts, exhibiting bald eagles and rattlesnakes, and they'd try to coax out of Dolores the history of her coyote. All of the men had gotten their tattoos when they were in the service, drunk on weekend leave and full of the spitfire[3] of young soldiers. Dolores had never been in the service and she'd never seen weekend leave and there wasn't a tattoo parlor anywhere near. They couldn't figure why or where

Did You Know?
Stan Laurel was the thin man with the long face; Oliver Hardy was his not-so-thin partner. The popular comedy team of Laurel and Hardy made movies together from the late 1920s to 1951.

PREDICT

What do you think the tattoo might be?

VISUALIZE

Can you picture what this tattoo would look like?

---

2. *Drywall compound* and *spackling paste* (mentioned in the next paragraph) are used to prepare walls before painting.
3. When soldiers are off duty and allowed to go off base, they're on *leave*. When they're full of *spitfire,* they're quick-tempered and ready to fight.

Vocabulary
speculation (spek´ yə lā´ shən) *n.* the act of forming an opinion or conclusion based on guesswork
taut (tôt) *adj.* stretched tight

any half-sober woman would have a howling coyote ground into the soft skin of her upper arm. But Dolores wasn't telling.

That the flowers in Stan's front window had anything to do with Dolores seemed completely <u>improbable</u>. As far as anyone knew, Dolores had never been in love nor had anyone ever been in love with her. Some believed it was the tattoo, of course, or the fine dark hair coating Dolores's upper lip which kept suitors away. Some felt it was because Dolores was just more of a man than most of the men in town, and fellows couldn't figure out how to court someone who knew more about the carburetor of a car or the back side of a washing machine than they did. Others thought Dolores simply didn't want love. This was a popular theory among the women in town who sold Avon and Mary Kay cosmetics. Whenever one of them ran into the hardware for a package of light bulbs or some batteries, she would mentally pluck every one of the black hairs above Dolores's lip. Then she'd wash that grease out of Dolores's hair, give her a good blunt cut, dress her in a decent silk-blend blouse with a nice Liz Claiborne skirt from the Sports line, and, finally, tone down that swarthy, longshoreman[4] look of Dolores's with a concealing beige foundation, some frosted peach lipstick, and a good gray liner for the eyes.

Dolores simply didn't want love, the Avon lady would think as she walked back to her car carrying her little bag of batteries. If she did, she'd fix herself up.

The man who was in love with Dolores and who brought her zinnias and cornflowers and nasturtiums[5] and marigolds and asters and four-o'clocks in clear mason jars did not know any of this. He did not know that men showed Dolores their tattoos. He did not know that Dolores understood how to use and to sell a belt sander. He did not know that Dolores needed some concealing beige foundation so she could get someone to love her. The man who brought flowers to Dolores on Wednesdays when the hardware opened its doors at 7:00 A.M. didn't care who Dolores had ever been or what anyone had ever thought of her. He loved her and he wanted to bring her flowers.

Ernie had lived in this town all of his life and had never before met Dolores. He was thirty-three years old, and for thirty-one of those years he had lived at home with his mother in a small, dark house on the edge of town near Beckwith's Orchards. Ernie had been a beautiful baby, with

EVALUATE

Does Rylant do a good job of supplying you with enough details to picture the character of Dolores?

RESPOND

Would you like to live in the same town with women like the Avon and Mary Kay ladies?

QUESTION

How could someone be in love with Dolores and know so little about her?

---

4. A *swarthy longshoreman* is a dark or sunburned dockworker.
5. *nasturtiums* (nä stur′ shəms)

Vocabulary
improbable (im prob′ ə bəl) *adj.* not likely

A Crush

ACTIVE READING MODEL

CONNECT

Do you know of any children or adults whose mental development happened this slowly?

REVIEW

Who are the major characters you have met so far?

VISUALIZE

How does the author help you picture this scene in your mind?

a shock of shining black hair and large blue eyes and a round, wise face. But as he had grown, it had become clearer and clearer that though he was indeed a perfectly beautiful child, his mind had not developed with the same perfection. Ernie would not be able to speak in sentences until he was six years old. He would not be able to count the apples in a bowl until he was eight. By the time he was ten, he could sing a simple song. At age twelve, he understood what a joke was. And when he was twenty, something he saw on television made him cry.

Ernie's mother kept him in the house with her because it was easier, so Ernie knew nothing of the world except this house. They lived, the two of them, in tiny dark rooms always <u>illuminated</u> by the glow of a television set, Ernie's bags of Oreos and Nutter Butters littering the floor, his baseball cards scattered across the sofa, his heavy winter coat thrown over the arm of a chair so he could wear it whenever he wanted, and his box of Burpee seed packages sitting in the middle of the kitchen table.

These Ernie cherished. The seeds had been delivered to his home by mistake. One day a woman wearing a brown uniform had pulled up in a brown truck, walked quickly to the front porch of Ernie's house, set a box down, and with a couple of toots of her horn, driven off again. Ernie had watched her through the curtains, and when she was gone, had <u>ventured</u> onto the porch and shyly, cautiously, picked up the box. His mother checked it when he carried it inside. The box didn't have their name on it but the brown truck was gone, so whatever was in the box was theirs to keep. Ernie pulled off the heavy tape, his fingers trembling, and found inside the box more little packages of seeds than he could count. He lifted them out, one by one, and examined the beautiful photographs of flowers on each. His mother was not interested, had returned to the television, but Ernie sat down at the kitchen table and quietly looked at each package for a long time, his fingers running across the slick paper and outlining the shapes of zinnias and cornflowers and nasturtiums and marigolds and asters and four-o'clocks, his eyes drawing up their colors.

Vocabulary
illuminated (i lōō′ mə nāt id) *adj.* lit up
venture (ven′ chər) *v.* to do something in spite of possible risk or danger

Cynthia Rylant ∿

Two months later Ernie's mother died. A neighbor found her at the mailbox beside the road. People from the county courthouse came out to get Ernie, and as they ushered him from the home he would never see again, he picked up the box of seed packages from his kitchen table and passed through the doorway.

Eventually Ernie was moved to a large white house near the main street of town. This house was called a group home, because in it lived a group of people who, like Ernie, could not live on their own. There were six of them. Each had his own room. When Ernie was shown the room that would be his, he put the box of Burpee seeds—which he had kept with him since his mother's death—on the little table beside the bed and then he sat down on the bed and cried.

Ernie cried every day for nearly a month. And then he stopped. He dried his tears and he learned how to bake refrigerator biscuits and how to dust mop and what to do if the indoor plants looked brown.

Ernie loved watering the indoor plants and it was this pleasure which finally drew him outside. One of the young men who worked at the group home—a college student named Jack—grew a large garden in the back of the house. It was full of tomato vines and the large yellow blossoms of healthy squash. During his first summer at the house, Ernie would stand at the kitchen window, watching Jack and sometimes a resident of the home move among the vegetables. Ernie was curious, but too afraid to go into the garden.

Then one day when Ernie was watching through the window, he noticed that Jack was ripping open several slick little packages and emptying them into the ground. Ernie panicked and ran to his room. But the box of Burpee seeds was still there on his table, untouched. He grabbed it, slid it under his bed, then went back through the house and out into the garden as if he had done this every day of his life.

He stood beside Jack, watching him empty seed packages into the soft black soil, and as the packages were emptied, Ernie asked for them, holding out his hand, his eyes on the photographs of red radishes and purple eggplant. Jack handed the empty packages over with a smile and with that gesture became Ernie's first friend.

Jack tried to explain to Ernie that the seeds would grow into vegetables but Ernie could not believe this until he saw it come true. And when it did, he looked all the more

---

Vocabulary
eventually (i ven′ choo ə lē) *adv.* in the end; finally

ACTIVE READING MODEL

PREDICT

Do you think someone like Ernie could live alone?

PREDICT

How long do you think it will take Ernie to go outdoors?

QUESTION

Do you think Ernie usually talks much to Jack or the other people in the group home?

Boulevard Diner–Worcester, MA, 1992. John Baeder. Oil on canvas, 30¼ x 48¼ in. O. K. Harris Works of Art, New York.

Viewing the painting: While Ernie was eating breakfast at the Big Boy restaurant, his life was changed. Whose life might be changed at the diner in this painting?

EVALUATE

Do you think the author has done a good job of showing the passage of time?

CONNECT

Have you ever been really frightened to try a new experience?

intently at the packages of zinnias and cornflowers and the rest hidden beneath his bed. He thought more deeply about them but he could not carry them to the garden. He could not let the garden have his seeds.

That was the first year in the large white house.

The second year, Ernie saw Dolores, and after that he thought of nothing else but her and of the photographs of flowers beneath his bed.

Jack had decided to take Ernie downtown for breakfast every Wednesday morning to ease him into the world outside that of the group home. They left very early, at 5:45 A.M., so there would be few people and almost no traffic to frighten Ernie and make him beg for his room. Jack and Ernie drove to the Big Boy restaurant which sat across the street from Stan's Hardware. There they ate eggs and bacon and French toast among those whose work demanded rising before the sun: bus drivers, policemen, nurses, mill workers. Their first time in the Big Boy, Ernie was too nervous to eat. The second time, he could eat but he couldn't look up. The third time, he not only ate everything on his

---

Vocabulary

intently (in tent′ lē) *adv.* in a firmly focused way; with concentration

Cynthia Rylant ~

plate, but he lifted his head and he looked out the window of the Big Boy restaurant toward Stan's Hardware across the street. There he saw a dark-haired woman in jeans and a black T-shirt unlocking the front door of the building, and that was the moment Ernie started loving Dolores and thinking about giving up his seeds to the soft black soil of Jack's garden.

Love is such a mystery, and when it strikes the heart of one as mysterious as Ernie himself, it can hardly be spoken of. Ernie could not explain to Jack why he went directly to his room later that morning, pulled the box of Burpee seeds from under his bed, then grabbed Jack's hand in the kitchen and walked with him to the garden where Ernie had come to believe things would grow. Ernie handed the packets of seeds one by one to Jack, who stood in silent admiration of the lovely photographs before asking Ernie several times, "Are you sure you want to plant these?" Ernie was sure. It didn't take him very long, and when the seeds all lay under the moist black earth, Ernie carried his empty packages inside the house and spent the rest of the day spreading them across his bed in different arrangements.

That was in June. For the next several Wednesdays at 7:00 A.M. Ernie watched every movement of the dark-haired woman behind the lighted windows of Stan's Hardware. Jack watched Ernie watch Dolores, and discreetly said nothing.

When Ernie's flowers began growing in July, Ernie spent most of his time in the garden. He would watch the garden for hours, as if he expected it suddenly to move or to impress him with a quick trick. The fragile green stems of his flowers stood uncertainly in the soil, like baby colts on their first legs, but the young plants performed no magic for Ernie's eyes. They saved their shows for the middle of the night and next day surprised Ernie with tender small blooms in all the colors the photographs had promised.

The flowers grew fast and hardy, and one early Wednesday morning when they looked as big and bright as their pictures on the empty packages, Ernie pulled a glass canning jar off a dusty shelf in the basement of his house. He washed the jar, half filled it with water, then carried it to the garden where he placed in it one of every kind of flower he had grown. He met Jack at the car and rode off to the Big Boy with the jar of flowers held tight between his small hands. Jack told him it was a beautiful bouquet.

ACTIVE READING MODEL

REVIEW

Go over in your mind what has happened so far in the story.

RESPOND

What would you like to ask the writer about this scene? Do you imagine that she knows someone like Ernie?

EVALUATE

Does Jack's behavior in the restaurant reflect what you know about him so far?

Vocabulary

discreetly (dis krēt′ lē) *adv.* in a manner showing good judgment; cautiously
hardy (här′ dē) *adj.* able to endure hardship; strong and healthy

A Crush

When they reached the door of the Big Boy, Ernie stopped and pulled at Jack's arm, pointing to the building across the street. "OK," Jack said, and he led Ernie to the front door of Stan's Hardware. It was 6:00 A.M. and the building was still dark. Ernie set the clear mason jar full of flowers under the sign that read "Closed," then he smiled at Jack and followed him back across the street to get breakfast.

When Dolores arrived at seven and picked up the jar of zinnias and cornflowers and nasturtiums and marigolds and asters and four-o'clocks, Ernie and Jack were watching her from a booth in the Big Boy. Each had a wide smile on his face as Dolores put her nose to the flowers. Ernie giggled. They watched the lights of the hardware store come up and saw Dolores place the clear mason jar on the ledge of the front window. They drove home still smiling.

All the rest of that summer Ernie left a jar of flowers every Wednesday morning at the front door of Stan's Hardware. Neither Dick Wilcox nor Dolores could figure out why the flowers kept coming, and each of them assumed somebody had a crush on the other. But the flowers had an effect on them anyway. Dick started spending more time out on the floor making conversation with the customers, while Dolores stopped wearing T-shirts to work and instead wore crisp white blouses with the sleeves rolled back off her wrists. Occasionally she put on a bracelet.

By summer's end Jack and Ernie had become very good friends, and when the flowers in the garden behind their house began to wither, and Ernie's face began to grow gray as he watched them, Jack brought home one bright day in late September a great long box. Ernie followed Jack as he carried it down to the basement and watched as Jack pulled a long glass tube from the box and attached this tube to the wall above a table. When Jack plugged in the tube's electric cord, a soft lavender light washed the room.

"Sunshine," said Jack.

Then he went back to his car for a smaller box. He carried this down to the basement where Ernie still stood staring at the strange light. Jack handed Ernie the small box, and when Ernie opened it he found more little packages of seeds than he could count, with new kinds of photographs on the slick paper.

"Violets," Jack said, pointing to one of them.

Then he and Ernie went outside to get some dirt.

Responding to Literature

PERSONAL RESPONSE

◆ What are your thoughts about the ending? Did you expect that Dolores would eventually find out who had a crush on her?

Active Reading Response

Look back at the **Active Reading Strategies** on pages 146–147. Choose one of the strategies and find three places in the story where you could apply it.

Analyzing Literature

RECALL

1. What makes Dolores different from the other women in town?
2. What are Ernie's most prized possessions?
3. Whom do Dolores and Dick Wilcox think the flowers are for?
4. What does Jack buy to help Ernie deal with the end of summer and the gardening season?

INTERPRET

5. In your opinion, why do the women in town judge Dolores the way they do?
6. Why does Ernie love his seed packages so much?
7. In your opinion, why did the bouquets affect the behavior of Dick and Dolores at the store?
8. What makes Jack a good caretaker and friend for Ernie?

EVALUATE AND CONNECT

9. Why do you think Cynthia Rylant chose to write a story about a character like Ernie?
10. Theme Connection   How did Ernie's crush change his life and the lives of the other three characters in the story?

LITERARY ELEMENTS

First- and Third-Person Point of View

Before Cynthia Rylant began to write "A Crush," she had to decide from which point of view to tell the story. In the **first-person point of view,** the narrator is one of the characters. He or she speaks to the reader and uses the pronouns *I, me,* and *we.* In a third-person narrative, the story is told by an unnamed person who may seem to know what every character is thinking. When the story is told from the **third-person point of view,** the narrator uses the pronouns *he, she,* and *they.*

1. Which point of view did Rylant choose for writing "A Crush"?

2. Choose one paragraph from the story and rewrite it from a different point of view.

● See **Literary Terms Handbook,** p. R8.

Literature and Writing

Writing About Literature

Detailed Description   In the beginning of "A Crush," Cynthia Rylant describes how the other men and women in town see Dolores. Write a paragraph describing Dolores in your own words.

Creative Writing

A Crush Revealed   Review your ideas from the **Reading Focus** on page 148. Then write a letter to an imaginary friend your age who has a secret crush on someone. Advise your friend on how to deal with the crush.

Extending Your Response

Literature Groups

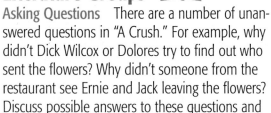

Asking Questions   There are a number of unanswered questions in "A Crush." For example, why didn't Dick Wilcox or Dolores try to find out who sent the flowers? Why didn't someone from the restaurant see Ernie and Jack leaving the flowers? Discuss possible answers to these questions and share them with the class.

Learning for Life

Job Description   Residents of group homes for the mentally handicapped often have jobs. If Jack thought Ernie was ready to have a job, he might try to find employment for him at a plant nursery. Write a job description for the kind of gardening work Ernie might do. Include the description in a letter to a local plant nursery, explaining Jack's connection to Ernie and Ernie's experience and potential.

Interdisciplinary Activity

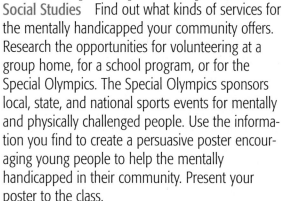

Social Studies   Find out what kinds of services for the mentally handicapped your community offers. Research the opportunities for volunteering at a group home, for a school program, or for the Special Olympics. The Special Olympics sponsors local, state, and national sports events for mentally and physically challenged people. Use the information you find to create a persuasive poster encouraging young people to help the mentally handicapped in their community. Present your poster to the class.

Reading Further

If you would like to read more of Cynthia Rylant's writings, try these books:

Short Stories: *A Couple of Kooks and Other Stories About Love*

Poetry: *Waiting to Waltz*

If you liked "The Crush," you might also enjoy: *A Racecourse for Andy* by Patricia Wrightson

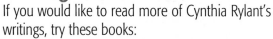 **Save your work for your portfolio.**

Skill Minilessons

GRAMMAR AND LANGUAGE • ADVERB CLAUSES

An **adverb clause** is a subordinate clause that modifies, or describes, the verb in the main clause of a complex sentence. An adverb clause tells *how, when, where, why,* or *under what conditions* the action occurs.

"*When the windows of Stan's Hardware started filling up with flowers,* everyone in town knew something had happened." In this sentence from the story, the italicized adverb clause modifies the verb *knew.* The adverb clause tells when everyone

knew. Adverb clauses are introduced by subordinating conjunctions such as *after, although, as, because, before, if, since, than, though, unless, until, when,* and *where.*

PRACTICE Review "A Crush" to find two other examples of sentences with adverb clauses. Copy each sentence. Then underline the adverb clause and double underline the verb it modifies.

● For more about adverb clauses, see **Language Handbook,** p. R37.

READING AND THINKING • INFERENCE

Clues in a piece of writing can help the reader infer, or figure out, information that is not stated directly. For example, in "A Crush," the writer never states that Ernie is mentally handicapped. The reader makes this inference from the description of Ernie's difficulty in learning to speak, his dependence on his mother, and his moving to a group home.

PRACTICE Does Dolores have any friends or boyfriends in town? Write a paragraph about what you can infer from the story about Dolores's social life. Refer to clues from the selection to support your inference.

● For more about inference, see **Reading Handbook,** pp. R92–R93.

VOCABULARY • THE SUFFIX *-ly*

A *quick* answer is given *quickly*. If you react *sadly*, it's because you are *sad.* The pattern you see in those words is one of the easy features of English. Adding *-ly* to the end of an adjective changes it to an adverb. Removing *-ly* from the end of an adverb changes it to an adjective. Not all adverbs end in *-ly,* and some words that end in *-ly* aren't adverbs, but if an adverb ends in *-ly,* you can usually make the adjective form of it by taking the *-ly* off. So, when you learn a new adverb, chances are you will also understand the adjective form of it, and vice versa.

The only tricky part about changing adjectives to adverbs involves spelling. If an adjective ends with *y,* you change the *y* to an *i* before adding *-ly. Creepy*

becomes *creepily,* not *creepyly*. If an adjective ends with *le,* you just change the *e* to *y. Lovable* becomes *lovably,* not *lovabley.*

PRACTICE Expand your vocabulary. If an adverb is given, write the adjective form of it. If an adjective is given, write the adverb form of it. Then use each word you've written in a sentence.

Adjectives	Adverbs
1. hardy	_____
2. _____	discreetly
3. taut	_____
4. _____	eventually
5. improbable	_____

Technology Skills

Spreadsheets: Creating a Spreadsheet

Accountants use spreadsheet software for budgets and other kinds of financial planning and record keeping. You can use one to help with your own financial planning and for other purposes. The terrific thing about electronic spreadsheets is that the mathematical work is all done by the computer.

When you open a new spreadsheet document, you'll see a worksheet and menus and toolbars similar to those on a word-processing document. Some of the icons, however, are found only on spreadsheet programs. Data is entered into small cells that make up rows and columns on the worksheet. A cell carries one piece of information. A column contains a category of data—for example, persons' names. A row contains a complete record for one person or thing. For example, a row might contain one person's name, address, job title, weekly salary, and other data.

You can also convert spreadsheet data into various kinds of graphs. (Spreadsheet software programs usually refer to graphs as charts.) The example on page 161 shows a bar graph that compares the estimated costs of the gifts listed on the left with their actual costs.

	A	B	C
1	**Gift List**	**Estimated Cost**	**Actual Cost**
2	New CD	$ 15.00	$ 12.95
3	Mall gift certificate	$ 25.00	$ 25.00
4	Scarf	$ 25.00	$ 27.50
5	Book	$ 10.00	$ 12.50
6	Movie gift certificate	$ 20.00	$ 20.00
7			
8	**Totals**	$ 95.00	$ 97.95

This shows a simple example of a spreadsheet. After the data was typed in, the computer found the total (or sum) of the costs. With a spreadsheet, you can do even difficult calculations quickly and easily.

TECHNOLOGY TIP

Be sure you check with your teacher or lab instructor about the spreadsheet program you are using. You may need to change these directions somewhat. In one popular spreadsheet program, for example, the formula for adding a group of cells uses two periods in place of a colon: =SUM(B2..B6).

Practice

1. Open your spreadsheet software.

2. Select **New** from the **File** menu. This will open a blank worksheet.

3. Without clicking, move your cursor over each item on the toolbars to get an idea of what functions are available. Use the program's Help if you want additional information about any of the tools.

4. Enter the gifts and estimated prices shown in the first spreadsheet example.

5. To get the computer to figure the sum, click in the cell where you want the sum to appear, but don't enter a figure into the cell.

6. Look at the top of your screen, and find the formula bar (look for an equal sign). Click on the = to begin the formula. An equal sign will appear in the space to the right of the formula bar. Without leaving any spaces, complete the

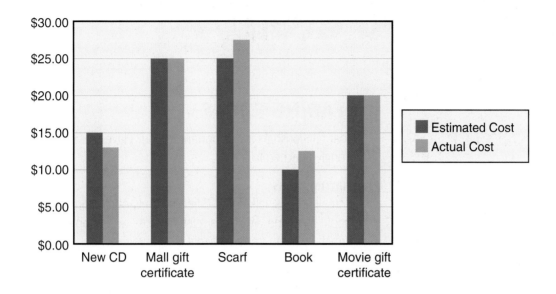

formula so that it looks like this: **=SUM(B2:B6)**. This tells the program that you want to add all the cells from B2 to B6. Hit the **Enter** key on your keyboard (the **Return** key on a Mac) when you finish your formula. The sum of the figures will appear in the highlighted cell.

ACTIVITIES

1. Working with a small group, find out how many hours per week each member spends: (a) studying for school and (b) watching television. Record the figures on a spreadsheet that looks something like this:

	A	B	C
1	**Student**	**Hours Studying**	**Hours Watching TV**
2	name		
3	name		
4	name		
5	name		
6			
7	**Averages**		

2. Have the spreadsheet figure the group's average time spent on studying for school and the average time spent watching television. The formula for computing an average is =SUM followed by the range of cells to be added, followed by a slash mark and the total number of students—for example, (B2:B5)/4.

3. Open a new worksheet. Add your data with the data of all the other groups in class. Have the computer calculate the class averages. Then make a bar graph to compare the averages for your class. Most programs will walk you through the steps in creating a chart. Use the Help feature if you need more help.

Before You Read

Last Cover

MEET PAUL ANNIXTER

Paul Annixter (a niks′ tər) is the pseudonym, or pen name, of Howard Sturtzel. Best known for his stories about nature and animal life, Sturtzel began writing at the age of nineteen. Asked why he became a writer, Sturtzel responded, "As a very young man I took up a timber claim in northern Minnesota. It was while proving up on the land that I began writing, mostly nature stories about the animals and elements I was up against." By 1950 he had written more than five hundred short stories.

Paul Annixter was born in 1894 in Minneapolis, Minnesota. He died in 1985.

READING FOCUS

What relationships are important to you? Have you ever felt strongly attached to a pet?

Sharing Ideas
In small groups, talk about different kinds of relationships people have and why close relationships—with people and animals—play an important role in everyone's life.

Setting a Purpose
Read to discover the relationships shared by the characters in this story.

BUILDING BACKGROUND

Did You Know?   Stories and fables have long portrayed the red fox as a clever and sly creature, always ready to trick an unsuspecting animal out of its food—or its life. Red foxes hunt small prey and do not hunt in packs. They are quick, solitary hunters.

VOCABULARY PREVIEW

bleak (blēk) *adj.* cheerless; depressing; p. 164
surly (sur′ lē) *adj.* rude and bad tempered; gruff; p. 164
invalid (in′ və lid) *n.* one who is disabled by disease or injury; p. 165
passive (pas′ iv) *adj.* not participating or active; p. 166
instinct (in′ stingkt) *n.* a way of knowing, behaving, or reacting that comes naturally rather than through learning; p. 167
sanction (sangk′ shən) *v.* to give support or encouragement to; approve; p. 168
wily (wī′ lē) *adj.* full of tricks; crafty; sly; p. 170
sanctuary (sangk′ choo er′ ē) *n.* a place of safety or protection; p. 170
incredulous (in krej′ ə ləs) *adj.* unwilling or unable to believe something; p. 170

Last Cover

Paul Annixter ～

I'm not sure I can tell you what you want to know about my brother; but everything about the pet fox is important, so I'll tell all that from the beginning.

It goes back to a winter afternoon after I'd hunted the woods all day for a sign of our lost pet. I remember the way my mother looked up as I came into the kitchen. Without my speaking, she knew what had happened. For six hours I had walked, reading signs, looking for a delicate print in the damp soil or even a hair that might have told of a red fox passing that way—but I had found nothing.

"Did you go up in the foothills?" Mom asked.

I nodded. My face was stiff from held-back tears. My brother, Colin, who was going on twelve, got it all from one look at me and went into a heartbroken, almost silent, crying.

Three weeks before, Bandit, the pet fox Colin and I had raised from a tiny kit,[1] had disappeared, and not even a rumor had been heard of him since.

"He'd have had to go off soon anyway," Mom comforted. "A big, lolloping fellow like him, he's got to live his life same as us. But he may come back. That fox set a lot of store by[2] you boys in spite of his wild ways."

---

1. Although it's a shortened form of kitten, *kit* refers to any young, fur-bearing animal, especially one that's smaller than normal.
2. *Lolloping* means "leaping or bounding," and to *set store by* means to "have trust or confidence in."

Last Cover

"He set a lot of store by our food, anyway," Father said. He sat in a chair by the kitchen window mending a piece of harness. "We'll be seeing a lot more of that fellow, never fear. That fox learned to pine for table scraps and young chickens. He was getting to be an egg thief, too, and he's not likely to forget that."

"That was only pranking[3] when he was little," Colin said desperately.

From the first, the tame fox had made tension in the family. It was Father who said we'd better name him Bandit, after he'd made away with his first young chicken.

"Maybe you know," Father said shortly. "But when an animal turns to egg sucking he's usually incurable. He'd better not come pranking around my chicken run again."

It was late February, and I remember the bleak, dead cold that had set in, cold that was a rare thing for our Carolina hills. Flocks of sparrows and snowbirds had appeared to peck hungrily at all that the pigs and chickens didn't eat.

"This one's a killer," Father would say of a morning, looking out at the whitened barn roof. "This one will make the shoats[4] squeal."

A fire snapped all day in our cookstove and another in the stone fireplace in the living room, but still the farmhouse was never warm. The leafless woods were bleak and empty, and I spoke of that to Father when I came back from my search.

"It's always a sad time in the woods when the seven sleepers are under cover," he said.

"What sleepers are they?" I asked. Father was full of woods lore.[5]

"Why, all the animals that have got sense enough to hole up and stay hid in weather like this. Let's see, how was it the old rhyme named them?

> *Surly bear and sooty bat,*
> *Brown chuck and masked coon,*
> *Chippy-munk and sly skunk,*
> *And all the mouses*
> *'Cept in men's houses.*

"And man would have joined them and made it eight, Granther Yeary always said, if he'd had a little more sense."

"I was wondering if the red fox mightn't make it eight," Mom said.

Father shook his head. "Late winter's a high time for foxes. Time when they're out deviling, not sleeping."

My chest felt hollow. I wanted to cry like Colin over our lost fox, but at fourteen a boy doesn't cry. Colin had squatted down on the floor and got out his small hammer and nails to start another new frame for a new picture. Maybe then he'd make a drawing for the frame and be able to forget his misery. It had been that way with him since he was five.

I thought of the new dress Mom had brought home a few days before in a heavy cardboard box. That box cover would be fine for Colin to draw on. I spoke of it, and Mom's glance thanked me as she went to

---

3. Here, *pranking* means "playfulness; mischief."
4. The *shoats* are young pigs.

5. The accumulated stories and beliefs about a subject are called *lore*.

Vocabulary

bleak (blēk) *adj.* cheerless; depressing
surly (sur' lē) *adj.* rude and bad tempered; gruff

get it. She and I worried a lot about Colin. He was small for his age, delicate and blond, his hair much lighter and softer than mine, his eyes deep and wide and blue. He was often sick, and I knew the fear Mom had that he might be predestined.[6] I'm just ordinary, like Father. I'm the sort of stuff that can take it—tough and strong—but Colin was always sort of special.

Mom lighted the lamp. Colin began cutting his white cardboard carefully, fitting it into his frame. Father's sharp glance turned on him now and again.

---

6. Mom fears that Colin has been chosen by God to die at a very young age.

"There goes the boy making another frame before there's a picture for it," he said. "It's too much like cutting out a man's suit for a fellow that's, say, twelve years old. Who knows whether he'll grow into it?"

Mom was into him then, quick. "Not a single frame of Colin's has ever gone to waste. The boy has real talent, Sumter, and it's time you realized it."

"Of course he has," Father said. "All kids have 'em. But they get over 'em."

"It isn't the pox we're talking of," Mom sniffed.

"In a way it is. Ever since you started talking up Colin's art, I've had an <u>invalid</u> for help around the place."

Vocabulary
invalid (in' və lid) *n.* one who is disabled by disease or injury

Fox Hunt, 1893. Winslow Homer. Oil on canvas, 38 x 68½ in. Museum of American Art, Pennsylvania Academy of Fine Art.

Viewing the painting: Do you think the painting captures Father's explanation that "winter's a high time for foxes"? Explain.

Last Cover

Father wasn't as hard as he made out, I knew, but he had to hold a balance against all Mom's frothing. For him the thing was the land and all that pertained to it. I was following in Father's footsteps, true to form, but Colin threatened to break the family tradition with his leaning toward art, with Mom "aiding and abetting[7] him," as Father liked to put it. For the past two years she had had dreams of my brother becoming a real artist and going away to the city to study.

It wasn't that Father had no understanding of such things. I could remember, through the years, Colin lying on his stomach in the front room making pencil sketches, and how a good drawing would catch Father's eye halfway across the room, and how he would sometimes gather up two or three of them to study, frowning and muttering, one hand in his beard, while a great pride rose in Colin, and in me too. Most of Colin's drawings were of the woods and wild things, and there Father was a master critic. He made out to scorn what seemed to him a <u>passive</u> "white-livered" interpretation of nature through brush and pencil instead of rod and rifle.

At supper that night Colin could scarcely eat. Ever since he'd been able to walk, my brother had had a growing love of wild things, but Bandit had been like his very own, a gift of the woods. One afternoon a year and half before, Father and Laban Small had been running a vixen through the hills with their dogs. With the last of her strength the she-fox had made for her den, not far from our house. The dogs had overtaken her and killed her just before she reached it. When Father and Laban came up, they'd found Colin crouched nearby holding her cub in his arms.

Father had been for killing the cub, which was still too young to shift for itself, but Colin's grief had brought Mom into it. We'd taken the young fox into the kitchen, all of us, except Father, gone a bit silly over the little thing. Colin had held it in his arms and fed it warm milk from a spoon.

"Watch out with all your soft ways," Father had warned, standing in the doorway. "You'll make too much of him. Remember, you can't make a dog out of a fox. Half of that little critter has to love, but the other half is a wild hunter. You boys will mean a whole lot to him while he's a kit, but there'll come a day when you won't mean a thing to him and he'll leave you shorn."[8]

For two weeks after that Colin had nursed the cub, weaning it from milk to bits of meat. For a year they were always together. The cub grew fast. It was soon following Colin and me about the barnyard. It turned out to be a patch fox, with a saddle of darker fur across its shoulders.

I haven't the words to tell you what the fox meant to us. It was far more wonderful owning him than owning any dog. There was something rare and secret like the spirit of the woods about him, and back of his calm, straw-gold eyes was the sense

---

7. *Abetting* means "encouraging."

8. To be left *shorn* is to be cut off, like hair, and left alone.

Vocabulary
passive (pas′ iv) *adj.* not participating or active

of a brain the equal of a man's. The fox became Colin's whole life.

Each day, going and coming from school, Colin and I took long side trips through the woods, looking for Bandit. Wild things' memories were short, we knew; we'd have to find him soon or the old bond would be broken.

Ever since I was ten I'd been allowed to hunt with Father, so I was good at reading signs. But, in a way, Colin knew more about the woods and wild things than Father or me. What came to me from long observation, Colin seemed to know by instinct.

It was Colin who felt out, like an Indian, the stretch of woods where Bandit had his den, who found the first slim, small fox-print in the damp earth. And then, on an afternoon in March, we saw him. I remember the day well, the racing clouds, the wind rattling the tops of the pine trees and swaying the Spanish moss. Bandit had just come out of a clump of laurel; in the maze of leaves behind him we caught a glimpse of a slim red vixen, so we knew he had found a mate. She melted from sight like a shadow, but Bandit turned to watch us, his mouth open, his tongue lolling as he smiled his old foxy smile. On his thin chops, I saw a telltale chicken feather.

Colin moved silently forward, his movements so quiet and casual he seemed to be standing still. He called Bandit's name, and the fox held his ground, drawn to us with all his senses. For a few moments he let Colin actually put an arm about him. It was then I knew that he loved us still, for all of Father's warnings. He really loved us back, with a fierce, secret love no tame thing ever gave. But the urge of his life just then was toward his new mate. Suddenly, he whirled about and disappeared in the laurels.

Colin looked at me with glowing eyes. "We haven't really lost him, Stan. When he gets through with his spring sparking[9] he may come back. But we've got to show ourselves to him a lot, so he won't forget."

"It's a go," I said.

"Promise not to say a word to Father," Colin said, and I agreed. For I knew by the chicken feather that Bandit had been up to no good.

A week later the woods were budding and the thickets were rustling with all manner of wild things scurrying on the love scent. Colin managed to get a glimpse of Bandit every few days. He couldn't get close though, for the spring running was a lot more important to a fox than any human beings were.

Every now and then Colin got out his framed box cover and looked at it, but he never drew anything on it; he never even picked up his pencil. I remember wondering if what Father had said about framing a picture before you had one had spoiled something for him.

I was helping Father with the planting now, but Colin managed to be in the woods every day. By degrees he learned Bandit's range, where he drank and rested and where he was likely to be according to the time of day. One day he told me how

---

9. *Spring sparking* refers to the mating season.

Vocabulary

instinct (in' stingkt) *n.* a way of knowing, behaving, or reacting that comes naturally rather than through learning

he had petted Bandit again, and how they had walked together a long way in the woods. All this time we had kept his secret from Father.

As summer came on, Bandit began to live up to the prediction Father had made. Accustomed to human beings he moved without fear about the scattered farms of the region, raiding barns and hen runs that other foxes wouldn't have dared go near. And he taught his wild mate to do the same. Almost every night they got into some poultry house, and by late June Bandit was not only killing chickens and ducks but feeding on eggs and young chicks whenever he got the chance.

Stories of his doings came to us from many sources, for he was still easily recognized by the dark patch on his shoulders. Many a farmer took a shot at him as he fled and some of them set out on his trail with dogs, but they always returned home without even sighting him. Bandit was familiar with all the dogs in the region, and he knew a hundred tricks to confound[10] them. He got a reputation that year beyond that of any fox our hills had known. His confidence grew, and he gave up wild hunting altogether and lived entirely off the poultry farmers. By September the hill farmers banded together to hunt him down.

It was Father who brought home that news one night. All time-honored rules of the fox chase were to be broken in this hunt; if the dogs couldn't bring Bandit down, he was to be shot on sight. I was stricken and furious. I remember the misery of Colin's face in the lamplight. Father, who took pride in all the ritual of the hunt, had refused to be a party to such an affair, though in justice he could do nothing but sanction any sort of hunt, for

---

10. Here, *confound* means "confuse."

Vocabulary
sanction (sangk′ shən) *v.* to give support or encouragement to; approve

Bandit, as old Sam Wetherwax put it, had been "purely getting in the Lord's hair."

The hunt began next morning, and it was the biggest turnout our hills had known. There were at least twenty mounted men in the party and as many dogs. Father and I were working in the lower field as they passed along the river road. Most of the hunters carried rifles, and they looked ugly.

Twice during the morning I went up to the house to find Colin, but he was nowhere around. As we worked, Father and I could follow the progress of the hunt by the distant hound music on the breeze. We could tell just where the hunters first caught sight of the fox and where Bandit was leading the dogs during the first hour. We knew as well as if we'd seen it how Bandit roused another fox along Turkey Branch and forced it to run for him, and how the dogs swept after it for twenty minutes before they sensed their mistake.

Noon came, and Colin had not come in to eat. After dinner Father didn't go back to the field. He moped about, listening to the hound talk. He didn't like what was going on any more than I did, and now and again I caught his smile of satisfaction when we heard the broken, angry notes of the hunting horn, telling that the dogs had lost the trail or had run another fox.

I was restless, and I went up into the hills in midafternoon. I ranged the woods for miles, thinking all the time of Colin. Time lost all meaning for me, and the short day was nearing an end, when I heard the horn talking again, telling that the fox had put over another trick. All day he had deviled the dogs and mocked the hunters. This new trick and the coming night would work to save him. I was wildly glad, as I moved down toward Turkey Branch and stood listening for a time by the deep, shaded pool where for years we boys had gone swimming, sailed boats, and dreamed summer dreams.

Suddenly, out of the corner of my eye, I saw the sharp ears and thin, pointed mask of a fox—in the water almost beneath me. It was Bandit, craftily submerged there, all but his head, resting in the cool water of the pool and the shadow of the two big beeches that spread above it. He must have run forty miles or more since morning. And he must have hidden in this place before. His knowing, crafty mask blended perfectly with the shadows and a mass of drift and branches that had collected by the bank of the pool. He was so still a pair of thrushes flew up from the spot as I came up, not knowing he was there.

Bandit's bright, harried[11] eyes were looking right at me. But I did not look at him direct. Some woods instinct, swifter than thought, kept me from it. So he and I met as in another world, indirectly, with feeling but without sign or greeting.

Suddenly I saw that Colin was standing almost beside me. Silently as a water snake, he had come out of the bushes and stood there. Our eyes met, and a quick and secret smile passed between us. It was a rare moment in which I really "met" my brother, when something of his essence[12] flowed into me and I knew all of him. I've never lost it since.

My eyes still turned from the fox, my heart pounding. I moved quietly away, and Colin moved with me. We whistled softly

---

11. Bandit's eyes show that he is troubled (harried).
12. Colin's essence is his most basic nature or spirit.

Last Cover

as we went, pretending to busy ourselves along the bank of the stream. There was magic to it, as if by will we wove a web of protection about the fox, a ring-pass-not that none might penetrate. It was so, too, we felt, in the brain of Bandit, and that doubled the charm. To us he was still our little pet that we had carried in our arms on countless summer afternoons.

Two hundred yards upstream, we stopped beside slim, fresh tracks in the mud where Bandit had entered the branch. The tracks angled upstream. But in the water the wily creature had turned down.

We climbed the far bank to wait, and Colin told me how Bandit's secret had been his secret ever since an afternoon three months before, when he'd watched the fox swim downstream to hide in the deep pool. Today he'd waited on the bank, feeling that Bandit, hard pressed by the dogs, might again seek the pool for sanctuary.

We looked back once we turned homeward. He still had not moved. We didn't know until later that he was killed that same night by a chance hunter, as he crept out from his hiding place.

That evening Colin worked a long time on his framed box cover that had lain about the house untouched all summer. He kept at it all the next day too. I had never seen him work so hard. I seemed to sense in the air the feeling he was putting into it, how he was *believing* his picture into being. It was evening before he finished it. Without a word he handed it to Father. Mom and I went and looked over his shoulder.

It was a delicate and intricate pencil drawing of the deep branch pool, and there was Bandit's head and watching, fear-filled eyes hiding there amid the leaves and shadows, woven craftily into the maze of twigs and branches, as if by nature's art itself. Hardly a fox there at all, but the place where he was—or should have been. I recognized it instantly, but Mom gave a sort of incredulous sniff.

"I'll declare," she said, "It's mazy as a puzzle. It just looks like a lot of sticks and leaves to me."

Long minutes of study passed before Father's eye picked out the picture's secret, as few men's could have done. I laid that to Father's being a born hunter. That was a picture that might have been done especially for him. In fact, I guess it was.

Finally he turned to Colin with his deep, slow smile. "So that's how Bandit fooled them all," he said. He sat holding the picture with a sort of tenderness for a long time, while we glowed in the warmth of the shared secret. That was Colin's moment. Colin's art stopped being a pox to Father right there. And later, when the time came for Colin to go to art school, it was Father who was his solid backer.

Vocabulary
wily (wī′ lē) *adj.* full of tricks; crafty; sly
sanctuary (sangk′ chōō er′ ē) *n.* a place of safety or protection
incredulous (in krej′ ə ləs) *adj.* unwilling or unable to believe something

Responding to Literature

PERSONAL RESPONSE

- ◆ Were you surprised by the outcome of the story? Explain.
- ◆ Think back to the group discussion in the **Reading Focus** on page 162. What, if any, new ideas did the story give you about relationships? Record your thoughts in your journal.

Analyzing Literature

RECALL

1. Who named Bandit? What does the name tell about this person's attitude toward the fox?
2. What is Colin's talent? At the beginning of the story, what is his father's attitude toward this talent?
3. According to the narrator, what are some differences between the two brothers?
4. Why does the hunt take place and what happens to Bandit?

INTERPRET

5. At the beginning, what effect does the fox have on the relationship between family members? Explain.
6. Why does Colin's father feel threatened by his son's talent? What tradition is Colin threatening? Explain.
7. What do the narrator's feelings about his brother and about the pet fox reveal about the narrator? Use details from the story to support your ideas.
8. Why does the father's attitude about Bandit change during the course of the story?

EVALUATE AND CONNECT

9. Trust is one of the **themes** of "Last Cover." What role do you think trust plays in the story? Explain.
10. Theme Connection How does the relationship between Colin and his father change over the course of the story? How does the relationship between the brothers change? Explain.

LITERARY ELEMENTS

Plot

The sequence of events in a story, novel, or play is called a **plot.** A good writer uses each event in a plot to cause or lead to the next event. The plot begins by introducing the story's characters, setting, and situation. This is called the **exposition.** It captures the reader's attention with a strong **conflict** between opposing forces. **Rising action** in the plot adds complications to the conflict that lead to a **climax,** or point when the reader's interest is at its highest. A **resolution** reveals the final outcome of the plot.

1. Briefly outline the plot of "Last Cover."

2. Use examples from the plot to show how Bandit at first causes tensions in the family but finally helps bring the family together.

● See **Literary Terms Handbook,** p. R8.

Extending Your Response

Writing About Literature

Characterization   The manner in which a writer develops the characters in a story is called **characterization**. Authors characterize in several ways. A narrator may describe each character at length as he or she is introduced. We also learn about characters through their actions and interactions with other characters, through what they say or think, and through what other characters say about them. Write a few paragraphs about the characters in "Last Cover." What does the author reveal to readers about his characters? How? Do the characters seem true to life? How do the characters change during the story? Which character do you like the most? Why? Use examples and quotations from the story to support your opinions.

Creative Writing

Changing Point of View   How would this story be different if Colin had narrated it? Imagine that you are Colin. Write a journal entry about Bandit's life, what happens to him, and your feelings about the whole situation. Be sure to include your attitude toward the other members of your family.

Literature Groups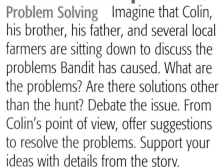

Problem Solving   Imagine that Colin, his brother, his father, and several local farmers are sitting down to discuss the problems Bandit has caused. What are the problems? Are there solutions other than the hunt? Debate the issue. From Colin's point of view, offer suggestions to resolve the problems. Support your ideas with details from the story.

Performing

With a small group, choose an important scene from the story and dramatize it for your classmates. Reread the section of the story several times and discuss each character's actions and feelings so that you understand what motivates each character in that scene.

Reading Further

If you would like to read more stories by Paul Annixter, try these books:
Pride of Lions, and Other Stories
The Best Nature Stories of Paul Annixter

For an animal story that has been popular for more than a hundred years, try:
Black Beauty by Anna Sewell

Save your work for your portfolio.

Skill Minilessons

GRAMMAR AND LANGUAGE • COMMAS USED WITH WORDS IN A SERIES

Commas make sentences easier to understand by signaling a pause or separation between parts of a sentence. Use commas to separate three or more words, phrases, or clauses in a series.

Example: Colin carried his pens, his pencils, and his paper to his desk.

PRACTICE Review "Last Cover" to find an example of a sentence that uses commas to separate three or more words or phrases in a series. Write this sentence in your journal, and then make up one of your own.

● For more about using commas in a series, see **Language Handbook,** p. R37.

READING AND THINKING • PREDICTING

Good readers make many types of inferences as they read. One type involves predicting outcomes. Readers may use details to predict the outcomes of conversations, actions, or events within a story. In other words, you may be able to figure out what will happen next in a story. Then, as you read, you can check your predictions by finding out what actually happened.

PRACTICE Reread "Last Cover" and find two examples of details that could help a reader predict what will happen next in the story. Share your findings with your classmates and see how many different details were found.

● For more about predicting, see **Reading Handbook,** pp. R86–R87.

VOCABULARY • ROOTS

The root of a word is the word part that is used as the base in making other words. Knowing the meaning of a root helps you understand other words with the same root. For example, *invalid* contains the root *val,* meaning "strong or well." An *invalid* is not strong or well. A *valid* argument is one that's well supported. *Valor* is the kind of bravery that comes from inner strength.

The word *incredulous* contains the root *cred,* which comes from a Latin word meaning "to believe." *Credit* can mean "approval or acknowledgment," but it can also mean "belief or trust." If you *credit* someone's statement, you believe it. By combining your understanding of the root *cred*

with any context clues that may exist, you can probably figure out the meaning of words in which this root appears.

PRACTICE Briefly state what you'd guess is the meaning of each underlined word.

1. I doubted his credibility.
2. She told an incredible story.
3. Don't give credence to such a ridiculous statement.
4. It's not fair to lie to an innocent, credulous child.
5. His lawyer tried to discredit the witnesses for the other side.

Before You Read

Birthday Box and *There Is No Word for Goodbye*

MEET
JANE YOLEN

Jane Yolen wrote her first two books before she was in high school. One was about pirates and the other about the pioneer west. Since then she has written more than 150 books.

Jane Yolen was born in 1939. This story was first published in 1995.

MEET
MARY TALLMOUNTAIN

Mary Tall-Mountain was born into the Koykon-Athabaskan tribe in Nulato, Alaska. It wasn't until she was in her fifties that TallMountain began to write poetry, sometimes for sixteen hours a day! Her poems recapture her Athabaskan childhood.

Mary TallMountain was born in 1918. "There Is No Word for Goodbye" was published in Continuum: Poems by Mary TallMountain in 1988.

READING FOCUS

What's the most memorable gift you ever unwrapped? Have you ever thought about the gifts you have been given that you can't hold in your hands—gifts like time, friendship, or love?

QuickWrite
Make a quick list of your favorite gifts—the kind you can and cannot hold in your hands.

Setting a Purpose
Read these selections to discover two views on love and separation.

BUILDING BACKGROUND

Sometimes writers don't have to spend days and weeks coming up with an idea for a story. In 1995 an editor named Johanna Hurwitz decided to invite ten writers, including Jane Yolen, to write about a child who receives a beautifully wrapped empty box for a birthday present. The writers were inspired to write fairy tales, fantasy, poetry, and realistic stories. Each writer's imagination was sparked by the same idea, and each writer wrote a completely original piece of literature.

VOCABULARY PREVIEW

insistent (in sis′ tənt) *adj.* demanding attention or notice; p. 176
stark (stärk) *adv.* completely; harshly or grimly; p. 177
infinite (in′ fə nit) *adj.* boundless; limitless; extremely great; p. 177
subtle (sut′ əl) *adj.* not open or direct; not obvious; p. 178

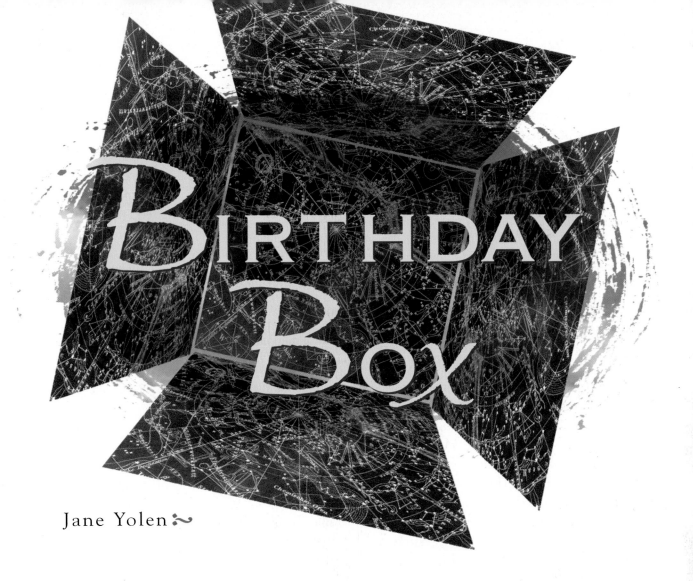

BIRTHDAY BOX

Jane Yolen ∿

I was ten years old when my mother died. Ten years old on that very day. Still she gave me a party of sorts. Sick as she was, Mama had seen to it, organizing it at the hospital. She made sure the doctors and nurses all brought me presents. We were good friends with them all by that time, because Mama had been in the hospital for so long.

The head nurse, V. Louise Higgins (I never did know what that V stood for), gave me a little box, which was sort of funny because she was the biggest of all the nurses there. I mean she was tremendous. And she was the only one who insisted on wearing all white. Mama had called her the great white shark when she was first admitted, only not to V. Louise's face. "All those needles," Mama had said. "Like teeth." But V. Louise was sweet, not sharklike at all, and she'd been so gentle with Mama.

I opened the little present first. It was a fountain pen, a real one, not a fake one like you get at Kmart.

"Now you can write beautiful stories, Katie," V. Louise said to me.

I didn't say that stories come out of your head, not out of a pen. That wouldn't have been polite, and Mama—even sick—was real big on politeness.

"Thanks, V. Louise," I said.

The Stardust Twins—which is what Mama called Patty and Tracey-Lynn because they reminded her of dancers in an old-fashioned ballroom—gave me a present together. It was a diary and had a picture of a little girl in pink, reading in a garden swing. A little young for me, a little too cute. I mean, I read Stephen King[1] and want to write like him. But as Mama always reminded me whenever Dad finally remembered to send me something, it was the thought that counted, not the actual gift.

"It's great," I told them. "I'll write in it with my new pen." And I wrote my name on the first page just to show them I meant it.

They hugged me and winked at Mama. She tried to wink back but was just too tired and shut both her eyes instead.

Lily, who is from Jamaica, had baked me some sweet bread. Mary Margaret gave me a gold cross blessed by the pope, which I put on even though Mama and I weren't churchgoers. That was Dad's thing.

Then Dr. Dann, the intern[2] who was on days, and Dr. Pucci, the oncologist (which is the fancy name for a cancer doctor), gave me a big box filled to the top with little presents, each wrapped up individually. All things they knew I'd love—paperback books and writing paper and erasers with funny animal heads and colored paper clips and a rubber stamp that printed FROM KATIE'S DESK and other stuff. They must have raided a stationery store.

There was one box, though, they held out till the end. It was about the size of a large top hat. The paper was deep blue and covered with stars; not fake stars but real stars, I mean, like a map of the night sky. The ribbon was two shades of blue with silver threads running through. There was no name on the card.

"Who's it from?" I asked.

None of the nurses answered, and the doctors both suddenly were studying the ceiling tiles with the kind of intensity they usually saved for X rays. No one spoke. In fact the only sound for the longest time was Mama's breathing machine going in and out and in and out. It was a harsh, horrible, insistent sound, and usually I talked and talked to cover up the noise. But I was waiting for someone to tell me.

At last V. Louise said, "It's from your mama, Katie. She told us what she wanted. And where to get it."

I turned and looked at Mama then, and her eyes were open again. Funny, but sickness had made her even more beautiful than good health had. Her skin was like that old paper, the kind they used to write on with quill pens, and stretched out over her bones so she looked like a model. Her

---

1. An extremely popular novelist, *Stephen King* writes mainly tales of horror and the supernatural.
2. An *intern* is a recent medical school graduate who works under the supervision of experienced doctors.

Vocabulary
insistent (in sis′ tənt) *adj.* demanding attention or notice

eyes, which had been a deep, brilliant blue, were now like the fall sky, bleached and softened. She was like a faded photograph of herself. She smiled a very small smile at me. I knew it was an effort.

"It's you," she mouthed. I read her lips. I had gotten real good at that. I thought she meant it was a present for me.

"Of course it is," I said cheerfully. I had gotten good at that, too, being cheerful when I didn't feel like it. "Of course it is."

I took the paper off the box carefully, not tearing it but folding it into a tidy packet. I twisted the ribbons around my hand and then put them on the pillow by her hand. It made the stark white hospital bed look almost festive.

Under the wrapping, the box was beautiful itself. It was made of a heavy cardboard and covered with a linen material that had a pattern of cloud-filled skies.

I opened the box slowly and . . .

"It's empty," I said. "Is this a joke?" I turned to ask Mama, but she was gone. I mean, her body was there, but she wasn't. It was as if she was as empty as the box.

Dr. Pucci leaned over her and listened with a stethoscope,[3] then almost absently patted Mama's head. Then, with infinite care, V. Louise closed Mama's eyes, ran her hand across Mama's cheek, and turned off the breathing machine.

---

3. A *stethoscope* (steth′ ə skōp′) is an instrument used to listen to sounds made by the internal organs of the body, especially the lungs and heart. The French doctor who invented the stethoscope in 1817 got the idea after seeing children making sounds through a hollow log.

"Mama!" I cried. And to the nurses and doctors, I screamed, "Do something!" And because the room had suddenly become so silent, my voice echoed back at me. "Mama, do something."

❋   ❋   ❋   ❋   ❋

I cried steadily for, I think, a week. Then I cried at night for a couple of months. And then for about a year I cried at anniversaries, like Mama's birthday or mine, at Thanksgiving, on Mother's Day. I stopped writing. I stopped reading except for school assignments. I was pretty mean to my half brothers and totally rotten to my stepmother and Dad. I felt empty and angry, and they all left me pretty much alone.

And then one night, right after my first birthday without Mama, I woke up remembering how she had said, "It's you." Not, "It's for you," just "It's you." Now Mama had been a high school English teacher and a writer herself. She'd had poems published in little magazines. She didn't use words carelessly. In the end she could hardly use any words at all. So—I asked myself in that dark room—why had she said, "It's you"? Why were they the very last words she had ever said to me, forced out with her last breath?

I turned on the bedside light and got out of bed. The room was full of shadows, not all of them real.

Pulling the desk chair over to my closet, I climbed up and felt along the top shelf, and against the back wall, there was the birthday box, just where I had thrown it the day I had moved in with my dad.

Vocabulary
stark (stärk) *adv.* completely; harshly or grimly
infinite (in′ fə nit) *adj.* boundless; limitless; extremely great

Emerging Angel. John S. Bunker. Mixed media, 8 x 11 in.
Viewing the painting: How is the subject of the painting like Katie? How is it like her writing?

I pulled it down and opened it. It was as empty as the day I had put it away.

"It's you," I whispered to the box.

And then suddenly I knew.

Mama had meant *I* was the box, solid and sturdy, maybe even beautiful or at least interesting on the outside. But I had to fill up the box to make it all it could be. And I had to fill me up as well. She had guessed what might happen to me, had told me in a <u>subtle</u> way. In the two words she could manage.

I stopped crying and got some paper out of the desk drawer. I got out my fountain pen. I started writing, and I haven't stopped since. The first thing I wrote was about that birthday. I put it in the box, and pretty soon that box was overflowing with stories. And poems. And memories.

And so was I.

And so was I.

Vocabulary
subtle (sut′ əl) *adj.* not open or direct; not obvious

There Is No Word for Goodbye

Mary TallMountain :~

Sokoya,° I said, looking through
    the net of wrinkles into
    wise black pools
    of her eyes.

5   What do you say in Athabaskan
    when you leave each other?
    What is the word
    for goodbye?

A shade of feeling rippled
10   the wind-tanned skin.
    Ah, nothing, she said,
    watching the river flash.

She looked at me close.
    We just say, Tlaa. That means,
15   See you.
    We never leave each other.
    When does your mouth
    say goodbye to your heart?

She touched me light
20   as a bluebell.
    You forget when you leave us,
    You're so small then.
    We don't use that word.

We always think you're coming back,
25   but if you don't,
    we'll see you some place else.
    You understand.
    There is no word for goodbye.

---

1 *Sokoya* means "aunt."

Female Figure, 1830. Haida, Queen Charlotte Islands, British Columbia. Hardwood (possibly crab apple), wool, red and black paint, 11 x 5 x 2⅞ in. The Thaw Collection, Fenimore House Museum, Cooperstown, NY.

Responding to Literature

PERSONAL RESPONSE

◆ Recall the list of gifts you made for the **Reading Focus** on page 174. Before reading the story did you imagine a gift that you both can and cannot hold?

◆ What kind of gift did the aunt in "There Is No Word for Goodbye" give the speaker of the poem?

Analyzing Literature

RECALL

1. How did Katie's mother manage to buy her the birthday box?

2. What happens to the family after Katie's mother dies?

3. What question does the speaker in "There Is No Word for Goodbye" ask the aunt in the beginning of the poem?

INTERPRET

4. What can you **infer** about the character of Katie's mother when you realize that, in spite of her serious illness, she had planned a party and presents for Katie?

5. How does the aunt in TallMountain's poem feel about saying goodbye to the people she loves?

EVALUATE AND CONNECT

6. Why do you think Jane Yolen tells the reader what happens to Katie's mother in the first sentence?

7. How does filling the box with her writing help Katie deal with her grief?

8. How would you react if someone you loved gave you an empty box? Explain your answer.

9. Think about a relationship you have with an older friend or relative. How would you feel if you had to say goodbye to each other?

10. Theme Connection   What do both "Birthday Box" and "There Is No Word for Goodbye" have to say about love between family members?

LITERARY ELEMENTS

Character

Characters are the actors in a work of literature. They can be people, animals, or whatever the writer chooses. In "Birthday Box," Katie and her mother are the main characters. The minor characters are the nurses and doctors in the hospital. In "There Is No Word for Goodbye," the characters are the speaker and the speaker's aunt.

1. Katie's mother hardly speaks in "Birthday Box." In what other ways does the author tell the reader about this character?

2. What do the aunt in "There Is No Word for Goodbye" and Katie's mother have in common?

● See **Literary Terms Handbook,** p. R2.

Extending Your Response

Writing About Literature

Setting   Most of the action in "Birthday Box" takes place in a hospital room. What details can you visualize about the hospital room from Yolen's description? Write a paragraph explaining how the hospital setting contributes to the effect of the story.

Creative Writing

Symbolic Gifts   Katie's box is a symbol of Katie herself and of her mother's love. The language lesson received by the speaker in "There Is No Word for Goodbye" is also a symbol of love. Write a short story about a character who receives a symbolic gift.

Literature Groups

The Empty Box   When Katie receives the empty box she thinks it is a joke. It takes her a year to understand what her mother meant by this gift. Do you think Katie's mother should have made sure Katie understood the meaning of the box from the beginning? Discuss your ideas and draw a conclusion. Be prepared to share your group's opinion with the whole class.

Learning for Life

Writing a Speech   Sometimes people who have lived through a painful experience want to help others in a similar situation. Imagine that five years after her mother has died, Katie is asked to speak to a group of children who have lost a parent. Write a speech for Katie that expresses what she has learned about overcoming grief and finding meaning in life after such a loss.

Art Activity

Wrap It!   Design your own wrapping paper. Decide what special occasion your paper will be used for. Then design a paper to suit that occasion. Draw your design at a smaller scale on regular 8½ x 11-inch paper, and share it with your class.

Reading Further

Check out these other books by Jane Yolen:
The Devil's Arithmetic
Here There Be Dragons

Save your work for your portfolio.

Skill Minilesson

VOCABULARY • NEGATIVE PREFIXES

How do you change *active, moral, regular,* and *legal* into words that mean the exact opposite? Add a prefix to each one, making *inactive, immoral, irregular,* and *illegal.* The basic prefix is *in-,* but its spelling changes to *im-, ir-,* or *il-* before certain letters. Be careful, though, because these prefixes have other meanings, and they don't always change a word into its opposite. When in doubt, use a dictionary for help.

PRACTICE   Write the five words from this list in which you think *in-, im-, ir-,* or *il-* is a negative prefix.

impress	income	inconsiderate
impure	injustice	impractical
irritate	indeed	irresponsible
	illustrate	

GRAMMAR LINK

Using Adjectives and Adverbs Correctly

Adjectives describe nouns or pronouns. The **comparative** form of an adjective compares two nouns or pronouns; the **superlative** form compares more than two.

Comparative: Maria is <u>younger</u> than Ricardo.

Superlative: Maria is her parents' <u>youngest</u> child.

Adverbs describe verbs, adjectives, or other adverbs. The comparative form of an adverb compares two actions; the superlative form compares more than two.

Comparative: Susan runs <u>faster</u> than Jeff.

Superlative: Of all the runners on the team, Susan runs the <u>fastest</u>.

The endings *-er* and *-est* are used to form the comparative and superlative forms of most short adjectives and adverbs. For longer adjectives and adverbs, the words *more* and *most* are usually used.

Adjectives: <u>dark</u> hair, <u>darker</u> hair, <u>darkest</u> hair

<u>curious</u> student, <u>more curious</u> student, <u>most curious</u> student

Adverbs: works <u>hard</u>, works <u>harder</u>, works <u>hardest</u>

smiles <u>happily</u>, smiles <u>more happily</u>, smiles <u>most happily</u>

Some adjectives and adverbs are *irregular.* Irregular adjectives and adverbs do not follow the same rules for forming comparatives and superlatives. Examples: good, better, best; badly, worse, worst.

● For more about using adjectives and adverbs, see **Language Handbook,** p. R27.

EXERCISE

Write the correct comparative or superlative form of the modifier shown in parentheses.

1. Ernie learned (slowly) than an average child.
2. Jack knew him (well) than anyone else and helped him (much) than anyone.
3. Of all the things in the world, Ernie was (fond) of his seed packets.
4. Ernie started feeling (strongly) about Dolores than he felt about his seeds.
5. Who was (curious) about the flowers—Dolores, Dick, or the Avon lady?

Writing Skills

Organizing Ideas for Comparison and Contrast

When you write to explore likenesses and differences, you are using **comparison and contrast**. Diagrams can help you organize a comparison-and-contrast essay.

Venn Diagram The Venn diagram below organizes details about Alfonso and his brother Ernie, from "Broken Chain" in Theme 1, pages 44–52. Each oval shows traits of one character. Traits shared by both characters appear where the ovals overlap.

Alfonso
seventh grade
smaller, with crooked teeth
wants to look good
considers others' feelings
keeps his things neat

Both
have bikes
want to impress girls
are easily embarrassed

Ernie
ninth grade
bigger and tougher
wants to be in charge
puts himself first
lets his things get messy

Comparison Chart A comparison chart helps when you know which features you will compare. List features as headings along the left side. List subjects as headings across the top. In the example, the features are literary elements of the Theme 1 stories "Broken Chain" and "Fish Cheeks."

	BROKEN CHAIN	**FISH CHEEKS**
SETTING	Fresno, California, in the 1980s	Oakland, California, in 1966
MAIN CHARACTERS	Alfonso, his brother Ernie, Sandra	Amy, her parents, Robert, and his parents

EXERCISES

1. Make a Venn diagram comparing and contrasting the main characters from two different stories in this theme. Then make a chart comparing the plots and themes of the stories.

2. Use information from your diagram and chart to write an essay comparing and contrasting the two stories.

Before You Read

Rip Van Winkle

MEET WASHINGTON IRVING

Washington Irving was the first American writer to win international fame. *The Sketch Book* (1820), a collection of stories admired throughout Europe, included Irving's two most famous tales, "Rip Van Winkle" and "The Legend of Sleepy Hollow." Like his famous fictional character Rip Van Winkle, Washington Irving was a born wanderer. Even as a child, he later wrote, "I began my travels, and made many tours into foreign parts and unknown regions of my native city, to the frequent alarm of my parents."

Washington Irving was born in New York City in 1783 and died in 1859.

READING FOCUS

How has the world changed since you were born? What about since your parents were born?

Think/Pair/Share
Take a moment to jot down your responses to the questions above. Then share your thoughts and feelings with a partner.

Setting a Purpose
Read this selection for the pleasure of discovering a story that readers have enjoyed for almost two hundred years.

BUILDING BACKGROUND

The Time and Place
The setting is the Hudson River valley and the Catskill Mountains, in southeastern New York State. The story takes place in the eighteenth century.

VOCABULARY PREVIEW

impunity (im pū′ nə tē) *n.* freedom from punishment, harm, or bad effects; p. 187

perseverance (pur′ sə vēr′ əns) *n.* continuation despite difficulty; determination; p. 187

incessantly (in ses′ ənt lē) *adv.* endlessly; constantly; p. 188

muse (mūz) *v.* to think or reflect; p. 190

singularity (sing′ gyə lar′ ə tē) *n.* that which is remarkable or out of the ordinary; unusualness; p. 191

incomprehensible (in′kom prē hen′ sə bəl) *adj.* not understandable; p. 191

perplexity (pər plek′ sə tē) *n.* doubt or uncertainty; puzzlement; p. 194

invariably (in vār′ ē ə blē) *adv.* without exception; p. 194

faltering (fôl′ tər ing) *adj.* shaky because of uncertainty; p. 199

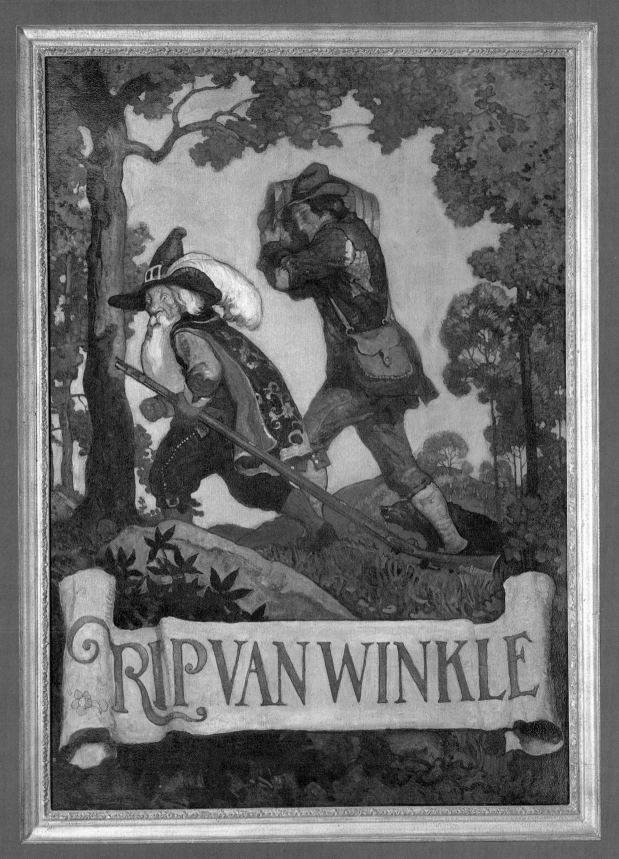

Title page from *Rip Van Winkle,* 1921. N. C. Wyeth.
Oil on canvas. Millport Conservancy, Lititz, PA.

Washington Irving

RIP VAN WINKLE

Whoever has made a voyage up the Hudson must remember the Kaatskill Mountains. They are a dismembered branch of the great Appalachian[1] family, and are seen away to the west of the river, swelling up to a noble height, and lording it over the surrounding country. Every change of season, every change of weather, indeed, every hour of the day, produces some change in the magical hues and shapes of these mountains, and they are regarded by all the good wives, far and near, as perfect barometers. When the weather is fair and settled, they are clothed in blue and purple, and print their bold outlines on the clear evening sky; but sometimes, when the rest of the landscape is cloudless, they will gather a hood of gray vapors about their summits, which, in the last rays of the setting sun, will glow and light up like a crown of glory.

At the foot of these fairy mountains, the voyager may have descried[2] the light smoke curling up from a village, whose shingled roofs gleam among the trees, just where the blue tints of the upland melt away into the fresh green of the nearer landscape. It is a little village, of great antiquity, having been founded by some of the Dutch colonists, in the early times of the province, just about the beginning of the government of the good Peter Stuyvesant[3] (may he rest in peace!) and there were some of the houses of the original settlers standing within a few years, built of small yellow bricks brought from Holland, having latticed windows and gable fronts, surmounted with weathercocks.

In that same village and in one of these very houses (which, to tell the precise truth, was sadly timeworn and weather-beaten), there lived many years since, while the country was yet a province of Great Britain, a simple good-natured fellow, of the name of Rip Van Winkle. He was a descendant of the Van Winkles who figured so gallantly in the chivalrous[4] days of Peter Stuyvesant. He inherited, however, but little of the martial[5] character of his ancestors. I have observed that he was a simple good-natured man; he was, moreover, a kind neighbor, and an obedient henpecked husband. Indeed, to the latter circumstance might be owing that meekness of spirit which gained him such universal popularity; for those men are most apt to be obsequious and conciliating abroad, who are under the discipline of shrews at home. Their tempers, doubtless, are rendered pliant and malleable in the fiery furnace of domestic tribulation, which

Did You Know?
A *latticed* (lat′ ist) window has small panes separated by crossed strips of wood or metal. A gable is the triangular section of wall between the sides of a sloping roof.

---

1. The Hudson is a river in New York, and the *Kaatskill* (now spelled *Catskill*) Mountains are part of the *Appalachian* mountain range.
2. *Descried* means "caught sight of."
3. *Peter Stuyvesant* (stī′ və sənt) was the last governor of the Dutch colony of New Netherland, which included parts of what are now Connecticut, Delaware, New Jersey, and New York. The narrator is poking fun at Stuyvesant, who was unpopular with the colonists.

4. A *chivalrous* (shiv′ əl rəs) person has the qualities of a knight, such as honor, courage, and skill in battle. The narrator again mocks Stuyvesant, who surrendered New Netherland to England in 1664, allowing it to become the British colony of New York.
5. *Martial* (mär′ shəl) means "warlike."

is worth all the sermons in the world for teaching the virtues of patience and long-suffering. A nagging wife may, therefore, in some respects, be considered a tolerable blessing; and if so, Rip Van Winkle was thrice blessed.[6]

Certain it is that he was a great favorite among all the good wives of the village, who took his part in all family squabbles; and never failed, whenever they talked those matters over in their evening gossipings, to lay all the blame on Dame[7] Van Winkle. The children of the village, too, would shout with joy whenever he approached. He assisted at their sports, made their playthings, taught them to fly kites and shoot marbles, and told them long stories of ghosts, witches, and Indians. Whenever he went dodging about the village, he was surrounded by a troop of them hanging on his coat skirts, clambering on his back, and playing a thousand tricks on him with <u>impunity</u>; and not a dog would bark at him throughout the neighborhood.

The great error in Rip's composition was an insuperable aversion[8] to all kinds of profitable labor. It could not be from the want of <u>perseverance</u>; for he would sit on a wet rock, with a rod as long and heavy as a Tartar's lance,[9] and fish all day without a murmur, even though he should not be encouraged by a single nibble. He would carry a fowling piece[10] on his shoulder for hours together, trudging through woods and swamps, and up hill and down dale, to shoot a few squirrels or wild pigeons. He would never refuse to assist a neighbor even in the roughest toil, and was a foremost man at all country frolics for husking Indian corn, or building stone fences. The women of the village, too, used to employ him to run their errands, and to do such little odds jobs as their less obliging husbands would not do for them. In a word, Rip was ready to attend to anybody's business but his own; but as to doing family duty, and keeping his farm in order, he found it impossible.

In fact, he declared it was of no use to work on his farm; it was the most pestilent little piece of ground in the whole country. Everything about it went wrong, and would go wrong, in spite of him. His fences were continually falling to pieces; his cow would either go astray or get among the cabbages; weeds were sure to grow quicker in his fields than anywhere else; the rain always made a point of setting in just as he had some outdoor work to do; so that though his estate had dwindled away under his management, acre by acre, until there was little more left than a mere patch of Indian corn and potatoes, yet it was the worst conditioned farm in the neighborhood.

His children, too, were as ragged and wild as if they belonged to nobody. His son Rip, an urchin begotten in his own

---

6. *[Indeed, to the latter . . . blessed]* The narrator suggests that dealing with nagging, bad-tempered wives makes men become better, more popular people. Rip, then, is especially blessed.

7. *Dame* is a title formerly used for the woman in charge of a household.

8. An *insuperable aversion* is a great dislike that cannot be overcome.

9. A *Tartar's lance* was a twelve-foot spear carried by thirteenth-century warriors in what is now Turkey.

---

10. A *fowling piece* is a shotgun used to hunt wild birds.

Vocabulary

impunity (im pū′ nə tē) *n.* freedom from punishment, harm, or bad effects

perseverance (pur′ sə vēr′ əns) *n.* continuation despite difficulty; determination

Termagant Wife, 1921. N. C. Wyeth. Oil on canvas. Millport Conservancy, Lititz, PA.

Viewing the painting: How does the painting reflect the relationship between Rip Van Winkle and his wife?

as a fine lady does her train in bad weather.

Rip Van Winkle, however, was one of those happy mortals, of foolish, well-oiled dispositions, who take the world easy, eat white bread or brown, whichever can be got with least thought or trouble, and would rather starve on a penny than work for a pound. If left to himself, he would have whistled life away in perfect contentment; but his wife kept continually dinning in his ears about his idleness, his carelessness, and the ruin he was bringing on his family. Morning, noon, and night, her tongue was <u>incessantly</u> going, and everything he said or did was sure to produce a torrent of household eloquence. Rip had but one way of replying to all lectures of the kind, and that, by frequent use, had grown into a habit. He shrugged his shoulders, shook his head, cast up his eyes, but said nothing. This, however, always provoked a fresh volley from his wife; so that he would take to the outside of the house—the only side which, in truth, belongs to a hen-pecked husband.

likeness, promised to inherit the habits, with the old clothes of his father. He was generally seen trooping like a colt at his mother's heels, equipped in a pair of his father's cast-off galligaskins[11], which he had much ado to hold up with one hand,

---

11. *Galligaskins* are the loose, baggy, knee-length trousers worn in the sixteenth and seventeenth centuries.

Vocabulary

incessantly (in ses′ ənt lē) *adv.* endlessly; constantly

Rip's sole domestic adherent[12] was his dog Wolf, who was as much henpecked as his master; for Dame Van Winkle regarded them as companions in idleness, and even looked upon Wolf with an evil eye, as the cause of his master's going so often astray. True it is, in all points of spirit befitting an honorable dog, he was as courageous an animal as ever scoured the woods—but what courage can withstand the ever-during and all-besetting terrors of a woman's tongue? The moment Wolf entered the house, his crest fell, his tail drooped to the ground, or curled between his legs, he sneaked about with a gallows air,[13] casting many a sidelong glance at Dame Van Winkle, and at the least flourish of a broomstick or ladle, he would fly to the door, yelping.

Times grew worse and worse with Rip Van Winkle as years of matrimony rolled on; a tart temper never mellows with age, and a sharp tongue is the only edged tool that grows keener with constant use. For a long while he used to console himself, when driven from home, by frequenting a kind of perpetual club of the sages, philosophers, and other idle personages[14] of the village; which held its sessions on a bench before a small inn, designated by a rubicund portrait of his Majesty George the Third. Here they used to sit in the shade through a long lazy summer's day, talking listlessly over village gossip, or telling endless sleepy stories about nothing. But it would have been worth any stateman's money to have heard the profound discussions that sometimes took place, when by chance an old newspaper fell into their hands from some passing traveler. How solemnly they would listen to the contents, as drawled out by Derrick Van Bummel, the schoolmaster, a dapper learned little man, who was not to be daunted by the most gigantic word in the dictionary; and how sagely they would deliberate upon public events some months after they had taken place.

The opinions of this junto[15] were completely controlled by Nicholas Vedder, a patriarch of the village, and landlord of the inn, at the door of which he took his seat from morning till night, just moving sufficiently to avoid the sun and keep in the shade of a large tree; so that the neighbors could tell the hour by his movements as accurately as by a sundial. It is true he was rarely heard to speak, but smoked his pipe incessantly. His adherents, however (for every great man has his adherents), perfectly understood him, and knew how to gather his opinions. When anything that was read or related displeased him, he was observed to smoke his pipe vehemently, and to send forth short, frequent, and angry puffs, but when pleased he would inhale the smoke slowly and tranquilly, and emit it in light and placid clouds. Sometimes, taking the pipe from his mouth, and letting the fragrant vapor curl about his nose, he would gravely nod his head in token of perfect approbation.[16]

From even this stronghold the unlucky Rip was at length routed by his wife, who would suddenly break in upon the tranquillity of the assemblage and call the members

---

12. An *adherent* is a firm supporter.
13. Having a *gallows air* is looking like one who is about to be hanged.
14. *Idle personages* are lazy persons.

---

15. A *junto* (jun′ tō) is a group with a common purpose.
16. *Approbation* means approval.

Rip With Dog Under Tree, 1921. N. C. Wyeth. Ink on paper. Stuart Kingston Gallery, Wilmington, DE.

Viewing the art: This drawing and those on pages 201–203 and 207 come from N. C. Wyeth's sketch books. They are early studies for the artist's Rip Van Winkle paintings. What parts of the story do they illustrate?

his master's face, and if dogs can feel pity, I verily believe he returned the sentiment with all his heart.

In a long ramble of the kind on a fine autumnal day, Rip had unconsciously scrambled to one of the highest parts of the Kaatskill Mountains. He was after his favorite sport of squirrel shooting, and the still solitudes had echoed and reechoed with the reports of his gun. Panting and fatigued, he threw himself, late in the afternoon, on a green knoll, covered with mountain herbage, that crowned the brow of a precipice.[19] From an opening between the trees he could overlook all the lower country for many a mile of rich woodland. He saw at a distance the lordly Hudson, far, far below him, moving on its silent but majestic course, with the reflection of a purple cloud, or the sail of a lagging bark,[20] here and there sleeping on its glassy bosom, and at last losing itself in the blue highlands.

On the other side he looked down into a deep mountain glen, wild, lonely, and shagged, the bottom filled with fragments from the impending[21] cliffs, and scarcely lighted by the reflected rays of the setting sun. For some time Rip lay <u>musing</u> on this

all to naught; nor was that august personage, Nicholas Vedder himself, sacred from the daring tongue of this terrible virago,[17] who charged him outright with encouraging her husband in habits of idleness.

Poor Rip was at last reduced almost to despair; and his only alternative, to escape from the labor of the farm and clamor of his wife, was to take gun in hand and stroll away into the woods. Here he would sometimes seat himself at the foot of a tree, and share the contents of his wallet[18] with Wolf, with whom he sympathized as a fellow sufferer in persecution. "Poor Wolf," he would say, "thy mistress leads thee a dog's life of it; but never mind, my lad, whilst I live thou shalt never want a friend to stand by thee!" Wolf would wag his tail, look wistfully in

---

17. A *virago* (və rä′ gō) is a scolding woman.
18. In Rip's time, *wallet* referred to a knapsack.

---

19. A *green knoll . . . precipice* (pres′ ə pis) refers to a high, steep cliff topped with a grassy hill.
20. A *lagging bark* is a slow-moving sailboat.
21. In this context, *impending* means overhanging.

Vocabulary
muse (mūz) *v.* to think or reflect

scene; evening was gradually advancing; the mountains began to throw their long blue shadows over the valleys; he saw that it would be dark long before he could reach the village, and he heaved a heavy sigh when he thought of encountering the terrors of Dame Van Winkle.

As he was about to descend, he heard a voice from a distance, hallooing, "Rip Van Winkle! Rip Van Winkle!" He looked round, but could see nothing but a crow winging its solitary flight across the mountain. He thought his fancy must have deceived him, and turned again to descend, when he heard the same cry ring through the still evening air: "Rip Van Winkle! Rip Van Winkle!"—at the same time Wolf bristled up his back, and, giving a loud growl, skulked to his master's side, looking fearfully down into the glen. Rip now felt a vague apprehension stealing over him; he looked anxiously in the same direction, and perceived a strange figure slowly toiling up the rocks, and bending under the weight of something he carried on his back. He was surprised to see any human being in this lonely and unfrequented place; but supposing it to be some one of the neighborhood in need of his assistance, he hastened down to yield it.

On nearer approach he was still more surprised at the <u>singularity</u> of the stranger's appearance. He was a short, square-built old fellow, with thick bushy hair and a grizzled beard. His dress was of the antique Dutch fashion—a cloth jerkin, strapped round the waist—several pair of breeches, the outer one of ample volume, decorated with rows of buttons down the sides, and bunches at the knees. He bore on his shoulder a stout keg, that seemed full of liquor, and made signs for Rip to approach and assist him with the load. Though rather shy and distrustful of this new acquaintance, Rip complied with his usual alacrity;[22] and mutually relieving each other, they clambered up a narrow gully, apparently the dry bed of a mountain torrent. As they ascended, Rip every now and then heard long rolling peals, like distant thunder, that seemed to issue out of a deep ravine, or rather cleft,[23] between lofty rocks, toward which their rugged path conducted. He paused for an instant, but supposing it to be the muttering of one of those transient thundershowers which often take place in mountain heights, he proceeded. Passing through the ravine, they came to a hollow, like a small amphitheater,[24] surrounded by perpendicular precipices, over the brinks of which impending trees shot their branches, so that you only caught glimpses of the azure sky and the bright evening cloud. During the whole time Rip and his companion had labored on in silence, for though the former marvelled greatly what could be the object of carrying a keg of liquor up this wild mountain; yet there was something strange and <u>incomprehensible</u> about the unknown, that inspired awe and checked familiarity.

---

22. *Alacrity* (ə lak′ rə tē) means "eager willingness."
23. A *cleft* is a wide crack or opening, as in a rock.
24. An *amphitheater* is a circular structure with rising rows of seats around a central open space.

Vocabulary

singularity (sing′ gyə lar′ ə tē) *n.* that which is remarkable or out of the ordinary; unusualness

incomprehensible (in′ kom prē hen′ sə bəl) *adj.* not understandable

On entering the amphitheater, new objects of wonder presented themselves. On a level spot in the center was a company of odd-looking personages playing at ninepins.[25] They were dressed in a quaint outlandish fashion; some wore short doublets, others jerkins,[26] with long knives in their belts, and most of them had enormous breeches, of similar style with that of the guide's. Their visages, too, were peculiar; one had a large head, broad face, and small piggish eyes; the face of another seemed to consist entirely of nose, and was surmounted by a white sugar-loaf hat, set off with a little red cock's tail. They all had beards, of various shapes and colors. There was one who seemed to be the commander. He was a stout old gentleman, with a weather-beaten countenance; he wore a laced doublet, broad belt and hanger, high-crowned hat and feather, red stockings, and high-heeled shoes, with roses in them. The whole group reminded Rip of the figures in an old Flemish painting, in the parlor of the village parson, which had been brought over from Holland at the time of the settlement.

25. *Ninepins* is a bowling game.
26. A *jerkin* is the close-fitting, hip-length jacket, usually sleeveless and collarless, worn by men in the sixteenth and seventeenth centuries. It was often worn over a *doublet*, a close-fitting, waist-length jacket, with or without sleeves.

What seemed particularly odd to Rip was, that though these folks were evidently amusing themselves, yet they maintained the gravest faces, the most mysterious silence, and were the most melancholy party of pleasure he had ever witnessed. Nothing interrupted the stillness of the scene but the noise of the balls, which, whenever they were rolled, echoed along the mountains like rumbling peals of thunder.

As Rip and his companion approached them, they suddenly desisted from their

Gnomes Bowling, 1921. N. C. Wyeth. Oil on canvas. Millport Conservancy, Lititz, PA.

Viewing the painting: How does the mood of the painting relate to the mood of Rip's night on the mountain?

they quaffed the liquor in profound silence, and then returned to their game.

By degrees Rip's awe and apprehension subsided. He even ventured, when no eye was fixed upon him, to taste the beverage, which he found had much of the flavor of excellent Holland ale. He was naturally a thirsty soul, and was soon tempted to repeat the draft. One taste provoked another; and he repeated his visits to the flagon so often, that at length his senses were overpowered, his eyes swam in his head, his head gradually declined, and he fell into a deep sleep.

On waking, he found himself on the green knoll whence he had first seen the old man of the glen. He rubbed his eyes—it was a bright sunny morning. The birds were hopping and twittering among the bushes, and the eagle was wheeling aloft, and breasting the pure mountain breeze. "Surely," thought Rip, "I have not slept here all night." He recalled the occurrences before he fell asleep. The strange man with a keg of liquor—the mountain ravine—the wild retreat among the rocks—the woebegone[29] party at ninepins—the flagon—"Oh! that flagon! that wicked flagon!" thought Rip; "what excuse shall I make to Dame Van Winkle?"

play, and stared at him with such fixed, statue-like gaze, and such strange, uncouth, lackluster countenances,[27] that his heart turned within him, and his knees smote together. His companion now emptied the contents of the keg into large flagons,[28] and made signs to him to wait upon the company. He obeyed with fear and trembling;

---

27. *Uncouth, lackluster countenances* means "crude and dull faces."
28. *Flagons* are containers with handles and spouts, used to hold liquids.

---

29. *Woebegone* means "sorrowful or mournful."

He looked round for his gun, but in place of the clean well-oiled fowling piece, he found an old firelock[30] lying by him, the barrel incrusted with rust, the lock falling off, and the stock worm-eaten. He now suspected that the grave roisters[31] of the mountain had put a trick upon him, and, having dosed him with liquor, had robbed him of his gun. Wolf, too, had disappeared, but he might have strayed away after a squirrel or partridge. He whistled after him, and shouted his name, but all in vain; the echoes repeated his whistle and shout, but no dog was to be seen.

He determined to revisit the scene of the last evening's gambol, and, if he met with any of the party, to demand his dog and gun. As he rose to walk he found himself stiff in the joints. "These mountain beds do not agree with me," thought Rip; "and if this frolic should lay me up with a fit of the rheumatism, I shall have a blessed time with Dame Van Winkle." With some difficulty he got down into the glen. He found the gully up which he and his companion had ascended the preceding evening; but to his astonishment, a mountain stream was now foaming down it— leaping from rock to rock, and filling the glen with babbling murmurs. He, however, made shift to scramble up its sides, working his toilsome way through thickets of birch, sassafras, and witch hazel, and sometimes tripped up or entangled by the wild grapevines that twisted their coils or tendrils from tree to tree, and spread a kind of network in his path.

At length he reached to where the ravine had opened through the cliffs to the amphitheater; but no traces of such opening remained. The rocks presented a high wall, over which the torrent came tumbling in a sheet of feathery foam, and fell into a broad, deep basin, black from the shadows of the surrounding forest. Here, then, poor Rip was brought to a stand. He again called and whistled after his dog; he was only answered by the cawing of a flock of idle crows, who seemed to look down and scoff at the poor man's perplexities. What was to be done? The morning was passing away, and Rip felt famished for want of his breakfast. He grieved to give up his dog and his gun; he dreaded to meet his wife; but it would not do to starve among the mountains. He shook his head, shouldered the rusty firelock, and, with a heart full of trouble and anxiety, turned his steps homeward.

As he approached the village he met a number of people, but none whom he knew, which somewhat surprised him, for he had thought himself acquainted with everyone in the country round. Their dress, too, was of a different fashion from that to which he was accustomed. They all stared at him with equal marks of surprise, and, whenever they cast their eyes upon him, invariably stroked their chins. The recurrence of this gesture induced[32] Rip,

---

30. A *firelock* is an early type of gun.
31. *Grave roisters* refers to the humorless partygoers of the previous night.

---

32. [*The recurrence . . . induced*] In other words, Rip repeated the gesture made by each of the people he met.

Vocabulary
perplexity (pər plek′ sə tē) *n.* doubt or uncertainty; puzzlement
invariably (in vār′ ē ə blē) *adv.* without exception

involuntarily, to do the same—when, to his astonishment, he found his beard had grown a foot long!

He had now entered the outskirts of the village. A troop of strange children ran at his heels, hooting after him, and pointing at his gray beard. The dogs, too, not one of which he recognized for an old acquaintance, barked at him as he passed. The very village was altered; it was larger and more populous. There were rows of houses which he had never seen before, and those which had been his familiar haunts[33] had disappeared. Strange names were over the doors—strange faces at the windows—everything was strange. His mind now misgave him; he began to doubt whether both he and the world around him were not bewitched. Surely this was his native village, which he had left but the day before. There stood the Kaatskill Mountains—there ran the silver Hudson at a distance—there was every hill and dale precisely as it had always been. Rip was sorely perplexed. "That flagon last night," thought he, "has addled my poor head sadly!"

Rip Van Winkle Returns Home, 1921 (detail). N. C. Wyeth. Oil on canvas. Millport Conservancy, Lititz, PA.

Viewing the painting: How does Wyeth's interpretation add to your understanding of the story?

---

33. *Haunts* are places often visited, or hangouts.

RIP VAN WINKLE

It was with some difficulty that he found the way to his own house, which he approached with silent awe, expecting every moment to hear the shrill voice of Dame Van Winkle. He found the house gone to decay—the roof fallen in, the windows shattered, and the doors off the hinges. A half-starved dog that looked like Wolf, was skulking about it. Rip called him by name, but the cur snarled, showed his teeth, and passed on. This was an unkind cut indeed—"My very dog," sighed poor Rip, "has forgotten me!"

He entered the house, which to tell the truth, Dame Van Winkle had always kept in neat order. It was empty, forlorn, and apparently abandoned. The desolateness overcame all his fears—he called loudly for his wife and children—the lonely chambers rang for a moment with his voice, and then all again was silence.

The Return of Rip Van Winkle, 1829. John Quidor. Oil on canvas, 39¼ x 49¾ in. Mellon Collection, National Gallery of Art, Washington, DC.

Viewing the painting: Look at the details in the painting. How are people responding to Rip's sudden appearance?

He now hurried forth, and hastened to his old resort, the village inn—but it too was gone. A large, rickety, wooden building stood in its place, with great gaping windows, some of them broken and mended with old hats and petticoats, and over the door was painted, "The Union Hotel, by Jonathan Doolittle." Instead of the great tree that used to shelter the quiet little Dutch inn of yore, there was now reared a tall naked pole, with something on the top that looked like a red nightcap,[34] and from it was fluttering a flag, on which was a singular assemblage of stars and stripes—all this was strange and incomprehensible. He recognized on the sign, however, the ruby face of King George, under which he had smoked so many a peaceful pipe; but even this was singularly changed. The red coat was changed for one of blue and buff, a sword was held in the hand instead of a scepter, the head was decorated with a cocked hat, and underneath was painted in large characters, GENERAL WASHINGTON.

There was, as usual, a crowd of folks about the door, but none that Rip recollected. The very character of the people seemed changed. There was a busy, bustling tone about it, instead of the accustomed drowsy tranquillity. He looked in vain for the sage Nicholas Vedder, with his broad face, double chin, and fair long pipe, uttering clouds of tobacco smoke instead of idle speeches; or Van Bummel, the schoolmaster, doling forth the contents of an ancient newspaper. In place of these, a lean, bilious-looking fellow, with his pockets full of handbills, was haranguing[35] vehemently about the rights of citizens—elections—members of Congress—liberty—Bunker's Hill—heroes of seventy-six—and other words, which were a perfect Babylonish jargon[36] to the bewildered Van Winkle.

The appearance of Rip, with his long grizzled beard, his rusty fowling piece, his uncouth dress, and an army of women and children at his heels, soon attracted the attention of the tavern politicians. They crowded round him, eyeing him from head to foot with great curiosity. The orator bustled up to him, and, drawing him partly aside, inquired "on which side he voted?" Rip stared in vacant stupidity. Another short but busy little fellow pulled him by the arm, and, rising on tiptoe, inquired in his ear, "Whether he was Federal or Democrat?"[37] Rip was equally at a loss to comprehend the question; when a knowing, self-important old gentleman, in a sharp cocked hat, made his way through the crowd, putting them to the right and left with his elbows as he passed, and planting himself before Van Winkle, with one arm akimbo, the other resting on his cane, his keen eyes and sharp hat penetrating, as it were, into his very soul, demanded in an austere tone, "What brought him to the election with a gun on his shoulder, and a mob at his heels, and whether he meant to breed a riot in the village?"—"Alas! gentlemen," cried Rip, somewhat dismayed, "I am a poor quiet man, a native of the place, and a loyal subject of the king, God bless him!"

---

34. A *red nightcap* is a "liberty cap," often worn as a symbol of independence during the American Revolution.
35. To be *bilious* is to be cross or bad-tempered; *haranguing* (hə rang′ ing) is making a long, noisy speech.

36. *Babylonish jargon* is confusing language.
37. *Federal or Democrat* refers to U.S. political parties following the Revolution.

Here a general shout burst from the bystanders—"A Tory! a Tory! a spy! a refugee![38] hustle him! away with him!" It was with great difficulty that the self-important man in the cocked hat restored order; and demanded again of the unknown culprit, what he came there for, and whom he was seeking? The poor man humbly assured him that he meant no harm, but merely came there in search of some of his neighbors, who used to keep about the tavern.

"Well—who are they?—name them."

Rip bethought himself a moment, and inquired, "Where's Nicholas Vedder?"

There was a silence for a little while, when an old man replied in a thin piping voice, "Nicholas Vedder! why, he is dead and gone these eighteen years! There was a wooden tombstone in the churchyard that used to tell all about him, but that's rotten and gone too."

"Where's Brom Dutcher?"

"Oh, he went off to the army in the beginning of the war; some say he was killed at the storming of Stony Point— others say he was drowned in a squall at the foot of Antony's Nose.[39] I don't know—he never came back again."

"Where's Van Bummel, the schoolmaster?"

"He went off to the wars too, was a great militia general, and is now in Congress."

Rip's heart died away at hearing of these sad changes in his home and friends, and finding himself thus alone in the world. Every answer puzzled him too, by treating of such enormous lapses of time, and of matters which he could not understand; war—Congress—Stony Point;—he had no courage to ask after any more friends, but cried out in despair, "Does nobody here know Rip Van Winkle?"

"Oh, Rip Van Winkle!" exclaimed two or three. "Oh, to be sure! that's Rip Van Winkle yonder, leaning against the tree."

Rip looked, and beheld a precise counterpart[40] of himself, as he went up the mountain: apparently as lazy, and certainly as ragged. The poor fellow was now completely confounded. He doubted his own identity, and whether he was himself or another man. In the midst of his bewilderment, the man in the cocked hat demanded who he was, and what was his name?

"God knows," exclaimed he, at his wits' end; "I'm not myself—I'm somebody else— that's me yonder—no—that's somebody else got into my shoes—I was myself last night, but I fell asleep on the mountain, and they've changed my gun, and everything's changed, and I'm changed, and I can't tell what's my name, or who I am!"

The bystanders began now to look at each other, nod, wink significantly, and tap their fingers against their foreheads. There was a whisper, also, about securing the gun, and keeping the old fellow from doing mischief, at the very suggestion of which the self-important man in the cocked hat retired quickly. At this critical moment a fresh, comely woman pressed through the throng to get a peep at the gray-bearded man. She had a chubby child in her arms, which, frightened at his looks, began to

---

38. A *Tory* was a person who supported the British during the Revolution. A *refugee* was a member of a group of British supporters who attacked the American revolutionaries.

39. *Stony Point* is a small bay on the Hudson River, and *Antony's Nose* is a mountain. Both are in southeastern New York.

40. A *precise counterpart* is a person who looks exactly like another.

cry. "Hush, Rip," cried she, "hush you little fool; the old man won't hurt you." The name of the child, the air of the mother, the tone of her voice, all awakened a train of recollections in his mind.

"What is your name, my good woman?" asked he.

"Judith Gardenier."

"And your father's name?"

"Ah, poor man, Rip Van Winkle was his name, but it's twenty years since he went away from home with his gun, and never has been heard of since—his dog came home without him; but whether he shot himself, or was carried away by the Indians, nobody can tell. I was then but a little girl."

Rip had but one question more to ask; but he put it with a <u>faltering</u> voice,—

"Where's your mother?"

"Oh, she too had died but a short time since; she broke a blood vessel in a fit of passion at a New England peddler."

There was a drop of comfort, at least, in this intelligence. The honest man could contain himself no longer. He caught his daughter and her child in his arms. "I am your father!" cried he—"Young Rip Van Winkle once—old Rip Van Winkle now!—Does nobody know poor Rip Van Winkle?"

All stood amazed, until an old woman, tottering out from among the crowd, put her hand to her brow, and peering under it in his face for a moment, exclaimed, "Sure enough! it is Rip Van Winkle—it is himself! Welcome home again, old neighbor—Why, where have you been these twenty long years?"

Rip's story was soon told, for the whole twenty years had been to him but as one night. The neighbors stared when they heard it; some were seen to wink at each other, and put their tongues in their cheeks; and the self-important man in the cocked hat, who, when the alarm was over, had returned to the field, screwed down the corners of his mouth, and shook his head—upon which there was a general shaking of the head throughout the assemblage.

It was determined, however, to take the opinion of old Peter Vanderdonk, who was seen slowly advancing up the road. He was a descendant of the historian of that name, who wrote one of the earliest accounts of the province. Peter was the most ancient inhabitant of the village, and well versed in all the wonderful events and traditions of the neighborhood. He recollected Rip at once, and corroborated[41] his story in the most satisfactory manner. He assured the company that it was a fact, handed down from his ancestor the historian, that the Kaatskill Mountains had always been haunted by strange beings. That it was affirmed that the great Henry Hudson, the first discoverer of the river and country, kept a kind of vigil there every twenty years, with his crew of the *Half-Moon;* being permitted in this way to revisit the scenes of his enterprise and keep a guardian eye upon the river and the great city called by his name. That his father had once seen them in their old Dutch dresses playing at ninepins in a hollow of the mountain; and that he himself

---

41. Something *corroborated* (kə rob′ ə rāt əd) is supported, or confirmed.

Vocabulary
faltering (fôl′ tər ing) *adj.* shaky because of uncertainty

had heard, one summer afternoon, the sound of their balls, like distant peals of thunder.

To make a long story short, the company broke up, and returned to the more important concerns of the election. Rip's daughter took him home to live with her; she had a snug, well-furnished house, and a stout cheery farmer for her husband, whom Rip recollected for one of the urchins that used to climb upon his back. As to Rip's son and heir, who was the ditto of himself, seen leaning against the tree, he was employed to work on the farm; but showed an hereditary disposition to attend to anything else but his business.

Rip now resumed his old walks and habits; he soon found many of his former cronies, though all rather the worse for the wear and tear of time; and preferred making friends among the rising generation, with whom he soon grew into great favor.

Having nothing to do at home, and being arrived at that happy age when a man can be idle with impunity, he took his place once more on the bench at the inn door, and was reverenced as one of the patriarchs of the village, and a chronicle of the old times "before the war." It was some time before he could get into the regular track of gossip, or could be made to comprehend the strange events that had taken place during his sleep. How that there had been a Revolutionary War—that the country had thrown off the yoke of Old England—and that, instead of being a subject of His Majesty George the Third, he was now a free citizen of the United States. Rip, in fact, was no politician; the changes of states and empires made but little impression on him; but there was one species of despotism[42] under which he had long groaned, and that was—petticoat government. Happily that was at an end; he had got his neck out of the yoke of matrimony, and could go in and out whenever he pleased without dreading the tyranny of Dame Van Winkle. Whenever her name was mentioned, however, he shook his head, shrugged his shoulders, and cast up his eyes; which might pass either for an expression of resignation to his fate, or joy at his deliverance.

He used to tell his story to every stranger that arrived at Mr. Doolittle's hotel. He was observed at first to vary on some points every time he told it, which was, doubtless, owing to his having so recently awaked. It at last settled down precisely to the tale I have related, and not a man, woman, or child in the neighborhood but knew it by heart. Some always pretended to doubt the reality of it, and insisted that Rip had been out of his head, and that this was one point on which he always remained flighty. The old Dutch inhabitants, however, almost universally gave it full credit. Even to this day they never hear a thunderstorm of a summer afternoon about the Kaatskills, but they say Henry Hudson and his crew are at their game of ninepins; and it is a common wish of all henpecked husbands in the neighborhood, when life hangs heavy on their hands, that they might have a quieting draft out of Rip Van Winkle's flagon.

---

42. A *despotism* (des′ pə tiz′ əm) is a government under a ruler who has unlimited authority.

Responding to Literature

PERSONAL RESPONSE

◆ What was your reaction to this story? Did you find it amusing, suspenseful, mysterious, or all three? Describe your impressions in your journal.

Analyzing Literature

RECALL

1. According to the narrator, what is the chief flaw in Rip's character? What is the chief flaw in his wife's character?

2. Briefly describe the strangers Rip meets in the mountains. What happens to him after he drinks their beverage?

3. What is the first change Rip notices after he wakes up? Describe one other change he notices once he returns to town.

4. According to the narrator, what is Rip's life like after his return?

INTERPRET

5. What sort of person is Rip Van Winkle? What conflict exists between him and his wife? Support your ideas with examples from the story.

6. The details used to describe the men and the atmosphere in the hollow intensify the mysterious **mood** Irving created in this part of the story. List details that helped you sense the mood of this scene.

7. In what way does Peter Vanderdonk confirm Rip's explanation of his absence?

8. In your opinion, is Rip's life better or worse after his twenty-year sleep? Explain.

EVALUATE AND CONNECT

9. Theme Connection   What historical events occurred during Rip's absence? Why do you think Irving chose that twenty-year period for Rip's long nap? Explain.

10. What is your reaction to what happens to Rip and his wife in this story? Explain.

LITERARY ELEMENTS

Setting

A **setting** is the time and place in which the events of a story, novel, or play occur. For example, the setting of "Rip Van Winkle" is the Hudson River valley in the late 1700s. Strong writers often use the setting to help create an atmosphere or mood for a story. Carefully chosen details help readers visualize the place being described.

1. Pick out details from "Rip Van Winkle" that helped you picture the setting in your mind. Explain how the details helped transport you into the time and place of the story.

2. Choose another story you've read, and describe its setting.

● See **Literary Terms Handbook,** p. R10.

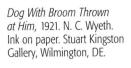

Dog With Broom Thrown at Him, 1921. N. C. Wyeth. Ink on paper. Stuart Kingston Gallery, Wilmington, DE.

Literature and Writing

Writing About Literature

Thinking About a Theme   What does "Rip Van Winkle" say about the passage of time and human nature? Write a paragraph or two explaining your ideas about the theme of this well-known story.

Rip as Old Man, 1921. N. C. Wyeth. Ink on paper. Stuart Kingston Gallery, Wilmington, DE.

Personal Writing

Sweet Dreams   Imagine if you were to fall asleep for the next twenty years. How do you think the world would change during that time? When you discovered these changes, how would you feel? Write a diary entry explaining what has happened, how things have changed, and how you feel.

Extending Your Response

Literature Groups

Debating Stereotypes   A stereotype has only a few, highly exaggerated character traits. Stereotypes are never fully believable. For example, the strong, silent cowboy is a stereotype; so is the wicked villain or the innocent heroine. Stereotypes often appear in folktales, legends, and literature that is meant to teach a lesson. Are both Rip and his wife stereotypes? Why or why not? How might Irving have made these two characters more believable? Debate the issue. Support your opinions with examples and quotations from the story.

Learning for Life

A Newspaper Account   Imagine that you are a journalist sent to interview Rip for the *Hudson River Valley Gazette.* Write an article about his mysterious experience. Include quotations and descriptions from Rip as well as other villagers.

Art Activity

Social Studies: Make a Timeline   Review the notes you made for the **Reading Focus** on page 184 to help you make a personal timeline starting at the year of your birth. Include important events in your own life, as well as the dates of important events and inventions in this country and around the world.

Reading Further

If you would like to read more by Washington Irving, try these works:

Diedrich Knickerbocker's History of New York

"The Legend of Sleepy Hollow" in *The Sketch Book of Geoffrey Crayon, Gent.*

📖 **Save your work for your portfolio.**

Skill Minilessons

GRAMMAR AND LANGUAGE • ADVERBS

An adverb is a word that modifies, or describes, a verb, an adjective, or another adverb. When modifying a verb, an adverb gives information about *when, where,* or *how* the action of a sentence takes place. Examples:

Rip slept **soundly.** (How?)

Later Rip woke up. (When?)

Rip looked **everywhere** for his dog. (Where?)

PRACTICE Write an adverb to modify the underlined word in each sentence.

1. Rip walked through the woods.
2. He looked into a deep mountain glen.
3. He listened to the voice in the distance.
4. The strange men stared at Rip.
5. Being quite thirsty, Rip drank the beverage.

● For more about adverbs, see **Language Handbook,** p. R27.

READING AND THINKING • EVALUATING

Evaluating characters and events in a story involves forming opinions and making judgments about what you read. Remember to evaluate *while* you are reading–not just after you have finished. As you read, ask yourself questions such as the following:

• Does this event make sense?

• Would this character really say or do this?

PRACTICE Review "Rip Van Winkle" and think about what happens to Rip once he wakes up from his sleep. Write questions about the events and trade your questions with a partner. Answer each other's questions and then talk about your answers.

● For more about reading strategies, see **Reading Handbook,** pp. R85–R100.

VOCABULARY • SYNONYMS AND ANTONYMS

As you probably know, *synonyms* are words with similar meanings, and *antonyms* are words with opposite meanings. A synonym for *loud* is *noisy,* and an antonym for *loud* is *quiet.* Although some words have no synonyms and some have no antonyms, many words have several of each.

PRACTICE Match each word below with its synonym and its antonym from the lists at the right.

Word

1. likely
2. delicate
3. invariably
4. incomprehensible
5. uncouth

Synonym	Antonym
A. fragile	a. doubtful
B. confusing	b. considerate
C. rude	c. never
D. probable	d. tough
E. constantly	e. clear

Rip Fishing, 1921. N. C. Wyeth. Ink on paper. Stuart Kingston Gallery, Wilmington, DE.

Before You Read

old age sticks

MEET
E. E. CUMMINGS

Edward Estlin Cummings (whose name has often been written as e. e. cummings) knew while still a child that he would become a poet. In fact, between the ages of eight and twenty-two he wrote a poem a day. By the time his first collection of poetry was published in 1923, his quirky use of grammar, capitalization, and punctuation was well established.

E. E. Cummings was born in Cambridge, Massachusetts, in 1894, and he died in 1962. This poem is from his Complete Poems.

READING FOCUS

Do most people take advice from people who are older than they are? Should they? Why or why not?

QuickWrite
What do you think older people can teach younger people? How about the reverse? Are there things younger people can teach their elders? Take a moment to jot down your thoughts and feelings about these questions.

Setting a Purpose
Read the poem to find out what the poet has to say about youth and old age.

BUILDING BACKGROUND

A famous French writer once defined poetry as "the music of the soul." Do you agree? Yet, no matter how much you enjoy poetry, a poem may sometimes be hard to read, especially when its format or punctuation is unusual. The following poem, "old age sticks," is just such a poem. Here are some tips on how to read it:

- Read the poem aloud, all the way through. Keep going, even if you come to a word or phrase you don't understand, or if the lack of punctuation confuses you.
- Don't feel that you need to pause at the end of a line, or even a stanza.
- Don't try to analyze the meaning of each line. Just think about your reactions to the whole poem.
- Read the poem again . . . and then again. Concentrate on the parts of the poem that seem confusing. Listen to how the poem sounds.
- Finally, think about the poem's meaning for you. Remember: reading a poem is a personal experience.

old age sticks

E. E. Cummings

Old Man Walking in a Rye Field. Lauris Anderson Ring.

old age sticks
up Keep
Off
signs)&

5   youth yanks them
down(old
age
cries No

Tres)&(pas)
10 youth laughs
(sing
old age

scolds Forbid
den Stop
15 Must
n't Don't

&)youth goes
right on
gr
20 owing old

Responding to Literature

PERSONAL RESPONSE

- ◆ Which lines from the poem did you find most memorable, powerful, or surprising? Why?
- ◆ What questions would you like to ask the poet if you could meet him?

Analyzing Literature

RECALL AND INTERPRET

1. What are the main images in this poem? Pick out the words and details that help you visualize the images.
2. What signs does Cummings include in this poem? Explain what each one means. Why do you think he uses signs?
3. According to the speaker of the poem, how does "youth" respond to the advice of "old age"?

EVALUATE AND CONNECT

4. What thoughts about life do you think Cummings is communicating in this poem? Explain.
5. Do you know someone who would enjoy reading this poem? Why would the poem appeal to that person?
6. **Theme Connection** How does this poem focus on the theme of change as a natural part of life?

LITERARY ELEMENTS

Style

Style includes the qualities that make a writer's work unlike the work of all other writers. Word choice, sentence length, sentence patterns, degree of formality, and use of imagery are a few of many factors that make up a style.

1. Suggest two characteristics that you think are part of E. E. Cummings's style.

2. Choose another poet from this book. Tell how that poet's style differs from Cummings's. Support your comparison with examples.

- ● See **Literary Terms Handbook,** pp. R10–R11.

Extending Your Response

Literature Groups

Readers Theater   In small groups, practice a readers theater dramatization of "old age sticks." You might divide your group into two parts—one half dramatizing "old age" and the other half "youth." Then think about the images that you want to portray from the poem. Use props such as signs to help your audience understand the main images.

Creative Writing

Writing an Advice Column   Do you feel there are topics about which you can give advice? For example, can you offer advice to younger students about what they should do on their first day at the middle school or junior high school? Write an advice column. Make up some questions, and then answer them with your best advice.

COMPARING SELECTIONS

RIP VAN WINKLE and old age sticks

COMPARE THEME CONNECTIONS

"Rip Van Winkle" and "old age sticks" focus on special kinds of journeys vividly described by two very different writers. The theme of change plays an important role in both of these selections.

- On what kind of journey does Rip Van Winkle go? By the end of the story, how has Rip changed?

- What is the special journey depicted in "old age sticks"? Who or what has changed by the end of the poem?

- How are these two journeys alike? How are they different?

Rip Hunting, 1921. N. C. Wyeth. Ink on paper. Stuart Kingston Gallery, Wilmington, DE.

COMPARE IDEAS

Plan a panel discussion about life and the problems of aging.

- With your group, brainstorm topics for the panel discussion. Review your **QuickWrite** from page 204 for ideas.

- Select a moderator to lead the discussion, and have group members take the roles of Rip, his wife, and people representing "old age" and "youth."

- Hold your panel discussion before your class. Encourage your classmates to ask the panel members questions.

COMPARE ENDINGS

Compare the endings of these two pieces of writing. How are they alike? How are they different? How else might each of these selections have ended?

- What else might have happened to Rip Van Winkle after he woke up from his sleep? Consider different possibilities.

- How else might the poem "old age sticks" end? In what other ways might "youth" respond to the advice of "old age"? Think about ideas for an alternative last stanza.

- Use your imagination to write an alternative ending to either the story or the poem. If you choose the poem, remember to use vivid verbs and colorful details to create strong images that communicate your ideas.

Writing WORKSHOP

Expository Writing: Compare-and-Contrast Essay

Think about a good friend. Then think about how the two of you are alike and how you are different. Thinking about your similarities and differences can give you insight into your friendship. Similarly, comparing and contrasting characters in literature can help you understand them better.

Assignment: Use the process shown in this Workshop to write a compare-and-contrast essay about two characters from stories in this theme.

● As you write your essay, refer to the **Writing Handbook,** pp. R48–R54.

> ### EVALUATION RUBRIC
> By the time you complete this Writing Workshop, you will have
> - compared and contrasted two fictional characters
> - included a thesis statement and developed it with supporting details
> - applied a consistent organizing strategy
> - used transitions that point out similarities and differences
> - presented an essay free of errors in grammar, usage, and mechanics

The Writing Process

PREWRITING

PREWRITING TIP
Choose characters who share at least one important quality. If they are completely different, your essay will fall flat.

● **Choose Your Characters**

You can compare two characters from the same selection or from two different selections. Try these strategies:

- Look through your reading journal for mention of characters who interest you.

- Skim the selections again. Then fill in your own choice of characters in sentences such as those below.

> The character I know the least about is Dick Wilcox from "A Crush."

> If Rip Van Winkle and Ernie ever met, they would probably understand each other.

> Dolores and Rip's wife probably would dislike each other.

> My favorite character from this theme is Dolores.

> Two characters who might like each other are Colin and Ernie.

> Two characters who appear to be different, but are really similar, are Colin and his father.

Explore Details

Use a Venn diagram, as in the **Writing Skills** activity on page 183, to organize details about your characters. List qualities you *can't* see as well as those you can.

Find Your Thesis

Think about how your details support your ideas about the two characters. What main point do your ideas add up to? Write this point, your **thesis,** as a sentence.

STUDENT MODEL • PREWRITING

Thesis statement: Although Ernie and Katie are different people from very different backgrounds, they both eventually find the strength to rebuild their lives. For each, the key to a new life is a cardboard box.

Complete Student Model on p. R105.

Consider Your Audience and Purpose

Your teacher and classmates will probably be the main audience for this essay. Your purpose is to explain similarities and differences between the two characters. You may need to include basic plot details if your audience has not read the stories.

Make a Plan

Your essay needs an introduction, a body, and a conclusion. To organize the body, you might choose one of the patterns shown below. (Both plans compare Ernie in the story "A Crush" with Katie, the daughter in "Birthday Box.") Fill in your own graphic to compare the two characters you have chosen. Choose details that support your thesis.

Subject-by-subject

With this plan, you begin by describing the qualities of one character. Then you go on to describe the same qualities of the other character in the same order.

Part 1: Describe Ernie
> What are his physical traits, his wishes or motivations, his inner weaknesses, and his inner strengths?

Part 2: Describe Katie
> What are her physical traits, her wishes or motivations, her inner weaknesses, and her inner strengths?

Feature-by-feature

With this plan, you write one paragraph for each feature you have selected. Within each paragraph, you describe a single feature in both of the characters you are comparing.

Paragraph	Feature
1 ⟶	physical traits (Ernie's, then Katie's)
2 ⟶	motivations or wishes (Ernie's, then Katie's)
3 ⟶	inner weaknesses (Ernie's, then Katie's)
4 ⟶	inner strengths (Ernie's, then Katie's)

DRAFTING

DRAFTING TIP
Cite details from the selection(s) to support each statement you make about a character. If you call a character kind, cite an action showing kindness.

DRAFTING TIP
Transition words such as *like, unlike, in the same way,* and *similarly* will help readers understand your comparisons.

● Start with the Basics

Use your first paragraph, the introduction, to build a clear framework for your readers.

- Name the *characters* you will compare, the *selection(s)* in which they appear, and the *author(s)* of the story or stories.

- State your thesis so that readers know what to expect from your essay.

● Draft Your Essay

Compare and contrast your characters, using your prewriting notes to guide you. Use transitions to help readers follow your ideas. To end your essay, restate your thesis. You might add a final thought from a slightly different perspective.

STUDENT MODEL • DRAFTING

> Ernie and Katie are two very different characters. They each learn a lesson from a box in a very different way.

Complete Student Model on p. R105.

REVISING

REVISING TIP
As you revise, make sure your ideas follow each other in logical order and that you are comparing and contrasting similar features of each character.

● Improve Your Draft

Let your draft sit for a few hours, or even overnight. Then come back to it with fresh eyes. As you read, mark the places where you could make improvements. Use the **Rubric for Revising** as a guide.

Now read your essay aloud to a friend. Have your friend see whether you have followed the **Rubric for Revising.**

RUBRIC FOR REVISING

Your revised compare-and-contrast essay should have

- an introduction that identifies the stories and the characters and states your thesis
- a subject-by-subject or feature-by-feature organization
- transitions that make your main ideas easy to follow
- details to support each statement made about the characters

Your revised comparison-and-contrast essay should be free of

- unnecessary plot details
- errors in grammar, usage, and mechanics

EDITING/PROOFREADING

When you are satisfied with the content of your essay, use the **Proofreading Checklist** to help you look for errors in grammar, usage, mechanics, and spelling. Be sure to use the correct comparative forms of modifiers, as shown in the **Grammar Link** on page 182.

PROOFREADING CHECKLIST

☑ Comparative forms of adjectives and adverbs are used correctly.

☑ Each sentence has a complete subject and predicate.

☑ Titles of selections are set off with quotation marks, italics, or underlining, as appropriate.

☑ Commas, end marks, and other punctuation marks are used correctly.

☑ Spelling is correct.

Grammar Hint

When you are writing by hand, underline titles of books, plays, and longer literary works. Use quotation marks to set off titles of short stories, poems, and essays.

I found the short story "A Crush" in Cynthia Rylant's book <u>A Couple of Kooks and Other Stories About Love</u>.

STUDENT MODEL • EDITING/PROOFREADING

Katie's situation in Birthday Box is similar to *both* and different from Ernie's.

Complete Student Model on p. R105.

Complete Student Model

For a complete version of the model developed in this Workshop, see **Writing Workshop Models**, p. R105.

PUBLISHING/PRESENTING

Share your essay with classmates. You might work in a small group to gather and bind your essays as models for future students. Essays might be grouped by subject or alphabetically by author or title.

PRESENTING TIP
People who have chosen the same characters can compare interpretations.

Reflecting

Consider the following question. Then write your response.

- How has comparing and contrasting your characters deepened your understanding of them?

📖 **Save your work for your portfolio.**

Theme Assessment

Responding to the Theme

1. Which story or poem in this theme most helped you think about how change, though often difficult, can be a powerful learning tool? Explain.

2. What new thoughts do you have about the following as a result of reading the stories and poems in this theme?
   - people's reactions to change in their lives
   - the importance of seeing change as a vital and powerful part of the journey of life

3. Present your theme project to the class.

Analyzing Literature

COMPARE SHORT STORIES

Compare two short stories from this theme. You may compare the stories in terms of characters, details chosen by the writers, or themes. Use examples and quotations from the stories to support your opinions.

Evaluate and Set Goals

1. Which of the following tasks was most rewarding for you? Which was most difficult?
   - reading and thinking about the stories and poems
   - writing independently
   - analyzing the stories and poems in discussions
   - making presentations
   - performing dramatizations
   - doing research

2. Using the following scale, how would you assess your work for this theme? Give at least two reasons for your assessment.

4 = outstanding	2 = fair
3 = good	1 = weak

Build Your Portfolio

SELECT

Look for the best pieces of work you did for this theme and add them to your portfolio. Ask yourself the following questions to help you decide:

- ✦ Is this my best work?
- ✦ Did I learn something from doing this?
- ✦ Did working on this piece stretch me?
- ✦ Did I enjoy doing this?

REFLECT

Write some notes to accompany the work you selected. Use the following questions to guide you:

- ✦ What do you like best about the piece?
- ✦ What did you learn from creating it?
- ✦ How would you revise the piece to make it even better?

Reading on Your Own

Have you enjoyed the stories and poems in this theme? If so, here are some other books you might enjoy.

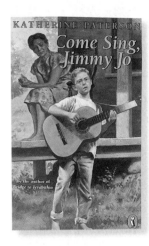

So Far from the Bamboo Grove

by Yoko Kawashima Watkins In this novel based on the author's experience, Yoko and her family must leave their home in North Korea and go through many hardships to get to Japan.

Come Sing, Jimmy Jo

by Katherine Paterson This novel tells the story of young James Johnson, who is discovered by a country music agent and thrust into a life on the road with his musical family.

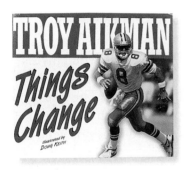

Things Change

by Troy Aikman Former Dallas Cowboys quarterback describes his life from childhood to three-time Superbowl champ, using his own experiences to show that change can provide an opportunity to grow.

The Autobiography of Miss Jane Pittman

by Ernest J. Gaines In this novel about a 110-year-old African American woman, Miss Jane Pittman recollects events in her life in the South from the Civil War to the Civil Rights movement of the 1960s.

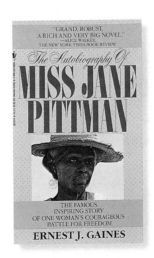

Standardized Test Practice

Read the following passage. Then read each question on page 215 and choose the best answer to each question. Mark the letter for that answer on your paper.

RealBaby is all Wrong

Here is a letter one student wrote to the company that made a product she bought, but was not satisfied with.

2342 North High St.
Montville, MS 02541
August 10, 1999

Mr. Ronald Wesson
ToyCo Customer Service
4532 Main St.
Lake Prima, NC 23687

Dear Mr. Wesson:

I am writing to you to express my dissatisfaction with your product, RealBaby. I bought the doll for my little sister because your commercial said that it was lifelike and acted like a real baby. However, when my sister opened the box to play with the RealBaby, I saw that the doll looked nothing like the doll on television. It was not lifelike at all. The arms and legs are supposed to move and the eyes are supposed to open and close. On the doll, only one eye opens and closes and one leg does not bend at all.

In addition, the doll does not make any sounds, even though in the commercial it seems to cry and say words. If you follow the directions and fill it with water, instead of small tears coming out of its eyes, the water pours out in a steady stream.

My sister was very disappointed with the toy, and I am too. I paid $19.99 for the doll with my own money, and I would like a full refund. I feel that this is a fair request. I am not interested in receiving another doll.

Sincerely,

Sheila Adams

1   The writer of the letter can best be described as —
    A   joyful.
    B   confused.
    C   displeased.
    D   rude.

2   Based on what the letter states, the reason the writer doesn't want a replacement doll is because —
    J   RealBaby doesn't do what the commercial said it would do.
    K   she wants the money to give back to her mother.
    L   all of the dolls' eyes are broken.
    M   her sister already has too many dolls.

3   Which of these sentences expresses an OPINION about the letter?
    A   The doll Sheila bought doesn't make sounds.
    B   RealBaby dolls are not good toys.
    C   Ronald Wesson works for ToyCo.
    D   Sheila gave the RealBaby doll to her sister.

4   Why is Sheila disappointed in the RealBaby doll?
    J   It doesn't work as advertised.
    K   Only the arms on RealBaby doll move as on television.
    L   Sheila's sister didn't want a RealBaby doll.
    M   The doll cost more than Sheila could afford.

5   How is Sheila's letter to ToyCo different from a letter she might write to a friend or a relative?
    A   It has the date written at the top.
    B   It contains several paragraphs.
    C   She asks for a refund on a product.
    D   She discusses her younger sister.

6   How does Sheila show that the doll does not do what the commercial said it would do?
    J   by referring to it as defective
    K   by saying that she never received it
    L   by complaining about how it was wrapped
    M   by describing the things that are wrong with it

Facing Challenge

66 Sooner or later, each of us must . . .
challenge our own monsters, with our
survival in the balance. **99**

—Joseph Bruchac, *Flying with the Eagle, Racing the Great Bear*

THEME
3

THEME CONTENTS

GENRE FOCUS NONFICTION

Exploring the Theme

Facing Challenge

We face challenges every day. Sometimes, outside forces put us in challenging situations. Sometimes, the challenges are inside ourselves. In this theme, you will meet real and imaginary characters who face a wide range of challenges. Try one of the options below to start your own thinking about the theme.

Starting Points

FACING THE MONSTER

If you remember the story of *The Three Little Pigs,* you'll appreciate Gary Larson's cartoon about the pigs' unlucky visitors.

- Role-play the situation in the cartoon, showing what happens next. Then expand your performance by role-playing a parody of another well-known story in which the characters face a challenge.

PERSONAL CHALLENGES

Think about a problem you faced in the past year and about how you prepared yourself for the challenge.

- Write a journal entry about a challenge you faced and what you learned from the experience.

The Far Side

1982

"Listen out there! We're George and Harriet Miller! We just dropped in on the pigs for coffee! We're coming out!... We don't want trouble!"

Theme Projects

As you read the selections in this theme, try your hand at one of these projects. Work on your own, with a partner, or with a group.

CRITICAL READING
Challenges in Fiction

1. Think about the main characters in your favorite books. Choose one character who faced a big challenge. You will pretend you are that character.

2. Plan how to portray your character. Take notes about the character's life and the special challenge that he or she faced.

3. Meet with four or five classmates for a chat. Stay in character as you talk about the ups and downs of your fictional life.

4. Compare your character's challenges and outcomes with those of your classmates. What similarities and differences did you notice?

inter**NET**
CONNECTION

Check out the Web for more project ideas. Brainstorm some keywords about facing challenges that you can enter in your search engine to locate suitable sites. You can also check out the Glencoe Literature site at lit.glencoe.com.

LEARNING FOR LIFE
Writing a Persuasive Memo

What are some challenges your community faces? Is there a park that needs repair, a river that is polluted, or a dangerous intersection that needs a stop sign?

1. Choose one problem that you feel strongly about solving, and brainstorm ways to involve the community in the solution.

2. Draft a memo to your town or city government that will persuade officials to help organize community volunteers to solve the problem.

MULTIMEDIA PROJECT
Newsmakers Facing Challenges

1. Read magazines and newspapers, browse the Web, listen to the radio, and watch television news to learn about people facing challenges.

2. Choose one person and write a make-believe interview with her or him about life's challenges.

3. With a small group, produce a news video or a radio news show using the interview as the basis for a presentation to the class.

Before You Read
New Directions

MEET
MAYA ANGELOU

uthor, poet, playwright,
editor, educator, profes-
sional stage and screen performer, and singer—each of
these words describes Maya
Angelou (mī′yə   an′jel ō).
Angelou's extraordinary career
has taken her to many places
around the world, including
Egypt and Ghana. She read
her poem "On the Pulse of
Morning," commissioned by
President Clinton, at the 1993
inauguration.

*Maya Angelou was born in 1928.
"New Directions" was published in*
Wouldn't Take Nothing for My
Journey Now *in 1993.*

READING FOCUS

Each person has his or her own method of problem solving.
How do you go about solving a problem?

Think/Pair/Share
Think about a problem you recently solved. Share your
problem-solving method with a partner. With your partner, put
together a list of three to five words that describe an approach
to solving a problem.

Setting a Purpose
As you read the selection, try to discover a problem and its
solution.

BUILDING BACKGROUND

The Time and Place   This selection is set in Arkansas in the
early 1900s.

Did You Know?   Many of Maya Angelou's most famous
books are autobiographical. Although Angelou spent some of
her childhood with her mother in large cities, she was raised
mainly by her grandmother in the small town of Stamps,
Arkansas. "New Directions" is based on the life of Angelou's
grandmother, a determined woman who had a vision and
then worked hard to reach her goal.

VOCABULARY PREVIEW

concede (kən sēd′) *v.* to admit to be true or proper; p. 221
meticulously (mi tik′yə ləs lē) *adv.* in a way that shows care-
    ful attention to details; p. 221
balmy (bä′ mē) *adj.* mild; soothing; p. 222
assess (ə ses′) *v.* to determine the meaning or importance of;
    analyze; p. 222
loom (lōōm) *v.* to appear to the mind as threatening; p. 222
ominous (om′ ə nəs) *adj.* threatening harm or evil; p. 222
unpalatable (un pal′ ə tə bəl) *adj.* not agreeable to the taste,
    mind, or feelings; unacceptable; p. 222

New Directions

Maya Angelou

In 1903 the late Mrs. Annie Johnson of Arkansas found herself with two toddling sons, very little money, a slight ability to read and add simple numbers. To this picture add a disastrous marriage and the burdensome fact that Mrs. Johnson was a Negro.

When she told her husband, Mr. William Johnson, of her dissatisfaction with their marriage, he conceded that he too found it to be less than he expected, and had been secretly hoping to leave and study religion. He added that he thought God was calling him not only to preach but to do so in Enid, Oklahoma. He did not tell her that he knew a minister in Enid with whom he could study and who had a friendly, unmarried daughter. They parted amicably,[1] Annie keeping the one-room house and William taking most of the cash to carry himself to Oklahoma.

Annie, over six feet tall, big-boned, decided that she would not go to work as a domestic[2] and leave her "precious babes" to anyone else's care. There was no possibility of being hired at the town's cotton gin or lumber mill, but maybe there was a way to make the two factories work for her. In her words, "I looked up the road I was going and back the way I come, and since I wasn't satisfied, I decided to step off the road and cut me a new path." She told herself that she wasn't a fancy cook but that she could "mix groceries well enough to scare hungry away and from starving a man."

She made her plans meticulously and in secret. One early evening to see if she was ready, she placed stones in two five-gallon pails and carried them three miles to the cotton gin. She rested a little, and then, discarding some rocks, she walked in the darkness to the saw mill five miles farther along the dirt road. On her way back to her little house and her babies, she dumped the remaining rocks along the path.

That same night she worked into the early hours boiling chicken and frying ham. She made dough and filled the rolled-out pastry with meat. At last she went to sleep.

---

1. Mr. and Mrs. Johnson parted on friendly terms (*amicably*).
2. A *domestic* (də mes′ tik) is a household servant.

Vocabulary

concede (kən sēd′) *v.* to admit to be true or proper
meticulously (mi tik′ yə ləs lē) *adv.* in a way that shows careful attention to details

New Directions

Did You Know?

A *brazier* (brā′ zhər) is a metal container that holds burning coals. It is used for cooking food.

The next morning she left her house carrying the meat pies, lard, an iron brazier, and coals for a fire. Just before lunch she appeared in an empty lot behind the cotton gin. As the dinner noon bell rang, she dropped the savors into boiling fat and the aroma rose and floated over to the workers who spilled out of the gin, covered with white lint, looking like specters.[3]

Most workers had brought their lunches of pinto beans and biscuits or crackers, onions and cans of sardines, but they were tempted by the hot meat pies which Annie ladled out of the fat. She wrapped them in newspapers, which soaked up the grease, and offered them for sale at a nickel each. Although business was slow, those first days Annie was determined. She balanced her appearances between the two hours of activity.

So, on Monday if she offered hot fresh pies at the cotton gin and sold the remaining cooled-down pies at the lumber mill for three cents, then on Tuesday she went first to the lumber mill presenting fresh, just-cooked pies as the lumbermen covered in sawdust emerged from the mill.

For the next few years, on <u>balmy</u> spring days, blistering summer noons, and cold, wet, and wintry middays, Annie never disappointed her customers, who could count on seeing the tall, brown-skin woman bent over her brazier, carefully turning the meat pies. When she felt certain that the workers had become dependent on her, she built a stall between the two hives of industry and let the men run to her for their lunchtime provisions.

She had indeed stepped from the road which seemed to have been chosen for her and cut herself a brand-new path. In years that stall became a store where customers could buy cheese, meal, syrup, cookies, candy, writing tablets, pickles, canned goods, fresh fruit, soft drinks, coal, oil, and leather soles for worn-out shoes.

Each of us has the right and the responsibility to <u>assess</u> the roads which lie ahead, and those over which we have traveled, and if the future road <u>looms</u> <u>ominous</u> or unpromising, and the roads back uninviting, then we need to gather our resolve and, carrying only the necessary baggage, step off that road into another direction. If the new choice is also <u>unpalatable</u>, without embarrassment, we must be ready to change that as well.

---

3. A *specter* (spek′ tər) is a ghost.

Vocabulary

balmy (bä′ mē) *adj.* mild; soothing

assess (ə ses′) *v.* to determine the meaning or importance of; analyze

loom (lo̅o̅m) *v.* to appear to the mind as threatening

ominous (om′ ə nəs) *adj.* threatening harm or evil

unpalatable (un pal′ ə tə bəl) *adj.* not agreeable to the taste, mind, or feelings; unacceptable

Responding to Literature

PERSONAL RESPONSE

- ◆ What went through your mind as you finished reading this selection?
- ◆ Think back to the **Reading Focus** on page 220. What words would you use to describe Mrs. Annie Johnson's method of problem solving? How does your method of problem solving compare with hers? Record your responses in a journal.

The Storyteller, 1995. Christian Pierre (b. 1962). Acrylic on Masonite, 48 x 32 in. Private collection.

Analyzing Literature

RECALL

1. What is the problem facing Mrs. Annie Johnson at the beginning of the narrative?
2. According to the narrator, what were Johnson's options for employment?
3. List the steps Johnson took to start her own business.
4. What became of Annie Johnson's stall?

INTERPRET

5. What is Johnson's attitude toward her problem? Explain.
6. Explain what Johnson means by the statement "I looked up the road I was going and back the way I come, and since I wasn't satisfied, I decided to step off the road and cut me a new path."
7. What does the title of the selection mean? How does it relate to Johnson's new career? Use quotations from the selection to support your ideas.
8. How did Annie Johnson's original vision become a thriving business?

EVALUATE AND CONNECT

9. The **theme** of a piece of writing is the message the writer hopes to communicate. What is the theme of this selection? Explain.
10. Theme Connection   Think of someone you know who faced a challenge and set out boldly in a new direction. Tell about the result of that person's action.

LITERARY ELEMENTS

Biography

A **biography** is a true story written by an author about the life of another person. The writer researches the person's life by conducting interviews and by reading letters, books, and diaries. A good biography tells more than what the subject said or did. A good biography makes its subject come alive for readers. A biography may cover a person's entire life, or it may focus on one period of time.

1. What details did you learn about Annie Johnson's life from reading this biographical essay?

2. What else would you like to learn about Annie Johnson's life?

● See **Literary Terms Handbook,** p. R2.

Extending Your Response

Writing About Literature

Finding Solutions "New Directions" focuses on one woman's imaginative solution to a difficult problem. Use the story and ideas you came up with in the **Reading Focus** on page 220 to write a paragraph about how to deal with a personal problem. Use examples from "New Directions" to support your ideas.

Literature Groups

A Vision of Success An entrepreneur is someone who has a vision for a business and then succeeds in creating that business. Many entrepreneurs are people like Annie Johnson, who follow their own unique paths to success. What personal qualities do you think Johnson had that enabled her to take charge of her life and start a successful business? In a small group, brainstorm a list of five important qualities necessary for achieving personal success. Support your ideas with details from the selection.

Creative Writing

A Journal Entry Imagine that you are Mrs. Annie Johnson the night before your first day selling food to the workers. How might you feel? What might you think? Describe your thoughts and feelings in a journal entry.

Art Activity

Design a Menu Design a menu for Mrs. Annie Johnson to hang on her food stall. Make your own drawings or cut out photographs of food from old magazines. Be sure to make up a catchy name for Johnson's food business.

📖 **Save your work for your portfolio.**

Skill Minilesson

VOCABULARY • ANALOGIES

Analogies compare relationships. Analogies are usually written in this form:

balmy : mild :: ominous : threatening

This analogy is read:

balmy is to *mild* as *ominous* is to *threatening.*

In this example, the words in each pair are synonyms, words that are similar in meaning. Analogies can state other kinds of relationships, such as antonyms (cold : hot); cause and effect (determination : success); or part and a whole (wheel : automobile). The relationship between the second pair of words must be the same as the relationship between the first pair.

PRACTICE Decide on the relationship of the first two words. Then apply that relationship to the second set of words.
1. smile : friendly :: frown : _____
   a. hostile   b. balmy   c. frighten
2. grumble : complain :: concede : _____
   a. refuse   b. acknowledge   c. assess
3. delicious : unpalatable :: meticulous : _____
   a. tasty   b. attentive   c. careless

Vo·cab·u·lar·y Skills

Using Homophones

Words that sound the same but have different meanings and spellings are called **homophones.** There are hundreds of homophones in the English language. A bad bird is a foul fowl. Rabbit fur might be called hare hair. A forbidden musical group is a banned band. A string that won't stay tied will not knot.

You have to be careful to write the right word. Even if you work on a computer that can check your spelling, you need to watch for homophone mistakes. If you type *brake* when you mean *break,* no computer spell-check program can fix your mistake because both *brake* and *break* are correctly spelled words.

EXERCISES

A. Read the passage below. If the underlined word is the correct one to use, write *Correct.* If it is a homophone for the correct word, write the correct word.

> When Annie Johnson's husband left her, she needed to <u>billed</u> a <u>new</u>
>   1   2
> life. She did not have a job, but she did have <u>two</u> children to take
>   3
> care of. Instead of feeling trapped by the <u>passed</u>, she moved with
>   4
> energy toward the future. With little education, she wondered if
> anyone <u>wood</u> <u>higher</u> her, <u>so</u> she created her own business. Every
>   5   6   7
> day, Annie <u>maid</u> food to <u>cell</u> to workers at nearby factories. The
>   8   9
> <u>scent</u> of the cooking pies guaranteed her success.
>   10

B. Complete each sentence by using two homophones. An example is provided.

Example: The bigger, better grinder could be called the *greater grater.*

1. A king's tossed chair is a _____.
2. If people take metal without paying for it, they _____.
3. If you chewed up seven grapes and then one more, you _____.
4. What the group of cows listened to is what the _____.
5. Buttons, snaps, and zippers are used to _____.

Before You Read

The Wreck of the Hesperus and I'll Walk the Tightrope

MEET HENRY WADSWORTH LONGFELLOW

Henry Wadsworth Longfellow was one of the first American writers to use the traditions of European writing to create a distinctly American form of literature.

Henry Wadsworth Longfellow was born in 1807 and died in 1882.

MEET MARGARET DANNER

Margaret Danner began writing poetry in junior high school. After college, Danner became the first African American assistant editor of *Poetry* magazine. In 1960 she published her first collection of poetry. Later, Danner became poet-in-residence at Wayne State University in Detroit.

Margaret Danner was born in 1915 and died in 1984.

READING FOCUS

Do you like to have adventures, or do you prefer to read about them?

Sharing Ideas

An adventure can be any experience or activity that is exciting for you, from traveling through a storm to learning to swim. In a small group, talk about adventures you have had or have read about. What did you learn from these adventures?

Setting a Purpose

Read to discover the adventure in each of these poems.

Shipwreck, 1833 (detail). Thomas Birch. Oil on canvas, 20 x 30 in.

BUILDING BACKGROUND

In December 1839, a series of winter storms swept New England. Two shipwrecks caused by the storms became the inspiration for Longfellow's "The Wreck of the Hesperus." Longfellow commented on the poem in a diary entry dated December 30, 1839.

"...I sat till twelve o'clock by my fire ..., when suddenly it came into my mind.... Then I went to bed, but could not sleep. New thoughts were running in my mind, and I got up to add them to the ballad. It was three by the clock. I then went to bed and fell asleep.... It did not come into my mind by lines, but by stanzas."

The Wreck of the Hesperus

Henry Wadsworth Longfellow

It was the schooner° Hesperus,
   That sailed the wintry sea;
And the skipper had taken his little daughter,
   To bear him company.

5   Blue were her eyes as the fairy-flax,
   Her cheeks like the dawn of day,
And her bosom white as the hawthorn buds,
   That ope° in the month of May.

The skipper he stood beside the helm,
10   His pipe was in his mouth,
And he watched how the veering flaw° did blow
   The smoke now West, now South.

Then up and spake an old Sailor,
   Had sailed to the Spanish Main,°
15   "I pray thee, put into yonder port,
   For I fear a hurricane.

"Last night, the moon had a golden ring,
   And tonight no moon we see!"
The skipper, he blew a whiff from his pipe,
20   And a scornful laugh laughed he.

---

1 A *schooner* is a ship with two or more masts. Masts are the tall, strong poles
   used to support the sails.
8 *Ope* (ōp) is an old, poetic form of *open*.
11 Here, *veering flaw* (vēr′ ing   flô) means "shifting, or changing, gusts of wind."
14 The *Spanish Main* refers to the Caribbean Sea along the coast of South
   America, where Spanish trading ships traveled in colonial times.

The Wreck of the Hesperus

Colder and louder blew the wind,
    A gale from the Northeast,
The snow fell hissing in the brine,
    And the billows frothed like yeast.

25   Down came the storm, and smote° amain°
        The vessel in its strength;
She shuddered and paused, like a frighted steed,
        Then leaped her cable's length.°

"Come hither! come hither! my little daughter,
30   And do not tremble so;
For I can weather the roughest gale
        That ever wind did blow."

He wrapped her warm in his seaman's coat
    Against the stinging blast;
35   He cut a rope from a broken spar,°
        And bound her to the mast.

"O father! I hear the church bells ring,
    Oh say, what may it be?"
"'Tis a fog bell on a rock-bound coast!"—
40   And he steered for the open sea.

"O father! I hear the sound of guns,
    Oh say, what may it be?"
"Some ship in distress, that cannot live
    In such an angry sea!"

45   "O father! I see a gleaming light,
       Oh say, what may it be?"
But the father answered never a word,
    A frozen corpse was he.

---

25 The storm struck *(smote)* with full force *(amain)*.
28 In sailing, *cable's length* is a unit of measurement equal to 720 feet
   (219.5 meters).
35 A *spar* is any of the strong poles used to support a ship's rigging (the ropes,
   cables, etc., that hold and control the sails).

Northeaster, 1895. Winslow Homer. Oil on canvas. Metropolitan Museum of Art, New York.

Viewing the painting: How is the mood of the painting similar to the mood of "The Wreck of the Hesperus"?

Lashed to the helm, all stiff and stark,
50   With his face turned to the skies,
The lantern gleamed through the gleaming snow
    On his fixed and glassy eyes.

Then the maiden clasped her hands and prayed
    That saved she might be;
55 And she thought of Christ, who stilled the wave,
    On the Lake of Galilee.

And fast through the midnight dark and drear,
    Through the whistling sleet and snow,
Like a sheeted ghost, the vessel swept
60 Tow'rds the reef of Norman's Woe.

The Wreck of the Hesperus

And ever the fitful gusts between
    A sound came from the land;
It was the sound of the trampling surf
    On the rocks and the hard sea sand.

65   The breakers were right beneath her bows,
    She drifted a dreary wreck,
And a whooping billow swept the crew
    Like icicles from her deck.

She struck where the white and fleecy waves
70   Looked soft as carded wool,°
But the cruel rocks, they gored her side
    Like the horns of an angry bull.

Her rattling shrouds,° all sheathed° in ice,
    With the masts went by the board;°
75 Like a vessel of glass, she stove° and sank,
    Ho! ho! the breakers roared!

At daybreak, on the bleak sea beach,
    A fisherman stood aghast,°
To see the form of a maiden fair,
80   Lashed close to a drifting mast.

The salt sea was frozen on her breast,
    The salt tears in her eyes;
And he saw her hair, like the brown seaweed,
    On the billows fall and rise.

85   Such was the wreck of the Hesperus,
    In the midnight and the snow!
Christ save us all from a death like this,
    On the reef of Norman's Woe!

---

70 *Carded wool* has been cleaned and combed to prepare it for spinning.

73–75 The ropes that support the masts *(shrouds)* were encased *(sheathed)* in heavy ice. After the shrouds and masts were torn away *(went by the board)*, the ship itself was smashed *(stove)* on the rocks.

78 Being *aghast* (ə gast′) means to be filled with horror and amazement.

I'll Walk the Tightrope

Fatima, 1994. Elizabeth Barakah Hodges. Acrylic, 23 x 18 in.

Margaret Danner ⌇

I'll walk the tightrope that's been stretched for me,
and though a wrinkled forehead, perplexed why,
will accompany me, I'll delicately
step along. For if I stop to sigh
at the earth-propped stride
of others, I will fall. I must balance high
without a parasol° to tide°
a faltering step, without a net below,
without a balance stick to guide.

---

7 A *parasol* is a small lightweight umbrella used as protection from the sun.
Here, *tide* means "to aid or assist."

Responding to Literature

PERSONAL RESPONSE

- ◆ Which image from each poem did you find the most dramatic or striking? Why?

Analyzing Literature

RECALL AND INTERPRET

1. According to the speaker of "The Wreck of the Hesperus," what happened to the ship, the skipper, and the skipper's young daughter?

2. Summarize what the speaker tells you in "I'll Walk the Tightrope."

3. What is the central **conflict** in the plot of "The Wreck of the Hesperus"? How is the conflict resolved?

4. What is the central image in the poem "I'll Walk the Tightrope"? What do you think the tightrope represents?

EVALUATE AND CONNECT

5. What attitude toward nature does the skipper express in "The Wreck of the Hesperus"? How does his attitude contrast with that of the old sailor? Explain.

6. Describe the relationship between the skipper and his daughter in "The Wreck of the Hesperus." Do you think the skipper should have taken his daughter on the voyage? Explain.

7. In "I'll Walk the Tightrope," what is the speaker's attitude about facing the challenges of life? Do you agree with that point of view? Explain.

8. How do you think the speaker in "I'll Walk the Tightrope" sees herself? What images are used to compare or contrast the speaker with other people?

9. Which poem do you prefer? Why?

10. **Theme Connection**   How is each of these poems related to the theme of facing challenges? Explain.

LITERARY ELEMENTS

Narrative Poetry

Narrative poetry is poetry that tells a story. "The Wreck of the Hesperus" is an example of a narrative poem. Like a short story or a novel, a narrative poem usually includes a setting, some characters, and a plot. The events in a narrative poem are often told in chronological order, the order in which they happen. In a narrative poem, the theme unfolds as the story is told.

1. Describe the setting, the plot, and the main characters of "The Wreck of the Hesperus."

2. Find another example of a narrative poem in this book or in another book. Tell why the poem is an example of narrative poetry.

- ● See **Literary Terms Handbook,** p. R7.

First Rate Man of War Foundering in a Gale, late 19th century. George Philip Reinagle. Oil on canvas. Royal Albert Memorial Museum, Exeter, England.

Extending Your Response

Writing About Literature

Looking at Imagery Both poems contain strong images that help readers "see" what is happening in the poems and understand the themes of the poems. Pick out an image from each poem. Then, describe how each image helps you understand the poem's message.

Creative Writing

News Flash Turn the plot of "The Wreck of the Hesperus" into a newspaper article. Add any details you need, including eyewitness interviews with other sailors and weather reports about the storm.

Literature Groups

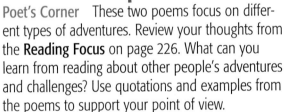

Poet's Corner These two poems focus on different types of adventures. Review your thoughts from the **Reading Focus** on page 226. What can you learn from reading about other people's adventures and challenges? Use quotations and examples from the poems to support your point of view.

Listening and Speaking

The Drama of Poetry Poetry should be read aloud to be fully appreciated. As a poem is read, listeners may close their eyes, picture the images, and hear the natural rhythm of the lines. With a partner or in a small group, choose one of the poems to read aloud. Perform your reading for the class.

Reading Further

If you would like to read more by these poets, try these books:

Selected Poems by Henry Wadsworth Longfellow, edited by Laurance Buell (many other editions available)

The Down of a Thistle by Margaret Danner

Save your work for your portfolio.

Skill Minilesson

READING AND THINKING • IDENTIFYING SPATIAL RELATIONSHIPS

One way to organize details is to use **spatial order**—that is, showing where things are located. When you read a poem, try to visualize where things are in relation to other things. For example, in the first scene of "The Wreck of the Hesperus," the skipper is standing by the helm. As you read, ask:

• What does this scene or image look like?
• Where is each thing in relation to the other things in the scene?

PRACTICE Reread each of the poems. As you do, try to think about the spatial order in the different scenes and images in each poem. For each poem, make a simple diagram (with labels) to illustrate one important scene or image. Show where each thing is in relation to the other things mentioned.

● For more about spatial order, see **Reading Handbook,** p. R91.

Before You Read
Too Soon a Woman

MEET DOROTHY M. JOHNSON

Dorothy M. Johnson was born in Iowa, but her experiences at the University of Montana inspired a lifelong love of the scenery and history of the American West. An honorary member of the Blackfoot Tribe, Johnson wrote vividly about Native Americans and cowboys, sheriffs and outlaws. Three of her short stories—"The Hanging Tree," "The Man Who Shot Liberty Valance," and "A Man Called Horse"—were made into classic Western movies.

Dorothy M. Johnson was born in 1905 and died in 1984.

READING FOCUS

What traits do you think pioneers needed to survive?

Think/Pair/Share
With a partner, list survival characteristics for a pioneer family traveling west 150 years ago.

Setting a Purpose
Read this story to discover what one family learns about survival.

BUILDING BACKGROUND

The Time and Place   This story takes place sometime in the 1800s, on the way west across the American prairie.

Did You Know?
Pioneers traveled west on overland routes such as the Oregon Trail. Pioneer wagon trains began traveling the Oregon Trail in the 1840s. The difficult trip lasted four to six months.

VOCABULARY PREVIEW

skimpy (skim′ pē) *adj.* lacking in quantity, fullness, or size; barely enough or not quite enough; p. 236

grudging (gruj′ ing) *adj.* given or allowed unwillingly or resentfully; p. 236

gaunt (gônt) *adj.* looking like skin and bones; p. 237

grim (grim) *adj.* fierce; severe; stern; forbidding; p. 237

endure (en door′) *v.* to put up with; undergo, as pain, stress, or other hardship; p. 238

savor (sā′ vər) *v.* to take great delight in; p. 239

gruffly (gruf′ lē) *adv.* in a rough, stern manner; p. 239

sedately (si dāt′ lē) *adv.* in a quiet, restrained style or manner; calmly; p. 239

Too Soon a Woman

Dorothy M. Johnson ~

A Back Road, 1884. Childe Hassam. 79.4 x 63.5 cm. The Brooklyn Museum, New York.

Too Soon a Woman

We left the home place behind, mile by slow mile, heading for the mountains, across the prairie where the wind blew forever.

At first there were four of us with the one-horse wagon and its skimpy load. Pa and I walked, because I was a big boy of eleven. My two little sisters romped and trotted until they got tired and had to be boosted up into the wagon bed.

That was no covered Conestoga, like Pa's folks came west in, but just an old farm wagon, drawn by one weary horse, creaking and rumbling westward to the mountains, toward the little woods town where Pa thought he had an old uncle who owned a little two-bit sawmill.

Did You Know?

A *Conestoga* (kon' is tō' gə) is a covered wagon with a canvas top and large wheels.

Two weeks we had been moving when we picked up Mary, who had run away from somewhere that she wouldn't tell. Pa didn't want her along, but she stood up to him with no fear in her voice.

"I'd rather go with a family and look after the kids," she said, "but I ain't going back. If you won't take me, I'll travel with any wagon that will."

Pa scowled at her, and her wide blue eyes stared back.

"How old are you?" he demanded.

"Eighteen," she said. "There's teamsters[1] come this way sometimes. I'd rather go with you folks. But I won't go back."

"We're prid'near out of grub," my father told her. "We're clean out of money. I got all I can handle without taking anybody else." He turned away as if he hated the sight of her. "You'll have to walk," he said.

So she went along with us and looked after the little girls, but Pa wouldn't talk to her.

On the prairie, the wind blew. But in the mountains, there was rain. When we stopped at little timber claims along the way, the homesteaders said it had rained all summer. Crops among the blackened stumps were rotted and spoiled. There was no cheer anywhere and little hospitality. The people we talked to were past worrying. They were scared and desperate.

So was Pa. He traveled twice as far each day as the wagon. He ranged through the woods with his rifle, but he never saw game. He had been depending on venison, but we never got any except as a grudging gift from the homesteaders.

He brought in a porcupine once; that was fat meat and good. Mary roasted it in chunks over the fire, half crying with the smoke. Pa and I rigged up the tarp sheet for a shelter to keep the rain from putting the fire clean out.

---

1. *Teamsters* are people who drive teams of horses or oxen.

Vocabulary

skimpy (skim' pē) *adj.* lacking in quantity, fullness, or size; barely enough or not quite enough

grudging (gruj' ing) *adj.* given or allowed unwillingly or resentfully

The porcupine was long gone, except for some of the tried-out[2] fat that Mary had saved, when we came to an old, empty cabin. Pa said we'd have to stop. The horse was wore out, couldn't pull anymore up those grades on the deep-rutted roads in the mountains.

At the cabin, at least there was shelter. We had a few potatoes left and some corn meal. There was a creek that probably had fish in it, if a person could catch them. Pa tried it for half a day before he gave up. To this day I don't care for fishing. I remember my father's sunken eyes in his gaunt, grim face.

He took Mary and me outside the cabin to talk. Rain dripped on us from branches overhead.

"I think I know where we are," he said. "I calculate to get to old John's and back in about four days. There'll be grub in the town, and they'll let me have some whether old John's still there or not."

He looked at me. "You do like she tells you," he warned. It was the first time he had admitted Mary was on earth since we picked her up two weeks before.

"You're my pardner," he said to me, "but it might be she's got more brains. You mind what she says."

He burst out with bitterness, "There ain't anything good left in the world, or people to care if you live or die. But I'll get grub in the town and come back with it."

He took a deep breath and added, "If you get too all-fired hungry, butcher the horse. It'll be better than starvin'."

He kissed the little girls good-bye and plodded off through the woods with one blanket and the rifle.

The cabin was moldy and had no floor. We kept a fire going under a hole in the roof, so it was full of blinding smoke, but we had to keep the fire so as to dry out the wood.

The third night, we lost the horse. A bear scared him. We heard the racket, and Mary and I ran out, but we couldn't see anything in the pitch dark.

In gray daylight I went looking for him, and I must have walked fifteen miles. It seemed like I had to have that horse at the cabin when Pa came or he'd whip me. I got plumb lost two or three times and thought maybe I was going to die there alone and nobody would ever know it, but I found the way back to the clearing.

That was the fourth day, and Pa didn't come. That was the day we ate up the last of the grub.

The fifth day, Mary went looking for the horse. My sisters whimpered, huddled in a quilt by the fire, because they were scared and hungry.

I never did get dried out, always having to bring in more damp wood and going out to yell to see if Mary would hear me and not get lost. But I couldn't cry like the little girls did, because I was a big boy, eleven years old.

It was near dark when there was an answer to my yelling, and Mary came into the clearing.

---

2. Here, *tried-out* refers to the melted fat from the roasted porcupine.

Vocabulary
gaunt (gônt) *adj.* looking like skin and bones
grim (grim) *adj.* fierce; severe; stern; forbidding

Too Soon a Woman

Mary didn't have the horse—we never saw hide nor hair of that old horse again—but she was carrying something big and white that looked like a pumpkin with no color to it.

She didn't say anything, just looked around and saw Pa wasn't there yet, at the end of the fifth day.

"What's that thing?" my sister Elizabeth demanded.

"Mushroom," Mary answered. "I bet it hefts ten pounds."

"What are you going to do with it now?" I sneered. "Play football here?"

"Eat it—maybe," she said, putting it in a corner. Her wet hair hung over her shoulders. She huddled by the fire.

My sister Sarah began to whimper again. "I'm hungry!" she kept saying.

"Mushrooms ain't good eating," I said. "They can kill you."

"Maybe," Mary answered. "Maybe they can. I don't set up to know all about everything, like some people."

"What's that mark on your shoulder?" I asked her. "You tore your dress on the brush."

"What do you think it is?" she said, her head bowed in the smoke.

"Looks like scars," I guessed.

"'Tis scars. They whipped me. Now mind your own business. I want to think."

Elizabeth whimpered, "Why don't Pa come back?"

"He's coming," Mary promised. "Can't come in the dark. Your pa'll take care of you soon's he can."

She got up and rummaged around in the grub box.

"Nothing there but empty dishes," I growled. "If there was anything, we'd know it."

Mary stood up. She was holding the can with the porcupine grease.

"I'm going to have something to eat," she said coolly. "You kids can't have any yet. And I don't want any squalling,[3] mind."

It was a cruel thing, what she did then. She sliced that big, solid mushroom and heated grease in a pan.

The smell of it brought the little girls out of their quilt, but she told them to go back in so fierce a voice that they obeyed. They cried to break your heart.

I didn't cry. I watched, hating her.

I endured the smell of the mushroom frying as long as I could. Then I said, "Give me some."

"Tomorrow," Mary answered. "Tomorrow, maybe. But not tonight." She turned to me with a sharp command: "Don't bother me! Just leave me be."

She knelt there by the fire and finished frying the slice of mushroom.

If I'd had Pa's rifle, I'd have been willing to kill her right then and there.

She didn't eat right away. She looked at the brown, fried slice for a while and said, "By tomorrow morning, I guess you can tell whether you want any."

---

3. *Squalling* is the screaming cries of complaint Mary expects from the hungry little girls.

Vocabulary

endure (en door´) *v.* to put up with; undergo, as pain, stress, or other hardship

The little girls stared at her as she ate. Sarah was chewing an old leather glove.

When Mary crawled into the quilts with them, they moved away as far as they could get.

I was so scared that my stomach heaved, empty as it was.

Mary didn't stay in the quilts long. She took a drink out of the water bucket and sat down by the fire and looked through the smoke at me.

She said in a low voice, "I don't know how it will be if it's poison. Just do the best you can with the girls. Because your pa will come back, you know. . . . You better go to bed, I'm going to sit up."

And so would you sit up. If it might be your last night on earth and the pain of death might seize you at any moment, you would sit up by the smoky fire, wide-awake, remembering whatever you had to remember, <u>savoring</u> life.

We sat in silence after the girls had gone to sleep. Once I asked, "How long does it take?"

"I never heard," she answered. "Don't think about it."

I slept after a while, with my chin on my chest. Maybe Peter dozed that way at Gethsemane[4] as the Lord knelt praying.

Mary's moving around brought me wide-awake. The black of night was fading.

"I guess it's all right," Mary said. "I'd be able to tell by now, wouldn't I?"

I answered <u>gruffly</u>, "I don't know."

Mary stood in the doorway for a while, looking out at the dripping world as if she found it beautiful. Then she fried slices of the mushroom while the little girls danced with anxiety.

We feasted, we three, my sisters and I, until Mary ruled, "That'll hold you," and would not cook any more. She didn't touch any of the mushroom herself.

That was a strange day in the moldy cabin. Mary laughed and was gay; she told stories, and we played "Who's Got the Thimble?" with a pine cone.

In the afternoon we heard a shout, and my sisters screamed, and I ran ahead of them across the clearing.

The rain had stopped. My father came plunging out of the woods leading a packhorse—and well I remember the treasures of food in that pack.

He glanced at us anxiously as he tore at the ropes that bound the pack.

"Where's the other one?" he demanded.

Mary came out of the cabin then, walking <u>sedately</u>. As she came toward us, the sun began to shine.

My stepmother was a wonderful woman.

---

4. The New Testament of the Christian Bible says that Jesus, knowing his death was near, went to the Garden of *Gethsemane* (geth sem′ ə nē) to pray. Although *Peter* and other disciples had come to pray with him, they all fell asleep.

Vocabulary

savor (sā′ vər) *v.* to take great delight in
gruffly (gruf′ lē) *adv.* in a rough, stern manner
sedately (si dāt′ lē) *adv.* in a quiet, restrained style or manner; calmly

Responding to Literature

PERSONAL RESPONSE

◆ Draw a picture that shows your interpretation of the situation in the cabin before the children eat the mushroom.

Analyzing Literature

RECALL

1. Who were the members of the original group who left the "home place"?
2. What is the most pressing problem the family and Mary have to solve?
3. What does Mary finally find to feed the children?
4. What do you find out about Mary at the very end of the story?

INTERPRET

5. What can you infer about the mother of the family?
6. In your opinion, why does Pa have such a hard time providing food for the family?
7. Why does Mary make the children wait so long before she lets them eat the mushroom? What does Mary's way of testing the mushroom reveal about her?
8. How does the last line of the story make you rethink the beginning?

EVALUATE AND CONNECT

9. Why, do you think, did Johnson choose "Too Soon a Woman" for her title?
10. Theme Connection   Would you have liked to experience a trek across the prairie? Does this story change the way you think about the challenges in your own life? Explain your answer.

LITERARY ELEMENTS

Dialect

In certain regions of America, particular groups speak variations of English called **dialects**. Dialects differ from Standard English because they contain different pronunciations, word forms, and meanings. The conversational language in "Too Soon a Woman" represents the author's idea of the dialect of Midwestern pioneers in the mid-1800s.

1. What do the phrases "We're prid'near out of grub" and "Just leave me be" mean?

2. Does the author's use of dialect add to the story? Why or why not?

● See **Literary Terms Handbook**, p. R3.

Extending Your Response

Writing About Literature

Surprise Ending   The last sentence in "Too Soon a Woman" comes as a surprise to the reader. Mary is a recent and, at first, unwelcome addition to the family. Then, suddenly, the narrator tells us she became his stepmother. Write a paragraph analyzing the effectiveness of the ending of the story.

Creative Writing

A Learning Experience   Recall the list you made for the **Reading Focus** on page 234. Using your list and what you learned from the story, write an introduction that explains the courage and survival techniques pioneers needed.

Literature Groups

A Caretaker's Responsibility   When Mary cooked the mushroom, she had no idea if she would survive eating it. Did she take too great a risk? What would have happened to the children if she became sick or died? Would you have eaten the mushroom? Discuss these questions, and be prepared to share your group's opinions with the whole class.

*inter*NET CONNECTION

Use the Web to learn more about pioneer life. Try typing words and phrases such as *Oregon Trail* and *Conestoga* into a search engine.

Learning for Life

Poison or Not   Write a report about mushrooms. In an encyclopedia or science book, look up mushrooms. Then choose an edible mushroom and draw a picture of it. List its characteristics, and form a conclusion about its nutritional value.

 Save your work for your portfolio.

Skill Minilesson

VOCABULARY • ANTONYMS

Antonyms are words with opposite, or nearly opposite, meanings.

PRACTICE   In each blank, write an antonym for the underlined word.

1. She had been <u>plump</u> before her illness, but afterwards she was quite _____.
2. The losers looked _____, but the winners looked <u>delighted</u>.
3. Some people react _____ to good news, while others jump up and down <u>excitedly</u>.
4. The portions that were served weren't <u>generous</u> at all; they were downright _____.
5. Successful salespeople treat customers <u>politely</u>, not _____.

Before You Read

A Boy and His Dog

MEET MARTHA BROOKS

Martha Brooks writes mainly about teenagers and their joys and disappointments. Her own childhood was spent at a tuberculosis sanatorium in rural Canada, where her parents were part of the medical staff. She and her sister grew up on the grounds with just a few other children. In her writing, Brooks has said that "what is important is that I try to be true to the characters I invent—listening to them, letting them tell their stories, and respecting the lives they live on the page."

Martha Brooks was born in 1944. This story was first published in 1988.

READING FOCUS

Human beings and their pets can become very dependent on each other. Do you have, or wish you had, a pet?

Chart It!

Choose a pet. Then create a two-column chart that shows what a pet needs from its owner and what the owner receives from the pet.

Setting a Purpose

Read this story to find out how one person feels about his dog.

BUILDING BACKGROUND

Did You Know?

Veterinary medicine deals with the diseases and injuries of animals. Animals can suffer from many of the same diseases that affect people, including heart disease and cancer.

VOCABULARY PREVIEW

spasm (spaz′ əm) *n.* a sudden uncontrollable tightening of a muscle; p. 243

obligingly (ə blī′ jing lē) *adv.* helpfully; agreeably; p. 244

slither (sli<u>th</u>′ ər) *v.* to move along with a sliding or gliding motion, as a snake; p. 246

frenzy (fren′ zē) *n.* a state of intense excitement or disturbance; p. 246

vigor (vig′ ər) *n.* strength and energy; p. 246

lolling (lol′ ing) *adj.* hanging down loosely; drooping; p. 246

saunter (sôn′ tər) *v.* to walk in a relaxed way; p. 246

reluctantly (ri luk′ tənt lē) *adv.* unwillingly; p. 247

A Boy and His Dog

Martha Brooks ∿

My dog is old. His eyes are constantly runny on account of he's going blind. Sometimes when we go for his walk he falls down. We'll be moving right along, I'll feel an unexpected tug at his leash, and bingo! he's over. The first time it happened he cried, sort of whimpered, and looked at his leg, the back one, the one that had betrayed him. I crouched in the tall grass (we take our walks in a sky-filled prairie field near the townhouses where we live) and felt the leg, which was in a <u>spasm</u>. I told him if it didn't work too well to just give up for a while. He seemed to know what I was telling him because he looked at me, whimpered some more, and finally flopped his head back on my leg. That's what kills me about dogs. They figure you're in charge of everything. Like if you pointed your finger, you could make a house fall down. Or if you told them everything's going to be okay, it would be.

After a couple of minutes he stood up and took off again in that businesslike, let's-get-the-show-on-the-road manner of his, sniffing, squatting to pee (he doesn't lift his leg anymore) near every bush in sight. Later, I found out he fell over because of arthritis. "Nothing you can do, really," said the vet, patting Alphonse's broad flat head. "He's just getting old, Buddy." She gave me some red pellet-shaped arthritis pills and sent us home.

Vocabulary

spasm (spaz′ əm) *n.* a sudden uncontrollable tightening of a muscle

A Boy and His Dog

After that, whenever he fell, he'd look quite cheerful. He'd lick the leg a bit, hang out his tongue, pant, and patiently wait. Just before stumbling to his feet, he'd look up like he was saying thank you—when I hadn't done anything!

I couldn't let him see how bad all this made me feel. He's so smart sometimes you have to put your hands over his ears and spell things so he won't know what you're talking about. Things like cheese, cookie, walk. All his favorites.

Mom said, "He can't last forever. Everybody dies sooner or later. It's the natural course of events. And big dogs don't live as long as little dogs."

Around our house, nobody put their hands over my ears.

Alphonse was a present for my first birthday. Dad brought him home, just a scruffy little brown pup someone was giving away. No special breed. I still have a snapshot of him and me at the party. I was this goopy-looking blond kid in blue corduroy overalls and a Donald Duck T-shirt. Alphonse was all over me in the way of puppies. I'd been startled by Dad's flash and also by Alphonse, who'd chosen that exact moment to paw me down and slurp strawberry ice cream off my face and hands. Dad says I didn't cry or anything! Just lay bug-eyed on the shag rug with Alphonse wiggling and slopping all over me. We got on like a house on fire after that.

Which is why it's so unfair that I'm fourteen going on fifteen and he's thirteen going on ninety-four.

I guess I thought we'd just go on forever with Alphonse being my dog. Listening when I tell him stuff. When he goes, who am I going to tell my secrets to? I tell him things I wouldn't even tell Herb Malken, who is my best friend now that we've been in this city a year. My dad's always getting transferred. He's in the army. When I grow up that's one thing I'm not going to be. In the army. I won't make my kids move every three years and leave all their friends behind. Which is one thing I *am* going to do: have more than one kid when I get married.

There's a big myth that only children are selfish and self-centered. I can say from personal experience that only children are more likely to feel guilty and be too eager to please. It's terrible when you are one kid having to be everything to two parents.

Which is why Alphonse is more than just a dog, you see. Mom even sometimes calls him "Baby." Like he's my brother. Which it sometimes feels like.

Last week he had bad gas. I always sleep with the windows open. Even so, it got pretty awful in my bedroom.

Alphonse doesn't make much sound when he has gas. Just a little "phhhht" like a balloon with a slow leak and there's no living with him. I swear when he gets like that it would be dangerous to light a match.

I sent him out. He went <u>obligingly</u>. He's always been a polite dog. I listened, first to his toenails clicking over the hardwood floors, then to the scratching of his dry bristly fur as he slumped against the other side of the bedroom door. When you can't be in the same room with someone who's shared your dreams for thirteen years, it's hard to get properly relaxed. It isn't the

---

Vocabulary
obligingly (ə blī′ jing lē) *adv.* helpfully; agreeably

Companions. James Charles (1851–1906). Oldham Art Gallery, Manchester, England.

Viewing the painting: How do you think the lives of this boy and his dog differ from the lives of the boy and dog in the story?

A Boy and His Dog

same when they aren't near you, breathing the same air.

For the next few days he lay around more than usual. I thought perhaps he was just overtired (even though I hadn't been able to stand it and had begun to let him back into my room, gas and all). By Sunday, Mom cocked her head at him and said to Dad and me, "I don't like the way Alphonse looks. Better take him back to the vet, Buddy."

Mom works at the army base too. It's late when she and Dad get home and by that time the vet is closed for the day. So I always take Alphonse right after school. It isn't far—three blocks past the field.

Monday was the kind of fall day that makes you breathe more deeply—the field all burning colors, far-off bushes little flames of magenta[1] and orange, dry wavy grass a pale yellow, and the big sky that kind of deep fire blue you see only once a year, in October. Alphonse didn't fall down once. Eyes half closed, he walked slowly, sniffing the air to take in messages.

A young ginger-colored cat slithered under a wooden fence and into the field. It saw Alphonse and suddenly crouched low, eyes dark, motionless. For a minute there I didn't think he would notice it. Then his ears went up and his head shot forward. Next thing, he was hauling me along at the end of his leash, barking himself into a frenzy. The cat parted the grass

---

1. *Magenta* is a purplish-red color.

like wildfire and, reaching the fence, dug its body gracelessly under at a spot where there seemed hardly an inch between wood and solid earth.

Alphonse has that effect on cats. They must think he's death on wheels the way they scatter to get out of his way. He stared proudly in the direction of the fence; his nose hadn't failed him. He walked on, a little more vigor in his step, his tongue lolling out, his ears nice and perky.

We reached the edge of the field where we usually turn around on our walks. This time, of course, we didn't. He lost some of his bounce and trailed slightly behind. I looked back. He lowered his head. "She's not going to do anything to you, you crazy dog," I told him. "She's going to shake her head again, and tell us to go home." He kept pace with me after that. Like I said, dogs believe everything you tell them.

The vet is the kind of person whose job runs her life. One minute she's smiling over a recovering patient, or one who's come in just for shots; the next, she's blowing her nose like the place is a funeral parlor. It must be murder to become so involved with your patients. She always looks as if she needs some place to hole up for a good sleep. And her legs are magnets for strays who are forever up for adoption.

At the clinic, I sat down with Alphonse resignedly backed up between my knees. To my astonishment, a resident cat sauntered over and actually rubbed against him. Alphonse sniffed its head and then ignored

---

Vocabulary

slither (slith′ ər) *v.* to move along with a sliding or gliding motion, as a snake

frenzy (fren′ zē) *n.* a state of intense excitement or disturbance

vigor (vig′ ər) *n.* strength and energy

lolling (lol′ ing) *adj.* hanging down loosely; drooping

saunter (sôn′ tər) *v.* to walk in a relaxed way

it (he only likes cats who run). He watched the door to the examining room and trembled. I wondered if his eyesight was improving. With one hand I held his leash; the other I bit away at because of hangnails.

When the vet, smiling, summoned us, I got to my feet and Alphonse <u>reluctantly</u> pattered after me. Inside the examining room he pressed against the door, willing it to open. I picked him up and lugged him over to the table.

"He's lost weight," said the vet, stroking, prodding gently.

"He was too fat," I said, patting his stomach.

She laughed, continuing her way down his body. "Has he been on a diet?"

"No. I guess older dogs don't eat as much—like older people."

She looked at his rectum. "How long has this been here?" she said softly, more to herself than to me.

"This what?" I looked.

"It's quite a small lump," she said, pressing it hard.

Alphonse stood politely on the table, shaking and puffing.

"Sometimes," she said, with a reassuring smile, "older dogs get these lumps and they usually aren't anything to worry about, Buddy."

Usually? What did she mean, *usually?* My heart began to race.

"Older neutered dogs," she continued, in the same even tone, "very often get benign[2] lumps in the anal region. But we'd better check this out, anyway. . . ."

My dog has cancer. What do I tell him now? What am I going to do? Mom and Dad have left it up to me. The vet, with strained sad eyes, says the little lump is just a symptom of what's going on inside. Why didn't I notice that he was so short of breath? That he was peeing more than usual? That he didn't eat much? That his bowels weren't working? She tells me that when dogs are old all of these things become a problem, it's the usual progress of aging. Except not in Alphonse's case. But how would I know that? I shouldn't blame myself. She says there was nothing I could have done to stop it, anyway.

So what do I tell him? Is he in pain? I couldn't stand it if he were in pain. Tonight Mom wanted to give me a sleeping pill. I refused it. Alphonse is here with me on my bed. He's going to sleep with me one last time. I'll hold him and tell him about me and what I plan to do with my life. I'll have to lie a little, fill in a few places, because I'm not *exactly* sure. But he has a right to know what he'll be missing. I'll have a good life, I know it, just like he's had. I'm going to tell him about it now, whisper it in his ear, and I won't leave out a single detail.

---

2. A *neutered* animal is one from which certain reproductive organs have been surgically removed, usually to prevent breeding. A *benign* (bi nīn′) lump is an abnormal growth that is not cancerous and, therefore, not usually dangerous.

Vocabulary
reluctantly (ri luk′ tənt lē) *adv.* unwillingly

Responding to Literature

PERSONAL RESPONSE

◆ Think back to the chart about humans and their pets you made in the **Reading Focus** on page 242. How would you change the chart now that you have read "A Boy and His Dog"?

Analyzing Literature

RECALL AND INTERPRET

1. What are some of the signs of old age in Alphonse?
2. Why did Buddy take Alphonse back to the vet?
3. What will happen to Alphonse after the story ends?
4. What is significant about the amount of time the boy and his dog have been together?
5. Why does the boy need to tell his dog about his future plans?

EVALUATE AND CONNECT

6. Why did the author choose the first-person point of view?
7. **Theme Connection** What challenges will Buddy face after the story ends?

LITERARY ELEMENTS

Foreshadowing

Clues that prepare readers for events that will happen later in a story are called **foreshadowing**. Foreshadowing can build suspense. For example, a weapon found in a drawer might foreshadow a future crime.

1. Does Alphonse's first visit to the vet foreshadow a later event? Explain your answer.

2. Find the paragraph in which Alphonse's death is foreshadowed by a casual statement.

● See **Literary Terms Handbook**, p. R5.

Extending Your Response

Literature Groups

A Last Good-bye   Have you ever lost a beloved pet–or person? How would you say good-bye to someone you loved? Discuss with your group how you think a person should act in such a situation.

Interdisciplinary Activity

Science   Invite a veterinarian or a vet student to your class. Prepare questions to ask–for example:
• Why did you choose to become a vet?
• How are vets trained?

• What subjects should students who are interested in a veterinary career study?

Then design a career-path chart that shows the steps a person needs to take to become a vet.

Reading Further

If you would like to read other stories written by Martha Brooks, try these:

Paradise Cafe and Other Stories

Two Moons in August

📖 **Save your work for your portfolio.**

COMPARING SELECTIONS

Too Soon a Woman   and   A Boy and His Dog

COMPARE **CHARACTERS**

The boy narrator and Mary, in "Too Soon a Woman,"
and Buddy, in "A Boy and His Dog," are young people who must deal with loss in their lives. Present
a skit in which, through time travel, the two boys
and Mary meet to talk about how life's challenges
have changed them and helped them grow. Present
two acts, a first act that takes place when the characters
are the same ages as they are in the stories, and a second
act that takes place ten years later.

COMPARE **TONE**

Both selections are written from the first-person point of view, but they differ
greatly in tone. Discuss these questions in small groups.

1. Which story uses elements of humor? Why do you think one writer chose to
   include humor and the other didn't?

2. How would you describe the tone of each story?

3. In what ways does the tone of each story suit the events the author is
   describing?

COMPARE **DESCRIPTIONS**

You probably noticed that Martha Brooks tells very little about how Buddy
looks, and that Dorothy M. Johnson tells almost nothing about her narrator's
appearance. Can you explain why these two writers did so little to describe how
their main characters look? Write a paragraph or two explaining what you think
these writers were most interested in telling us about their characters. Use
examples from the story to back up your ideas.

Reading and Thinking Skills

Visualizing

Good writers use exact, vivid words and strong, colorful details so that their readers can **visualize,** or picture, what is going on as they read. For example, consider the following passage from "New Directions." As you read the passage, notice how the exact words and the vivid details add to your ability to picture the scene.

> The next morning she left her house carrying the meat pies, lard, an iron brazier, and coals for a fire. Just before lunch she appeared in an empty lot behind the cotton gin. As the dinner noon bell rang, she dropped the savors into boiling fat and the aroma rose and floated over to the workers who spilled out of the gin, covered with white lint, looking like specters.

As a skillful reader, use your own experiences to help you understand as well as imagine the scene. For example, have you ever felt the weight of a heavy load, such as your schoolbooks as you walked to school?

● For more about visualizing, see **Reading Handbook,** pp. R87–R88.

EXERCISES

Read the opening paragraphs from "Too Soon a Woman" by Dorothy M. Johnson. Then answer the questions at the right.

> We left the home place behind, mile by slow mile, heading for the mountains, across the prairie where the wind blew forever.
> At first there were four of us with the one-horse wagon and its skimpy load. Pa and I walked, because I was a big boy of eleven. My two little sisters romped and trotted until they got tired and had to be boosted up into the wagon bed.

1. Where are the characters in relation to one another and their surroundings in this scene? Pick out the words and details that tell where they are.

2. Find another descriptive passage in the story. Write a paragraph describing how the author's use of details helps readers visualize the scene. Quote examples from the story.

Before You Read
The Women's 400 Meters and *To James*

MEET LILLIAN MORRISON

A full-time author and poet, Lillian Morrison is an avid sports fan who has written entire collections of poems about sports. Morrison's connection to teenagers comes from her experience as coordinator of young adult services at the New York Public Library. She has also collected and published collections of folk rhymes and folk sayings.

Lillian Morrison was born in 1917.

MEET FRANK HORNE

Frank Horne's love of track began when he ran the quarter mile as a college student. Later, after becoming an optometrist, he coached a championship high school track team. "To James" was inspired by his coaching experiences.

Frank Horne was born in 1899. "To James" is from a 1963 collection of Horne's poetry titled Haverstraw.

READING FOCUS

Have you ever tried to run as fast and as long as you could or push your body all the way to the edge in some other way? How did it feel?

Journal
Write an entry about how your body and mind feel when you test your physical endurance. If you have ever been in a race, write about that experience.

Setting a Purpose
The first time through, just read to enjoy the poems and get an idea of what they are about. Read them aloud and listen to their sounds. Then you can read the poems more carefully to see how the poets use sounds and images to express their ideas.

BUILDING BACKGROUND

Track-and-field events, held since the Olympic Games in 776 B.C., are the oldest organized sports. These athletic meets include running and walking races, and jumping and throwing events. Track meets are usually held in a field or stadium built around a 400-meter (437-yard) oval track. The fastest, shortest races are dashes that range from 50 to 400 meters. The racers begin in a crouch at the starting line. When the starter fires a pistol, the runners leap into a full stride and run at top speed to the finish line. A fast start can often mean the difference between winning and losing the race.

The Women's 400 Meters

Lillian Morrison

Skittish,°
they flex knees, drum heels and
shiver at the starting line

waiting the gun
to pour them over the stretch
like a breaking wave.

Bang! they're off
careening° down the lanes,
each chased by her own bright tiger.

---

1 The word *skittish* means "easily frightened or excited."
8 *Careening* is rushing along, perhaps swaying from side
  to side as if out of control.

To James

Frank Horne

Do you remember
how you won
that last race . . . ?
how you flung your body
5   at the start . . .
how your spikes
ripped the cinders
in the stretch . . .
how you catapulted°
10   through the tape . . .
do you remember . . . ?
Don't you think
I lurched° with you
out of those starting holes . . . ?

---

9 To *catapult* is to leap or hurl oneself, as if from a giant slingshot.

13 To *lurch* is to plunge forward suddenly in a jerky manner.

15 Don't you think
    my sinews° tightened
    at those first
    few strides . . .
    and when you flew into the stretch
20 was not all my thrill
    of a thousand races
    in your blood . . . ?
    At your final drive
    through the finish line
25 did not my shout
    tell of the
    triumphant ecstasy°
    of victory . . . ?

    Live
30 as I have taught you
    to run, Boy—
    it's a short dash.
    Dig your starting holes
    deep and firm
35 lurch out of them
    into the straightaway
    with all the power
    that is in you
    look straight ahead
40 to the finish line
    think only of the goal
    run straight
    run high
    run hard
45 save nothing
    and finish
    with an ecstatic burst
    that carries you
    hurtling
50 through the tape
    to victory . . .

---

16 The cords of tissue that connect muscles to bones are
   called tendons or *sinews* (sin′ ūz).
27 *Ecstasy* is a state of overwhelming joy or delight.

Responding to Literature

PERSONAL RESPONSE

◆ Choose an image from each poem that stays in your mind's eye. How did the poetry affect the way you picture a track event?

Analyzing Literature

RECALL

1. What part of a race is described in "The Women's 400 Meters"?

2. Who are the two characters in the poem "To James"?

INTERPRET

3. How does the rhythm of "The Women's 400 Meters" make you feel as if you are at the start of a race?

4. How does the speaker in "To James" feel about the runner? How can you tell?

EVALUATE AND CONNECT

5. What does the first stanza of "The Women's 400 Meters" compare the racers to? Why is this an effective comparison?

6. Describe the image in the second stanza of "The Women's 400 Meters." How effective is this image?

7. In the third stanza of "The Women's 400 Meters," the poet suggests that each runner is being chased by a tiger. What does she mean by that?

8. Imagine that the speaker in "To James" had given you similar advice before a race. Would you agree or disagree? Explain.

9. Much of the advice in "To James" applies to life as well as to running. Find one line from the poem that you think people your age could use to help them succeed in school.

10. Theme Connection   How do you think the runners in each poem could use their experience to inspire other young people?

LITERARY ELEMENTS

Free Verse

Poetry without a fixed pattern of rhyme, rhythm, line length, or stanza arrangement is called **free verse.** Both "To James" and "The Women's 400 Meters" are written in free verse. Some poets use free verse to give their poems the natural, realistic rhythms of conversation. Repetition and strong images are often the main poetic devices in free verse poetry.

1. Read the first stanza of "To James" aloud. Notice how Horne uses repetition to give some rhythm to the free verse. Write the phrases that are repeated.

2. Describe three examples of strong imagery in "The Women's 400 Meters."

● See **Literary Terms Handbook,** p. R5.

Extending Your Response

Writing About Literature

Theme Consider how these poems connect to the theme of "Facing Challenge." What are some other ways in which people face challenge in their every-day lives? What can each poem teach people about facing challenges? What have the poems taught you about facing your own challenges? Write a short essay answering these questions. Include specific references to or quotations from the poems.

Personal Writing

Journal Recall your response to the **Reading Focus** on page 251. How does your description of pushing your body to the edge compare with the descriptions in the two poems? Write a more poetic description of your experience in your journal.

Literature Groups

Experience the Words! Run once around the schoolyard or the sports field with your group. Then sit down and compare your experiences with the descriptions of running in each poem.

Listening and Speaking

Why Run? Interview a student athlete about the reasons he or she chooses to run. Be sure to ask about the physical and psychological benefits and any negative aspects of running and competing.

Reading Further

If you would like to read more poems about sports, try these books by Lillian Morrison:

Sprints and Distances

At the Crack of the Bat

Other books of poetry you might like are:

Don't You Turn Back by Langston Hughes

On City Streets: An Anthology of Poetry edited by Nancy Larrick

Save your work for your portfolio.

Skill Minilesson

GRAMMAR AND LANGUAGE • ELLIPSIS

An **ellipsis** is the omission, or leaving out, of one or more words. In writing, three spaced periods are used to show an ellipsis. These periods are called *ellipses* (the plural of *ellipsis*). For example, the sentence "The team, without a great deal of talent or effort, won the track-and-field event" could be shortened (if you were interested only in the *result* of the event) to "The team . . . won the track-and-field event." Ellipsis marks are also used to indicate a pause in dialogue, such as: "The reason I was late for practice, Coach, is that I . . . uh . . . I needed to go home and . . . check on my sick dog."

PRACTICE Reread "To James," and find two places where the poet has used an ellipsis. Write the examples and then explain why, in your opinion, the poet has used them.

Measurement Systems

In Lillian Morrison's poem, runners anxiously wait at the starting line of a 400-meter race. The meter is the primary unit of measure for length in the metric system. However, before standardized measurements were invented, people used their bodies to measure distances and lengths.

Systems of Measure–Length	
Metric Unit	**U.S. Equivalent**
1 kilometer = 1000 meters	0.62 mile
1 meter = 10 decimeters	39.37 inches
1 decimeter = 10 centimeters	3.94 inches
1 centimeter = 10 millimeters	0.39 inch

Kingly Feet

Hundreds and hundreds of years ago, the width of a man's thumb and the length of his foot were commonly used as standard measurements for the inch and the foot. Of course, not many thumbs or feet were of equal length, which caused great frustration between merchants and buyers in the marketplace.

In Egypt, one king attempted to set a standard for the foot by distributing official measuring sticks of his own foot length. Each new king, however, wanted to use the length of *his* foot for the official standard, so the problem continued. In the fourteenth century, an English king set the standard for the length of the yard based upon the measurement of his rather rotund waist. During Queen Elizabeth's reign, the standard for the yard was the measurement from the queen's nose to the tip of her longest finger.

All Thumbs

People still sometimes use a thumb's width to guess the equivalent of an inch. Measure the width of your desktop with your thumb. Then share your answer with a classmate. Do your estimates match? Probably not.

Although your thumb won't measure an inch very accurately, it can help you estimate distances you might not be able to judge accurately with your eyes. For instance, look at the two lines drawn below. Which line is longer? Take a guess, then measure each line in thumb widths to see if you were right.

ACTIVITY

Walking heel to toe, count the "feet" between opposite walls of your classroom. Now measure the same distance with a reliable tool for measuring feet. How do the two units of measurement— your own foot versus a standard "foot"–compare?

Before You Read

a poem (for langston hughes) and *Dreams*

MEET
NIKKI GIOVANNI

In addition to being a poet, Nikki Giovanni is a professor of English at Virginia Polytechnic Institute, a recording artist, a writer, a scholar, and a political and social activist.

Nikki Giovanni was born in 1943. "a poem (for langston hughes)" is from Shimmy Shimmy Shimmy Like My Sister Kate.

MEET
LANGSTON HUGHES

Called the leading African American poet of the twentieth century, Langston Hughes wrote poetry, fiction, children's books, scripts, song lyrics, and works about history and music. (For more about Langston Hughes, see page 340.)

Langston Hughes was born in 1902 and died in 1967. "Dreams" can be found in his Collected Poems.

READING FOCUS

If you were given an assignment to write a poem, what would you write about?

Sharing Ideas
Make a quick list of topics that are special to you and that might make good subjects for poems. Share your list with your classmates.

Setting a Purpose
The Nikki Giovanni selection includes a poem and a nonfiction prose piece. Read to see how those two parts relate and how both parts relate to the Langston Hughes poem.

BUILDING BACKGROUND

According to Nikki Giovanni, if you're going to do anything about poetry, you should begin with Langston Hughes. Hughes remains the most important and respected African American poet of his time. In a simple yet powerful voice alive with the rhythm of jazz, he deals with racial injustice, social issues, and the human struggle for a life with dignity.

a poem
(for langston hughes)

Nikki Giovanni

diamonds are mined . . . oil is discovered
gold is found . . . but thoughts are uncovered

wool is sheared . . . silk is spun
weaving is hard . . . but words are fun

5 highways span . . . bridges connect
country roads ramble . . . but i suspect

if i took a rainbow ride
i could be there by your side

metaphor° has its point of view
10 allusion° and illusion° . . . too

meter . . . verse . . . classical . . . free
poems are what you do to me

let's look at this one more time
since i've put this rap to rhyme

15 when i take my rainbow ride
you'll be right there at my side

hey bop hey bop hey re re bop

---

9 In a *metaphor,* two unlike things are compared (without using *like* or *as*).

10 An *allusion* is a reference that is not directly identified or explained, like
the poet's reference to rap in line 14. The poet assumes the reader knows
what a rap is. An *illusion* is a false idea or a misleading appearance, like a
magician's trick.

a poem (for langston hughes)

USA Today called my office one day. It was a Tuesday, a pretty day. I remember sitting there, the phone rang, I said, "Giovanni," because that's the way I answer the phone. A woman said, "I'm from *USA Today* and we're going to do a feature on poetry and we'd like to know if you could contribute to it."

I said, "Sure," thinking they want an interview or something of that nature. The woman said, "We really would like a poem from you." I said, "You'd like a poem from me?" Great. And she said, "We'd like it on Wednesday or Thursday." I said, "Wednesday and Thursday when?" "No, no," she said. "We want it within two days." I said, "You're kidding."

But I thought about it and thought, "Okay, okay, I'm not going to say I can't do it." So I said, "Well, okay, I'll do it. I'll mail it over." And she said, "No, no, I want to give you the fax number and you have to fax it over because we'll be just putting it right in the paper and we need it at once. Not only by Thursday, but by Thursday at ten o'clock in the morning." The fax is not your friend, because in the old days of the post office you could always say, "Gee, I put it in the mail yesterday, I'm surprised you don't have it," one of those kind of things. But with a fax, you fax it over at 9:00, it's supposed to be there at 9:05.

I was sitting in my office brooding. I have a small office. Actually I'm quite fortunate because at least it's mine, I don't have to share it. It overlooks Virginia Tech;[1] we have a drill field and my office overlooks the drill field. I was just sitting, looking out my window, pouting. I said to myself, and I think it's a human kind of thing, "It isn't that *I* couldn't write a poem and have it there overnight practically; nobody could." And then a little voice said, "Langston Hughes could have done it."

It's true, Langston Hughes could have done it. I was still pouting, but now it was okay, and I said, "If Langston Hughes could have done it, what would he have done it on?" By now I'm trying to think really, really hard. Langston said, "Always write a love poem no matter what you're doing. Always write a love poem." That made sense. You should always love what you're doing. That's all he meant. . . .

So I wrote *a poem (for langston hughes)*. If you're going to do anything on poetry it ought to start, in all fairness, with Langston Hughes.

---

1. *Virginia Tech* is Virginia Polytechnic Institute, the university where Giovanni teaches.

DREAMS

Langston Hughes ∿

Hold fast to dreams
For if dreams die
Life is a broken-winged bird
That cannot fly.

Hold fast to dreams
For when dreams go
Life is a barren field
Frozen with snow.

Portrait of Langston Hughes, 1902–1967, Poet. Winold Reiss (1886–1953). Pastel on artist board, 76.3 x 54.9 cm. National Portrait Gallery, Washington, DC.

Responding to Literature

PERSONAL RESPONSE

- ◆ Could you feel Giovanni's connection to Langston Hughes and to the subject of poetry as you read these two poems? Explain.

Analyzing Literature

RECALL

1. What circumstances led Giovanni to write her poem?
2. What advice does Langston Hughes give in "Dreams"?

INTERPRET

3. How do you think the title of Giovanni's poem relates to her poem's theme?
4. What do you think Giovanni means by these lines?

    meter . . . verse . . . classical . . . free
    poems are what you do to me

5. What two **metaphors** (figures of speech that compare two unlike things) does the poet use in "Dreams"?

EVALUATE AND CONNECT

6. What advice by Langston Hughes does Giovanni mention? Does she follow it? Do you think it is good advice? Explain.
7. What do you think Giovanni means when she uses the expression "my rainbow ride"?
8. In your opinion, what does Hughes mean by "broken-winged bird"?
9. Theme Connection   What challenge did Nikki Giovanni face? How did she respond to it?
10. What did you learn about poetry from reading the two poems?

LITERARY ELEMENTS

Rhyme Scheme

The most common type of rhyme in poetry is called end rhyme, so called because it occurs at the ends of lines. To find the **rhyme scheme,** or pattern, of a poem that uses end rhymes, mark each line according to the sound at the end. Mark the first line with an *a*. Whenever you find another line that ends with the same sound, mark that line with an *a* also. Then mark the next end-of-the-line sound with a *b* and so on.

Mary had a little lamb	*a*
Its fleece was white as snow,	*b*
And everywhere that Mary went	*c*
The lamb was sure to go.	*b*

1. Copy "a poem (for langston hughes)" and mark the end of each line as shown above. Then describe the rhyme scheme.
2. Find another poem in this book that has end rhymes. Copy it and mark its rhyme scheme.

- ● See **Literary Terms Handbook,** p. R9.

Extending Your Response

Writing About Literature

Sensory Imagery The poems by Giovanni and Hughes are filled with images that appeal to the senses. Pick out your favorite image from one of the poems. Write a paragraph explaining the image and telling why you find it particularly effective.

Creative Writing

For Whom? Think about the ideas you discussed for the **Reading Focus** on page 258. Were any of these ideas based on some special person? Write a short poem for a person in your life. Focus on one special thing that is important to this person, as Giovanni does in "a poem (for langston hughes)."

Literature Groups

Poet's Corner In her poem, Nikki Giovanni states, "i've put this rap to rhyme." Could this poem be performed as a rap? What do you think the last line of the poem means? In small groups, talk about the connection between music and poetry. Then decide what kind of music would best suit each of the two poems.

Listening and Speaking

Appreciating Poetry Take turns sharing your group's musical interpretations of the poems with your classmates. Notice how different readings and different music affect your experience of the poems.

Reading Further

To read more by Nikki Giovanni, try:

Ego-Tripping and Other Poems for Young People

For more of Langston Hughes's poetry, try:

The Dream Keeper and Other Poems

Save your work for your portfolio.

Skill Minilessons

READING AND THINKING • IDENTIFYING ASSUMPTIONS

An **assumption** is a piece of information that a writer assumes, or takes for granted, the reader knows. For example, Nikki Giovanni assumes that her readers know about Langston Hughes and his importance to the world of poetry. She also assumes that her readers know what a rap is. As you read, identify the assumptions the writer is making about your knowledge about a topic. Ask yourself: *Is there something I should know more about*

in order to understand this poem clearly? How can I learn more about this topic?

PRACTICE Reread the poem "Slam, Dunk, & Hook" in Theme 2. What assumptions does the poet make about his readers' prior knowledge? In a paragraph, identify one or two of these assumptions.

● For more about related reading strategies, see **Reading Handbook,** p. R86.

Technology Skills

E-mail: Online Safety

When you communicate via the Internet, you have the chance to talk with people from all over the world. You can learn about other cultures, get homework help, and share messages with kids your own age. But you may also run into people who do not have your best interests at heart. It's important that you follow a few simple rules to keep yourself safe as you cruise along the information superhighway.

Talk About It

In a small group, spend five minutes brainstorming some safety rules you think may apply to e-mail communication. Record each rule your group comes up with. Share your rules and the reasons behind them with your classmates. Decide as a class which rules are the most helpful. Then compare your findings with the following rules.

Rules for Online Safety

1. Never give out personal information, such as your address, telephone number, or a parent's work address or phone number, in a public message—like a chat room, bulletin board, or message to an e-mail pal—without the permission of your parent or guardian.

2. Never share your Internet password with anyone, not even your best friend. Only you and your parents should know it.

3. Never give the name and location of your school to anyone on the Internet.

4. Never agree to a face-to-face meeting with someone you've encountered on the Internet without informing your parent or guardian. If your parent or guardian agrees to a meeting, it should be in a public place, and your parent or guardian should go with you.

5. If you receive an e-mail message that is threatening or belligerent, or if anyone sends you mail or files that make you feel uncomfortable in any way, tell a responsible adult immediately. Do not respond to such a message.

6. Never send your picture or anything else to someone on the Internet without the permission of your parent or guardian.

7. If an e-mail mentor claims to work for a certain company, verify that by logging on to the company's Web site and searching for her or his name and title. If the company doesn't have a Web site, ask an adult to call the company's personnel office to confirm her or his employment.

8. Remember that people online may not be who they claim to be.

9. Don't get involved in chain letters, especially those that require you to send anyone money.

10. Don't respond to spam offers that sound too good to be true. They almost certainly *are* too good to be true.

Spam

Spam is unsolicited mass mailings by way of e-mail. It's the Internet version of junk mail. If you get on a mailing list, you may end up getting spammed. One reason the rules above warn you against giving out information about yourself or your family is that it could fall into the hands of people who will send you spam. They can also sell or trade information about you to other spammers. While much of the spam that circulates on the Net is legitimate advertising, there are also scam artists out there trying to make money (maybe your money) dishonestly. Remember, you don't have to give anyone any information you don't want to share.

All these warnings do not mean that you can't trust anyone on the Net. What they do mean is that you ought to exercise caution anytime you're in contact with someone you don't know.

ACTIVITIES

1. In your journal, keep a list of the names and e-mail addresses of people with whom you communicate regularly. If you start receiving e-mail that is threatening or inappropriate, cross that person's name and address from your list and notify a responsible adult.

2. Log on to the World Wide Web and search for sites that address Internet safety. You may want to begin your search at www.safeteens.com.

3. Go to the Federal Trade Commission's Web site (www.ftc.gov) to find out more about the kinds of scams that can reach people's e-mail boxes. Look for the FTC's "Dirty Dozen" list. Share what you learn with your classmates.

4. Share your knowledge of e-mail safety with the computer club at a local elementary school.

5. What non-Web resources can you use to learn more about online safety? Identify possible sources of information in your school or local library and share what you learned with the class.

MEDIA Connection

WEB SITE

On the Internet, you'll often find something unexpected. The following Native American folktale came from a Web site devoted to information about skunks and opossums.

Why 'Possum Has a Large Mouth: A Choctaw Folktale

Address: ▼ The Wonderful Skunk and Opossum Web Site

As Told by Bayou Lacomb

Very little food there was for Deer one dry season. He became thin and weak. One day he met 'Possum. Deer at once exclaimed, "Why, 'Possum, how fat you are! How do you keep so fat when I cannot find enough to eat?"

'Possum said, "I live on persimmons. They are very large this year, so I have all I want to eat."

"How do you get the persimmons?" asked Deer. "They grow so high!"

"That is easy," said 'Possum. "I go to the top of a high hill. Then I run down and strike a large persimmon tree so hard with my head that all the ripe persimmons

drop to the ground. Then I sit there and eat them."

"That is easily done," said Deer. "I will try it. Now watch me."

'Possum waited. Deer went to the top of a nearby hill. He ran down and struck the tree with his head. 'Possum watched him, laughing. He opened his mouth so wide while he laughed that he stretched it out. That is why 'Possum has such a large mouth.

Analyzing Media

1. What characteristic of 'Possum can you identify from his behavior in this folktale?

2. There are many folktales and myths that tell how some animal or plant got to be the way it is. Look on the Internet or in a library for another one that you can share with the class.

Before You Read
Racing the Great Bear

MEET JOSEPH BRUCHAC

Joseph Bruchac (broo′ shak) grew up in the Adirondack region of New York. As a member of the Abenaki tribe, he has drawn on his own life and Native American legends for many of his more than sixty books. He writes, "One of the reasons I have devoted so much of my own life to the understanding and the respectful telling of traditional Native stories is my strong belief that now, more than ever, these tales have much to teach us."

Joseph Bruchac was born in 1942. This story was first published in 1993.

READING FOCUS

How do people become leaders? Is it because they are intelligent, ambitious, compassionate, or brave?

Discuss
Talk with your classmates about the traits and experiences that make some men and women stand out as leaders.

Setting a Purpose
Read to see what you can learn about how some people become leaders.

BUILDING BACKGROUND

The Time and Place   This story takes place in an unknown time in the ancient past.

Did You Know?   When the early Europeans came to America, the Iroquois lived south of Lake Ontario in the area that is now New York State. The Iroquois referred to themselves with a name that means "people of the longhouse," the longhouse being their traditional dwelling.

VOCABULARY PREVIEW

clan (klan) *n.* a group of families descended from a common ancestor; p. 270
keen (kēn) *adj.* highly sensitive; sharp; p. 272
pursue (pər soo′) *v.* to chase; p. 273
spare (spār) *v.* to treat with mercy; hold back from harming or injuring; p. 274
sinewy (sin′ū ē) *adj.* physically tough, or powerful; p. 274
embrace (em brās′) *v.* to hug or hold in the arms, especially as a sign of love or affection; p. 275

Racing the Great Bear

Retold by Joseph Bruchac ∿

NE ONENDJI. Hear my story, which happened long ago. For many generations, the five nations of the Haudenosaunee, the People of the Longhouse, had been at war with one another. No one could say how the wars began, but each time a man of one nation was killed, his relatives sought revenge in the blood feud,[1] and so the fighting continued. Then the Creator took pity on his people and sent a messenger of peace.

---

1. A *feud* (fūd) is a bitter, long-running quarrel or clash between two individuals or groups. A *blood feud* involves members of the same group. Here, that group is the Five Nations.

Grizzly Bear in a Mountainous Landscape (detail). Carl Rungius (1869–1959). Oil on canvas, 47 x 52 in. Private collection.

The Peacemaker traveled from nation to nation, convincing the people of the Five Nations—the Mohawk, the Oneida, the Onondaga, the Cayuga, and the Seneca[2]— that it was wrong for brothers to kill one another. It was not easy, but finally the nations agreed and the Great Peace began. Most welcomed that peace, though there were some beings with bad hearts who wished to see the return of war.

One day, not long after the Great Peace had been established, some young men in a Seneca village decided they would pay a visit to the Onondaga people.

2. **Pronunciations:** *Oneida* (ō nī′ də), *Onondaga* (on′ ən dô′ ga), *Cayuga* (kā ū′ gə), *Seneca* (sen′ ə kə)

"It is safe now to walk the trail between our nations," the young men said. "We will return after the sun has risen and set seven times."

Then they set out. They walked toward the east until they were lost from sight in the hills. But many more than seven days passed, and those young men never returned. Now another group of young men left, wanting to find out where their friends had gone. They, too, did not return.

The people grew worried. Parties were sent out to look for the vanished young men, but no sign was found. And the searchers who went too far into the hills did not return, either.

The old chief of the village thought long and hard. He asked the clan mothers, those wise women whose job it was to choose the chiefs and give them good advice, what should be done.

"We must find someone brave enough to face whatever danger is out there," the clan mothers said.

So the old chief called the whole village to a council meeting. He held up a white strand of wampum beads made from quahog[3] clamshells as he spoke.

"Hear me," he said. "I am of two minds about what has happened to our people. It may be that the Onondaga have broken the peace and captured them. It may be there is something with an evil mind that wishes to destroy this new peace and so has killed our people. Now someone must go and find out. Who is brave enough? Who will come and take this wampum from my hand?"

Many men were gathered in that

Did You Know?

Wampum is a shortened form of the Algonquian word *wampumpeag,* or *wampumpeake,* which means "a string of white shell beads." These small, polished beads were used to decorate headbands, belts, collars, or necklaces. Some Native Americans in the Northeast used wampum as a form of money, but its most significant use was in rituals of kinship and mourning and to record history. White wampum, the most precious of all, symbolizes a state of well-being and truth.

council. Some were known to speak of themselves as brave warriors. Still, though they muttered to one another, no man stepped forward to take the strand of wampum. The old chief began to walk about the circle, holding the wampum in front of each man in turn. But each man only lowered his eyes to the ground. No man lifted his hand to take the wampum.

Just outside the circle stood a boy who had not yet become a man. His parents were dead, and he lived with his grandmother in her old lodge at the edge of the village. His clothing was always torn and his face dirty because his grandmother was too old to care for him as a mother would. The other young men made fun of him, and as a joke they called him Swift Runner—even though no one had ever seen him run and it was thought that he was weak and lazy. All he ever seemed to do was play with his little dog or sit by the fire and listen when the old people were talking.

"Our chief has forgotten our greatest warrior," one of the young men said to another, tilting his head toward Swift Runner.

"*Nyoh,*" the other young man said, laughing. "Yes. Why does he not offer the wampum to Swift Runner?"

The chief looked around the circle of men, and the laughing stopped. He walked out of the circle to the place where the small boy in torn clothes stood. He held out the wampum and Swift Runner took it without hesitating.

"I accept this," Swift Runner said. "It is right that I be the one to face the danger.

---

3. The *quahog* (kwô′ hôg) is a type of clam found on the Atlantic coast of North America.

Vocabulary
clan (klan) *n.* a group of families descended from a common ancestor

In the eyes of the people I am worthless, so if I do not return, it will not matter. I will leave when the sun rises tomorrow."

When Swift Runner arrived home at his grandmother's lodge, the old woman was waiting for him.

"Grandson," she said, "I know what you have done. The people of this village no longer remember, but your father was a great warrior. Our family is a family that has power."

Then she reached up into the rafters and took down a heavy bow. It was blackened with smoke and seemed so thick that no man could bend it.

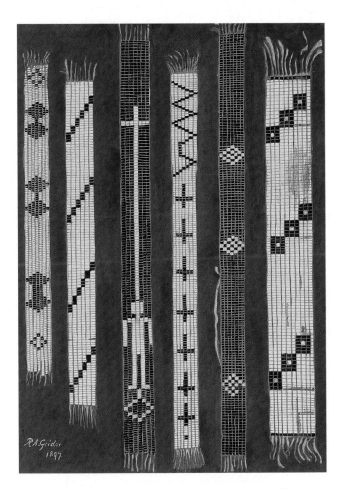

Iroquois Wampum Belts. Rufus Grider. Newberry Library, Chicago.

"If you can string this bow, Grandson," the old woman said, "you are ready to face whatever waits for you on the trail."

Swift Runner took the bow. It was as thick as a man's wrist, but he bent it with ease and strung it.

"Wah-hah!" said his grandmother. "You are the one I knew you would grow up to be. Now you must sleep. At dawn we will make you ready for your journey."

It was not easy for Swift Runner to sleep, but when he woke the next morning, he felt strong and clearheaded. His grandmother was sitting by the fire with a cap in her hand.

"This was your grandfather's cap," she said. "I have sewed four hummingbird feathers on it. It will make your feet more swift."

Swift Runner took the cap and placed it on his head.

His grandmother held up four pairs of moccasins.

"Carry these tied to your waist. When one pair wears out, throw them aside and put on the next pair."

Swift Runner took the moccasins and tied them to his belt.

Next his grandmother picked up a small pouch. "In this pouch is cornmeal mixed with maple sugar," she said. "It is the only food you will need as you travel. It will give you strength when you eat it each evening."

Swift Runner took the pouch and hung it from his belt by the moccasins.

"The last thing I must give you," said the old woman, "is this advice. Pay close attention to your little dog. You have treated him well and so he is your great friend. He is small, but his eyes and nose are <u>keen</u>. Keep him always in front of you. He will warn you of danger before it can strike you."

Then Swift Runner set out on his journey. His little dog stayed ahead of him, sniffing the air and sniffing the ground. By the time the sun was in the middle of the sky, they were far from the village. The trail passed through deep woods, and it seemed to the boy as if something was following them among the trees. But he could see nothing in the thick brush.

The trail curved toward the left, and the boy felt even more the presence of something watching. Suddenly his little dog ran into the brush at the side of the trail, barking loudly. There were the sounds of tree limbs breaking and heavy feet running. Then out of the forest came a Nyagwahe, a monster bear. Its great teeth were as long as a man's arm. It was twice as tall as a moose. Close at its heels was Swift Runner's little dog.

"I see you," Swift Runner shouted. "I am after you. You cannot escape me."

Swift Runner had learned those words by listening to the stories the old people told. They were the very words a monster bear speaks when it attacks, words that terrify anyone who hears them. On hearing those words, the great bear turned and fled from the boy.

Beaded Pouch. Iroquois. Velvet, metal, beads, cloth, length: 6½ in.

"You cannot escape me," Swift Runner shouted again. Then he ran after the bear.

The Nyagwahe turned toward the east, with Swift Runner and his dog close behind. It left the trail and plowed through the thick forest, breaking down great trees and leaving a path of destruction like that of a whirlwind. It ran up the tallest hills and down through the swamps, but the boy and the dog stayed at its heels. They ran past a great cave in the rocks. All around the cave were the bones of people the bear had caught and eaten.

"My relatives," Swift Runner called as he passed the cave, "I will not forget you. I am after the one who killed you. He will not escape me."

Throughout the day, the boy and his dog chased the great bear, growing closer bit by bit. At last, as the sun began to set, Swift Runner stopped at the head of a small valley and called his small dog to him.

"We will rest here for the night," the boy said. He took off his first pair of moccasins, whose soles were worn away to nothing. He threw them aside and put on a new pair. Swift Runner made a fire and

Vocabulary
keen (kēn) *adj.* highly sensitive; sharp

sat beside it with his dog. Then he took out the pouch of cornmeal and maple sugar, sharing his food with his dog.

"Nothing will harm us," Swift Runner said. "Nothing can come close to our fire." He lay down and slept.

In the middle of the night, he was awakened by the growling of his dog. He sat up with his back to the fire and looked into the darkness. There, just outside the circle of light made by the flames, stood a dark figure that looked like a tall man. Its eyes glowed green.

"I am Nyagwahe," said the figure. "This is my human shape. Why do you pursue me?"

"You cannot escape me," Swift Runner said. "I chase you because you killed my people. I will not stop until I catch you and kill you."

The figure faded back into the darkness.

"You cannot escape me," Swift Runner said again. Then he patted his small dog and went to sleep.

As soon as the first light of the new day appeared, Swift Runner rose. He and his small dog took the trail. It was easy to follow the monster's path, for trees were uprooted and the earth torn by its great paws. They ran all through the morning. When the sun was in the middle of the sky, they reached the head of another valley. At the other end they saw the great bear running toward the east. Swift Runner pulled off his second pair of moccasins, whose soles were worn away to nothing. He put on his third pair and began to run again.

All through that day, they kept the Nyagwahe in sight, drawing closer bit by bit. When the sun began to set, Swift Runner stopped to make camp. He took off the third pair of moccasins, whose soles were worn away to nothing, and put on the last pair.

"Tomorrow," he said to his small dog, "we will catch the monster and kill it." He reached for his pouch of cornmeal and maple sugar, but when he opened it, he found it filled with worms. The magic of the Nyagwahe had done this. Swift Runner poured out the pouch and said in a loud voice, "You have spoiled our food, but it will not stop me. I am on your trail. You cannot escape me."

That night, once again, he was awakened by the growling of his dog. A dark figure stood just outside the circle of light.

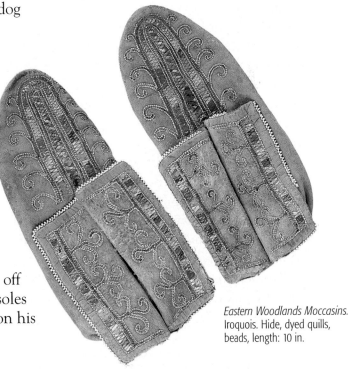

Eastern Woodlands Moccasins. Iroquois. Hide, dyed quills, beads, length: 10 in.

Vocabulary
pursue (pər sōō′) *v.* to chase

It looked smaller than the night before, and the glow of its eyes was weak.

"I am Nyagwahe," the dark figure said. "Why do you pursue me?"

"You cannot escape me," Swift Runner said. "I am on your trail. You killed my people. You threatened the Great Peace. I will not rest until I catch you."

"Hear me," said the Nyagwahe. "I see your power is greater than mine. Do not kill me. When you catch me, take my great teeth. They are my power, and you can use them for healing. Spare my life and I will go far to the north and never again bother the People of the Longhouse."

"You cannot escape me," Swift Runner said. "I am on your trail."

The dark figure faded back into the darkness, and Swift Runner sat for a long time, looking into the night.

At the first light of day, the boy and his dog took the trail. They had not gone far when they saw the Nyagwahe ahead of them. Its sides puffed in and out as it ran. The trail was beside a big lake with many alder trees close to the water. As the great bear ran past, the leaves were torn from the trees. Fast as the bear went, the boy and his dog came closer, bit by bit. At last, when the sun was in the middle of the sky, the giant bear could run no longer. It fell heavily to the earth, panting so hard that it stirred up clouds of dust.

Swift Runner unslung his grandfather's bow and notched an arrow to the sinewy string.

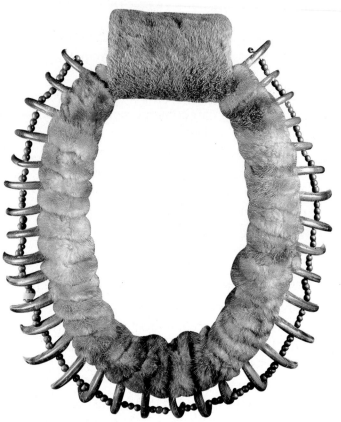

Bear Claw Necklace. Native American. Bear claws, metal beads, otter or fisher tail, length: 57½ in.

"Shoot for my heart," said the Nyagwahe. "Aim well. If you cannot kill me with one arrow, I will take your life."

"No," Swift Runner said. "I have listened to the stories of my elders. Your only weak spot is the sole of your foot. Hold up your foot and I will kill you."

The great bear shook with fear. "You have defeated me," it pleaded. "Spare my life and I will leave forever."

"You must give me your great teeth," Swift Runner said. "Then you must leave and never bother the People of the Longhouse again."

Vocabulary
spare (spâr) *v.* to treat with mercy; hold back from harming or injuring
sinewy (sin′ ū ē) *adj.* physically tough, strong, or powerful

"I shall do as you say," said the Nyagwahe. "Take my great teeth."

Swift Runner lowered his bow. He stepped forward and pulled out the great bear's teeth. It rose to its feet and walked to the north, growing smaller as it went. It went over the hill and was gone.

Carrying the teeth of the Nyagwahe over his shoulder, Swift Runner turned back to the west, his dog at his side. He walked for three moons before he reached the place where the bones of his people were piled in front of the monster's empty cave. He collected those bones and walked around them four times. "Now," he said, "I must do something to make my people wake up." He went to a big hickory tree and began to push it over so that it would fall on the pile of bones.

"My people," he shouted, "get up quickly or this tree will land on you."

The bones of the people who had been killed all came together and jumped up, alive again and covered with flesh. They were filled with joy and gathered around Swift Runner.

"Great one," they said, "who are you?"

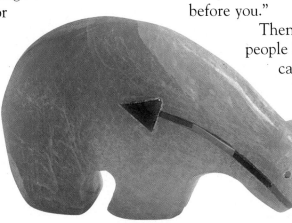

Alabaster Bear with Heartline. Contemporary Zuni. Alabaster, 1⅝ x 2¾ in. Private collection.

"I am Swift Runner," he said.

"How can that be?" one of the men said. "Swift Runner is a skinny little boy. You are a tall, strong man."

Swift Runner looked at himself and saw that it was so. He was taller than the tallest man, and his little dog was bigger than a wolf.

"I am Swift Runner," he said. "I was that boy and I am the man you see before you."

Then Swift Runner led his people back to the village. He carried with him the teeth of the Nyagwahe, and those who saw what he carried rejoiced. The trails were safe again, and the Great Peace would not be broken. Swift Runner went to his grandmother's lodge and embraced her.

"Grandson," she said, "you are now the man I knew you would grow up to be. Remember to use your power to help the people."

So it was that Swift Runner ran with the great bear and won the race. Throughout his long life, he used the teeth of the Nyagwahe to heal the sick, and he worked always to keep the Great Peace.

Da neho. I am finished.

Vocabulary

embrace (em brās´) *v.* to hug or hold in the arms, especially as a sign of love or affection

Responding to Literature

PERSONAL RESPONSE

◆ Think back to the discussion you had about leaders in the **Reading Focus** on page 267. Which traits make Swift Runner a leader of his tribe?

Analyzing Literature

RECALL

1. What happened in the village that causes the chief to seek a brave person?
2. Why was Swift Runner an unlikely candidate for the journey?
3. Who did Swift Runner discover had been killing the villagers? Describe the killer.
4. How is Swift Runner changed when he returns from his journey?

INTERPRET

5. Why was it so important to find out if the Onondaga had broken the peace?
6. How does Swift Runner's grandmother reassure him that he is ready to face the danger?
7. What does the Great Bear symbolize?
8. Why is "Racing the Great Bear" called a "coming of age" story?

EVALUATE AND CONNECT

9. How does the writer show that the character of Swift Runner changes during the story?
10. A number of times in the story, Swift Runner knows what to do because he has listened well to the stories of his elders. How have the stories and legends you've heard at home and in school affected your behavior?

LITERARY ELEMENTS

Oral Tradition

Stories that are passed from generation to generation by retelling them aloud are part of an **oral tradition.** "Racing the Great Bear" is part of the Iroquois oral tradition. As Joseph Bruchac has written, "When I first began telling the traditional stories that were part of my own Native heritage, it was to share them with my own children. . . . That is how the circle of stories works, linking the generations."

1. Stories in the oral tradition are often inspired by a group's values. What are some of the values reinforced in "Racing the Great Bear"?

2. Find and explain a place in the story where the oral tradition helps Swift Runner scare away the bear.

● See **Literary Terms Handbook,** p. R7.

Literature and Writing

Writing About Literature

Dialogue   The dialogue in this story—the words spoken by the characters—does not sound like everyday speech. That is because the words are part of an ancient legend that has been repeated from generation to generation. Analyze the effectiveness of the dialogue in the story. Use examples in your analysis.

Personal Writing

Journeys   Swift Runner traveled from the village to the woods to find the bear. He also went on a personal journey from childhood to adulthood. Write a journal entry about a personal journey of growth you or someone you know has taken.

Extending Your Response

Literature Groups

Storytelling   The story of Swift Runner is part of the oral tradition of the Iroquois. Work with your group to retell the story to another class. Discuss which parts are most important and which parts are most exciting. Choose whether to use a single narrator or several voices to tell the story. Rehearse and critique the performance before presenting it.

_inter_NET
CONNECTION

Use your search engine to locate sites devoted to Native Americans. Library and bookstore sites have information about books and audio- or videotapes. Many museums have Native American collections, and most of them have their own Web sites.

Interdisciplinary Activity

Art   Using natural materials, build a model longhouse. First, research the traditional design of an Iroquois longhouse. Then decide what materials to use that will recreate the look. Make sure your model is in the correct proportion to the actual structures.

Reading Further

If you would like to read more about the Iroquois, try these books:

Iroquois Stories: Heroes and Heroines, Monsters and Magic by Joseph Bruchac

The Iroquois by Craig and Katherine Doherty

Some other books about Native Americans you might enjoy are:

The Owl's Song by Janet C. Hale

Sequoyah by Robert Cwiklik

Indian Chiefs by Russell Freedman

Save your work for your portfolio.

Skill Minilessons

GRAMMAR AND LANGUAGE • POSSESSIVE PRONOUNS

A **possessive pronoun** shows who or what has or owns something. A possessive pronoun can be used in place of one or more possessive nouns. For example, "The brother's and sister's pets" can be replaced by "Their pets." *Their* is a plural possessive pronoun.

PRACTICE Write each sentence, replacing each underlined word or words with the correct possessive pronoun.

1. Then Swift Runner set out on <u>Swift Runner's</u> journey.

2. When the monster bear came out of the forest, <u>the monster bear's</u> teeth were as long as a man's arm.

3. The old people had told <u>the old people's</u> stories to Swift Runner.

4. The boy and <u>the boy's</u> dog chased the bear.

5. Swift Runner said, "I chase you because you killed <u>Swift Runner's</u> people."

● For more about pronouns, see **Language Handbook,** p. R31.

READING AND THINKING • SETTING A READING PURPOSE

Before you begin reading a story or an article, it often helps to set a purpose for reading. What do you want to learn from the selection? Will you have to remember ideas in order to discuss the piece or answer questions? Do you want to better understand the subject or the type of writing? Do you want to be entertained?

PRACTICE Choose a selection in this book that you haven't read. Set a purpose for reading the selection before you begin reading. The title, author, and the art may help give you an idea for a purpose. After setting a purpose, write a few sentences that explain how the purpose you set might help you better enjoy or understand the selection.

● For more about setting a reading purpose, see **Reading Handbook,** p. R86.

VOCABULARY • MULTIPLE-MEANING WORDS

Many words have more than one meaning, which usually doesn't cause a problem if both meanings are familiar. You are unlikely to mistake the bark of a tree for the bark of a dog. However, when one meaning is familiar but another one isn't, the situation can be confusing.

In "Racing the Great Bear," *spare* means "to treat with mercy." It can also have several other meanings:

a. *v.* to treat with mercy; hold back from harming
b. *v.* to keep from using or use only with care
c. *adj.* not in regular use; extra

d. *adj.* small in amount; barely enough or not enough
e. *adj.* lean or thin

PRACTICE For each sentence, write the letter of the corresponding meaning of *spare*.

1. Abraham Lincoln was a tall, spare man.
2. After their spare meal, the soldiers were still hungry.
3. Wait for a sale and spare your bank account.
4. The company stayed in our spare room.
5. Is it wrong to tell a lie in order to spare someone's feelings?

LISTENING, SPEAKING, and VIEWING

LUNGS AT WORK
NO SMOKING!
Your Lung Association

Analyzing Persuasion

A friend talks you into sharing your lunch. A television commercial urges you to try a new shampoo. A magazine ad asks you to support a charity. A billboard warns you against smoking. In these ways, and many more, you encounter persuasion every day.

Persuasion is based on appeals to emotion and appeals to reason. Appeals to emotion involve words, sounds, or images that create strong feelings. Appeals to reason involve logic or factual evidence.

When you encounter persuasion, identify the kinds of appeals being used. Then decide whether they are used responsibly. Ask yourself questions like those below.

VOTE YES!

ON PROPOSITION 2

Appeals to Emotion

- Which images catch my interest? What feelings do they create?
- Which words suggest feelings? What feelings do they suggest?
- Are the appeals straightforward? Or do they reflect a "hidden agenda"—an attempt to manipulate the audience?

Appeals to Reason

- What conclusion is the audience asked to draw? What evidence supports the conclusion?
- What is the general line of reasoning used here? Does it make sense?
- Is the reasoning supported with facts, statistics, or other solid evidence?

EXERCISES

1. Use the questions above to analyze your favorite (or least favorite) television commercial. Look for appeals to emotion and appeals to reason.
2. Write a short persuasive essay.
   a. Ask a classmate to analyze it.

   b. List the appeals to emotion and the appeals to reason that you notice in your classmate's essay.
   c. Discuss your analyses with your classmate.
   d. Revise your essay.

Before You Read

Beyond the Limits

MEET STACY ALLISON

Stacy Allison, a gifted mountain climber, author, businessperson, and public speaker, certainly knows about challenges and dreams. In 1987 she took part in an unsuccessful attempt to reach the top of Mount Everest. The following year, she returned to the mountain and reached its peak. Allison later led a team to the top of K2, the world's second-highest mountain— and an even greater challenge than Mount Everest.

This story is part of an autobiographical account, Beyond the Limits: A Woman's Triumph on Everest, *first published in 1993.*

READING FOCUS

Think of a time when you faced a big challenge that resulted in disappointment.

Sharing Ideas

In small groups, share stories about your own experiences in facing challenges that ended in disappointment.

Setting a Purpose

Why would anyone want to climb a mountain on which more than a hundred climbers have been killed? See if you can discover an answer as you read.

BUILDING BACKGROUND

The Time and Place   It is the fall of 1987 in a small tent on the jagged North Face of Mount Everest, in the Himalayas.

Did You Know?
At 29,028 feet (about 5.5 miles) above sea level, Mount Everest is the world's highest mountain. In May 1953, Edmund Hillary and his Nepalese guide, Tenzing Norgay, became the first climbers to reach its peak.

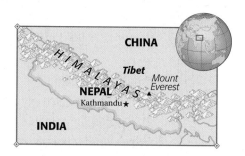

VOCABULARY PREVIEW

agility (ə jil′ ə tē) *n.* quickness and ease in motion or thought; p. 282

brink (bringk) *n.* the point at which something may begin; p. 282

charismatic (kar′ iz mat′ ik) *adj.* having personal qualities that enable one to inspire loyalty and devotion; p. 283

pinnacle (pin′ ə kəl) *n.* a high point, or peak; p. 285

distinct (dis tingkt′) *adj.* different in quality or kind; p. 285

anguished (ang′ gwisht) *adj.* having or showing extreme mental or physical suffering; p. 286

from

Beyond the Limits

A Woman's Triumph on Everest

Stacy Allison ∾
with Peter Carlin

We were so close. From where we were sitting, curled in the dim light of a snow cave, the top of the world was only 3,000 feet away. Less than two days of climbing on the jagged North Face. But we weren't climbing.

We were hiding. Four American mountain climbers—Scott Fischer, Wes Krause, Samuel "Q" Belk, and me—tunneled into the side of Mount Everest, listening to the roar of the jet stream[1] wind. It was late in the climbing season and the winter winds had descended, tearing across the top of the mountain at 150 miles an hour. But for how long?

---

1. The *jet stream* is the high-speed air current several miles above the earth's surface.

Sitting up in my sleeping bag, balancing a cup of hot chocolate in my lap, I could imagine that the hurricane outside would vanish. In the dim light of the cave, I could overlook the life-squeezing pressure of life at 25,500 feet.

I could almost convince myself we wouldn't have to turn around when morning came. *Turn around?* Not after I had devoted years of my life to get here. Years spent dreaming of scaling this massive hill and then leaving my footprint on the crown of the earth. Now I was two-thirds of the way there—25,500 feet up the North Face of Everest. Stranded in a snow cave . . . but so close.

I was determined to get to the top.

Hunched beneath the snow, I could imagine the grace of those final steps. Beyond the limits of gravity, human strength, and mental <u>agility</u>—out to where there are no limits. Nothing but the snow-covered mountain, the sky, and me, and right then it would be hard to tell where one ended and another began. I could have it all, but only if the jet stream rose off the mountain for one more day. Everything depends on the weather: even the best climber in the world won't get very high on a mountain shrouded[2] in a storm or belted by gale-force winds. We'd worked so hard for so long, but on that cold night in the fall of 1987, I knew our entire expedition was on the <u>brink</u>.

The fifteen climbers on the 1987 American Everest North Face Expedition each had more than a decade of climbing experience. For two years most of us had committed our lives to climbing this one mountain. We spent two years maneuvering the bureaucracies[3] of two governments, scraping for the money to cover airplane tickets, freight, climbing permits, and fees, convincing manufacturers to give us equipment and food. Two years planning and preparing and then three months on the expedition itself—the flight into Nepal, the trek from Kathmandu into Tibet and the yak-powered climb to Advance Base Camp, then the weeks of mountainside preparation. We built Advance Base Camp at the foot of the North Face, and then set up four intermediate camps on the mountain. We fixed our route up the mountain using ice screws, aluminum stakes, and rope to anchor a safety line up the steep sections, then dug snow caves in the steep mountainside and hauled up loads of food and gear to stock them. Only then could we set our sights on the summit. Set our sights, and hope the mountain would be kind to us as we tried to creep up her icy shoulders.

Kindness was a lot to hope for this high in the world. More, in fact, than what we'd been able to secure for ourselves. By the time the second summit team—our

Did You Know?
The *yak* is a long-haired ox, native to central Asia. Yaks are often used to carry heavy loads.

---

2. Here, *shrouded* means "covered" or "concealed."

3. *Bureaucracies* (byoo rok′ rə sēz) refers to all of the departments, officials, rules, and paperwork that one must deal with to get government approval for a project or program.

Vocabulary
agility (ə jil′ ə tē) *n.* quickness and ease in motion or thought
brink (bringk) *n.* the point at which something may begin

charismatic, blond team leader Scott Fischer, our more reserved deputy leader Wes Krause, the hyperkinetic[4] young bond trader Samuel "Q" Belk, and me—set out for the mountaintop, an ugly wind was blowing through the expedition tents at base camp. So we moved with a redoubled sense of purpose. *I just want to climb*, Scott said when we left our Advance Base Camp. *Forget everything else and climb the mountain.*

The mountain cooperated for thirty-six hours. On the first day we climbed under calm, clear skies, moving from Camp 1 at 19,500 feet to Camp 2 at 23,500 feet by midday. We spent the night in the snow cave, then headed up again the next morning, climbing halfway up the White Limbo snowfield before a gathering snowstorm sent us scurrying back to Camp 2. The blizzard ravaged[5] the mountain for four long days and nights, and when the sky finally cleared we scaled the 2,000 feet to Camp 3. But then the stubborn blasting wind descended and we were pinned down again.

We were running out of time. Climbers call the upper reaches of the world the Death Zone— above 19,000 feet the earth's atmosphere is too thin to support life. No matter how much you eat, your digestive system can't assimilate enough nourishment to keep you alive. After a few days your muscles

start to atrophy.[6] You grow weaker. Most climbers start to fade after a week, although some can hold on for two or even three weeks. Soon I'd discover how strong I was—this was our second night above 25,000 feet. It was our seventh night in the Death Zone.

A shower of loose snow tumbled in through the tunnel entry, settling onto my head, my shoulders, melting cold down my neck. As the empty hours passed I sat in silence, sharing the same thought as my three companions. *This can't be happening.* I needed success too much this year.

When the storm first pinned us down at Camp 2, we tried not to seem concerned. Snowstorms never last forever, not even in the Himalayas. We had enough food in the cave to hold out for days, and then once

> ## Climbers call the upper reaches of the world the Death Zone . . .

the sky did clear nothing would hold us back. As it turned out, that storm was the worst autumn blizzard to hit Everest in more than forty years. But it did clear one night, and by the next afternoon we were

---

4. Being *hyperkinetic,* Belk likes to be always moving about or doing something.

5. *Ravaged* (rav′ ijd) means "destroyed violently; ruined."

6. To *assimilate* food is to absorb it and use it to create living tissue. If this doesn't happen, the body will waste away, or *atrophy.*

Vocabulary
charismatic (kar′ iz mat′ ik) *adj.* having personal qualities that enable one to inspire loyalty and devotion

in Camp 3. By then, the summit was only two days away . . . until we woke up the next morning and saw the gale-force winds ripping across the top of the mountain. So we went back to the cave, the four of us, back to talking and waiting. Two days passed and eventually we ran out of words. The wind kept blowing.

Then there was silence—the sound of breathing, the sputtering of the stove, the dry stuttering of the spindrift[7] blowing in the tunnel. After seven days the altitude had weakened us, and it was too late in the season to retreat to base camp and wait for better weather. If we didn't get to the summit now, we couldn't try again. Unless the jet stream lifted by morning, we would have to go down. *Two years of work. A decade of training. A lifetime of hope.* Blown away.

Sleep wouldn't come. The cold air sank down through the tunnel, covering us like a dark, wet blanket. Lying closest to the entry, Q was curled into a ball, trembling under three layers of down. Scott flopped around in his bag, occasionally heaving up a great dispirited[8] sigh. Wes lay still, his eyes burning. The minutes crept past. I swam in my sleeping bag, searching for the comfortable spot. But my body had been whittled away by the months of high-altitude effort, and comfort was beyond me. I was a stick figure of a woman, fragile bones jutting against pale flesh, muscles stretched taut like rubber bands: a body pulled to the breaking point.

Come on, morning. Our last chance would come with the daylight. I tried to push the hours along, pulling up the dawn by force of willpower. *Give me this one*

---

7. Here, *spindrift* refers to light, misty, blowing snow.
8. *Dispirited* (dis pir′ ə tid) means "discouraged; depressed."

chance. The dawn, and calm skies. Just two more days without the jet stream. *Please, please, I need this now.*

When life gets tangled there's something so reassuring about climbing a mountain. The challenge is unambiguous.[9] Ice and snow and rock. Self-discipline. Concentration. Focus. As you push higher you work yourself into a trance. Can I reach that ledge? Are my fingers strong enough to hold on to this crack? Will this ice screw hold? Eventually the weight of the world slides away. For those moments when it's just you and the rock and the ice and the snow, life always makes sense.

Climbing has always been more than a physical pursuit for me. Each mountain I face is another <u>pinnacle</u> in an internal adventure. An exploration of myself, an expression of my spirit. For ten years I had climbed, from desert cliffs in Utah to small mountains in the Cascade Range of the Pacific Northwest. Looking higher, I reached up into the clouds, then past the clouds. To larger mountains, and more complex climbs: Mount McKinley in Alaska, Ama Dablam in Nepal, Pik Kommunizma in the Soviet Union. I reached up, step by step, until I could see myself standing on the peak of the world's tallest mountain.

Mount Everest. Chomolungma to the Tibetans. Sagarmatha to the Nepali. The Mother Goddess of the Earth to everyone living in its shadow. The top of Everest is the top of the world—29,028 feet up into the empty Himalayan sky. The only spot on earth where you can't climb any higher.

I had to get up there. Usually I don't get obsessed about mountaintops—I had learned long ago that the time spent climbing in life means more than the time spent standing on a summit. But when my life turned sour, the tip of Everest gained significance. It was the top of the world! Reaching that windswept perch, I decided, would cleanse my spirit and heal my wounds. More than that, it would send me home with a title: The First American Woman to Climb Everest.

For so many years I wouldn't even allow myself to think I could get this far. Everest was for the big boys, and I was a very small woman. The climbing community has never had a lot of patience with women. It draws a <u>distinct</u> crowd—generally men equipped with a surplus of money, opinions, and muscle.

It came a step at a time, a decade of effort leading up to this one summit attempt, this journey to the top of the world. And now the world wasn't cooperating. Why did I think it would? I knew Everest wasn't like any other mountain. Only one of ten climbers who attempt the mountain stands on the summit. And for every three climbers who do scale the mountain, one dies trying. The facts aren't welcoming. But you don't plan a trip to Everest believing those facts will apply to you.

---

9. Something that's *unambiguous* is perfectly clear, leaving no room for doubt or confusion.

Vocabulary
pinnacle (pin′ ə kəl) *n.* a high point, or peak
distinct (dis tingkt′) *adj.* different in quality or kind

Viewing the photograph: How are the conditions here similar to those faced by the climbers in the selection?

When dawn finally came we got dressed for the summit—pulling our down climbing suits over the layers of polypropylene long underwear, polypro socks, plastic climbing boots, polypro and down gloves, a heavy pile hat, a neoprene[10] face mask—then crawled out of the cave, pulled along by a fine thread of hope, and walked gingerly[11] to the side of the ice tower that stood above our cave. Above us we'd see the summit, that great crooked pyramid on top of the world, the crown for the Mother

Goddess. If she rose straight into a clean blue sky, we could try to push ourselves higher. But if she sent off a tail of white, if the winds were still ripping the snow from the hillside, we had to go down.

Wes turned the corner first. I didn't have to look up. I could read it in his shoulders. Wes slumped, then turned to see Scott, coming around the corner after us. I saw it in Scott's eyes, then heard his voice, shouting above the constant roar of the wind.

"Well, that's the ballgame."

Scott stomped back toward the snow cave, <u>anguished</u>, shaking his head. Wes stayed, staring into the sky. I turned my face

---

10. *Polypropylene, pile,* and *neoprene* are human-made fabrics that provide insulation from cold temperatures.
11. *Gingerly* (jin′ jər lē) means "with extreme caution; carefully."

Vocabulary

anguished (ang′ gwisht) *adj.* having or showing extreme mental or physical suffering

upward and saw it, too. The thick plume of spindrift sailing from the mountain-top. The jet stream had not lifted. It was slamming against the mountain at 150 miles an hour for the third day in a row. And the thin thread of hope snapped.

Back in the cave Scott's blond hair hung lank over dim eyes, his usually rosy cheeks looked pale and sunken. His chest caved in beneath his shoulders.

"If you guys want to wait another day," I said, "I can wait." Q looked up dimly and coughed. I was grasping at thin air. We had failed. It was over. Even so, Scott flashed a look at the rest of us, measuring reactions.

"One more day? Give it a shot?"

Q shook his head. The Death Zone was wreaking its havoc[12] on him. He was losing wattage with every passing hour. "I can't stay up here another day," Q said. He'd been barely able to eat breakfast that morning. "If I don't go down today, I'm not going to get down."

Now just the sound of breathing, and outside the wind and then occasionally a light cloud of spindrift, floating through the tunnel and down into the cave. The cold drifted down my spine until I could feel it in my toes.

Scott picked up the walkie-talkie and called to our expedition mates waiting at base camp. *We're finished. We're coming down.* The message was received, tenderly, and we started packing. Sleeping bags,

Thinsulate[13] pads, ice screws, rope, and cook gear over here, stoves, food, fuel over there. We'd carry the fragile gear, but the really soft and really hard gear could take the fast way down the Great Couloir, the chutelike valley just to the left of our route on the North Face. Camp 1 was just below the bottom of the chute; once the gear rocketed down, the other climbers would try to collect it.

We went back to the cave entry and slung on our packs. And we stood there for a moment, not looking at each other. Just stood there in the cold and the wind before taking the first step down. And then Wes moved, and Q followed, and then we were all moving. After two long years of planning and working and hoping, we were walking away from the summit. I could barely fathom[14] the disappointment. I couldn't, not with the descent ahead of us. I still had to focus on getting down in one piece.

I turned to take a last look and my eyes fell on Scott's face. Tears were sliding down his cheeks. Did he see me watching him? It was only a moment, and he was wearing reflecting shades so it was impossible to tell. I turned around again and continued down dry-eyed. Whatever anguish I felt, I'd deal with it when we got down to safe terrain.[15]

---

12. The expression *wreaking havoc* means "causing destruction."

13. *Thinsulate* is the brand name of an insulating material.
14. Here, *fathom* (fa<u>th</u>′ əm) means "to understand fully."
15. Scott Fischer successfully reached Everest's peak in 1994. Two years later, he and seven other climbers died in another attempt to reach the top.

Responding to Literature

PERSONAL RESPONSE

◆ Suppose you had a chance to interview Stacy Allison. What questions would you like to ask her about the challenges she faced? Record your questions in your journal.

Analyzing Literature

RECALL

1. What problems did the climbers face as they sat stranded in their snow cave?
2. What does the writer find reassuring about climbing a mountain?
3. Why didn't the team of climbers reach the summit?

INTERPRET

4. According to the writer, "Kindness was a lot to hope for this high in the world." Explain what she means.
5. How would you describe the writer's attitude about the challenge she and the other climbers faced?
6. Why was it so important that the mountain be "kind" to the climbers?
7. According to the writer, mountain climbing was "an exploration of myself." What do you think she means?
8. What was the conflict the climbers faced on their final morning at Camp 3? How did they resolve it?

EVALUATE AND CONNECT

9. How might the account of this adventure be different if it had been written by someone who wasn't a part of the expedition? Explain.
10. **Theme Connection** What "summit" would you like to face? Why is that particular goal important to you?

LITERARY ELEMENTS

Autobiography

Have you ever written an account of your own life? If so, you have written an autobiography. The word part *auto* means "self," *bio* means "life," and *graphy* means "something written." A **biography** is the story of someone's life. An **autobiography** is the story of a person's life written by that person. An autobiography may cover a person's entire life, or it may focus on one aspect of that life, such as an important event or a childhood experience. Such works are sometimes called **memoirs.** Autobiography is almost always written from the first-person point of view.

1. What details did you learn about Stacy Allison's life from reading this autobiographical selection?

2. What else would you like to learn about her life?

● See **Literary Terms Handbook,** p. R2.

Extending Your Response

Writing About Literature

Comparing Challenges   *Beyond the Limits* is an account of one person's experience in facing a difficult challenge. Think about the challenges you discussed for the **Reading Focus** on page 280. Write a paragraph comparing your or your group's challenges with those of the author.

If you are interested in learning more about mountain climbing, use a Web browser, and type in the phrase "mountain climbing" to search for Web sites about this challenging sport.

Creative Writing

Entry from the Top of the World   Imagine that you are one of the members of the 1987 North Face expedition. You are stranded in a sleeping bag in a snow cave at Camp 3. Think about how you would feel. Write a journal entry describing your thoughts and feelings.

Literature Groups

Debate It!   Mountain climbing demands physical fitness, skill, self-discipline, and courage. Critics of the sport claim that climbing is costly, dangerous, and often destructive to the natural environment. Choose one point of view, and defend your position in a small group discussion.

Interdisciplinary Activity

Social Studies/Art   Reread the selection, and take notes on each place in the expedition. Use a real map to give you an outline of the journey. Then draw your own map of the area and label each site. Use your map to retell the story to a family member or a friend.

💼 **Save your work for your portfolio.**

Skill Minilesson

VOCABULARY • GREEK WORD PARTS

Allison describes team member Samuel "Q" Belk as *hyperkinetic.* That word, like many scientific, technical, and medical words, is made up of Greek roots— *hyper* (meaning "more" or "excessive") and *kinetic* ("motion" or "energy"). Belk was a person who couldn't stay still. Following are some additional Greek roots and their meanings.

bio (life)	*phone* (sound, speak)
gram, graph (write)	*psych* (mind)
log, logy (study of)	*scope* (view)
meter (measure)	*tele* (far, distant)
micro (small)	*thermo* (heat)

PRACTICE   Combine the Greek roots above to make ten English words.

NONFICTION

Nonfiction is writing that tells about real-life people, places, events, and ideas. Fiction, too, can deal with real-life stories, but authors of fiction can invent characters, situations, and dialogue. Writers of nonfiction, on the other hand, write about real people, events, and situations. To do so, they use special text structures that help them organize their material for readers.

Narrative Nonfiction

Some nonfiction follows a narrative text structure similar to that used by writers of fiction. Autobiography, biography, and historical accounts are the main types of narrative nonfiction. They tell stories that have settings, characters, plots, and themes. The stories are most often told in chronological (time) order. Unlike fiction, however, the stories of narrative nonfiction are true, and the people are real.

Expository Writing

The main purpose of expository writing is to explain or to inform. Newspaper and magazine articles, how-to books, instruction manuals, and books on topics such as science and technology are some types of expository writing. The textbooks you use in science, math, or social studies classes are familiar examples of exposition.

MODEL

Breathing and Respiration

People often get the terms *breathing* and *respiration* mixed up. Breathing is the process whereby fresh air moves into and stale air moves out of lungs. Fresh air contains oxygen, which passes from the lungs into your circulatory system. Blood then carries the oxygen to your individual cells. At the same time, your digestive system has prepared a supply of glucose in your cells from digested food. Now the oxygen plays a key role in the chemical action that releases energy from glucose. This chemical reaction is called respiration. Carbon dioxide is a waste product of respiration. At the end of this reaction, carbon dioxide wastes are carried back to your lungs in your blood. There, it is expelled from your body in the stale air.

To help readers understand their ideas, writers of exposition use one or more text structures to organize their writing. The following are the most common of these text structures.

- **Description** Writers of expository non-fiction often draw on description to help readers understand their topics. The writer of a book on astronomy, for example, needs to describe planets, satellites, stars, nebulas, and so on, as well as provide explanations about how the universe works.

- **Time Order** Writers often help readers by using time order to show the stages in which something happened or should be done. A history book, for example, will present events in chronological order. A how-to book will give a series of directions in the order in which they must be done.

- **Compare-Contrast** Comparing looks at how two or more things are similar. Contrasting examines how things are different. The compare-contrast text structure might be used in a science book to show the similarities and differences in two particular animals. A social studies book might compare regions, cultures, presidents, or the views of two political parties or candidates.

- **Cause-Effect** In this structure, the text is arranged to show the relationship between outcomes and their causes. For example, a drop in temperature (cause) results in the freezing of water (effect). A long drought results in decreased crops. That decrease, in turn, may lead to higher food prices. Cause-effect structures are used often in science, social science, and history materials.

- **Problem-Solution** In this text structure, a writer presents a problem and offers one or more solutions to it. Books and articles on science often make use of the problem-solution structure.

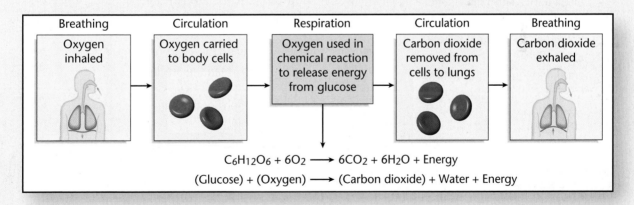

What is the main text structure used in this passage from a science textbook? What key words can you find in the passage that point to that particular text structure? Does the diagram have the same organizational structure?

Active Reading Strategies

Strategies for Informative Nonfiction

Do you enjoy reading about real life, about factual events in the past or present? Nonfiction writing deals with real people, places, and events. Literary nonfiction includes autobiography, biography, and essays. Informative nonfiction includes encyclopedias, textbooks, books on topics such as history and science, and most articles in newspapers and magazines. Informative nonfiction is written primarily to inform readers. Facts, therefore, are extremely important.

When reading informative nonfiction, active readers use strategies like those below to increase their understanding.

● For more about these and other reading strategies, see **Reading Handbook,** pp. R82–R101.

PREVIEW

Ask Yourself . . .

Previewing a selection by looking at the title, headings, bold-faced terms, illustrations, and any diagrams or charts will give you an idea of what it will be about. Previewing may also help you figure out what text structure the author has used to organize the work.

● How has the author organized this information? How can I use the text structure to find the most important ideas?

● Will I need to understand this chart (or other graphic) before I read the article?

● What do the photographs or illustrations tell me about the subject?

QUESTION

Ask Yourself . . .

Questioning helps you clarify the facts in the text.

● What do I know about this subject that will help me understand this information?

● Can I turn these section headings into questions that will guide my reading?

● Do I understand why the writer has included this specific information?

REVIEW

Think about what you read. Summarize and rephrase the information. Look back at bold-faced terms and section headings.

Say to Yourself . . .

- In other words, the author means _____.

- So far in this work _____.

- The most important information I have learned about this subject is _____.

EVALUATE

Form opinions and make judgments about what you have read.

Ask Yourself . . .

- Is this writer qualified to write on this topic?

- Are the sources for these facts reliable?

- Is this actually an opinion that the writer is presenting as a fact?

- If I wrote an essay on this subject, what would I include that this author hasn't included?

APPLYING THE STRATEGIES

Read "The Fish Crisis." Use the Active Reading Model notes in the margins as you read. Write your own responses on a separate piece of paper or use self-stick notes.

Before You Read
The Fish Crisis

MEET
J. MADELEINE NASH

Starting her career in journalism in 1966 as a researcher at *Time* magazine, J. Madeleine Nash went on to become a reporter for the magazine. Nash has also used her experience as a journalist to research and write a book about parent involvement in education called *Schools Where Parents Make a Difference*.

J. Madeleine Nash was born in 1943. This article was published in the August 11, 1997, issue of Time.

READING FOCUS

When you eat a tuna sandwich for lunch, do you ever think about where the tuna fish came from?

List Ideas
Work in a small group to list all the edible fish you have heard about or tasted. Then try to guess where the fish originate—in fresh water (lakes, rivers) or the ocean.

Setting a Purpose
Read the following article to learn about the world's supply of fish.

BUILDING BACKGROUND

Did You Know?   The waters where fishing takes place are called *fisheries.* The most productive fisheries are in oceans, especially areas near coastlines.

VOCABULARY PREVIEW

contemplate (kon′ təm plāt′) *v.* to give intense attention to; consider carefully; p. 296

plummet (plum′ it) *v.* to fall or drop straight downward; plunge; p. 296

depleted (di plēt′ id) *adj.* greatly reduced in amount; p. 296

undermine (un′ dər mīn′) *v.* to weaken, wear away, or destroy slowly; p. 298

exploit (iks ploit′) *v.* to use or develop for profit, often in a selfish, unjust, or unfair way; p. 299

converge (kən vurj′) *v.* to come together at a place; p. 299

amplify (am′ plə fī′) *v.* to increase; extend; p. 300

indiscriminately (in′ dis krim′ ə nit lē) *adv.* in a way that does not pay attention to differences; carelessly; p. 300

diligently (dil′ ə jənt lē) *adv.* in a way that shows great attention, care, and effort; p. 301

subsidize (sub′ sə dīz′) *v.* to aid or support with a contribution of money; p. 301

The Fish Crisis

J. Madeleine Nash ∿

THICK SWORDFISH STEAKS. Orange roughy fillets. Great mounds of red-fleshed tuna. Judging from the seafood sections of local supermarkets, there would seem to be plenty of fish left in the oceans. But this appearance of abundance is an illusion, says Sylvia Earle, former chief scientist for the National Oceanic and Atmospheric Administration.

The Fish Crisis

ACTIVE READING MODEL

Already, Earle fears, an international armada of fishing vessels is on the verge of exhausting a storehouse of protein so vast that it once appeared to be infinite. "It's a horrible thing to contemplate," shudders Earle. "What makes it even worse is that we know better. Yet here we go, making the same mistake over and over again."

If fishermen around the world soon start hauling back empty nets and fishing lines, it will not be for lack of warning. In the 1990s, after increasing for nearly four decades, the wild catch of marine fish leveled off worldwide and in some years actually declined. "We are reaching, and in many cases have exceeded, the oceans' limits," declare the authors of a sobering report released by the Natural Resources Defense Council earlier this year. "We are no longer living off the income but eating deeply into the capital."[1]

QUESTION

Is the author stating a fact here, or her opinion?

Fights have already started to break out over the dwindling supply. Two weeks ago, hundreds of Canadian fishermen blockaded a British Columbia port for several days to keep an Alaskan ferry from leaving. The reason for their protest? Alaskan trawlers[2] were sweeping up the salmon that spawn in Canada's rivers. Now the Canadians are threatening to do to the salmon runs of Washington State what U.S. fishermen have done to theirs.

Of course, overfishing is not the only human activity that is jeopardizing life in the oceans. Coastal pollution and habitat destruction—filling in wetlands, building dams—are contributing to the crisis. But it is overfishing, the NRDC report makes plain, that constitutes[3] the most urgent threat and demands the most immediate action.

PREDICT

What could be a worse threat than this?

Until now, the worst threat most creatures of the sea had faced at fishermen's hands was so-called commercial extinction.[4] Whenever local populations of a particular fish plummeted, boats simply targeted some other species or moved to more distant waters. The depleted stocks almost always recovered. But now, experts warn,

---

1. In financial terms, *capital* is wealth that is used to produce more wealth. A savings account, for example, adds to your income by earning interest. However, if you spend the savings (your capital), you earn less interest and gradually use up all your savings.
2. *Trawlers* are boats that catch fish by towing strong, bag-shaped nets across the ocean bottom.
3. Here, *constitutes* means "forms; makes up."
4. An *extinction* is the permanent elimination of something.

Vocabulary

contemplate (kon′ təm plāt′) v. to give intense attention to; consider carefully
plummet (plum′ it) v. to fall or drop straight downward; plunge
depleted (di plēt′ id) adj. greatly reduced in amount

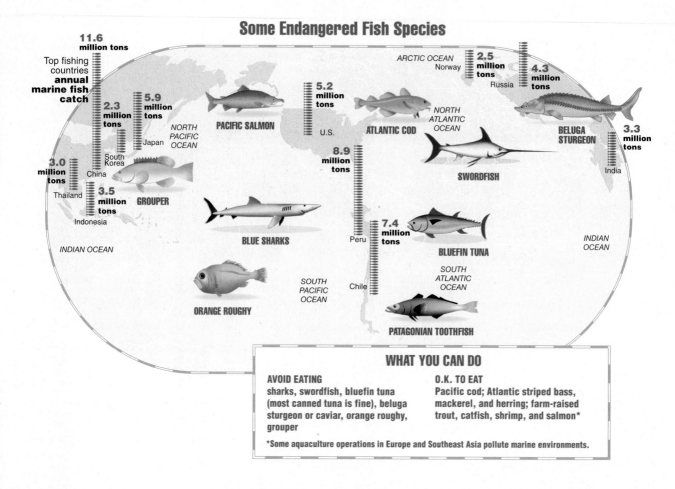

Some Endangered Fish Species

11.6 million tons
Top fishing countries **annual marine fish catch**

2.3 million tons South Korea, Japan

5.9 million tons Japan

3.0 million tons Thailand, China

3.5 million tons Indonesia

NORTH PACIFIC OCEAN

INDIAN OCEAN

GROUPER

PACIFIC SALMON

5.2 million tons U.S.

8.9 million tons Peru

BLUE SHARKS

ORANGE ROUGHY

SOUTH PACIFIC OCEAN

ATLANTIC COD

ARCTIC OCEAN
Norway **2.5 million tons**
Russia

4.3 million tons

NORTH ATLANTIC OCEAN

SWORDFISH

BELUGA STURGEON

India **3.3 million tons**

7.4 million tons Chile

BLUEFIN TUNA

SOUTH ATLANTIC OCEAN

INDIAN OCEAN

PATAGONIAN TOOTHFISH

WHAT YOU CAN DO

AVOID EATING
sharks, swordfish, bluefin tuna (most canned tuna is fine), beluga sturgeon or caviar, orange roughy, grouper

O.K. TO EAT
Pacific cod; Atlantic striped bass, mackerel, and herring; farm-raised trout, catfish, shrimp, and salmon*

*Some aquaculture operations in Europe and Southeast Asia pollute marine environments.

PREDICT

Do you think the author will explain more about the kind of fishing gear that is depleting fish?

unprecedented forces—among them, industrial-scale fishing gear and a burgeoning[5] global seafood market—are altering this age-old cycle. The economic and technological barriers that have kept overfishing within bounds appear increasingly shaky, like dikes along a river that floodwaters have <u>undermined</u>. Should these barriers collapse, commercial extinction could escalate into biological catastrophe.[6]

In most imminent peril[7] are the giant predators of the oceans—sharks, of course, but also marlin, sailfish, swordfish, and bluefin tuna, the magnificent swimming machines that have earned the nickname "Porsches of the sea." In the western Atlantic, the breeding population of northern bluefin, the largest tuna species, is thought to consist of perhaps 40,000

---

5. When something is *unprecedented,* there has never before been anything like it. When something is *burgeoning,* it is growing rapidly.
6. The gradual wiping out of food fish could increase by stages *(escalate)* into a sudden, terrible disaster for all sea creatures *(biological catastrophe).*
7. *In most imminent peril* could be restated as: "Likely to be in danger first."

Vocabulary
undermine (un´ dər mīn´) *v.* to weaken, wear away, or destroy slowly

J. Madeleine Nash

adults, down from some 250,000 two decades ago. Reason: the flourishing airfreight industry that allows fish brokers to deliver Atlantic Ocean bluefin overnight to Tokyo's sashimi[8] market, where a single fish can fetch $80,000 or more at auction. "To a fisherman, catching a bluefin is a lot like winning the lottery," sighs Stanford University marine biologist Barbara Block.

The crash of commercially important fisheries is not new. What is new is how quickly fisheries arise and how quickly they are exploited. In recent years, piked dogfish, a small spiny shark, has begun to stand in for cod in the fish and chips served by British pubs, and the Patagonian toothfish has become a popular substitute for sablefish in Japan. But environmental groups are concerned about the long-term viability of the fisheries that are serving up these quaintly named piscine[9] treats. This year, for example, ships from around the world have converged on the Southern Ocean, where the toothfish makes its home. "At this rate," predicts Beth Clark, a scientist with the Antarctica Project, "the entire fishery will be gone in 18 months."

Unfortunately, it takes longer to rebuild a fishery than it does to ruin one. Consider the present state of the orange roughy on New Zealand's Challenger Plateau. Discovered in 1979, this deep-water fishing hole took off in the 1980s when the mild-tasting, white-fleshed fish became popular with U.S. chefs. Happy to stoke the surging demand, fishermen are believed to have reduced the biomass of orange roughy as much as 80% before officials stepped in. Now, says Yale University ichthyologist[10] Jon Moore, it may take centuries before the fishery rebounds. As scientists have belatedly learned, orange roughy grow extremely slowly, live 100 years or more and take 25 to 30 years to reach sexual maturity.

How can a fishing fleet do so much damage so quickly? Until recently, many fish, especially deep-water fish, were too hard to find to make tempting commercial targets. But technical advances have given fishermen the power to peer beneath the waves and plot their position

---

ACTIVE READING MODEL**

EVALUATE

How does the author's use of the word *sighs* affect your sense of the scientist's statement?

REVIEW

Try to rephrase this paragraph in your own words.

QUESTION

Why is the author referring to the slow growth rate of these fish?

---

8. This is the market where Tokyo's restaurants buy their fish. *Sashimi* is raw fish.
9. To have *viability* is to be able both to survive and to work as intended. *Piscine* (pī′ sēn) means "of or relating to fish."
10. *Biomass* is the total amount of living matter within a given environmental area. It's a term that might be used by an *ichthyologist,* a scientist who specializes in the study of fish.

Vocabulary
exploit (iks ploit′) *v.* to use or develop for profit, often in a selfish, unjust, or unfair way
converge (kən vurj′) *v.* to come together at a place

The Fish Crisis

with unprecedented accuracy. Sonar makes it possible to locate large shoals of fish that would otherwise remain concealed beneath tens, even hundreds of feet of water. And once a fishing hot spot is pinpointed by sonar, satellite-navigation systems enable vessels to return unerringly to the same location year after year. In this fashion, fishermen from New Zealand to the Philippines have been able to home in on orange roughy and giant groupers as they gather to spawn, in some cases virtually eliminating entire generations of reproducing adults.

EVALUATE

Does the author do a good job describing how these technical advances work?

But what has <u>amplified</u> the destructive power of modern fishing more than anything else is its gargantuan[11] scale. Trawling for pollock in the Bering Sea and the Gulf of Alaska, for example, are computerized ships as large as football fields. Their nets—wide enough to swallow a dozen Boeing 747s—can gather up 130 tons of fish in a single sweep. Along with pollock and other groundfish, these nets <u>indiscriminately</u> draw in the creatures that swim or crawl alongside, including halibut, Pacific herring, Pacific salmon, and king crab. In similar fashion, so-called longlines—which stretch for tens of miles and bristle with thousands of hooks—snag not just tuna and swordfish but also hapless sea turtles and albatrosses, marlin and sharks.

QUESTION

Is this some of the industrial fishing gear the author mentioned earlier?

What happens to the dead and dying animals that constitute this so-called "by-catch"? Most are simply dumped overboard, either because they are unwanted or because fishery regulations require it. In 1993, for example, shrimp trawlers in the Gulf of Mexico caught and threw away an estimated 34 million red snappers, including many juveniles. By contrast, the annual catch of red snapper from the Gulf averages only around 3 million fish. Indeed, so many snappers are being scooped up as by-catch that the productivity of the fishery has been compromised. Fortunately, there is a solution. Shrimp nets can be outfitted with devices that afford larger animals like snappers and sea turtles a trapdoor escape hatch.

RESPOND

How did you feel when you read that something positive could be done to help solve part of the overfishing problem?

To a surprising extent, solutions to the problem of overfishing also exist, at least on paper, and that's what critics of the fishing industry find so encouraging—and so frustrating. Last year, for example, Congress passed landmark legislation that requires fishery managers to crack down on overfishing in U.S. waters. Perhaps even more impressive, the

---

11. From the name of a fictional giant, Gargantua, *gargantuan* means "enormous; huge."

Vocabulary

amplify (am′ plə fī′) *v.* to increase; extend
indiscriminately (in′ dis krim′ ə nit lē) *adv.* in a way that does not pay attention to differences; carelessly

J. Madeleine Nash ~

U.N. has produced a tough-minded treaty that promises to protect stocks of fish that straddle the coastal zones of two or more countries or migrate, as bluefin tuna and swordfish do, through international waters in the wide-open oceans. The treaty will take effect, however, only after 30 or more nations ratify[12] it—and even then, some question how <u>diligently</u> its provisions will be enforced.

QUESTION

Why didn't the author tell us how many nations have ratified the treaty so far?

What has been missing is a willingness to take action. Consumers no less than politicians bear some of the blame. Simply by refusing to buy bluefin tuna in Tokyo, grouper in Hong Kong or swordfish in Chicago, consumers could relieve the pressure on some of the world's most beleaguered[13] fisheries and allow them the time they need to recover. To help shoppers become more selective about what they put on the dinner table, the Worldwide Fund for Nature and Unilever, one of the world's largest purveyors of frozen seafood, have launched a joint venture[14] that in 1998 will start putting labels on fish and fish products caught in environmentally responsible ways.

CONNECT

Would you or your family be willing to take a stand about these fish?

A sign that consumers are worried about the world's fisheries could provide the jolt political leaders need. For the past half-century, billions of dollars have been spent by maritime nations to expand their domestic fishing fleets, <u>subsidizing</u> everything from fuel costs to the construction of factory trawlers. And until countries like Canada, China, Japan, South Korea, New Zealand, Norway, Spain, and, yes, the U.S. are willing to confront this monster of their own making, attempts to control overfishing are likely to prove ineffectual.[15] The problem, as Carl Safina, director of the National Audubon Society's Living Oceans Program, observes, is this: there is just too much fishing power chasing too few fish.

EVALUATE

Does Nash supply you with enough information to form your own opinion about overfishing?

12. To *ratify* means to approve a document and agree to obey its rules.
13. The most *beleaguered* fisheries are those in the greatest trouble.
14. These food suppliers *(purveyors)* have formed a partnership *(joint venture)*.
15. If the attempts are *ineffectual,* they will fail to produce the desired result.

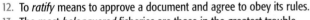

Vocabulary

diligently (dil′ ə jənt lē) *adv.* in a way that shows great attention, care, and effort
subsidize (sub′ sə dīz′) *v.* to aid or support with a contribution of money

Responding to Literature

PERSONAL RESPONSE

◆ Did you discover the author's purpose, as suggested in the **Reading Focus** on page 294? Were you convinced by the author's arguments about the "fish crisis"? Explain why or why not.

Active Reading Response

Look back at the strategies described in the **Active Reading Model** notes on pages 292–293. Choose one of the strategies and find three places in the article where you could apply it.

Analyzing Literature

RECALL

1. Summarize what has happened to the world's ocean fish supply in the 1990s.
2. Which takes longer, ruining a fishery or rebuilding one?
3. List the technical advances that have affected fishing.
4. What have the U.S. Congress and the United Nations done to solve the problem of overfishing?

INTERPRET

5. In your opinion, what is the leading cause of the depleted fish supply?
6. Why, do you think, do fishers converge at a fishery when a new fish becomes popular?
7. Which do you think has caused the most damage to the fish population, technical advances or the huge scale of the fishing industry? Explain your answer.
8. Do you think the fishing industry or consumers will ever take action on their own to prevent overfishing? Why or why not?

EVALUATE AND CONNECT

9. Do you think the writer presented both sides of the debate on overfishing? Use examples to support your answer.
10. How would your life be changed if the supply of ocean fish dwindled to almost nothing?

LITERARY ELEMENTS

Essay

An **essay** is a short piece of non-fiction writing on any topic. The purpose of an essay is to communicate an idea or opinion. In a **persuasive essay,** such as "The Fish Crisis," the author tries to convince the reader of an opinion. One persuasive technique essayists use is the addition of emotional words, as in this sentence from "The Fish Crisis": "[Overfishing is] a horrible thing to contemplate."

1. What is J. Madeleine Nash trying to persuade the reader to believe?

2. Give three examples in which the writer uses emotional words to persuade the reader.

● See **Literary Terms Handbook,** p. R4.

Literature and Writing

Writing About Literature

Looking at Sources   A powerful persuasive essay or article like "The Fish Crisis" should contain facts and quotations from a number of trustworthy sources. Write a list of the major sources Nash uses in her article. Does the use of these sources help convince you that the author is right?

Creative Writing

Letter to the Editor   On the editorial pages of newspapers, both professional journalists and local readers can express their opinions in print. Write a persuasive letter alerting the people in your community to the dangers of overfishing in the world's oceans. Read your letter aloud to your group or class.

Extending Your Response

Literature Groups

Persuade the Public!   Your group has decided that everyone needs to know about the danger to the ocean fish supply. Brainstorm a slogan, and then design a poster that includes your warning and an illustration that calls attention to your cause.

Interdisciplinary Activity

Science/Math: Diagram   Study the selection and take notes on the statistics listed in different parts of the essay. Then find a way to represent these facts in a graph or chart.

Reading Further

If you would like to read more about fish, try these:

Fish by Steve Parker

Threatened Oceans by Jenny T. Tesar

Save your work for your portfolio.

Skill Minilesson

VOCABULARY • SUFFIXES

If you *purify* something, you make it more *pure*. If you *electrify* a car, you make it *electric*. As you can see, the suffix *-fy* means "to make or cause to be." When the *-fy* suffix is added, an *e* or a *y* at the end of the original word will change to *i*. Sometimes an *i* is inserted to make the new word easier to pronounce.

PRACTICE   Complete each sentence without using a form of the underlined word.
1. You might beautify a room by . . .
2. You could solidify water by . . .
3. You might simplify a statement by . . .
4. You could signify that you were happy by . . .
5. You could intensify your cheering by . . .

Americans Continue to Worry About the Decline of the Oceans

A Seaway Ocean Update, February 1998

As the International Year of the Ocean dawns, a new poll shows that more than half (59%) of Americans continue to view the health of the oceans today negatively, with 17% saying the oceans are in poor condition. Only one-fifth say the oceans are in good shape, while a mere 1% call the oceans' health "excellent."

The poll, conducted by the Washington, D.C.–based Mellman Group for SeaWeb, shows also that a majority (60%) believe the condition of the seas has become worse over the past few years, while only 11% say it has improved.

Nearly three-quarters (72%) agree that human beings are also in trouble as a result of the seas' problems, while 53% say that the destruction of the oceans represents a "very serious" threat to the quality of life today. Fifty percent believe we are currently taking too much out of the ocean in the form of commercial fishing and oil drilling, while 80% say we are dumping too much into the ocean in the form of waste, oil, and agricultural runoff.

"When a mere 1% call the condition of the ocean 'excellent,' it is obvious that Americans understand that we are doing more harm than good to our ocean," says Vikki Spruill, executive director of SeaWeb.

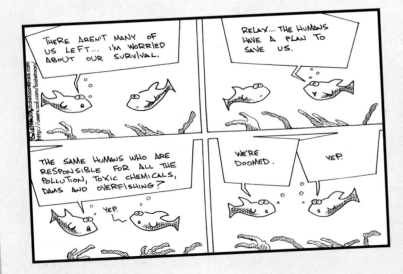

Analyzing Media

1. From the reported results, figure out what questions the people were asked. Then answer them yourself. Total the results for your class, and see how your class's opinions compare with those of the public.

2. Take your class's results and the statistics from the report, and put them into some graphic form—for example, a bar graph.

Before You Read

Hurricanes

MEET PATRICIA LAUBER

A person who is setting out to tell a story offers a hand and says, 'Come with me and I will show you many wondrous things.'" So says award-winning writer Patricia Lauber, who has written more than ninety non-fiction books for young people. Her book, *Volcano: The Eruption and Healing of Mount St. Helens*, was named a Newbery Honor Book. Lauber was awarded the Washington Post/Children's Book Guild Award for her contribution to nonfiction for children.

Patricia Lauber was born in 1924. She lives in Connecticut, where she has experienced several hurricanes. "Hurricanes" comes from her 1996 book Hurricanes: Earth's Mightiest Storms.

READING FOCUS

Close your eyes and imagine this scene. You are at home, in the dark. The howling wind sounds like a rushing freight train hurtling toward the walls of your house. What are you thinking? How do you feel?

QuickWrite
Jot down at least three words that describe your thoughts and feelings as the storm heads your way.

Setting a Purpose
Read to find out about one of nature's most powerful storms.

BUILDING BACKGROUND

Did You Know? Hurricanes and typhoons are tropical cyclones that have steady winds of at least seventy-five miles per hour. Storms that occur in the Atlantic and Pacific oceans are called hurricanes. Storms that take place in the western Pacific are called typhoons. The main energy source for these kinds of storms is the heat released when water vapor condenses. Because only very moist air can supply the energy necessary for one of these storms, tropical cyclones can only form over oceans with water temperatures of at least 80 degrees Fahrenheit. After forming, these types of storms intensify as they pass over warmer water and weaken as they pass over colder water or land.

VOCABULARY PREVIEW

compact (kəm pakt′) *adj.* occupying a relatively small space or area; tightly packed; p. 306

evacuate (i vak′ ū āt′) *v.* to leave or clear an area; p. 307

ecology (ē kol′ ə jē) *n.* the relationship of living things to their environment and to each other; p. 309

unique (ū nēk′) *adj.* highly uncommon; rare; one-of-a-kind; p. 309

Hurricanes:
Big Winds and Big Damage

Patricia Lauber

In mid-August of 1992, satellite pictures showed a low-pressure area of wind and rain moving west across the Atlantic. Though the storm did not seem to amount to much, the National Hurricane Center in Miami, Florida, tracked it carefully.

By August 20 the storm was about 400 miles east of Puerto Rico. Here it weakened so much that it almost disappeared. The lower part of the storm was moving northwest, but the upper part was being blown northeast by strong high-altitude winds. For a time, it seemed the storm might be torn apart. Instead, the high-altitude winds began to flow around the storm. It charged ahead, with all its parts moving in the same direction.

By then scientists at the Hurricane Center were working with computer models of storms. They were trying to predict the storm's behavior and decide whether people should be told to leave coastal areas. The scientists fed their computers all the data they had received from satellites, radar, and airplane flights into the storm.

By 4:00 A.M. of August 22, winds within the storm were blowing at more than 75 miles an hour. The storm had become a hurricane. First of the season, it was named Andrew.[1]

As its winds swirled ever faster, Andrew churned across the Bahamas. It was a furious and <u>compact</u> storm, with an eye[2] only eight miles wide and winds that reached out for 60 miles. It was heading for the east coast of Florida.

---

1. In North America, hurricanes tend to occur from June through November, with most striking in September. Each season's first storm is given a name beginning with an *A*. Male and female names are used alternately through the alphabet.
2. A hurricane's *eye,* or center, has very light winds and can be as much as several miles across. If you were caught in a hurricane as the eye passed over, you might well see clear, blue sky overhead.

Vocabulary
compact (kəm pakt′) *adj.* occupying a relatively small space or area; tightly packed

The computer models could not predict exactly where Andrew would come ashore. For 250 miles, from Fort Lauderdale to Key West, people were ordered to <u>evacuate</u> all low-lying areas along the coast.

Sunday, August 23, dawned clear and fair in south Florida. The sky was blue with fleecy clouds. Temperatures rose into the 90s. The air was damp and salty. Herons and frigate birds drifted over blue waters.

Vocabulary
evacuate (i vak′ ū āt′) *v.* to leave or clear an area

Hurricanes

It could have been any summer day, except that roads were jammed with cars as people fled inland and north.

By evening, wind and sea were rising. Shortly after midnight, in the early hours of August 24, Andrew came ashore south of Miami, with winds gusting to 195 miles an hour.

People woke in terror to dark houses, without electricity. The wind, sometimes shrieking, sometimes growling like a rushing freight train, snatched at shutters and shingles and pounded the sides of houses. Walls bulged in, then out. Howling winds toppled trees, ripped off roofs, blew in windows and doors, and knocked down houses. Where roofs or walls were gone, rain poured in. Inside their houses, people huddled together, held hands, and prayed.

The eye of the storm passed quickly through, bringing only minutes of calm and silence. Then the second half of the storm arrived, with winds howling from the opposite direction.

Moving west, Andrew cut a 25-mile-wide path through Everglades National Park, flattening trees, tearing out board-walks, and leveling the visitors center.

The storm moved out over the Gulf of Mexico and made a second landfall, west of Baton Rouge, Louisiana, where it died out over the swamps and marshes.

The sun rose on a strange landscape. In Miami large boats, hurled ashore, now

Workers prepare for Hurricane Andrew by boarding up windows.

Viewing the photograph: How successful do you think efforts like these were against Andrew?

leaned against lampposts and lay across highways. Wind had stripped the signs off posts and the fronds off palm trees. Fallen trees, telephone poles, and cables blocked streets. Traffic lights had disappeared.

But Miami had been at the edge of the hurricane. The center of the storm had hit to the south, bulldozing the towns of Homestead and Florida City. Twenty miles inland, they had been crushed not by the sea but by the wind. They looked as if they had been bombed, and 22 people had died.

The people in this area were not wealthy. Most were fishermen, small farmers, migrant workers, retired couples, people with low-paying jobs in Miami. They had just enough money to buy or rent a small home. Many lived in trailer parks. Some had no insurance. Now their houses were kindling wood. Their trailer homes looked like crushed soda cans. And with their homes had gone everything they owned, from clothes and furniture to toys and family photographs. Of the houses still standing, most had serious damage.

Shopping centers, warehouses, churches, and schools were ripped out of the ground or hammered into piles of twisted steel beams and splintered wood. Trees littered the ground. Lampposts were bent in two. Street signs were gone, and streets were buried under wreckage. Dogs and cats, horses and cows wandered about, lost.

Help was slow to arrive. The armed forces had planned ahead and were ready to move even before Andrew hit. But civilian leaders were slow to realize how great the damage was, slow to ask for help, slow to give orders.

Meanwhile, in South Florida some 250,000 people camped out in the ruins as best they could, living with rain and mosquitoes. In all, Andrew had destroyed 20,000 houses and badly damaged another 90,000.

Finally, the troops were given their orders and arrived. Tent cities sprang up. Generators hummed, bringing back electricity. Food and water were supplied. Troops patrolled against looters and directed traffic. Bulldozers and cranes began a giant cleanup. But it would be years before Homestead and Florida City looked like towns again, years before people could put their lives together again.

It would also be years before anyone could tell how plant and animal life had been affected. In the past, many hurricanes have roared across South Florida. Each time, plant and animal life recovered. But in recent years, people have made many changes in the region. Because of these changes, the effects of Andrew's pounding may pose a long-term threat to the ecology of Everglades National Park.

Like other national parks, Everglades is a piece of wilderness set aside to be preserved in its natural state. But in one way Everglades is unique. Other parks were chosen to preserve landforms. Everglades National Park was to preserve lifeforms. It is a park of birds, mammals, fish, reptiles, and amphibians, and of plants.

Andrew cut through the heart of the park, felling[3] everything in its path. Animals

---

3. To *fell* is to strike and knock down, as a lumberjack chops down a tree.

Vocabulary

ecology (ē kol′ ə jē′) *n.* the relationship of living things to their environment and to each other

unique (ū nēk′) *adj.* highly uncommon; rare; one-of-a-kind

in the park survived well. But in Andrew's winds, slash pines snapped like matchsticks. Gumbo-limbo, wild tamarind, and ancient mahogany trees were uprooted. The storm left behind a tangled mass of dead and dying plants, lying in torn-up ground.

The last hurricane that seriously damaged Everglades swept through in 1960. That time the park recovered well. Some fallen trees resprouted. Seeds from similar plants blew in on the winds or were carried in by animals.

Since then many changes have taken place in areas around the park. To the north, land has been drained and cleared for towns, ranches, and farms. The natural flow of water through the park has changed, and

Mangrove trees have a system of exposed roots that help support the plant.

chemicals seep into the water. Housing developments have gone up right next to the park. And foreign plants have been brought in and planted just outside the park. Among these are Australian pines, Brazilian pepper shrubs, and melaleuca trees. All were brought in as ornamental plants. But they are a problem. Their seeds spread like wildfire, grow fast, and thrive in disturbed soil. Once they take hold, they are nearly impossible to get rid of.

Before Andrew, the park was under stress because of changes to the north. Now park scientists fear that foreign plants will invade the hurricane-damaged areas, take hold, and drive out native plants. This would change the park's plant life. It would also change the animal life, because animals depend on native plants for food and for places to nest and raise their young.

No one knows how big a change will take place or how it will affect the songbirds and wading birds, the raccoons, bobcats, deer, alligators, snakes, and tree frogs. Park scientists can only wait and see.

Natural scientists are also concerned about damage to mangrove swamps along southern Biscayne Bay, where Andrew came ashore.

The storm surge spent itself on a string of small barrier islands.[4] But the hurricane's winds and waves battered the shore, which was lined with swamps of mangrove trees. The raging winds shredded the mangroves. When mangroves are lost, many food chains and food webs are affected.

Mangroves are umbrella-shaped trees that can grow in salty water. There are

---

4. *Barrier islands* are long, narrow islands that lie in the shallow waters along a shore. They are made of sand and gravel piled up into ridges and dunes by waves and winds.

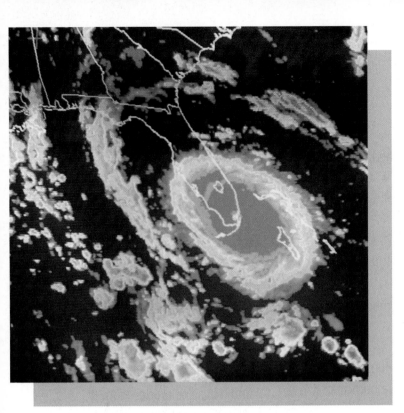

Satellite images help scientists track hurricanes. In this image of a hurricane over the state of Florida, the land areas are outlined by computer.

trout, and others, all of which grow up into big fishes that are at or near the head of food chains. These chains also include other fish eaters, among them alligators, herons, egrets, eagles, wood storks, white ibises, and humans.

Because of the mangroves, the shores are rich in food for many animals. They are also a nursery for the young of many fishes and other sea creatures. They are important to the lives of animals and also to the lives of humans—to those who take their living from the sea and to those who eat food from the sea.

It will be years before anyone can tell how badly Andrew damaged the mangrove swamps and the food chains that begin in them. Florida has lost many miles of mangrove swamps in the past 30 years. They have been filled, cleared, and built on. The remaining ones are precious.

Hurricanes are part of nature. They are natural events. And they have been making landfalls for a very long time. In the past, nature always healed itself after a big blow—plant and animal life came back quickly to damaged areas. Today human activities may have changed the ways in which nature can heal itself. Scientists are concerned about these changes.

They are also concerned about another kind of change: the huge number of people who have moved to coastal areas. The years ahead, scientists say, may see more and more of earth's mightiest storms roaring in from the sea and putting these people at risk.

three kinds—the red, the black, and the white. The red is the kind most people are familiar with, because much of its root system is above ground. The roots arch out, like the legs of a crab, around the trunk. They protect the land against ocean storms.

Mangroves are the start of many food chains. These trees shed leaves heavily. The leaves fall in the water, where they become food for bacteria and fungi. The bacteria and fungi are grazed, or fed on, by one-celled animals. All three are eaten by tiny crabs, shrimp, worms, insect young, and small fishes. These animals are in turn eaten by bigger ones—blue crabs, sardines, anchovies, eels, sunfish. They are also eaten by young tarpon, snook, gray snapper, spotted sea

Active Reading and Critical Thinking

Responding to Literature

PERSONAL RESPONSE

- ◆ What went through your mind as you finished reading "Hurricanes"?
- ◆ What images from this selection linger in your mind?

Analyzing Literature

RECALL

1. Why were scientists working with computer models of storms? What were they hoping to predict?
2. Where and when did Andrew come ashore?
3. Describe the path of destruction caused by Hurricane Andrew.
4. How was plant and animal life affected by the hurricane?

INTERPRET

5. Why is the path of a storm so difficult to predict? Explain.
6. Why did people awake in terror?
7. The writer states that the storm had "bulldozed" the towns of Homestead and Florida City. Why do you think the writer used this image?
8. Summarize the changes that have taken place around Everglades National Park since the hurricane.

EVALUATE AND CONNECT

9. What questions would you like to ask the writer of this selection?
10. Theme Connection   What challenges would you face if a hurricane or some other severe storm hit your community?

LITERARY ELEMENTS

Informative Nonfiction

All types of writing have a main purpose, or an objective, to achieve. A major purpose of most fiction is to entertain by telling a story. Nonfiction tells about real people, events, and places. **Informative nonfiction** is one type of nonfiction. This type of writing—for example, textbooks and magazine articles—conveys facts and information. Its main purpose is to inform readers about a topic. However, few pieces of writing are confined to a single purpose. A single article may inform, persuade, and enter-tain all at the same time, but usu-ally it will have one main purpose.

1. In your opinion, what was the writer's main purpose in writ-ing "Hurricanes"? Support your opinion with examples.

2. What secondary purpose or purposes do you observe in "Hurricanes"? Give examples.

● See **Literary Terms Handbook,** pp. R5–R6.

Literature and Writing

Writing About Literature

Summarizing   A **summary** is a brief account that contains the main ideas and only the most important details. Write a summary of what you have learned about the power of hurricanes from reading this selection. Present your summary orally to a small group, using your own words except for any direct quotations you use from the article.

Personal Writing

A Postcard Home   Imagine that you were visiting relatives in southern Florida when Hurricane Andrew struck. Write a postcard home, explaining what you witnessed and how you felt. Try to use the descriptive words you listed for the **Reading Focus** on page 305.

Extending Your Response

Literature Groups

A Natural Disaster   How would local officials respond to a natural disaster if one occurred in your area? In small groups, talk about the steps that should be taken to safeguard your community. Make a chart outlining the steps. If possible, invite a local representative from the Red Cross or the fire department to speak about the kinds of precautions that are already in place in preparation for a major emergency.

Interdisciplinary Activity

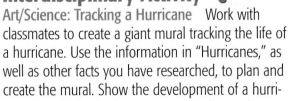

Art/Science: Tracking a Hurricane   Work with classmates to create a giant mural tracking the life of a hurricane. Use the information in "Hurricanes," as well as other facts you have researched, to plan and create the mural. Show the development of a hurricane from its beginnings at sea to its destructive path across land. Display your mural on a classroom wall or a hall bulletin board.

Learning for Life

News Broadcast   Imagine that you were part of the first group of reporters on the scene to witness Hurricane Andrew's destruction. Use the information in the selection as well as your imagination to create a news broadcast detailing the hurricane story. In small groups, work on different parts of the story, such as providing background information, following the progress of the hurricane, or interviewing disaster victims or a scientist in the Everglades. Share your broadcast with your classmates in a class presentation.

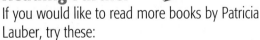

Reading Further

If you would like to read more books by Patricia Lauber, try these:

Furs, Feathers, and Flippers: How Animals Live Where They Do

Volcano: The Eruption and Healing of Mount St. Helens

An exciting novel about another kind of natural disaster—a tornado—is:

Night of the Twisters by Ivy Rickman

 Save your work for your portfolio.

Skill Minilessons

GRAMMAR AND LANGUAGE • SPELLING PLURALS

The usual way to form plurals in English is to add -s or -es. However, there are some other general rules for forming plurals.

- If the noun ends in s, sh, ch, x, or z, then add -es. (bus/buses, tax/taxes, buzz/buzzes)
- If the noun ends in a consonant + y, then change y to i and add -es. (candy/candies)
- If the noun ends in lf, then change the f to v and add -es. (calf/calves)

- If the noun ends in fe, then change the f to v and add -s. (wife/wives)

PRACTICE Write a paragraph describing the different kinds of animals found at Everglades National Park. Underline each plural noun used in your paragraph. Check that each plural form is spelled correctly.

● For more about forming plurals, see **Language Handbook,** pp. R46–R47.

READING AND THINKING • DISTINGUISHING FACT AND OPINION

A fact is something that can be proved to be true. An opinion, on the other hand, is someone's point of view about a topic.

> **Fact:** Hurricane Andrew came ashore south of Miami, Florida, in the early hours of August 24, 1992.
>
> **Opinion:** Hurricanes are scary.

When you include your opinion in a piece of writing, support it with facts and examples.

PRACTICE Reread "Hurricanes," and find two examples of facts. Then write two sentences of your own, expressing opinions about the topic of hurricanes. Share the facts and the opinions with your classmates. Write the sentences on the board, and ask classmates to tell whether each statement is a fact or an opinion.

● For more about distinguishing fact and opinion, see **Reading Handbook,** pp. R93–R94.

VOCABULARY • PREFIXES THAT EXPRESS NUMBER

Unique comes from a Latin word that means "one." Something unique is one-of-a-kind. *Unity, unite,* and *unit* come from that same Latin word. Many other words use *uni-* as a prefix meaning "one." For example, the word *uniform* means "one form."

Here are some prefixes that express number:

one	*uni-, mono-*
two	*bi-, di-*
three	*tri-*
four	*quadri-, tetra-*

PRACTICE Use the list of prefixes that express number to answer the questions. A few hints are provided.

1. What common shape is a quadrilateral? (Hint: The word *lateral* means "side.")
2. Name an animal that is a biped. (Hint: *Ped* means "foot.")
3. Write down a word that is a monosyllable.
4. Name an animal that is a tetrapod. (Hint: *Pod* also means "foot.")
5. To divide something into two parts, you bisect it. What do you do if you divide it into three parts?

Subject-Verb Agreement

The **subject** of a sentence tells who or what is doing something. The **verb** tells what the subject is doing. These two parts of a sentence must match or "agree."

Singular: A **hurricane is** a big storm.　**Plural:** **Hurricanes are** dangerous.

Problem 1　A subject is separated from the verb by an intervening phrase.

> *The hurricane, with its mighty winds, were terrifying.*

Solution　Ignore a prepositional phrase between a subject and a verb.

> *The <u>hurricane</u>, with its mighty winds, <u>was</u> terrifying.*

Problem 2　A sentence begins with *here* or *there*.

> *Here is a writer's impressions of a hurricane's power.*

Solution　The subject is never *here* or *there*. In sentences beginning with *here* or *there*, the subject always comes after the verb.

> *Here <u>are</u> a writer's <u>impressions</u> of a hurricane's power.*

Problem 3　A compound subject is joined by *or* or *nor*.

> *Neither mangrove swamps nor the food chain survive such a storm undamaged.*

Solution　If a compound subject is joined by *or* or *nor*, the verb agrees with the subject closest to it.

> *Neither mangrove swamps nor the <u>food chain</u> <u>survives</u> such a storm undamaged.*

● For more about subject-verb agreement, see **Language Handbook,** pp. R14–R15.

EXERCISES

For each sentence, write the correct form of the verb in parentheses.

1. Mountain climbers on Mount Everest (faces, face) life-and-death challenges.
2. There (is, are) frequent storms late in the climbing season.
3. Years of planning (goes, go) into such a climb.
4. Neither careful planning nor the climbers' efforts (affects, affect) the force of nature.
5. There (is, are) no choice but to give up the climb.

Writing WORKSHOP

Persuasive Writing: Editorial

You probably have strong opinions about many of the challenges that you face. When you write about your opinions, you clarify them for yourself. You may also convince others to share your opinions or spur your readers to take action.

Assignment: Follow the process explained in these pages to develop a persuasive editorial about an issue that matters to you.

● As you write your editorial, see the **Writing Handbook,** pp. R48–R53.

> ### EVALUATION RUBRIC
> By the time you complete this Writing Workshop, you will have
> - written a persuasive editorial about an issue of interest to you
> - developed an introduction that introduces your issue and includes a position statement
> - presented at least three reasons in support of your position
> - addressed potential objections to your position
> - created a conclusion that motivates your readers to take action
> - presented an editorial that is free of errors in grammar, usage, and mechanics

The Writing Process

PREWRITING

PREWRITING TIP
Try working in a group, brainstorming about different ways to complete each sentence.

● Gather Ideas

Look through your reading journal for your views on issues raised in this unit. For example, you might wish for more concern for the environment and its inhabitants or more awareness of the struggles that young people or homeless people experience. To find other ideas, try completing the following sentences:

- I really think it's unfair that . . .

- One of the most helpful things that people today can do is . . .

- I don't think many people care enough about . . .

● Focus Your Views

Filling in a pro/con chart can help you see both sides of an issue. As you look over your chart, ask yourself what underlying issue(s) your chart reveals. You might choose to explore your original issue or an underlying issue that you discover.

Issue: Whether our town should set a 10:00 P.M. curfew for young people

Pros:
- May result in fewer troublemakers on the street
- May cut back on graffiti

Cons:
- Would not affect troublemakers
- Would be unfair to good kids and their parents
- Would be hard to enforce

Underlying Issue: Getting at the real causes of crime

● Ask Yourself About Audience and Purpose

You might choose to write your persuasive editorial as a letter to a friend, as a newspaper or magazine editorial, or even as an op-ed piece for local TV. Because your purpose is to persuade, you must think carefully about your audience. Ask yourself the following questions:

- What are the ages, experience, and concerns of my audience?
- How can I best appeal to my audience?
- What facts should I give them?
- What objections might my audience raise, and how can I best respond?

● Plan Your Strategy

Sum up your opinion in a sentence. This single-sentence position statement will guide your draft. Opinions need support, so plan several supporting points that can be backed up with reliable, convincing evidence (facts, examples, statistics).

Position Statement: Setting a curfew is a bad idea.

Point 1: A curfew would not affect troublemakers.

Evidence ⟶ Fact: Older teens and adults cause more crime than young people.

Point 2: There are few teenagers out on the streets after 10:00 P.M.

Evidence ⟶ Statistics (poll of my English class): None of us are allowed to stay out late.

Point 3: A curfew would be hard for the police to enforce.

Evidence ⟶ Example: The police would have to guess kids' ages.

Writing WORKSHOP

DRAFTING

DRAFTING TIP
Don't ignore valid objections that your audience might raise. Acknowledge them. Then offer reasonable responses.

● Start Your Draft

Try opening with a question or a description that alerts your audience to your issue. For clarity, put a version of your position statement in this first paragraph.

● Follow Through

With your prewriting notes for reference, write at least one paragraph about each supporting point. Include your evidence.

STUDENT MODEL · DRAFTING

I don't know anyone my age who is allowed to be out late at night. Our parents already set curfews for us. In fact, we took a poll in my English class about how late our parents let us stay out, and not one of the twenty-three students polled was allowed out alone after 9:30.

Complete Student Model on pp. R106–R107.

REVISING

REVISING TIP
To avoid generalizing, consider adding qualifiers—words such as *often, seldom, sometimes, few, many,* or *most.*

● Plan Improvements

Take a break. After a few hours, reread your draft. Mark places where you could make improvements, such as clarifying a point or providing stronger evidence.

Use the **Rubric for Revising** as a guide for revising your draft. If you wish, read your editorial aloud to someone who disagrees with you. This will test its persuasive power.

RUBRIC FOR REVISING

Your revised persuasive editorial should have
- an introduction that clearly states the issue and your position on it
- a body that consists of at least three logical supporting points
- reliable evidence to support each point
- reasonable responses to objections that your readers might raise
- a motivating conclusion

Your revised persuasive editorial should be free of
- overgeneralizations
- errors in grammar, usage, and mechanics

EDITING/PROOFREADING

When you finish revising, go over your draft once more to correct errors in grammar, usage, and mechanics. Use the **Proofreading Checklist**.

Grammar Hint

One way to fix a run-on sentence is to use a semicolon between the two main clauses.

A curfew wouldn't stop troublemakers; they would just find a way around it.

PROOFREADING CHECKLIST

☑ There are no sentence fragments or run-on sentences.

☑ Verb forms are correct, and verb tenses are consistent.

☑ Verbs agree with their subjects.

☑ Comparative forms of modifiers are correct.

☑ Commas, semicolons, and end marks are used correctly.

☑ All words are spelled correctly.

STUDENT MODEL · EDITING/PROOFREADING

I would never say that graffiti isn't a problem, it is.

Complete Student Model on pp. R106–107.

Complete Student Model

For a complete version of the model developed in this Workshop, see **Writing Workshop Models**, pp. R106–R107.

PUBLISHING/PRESENTING

Consider submitting your editorial, letter to the editor, or op-ed piece to your school or local newspaper. As an alternative, you may wish to audiotape or videotape your persuasive editorial. Working with friends, prepare a taped "commentary session" that presents several opinion pieces and play it for your class.

TECHNOLOGY TIP
With desktop publishing software, you can design, lay out, and print your opinion piece in a newspaper format.

Reflecting

- What grade would you give yourself on this piece of writing? Why does your work merit that grade?

- What other topic might you address in a persuasive piece? How might your writing process differ from the process you followed this time?

📖 **Save your work for your portfolio.**

Theme Assessment

Responding to the Theme

1. Which piece of fiction, nonfiction, or poetry in this theme most helped you think about how facing challenges can be a powerful experience? Explain your answer.

2. As a result of your reading in this unit, what new thoughts do you have about the following?
   - the kinds of challenges people face in their everyday lives
   - people's feelings and thoughts about facing those challenges
   - the importance of seeing challenge as a necessary part of life

3. Present your theme project to the class.

Analyzing Literature

COMPARE NONFICTION

Compare two pieces of nonfiction writing from this theme. Use examples and quotes from the selections to support your opinions.

Evaluate and Set Goals

1. Which of the following was most rewarding to you? Which was most difficult?
   - reading and thinking about the fiction, nonfiction, and poetry
   - doing independent writing
   - analyzing the selections in discussions
   - making presentations
   - doing research

2. Using the following scale, how would you assess your work in this theme? Give at least two reasons for your assessment.
   4 = outstanding   2 = fair
   3 = good   1 = weak

3. Based on what you found difficult in this theme, choose a goal to work toward in the next theme.
   - Write down your goal and three steps you will take to reach it.
   - Meet with your teacher to review your goal and your plan for achieving it.

Build Your Portfolio

SELECT

Select two pieces of work you did during this theme to include in your portfolio. Use the following questions to help you decide.

- Which work do you think is your best work?
- From which work did you learn the most?
- Which work "stretched" you the most?
- Which work did you enjoy the most?

REFLECT

Write some notes to accompany the work you selected. Use the following questions to guide you.

- What do you like best about the piece?
- What did you learn from creating it?
- What might you do differently if you were beginning this piece again?

Reading on Your Own

Have you liked reading the stories and poems in this theme?
If you have, here are some other books you might enjoy.

Where the Red Fern Grows
by Wilson Rawls
This story of a young boy living in the Oklahoma Ozarks and the pair of hunting dogs he trains has become a favorite with young readers.

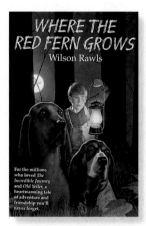

Hostage
by Edward Myers
Alyssa and Rob must use their wits and survival techniques after a fossil thief takes them hostage on a trek through the Utah desert.

Reach Higher
by Scottie Pippen Pippen tells about his life and the challenges he faced to become an NBA champion with the Chicago Bulls. The title describes his advice to his young readers.

The Outsiders
by S. E. Hinton Fourteen-year-old Ponyboy is proud to be a "greaser," until a friend kills a member of a rival gang and starts a chain of events that causes him to question his outsider status.

Standardized Test Practice

Read the sentences in each numbered item. Choose the sentence that DOES NOT have a mistake in sentence structure.

1 A Badly I played the piano at the recital.
   B I played the piano badly at the recital.
   C At the recital, I badly played the piano.
   D I badly played the piano at the recital.

2 J When you finish eating the cereal, put it away.
   K Put it away, when the cereal is finished being eaten by you.
   L When you finished putting away the cereal, it is eaten.
   M When the cereal is finished being eaten by you, put it away.

3 A Liking to play fetch, the dog over there.
   B The dog over there likes to play fetch.
   C There is a dog over there, it likes to play fetch.
   D The dog over there. It likes to play fetch.

4 J Herbert wants to go. Outside it is really nice out today.
   K Herbert wants to go outside because it was really nice out today.
   L Herbert wants to go outside. It is really nice out today.
   M Herbert wants to go outside, it is really nice out today.

5 A In puddles I like to jump on rainy days.
   B I like to jump on rainy days in puddles.
   C On rainy days, in puddles I like to jump.
   D I like to jump in puddles on rainy days.

6 J The flashlight helped Juan find his way in the dark.
   K The flashlight in the dark helping Juan find his way.
   L In the dark helping Juan find his way was the flashlight.
   M In the dark the flashlight helped Juan find his way.

Read the sentences in each numbered item and look at the underlined words. The underlined words in each sentence may contain a mistake in word usage. Find the sentence in which the underlined words have CORRECT word usage.

7   A   The flowers will soon <u>lose her</u> petals.
     B   The flowers will soon <u>lose their</u> petals.
     C   The flowers will soon <u>lose his</u> petals.
     D   The flowers will soon <u>lose its</u> petals.

8   J   Sheila <u>likes to mowing</u> the grass.
     K   Sheila <u>likes mow</u> the grass.
     L   Sheila <u>likes to mowed</u> the grass.
     M   Sheila <u>likes to mow</u> the grass.

9   A   The <u>burning, hot coals</u> cooked the meat.
     B   The <u>burned, hot coals</u> cooked the meat.
     C   The <u>burning, hotting coals</u> cooked the meat.
     D   The <u>burn, hot coals</u> cooked the meat.

10   J   After we left the house, <u>we are going</u> to the dentist.
     K   After we left the house, <u>we go</u> to the dentist.
     L   After we left the house, <u>we went</u> to the dentist.
     M   After we left the house, <u>we will go</u> to the dentist.

11   A   Brian spends a lot of time <u>at their grandfather's</u> house.
     B   Brian spends a lot of time <u>at his grandfather's</u> house.
     C   Brian spends a lot of time <u>at its grandfather's</u> house.
     D   Brian spends a lot of time <u>at him grandfather's</u> house.

12   J   The movie <u>I will see last night</u> was great.
     K   The movie <u>I seen last night</u> was great.
     L   The movie <u>I saw last night</u> was great.
     M   The movie <u>I see last night</u> was great.

Where the Heart Is

66 *Home is where one starts from.* 99

—*T. S. Eliot*

Lugar Natal, 1989. Eduardo Kingman. Oil on canvas, 40 x 53 in. Inter-American Development Bank Art Collection, Washington, D.C. Reproduced by permission of the IDB.

THEME
4

THEME CONTENTS

GENRE FOCUS ESSAY

Exploring the Theme

Where the Heart Is

What would life be like without the love of your family and friends? How would you feel without the warmth and security of a place called home? In the stories, poems, and essays in this theme, you will meet characters who face these questions. To begin your own thinking about the theme, try one of the options below.

Starting Points

HOME IS WHERE THE HEART IS

Do you ever feel like the pair of birds in the cartoon—staying home with your family and doing something fun, like playing a game or baking something delicious?

- Brainstorm a list of things that you enjoy doing at home. Then, as a class, create a "top ten" list of favorite things to do at home.

WITHIN YOUR OWN HEART

Think about the people and places that are most important to you.

- What do you love most about your family members and friends? What makes your home special to you? Write a few notes about your feelings.

"I don't feel like going out. Why don't just the two of us stay in and open a can of worms?"

Theme Projects

As you read the selections in this theme, try your hand at one of the projects below. Work on your own, with a partner, or with a group.

CRITICAL VIEWING
Families in Books and on Screen

1. Keep a journal about how families are portrayed in your favorite books and on your favorite television shows. How do the average fictional families look and act? What conclusions can you draw from your observations?

2. Organize your findings in a chart. Choose headings to represent the various categories of behavior you have found. You can use drawings or pictures from old magazines and newspapers to illustrate your chart.

interNET
CONNECTION

To learn more about many of the authors in this and other themes, type an author's name into a search engine. For links relating to the selections, practice exercises, games, and more, visit the Glencoe Literature site at lit.glencoe.com.

LEARNING FOR LIFE
Writing a Policy Statement

Some of the characters in this unit are fortunate enough to speak two languages—the language of their parents' native country and English. In today's global economy, the ability to speak more than one language has great advantages.

1. Develop a policy statement for the establishment of a school-wide second-language program that would begin in kindergarten. Start with your own ideas about why knowing more than one language is important.

2. Draft a series of questions to obtain the information you want. Then gather information from teachers, bilingual students, librarians, and your family. Draft your policy statement and share it with the class.

MULTIMEDIA PROJECT
Homes Around the World

1. Gather data about the different kinds of homes people live in around the world. The **Interdisciplinary Connection** on page 332 shows some examples; see what others you can find. Look for information about architecture, life in other countries, and traditional cultures on the Web and in books and magazines.

2. Choose a kind of housing that interests you. Consider how it differs from the housing you are familiar with in such matters as size, architectural style, and building materials.

3. Build a model or draw pictures and diagrams of your chosen house. Present your finished project to the class.

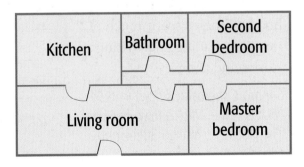

Before You Read

Bums in the Attic

MEET SANDRA CISNEROS

Sandra Cisneros (sis nā′ rōs′) was born in Chicago, the only daughter in a family with seven children. Her family frequently moved between the United States and Mexico because of her father's homesickness for Mexico. As a result, Cisneros often felt lonely and unsettled. "Because we moved so much," Cisneros said, ". . . I retreated inside myself." Throughout her childhood, Cisneros spent much of her time reading and writing stories and poems.

Sandra Cisneros was born in 1954. "Bums in the Attic" is from her book The House on Mango Street, *published in 1983.*

READING FOCUS

What are your dreams for the future? What will you do? Where will you live—in a house, in an apartment, on a farm?

QuickWrite

Describe in a few sentences how and where you imagine yourself living in the future.

Setting a Purpose

Read to find out what dream for the future is expressed in this selection.

BUILDING BACKGROUND

The Time and Place   This selection is set in our time in Chicago, Illinois.

Did You Know?   Organized in a series of vignettes, or brief scenes, *The House on Mango Street* tells the story of Esperanza Cordero, a young girl growing up in Chicago, who longs for a room of her own and a house of which she can be proud. When asked about her style of writing in *The House on Mango Street,* Sandra Cisneros commented, "I wanted to write stories that were a cross between poetry and fiction. . . . [I] wanted to write a collection which could be read at any random point without having any knowledge of what came before or after. Or, that could be read in a series to tell one big story."

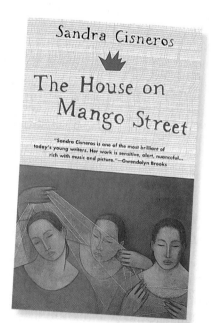

Sandra Cisneros

The House on Mango Street

"Sandra Cisneros is one of the most brilliant of today's young writers. Her work is sensitive, alert, nuanceful... rich with music and picture."—Gwendolyn Brooks

Bums in the Attic

Sandra Cisneros

I want a house on a hill like the ones with the gardens where Papa works. We go on Sundays, Papa's day off. I used to go. I don't anymore. You don't like to go out with us, Papa says. Getting too old? Getting too stuck-up, says Nenny. I don't tell them I am ashamed—all of us staring out the window like the hungry. I am tired of looking at what we can't have. When we win the lottery . . . Mama begins, and then I stop listening.

People who live on hills sleep so close to the stars they forget those of us who live too much on earth. They don't look down at all except to be content to live on hills. They have nothing to do with last week's garbage or fear of rats. Night comes. Nothing wakes them but the wind.

One day I'll own my own house, but I won't forget who I am or where I came from. Passing bums will ask, Can I come in? I'll offer them the attic, ask them to stay, because I know how it is to be without a house.

Some days after dinner, guests and I will sit in front of a fire. Floorboards will squeak upstairs. The attic grumble.

Rats? they'll ask.

Bums, I'll say, and I'll be happy.

Responding to Literature

PERSONAL RESPONSE

- ◆ What do you think about the narrator's hopes and dreams for the future?
- ◆ Think back to your QuickWrite for the **Reading Focus** on page 328. How do your dreams for the future compare to the thoughts and feelings described in this selection? Write your response in your journal.

Analyzing Literature

RECALL

1. What does the narrator's family do on Sundays? Why doesn't the narrator go anymore?
2. According to the narrator, why do the people in the houses on the hill forget about other people?
3. What does the narrator intend to own when she grows up?
4. Describe how bums will end up in the narrator's attic.

INTERPRET

5. What is the narrator's attitude toward her family's Sunday activity? Why?
6. How does the narrator feel about the people who live on the hill? Explain.
7. What does the narrator mean when she says, "I won't forget who I am or where I came from"? Use quotations from the story to support your ideas.
8. How do you imagine the narrator will feel when she tells her guests that she has bums in the attic?

EVALUATE AND CONNECT

9. The **theme** of a piece of writing is the message that the writer hopes to communicate. What is the theme of this selection? Explain why you think so.
10. Do you think the narrator knows how it feels to be homeless, like the bums she mentions in her writing? Explain.

LITERARY ELEMENTS

First-Person Point of View

In a story, a book, or an essay, the **point of view** is the relationship of the narrator, or storyteller, to the story. In a story with **first-person point of view,** the story is always told by one of the characters, who refers to himself or herself as "I." All information about the story must come from this character. Readers can only know what this character knows and can only feel what this character feels. "Bums in the Attic" is an example of writing told from a first-person point of view.

1. Why do you think Cisneros wrote "Bums in the Attic" from a first-person point of view?

2. How would this piece be different if it were told from a third-person point of view? (See page 157.) Explain.

● See **Literary Terms Handbook,** p. R8.

Extending Your Response

Writing About Literature

Analyzing Style   How would you describe the writer's style in this piece of writing? How does Cisneros create a response in her readers to the idea of bums in an attic? Does she use humor? Realism? Emotional situations? Write a paragraph explaining how Cisneros weaves together a style that makes her story effective. Support your conclusions with examples.

Creative Writing

Changing Point of View   How would this selection be different if another character had narrated it? Choose a different character: Papa, Nenny, Mama, or one of the bums. Write a journal entry from the point of view of that person. Tell about the character's life and dreams for the future. Make up any details you wish.

Literature Groups

Home Is Where the Heart Is   In a small group discussion, compare the details about the narrator's present life with her dreams for the future. How does the narrator hope her life will change? How does she intend to hang on to her identity? Do you think the narrator will one day live in a house on the hill? Why or why not? Support your ideas with details and quotations.

Art Activity

The House on the Hill   Work with classmates to create a large floor plan of the house on the hill. Before drawing the house, make a list of all the necessary details, such as the fireplace, the garden, and the attic. Use your imagination for details the selection does not include. Display your plan.

Save your work for your portfolio.

Skill Minilesson

GRAMMAR AND LANGUAGE • PRONOUN-ANTECEDENT AGREEMENT

A **pronoun** is a word used in place of a noun or noun phrase. An **antecedent** is the word or words the pronoun refers to. A pronoun and its antecedent must agree in number and gender.

Mario brought his mother flowers. *She* was pleased with *them.*

She, a singular feminine pronoun, refers to *mother. Them,* a plural neuter (neither masculine nor feminine) pronoun, refers to *flowers.*

PRACTICE   Write the appropriate pronoun for each numbered blank. After the pronoun, write its antecedent.

Sandra Cisneros wrote *The House on Mango Street* when (1) _____ was in her twenties. "Bums in the Attic" is from (2) _____ book. (3) _____ is one of a number of short pieces that make up the book. Each of these brief vignettes can stand on (4) _____ own, but together, Cisneros says, (5) _____ "tell one big story."

● For more about pronoun-antecedent agreement, see **Language Handbook,** p. R17.

Architecture

No matter how similar the floor plans, no two homes are ever *exactly* the same. Throughout the world, the technology and design used in home construction varies greatly. However, all people build homes for the same reason: to feel comfortable and safe.

In Zimbabwe, villagers use wood, grass, or dried mud to construct a hut with circular walls. Inside, the hut remains cool and dry because of its thatched grass or corrugated metal roof. Zimbabweans build their huts close together to create a village.

Mexican villagers often build their own houses, too, shaping and drying clay into adobe bricks. The villagers typically whitewash their houses to deflect the hot sun. Sometimes colorful tiles add decoration to the roof or around windows and over the door frame.

Traditional Japanese houses use latticed paper walls to divide the living space into rooms. These sliding screens can be easily rearranged to add more space or to let summer breezes in. At night, the family unrolls futons onto woven grass mats (*tatami*) that cover the floor, and the rooms convert to bedrooms.

In Mongolia, nomadic families live in portable homes, similar to tents. This type of house, called a *yurt,* looks simple, but underneath its felt walls, a complex wooden frame keeps the structure from collapsing in desert winds. The family adds carpets and furniture to the single room to make it cozy.

ACTIVITY

With a partner or a group, research one of the home styles mentioned above or another style. Use both library and Internet sources. Put together an illustrated oral report on that style of housing.

Before You Read

En un Barrio de Los Angeles /
In a Neighborhood in Los Angeles

MEET FRANCISCO X. ALARCÓN

F rancisco X. Alarcón
(al är kōn') arrived in this
country from Mexico with
only five dollars in his pocket.
After working as a dishwasher
and a migrant laborer, he
began taking classes in an
adult-education program in
Los Angeles. By the time he
had completed his education,
Alarcón had received three
college degrees. Today, as a
poet, a professor, and a performer, Alarcón's mission is to
bring his poetry to the widest
possible audience.

*Francisco X. Alarcón was born in
1954. This poem comes from his
collection of poems* Body in Flames,
published in 1990.

READING FOCUS

Think of a family member you love. What is special about your
relationship with this person?

Sharing Ideas
Jot down a list of things you love about this person. Share
your list with your classmates.

Setting a Purpose
Read the poem to discover how the speaker feels about his
grandmother and why he feels that way.

BUILDING BACKGROUND

The Language of the Poem   "In a Neighborhood in Los
Angeles" was originally written in Spanish. It was then translated into English. Both versions are presented here. If you or
one of your classmates can read Spanish, read "En un Barrio
de Los Angeles" aloud so that you can hear how it sounds in
the original language.

Spanish-Speaking Californians   Francisco X. Alarcón
came to Los Angeles from Mexico. Spanish-speaking people,
however, have been in California for a long time. Seven years
before thirteen British colonies declared themselves the United
States of America, Spanish missionaries founded the first of
twenty-one missions they would build in California between
1769 and 1823. One of them was located in what is now Los
Angeles. The Spanish also built a number of presidios—military
posts—in California. When Mexico won its independence from
Spain in 1821, California became part of Mexico. California
didn't belong to the United States until the middle 1800s.

En un Barrio de Los Angeles

In a Neighborhood in Los Angeles

Francisco X. Alarcón ～
Translated by Francisco Aragon

el español	I learned
lo aprendí	Spanish
de mi abuela	from my grandma
mijito	*mijito*°
5 no llores	5 don't cry
me decía	she'd tell me
en las mañanas	on the mornings
cuando salían	my parents
mis padres	would leave
10 a trabajar	10 to work
en las canerías	at the fish
de pescado	canneries
mi abuela	my grandma
platicaba	would chat
15 con las sillas	15 with chairs
les cantaba	sing them
canciones	old
antiguas	songs
les bailaba	dance
20 valses en	20 waltzes with them
la cocina	in the kitchen

----
4 *Mijito* (mē hē′ tō) means "my little child."

cuando decía
niño barrigón
se reía

25 con mi abuela
aprendí
a contar nubes

a reconocer
en las macetas
30 la yerbabuena

mi abuela
llevaba lunas
en el vestido

la montaña
35 el desierto
el mar de México

en sus ojos
yo las veía
en sus trenzas

40 yo los tocaba
con su voz
yo los olía

un día
me dijeron:
45 se fue muy lejos

pero yo aún
la siento
conmigo

diciéndome
50 quedito al oído
mijito

---

when she'd say
niño barrigón°
she'd laugh

25 with my grandma
I learned
to count clouds

to point out
in flowerpots
30 mint leaves

my grandma
wore moons
on her dress

Mexico's mountains
35 deserts
ocean

in her eyes
I'd see them
in her braids

40 I'd touch them
in her voice
smell them

one day
I was told:
45 she went far away

but still
I feel her
with me

whispering
50 in my ear
mijito

---

23 The grandmother was teasing the speaker by
calling him niño barrigón (nēn′ yō   bär′ rē gōn′),
which means "big-bellied boy."

Responding to Literature

PERSONAL RESPONSE

◆ What images from the poem linger in your mind?

Analyzing Literature

RECALL

1. Why did the speaker spend so much time with his grandmother as a child?

2. What are some special memories of his grandmother that the speaker shares with his readers?

INTERPRET

3. Do you think the speaker enjoyed being with his grandmother? Why or why not?

4. What does the speaker tell us in the last three stanzas of the poem?

EVALUATE AND CONNECT

5. How well does the poet succeed in making the grandmother in this poem seem real to you? Explain.

6. Do any of the details in this poem remind you of experiences you have had with a grandparent or another older relative? Explain.

7. What message about human relationships does this poem express? Use words from the poem to support your opinion.

8. Describe the special role the grandmother played in the speaker's life.

9. A good translator tries to put the style, meaning, and feeling of the original work into a different language. If you are bilingual in Spanish and English or can find someone who can translate each Spanish word of "En un Barrio de Los Angeles" for you, compare the two versions of the poem. Do both versions create the same feeling? Why or why not?

10. **Theme Connection**   Think of someone you know who would enjoy reading this poem. Why would he or she enjoy it?

LITERARY ELEMENTS

Imagery

Imagery is language that creates vivid pictures and sensory impressions. Poets use words and phrases to create images that appeal to readers' senses. For example, in the poem "In a Neighborhood in Los Angeles," the poet uses several sensory images so that readers can visualize clearly the grandmother in the poem: "my grandma / would chat / with chairs / sing them / old / songs / dance / waltzes with them / in the kitchen." For readers, being able to "see" the grandmother talking, singing, and dancing with chairs leaves a wonderful sensory impression.

1. Pick out your favorite example of imagery in the poem and explain why you like it.

2. Select an especially effective image from another poem in this book and describe how details helped you to visualize the image.

● See **Literary Terms Handbook,** p. R5.

Extending Your Response

Writing About Literature

Character Sketch In this poem, the speaker describes his grandmother and the special relationship he shared with her. Write a paragraph describing how you picture the grandmother.

Creative Writing

Poem Write a short poem about a person who is, or was, important in your life. As a starting point, you may want to look back at the list you created in the **Reading Focus** on page 333. Use vivid images to describe the special nature of the relationship you and this person have shared together.

Performing

Tableau Select a dramatic moment from this poem. With a partner, create a tableau of that moment by getting into, freezing, and holding the exact pose of the characters in that scene. Choose a third person to tap each character one at a time. As each character is tapped, that person comes to life and speaks and acts just as that character would in the poem.

Literature Groups

Vivid Descriptions To the speaker of "In a Neighborhood in Los Angeles," time spent with his grandmother was an unforgettable part of his childhood. Pick out one or more descriptions that focus on the special nature of the speaker's relationship with his grandmother. Discuss how the descriptions explain the importance of the relationship. Then talk about the ways in which older people can be important in the lives of young people.

Reading Further

For more poetry, try these books:

Imaginary Gardens: American Poetry and Art for Young People edited by Charles Sullivan

Tortillitas Para Mamma: and Other Spanish Nursery Rhymes by Margot C. Griego

For biographies of some important Mexican Americans, try:

Famous Mexican Americans by Clarke Newlon

Cesar Chavez by Ruth Franchere

Save your work for your portfolio.

Skill Minilesson

READING AND THINKING • DRAWING CONCLUSIONS

As a skillful reader, you should always ask questions about what you read. Evaluate the characters, actions, and events. By using the details and the information in a piece of writing, you can draw conclusions that will help you understand the story or the poem.

- For more about drawing conclusions, see **Reading Handbook,** pp. R92–R93.

PRACTICE Reread "In a Neighborhood in Los Angeles." As you do, pay attention to the details and images that Alarcón includes about the speaker's special experiences with his grandmother. In a short paragraph, use the clues in the poem to draw your own conclusions about the speaker's feelings about his grandmother's death.

Technology Skills

Internet: Judging Online Information

It's sometimes difficult to distinguish fact from opinion. A fact is a statement that can be supported by evidence. An opinion, on the other hand, represents a personal viewpoint, one that really can't be proved. When an opinion is stated strongly, it might be hard to recognize it for what it is: only one point of view.

Because the Internet is based on the free exchange of ideas, anyone can write and publish anything. It's up to you to decide whether a posting is fact or opinion. Remember: something isn't true just because you read about it on the Internet.

Fact or Opinion?

With a partner, decide which of the following statements are facts and which are opinions. How can you tell? Discuss your answers with the rest of the class.

1. Chickadee Net is a fun place for kids.
2. Owl Kids Online won the 1997 Internet Impact Award.
3. There will be 20.9 million kids online by the year 2002.
4. Kids go online to learn and have fun.
5. As the Internet becomes more user-friendly and accessible to the public at large, the number of schools and homes going online continues to grow.
6. SafeTeens.com is a site dedicated to keeping teens safe in cyberspace.
7. As of today, less than one percent of kids access the Internet from school.
8. The Internet can be viewed as one giant encyclopedia, but one important difference is obvious: the bulk of the Internet is written by unreliable sources.
9. The *Cool Site of the Day* crew selects an outstanding Web site each day of the year.
10. This slick Webzine with neon-bright, pop-art graphics dishes the best daily buzz about the alternative-music scene.

How Can You Tell?

One way to determine whether something you read on the Internet is true is to look for the name of the author. Is it someone whose name you recognize as an authority on the topic? An article about the movies written by a well-known movie reviewer, for example, is more believable than one written by someone you've never heard of. (Remember, however, that people you've never heard of may be experts in their fields.)

Another clue lies in the site's host. Information found at university or government sites can often be verified, whereas statements posted on Internet service providers may be difficult to confirm. You can tell a university sponsors a site because the URL (Net address) ends with an *.edu* extension. Similarly, government sites end with *.gov.* Of course, just because something is posted from a college's Web site doesn't automatically make it true.

You can also determine the truthfulness of a posting if statements are backed up with sources. Sources may be noted directly in the text, in parentheses, or in hyperlinks. If the reference is hyperlinked, you can go to the original document to see for yourself whether the statement is a fact.

In many cases, time may be a factor in determining how accurate something is. An article about the current state of the Internet, for example, wouldn't be very reliable if it was posted three years ago. Look for information about when the document was published or last revised. (Such information, if it's given, usually comes at the beginning or the end of a site's home page.)

In many cases, you will have to rely on your own judgment. As you examine information on the Web, always ask yourself: Is this a fact or an opinion? Don't be misled because you agree totally with what an author says. Sharing an author's opinion doesn't make that opinion a fact.

On the other hand, don't think that a Web document is useless just because it contains someone's opinions. Very often, opinions are just what you want. You read editorials and essays for their authors' opinions. Reviews of books, movies, plays, and CDs can help you decide whether to spend your time and money on something. It's when opinions are based on faulty reasoning or prejudice that we need to mistrust them.

Practice

1. Log on to the World Wide Web.

2. Browse through at least five sites that interest you. Look for examples of fact and opinion.

3. For each site, determine how believable the information offered is. Write down the name and URL of the site and the criteria you used to determine whether it is trustworthy.

4. Share your findings in a class-wide discussion.

TECHNOLOGY TIP

A good way to avoid misinformation on the Internet is to keep the addresses of sites you've found trustworthy in your favorites (or bookmarks) folder. Here are a few sites you might find useful. For news, try *CNN* (www.cnn.com) and Yahooligans! News (www.yahooligans.com/content/news). For science topics, visit Discovery News Online (www.discovery. com/online). The National Geographic site (www. nationalgeographic.com) is useful for science and social studies topics. ESPN Sports Zone (espn.go. com) is excellent for sports news. Some of these sites also include fun activities or games.

ACTIVITIES

1. Start a class list of sites divided into *Mostly Fact* and *Mostly Opinion* categories. Add to the list as you discover new sites.

2. In your journal, keep a list of questionable "facts" you find on the Internet.

3. Write a letter to the editor of your school newspaper or to a Web site that accepts student contributions. In your letter, emphasize the importance of not believing everything you read. Include examples from your own research.

Before You Read

The Courage That My Mother Had and Mother to Son

MEET EDNA ST. VINCENT MILLAY

Edna St. Vincent Millay dreamed of becoming a pianist, but the Pulitzer Prize–winning poet focused her energies on writing. Millay wrote not only poetry, but also dramatic works, and even librettos for operas.

Edna St. Vincent Millay was born in Maine in 1892 and died in New York in 1950.

MEET LANGSTON HUGHES

During his career, Langston Hughes worked as a cook, busboy, seaman, reporter, and teacher. He produced poetry, novels, collections of short stories, works of nonfiction, plays, and nine children's books.

Langston Hughes was born in Joplin, Missouri, in 1902. He died in 1967 in New York City. "Mother to Son" appeared in his 1932 book The Dream Keeper and Other Poems.

READING FOCUS

What important kinds of nonmaterial "gifts," such as love and confidence, do parents try to give to their children?

Sharing Ideas

In small groups, talk about the many nonmaterial gifts that parents give to their children. Put together a list of these gifts. Why are they important?

Setting a Purpose

Reading these poems might help you to discover the kinds of gifts parents can give their children.

BUILDING BACKGROUND

Did You Know?   Edna St. Vincent Millay and Langston Hughes shared some interesting similarities in their lives. Both came from single-parent homes. Both began writing poetry early. Millay saw her first verses published at age fourteen. Hughes had poems published in his high school's monthly magazine. Each later published one poem that made the critics take notice. Millay's breakthrough came with "Renascence," which she entered in a poetry contest at age twenty. Hughes began attracting attention after publishing "The Negro Speaks of Rivers" at age nineteen.

Each poet attended college, traveled a great deal overseas, lived for a time in Paris, and settled in New York City—Millay downtown in Greenwich Village, Hughes uptown in Harlem. Both were interested in the theater. Millay wrote a verse play and joined a theater company as an actress. Hughes wrote a play that had a successful run on Broadway. Both poets also wrote texts for operas.

In addition, the two poets worked all their adult lives for causes that were important to them—Millay for women's rights and Hughes for the rights of African Americans.

The Courage That My Mother Had

Edna St. Vincent Millay

The courage that my mother had
Went with her, and is with her still:
Rock from New England quarried;°
Now granite in a granite hill.

5   The golden brooch° my mother wore
She left behind for me to wear;
I have no thing I treasure more:
Yet, it is something I could spare.

Oh, if instead she'd left to me
10   The thing she took into the grave!—
That courage like a rock, which she
Has no more need of, and I have.

3 **quarry:** to cut or blast rock from the earth for use in construction.

5 **brooch:** a piece of jewelry fastened by a clasp; an ornamental pin worn on clothing.

The Way It Is (detail). GG Kopilak. Private collection. Do you think the artist has captured in this woman's face the quality that Millay speaks of in her poem? Why or why not?

Mother to Son

Langston Hughes

Well, son, I'll tell you:
Life for me ain't been no crystal stair.
It's had tacks in it,
And splinters,
5 And boards torn up,
And places with no carpet on the floor—
Bare.
But all the time
I'se been a-climbin' on,
10 And reachin' landin's,
And turnin' corners,
And sometimes goin' in the dark
Where there ain't been no light.
So, boy, don't you turn back.
15 Don't you set down on the steps
'Cause you finds it kinder hard.
Don't you fall now—
For I'se still goin', honey,
I'se still climbin',
20 And life for me ain't been no crystal stair.

Survivor, 1978. Elizabeth Catlett. Linocut, 10⅞ x 9⅞ in. Armistad Research Center, Tulane University, New Orleans.

Responding to Literature

PERSONAL RESPONSE

◆ Which lines from each poem did you find most memorable? Why?

Analyzing Literature

RECALL

1. In "The Courage That My Mother Had," what did the mother leave the speaker of the poem when the mother died?
2. What does the speaker of "The Courage That My Mother Had" wish she had inherited? Why?
3. What advice does the speaker give her son in "Mother to Son"?

INTERPRET

4. What two unlike things are compared in "The Courage That My Mother Had"?
5. To what does the mother in "Mother to Son" compare her life?
6. What is the **theme** of "Mother to Son"?

EVALUATE AND CONNECT

7. How can parents leave their children gifts such as courage or confidence?
8. How are the mothers in the two poems alike?

LITERARY ELEMENTS

Figurative Language

Figurative language is imaginative language used by writers for descriptive effect. Instances of figurative language are called figures of speech. An **analogy** is a figure of speech in which two unlike things are compared on the basis of some characteristic they share. Similes and metaphors are types of analogies often used in literature. A **simile** uses the words *like* or *as* to compare two things. Have you ever heard someone described as being "pretty as a picture"? That's a simile. In a **metaphor,** one thing is described as if it *were* another. "This test is a breeze" is a metaphor.

1. Find an example of a simile in either poem. Explain what two things are being compared and why.

2. Find an example of a metaphor in either poem. What two things are being compared? How does the metaphor enrich the poem?

● See **Literary Terms Handbook,** pp. R1 and R4.

Extending Your Response

Literature Groups

Dad's Turn   Suppose these two poems had been called "The Courage That My Father Had" or "Father to Son." How would these poems be similar to or different from the poems you just read? Talk about the reasons for any similarities and differences you suggest.

Writing About Literature

Poetry and Ideas   Mothers play an important role in both poems. These poets believe that parents give their children many things besides shelter, food, and clothing. Do you agree or disagree? What do children hope to learn from their parents? Review your list from the **Reading Focus** on page 340. Use examples from the poems to support your ideas.

Listening and Speaking

Appreciating Poetry   Most poetry should be read aloud to be fully appreciated. As a poem is read, listeners may close their eyes, picture the images, and hear the natural rhythm of the lines. With a partner, take turns reading these poems to each other.

Creative Writing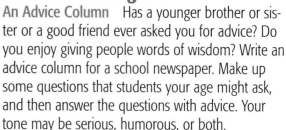

An Advice Column   Has a younger brother or sister or a good friend ever asked you for advice? Do you enjoy giving people words of wisdom? Write an advice column for a school newspaper. Make up some questions that students your age might ask, and then answer the questions with advice. Your tone may be serious, humorous, or both.

Reading Further

If you would like to read more by these poets, try these books:

The Block: Poems and *Black Misery* by Langston Hughes

Collected Sonnets of Edna St. Vincent Millay

Other books of poetry you might enjoy are:

Rainbows Are Made: Poems by Carl Sandburg

The Covered Bridge House and Other Poems by Kay Starbird

📖 **Save your work for your portfolio.**

Skill Minilesson

READING AND THINKING • VISUALIZING

When you read or listen to a poem, remember to form pictures in your mind. Pay attention to the wide range of details in the poem, and make each detail a part of your sensory experience of the poem. Keep asking yourself:

• How does this (person, place, thing) look?
• What sounds does this poem make me think of?
• How does this detail feel, smell, or taste?

PRACTICE Reread each of the poems. As you do, try to visualize the different images in each poem. Draw a sketch that shows an important image in each poem. Then write a paragraph explaining why you chose those two images.

● For more about visualizing, see **Reading Handbook,** pp. R87–R88.

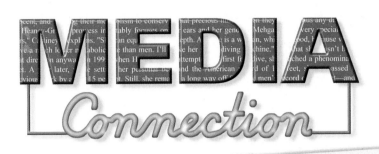

NEWSPAPER STORY

What happens when you take a city person to the country? Sometimes, as you'll discover in this news story, the person will learn something that can be useful back in the city.

Kids from Chicago's Cabrini Green Learn Urban Farming in Arkansas

by Paisley Dodds—Associated Press, Tuesday, August 19, 1997

PERRYVILLE, Ark.—No overalls or straw hats in this crowd.

Fresh from Chicago's Cabrini Green housing complex and another development in Milwaukee, a dozen kids are visiting Arkansas to learn how to become inner-city farmers.

Growing cucumbers may keep 16-year-old Helen Marshbanks from joining a gang. Raising catfish under an apartment window sill may put more food on the table for the family of 14-year-old Darius Moore.

For 19-year-old Eric Brown, urban farming is a "cool" complement to playing basketball and watching television. "I want to be a writer when I grow up," Brown said. "But this thing, yeah, it's been real cool."

"For me, doing these kinds of projects has kept me out of trouble and out of gangs that are in my neighborhood," Marshbanks said Monday.

All are at a four-day, inner-city farming seminar at the Heifer International Project, an international grassroots organization.

The seminar, held on Heifer's 1,100-acre ranch in central Arkansas, provides some of the budding farmers their first time out of the city. They stay at the "Heifer Hilton"—a barn that sleeps about two dozen.

The seminar aims to show how to boost inner-city crops and expand into rooftop beekeeping, catfish harvesting, worm composting, goat-cheese making, and organic farming.

"We feel really good about doing this," Moore said. "There are a lot of people who can't afford things in our neighborhood. I think when people see what we're doing, they'll want to get involved too."

Learning professional techniques could help the gardening projects already running and encourage donors to keep them afloat, Marshbanks said.

"We can see what a difference it's made in our neighborhood," she said. "It makes people happy."

Analyzing Media

1. What kinds of skills will city kids learn from the Heifer International Project?

2. Suppose a similar project brought country kids to the city. What might they learn that would be helpful back on the farm?

Before You Read

Antaeus

MEET
BORDEN DEAL

The son of Mississippi farmers, Borden Deal explored the places of his childhood again and again in his writings. A prize-winning author, Deal wrote several novels and over one hundred short stories. The central themes running through much of Deal's work are the search for identity as well as the need for land of one's own. His story "Antaeus" focuses on both of these themes.

Borden Deal was born in 1922 in Mississippi. He died in Florida in 1985.

READING FOCUS

Do you feel a special bond to the world of nature? Do you enjoy hiking, gardening, or walking in the park?

Sharing Ideas
In small groups, talk about why many people need to feel connected in some way to nature. Make a list of ways that people of all ages enjoy the outdoors.

Setting a Purpose
Read to discover how some city boys learn about being connected to the land.

BUILDING BACKGROUND

The Time and Place   The setting of this story is a northern city in the United States, sometime during World War II.

Did You Know?   The title "Antaeus" refers to the name of a mighty wrestler from Greek mythology. Antaeus was a son of Gaia (jē′ ə), the goddess of the earth. His enormous strength came from contact with the earth, and he remained unbeatable as long as his feet touched the ground. The Greek hero Hercules learned of the source of Antaeus's strength and defeated him by lifting him off the ground.

VOCABULARY PREVIEW

robust (rō bust′) *adj.* strong and full of energy; p. 348
resolute (rez′ ə lōōt′) *adj.* determined; stubborn; p. 348
obscure (əb skyoor′) *adj.* difficult to understand; p. 350
awe (ô) *n.* wonder combined with respect; p. 351
inert (i nurt′) *adj.* without power to move or act; p. 352
bravado (brə vä′ dō) *n.* a false show of bravery; p. 353
principle (prin′ sə pəl) *n.* a basic law, truth, or belief; rule of personal conduct; p. 354
flourishing (flur′ ish ing) *adj.* growing or developing successfully; doing very well; p. 354
nurture (nur′ chər) *v.* to care for and help grow; p. 356

Antaeus

Borden Deal

This was during the wartime, when lots of people were coming North for jobs in factories and war industries,[1] when people moved around a lot more than they do now, and sometimes kids were thrown into new groups and new lives that were completely different from anything they had ever known before. I remember this one kid, T. J. his name was, from somewhere down South, whose family moved into our building during that time. They'd come North with everything they owned piled into the back seat of an old-model sedan that you wouldn't expect could make the trip, with T. J. and his three younger sisters riding shakily on top of the load of junk.

Our building was just like all the others there, with families crowded into a few rooms, and I guess there were twenty-five or thirty kids about my age in that one building. Of course, there were a few of us who formed a gang and ran together all the time after school, and I was the one who brought T. J. in and started the whole thing.

---

1. *[war industries]* During World War II (1939–1945), many U.S. industries switched from making consumer goods to producing weapons and equipment for the military.

Did You Know?

A *parapet* is a low, protective wall along the edge of a roof or balcony.

The building right next door to us was a factory where they made walking dolls. It was a low building with a flat, tarred roof that had a parapet all around it about head-high, and we'd found out a long time before that no one, not even the watchman, paid any attention to the roof because it was higher than any of the other buildings around. So my gang used the roof as a headquarters. We could get up there by crossing over to the fire escape from our own roof on a plank and then going on up. It was a secret place for us, where nobody else could go without our permission.

I remember the day I first took T. J. up there to meet the gang. He was a stocky, robust kid with a shock of white hair, nothing sissy about him except his voice; he talked in this slow, gentle voice like you never heard before. He talked different from any of us and you noticed it right away. But I liked him anyway, so I told him to come on up.

We climbed up over the parapet and dropped down on the roof. The rest of the gang were already there.

"Hi," I said. I jerked my thumb at T. J. "He just moved into the building yesterday."

He just stood there, not scared or anything, just looking, like the first time you see somebody you're not sure you're going to like.

"Hi," Blackie said. "Where are you from?"

"Marion County," T. J. said.

We laughed. "Marion County?" I said. "Where's that?"

He looked at me for a moment like I was a stranger, too. "It's in Alabama," he said, like I ought to know where it was.

"What's your name?" Charley said.

"T. J.," he said, looking back at him. He had pale blue eyes that looked washed-out, but he looked directly at Charley, waiting for his reaction. He'll be all right, I thought. No sissy in him, except that voice. Who ever talked like that?

"T. J.," Blackie said. "That's just initials. What's your real name? Nobody in the world has just initials."

"I do," he said. "And they're T. J. That's all the name I got."

His voice was resolute with the knowledge of his rightness, and for a moment no one had anything to say. T. J. looked around at the rooftop and down at the black tar under his feet. "Down yonder where I come from," he said, "we played out in the woods. Don't you-all have no woods around here?"

"Naw," Blackie said. "There's the park a few blocks over, but it's full of kids and cops and old women. You can't do a thing."

T. J. kept looking at the tar under his feet. "You mean you ain't got no fields to raise nothing in? . . . no watermelons or nothing?"

Vocabulary

robust (rō bust′) *adj.* strong and full of energy
resolute (rez′ ə lōōt′) *adj.* determined; stubborn

Early New York Evening, 1954. Jane Freilicher. Oil on canvas, 51½ x 31¾ in. Private collection. Courtesy Tibor de Nagy Gallery, New York.

Viewing the painting: How does putting a few flowers on a window sill compare with T. J.'s need for plant life?

"Naw," I said scornfully. "What do you want to grow something for? The folks can buy everything they need at the store."

He looked at me again with that strange, unknowing look. "In Marion County," he said, "I had my own acre of cotton and my own acre of corn. It was mine to plant and make ever' year."

He sounded like it was something to be proud of, and in some obscure way it made the rest of us angry. Blackie said, "Who'd want to have their own acre of cotton and corn? That's just work. What can you do with an acre of cotton and corn?"

T. J. looked at him. "Well, you get part of the bale offen[2] your acre," he said seriously. "And I fed my acre of corn to my calf."

We didn't really know what he was talking about, so we were more puzzled than angry; otherwise, I guess, we'd have chased him off the roof and wouldn't let him be part of our gang. But he was strange and different, and we were all attracted by his stolid[3] sense of rightness and belonging, maybe by the strange softness of his voice contrasting our own tones of speech into harshness.

He moved his foot against the black tar. "We could make our own field right here," he said softly, thoughtfully. "Come spring we could raise us what we want to—watermelons and garden truck[4] and no telling what all."

"You'd have to be a good farmer to make these tar roofs grow any watermelons," I said. We all laughed.

But T. J. looked serious. "We could haul us some dirt up here," he said. "And spread it out even and water it, and before you know it, we'd have us a crop in here." He looked at us intently. "Wouldn't that be fun?"

"They wouldn't let us," Blackie said quickly.

"I thought you said this was you-all's roof," T. J. said to me. "That you-all could do anything you wanted to up here."

"They've never bothered us," I said. I felt the idea beginning to catch fire in me. It was a big idea, and it took a while for it to sink in; but the more I thought about it, the better I liked it. "Say," I said to the gang. "He might have something there. Just make us a regular roof garden, with flowers and grass and trees and everything. And all ours, too," I said. "We wouldn't let anybody up here except the ones we wanted to."

"It'd take a while to grow trees," T. J. said quickly, but we weren't paying any attention to him. They were all talking about it suddenly, all excited with the idea after I'd put it in a way they could catch hold of it. Only rich people had roof gardens, we knew, and the idea of our own private domain[5] excited them.

"We could bring it up in sacks and boxes," Blackie said. "We'd have to do it while the folks weren't paying any attention to us, for we'd have to come up to the

2. *[offen]* This is an informal way of saying *off of.* T. J. is describing the situation of a sharecropper, who farms land owned by someone else and shares the crop or the profit from its sale with the landowner.

3. *Stolid* means "firm and unemotional."

4. Here, *truck* refers to vegetables, especially those driven by truck from farms to markets.

5. A *domain* is the area under the rule or control of a person or group.

Vocabulary

obscure (əb skyoor´) *adj.* difficult to understand

roof of our building and then cross over with it."

"Where could we get the dirt?" somebody said worriedly.

"Out of those vacant lots over close to school," Blackie said. "Nobody'd notice if we scraped it up."

I slapped T. J. on the shoulder. "Man, you had a wonderful idea," I said, and everybody grinned at him, remembering that he had started it. "Our own private roof garden."

He grinned back. "It'll be ourn," he said. "All ourn." Then he looked thoughtful again. "Maybe I can lay my hands on some cotton seed, too. You think we could raise us some cotton?"

We'd started big projects before at one time or another, like any gang of kids, but they'd always petered out for lack of organization and direction. But this one didn't; somehow or other T. J. kept it going all through the winter months. He kept talking about the watermelons and the cotton we'd raise, come spring, and when even that wouldn't work, he'd switch around to my idea of flowers and grass and trees, though he was always honest enough to add that it'd take a while to get any trees started. He always had it on his mind, and he'd mention it in school, getting them lined up to carry dirt that afternoon, saying in a casual way that he reckoned a few more weeks ought to see the job through.

Our little area of private earth grew slowly. T. J. was smart enough to start in one corner of the building, heaping up the carried earth two or three feet thick so that we had an immediate result to look at, to contemplate with awe. Some of the evenings T. J. alone was carrying earth up to the building, the rest of the gang distracted by other enterprises[6] or interests, but T. J. kept plugging along on his own, and eventually we'd all come back to him again, and then our own little acre would grow more rapidly.

He was careful about the kind of dirt he'd let us carry up there, and more than once he dumped a sandy load over the parapet into the areaway below because it wasn't good enough. He found out the kinds of earth in all the vacant lots for blocks around. He'd pick it up and feel it and smell it, frozen though it was sometimes, and then he'd say it was good growing soil or it wasn't worth anything, and we'd have to go on somewhere else.

Thinking about it now, I don't see how he kept us at it. It was hard work, lugging paper sacks and boxes of dirt all the way up the stairs of our own building, keeping out of the way of the grown-ups so they wouldn't catch on to what we were doing. They probably wouldn't have cared, for they didn't pay much attention to us, but we wanted to keep it secret anyway. Then we had to go through the trap door to our roof, teeter over a plank to the fire escape, then climb two or three stories to the parapet, and drop them down onto the roof. All that for a small pile of earth that sometimes didn't seem worth the effort.

---

6. Here, *enterprises* means "projects or activities."

Vocabulary
awe (ô) *n.* wonder combined with respect

New Chicago Athletic Club, 1937. Antonio Berni. Oil on canvas, 184.3 x 300.3 cm. Museum of Modern Art, New York.

Viewing the painting: In what ways do these boys seem similar to those in the story?

But T. J. kept the vision bright within us, his words shrewd and calculated[7] toward the fulfillment of his dream; and he worked harder than any of us. He seemed driven toward a goal that we couldn't see, a particular point in time that would be definitely marked by signs and wonders that only he could see.

The laborious[8] earth just lay there during the cold months, inert and lifeless, the clods lumpy and cold under our feet when we walked over it. But one day it rained, and afterward there was a softness in the air, and the earth was live and giving again with moisture and warmth.

That evening T. J. smelled the air, his nostrils dilating with the odor of the earth under his feet. "It's spring," he said, and there was a gladness rising in his voice that filled us all with the same feeling. "It's mighty late for it, but it's spring. I'd just about decided it wasn't never gonna get here at all."

We were all sniffing at the air, too, trying to smell it the way that T. J. did, and I can still remember the sweet odor of the earth under our feet. It was the first time in my life that spring and spring earth had meant anything to me. I looked at T. J. then, knowing in a faint way the hunger within

---

7. T. J.'s words are clever and practical *(shrewd)* and reasoned out beforehand *(calculated).*
8. The earth is *laborious* in that getting it to the roof required difficulty and hard labor.

Vocabulary

inert (i nurt′) *adj.* without power to move or act

352

him through the toilsome[9] winter months, knowing the dream that lay behind his plan. He was a new Antaeus, preparing his own bed of strength.

"Planting time," he said. "We'll have to find us some seed."

"What do we do?" Blackie said. "How do we do it?"

"First we'll have to break up the clods," T. J. said. "That won't be hard to do. Then we plant the seed, and after a while they come up. Then you got you a crop." He frowned. "But you ain't got it raised yet. You got to tend it and hoe it and take care of it, and all the time it's growing and growing, while you're awake and while you're asleep. Then you lay it by when it's growed and let it ripen, and then you got you a crop."

"There's these wholesale seed houses over on Sixth," I said. "We could probably swipe some grass seed over there."

T. J. looked at the earth. "You-all seem mighty set on raising some grass," he said. "I ain't never put no effort into that. I spent all my life trying not to raise grass."

"But it's pretty," Blackie said. "We could play on it and take sunbaths on it. Like having our own lawn. Lots of people got lawns."

"Well," T. J. said. He looked at the rest of us, hesitant for the first time. He kept on looking at us for a moment. "I did have it in mind to raise some corn and vegetables. But we'll plant grass."

He was smart. He knew where to give in. And I don't suppose it made any

difference to him, really. He just wanted to grow something, even if it was grass.

"Of course," he said. "I do think we ought to plant a row of watermelons. They'd be mighty nice to eat while we was a-laying on that grass."

We all laughed. "All right," I said. "We'll plant us a row of watermelons."

Things went very quickly then. Perhaps half the roof was covered with the earth, the half that wasn't broken by ventilators, and we swiped pocketfuls of grass seed from the open bins in the wholesale seed house, mingling among the buyers on Saturdays and during the school lunch hour. T. J. showed us how to prepare the earth, breaking up the clods and smoothing it and sowing the grass seed. It looked rich and black now with moisture, receiving of the seed, and it seemed that the grass sprang up overnight, pale green in the early spring.

We couldn't keep from looking at it, unable to believe that we had created this delicate growth. We looked at T. J. with understanding now, knowing the fulfillment of the plan he had carried alone within his mind. We had worked without full understanding of the task, but he had known all the time.

We found that we couldn't walk or play on the delicate blades, as we had expected to, but we didn't mind. It was enough just to look at it, to realize that it was the work of our own hands, and each evening, the whole gang was there, trying to measure the growth that had been achieved that day.

One time a foot was placed on the plot of ground, one time only, Blackie stepping onto it with sudden bravado. Then he

---

9. The months are *toilsome* (a synonym for *laborious*) in that they are difficult and tiresome.

Vocabulary
bravado (brə vä′ dō) *n.* a false show of bravery

looked at the crushed blades and there was shame in his face. He did not do it again. This was his grass, too, and not to be desecrated.[10] No one said anything, for it was not necessary.

T. J. had reserved a small section for watermelons, and he was still trying to find some seed for it. The wholesale house didn't have any watermelon seed, and we didn't know where we could lay our hands on them. T. J. shaped the earth into mounds, ready to receive them, three mounds lying in a straight line along the edge of the grass plot.

We had just about decided that we'd have to buy the seed if we were to get them. It was a violation of our <u>principles</u>, but we were anxious to get the watermelons started. Somewhere or other, T. J. got his hands on a seed catalog and brought it one evening to our roof garden.

"We can order them now," he said, showing us the catalog. "Look!"

We all crowded around, looking at the fat, green watermelons pictured in full color on the pages. Some of them were split open, showing the red, tempting meat, making our mouths water.

"Now we got to scrape up some seed money," T. J. said, looking at us. "I got a quarter. How much you-all got?"

We made up a couple of dollars among us and T. J. nodded his head. "That'll be more than enough. Now we got to decide what kind to get. I think them Kleckley Sweets. What do you-all think?"

He was going into esoteric[11] matters beyond our reach. We hadn't even known there were different kinds of melons. So we just nodded our heads and agreed that yes, we thought the Kleckley Sweets too.

"I'll order them tonight," T. J. said. "We ought to have them in a few days."

"What are you boys doing up here?" an adult voice said behind us.

It startled us, for no one had ever come up here before, in all the time we had been using the roof of the factory. We jerked around and saw three men standing near the trap door at the other end of the roof. They weren't policemen, or night watchmen, but three men in plump business suits, looking at us. They walked toward us.

"What are you boys doing up here?" the one in the middle said again.

We stood still, guilt heavy among us, levied[12] by the tone of voice, and looked at the three strangers.

The men stared at the grass <u>flourishing</u> behind us. "What's this?" the man said. "How did this get up here?"

"Sure is growing good, ain't it?" T. J. said conversationally. "We planted it."

The men kept looking at the grass as if they didn't believe it. It was a thick carpet over the earth now, a patch of deep greenness startling in the sterile[13] industrial surroundings.

---

10. To treat something holy with disrespect is to *desecrate* (des′ ə krāt′) it.

11. *Esoteric* (es′ ə ter′ ik) matters are beyond the understanding or knowledge of most people. T. J.'s knowledge of melons and farming seems esoteric to the other boys.
12. Here, *levied* means "enforced."
13. Most often, *sterile* (ster′ əl) is used to mean free from bacteria—like a surgeon's instruments. Here, the meaning is "having little or no plant life."

Vocabulary

principle (prin′ sə pəl) *n.* a basic law, truth, or belief; rule of personal conduct
flourishing (flur′ ish ing) *adj.* growing or developing successfully; doing very well

"Yes, sir," T. J. said proudly. "We toted that earth up here and planted that grass." He fluttered the seed catalog. "And we're just fixing to plant us some watermelon."

The man looked at him then, his eyes strange and faraway. "What do you mean, putting this on the roof of my building?" he said. "Do you want to go to jail?"

T. J. looked shaken. The rest of us were silent, frightened by the authority of his voice. We had grown up aware of adult authority, of policemen and night watchmen and teachers, and this man sounded like all the others. But it was a new thing to T. J.

"Well, you wasn't using the roof," T. J. said. He paused a moment and added shrewdly, "So we just thought to pretty it up a little bit."

"And sag it so I'd have to rebuild it," the man said sharply. He started turning away, saying to another man beside him, "See that all that junk is shoveled off by tomorrow."

"Yes, sir," the man said.

T. J. started forward. "You can't do that," he said. "We toted it up here, and it's our earth. We planted it and raised it and toted it up here."

The man stared at him coldly. "But it's my building," he said. "It's to be shoveled off tomorrow."

"It's our earth," T. J. said desperately. "You ain't got no right!"

The men walked on without listening and descended clumsily through the trap door. T. J. stood looking after them, his body tense with anger, until they had disappeared. They wouldn't even argue with him, wouldn't let him defend his earth rights.

He turned to us. "We won't let 'em do it," he said fiercely. "We'll stay up here all

day tomorrow and the day after that, and we won't let 'em do it."

We just looked at him. We knew that there was no stopping it.

He saw it in our faces, and his face wavered for a moment before he gripped it into determination. "They ain't got no right," he said. "It's our earth. It's our land. Can't nobody touch a man's own land."

We kept looking at him, listening to the words but knowing that it was no use. The adult world had descended on us even in our richest dream, and we knew there was no calculating the adult world, no fighting it, no winning against it.

We started moving slowly toward the parapet and the fire escape, avoiding a last look at the green beauty of the earth that T. J. had planted for us, had planted deeply in our minds as well as in our experience. We filed slowly over the edge and down the steps to the plank, T. J. coming last, and all of us could feel the weight of his grief behind us.

"Wait a minute," he said suddenly, his voice harsh with the effort of calling.

We stopped and turned, held by the tone of his voice, and looked up at him standing above us on the fire escape.

"We can't stop them?" he said, looking down at us, his face strange in the dusky light. "There ain't no way to stop 'em?"

"No," Blackie said with finality.[14] "They own the building."

We stood still for a moment, looking up at T. J., caught into inaction by the decision working in his face. He stared back at us, and his face was pale and mean in the poor light, with a bald nakedness in his skin like cripples have sometimes.

---

14. **Blackie speaks with decisiveness *(finality)*;** the issue is settled.

"They ain't gonna touch my earth," he said fiercely. "They ain't gonna lay a hand on it! Come on."

He turned around and started up the fire escape again, almost running against the effort of climbing. We followed more slowly, not knowing what he intended to do. By the time we reached him, he had seized a board and thrust it into the soil, scooping it up and flinging it over the parapet into the areaway below. He straightened and looked at us.

"They can't touch it," he said. "I won't let 'em lay a dirty hand on it!"

We saw it then. He stooped to his labor again, and we followed, the gusts of his anger moving in frenzied labor among us as we scattered along the edge of earth, scooping it and throwing it over the parapet, destroying with anger the growth we had <u>nurtured</u> with such tender care. The soil carried so laboriously upward to the light and the sun cascaded swiftly into the dark areaway, the green blades of grass crumpled and twisted in the falling.

It took less time than you would think; the task of destruction is infinitely easier than that of creation. We stopped at the end, leaving only a scattering of loose soil, and when it was finally over, a stillness stood among the group and over the factory building. We looked down at the bare sterility of black tar, felt the harsh texture of it under the soles of our shoes, and the anger had gone out of us, leaving only a sore aching in our minds, like over-stretched muscles.

T. J. stood for a moment, his breathing slowing from anger and effort, caught into the same contemplation of destruction as all of us. He stooped slowly, finally, and picked up a lonely blade of grass left trampled under our feet and put it between his teeth, tasting it, sucking the greenness out of it into his mouth. Then he started walking toward the fire escape, moving before any of us were ready to move, and disappeared over the edge.

We followed him, but he was already halfway down to the ground, going on past the board where we crossed over, climbing down into the areaway. We saw the last section swing down with his weight, and then he stood on the concrete below us, looking at the small pile of anonymous[15] earth scattered by our throwing. Then he walked across the place where we could see him and disappeared toward the street without glancing back, without looking up to see us watching him.

They did not find him for two weeks.

Then the Nashville police caught him just outside the Nashville freight yards. He was walking along the railroad track, still heading South, still heading home.

As for us, who had no remembered home to call us, none of us ever again climbed the escapeway to the roof.

---

15. The word *anonymous* has two main meanings: "of unknown authorship or origin" and "lacking personality or special features." Here, the scattered soil looks as though it could have come from anywhere. Without grass growing on it, it's just ordinary dirt.

Vocabulary
nurture (nur´ chər) *v.* to care for and help grow

Responding to Literature

PERSONAL RESPONSE

- ◆ Were you surprised by the outcome of the story? Explain why or why not.
- ◆ Look back at your notes from the **Reading Focus** on page 346. Do any of the characters in the story connect to the world of nature in ways you discussed? Explain.

Analyzing Literature

RECALL

1. Where does the narrator take T. J. to meet his gang?
2. What does T. J. convince the gang to do?
3. Why does the narrator believe that the roof garden project did not fade away like other big projects the boys had started? Explain.
4. What happens after the roof garden is discovered? According to the narrator, where was T. J. going when he was found?

INTERPRET

5. At the beginning, how does the gang react to T. J.? What do readers learn about T. J. from his reaction to them?
6. Why do the boys become so excited by the thought of a roof garden? Explain.
7. What does the narrator mean when he says, "We were all sniffing at the air, too, trying to smell it the way that T. J. did"?
8. Why does T. J. react as he does to the discovery of the garden?

EVALUATE AND CONNECT

9. In your opinion, what was the most important thing T. J. taught the members of the gang? Explain.
10. Theme Connection   State the theme, or main idea, of "Antaeus" in a single sentence. Then write a paragraph telling how the theme of this story relates to the general theme of this group of selections.

LITERARY ELEMENTS

Allusion

An **allusion** is a reference to a well-known character, place, or situation from another work of literature, music, art, history, politics, or science. When readers recognize an allusion, it enriches their understanding of the piece of writing by making a connection between two characters, places, or situations.

1. Explain the connection between T. J. and the mythical Antaeus. Is T. J. a modern-day hero? Why or why not? Support your ideas with examples from the story.

2. In your opinion, in what ways is the story strengthened by the allusion to Greek mythology? Explain.

● See **Literary Terms Handbook**, p. R1.

Literature and Writing

Writing About Literature

Character Review   Write a paragraph or two reviewing either T. J. or the narrator. In your opinion, does this person seem true to life? Why or why not? How does the character change over the course of the story? What obstacles does the character have to overcome to reach his goals? Support your opinions with examples and quotations from the story.

Creative Writing

Epilogue   What do you think happens to T. J. after the final scene in the story? An **epilogue** is a brief concluding section to a novel, a story, or a poem. Write an epilogue to "Antaeus." Your epilogue might take place weeks, months, or many years after the end of the story.

Extending Your Response

Literature Groups

Home Is Where the Heart Is   Talk about T. J.'s connection to nature. What does the earth represent to him? Why does he need to create a garden in the city? Do you think T. J. could ever be happy living in a city? Debate the question: Can country people and city people ever be happy living in the other's environment? Support your ideas with examples from the story and details from your own experience.

Learning for Life

Community Garden Proposal   Is there a vacant lot near your school or somewhere in your town or city? Write a proposal to convince public officials to allow you to transform the vacant lot into a community garden. Describe how important a garden would be to the neighborhood. Outline a plan to complete the project, using students and other volunteers to do the work.

Interdisciplinary Activity

Art/Science   Work with classmates to create a community garden in honor of T. J.'s vision. Find out which flowers or vegetables will thrive in your location and decide which ones to include in the garden. Decide on the size of the garden, the location of the plants within the garden, and additional items such as paths, benches, and lights. Make a mural of the garden to display on a classroom wall.

Reading Further

If you would like to read more stories about nature, try these books:

A Day No Pigs Would Die by Robert Newton Peck

The Island Keeper by Harry Mazer

📖 **Save your work for your portfolio.**

Skill Minilessons

GRAMMAR AND LANGUAGE • COMMAS IN COMPOUND SENTENCES

If the main clauses in a compound sentence are connected by a conjunction (*and, but,* or *or*), a comma should come before the conjunction.

Example: The soil was heavy, **but** the boys carried it up to the rooftop nevertheless.

PRACTICE Review "Antaeus" to find and copy two examples of compound sentences containing commas. Then write two compound sentences of your own, using commas and conjunctions correctly.

● For more about commas, see **Language Handbook,** pp. R37–R38.

READING AND THINKING • STEREOTYPE

A **stereotype** is an oversimplified or generalized opinion or prejudice about a particular group or issue. For example, someone who thinks that all Texans are either ranchers or oil drillers is using a stereotype. **Bias**–favoritism toward or against something–may lead people to use stereotypes. Stereotypes in writing can show a writer's bias. In fiction, they can show a character's bias.

PRACTICE Identify the following stereotypes from "Antaeus." Look back at the story if you need help.

1. In "Antaeus," the narrator says that there was "nothing sissy" about T. J. "except his voice." What stereotype does that comment demonstrate?
2. What stereotype do you think the man who ordered the boys off his roof had about teenagers?
3. What stereotype did the gang members probably have about grown-ups?

● For more about stereotypes, see **Literary Terms Handbook,** p. R10.

VOCABULARY • ANALOGIES: LEVELS OF INTENSITY

Analogies compare the relationships between things or ideas. One kind of analogy deals with levels of intensity. That is, the words in each pair have similar meanings, but one word is stronger, more intense than the other.

angry : furious :: happy : overjoyed

Angry and *furious* are similar in meaning, and so are *happy* and *overjoyed.* But in each pair, the second word describes a feeling that is more intense than the first word suggests. Someone who is extremely *angry* is *furious,* just as someone who is extremely *happy* is *overjoyed.*

To finish an analogy, think of the relationship between the first pair of words. Then find another pair of words that have the same relationship.

PRACTICE Complete each analogy.
1. surviving : flourishing ::
   a. thankful : grateful   d. large : old
   b. sad : lonely   e. damp : soaked
   c. cautious : careless
2. well : robust ::
   a. wrong : mistaken   d. poetic : musical
   b. weak : small   e. muscular : healthy
   c. pretty : beautiful

● For more about analogies, see **Communications Skills Handbook,** p. R67.

Before You Read

Home and *the 1st*

MEET GWENDOLYN BROOKS

Gwendolyn Brooks's advice to young poets was "Tell your truth. Don't try to sugar it up." In 1950 Brooks became the first African American author to win the Pulitzer Prize for Poetry.

Gwendolyn Brooks was born in 1917 and died in 2000. Maud Martha, the novel from which "Home" is taken, was published in 1953.

MEET LUCILLE CLIFTON

Lucille Clifton now lives in Columbia, Maryland, where she is Distinguished Professor of Humanities at Saint Mary's College. Clifton is a former poet laureate of Maryland and has received numerous awards and prizes for her poetry.

Lucille Clifton was born in 1936. "the 1st" comes from Good Woman: Poems and a Memoir 1969–1980, *published in 1987.*

READING FOCUS

When you hear the word *home,* what do you think about? What are some things that make a home important to the people who live there?

Think/Pair/Share
Jot down your thoughts and feelings about the word *home.* Then share your ideas with a partner.

Setting a Purpose
As you read, look for what makes their home important to the characters in these selections.

Children Dancing, 1948. Robert Gwathmey (1903–1988). Oil on canvas, 32 x 40 in. The Butler Institute of American Art, Youngstown, OH.

VOCABULARY PREVIEW

obstinate (ob′ stə nit) *adj.* stubborn; difficult to overcome or control; p. 361

emphatic (em fat′ ik) *adj.* strongly expressive; forceful; p. 361

possessively (pə zes′ iv lē) *adv.* in a way that shows ownership or control; p. 361

staccato (stə kä′ tō) *adj.* made of short, sharp sounds or movements; p. 362

casually (kazh′ o͞o əl lē) *adv.* in a relaxed, informal way; p. 362

Home

Gwendolyn Brooks ✿

What had been wanted was this always, this always to last, the talking softly on this porch, with the snake plant in the jardiniere[1] in the southwest corner, and the obstinate slip from Aunt Eppie's magnificent Michigan fern at the left side of the friendly door. Mama, Maud Martha and Helen rocked slowly in their rocking chairs, and looked at the late afternoon light on the lawn, and at the emphatic iron of the fence and at the poplar tree. These things might soon be theirs no longer. Those shafts and pools of light, the tree, the graceful iron, might soon be viewed possessively by different eyes.

Papa was to have gone that noon, during his lunch hour, to the office of the Home Owners' Loan. If he had not succeeded in getting another extension, they would be leaving this house in which they had lived for more than fourteen years. There was little hope. The Home Owners'

Woman Holding a Jug, 1932–1933. James A. Porter. Oil on canvas. Carl Van Vechten Gallery of Fine Arts, Fisk University, Nashville, TN.

Loan was hard. They sat, making their plans.

"We'll be moving into a nice flat[2] somewhere," said Mama. "Somewhere on South Park, or Michigan, or in Washington Park Court." Those flats, as the girls and Mama knew well, were burdens on wages twice the size of Papa's. This was not mentioned now.

"They're much prettier than this old house," said Helen. "I have friends I'd just as soon not bring here. And I have other friends that wouldn't come down this far for anything, unless they were in a taxi."

Yesterday, Maud Martha would have attacked her. Tomorrow she might. Today she said nothing. She merely gazed at a little hopping robin in the tree, her tree, and tried to keep the fronts of her eyes dry.

"Well, I do know," said Mama, turning her hands over and over, "that I've been getting tireder and tireder of doing that

---

1. A *jardiniere* (järd′ ən ēr′) is an ornamental pot or plant stand.

2. Here, *flat* means "apartment."

Vocabulary
obstinate (ob′ stə nit) *adj.* stubborn; difficult to overcome or control
emphatic (em fat′ ik) *adj.* strongly expressive; forceful
possessively (pə zes′ iv lē) *adv.* in a way that shows ownership or control

Home

firing. From October to April, there's firing to be done."

"But lately we've been helping, Harry and I," said Maud Martha. "And sometimes in March and April and in October, and even in November, we could build a little fire in the fireplace. Sometimes the weather was just right for that."

She knew, from the way they looked at her, that this had been a mistake. They did not want to cry.

But she felt that the little line of white, somewhat ridged with smoked purple, and all that cream-shot saffron,[3] would never drift across any western sky except that in back of this house. The rain would drum with as sweet a dullness nowhere but here. The birds on South Park were mechanical birds, no better than the poor caught canaries in those "rich" women's sun parlors.

"It's just going to kill Papa!" burst out Maud Martha. "He loves this house! He *lives* for this house!"

"He lives for us," said Helen. "It's us he loves. He wouldn't want the house, except for us."

"And he'll have us," added Mama, "wherever."

"You know," Helen sighed, "if you want to know the truth, this is a relief. If this hadn't come up, we would have gone on, just dragged on, hanging out here forever."

---

3. The orange-yellow color *(saffron)* is streaked or mixed *(shot)* with a cream color.

"It might," allowed Mama, "be an act of God. God may just have reached down, and picked up the reins."

"Yes," Maud Martha cracked in, "that's what you always say—that God knows best."

Her mother looked at her quickly, decided the statement was not suspect, looked away.

Helen saw Papa coming. "There's Papa," said Helen.

They could not tell a thing from the way Papa was walking. It was that same dear little <u>staccato</u> walk, one shoulder down, then the other, then repeat, and repeat. They watched his progress. He passed the Kennedys', he passed the vacant lot, he passed Mrs. Blakemore's. They wanted to hurl themselves over the fence, into the street, and shake the truth out of his collar. He opened his gate—the gate—and still his stride and face told them nothing.

"Hello," he said.

Mama got up and followed him through the front door. The girls knew better than to go in too.

Presently Mama's head emerged. Her eyes were lamps turned on.

"It's all right," she exclaimed. "He got it. It's all over. Everything is all right."

The door slammed shut. Mama's footsteps hurried away.

"I think," said Helen, rocking rapidly, "I think I'll give a party. I haven't given a party since I was eleven. I'd like some of my friends to just <u>casually</u> see that we're homeowners."

Vocabulary

staccato (stə kä′ tō) *adj.* made of short, sharp sounds or movements
casually (kazh′ o͞o əl lē) *adv.* in a relaxed, informal way

the 1st

Lucille Clifton

what i remember about that day
is boxes stacked across the walk
and couch springs curling through the air
and drawers and tables balanced on the curb
and us, hollering,
leaping up and around
happy to have a playground;

nothing about the emptied rooms
nothing about the emptied family

The Apartment, 1943. Jacob Lawrence. Gouache on paper, 21.25 x 29.25 in. The Hunter Museum of American Art, Chattanooga, TN.

Responding to Literature

PERSONAL RESPONSE

- ◆ What is your response to these selections? Explain.
- ◆ Review your notes from the **Reading Focus** on page 360. How do your thoughts and feelings about the word *home* compare with the thoughts and feelings of the characters in these selections?

Analyzing Literature

RECALL

1. What problem does the family in "Home" face? Near the end of the story, what news does Papa bring home?

2. In the poem "the 1st," what event is the speaker recalling from her childhood? What does she remember about her feelings? Explain.

INTERPRET

3. How does the family in "Home" feel about their home? Support your opinion with examples from the story.

4. What are the two conflicting images and emotions in the poem "the 1st"? Why, do you think, are the last two lines almost the same? Explain.

EVALUATE AND CONNECT

5. Both of these selections deal with the subject of moving and loss. How do the forms—a short story and a poem—allow the writers to deal differently with the same topic? Explain.

6. How does the dialogue between the characters in "Home" contribute to the story's suspense? Give examples.

7. In what ways do these selections seem true to life? Explain.

8. How do you feel about what happens to these families?

9. **Theme Connection** Why is a place to call home important to the characters in these selections? Explain.

10. Which of these selections do you prefer? Why? Use quotations from the selections to support your ideas.

LITERARY ELEMENTS

Theme

A **theme** is the message that is expressed in a work of literature. A story, a novel, a play, or a poem may have more than one theme, but one message will usually be the strongest. A theme may be stated directly, but more often it is revealed gradually, through the words, thoughts, and actions of the characters. Since readers usually need to *infer* the theme—that is, figure it out through reasoning—it is always open to interpretation. A strong piece of literature may mean different things to different people.

1. What is the theme of the story "Home"? Use examples from the story to support your ideas.

2. Summarize the central theme of the poem "the 1st."

● See **Literary Terms Handbook,** p. R11.

Extending Your Response

Writing About Literature

Dialogue Dialogue is conversation between characters. Readers learn a great deal of information through the dialogue in a story. Write a paragraph or two explaining what you learned from the dialogue in "Home" about the thoughts and feelings of the different characters.

Creative Writing

One-Act Play With a partner, write a one-act play based on "the 1st." Think about the poem's central images and the different emotions they evoke. Make up any details you wish, including dialogue for the characters and stage directions that describe the setting and action. If you wish, perform your play. Use props to make the dramatization seem real.

Literature Groups

Home Sweet Home According to the writer, what is the true meaning of the word *home?* What is your own definition? Review your notes from the **Reading Focus** on page 360. Discuss the meaning of the word *home* and what makes a place a home.

Learning for Life

A Persuasive Memo Imagine you are Papa in the story "Home." The Home Owners' Loan Association has asked you to write them a memo explaining why you need another extension on your loan, how you intend to repay the loan, and what the house means to you and your family. Be persuasive!

Save your work for your portfolio.

Skill Minilesson

VOCABULARY • WORDS USED IN UNUSUAL WAYS

In "Home," Gwendolyn Brooks calls the iron of a fence *emphatic.* A fence can't really be emphatic. Brooks uses a figure of speech to suggest that the iron of the fence is strong and not flexible. This literary device, called **personification,** gives human qualities such as actions or feelings to an object, an idea, or an animal.

PRACTICE To complete each sentence, think about what is suggested by the underlined word.

1. A <u>tired</u> roof is probably
   a. sagging   c. flat
   b. leaking

2. A <u>bold</u> flower probably has
   a. thorns   c. bright colors
   b. a sweet smell

3. A <u>heavy</u> sky probably has many
   a. stars   c. puffy clouds
   b. dark clouds

4. A <u>forgiving</u> rug doesn't
   a. look new   c. show stains easily
   b. fit the room

5. An <u>undecided</u> path probably
   a. twists   c. goes uphill
   b. is narrow

Making Connections

When you get involved in a story, you may identify with one or more of its characters. Skillful readers put themselves in a story by **making connections** between their own life experiences and the experiences of the characters. Thinking about these connections while you read makes a story more meaningful.

Read the following passage from "Home" by Gwendolyn Brooks. As you read, try to connect the situation in the story with a situation in your own life.

> "We'll be moving into a nice flat somewhere," said Mama. "Somewhere on South Park, or Michigan, or in Washington Park Court." Those flats, as the girls and Mama knew well, were burdens on wages twice the size of Papa's. This was not mentioned now.
>
> "They're much prettier than this old house," said Helen. "I have friends I'd just as soon not bring here. And I have other friends that wouldn't come down this far for anything, unless they were in a taxi."

Were you able to make a connection between your life and the characters and situation described in this excerpt? Perhaps you remembered a time when a relative or friend tried to comfort you after you did not make the team or the cast of the school play. Or, perhaps you recalled a time when you helped a friend see the brighter side of a difficult situation. Connecting your personal experiences with the actions, emotions, motivations, and situations of the characters in a story makes fiction come alive.

● For more about reading strategies, see **Reading Handbook,** pp. R73–R102.

ACTIVITY

Reread "Antaeus," by Borden Deal, or another short story of your choosing. Then answer the following questions.

1. Which character or event in the story reminded you of a person or situation in your own life?

2. How are the two characters or events alike? How are they different?

3. How did connecting the people and experiences in your own life to those in the story help you better understand the characters' emotions and motivations?

Before You Read
The Teacher Who Changed My Life

MEET NICHOLAS GAGE

When Nicholas Gage first came to America, he was nine years old and did not speak English. Thirty years later, when he left America for Greece, Gage was a top investigative reporter for *The New York Times*. He returned to Lia, the tiny remote village of his birth, to find his mother's murderers. The best-selling book he wrote about his search was named after his mother, *Eleni*. This autobiographical essay begins in 1953, when the author was a fourteen-year-old refugee from war-torn Greece.

Nicholas Gage was born in 1939. This story is part of his memoir, A Place for Us, published in 1989.

READING FOCUS

How can one person positively influence another's life? What people do you think of when it comes to making a difference?

Journal
Write a paragraph in your journal about a person who has been a big influence in your life.

Setting a Purpose
Read about one person who made a difference in a young person's life.

BUILDING BACKGROUND

Did You Know?   Between 1940 and 1949, Greeks fought in two wars—World War II and a civil war. During this time, 600,000 Greeks were killed, including Nicholas Gage's mother. The civil war was mostly fought in the northern mountain villages, where Greek Communist guerrillas, who had fought the Germans in World War II, plotted to take over the Greek government. Their policy was to abduct over twenty-eight thousand Greek children and send them to Albania, Yugoslavia, and Bulgaria to grow up as Communists.

VOCABULARY PREVIEW

portly (pôrt′ lē) *adj.* having a stout but dignified appearance; p. 369

authoritarian (ə thôr′ ə tār′ ē ən) *adj.* having or expecting complete obedience to authority; p. 369

ultimately (ul′ tə mit lē) *adv.* in the end; finally; p. 369

perspective (pər spek′ tiv) *n.* point of view; p. 370

impoverished (im pov′ ər isht) *adj.* reduced to poverty; made very poor; p. 370

mortified (môr′ tə fīd′) *adj.* greatly embarrassed; p. 370

tact (takt) *n.* the ability to handle people or situations without causing displeasure or resentment; p. 370

ecstatic (ek stat′ ik) *adj.* overwhelmed with joy; p. 371

avidly (av′ id lē) *adv.* eagerly; enthusiastically; p. 372

consolation (kon′ sə lā′ shən) *n.* a comfort; p. 373

The Teacher Who Changed My Life

Nicholas Gage

The grown-up Nicholas and his former teacher, Marjorie Hurd Rabidou.

The person who set the course of my life in the new land I entered as a young war refugee—who, in fact, nearly dragged me onto the path that would bring all the blessings I've received in America—was a salty-tongued,[1] no-nonsense schoolteacher named Marjorie Hurd. When I entered her classroom in 1953, I had been to six schools in five years, starting in the Greek village where I was born in 1939.

When I stepped off a ship in New York Harbor on a gray March day in 1949, I was an undersized 9-year-old in short pants who had lost his mother and was coming to live with the father he didn't know. My mother, Eleni Gatzoyiannis, had been imprisoned, tortured, and shot

---

1. A *salty-tongued* person speaks in a sharp, witty, and often sarcastic way.

by Communist guerrillas[2] for sending me and three of my four sisters to freedom. She died so that her children could go to their father in the United States.

The portly, bald, well-dressed man who met me and my sisters seemed a foreign, authoritarian figure. I secretly resented him for not getting the whole family out of Greece early enough to save my mother. Ultimately, I would grow to love him and appreciate how he dealt with becoming a single parent at the age of 56, but at first our relationship was prickly,[3] full of hostility.

As Father drove us to our new home—a tenement in Worcester,[4] Mass.—and pointed out the huge brick building that would be our first school in America, I clutched my Greek notebooks from the refugee camp, hoping that my few years of schooling would impress my teachers in this cold, crowded country. They didn't. When my father led me and my 11-year-old sister to Greendale Elementary School, the grim-faced Yankee principal put the two of us in a class for the mentally retarded. There was no facility in those days for non-English-speaking children.

By the time I met Marjorie Hurd four years later, I had learned English, been placed in a normal, graded class and had even been chosen for the college preparatory track in the Worcester public school system. I was 13 years old when our father moved us yet again, and I entered Chandler Junior High shortly after the beginning of seventh grade. I found myself surrounded by richer, smarter and better-dressed classmates who looked askance[5] at my strange clothes and heavy accent. Shortly after I arrived, we were told to select a hobby to pursue during "club hour" on Fridays. The idea of hobbies and clubs made no sense to my immigrant ears, but I decided to follow the prettiest girl in my class—the blue-eyed daughter of the local Lutheran minister. She led me through the door marked "Newspaper Club" and into the presence of Miss Hurd, the newspaper adviser and English teacher who would become my mentor and my muse.[6]

A formidable, solidly built woman with salt-and-pepper hair, a steely eye and a flat Boston accent, Miss Hurd had no patience with layabouts. "What are all you goof-offs doing here?" she bellowed at the would-be journalists. "This is the Newspaper Club! We're going to put out a *newspaper*. So if there's anybody in this room who doesn't like work, I suggest you go across to the Glee Club now, because you're going to work your tails off here!"

I was soon under Miss Hurd's spell. She did indeed teach us to put out a newspaper, skills I honed during my next 25 years as a journalist. Soon I asked the principal

---

2. *Guerrillas* (gə ril′ əz) are members of small, organized forces, usually made up of volunteers who are not soldiers in a regular army.
3. Here, *prickly* means "difficult; troublesome."
4. [*Worcester*] This city's founders brought its oddly pronounced name with them from England. It's pronounced as if it were spelled *Wooster,* with an *o* sound as in *wood.*

5. The expression *looked askance* (ə skans′) means "viewed with suspicion or disapproval."
6. A *mentor* is a wise and trusted counselor, and a *muse* is a source of artistic inspiration.

Vocabulary

portly (pôrt′ lē) *adj.* having a stout but dignified appearance
authoritarian (ə thôr′ ə tār′ ē ən) *adj.* having or expecting complete obedience to authority
ultimately (ul′ tə mit lē) *adv.* in the end; finally

to transfer me to her English class as well. There, she drilled us on grammar until I finally began to understand the logic and structure of the English language. She assigned stories for us to read and discuss; not tales of heroes, like the Greek myths I knew, but stories of underdogs—poor people, even immigrants, who seemed ordinary until a crisis drove them to do something extraordinary. She also introduced us to the literary wealth[7] of Greece— giving me a new perspective on my war-ravaged, impoverished homeland. I began to be proud of my origins.

One day, after discussing how writers should write about what they know, she assigned us to compose an essay from our own experience. Fixing me with a stern look, she added, "Nick, I want you to write about what happened to your family in Greece." I had been trying to put those painful memories behind me and left the assignment until the last moment. Then, on a warm spring afternoon, I sat in my room with a yellow pad and pencil and stared out the window at the buds on the trees. I wrote that the coming of spring always reminded me of the last time I said goodbye to my mother on a green and gold day in 1948.

I kept writing, one line after another, telling how the Communist guerrillas occupied our village, took our home and food, how my mother started planning our escape when she learned that the children were to be sent to re-education camps behind the Iron Curtain[8] and how, at the last moment, she couldn't escape with us because the guerrillas sent her with a group of women to thresh wheat in a distant village. She promised she would try to get away on her own, she told me to be brave and hung a silver cross around my neck, and then she kissed me. I watched the line of women being led down into the ravine and up the other side, until they disappeared around the bend—my mother a tiny brown figure at the end who stopped for an instant to raise her hand in one last farewell.

I wrote about our nighttime escape down the mountain, across the minefields, and into the lines of the Nationalist soldiers, who sent us to a refugee camp. It was there that we learned of our mother's execution. I felt very lucky to have come to America, I concluded, but every year, the coming of spring made me feel sad because it reminded me of the last time I saw my mother.

I handed in the essay, hoping never to see it again, but Miss Hurd had it published in the school paper. This mortified me at first, until I saw that my classmates reacted with sympathy and tact to my family's story. Without telling me, Miss

---

7. Greece's *literary wealth,* dating from about 750 to 300 B.C., includes plays, poems, and other texts that greatly influenced the development of European and American civilization.

8. During the years following World War II, the *Iron Curtain* was an imaginary barrier separating the former Soviet Union and its allies from the non-Communist world.

Vocabulary

perspective (pər spek′ tiv) *n.* point of view
impoverished (im pov′ ər isht) *adj.* reduced to poverty; made very poor
mortified (môr′ tə fīd′) *adj.* greatly embarrassed
tact (takt) *n.* the ability to handle people or situations without causing displeasure or resentment

Hurd also submitted the essay to a contest sponsored by the Freedoms Foundation at Valley Forge, Pa., and it won a medal. The Worcester paper wrote about the award and quoted my essay at length. My father, by then a "five-and-dime-store chef," as the paper described him, was <u>ecstatic</u> with pride, and the Worcester Greek community celebrated the honor to one of its own.

For the first time I began to understand the power of the written word. A secret ambition took root in me. One day, I vowed, I would go back to Greece, find out the details of my mother's death and write about her life, so her grandchildren would know of her courage. Perhaps I would even track down the men who killed her and write of their crimes. Fulfilling that ambition would take me 30 years.

Meanwhile, I followed the literary path that Miss Hurd had so forcefully set me on. After junior high, I became the editor of my school paper at Classical High School and got a part-time job at the Worcester *Telegram and Gazette*. Although my father could only give me $50 and encouragement toward a college education, I managed to finance four years at Boston University with scholarships and part-time jobs in journalism. During my last year of college, an article I wrote about a friend who had died in the Philippines—the first person to lose his life working for the Peace Corps[9]—led to my winning the Hearst Award for College

---

9. A *scholarship* is money given to help a student continue his or her education. The *Peace Corps* is a U.S. program that sends volunteers to help people in poorer countries to improve their living conditions. It was begun by President Kennedy in 1961.

Vocabulary
ecstatic (ek stat′ ik) *adj.* overwhelmed with joy

Nicholas Gage's third-grade class. Nicholas is in the back row, second from the left.

Viewing the photograph: Compare this class photo with the one on page 69. How did students change between the early 1900s and the middle 1900s? How do today's students differ from both earlier groups?

Young Nicholas with his sister and his father in 1950.

Journalism. And the plaque was given to me in the White House by President John F. Kennedy.

For a refugee who had never seen a motorized vehicle or indoor plumbing until he was 9, this was an unimaginable honor. When the Worcester paper ran a picture of me standing next to President Kennedy, my father rushed out to buy a new suit in order to be properly dressed to receive the congratulations of the Worcester Greeks. He clipped out the photograph, had it laminated in plastic and carried it in his breast pocket for the rest of his life to show everyone he met. I found the much-worn photo in his pocket on the day he died 20 years later.

In our isolated Greek village, my mother had bribed a cousin to teach her to read, for girls were not supposed to attend school beyond a certain age. She had always dreamed of her children receiving an education. She couldn't be there when I graduated from Boston University, but the person who came with my father and shared our joy was my former teacher, Marjorie Hurd. We celebrated not only my bachelor's degree but also the scholarships that paid my way to Columbia's Graduate School[10] of Journalism. There, I met the woman who would eventually become my wife. At our wedding and at the baptisms of our three children, Marjorie Hurd was always there, dancing alongside the Greeks.

By then, she was Mrs. Rabidou, for she had married a widower when she was in her early 40s. That didn't distract her from her vocation[11] of introducing young minds to English literature, however. She taught for a total of 41 years and continually would make a "project" of some balky student in whom she spied a spark of potential.[12] Often these were students from the most troubled homes, yet she would alternately bully and charm each one with her own special brand of tough love until the spark caught fire. She retired in 1981 at the age of 62 but still avidly follows the lives and careers of former students while overseeing her adult stepchildren and driving her husband on camping trips to New Hampshire.

---

10. Upon completing four years (usually) of study, college students receive an honor called a *bachelor's degree.* Some then go on to *graduate schools* for more advanced training.
11. Besides referring to an occupation, the word *vocation* can mean the particular work one feels called to do or is especially suited for.
12. A *balky* student is one who tends to stop short and refuse to go on. A student with *potential* has qualities or abilities capable of being developed.

Vocabulary
avidly (av′ id lē) *adv.* eagerly; enthusiastically

Miss Hurd was one of the first to call me on Dec. 10, 1987, when President Reagan, in his television address after the summit meeting with Gorbachev, told the nation that Eleni Gatzoyiannis' dying cry, "My children!" had helped inspire him to seek an arms agreement[13] "for all the children of the world."

"I can't imagine a better monument for your mother," Miss Hurd said with an uncharacteristic catch in her voice.

Did You Know?
Shish kebab (shish′ kə bob′) consists of chunks of meat and vegetables threaded on a long, thin skewer and broiled.

Although a bad hip makes it impossible for her to join in the Greek dancing, Marjorie Hurd Rabidou is still an honored and enthusiastic guest at all our family celebrations, including my 50th birthday picnic last summer, where the shish kebab was cooked on spits, clarinets and *bouzoukis* wailed, and costumed dancers led the guests in a serpentine[14] line around our colonial farmhouse, only 20 minutes from my first home in Worcester.

My sisters and I felt an aching void because my father was not there to lead the line, balancing a glass of wine on his head while he danced, the way he did at every celebration during his 92 years. But Miss Hurd was there, surveying the scene with quiet satisfaction. Although my parents are gone, her presence was a <u>consolation</u>, because I owe her so much.

This is truly the land of opportunity, and I would have enjoyed its bounty even if I hadn't walked into Miss Hurd's classroom in 1953. But she was the one who directed my grief and pain into writing, and if it weren't for her I wouldn't have become an investigative reporter and foreign correspondent, recorded the story of my mother's life and death in *Eleni* and now my father's story in *A Place for Us*, which is also a testament to the country that took us in. She was the catalyst[15] that sent me into journalism and indirectly caused all the good things that came after. But Miss Hurd would probably deny this emphatically.

A few years ago, I answered the telephone and heard my former teacher's voice telling me, in that won't-take-no-for-an-answer tone of hers, that she had decided I was to write and deliver the eulogy[16] at her funeral. I agreed (she didn't leave me any choice), but that's one assignment I never want to do. I hope, Miss Hurd, that you'll accept this remembrance instead.

---

13. In 1987 Mikhail *Gorbachev* was the leader of the Soviet Union. An *arms agreement* is a treaty in which nations agree to limits on certain kinds of weapons.
14. A *bouzouki* (boo zoo′ kē) is a stringed instrument similar to a mandolin; a *serpentine* (sur′ pən tēn′) line winds around, like a snake's body.

---

15. Here, the *testament* is a statement of gratitude and respect. A *catalyst* is one who stirs to action.
16. At a funeral, the *eulogy* (ū′ lə jē) is a speech praising the dead.

Vocabulary
consolation (kon′ sə lā′ shən) *n.* a comfort

Responding to Literature

PERSONAL RESPONSE

◆ What reactions and thoughts did you experience while reading this story?

Analyzing Literature

RECALL

1. According to the selection, how did the Worcester, Massachusetts, school system handle the education of non-English speakers in the 1950s?
2. Describe the "spell" that the author fell under as one of Miss Hurd's pupils.
3. What painful memories was the author trying to forget?
4. Give two examples of ways Miss Hurd became a part of the author's family.

INTERPRET

5. How did the author's first school experience in America shape him?
6. Miss Hurd assigned Nicholas Gage to write an essay about what happened to his family in Greece. What effect did that assignment have on the rest of his life?
7. In what ways did Gage live up to his mother's dreams for him?
8. In your opinion, why did Miss Hurd become such an important presence in Nicholas Gage's family life?

EVALUATE AND CONNECT

9. Theme Connection   In Gage's **narrative,** he refers to his teacher as "my mentor and my muse." What do those words mean? Why do you think Gage chose those words?
10. There are children in this country today who are war refugees like Nicholas Gage. How do you imagine they are adjusting to life in America? Do you think it would be easier or harder than it was for Gage? Give reasons for your opinions.

LITERARY ELEMENTS

Main Idea

The most important idea expressed in a paragraph or an essay is called the **main idea.** The main idea in a paragraph may or may not be directly stated in a topic sentence. Sometimes the reader has to study all the details in the paragraph and make an educated guess about its main idea. The main idea of an essay might be stated in the title or in an introductory or concluding paragraph.

1. Does the title of this selection express the main idea? Support your opinion.

2. Imagine you wanted to tell someone about the essay "The Teacher Who Changed My Life." Write one or two sentences that express the main idea of the selection.

● See **Literary Terms Handbook,** p. R6.

Extending Your Response

Writing About Literature

Author's Purpose   In the midst of describing his teacher, Nicholas Gage summarizes a book he wrote about his mother's tragic death. Write a paragraph analyzing why the author chose to include this information. What emotional impact did he hope to create?

Creative Writing

Autobiographical Essay   Develop your journal entry for the **Reading Focus** on page 367 into a personal narrative.

Listening and Speaking

Storyteller   In ancient Greece, storytellers taught the Greek people their history and legends. Play the part of a modern storyteller and tell the story of someone who has had an influence on you or on society.

Literature Groups

Award Winner!   Imagine that you and the other members of your group are among Miss Hurd's students. A national award is being presented to "The Teacher Who Changed My Life," and you have nominated Miss Hurd. With your group, develop a list of her qualities that would convince the judges to vote for Miss Hurd. Make your presentation to the class.

Reading Further

If you would like to read more about young people and their families caught in political turmoil, try these books:

The Endless Steppe by Esther Hautzig

My Brother Sam Is Dead by James Lincoln Collier

Farewell to Manzanar by Jeanne W. and James Houston

💼 **Save your work for your portfolio.**

Skill Minilesson

VOCABULARY • THE SUFFIX *-arian*

Young Nicholas Gage's first impression of his father was of someone who seemed *authoritarian,* someone who believes in the use of *authority.* The suffix *-arian* means "one who or one that." It may mean "one who believes in," "one who supports," or "one who works in or with."

Understanding the suffix *-arian* may help you with some new words. For example, if you know that *utility* means "usefulness," you can figure out that a *utilitarian* kitchen contains things that are definitely useful.

PRACTICE   Look carefully at the familiar part of each word on the left to match it to its meaning.

One who works with, believes in, or supports:
1. disciplinarian   a. people's right to be free
2. libertarian   b. system of rules and correction
3. grammarian   c. same treatment and rights for all
4. humanitarian   d. welfare of all people
5. equalitarian   e. rules for speaking and writing

Before You Read

How I Learned English

MEET GREGORY DJANIKIAN

Gregory Djanikian (jə nik′ ē ən) is an American who was born and raised in Egypt. Djanikian is an award-winning poet who has published several collections of his poems. He is currently the Director of Creative Writing at the University of Pennsylvania.

Gregory Djanikian was born in 1949. "How I Learned English" was published in 1987.

READING FOCUS

Imagine moving to a new school in a new country. How would you meet friends?

Chart It!
Work with your classmates to make a chart that shows the different ways you have made your current friends.

At School	In Sports or Clubs	At a Friend's House

Setting a Purpose
Read this poem to discover what bonds connect people.

BUILDING BACKGROUND

The Time and Place   The poem is set sometime in the later half of the twentieth century in the town of Williamsport, Pennsylvania.

Did You Know?   Baseball, or an English variation of the modern game called "rounders," has been around since the 1700s. In 1845 an amateur New York City player suggested a few changes in the game rules, including tagging the runner out. The new rules were adopted by many amateur New York City club teams, and the game's popularity grew. During the Civil War, soldiers from New York and New Jersey taught the game to other Americans.

Union Prisoners at Salisbury, N.C., 1863. Otto Boetticher. Colored stone lithograph with buff and blue tints, 21 x 37½ in. Lithographer: Sarony, Major and Knapp. The Stokes Collection. The New York Public Library.

How I Learned English

Gregory Djanikian

It was in an empty lot
Ringed by elms and fir and honeysuckle.
Bill Corson was pitching in his buckskin jacket,
Chuck Keller, fat even as a boy, was on first,
5   His t-shirt riding up over his gut,
Ron O'Neill, Jim, Dennis, were talking it up
In the field, a blue sky above them
Tipped with cirrus.
                   And there I was,
Just off the plane and plopped in the middle
10   Of Williamsport, Pa. and a neighborhood game,
Unnatural and without any moves,
My notions of baseball and America
Growing fuzzier each time I whiffed.

How I Learned English

So it was not impossible that I,
15 Banished° to the outfield and daydreaming
Of water, or a hotel in the mountains,
Would suddenly find myself in the path
Of a ball stung by Joe Barone.
I watched it closing in
20 Clean and untouched, transfixed°
By its easy arc before it hit
My forehead with a thud.
          I fell back,
Dazed, clutching my brow,
Groaning, "Oh my shin, oh my shin,"
25 And everybody peeled away from me
And dropped from laughter, and there we were,
All of us writhing on the ground for one reason
Or another.
          Someone said "shin" again,
There was a wild stamping of hands on the ground,
30 A kicking of feet, and the fit
Of laughter overtook me too,
And that was important, as important
As Joe Barone asking me how I was
Through his tears, picking me up
35 And dusting me off with hands like swatters,
And though my head felt heavy,
I played on till dusk
Missing flies and pop-ups and grounders
And calling out in desperation things like
40 "Yours" and "take it," but doing all right,
Tugging at my cap in just the right way,
Crouching low, my feet set,
"Hum baby" sweetly on my lips.

---

15 To be *banished* is to be expelled or driven away—in this case, from
the infield.
20 To be *transfixed* is to be made motionless, as from wonder or fear.

Responding to Literature

PERSONAL RESPONSE

◆ Return to the **Reading Focus** on page 376. How does the speaker's experience connect with your ideas about making friends?

Analyzing Literature

RECALL AND INTERPRET

1. Why are the speaker's notions of America and baseball fuzzy?

2. Why do all the players end up on the ground when the speaker groans, "my shin, my shin"?

3. Why does the speaker mention the other players by name? Do you think they are still friends? Explain your answer.

EVALUATE AND CONNECT

4. At what point in the poem do you know that the boys have become friends? How does this experience connect with your own?

5. How does the poet bring to life the experience of playing a lighthearted baseball game?

6. Have you ever attempted to play a new game with strangers, or had a stranger join your own game? Describe your experience.

LITERARY ELEMENTS

Setting

The **setting** of a story, poem, or play is the time and place in which the events take place. The setting can include the geographic location, the time period, the season of the year, and even the time of day. Sometimes the writer describes all or part of the setting. For example, the poet tells the reader that the events in "How I Learned English" take place during a baseball game in the town of Williamsport, Pennsylvania.

1. How can you tell what time of day the baseball game started?

2. Why would a newly arrived immigrant find the setting of the poem meaningful?

● See **Literary Terms Handbook,** p. R10.

Extending Your Response

Literature Groups

Changing Places   Imagine that you are the speaker of "How I Learned English." Work with your group to write a series of letters about your new life in America to people in your old home town.

Writing About Literature

Point of View   "How I Learned English" is told from the point of view of a young boy who has recently immigrated to the United States. Write a brief poem or a prose paragraph from another character's point of view.

COMPARING SELECTIONS

The Teacher Who Changed My Life **and** How I Learned English

COMPARE **RESPONSES**

Both Nicholas Gage's personal narrative and Gregory Djanikian's poem focus on the experiences of a new immigrant.

1. Which selection did you prefer—the narrative or the poem? Give reasons for your answer.

2. From which selection did you learn more about the immigrant experience? What did you learn?

COMPARE **CHARACTERS**

In both selections, the narrator or speaker tells of his experience learning English. If Nicholas Gage and the speaker in "How I Learned English" could meet, what do you think they might tell each other? Write an imaginary conversation between the two characters as they compare their experiences of learning English.

COMPARE **EXPERIENCES**

The essay and the poem each give the reader a different sense of how it feels to be a new immigrant in this country.

- Think of a non-English-speaking country you would like to visit someday. Find pictures of the places that interest you. Try to find out a bit about the language and the customs.

- Close your eyes and imagine traveling to this country and meeting students your age. What would be a typical activity for them? Think about how you would communicate with your new friends.

- Share your ideas with a partner or a small group.

Using Irregular Verbs Correctly

For **regular verbs,** the past form is made by adding *-ed* to the base. The past participle form is the same as the past form, but with a "helping" verb such as *has.*

Base form: I *like* poems.   **Past form:** I *liked* the poem by Lucille Clifton.
Past participle form: I *have liked* most of the poems in this book.

Many **irregular verbs** use the same form for the past and the past participle.

Base form: *catch*   **Past form:** *caught*
Past participle form: *has caught*

Some irregular verbs, however, have two different forms—one for use without a helping verb and another for use with a helping verb.

Base form: *grows*   **Past form:** *grew*
Past participle form: *had grown*

Problem 1 an improperly formed irregular verb

> *The player **standed** in the outfield.*

> Solution   *The player **stood** in the outfield.*

Problem 2 use of the past form when the past participle is needed

> *He **seen** the ball before it hit him.*

> Solution   *He **had seen** the ball before it hit him.*

Here are the base form, past form, and past participle form of some irregular verbs.

begin, began, begun   do, did, done   know, knew, known
give, gave, given   tell, told, told   write, wrote, written

● For more about irregular verbs, see **Language Handbook,** p. R16.

EXERCISE

Write the correct form of each verb in parentheses.

1. Marjorie Hurd (give) Nicholas Gage an assignment.

2. He (write) the first essay he had ever (write).

3. He (tell) about how his journey had (begin) in a nighttime escape.

4. His classmates had not (knew) the difficulties Gage had (go) through.

Before You Read

Oh Broom, Get to Work and *Anansi and His Visitor, Turtle*

MEET
YOSHIKO UCHIDA

Yoshiko Uchida (yō shē′ kō ū′ chē dä) was born in California to Japanese parents. As a child and young adult, she did not feel accepted as an American. She expressed her thoughts in journals in which she "was trying to . . . preserve the . . . joy and sadness of certain moments."

Yoshiko Uchida was born in 1921 and died in 1992. This story was first published in 1977.

MEET
EDNA MASON KAULA

Born in Australia, Edna Mason Kaula (kä ōō′ lä) has lived in several countries. Kaula has written and illustrated books for children and adults, based on her travels around the world.

Edna Mason Kaula was born in 1906. The story about Anansi and Turtle comes from her book African Village Folktales, *published in 1968.*

READING FOCUS

How should hosts and their guests behave toward each other?

QuickWrite

List ways to deal with guests who don't behave properly.

Setting a Purpose

Read these two stories to discover ways to deal with an awkward guest-host situation.

BUILDING BACKGROUND

Did You Know? The traditional tales of West Africa include a trickster named Anansi. Anansi is often a spider who is a smart and funny mischief-maker. His tricks can be nasty, but his victims usually get even in the end.

VOCABULARY PREVIEW

intrusion (in trōō′ zhən) *n.* a sudden interruption; p. 384
devise (di vīz′) *v.* to think out; invent; plan; p. 384
pious (pī′ əs) *adj.* having either genuine or pretended religious devotion; p. 385
pompous (pom′ pəs) *adj.* showing an exaggerated sense of self-importance; p. 385
dispense (dis pens′) *v.* to give out in portions; p. 385
indifferent (in dif′ ər ənt) *adj.* having or showing a lack of feeling, concern, or care; p. 385
laden (lād′ ən) *adj.* loaded; weighed down; burdened; p. 386
meek (mēk) *adj.* patient and mild in manner; gentle; p. 389
delectable (di lek′ tə bəl) *adj.* highly pleasing or delightful, especially to the taste; delicious; p. 389
ravenous (rav′ ə nəs) *adj.* extremely hungry; p. 390
cunning (kun′ ing) *adj.* crafty; sly; p. 390
anticipation (an tis′ ə pā′ shən) *n.* a feeling of excited expectation; p. 390

Oh Broom, Get to Work

Yoshiko Uchida

Fuji from Lava Beach. Lilla Cabot Perry (1848–1933). Oil on canvas, 7 x 21¾ in. Collection of Mrs. Lilla Cabot Levitt.

I was on my way home from school when I found it. A little dead sparrow. It lay still and stiff, its legs thrust in the air like two sticks. It was the first dead creature I had seen close up, and it filled me with both dread and fascination.

I knew what I would do. I would give the bird a nice funeral. Mama would find a piece of soft red silk for me from her bag of sewing scraps. I would wrap the bird in a silken shroud,[1] put it in a candy box, and bury it beneath the peach tree. Maybe I would have Mama say a prayer for it, like the minister did at real funerals.

---

1. Here, *shroud* means "a cloth used to wrap a body for burial."

Oh Broom, Get to Work

I picked up the bird carefully, cupping it in both hands, and ran home. I rushed through the kitchen and flung open the swinging door to the dining room.

"Look, Mama! I found a dead sparrow!"

But Mama was busy. She was sitting in the easy chair, knitting quietly. Sitting across from her on the sofa was a squat blob of a man—balding and gray—as silent as a mushroom.

The only sound was the soft ticking of the Chelsea clock on the mantel above the fireplace. I could see dust motes floating in the shaft of late afternoon sun that filtered in from the small west window.

Poor Mama was stuck with company again. She and the guest had both run out of things to say, but the visitor didn't want to leave.

"Hello, Yo Chan," my mother called. She seemed happy for the intrusion. "How was school today?"

But all I thought was, company again! It wasn't the first time a visitor had deprived me of my mother's time and attention, and I was tired of having them intrude into our lives uninvited. I stomped out of the living room without even a word of greeting to our guest, and knew I would have to bury the sparrow by myself.

Mama might have sung a Japanese hymn for me in her high, slightly off-key voice, and she certainly would have offered a better prayer than I could devise. But I did the best I could.

"Dear Heavenly Father," I began. "Please bless this little bird. It never hurt anybody. Thank you. Amen."

I buried the box beneath a mound of soft, loose dirt, picked a few nasturtiums to lay on top, and made a cross out of two small twigs.

The gray-blob mushroom was just another of the countless visitors, usually from Japan, who came to see my parents. They were both graduates of Doshisha, one of Japan's leading Christian universities, and had close ties with many of its professors. This meant that many of our visitors were ministers or young men studying to become ministers at the Pacific School of Religion in Berkeley.[2]

Once in a while, one of the visitors would be a pleasant surprise. Like the Reverend Kimura, who sang the books of the Bible to the tune of an old folk song.

"*Mah-tai, Mah-ko, Luka, Yoha-neh-deh-un* . . ." he sang out in a loud, clear voice. "*Shito, Roma, Corinto, Zen-ko-sho* . . ." He clapped in time as he sang.

I saw Mama's eyes light up as she listened, and soon she joined in, clapping and singing and laughing at the pure joy of it.

Mama surprised me sometimes. She could be a lot of fun depending on whom she was with. It was too bad, I thought, that so much of the time she had to be

Did You Know?
The *nasturtium* is a common funnel-shaped flower that grows in a variety of colors.

---

2. This school is in *Berkeley*, California.

Vocabulary
intrusion (in tr$\overline{oo}'$ zhən) *n.* a sudden interruption
devise (di vīz') *v.* to think out; invent; plan

serious and proper, while visiting ministers smothered her with their pious attitudes.

To me they were all achingly and endlessly boring. It was only once in a great while that a Reverend Kimura turned up, like a bright red jelly bean in a jar full of black licorice.

One pompous minister from Japan not only stayed overnight, which was bad enough, but left his dirty bathwater in the tub for Mama to wash out.

"What nerve!" Keiko fumed.[3]

"I'll say!" I echoed.

But Mama explained that in Japan everyone washed and rinsed outside the tub and got in just to soak. "That way the water in the tub stays clean, and you leave it for the next person."

Mama got down on her knees to wash out the tub, saying, "We're lucky he didn't try to wash himself outside the tub and flood the bathroom."

Some kind of luck, I thought.

I didn't feel at all lucky about the seminary[4] students who often dropped in, plunked themselves down on our sofa, and stayed until they were invited to have supper with us.

"Poor boys, they're lonely and homesick," Mama would say.

"They just need some of Mama's kind heart and good cooking," Papa would add. And if they needed some fatherly advice,

he was more than willing to dispense plenty of that as well.

Both my parents had grown up poor, and they also knew what it was to be lonely. They cared deeply about other people and were always ready to lend a helping hand to anyone. Mama couldn't bear to think of her children ever being less than kind and caring.

"Don't ever be indifferent," she would say to Keiko and me. "That is the worst fault of all."

It was a fault she certainly never had. She would even send vitamins or herbs to some ailing person she had just met in the dentist's waiting room.

On holidays all the Japanese students from the Pacific School of Religion—sometimes as many as five or six—were invited to dinner. Keiko and I always complained shamelessly when they came.

"Aw, Mama . . . do you *have* to invite them?"

But we knew what we were expected to do. We flicked the dust cloth over the furniture, added extra boards to the dining room table so it filled up the entire room, and set it with Mama's good linen tablecloth and the company china.

If it was to be a turkey dinner, we put out the large plates and good silverware. If it was a sukiyaki dinner, we put out the rice bowls, smaller dishes, and black lacquer chopsticks.

The men came in their best clothes, their squeaky shoes shined, their hair smelling of camellia hair oil. Papa didn't

---

3. Here, *fume* means "to be filled with or show anger or irritation."
4. A *seminary* is a school that trains ministers, priests, or rabbis.

Vocabulary
pious (pī′ əs) *adj.* having either genuine or pretended religious devotion
pompous (pom′ pəs) *adj.* showing an exaggerated sense of self-importance
dispense (dis pens′) *v.* to give out in portions
indifferent (in dif′ ər ənt) *adj.* having or showing a lack of feeling, concern, or care

cook much else, but he was an expert when it came to making sukiyaki,[5] and he cooked it right at the table with gas piped in from the kitchen stove. As the men arrived, he would start the fat sizzling in the small iron pan.

Soon Mama would bring out huge platters <u>laden</u> with thin slivers of beef, slices of bean curd cake, scallions, bamboo shoots, spinach, celery, and yam noodle threads. Then Papa would combine a little of everything in broth flavored with soy sauce,[6] sugar, and wine, and the mouth-watering smells would drift through the entire house.

One evening in the middle of a sukiyaki dinner, one of the guests, Mr. Okada, suddenly rose from the table and hurried into the kitchen. We all stopped eating as the scholarly Mr. Okada vanished without explanation.

"Mama," I began, "he's going the wrong way if he has to . . ."

Mama stopped me with a firm hand on my knee. My sister and I looked at each other. What did he want in the kitchen anyway? More rice? Water? What?

It seemed a half hour before Mr. Okada finally reappeared. But he was smiling and seemed much happier.

"I'm sorry," he murmured, "but it was so warm I had to remove my winter undershirt." He wiped his face with a big handkerchief and added, "I feel much better now."

I knew if I looked at Keiko we would both explode. But I did. And we did. We laughed so hard we had to leave the table and rush into the kitchen holding our sides. Keiko and I often got the giggles at company dinners, and the harder we tried to stop, the harder we laughed. The only solution was for us not ever to glance at each other if we felt the giggles coming on.

In spite of all our grumbling, Keiko and I often enjoyed ourselves at these dinners. Sometimes it was Papa who provided the laughs. He loved to talk, and everyone always liked listening to his stories. Sometimes he would tell a joke he had heard at the office:

A visitor from Japan looked up at the sky. "Beautiful pigeons!" he says to a native San Franciscan.

"No, no," answers the native. "Those aren't pigeons, they're gulls."

---

5. This Japanese dish consists of thin strips of meat, vegetables, and other ingredients cooked together, usually at the dining table.
6. *Bean curd,* also known as tofu (tō′ fōō), is a food made from soybeans. *Scallions* are young green onions. *Soy sauce,* another soybean product, is a salty, dark-brown sauce used in Japanese and Chinese cooking.

Vocabulary
laden (lād′ ən) *adj.* loaded; weighed down; burdened

The visitor replies, smiling, "Well, gulls or boys, they're beautiful pigeons!"

Much laughter all around.

After dinner Papa liked to gather everyone around the piano. He had a good baritone voice, often sang solos at church, and even organized the church choir. Keiko played the piano, and we sang everything from "Old Black Joe" to "In the Good Old Summertime."

Sometimes Keiko and I added to the entertainment by playing duets for our guests—a fairly audacious[7] act since most of the time I hadn't practiced all week. It never occurred to me then, but I suppose we were just as boring to them as they so often seemed to us.

I once thought I'd found the perfect solution for getting rid of unwanted guests. Mrs. Wasa, who was like an adopted grandmother, told me one day of an old Japanese superstition.

"If you want someone to leave," she said, "just drape a cloth over the bristles of a broom and stand it upside down. It always works!"

I filed that wonderful bit of information inside my head, and the very next time Mama was trapped in the living room with another silent mushroom, I gave it a try. I did just as Mrs. Wasa instructed and stood the broom at the crack of a swinging door leading to the dining and living rooms.

"Oh broom," I murmured. "Get to work!"

I kept a watchful eye on our visitor, and before too long, he actually got up and left.

"Mama, it worked! It worked!" I shouted, dancing into the living room with the broom. "He left! I got him to leave!"

But Mama was horrified.

"*Mah*, Yo Chan," she said. "You put the broom at the doorway where he could see?"

I nodded. "I didn't think he'd notice."

Only then did I realize that our visitor had not only seen the broom, but had probably left because he knew a few Japanese superstitions himself.

I'd always thought the seminary on the hill was bent on endlessly churning out dull ministers to try my soul. But that afternoon I felt as though I'd evened the score just a little.

---

7. An *audacious* (ô dā' shəs) act is recklessly or shamelessly bold and daring.

Anansi and His Visitor, Turtle
A Story from the Ashanti People

Retold by Edna Mason Kaula ৵

It was almost time for Sun to sink to his resting place when Turtle, tired and dusty from hours of wandering, came to Anansi's house in the middle of a clearing in the woods. Turtle was hungry and the appetizing aroma of freshly cooked fish and yams drew him to approach Anansi's door and to knock. Anansi jerked the door open. When he saw the tired stranger he was inwardly annoyed, but it was an unwritten law of his country that one must never, no never, refuse hospitality to a passer-by.

Anansi smiled grimly and said, "Come in, come in, and share my dinner, Mr. Turtle."

As Turtle stretched out one paw to help himself from the steaming platter Anansi almost choked on a mouthful of food. In a shocked voice he said, "Turtle, I must remind you that in my country it is ill-mannered to come to the table without first washing. Please go to the stream at the foot of the hill and wash your dusty paws."

Turtle waddled down the hill and waded in the water for a while. He even washed his face. By the time he had trudged back up the trail to Anansi's house, the platter of fish was half empty. Anansi was eating at a furious rate.

Turtle stretched out one paw to help himself to food, but again Anansi stopped him. "Turtle, your paws are still dusty. Please, go wash them."

"It is the dust from the long trail up the hill," Turtle explained in a <u>meek</u> voice. Clearly, it was not Turtle's place to argue if he expected to share the <u>delectable</u> meal,

Viewing the painting: How does the artist combine animal and human characteristics in artwork here and on page 388? Why does he do so?

Vocabulary

meek (mēk) *adj.* patient and mild in manner; gentle
delectable (di lek′ tə bəl) *adj.* highly pleasing or delightful, especially to the taste; delicious

so he crawled down the hill a second time and rewashed his paws. Turtle was careful to walk on the grass beside the dusty trail on the climb back to Anansi's house. He hurried, for by now he was <u>ravenous</u>.

But, oh dear! Anansi had scraped the platter bare of fish and yams. "My, that was a good dinner," he said, wiping the last drop of gravy from his chin.

"Thank you for your wonderful hospitality, Anansi. Some day you must visit me." And Turtle, in a huff, went on home.

Some months later Anansi visited Turtle. After creepy-crawling all day from one tall grass stem to the next, he found Turtle snoozing beside the river.

"Well, well," exclaimed Turtle. "So you have come to share my dinner. Make yourself comfortable, my dear Anansi, while I go below and prepare the food." He plunged into the river with a splash. Anansi was hungry. He paced the shore line and watched for Turtle's reappearance.

At last Turtle's head popped above the water. "Dinner is ready," he called as he bit into a huge clam. "Come on down." Then he disappeared from sight.

Anansi dived head first into the water, sank a few inches, then floated to the surface. His spindly legs and tiny body prevented him from sinking. He flipped and flapped his puny[1] arms, tried swallow dives

---

1. *Puny* (pyōō′ nē) means "small and weak."

and belly flops, but he could not reach the bed of the river.

Then that <u>cunning</u> spider schemed. He filled the pockets of his jacket with small round pebbles, dived into the river, and sank with a bump that landed him right at the dinner table. Before him was spread the most delicious meal he had ever seen. There were oysters and clams, mussels, slices of eel, and crabs. As a centerpiece, sprays of watercress rested against large pink shrimp. Anansi's eyes widened with pleasure, his stomach rumbled in <u>anticipation</u>.

Did You Know?

Watercress is a floating water plant bearing long clusters of small white flowers. Its leaves are eaten as salad greens.

Turtle, already seated at the table, swallowed a piece of eel, looked at Anansi and said, "Oh, Anansi, I must remind you that in my country it is ill-mannered to come to the table wearing a jacket. Please take it off."

Very slowly Anansi removed his jacket. Very slowly Anansi left the table. Without the weight of the pebbles to hold him down, he floated straight up through the green water and out of sight.

When you set out to outsmart another person to your own advantage, there is usually someone who can outsmart you.

Vocabulary
ravenous (rav′ ə nəs) *adj.* extremely hungry
cunning (kun′ ing) *adj.* crafty; sly
anticipation (an tis′ ə pā′ shən) *n.* a feeling of excited expectation

Responding to Literature

Oh Broom, Get to Work and *Anansi and His Visitor, Turtle*

PERSONAL RESPONSE

◆ Take another look at your list of ways to deal with guests from the **Reading Focus** on page 382. How do your ideas compare with the methods of the narrator in "Oh Broom, Get to Work" or Anansi in "Anansi and His Visitor, Turtle"?

Analyzing Literature

RECALL

1. What is Yo Chan's opinion about most of the visiting students?

2. What are the two meals served on holidays at Yo Chan's house?

3. What is the Japanese superstition about getting rid of guests who stay too long?

4. How does Anansi get rid of Turtle? What does Turtle do to Anansi to get even?

INTERPRET

5. Do you think Yo Chan appreciates her mother's hospitality to the young men? How can you tell?

6. From the description of cooking sukiyaki, what can you **infer** about Yo Chan's feelings toward her father and her heritage?

7. Does Yo Chan or Anansi feel guilty for sending the guests away? Support your opinion with evidence from the stories.

8. Why do you think the storyteller ends "Anansi and His Visitor, Turtle" with a moral?

EVALUATE AND CONNECT

9. The characters in "Anansi and His Visitor, Turtle" talk and act like people. How would your response to the story change if the characters were real human beings?

10. Do you think Yo Chan's reaction to her parents' guests is hospitable? How would you have behaved in her situation?

LITERARY ELEMENTS

Metaphors

Think about what you have learned about **figurative language**. A **metaphor** compares two seemingly different things by saying one thing is the other thing. A **simile** uses the words *like* or *as* to compare two things. In "Oh Broom, Get to Work," Yo Chan uses a metaphor when she calls the first uninvited guest "the gray-blob mushroom." He isn't actually a mushroom, but Yo Chan thinks he looks and acts like one.

1. Reread or skim "Oh Broom, Get to Work" to find another example of a metaphor and one of a simile. Write a sentence explaining what two things are being compared in each example.

2. Find and copy an example of a metaphor or a simile from any other selection in this theme. Tell what two things are being compared in it.

● See **Literary Terms Handbook,** p. R6.

Literature and Writing

Writing About Literature

Comparing Characters Write a paragraph or two comparing the way the narrator in "Oh Broom, Get to Work" deals with uninvited guests with the way Anansi and Turtle treat each other in "Anansi and His Visitor, Turtle."

Creative Writing

The Next Meal What happened to the jacket that Anansi left at the bottom of the river with Turtle? Write a sequel to "Anansi and His Visitor, Turtle" in which Turtle returns the jacket and manages to drop in during another delicious meal at Anansi's house.

Extending Your Response

Literature Groups

Debating Indifference In the story, Yo Chan's mother says, "Don't ever be indifferent. That's the worst fault of all." Do you agree with this philosophy? Choose to be for or against this belief and hold a group debate.

Interdisciplinary Activity

Art The characters of Yo Chan and Anansi have been taught by their families and community that polite people (or animals) invite guests into their homes and treat them well. Yet both characters have trouble being kind hosts. Using the character of Yo Chan or Anansi as a narrator, create a comic book for younger children about the proper way to be a host. Include humorous drawings or cartoons to illustrate your rules.

Learning for Life

Letter of Introduction Imagine you are a Japanese student planning to study in Berkeley, California. You have heard from another student that the Uchidas are wonderful hosts who might let you stay at their home until you find a place of your own. Write a letter to the Uchidas introducing yourself and explaining your needs.

Reading Further

To read more by these two writers, try:
A Jar of Dreams and *Journey Home* by Yoshiko Uchida

African Village Folktales by Edna Mason Kaula

To learn more about Japanese Americans, try:

Japanese-American Journey: The Story of a People edited by Florence M. Hongo

📖 **Save your work for your portfolio.**

Skill Minilessons

GRAMMAR AND LANGUAGE • SUFFIXES AND THE SILENT *e*

For words ending with a silent *e,* remember to drop the final *e* when you add a suffix. For example, in the sentence: "The dead bird continued to *fascinate* Yo Chan," the word *fascinate* is a verb. The suffix *-ion* is added to *fascinate* to create the noun form in this sentence: "The dead sparrow filled me with dread and *fascination.*"

● For more about suffixes and spelling, see
Language Handbook, pp. R44–R45.

PRACTICE Identify each word in the list as either the noun form or the verb form. Then use the other form of each word in a sentence.
1. confuse
2. invention
3. narrate
4. correction
5. protection

READING AND THINKING • PROBLEM/SOLUTION

The plots in most short stories contain one or more problems that the characters try to solve. In many stories, character development is revealed in the way characters respond to problems in their lives. In "Oh, Broom, Get to Work," the narrator tries to solve her major problem (too many guests) in a variety of ways until she comes upon the solution of the broom.

PRACTICE Reread "Anansi and His Visitor, Turtle," and find two problems that are solved by the end of the story.

● For more about helpful reading strategies, see
Reading Handbook, p. R89.

VOCABULARY • SYNONYMS

Synonyms are words with similar meanings. That does not mean that they have the *same* meaning. For example, *neutral* and *indifferent* are synonyms. However, a judge, an umpire, or a referee should be neutral but not indifferent. *Neutral* suggests not taking sides, while *indifferent* suggests not caring.

PRACTICE Think about what the underlined word means in each sentence. Then choose the better synonym for that word *as it is used in the sentence.*

1. A friend who telephones during dinner might apologize for the intrusion.
   a. invasion   b. interruption
2. There's no excuse for being pompous about your school or family.
   a. proud   b. conceited
3. The pickup truck pulled into the parking lot, laden with gifts for the children.
   a. loaded   b. burdened

Vo·cab·u·lar·y Skills

Roots

A **root** is a word part that is the base of many words. A root may be a whole word, such as *place.* A root that is a whole word is also called a "base word." When prefixes or suffixes are attached to a root, new words are formed, for example *placement, replace,* and *displaced.*

Many roots come from Anglo-Saxon, or Old English—for example, *burn, dear, drink, knob, spell, spin,* and *wring.* Even with prefixes and suffixes added to them, you can usually recognize and understand words with these roots. Some words with Latin or Greek roots, on the other hand, may be difficult to interpret. For example, the Latin root *vers,* meaning "to turn," is the basis of the words *reverse* and *versatile.*

If you know the meaning of a root, you may notice it in an unfamiliar word and be able to get some idea of the word's meaning. The chart here shows some common Latin roots.

Root	Meaning	Examples
dic, dict	say	predict
fac, fact	make, do	factory
mort	die	mortal
port	carry	portable
rupt	break	interrupt
sol	alone	sole
terr	land	territory
tort	twist, turn	torture
var	different	variety
viv	live	survive

EXERCISES

A. Use the list of roots above to figure out the answer that completes each sentence.
1. If Anansi preferred solitude, then he would probably prefer to eat
    a. quickly   b. with company   c. alone
2. If Turtle followed a tortuous path to get to Anansi's house, the path was
    a. twisting   b. low   c. narrow
3. Anansi's edict to Turtle is something that he
    a. offers him   b. shows him   c. says to him
4. If Turtle needed some dinner in order to feel vivacious, food would make him
    a. happy   b. lively   c. grateful
5. Anansi's problems with the terrain in Turtle's country were problems with the
    a. land   b. language   c. rules

B. Use the list of roots to match each word on the left with its definition.
1. facsimile   a. burst
2. mortal   b. a copy
3. invariable   c. lonely
4. ruptured   d. unchanging
5. desolate   e. causing death

Writing Skills

Describing with Sensory Details

Do you remember this description from Yoshiko Uchida's story "Oh Broom, Get to Work"?

> "... on the sofa was a squat blob of a man—balding and gray—silent as a mushroom."

Suppose Uchida had written only, "On the sofa sat a very boring man." You would have understood what she meant, but you would not have been able to picture the man or hear his silence. Uchida uses **sensory details**–details appealing to the senses–to bring her description to life.

When you write descriptions, rely on sensory details. They fill your writing with vivid, memorable images. The chart below shows some sensory details from "Oh, Broom, Get to Work." Use a similar chart to list sensory details for your own descriptive writing.

Chris's Apartment

Start:	Front Door
Details:	sticks slams good smells come out
↓	
Straight ahead:	Living Room
Details:	TV window to street comfy sofa
↓	
To Left:	Kitchen
Details:	Chris's dad bright light always hot

ACTIVITY

1. Create and fill in a sensory detail chart about a place where you like to be. Include at least two details for each of as many of the five senses as you can.

2. Using details from your chart, write a paragraph describing this place.

ESSAY

The word *essay* comes from a French verb meaning "to try." The noun *essay* refers to a particular kind of writing. In an **essay,** an author "tries out" an idea in a short work of nonfiction focusing on a single subject. All essays contain the basic elements described on this page.

THEME refers to the main point or message of the essay. The theme of an essay may be stated directly in a thesis statement that appears in the introduction. The **thesis statement**—usually a single sentence—gives the main idea of the essay.

PURPOSE refers to an author's reason for writing an essay. An essayist usually has one or more purposes in mind—to inform, to entertain, to persuade, or to tell about real people, places, and events.

TEXT STRUCTURE is the way a piece of writing is organized. A narrative essay such as Thurber's "The Night the Bed Fell" is meant to entertain. It is usually organized like a story, with a setting, characters, plot (in chronological order), and theme.

STYLE is an author's personal way of using language. You can see an essayist's style in his or her word choice, sentence patterns, and ways of moving from idea to idea.

TONE is the author's attitude toward his or her subject. An essayist's tone may be witty or serious, sad or upbeat, scholarly or sarcastic, admiring or angry.

MODEL

"Bums in the Attic" begins with a clear, direct thesis statement: "I want a house on a hill like the ones with the gardens where Papa works."

The purpose of Nicholas Gage's "The Teacher Who Changed My Life" is to tell you about a remarkable person, ". . . a salty-tongued, no-nonsense school teacher named Marjorie Hurd."

In "The Night the Bed Fell," Thurber's style comes through in his lively, surprising language, ". . . it is almost necessary to throw furniture around, shake doors, and bark like a dog, to lend the proper atmosphere . . . to what is admittedly a somewhat incredible tale."

In "The Dog Diaries," Markoe describes her dogs with humor and honesty, "I pick dogs that remind me of myself—scrappy, mutt-faced, with a hint of mange."

Active Reading Strategies

Tips for Reading an Essay

When reading an essay, active readers use strategies like the ones below to build on their understanding of the essay and to evaluate what they have read.

- For more about these and other reading strategies, see **Reading Handbook,** pp. R85–R99.

PREDICT

While reading, ask yourself questions such as, "What does the title mean?" or "How will the author respond?" Combine clues in the text with what you already know to predict what will happen next.

QUESTION

Questioning helps you separate facts from opinions. Facts are statements that can be proved. Opinions express a person's beliefs and cannot be proved. Writers sometimes present strong opinions as if they were facts. Questioning will help you recognize the difference.

VISUALIZE

Use the details the essayist gives you to form pictures in your mind. As you read a descriptive passage in an essay, ask yourself, "What does this person look like?" or "Can I picture the scene the writer is describing?"

EVALUATE

After you finish reading an essay and reflecting on its ideas, think about what it means to you. Discuss it with your classmates. Listening to the observations of others will give you a deeper understanding of the essay.

APPLYING THE STRATEGIES

Read the following essay, "The Night the Bed Fell." Use the **Active Reading Model** notes in the margins as you read. Write your responses on a separate piece of paper or use self-stick notes.

Before You Read

The Night the Bed Fell

MEET JAMES THURBER

James Thurber is considered one of America's greatest humorists. He was born in Columbus, Ohio, the middle child in an eccentric family of three boys. He wrote hilarious-but-true stories about his unusual childhood home, but, as he explained, "all truths in that house were peculiar." He also used his wit and his artistic talent to create well-loved cartoons that were published in magazines and collected in books.

James Thurber was born in 1894 and died in 1961. This story was first published in 1933.

READING FOCUS

What stories about unusual relatives or humorous situations are retold again and again in your family?

QuickWrite

Write about a funny family incident—for example, a holiday meal that didn't turn out right, or a visit from a relative.

Setting a Purpose

Some titles tease your imagination. You might want to read this essay to find out what happened the night the bed fell.

BUILDING BACKGROUND

Did You Know?   James Thurber was successful in nearly every category of writing. He was a newspaper reporter, magazine writer and editor, cartoonist, children's book writer, essayist, humorist, novelist, playwright, and screenwriter for movies and television!

VOCABULARY PREVIEW

premonition (prē′ mə nish′ ən) *n.* a feeling that something is about to happen; warning or sign; p. 400

destine (des′ tin) *v.* to determine beforehand; p. 400

avert (ə vurt′) *v.* to keep from happening; prevent; p. 401

fortitude (fôr tə tōod′) *n.* firm courage or strength of mind in the face of pain or danger; p. 401

perilous (per′ə ləs) *adj.* dangerous; risky; p. 403

uncanny (un kan′ ē) *adj.* so strange as to cause fear or wonder; weird; p. 404

endeavor (en dev′ ər) *n.* a serious attempt to accomplish something; undertaking; p. 404

extricate (eks′ trə kāt′) *v.* to release from entanglement or difficulty; set free; p. 404

culprit (kul′ prit) *n.* one guilty of some offense; p. 405

The Night the Bed Fell

James Thurber

I suppose that the high-water mark of my youth in Columbus, Ohio, was the night the bed fell on my father. It makes a better recitation (unless, as some friends of mine have said, one has heard it five or six times) than it does a piece of writing, for it is almost necessary to throw furniture around, shake doors, and bark like a dog, to lend the proper atmosphere and verisimilitude[1] to what is admittedly a somewhat incredible tale. Still, it did take place.

---

1. If something has *verisimilitude* (ver′ ə si mil′ ə tood′), it has the appearance of being true.

The Night the Bed Fell

ACTIVE
READING
MODEL

QUESTION

What do these details tell you about Grandfather's character?

It happened, then, that my father had decided to sleep in the attic one night, to be away where he could think. My mother opposed the notion strongly because, she said, the old wooden bed up there was unsafe: it was wobbly and the heavy headboard would crash down on father's head in case the bed fell, and kill him. There was no dissuading[2] him, however, and at a quarter past ten he closed the attic door behind him and went up the narrow twisting stairs. We later heard ominous creakings as he crawled into bed. Grandfather, who usually slept in the attic bed when he was with us, had disappeared some days before. (On these occasions he was usually gone six or eight days and returned growling and out of temper, with the news that the federal Union was run by a passel of blockheads and that the Army of the Potomac[3] didn't have a chance.)

We had visiting us at this time a nervous first cousin of mine named Briggs Beall, who believed that he was likely to cease breathing when he was asleep. It was his feeling that if he were not awakened every hour during the night, he might die of suffocation. He had been accustomed to setting an alarm clock to ring at intervals until morning, but I persuaded him to abandon this. He slept in my room and I told him that I was such a light sleeper that if anybody quit breathing in the same room with me, I would wake instantly. He tested me the first night—which I had suspected he would—by holding his breath after my regular breathing had convinced him I was asleep. I was not asleep, however, and called to him. This seemed to allay his fears a little, but he took the precaution of putting a glass of spirits of camphor[4] on a little table at the head of his bed. In case I didn't arouse him until he was almost gone, he said, he would sniff the camphor, a powerful reviver. Briggs was not the only member of his family who had his crotchets.[5] Old Aunt Melissa Beall (who could whistle like a man, with two fingers in her mouth) suffered under the premonition that she was destined to die on South High Street, because she had been born on South High Street and married on South High Street. Then there was Aunt Sarah

PREDICT

What might happen to Briggs Beall later in the essay?

---

2. To *dissuade* is to argue or advise against an action or belief.
3. The *Army of the Potomac* was the eastern branch of the Union army during the Civil War.
4. To *allay* is to calm or relieve. *Spirits of camphor* is a strong-smelling, distilled mixture that is used to soothe aches.
5. The family members' *crotchets* are their peculiar ideas or beliefs.

Vocabulary

premonition (prē′ mə nish′ ən) *n.* a feeling that something is about to happen; warning or sign

destine (des′ tin) *v.* to determine beforehand

Shoaf, who never went to bed at night without the fear that a burglar was going to get in and blow chloroform under her door through a tube. To avert this calamity—for she was in greater dread of anesthetics[6] than of losing her household goods—she always piled her money, silverware, and other valuables in a neat stack just outside her bedroom, with a note reading: "This is all I have. Please take it and do not use your chloroform, as this is all I have." Aunt Gracie Shoaf also had a burglar phobia,[7] but she met it with more fortitude. She was confident that burglars had been getting into her house every night for forty years. The fact that she never missed anything was to her no proof to the contrary. She always claimed that she scared them off before they could take anything, by throwing shoes down the hallway. When she went to bed she piled, where she could get at them handily, all the shoes there were about her house. Five minutes after she had turned off the light, she would sit up in bed and say "Hark!" Her husband, who had learned

CONNECT

How does the description of Aunt Gracie Shoaf's actions connect to the first paragraph, where the narrator says that to tell the story "it is almost necessary to throw furniture"?

6. The sweet-smelling fumes of *chloroform* used to be a common *anesthetic*—a substance used to put patients to sleep before surgery.
7. A *phobia* is a strong, continuing, and unreasonable fear.

Vocabulary

avert (ə vurt′) *v.* to keep from happening; prevent
fortitude (fôr′ tə tood′) *n.* firm courage or strength of mind in the face of pain or danger

to ignore the whole situation as long ago as 1903, would either be sound asleep or pretend to be sound asleep. In either case he would not respond to her tugging and pulling, so that presently she would arise, tiptoe to the door, open it slightly and heave a shoe down the hall in one direction, and its mate down the hall in the other direction. Some nights she threw them all, some nights only a couple of pair.

But I am straying from the remarkable incidents that took place during the night that the bed fell on father. By midnight we were all in bed. The layout of the rooms and the disposition of their occupants is important to an understanding of what later occurred. In the front room upstairs (just under father's attic bedroom) were my mother and my brother Herman, who sometimes sang in his sleep, usually "Marching Through Georgia" or "Onward, Christian Soldiers." Briggs Beall and myself were in a room adjoining this one. My brother Roy was in a room across the hall from ours. Our bull terrier, Rex, slept in the hall.

My bed was an army cot, one of those affairs which are made wide enough to sleep on comfortably only by putting up, flat with the middle section, the two sides which ordinarily hang down like the sideboards of a drop-leaf table. When these sides are up, it is <u>perilous</u> to roll too far toward the edge, for then the cot is likely to tip completely over, bringing the whole bed down on top of one, with a tremendous banging crash. This, in fact, is precisely what happened, about two o'clock in the morning. (It was my mother who, in recalling the scene later, first referred to it as "the night the bed fell on your father.")

Did You Know?
A *canopy* is an overhanging covering, such as on a bed, throne, or building entrance.

Always a deep sleeper, slow to arouse (I had lied to Briggs), I was at first unconscious of what had happened when the iron cot rolled me onto the floor and toppled over on me. It left me still warmly bundled up and unhurt, for the bed rested above me like a canopy. Hence I did not wake up, only reached the edge of consciousness and went back. The racket, however, instantly awakened my mother, in the next room, who came to the immediate conclusion that her worst dread was realized: the big wooden bed upstairs had fallen on father. She therefore screamed, "Let's go to your poor father!" It was this shout, rather than the noise of my cot falling, that awakened Herman, in the same room with her. He thought that mother had become, for no apparent reason, hysterical.

Vocabulary
perilous (per′ ə ləs) *adj.* dangerous; risky

ACTIVE READING MODEL

REVIEW

What does each of the narrator's relatives fear?

PREDICT

Thurber is very precise about the layout of the rooms. Why do you think he wants you to know this information?

VISUALIZE

How does Thurber help you visualize this kind of bed?

RESPOND

Do you know anyone who sleeps this soundly? Is Thurber exaggerating? Why or why not?

The Night the Bed Fell

ACTIVE READING MODEL

PREDICT

What do you think will happen to Briggs in all the confusion?

QUESTION

What do you learn about camphor from this description?

CONNECT

Have you ever been in a situation where simple misunderstandings caused comic complications?

EVALUATE

Take a minute to ask yourself if you think the father would really respond this way to the battering on the door.

"You're all right, Mamma!" he shouted, trying to calm her. They exchanged shout for shout for perhaps ten seconds: "Let's go to your poor father!" and "You're all right!" That woke up Briggs. By this time I was conscious of what was going on, in a vague way, but did not yet realize that I was under my bed instead of on it. Briggs, awakening in the midst of loud shouts of fear and apprehension, came to the quick conclusion that he was suffocating and that we were all trying to "bring him out." With a low moan, he grasped the glass of camphor at the head of his bed and instead of sniffing it poured it over himself. The room reeked of camphor. "Ugf, ahfg," choked Briggs, like a drowning man, for he had almost succeeded in stopping his breath under the deluge of pungent[8] spirits. He leaped out of bed and groped toward the open window, but he came up against one that was closed. With his hand, he beat out the glass, and I could hear it crash and tinkle on the alleyway below. It was at this juncture that I, in trying to get up, had the uncanny sensation of feeling my bed above me! Foggy with sleep, I now suspected, in my turn, that the whole uproar was being made in a frantic endeavor to extricate me from what must be an unheard-of and perilous situation. "Get me out of this!" I bawled. "Get me out!" I think I had the nightmarish belief that I was entombed in a mine. "Gugh," gasped Briggs, floundering in his camphor.

By this time my mother, still shouting, pursued by Herman, still shouting, was trying to open the door to the attic, in order to go up and get my father's body out of the wreckage. The door was stuck, however, and wouldn't yield. Her frantic pulls on it only added to the general banging and confusion. Roy and the dog were now up, the one shouting questions, the other barking.

Father, farthest away and soundest sleeper of all, had by this time been awakened by the battering on the attic door. He decided that the house was on fire. "I'm coming, I'm coming!" he wailed in a slow, sleepy voice—it took him many minutes to regain full consciousness. My mother, still believing he was caught under the bed, detected in his "I'm coming!" the mournful, resigned note of one who is preparing to meet his Maker. "He's dying!" she shouted.

---

8. Briggs is overwhelmed by a flood *(deluge)* of strong-smelling, sharp-tasting *(pungent)* fumes.

Vocabulary

uncanny (un kan′ ē) *adj.* so strange as to cause fear or wonder; weird
endeavor (en dev′ ər) *n.* a serious attempt to accomplish something; undertaking
extricate (eks′ trə kāt′) *v.* to release from entanglement or difficulty; set free

"I'm all right!" Briggs yelled to reassure her. "I'm all right!" He still believed that it was his own closeness to death that was worrying mother. I found at last the light switch in my room, unlocked the door, and Briggs and I joined the others at the attic door. The dog, who never did like Briggs, jumped for him—assuming that he was the culprit in whatever was going on—and Roy had to throw Rex and hold him. We could hear father crawling out of bed upstairs. Roy pulled the attic door open, with a mighty jerk, and father came down the stairs, sleepy and irritable but safe and sound. My mother began to weep when she saw him. Rex began to howl. "What in the name of God is going on here?" asked father.

The situation was finally put together like a gigantic jigsaw puzzle. Father caught a cold from prowling around in his bare feet but there were no other bad results. "I'm glad," said mother, who always looked on the bright side of things, "that your grandfather wasn't here."

❖

Vocabulary
culprit (kul′ prit) *n.* one guilty of some offense

Responding to Literature

PERSONAL RESPONSE

◆ Take a look at your responses to the **Reading Focus** on page 398. Which of your family stories do you think Thurber would have most enjoyed hearing? Why?

Active Reading Response
Look back at the **Active Reading Strategies** described on page 397. Choose one of the strategies and find three places in the selection where you could apply it.

Analyzing Literature

RECALL

1. What did Thurber call "the high-water mark" of his youth?
2. Which relatives with "crotchets" or strange ideas does Thurber describe?
3. What starts the chain of events that Thurber narrates?
4. What does Mrs. Thurber think happened?
5. What does Father think is happening when he is awakened by all the noise?

INTERPRET

6. What can you tell from the first paragraph about Thurber's purpose for this essay?
7. How does the introduction of Thurber's strange relatives prepare you for the rest of the essay?
8. In what way is Mother's conclusion that Father is dying characteristic of her personality?

EVALUATE AND CONNECT

9. How does Thurber prepare readers that this essay, though based on fact, is going to be exaggerated and humorous?
10. Theme Connection   How has this selection changed the way you think about your own family stories? What parts of your own family history might you use to write a humorous essay?

LITERARY ELEMENTS

Characterization

The methods a writer uses to develop the personality of a character are called **characterization.** In direct characterization, a writer makes direct statements about a character's personality, as in this description: "We had visiting us at this time a nervous first cousin of mine named Briggs Beall, who believed that he was likely to cease breathing when he was asleep." Characterization can also be indirect. Thurber does not directly state that his grandfather was eccentric. Rather, he describes the man's strange behavior to give readers that impression. Writers often characterize through a character's words, actions, and interactions with other characters.

1. Choose one of the characters in the essay. Then find and list all of the descriptions Thurber uses to characterize that person.

2. Write a sentence or two of your own describing that character's personality.

● See **Literary Terms Handbook,** p. R2.

Literature and Writing

Writing About Literature

Recognizing Climax   The **climax** is a story's point of highest interest, or turning point. Ask yourself, at what point is the conflict of the evening at Thurber's house resolved? When does the outcome of the essay become clear? Write a paragraph that describes the story's climax.

Creative Writing

Another Point of View   Choose one of the characters in the essay. Retell the events from that character's point of view. Remember to begin this version from the moment in the evening where your character would have been aware of the strange happenings.

Extending Your Response

Literature Groups

Diagramming the Confusion   The sequence of events in "The Night the Bed Fell" is quite elaborate. One way to help recall all the "remarkable incidents" is to make a chain-of-events diagram showing how each event caused the next event. Share your group's diagram with those of the other groups.

Interdisciplinary Activity

Art: A Cartoonist at Heart   James Thurber is well known as a cartoonist. His cartoons were published for many years in magazines and books. Look at some examples of his cartoons. Then, in either his style or your own style, draw a series of cartoons about some of the events or characters in "The Night the Bed Fell."

Listening and Speaking

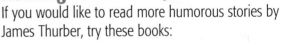

Oral Reading   Take turns reading the essay aloud to the rest of the class. Pay attention to how your voice can reflect the selection's humorous events.

Reading Further

If you would like to read more humorous stories by James Thurber, try these books:

Fables for Our Time and Famous Poems

The 13 Clocks

 Save your work for your portfolio.

Skill Minilessons

GRAMMAR AND LANGUAGE • PARENTHESES

Writers use parentheses to set off words that define, add information, or helpfully explain a word in the sentence. For example, in "The Night the Bed Fell," Thurber uses parentheses to set off a description: "Old Aunt Melissa Beall (who could whistle like a man, with two fingers in her mouth) suffered under the premonition that she was destined to die on South High Street." Parentheses can also be used around an entire sentence that adds extra information to a paragraph.

PRACTICE Skim "The Night the Bed Fell" to find three other examples of parentheses within sentences and two complete sentences that are enclosed in parentheses. Choose one of the examples and write about why you think Thurber chose to include the information within parentheses.

● For more about parentheses, see **Language Handbook,** pp. R41–R42.

READING AND THINKING • EXAGGERATION

Much of the humor in "The Night the Bed Fell" comes from Thurber's exaggeration of his characters' actions. He stretches the truth until his essay is much funnier than everyday life.

PRACTICE Think of something from your own life that you can tell as an **anecdote,** a short account of an interesting event or incident. First write your anecdote in a straightforward way, without humor. Then write it a second time, using exaggeration to make it humorous.

VOCABULARY • ANTONYMS

Finding synonyms is usually easier than finding **antonyms,** or opposites. You often have to think about what a word really means before you can figure out a good antonym for it. When you need to choose an antonym for a given word, don't give up just because the answer is not obvious right away. You might have to think about it.

PRACTICE Choose the word that is most closely opposite in meaning to the first word in each item.

1. **avert**
   a. cause   b. discourage   c. attempt
2. **uncanny**
   a. lovely   b. pleasant   c. normal
3. **perilous**
   a. safe   b. boring   c. fortunate
4. **fortitude**
   a. sadness   b. playfulness   c. weakness
5. **extricate**
   a. search   b. trap   c. irritate

COMIC STRIP

Cartoon strips, or comic strips, are among the most popular newspaper features. Few comic strips have been as well liked or as long lasting as Charles Schulz's *Peanuts,* which began in 1950.

Analyzing Media

1. Why does the cartoonist have Snoopy respond with "Au revoir," the French words for "See you later"? How does that response contrast with what Charlie Brown has been saying to his dog?

2. Snoopy and many other animal characters used in cartoon strips speak and often do the same kinds of things humans do. How does this add to the humor of the strip?

Before You Read

The Dog Diaries

MEET MERRILL MARKOE

When Merrill Markoe's neighbors see her outside with Lewis and Beau, her two dogs, they must wonder if she is about to start barking. The Emmy-award-winning comedy writer has been known to imitate her dogs in an effort to understand them. Markoe has written humor for *Late Night with David Letterman*, a number of television specials, and popular magazines.

Merrill Markoe was born in 1949. This essay was first published in 1992.

READING FOCUS

Have you ever wondered why dogs chase their tails or why cats claw couches?

Think/Pair/Share
What is your personal theory about pet behavior? With a partner, discuss your thoughts on why pets do the strange things they do. Use examples from pets you know.

Setting a Purpose
Read this essay to find out what one dog owner discovers about the behavior of her dogs.

BUILDING BACKGROUND

Did You Know? The dog family includes wolves, foxes, jackals, and wild and domestic dogs. All members of the dog family have teeth adapted to kill their prey, chew meat, and gnaw bones. Whether they live in packs in the wild or alone in a home, they rely upon their alert ears and sensitive noses for survival.

VOCABULARY PREVIEW

infantile (in′ fən tīl′) *adj.* like an infant; childish; p. 413

comprehend (kom′ pri hend′) *v.* to grasp mentally; understand fully; p. 413

ascertain (as′ ər tān′) *v.* to find out with certainty; determine; p. 413

obsession (əb sesh′ ən) *n.* a single emotion or idea that occupies or troubles the mind; p. 414

murky (mur′ kē) *adj.* dark; not clear; p. 414

etiquette (et′ i kit) *n.* the rules of good manners and polite behavior; p. 414

collaborator (kə lab′ ə rā′ tər) *n.* one who works or cooperates with another; p. 415

confront (kən frunt′) *v.* to come face to face with; stand facing; p. 416

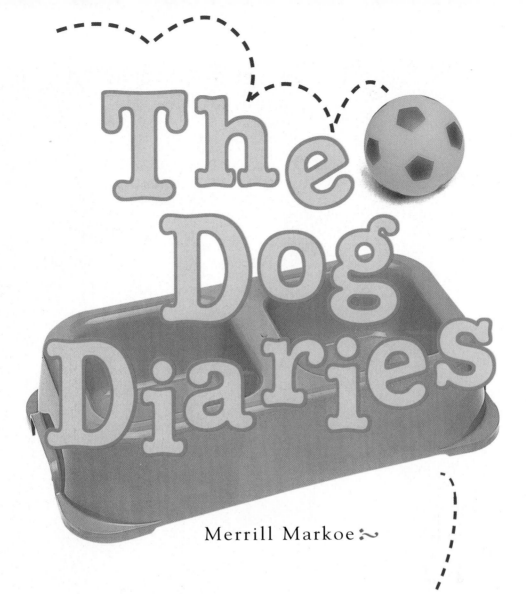

The Dog Diaries

Merrill Markoe

I pick dogs that remind me of myself—scrappy, mutt-faced, with a hint of mange.[1] People look for a reflection of their own personalities or the person they dream of being in the eyes of an animal companion. That is the reason I sometimes look into the face of my dog Stan and see wistful sadness and existential angst,[2] when all he is actually doing is slowly scanning the ceiling for flies.

---

1. *Mange* (mānj) is a disease that produces scaly skin and loss of hair in domestic animals.
2. *Existential angst* (eg′ zis ten′ shəl   ängst) involves feelings of depression or worry over the value and meaning of one's life.

My Favorite Part of Town, 1990. George Rodrigue. Oil on canvas, 30 x 24 in. Private collection.

Viewing the painting: Why do you think the artist painted the dog blue?

We pet owners demand a great deal from our pets. When we give them the job, it's a career position. Pets are required to listen to us blithely,[3] even if we talk to them in infantile and goofy tones of voice that we'd never dare use around another human being for fear of being forced into psychiatric observation. On top of that, we make them wear little sweaters or jackets, and not just the cool kind with the push-up sleeves, either, but weird little felt ones that say, *It's raining cats and dogs.*

We are pretty sure that we and our pets share the same reality, until one day we come home to find that our wistful, intelligent friend who reminds us of our better self has decided a good way to spend the day is to open a box of Brillo pads, unravel a few, distribute some throughout the house, and eat or wear all the rest. And we shake our heads in an inability to comprehend what went wrong here.

Is he bored or is he just out for revenge? He certainly can't be as stupid as this would indicate. In order to answer these questions more fully, I felt I needed some kind of new perspective, a perspective that comes from really knowing both sides of the story.

Thus, I made up my mind to live with my pets as one of them: to share their hopes, their fears, their squeaking vinyl lamb chops, their drinking space at the toilet.

What follows is the revealing, sometimes shocking, sometimes terrifying, sometimes really stupid diary that resulted.

8:45 A.M. We have been lying on our sides in the kitchen for almost an hour now. We started out in the bedroom with just our heads under the bed. But then one of us heard something, and we all ran to the back door. I think our quick response was rather effective because, although I never ascertained exactly what we heard to begin with, I also can't say I recall ever hearing it again.

9:00 A.M. We carefully inspected the molding in the hallway, which led us straight to the heating duct by the bedroom. Just a coincidence? None of us was really sure. So we watched it suspiciously for a while. Then we watched it for a little while longer.

Then, never letting it out of our sight, we all took a nap.

10:00 A.M. I don't really know whose idea it was to yank back the edge of the carpet and pull apart the carpet pad, but talk about a rousing good time! How strange that I could have lived in this house for all these years, and never before felt the fur of a carpet between my teeth. Or actually bit into a moist, chewy chunk of carpet padding. I will never again think of the carpet as simply a covering for the floor.

11:15 A.M. When we all wound up in the kitchen, the other two began to stare at me eagerly. Their meaning was clear. The pressure was on for me to produce snacks. They remembered the old me—the one with the prehensile[4] thumb, the one who could

---

3. To listen *blithely* is to do so in a lighthearted and carefree way.

4. A thumb that can grasp something by folding around it is *prehensile* (prē hen′ sil). Some monkeys have prehensile fingers and tails.

Vocabulary

infantile (in′ fən tīl′) *adj.* like an infant; childish
comprehend (kom′ pri hend′) *v.* to grasp mentally; understand fully
ascertain (as′ ər tān′) *v.* to find out with certainty; determine

Viewing the image: Is it a dream or a nightmare? Evaluate the image from the viewpoint of a dog-lover.

open refrigerators and cabinets. I saw they didn't yet realize that today, I intended to live as their equal. But as they continued their staring, I soon became caught up in their <u>obsession</u>. That is the only explanation I have as to why I helped them topple over the garbage. At first I was nervous, watching the <u>murky</u> fluids soak into the floor. But the heady sense of acceptance

I felt when we all dove headfirst into the can more than made up for my compromised sense of right and wrong. Pack <u>etiquette</u> demanded that I be the last in line. By the time I really got my head in there, the really good stuff was gone. But wait! I spied a tiny piece of tinfoil hidden in a giant clump of hair, and inside, a wad of previously chewed gum, lightly coated with

Vocabulary
obsession (əb sesh′ ən) *n.* a single emotion or idea that occupies or troubles the mind
murky (mur′ kē) *adj.* dark; not clear
etiquette (et′ i kit) *n.* the rules of good manners and polite behavior

sugar or salt. I was settling down to my treasure when I had the sense that I was being watched. Raising my head just slightly, I looked into the noses of my companions. Their eyes were glued to that hard rubber mass. Their drools were long and elastic, and so, succumbing to peer[5] pressure, I split up my gum wad three ways. But I am not sure that I did the right thing. As is so often the case with wanting popularity, I may have gained their short-term acceptance. But I think that in the long run, I lost their real respect. No dog of reasonable intelligence would ever divide up something that could still be chewed.

11:50 A.M. Someone spotted a fly, and all three of us decided to catch him in our teeth. I was greatly relieved when one of the others got to him first.

12:20 P.M. Someone heard something, and in a flash, we were all in the backyard, running back and forth by the fence, periodically hooting. Then one of us spotted a larger-than-usual space between two of the fence boards, and using both teeth and nails, began to make the space larger. Pretty soon, all three of us were doing everything in our power to help. This was a case where the old prehensile thumb really came in handy. Grabbing hold of one of the splinters, I was able to enlarge the hole immediately. Ironically, I alone was unable to squeeze through to freedom, and so I watched with envy as the others ran in pointless circles in the lot next door. What was I going to do? All of my

choices were difficult. Sure, I could go back into the house and get a hacksaw, or I could simply let myself out the back gate, but if I did that, did I not betray my companions? And would I not then be obligated to round us all up and punish us? No, I was a collaborator, and I had the lip splinters to prove it. So I went back to the hole and continued chewing. Only a few hundred dollars' worth of fence damage later, I was able to squeeze through that darn hole myself.

1:30 P.M. The extra time I took was just enough for me to lose sight of my two companions. And so, for the first time, I had to rely on my keen, new animal instincts. Like the wild creature I had become, I was able to spot their tracks immediately. They led me in a series of ever-widening circles, then across the lot at a forty-five-degree angle, then into a series of zigzags, then back to the hole again. Finally, I decided to abandon the tracking and head out to the sidewalk. Seconds later, I spotted them both across the street, where they were racing up and back in front of the neighbor's house. They seemed glad to see me, and so I eagerly joined them in their project. The three of us had only been running and hooting for less than an hour when the apparent owner of the house came to the front door. And while I admit this may not have been the best of circumstances for a first introduction, nevertheless I still feel the manner in which he threatened to turn the hose on us was both excessively violent and unnecessarily vulgar.

---

5. To *succumb* (sə kum′) is to give in or yield. One's *peers* are those who are equal in age, social status, ability, and so on.

Vocabulary
collaborator (kə lab′ ə rā′ tər) *n.* one who works or cooperates with another

The Dog Diaries

Clearly, it was up to me to encourage our group to relocate, and I was shocked at how easily I could still take command of our unit. A simple "Let's go, boys," and everyone was willing to follow me home. (It's such a power-packed phrase. That's how I met my last boyfriend!)

3:00 P.M. By the time we had moved our running and hooting activities into our own front yard, we were all getting a little tired. So we lay down on our sides on the porch.

4:10 P.M. We all changed sides.

4:45 P.M. We all changed sides again.

5:20 P.M. We all lay on our backs. (What a nice change of pace!)

6:00 P.M. Everyone was starting to grow restless. Occasionally, one of us would get up, scratch the front door, and moan. I wrestled silently with the temptation simply to let us all in. But then I realized I didn't have any keys on me. Of course, it occurred to me that we could all go back through the new hole in the fence, but everyone else seemed to have forgotten about the entire fence incident by this time. As they say, "a word to the wise." And so, taking a hint from my friends, I began to forget about the whole thing myself.

6:30 P.M. The sound of an approaching car as it pulls into the driveway. The man who shares this house with us is coming home. He is both surprised and perplexed to see us all out in the front yard running in circles. He is also quickly irritated by the fact that no one offers any explanations. And once he opens the front door, he unleashes a furious string of harsh words as he <u>confronts</u> the mounds of garbage someone has strewn all over the house. We have nothing but sympathy for him in his tragic misfortune. But since none of us knows anything about it, we all retire to the coat closet until the whole thing blows over. And later, as he eats his dinner, I sit quietly under the table. As I watch him, a pleasant feeling of calm overtakes me as I realize just how much I have grown as a person. Perhaps that is why the cruel things he says to me seem to have no effect. And so, when he gets up to pour himself another beverage, I raise my head up to his plate, and, with my teeth, I lift off his sandwich.

Vocabulary
confront (kən frunt′) *v.* to come face to face with; stand facing

Responding to Literature

PERSONAL RESPONSE

◆ Can you imagine spending your day acting like a dog? What do you think the author has actually learned about dog behavior?

Analyzing Literature

RECALL

1. According to the author, what kinds of demands do pet owners put on their pets?
2. What does the author decide to do to gain a new perspective on dog behavior?
3. What choices did the author have to make about getting through the fence?
4. How did the man of the house react to the actions of "all" the dogs?

INTERPRET

5. What can you tell from the first two paragraphs about the author's opinion of dogs?
6. Why, do you think, does the author decide to "live with my pets as one of them"?
7. How does the author use exaggeration to add humor to the episode about chewing through the fence?
8. How, do you think, will the man react to his sandwich being stolen by the narrator?

EVALUATE AND CONNECT

9. Why did Merrill Markoe choose a diary format for this story? Do you think she actually did any of the things she described?
10. **Theme Connection**   Scientists have proved that having pets is good for your health because pets are such loving companions. How do you think a pet can improve a family's life?

LITERARY ELEMENTS

Point of View

When an author uses the pronouns *I, we, me,* and *us,* the reader knows the story is told from the first-person **point of view.** In "The Dog Diaries," Merrill Markoe does something unusual; she uses a first-person point of view throughout the essay, but the antecedent of *we* and *us* changes.

1. Reread "The Dog Diaries" with point of view in mind. In the introduction, to whom does *we* refer? To whom does *he* refer?

2. Once the actual diary begins, when the author writes, "We have been lying on our sides," to whom is she referring? Who is the *he* in this section of the essay? How does Markoe's point of view in the diary section add to the humor of the essay?

● See **Literary Terms Handbook,** p. R8.

Literature and Writing

Writing About Literature

Recognizing Humor   One reason "The Dog Diaries" is funny is that the author describes very silly behavior in a serious way. Imagine that you are the writer's husband returning from work on the day the author is acting like a dog. In the same humorous tone as the essay, write about what you saw and felt when the sandwich was stolen from your plate.

Personal Writing

A Learning Experience   Recall your discussion about pet behavior in the **Reading Focus** on page 410. Write a paragraph about how to test your theories the way Merrill Markoe wrote about testing her ideas. Try to include humor and exaggeration in your writing. Read your paragraph aloud to your group or class.

Extending Your Response

Literature Groups

Now *That's* Funny!   Discuss with your group members which image from the story is the most humorous. Work together to draw a sketch of that scene and share it with the rest of the class.

There is a wealth of information about dogs on the Web. You can find descriptions of different breeds, questions about health and training, and funny stories about people's beloved pets! Find some Web sites on the type of pet you have or would like to have.

Performing

The Talking Dog Talk Show
Imagine that the two dogs from the story are guests on a dog talk show. They are complaining to the host about the strange day they spent with their eccentric owner. For some reason she followed them wherever they went. Have the dogs discuss their reactions to her nonhuman-like behavior. Write a television script with a partner, and then act it out for the class.

Reading Further

Check out these other books about animals and their behaviors:

All Things Bright and Beautiful by James Herriot

The Gorilla Signs Love by Barbara Brenner

 Save your work for your portfolio.

Skill Minilessons

GRAMMAR AND LANGUAGE • PRINCIPAL PARTS OF VERBS

Verbs have four principal parts that are used to form all tenses. The chart below shows how the principal parts of most verbs are formed.

Principal Parts of the Verb *bark*
Base Form: bark
Present Participle: barking
Past Form: barked
Past Participle: (has or have) barked

The principal parts of a verb are often combined with helping verbs such as *be, have,* and *do* to form verb phrases. Look at this sentence:

My dogs **are barking** at the neighbors.

In this sentence the word *are* is the helping verb and the present participle *barking* is the main verb. Together they form a verb phrase.

PRACTICE Copy the "Principal Parts" chart. Then fill in the four principal parts for these verbs from "The Dog Diaries."

1. demand   4. chew
2. require   5. punish
3. remember

● For more about verbs, see **Language Handbook,** pp. R32–R33.

READING AND THINKING • AUTHOR'S PURPOSE

Before authors choose what to write about, they need to decide their purpose. Do they want to inform the reader about a certain subject? Do they want to persuade the reader to do or believe something? Do they want to entertain the reader?

PRACTICE Write a paragraph stating what you think Markoe's purpose was in "The Dog Diaries." Use examples from the essay to support your opinion. Conclude your thoughts by explaining how well you think the author achieved her purpose.

● For more about author's purpose, see **Reading Handbook,** p. R99.

VOCABULARY • PREFIXES

Co-, com-, con-, and *col-* are different spellings of the same prefix, which means "together" or "with." The spelling depends on what letter follows the prefix. *Comprehend, collaborator,* and *confront* are words with this prefix in "The Dog Diaries."

Even if you understand the prefix, *comprehend* is not clear unless you know that the Latin word *prehendere* means "to grasp." *Confront* is easier. If you *confront* someone, you come face to face (or "front to front") with the person or a situation. *Collaborator* is quite clear if you see *labor* in the word. A *collaborator* "labors with," or works with, someone else.

PRACTICE Think about the prefixes *co-, com-, con-,* and *col-* and the base words they are attached to in the list of words. Then match each word to its definition.

1. context   a. to blend or mix together
2. coexist   b. a member of the same group; fellow worker
3. colleague   c. to understand fully
4. commingle   d. the words that occur with or near another word
5. comprehend   e. to live together at the same time or in the same place

Writing WORKSHOP

Descriptive Writing: A Photo in Words

What says "home" to you? Picture a place where you feel truly at home. Now imagine taking a photo of it—a photo that shows what makes it special.

Assignment: Write a description of an important place or person in your life. Follow the process on these pages to create a description as striking as a sharp photograph.

● As you write your description, refer to the **Writing Handbook**, pp. R48–R54.

EVALUATION RUBRIC

By the time you complete this Writing Workshop, you will have
- written a descriptive essay about a special person or place
- used vivid images that state your main impression and supported that impression with vivid sensory details
- organized the description in spatial order or order of importance
- created a conclusion that supports and reflects on your main impression
- presented a descriptive essay free of errors in grammar, usage, and mechanics

The Writing Process

PREWRITING

PREWRITING TIP
Close your eyes to mentally "observe" the person or place you choose. Recall obvious things as well as small details that only you may have noticed.

● Find a Topic

Think of people and places described in this unit: Miss Hurd, who changed Nicholas Gage's life; James Thurber's wacky family; T. J.'s rooftop garden; Maud Martha's home. For your own description, try brainstorming to create two lists. Title them "My Most Unforgettable People" and "My Most Unforgettable Places."

● Zoom In on Details

A cluster can help you remember details about a person or place. For a person, cluster physical traits as well as inner qualities. For a place, cluster physical details as well as details about how you feel there. Search your memory for sensory images, as shown in the **Writing Skills** activity on page 395.

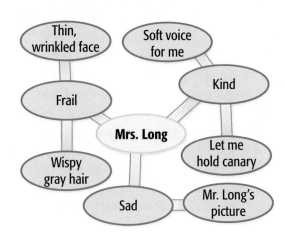

● Choose Your Angle: Audience and Purpose

Who will read your description? Some of your readers may already know the person or place you are describing. However, no one sees exactly as you do, so plan to show your unique view. Decide on your purpose. Do you want readers to chuckle with you, to appreciate a special place or person, or perhaps to wonder at someone or some place mysterious?

● Focus and Frame

To focus your description, choose one main impression that you want to convey. Write your main impression as a phrase or sentence. For example: *My childhood home is a beautiful place.* Then try using a graphic to frame your organization, as shown below. Fill in details that will illustrate your main impression.

My House, Woodstock, 1924. George Bellows. Oil on panel, 17¾ x 22 in. Sid and Diana Avery Trust.

Spatial Order	
To describe a place, you might use **spatial order**—the order in which things exist in space. Start at a given point. From there, describe things in order, moving from closest to farthest, from right or left, or from top to bottom.	
My Childhood Home	
Start (closest):	**Meadow in front of house**
Details:	golden color tickle of grass hard, dry ground
Straight ahead:	**House**
Details:	white wood red roof blue door
Behind (farthest):	**Woods and pond in back**
Details:	crunchy, brightly colored leaves shadowy, peaceful water deer, ducks, and squirrels

Order of Importance	
To describe a person, you might discuss the person's traits in **order of importance.** You can either begin with the traits that mean the most to you or begin with less important traits and gradually work up to the most important ones.	
Mrs. Long	
Trait:	**Frailty**
Details:	thin, wrinkled face wispy gray hair shaky hands
Trait:	**Sadness**
Details:	Mr. Long's picture faraway look
Trait:	**Kindness**
Details:	soft voice for me let me hold canary fed blue jays

Writing WORKSHOP

DRAFTING

DRAFTING TIP
If you get a new idea while drafting, go ahead and try it. If it leads you off track, your prewriting notes can bring you back.

TECHNOLOGY TIP
On a computer, copy your draft before you revise. By saving the original, you are free to experiment. If an experiment doesn't turn out well, you can return to your original draft and try again.

● Catch Your Reader's Eye

Try beginning with a single vivid image. Show the person in a characteristic pose. Show the place at one specific time. You might go on to state your main impression near the end of this first paragraph.

> **STUDENT MODEL** • DRAFTING
>
> From the window of the bus, I can see the golden meadow, the big white house with the red roof, and the trees that circle the hidden pond. Behind them are the mountains that tower over everything like giants.

Complete Student Model on p. R108.

● Work with Details

Follow your prewriting plan, using sensory details to illustrate your statements. Include details that show your feelings so that readers can tell what the place or person means to you. To conclude, you might refer again to your main impression and reflect on the role that this place or person plays in your life.

REVISING

REVISING TIP
If you reword your main impression to make it more precise, adjust your paragraphs to illustrate the revised version.

● Take Another Look

Read over your description. Did your main impression change as you drafted? If so, reword it now to reflect your new insights. Use the **Rubric for Revising** to plan other changes, or trade papers with a partner and go over the rubric with each other. Keep revising until your description is as good as you can make it.

RUBRIC FOR REVISING
Your revised descriptive essay should have
- a vivid introduction that captures readers' attention and that states your main impression
- a consistent pattern of organization
- details that appeal to the senses
- a conclusion that restates and reflects on your main impression

Your revised essay should be free of
- irrelevant details
- errors in grammar, usage, and mechanics

EDITING/PROOFREADING

Before you make a final copy of your description, use the **Proofreading Checklist** to spot errors. Correct any that you find.

Grammar Hint

In a compound sentence, you can use *however* to join two clauses. Put a semicolon before *however* and a comma after it.

I liked winters there; however, I think summer was my favorite season.

PROOFREADING CHECKLIST

☑ Each sentence has at least one complete subject and predicate.

☑ Compound sentences are structured correctly. (Double-check sentences joined with *however*.)

☑ Punctuation is correct. (Double-check compound sentences.)

☑ Capitalization and spelling are correct.

STUDENT MODEL · EDITING/PROOFREADING

I no longer live near the Pond; however, I often visited it in my mind.

Complete Student Model on p. R108.

Complete Student Model

For a complete version of the model developed in this Workshop, see **Writing Workshop Models**, p. R108.

PUBLISHING/PRESENTING

PRESENTING TIP

Some magazines have Web sites that tell you how to submit manuscripts.

Consider submitting your description to a magazine that publishes young people's writing. Your teacher or a librarian can suggest magazines, show you how to find their addresses, and help you prepare your manuscript for submission.

Reflecting

Take time to think about the following questions; then write your responses.

- Did your view of your subject change as you worked on this description? If so, explain how. If not, offer some ideas about why it did not.

- Which aspects of your subject come through best in your description? Which aspects come through only faintly or are left out?

Save your work for your portfolio.

Theme Assessment

Responding to the Theme

1. Which story, poem, or essay in this theme most helped you think about what home and family mean to you? Explain your answer.

2. What new ideas do you have about the following as a result of reading the literature in this theme?
   - How the people and places you love affect your life
   - The importance of seeing warmth and humor in family situations

3. Present your theme project to the class.

Analyzing Literature

COMPARE ESSAYS
Compare two essays from this theme. You may compare them in terms of point of view, use of humor, vividness of characters, or the author's purpose. Remember to support your opinions with quotations from the essays.

Evaluate and Set Goals

1. Which of the following tasks was most rewarding to you? Which was most difficult?
   - reading and thinking about the stories, poems, and essays
   - doing independent writing
   - analyzing the stories, poems, and essays in discussions
   - performing dramatizations
   - doing research

2. Using the following scale, how would you assess your work in this theme? Give at least two reasons for your assessment.

   | 4 = outstanding | 2 = fair |
   | 3 = good | 1 = weak |

3. Based on what you found difficult in this theme, choose a goal to work toward in the next theme.
   - Write down your goal and three steps you will need to take to help you reach it.
   - Meet with your teacher to review your goal and your plan for achieving it.

Build Your Portfolio

SELECT
Select two pieces of work you did during this theme to include in your portfolio. Use the following questions to help you decide.

- Which work do you consider your best?
- From which work did you learn the most?
- Which work did you enjoy the most?

REFLECT
Write some notes to accompany the work you selected. Use these questions to guide you.

- What do you like best about the piece?
- What did you learn from creating it?
- What might you do differently if you were beginning this piece again?

Reading on Your Own

Have you enjoyed reading the essays, stories, and poems in this theme? Here are some other books you might like.

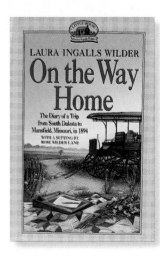

Dragonwings
by Laurence Yep A Chinese immigrant father and son build a flying machine in the era of the Wright brothers and the San Francisco earthquake.

On the Way Home
by Laura Ingalls Wilder and Rose Wilder Lane The diary of the author of *Little House on the Prairie* describes her family's exciting 1894 journey from South Dakota to a new home in the Missouri Ozarks. Her daughter adds her own memories of the trip.

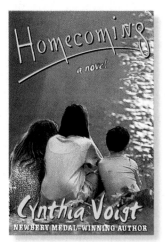

Homecoming
by Cynthia Voigt This poignant story focuses on the four Tillerman kids, left parentless when they are abandoned by their mother. They must struggle to stay together and to find someone to shelter them and love them.

Where Angels Glide at Dawn: New Stories from Latin America
edited by Lori M. Carlson and Cynthia L. Ventura Homes and families provide a background in several of these ten stories from Latin America. The stories display a variety of cultures and writing styles.

Standardized Test Practice

Read the passage. Then read each question on page 427. Decide which is the best answer to each question. Mark the letter for that answer on your paper.

Learning the Game

Rita stared ahead at the green grass curving out before her. She could make out the fluttering orange tongue of the flag 250 yards away. She was on the shortest hole at the Shady Views Golf Course, but Rita knew that she was no expert at the first swing off the tee.

Her father sensed her apprehension and gave her a little smile. "It's OK," he said. "I've got a feeling this one is going to work out for you just fine."

"I just can't use this driver," Rita complained, holding up the club in question as if it were a poisonous snake. "I can hit pretty well with the shorter clubs, but I need more practice with the drivers."

"Nothing to it," her father shrugged. "You've got the basics down. Take a wide stance, relax your shoulders, and breathe through the swing. I've seen you do it before. Stop worrying about it and just try it."

"All right," Rita sighed, planting her feet. She limbered her knees and loosely shook her head back and forth. "Talk me through it, okay?"

Her father moved around her and studied her form with a practiced eye. He remembered the first time he had taken Rita golfing after she had expressed interest in the sport—she had been ten years old, but she hadn't been all that bad!

True, she needed more work with the bigger clubs, especially the drivers. But he was certain that once she crossed that hurdle, she could be a great player.

"Take a few practice swings . . . very nice. A little wider in your stance . . ."

Rita adjusted her feet accordingly.

"Good!" her father said. "No, no. Straighten the left elbow."

Rita made the correction.

"Yes! Now remember to keep your head tucked. Don't look up until after you've swung through."

"OK. You've helped," Rita mumbled. "Now let me swing."

There was silence for a moment while Rita and her golf ball held quiet commerce with each other. Rita's father knew that golf might not be a game for folks who thought too much, but it surely was a game for those who could concentrate. He knew that Rita could focus with amazing intensity.

Rita took in a sharp breath and slowly released it. Her arms drew back the golf club like a ballet dancer moving through heavy water, graceful and poised. The head of the club rose like a new moon until it crested over her ear. Then the swing came down, rocketing the club around like a whipcord, slicing through the air with a sizzling *huwuuuff!* The ball exploded forward like a rifle shot, bolting through the air. Rita and her father watched it fly straight as an arrow toward the flag pin so many yards away.

"That's a keeper—" Rita's father started to say, but then he cut himself off. Suddenly he spun on his heel and dove for his golf bag, digging through a pocket until he found his field glasses. Holding the binoculars up to his eyes for a brief moment, he held his breath before letting out a huge shout.

"What? What is it?" Rita demanded.

"See for yourself," her father laughed, pressing the glasses into her hand.

Rita held the binoculars up to her own eyes and scanned the distant putting green for a sign of her ball. She couldn't find it anywhere. "Did I sink it in the water trap?" she asked. "Why can't I see it?"

Her father's grin was so huge it nearly fell off his face. "Because it's in the cup, Rita," he laughed. "Congratulations! That's your first hole-in-one!"

---

1   The author refers to the flag as a "fluttering orange tongue" because —
   A   the flag was very far away.
   B   the flag looked and moved like a tongue.
   C   Rita wasn't exactly sure what the flag was.
   D   that's what flags are called on golf courses.

2   The main purpose of the story is to show that —

J   sometimes it's better to ask for advice rather than feel discouraged.
K   golf can be a great sport for fathers and daughters to play together.
L   a hole-in-one is one of the rarest events in all sports.
M   hitting with a driver in golf is a difficult skill to master.

3   How does the way Rita feels at the beginning of the story differ from the way her father feels?
   A   Rita feels nervous. Her father feels uncertain.
   B   Rita feels excited. Her father feels confident.
   C   Rita feels uncertain. Her father feels confident.
   D   Rita feels confident. Her father feels nervous.

4   Rita wanted her father to talk her through the swing with the driver because —
   J   she knew that she was good.
   K   she had been playing since she was ten.
   L   she was uncertain of her own ability to swing the driver.
   M   she wanted to hit a hole-in-one.

5   What literary device does the author use to show Rita and her father's interactions?
   A   Flashback
   B   Humor
   C   Repetition
   D   Dialogue

At the Crossroads

THEME 5

> **"** *Two roads diverged in a wood, and I— I took the one less traveled by, And that has made all the difference.* **"**
>
> —Robert Frost
> "The Road Not Taken"

THEME CONTENTS

GENRE FOCUS DRAMA

Exploring the Theme

At the Crossroads

Have you ever been at a point in your life where you had a difficult problem to solve or a decision to make? In this theme's stories, poems, and play, you will meet characters who confront their problems by making courageous or difficult decisions. Begin thinking about the theme by trying one of the activities below.

Starting Points

A TOUGH DECISION

Can you identify with Charlie Brown's difficult situation?

- What other decisions could Charlie Brown have made? With a partner or in a small group, write and then dramatize a dialogue between Charlie Brown and his friends, discussing the different decisions he might have made.

WHICH WAY TO TURN

You have to make choices and decisions every day of your life. Sometimes the decision is easy. Which movie should you see next Saturday? Other times the decision is more difficult. Should you stand up for an unpopular cause in which you believe strongly?

- Write a list of some decisions you have made today. Explain which decisions were more difficult for you to make and why.

PEANUTS
by Charles M. Schulz

PEANUTS reprinted by permission of United Features Syndicate, Inc.

Theme Projects

As you read the selections in this theme, complete one of the projects below. Work on your own, with a partner, or with a group.

LEARNING FOR LIFE

Interview Questions

People make personal decisions every day about many small and large problems. Some people make decisions that affect many other people. Think about doctors, school principals, mayors, presidents of corporations, and the president of the United States.

1. Develop a list of questions to ask a local decision maker about how she or he solves problems.
2. Interview the person—on the phone, by e-mail, by regular mail, or in person.
3. Write a memo to summarize the results of your interview for your class.

MULTIMEDIA PROJECT

A Decision Maker

Select a person who has come to a crossroads in life and has made a difficult or important decision.

1. Find people through biographies, magazine articles, other library research, or personal contact.
2. Using a tape recorder or video camera, interview the person you have chosen to report on or other people who can comment on that person's decision.
3. Gather information from a variety of sources to add to your presentation—for example, photos, newspaper clippings, or objects that are connected to the person's decision. Use these objects along with your audio or video interviews to create a multimedia presentation for the class.

As you think about your project, visit the Glencoe Web site at lit.glencoe.com. While you are there, you can find out more about the authors and selections in this theme.

CRITICAL THINKING

Personal Problem-Solving Techniques

1. Think about a problem you have had and about how you tried to solve it.
2. Create a flowchart that illustrates your problem-solving process. On the chart, indicate the steps you took to solve the problem, the point where you had to make an important decision, and the end solution.

Before You Read

Amigo Brothers

MEET PIRI THOMAS

Piri Thomas first began writing while serving a prison term for attempted armed robbery. For Thomas, creative writing was a way to escape his prison surroundings, break down stereotypes used to judge people of African American and Puerto Rican descent, and change his life. After his release from prison, Thomas began working in drug rehabilitation centers. His autobiography and novels are known for their use of the Spanish Harlem dialect and for the tough reality they portray.

Piri Thomas was born in 1928. This story was first published in 1978 in the collection Stories from El Barrio.

READING FOCUS

Think about your closest friend. What qualities make that person such a good friend?

Chart It!
Create a chart that shows the character traits that you feel make a good friend.

Setting a Purpose
Read to find out how two friends respond to a test of their friendship.

BUILDING BACKGROUND

In the ancient Greek Olympic games, boxers were not classified in different weight divisions. The strongest and largest boxers held the greatest advantage in competition. Today, professional boxers compete in eight different weight divisions, so that they are evenly matched in size. The divisions range from flyweight, 112 pounds or less, to heavyweight, 195 pounds and over.

VOCABULARY PREVIEW

devastating (dev′ əs tāt′ ing) *adj.* causing great pain, damage, or destruction; overwhelming; p. 434

wary (wār′ ē) *adj.* cautious; on the alert; p. 437

perpetual (pər pech′ ōō əl) *adj.* constant; unceasing; p. 437

improvise (im′ prə vīz′) *v.* to invent, compose, or do without much preparation; p. 438

nimble (nim′ bəl) *adj.* light and quick in movement; p. 439

flail (flāl) *v.* to wave or swing, especially swiftly or violently; p. 440

evading (i vād′ ing) *adj.* escaping or avoiding; p. 440

surge (surj) *v.* to rise or increase suddenly; move with a violent swelling motion, as waves; p. 441

Amigo Brothers

Piri Thomas

Antonio Cruz and Felix Varga were both seventeen years old. They were so together in friendship that they felt themselves to be brothers. They had known each other since childhood, growing up on the lower east side of Manhattan in the same tenement building on Fifth Street between Avenue A and Avenue B.

Antonio was fair, lean, and lanky, while Felix was dark, short, and husky. Antonio's hair was always falling over his eyes, while Felix wore his black hair in a natural Afro style.

Each youngster had a dream of someday becoming lightweight[1] champion of the world. Every chance they had the boys worked out, sometimes at the Boys Club on 10th Street and Avenue A and sometimes at the pro's gym on 14th Street. Early morning sunrises would find them running along the East River Drive, wrapped in sweat shirts, short towels around their necks, and handkerchiefs Apache style around their foreheads.

While some youngsters were into street negatives, Antonio and Felix slept, ate, rapped, and dreamt positive. Between them, they had a collection of *Fight* magazines second to none, plus a scrapbook filled with torn tickets to every boxing match they had ever attended, and some clippings of their own. If asked a question about any given fighter, they would immediately zip out from their memory banks divisions, weights, records of fights, knock-outs, technical knock-outs,[2] and draws or losses.

Each had fought many bouts representing their community and had won two gold-plated medals plus a silver and bronze medallion. The difference was in their style. Antonio's lean form and long reach made him the better boxer, while Felix's short and muscular frame made him the better slugger. Whenever they had met in the ring for sparring sessions,[3] it had always been hot and heavy.

---

1. Boxers compete in classes, or divisions, based on their weight. In professional boxing, the *lightweight* division is 131–135 pounds.
2. In a *technical knock-out*, the boxer is judged to be physically unable to go on fighting. A TKO can be called by an official, the fighter, or the fighter's coach.
3. *Sparring sessions* are practice fights.

Amigo Brothers

Now, after a series of elimination bouts,[4] they had been informed that they were to meet each other in the division finals that were scheduled for the seventh of August, two weeks away—the winner to represent the Boys Club in the Golden Gloves Championship Tournament.

The two boys continued to run together along the East River Drive. But even when joking with each other, they both sensed a wall rising between them.

One morning less than a week before their bout, they met as usual for their daily work-out. They fooled around with a few jabs at the air, slapped skin, and then took off, running lightly along the dirty East River's edge.

Antonio glanced at Felix who kept his eyes purposely straight ahead, pausing from time to time to do some fancy leg work while throwing one-twos followed by upper cuts to an imaginary jaw. Antonio then beat the air with a barrage of body blows and short <u>devastating</u> lefts with an overhand jaw-breaking right.

After a mile or so, Felix puffed and said, "Let's stop a while, bro. I think we both got something to say to each other."

Antonio nodded. It was not natural to be acting as though nothing unusual was happening when two ace-boon buddies[5] were going to be blasting each other within a few short days.

They rested their elbows on the railing separating them from the river. Antonio wiped his face with his short towel. The sunrise was now creating day.

Felix leaned heavily on the river's railing and stared across to the shores of Brooklyn. Finally, he broke the silence.

"Man, I don't know how to come out with it."

Antonio helped. "It's about our fight, right?"

"Yeah, right." Felix's eyes squinted at the rising orange sun.

"I've been thinking about it too, *panin*. In fact, since we found out it was going to be me and you, I've been awake at night, pulling punches[6] on you, trying not to hurt you."

"Same here. It ain't natural not to think about the fight. I mean, we both are *cheverote*[7] fighters and we both want to win. But only one of us can win. There ain't no draws in the eliminations."

Felix tapped Antonio gently on the shoulder. "I don't mean to sound like I'm bragging, bro. But I wanna win, fair and square."

Antonio nodded quietly. "Yeah. We both know that in the ring the better man wins. Friend or no friend, brother or no . . ."

Felix finished it for him. "Brother. Tony, let's promise something right here. Okay?"

"If it's fair, *hermano*, I'm for it." Antonio admired the courage of a tug boat pulling a barge five times its welterweight[8] size.

---

4. *[elimination bouts]* These are fights in a tournament; the winners advance to fight again, but the losers are eliminated from competition.

5. Here, *ace* means "best" and *boon* means "merry," so *ace-boon buddies* are best friends who share fun and good times.

6. In American Spanish slang, *panin* (pä′ nēn) means "pal; buddy." *Pulling punches* is holding back from delivering full-strength blows.

7. *Cheverote* (che ve rō′ tä) is American Spanish slang for "really cool; fine."

8. *Hermano* (är män′ ō) means "brother." A professional *welterweight* boxer weighs between 141 and 147 pounds.

Vocabulary
devastating (dev′ əs tāt′ ing) *adj.* causing great pain, damage, or destruction; overwhelming

Vinny Pazienza, 1996. Bill Angresano. Oil on canvas, 24 x 20 in. Big Fights Boxing Memorabilia, New York.

Viewing the painting: Does this fighter seem to have the same determination as the *amigo* brothers? Explain your opinion.

Amigo Brothers

"It's fair, Tony. When we get into the ring, it's gotta be like we never met. We gotta be like two heavy strangers that want the same thing and only one can have it. You understand, don'tcha?"

"*Si*, I know." Tony smiled. "No pulling punches. We go all the way."

"Yeah, that's right. Listen, Tony. Don't you think it's a good idea if we don't see each other until the day of the fight? I'm going to stay with my Aunt Lucy in the Bronx. I can use Gleason's Gym for working out. My manager says he got some sparring partners with more or less your style."

Tony scratched his nose pensively.[9] "Yeah, it would be better for our heads." He held out his hand, palm upward. "Deal?"

"Deal." Felix lightly slapped open skin.

"Ready for some more running?" Tony asked lamely.

"Naw, bro. Let's cut it here. You go on. I kinda like to get things together in my head."

"You ain't worried, are you?" Tony asked.

"No way, man." Felix laughed out loud. "I got too much smarts for that. I just think it's cooler if we split right here. After the fight, we can get it together again like nothing ever happened."

The amigo brothers were not ashamed to hug each other tightly.

"Guess you're right. Watch yourself, Felix. I hear there's some pretty heavy dudes up in the Bronx. *Sauvecito*,[10] okay?"

"Okay. You watch yourself too, *sabe*?"[11]

Tony jogged away. Felix watched his friend disappear from view, throwing rights and lefts. Both fighters had a lot of psyching[12] up to do before the big fight.

The days in training passed much too slowly. Although they kept out of each other's way, they were aware of each other's progress via the ghetto grapevine.

The evening before the big fight, Tony made his way to the roof of his tenement. In the quiet early dark, he peered over the ledge. Six stories below the lights of the city blinked and the sounds of cars mingled with the curses and the laughter of children in the street. He tried not to think of Felix, feeling he had succeeded in psyching his mind. But only in the ring would he really know. To spare Felix hurt, he would have to knock him out, early and quick.

Up in the South Bronx, Felix decided to take in a movie in an effort to keep Antonio's face away from his fists. The flick was *The Champion* with Kirk Douglas, the third time Felix was seeing it.

The champion was getting the daylights beat out of him. He was saved only by the sound of the bell.

Felix became the champ and Tony the challenger.

The movie audience was going out of its head. The champ hunched his shoulders grunting and sniffing red blood back into his broken nose. The challenger, confident that he had the championship in the bag, threw a left. The champ countered with a dynamite right.

Felix's right arm felt the shock. Antonio's face, superimposed on the screen, was hit by the awesome force of the blow. Felix saw himself in the ring, blasting

---

9. Doing a thing *pensively* is doing it in a deeply thoughtful and, perhaps, sad way.
10. This American Spanish slang expression translates as "Take it easy" or "Be cool." Pronunciation: *sauvecito* (sä′ vä sē′ tō)
11. *Sabe?* (sä′ bā) means "You know?"

12. *Psyching* (sī′ king) *up* is getting into the right mental or emotional state.

Antonio against the ropes. The champ had to be forcibly restrained. The challenger fell slowly to the canvas.

When Felix finally left the theatre, he had figured out how to psyche himself for tomorrow's fight. It was Felix the Champion vs. Antonio the Challenger.

He walked up some dark streets, deserted except for small pockets of <u>wary</u>-looking kids wearing gang colors. Despite the fact that he was Puerto Rican like them, they eyed him as a stranger to their turf. Felix did a fast shuffle, bobbing and weaving, while letting loose a torrent of blows that would demolish whatever got in its way. It seemed to impress the brothers, who went about their own business.

Finding no takers, Felix decided to split to his aunt's. Walking the streets had not relaxed him, neither had the fight flick. All it had done was to stir him up. He let himself quietly into his Aunt Lucy's apartment and went straight to bed, falling into a fitful sleep with sounds of the gong for Round One.

Antonio was passing some heavy time on his rooftop. How would the fight tomorrow affect his relationship with Felix? After all, fighting was like any other profession. Friendship had nothing to do with it. A gnawing doubt crept in. He cut negative thinking real quick by doing some speedy fancy dance steps, bobbing and weaving like mercury.[13] The night air was blurred with <u>perpetual</u> motions of left hooks and right crosses. Felix, his *amigo*

brother, was not going to be Felix at all in the ring. Just an opponent with another face. Antonio went to sleep, hearing the opening bell for the first round. Like his friend in the South Bronx, he prayed for victory, via a quick clean knock-out in the first round.

Large posters plastered all over the walls of local shops announced the fight between Antonio Cruz and Felix Vargas as the main bout.

The fight had created great interest in the neighborhood. Antonio and Felix were well liked and respected. Each had his own loyal following.

Antonio's fans had unbridled[14] faith in his boxing skills. On the other side, Felix's admirers trusted in his dynamite-packed fists.

Felix had returned to his apartment early in the morning of August 7th and stayed there, hoping to avoid seeing Antonio. He turned the radio on to *salsa*[15] music sounds and then tried to read while waiting for word from his manager.

The fight was scheduled to take place in Tompkins Square Park. It had been decided that the gymnasium of the Boys Club was not large enough to hold all the people who were sure to attend. In Tompkins Square Park, everyone who wanted could view the fight, whether from ringside or window fire escapes or tenement rooftops.

The morning of the fight Tompkins Square was a beehive of activity with

---

13. *Mercury* is a metal that is liquid at room temperature and moves about as if it were alive.

14. Here, *unbridled* means "uncontrolled."
15. *Salsa* is lively Latin American dance music that uses elements of rhythm and blues, jazz, and rock.

Vocabulary
wary (wār′ē) *adj.* cautious; on the alert
perpetual (pər pech′ōō əl) *adj.* constant; unceasing

numerous workers setting up the ring, the seats, and the guest speakers' stand. The scheduled bouts began shortly after noon and the park had begun filling up even earlier.

The local junior high school across from Tompkins Square Park served as the dressing room for all the fighters. Each was given a separate classroom with desk tops, covered with mats, serving as resting tables. Antonio thought he caught a glimpse of Felix waving to him from a room at the far end of the corridor. He waved back just in case it had been him.

The fighters changed from their street clothes into fighting gear. Antonio wore white trunks, black socks, and black shoes. Felix wore sky blue trunks, red socks, and white boxing shoes. Each had dressing gowns to match their fighting trunks with their names neatly stitched on the back.

The loudspeakers blared into the open windows of the school. There were speeches by dignitaries, community leaders, and great boxers of yesteryear. Some were well prepared, some improvised on the spot. They all carried the same message of great pleasure and honor at being part of such a historic event. This great day was in the tradition of champions emerging from the streets of the lower east side.

Interwoven with the speeches were the sounds of the other boxing events. After the sixth bout, Felix was much relieved when his trainer Charlie said, "Time change. Quick knock-out. This is it. We're on."

Waiting time was over. Felix was escorted from the classroom by a dozen fans in white T-shirts with the word FELIX across their fronts.

Antonio was escorted down a different stairwell and guided through a roped-off path.

As the two climbed into the ring, the crowd exploded with a roar. Antonio and Felix both bowed gracefully and then raised their arms in acknowledgment.

Antonio tried to be cool, but even as the roar was in its first birth, he turned slowly to meet Felix's eyes looking directly into his. Felix nodded his head and Antonio responded. And both as one, just as quickly, turned away to face his own corner.

Bong—bong—bong. The roar turned to stillness.

"Ladies and Gentlemen, *Señores y Señoras.*"[16]

The announcer spoke slowly, pleased at his bilingual[17] efforts.

"Now the moment we have all been waiting for—the main event between two fine young Puerto Rican fighters, products of our lower east side.

"In this corner, weighing 134 pounds, Felix Vargas. And in this corner, weighing 133 pounds, Antonio Cruz. The winner will represent the Boys Club in the tournament of champions, the Golden Gloves. There will be no draw. May the best man win."

The cheering of the crowd shook the window panes of the old buildings surrounding Tompkins Square Park. At the center of the ring, the referee was giving instructions to the youngsters.

"Keep your punches up. No low blows. No punching on the back of the head. Keep your heads up. Understand. Let's

---

16. Pronunciation: *Señores y Señoras* (sen yôr′ ās ē sen yôr′ əs)
17. A *bilingual* person can use two languages.

Vocabulary
improvise (im′ prə vīz′) *v.* to invent, compose, or do without much preparation

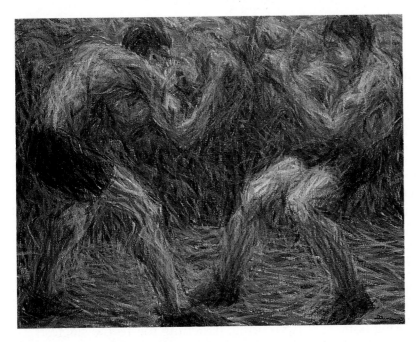

Boxing. G. Cominetti. 75.3 x 92 cm. Private collection.

Viewing the painting: Is the artist's style of painting appropriate to the subject? Why or why not?

have a clean fight. Now shake hands and come out fighting."

Both youngsters touched gloves and nodded. They turned and danced quickly to their corners. Their head towels and dressing gowns were lifted neatly from their shoulders by their trainers' <u>nimble</u> fingers. Antonio crossed himself. Felix did the same.

BONG! BONG! ROUND ONE. Felix and Antonio turned and faced each other squarely in a fighting pose. Felix wasted no time. He came in fast, head low, half hunched toward his right shoulder, and lashed out with a straight left. He missed a right cross as Antonio slipped the punch and countered with one-two-three lefts that snapped Felix's head back, sending a mild shock coursing through him. If Felix had any small doubt about their friendship

affecting their fight, it was being neatly dispelled.[18]

Antonio danced, a joy to behold. His left hand was like a piston pumping jabs one right after another with seeming ease. Felix bobbed and weaved and never stopped boring in. He knew that at long range he was at a disadvantage. Antonio had too much reach on him. Only by coming in close could Felix hope to achieve the dreamed-of knockout.

Antonio knew the dynamite that was stored in his *amigo* brother's fist. He ducked a short right and missed a left hook. Felix trapped him against the ropes just long enough to pour some punishing rights and lefts to Antonio's hard midsection. Antonio slipped away from Felix, crashing two lefts to his head, which set Felix's right ear to ringing.

Bong! Both *amigos* froze a punch well on its way, sending up a roar of approval for good sportsmanship.

Felix walked briskly back to his corner. His right ear had not stopped ringing. Antonio gracefully danced his way toward his stool none the worse, except for glowing glove burns, showing angry red against the whiteness of his midribs.

"Watch that right, Tony." His trainer talked into his ear. "Remember Felix

---

18. To *dispel* something is to make it go away or disappear.

Vocabulary
nimble (nim′ bəl) *adj.* light and quick in movement

always goes to the body. He'll want you to drop your hands for his overhand left or right. Got it?"

Antonio nodded, spraying water out between his teeth. He felt better as his sore midsection was being firmly rubbed.

Felix's corner was also busy.

"You gotta get in there, fella." Felix's trainer poured water over his curly Afro locks. "Get in there or he's gonna chop you up from way back."

Bong! Bong! Round two. Felix was off his stool and rushed Antonio like a bull, sending a hard right to his head. Beads of water exploded from Antonio's long hair.

Antonio, hurt, sent back a blurring barrage of lefts and rights that only meant pain to Felix, who returned with a short left to the head followed by a looping right to the body. Antonio countered with his own flurry, forcing Felix to give ground. But not for long.

Felix bobbed and weaved, bobbed and weaved, occasionally punching his two gloves together.

Antonio waited for the rush that was sure to come. Felix closed in and feinted[19] with his left shoulder and threw his right instead. Lights suddenly exploded inside Felix's head as Antonio slipped the blow and hit him with a pistonlike left, catching him flush on the point of his chin.

Bedlam[20] broke loose as Felix's legs momentarily buckled. He fought off a series of rights and lefts and came back with a strong right that taught Antonio respect.

Antonio danced in carefully. He knew Felix had the habit of playing possum when hurt, to sucker an opponent within reach of the powerful bombs he carried in each fist.

A right to the head slowed Antonio's pretty dancing. He answered with his own left at Felix's right eye that began puffing up within three seconds.

Antonio, a bit too eager, moved in too close and Felix had him entangled into a rip-roaring, punching toe-to-toe slugfest that brought the whole Tompkins Square Park screaming to its feet.

Rights to the body. Lefts to the head. Neither fighter was giving an inch. Suddenly a short right caught Antonio squarely on the chin. His long legs turned to jelly and his arms flailed out desperately. Felix, grunting like a bull, threw wild punches from every direction. Antonio, groggy, bobbed and weaved, evading most of the blows. Suddenly his head cleared. His left flashed out hard and straight catching Felix on the bridge of his nose.

Felix lashed back with a haymaker, right off the ghetto streets. At the same instant, his eye caught another left hook from Antonio. Felix swung out trying to clear the pain. Only the frenzied screaming of those along ringside let him know that he had dropped Antonio. Fighting off the growing haze, Antonio struggled to his feet, got up, ducked, and threw a smashing right that dropped Felix flat on his back.

---

19. To *feint* is to make a movement intended to fool an opponent.
20. Noisy uproar and confusion is *bedlam*.

Vocabulary

flail (flāl) *v.* to wave or swing, especially swiftly or violently
evading (i vād′ ing) *adj.* escaping or avoiding

Felix got up as fast as he could in his own corner, groggy but still game. He didn't even hear the count. In a fog, he heard the roaring of the crowd, who seemed to have gone insane. His head cleared to hear the bell sound at the end of the round. He was very glad. His trainer sat him down on the stool.

In his corner, Antonio was doing what all fighters do when they are hurt. They sit and smile at everyone.

The referee signaled the ring doctor to check the fighters out. He did so and then gave his okay. The cold water sponges brought clarity to both *amigo* brothers. They were rubbed until their circulation ran free.

Bong! Round three—the final round. Up to now it had been tic-tac-toe, pretty much even. But everyone knew there could be no draw and that this round would decide the winner.

This time, to Felix's surprise, it was Antonio who came out fast, charging across the ring. Felix braced himself but couldn't ward off the barrage of punches. Antonio drove Felix hard against the ropes.

The crowd ate it up. Thus far the two had fought with *mucho corazón.*[21] Felix tapped his gloves and commenced his attack anew. Antonio, throwing boxer's caution to the winds, jumped in to meet him.

Both pounded away. Neither gave an inch and neither fell to the canvas. Felix's left eye was tightly closed. Claret[22] red blood poured from Antonio's nose. They fought toe-to-toe.

The sounds of their blows were loud in contrast to the silence of a crowd gone completely mute.

Bong! Bong! Bong! The bell sounded over and over again. Felix and Antonio were past hearing. Their blows continued to pound on each other like hailstones.

Finally the referee and the two trainers pried Felix and Antonio apart. Cold water was poured over them to bring them back to their senses.

They looked around and then rushed toward each other. A cry of alarm <u>surged</u> through Tompkins Square Park. Was this a fight to the death instead of a boxing match?

The fear soon gave way to wave upon wave of cheering as the two *amigos* embraced.

No matter what the decision, they knew they would always be champions to each other.

BONG! BONG! BONG! "Ladies and Gentlemen. *Señores* and *Señoras.* The winner and representative to the Golden Gloves Tournament of Champions is . . ."

The announcer turned to point to the winner and found himself alone. Arm in arm the champions had already left the ring.

---

21. They fought with "great heart." Pronunciation: *mucho corazón* (mōō′ chō   kō′ rə zōn′)

22. *Claret* (klar′ it) is a dark, purplish-red color.

Vocabulary
surge (surj) *v.* to rise or increase suddenly; move with a violent swelling motion, as waves

Responding to Literature

PERSONAL RESPONSE

◆ Do the characters in the story have any of the qualities you charted in the **Reading Focus** on page 432? Which ones?

Analyzing Literature

RECALL

1. What dream do Antonio and Felix share?
2. What causes the wall between the two friends?
3. How does each boxer prepare the night before for the fight?
4. How does the fight end?

INTERPRET

5. What do the efforts of Antonio and Felix to achieve their dream tell you about them?
6. Why do you think Felix moves to his aunt's house before the fight?
7. Do you think the fighters were evenly matched? Explain your opinion.
8. Why do you think the two friends embrace before they hear the results of the match?

Bokszolok. Sandor Botnyik (1893–1976). Gouache on paper, 9¼ x 11½ in. Private collection.

EVALUATE AND CONNECT

9. In your opinion, why did the author choose not to reveal the result of the fight? How does this affect the ending of the story?
10. Theme Connection   If you were one of the characters, do you think the fight would change your relationship with your friend? Explain your answer.

LITERARY ELEMENTS

Internal/External Conflict

A struggle between two opposing forces is usually at the center of a plot. This struggle is called the **conflict.** There are two basic kinds of conflict, and a plot may include either one or both. An **external conflict** exists when a character struggles against some outside force, such as another person, nature, society, or fate. An **internal conflict** takes place within a character's mind when the character is torn between opposing feelings or goals—for example, loyalty vs. pride.

1. What is the external conflict that drives the plot of "Amigo Brothers"?

2. Write two or three sentences explaining the internal conflicts with which Felix and Antonio struggle.

● See **Literary Terms Handbook,** p. R3.

Extending Your Response

Writing About Literature

Analysis Do you agree with the author's decision to end "Amigo Brothers" as he did? Explain with examples from the story.

Creative Writing

Sports Pages Write a newspaper article about the upcoming battle of two "amigos" and the fighting styles of the opponents. Choose a headline for your article.

Literature Groups

Friend or Foe? Antonio and Felix came to realize that their upcoming fight was causing a problem in their friendship. They decided to train separately and be friends again. List other solutions they could have chosen and present them to the class.

Performing

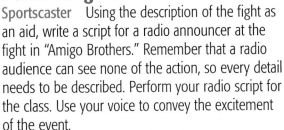

Sportscaster Using the description of the fight as an aid, write a script for a radio announcer at the fight in "Amigo Brothers." Remember that a radio audience can see none of the action, so every detail needs to be described. Perform your radio script for the class. Use your voice to convey the excitement of the event.

Reading Further

Check out these other books about boxing:
Muhammad Ali by Norman Macht
Shadow Boxer by Chris Lynch

Save your work for your portfolio.

Skill Minilesson

VOCABULARY • UNLOCKING MEANING

If you know what *nimble* means, you can guess that *nimbleness* is the quality of being light and quick in movement. *Nimbleness* is the noun form of the adjective *nimble*.

PRACTICE Use what you know about the *italicized* words to complete the statements.

1. *improvise* A group that does improvisational theater performs without
   a. an audience
   b. any rehearsal
   c. getting paid
2. *surge* If your hopes are resurgent, they are
   a. foolish
   b. brand new
   c. increasing again
3. *perpetual* An agreement that lasts in perpetuity lasts
   a. forever
   b. a short time
   c. for a few years
4. *devastate* The devastation of a house could result from
   a. fire
   b. painting it
   c. mowing the lawn
5. *wary* A person shows his or her wariness by being very
   a. brave
   b. polite
   c. careful

Before You Read
Your World

MEET GEORGIA DOUGLAS JOHNSON

Georgia Douglas Johnson inspired younger African American writers in the early 1900s. From her home in Washington, D.C., she hosted weekly meetings with Harlem Renaissance writers such as Countee Cullen and Langston Hughes. Johnson was one of the first African American female poets to gain wide recognition. Born in Georgia, she studied at Atlanta University and Oberlin Conservatory in Ohio. Johnson's works often advocated greater rights for women and minorities.

Georgia Douglas Johnson was born in 1877 and died in 1966.

READING FOCUS

Think of a challenge you face now or will face in the near future. Does it seem a bit scary, or even overwhelming?

Journal
Describe the challenge and what makes it seem frightening or overwhelming.

Setting a Purpose
Read to discover what one poet has to say about meeting new challenges.

BUILDING BACKGROUND

Did You Know?   From 1920 to 1930, in Harlem, a mostly African American part of New York City, a group of writers, artists, and composers took part in a cultural movement that came to be known as the Harlem Renaissance. In their poems, novels, plays, and music, these men and women expressed a renewed pride in their heritage and their community.

The Ascent of Ethiopia, 1932. Loïs Mailou Jones. Oil on canvas, 23½ x 17¼ in. Milwaukee Art Museum, Purchase, African-American Acquisition Fund, matching funds from Suzanne and Richard Pieper, with additional funds from Arthur and Dorothy Nelle Sanders.

Your World

Georgia Douglas Johnson

Your world is as big as you make it.
I know, for I used to abide
In the narrowest nest in a corner,
My wings pressing close to my side.

5   But I sighted the distant horizon
Where the sky line encircled the sea
And I throbbed with a burning desire
To travel this immensity.

I battered the cordons around me
10 And cradled my wings on the breeze
Then soared to the uttermost reaches
With rapture, with power, with ease!

---

2 Here, *abide* may mean either "dwell" or "remain."
8 Anything of great size or extent is an *immensity*.
9 *Cordons* are barriers.
12 *Rapture* is the condition of being carried away
    by strong emotion, such as joy or love.

Active Reading and Critical Thinking

Responding to Literature

PERSONAL RESPONSE

◆ How might this poem inspire you to face the challenge you described for the **Reading Focus** on page 444?

Analyzing Literature

RECALL AND INTERPRET

1. To what creature does the speaker compare himself or herself? Do you think the **metaphor** works in the poem? Why or why not?

2. **Alliteration** is the repetition of the consonant sounds at the beginnings of words. Find an example of alliteration in the first stanza of "Your World." How does it contribute to the poem's effect?

3. What does the speaker see in the second stanza? How does this change the direction of his or her life?

EVALUATE AND CONNECT

4. Do you agree with the speaker's belief that "Your world is as big as you make it"? Explain your answer.

5. How does the speaker change during the poem? Summarize the differences in the speaker at the beginning and end of the poem.

6. Read the last two lines of the poem aloud. How does the rhythm contribute to the poem's emotional effect?

LITERARY ELEMENTS

Symbol

In literature, when a person, a place, an object, or an action stands for something else, it becomes a **symbol.** For example, a dove is a symbol for peace. Writers use symbols in stories and poems to add meaning and to emphasize the theme. In "Your World," the poet uses a bird's nest as a symbol of a life with no room to grow.

1. What do the speaker's wings symbolize in the first and third stanzas?

2. What does "battered the cordons" mean? How does the poet use this image as a symbol?

● See **Literary Terms Handbook,** p. R11.

Extending Your Response

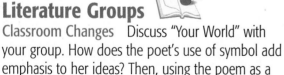

Literature Groups

Classroom Changes Discuss "Your World" with your group. How does the poet's use of symbol add emphasis to her ideas? Then, using the poem as a model, work together to compose a new short poem, "Our World."

Writing About Literature

Imagery and Theme What is the **theme**—the poet's main idea or message—of "Your World"? Write a paragraph analyzing how the poet's use of imagery supports the poem's theme.

COMPARING SELECTIONS

Amigo Brothers **and** *Your World*

COMPARE **THEMES**

In "Amigo Brothers" and "Your World," people arrive at crossroads in their lives. Think about the decisions or changes they make to open up new directions and possibilities.

1. At what crossroads do Antonio and Felix find themselves? What decisions do they each make?

2. What advice does the speaker of "Your World" have for others who stand at the crossroads?

3. The speaker in "Your World" was inspired to leave "the narrowest nest" and soar "to the uttermost reaches." What dreams are calling Antonio and Felix away from their current lives toward a larger world?

COMPARE **RESPONSES**

"Amigo Brothers" and "Your World" offer inspiring messages in different forms—one a short story, the other a poem.

1. Which selection do you find more inspiring? Why?

2. What life lesson is reinforced in "Amigo Brothers"?

3. The speaker in "Your World" believes that people must break through certain barriers in order to change. What barriers do the characters in "Amigo Brothers" break through?

COMPARE **ACTIONS**

The poem "Your World" is a call to action. The speaker breaks the bonds of a narrow life and finds opportunities in the larger world. It is a poem that could inspire young people to think differently about their own lives.

• What do you think would happen to Antonio or Felix if they read "Your World" and took it to heart?

• Write a letter from one *amigo* brother to the other about what the poem meant to him, and how he thinks the philosophy in the poem could benefit each of their lives.

Physical Fitness

In the short story "Amigo Brothers," Antonio and Felix keep themselves physically fit by working out at the gym and by running. However, you don't need to be a sports pro or have special training to enjoy being physically active and fit. In fact, you don't even need to be particularly athletic to have fun that's good for your body.

One family, the Kuntzelmans, planned a unique "walk across America" to see how far they could travel as a team. They totaled the miles they walked near home, then marked those distances across a United States map each week. After walking enough miles to reach Mexico, the whole family celebrated by eating at a local Mexican restaurant.

At a middle school in Naperville, Illinois, students discovered a way everyone could track his or her personal best. Rather than competing against each other, each student individually decided how far to run, then recorded the distance, using a heart monitor to watch for an improved heart rate.

Changing everyday habits can get your body moving and increase your fitness, too. Here are a few tips:

- Ride your bike or walk when you visit a friend or go on an errand.

- Whenever possible, take the stairs instead of an elevator or escalator.

- Dance to your favorite CD, jump rope, swim, build a snow fort, or just stretch your muscles after sitting through a movie or TV show—or an English class.

- Go outside for a game of kickball, baseball, basketball, soccer, or even a short walk.

ACTIVITY

Find an article or chapter on exercise or physical fitness that you consider interesting. Search on the Internet, in magazines, or in books. Write a summary of the article to read to the class. Remember, a summary should be in your own words and should include only the most important ideas and details. It should demonstrate your understanding of the material summarized.

LISTENING, SPEAKING, and VIEWING

Small-Group Discussions

In "Amigo Brothers," Antonio and Felix need to talk before their bout, but it's difficult. They make the discussion work by helping each other. They listen carefully, suggest phrases, and check to make sure they have understood each other. When you join a small-group discussion, you can use the same strategies to help make the discussion work. Try these tips.

Group Discussion Tips

- Take turns talking. Help everyone get a chance to be heard. If there is a group leader, follow his or her directions.
- Listen carefully. Try repeating others' points in your own words to be sure you understand them.
- To keep the discussion on track, make only comments that deal directly with the topic.
- Avoid interrupting or raising your voice. If you are interrupted, resume in an even tone after the interruption ends.

- Disagree with ideas, not with people. Avoid personal comments or put-downs.
- When someone criticizes your ideas, listen quietly. Give the criticism careful thought before you respond.

ACTIVITIES

1. Watch a group discussion on television, in a film or video, or in real life. Note how group members follow (or ignore) the tips listed above. Then share your observations with classmates.

2. Join a small-group discussion of ideas that group members have written about. Afterwards, rate your own performance on each tip listed above.

Before You Read

The Scholarship Jacket

MEET MARTA SALINAS

Marta Salinas is the author of many short stories. Her short story "The Scholarship Jacket" was first published in *Cuentos Chicanos: A Short Story Anthology*. Her work has also appeared in the *Los Angeles Herald Examiner* and in *California Living* magazine.

READING FOCUS

Think about an award you have earned or would like to earn.

Think/Pair/Share

For what did you receive an award? What did you do to prepare for it? Or, what award would you be pleased to get? What would you have to do to earn it? Describe what receiving it was like (or would be like) for you.

Setting a Purpose

Read the story to find out what a school award means to a young girl.

BUILDING BACKGROUND

The Time and Place   This story takes place in recent time in a small town in Texas.

Did You Know?   Have you ever heard of the word *valedictorian*? The word comes from the Latin word *valedicere,* which means "to say farewell." A valedictorian is the student who has achieved the highest grades in a graduating class during all his or her years at school. This person is usually given the honor of giving the farewell address at the graduation ceremony.

VOCABULARY PREVIEW

coincidence (kō in′ si dəns) *n.* an accidental occurrence of events, ideas, or circumstances at the same time, without one causing the other; p. 452

dismay (dis mā′) *n.* a feeling of alarm or uneasiness; p. 453

muster (mus′ tər) *v.* to find and gather together; collect; p. 453

withdrawn (with drôn′) *adj.* shy, reserved, or unsociable; p. 454

vile (vīl) *adj.* very bad; unpleasant; foul; p. 455

The Scholarship Jacket

Marta Salinas ﹋

The small Texas school that I attended carried out a tradition every year during the eighth grade graduation; a beautiful gold and green jacket, the school colors, was awarded to the class valedictorian, the student who had maintained the highest grades for eight years. The scholarship jacket had a big gold S on the left front side and the winner's name was written in gold letters on the pocket.

My oldest sister Rosie had won the jacket a few years back and I fully expected to win also. I was fourteen and in the eighth grade. I had been a straight A student since the first grade, and the last year I had looked forward to owning that jacket. My father was a farm laborer who couldn't earn enough money to feed eight children, so when I was six I was given to my grandparents to raise. We couldn't participate in sports at school because there were registration fees, uniform costs, and trips out of town; so even though we were quite agile and athletic, there would never be a sports school jacket for us. This one, the scholarship jacket, was our only chance.

In May, close to graduation, spring fever struck, and no one paid any attention in class; instead we stared out the windows and at each other, wanting to speed up the last few weeks of school. I despaired every time I looked in the mirror. Pencil thin, not a curve anywhere, I was called "Beanpole" and "String Bean" and I knew that's what I looked like.

The Scholarship Jacket

A flat chest, no hips, and a brain, that's what I had. That really isn't much for a fourteen-year-old to work with, I thought, as I absentmindedly wandered from my history class to the gym. Another hour of sweating in basketball and displaying my toothpick legs was coming up. Then I remembered my P.E. shorts were still in a bag under my desk where I'd forgotten them. I had to walk all the way back and get them. Coach Thompson was a real bear if anyone wasn't dressed for P.E. She had said I was a good forward and once she even tried to talk Grandma into letting me join the team. Grandma, of course, said no.

I was almost back at my classroom's door when I heard angry voices and arguing. I stopped. I didn't mean to eavesdrop; I just hesitated, not knowing what to do. I needed those shorts and I was going to be late, but I didn't want to interrupt an argument between my teachers. I recognized the voices: Mr. Schmidt, my history teacher, and Mr. Boone, my math teacher. They seemed to be arguing about me. I couldn't believe it. I still remember the shock that rooted me flat against the wall as if I were trying to blend in with the graffiti written there.

"I refuse to do it! I don't care who her father is, her grades don't even begin to compare to Martha's. I won't lie or falsify records. Martha[1] has a straight A plus average and you know it." That was Mr. Schmidt

and he sounded very angry. Mr. Boone's voice sounded calm and quiet.

"Look, Joann's father is not only on the Board, he owns the only store in town; we could say it was a close tie and—"

The pounding in my ears drowned out the rest of the words, only a word here and there filtered through. ". . . Martha is Mexican. . . . resign. . . . won't do it. . . ." Mr. Schmidt came rushing out, and luckily for me went down the opposite way toward the auditorium, so he didn't see me. Shaking, I waited a few minutes and then went in and grabbed my bag and fled from the room. Mr. Boone looked up when I came in but didn't say anything. To this day I don't remember if I got in trouble in P.E. for being late or how I made it through the rest of the afternoon. I went home very sad and cried into my pillow that night so grandmother wouldn't hear me. It seemed a cruel <u>coincidence</u> that I had overheard that conversation.

The next day when the principal called me into his office, I knew what it would be about. He looked uncomfortable and unhappy. I decided I wasn't going to make it any easier for him so I looked him straight in the eye. He looked away and fidgeted with the papers on his desk.

"Martha," he said, "there's been a change in policy this year regarding the scholarship jacket. As you know, it has always been free." He cleared his throat and continued. "This year the Board decided to charge fifteen dollars—which still won't cover the complete cost of the jacket."

---

1. The main character is called "Martha" at school and "Marta" at home. Martha is an English version of the main character's Spanish name.

Vocabulary

coincidence (kō in′ si dəns) *n.* an accidental occurrence of events, ideas, or circumstances at the same time, without one causing the other

I stared at him in shock and a small sound of <u>dismay</u> escaped my throat. I hadn't expected this. He still avoided looking in my eyes.

"So if you are unable to pay the fifteen dollars for the jacket, it will be given to the next one in line."

Standing with all the dignity I could <u>muster</u>, I said, "I'll speak to my grandfather about it, sir, and let you know tomorrow." I cried on the walk home from the bus stop. The dirt road was a quarter of a mile from the highway, so by the time I got home, my eyes were red and puffy.

"Where's Grandpa?" I asked Grandma, looking down at the floor so she wouldn't ask me why I'd been crying. She was sewing on a quilt and didn't look up.

"I think he's out back working in the bean field."

I went outside and looked out at the fields. There he was. I could see him walking between the rows, his body bent over the little plants, hoe in hand. I walked slowly out to him, trying to think how I could best ask him for the money. There was a cool breeze blowing and a sweet smell of mesquite in the air, but I didn't appreciate it. I kicked at a dirt clod. I wanted that jacket so much. It was more than just being a valedictorian and giving a little thank you speech for the jacket on graduation night. It represented eight years of hard work and expectation. I knew I had to be honest with Grandpa; it was my only chance. He saw me and looked up.

He waited for me to speak. I cleared my throat nervously and clasped my hands behind my back so he wouldn't see them shaking. "Grandpa, I have a big favor to ask you," I said in Spanish, the only language he knew. He still waited silently. I tried again. "Grandpa, this year the principal said the scholarship jacket is not going to be free. It's going to cost fifteen dollars and I have to take the money in tomorrow, otherwise it'll be given to someone else." The last words came out in an eager rush. Grandpa straightened up tiredly and leaned his chin on the hoe handle. He looked out over the field that was filled with the tiny green bean plants. I waited, desperately hoping he'd say I could have the money.

He turned to me and asked quietly, "What does a scholarship jacket mean?"

I answered quickly; maybe there was a chance. "It means you've earned it by having the highest grades for eight years and that's why they're giving it to you." Too late I realized the significance of my words. Grandpa knew that I understood it was not a matter of money. It wasn't that. He went back to hoeing the weeds that sprang up between the delicate little bean plants. It was a time consuming job; sometimes the small shoots were right

Did You Know?
Mesquite (mes kēt′) is a small thorny tree. Its pleasant-smelling wood is a favored barbecue fuel in the Southwest.

Vocabulary
dismay (dis mā′) *n.* a feeling of alarm or uneasiness
muster (mus′ tər) *v.* to find and gather together; collect

New Mexico Peon, 1942. Ernest L. Blumenschein. Oil on canvas, 40 x 25 in. Gerald Peters Gallery, Sante Fe.

Viewing the painting: Does the person in the painting remind you of any character in the story? Explain.

next to each other. Finally he spoke again.

"Then if you pay for it, Marta, it's not a scholarship jacket, is it? Tell your principal I will not pay the fifteen dollars."

I walked back to the house and locked myself in the bathroom for a long time. I was angry with grandfather even though I knew he was right, and I was angry with the Board, whoever they were. Why did they have to change the rules just when it was my turn to win the jacket?

It was a very sad and <u>withdrawn</u> girl who dragged into the principal's office the next day. This time he did look me in the eyes.

"What did your grandfather say?"

I sat very straight in my chair.

"He said to tell you he won't pay the fifteen dollars."

The principal muttered something I couldn't understand under his breath, and walked over to the window. He stood looking out at something outside. He looked bigger than usual when he stood up; he was a tall gaunt[2]

---

2. A *gaunt* person is thin and bony.

Vocabulary
withdrawn (with drôn′) *adj.* shy, reserved, or unsociable

man with gray hair, and I watched the back of his head while I waited for him to speak.

"Why?" he finally asked. "Your grandfather has the money. Doesn't he own a small bean farm?"

I looked at him, forcing my eyes to stay dry. "He said if I had to pay for it, then it wouldn't be a scholarship jacket," I said and stood up to leave. "I guess you'll just have to give it to Joann." I hadn't meant to say that; it had just slipped out. I was almost to the door when he stopped me.

"Martha—wait."

I turned and looked at him, waiting. What did he want now? I could feel my heart pounding. Something bitter and <u>vile</u> tasting was coming up in my mouth; I was afraid I was going to be sick. I didn't need any sympathy speeches. He sighed loudly and went back to his big desk. He looked at me, biting his lip, as if thinking.

"Okay. We'll make an exception in your case. I'll tell the Board, you'll get your jacket."

I could hardly believe it. I spoke in a trembling rush. "Oh, thank you sir!" Suddenly I felt great. I didn't know about adrenalin[3] in those days, but I knew something was pumping through me, making me feel as tall as the sky. I wanted to yell, jump, run the mile, do something. I ran out so I

---

3. A chemical released into the blood in times of stress or excitement, *adrenalin* (ə dren' əl in) increases the body's energy.

could cry in the hall where there was no one to see me. At the end of the day, Mr. Schmidt winked at me and said, "I hear you're getting a scholarship jacket this year."

His face looked as happy and innocent as a baby's, but I knew better. Without answering I gave him a quick hug and ran to the bus. I cried on the walk home again, but this time because I was so happy. I couldn't wait to tell Grandpa and ran straight to the field. I joined him in the row where he was working and without saying anything I crouched down and started pulling up the weeds with my hands. Grandpa worked alongside me for a few minutes, but he didn't ask what had happened. After I had a little pile of weeds between the rows, I stood up and faced him.

"The principal said he's making an exception for me, Grandpa, and I'm getting the jacket after all. That's after I told him what you said."

Grandpa didn't say anything, he just gave me a pat on the shoulder and a smile. He pulled out the crumpled red handkerchief that he always carried in his back pocket and wiped the sweat off his forehead.

"Better go see if your grandmother needs any help with supper."

I gave him a big grin. He didn't fool me. I skipped and ran back to the house whistling some silly tune.

Vocabulary
vile (vīl) *adj.* very bad; unpleasant; foul

Responding to Literature

PERSONAL RESPONSE

- ◆ Think back to the notes you wrote in the **Reading Focus** on page 450. How would you feel if someone who didn't work for an award received it? What would you do?

Analyzing Literature

RECALL

1. What is the scholarship jacket?
2. What does Marta learn when she accidentally overhears two teachers arguing?
3. What does the principal tell Marta when she is called into his office the next day?
4. What is Grandpa's reaction when Marta asks him for the money?

INTERPRET

5. As the story begins, why does Marta expect to receive the jacket? Why is the jacket so important to her?
6. Why are Mr. Schmidt and Mr. Boone arguing? Why might Mr. Schmidt have sounded so angry?
7. In your opinion, why was the policy regarding the scholarship jacket changed? Explain.
8. Theme Connection   What was Grandpa's decision concerning the jacket? What does Grandpa mean when he says, "If you pay for it, Marta, it's not a scholarship jacket, is it?"

EVALUATE AND CONNECT

9. A conclusion based on known information is called an **inference.** What can you infer about the character of the principal in this story? How does his attitude about the jacket change? Explain.
10. Should the jacket be so important to Marta? Why or why not?

LITERARY ELEMENTS

Resolution

In a story, novel, or play, the **resolution** is the part of the plot that presents the final outcome of the story. At that time, the plot's conflicts are resolved and the story ends. For example, in "Amigo Brothers" the resolution occurs once the final bell sounds and the two champions leave the ring, arm in arm.

1. What happens at the resolution of "The Scholarship Jacket"? What problem is solved? How do the main characters feel?

2. Think about one of your favorite stories from this book. What happens at the resolution of the story?

● See **Literary Terms Handbook,** p. R9.

Literature and Writing

Writing About Literature

Critical Review   A **critical review** of a story evaluates it. Is the story good, bad, or somewhere in between? The review supports its opinions with examples or quotations from the work. Write a critical review of "The Scholarship Jacket," concentrating on its plot, characters, and theme.

Creative Writing

Journal   Imagine you are Marta. You have just learned that you will be given the scholarship jacket after all. At this moment, how do you, as Marta, feel? In your journal, describe the events of the last few days and your feelings about those events.

Extending Your Response

Literature Groups

Keeping Promises   Discuss what it means to keep a promise. What promise in the story is broken? What message does a student, such as Marta, receive when a promise is broken? Which characters in the story understand what it means to keep a promise? Together, write a statement explaining why it is important to keep a promise. Share your statement with the other literature groups.

Learning for Life

Graduation Speech   As the valedictorian of her graduating class, Marta will probably give a speech at the graduation ceremony. Write a speech for Marta that expresses her feelings about her award and what it represents to her and to her family. Perform your speech before a small group and ask them to comment on its effectiveness.

Interdisciplinary Activity

Art   Design and create an award for someone special in your life. Choose a person to honor. You might pick a friend, a relative, or a teacher. Make the award out of any available materials. Be sure the award includes a descriptive title, such as Best Listener or Our Family's Finest Pizza Maker.

Reading Further

Here are some narratives and essays you might enjoy:
A Summer Life by Gary Soto
The Anaya Reader by Rudolfo Anaya

📖 **Save your work for your portfolio.**

Skill Minilessons

GRAMMAR AND LANGUAGE • USING ADVERBS AND ADJECTIVES

Good and *bad* are adjectives. Use them after linking verbs. *Well* and *badly* are adverbs. Use them to describe action verbs. *Well* may also be used as an adjective when describing someone's health. In this case it will follow a linking verb. Here are some examples.

The Sanchez sisters were **good** dancers. (adjective)
The rainy weather was **bad** for a picnic. (predicate adjective)
Rain **badly** damaged the crops. (adverb)

My grandmother sings **well.** (adverb)
After a long illness, Grandpa is finally **well.** (adjective)

PRACTICE Write a paragraph reviewing one of the stories you have read in this book. In the paragraph, include the words *good, bad, badly,* and *well.* Trade paragraphs with a partner and edit each other's work.

● For more about adverbs and adjectives, see **Language Handbook,** pp. R18 and R27.

READING AND THINKING • QUESTIONING/CLARIFYING

Questioning what you are reading helps you understand more clearly the characters and events in a short story or a novel. As you read, ask yourself questions such as these:
• What's really going on here?
• Why did she or he say that?
• Why is the writer describing this?

PRACTICE Reread "The Scholarship Jacket." Write two or three questions about the story that help clarify what is happening. Trade questions with a partner and answer each other's questions.

● For more about these and other reading strategies, see **Reading Handbook,** p. R87.

VOCABULARY • MORE NEGATIVE PREFIXES

A negative prefix, such as the Latin prefix *dis-* and the Anglo-Saxon prefixes *un-* and *mis-*, can change some words into their antonyms. *Disapproval* is the opposite of *approval. Undo* is the opposite of *do.* To *misbehave* is to behave badly.

Sometimes a base word can take either of two of these prefixes. For example, *mistrust* and *distrust* are both proper forms of words with the base word *trust.* Often, however, only one negative prefix can be used correctly with a particular base word. For example, you can *misbehave,* but you can't *un-behave* or *disbehave.*

PRACTICE Add one of the prefixes *un-, dis-,* or *mis-* to each underlined word to create a word that reflects the meaning of each phrase. Use a dictionary to check whether you have used the correct prefix.
1. to <u>communicate</u> badly
2. to <u>quote</u> wrongly
3. to take away someone's <u>illusion</u>
4. not <u>known</u>
5. to <u>focus</u> badly
6. to not <u>trust</u> someone
7. to make someone not <u>qualify</u>
8. not <u>selfish</u>

MEDIA Connection

WEB SITE

Sites on the World Wide Web can keep you informed about the latest developments in space exploration. Spacecraft images have shown a Venus far different from what early writers of science fiction described.

The Face of Venus

Address: ▼ www.hawastsoc.org/solar/eng/homepage.htm

Astronomers refer to Venus as Earth's sister planet. Both are similar in size, mass, density and volume. Both formed about the same time and condensed out of the same nebula. However, during the last few years scientists have found that the kinship ends here. Venus is very different from the Earth. It has no oceans and is surrounded by a heavy atmosphere composed mainly of carbon dioxide with virtually no water vapor. Its clouds are composed of sulfuric acid droplets. At the surface, the atmospheric pressure is 92 times that of Earth at sea level.

Venus is scorched with a surface temperature of about 482°C (900°F). This high temperature is primarily due to a runaway greenhouse effect caused by the heavy atmosphere of carbon dioxide. Sunlight passes through the atmosphere to heat the surface of the planet. Heat is radiated out, but is trapped by the dense atmosphere and not allowed to escape into space. This makes Venus hotter than Mercury.

A Venusian day is 243 Earth days and is longer than its year of 225 days. Oddly, Venus rotates from east to west. To an observer on Venus, the Sun would rise in the west and set in the east.

Until just recently, Venus's dense cloud cover has prevented scientists from uncovering the geological nature of the surface. Developments in radar telescopes and radar imaging systems orbiting the planet have made it possible to see through the cloud deck to the surface below. As spacecraft began mapping the planet, a new picture of Venus emerged.

Analyzing Media

1. What conditions would make it difficult for us to live on Venus? Do you think it will ever happen? Explain your answer.

2. How does the writing on this Web page differ from other nonfiction writing in this book?

Before You Read

All Summer in a Day

MEET
RAY BRADBURY

R ay Bradbury has been writing since he was a boy. "My parents had given me a toy typewriter for Christmas," Bradbury wrote, "and I stormed it with words. Anytime I liked I could turn a faucet on each finger and let the miracles out, yes, into machines and onto paper where I might freeze and control them forever. I haven't stopped writing since." Besides his novels and short stories, Bradbury has written poetry and plays for stage, screen, and television.

Ray Bradbury was born in Waukegan, Illinois, in 1920. This story was first published in 1954.

READING FOCUS

Imagine living where it rains continuously and the sun shines only once every seven years.

Think/Pair/Share
Take a moment to jot down how life would be different. How would nonstop rain make you feel? Share your thoughts and feelings with a partner.

Setting a Purpose
Read the story to discover one version of life on another planet.

BUILDING BACKGROUND

The Time and Place   The story takes place at a school on the planet Venus, sometime in the future.

Did You Know?   Some science-fiction writers try to be as scientifically correct as they can. Ray Bradbury is not one of those writers. Character, style, and theme are far more important to him than scientific accuracy. Today, we know much more about Venus than anyone knew when Bradbury wrote this story. Still, the story remains fascinating in spite of its outdated science.

VOCABULARY PREVIEW

frail (frāl) *adj.* lacking in strength; weak; p. 463
vital (vīt′ əl) *adj.* of primary importance; essential; p. 464
consequence (kon′ sə kwens′) *n.* importance; significance; p. 464
apparatus (ap′ ə rat′ əs) *n.* something created or invented for a particular purpose; p. 465
tumultuously (too mul′ choo əs lē) *adv.* in a wildly excited, confused, or disturbed way; p. 465
resilient (ri zil′ yənt) *adj.* capable of springing back into shape or position after being bent, stretched, or compressed; p. 465

All Summer in a Day

Ray Bradbury

"READY?"

"Ready."

"Now?"

"Soon."

"Do the scientists really know? Will it happen today, will it?"

"Look, look; see for yourself!"

The children pressed to each other like so many roses, so many weeds, intermixed, peering out for a look at the hidden sun.

It rained.

It had been raining for seven years; thousand upon thousands of days compounded and filled from one end to the other with rain, with the drum and gush of water, with the sweet crystal fall of showers and the concussion[1] of storms so heavy they were tidal waves come over the islands. A thousand forests had been crushed under the rain and grown up a thousand times to be crushed again. And this was the way life was forever on the planet Venus, and this was the schoolroom of the children of the rocket men and women who had come to a raining world to set up civilization and live out their lives.

---

1. Here, *concussion* refers to a violent shaking or pounding.

"It's stopping, it's stopping!"

"Yes, yes!"

Margot stood apart from them, from these children who could never remember a time when there wasn't rain and rain and rain. They were all nine years old, and if there had been a day, seven years ago, when the sun came out for an hour and showed its face to the stunned world, they could not recall. Sometimes, at night, she heard them stir, in remembrance, and she knew they were dreaming and remembering gold or a yellow crayon or a coin large enough to buy the world with. She knew they thought they remembered a warmness, like a blushing in the face, in the body, in the arms and legs and trembling hands. But then they always awoke to the tatting drum, the endless shaking down of clear bead necklaces upon the roof, the walk, the gardens, the forests, and their dreams were gone.

All day yesterday they had read in class about the sun. About how like a lemon it was, and how hot. And they had written small stories or essays or poems about it:

> *I think the sun is a flower,*
> *That blooms for just one hour.*

That was Margot's poem, read in a quiet voice in the still classroom while the rain was falling outside.

"Aw, you didn't write that!" protested one of the boys.

"I did," said Margot. "I *did*."

"William!" said the teacher.

But that was yesterday. Now the rain was slackening, and the children were crushed in the great thick windows.

"Where's teacher?"

"She'll be back."

"She'd better hurry, we'll miss it!"

They turned on themselves, like a feverish wheel, all tumbling spokes.

Midnight Sun, Lofoten, 1937 (detail). William H. Johnson. Oil on burlap, 41½ x 59⅛ in. National Museum of American Art, Washington, DC.

Viewing the painting: In what way does this painting reflect the emotions in this story?

hair. She was an old photograph dusted from an album, whitened away, and if she spoke at all her voice would be a ghost. Now she stood, separate, staring at the rain and the loud wet world beyond the huge glass.

"What're *you* looking at?" said William.

Margot said nothing.

"Speak when you're spoken to." He gave her a shove. But she did not move; rather she let herself be moved only by him and nothing else.

They edged away from her, they would not look at her. She felt them go away. And this was because she would play no games with them in the echoing tunnels of the underground city. If they tagged her and ran, she stood blinking after them and did not follow. When the class sang songs about happiness and life and games her lips barely moved. Only when they sang about the sun and the summer did her lips move as she watched the drenched windows.

And then, of course, the biggest crime of all was that she had come here only five

Margot stood alone. She was a very <u>frail</u> girl who looked as if she had been lost in the rain for years and the rain had washed out the blue from her eyes and the red from her mouth and the yellow from her

---

Vocabulary

frail (frāl) *adj.* lacking in strength; weak

years ago from Earth, and she remembered the sun and the way the sun was and the sky was when she was four in Ohio. And they, they had been on Venus all their lives, and they had been only two years old when last the sun came out and had long since forgotten the color and heat of it and the way it really was. But Margot remembered.

"It's like a penny," she said once, eyes closed.

"No it's not!" the children cried.

"It's like a fire," she said, "in the stove."

"You're lying, you don't remember!" cried the children.

But she remembered and stood quietly apart from all of them and watched the patterning windows. And once, a month ago, she had refused to shower in the school shower rooms, had clutched her hands to her ears and over her head, screaming the water mustn't touch her head. So after that, dimly, dimly, she sensed it, she was different and they knew her difference and kept away.

There was talk that her father and mother were taking her back to Earth next year; it seemed <u>vital</u> to her that they do so, though it would mean the loss of thousands of dollars to her family. And so, the children hated her for all these reasons of big and little <u>consequence</u>. They hated her pale snow face, her waiting silence, her thinness, and her possible future.

"Get away!" The boy gave her another push. "What're you waiting for?"

Then, for the first time, she turned and looked at him. And what she was waiting for was in her eyes.

"Well, don't wait around here!" cried the boy savagely. "You won't see nothing!"

Her lips moved.

"Nothing!" he cried. "It was all a joke, wasn't it?" He turned to the other children. "Nothing's happening today. Is it?"

They all blinked at him and then, understanding, laughed and shook their heads. "Nothing, nothing!"

"Oh, but," Margot whispered, her eyes helpless. "But this is the day, the scientists predict, they say, they *know*, the sun . . ."

"All a joke!" said the boy, and seized her roughly. "Hey, everyone, let's put her in a closet before teacher comes!"

"No," said Margot, falling back.

They surged about her, caught her up and bore her, protesting, and then pleading, and then crying, back into a tunnel, a room, a closet, where they slammed and locked the door. They stood looking at the door and saw it tremble from her beating and throwing herself against it. They heard her muffled cries. Then, smiling, they turned and went out and back down the tunnel, just as the teacher arrived.

Vocabulary
vital (vīt′ əl) *adj.* of primary importance; essential
consequence (kon′ sə kwens′) *n.* importance; significance

"Ready, children?" She glanced at her watch.

"Yes!" said everyone.

"Are we all here?"

"Yes!"

The rain slackened still more.

They crowded to the huge door.

The rain stopped.

It was as if, in the midst of a film concerning an avalanche, a tornado, a hurricane, a volcanic eruption, something had, first, gone wrong with the sound apparatus, thus muffling and finally cutting off all noise, all of the blasts and repercussions[2] and thunders, and then, second, ripped the film from the projector and inserted in its place a peaceful tropical slide which did not move or tremor. The world ground to a standstill. The silence was so immense and unbelievable that you felt your ears had been stuffed or you had lost your hearing altogether. The children put their hands to their ears. They stood apart. The door slid back and the smell of the silent, waiting world came in to them.

The sun came out.

It was the color of flaming bronze and it was very large. And the sky around it was a blazing blue tile color. And the jungle burned with sunlight as the children, released from their spell, rushed out, yelling, into the springtime.

"Now, don't go too far," called the teacher after them. "You've only two hours, you know. You wouldn't want to get caught out!"

But they were running and turning their faces up to the sky and feeling the sun on their cheeks like a warm iron; they were taking off their jackets and letting the sun burn their arms.

"Oh, it's better than the sun lamps, isn't it?"

"Much, much better!"

They stopped running and stood in the great jungle that covered Venus, that grew and never stopped growing, tumultuously, even as you watched it. It was a nest of octopi, clustering up great arms of fleshlike weed, wavering, flowering in this brief spring. It was the color of rubber and ash, this jungle, from the many years without sun. It was the color of stones and white cheeses and ink, and it was the color of the moon.

Did You Know?
Octopi (ok′ tə pī) is the plural of *octopus.* An octopus is a sea creature that has, as the prefix *octo-* indicates, eight arms.

The children lay out, laughing, on the jungle mattress, and heard it sigh and squeak under them, resilient and alive. They ran among the trees, they slipped and fell, they pushed each other, they played hide-and-seek and tag, but most of all they squinted at the sun until tears ran down their faces, they put their hands up to that yellowness and that amazing blueness and breathed of the fresh, fresh air

---

2. As used here, the *repercussions* are echoes or vibrations.

Vocabulary

apparatus (ap′ ə rat′ əs) *n.* something created or invented for a particular purpose

tumultuously (too mul′ choo əs lē) *adv.* in a wildly excited, confused, or disturbed way

resilient (ri zil′ yənt) *adj.* capable of springing back into shape or position after being bent, stretched, or compressed

and listened and listened to the silence which suspended them in a blessed sea of no sound and no motion. They looked at everything and savored everything. Then, wildly, like animals escaped from their caves, they ran and ran in shouting circles. They ran for an hour and did not stop running.

And then—

In the midst of their running one of the girls wailed.

Everyone stopped.

The girl, standing in the open, held out her hand.

"Oh, look, look," she said, trembling.

They came slowly to look at her opened palm.

In the center of it, cupped and huge, was a single raindrop.

She began to cry, looking at it.

They glanced quietly at the sky.

"Oh. Oh."

A few cold drops fell on their noses and their cheeks and their mouths. The sun faded behind a stir of mist. A wind blew cool around them. They turned and started to walk back toward the underground house, their hands at their sides, their smiles vanishing away.

A boom of thunder startled them and like leaves before a new hurricane, they tumbled upon each other and ran. Lightning struck ten miles away, five miles away, a mile, a half mile. The sky darkened into midnight in a flash.

They stood in the doorway of the underground for a moment until it was raining hard. Then they closed the door and heard the gigantic sound of the rain falling in tons and avalanches, everywhere and forever.

Behind the closet door was only silence.

"Will it be seven more years?"

"Yes. Seven."

Then one of them gave a little cry.

"Margot!"

"What?"

"She's still in the closet where we locked her."

"Margot."

They stood as if someone had driven them, like so many stakes, into the floor. They looked at each other and then looked away. They glanced out at the world that was raining now and raining and raining steadily. They could not meet each other's glances. Their faces were solemn and pale. They looked at their hands and feet, their faces down.

"Margot."

One of the girls said, "Well . . . ?"

No one moved.

"Go on," whispered the girl.

They walked slowly down the hall in the sound of cold rain. They turned through the doorway to the room in the sound of the storm and thunder, lightning on their faces, blue and terrible. They walked over to the closet door slowly and stood by it.

Behind the closet door was only silence.

They unlocked the door, even more slowly, and let Margot out.

Responding to Literature

PERSONAL RESPONSE

◆ If you were Margot, how would you feel about missing the sun? What would you say to those who put you in the closet?

◆ What should be done to the students who locked Margot in the closet?

Analyzing Literature

RECALL

1. As the story begins, where are the children and what are they doing?
2. Why is the day a special one? How long has it rained?
3. Who is Margot, and why do the other children dislike her?
4. What do the children do when the rain stops? Why doesn't Margot go with them?

INTERPRET

5. How do you think the children felt as the special time approached? Support your opinion with details from the story.
6. What effect has the rain had on the planet?
7. Why is Margot different from the other children? Do you think her parents will take her back to Earth? Why or why not?
8. According to the author, when the children are playing outside, they act "like animals escaped from their caves." Why?

EVALUATE AND CONNECT

9. What do you think the title of the story means?
10. Theme Connection Do you know of situations in which children acted as cruelly as Margot's classmates do? How *should* young people behave with someone who is new to their school or neighborhood or who is in some way different from them?

LITERARY ELEMENTS

Science Fiction

Science fiction is a form of literature that explores imaginary worlds of the past, the present, and the future. Science fiction often has characters living in the future or shows people using technology that is not available today. Nevertheless, these characters deal with current issues and problems, such as prejudice, fear, and isolation.

1. What is the current problem faced by the main character in "All Summer in a Day"?

2. Describe a setting for a science-fiction story you might write someday.

● See **Literary Terms Handbook,** p. R9.

Literature and Writing

Writing About Literature

Setting How does the setting of "All Summer in a Day" play an important part in the story? Review your notes from the **Reading Focus** on page 460 and think about the effect such a setting would have on your own actions and moods. Then consider what effect the setting has on the story's events and on the actions of the characters. Write a paragraph explaining why the setting of "All Summer in a Day" is so important to the story.

Creative Writing

A Sequel What will the children say to Margot after they let her out? What will happen to Margot in the days, months, or years ahead? Write a sequel to the story, starting with the unlocking of the door. Set the scene carefully, and use dialogue as well as narrative text. Be sure to describe the characters' facial expressions and gestures to help your readers understand what they are feeling.

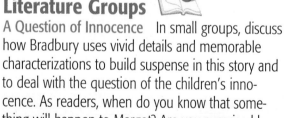

Until very recently, this is all people could see of cloud-covered Venus. New radar imaging has allowed us to see through this cloud cover.

Extending Your Response

Literature Groups

A Question of Innocence In small groups, discuss how Bradbury uses vivid details and memorable characterizations to build suspense in this story and to deal with the question of the children's innocence. As readers, when do you know that something will happen to Margot? Are you surprised by the children's cruelty? Why do the children treat Margot as an outsider? What do you think Bradbury is saying about children?

Learning for Life

A Brochure Imagine that you work for a travel agency that plans trips to Venus. Create a brochure describing the trip and what life is like on Venus. Use details from the story as a starting point, but make up any added details you need.

Art Activity

Make a Map Think about the setting of "All Summer in a Day." What do you think the school looks like? As the children look through the classroom window, what do they see? Draw a map of the schoolyard setting of this story. Use the story details and descriptions to help you, but feel free to use your imagination to add new details.

Reading Further

If you would like to read more by Ray Bradbury, try these books:
The Martian Chronicles
Twice Twenty-Two

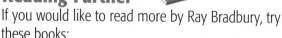 **Save your work for your portfolio.**

Skill Minilessons

GRAMMAR AND LANGUAGE • AVOIDING DOUBLE NEGATIVES

Negative words express the idea of "no." *Not* is a negative word. *Not* often appears in a shortened form as part of a contraction, such as *isn't* ("is not"). Other words—for example, *never, none, nobody, nowhere,* and *nothing*—may be used to express the negative. Two negatives used together in the same sentence create a **double negative.** Avoid using double negatives in your writing.

Nonstandard: You **shouldn't never** swim alone.

You can correct a sentence with a double negative in two ways:

1. Remove one of the negative words:
   Improved: You shouldn't swim alone.

2. Replace one of the negative words with a positive word:
   Improved: You shouldn't ever swim alone.

PRACTICE Revise the following paragraph by correcting each double negative you find.

The rain didn't never stop. It rained and rained until nobody could not remember the color of the sky. Plants couldn't never grow because they didn't never receive the warmth of the sun. Neither humans nor animals nor plants could never thrive in this rain-swept place.

● For more about negative adverbs, see **Language Handbook,** p. R27.

READING AND THINKING • INFERENCE FROM SETTING

You can use what you know about the setting to help you infer other details about life for the characters in this story. For example, since you know from the setting that it rains all the time, you can infer that most aspects of life take place indoors.

PRACTICE Reread "All Summer in a Day" and think about what you can infer about the kinds of activities and games the children in this story enjoy. Write a paragraph explaining your conclusions and how you arrived at them.

● For more about making inferences, see **Reading Handbook,** pp. R92–R93.

VOCABULARY • THE LATIN ROOTS *vit* AND *viv*

The root of *vital* is *vit,* which comes from a Latin word meaning "life." People must meet their *vital* needs, such as their needs for air, food, and water. *Vitamins* have that name because they are necessary for life. Over time, *vit* has come to have the somewhat broader meaning of "extremely important; absolutely necessary." Something of *vital* concern should receive immediate attention. The root *viv* is similar to *vit;* it means "live."

PRACTICE Use what you know about the roots *vit* and *viv* to answer each question.

1. Would someone show *vivacity* by leaping, coughing, or stumbling?
2. Does a *vivid* description of something make it seem frightening, boring, or real?
3. If there is a *revival* of an old-fashioned style, does it die out or become popular again?
4. What is the best synonym for *vitality—energy, hunger,* or *luck?*
5. Do people tend to feel *revitalized* after doing hard work, hearing a lullaby, or getting a good night's sleep?

Reading and Thinking Skills

Drawing Conclusions

As a skillful reader, you are always **drawing conclusions,** or figuring out much more than an author states directly. To do this, you often must combine clues about characters and events in the text with your own knowledge and experience. For example, read the following passage from "The Scholarship Jacket."

> The next day when the principal called me into his office, I knew what it would be about. He looked uncomfortable and unhappy. I decided I wasn't going to make it any easier for him so I looked him straight in the eye. He looked away and fidgeted with the papers on his desk.

Details in this passage help you draw some conclusions about the feelings of the principal and the narrator. From the description of the principal looking "uncomfortable and unhappy" and fidgeting with his papers, you can draw the conclusion that he is nervous. From the description of the narrator, who "looked him straight in the eye," you can draw the conclusion that she is unwilling to be treated unfairly.

● For more about drawing conclusions, see **Reading Handbook,** p. R93.

EXERCISE

Read the following passage from "Amigo Brothers." Then answer the questions.

> Every chance they had, the boys worked out, sometimes at the Boys Club on 10th Street and Avenue A and sometimes at the pro's gym on 14th Street. Early morning sunrises would find them running along the East River Drive, wrapped in sweat shirts, short towels around their necks, and handkerchiefs Apache style around their foreheads.

1. What clues help you draw conclusions about how seriously the boys take their dreams?

2. How does your own experience, as well as the details in the passage, help you draw that conclusion?

Before You Read

Primer Lesson and *The Bird Like No Other*

MEET CARL SANDBURG

Carl Sandburg first saw Chicago when he was eighteen. Those images of city life would later appear in his *Chicago Poems*. Most of his poems echo the poet's Midwestern values.

Carl Sandburg was born in 1878 in Galesburg, Illinois. He died in 1967.

MEET DOROTHY WEST

Just nineteen years old when she arrived in New York City, Dorothy West was known as "the Kid" by the other Harlem Renaissance writers. Her writing career has spanned eight decades. Her second novel, *The Wedding*, was published in 1995, when she was eighty-seven years old.

Dorothy West was born in 1907 in Boston, Massachusetts. She died in 1998.

READING FOCUS

Have you ever said something in anger or frustration that you later regretted? What advice might you give to someone who is feeling angry or frustrated?

Journal

Take a moment to write your responses to these questions in your journal.

Setting a Purpose

Read these selections to discover what the writers have to say about the power of words.

BUILDING BACKGROUND

Did You Know?   A great surge of artistic activity took place in Harlem during the 1920s. This area in New York City became a magnet, attracting African American writers, artists, actors, musicians, and dancers. This artistic movement became known as the Harlem Renaissance.

VOCABULARY PREVIEW

obligation (ob′ lə gā′ shən) *n.* a sense of duty; a responsibility; p. 474

uncommitted (un′ kə mit′ id) *adj.* not having or showing a particular opinion, view, or course of action; p. 474

woe (wō) *n.* great sadness or suffering; great trouble or misfortune; p. 474

initiative (i nish′ ə tiv) *n.* the action of taking the first step; p. 476

soberly (sō′ bər lē) *adv.* very seriously; p. 476

pretentious

selfish

foolish

vain

impolite

PRIMER LESSON

Carl Sandburg :~

Look out how you use proud words.
When you let proud words go, it is
  not easy to call them back.
They wear long boots, hard boots; they
  walk off proud; they can't hear you
  calling—
Look out how you use proud words.

egotistic

phoney

shallow

arrogant

rude

lazy

thoughtless

inconsiderate

THE BIRD LIKE NO OTHER

Dorothy West ∾

Colby ran through the woods. He ran hard, as if he were putting his house and family behind him forever. The woods were not a dark forest of towering trees. They were just scrub oak and stunted pine with plenty of room for the sun to dapple[1] the road. The road, really a footpath worn by time, was so much a part of Colby's summers that at any point he knew how many trees to count before he reached the one with the hollow that caught the rain and gave the birds a drinking cup.

As the clearing came in sight with its cluster of cottages, Colby began to call Aunt Emily, the stridency[2] in his voice commanding her to shut out the sweeter sounds of summer.

Whatever Aunt Emily was doing, Colby knew, she would stop what she was

Haunted House, Aspen, 1996 (detail). Debby West. Acrylic on canvas, 24 x 18 in. Gallery Contemporanea, Jacksonville, FL.

doing. Wherever she was, she would start for the porch, so that by the time Colby pounded up the stairs, she would be sitting on her old porch glider, waiting for him to fling himself down beside her and cool his hot anger in her calm.

Aunt Emily was a courtesy aunt, a family friend of many years. When Colby's mother was a little girl, she played with Aunt Emily's little boy when they came on holiday from their separate cities. Then Aunt Emily lost her little boy in a winter accident on an icy street. When vacation time came again, it took all her courage to reopen her cottage. But she knew she must do it this saddest summer of all if she was ever to learn to live in a world that could not bend its tempo to the slow cadence[3] of grief.

---

1. The sun would *dapple* the road by casting spots of light into the shadows.
2. *Stridency* is a quality of being loud and harsh.

---

3. *Tempo* means "pace" or "speed," and *cadence* means "rhythm" or "beat."

Colby's sister made frequent visits with her dolls. She brought the dolls that didn't cry or didn't wet because they were always rewarded with a tea party for their good behavior. She eased the summer's sorrow for Aunt Emily, who felt an obligation to show this trusting child a cheerful face and to take an interest in her eager talk.

All the same, though Aunt Emily felt a bit ungrateful thinking it, a little girl dressing her dolls for a tea party is no substitute for a little boy playing cowboys and Indians at the top of his lungs.

Colby's family would have agreed with her. His mother adored him because he was her long-awaited son, five years younger than the youngest of his three sisters. His father was pleased and proud to have another male aboard.

But Colby couldn't see where he came first with anybody. As far as he was concerned he was always at the bottom of a heap of scrapping sisters. No matter how good he tried to be, his day most generally depended on how good his sisters decided to be. His rights were never mightier than their wrongs.

Aunt Emily had been Colby's sounding board[4] ever since the summer he was four. One day that summer, his mother postponed a promised boat ride because his sisters had fought with each other all morning over whose turn it was to use the paint box that somebody had given them together. When they began to make each other cry, they were sent upstairs as punishment, and the outing was postponed.

Colby felt he was being punished for blows he hadn't struck and tears he hadn't caused. He had to tell somebody before he burst. Since he knew the way to Aunt Emily's, he went to tell her.

She took a look at his clouded-over face, plumped him down on her old porch glider, then went inside to telephone his mother that Colby wasn't lost, just decamped. His mother told her what had happened, and Aunt Emily listened with uncommitted little clucks. She wasn't any Solomon[5] to decide if it was more important to punish the bad than to keep a promise to the good.

She could hear him banging back and forth on the glider, waiting in hot impatience to tell his tale of woe. The old glider screeched and groaned at his assault on its unoiled joints.

Standing inside her screen door, wincing in sympathy, Aunt Emily knew that neither she nor any nearby neighbor could take that tortured sound much longer. She tried to think of something to distract Colby's mind until he calmed down. A blue jay flew across her line of vision, a bird familiar to the landscape, but the unexciting sight bloomed into an idea.

Shutting the screen door soundlessly, approaching Colby on whispering feet, she put her finger to her lips and sat down beside him.

---

4. A *sounding board* can be a person to whom one expresses opinions or ideas as a way of testing, or sounding them out.

5. Here, *decamped* refers to having run away, quickly and secretly. Famous for his great wisdom, *Solomon* was a king of Israel in the tenth century B.C.

Vocabulary

obligation (ob′ lə gā′ shən) *n.* a sense of duty; a responsibility

uncommitted (un′ kə mit′ id) *adj.* not having or showing a particular opinion, view, or course of action

woe (wō) *n.* great sadness or suffering; great trouble or misfortune

Full Moon Gossip, 1997. Gustavo Novoa. Acrylic on canvas, 36 x 36 in. Wally Findlay Galleries, New York.

Viewing the painting: Which aspects of this painting are realistic? Which are imaginative? Could any of these birds be "the bird like no other"? Explain your answer.

As he stared at her round-eyed, his swinging suspended, she said softly, "Colby, before you came the most beautiful bird I ever saw was sitting on my hydrangea bush. He almost took my breath. I never saw a bird of so many colors. When you came running, he flew away. But if we don't talk or make any noise, he may come back."

After a moment of reflection,[6] Colby's curiosity pulled out the plug in his sea of troubles, and he settled back.

That was the way this gentle fiction began. When Aunt Emily decided that the beautiful bird was gone for the day, Colby was wearing an agreeable face of a normal color. Taking the <u>initiative</u>, a shameless triumph over a small boy, Aunt Emily plunged into a story before Colby could get his mouth open to begin his own.

For the rest of that summer, and in the summers that followed, when Colby came glad or when Colby came only a little bit mad, the right to speak first was his automatically. But when Colby came breathing fire, by uncanny coincidence,[7] the bird like no other had just left the yard.

It was soon routine for Colby to seal his lips and settle down to wait.

Now he was eight, and on this angry morning when he flung himself up Aunt Emily's stairs, and flung himself down beside her on the poor old glider that responded as expected to a sudden shock, it was plainly a morning to search the sky for the bird like no other.

Before Aunt Emily could comb a fresh story out of her memory, Colby got a speech in ahead of her. He said in an excited whisper, "I see it, I see it. I see the bird you said was so beautiful. I guess he's every color in the world."

Jerking upright in stunned surprise, making the glider wearily protest, Aunt Emily asked in a shaken voice, "Where?"

"On that tree over there, see, over there."

By a confluence[8] of golden sunlight and blue sky and green leaves and shimmering summer air, a bird on a swinging bough took on an astonishing beauty.

For a moment Aunt Emily couldn't believe her eyes. But in another moment her eyes stopped playing tricks. And suddenly she wanted to stop playing tricks, too.

"Colby, look again. That's a jay. There never was a bird like the one I told you about. I made him up."

As if to give credence[9] to her confession, the bird on the bough released itself from its brief enchantment and flew away in the dress of a blue jay.

Colby spoke slowly. "Why did you make up a bird to tell me about?"

Aunt Emily started to answer, but asked instead, "Don't you know why, Colby?"

"I think so," he said <u>soberly</u>.

"Will you tell me?"

---

6. *Reflection* is serious and careful thinking.
7. An *uncanny coincidence* is a really strange occurrence of two things happening at the same time.
8. A *confluence* is a flowing together, or meeting, of two or more things.
9. Although *credence* (krēd′ əns) usually means "belief," here, the author is using the very old meaning of "believability" or "deserving trust."

Vocabulary
initiative (i nish′ ə tiv) *n.* the action of taking the first step
soberly (sō′ bər lē) *adv.* very seriously

When I Was a Child, 1996. Dr. Samella Lewis. Oil on canvas, 39¾ x 30 in. Stella Jones Gallery, New Orleans, LA.

Viewing the painting: How is the boy in the painting like or unlike Colby?

"To make me sit still so I wouldn't say bad things about my family when I was mad. But you didn't want to make me sit still like a punishment. So you made me sit still like we were waiting to see something wonderful."

"I see the wonderful thing I've been waiting for. I see a little boy who's learned about family loyalty. It's as beautiful to look at as that bird."

Colby got up. He scuffed his sneakers. "Well, I guess I'll go home now. See you, Aunt Emily."

He bounded down the stairs and began to run home, running faster and faster. Aunt Emily's eyes filled with sentimental tears. He was trying to catch up with the kind of man he was going to be. He was rushing toward understanding.

Responding to Literature

PERSONAL RESPONSE

◆ Think back to the **Reading Focus** on page 471. How does your advice compare or contrast with the advice suggested in "Primer Lesson" or "The Bird Like No Other"? Add your latest thoughts to your journal.

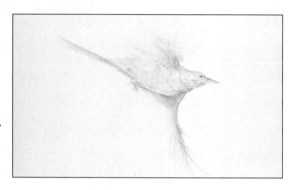

Bird in Flight–Bird Series II, 1981. Freshman Brown. Prisma colors on bfk rives. Private collection.

Analyzing Literature

RECALL

1. About what kind of words does the speaker of "Primer Lesson" warn the reader?
2. What usually causes Colby to run to Aunt Emily's cottage?
3. What does Aunt Emily tell Colby whenever he arrives angry?

INTERPRET

4. What does the speaker in "Primer Lesson" mean by "proud words"?
5. According to "Primer Lesson," why is it not easy to call back proud words?
6. What is the central image of "Primer Lesson"? What does this image suggest?
7. How would you describe the relationship between Aunt Emily and Colby? Why do they share this relationship?
8. Why does Aunt Emily admit to Colby that she made up the story about the bird?

EVALUATE AND CONNECT

9. Do you agree that it isn't easy to call back proud words? Why or why not?
10. Theme Connection   In your opinion, what valuable lessons does Colby learn from Aunt Emily? Explain why those lessons are important.

LITERARY ELEMENTS

Descriptive Details

Writers use **descriptive details** to create memorable portraits of characters, places, objects, and events. Good writers help readers imagine what they describe by choosing details carefully and expressing them in vivid language. Dorothy West, for example, tells us that Colby "pounded up the stairs," and that Aunt Emily waited "for him to fling himself down beside her and cool his hot anger in her calm."

1. Describe two details in "The Bird Like No Other" that create a picture of the road leading to Aunt Emily's cottage.

2. Pick out a detail describing Colby that helps you imagine him more clearly.

● See **Literary Terms Handbook,** p. R3.

Extending Your Response

Writing About Literature

The Poet's Theme Do you think that Sandburg was effective in getting across his **theme,** or central idea, in "Primer Lesson"? Write a paragraph or two explaining your opinion. Use details from the poem to support your assessment.

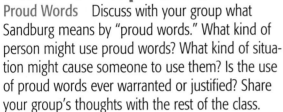

Literature Groups

Proud Words Discuss with your group what Sandburg means by "proud words." What kind of person might use proud words? What kind of situation might cause someone to use them? Is the use of proud words ever warranted or justified? Share your group's thoughts with the rest of the class.

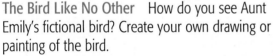

Art Activity

The Bird Like No Other How do you see Aunt Emily's fictional bird? Create your own drawing or painting of the bird.

Creative Writing

Letter to Aunt Emily Imagine that you are Colby as a teenager. Write a letter to Aunt Emily from Colby's point of view, describing some of the problems you now face. Express to Aunt Emily what her relationship has come to mean to you over the years and what advice you wish she could offer you now. Then trade letters with a partner. Next, imagine yourself as Aunt Emily, and answer your partner's letter.

Reading Further

Here are some other works by Carl Sandburg and Dorothy West you might enjoy:
The Complete Poems of Carl Sandburg
The Richer, the Poorer by Dorothy West

📖 **Save your work for your portfolio.**

Skill Minilesson

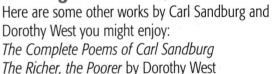

VOCABULARY • ANALOGIES: DEFINING CHARACTERISTICS

One kind of **analogy** deals with "defining characteristics," that is, characteristics that are a necessary part of what makes the person or thing what it is.

> fur : rabbit :: wool : sheep

Fur is a characteristic of a *rabbit* just as *wool* is a characteristic of a *sheep.* Every analogy contains two pairs of words. Decide what the relationship is between the first pair of words. Then find the word that will complete the second pair and show the same relationship.

PRACTICE Choose the word that best completes each analogy.

1. wings : fly :: feet :
   a. legs   b. walk   c. person
2. dishonesty : thief :: initiative :
   a. leader   b. judge   c. coward
3. wall : house :: page :
   a. turn   b. book   c. read
4. displeasure : fury :: gloominess :
   a. delight   b. anger   c. woe
5. gift : present :: obligation :
   a. duty   b. decision   c. fault

Technology Skills

Becoming an Active Viewer

Did you know that directors of movies and television shows use many of the same storytelling elements that writers of novels and short stories do? Movies and television dramas are set in a particular time and place, or **setting.** They generally have a story line, or **plot,** that probably includes a **conflict** that leads to a **climax.** The actors help give the **characters** they play certain traits, which become part of their **characterization.** Camera work and lighting help establish the **mood** of the story, which may also include **suspense.** Even such literary elements as **symbolism, theme,** and **imagery** may be part of a movie or teleplay. (If any of the bold-faced terms above puzzle you, look for them in your **Literary Terms Handbook,** starting on page R1.)

Practice Active Viewing Strategies

As you begin to recognize the techniques filmmakers use, you will need to practice active viewing strategies. For example, look at this still photo of a shot from the classic film *Citizen Kane.* In this shot, young Charles Foster Kane (the boy) is being introduced to the man who is about to become his guardian. Study the scene to answer the following questions.

Connect

◆ What emotion is the boy expressing? How can you tell? Have you ever felt this way?

Question

◆ Why is the guardian positioned between the boy and his father?
◆ Why do you think the boy is being sent away? What do you see in the scene that might suggest a reason?

TECHNOLOGY TIP

To discuss film, you need to know some of the vocabulary of filmmaking. A movie is made up of many—probably hundreds of—shots. A **shot** is a single sequence in which the camera films without interruption. The switch from one shot to another is called a **cut.** Cutting is the responsibility of the film editor. A **scene** in a movie is all the consecutive shots in a single setting. Movie cameras can **pan** (swing from one side to another), **zoom** (use a special lens to move toward or away from a subject), or move in a number of other ways, either carried by hand or on various mechanisms. As you learn more about filmmaking, your appreciation of the art will grow.

Predict

◆ How might this scene relate to what will happen later in the movie?

Evaluate

◆ Why is this scene set outdoors on a cold winter day? Is there some connection between the setting and the action?

◆ What is your impression of the guardian? What gives you that impression?

◆ What do you think of the mother? Why?

Respond

◆ Can you identify with any of these characters? Why or why not?

The Art of Film

When you view a movie or TV drama, you should be aware of the filmmaker's art. Notice how a scene is framed, and how the actors are arranged. Looking at a single picture from a movie can start you thinking, but you need to remember that movies are *motion* pictures. How actors move may tell you something about their character. How they move in relation to one another can reveal relationships.

The camera can also move. It may pan from one character to another or from one place to another. It can follow a character as he or she moves. It can zoom in on something, drawing your attention to it, or zoom out to show you where something is taking place.

Look at camera angles. The camera can make a character seem smaller or weaker by looking down. Looking upward, it can make a person seem stronger or domineering. Tilted at an angle, it gives the viewer a sense of unease.

Watch for how a scene is edited. For example, cutting quickly from shot to shot can create excitement. A long scene with few or no cuts can create a sense of calm.

Listen to the background music. Does it add to or detract from the mood of what you're seeing? How?

All this doesn't mean that you need to strain to find meaning in everything you see. Viewing a situation comedy on TV doesn't require much care. But when you view a serious movie made by a good filmmaker, you'll find it a much richer experience if you view actively.

TECHNOLOGY TIP

When you see a movie on a television screen, you may not be seeing the movie as it was meant it to be seen. Most movies today are made in a wide-screen format. To fit the shape of a TV screen, the sides of the movie are cut off. Sometimes the movie may cut or pan back and forth between two characters who were originally shown on opposite sides of the wide screen. This adds cuts or pans that were not intended by the director, the film editor, or the director of photography. Until wide-screen digital TV becomes widely available, or unless you watch a wide-screen VHS or DVD version, keep in mind that you're not seeing exactly what the filmmakers intended.

ACTIVITIES

1. Practice active viewing strategies when you watch television or a movie. What methods do directors and actors use to get their messages across? Write your conclusions in your journal.

2. Do an Internet search to find tips on screenwriting.

3. Rewrite a scene from one of the stories in this book as a screenplay. Describe how the scene should look, where actors should be, how they will move, and what sound effects or music should accompany the scene.

Before You Read
The Old Demon *and* The Boy and His Grandfather

MEET
PEARL S. BUCK

Pearl S. Buck was the first American woman to win the Nobel Prize for Literature. Many of her novels, stories, plays, and essays reflect her experience of growing up, living, and working in China for nearly forty years.

Pearl S. Buck was born in 1892 and died in 1973.

MEET
RUDOLFO A. ANAYA

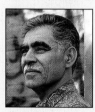

One of the founding fathers of modern Hispanic American literature, Rudolfo Anaya (rōō dôl′ fō   ä nä′ yä) has written fiction, plays, and essays, mostly set in his native New Mexico. Anaya often weaves Hispanic legends and folktales into his work.

Rudolfo A. Anaya was born in 1937.

READING FOCUS

Do you ever wonder how you would react in a time of danger or need? Could you be as courageous as you had to be?

Discuss
With a small group, discuss how you and people you know might respond to the needs of the sick or neglected.

Setting a Purpose
Read these stories to discover how others respond to danger or the needs of others.

BUILDING BACKGROUND

The Time and Place   "The Old Demon" takes place in China in the late 1930s, after Japan invaded China.

Did You Know?   The Yellow River (Huang Ho in Chinese) got its name from the yellow silt that is carried with the current and gives the river a yellowish color. Once every twenty-five years or so, the river overflows its banks, and a massive flood destroys villages, livestock, and people. For this reason, the Yellow River is often referred to as "China's Sorrow."

VOCABULARY PREVIEW

malicious (mə lish′ əs) *adj.* having or showing a desire to harm another; p. 484
quavering (kwā′ vər ing) *adj.* trembling or shaking; p. 484
somberly (som′ bər lē) *adv.* in a gloomy manner; p. 490
tentatively (ten′ tə tiv lē) *adv.* hesitantly; uncertainly; p. 492
discern (di surn′) *v.* to detect or recognize; p. 492
acutely (ə kūt′ lē) *adv.* sharply and with intensity; p. 493
impetuous (im pech′ ōō əs) *adj.* marked by force or violent action; p. 494

The Old Demon

Pearl S. Buck ~

Old Mrs. Wang knew, of course, that there was a war. Everybody had known for a long time that there was war going on and that Japanese were killing Chinese. But still it was not real and no more than hearsay since none of the Wangs had been killed. The Village of Three Mile Wangs on the flat banks of the Yellow River, which was old Mrs. Wang's clan village, had never seen a Japanese. This was how they came to be talking about Japanese at all.

Emperor Kuang Wu, of the Western Han Dynasty, Fording a River. Ch'iu Ying (active 1510–1551). Hanging scroll, ink and color on silk, height: 67¼ in. National Gallery of Canada, Ottawa.

The Old Demon

It was evening and early summer, and after her supper Mrs. Wang had climbed the dike steps, as she did every day, to see how high the river had risen. She was much more afraid of the river than of the Japanese. She knew what the river would do. And one by one the villagers had followed her up the dike, and now they stood staring down at the <u>malicious</u> yellow water, curling along like a lot of snakes, and biting at the high dike banks.

"I never saw it as high as this so early," Mrs. Wang said. She sat down on a bamboo stool that her grandson, Little Pig, had brought for her, and spat into the water.

"It's worse than the Japanese, this old devil of a river," Little Pig said recklessly.

"Fool!" Mrs. Wang said quickly. "The river god will hear you. Talk about something else."

So they had gone on talking about the Japanese. . . . How, for instance, asked Wang, the baker, who was old Mrs. Wang's nephew twice removed, would they know the Japanese when they saw them?

Mrs. Wang at this point said positively, "You'll know them. I once saw a foreigner. He was taller than the eaves of my house and he had mud-colored hair and eyes the color of a fish's eyes. Anyone who does not look like us—that is a Japanese."

Then Little Pig spoke up in his disconcerting[1] way. "You can't see them, Grandmother. They hide up in the sky in airplanes."

Mrs. Wang did not answer immediately. Once she would have said positively, "I shall not believe in an airplane until I see it." But so many things had been true which she had not believed—the Empress, for instance, whom she had not believed dead, was dead. The Republic, again, she had not believed in because she did not know what it was. She still did not know, but they had said for a long time there had been one. So now she merely stared quietly about the dike where they all sat around her. It was very pleasant and cool, and she felt nothing mattered if the river did not rise to flood.

"I don't believe in the Japanese," she said flatly.

They laughed at her a little, but no one spoke. Someone lit her pipe—it was Little Pig's wife, who was her favorite, and she smoked it.

"Sing, Little Pig!" someone called.

So Little Pig began to sing an old song in a high <u>quavering</u> voice, and old Mrs. Wang listened and forgot the Japanese. The evening was beautiful, the sky so clear and still that the willows overhanging the dike were reflected even in the muddy water. Everything was at peace. The thirty-odd houses which made up the village straggled along beneath them. Nothing could break this peace. After all, the Japanese were only human beings.

"I doubt those airplanes," she said mildly to Little Pig when he stopped singing.

But without answering her, he went on to another song.

---

1. Little Pig's *disconcerting* way of speaking causes embarrassment, confusion, or frustration.

Vocabulary

malicious (mə lish′ əs) *adj.* having or showing a desire to harm another
quavering (kwā′ vər ing) *adj.* trembling or shaking

Year in and year out she had spent the summer evenings like this on the dike. The first time she was seventeen and a bride, and her husband had shouted to her to come out of the house and up the dike, and she had come, blushing and twisting her hands together, to hide among the women while the men roared at her and made jokes about her. All the same, they had liked her. "A pretty piece of meat in your bowl," they had said to her husband. "Feet a trifle big," he had answered deprecatingly.[2] But she could see he was pleased, and so gradually her shyness went away.

He, poor man, had been drowned in a flood when he was still young. And it had taken her years to get him prayed out of Buddhist purgatory.[3] Finally she had grown tired of it, what with the child and the land all on her back, and so when the priest said coaxingly, "Another ten pieces of silver and he'll be out entirely," she asked, "What's he got in there yet?"

"Only his right hand," the priest said, encouraging her.

Well, then, her patience broke. Ten dollars! It would feed them for the winter. Besides, she had had to hire labor for her share of repairing the dike, too, so there would be no more floods.

"If it's only one hand, he can pull himself out," she said firmly.

She often wondered if he had, poor silly fellow. As like as not, she had often thought gloomily in the night, he was still lying there, waiting for her to do

something about it. That was the sort of man he was. Well, some day, perhaps, when Little Pig's wife had had the first baby safely and she had a little extra, she might go back to finish him out of purgatory. There was no real hurry, though. . . .

"Grandmother, you must go in," Little Pig's wife's soft voice said. "There is a mist rising from the river now that the sun is gone."

"Yes, I suppose I must," old Mrs. Wang agreed. She gazed at the river a moment. The river—it was full of good and evil together. It would water the fields when it was curbed and checked, but then if an inch were allowed it, it crashed through like a soaring dragon. That was how her husband had been swept away—careless, he was, about his bit of the dike. He was always going to mend it, always going to pile more earth on top of it, and then in a night the river rose and broke through. He had run out of the house, and she had climbed on the roof with the child and had saved herself and it while he was drowned. Well, they had pushed the river back again behind its dikes, and it had stayed there this time. Every day she herself walked up and down the length of the dike for which the village was responsible and examined it. The men laughed and said, "If anything is wrong with the dikes, Granny will tell us."

It had never occurred to any of them to move the village away from the river. The Wangs had lived there for generations, and some had always escaped the floods and had fought the river more fiercely than ever afterward.

Little Pig suddenly stopped singing.

---

2. To speak *deprecatingly* is to express mild disapproval.

3. *Buddhism* is one of the major religions of the world. It grew out of the teachings of Gautama, called the Buddha. *Purgatory*, according to Roman Catholic doctrine, is a place where the souls of dead sinners are kept until they have been purged of sin and can enter heaven.

The Old Demon

"The moon is coming up!" he cried. "That's not good. Airplanes come out on moonlight nights."

"Where do you learn all this about airplanes?" old Mrs. Wang exclaimed. "It is tiresome to me," she said, so severely that no one spoke. In this silence, leaning upon the arm of Little Pig's wife she descended slowly the earthen steps which led down into the village, using her long pipe in the other hand as a walking stick. Behind her the villagers came down, one by one, to bed. No one moved before she did, but none stayed long after her.

And in her own bed at last, behind the blue cotton mosquito curtains which Little Pig's wife fastened securely, she fell peacefully asleep. She had lain awake a little while thinking about the Japanese and wondering why they wanted to fight. Only very coarse persons wanted wars. In her mind she saw large coarse persons. If they came one must wheedle them, she thought, invite them to drink tea, and explain to

Exiles, 1939. Chen Baoyi. Oil. Courtesy Dr. Michael Sullivan, St. Catherine's College, Oxford, England.
Viewing the painting: What story does the painting tell? What connection could you make between the painting and "The Old Demon"?

them, reasonably—only why should they come to a peaceful farming village . . . ?

So she was not in the least prepared for Little Pig's wife screaming at her that the Japanese had come. She sat up in bed muttering, "The tea bowls—the tea—"

"Grandmother, there's no time!" Little Pig's wife screamed. "They're here—they're here!"

"Where?" old Mrs. Wang cried, now awake.

"In the sky!" Little Pig's wife wailed.

They had all run out at that, into the clear early dawn, and gazed up. There, like wild geese flying in autumn, were great bird-like shapes.

"But what are they?" old Mrs. Wang cried.

And then, like a silver egg dropping, something drifted straight down and fell at the far end of the village in a field. A fountain of earth flew up, and they all ran to see it. There was a hole thirty feet across, as big as a pond. They were so astonished they could not speak, and then, before anyone could say anything, another and another egg began to fall and everybody was running, running . . .

Everybody, that is, but Mrs. Wang. When Little Pig's wife seized her hand to drag her along, old Mrs. Wang pulled away and sat down against the bank of the dike.

"I can't run," she remarked. "I haven't run in seventy years, since before my feet were bound.[4] You go on. Where's Little Pig?" She looked around. Little Pig was

already gone. "Like his grandfather," she remarked, "always the first to run."

But Little Pig's wife would not leave her, not, that is, until old Mrs. Wang reminded her that it was her duty.

"If Little Pig is dead," she said, "then it is necessary that his son be born alive." And when the girl still hesitated, she struck at her gently with her pipe. "Go on—go on," she exclaimed.

So unwillingly, because now they could scarcely hear each other speak for the roar of the dipping planes, Little Pig's wife went on with the others.

By now, although only a few minutes had passed, the village was in ruins and the straw roofs and wooden beams were blazing. Everybody was gone. As they passed they had shrieked at old Mrs. Wang to come on, and she had called back pleasantly:

"I'm coming—I'm coming!"

But she did not go. She sat quite alone watching now what was an extraordinary spectacle. For soon other planes came, from where she did not know, but they attacked the first ones. The sun came up over the fields of ripening wheat, and in the clear summery air the planes wheeled and darted and spat at each other. When this was over, she thought, she would go back into the village and see if anything was left. Here and there a wall stood, supporting a roof. She could not see her own house from here. But she was not unused to war. Once bandits had looted their village, and houses had been burned then, too. Well, now it had happened again. Burning houses one could see often, but not this darting silvery shining battle in the air. She understood none of it—not what those things were, nor how they

4. *[feet were bound]* The Chinese once believed that tiny feet added to a woman's beauty, so the feet of many Chinese girls were tightly wrapped to limit their growth. This painful process resulted in small but badly deformed feet. The practice was ended in the early 1900s.

Beneficent Rain DETAIL #5 and #6. Chang Yu-ts'ai (1295–1316). Handscroll. Ink on silk. 10⅝ x 106¾ in. The Metropolitan Museum of Art, New York.

Viewing the painting: *Beneficent* means "doing or resulting in good." Do you find the details in the painting beneficent? Is the river in the story beneficent? Why or why not?

stayed up in the sky. She simply sat, growing hungry, and watching.

"I'd like to see one close," she said aloud. And at that moment, as though in answer, one of them pointed suddenly downward, and, wheeling and twisting as though it were wounded, it fell head down in a field which Little Pig had ploughed only yesterday for soybeans. And in an instant the sky was empty again, and there was only this wounded thing on the ground and herself.

She hoisted herself carefully from the earth. At her age she need be afraid of nothing. She could, she decided, go and see what it was. So, leaning on her bamboo pipe, she made her way slowly across the fields. Behind her in the sudden stillness two or three village dogs appeared and followed, creeping close to her in their terror. When they drew near to the fallen plane, they barked furiously. Then she hit them with her pipe.

"Be quiet," she scolded, "there's already been noise enough to split my ears!"

She tapped the airplane.

"Metal," she told the dogs. "Silver, doubtless," she added. Melted up, it would make them all rich.

She walked around it, examining it closely. What made it fly? It seemed dead. Nothing moved or made a sound within it. Then, coming to the side to which it tipped, she saw a young man in it, slumped into a heap in a little seat. The dogs growled, but she struck at them again and they fell back.

"Are you dead?" she inquired politely.

The young man moved a little at her voice, but did not speak. She drew nearer and peered into the hole in which he sat. His side was bleeding.

"Wounded!" she exclaimed. She took his wrist. It was warm, but inert, and when she let it go, it dropped against the side of the hole. She stared at him. He had black hair and a dark skin like a Chinese and still he did not look like a Chinese.

"He must be a Southerner," she thought. Well, the chief thing was, he was alive.

"You had better come out," she remarked. "I'll put some herb plaster on your side."

The young man muttered something dully.

"What did you say?" she asked. But he did not say it again.

"I am still quite strong," she decided after a moment. So she reached in and seized him about the waist and pulled him out slowly, panting a good deal. Fortunately he was rather a little fellow and very light. When she had him on the ground, he seemed to find his feet; and he stood shakily and clung to her, and she held him up.

"Now if you can walk to my house," she said, "I'll see if it is there."

Then he said something, quite clearly. She listened and could not understand a word of it. She pulled away from him and stared.

"What's that?" she asked.

He pointed at the dogs. They were standing growling, their ruffs up. Then he spoke again, and as he spoke he crumpled to the ground. The dogs fell on him, so that she had to beat them off with her hands.

"Get away!" she shouted. "Who told *you* to kill him?"

And then, when they had slunk back, she heaved him somehow onto her back; and, trembling, half carrying, half pulling him, she dragged him to the ruined village and laid him in the street while she went to find her house, taking the dogs with her.

Her house was quite gone. She found the place easily enough. This was where it should be, opposite the water gate into the dike. She had always watched that gate herself. Miraculously it was not injured now, nor was the dike broken. It would be easy enough to rebuild the house. Only, for the present, it was gone.

So she went back to the young man. He was lying as she had left him, propped against the dike, panting and very pale. He had opened his coat and he had a little bag from which he was taking out strips of cloth and a bottle of something. And again he spoke, and again she understood nothing. Then he made signs and she saw it was water he wanted, so she took up a broken pot from one of many blown about the street, and, going up the dike, she filled it with river water and brought it down again and washed his wound, and she tore off the strips he made from the rolls of bandaging. He knew how to put the cloth over the gaping wound and he made signs to her, and she followed these signs. All the time he was trying to tell her something, but she could understand nothing.

"You must be from the South, sir," she said. It was easy to see that he had education. He looked very clever. "I have heard your language is different from ours." She laughed a little to put him at his ease, but he only stared at her <u>somberly</u> with dull eyes. So she said brightly, "Now if I could find something for us to eat, it would be nice."

He did not answer. Indeed he lay back, panting still more heavily, and stared into space as though she had not spoken.

"You would be better with food," she went on. "And so would I," she added. She was beginning to feel unbearably hungry.

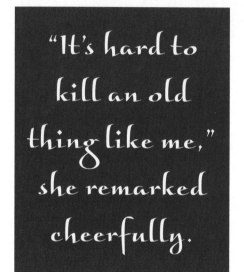

"It's hard to kill an old thing like me," she remarked cheerfully.

It occurred to her that in the baker's shop there might be some bread. Even if it were dusty with fallen mortar, it would still be bread. She would go and see. But before she went she moved the soldier a little so that he lay in the edge of shadow cast by a willow tree that grew in the bank of the dike. Then she went to the baker's shop. The dogs were gone.

The baker's shop was, like everything else, in ruins. No one was there. At first she saw nothing but the mass of crumpled earthen walls. But then she remembered that the oven was just inside the door, and the door frame still stood erect, supporting one end of the roof. She stood in this frame, and, running her hand in underneath the fallen roof inside, she felt the wooden cover of the iron caldron.[5] Under this there might be steamed bread. She worked her arm delicately and carefully in. It took quite a long time, but, even so, clouds of lime and dust almost choked her. Nevertheless she was right. She squeezed her hand under the cover and felt the firm smooth skin of the big steamed bread rolls, and one by one she drew out four.

"It's hard to kill an old thing like me," she remarked cheerfully to no one, and she began to eat one of the rolls as she walked

---

5. A *caldron* is a large kettle.

Vocabulary
somberly (sŏm′ bər lē) *adv.* in a gloomy manner

back. If she had a bit of garlic and a bowl of tea—but one couldn't have everything in these times.

It was at this moment that she heard voices. When she came in sight of the soldier, she saw surrounding him a crowd of other soldiers, who had apparently come from nowhere. They were staring down at the wounded soldier, whose eyes were now closed.

"Where did you get this Japanese, Old Mother?" they shouted at her.

"What Japanese?" she asked, coming to them.

"This one!" they shouted.

"Is he a Japanese?" she cried in the greatest astonishment. "But he looks like us—his eyes are black, his skin—"

"Japanese!" one of them shouted at her.

"Well," she said quietly, "he dropped out of the sky."

"Give me that bread!" another shouted.

"Take it," she said, "all except this one for him."

"A Japanese monkey eat good bread?" the soldier shouted.

"I suppose he is hungry also," old Mrs. Wang replied. She began to dislike these men. But then, she had always disliked soldiers.

"I wish you would go away," she said. "What are you doing here? Our village has always been peaceful."

"It certainly looks very peaceful now," one of the men said, grinning, "as peaceful as a grave. Do you know who did that, Old Mother? The Japanese!"

"I suppose so," she agreed. Then she asked, "Why? That's what I don't understand."

"Why? Because they want our land, that's why!"

"Our land!" she repeated. "Why, they can't have our land!"

"Never!" they shouted.

But all this time while they were talking and chewing the bread they had divided among themselves, they were watching the eastern horizon.

"Why do you keep looking east?" old Mrs. Wang now asked.

"The Japanese are coming from there," the man replied who had taken the bread.

"Are you running away from them?" she asked, surprised.

"There are only a handful of us," he said apologetically. "We were left to guard a village—Pao An, in the county of—"

"I know that village," old Mrs. Wang interrupted. "You needn't tell me. I was a girl there. How is the old Pao who keeps the tea shop in the main street? He's my brother."

"Everybody is dead there," the man replied. "The Japanese have taken it—a great army of men came with their foreign guns and tanks, so what could we do?"

"Of course, only run," she agreed. Nevertheless she felt dazed and sick. So he was dead, that one brother she had left! She was now the last of her father's family.

But the soldiers were straggling away again leaving her alone.

"They'll be coming, those little black dwarfs," they were saying. "We'd best go on."

Nevertheless, one lingered a moment, the one who had taken the bread, to stare down at the young wounded man, who lay with his eyes shut, not having moved at all.

"Is he dead?" he inquired. Then, before Mrs. Wang could answer, he pulled a short knife out of his belt. "Dead or not, I'll give him a punch or two with this—"

Carte Blanche, 1990. Bonnie Kwan Huo. Watercolor, 23.5 x 36.5 cm. Private collection.

Viewing the painting: Look up the meaning of this painting's title and discuss whether you think it is appropriate. How does this landscape differ from the one in the story?

But old Mrs. Wang pushed his arm away.

"No, you won't," she said with authority. "If he is dead, then there is no use in sending him into purgatory all in pieces. I am a good Buddhist myself."

The man laughed. "Oh well, he is dead," he answered; and then, seeing his comrades already at a distance, he ran after them.

A Japanese, was he? Old Mrs. Wang, left alone with this inert figure, looked at him <u>tentatively</u>. He was very young, she could see, now that his eyes were closed. His hand, limp in unconsciousness, looked like a boy's hand, unformed and still growing. She felt his wrist but could <u>discern</u> no pulse. She leaned over him and held to his lips the half of her roll which she had not eaten.

"Eat," she said very loudly and distinctly. "Bread!"

Vocabulary
tentatively (ten′ tə tiv lē) *adv.* hesitantly; uncertainly
discern (di surn′) *v.* to detect or recognize

But there was no answer. Evidently he was dead. He must have died while she was getting the bread out of the oven.

There was nothing to do then but to finish the bread herself. And when that was done, she wondered if she ought not to follow after Little Pig and his wife and all the villagers. The sun was mounting and it was growing hot. If she were going, she had better go. But first she would climb the dike and see what the direction was. They had gone straight west, and as far as the eye could look westward was a great plain. She might even see a good-sized crowd miles away. Anyway, she could see the next village, and they might all be there.

So she climbed the dike slowly, getting very hot. There was a slight breeze on top of the dike and it felt good. She was shocked to see the river very near the top of the dike. Why, it had risen in the last hour!

"You old demon!" she said severely. Let the river god hear it if he liked. He was evil, that he was—to threaten flood when there had been all this other trouble.

She stooped and bathed her cheeks and her wrists. The water was quite cold, as though with fresh rains somewhere. Then she stood up and gazed around her. To the west there was nothing except in the far distance the soldiers still half-running, and beyond them the blur of the next village, which stood on a long rise of ground. She had better set out for that village. Doubtless Little Pig and his wife were there waiting for her.

Just as she was about to climb down and start out, she saw something on the eastern horizon. It was at first only an immense cloud of dust. But, as she stared at it, very quickly it became a lot of black dots and shining spots. Then she saw what it was. It was a lot of men—an army. Instantly she knew what army.

"That's the Japanese," she thought. Yes, above them were the buzzing silver planes. They circled about, seeming to search for someone.

"I don't know who you're looking for," she muttered, "unless it's me and Little Pig and his wife. We're the only ones left. You've already killed my brother Pao."

She had almost forgotten that Pao was dead. Now she remembered it <u>acutely</u>. He had such a nice shop—always clean, and the tea good and the best meat dumplings to be had and the price always the same. Pao was a good man. Besides, what about his wife and his seven children? Doubtless they were all killed, too. Now these Japanese were looking for her. It occurred to her that on the dike she could easily be seen. So she clambered hastily down.

It was when she was about halfway down that she thought of the water gate. This old river—it had been a curse to them since time began. Why should it not make up a little now for all the wickedness it had done? It was plotting wickedness again, trying to steal over its banks. Well, why not? She wavered a moment. It was a pity, of course, that the young dead Japanese would be swept into the flood. He was a nice-looking boy, and she had saved him from being stabbed. It was not quite the same as saving his life, of course, but still it was a little the same. If he had been

---

Vocabulary
acutely (ə kūt′ lē) *adv.* sharply and with intensity

Did You Know?

A *sluice* is a gate or valve used to control the flow of water through an artificial channel, which is also called a sluice.

alive, he would have been saved. She went over to him and tugged at him until he lay well under the top of the bank. Then she went down again.

She knew perfectly how to open the water gate. Any child knew how to open the sluice for crops. But she knew also how to swing open the whole gate. The question was, could she open it quickly enough to get out of the way?

"I'm only one old woman," she muttered. She hesitated a second more. Well, it would be a pity not to see what sort of a baby Little Pig's wife would have, but one could not see everything. She had seen a great deal in this life. There was an end to what one could see, anyway.

She glanced again to the east. There were the Japanese coming across the plain. They were a long clear line of black, dotted with thousands of glittering points. If she opened this gate, the <u>impetuous</u> water would roar toward them, rushing into the plains, rolling into a wide lake, drowning them, maybe. Certainly they could not

keep on marching nearer and nearer to her, and to Little Pig and his wife who were waiting for her. Well, Little Pig and his wife—they would wonder about her—but they would never dream of this. It would make a good story—she would have enjoyed telling it.

She turned resolutely to the gate. Well, some people fought with airplanes and some with guns, but you could fight with a river, too, if it were a wicked one like this one. She wrenched out a huge wooden pin. It was slippery with silvery green moss. The rill[6] of water burst into a strong jet. When she wrenched one more pin, the rest would give way themselves. She began pulling at it, and felt it slip a little from its hole.

"I might be able to get myself out of purgatory with this," she thought, "and maybe they'll let me have that old man of mine, too. What's a hand of his to all this? Then we'll—"

The pin slipped away suddenly, and the gate burst flat against her and knocked her breath away. She had only time to gasp, to the river:

"Come on, you old demon!"

Then she felt it seize her and lift her up to the sky. It was beneath her and around her. It rolled her joyfully hither and thither, and then, holding her close and enfolded, it went rushing against the enemy.

---

6. A *rill* is a small stream.

Vocabulary

impetuous (im pech′ oo əs) *adj.* marked by force or violent action

The Boy and His Grandfather

Rudolfo A. Anaya

In the old days it was not unusual to find several generations living together in one home. Usually, everyone lived in peace and harmony, but this situation caused problems for one man whose household included, besides his wife and small son, his elderly father.

It so happened that the daughter-in-law took a dislike to the old man. He was always in the way, she said, and she insisted he be removed to a small room apart from the house.

Because the old man was out of sight, he was often neglected. Sometimes he even went hungry. They took poor care of him, and in winter the old man often suffered from the cold. One day the little grandson visited his grandfather.

"My little one," the grandfather said, "go and find a blanket and cover me. It is cold and I am freezing."

The small boy ran to the barn to look for a blanket, and there he found a rug.

"Father, please cut this rug in half," he asked his father.

"Why? What are you going to do with it?"

"I'm going to take it to my grandfather because he is cold."

"Well, take the entire rug," replied his father.

"No," his son answered, "I cannot take it all. I want you to cut it in half so I can save the other half for you when you are as old as my grandfather. Then I will have it for you so you will not be cold."

His son's response was enough to make the man realize how poorly he had treated his own father. The man then brought his father back into his home and ordered that a warm room be prepared. From that time on he took care of his father's needs and visited him frequently every day.

Responding to Literature

PERSONAL RESPONSE

- ◆ Do you think Mrs. Wang took the correct action at the end of the story? Why or why not?
- ◆ Do you think the grandson in "The Boy and His Grandfather" did the right thing? Why or why not?

Analyzing Literature

RECALL

1. What two forces endanger the village in "The Old Demon"?
2. What do all the villagers do when the bombs begin to fall?
3. What is Mrs. Wang's final action?
4. What makes the father in "The Boy and His Grandfather" change his attitude about the grandfather?

INTERPRET

5. What does Mrs. Wang fear more—the river or the Japanese? Explain your answer.
6. In your opinion, why does Mrs. Wang choose to stay after the village is bombed?
7. In your opinion, why does Mrs. Wang make the decision she makes at the end of the story?
8. "The Boy and His Grandfather" is a story that teaches a lesson. Write that lesson in one sentence.

EVALUATE AND CONNECT

9. Why is the title "The Old Demon" appropriate for the story?
10. **Theme Connection**   Do you think that decisions you have had to make in your life have prepared you to face an enemy with courage, as Mrs. Wang does in "The Old Demon"? Explain.

LITERARY ELEMENTS

Theme

Some stories, poems, or novels have a stated **theme** in which the main idea is expressed as a general statement. More frequently, however, literary works have an **implied theme,** which is revealed through such elements as plot, character, setting, and point of view. In "The Old Demon," the implied theme is revealed through the character of Mrs. Wang.

1. How do Mrs. Wang's actions throughout the story show that she feels it is her duty to protect her family and village?

2. What do you think is the implied theme of "The Old Demon"? What is the implied theme of "The Boy and His Grandfather"?

● See **Literary Terms Handbook,** p. R11.

Literature and Writing

Writing About Literature

Analyzing Descriptions   Pearl S. Buck knew the force of the Yellow River. She wanted to portray its power in her story. Write a paragraph that expresses your opinion about the effectiveness of her descriptions. Use examples from the story.

Personal Writing

Reflection on Personal Courage   Recall the discussion you had in the **Reading Focus** on page 482. Then write a brief essay reflecting upon how you imagine you would respond to a needy person.

Chinese cities as well as the countryside were affected by this flood in the 1930s.

Extending Your Response

Literature Groups

Debating a Plan of Action   Did Mrs. Wang make the right decision? Work with your group to decide whether you are for or against her action. Find another group that has chosen the opposite stand and hold a debate.

Interdisciplinary Activity

Social Studies   Find out all you can about China's major rivers—their names, locations, tributaries (smaller rivers that flow into them), and how they are used by the Chinese. Use both library resources and the Internet for your research. Then draw a map of the river systems for the class. Include the names of the rivers and any major cities along them.

Listening and Speaking

The Art of Storytelling   "The Boy and His Grandfather" is the kind of story that one generation passes on to the next orally. Prepare your own telling of the story. Practice telling it until you no longer need notes. Then invite family, friends, or young children to hear your version.

Reading Further

To read more about China, try these books:

Homesick: My Own Story by Jean Fritz

The Remarkable Journey of Prince Jen by Lloyd Alexander

Save your work for your portfolio.

Skill Minilesson

GRAMMAR AND LANGUAGE • PARTICIPLES AND PARTICIPIAL PHRASES

A **present participle** is formed by adding *-ing* to a verb. A **past participle** is formed by adding *-ed* to a verb.

A participle often functions as an adjective to modify nouns or pronouns.

the ruined village
burning houses

A **participial phrase** is a group of words that includes a participle and other words that complete its meaning. For example:

So, *leaning on her bamboo pipe,* she made her way slowly across the fields.

The participial phrase *leaning on her bamboo pipe* modifies the pronoun *she.*

PRACTICE Review "The Old Demon" to find two sentences having participial phrases. Copy each sentence, underline the participial phrase, and tell what word or words it modifies.

● For more about participles, see **Language Handbook,** pp. R29–R30.

READING AND THINKING • SUMMARIZING

When you summarize a piece of writing, you state the main ideas of the selection in your own words. You omit unimportant details so that the summary is much briefer than the original piece. For example, in a summary of "The Old Demon," you would be sure to include that the pilot was a wounded Japanese soldier. You would not need to mention that he pointed to the dogs before he fell on the ground.

PRACTICE Write a summary of "The Boy and His Grandfather." Be sure to include all the key events in chronological order. When you edit your writing, check that you have written everything in your own words and that you have deleted any unimportant details.

● For more about summarizing, see **Reading Handbook,** p. R92.

VOCABULARY • THE PREFIXES *mal-* AND *mis-*

Something *malicious* always involves an effort to cause harm. The Latin prefix *mal-,* which means "evil" or "bad," gives this word its meaning. It is similar to the Anglo-Saxon prefix *mis-,* which means "bad" or "wrong."

PRACTICE Use what you know about the prefixes *mal-* and *mis-* and familiar base words to match each word on the left with its meaning.

1. malnutrition	a. dissatisfied
2. malcontent	b. poor nourishment
3. misdeed	c. bad luck
4. malodorous	d. broken; not working
5. misshapen	e. bad act
6. maltreatment	f. say incorrectly
7. misguided	g. bad-smelling
8. malfunctioning	h. badly shaped
9. misfortune	i. led astray
10. mispronounce	j. abuse; injury

Using Pronouns

Every pronoun gets its meaning from a noun, or another pronoun, called its antecedent. It must be clear exactly *which* antecedent a pronoun refers to. In addition, personal pronouns have different forms depending on whether they are used in a sentence as its subject or as the object of a verb or a preposition.

Subjective form: I he she we they
Objective form: me him her us them

Problem 1 A pronoun that can refer to more than one antecedent

Before Felix's fight with Antonio, he goes to stay with his aunt.

[Who goes to stay with Aunt Lucy? *He* could refer to *Felix* or *Antonio.*]

Solution A Use a noun in place of the pronoun.

Before his fight with Antonio, Felix goes to stay with his aunt.

Solution B Rewrite the sentence so that any pronoun reference is clear.

Felix goes to stay with his aunt before his fight with Antonio.

Problem 2 Confusion between subject pronouns and object pronouns

Him and Antonio know they must forget their friendship during the fight. After the bell, the trainers must pull Antonio and he apart.

Solution In the first sentence, use the subject pronoun *he* in the subject of the sentence. In the second sentence, "Antonio and he" is the object of the verb *pull.* Use the object pronoun *him.*

He and Antonio know they must forget their friendship during the fight. After the bell, the trainers must pull Antonio and him apart.

● For more about pronouns, see **Language Handbook,** p. R17.

EXERCISE

Rewrite each sentence as needed. If a sentence has no pronoun problems, write *C.*

1. The children saw raindrops as they fell from the sky.
2. The teacher assumed that Margot and them had gone outside.
3. As the children lay down on the jungle plants, they sighed and squeaked.
4. "All Summer in a Day" caused a disagreement between my friend Lucy and I.

GENRE FOCUS

DRAMA

If you've ever seen a live **drama,** you know that it can "grab" you. Drama, whether a stage play, a movie, or a TV show, brings literature to life. When you *read* a drama, you need to recognize its special features, and you must use your imagination to make up for the lack of a stage, scenery, and the actions of actors.

FEATURES OF DRAMA

From ancient times through the eighteenth century, most plays were written, partly or wholly, as verse. Most modern plays, including those written for movies or television, are written in prose, the language of ordinary conversation.

On the printed page, drama looks different from other literature. A drama appears as a **script**—a set of words and instructions to be used by actors. Longer scripts are divided into sections called **acts,** and each act may be divided into smaller sections called **scenes.** Each act or scene usually includes the following features:

DIALOGUE—lines spoken by characters. Each line of dialogue is preceded by the name of the character who speaks it. The names are printed in all capital letters, bold type, italic type, or some combination of those features. Each name may be followed by a period, a colon, or no punctuation.

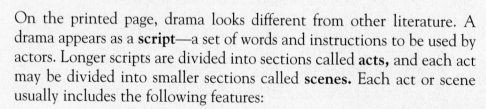

MODEL: "The Monsters Are Due on Maple Street"

STEVE. What do you mean? What are you talking about?

TOMMY. They don't want us to leave. That's why they shut everything off.

ELEMENTS OF DRAMA

Dramatic Conflicts in *Star Wars*		
Internal		
Luke Skywalker's obligation to stay home and help his uncle	vs.	his need to "try his wings"
Luke's desire to master the Force	vs.	his inexperience and lack of confidence
External		
Rebel Alliance	vs.	the Galactic Empire
Obi Wan Kenobe	vs.	Darth Vader
Han Solo's Millennium Falcon	vs.	the Storm Troopers' tie-fighters

The elements of drama, like the elements of fiction, include character, setting, theme, and plot. (For more about these elements, see **Literary Terms Handbook,** pages R1–R11.) In a dramatic plot, look especially for **conflicts,** or problems that characters must deal with. Some conflicts are **external**—clashes between two characters, or between a character and an outside force. Other conflicts are **internal**—clashes between opposing feelings within a character. The chart shows some external and internal conflicts from a movie that you probably know.

STAGE DIRECTIONS—words—often in italics and enclosed within brackets—describing characters and telling actors how to move or speak; indicating settings, props, sound effects, and lighting; and, for films and teleplays, giving camera directions. Some playwrights give very brief stage directions; others write extremely long ones, specifying, for example, every aspect of a character's appearance, actions, and even his or her thoughts

STEVE. [*Raising his voice and looking toward porch.*] Guess it was a meteor, honey. Came awful close, didn't it?

MRS. BRAND. Too close for my money! Much too close.

[*The camera pans across the various porches to people who stand there watching and talking in low tones.*]

CAST OF CHARACTERS—a list at the beginning of a play naming, and sometimes giving brief descriptions of, the characters. The cast of characters may also give readers information about how characters are related, for example:

John, Sarah's husband
Timmy, their son

CHARACTERS

NARRATOR

STEVE BRAND

MRS. BRAND

DON MARTIN

TOMMY

Active Reading Strategies

Tips for Reading a Drama

When reading a drama, skillful readers use strategies that help them follow the action of the play. These strategies also help readers by prompting them to question and evaluate what they read.

● For more about these and other reading strategies, see **Reading Handbook**, pp. R82–R96.

PREDICT

Combine clues in the play with what you already know to make educated guesses about what will happen next.

Ask Yourself . . .

● What action will this character take?

● What will happen next?

VISUALIZE

Reading the stage directions carefully will help you visualize the action of the play.

Ask Yourself . . .

● How does this scene look?

QUESTION

Keep asking yourself questions to help you clarify what is happening. Ask questions about the motivations of the characters.

Ask Yourself . . .

● What is really happening in this scene?

● What causes that character to act this way?

RESPOND

Don't wait until the play is over to respond to it. Think about what the play means to you while you are still reading it.

Say to Yourself . . .

● If I were this character, I would _____ .

● I'd like to ask the playwright why _____ .

REVIEW

Pause every page or two to think about what you have read. Summarize what is happening so you are sure you understand what has happened so far in the drama.

Ask Yourself . . .

- What happened in this scene?

- Do I understand what the playwright has written here?

EVALUATE

To evaluate means to make judgments. You can evaluate what the playwright has done during your reading as well as after you have finished the play.

Ask Yourself . . .

- Are these characters believable?

- Why did the playwright decide to have the plot take this turn?

- Would I enjoy seeing this play?

APPLYING THE STRATEGIES

Read the following teleplay, "The Monsters Are Due on Maple Street." Use the **Active Reading Model** notes in the margins as you read. Write your responses on a separate piece of paper or use stick-on notes.

Before You Read

The Monsters Are Due on Maple Street

MEET ROD SERLING

Although Rod Serling became best known as the creator and host of *The Twilight Zone*, a popular fantasy and science-fiction television series, he was first and foremost a writer. Between 1951 and 1955, he wrote more than seventy TV dramas. Three of Serling's six Emmy Awards were for pre-*Twilight Zone* plays. In the five seasons *The Twilight Zone* was on the air from 1959 to 1964, Serling wrote nearly two out of every three of the show's 156 plays. The following selection was one of those plays.

Rod Serling was born in New York in 1924 and died in 1975.

READING FOCUS

Lights flicker on and off. Cars start and stop. Telephones ring and go dead. Imagine these things happening in your town.

Journal
Describe how you think your neighbors would react to a series of strange occurrences on your street.

Setting a Purpose
Read to find out what happens on Maple Street.

BUILDING BACKGROUND

Did You Know? "The Monsters Are Due on Maple Street" is a play written especially for television. The stage notes, written specifically for the television camera, include
- *pan* to turn the camera to follow a moving person or object
- *cut* to switch from one scene to another
- *close-up* to move the camera close to the subject, such as a person's face
- *long shot* to film a subject from a long distance away

VOCABULARY PREVIEW

reflective (ri flek′ tiv) *adj.* showing serious and careful thinking; thoughtful; p. 507

intimidated (in tim′ ə dāt′ əd) *adj.* made timid or fearful; bullied; p. 510

instill (in stil′) *v.* to put in gradually, little by little; p. 510

validity (və lid′ ə tē) *n.* state of being supported by facts; truth; p. 511

defiant (di fī′ ənt) *adj.* showing bold resistance to authority or an opponent; p. 511

antagonism (an tag′ ə niz′ əm) *n.* hostility; p. 511

incriminate (in krim′ ə nāt′) *v.* to show the guilt of; p. 515

legitimate (li jit′ ə mit) *adj.* that which follows the rules; lawful; p. 517

explicit (eks plis′ it) *adj.* clearly expressed; p. 524

prejudice (prej′ ə dis) *n.* an unfavorable opinion or judgment formed unfairly; p. 524

THE MONSTERS
ARE DUE ON MAPLE STREET

Rod Serling

CHARACTERS

NARRATOR　　　　**FIGURE ONE**　　　　　**FIGURE TWO**

Residents of Maple Street:

STEVE BRAND　　　　**CHARLIE'S WIFE**　　　　**MRS. GOODMAN**

MRS. BRAND　　　　**TOMMY**　　　　　　**WOMAN**

DON MARTIN　　　　**SALLY, TOMMY'S MOTHER**　**MAN ONE**

PETE VAN HORN　　　**LES GOODMAN**　　　　**MAN TWO**

CHARLIE

ACT I

[*Fade in on a shot of the night sky. The various nebulae[1] and planet bodies stand out in sharp, sparkling relief, and the camera begins a slow pan across the Heavens.*]

NARRATOR'S VOICE.　There is a fifth dimension beyond that which is known to man. It is a dimension as vast as space, and as timeless as infinity. It is the middle ground between light and shadow—between science and superstition. And it lies between the pit of man's fears and the summit of his knowledge. This is the dimension of imagination. It is an area which we call The Twilight Zone.

QUESTION

Why does the play begin with a shot of the night sky? What do the narrator's words tell you about the play that is about to begin?

---

1. The word *nebulae* (neb′ yə lē′) refers to bright, cloudlike masses of dust and gases that are visible in the night sky.

The Monsters Are Due On Maple Street

[*The camera has begun to pan down until it passes the horizon and is on a sign which reads "Maple Street." Pan down until we are shooting down at an angle toward the street below. It's a tree-lined, quiet residential American street, very typical of the small town. The houses have front porches on which people sit and swing on gliders, conversing across from house to house. STEVE BRAND polishes his car parked in front of his house. His neighbor, DON MARTIN, leans against the fender watching him. A Good Humor man rides a bicycle and is just in the process of stopping to sell some ice cream to a couple of kids. Two women gossip on the front lawn. Another man waters his lawn.*]

NARRATOR'S VOICE. Maple Street, U.S.A., late summer. A tree-lined little world of front porch gliders, hop scotch, the laughter of children, and the bell of an ice cream vendor.

[*There is a pause and the camera moves over to a shot of the Good Humor man and two small boys who are standing alongside, just buying ice cream.*]

NARRATOR'S VOICE. At the sound of the roar and the flash of light it will be precisely 6:43 P.M. on Maple Street.

[*At this moment one of the little boys, TOMMY, looks up to listen to a sound of a tremendous screeching roar from overhead. A flash of light plays on both their faces and then it moves down the street past lawns and porches and rooftops and then disappears.*
Various people leave their porches and stop what they're doing to stare up at the sky. STEVE BRAND, the man who's been polishing his car, now stands there transfixed,[2] staring upwards. He looks at DON MARTIN, his neighbor from across the street.]

STEVE. What was that? A meteor?

DON. [*Nods.*] That's what it looked like. I didn't hear any crash though, did you?

STEVE. [*Shakes his head.*] Nope. I didn't hear anything except a roar.

MRS. BRAND. [*From her porch.*] Steve? What was that?

STEVE. [*Raising his voice and looking toward porch.*] Guess it was a meteor, honey. Came awful close, didn't it?

MRS. BRAND. Too close for my money! Much too close.

[*The camera pans across the various porches to people who stand there watching and talking in low tones.*]

---

2. To be *transfixed* is to be made motionless, as from wonder or fear.

Portrait of Orleans, 1950. Edward Hopper. Oil on canvas, 26 x 40 in. Fine Arts Museum of San Francisco.

Viewing the painting: In what ways is this street like the street in the teleplay?

NARRATOR'S VOICE. Maple Street. Six-forty-four P.M. on a late September evening. [*A pause.*] Maple Street in the last calm and <u>reflective</u> moment . . . before the monsters came!

[*The camera slowly pans across the porches again. We see a man screwing a light bulb on a front porch, then getting down off the stool to flick the switch and finding that nothing happens.*
Another man is working on an electric power mower. He plugs in the plug, flicks on the switch of the power mower, off and on, with nothing happening. Through the window of a front porch, we see a woman pushing her finger back and forth on the dial hook. Her voice is indistinct and distant, but intelligible and repetitive.]

WOMAN. Operator, operator, something's wrong on the phone, operator!

[*MRS. BRAND comes out on the porch and calls to STEVE.*]

MRS. BRAND. [*Calling.*] Steve, the power's off. I had the soup on the stove and the stove just stopped working.

WOMAN. Same thing over here. I can't get anybody on the phone either. The phone seems to be dead.

QUESTION

What do these word-less actions suggest to you? What do you think is happening on Maple Street?

Vocabulary
reflective (ri flek′ tiv) *adj.* showing serious and careful thinking; thoughtful

The Monsters Are Due
On Maple Street

ACTIVE READING MODEL

PREDICT

Do you think it's just a power failure? What will happen next?

[*We look down on the street as we hear the voices creep up from below, small, mildly disturbed voices highlighting these kinds of phrases:*]

VOICES.
Electricity's off.
Phone won't work.
Can't get a thing on the radio.
My power mower won't move, won't work at all.
Radio's gone dead!

[*PETE VAN HORN, a tall, thin man, is seen standing in front of his house.*]

VAN HORN. I'll cut through the back yard . . . See if the power's still on on Floral Street. I'll be right back!

[*He walks past the side of his house and disappears into the back yard. The camera pans down slowly until we're looking at ten or eleven people standing around the street and overflowing to the curb and sidewalk. In the background is STEVE BRAND's car.*]

STEVE. Doesn't make sense. Why should the power go off all of a sudden, and the phone line?

DON. Maybe some sort of an electrical storm or something.

CHARLIE. That don't seem likely. Sky's just as blue as anything. Not a cloud. No lightning. No thunder. No nothing. How could it be a storm?

WOMAN. I can't get a thing on the radio. Not even the portable.

[*The people again murmur softly in wonderment and question.*]

CHARLIE. Well, why don't you go downtown and check with the police, though they'll probably think we're crazy or something. A little power failure and right away we get all flustered[3] and everything.

---

3. To be *flustered* is to be embarrassed, nervous, or confused.

Rod Serling ❧

STEVE. It isn't just the power failure, Charlie. If it was, we'd still be able to get a broadcast on the portable.

[*There's a murmur of reaction to this.* STEVE *looks from face to face and then over to his car.*]

STEVE. I'll run downtown. We'll get this all straightened out.

[*He walks over to the car, gets in it, turns the key. Looking through the open car door, we see the crowd watching him from the other side.* STEVE *starts the engine. It turns over sluggishly and then just stops dead. He tries it again and this time he can't get it to turn over. Then, very slowly and reflectively, he turns the key back to "off" and slowly gets out of the car. The people stare at* STEVE. *He stands for a moment by the car, then walks toward the group.*]

STEVE. I don't understand it. It was working fine before . . .

DON. Out of gas?

STEVE. [*Shakes his head.*] I just had it filled up.

WOMAN. What's it mean?

CHARLIE. It's just as if . . . as if everything had stopped. [*Then he turns toward* STEVE.] We'd better walk downtown. [*Another murmur of assent*[4] *at this.*]

STEVE. The two of us can go, Charlie. [*He turns to look back at the car.*] It couldn't be the meteor. A meteor couldn't do *this*.

[*He and* CHARLIE *exchange a look, then they start to walk away from the group.*
We see TOMMY, *a serious-faced fourteen-year-old in spectacles who stands a few feet away from the group. He is halfway between them and the two men, who start to walk down the sidewalk.*]

TOMMY. Mr. Brand . . . you better not!

STEVE. Why not?

TOMMY. They don't want you to.

[STEVE *and* CHARLIE *exchange a grin, and* STEVE *looks back toward the boy.*]

STEVE. Who doesn't want us to?

TOMMY. [*Jerks his head in the general direction of the distant horizon.*] Them!

STEVE. Them?

CHARLIE. Who are them?

---

4. An expression of agreement is *assent.*

ACTIVE READING MODEL

RESPOND

Would you walk downtown if you were Steve or Charlie?

QUESTION

Who is the "them" Tommy refers to? What makes you think so?

The Monsters Are Due
On Maple Street

ACTIVE READING MODEL

TOMMY. [*Very intently.*] Whoever was in that thing that came by overhead.

[STEVE *knits his brows for a moment, cocking his head questioningly. His voice is intense.*]

STEVE. What?

TOMMY. Whoever was in that thing that came over. I don't think they want us to leave here.

[STEVE *leaves* CHARLIE *and walks over to the boy. He kneels down in front of him. He forces his voice to remain gentle. He reaches out and holds the boy.*]

STEVE. What do you mean? What are you talking about?

TOMMY. They don't want us to leave. That's why they shut everything off.

STEVE. What makes you say that? Whatever gave you that idea?

WOMAN. [*From the crowd.*] Now isn't that the craziest thing you ever heard?

QUESTION

Why do you think Tommy is being so persistent?

TOMMY. [*Persistently but a little intimidated by the crowd.*] It's always that way, in every story I ever read about a ship landing from outer space.

WOMAN. [*To the boy's mother,* SALLY, *who stands on the fringe of the crowd.*] From outer space, yet! Sally, you better get that boy of yours up to bed. He's been reading too many comic books or seeing too many movies or something.

SALLY. Tommy, come over here and stop that kind of talk.

STEVE. Go ahead, Tommy. We'll be right back. And you'll see. That wasn't any ship or anything like it. That was just a . . . a meteor or something. Likely as not— [*He turns to the group, now trying to weight his words with an optimism[5] he obviously doesn't feel but is desperately trying to instill in himself as well as the others.*] No doubt it did have something to do with all this power failure and the rest of it. Meteors can do some crazy things. Like sunspots.

DON. [*Picking up the cue.*] Sure. That's the kind of thing—like sunspots. They raise Cain[6] with radio reception all over the world. And this thing being so close—why, there's no telling the sort of stuff

---

5. *Optimism* means "a hopeful or cheerful view of things."
6. *[raise Cain]* This expression means "cause trouble."

Vocabulary
intimidated (in tim′ ə dāt′ əd) *adj.* made timid or fearful; bullied
instill (in stil′) *v.* to put in gradually, little by little

it can do. [*He wets his lips, smiles nervously.*] Go ahead, Charlie. You and Steve go into town and see if that isn't what's causing it all.

[*STEVE and CHARLIE again walk away from the group down the sidewalk. The people watch silently.*
TOMMY stares at them, biting his lips, and finally calling out again.]

TOMMY. Mr. Brand!

[*The two men stop again.* TOMMY *takes a step toward them.*]

TOMMY. Mr. Brand . . . please don't leave here.

[*STEVE and CHARLIE stop once again and turn toward the boy. There's a murmur in the crowd, a murmur of irritation and concern as if the boy were bringing up fears that shouldn't be brought up; words which carried with them a strange kind of validity that came without logic but nonetheless registered and had meaning and effect. Again we hear a murmur of reaction from the crowd.*
TOMMY is partly frightened and partly defiant as well.]

TOMMY. You might not even be able to get to town. It was that way in the story. Nobody could leave. Nobody except—

STEVE. Except who?

TOMMY. Except the people they'd sent down ahead of them. They looked just like humans. And it wasn't until the ship landed that—

[*The boy suddenly stops again, conscious of the parents staring at them and of the sudden hush of the crowd.*]

SALLY. [*In a whisper, sensing the antagonism of the crowd.*] Tommy, please son . . . honey, don't talk that way—

MAN ONE. That kid shouldn't talk that way . . . and we shouldn't stand here listening to him. Why this is the craziest thing I ever heard of. The kid tells us a comic book plot and here we stand listening—

[*STEVE walks toward the camera, stops by the boy.*]

STEVE. Go ahead, Tommy. What kind of story was this? What about the people that they sent out ahead?

TOMMY. That was the way they prepared things for the landing. They sent four people. A mother and a father and two kids who looked just like humans . . . but they weren't.

Vocabulary
validity (və lid′ ə tē) *n.* state of being supported by facts; truth
defiant (di fī′ ənt) *adj.* showing bold resistance to authority or an opponent
antagonism (an tag′ ə niz′ əm) *n.* unfriendliness; hostility

The Monsters Are Due
On Maple Street

ACTIVE READING MODEL

[*There's another silence as* STEVE *looks toward the crowd and then toward* TOMMY. *He wears a tight grin.*]

STEVE. Well, I guess what we'd better do then is to run a check on the neighborhood and see which ones of us are really human.

[*There's laughter at this, but it's a laughter that comes from a desperate attempt to lighten the atmosphere. It's a release kind of laugh. The people look at one another in the middle of their laughter.*]

CHARLIE. There must be somethin' better to do than stand around makin' bum jokes about it. [*Rubs his jaw nervously.*] I wonder if Floral Street's got the same deal we got. [*He looks past the houses.*] Where is Pete Van Horn anyway? Didn't he get back yet?

[*Suddenly there's the sound of a car's engine starting to turn over. We look across the street toward the driveway of* LES GOODMAN's *house. He's at the wheel trying to start the car.*]

SALLY. Can you get it started, Les?

[*He gets out of the car, shaking his head.*]

GOODMAN. No dice.

[*He walks toward the group. He stops suddenly as behind him, inexplicably[7] and with a noise that inserts itself into the silence, the car engine starts up all by itself.* GOODMAN *whirls around to stare toward it.
The car idles roughly, smoke coming from the exhaust, the frame shaking gently.*
GOODMAN's *eyes go wide, and he runs over to his car.
The people stare toward the car.*]

MAN ONE. He got the car started somehow. He got his car started!

[*The camera pans along the faces of the people as they stare, somehow caught up by this revelation and somehow, illogically, wildly, frightened.*]

WOMAN. How come his car just up and started like that?

SALLY. All by itself. He wasn't anywheres near it. It started all by itself.

[DON *approaches the group, stops a few feet away to look toward* GOODMAN's *car and then back toward the group.*]

DON. And he never did come out to look at that thing that flew overhead. He wasn't even interested. [*He turns to the faces in the group, his face taut and serious.*] Why? Why didn't he come out with the rest of us to look?

PREDICT

How will the group react to the car's starting by itself?

---

7. Something that happens *inexplicably* (in′ iks plik′ ə blē) is impossible to understand or explain.

Did You Know?

A *metamorphosis* is a complete change, as when a caterpillar becomes a butterfly.

CHARLIE. He always was an oddball. Him and his whole family. Real oddball.

DON. What do you say we ask him?

[*The group suddenly starts toward the house. In this brief fraction of a moment they take the first step toward performing a metamorphosis that changes people from a group into a mob. They begin to head purposefully across the street toward the house at the end.* STEVE *stands in front of them. For a moment their fear almost turns their walk into a wild stampede, but* STEVE's *voice, loud, incisive,*[8] *and commanding, makes them stop.*]

VISUALIZE

Take a minute to picture this scene as if you were on the street but apart from the group.

STEVE. Wait a minute . . . wait a minute! Let's not be a mob!

[*The people stop as a group, seem to pause for a moment, and then much more quietly and slowly start to walk across the street.* GOODMAN *stands alone facing the people.*]

GOODMAN. I just don't understand it. I tried to start it and it wouldn't start. You saw me. All of you saw me.

[*And now, just as suddenly as the engine started, it stops and there's a long silence that is gradually intruded upon by the frightened murmuring of the people.*]

GOODMAN. I don't understand. I swear . . . I don't understand. What's happening?

DON. Maybe you better tell us. Nothing's working on this street. Nothing. No lights, no power, no radio. [*And then meaningfully*] Nothing except one car—yours!

[*The people pick this up and now their murmuring becomes a loud chant filling the air with accusations and demands for action. Two of the men pass* DON *and head toward* GOODMAN, *who backs away, backing into his car and now at bay.*][9]

REVIEW

What has happened up to this point? How have the characters reacted to these events? Can you tell yet who the main characters are?

GOODMAN. Wait a minute now. You keep your distance—all of you. So I've got a car that starts by itself—well, that's a freak thing, I admit it. But does that make me some kind of a criminal or something? I don't know why the car works—it just does!

---

8. Steve's *incisive* voice is sharp and forceful.

9. *[at bay]* This describes the position of a cornered animal that is forced to turn and face its pursuers.

Room for Tourists, 1945. Edward Hopper. Oil on canvas, 30¼ x 42⅛ in. Yale University Art Gallery, New Haven, CT.

Viewing the painting: What mood does the artist create in this painting? How might a playwright create a similar mood?

[*This stops the crowd momentarily and now* GOODMAN, *still backing away, goes toward his front porch. He goes up the steps and then stops to stand facing the mob.*

We see a long shot of STEVE *as he comes through the crowd.*]

STEVE. [*Quietly.*] We're all on a monster kick, Les. Seems that the general impression holds that maybe one family isn't what we think they

QUESTION

What's a "monster kick"? Why does Steve say that?

are. Monsters from outer space or something. Different than us. Fifth columnists[10] from the vast beyond. [*He chuckles.*] You know anybody that might fit that description around here on Maple Street?

GOODMAN. What is this, a gag or something? This a practical joke or something?

[*We see a close-up of the porch light as it suddenly goes out. There's a murmur from the group.*]

GOODMAN. Now I suppose that's supposed to incriminate me! The light goes on and off. That really does it, doesn't it?

[*He looks around the faces of the people.*] I just don't understand this— [*He wets his lips, looking from face to face.*] Look, you all know me. We've lived here five years. Right in this house. We're no different from any of the rest of you! We're no different at all. Really . . . this whole thing is just . . . just weird—

WOMAN. Well, if that's the case, Les Goodman, explain why— [*She stops suddenly, clamping her mouth shut.*]

GOODMAN. [*Softly.*] Explain what?

STEVE. [*Interjecting.*] Look, let's forget this—

CHARLIE. [*Overlapping him.*] Go ahead, let her talk. What about it? Explain what?

WOMAN. [*A little reluctantly.*] Well . . . sometimes I go to bed late at night. A couple of times . . . a couple of times I'd come out on the porch and I'd see Mr. Goodman here in the wee hours of the morning standing out in front of his house . . . looking up at the sky. [*She looks around the circle of*

RESPOND

How would you feel at this point if you were Goodman?

---

10. *Fifth columnists* are traitors.

Vocabulary
incriminate (in krim′ ə nāt′) *v.* to show the guilt of

**ACTIVE
READING
MODEL**

EVALUATE

Would a person
really say something
like this about a
neighbor?

REVIEW

So far, what has
actually happened?

faces.] That's right, looking up at the sky as if . . . as if he were waiting for something. [*A pause.*] As if he were looking for something.

[*There's a murmur of reaction from the crowd again.
We cut suddenly to a group shot. As* GOODMAN *starts toward them,
they back away frightened.*]

GOODMAN. You know really . . . this is for laughs. You know what I'm guilty of? [*He laughs.*] I'm guilty of insomnia.[11] Now what's the penalty for insomnia? [*At this point the laugh, the humor, leaves his voice.*] Did you hear what I said? I said it was insomnia. [*A pause as he looks around, then shouts.*] I said it was insomnia! You fools. You scared, frightened rabbits, you. You're sick people, do you know that? You're sick people—all of you! And you don't even know what you're starting because let me tell you . . . let me tell you—this thing you're starting—that should frighten you. As God is my witness . . . you're letting something begin here that's a nightmare!

ACT II

[*We see a medium shot of the Goodman entry hall at night. On the side table rests an unlit candle.* MRS. GOODMAN *walks into the scene, a glass of milk in hand. She sets the milk down on the table, lights the candle with a match from a box on the table, picks up the glass of milk, and starts out of scene.*

MRS. GOODMAN *comes through her porch door, glass of milk in hand. The entry hall, with table and lit candle, can be seen behind her.*

Outside, the camera slowly pans down the sidewalk, taking in little knots of people who stand around talking in low voices. At the end of each conversation they look toward LES GOODMAN'S *house. From the various houses we can see candlelight but no electricity, and there's an all-pervading quiet that blankets the whole area, disturbed only by the almost whispered voices of the people as they stand around. The camera pans over to one group where* CHARLIE *stands. He stares across at* GOODMAN'S *house.*

We see a long shot of the house. Two men stand across the street in almost sentry-like poses. Then we see a medium shot of a group of people.]

QUESTION

How much time has
passed since the end
of act 1? How can
you tell?

SALLY. [*A little timorously.*][12] It just doesn't seem right, though, keeping watch on them. Why . . . he was right when he said he was one of our neighbors. Why, I've known Ethel Goodman ever since they moved in. We've been good friends—

---

11. *Insomnia* is restless sleep or the inability to fall asleep.
12. *Timorously* (tim′ r s lē) means "lacking courage or self-confidence; timidly."

CHARLIE. That don't prove a thing. Any guy who'd spend his time lookin' up at the sky early in the morning—well, there's something wrong with that kind of person. There's something that ain't legitimate. Maybe under normal circumstances we could let it go by, but these aren't normal circumstances. Why, look at this street! Nothin' but candles. Why, it's like goin' back into the dark ages or somethin'!

[*STEVE walks down the steps of his porch, walks down the street over to LES GOODMAN's house, and then stops at the foot of the steps. GOODMAN stands there, his wife behind him, very frightened.*]

GOODMAN. Just stay right where you are, Steve. We don't want any trouble, but this time if anybody sets foot on my porch, that's what they're going to get—trouble!

STEVE. Look, Les—

GOODMAN. I've already explained to you people. I don't sleep very well at night sometimes. I get up and I take a walk and I look up at the sky. I look at the stars!

MRS. GOODMAN. That's exactly what he does. Why this whole thing, it's . . . it's some kind of madness or something.

STEVE. [*Nods grimly.*] That's exactly what it is—some kind of madness.

CHARLIE'S VOICE. [*Shrill, from across the street.*] You best watch who you're seen with, Steve! Until we get this all straightened out, you ain't exactly above suspicion yourself.

STEVE. [*Whirling around toward him.*] Or you, Charlie. Or any of us, it seems. From age eight on up.

WOMAN. What I'd like to know is—what are we gonna do? Just stand around here all night?

CHARLIE. There's nothin' else we can do! [*He turns back looking toward STEVE and GOODMAN again.*] One of 'em'll tip their hand. They got to.

STEVE. [*Raising his voice.*] There's something you can do, Charlie. You could go home and keep your mouth shut. You could quit strutting around like a self-appointed hanging judge and just climb into bed and forget it.

CHARLIE. You sound real anxious to have that happen, Steve. I think we better keep our eye on you too!

PREDICT

Toward what do events appear to be moving? What is going to happen next?

RESPOND

If you were Steve, how would you be feeling now?

Vocabulary
legitimate (li jit′ ə mit) *adj.* that which follows the rules; lawful

The Monsters Are Due
On Maple Street

DON. [*As if he were taking the bit in his teeth, takes a hesitant step to the front.*] I think everything might as well come out now. [*He turns toward STEVE.*] Your wife's done plenty of talking, Steve, about how odd you are!

CHARLIE. [*Picking this up, his eyes widening.*] Go ahead, tell us what she's said.

[*We see a long shot of STEVE as he walks toward them from across the street.*]

STEVE. Go ahead, what's my wife said? Let's get it all out. Let's pick out every idiosyncrasy of every single man, woman, and child on the street. And then we might as well set up some kind of kangaroo court.[13] How about a firing squad at dawn, Charlie, so we can get rid of all the suspects? Narrow them down. Make it easier for you.

DON. There's no need gettin' so upset, Steve. It's just that . . . well . . . Myra's talked about how there's been plenty of nights you spent hours down in your basement workin' on some kind of radio or something. Well, none of us have ever seen that radio—

[*By this time STEVE has reached the group. He stands there defiantly close to them.*]

How would you react at this point if you were Steve?

CHARLIE. Go ahead, Steve. What kind of "radio set" you workin' on? I never seen it. Neither has anyone else. Who you talk to on that radio set? And who talks to you?

STEVE. I'm surprised at you, Charlie. How come you're so dense all of a sudden? [*A pause.*] Who do I talk to? I talk to monsters from outer space. I talk to three-headed green men who fly over here in what look like meteors.

[*STEVE's wife steps down from the porch, bites her lip, calls out.*]

MRS. BRAND. Steve! Steve, please. [*Then looking around, frightened, she walks toward the group.*] It's just a ham radio[14] set, that's all. I bought him a book on it myself. It's just a ham radio set. A lot of people have them. I can show it to you. It's right down in the basement.

STEVE. [*Whirls around toward her.*] Show them nothing! If they want to look inside our house—let them get a search warrant.

CHARLIE. Look, buddy, you can't afford to—

---

13. An *idiosyncrasy* (id´ ē ə sing´ krə sē) is a personal way of acting; an odd mannerism. A *kangaroo court* is an unofficial, irregular trial in which the verdict is often decided beforehand and fair legal procedures are ignored.
14. *Ham radio* is a hobby in which a person operates his or her own radio station, sending messages by voice or Morse code.

STEVE. [*Interrupting.*] Charlie, don't tell me what I can afford! And stop telling me who's dangerous and who isn't and who's safe and who's a menace. [*He turns to the group and shouts.*] And you're with him, too—all of you! You're standing here all set to crucify—all set to find a scapegoat[15]—all desperate to point some kind of a finger at a neighbor! Well now look, friends, the only thing that's gonna happen is that we'll eat each other up alive—

[*He stops abruptly as* CHARLIE *suddenly grabs his arm.*]

CHARLIE. [*In a hushed voice.*] That's not the only thing that can happen to us.

[*Cut to a long shot looking down the street. A figure has suddenly materialized in the gloom and in the silence we can hear the clickety-clack of slow, measured footsteps on concrete as the figure walks slowly toward them. One of the women lets out a stifled cry. The young mother grabs her boy as do a couple of others.*]

TOMMY. [*Shouting, frightened.*] It's the monster! It's the monster!

[*Another woman lets out a wail and the people fall back in a group, staring toward the darkness and the approaching figure.*
We see a medium group shot of the people as they stand in the shadows watching. DON MARTIN *joins them, carrying a shotgun. He holds it up.*]

DON. We may need this.

STEVE. A shotgun? [*He pulls it out of* DON's *hand.*] Good Lord—will anybody think a thought around here? Will you people wise up? What good would a shotgun do against—

[*Now* CHARLIE *pulls the gun from* STEVE's *hand.*]

CHARLIE. No more talk, Steve. You're going to talk us into a grave! You'd let whatever's out there walk right over us, wouldn't yuh? Well, some of us won't!

[*He swings the gun around to point it toward the sidewalk.*
The dark figure continues to walk toward them.
The group stands there, fearful, apprehensive, mothers clutching children, men standing in front of wives. CHARLIE *slowly raises the gun. As the figure gets closer and closer he suddenly pulls the trigger. The sound of it explodes in the stillness. There is a long angle shot looking down at the figure, who suddenly lets out a small cry, stumbles forward onto his knees and then falls forward on his face.* DON, CHARLIE, *and* STEVE *race*

PREDICT

Who do you think the dark figure down the street is?

EVALUATE

Take a minute to ask yourself if you think Charlie would really do this.

---

15. A *scapegoat* is someone who is made to take the blame and suffer for the mistakes or misfortunes of another person or a group.

Stormy Midnight, 1995. Jane Wilson. Oil on linen, 18 x 18 in. Courtesy Fischbach Gallery, New York.

Viewing the painting: If you were to add people to this scene, what would they be doing? Why? How does the mood of the painting compare with the mood of the play?

forward over to him. STEVE is there first and turns the man over. Now the crowd gathers around them.]

STEVE. [*Slowly looks up.*] It's Pete Van Horn.

DON. [*In a hushed voice.*] Pete Van Horn! He was just gonna go over to the next block to see if the power was on—

WOMAN. You killed him, Charlie. You shot him dead!

CHARLIE. [*Looks around at the circle of faces, his eyes frightened, his face contorted.*] But . . . but I didn't know who he was. I certainly didn't know who he was. He comes walkin' out of the darkness—how am I supposed to know who he was? [*He grabs STEVE.*] Steve—you know why I shot! How was I supposed to know he wasn't a monster or something? [*He grabs DON now.*] We're all scared of the same thing, I was just tryin' to . . . tryin' to protect my home, that's all! Look, all of you, that's all I was tryin' to do. [*He looks down wildly at the body.*] I didn't know it was somebody we knew! I didn't know—

[*There's a sudden hush and then an intake of breath. We see a medium shot of the living room window of CHARLIE's house. The window is not lit, but suddenly the house lights come on behind it.*]

WOMAN. [*In a very hushed voice.*] Charlie . . . Charlie . . . the lights just went on in your house. Why did the lights just go on?

DON. What about it, Charlie? How come you're the only one with lights now?

GOODMAN. That's what I'd like to know.

[*A pause as they all stare toward CHARLIE.*]

GOODMAN. You were so quick to kill, Charlie and you were so quick to tell us who we had to be careful of. Well, maybe you had to kill. Maybe Peter there was trying to tell us something. Maybe he'd found out something and came back to tell us who there was amongst us we should watch out for—

[*CHARLIE backs away from the group, his eyes wide with fright.*]

CHARLIE. No . . . no . . . it's nothing of the sort! I don't know why the lights are on, I swear I don't. Somebody's pulling a gag or something.

[*He bumps against STEVE, who grabs him and whirls him around.*]

STEVE. A gag? A gag? Charlie, there's a dead man on the sidewalk and you killed him. Does this thing look like a gag to you?

[*CHARLIE breaks away and screams as he runs toward his house.*]

CHARLIE. No! No! Please!

ACTIVE READING MODEL

VISUALIZE

Can you picture this scene?

REVIEW

How would you summarize what has happened so far?

The Monsters Are Due
On Maple Street

[*A man breaks away from the crowd to chase* CHARLIE. *We see a long angle shot looking down as the man tackles* CHARLIE *and lands on top of him. The other people start to run toward them.* CHARLIE *is up on his feet, breaks away from the other man's grasp, lands a couple of desperate punches that push the man aside. Then he forces his way, fighting, through the crowd to once again break free, jumps up on his front porch. A rock thrown from the group smashes a window alongside of him, the broken glass flying past him. A couple of pieces cut him. He stands there perspiring, rumpled, blood running down from a cut on the cheek. His wife breaks away from the group to throw herself into his arms. He buries his face against her. We can see the crowd converging on the porch now.*]

VOICES.
It must have been him.
He's the one.
We got to get Charlie.

[*Another rock lands on the porch. Now* CHARLIE *pushes his wife behind him, facing the group.*]

CHARLIE. Look, look I swear to you . . . it isn't me . . . but I do know who it is . . . I swear to you, I do know who it is. I know who the monster is here. I know who it is that doesn't belong. I swear to you I know.

GOODMAN. [*Shouting.*] What are you waiting for?

WOMAN. [*Shouting.*] Come on, Charlie, come on.

MAN ONE. [*Shouting.*] Who is it, Charlie, tell us!

DON. [*Pushing his way to the front of the crowd*] All right, Charlie, let's hear it!

[CHARLIE's *eyes dart around wildly.*]

CHARLIE. It's . . . it's . . .

MAN TWO. [*Screaming.*] Go ahead, Charlie, tell us.

CHARLIE. It's . . . it's the kid. It's Tommy. He's the one.

[*There's a gasp from the crowd as we cut to a shot of* SALLY *holding her son* TOMMY. *The boy at first doesn't understand and then, realizing the eyes are all on him, buries his face against his mother.*]

SALLY. [*Backs away.*] That's crazy! That's crazy! He's a little boy.

WOMAN. But he knew! He was the only one who knew! He told us all about it. Well, how did he know? How *could* he have known?

[*The various people take this up and repeat the question aloud.*]

VOICES.
How could he know?

Who told him?
Make the kid answer.

DON.   It was Charlie who killed old man Van Horn.

WOMAN.   But it was the kid here who knew what was going to happen all the time. He was the one who knew!

[*We see a close-up of* STEVE.]

STEVE.   Are you all gone crazy? [*Pause as he looks about.*] Stop.

[*A fist crashes at* STEVE's *face, staggering him back out of the frame of the picture.*
There are several close camera shots suggesting the coming of violence. A hand fires a rifle. A fist clenches. A hand grabs the hammer from VAN HORN's *body, etc. Meanwhile, we hear the following lines.*]

DON.   Charlie has to be the one—Where's my rifle—

WOMAN.   Les Goodman's the one. His car started! Let's wreck it.

MRS. GOODMAN.   What about Steve's radio—He's the one that called them—

MR. GOODMAN.   Smash the radio. Get me a hammer. Get me something.

STEVE.   Stop—Stop—

CHARLIE.   Where's that kid—Let's get him.

MAN ONE.   Get Steve—Get Charlie—They're working together.

[*The crowd starts to converge around the mother, who grabs the child and starts to run with him. The crowd starts to follow, at first walking fast, and then running after him.*
We see a full shot of the street as suddenly CHARLIE's *lights go off and the lights in another house go on. They stay on for a moment, then from across the street other lights go on and then off again.*]

MAN ONE.   [*Shouting.*] It isn't the kid . . . it's Bob Weaver's house.

WOMAN.   It isn't Bob Weaver's house, it's Don Martin's place.

CHARLIE.   I tell you it's the kid.

DON.   It's Charlie. He's the one.

[*We move into a series of close-ups of various people as they shout, accuse, scream, interspersing these shots with shots of houses as the lights go on and off, and then slowly in the middle of this nightmarish morass¹⁶ of sight and sound the camera starts to pull away, until once again we've*

---

16. *Interspersing* means "scattering or mixing in over brief periods." A *morass* (mə ras′) is any difficult, confused, or entangling condition or situation.

EVALUATE

Has the playwright kept the character of Steve consistent throughout the story? How would you describe Steve?

EVALUATE

What mood does the playwright create with this scene? How does he create that mood?

The Monsters Are Due
On Maple Street

reached the opening shot looking at the Maple Street sign from high above. The camera continues to move away until we dissolve to a shot looking toward the metal side of a space craft, which sits shrouded in darkness. An open door throws out a beam of light from the illuminated interior. Two figures silhouetted against the bright lights appear. We get only a vague feeling of form, but nothing more <u>explicit</u> than that.]

FIGURE ONE.   Understand the procedure now? Just stop a few of their machines and radios and telephones and lawn mowers . . . Throw them into darkness for a few hours, and then you just sit back and watch the pattern.

FIGURE TWO.   And this pattern is always the same?

FIGURE ONE.   With few variations. They pick the most dangerous enemy they can find . . . and it's themselves. And all we need do is sit back . . . and watch.

FIGURE TWO.   Then I take it this place . . . this Maple Street . . . is not unique.

FIGURE ONE.   [*Shaking his head.*] By no means. Their world is full of Maple Streets. And we'll go from one to the other and let them destroy themselves. One to the other . . . one to the other . . . one to the other—

[*Now the camera pans up for a shot of the starry sky and over this we hear the* NARRATOR'S VOICE.]

NARRATOR'S VOICE.   The tools of conquest do not necessarily come with bombs and explosions and fallout.[17] There are weapons that are simply thoughts, attitudes, <u>prejudices</u>—to be found only in the minds of men. For the record, prejudices can kill and suspicion can destroy and a thoughtless frightened search for a scapegoat has a fallout all its own for the children . . . and the children yet unborn. [*A pause.*] And the pity of it is . . . that these things cannot be confined to . . . The Twilight Zone!

---

17. *Fallout* is the radioactive dust particles that result from a nuclear explosion and fall to earth from the atmosphere.

Vocabulary
explicit (eks plis′ it) *adj.* clearly expressed
prejudice (prej′ ə dis) *n.* an unfavorable opinion or judgment formed unfairly

Responding to Literature

PERSONAL RESPONSE

- ◆ What is your reaction to this play? Recall the **Reading Focus** on page 504. How do the reactions of the neighbors in the teleplay compare or contrast with how you imagined your own neighbors reacting to strange occurrences?

Active Reading Response

Review the strategies described in the **Active Reading Model** on pages 502–503. Choose one of the strategies and find three additional places in the teleplay where you could apply it.

Analyzing Literature

RECALL

1. What is the first sign of trouble on Maple Street?
2. Who is Tommy? Describe him and explain what he tells Steve.
3. Who is the first person the neighbors begin to suspect?
4. What events lead to the shooting?

INTERPRET

5. At the beginning of the play, what is the **mood** on Maple Street? What causes the mood to change?
6. What role do you think Tommy plays in this drama?
7. Why do the people on Maple Street begin to turn on each other?
8. At what point do the neighbors become a "mob"? Why does this happen? Use quotations from the play to support your ideas.

EVALUATE AND CONNECT

9. How do the aliens use their understanding of human nature to accomplish their goal? Explain.
10. The narrator says, "The tools of conquest do not necessarily come with bombs." How does the play portray that idea?

LITERARY ELEMENTS

Teleplay

"The Monsters Are Due on Maple Street" is a **teleplay,** or a play written especially for television. Its format is similar to that of a stage play. Like a play, the teleplay is divided into **scenes** and **acts.** Stage directions, meant for the actors and the studio crew, are in italic type and are enclosed in brackets. The main difference between the format of a play and a teleplay is the addition of camera directions.

1. Identify a stage direction that describes the setting of the teleplay.
2. Find where Act II begins. Tell why you think Serling divided the play at that particular point.

● See **Literary Terms Handbook,** p. R11.

Literature and Writing

Writing About Literature

Thinking About Conflict   **Conflict** is the struggle between two opposing forces at the center of a plot in a story or drama. What do you think is the main conflict in this teleplay? What other conflicts are portrayed? Write one or two paragraphs describing your ideas. Support your ideas with examples from the teleplay.

Creative Writing

From an Alien's Point of View   Imagine that you are one of the aliens on the spacecraft. You are sending home a message about the events on Maple Street. Describe what you and your fellow aliens did and what happened as a result. Explain how you were able to get the "Earthlings" to accomplish your goals.

Extending Your Response

Learning for Life

News Broadcast   Work with a group to prepare a television news report about the events on Maple Street. Decide at which point in the play your "live" report will take place. Divide the group into a TV anchor person, on-the-spot reporters, and characters from the play who will be interviewed. After rehearsing it, present your newscast to the class.

*inter*NET
CONNECTION

You can find out more about "The Twilight Zone," Rod Serling, and science fiction in general at many sites on the World Wide Web. Just type "twilight zone," "rod serling," or "science fiction" in the subject window of your search engine.

Literature Groups

Who Are the *Real* Monsters?   "The Monsters Are Due on Maple Street" describes a neighborhood changed by fear. Do you agree with the author that human beings can be turned into "monsters"? Talk about the central question raised in this play: Who are the real monsters on Maple Street? How does fear change people? Support your ideas with examples from the play.

Reading Further

If you would like to read more by Rod Serling, try this book:
Stories from The Twilight Zone

 Save your work for your portfolio.

Skill Minilesson

GRAMMAR AND LANGUAGE • APOSTROPHES

Do you know the difference between *its* and *it's*? The pronoun *its* shows possession. The word *it's* is a contraction of *it is.* The apostrophe (') in *it's* is used to indicate where the letter *i* has been left out.

Its setting is a typical American town. [possessive pronoun]

It's a drama about how fear destroys people's lives. [contraction of *it is*]

PRACTICE Write a paragraph describing "The Monsters Are Due on Maple Street" for someone who hasn't read it. Use the possessive pronoun *its* as well as the contraction *it's* in your paragraph.

● For more about using apostrophes, see **Language Handbook,** p. R19.

READING AND THINKING • VISUALIZING

A teleplay is meant to be seen on a screen. Therefore, when you read a teleplay, imagine that you are seeing the drama in your mind. Use the details to help you picture the different scenes as you read. Keep asking yourself:

How does this scene look? What is going on here? What is each character doing?

PRACTICE Work with a partner. Pick out one scene to read to your partner. As you read, your partner should draw a sketch showing what is going on in the scene. Then trade roles and draw a sketch as you listen to your partner read a different scene.

● For more about visualizing, see **Reading Handbook,** pp. R87–R88.

VOCABULARY • BASE WORDS

Base words are whole words that form the "base" of new words when prefixes or suffixes (or both) are attached to them. For example, *drama* is the base word in *dramatic* and *dramatize. Sure* is the base word in *unsure* and *surely.* Familiar base words can help you unlock the meanings of unfamiliar words. For example, *construct* is a good clue to the meaning of *unreconstructed,* and knowing the meaning of *specific* can help you understand *specification.*
Spelling tip: When a silent *e* comes at the end of a base word, the *e* is sometimes dropped when a suffix is added. For example: *judge* → *judging*

PRACTICE Use what you know about base words and familiar prefixes and suffixes to match each word on the left to its meaning.

1. undesirable
2. inescapable
3. illogical
4. nonexistent
5. revaluation
6. presuppose
7. encirclement
8. unpredictable

a. cannot be avoided
b. not wanted
c. unable to be foretold
d. determining worth again
e. that which surrounds
f. senseless
g. found nowhere
h. assume beforehand

MEDIA Connection

WEB SITE

"The Monsters Are Due on Maple Street" was written for the TV series *The Twilight Zone*. On some Web sites devoted to the series, you can find plot summaries of all the episodes. Here's an example.

The Eye of the Beholder

Address: http://www.the5thdimension.com/shows/

TWILIGHT ZONE

**Episode 42 •
November 11, 1960**

Janet Tyler is having her eleventh state-sponsored operation, the maximum allowed. The surgery is necessary because she is an outcast with a hideous face. The nurses commiserate with her, and her doctor is quite sympathetic. Janet believes the situation is hopeless and takes comfort in the bandages covering her face.

While talking with her doctor, Janet breaks down and starts crying because she just wants to look like everybody else and therefore enjoy the same privileges. However, if the surgery fails she will be forced to live in a village with other "freaks" away from normal society, which doesn't sit well with Janet, who calls it a "ghetto." She starts crying out against the state and pleads for her doctor to take off the bandages to see if the last experiment worked. He agrees to do so.

Slowly, the doctor starts to take off the bandages, layer by layer. The last layer is removed, the nurses cover their faces in horror, and the doctor drops his scissors: there has been no change. Janet Tyler raises her head, and appears to us to be quite beautiful. She tries to run and is pinned against the wall by her doctor and nurse, who turns on the light. The faces of the others are revealed: pig-like nose, protruding lips, bone outlines, they are the ones that are "normal." Janet escapes their grasps and runs down many hallways, eventually stopping in front of Walter Smith, a similar outcast who has come to take her to the village. He tries to remind her to always remember that beauty is in the eye of the beholder.

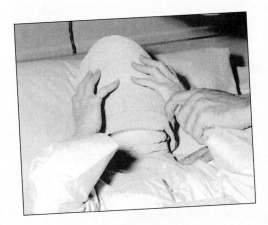

Analyzing Media

1. In your opinion, why did the scriptwriter keep all the characters' faces hidden from viewers until the end of the teleplay?

2. Write a summary of a TV drama or movie you have recently seen.

Vo·cab·u·lar·y *Skills*

Idioms

When you step off a ladder, you put your foot down. When you firmly refuse to allow something, you put your foot down. In the first sentence, the words *put your foot down* have their ordinary, literal meaning. In the second, they do not. To "put one's foot down" is often used as an **idiom**—a word or phrase that has a special meaning different from the ordinary meaning of the word or words.

The English language contains many idioms. "He's on the ball." "She's really steamed." "They jumped the gun." "I'm all tied up." Many of them are so familiar they cause no problems. Unfamiliar idioms, however, can cause confusion.

There are two useful ways to figure out the meaning of an unfamiliar idiom. One is to think about what the ordinary meanings of the words suggest.

 ♦ If the father in "The Boy and His Grandfather" tried to defend his bad treatment of his own father, he <u>wouldn't have a leg to stand on</u>.

Even if you had never seen the underlined idiom, you could understand that it means not having any support. The father would have no basis for such a defense.

A second way to approach idioms is to use context clues.

 ♦ Mrs. Wang had never worked out a plan for using the river's power against the enemy; her action resulted from a <u>spur of the moment</u> decision.

Context clues in the sentence suggest that "spur of the moment" means the opposite of "planned in advance."

EXERCISE

Write a short definition of each underlined idiom.

1. The villagers know that their only hope for survival is to flee, so they <u>get out while the getting is good</u>.

2. It is useless to argue with the <u>hard-nosed</u> Mrs. Wang.

3. Once Mrs. Wang has decided to open the sluice, she <u>lets no grass grow under her feet</u>.

4. It isn't easy for Mrs. Wang to rescue the injured pilot, but she <u>sees it through</u>.

5. Who would expect a sudden flood across dry land? When the enemy soldiers see the mighty river boiling toward them, the sight will <u>throw them for a loop</u>.

Writing WORKSHOP

Expository Writing: Definition Essay

What does loyalty mean to you? How would you define courage or cowardice, cruelty or compassion? To define a concept, you explain what it is and why it's important. You use examples to show your audience exactly what you mean.

Assignment: Follow the process explained in these pages to write an essay in which you define a personal quality. Use one or more of the characters from selections you've read in this book as examples to support your definition.

● As you write your expository essay, refer to the **Writing Handbook,** pp. R48–R61.

EVALUATION RUBRIC
By the time you complete this Writing Workshop, you will have

- written an essay that defines a personal quality
- captured readers' attention and stated your thesis in your introduction
- used real-life or fictional examples to explain the quality
- linked ideas with clear transitions
- restated your thesis in your conclusion
- written an essay free of errors in grammar, usage, and mechanics

The Writing Process

PREWRITING

PREWRITING TIP
To narrow down your selection of a quality to write about, look at the titles of the selections in the table of contents. As you glance at each title, try to recall the character or characters involved in the selection. Which ones can you remember most vividly? Which stand out as having a character trait you find appealing or especially interesting?

● Choose a Character and a Quality

To find a topic for your essay, you can look through your journal or brainstorm with classmates. You can also ask yourself questions such as the following:

- What quality in a friend means the most to me? Which character shows that quality most or least?

- Which character do I remember best?

- Why has he or she stayed in my mind?

- What are his or her main qualities?

Choose one quality that you understand, admire, or consider important.

Rosa Parks

● Explore Your Ideas

You might start with a dictionary. Look up the quality you have chosen and copy the dictionary definition into your journal. Then, in a focused freewriting, move beyond that definition, using your own words. Explore what the quality means to you and how you've seen it demonstrated. Write about people or characters who show that quality.

Stacy Allison

Lou Gehrig

● Think About Audience and Purpose

Your teacher and classmates will read your essay, and you might aim at a wider audience as well. Your essay might interest a newspaper or magazine columnist exploring teens' viewpoints. It might inspire members of a special-interest group, or it might help a younger person learn about behavior choices. Target your chosen readers with writing that will appeal to them. Your purpose is to communicate to your audience what a certain personal quality means to you.

● Plan Your Approach

Look over your prewriting notes and then create a sentence or two summing up your definition. This **thesis statement** will guide you as you plan and draft. Rough out the main points that will support your thesis statement. You might discuss what the quality is and isn't, how it affects people's lives, and what it means to you. To illustrate each point, write notes on examples of actions by a character in this theme and by people in real life.

Stacy Allison—Courageously climbed to top of Mount Everest on second attempt in spite of disappointing defeat on first try

Lou Gehrig—Showed courage in facing a life-threatening disease. Gave "lucky man" speech in Yankee Stadium when forced to quit baseball while still a young man

Rosa Parks—African American woman who showed courage in fighting against segregation in the early days of the Civil Rights movement

DRAFTING

DRAFTING TIP

If you get a new idea for your definition while drafting, try it out. You can always go back to your original prewriting plan if the new idea doesn't work out.

● Start with Flair

Capture your readers' interest with an intriguing statement, a meaningful quotation, or an anecdote illustrating the quality you will define. To let your readers know what to expect from your essay, include your thesis statement in your first paragraph.

> **STUDENT MODEL • DRAFTING**
>
> Are you courageous? According to *Webster's Dictionary*, you are courageous if you have the "mental or moral strength to venture, persevere, and withstand danger, fear, or difficulty."

Complete Student Model on pp. R109–R110.

● Follow Through

Each of your main points might be the topic sentence for a paragraph. The examples you have chosen can provide some of the supporting details. Link your sentences and paragraphs with appropriate transitions, such as *for example, for instance,* or *in this way.* Wrap up your essay by restating your thesis.

REVISING

REVISING TIP

As you revise, picture your readers. Choose words and images that you can imagine them responding to.

● Plan Changes

After a break, come back to your draft, perhaps with a partner. Use the **Rubric for Revising** to plan improvements. You might write your planned changes in the margins of your first draft. Or you might set your first draft aside and write a fresh second draft that incorporates your ideas for improvement.

RUBRIC FOR REVISING

Your revised essay should have
- an introduction that engages your readers' interest and states your thesis
- details, examples, or other evidence that supports your thesis
- transitions that smoothly connect ideas
- a conclusion that restates your thesis
- no errors in grammar, usage, and mechanics

EDITING/PROOFREADING

Before writing your final draft, go over your essay once more to fix errors in grammar, usage, and mechanics. Pay special attention to your use of pronouns, as shown in the **Grammar Link** on page 499.

Grammar Hint

Use the comparative form of a modifier when comparing only two things. Use the superlative when comparing more than two things.

Which of the two emotions is stronger?
Which of the four people is bravest?

PROOFREADING CHECKLIST

☑ Modifiers are correctly used. (Double-check comparative forms.)
☑ Sentences are complete. There are no fragments or run-ons.
☑ Verbs agree with their subjects.
☑ Pronouns are in the correct form and agree with their antecedents.
☑ Spelling, capitalization, and punctuation are correct.

STUDENT MODEL · EDITING/PROOFREADING

Lou Gehrig and Rosa Parks were both brave, but I think Rosa Parks was braver.

Complete Student Model on pp. R109–R110.

Complete Student Model

For a complete version of the model developed in this Workshop, see **Writing Workshop Models**, pp. R109–R110.

PUBLISHING/PRESENTING

PRESENTING TIP
When reading aloud, pause at the ends of sentences and paragraphs to make eye contact with your listeners.

In a small group, read your essay aloud and listen to other group members' essays. Then discuss your definitions. Use the group discussion guidelines in the **Communications Skills Handbook,** pages R71–R72, to explore areas of agreement and disagreement with one another's views.

Reflecting

Take a few minutes to think about the questions below. Write your responses in your journal.

- How is your definition like and unlike the dictionary definition?
- Which part(s) of your essay do you consider especially effective? Why?

Save your work for your portfolio.

Theme Assessment

Responding to the Theme

1. Which story, poem, or play in this theme most helped you think about the kinds of crossroads people face at certain times in their lives? Explain your answer.

2. What new ideas do you have about the following as a result of reading the literature in this theme?
   - the points in people's lives when they must make difficult choices
   - how people go about making decisions when faced with a problem

3. Present your theme project to the class.

Analyzing Literature

COMPARE CHARACTERS

Compare two characters from this theme. You may compare the problems they encounter and how they respond to those problems. Remember to support your opinions with examples and quotations from the selections.

Evaluate and Set Goals

1. Which of the following tasks was most rewarding to you? Which was most difficult?
   - reading and thinking about selections
   - doing independent writing
   - analyzing the stories, poems, and teleplay in discussions
   - performing dramatizations
   - making presentations
   - doing research

2. Using the following scale, how would you assess your work in this unit? Give at least two reasons for your assessment.

   4 = outstanding   2 = fair
   3 = good   1 = weak

3. Based on what you found difficult in this theme, choose a goal to work toward in the next theme.
   - Write down your goal and three steps you will take to help you reach it.
   - Meet with your teacher to review your goal and your plan for achieving it.

Build Your Portfolio

SELECT

Select two pieces of work you did during this theme to include in your portfolio. Use the following questions to help you decide.

- ✦ Which work do you consider your best?
- ✦ From which work did you learn the most?
- ✦ Which work did you enjoy the most?

REFLECT

Write some notes to accompany the work you selected. Use these questions as guides.

- ✦ What do you like best about the piece?
- ✦ What did you learn from creating it?
- ✦ What might you do differently if you were beginning this piece again?

Reading on Your Own

Have you enjoyed reading the literature in this theme?
If so, here are some other books you might like.

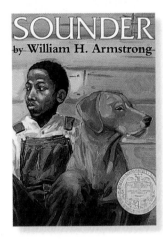

The Slave Dancer
by Paula Fox Jesse is kidnapped and forced to serve on a slave ship. He witnesses the horrors of slavery while providing music as the slaves are forced to exercise to keep themselves strong so they will remain "profitable investments."

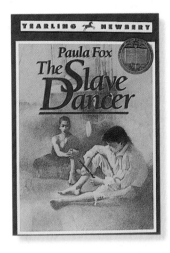

Sounder
by William Armstrong
This award-winning novel deals with the hard lives of African American sharecroppers in the rural South a century ago and with a young boy's growth in understanding with the help of the family's devoted dog.

Father Figure
by Richard Peck Jim's role as a substitute father for his younger brother is threatened when, after their mother's death, the boys are sent to spend the summer with their long-absent father.

Running Out of Time
by Margaret Peterson Haddix This exciting thriller tells the story of a thirteen-year-old girl who makes a decision to escape from her community in order to save her family and friends.

Standardized Test Practice

Read the phrase in each numbered item. Choose the phrase in which the italicized word is NOT spelled correctly.

1   A   the *librarian's* desk
    B   to wait *patiently*
    C   a broken *microphon*
    D   pieces of *unlined* paper

2   J   *boyish* charm
    K   *inscribed* her name
    L   an *unatural* color
    M   *rebuild* the shed

3   A   told an *unbelieveable* story
    B   good *insulation* in the attic
    C   known for his *kindness*
    D   ate only *nonfat* desserts

4   J   made an *ilegal* play
    K   to *repay* completely
    L   a *valuable* painting
    M   *reappearing* in an instant

5   A   *superhuman* efforts
    B   a *terrific* sport
    C   *semisweet* chocolate
    D   the *deccimal* system

6   J   on a *tripod*
    K   riding a *unicycle*
    L   to sleep *peacefuly*
    M   a talented *violinist*

7   A   *prettyest* time of year
    B   *exchange* this blouse
    C   a *childhood* friend
    D   passed the *examination*

8   J   making *inconsiderate* remarks
    K   *tropical* plants in the garden
    L   to *missdial* a number
    M   *unforgivable* behavior

9 A a *mercyless* judge
   B end of the *decade*
   C *rewrite* this paragraph
   D *antibacterial* soap

10 J *leadership* training
   K *accidently* broke the vase
   L musical *conductor*
   M an *inactive* account

11 A *biweekly* meetings
   B *global* warming
   C near the Bermuda *Triangle*
   D *preveiws* of coming
      attractions

12 J going on *vacasion*
   K watch *television*
   L good *nutrition*
   M on a *mission*

13 A a *sensible* shoe
   B an unfortunate
      dissagreement
   C *darkness* descended
   D *returning* at noon

14 J a bowl of *indigestible*
      noodles
   K drawn with a *superfine* point
   L out of *alinement*
   M *copiloting* the plane

15 A an *extrordinary* idea
   B *biography* of a hero
   C to a painless *dentist*
   D in a yellow *submarine*

16 J *flexible* rules
   K through a powerful *telescope*
   L a *pleasureable* afternoon
   M *postponing* the race again

STOP

Twists and Turns

> " . . . life is a water wheel. It turns. The trick is to hold your nose when you're under and not get dizzy when you're up. "
>
> —James Baldwin, *Nobody Knows My Name*

THEME
6

THEME CONTENTS

GENRE FOCUS *POETRY*

Exploring the Theme

Twists and Turns

What makes literature interesting? The same twists and turns that make life interesting. In this theme, you will discover the surprising actions that characters take in order to deal with life's unexpected events. To begin your own thinking about the theme, choose one of the options below.

Starting Points

A VIEW WITH A TWIST

How often do you try looking at, reading, or thinking about something from a different point of view? Sometimes, by simply trying another viewpoint, your impression of reality can change dramatically.

- In Charlie Chaplin's classic comedy film *Modern Times,* his character gets pulled into the gears of a huge machine. How do you think he felt about this plot twist? How would you feel?

APPRECIATING LIFE'S BUMPS

Life doesn't always go smoothly. Sometimes, however, difficulties turn out to be surprise blessings. At other times, events you look forward to can turn out to be disasters. These all become the life experiences that make good stories.

- Think about an entertaining or dramatic event in your life that you have described more than once to

your family and friends. Draw a picture of this moment when, out of the blue, life surprised you in a positive or negative way.

Charlie Chaplin in the movie *Modern Times.*

Theme Projects

As you read the selections in this theme, complete one of the projects below. Work on your own, with a partner, or with a group.

LEARNING FOR LIFE
Writing an Incident Report
Events in real life are often the inspiration for events in fiction. Take notes about an actual news event that you have read or heard about.

1. Write a report as if you were an official investigating the incident. Describe the people involved, the series of events that led to the incident, the incident itself, and the outcome.
2. Share your report with the class. Ask classmates to help you check for any missing information.

PERFORMING
Storytelling
1. Choose a story with an unusual twist in the plot.
2. To learn the story, read it more than once. Then make an outline using your own words.
3. Practice telling the story in front of a mirror. Remember that facial expressions and gestures are important parts of the storyteller's art.
4. Perform your story in front of an audience. Make sure to use your voice to emphasize any surprises in the plot.

CRITICAL READING
Discovering the Unexpected
1. Review the plots of the stories and poems you have read recently.
2. Choose a plot with a turn of events that surprised you.
3. Rewrite the climax of the plot so that the outcome changes. Share your new story with your classmates.

Look for other literature selections on the theme "Twists and Turns." For example, try short stories by O. Henry or H. H. Munro (Saki). Search by author on the On-Line Books Page: http://digital.library.upenn.edu/books.

MULTIMEDIA PROJECT
Dramatizing
1. Working with a large group or the whole class, choose a story with a plot twist. It can be a story from this theme, from another theme, or from a source other than your literature book.
2. Discuss the story. Then work together to turn it into a script for a radio or television play.
3. Assign tasks to group members. You will need actors, a director, people to provide sound effects (for a radio play), scenery and perhaps costumes (for television), and background music. If you want to present your dramatization on audiotape or videotape, you will also need a technical crew to run the equipment.
4. Rehearse your script carefully. Then perform your story in front of an audience, or record it for presentation on audiotape or videotape.

COMIC STRIP

This comic strip comes from one of Bill Watterson's *Calvin and Hobbes* collections. As in most humorous comic strips, the humor arises from an unexpected twist.

Analyzing Media

1. What does Calvin's self-portrait suggest about his behavior at school?

2. Rewrite the cartoon strip as a words-only anecdote. Then discuss the differences between your version and the cartoon strip.

Before You Read

Charles and *No News*

MEET SHIRLEY JACKSON

Shirley Jackson's fiction is filled with strange twists and turns. In most of her novels and short stories, she explores the darker side of human life. However, Jackson also wrote humorously about family life, as she does in "Charles."

Shirley Jackson was born in 1919 and died in 1965.

MEET CONNIE REGAN-BLAKE AND BARBARA FREEMAN

Regan-Blake and Freeman are cousins who started telling stories as children. They have traveled around the country collecting and telling stories for more than twenty years. Many of their stories, like "No News," are set in the rural South.

Connie Regan-Blake was born in 1947; Barbara Freeman was born in 1944.

READING FOCUS

Have you ever heard the expression *read between the lines?*

Sharing Ideas
In a small group, talk about the meaning of the expression and give examples of moments when the expression might be used in conversation.

Setting a Purpose
Try to read between the lines to discover the twists and turns in these two selections.

BUILDING BACKGROUND

Did You Know?   Children entering school must learn to get along with each other, follow directions, and help with classroom routines. In kindergarten, children become accustomed to a school setting and learn to play together.

VOCABULARY PREVIEW

raucous (rô′ kəs) *adj.* loud and rough-sounding; p. 544
insolently (in′ sə lənt lē) *adv.* in a boldly rude manner; p. 544
simultaneously (sī′ məl tā′ nē əs lē) *adv.* at the same time; p. 546
solemnly (sol′ əm lē) *adv.* seriously; p. 546
reformation (ref′ ər mā′ shən) *n.* a change for the better; improvement; p. 547
cynically (sin′ ə kəl lē) *adv.* in a way that shows doubt or disbelief; doubtfully; p. 547
primly (prim′ lē) *adv.* in a stiffly formal manner; p. 548
lapse (laps) *n.* a slipping or falling away; p. 548

Charles

Shirley Jackson

The day my son Laurie started kindergarten he renounced corduroy overalls with bibs and began wearing blue jeans with a belt; I watched him go off the first morning with the older girl next door, seeing clearly that an era of my life was ended, my sweet-voiced nursery-school tot replaced by a long-trousered, swaggering character who forgot to stop at the corner and wave good-bye to me.

He came home the same way, the front door slamming open, his cap on the floor, and the voice suddenly become <u>raucous</u> shouting, "Isn't anybody *here?*"

At lunch he spoke <u>insolently</u> to his father, spilled his baby sister's milk, and remarked that his teacher said we were not to take the name of the Lord in vain.

"How *was* school today?" I asked, elaborately casual.

"All right," he said.

"Did you learn anything?" his father asked.

Laurie regarded his father coldly. "I didn't learn nothing," he said.

"Anything," I said. "Didn't learn anything."

"The teacher spanked a boy, though," Laurie said, addressing his bread and butter. "For being fresh," he added, with his mouth full.

Vocabulary
raucous (rô′ kəs) *adj.* loud and rough-sounding
insolently (in′ sə lənt lē) *adv.* in a boldly rude manner

Viewing the photograph: What words would you use to describe this boy's personality? Would you use similar words to describe anyone in the story?

"What did he do?" I asked. "Who was it?"

Laurie thought. "It was Charles," he said. "He was fresh. The teacher spanked him and made him stand in a corner. He was awfully fresh."

"What did he do?" I asked again, but Laurie slid off his chair, took a cookie, and left, while his father was still saying, "See here, young man."

The next day Laurie remarked at lunch, as soon as he sat down, "Well, Charles was bad again today." He grinned enormously and said, "Today Charles hit the teacher."

"Good heavens," I said, mindful of the Lord's name, "I suppose he got spanked again?"

"He sure did," Laurie said. "Look up," he said to his father.

"What?" his father said, looking up.

"Look down," Laurie said. "Look at my thumb. Gee, you're dumb." He began to laugh insanely.

"Why did Charles hit the teacher?" I asked quickly.

"Because she tried to make him color with red crayons," Laurie said. "Charles wanted to color with green crayons so he hit the teacher and she spanked him and said nobody play with Charles but everybody did."

The third day—it was Wednesday of the first week—Charles bounced a see-saw on to the head of a little girl and made her bleed, and the teacher made him stay inside all during recess. Thursday Charles had to stand in a corner during story-time because he kept pounding his feet on the floor. Friday Charles was deprived of blackboard privileges because he threw chalk.

On Saturday I remarked to my husband, "Do you think kindergarten is too unsettling for Laurie? All this toughness, and bad grammar, and this Charles boy sounds like such a bad influence."

"It'll be all right," my husband said reassuringly. "Bound to be people like Charles in the world. Might as well meet them now as later."

On Monday Laurie came home late, full of news. "Charles," he shouted as he came up the hill; I was waiting anxiously on the front steps. "Charles," Laurie yelled all the way up the hill, "Charles was bad again."

"Come right in," I said, as soon as he came close enough. "Lunch is waiting."

"You know what Charles did?" he demanded, following me through the door. "Charles yelled so in school they sent a boy in from first grade to tell the teacher she had to make Charles keep quiet, and so Charles had to stay after school. And so all the children stayed to watch him."

"What did he do?" I asked.

"He just sat there," Laurie said, climbing into his chair at the table. "Hi, Pop, y'old dust mop."

"Charles had to stay after school today," I told my husband. "Everyone stayed with him."

"What does this Charles look like?" my husband asked Laurie. "What's his other name?"

"He's bigger than me," Laurie said. "And he doesn't have any galoshes and he doesn't ever wear a jacket."

Monday night was the first Parent-Teachers meeting, and only the fact that the baby had a cold kept me from going; I wanted passionately to meet Charles's mother. On Tuesday Laurie remarked suddenly, "Our teacher had a friend come to see her in school today."

"Charles's mother?" my husband and I asked <u>simultaneously</u>.

"Naaah," Laurie said scornfully. "It was a man who came and made us do exercises, we had to touch our toes. Look." He climbed down from his chair and squatted down and touched his toes. "Like this," he said. He got <u>solemnly</u> back into his chair and said, picking up his fork, "Charles didn't even *do* exercises."

"That's fine," I said heartily. "Didn't Charles want to do exercises?"

"Naaah," Laurie said. "Charles was so fresh to the teacher's friend he wasn't *let* do exercises."

"Fresh again?" I said.

"He kicked the teacher's friend," Laurie said. "The teacher's friend told Charles to

Vocabulary
simultaneously (sī′ məl tā′ nē əs lē) *adv.* at the same time
solemnly (sol′ əm lē) *adv.* seriously

touch his toes like I just did and Charles kicked him."

"What are they going to do about Charles, do you suppose?" Laurie's father asked him.

Laurie shrugged elaborately. "Throw him out of school, I guess," he said.

Wednesday and Thursday were routine; Charles yelled during story hour and hit a boy in the stomach and made him cry. On Friday Charles stayed after school again and so did all the other children.

With the third week of kindergarten Charles was an institution[1] in our family; the baby was being a Charles when she cried all afternoon; Laurie did a Charles when he filled his wagon full of mud and pulled it through the kitchen; even my husband, when he caught his elbow in the telephone cord and pulled telephone, ashtray, and a bowl of flowers off the table, said, after the first minute, "Looks like Charles."

During the third and fourth weeks it looked like a reformation in Charles; Laurie reported grimly at lunch on Thursday of the third week, "Charles was so good today the teacher gave him an apple."

"What?" I said, and my husband added warily, "You mean Charles?"

"Charles," Laurie said. "He gave the crayons around and he picked up the books afterward and the teacher said he was her helper."

"What happened?" I asked incredulously.

"He was her helper, that's all," Laurie said, and shrugged.

"Can this be true, about Charles?" I asked my husband that night. "Can something like this happen?"

"Wait and see," my husband said cynically. "When you've got a Charles to deal with, this may mean he's only plotting."

He seemed to be wrong. For over a week Charles was the teacher's helper; each day he handed things out and he picked things up; no one had to stay after school.

"The P.T.A. meeting's next week again," I told my husband one evening. "I'm going to find Charles's mother there."

"Ask her what happened to Charles," my husband said. "I'd like to know."

"I'd like to know myself," I said.

On Friday of that week things were back to normal. "You know what Charles did today?" Laurie demanded at the lunch table, in a voice slightly awed. "He told a little girl to say a word and she said it and the teacher washed her mouth out with soap and Charles laughed."

"What word?" his father asked unwisely, and Laurie said, "I'll have to whisper it to you, it's so bad." He got down off his chair and went around to his father. His father bent his head down and Laurie whispered joyfully. His father's eyes widened.

"Did Charles tell the little girl to say *that*?" he asked respectfully.

"She said it *twice*," Laurie said. "Charles told her to say it *twice*."

___
1. Here, *institution* means "a regular feature or tradition."

Vocabulary
reformation (ref′ ər mā′ shən) *n.* a change for the better; improvement
cynically (sin′ ə kəl lē) *adv.* in a way that shows doubt or disbelief; doubtfully

Charles

"What happened to Charles?" my husband asked.

"Nothing," Laurie said. "He was passing out the crayons."

Monday morning Charles abandoned the little girl and said the evil word himself three or four times, getting his mouth washed out with soap each time. He also threw chalk.

My husband came to the door with me that evening as I set out for the P.T.A. meeting. "Invite her over for a cup of tea after the meeting," he said. "I want to get a look at her."

"If only she's there," I said prayerfully.

"She'll be there," my husband said. "I don't see how they could hold a P.T.A. meeting without Charles's mother."

At the meeting I sat restlessly, scanning each comfortable matronly[2] face, trying to determine which one hid the secret of Charles. None of them looked to me haggard[3] enough. No one stood up in the meeting and apologized for the way her son had been acting. No one mentioned Charles.

After the meeting I identified and sought out Laurie's kindergarten teacher. She had a plate with a cup of tea and a piece of chocolate cake; I had a plate with a cup of tea and a piece of marshmallow cake. We maneuvered up to one another cautiously, and smiled.

"I've been so anxious to meet you," I said. "I'm Laurie's mother."

"We're all so interested in Laurie," she said.

"Well, he certainly likes kindergarten," I said. "He talks about it all the time."

"We had a little trouble adjusting, the first week or so," she said primly, "but now he's a fine little helper. With occasional lapses, of course."

"Laurie usually adjusts very quickly," I said. "I suppose this time it's Charles's influence."

"Charles?"

"Yes," I said, laughing, "you must have your hands full in that kindergarten, with Charles."

"Charles?" she said. "We don't have any Charles in the kindergarten."

---

2. Another word for *matronly* would be "motherly." It refers to a mature woman, especially one who is married and has children.
3. A *haggard* person looks worn out as a result of grief, worry, illness—or dealing with a boy like Charles.

Vocabulary
primly (prim′ lē) *adv.* in a stiffly formal manner
lapse (laps) *n.* a slipping or falling away

No News

Retold by Connie Regan-Blake and Barbara Freeman

A certain Southern lady was returning home after recuperating[1] in the mountains for three months. Her friend Georgeanne met her at the railway station.

"Georgeanne, has there been any news while I've been away?"

"Oh, no, there's no news."

"No news? Surely something has occurred in my absence. Why, I've been gone for nearly three months, and I'm anxious for any little bit of news you may have."

"Oh, now, since you mentioned it—'course it don't amount to much—but since you've been away, your dog died."

"My dog died? How did my dog die?"

"He ate some of the burnt horseflesh, and that's what killed the dog."

"Burnt horseflesh?"

"Well, after the fire cooled off, the dog ate some of the burnt horseflesh, and that's what killed the dog."

"Fire cooled off?"

"Well, the barn burned down, burned up all of the cows and horses, and when the fire cooled down, the dog ate some of the burnt horseflesh, and that's what killed the dog."

"My barn burned down? How did my barn burn down?"

"Oh, it was a spark from the house. Blew over, lit the roof of the barn, burned down the barn, burned up all the cows and horses, and when the fire cooled off, the dog ate some of the burnt horseflesh, and that's what killed the dog."

"A spark from the house?"

"Oh, yes, now that's completely burned down."

"But how did my house burn down?"

"It was the candle flame that lit the curtains, shot up the side of the wall, and burned down the house; a spark flew over on the roof of the barn, burned down the barn, burned up all of the cows and horses, and when the fire cooled off, the dog ate some of the burnt horseflesh, and that's what killed the dog."

"Candles? I don't even allow candles in my house. How did the candles get into my house?"

"Oh, they were around the coffin."

"Coffin? Who died?"

"Oh, now you needn't worry about that. Since you've been away, your mother-in-law died."

"Oh, my mother-in-law. What a pity. How did she die?"

"Well, some folks say that it was the shock of hearing that your husband had run away with the choir leader. But other than that, there ain't been no news."

---

1. To *recuperate* (ri kōō′ pə rāt′) is to regain health or strength.

Responding to Literature

PERSONAL RESPONSE

◆ Recall the **Reading Focus** on page 543. In each story, when did you first decide that you needed to read between the lines?

Analyzing Literature

RECALL

1. How does Laurie change when he starts kindergarten?
2. Compare Laurie's behavior at home with Charles's actions at school. How are their behaviors similar? How are they different?
3. According to Laurie, why do he and all the other children stay after school with Charles?
4. What does the Southern lady find out after her friend assures her that "there's no news"?

INTERPRET

5. Why do you think Laurie turns into a "swaggering character" when he begins kindergarten? Explain.
6. In your opinion, why does Laurie tell stories about Charles at home?
7. Why is Charles such a fascination in Laurie's household?
8. An *understatement* is a statement that plays down the importance of something. How does "No News" illustrate the word *understatement?*

EVALUATE AND CONNECT

9. Theme Connection   How do the **plots** of both selections reflect the theme of this unit? (For more about plot, see page R8.)
10. Which story do you prefer? Why?

LITERARY ELEMENTS

Plot Twist

The sequence of events in a story is called the **plot.** Usually the plot is built around a central **conflict** in which opposing sides are involved in a struggle or a problem that must be resolved. The turning point of the plot is called the **climax,** the point of highest interest. This is the point where the outcome of the conflict is determined. In some plots, the climax includes an unexpected turn of events, called a **plot twist.** "Charles" is an example of a story with a plot twist.

1. What is the plot twist in "Charles"?

2. In one or two sentences, describe the plot twist in "No News."

3. What does the plot twist at the end add to the story "No News"?

● See **Literary Terms Handbook,** p. R8.

Literature and Writing

Writing About Literature

Foreshadowing   When writers give clues or hints about something that will occur later, they are **fore-shadowing** the later event or development. Reread "Charles" carefully. Identify the details that fore-shadow the plot twist at the end. Write a paragraph describing how Jackson foreshadows the ending of her story.

Personal Writing

Time Travel   Think about yourself in your kinder-garten or preschool days. Did you ever tell an exag-gerated story—to your parents, your friends, or a teacher? Did you ever have a problem in school? How was it resolved? Write a narrative describing an early school experience.

Extending Your Response

Performing

Dramatization   With a partner or in a small group, choose either story to dramatize. If you choose "Charles," pick out one or two scenes to perform. Think about what Laurie says and does as well as how his body looks and moves.

Listening and Speaking

Interview   Interview a kindergarten student, a teacher, or someone else who works with young children. Find out what kindergarteners are like. Before the interview, make a list of questions that will help you find out about the thoughts, interests, and daily activities of a five- or six-year-old child.

Literature Groups

Turning Real Life into Fiction   How do you think authors turn real life into stories? In small groups, make a list of real-life events at your school. Work together to turn one or more of these events into a work of fiction. Share your story with your classmates.

📖 **Save your work for your portfolio.**

Skill Minilessons

GRAMMAR AND LANGUAGE • CORRECT PRONOUN USE

A **subject pronoun** is used as the subject of a sentence. An **object pronoun** is used as the object of a verb or a preposition. If you are unsure of which form of the pronoun to use, say the sentence aloud with only the pronoun as the subject or the object. Your ear should tell you which form is right.

He and his mother walked home. *(subject)*
Tell Laurie and **me** about school. *(object of verb)*
Mother read a story to **him.** *(object of preposition)*

   Be especially careful when a sentence has two subjects or two objects.

Laurie and **I** played together. *(subject)*
Those games were fun for **Laurie** and **me.** *(object of preposition)*

PRACTICE Choose the correct form of the pronoun.
1. Laurie and (I, me) were in the same class.
2. Laurie told my husband and (I, me) story after story about Charles.
3. She and (I, me) were amazed at Charles's behavior.
4. The teacher asked for the crayon, but Charles refused to give it to (she, her).
5. Just between you and (I, me), I don't think Charles really existed.

● For more about pronouns, see **Language Handbook,** p. R17.

READING AND THINKING • DRAWING CONCLUSIONS

Stories include details about characters and events. By combining these details with your own knowledge and experience, you can draw conclusions that will help you understand a story.

● For more on drawing conclusions, see **Reading Handbook,** pp. R92–R104.

PRACTICE The author doesn't reveal why Laurie told stories about a boy that didn't exist. You have to draw conclusions to figure it out for yourself. Write a paragraph giving your conclusions about Laurie's tales about Charles.

VOCABULARY • THE PREFIX *re-*

Some prefixes have more than one meaning. The prefix *re-* can mean either "again" or "back."

   When Charles's behavior improved, it looked like a *reformation.* It seemed that Charles had been "formed again." However, if you *recall* something, you don't call it again, you call it back. A ball that *rebounds* bounces back. When *re-* is attached to a word, think about the meaning of the word without the prefix and then add either "again" or "back."

PRACTICE Use what you know about the prefix *re-* to match each word to its definition.
1. repress   a. to say again
2. recoil   b. to copy or make again
3. restate   c. a coming back inside
4. reproduce   d. to push or hold back
5. reentry   e. to spring back when let go

GRAMMAR LINK

Using Commas Correctly

Speakers use their voices to make their meanings clear. In writing, commas separate words or parts of sentences to make the meaning clear.

Problem 1 Missing commas in a series

Georgeanne met her friend answered questions and provided news.

Solution Use commas to separate three or more items in a series.

Georgeanne met her friend, answered questions, and provided news.

Problem 2 Missing commas with direct quotations

"If the story weren't so funny" I said "it would be sad."

Solution Use commas before and after words that interrupt a quotation.

"If the story weren't so funny," I said, "it would be sad."

Problem 3 Missing commas with nonessential appositives

The barn a wooden structure burned down.

Solution Use commas to set off the nonessential appositive.

The barn, a wooden structure, burned down.

The **appositive,** *a wooden structure,* gives more information about the noun *barn.* Since it doesn't change the meaning of the sentence, it is a **nonessential appositive** and should be set off by commas.

● For more about commas, see **Language Handbook,** p. R19.

EXERCISE

Rewrite the sentences, adding commas wherever they are needed.

1. Laurie a kindergarten student told stories about Charles.
2. Charles sassed the teacher yelled pounded his feet and threw chalk.
3. "Charles" said Laurie "didn't do exercises hit a child and had to stay after school."
4. The narrator of the story Laurie's mother was eager to meet Charles's mother.
5. "When I got a chance to speak with his teacher" Laurie's mother said to her husband "I asked her about Charles."

Before You Read

Who's on First?

MEET ABBOTT AND COSTELLO

Bud Abbott and Lou Costello were a slapstick comedy team who became two of the most popular film and television entertainers of the 1940s and 1950s. Their comedy routines featured Abbott as the witty straight man and Costello as the bumbling innocent. Their comedy skits were based on old vaudeville routines, but the comics freshened the material by ad-libbing, making up lines on the spot. Some say that they never performed a scene the same way twice.

Bud Abbott was born in 1895 and died in 1974. Lou Costello was born in 1906 and died in 1959.

READING FOCUS

What makes you laugh? Do you like jokes, slapstick, plays on words?

Ask It!
Create a questionnaire about humor. Ask questions such as
• What different kinds of humor can you name?
• Which type of humor do you prefer? Why?
• What good examples of humor have you read or seen recently?
• Why is humor important to humans?
Make copies of your questionnaire, and have friends and family members fill it out. Compile your results, and share the information with others in your class.

Setting a Purpose
Read this comedy sketch for enjoyment. Then read it again to discover why it's funny.

BUILDING BACKGROUND

Did You Know?   "Who's on First?" is a comedy sketch created, performed, and made famous by the comedy team of Abbott and Costello. The team first performed this hilarious baseball skit on the Kate Smith Show, a radio program of the early 1940s. They performed it many, many times after that, including in a movie and on their television series *The Abbott and Costello Show.* The routine is memorialized on a plaque in the Baseball Hall of Fame in Cooperstown, New York.

Abbott and Costello with the Andrews Sisters, a popular singing trio, in the 1941 film *Buck Privates.*

Who's on First?

Bud Abbott and Lou Costello ∾

SEBASTIAN. Peanuts!

DEXTER. Peanuts!

SEBASTIAN. Popcorn!

DEXTER. Popcorn!

SEBASTIAN. Crackerjack!

DEXTER. Crackerjack!

SEBASTIAN. Get your packages of Crackerjack here!

DEXTER. —Crackerjack—will you keep quiet? Sebastian! Sebastian, please! Don't interrupt my act!

SEBASTIAN. Ladies and gentlemen and also the children—will you excuse me for a minute, please? Thank you.

DEXTER. What do you want to do?

SEBASTIAN. Look, Mr. Broadhurst—

DEXTER. What are you doing?

Who's on First?

SEBASTIAN. I love baseball!

DEXTER. Well, we all love baseball.

SEBASTIAN. When we get to St. Louis, will you tell me the guys' names on the team so when I go to see them in that St. Louis ballpark I'll be able to know those fellows?

DEXTER. Then you'll go and peddle your popcorn and won't interrupt the act anymore?

SEBASTIAN. Yes, sir.

DEXTER. All right. But you know, strange as it may seem, they give ballplayers nowadays very peculiar names.

SEBASTIAN. Funny names?

DEXTER. Nicknames. Nicknames.

SEBASTIAN. Not—not as funny as my name—Sebastian Dinwiddie.

DEXTER. Oh, yes, yes, yes!

SEBASTIAN. Funnier than that?

DEXTER. Oh, absolutely. Yes. Now on the St. Louis team we have Who's on first, What's on second, I Don't Know is on third—

SEBASTIAN. That's what I want to find out. I want you to tell me the names of the fellows on the St. Louis team.

DEXTER. I'm telling you. Who's on first, What's on second, I Don't Know is on third—

SEBASTIAN. You know the fellows' names?

DEXTER. Yes.

SEBASTIAN. Well, then, who's playin' first?

DEXTER. Yes!

SEBASTIAN. I mean the fellow's name on first base.

DEXTER. Who.

SEBASTIAN. The fellow playin' first base for St. Louis.

DEXTER. Who.

SEBASTIAN. The guy on first base.

DEXTER. Who is on first.

SEBASTIAN. Well, what are you askin' me for?

DEXTER. I'm not asking you—I'm telling you. *Who is on first.*

SEBASTIAN. I'm asking you—who's on first?

DEXTER. That's the man's name!

SEBASTIAN. That's whose name?

DEXTER. Yes.

SEBASTIAN. Well, go ahead and tell me!

DEXTER. Who.

SEBASTIAN. The guy on first.

DEXTER. Who.

SEBASTIAN. The first baseman.

DEXTER. Who is on first.

SEBASTIAN. Have you got a first baseman on first?

DEXTER. Certainly.

SEBASTIAN. Then who's playing first?

DEXTER. Absolutely.

SEBASTIAN. When you pay off the first baseman every month, who gets the money?

DEXTER. Every dollar of it. And why not, the man's entitled to it.

SEBASTIAN. Who is?

DEXTER. Yes.

SEBASTIAN. So who gets it?

DEXTER. Why shouldn't he? Sometimes his wife comes down and collects it.

SEBASTIAN. Whose wife?

DEXTER. Yes. After all, the man earns it.

SEBASTIAN. Who does?

DEXTER. Absolutely.

SEBASTIAN. Well, all I'm trying to find out is what's the guy's name on first base.

DEXTER. Oh, no, no. What is on second base.

SEBASTIAN. I'm not asking you who's on second.

DEXTER. Who's on first.

SEBASTIAN. That's what I'm trying to find out.

DEXTER. Well, don't change the players around.

SEBASTIAN. I'm not changing nobody.

DEXTER. Now, take it easy.

SEBASTIAN. What's the guy's name on first base?

DEXTER. What's the guy's name on second base.

SEBASTIAN. I'm not askin' ya who is on second.

DEXTER. Who's on first.

SEBASTIAN. I don't know.

DEXTER. He's on third. We're not talking about him.

SEBASTIAN. How could I get on third base?

DEXTER. You mentioned his name.

SEBASTIAN. If I mentioned the third baseman's name, who did I say is playing third?

DEXTER. No, Who's playing first.

SEBASTIAN. Stay offa first, will ya?

DEXTER. Well, what do you want me to do?

SEBASTIAN. Now what's the guy's name on first base?

DEXTER. What's on second.

SEBASTIAN. I'm not asking ya who's on second.

DEXTER. Who's on first.

SEBASTIAN. I don't know.

DEXTER. He's on third.

SEBASTIAN. There I go back on third again.

DEXTER. Well, I can't change their names.

SEBASTIAN. Say, will you please stay on third base, Mr. Broadhurst.

DEXTER. Please. Now, what is it you want to know?

SEBASTIAN. What is the fellow's name on third base?

DEXTER. What is the fellow's name on second base.

SEBASTIAN. I'm not askin' ya who's on second.

DEXTER. Who's on first.

SEBASTIAN. I don't know.

DEXTER AND SEBASTIAN. *Third base!*

SEBASTIAN. You got a pitcher on the team?

Who's on First?

DEXTER. Wouldn't this be a fine team without a pitcher?

SEBASTIAN. I don't know. Tell me the pitcher's name.

DEXTER. Tomorrow.

SEBASTIAN. You don't want to tell me today?

DEXTER. I'm telling you, man.

SEBASTIAN. Then go ahead.

DEXTER. Tomorrow.

SEBASTIAN. What time?

DEXTER. What time what?

SEBASTIAN. What time tomorrow are you gonna tell me who's pitching?

DEXTER. Now listen, Who is not pitching. Who is on—

SEBASTIAN. I'll break your arm if you say who's on first.

DEXTER. Then why come up here and ask?

SEBASTIAN. I want to know what's the pitcher's name.

DEXTER. What's on second.

SEBASTIAN. I don't know.

SEBASTIAN AND DEXTER. *Third base!*

SEBASTIAN. Gotta catcher?

DEXTER. Yes.

SEBASTIAN. I'm a good catcher, too, you know.

DEXTER. I know that.

SEBASTIAN. I would like to play for the St. Louis team.

DEXTER. Well, I might arrange that.

SEBASTIAN. I would like to catch.

Now, I'm being a good catcher, Tomorrow's pitching on the team, and I'm catching.

DEXTER. Yes.

SEBASTIAN. Tomorrow throws the ball and the guy up bunts the ball.

DEXTER. Yes.

SEBASTIAN. Now, when he bunts the ball—me being a good catcher—I want to throw the guy out at first base, so I pick up the ball and throw it to who?

DEXTER. Now that's the first thing you've said right.

SEBASTIAN. I DON'T EVEN KNOW WHAT I'M TALKING ABOUT.

DEXTER. Well, that's all you have to do.

SEBASTIAN. Is to throw it to first base.

DEXTER. Yes.

SEBASTIAN. Now who's got it?

DEXTER. Naturally.

SEBASTIAN. Who has it?

DEXTER. Naturally.

SEBASTIAN. Naturally.

DEXTER. Naturally.

SEBASTIAN. O.K.

DEXTER. Now you've got it.

SEBASTIAN. I pick up the ball and I throw it to Naturally.

DEXTER. No you don't, you throw the ball to first base.

SEBASTIAN. Then who gets it?

DEXTER. Naturally.

SEBASTIAN. O.K.

DEXTER. All right.

SEBASTIAN. I throw the ball to Naturally.

DEXTER. You don't. You throw it to Who.

SEBASTIAN. Naturally.

DEXTER. Well, naturally. Say it that way.

SEBASTIAN. That's what I said.

DEXTER. You did not.

SEBASTIAN. I said I'd throw the ball to Naturally.

DEXTER. You don't. You throw it to Who.

SEBASTIAN. Naturally.

DEXTER. Yes.

SEBASTIAN. So I throw the ball to first base and Naturally gets it.

DEXTER. No. You throw the ball to first base—

SEBASTIAN. Then who gets it?

DEXTER. Naturally.

SEBASTIAN. That's what I'm saying.

DEXTER. You're not saying that.

SEBASTIAN. Excuse me, folks.

DEXTER. Now, don't get excited. Now, don't get excited.

SEBASTIAN. I throw the ball to first base.

DEXTER. Then Who gets it.

SEBASTIAN. He better get it.

DEXTER. That's it. All right now, don't get excited. Take it easy.

SEBASTIAN. Now I throw the ball to first base, whoever it is grabs the ball, so the guy runs to second.

DEXTER. Uh-huh.

SEBASTIAN. Who picks up the ball and throws it to What. What throws it to I Don't Know. I Don't Know throws it back to Tomorrow—a triple play.

DEXTER. Yeah. It could be.

SEBASTIAN. And I don't care.

DEXTER. What was that?

SEBASTIAN. I said, *I don't care.*

DEXTER. Oh, that's our shortstop!

Responding to Literature

PERSONAL RESPONSE

◆ Take a look at your questionnaire results from the **Reading Focus** on page 554. Does "Who's on First?" fit into any of the categories you listed? Which ones?

◆ Who's your favorite comic or comedy team? How do Abbott and Costello compare with your favorite?

Analyzing Literature

RECALL

1. To what is Dexter referring when he says, "Don't interrupt my act"?

2. Why does Sebastian want to know the names of the players on the St. Louis team?

3. What is Sebastian's reaction to Dexter's information about the players? Does his reaction change by the end of the skit?

4. Does Sebastian ever understand any of the player's names? Give an example.

INTERPRET

5. What do you learn about Sebastian's personality from the opening of the skit? What do you learn about Dexter's personality?

6. What knowledge about baseball does the audience need in order to fully appreciate the skit?

7. On what does the humor of "Who's on First?" depend? Explain.

EVALUATE AND CONNECT

8. Do you think the skit is as funny today as it was in the 1940s? Why or why not?

9. "Who's on First?" has been included in a number of anthologies of great American humor. If you were an editor of such a book, would you include it? Why or why not?

10. Have you ever tried to explain something but had no luck in communicating your information? Describe the situation.

LITERARY ELEMENTS

Dialogue

In a play, the plot and the characters' personalities are revealed through the conversations between characters. These conversations are called **dialogue.** In the written form of a play, the dialogue appears following the characters' names. Quotation marks are not used around the characters' words.

Dialogue is not limited to drama. In fiction, writers move a plot along through the characters' own words and interactions. Dialogue also gives readers a break from writing in which a narrator tells everything.

1. What can you tell about Sebastian and Dexter from the dialogue?

2. Would "Who's on First?" be as funny if it were written as a story without dialogue? Why or why not?

● See **Literary Terms Handbook,** p. R3.

Extending Your Response

Writing About Literature

Puns Most of the humor in "Who's on First?" is based on puns. A **pun** is a play on words based on two different meanings of the same word or two different words with the same pronunciation. For example, *who* is used both as a pronoun that asks a question and as a player's name. Choose one section of the routine and write a paragraph explaining how the puns create humor.

Literature Groups

Who's Where? One way to make the positions of the players and their names clearer is to draw a diagram of the team on the field. Work together to create a large baseball diamond on chart paper, and place an "X" at each of the nine positions. Label the positions and add the players' names from the routine. Make up confusing names for the three outfield positions—left, right, and center field—not mentioned in the script. Share your chart with the class.

Creative Writing

Further Confusion Choose a team sport other than baseball. Write a comedy routine using the same names as "Who's on First?" but with positions and action to match the new sport.

Performing

Vaudeville Timing Read "Who's on First?" with a partner, each of you taking one of the parts. You will soon find out that to make the skit truly funny, the dialogue must be spoken with split-second timing. Practice with the script until you feel you can make people laugh at every funny line. Then perform your routine for your classmates or another class.

Reading Further

Check out these other books full of puns:

The Laugh Book compiled by Joanna Cole and Stephanie Calmenson

Incognito Mosquito by E. A. Hass

💼 **Save your work for your portfolio.**

Skill Minilesson

VOCABULARY • HOMONYMS

The puns in "Who's on First?" are **homonyms,** words that sound or look alike. Here's another pun.

How do you get down off an elephant?
You don't. You get down off a duck.

To appreciate the pun, you must recognize that *down* can mean "from a higher to a lower place" or "the soft feathers of a duck." Puns have been used in literature dating back at least as far as biblical times. Some of the greatest writers have used them.

Puns are also used in jokes, everyday conversation, newspaper headlines, and advertising.

PRACTICE Work alone or with a partner to practice punning.

1. Make a list of at least five pairs of homonyms. (Remember, many homonyms are spelled differently—for example *peace* and *piece*.)
2. Choose at least one pair of homonyms on your list to make a humorous pun. Share your pun with the class.

Technology Skills

Multimedia: Using Hypertext

When you learned to read, you trained your eyes to focus on letters that form words and words that form sentences. As you read, your eyes move from left to right and top to bottom on a page. But your mind may not always want to go along with your eyes. That's because the mind is capable of processing a lot of information at once. Suppose you're reading an article about cats. You may run across the line, "Cats, considered sacred by the ancient Egyptians, were often featured in Egyptian art." Before reading the next sentence, you may wonder briefly what such art looked like. But if the article doesn't have pictures, you have to put the thought out of your mind and continue reading.

Hypertext is a computer feature that allows you to follow such trains of thought by linking keywords with related data. You can click on words or phrases that will take you to more information. These clickable words are known as **hyperlinks,** or hotlinks, and they are usually differentiated from regular text through color, bold type, or underlining. If the story about cats were written on a computer in hypertext, it might look something like this:

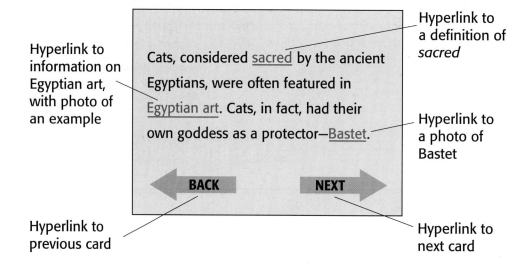

Hyperlink to a definition of *sacred*

Hyperlink to information on Egyptian art, with photo of an example

Cats, considered sacred by the ancient Egyptians, were often featured in Egyptian art. Cats, in fact, had their own goddess as a protector—Bastet.

Hyperlink to a photo of Bastet

BACK   NEXT

Hyperlink to previous card

Hyperlink to next card

Hypertext Software

Hypertext software programs and presentation software allow *you* to write stories, reports, or essays that contain many pages of linked text, graphics, sounds, and even animation! Each page is known as a card, and a group of cards is known as a stack.

To familiarize yourself with your hypertext software, open the program and click on its tutorial. The computer will lead you through the steps of creating a simple stack. (If your software lacks a tutorial, its manufacturer may offer one at its Web site on the Net. Otherwise, find the program's manual, ask your teacher or lab instructor for help, or use the topics in the Help index to learn how to use the program.)

Practice

Hypertext programs are fairly "intuitive." That means that you can figure out the items on their menus and toolbars from their names or by trying them out yourself. Many items and procedures are similar to those you will be familiar with from other software you use—word processing programs, for example.

The following chart may be useful. It tells you how to do some basic operations. The steps are separated by slash marks. For example, *File/New* means pull down the File menu and select New from the options on the menu.

To change a font size or style	Options/Text Style
To include a button that moves the reader to another card	Objects/Add a Button/Actions/Places to Go
To add graphics	File/Add Clip Art [or Photo, Movie]
To add sounds	Objects/Add a Button/Actions/Things to Do/ Play a Sound

1. To create your own hypertext stack, click on **File/New** and follow the prompts.

2. Explore the program by creating a stack that contains at least four linked cards. The stack can be about whatever you like: a short story, an autobiographical sketch, a review, essay, or article about literature, music, television, movies, or any other topic you wish.

3. If you have access to files of clip art, photos, or sounds (including music), add hyperlinks to appropriate graphics or sounds to your stack.

4. Save the stack when you have finished. (Your teacher or lab instructor will tell you where to save it.) Also, print out a copy to put in your portfolio.

ACTIVITIES

1. Complete one of the writing assignments from this unit using hypertext software. Present your work to your classmates.

2. Post your stack to your school's Web site or Intranet.

3. Volunteer to create stacks that describe your school's extracurricular activities. These stacks can be kept in the library and accessed by students who want to learn more about clubs and sports.

Before You Read

After Twenty Years

MEET
O. HENRY

William Sydney Porter, who used the pen name O. Henry, led a varied but difficult life. Many of his life experiences became material for his stories. He first worked in his uncle's drugstore in North Carolina, then as a sheepherder on a ranch in Texas. He was also a bank teller, a fugitive in Honduras, a prisoner, a magazine editor, and a newspaper writer before he began writing the stories that made him famous. Many of his stories contain a surprise ending or an ironic twist.

William Sydney Porter was born in 1862 and died in 1910.

READING FOCUS

How do you feel about loyalty between friends?

QuickWrite
Write about whether you think a person should always expect loyalty from a friend, no matter what the situation.

Setting a Purpose
Read this story to find out what tests the loyalty of two old friends.

BUILDING BACKGROUND

The Time and Place   This story takes place in New York City in the late 1800s.

Did You Know?   William Sydney Porter, writing under the name O. Henry, became one of America's most loved writers. Porter's first published stories were written in prison. He spent three years in prison for stealing money from the bank where he worked. He claimed he was innocent, but by using a pseudonym, he made sure his readers would not know about his past.

VOCABULARY PREVIEW

habitual (hə bich′ ōō əl) *adj.* done by habit; p. 565
intricate (in′ tri kit) *adj.* full of complicated detail; p. 565
artful (ärt′ fəl) *adj.* done with skill or cleverness; p. 565
correspond (kôr′ ə spond′) *v.* to communicate by exchanging letters; p. 567
dismally (diz′ məl lē) *adv.* in a gloomy, cheerless way; p. 567
absurdity (ab sur′ də tē) *n.* the state of being ridiculous, senseless, or irrational; p. 567
moderately (mod′ ər it lē) *adv.* neither too great nor too small; within limits; p. 568

After Twenty Years

O. Henry

The policeman on the beat moved up the avenue impressively. The impressiveness was <u>habitual</u> and not for show, for spectators were few. The time was barely 10 o'clock at night, but chilly gusts of wind with a taste of rain in them had well nigh depeopled the streets.

Trying doors as he went, twirling his club with many <u>intricate</u> and <u>artful</u> movements, turning now and then to cast his watchful eye adown the pacific thoroughfare, the officer, with his stalwart[1] form and slight swagger, made a fine picture of a guardian of the peace. The vicinity was one that kept early hours. Now and then you might see the lights of a cigar store or of an all-night lunch counter; but the majority of the doors belonged to business places that had long since been closed.

When about midway of a certain block the policeman suddenly slowed his walk. In the doorway of a darkened hardware store a man leaned, with an unlighted cigar in his mouth. As the policeman walked up to him the man spoke up quickly.

"It's all right, officer," he said, reassuringly. "I'm just waiting for a friend. It's an appointment made twenty years ago. Sounds a little funny to you, doesn't it? Well, I'll explain if you'd like to make certain it's all straight. About that long ago there used to be a restaurant where this store stands—'Big Joe' Brady's restaurant."

"Until five years ago," said the policeman. "It was torn down then."

---

1. *Pacific* means "calm; peaceful," and *stalwart* means "physically strong."

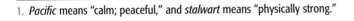

Vocabulary
habitual (hə bich′ ōō əl) *adj.* done by habit
intricate (in′ tri kit) *adj.* full of complicated detail
artful (ärt′ fəl) *adj.* done with skill or cleverness

Rainy Night, 1939. Charles Burchfield. Watercolor over pencil, 30 x 42 in. San Diego Museum of Art.

Viewing the painting: What mood does the painting create? What details help create that mood? What details does O. Henry use to create a mood in the story?

The man in the doorway struck a match and lit his cigar. The light showed a pale, square-jawed face with keen eyes, and a little white scar near his right eyebrow. His scarfpin was a large diamond, oddly set.

"Twenty years ago tonight," said the man, "I dined here at 'Big Joe' Brady's with Jimmy Wells, my best chum, and the finest chap in the world. He and I were raised here in New York, just like two brothers, together. I was eighteen and Jimmy was twenty. The next morning I was to start for the West to make my fortune. You couldn't have dragged Jimmy out of New York; he thought it was the only place on earth. Well, we agreed that night that we would

meet here again exactly twenty years from that date and time, no matter what our conditions might be or from what distance we might have to come. We figured that in twenty years each of us ought to have our destiny worked out and our fortunes made, whatever they were going to be."

"It sounds pretty interesting," said the policeman. "Rather a long time between meets, though, it seems to me. Haven't you heard from your friend since you left?"

"Well, yes, for a time we corresponded," said the other. "But after a year or two we lost track of each other. You see, the West is a pretty big proposition, and I kept hustling around over it pretty lively. But I know Jimmy will meet me here if he's alive, for he always was the truest, staunchest[2] old chap in the world. He'll never forget. I came a thousand miles to stand in this door tonight, and it's worth it if my old partner turns up."

The waiting man pulled out a handsome watch, the lids of it set with small diamonds.

"Three minutes to ten," he announced. "It was exactly ten o'clock when we parted here at the restaurant door."

"Did pretty well out West, didn't you?" asked the policeman.

"You bet! I hope Jimmy has done half as well. He was a kind of plodder,[3] though, good fellow as he was. I've had to compete with some of the sharpest wits going to get my pile. A man gets in a groove in New York. It takes the West to put a razor-edge on him."

The policeman twirled his club and took a step or two.

"I'll be on my way. Hope your friend comes around all right. Going to call time on him sharp?"

"I should say not!" said the other. "I'll give him half an hour at least. If Jimmy is alive on earth he'll be here by that time. So long, officer."

"Good-night, sir," said the policeman, passing on along his beat, trying doors as he went.

There was now a fine, cold drizzle falling, and the wind had risen from its uncertain puffs into a steady blow. The few foot passengers astir in that quarter hurried dismally and silently along with coat collars turned high and pocketed hands. And in the door of the hardware store the man who had come a thousand miles to fill an appointment, uncertain almost to absurdity, with the friend of his youth, smoked his cigar and waited.

---

2. Here, *proposition* means "a challenging opportunity" and *staunchest* means "most loyal and dependable."

3. A *plodder* is someone who moves slowly, but the man means that Jimmy was not a quick thinker.

Vocabulary
correspond (kôr′ ə spond′) *v.* to communicate by exchanging letters
dismally (diz′ məl lē) *adv.* in a gloomy, cheerless way
absurdity (ab sur′ də tē) *n.* the state of being ridiculous, senseless, or irrational

After Twenty Years

About twenty minutes he waited, and then a tall man in a long overcoat, with collar turned up to his ears, hurried across from the opposite side of the street. He went directly to the waiting man.

"Is that you, Bob?" he asked, doubtfully.

"Is that you, Jimmy Wells?" cried the man in the door.

"Bless my heart!" exclaimed the new arrival, grasping both the other's hands with his own. "It's Bob, sure as fate. I was certain I'd find you here if you were still in existence. Well, well, well!—twenty years is a long time. The old restaurant's gone, Bob; I wish it had lasted, so we could have had another dinner there. How has the West treated you, old man?"

"Bully;[4] it has given me everything I asked it for. You've changed lots, Jimmy. I never thought you were so tall by two or three inches."

"Oh, I grew a bit after I was twenty."

"Doing well in New York, Jimmy?"

"<u>Moderately</u>. I have a position in one of the city departments. Come on, Bob; we'll go around to a place I know of, and have a good long talk about old times."

The two men started up the street, arm in arm. The man from the West, his egotism[5] enlarged by success, was beginning to outline the history of his career. The other, submerged in his overcoat, listened with interest.

At the corner stood a drug store, brilliant with electric lights. When they came into this glare each of them turned simultaneously to gaze upon the other's face.

The man from the West stopped suddenly and released his arm.

"You're not Jimmy Wells," he snapped. "Twenty years is a long time, but not long enough to change a man's nose from a Roman to a pug."[6]

"It sometimes changes a good man into a bad one," said the tall man. "You've been under arrest for ten minutes, 'Silky' Bob. Chicago thinks you may have dropped over our way and wires us she wants to have a chat with you. Going quietly, are you? That's sensible. Now, before we go on to the station here's a note I was asked to hand you. You may read it here at the window. It's from Patrolman Wells."

The man from the West unfolded the little piece of paper handed him. His hand was steady when he began to read, but it trembled a little by the time he had finished. The note was rather short.

BOB: I was at the appointed place on time. When you struck the match to light your cigar I saw it was the face of the man wanted in Chicago. Somehow I couldn't do it myself, so I went around and got a plain clothes[7] man to do the job.

JIMMY.

---

4. *Bully* is slang for "excellent; first-rate."
5. Here, *egotism* refers to an exaggerated sense of self-importance.

---

6. A *Roman nose* is long and bold, while a *pug* is short, thick, and turned-up.
7. *Plain clothes* refers to a police officer who does not wear a uniform while on duty.

Vocabulary
moderately (mod′ ər it lē) *adv.* neither too great nor too small; within limits

Responding to Literature

PERSONAL RESPONSE

- ◆ What surprised you most about the ending of the story?
- ◆ Can you think of an alternative ending for the story?

Analyzing Literature

RECALL

1. For whom is the man from the West waiting? What promise did he make twenty years ago?
2. What does the Westerner tell the police officer about Jimmy's character?
3. After the police officer leaves, who approaches the Westerner?
4. What does Jimmy reveal in his note?

INTERPRET

5. Why does the man from the West try so hard to reassure the police officer?
6. What is Jimmy Wells's internal conflict in the story?
7. What does the Westerner's physical reaction to the note tell you about his emotional state?
8. What do you think motivated Jimmy to do what he did to his old friend at the end?

EVALUATE AND CONNECT

9. In your opinion, what is the author saying about measuring success in a person's life? How has Jimmy been both more successful and less successful than Bob?
10. **Theme Connection** Did O. Henry surprise you? Why or why not?

LITERARY ELEMENTS

Short Story

A **short story** is a brief work of fiction that usually can be read in one sitting. Short stories have the usual elements of fiction—plot, character, setting, and theme. These are the events, people, places, and ideas that make a short story complete. The combination of these elements determines the story's overall impact on the reader.

1. What surprising facts do you learn about each character at the end of O. Henry's story?

2. What theme does the story communicate about the twists and turns of life and the way people can change?

● See **Literary Terms Handbook,** p. R10.

Night Shadows. Edward Hopper (1882–1967). Etching, sheet: 12³⁄₁₆ x 15¹⁵⁄₁₆ in., plate: 7 x 8¼ in. Whitney Museum of American Art, New York. Josephine N. Hopper bequest.

Extending Your Response

Personal Writing

Judging Loyalty Look back at what you wrote about loyalty in the **Reading Focus** on page 564. Then write a response to Jimmy's choice in choosing between personal loyalty to a friend and loyalty to his duty as a police officer.

Literature Groups

Friend or Foe? Use examples from the story to create a chart that compares and contrasts Jimmy and Bob. Consider their physical and emotional characteristics and their past and future lives.

Characteristics	Jimmy	Bob
Physical		
Emotional		
Career		

Learning for Life

Crime Column Write a report for the crime section of the newspaper to inform the public of the arrest of "Silky" Bob. Include a description of the suspect and a tribute to the quick thinking of Officer Jimmy Wells.

Writing About Literature

Irony **Irony** is a difference between appearance and reality. A story is ironic when it focuses on the differences between the way things seem to be and the way they actually are. In a paragraph, identify two specific examples of irony in "After Twenty Years" and explain what is ironic about each.

Reading Further

If you would like to read other stories by O. Henry, try these books:

The Best Short Stories of O. Henry

The Gift of the Magi and Other Stories

📖 **Save your work for your portfolio.**

Skill Minilesson

VOCABULARY • THE SUFFIX *-ity*

When *-ity* is added to the end of a word, it adds the meaning "state or condition." *Absurd* means "ridiculous," and *absurdity* means "the state of being ridiculous." Adding the suffix *-ity* usually changes the way the base word sounds. For example, the first syllable is stressed in *rapid,* but the second syllable is stressed in *rapidity.* Remember that when a suffix is added to most words ending with a silent *e,* the *e* is dropped: *antique + -ity = antiquity.*

PRACTICE Use what you know about familiar words and the suffix *-ity* to match each word with a word that has a similar meaning.

1. solidity   a. lawlessness
2. illegality   b. oldness
3. abnormality   c. hardness
4. antiquity   d. roundness
5. circularity   e. oddness

LISTENING, SPEAKING, and VIEWING

Storytelling

Is there a trick to telling a story aloud to an audience? Not really. All you have to do is practice. Learn your story well enough so that, even if you use notes, you don't have to read them word-for-word. Above all, practice. Practice in front of a mirror to be comfortable with yourself. Practice in front of a friend, and ask for feedback. Practice with a tape recorder or video camera to experiment with your voice and body language.

Whether you're spinning a tale you know by heart or telling a story you've written yourself, the following guidelines can help.

Storytelling Guidelines

- Stand or sit with good posture; it helps your voice to carry.
- Look at your listeners. When they return your gaze, you have their attention. Maintain eye contact as you speak.
- Change positions from time to time so that you don't tense up.
- Vary your volume and pacing to fit the story.
- Keep checking your listeners' responses. If they fidget, ask yourself why.
- Feel free to "talk with your hands." If you wish, take on characters' roles by changing your posture, gestures, and tone of voice.

ACTIVITIES

1. With a classmate, practice and take turns telling a story you both know well. Follow the above guidelines.

2. Tell classmates a story you have written. Score yourself afterward on how well you followed the **Storytelling Guidelines.**

Before You Read
The Million-Pound Bank Note

MEET MARK TWAIN

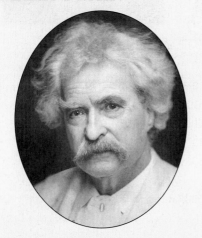

Mark Twain found inspiration for his writing in childhood experiences along the Mississippi River, as well as from being a riverboat pilot, a gold panner, and a journalist. Generations of readers worldwide have enjoyed his work as a novelist, short-story writer, essayist, humorist, journalist, and literary critic. He is one of the great figures of American literature.

Samuel Langhorne Clemens, better known as Mark Twain, was born in 1835 and died in 1910.

READING FOCUS

What would you do with a million dollars?

Graph It!
Gather suggestions from your classmates and work together to graph the class's responses.

Setting a Purpose
Read this play to find out how one man is affected by having a banknote worth a million British pounds.

BUILDING BACKGROUND

The Time and Place   The story takes place in the late 1800s.

This scene is from the 1954 film version of Twain's story, titled *Man with a Million.*

VOCABULARY PREVIEW

proposition (prop′ ə zish′ ən) *n.* something offered for consideration; proposal; p. 573

conceive (kən sēv′) *v.* to form an image or idea of; p. 577

competent (kom′ pət ənt) *adj.* having enough ability for the purpose; capable; p. 577

rebuke (ri būk′) *n.* an expression of sharp criticism or disapproval; p. 578

eccentric (ik sen′ trik) *adj.* not usual or normal in behavior; peculiar; p. 578

benefactor (ben′ ə fak′ tər) *n.* one who gives financial assistance; p. 584

shrewd (shrood) *adj.* sharp, clever, and practical; p. 584

The Million-Pound Bank Note

Mark Twain

Dramatized for radio by Walter Hackett

CAST OF CHARACTERS

HENRY ADAMS	SERVANT	SECOND MAN
LLOYD HASTINGS	TOD	WOMAN
FIRST COCKNEY	MR. SMEDLEY	THIRD MAN
GORDON FEATHERSTONE	HOTEL MANAGER	BUTLER
ABEL FEATHERSTONE	SECOND COCKNEY	PORTIA LANGHAM
ALBERT HAWKINS	FIRST MAN	SIR ALFRED

HENRY. When I was twenty-seven years old, I was a mining broker's clerk in San Francisco. I was alone in the world, and had nothing to depend upon but my wits and a clean reputation. These were setting my feet in the road to eventual fortune, and I was content with the prospect. During my spare time, I did outside work. One of my part-time employers was Lloyd Hastings, a mining broker. During this period I was helping Hastings to verify[1] the Gould and Curry Extension papers, covering what seemed to be a highly valuable gold mine. One morning at two, after six hard hours of work on these papers, Lloyd Hastings and I went to the What Cheer restaurant in Frisco. As we lingered over our coffee, he offered me a <u>proposition</u>.

HASTINGS. Henry, how would you like to go to London?

HENRY. Thank you, no.

HASTINGS. Listen to me. I'm thinking of taking a month's option[2] on the Gould and Curry Extension for the locators.

HENRY. And—?

HASTINGS. They want one million dollars for it.

HENRY. Not too much—if the claim works out the way it appears it may.

HASTINGS. I'm going to try to sell it to London interests, which means a trip there, and I want you to go with me, because you know more about these papers than I.

---

1. Here, *prospect* means "possibility of future success." To *verify* the papers is to check the accuracy of their information.

2. In financial terms, an *option* is a right to buy or sell something for a certain price and within a certain time.

Vocabulary

proposition (prop′ ə zish′ ən) *n.* something offered for consideration; proposal

HENRY. No, thanks.

HASTINGS. I'll make it well worth your while. I'll pay all your expenses, and give you something over if I make the sale.

HENRY. I have a job.

HASTINGS. I'll arrange for you to get a leave of absence. What do you say?

HENRY. No.

HASTINGS. Why?

HENRY. If I go to London, I'll get out of touch with my work and with mining conditions here, and that means months getting the hang of things again.

HASTINGS. That's a pretty slim excuse, Henry.

HENRY. More important, perhaps, I think you're doomed to failure.

HASTINGS. But you just said the claim is valuable.

HENRY. It may well turn out that way, but right now its real value can't be proved. And even so, a month's option may leave you too little time to sell it; unless you sell it within the option time, you'll go stone broke.

HASTINGS. I'm willing to gamble.

HENRY. Well, I'm not.

HASTINGS. Think—a free trip to London.

HENRY. I've no desire to go to London. I'll remain right here in Frisco.

HASTINGS. [*Fading.*][3] Very well, but I know you're making a mistake, Henry.

HENRY. One of my few diversions[4] was sailing in the bay. One day I ventured too far, and was carried out to sea. Late that night, I was picked up by a freighter which was bound for London. It was a long voyage, and the captain made me work my passage without pay, as a common sailor. When I stepped ashore at London my clothes were ragged and shabby, and I had only a dollar in my pocket. This money fed and sheltered me for twenty-four hours. During the next twenty-four I went without food and shelter. I tried to get a job, doing manual labor. But the reply was always the same.

COCKNEY.[5] I'm not sure you'd do. You ain't the sort. [*Suspiciously.*] Look, 'ere, you're a Yank, ain't you?

HENRY. The next morning, seedy and hungry, I was dragging myself along Portland Place, when my desiring eye fell on a tempting treasure lying in the gutter. It was a luscious big pear—minus one bite. My mouth watered for it. But every time I made a move to get it, some passing eye detected my purpose. I was just getting desperate enough to brave all the shame, when a window behind me was raised.

GORDON. [*Away.*] I say, you there, will you step in here, please?

HENRY. It was a very sumptuous[6] house and an equally sumptuous room into which I was ushered by a servant. A couple of elderly gentlemen were sitting by the window. At that moment if I had known what they had in mind, undoubtedly I would have bolted for the door. They looked me over very thoroughly.

---

3. The *fading* of Hastings's voice indicates the end of the scene.
4. *Diversions* are activities that amuse and take one's mind away from work or worries.

5. A *cockney* is a person who speaks with an accent found only in a certain district of London.
6. Things that are *sumptuous* (sump′ chōō əs) are expensive, showy, and magnificent.

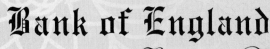

GORDON. He looks poor enough, don't you think, brother?

ABEL. Very. Er, young man, you are poor?

HENRY. Extremely!

ABEL. Good! And honest, too?

HENRY. Honesty is about all I have left; that, and character.

ABEL. Splendid!

GORDON. If my brother and I are judges of people, we'd say you are just the man for whom we have been searching. By the way, you are also intelligent, I would say.

HENRY. Yes, sir, I am. But what do you mean by saying that I appear to be just the man for whom you have been searching?

GORDON. And we don't know you. You're a perfect stranger. And better still, an American.

HENRY. It's very kind of you gentlemen to call me into your home, but I'm a bit puzzled. Could you tell me what you have in mind?

ABEL. Might we inquire into your background?

HENRY. Pretty soon they had my full story. Their questions were complete and searching, and I gave them straightforward answers. Finally one said:

GORDON. Oh, yes, we're certain you will do, eh, brother?

ABEL. Definitely! He is elected.

HENRY. To what am I elected, please?

GORDON. This envelope will explain everything. Here, take it. [*Hastily.*] No, don't open it now. Take it to your lodgings and look it over carefully.

ABEL. Being sure not to be rash[7] or hasty.

HENRY. I'd like to discuss the matter.

GORDON. There is nothing to discuss at the moment.

HENRY. Is this a joke?

ABEL. Not at all. And now good day.

GORDON. And good luck.

ABEL. Cheerio!

HENRY. As soon as I was out of sight of the house I opened my envelope and saw it contained money. I lost not a moment, but shoved note and money into my pocket, and broke for the nearest cheap eating house. How I did eat! Finished, I took out my money and unfolded it. I took one glimpse and nearly fainted. It was a single million-pound bank note. Five millions of dollars! It made my head swim. The next

---

7. To be *rash* is to act without thought or preparation.

thing I noticed was the owner of the eating house. His eyes were on the note, and he was petrified.[8] He couldn't stir hand or foot. I tossed the note toward him in careless fashion.

HAWKINS.   I-is it real, sir! A million-pound note?

HENRY.   [*Casually.*] Certainly. Let me have my change, please.

HAWKINS.   Oh, I'm very sorry, sir, but I can't break the bill.

HENRY.   Look here—

HAWKINS.   Hawkins is the name, Albert Hawkins, proprietor.[9] It's only a matter of two shillings you owe, a trifling sum. Please owe it to me.

HENRY.   I may not be in this neighborhood again for a good time.

HAWKINS.   It's of no consequence, sir. And you can have anything you want, any time you choose, and let the account run as long as you please. I'm not afraid to trust as rich a gentleman as you, just because you choose to play larks[10] by dressing as a tramp.

HENRY.   Well, thank you. I shall take advantage of your kindness.

HAWKINS.   Not at all, sir, [*Fading.*] and please, sir, enter my humble restaurant place any time you wish. I shall be honored to receive you.

HENRY.   I was frightened, afraid that the police might pick me up. I was afraid of the two brothers' reaction when they

discovered they had given me a million-pound note instead of what they must have intended giving—a one-pound note. I hurried to their house and rang the bell. The same servant appeared. I asked for the brothers.

SERVANT.   They are gone.

HENRY.   Gone! Where?

SERVANT.   On a journey.

HENRY.   But whereabouts?

SERVANT.   To the Continent,[11] I think.

HENRY.   The Continent?

SERVANT.   Yes, sir.

HENRY.   Which way—by what route?

SERVANT.   I can't say, sir.

HENRY.   When will they be back?

SERVANT.   In a month, they said.

HENRY.   A month! This is awful! Tell me how to get word to them. It's of great importance.

SERVANT.   I can't, indeed. I've no idea where they've gone, sir.

HENRY.   Then I must see some member of the family.

SERVANT.   Family's been away too; been abroad months—in Egypt and India, I think.

HENRY.   There's been an immense mistake made. They'll be back before night. Tell them I've been here, and that I'll keep coming till it's all made right, and they needn't worry.

SERVANT.   I'll tell them, if they come back, but I'm not expecting them. They said you'd be here in an hour to make inquiries,

---

8. *Petrified* means "turned to stone." The man is struck rigid with astonishment.
9. As a *proprietor* (prə prī′ ə tər), Hawkins is the owner and operator of a small business.
10. The British expression *play larks* means "joke around."

11. *The Continent* is how the British often refer to mainland Europe.

but I must tell you it's all right, they'll be here on time to meet you. [*Fading.*] And that's all they said.

HENRY. [*Slowly.*] I had to give it up and go away. What a riddle it all was! They would be here "on time." What could that mean? Then I thought of the letter. I got it out and read it. It said: "You are an intelligent and honest man, as one can see by your face. We conceive you to be poor and a stranger. Enclosed you will find a sum of money. It is lent to you for thirty days, without interest. Report to this house at the end of that time. I have a bet on you. If I win it you shall have any situation[12] that is in my gift, any, that is, that you shall be able to prove yourself familiar with and competent to fill." That was all. No signature, no address, no date. I hadn't the least idea what the game was, nor whether harm was meant me or kindness. The letter said there was a bet on me. What kind of a bet? Was the bet that I would abscond[13] with the million-pound bank note? Which brother was betting on my honesty? I reasoned this way: if I ask the Bank of England to deposit it to the credit of the man it belongs to, they'll ask me how I came by it, and if I tell the truth, they'll put me in the asylum; on the other hand, if I lie, they'll put me in jail. The same result would follow if I try to bank it anywhere or borrow money on it. Therefore, I have to carry this burden around until those men come back. A month's suffering without wages or profit—

unless I help win that bet, whatever it may be. If I do, I will get the situation I am promised. My hopes began to rise high. Then I looked at my rags. Could I afford a new suit? No, for I had nothing in the world but a million pounds. Finally I gave in and entered a fashionable tailor shop. The clerk looked at me very arrogantly.[14]

TOD. [*Icily.*] No chores to be done here. Get out!

HENRY. Perhaps you have a misfit suit.

TOD. We don't give away suits, even misfits.

HENRY. I can pay for it.

TOD. Follow me.

HENRY. He took me into a back room, and overhauled a pile of rejected suits. He tossed the rattiest looking one at me. I put it on. It didn't fit. It wasn't in any way attractive.

TOD. You may have that for four pounds, cash.

HENRY. It would be an accommodation to me if you could wait some days for the money. I haven't any small change about me.

TOD. [*Sarcastically.*][15] Oh, you haven't? Well, of course, I didn't expect it. I'd only expect gentlemen like you to carry large change.

HENRY. My friend, you shouldn't judge a stranger always by the clothes he wears. I am quite able to pay for this suit.

---

12. Here, *situation* means "a job or position of employment."
13. If Henry were to *abscond,* he would flee secretly and hide.

14. *Arrogantly* means "in a self-important way; proudly."
15. Tod speaks in a sharp, mocking way *(sarcastically).*

Vocabulary
conceive (kən sēv′) *v.* to form an image or idea of
competent (kom′ pət ənt) *adj.* having enough ability for the purpose; capable

West Front of St. Paul's from Ludgate Hill. Joseph Pennell (1857–1926). Gouache en grisaille on paper laid down on board, 20 x 13¾ in. Private collection.

Viewing the painting: What would you want to see or do if you were in this scene with a million-pound bank note?

TOD. Hah!

HENRY. I simply don't wish to put you to the trouble of changing a large note.

TOD. As long as <u>rebukes</u> are going around, I might say that it wasn't quite

your affair to infer[16] that we couldn't change any note that you might happen to be carrying around. On the contrary, we *can*.

HENRY. Oh, very well. I apologize. Here you are.

TOD. Thank you. [*A complete change. He stutters and fumbles.*] Ah—it's—ah— that is—we—ah—you see— It's— [*Quickly.*] take it back, please. [*Raising voice.*] Mr. Smedley! Mr. Smedley! Help! Oh, Mr. Smedley.

SMEDLEY. [*Coming in. A fussy man.*] What is it, Tod, what is it? Stop shouting!

TOD. Oh, but Mr. Smedley, I can't control myself.

SMEDLEY. What's up? What's the trouble? What's wanting? Who's this?

HENRY. I am a customer and I am waiting for my change.

SMEDLEY. Change, change! Tod, give him his change. Get it for him.

TOD. Get him his change! It's easy for you to say that, Mr. Smedley, but look at the bill yourself.

SMEDLEY. Bill, bill! Let me see it! [*Pause.*] Tod, you ass, selling an <u>eccentric</u> millionaire

---

16. Here, *infer* means "to come to a conclusion based on something assumed."

Vocabulary
rebuke (ri būk´) *n.* an expression of sharp criticism or disapproval
eccentric (ik sen´ trik) *adj.* not usual or normal in behavior; peculiar

such an unspeakable suit as that. Tod, you're a fool—a born fool! Drives every millionaire away from this place, because he can't tell a millionaire from a tramp. Here, sir, are some suits more in keeping with your position.

HENRY. Thank you, but this one will do.

SMEDLEY. Of course it won't do! I shall burn it. Tod, burn this suit at once.

TOD. Yes, Mr. Smedley.

SMEDLEY. We shall be honored to outfit you completely, sir . . . morning clothes, evening dress, sack suits, tweeds, shetlands—everything you need. Come, Tod, book and pen. Now—length of leg, 32 inches; sleeve—

HENRY. But look here, I can't give you an order for suits, unless you can wait indefinitely,[17] or change this bill.

SMEDLEY. Indefinitely, sir. It's a weak word, a weak word. *Eternally,* that's the word, sir. Tod, rush these things through. Let the minor customers wait. Set down the gentleman's address and—

HENRY. I'm changing my quarters. I'll drop in and leave the new address.

SMEDLEY. Quite right, sir, quite right. One moment—allow me to show you out, sir. And don't worry about paying us. [*Fading.*] Your credit is the highest. Good day, sir, good day. You honor us greatly, sir.

HENRY. [*As though sighing.*] Well, don't you see what was bound to happen? I drifted naturally into whatever I wanted. Take my hotel, for example. I merely showed the resident manager my million-pound note, and he said:

MANAGER. We are honored to have you as a guest, sir. Now, I have just the suite for you. It consists of a bedroom, sitting room, a dressing room, a dining room, two baths and—

HENRY. I'll pay you a month in advance with this.

MANAGER. [*Laughing.*] You honor our simple hotel, sir. Pray, don't worry about the bill.

HENRY. But it may be several months before I can pay you.

MANAGER. We're not worried, Mr.—er—

HENRY. Henry Adams.

MANAGER. Mr. Adams, you are a most distinguished guest. [*Fading.*] Anything you desire, please name it and we shall procure it for you immediately. Thank you, sir.

HENRY. And there I was, sumptuously housed in an expensive hotel in Hanover Square. I took my dinners there, but for breakfast I stuck by Hawkins' humble feeding-house, where I had got my first meal on my million-pound bank note. I was the making of Hawkins.

[*SOUND. Rattle of dishes and silver, customers' voices ad-libbing[18] in background.*]

HAWKINS. Business is brisk, sir, very brisk, indeed, and has been ever since you and your million-pound bank note became patrons of my humble establishment. I've had to hire extra help, put in additional tables. Look for yourself, sir. There's a long line waiting to get in. Why, I'm famous and fair on my way to becoming wealthy.

---

17. To wait *indefinitely* would be for an unlimited length of time.

18. *Ad libbing* is saying things that are not written in a script.

COCKNEY 2. Pardon me, Guv'ner,[19] but aren't you the gentleman what owns the million-pound bank note?

HAWKINS. Look here, you, go away and stop bothering Mr.— Mr.—

HENRY. Adams.

HAWKINS. Mr. Adams.

COCKNEY 2. I was just anxious to get a look at him.

HAWKINS. Who? Mr. Adams?

COCKNEY 2. No. The bank note.

HENRY. Glad to oblige. There you are.

COCKNEY 2. By George, it *is* real. [*Fading.*] Now I can go home and tell me old lady I've seen it with me own eyes. I hopes she believes me, but she won't.

HAWKINS. Mr. Adams, I wonder if I couldn't force upon you a small loan— even a large one.

HENRY. Oh, no.

HAWKINS. Please allow me, sir.

HENRY. [*Relenting.*][20] Well, as a matter of fact, I haven't gotten around to changing this note.

HAWKINS. Fifty pounds might help tide you over. You know, a little spending money?

HENRY. It would help, a bit.

HAWKINS. I consider it a great honor. [*Fading.*] Indeed, a very great honor. Here you are, Mr. Adams, fifty pounds it is. [*Fading.*] And don't worry about repaying me.

HENRY. I was in, now, and must sink or swim. I walked on air. And it was natural, for I had become one of the notorieties[21] of London. It turned my head, not just a little, but a great deal. The newspapers referred to me as the "Vest-Pocket Millionaire." Then came the climaxing stroke: "Punch" caricatured[22] me! Wherever I went, people cried:

MAN 1. There he goes!

MAN 2. That's him!

WOMAN 1. Morning, Guv'ner.

MAN 3. He's a bit of all right, he is.

HENRY. Why, I just swam in glory all day long. About the tenth day of my fame I fulfilled my duty to my country by calling upon the American Ambassador. He received me with enthusiasm, and insisted that I attend a dinner party he was giving the following night. Two important things happened at that dinner. I met two people who were to play important roles in the little drama I was living. Among the guests was a lovely English girl, named Portia Langham, whom I fell in love with in two minutes, and she with me; I could see it without glasses. And just before dinner, the butler announced:

[BIZ. *Guests ad-libbing in background, very politely.*]

BUTLER. [*Calling out.*] Mr. Lloyd Hastings.

HENRY. I stared at Hastings and he at me, his mouth open in surprise.

HASTINGS. I, er—pardon me, but are you? No, of course you can't be.

HENRY. [*Chuckling.*] But I am, Lloyd.

HASTINGS. Henry, I'm speechless. [*Suddenly.*] Don't tell me that you're also the Vest-Pocket Millionaire?

---

19. *Guv'ner* ("Governor") is Cockney dialect for addressing a man in authority or of a higher social class.
20. Here, *relenting* means "giving in."

21. A *notoriety* is someone who has become a celebrity.
22. *Punch* is a British humor magazine. It *caricatured* Henry in a cartoon that ridiculously exaggerated his features.

HENRY. Correct!

HASTINGS. I've seen your own name coupled with the nickname, but it never occurred to me you were *the* Henry Adams. Why, it isn't six months since you were clerking in Frisco, and sitting up nights helping me verify the Gould and Curry Extension papers. The idea of your being in London, and a vast millionaire, and a colossal celebrity! It's out of the Arabian Nights!

HENRY. I can't realize it myself.

HASTINGS. It was just three months ago that we were eating together, and I tried to persuade you to come to London with me. You turned me down and now here you are. How did you happen to come, and what gave you this incredible start?

HENRY. I'll tell you all about it, but not now.

HASTINGS. When?

HENRY. The end of this month.

HASTINGS. Make it a week.

HENRY. I can't. How's your business venture coming along?

HASTINGS. [*Sighing.*] You were a true prophet, Henry. I wish I hadn't come.

HENRY. Stop with me, when we leave here, and tell me all about it. I want to hear the whole story.

HASTINGS. You'll hear it, every last dismal word. [*Fading a bit.*] I'm so grateful to find a willing and sympathetic ear.[23]

[BIZ. *Background ad-libbing out. A pause, then:*]

---

23. One who listens in a caring way is said to have a *sympathetic ear.*

[PIANO. *Playing semi-classical tune in background.*]

HENRY. After dinner there was coffee and an informal piano recital and dear Miss Langham—lovely Portia Langham, the English girl. I eased her away from the music and the guests, to the library, where we talked.

[PIANO. *Out.*]

PORTIA. I'm really quite excited, Mr. Adams, meeting you like this. A millionaire!

HENRY. But I'm not one.

PORTIA. B-but of course you are.

HENRY. You're wrong.

PORTIA. I don't understand.

HENRY. You will! You will, that is, if you allow me to see you tomorrow.

PORTIA. [*As though smiling.*] Well, Mr. Adams—

HENRY. Henry.

PORTIA. Henry, then. I will give the invitation serious thought.

HENRY. Tomorrow is going to be a sunny day, just right for a picnic in the country. Yes?

PORTIA. Yes.

HENRY. I'll tell you the whole story then.

PORTIA. Do you think you should?

HENRY. Certainly! After all, we're going to be married.

PORTIA. [*Amazed.*] We—we're—going to—marry!

HENRY. Absolutely! I'll call for you at noon. Where?

PORTIA. Meet me here.

HENRY. You're a guest here?

PORTIA. N—no, but it will be more convenient.

HENRY. Do you like me?

PORTIA. Yes, Henry. [*Fading.*] You're a very unusual young man, even if you are a millionaire, and even if you claim you aren't.

HENRY. All the way home I was in the clouds, Hastings talking, and I not hearing a word. When we reached my suite, he said to me:

HASTINGS. This luxury makes me realize how poor, how defeated I am. Even the drippings of your daily income would seem like a tremendous fortune to me.

HENRY. Unreel your story, Lloyd.

HASTINGS. I told you the whole story on the way over here.

HENRY. You did?

HASTINGS. Yes.

HENRY. I'll be hanged if I heard a word of it.

HASTINGS. Are you well?

HENRY. Yes. I'm in love.

HASTINGS. That English girl you were speaking to?

HENRY. Yes. I'm going to marry her.

HASTINGS. Small wonder you didn't hear a word I said.

HENRY. Now I'm all attention.

HASTINGS. I came here with what I thought was a grand opportunity. I have an option to sell the Gould and Curry Mine and keep all I can get over a million dollars.

HENRY. Sounds like a good proposition.

HASTINGS. Yes, it's a fine claim.

HENRY. Well?

HASTINGS. The parties here whom I tried to interest have backed down. And so here I am trying to peddle a gold mine, but with nary a buyer in sight. In addition, I am almost penniless.

HENRY. Surely you'll find a buyer.

HASTINGS. My option on the mine expires in a matter of days; in fact, at the end of this month.

HENRY. You *are* in a fix.

HASTINGS. Henry, you can save me. Will you do it?

HENRY. I? How?

HASTINGS. Give me a million dollars and my passage home for my option.

HENRY. I can't.

HASTINGS. But you're wealthy.

HENRY. I—I—not really.

HASTINGS. You have a million pounds—five millions of dollars. Buy the mine and you'll double, maybe triple your investment.

HENRY. I'd like to help, but I can't.

HASTINGS. You know the value of this mine, as well as I do.

HENRY. [*Tired.*] Oh, Lloyd, I wish I could explain, but I can't. What you ask is impossible.

HASTINGS. That's quite all right. I'm sorry to have bothered you, Henry. [*Fading.*] You must have a good reason in turning me down, I'm sure.

HENRY. It hurt me to have to refuse Lloyd, but it made me comprehend my delicate and precarious[24] position. Here I was, deep in debt, not a cent in the world, in love

---

24. *Precarious* means "exposed to risk or danger."

with a lovely girl, and nothing in front of me but a promise of a position, if, *if* I won the bet for the nameless brother. Nothing could save me. The next day, Portia and I went on our picnic in the country. I told her the whole story, down to the last detail. Her reaction wasn't exactly what I thought it would be.

[SOUND. *Bird singing in background. Weave in and out of this scene.*]

PORTIA. [*Laughs.*] Oh, Henry, that's priceless.

HENRY. [*A bit stiffly.*] I fail to see the humor.

PORTIA. But I do, more than you can imagine.

HENRY. Here I am mixed up in a bet between two eccentric old men, and for all they care I might well be in jail.

PORTIA. [*Still laughing.*] Wonderful, the funniest thing I've ever heard.

HENRY. Pardon me if I don't laugh.

PORTIA. [*Stops laughing.*] Sorry, but it is both funny and pathetic.[25] But you say that one of the men is going to offer you a position?

HENRY. If I win the bet.

PORTIA. Which one is he?

HENRY. I don't know. But I have one solution. If I win, I get the position. Now, I've kept a very careful track of every cent I either owe or have borrowed, and I'm going to pay it back from my salary. If the position pays me six hundred pounds a year, I'll—I'll—

PORTIA. You'll what?

HENRY. I'll— [*He whistles.*] To date I owe exactly six hundred pounds, my whole year's salary.

PORTIA. And the month isn't ended.

HENRY. If I'm careful, my second year's salary may carry me through. Oh, dear, that *is* going to make it difficult for us to get married immediately, isn't it?

PORTIA. [*Dreamily.*] Yes, it is. [*Suddenly.*] Henry, what are you talking about? Marriage! You don't know me.

HENRY. I know your name, your nationality, your age, and, most important, I know that I love you. I also know that you love me.

PORTIA. Please be sensible.

HENRY. I can't. I'm in love.

PORTIA. All this sounds like a play.

HENRY. It is—a wonderful one. I'll admit my owing my first two years' pay is going to pose a problem insofar as our getting married is concerned. [*Suddenly.*] I have it! The day I confront those two old gentlemen, I'll take you with me.

PORTIA. Oh, no. It wouldn't be proper.

HENRY. But so much depends upon that meeting. With you there, I can get the old boys to raise my salary—say, to a thousand pounds a year. Perhaps fifteen hundred. Say you'll go with me.

PORTIA. I'll go.

HENRY. In that case, I'll demand two thousand a year, so we can get married immediately.

PORTIA. Henry.

HENRY. Yes?

PORTIA. Keep your expenses down for the balance of the month. Don't dip into your third year's salary.

---

25. Something that's *pathetic* inspires pity or sadness.

HENRY.   And that is how matters stood at that point. Thoughts raced through my mind. What if I lost the bet for my nameless benefactor? What if he failed to give me a position? Then the answer came to me, like a flash of lightning. I roused Lloyd Hastings from bed. He was a bit bewildered.

HASTINGS.   I don't understand you. What are you getting at?

HENRY.   Lloyd, I'm going to save you. Save you—understand!

HASTINGS.   No.

HENRY.   I'll save you, but not in the way you ask, for that wouldn't be fair, after your hard work and the risks you've run. Now, I don't need to buy a mine. I can keep my capital moving without that; it's what I'm doing all the time. I know all about your mine; I know its immense value and can swear to it if anybody wishes it. You shall sell it inside of the fortnight[26] for three million cash.

HASTINGS.   Three million!

HENRY.   Right!

HASTINGS.   But how?

HENRY.   By using my name freely—and right now my name is on the tip of everybody's tongue. We'll divide the profits, share and share alike.

HASTINGS.   [*Overjoyed.*] I may use your name! Your name—think of it! Man, they'll flock in droves, these rich English. They'll fight for that stock. I'm a made man,[27] a made man forever. [*Fading.*] I'll never forget you as long as I live . . . never, never . . .

HENRY.   In less than twenty-four hours London was abuzz! I hadn't anything to do, day after day, but sit home, and wait for calls.

SIR ALFRED.   Then I may assume, Mr. Adams, that you consider this mining property a sound investment?

HENRY.   A very sound investment, Sir Alfred.

SIR ALFRED.   And what of this American chap, Hastings?

HENRY.   I know him very well, and he is as sound as the mine.

SIR ALFRED.   Then I think I shall invest in this property. Your recommendation does it.

   [*SOUND. Telephone bell.*]

HENRY.   Excuse me, Sir Alfred.

   [*SOUND. Receiver lifted from hook.*]

HENRY.   [*Into phone.*] Yes, this is Henry Adams. Who? Sir John Hardcastle. Yes, Sir John. The Gould and Curry Extension? Yes, I know a great deal about it. I certainly would recommend it as a shrewd investment. The mine is worth far more than the asking price. Yes, Mr. Hastings is very well known in the States. Honest as the day is long, as they say. Yes, I suggest you contact Mr. Hastings. Thank you. Not at all. Good day, Sir John.

---

26. In financial terms, *capital* is wealth that is used to produce more wealth. A *fortnight* is two weeks.

27. A *made man* is one who is assured of success.

Vocabulary
benefactor (ben′ ə fak′ tər) *n.* one who gives financial assistance
shrewd (shro͞od) *adj.* sharp, clever, and practical

Indeed! Edward C. Clifford (1858–1910). Christopher Wood Gallery, London.

Viewing the painting: Compare this picture with the scene from the movie on page 572. Which do you think is truer to the story? Why?

[SOUND. *Receiver replaced onto hook.*]

SIR ALFRED.   That clinches it. If Sir John is in, so am I. Do you suppose that your Mr. Hastings would mind if I brought in a few discreet friends on this venture?

HENRY.   Er, no, in fact I'm sure he wouldn't. Mr. Hastings is a very democratic chap.

SIR ALFRED.   Directly I shall go and call upon Mr. Hastings. By the way, exactly where is this mine?

HENRY.   California.

SIR ALFRED.   Is that near Washington, D.C.?

HENRY.   Not exactly.

SIR ALFRED.   A pity, for I had thought of asking the British Ambassador to look at it. [*Fading.*] Well, I'm off. Thank you for your advice. Good day, Mr. Adams.

HENRY.   And that's the way it went—a steady stream of wealthy Londoners asking my advice, which, of course, I gave freely. Meanwhile I said not a word to Portia about the possible sale of the mine. I wanted to save it as a surprise; and then there always was the possibility the sale might fall through. The day the month was up, she and I, dressed in our best, went to the house on Portland Place. As we waited for the two old gentlemen to enter, we talked excitedly.

PORTIA.   You're certain you have the bank note with you?

HENRY. Right here. Portia, dearest, the way you look it's a crime to ask for a salary a single penny under three thousand a year.

PORTIA. You'll ruin us.

HENRY. Just trust in me. It'll come out all right.

PORTIA. [*Worried.*] Please remember if we ask for too much we may get no salary at all; and then what will become of us, with no way in the world to earn our living? [*Fading.*] Please handle this delicately, Henry.

HENRY. When the two old gentlemen entered, of course they were surprised to see Portia with me. I asked them to introduce themselves, which they did.

GORDON. I am Gordon Featherstone.

ABEL. And I am Abel Featherstone.

HENRY. Gentlemen, I am ready to report, but first may I ask which of you bet on me?

GORDON. It was I. Have you the million-pound note?

HENRY. Here it is, sir.

GORDON. Ah! I've won. *Now* what do you say, Abel?

ABEL. I say he did survive, and I've lost twenty thousand pounds. I never would have believed it.

HENRY. Perhaps you might enlighten[28] me as to the terms of the bet.

GORDON. Gladly! The Bank of England once issued two notes of a million pounds each. Only one of these had been used and cancelled; the other lay in the vaults. Well, Abel and I got to wondering what would happen to a perfectly honest and intelligent stranger turned adrift in London without a friend and with no money in the world but the million-pound bank note. Abel said he would starve to death, and I claimed he wouldn't. My brother said he would be arrested if he offered the note at a bank. Well, we went on arguing until I bet him twenty thousand pounds that the man would live thirty days, *anyway*, on that million, and keep out of jail, too.

ABEL. And I took him up.

HENRY. How did you know I was the right choice?

ABEL. After talking with you, we decided you had all the qualifications.

GORDON. And that pear incident, if you had picked it up very boldly, it would have proved to us you were nothing but a tramp.

HENRY. You don't know how tempted I was to do just that.

GORDON. And so you shall receive your reward—a choice of any position you can fill.

HENRY. First I ask that you look at this scrap of paper, all of you. You, too, Portia.

GORDON. A certificate of deposit in the London and County Bank—

ABEL. In the sum of—

GORDON. Two hundred thousand pounds.

PORTIA. Henry, is it yours?

HENRY. It is. It represents my share of the sale of a mining property in California, sold by my friend Lloyd Hastings; a sort of commission, as it were. It all came about by thirty days' judicious[29] use of that little loan you gentlemen let me have. And the only use I made of it was to buy trifles and offer the bill in change.

---

28. To *enlighten* is to give or reveal knowledge or wisdom.

29. *Judicious* means "showing good judgment."

ABEL. Come, this is astonishing.

GORDON. It's incredible.

HENRY. [*Laughing.*] I can prove it.

PORTIA. Henry, is that really your money? Have you been fibbing to me?

HENRY. I have, indeed. But you'll forgive me, I know.

PORTIA. [*Half-smiling.*] Don't you be so sure.

HENRY. Oh, you'll get over it. Come, let's be going.

GORDON. Wait! I promised to give you a situation, you know.

HENRY. Thank you, but I really don't want one.

PORTIA. Henry, I'm ashamed of you. You don't even thank the good gentleman. May I do it for you?

HENRY. If you can improve upon it.

PORTIA. I shall. Uncle Abel, first, thank you for making this possible. And, dear Father—

HENRY. Hold on. You're her uncle?

ABEL. I am.

HENRY. And you—

GORDON. Yes, I'm her step-father.

PORTIA. And the dearest one that ever was. You understand now, don't you, Henry, why I was able to laugh when you told me the story of the bet with the two nameless gentlemen. Of course I couldn't miss knowing that it was this house and that the two men were Father and Uncle Abel.

HENRY. Sir, you *have* got a situation open that I want.

GORDON. Name it.

HENRY. Son-in-law.

GORDON. Well, well, well! But if you haven't ever served in that capacity, you of course can't furnish satisfactory recommendations to satisfy the conditions of the contract.

HENRY. Only just try me for thirty or forty years.

GORDON. What do you think, Abel?

ABEL. Well, he does look to be a satisfactory sort.

GORDON. And you, Portia?

PORTIA. I agree—heartily.

GORDON. Very well. Take her along. If you hurry, you can reach the license bureau before it closes. [*Fading.*] Hop to it now.

HENRY. Happy, we two? Indeed, yes! And when London got the whole history of my adventure for a month, how it did talk. My Portia's father took the million-pound bank note to the Bank of England, cashed it, had it cancelled, and he gave it to us at our wedding. Framed, it now hangs in our home. It gave me my Portia, but for it I could not have remained in London, would not have appeared at the American Ambassador's, never should have met her. And so I always say: Yes, it's a million-pounder; but it made but one purchase in its life, and then got the article for only about a tenth part of its value.

THE END

Responding to Literature

PERSONAL RESPONSE

◆ Take a look at the graph you created in the **Reading Focus** on page 572. How do your ideas of what to do with a million dollars compare with how Henry uses the million-pound note?

Analyzing Literature

RECALL

1. Why did Hastings want Henry to travel to London, England?
2. What do the two wealthy gentlemen offer Henry? What is his response when he realizes the value of the bill?
3. How do the shop people respond to the million-pound note? How do they contribute to Henry's fame?
4. How does Henry manage to earn his own fortune?

INTERPRET

5. Why is it ironic that Henry finds himself on a freighter bound for London?

6. What do you think Gordon and Abel are trying to test?

7. Why does Henry achieve fame as the "Vest-Pocket Millionaire"?

8. What does Henry's success with the uncashed million-pound note tell you about his personality and business skills?

EVALUATE AND CONNECT

9. Were you surprised by the climax of the story? Do you think Twain gave enough clues to make the gentlemen's bet and Portia's connection to the two men believable? Explain.

10. **Theme Connection** How does having a million-pound bank note affect Henry? How would it affect you?

LITERARY ELEMENTS

Stage Directions

Mark Twain originally wrote "The Million-Pound Bank Note" as a short story. Many years later, Walter Hackett adapted the story as a radio play. Like a traditional play, a radio play includes **stage directions** written in italic type and set in brackets. However, directions about scenery, movement, lighting, or props are unnecessary. In a radio play, the audience must use its imagination to visualize the characters and the setting. The only stage directions deal with sound effects and how the actors should say their lines.

1. Compare Henry's first meal at Hawkins's restaurant on pages 575–576 with the stage directions on page 579 when he returns there. What difference would the addition of sound effects make to the listener?

2. A number of times in the play the word *fading* appears within a character's speech. What effect do you think the dramatist is trying to achieve in these places? What would the speech sound like?

● See **Literary Terms Handbook,** p. R10.

Extending Your Response

Writing About Literature

Dialogue and Monologue   This dramatization contains **dialogue**–conversations between characters–and **monologues**–speeches Henry directs to the audience. From which of these do you learn more about Henry? From which do you learn more about the action in the play? Support your ideas with quotations from the play.

Creative Writing

Henry's Headlines   Write a series of brief newspaper articles from the point of view of a London journalist hot on the trail to describe Henry's wealth, adventures, and romance.

Literature Groups

Making Judgments   Discuss the assumptions people make about Henry when they see his shabby clothes and how those assumptions change when they see his million-pound note. What conclusions can be drawn about how the appearance of wealth affects our judgment of people?

inter**NET**
C O N N E C T I O N

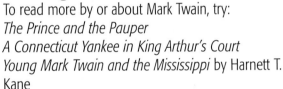

You can find out more about Mark Twain and his writings on the Internet. Just type *Mark Twain* or *Samuel Clemens* in the subject window of a search engine. You can even find the entire text of some of his novels and short stories if you'd like to read them.

Reading Further

To read more by or about Mark Twain, try:
The Prince and the Pauper
A Connecticut Yankee in King Arthur's Court
Young Mark Twain and the Mississippi by Harnett T. Kane

Save your work for your portfolio.

Skill Minilesson

VOCABULARY • ETYMOLOGY

Words have histories. Knowing where a word comes from can help you understand what it means now and why it means that. For example, *eccentric* comes from the Greek words *ek,* meaning "out of," and *kentron,* meaning "center." So an *eccentric* millionaire is one who is sort of "off center," or odd.

The history of a word is called its **etymology.** Here are the etymologies of some other words from "The Million-Pound Bank Note."

proposition: from the Latin *pro-* ("forward") and *positio* ("to place")
benefactor: from the Latin *bene-* ("well") and *facere* ("to do").
rebuke: from the Latin *re-* ("back") and the Old French *buchier* ("to beat")

PRACTICE   Choose one of the words from the above list and briefly explain how the etymology of that word is connected to its present-day meaning.

Before You Read
The Force of Luck

MEET
RUDOLFO A. ANAYA

The land and culture of his native New Mexico has inspired Rudolfo A. Anaya (rōō dôl′ fō ä nä′yä) since he was a child. Anaya was born in Pastura, a village on a vast plain covered with small farming communities. He has written that "the most important elements of my childhood are the people of those villages and the wide open plains." In his short stories, novels, and plays, Anaya draws upon Mexican legends, myths, and symbolism to create an insight into the Mexican American community.

Rudolfo A. Anaya was born in 1937. This story is part of a collection called Cuentos: Tales from the Hispanic Southwest.

READING FOCUS

Do you believe good fortune comes to those who are hard-working and honest or to those who are simply lucky?

Journal
In your journal, write your own ideas about good fortune.

Setting a Purpose
Read this story to find out what roles hard work and luck play in the life of one character.

BUILDING BACKGROUND

Time and Place   This story, like many folktales, takes place in a small village sometime in the past.

Did You Know?   "The Force of Luck" is part of the oral tradition of the Hispanic people who lived in the American Southwest. The *cuentistas,* or oral storytellers, played an important role in the life of writer Rudolfo A. Anaya. Anaya comments, "[Storytelling] is a tradition one often loses when one moves into print, but its elements are strong and as valuable today as they have been historically."

VOCABULARY PREVIEW

prosperous (pros′ pər əs) *adj.* having wealth or good fortune; successful; p. 592
squander (skwon′ dər) *v.* to spend or use in a reckless or wasteful manner; p. 593
spendthrift (spend′ thrift′) *n.* one who spends money generously or wastefully; p. 594
novelty (nov′ əl tē) *n.* anything new and unusual; p. 595
jest (jest) *v.* to speak or act in a playful manner; joke; p. 596
intact (in takt′) *adj.* undamaged and whole; p. 598

The Force of Luck

Retold by Rudolfo A. Anaya ⁓

Farmers (Agricultores), 1935. Antonio Gattorno. Gouache and ink on paper laid down on board, 17½ x 19½ in. Private collection.

The Force of Luck

Once two wealthy friends got into a heated argument. One said that it was money which made a man prosperous, and the other maintained that it wasn't money, but luck, which made the man. They argued for some time and finally decided that if only they could find an honorable man then perhaps they could prove their respective points of view.[1]

One day while they were passing through a small village they came upon a miller who was grinding corn and wheat. They paused to ask the man how he ran his business. The miller replied that he worked for a master and that he earned only four bits a day, and with that he had to support a family of five.

The friends were surprised. "Do you mean to tell us you can maintain a family of five on only fifteen dollars a month?" one asked.

"I live modestly to make ends meet," the humble miller replied.

The two friends privately agreed that if they put this man to a test perhaps they could resolve their argument.

"I am going to make you an offer," one of them said to the miller. "I will give you two hundred dollars and you may do whatever you want with the money."

"But why would you give me this money when you've just met me?" the miller asked.

"Well, my good man, my friend and I have a long standing argument. He contends that it is luck which elevates a man to high position, and I say it is money. By giving you this money perhaps we can settle our argument. Here, take it, and do with it what you want!"

So the poor miller took the money and spent the rest of the day thinking about the strange meeting which had presented him with more money than he had ever seen. What could he possibly do with all this money? Be that as it may, he had the money in his pocket and he could do with it whatever he wanted.

When the day's work was done, the miller decided the first thing he would do would be to buy food for his family. He took out ten dollars and wrapped the rest of the money in a cloth and put the bundle in his bag. Then he went to the market and bought supplies and a good piece of meat to take home.

On the way home he was attacked by a hawk that had smelled the meat which the miller carried. The miller fought off the bird but in the struggle he lost the bundle of money. Before the miller knew what was happening the hawk grabbed the bag and flew away with it. When he realized what had happened he fell into deep thought.

"Ah," he moaned, "wouldn't it have been better to let that hungry bird have the meat! I could have bought a lot more meat with the money he took. Alas, now I'm in the same poverty as before! And worse, because now those two men will say I am a thief! I should have thought carefully and bought nothing. Yes, I should have gone straight home and this wouldn't have happened!"

---

1. *Prove their respective points of view* means that each man was interested in proving his opinion the correct one.

Vocabulary

prosperous (pros′ pər əs) *adj.* having wealth or good fortune; successful

So he gathered what was left of his provisions[2] and continued home, and when he arrived he told his family the entire story.

When he was finished telling his story his wife said, "It has been our lot[3] to be poor, but have faith in God and maybe someday our luck will change."

The next day the miller got up and went to work as usual. He wondered what the two men would say about his story. But since he had never been a man of money he soon forgot the entire matter.

Three months after he had lost the money to the hawk, it happened that the two wealthy men returned to the village. As soon as they saw the miller they approached him to ask if his luck had changed. When the miller saw them he felt ashamed and afraid that they would think that he had squandered the money on worthless things. But he decided to tell them the truth and as soon as they had greeted each other he told his story. The men believed him. In fact, the one who insisted that it was money and not luck which made a man prosper took out another two hundred dollars and gave it to the miller.

"Let's try again," he said, "and let's see what happens this time."

The miller didn't know what to think. "Kind sir, maybe it would be better if you put this money in the hands of another man," he said.

"No," the man insisted, "I want to give it to you because you are an honest man,

and if we are going to settle our argument you have to take the money!"

The miller thanked them and promised to do his best. Then as soon as the two men left he began to think what to do with the money so that it wouldn't disappear as it had the first time. The thing to do was to take the money straight home. He took out ten dollars, wrapped the rest in a cloth, and headed home.

When he arrived his wife wasn't at home. At first he didn't know what to do with the money. He went to the pantry where he had stored a large earthenware jar filled with bran. That was as safe a place as any to hide the money, he thought, so he emptied out the grain and put the bundle of money at the bottom of the jar, then covered it up with the grain. Satisfied that the money was safe he returned to work.

That afternoon when he arrived home from work he was greeted by his wife.

"Look, my husband, today I bought some good clay with which to whitewash the entire house."

"And how did you buy the clay if we don't have any money?" he asked.

"Well, the man who was selling the clay was willing to trade for jewelry, money, or anything of value," she said. "The only thing we had of value was the jar full of bran, so I traded it for the clay. Isn't it wonderful, I think we have enough clay to whitewash these two rooms!"

The man groaned and pulled his hair.

"Oh, you crazy woman! What have you done? We're ruined again!"

---

2. The miller's *provisions* are his food supplies.
3. Here, *lot* means "fate; final outcome."

Vocabulary
squander (skwon′ dər) v. to spend or use in a reckless or wasteful manner

La Molendera I, 1924. Diego Rivera. *Encaustica sobre tela,* 90 x 117 cm. Museo de Arte Moderno, Bosque de Chapultepec, Mexico.

Viewing the painting: Which character in the story does this woman come closest to illustrating?

"But why?" she asked, unable to understand his anguish.

"Today I met the same two friends who gave me the two hundred dollars three months ago," he explained. "And after I told them how I lost the money they gave me another two hundred. And I, to make sure the money was safe, came home and hid it inside the jar of bran—the same jar you have traded for dirt! Now we're as poor as we were before! And what am I going to tell the two men? They'll think I'm a liar and a thief for sure!"

"Let them think what they want," his wife said calmly. "We will only have in our lives what the good Lord wants us to have. It is our lot to be poor until God wills it otherwise."

So the miller was consoled and the next day he went to work as usual. Time came and went, and one day the two wealthy friends returned to ask the miller how he had done with the second two hundred dollars. When the poor miller saw them he was afraid they would accuse him of being a liar and a spendthrift. But he

---

Vocabulary

spendthrift (spend′ thrift′) *n.* one who spends money generously or wastefully

decided to be truthful and as soon as they had greeted each other he told them what had happened to the money.

"That is why poor men remain honest," the man who had given him the money said. "Because they don't have money they can't get into trouble. But I find your stories hard to believe. I think you gambled and lost the money. That's why you're telling us these wild stories."

"Either way," he continued, "I still believe that it is money and not luck which makes a man prosper."

"Well, you certainly didn't prove your point by giving the money to this poor miller," his friend reminded him. "Good evening, you luckless man," he said to the miller.

"Thank you, friends," the miller said.

"Oh, by the way, here is a worthless piece of lead I've been carrying around. Maybe you can use it for something," said the man who believed in luck. Then the two men left, still debating their points of view on life.

Since the lead was practically worthless, the miller thought nothing of it and put it in his jacket pocket. He forgot all about it until he arrived home. When he threw his jacket on a chair he heard a thump and he remembered the piece of lead. He took it out of the pocket and threw it under the table. Later that night after the family had eaten and gone to bed, they heard a knock at the door.

"Who is it? What do you want?" the miller asked.

"It's me, your neighbor," a voice answered. The miller recognized the

fisherman's wife. "My husband sent me to ask you if you have any lead you can spare. He is going fishing tomorrow and he needs the lead to weight down the nets."

The miller remembered the lead he had thrown under the table. He got up, found it, and gave it to the woman.

"Thank you very much, neighbor," the woman said. "I promise you the first fish my husband catches will be yours."

"Think nothing of it," the miller said and returned to bed. The next day he got up and went to work without thinking any more of the incident. But in the afternoon when he returned home he found his wife cooking a big fish for dinner.

"Since when are we so well off we can afford fish for supper?" he asked his wife.

"Don't you remember that our neighbor promised us the first fish her husband caught?" his wife reminded him. "Well this was the fish he caught the first time he threw his net. So it's ours, and it's a beauty. But you should have been here when I gutted him! I found a large piece of glass in his stomach!"

"And what did you do with it?"

"Oh, I gave it to the children to play with," she shrugged.

When the miller saw the piece of glass he noticed it shone so brightly it appeared to illuminate the room, but because he knew nothing about jewels he didn't realize its value and left it to the children. But the bright glass was such a novelty that the children were soon fighting over it and raising a terrible fuss.

Now it so happened that the miller and his wife had other neighbors who were

---

Vocabulary
novelty (nov′ əl tē) *n.* anything new and unusual

jewelers. The following morning when the miller had gone to work the jeweler's wife visited the miller's wife to complain about all the noise her children had made.

"We couldn't get any sleep last night," she moaned.

"I know, and I'm sorry, but you know how it is with a large family," the miller's wife explained. "Yesterday we found a beautiful piece of glass and I gave it to my youngest one to play with and when the others tried to take it from him he raised a storm."

The jeweler's wife took interest. "Won't you show me that piece of glass?" she asked.

"But of course. Here it is."

"Ah, yes, it's a pretty piece of glass. Where did you find it?"

"Our neighbor gave us a fish yesterday and when I was cleaning it I found the glass in its stomach."

"Why don't you let me take it home for just a moment. You see, I have one just like it and I want to compare them."

"Yes, why not? Take it," answered the miller's wife.

So the jeweler's wife ran off with the glass to show it to her husband. When the jeweler saw the glass he instantly knew it was one of the finest diamonds he had ever seen.

"It's a diamond!" he exclaimed.

"I thought so," his wife nodded eagerly. "What shall we do?"

"Go tell the neighbor we'll give her fifty dollars for it, but don't tell her it's a diamond!"

"No, no," his wife chuckled, "of course not." She ran to her neighbor's house. "Ah yes, we have one exactly like this," she told the miller's wife. "My husband is willing to buy it for fifty dollars—only so we can have a pair, you understand."

"I can't sell it," the miller's wife answered. "You will have to wait until my husband returns from work."

That evening when the miller came home from work his wife told him about the offer the jeweler had made for the piece of glass.

"But why would they offer fifty dollars for a worthless piece of glass?" the miller wondered aloud. Before his wife could answer they were interrupted by the jeweler's wife.

"What do you say, neighbor, will you take fifty dollars for the glass?" she asked.

"No, that's not enough," the miller said cautiously. "Offer more."

"I'll give you fifty thousand!" the jeweler's wife blurted out.

"A little bit more," the miller replied.

"Impossible!" the jeweler's wife cried, "I can't offer any more without consulting my husband." She ran off to tell her husband how the bartering[4] was going, and he told her he was prepared to pay a hundred thousand dollars to acquire the diamond.

He handed her seventy-five thousand dollars and said, "Take this and tell him that tomorrow, as soon as I open my shop, he'll have the rest."

When the miller heard the offer and saw the money he couldn't believe his eyes. He imagined the jeweler's wife was jesting with him, but it was a true offer and

---

4. **Bartering** is trading goods for other goods without using money.

Vocabulary
jest (jest) v. to speak or act in a playful manner; joke

he received the hundred thousand dollars for the diamond. The miller had never seen so much money, but he still didn't quite trust the jeweler.

"I don't know about this money," he confided to his wife. "Maybe the jeweler plans to accuse us of robbing him and thus get it back."

"Oh no," his wife assured him, "the money is ours. We sold the diamond fair and square—we didn't rob anyone."

"I think I'll still go to work tomorrow," the miller said. "Who knows, something might happen and the money will disappear, then we would be without money and work. Then how would we live?"

So he went to work the next day, and all day he thought about how he could use the money. When he returned home that afternoon his wife asked him what he had decided to do with their new fortune.

"I think I will start my own mill," he answered, "like the one I operate for my master. Once I set up my business we'll see how our luck changes."

The next day he set about buying everything he needed to establish his mill and to build a new home. Soon he had everything going.

Six months had passed, more or less, since he had seen the two men who had given him the four hundred dollars and the piece of lead. He was eager to see them again and to tell them how the piece of lead had changed his luck and made him wealthy.

Time passed and the miller prospered. His business grew and he even built a summer cottage where he could take his family on vacation. He had many employees who worked for him. One day while he was at his store he saw his two benefactors riding by. He rushed out into the street to greet them and ask them to come in. He was overjoyed to see them, and he was happy to see that they admired his store.

"Tell us the truth," the man who had given him the four hundred dollars said. "You used that money to set up this business."

The miller swore he hadn't, and he told them how he had given the piece of lead to his neighbor and how the fisherman had in return given him a fish with a very large diamond in its stomach. And he told them how he had sold the diamond.

"And that's how I acquired this business and many other things I want to show you," he said. "But it's time to eat. Let's eat first then I'll show you everything I have now."

The men agreed, but one of them still doubted the miller's story. So they ate and then the miller had three horses saddled and they rode out to see his summer home. The cabin was on the other side of the river where the mountains were cool and beautiful. When they arrived the men admired the place very much. It was such a peaceful place that they rode all afternoon through the forest. During their ride they came upon a tall pine tree.

"What is that on top of the tree?" one of them asked.

"That's the nest of a hawk," the miller replied.

"I have never seen one; I would like to take a closer look at it!"

"Of course," the miller said, and he ordered a servant to climb the tree and bring down the nest so his friend could see how it was built. When the hawk's nest was on the ground they examined it carefully.

The Force of Luck

They noticed that there was a cloth bag at the bottom of the nest. When the miller saw the bag he immediately knew that it was the very same bag he had lost to the hawk which fought him for the piece of meat years ago.

"You won't believe me, friends, but this is the very same bag in which I put the first two hundred dollars you gave me," he told them.

"If it's the same bag," the man who had doubted him said, "then the money you said the hawk took should be there."

"No doubt about that," the miller said. "Let's see what we find."

The three of them examined the old, weatherbeaten bag. Although it was full of holes and crumbling, when they tore it apart they found the money intact. The two men remembered what the miller had told them and they agreed he was an honest and honorable man. Still, the man who had given him the money wasn't satisfied. He wondered what had really happened to the second two hundred he had given the miller.

They spent the rest of the day riding in the mountains and returned very late to the house.

As he unsaddled their horses, the servant in charge of grooming and feeding the horses suddenly realized that he had no grain for them. He ran to the barn and checked, but there was no grain for the hungry horses. So he ran to the neighbor's granary and there he was able to buy a large clay jar of bran. He carried the jar home and emptied the bran into a bucket to wet it before he fed it to the horses. When he got to the bottom of the jar he noticed a large lump which turned out to be a rag covered package. He examined it and felt something inside. He immediately went to give it to his master who had been eating dinner.

"Master," he said, "look at this package which I found in an earthenware jar of grain which I just bought from our neighbor!"

The three men carefully unraveled the cloth and found the other one hundred and ninety dollars which the miller had told them he had lost. That is how the miller proved to his friends that he was truly an honest man.

And they had to decide for themselves whether it had been luck or money which had made the miller a wealthy man!

❖

Eagle (Aquila), (detail). Diego Rivera (1886–1957). Overdoor mural, fresco. Secretaria de Education Publica, Mexico City.

Vocabulary
intact (in takt') *adj.* undamaged and whole

Responding to Literature

PERSONAL RESPONSE

◆ Look back at the **Reading Focus** on page 590. Did your ideas about hard work and luck change as you read the story? How?

Analyzing Literature

RECALL AND INTERPRET

1. What are the two wealthy men trying to prove? Is the miller a good test case for the men's theories? Explain your answers.
2. How does the miller lose his first and second gifts of two hundred dollars? Is his response to these events believable?
3. How does the miller's luck change? Why do the two benefactors assume he used their money to start his business?

EVALUATE AND CONNECT

4. Compare the responses of the miller and his wife to losing the first amount of money. Why does the storyteller include both responses?
5. What do you think you would do if you suddenly had an extra two hundred dollars to spend?
6. Theme Connection   Reread the last line of the story. What is your opinion about the source of the twists and turns in the miller's fortunes?

LITERARY ELEMENTS

Folktales

Folktales, the world's most popular stories, have no known original authors. These stories have been passed down from person to person, generation to generation by word of mouth. Often folktales are told to reinforce the traditions and values of the culture that preserves them. The characters in folktales can be animals, people who have extraordinary powers, or ordinary people who have unusual or seemingly impossible experiences.

1. What values do you think the miller's story reinforces?
2. List two things that happen to the miller that would not occur in a more realistic story.

● See **Literary Terms Handbook,** p. R4.

Extending Your Response

Literature Groups

Plot   With a group, create a chart that shows each twist and turn of the plot. Then color code each event according to whether you think it was caused by good luck, bad luck, plenty of money, or not enough money. Present your chart to the other groups.

Writing About Literature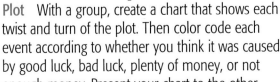

Monologues   Write two monologues for the miller. First, create a speech in which he describes his life at the beginning of the story. Then write a speech in which he explains how his life has changed since he opened his own mill. Perform your monologues for your group.

COMPARING SELECTIONS

The Million-Pound Bank Note **and** The Force of Luck

COMPARE **GENRES**

"The Million-Pound Bank Note" is a dramatization of Twain's original story in the form of a radio play. "The Force of Luck" is a folktale. Both genres can be appreciated by either listening to the words or speaking them aloud. Working with a group, rewrite "The Force of Luck" as a radio play and shorten "The Million-Pound Bank Note" so that it can be told by a storyteller using just a few notes. Then present each new version to the class.

COMPARE **CHARACTERS AND PLOTS**

The plots of "The Million-Pound Bank Note" and "The Force of Luck" are similar in a number of ways. Both stories are about two men who decide to test a third person by giving him money.

1. What do the two men in "The Million-Pound Bank Note" and the two men in "The Force of Luck" have in common? How do the pairs differ?

2. What is the first thing Henry and the miller do with their gifts of money? What do their actions tell you about the state of their lives at the time?

3. What do you think would have happened to the miller if he had a million-pound bank note to cash? What do you think would have happened to Henry Adams if he had lost his bank note?

Indeed! (detail).

COMPARE **IDEAS**

Henry Adams and the miller both prove to be good, honest persons. Imagine that Henry and the miller became very rich. How do you think each might choose to give back to his community? What causes might they support? For each man, write a plan outlining his charity donations. Have each man's plan reflect the setting of the story as well as his previous experience.

Money Matters

Historically, paper money is a fairly recent development. At first, people traded or bartered for the things they wanted. Eventually, people needed a neutral item to trade, something they could use to buy anything, at any time. Shells were one of the early forms of money. They were used by both ancient Chinese people and Native Americans. In ancient Mexico, cacao beans served as money. In some parts of Africa, people exchanged salt. In the Caroline Islands of the western Pacific, people once traded giant stone rings.

Most of these early kinds of money wore out quickly or were awkward to carry. In what is now known as Turkey, people made the first coins. The idea spread to other places, and coins of gold or silver remained the most widely accepted form of money for centuries.

Eventually banks and governments issued "notes" and paper money. Paper money had the advantage of being easy to carry from place to place. However, whether money takes the form of shells, paper, or feathers, it all stands for the same thing—a symbol of value that you're willing to exchange for something else of value.

ACTIVITY

When Mark Twain's "The Million-Pound Bank Note" was published in 1893, a million British pounds was worth about $4,850,000 in U.S. currency.

1. Use a local bank, the travel section of a major newspaper, or the Internet to find out how much a million British pounds is worth in U.S. dollars today.

2. Using one of the same sources, find the exchange rate for at least two other countries listed at the right.

The United States, Canada, Australia, New Zealand, Zimbabwe, and more than a dozen other countries each have their own kind of dollar as a unit of exchange. Here are the units of exchange used by some other countries.

Brazil	cruzeiro
China	yuan
France	franc
Germany	mark
Great Britain	pound
Greece	drachma
Japan	yen
Mexico	peso
Russia	ruble
South Africa	rand

Before You Read

Beware of the Dog

MEET ROALD DAHL

British author Roald Dahl (rōō äl′ dol′) is best known for his children's fiction. Dahl's stories and books—such as *James and the Giant Peach* and *Matilda*—are modern classics, loved by children throughout the world. About writing for children, Dahl said, "Children are a great discipline because they are highly critical. And they lose interest so quickly. You have to keep things ticking along. And if you think a child is getting bored, you must think up something that jolts it back. Something that tickles. You have to know what children like."

Roald Dahl was born in South Wales in 1916 and died in 1990.

READING FOCUS

How would you feel if you woke up in an unfamiliar place?

Think/Pair/Share
Take a moment to jot down your thoughts and feelings about the question. Then share your ideas with a partner.

Setting a Purpose
The title of this story refers to something the main character discovers. Read the story to find out what it means.

BUILDING BACKGROUND

The Time and Place   The story takes place in Europe during World War II, in the early 1940s. The British were at war with Germany, and German troops occupied France.

Did You Know?   The following story is fiction, but Roald Dahl's wartime experiences gave him plenty of background information for his story's plot. In 1939, at the beginning of World War II, Dahl joined the British Royal Air Force and was trained as a fighter pilot. His plane was brought down by enemy fire over Egypt, and Dahl crawled from the wreckage as the plane exploded. It took him six months to recuperate from his injuries.

A British fighter pilot of the early 1940s.

VOCABULARY PREVIEW

undulating (un′ jə lāt′ ing) *adj.* moving in waves; rippling; p. 603

giddy (gid′ dē) *adj.* dizzy or light-headed; p. 604

precise (pri sīs′) *adj.* strictly accurate or clearly defined; exact; p. 604

intellectual (int′ əl ek′ chōō əl) *adj.* appealing to or involving mental ability; p. 608

intense (in tens′) *adj.* of a very high degree; very strong; p. 610

BEWARE OF THE DOG

Roald Dahl

Down below there was only a vast white undulating sea of cloud. Above there was the sun, and the sun was white like the clouds, because it is never yellow when one looks at it from high in the air.

He was still flying the Spitfire. His right hand was on the stick and he was working the rudder-bar[1] with his left leg alone. It was quite easy. The machine was flying well. He knew what he was doing.

Everything is fine, he thought. I'm doing all right. I'm doing nicely. I know my way home. I'll be there in half an hour. When I land I shall taxi in and switch off my engine and I shall say, help me to get out, will you. I shall make my voice sound ordinary and natural and none of them will take any notice. Then I shall say, someone help me to get out. I can't do it alone because I've lost one of my legs. They'll all laugh and think that I'm joking and I shall say, all right, come and have a look. Then Yorky will climb up onto the wing and look inside. He'll probably be sick because of all the blood and the mess. I shall laugh and say, for God's sake, help me get out.

---

1. The *Spitfire* was a British fighter plane used during World War II. Its *rudder-bar* controlled the movement of the tail rudder, which turned the plane left or right.

Vocabulary
undulating (un′ jə lāt′ ing) *adj.* moving in waves; rippling

He glanced down again at his right leg. There was not much of it left. The cannon-shell had taken him on the thigh, just above the knee, and now there was nothing but a great mess and a lot of blood. But there was no pain.

He really felt fine, and because he still felt fine, he felt excited and unafraid.

Then he saw the sun shining on the engine cowling[2] of his machine. He saw the sun shining on the rivets in the metal, and he remembered the airplane and he remembered where he was. He realized that he was no longer feeling good; that he was sick and giddy. His head kept falling forward onto his chest because his neck seemed no longer to have any strength. But he knew that he was flying the Spitfire. He could feel the handle of the stick between the fingers of his right hand.

I'm going to pass out, he thought. Any moment now I'm going to pass out.

He looked at his altimeter. Twenty-one thousand. To test himself he tried to read the hundreds as well as the thousands. Twenty-one thousand and what? As he looked the dial became blurred and he could not even see the needle. He knew then that he must bail out; that there was not a second to lose, otherwise he would become unconscious. Quickly, frantically, he tried to slide back the hood with his left hand, but he had not the strength. For a second he took his right hand off the stick and with both hands he managed to push the hood back. The rush of cold air

on his face seemed to help. He had a moment of great clearness. His actions became orderly and precise. That is what happens with a good pilot. He took some quick deep breaths from his oxygen mask, and as he did so, he looked out over the side of the cockpit. Down below there was only a vast white sea of cloud and he realized that he did not know where he was.

It'll be the Channel, he thought. I'm sure to fall in the drink.[3]

He throttled back,[4] pulled off his helmet, undid his straps, and pushed the stick hard over to the left. The Spitfire dripped its port wing and turned smoothly over onto its back. The pilot fell out.

As he fell, he opened his eyes, because he knew that he must not pass out before he had pulled the cord. On one side he saw the sun; on the other he saw the whiteness of the clouds, and as he fell, as he somersaulted in the air, the white clouds chased the sun and the sun chased the clouds. They chased each other in a small circle; they ran faster and faster and there was the sun and the clouds and the clouds and the sun and the clouds came nearer until suddenly there was no longer any sun but only a great whiteness. The whole world was white and there was nothing in it. It was so white that sometimes it looked black, and after a time it was either white or black, but mostly it was white. He watched it as it turned from white

---

2. A *cowling* is a streamlined covering for the engine or another section of an airplane.

3. The *Channel* is the English Channel, a narrow part of the ocean, which separates the British Isles from France. To *fall in the drink* means to fall into the water.

4. When he *throttled back,* he "took his foot off the gas," so that the plane would slow down. The *throttle* is a valve that controls the supply of fuel to an engine.

Vocabulary
giddy (gid′ dē) *adj.* dizzy or light-headed
precise (pri sīs′) *adj.* strictly accurate or clearly defined; exact

to black, then back to white again, and the white stayed for a long time, but the black lasted only for a few seconds. He got into the habit of going to sleep during the white periods, of waking up just in time to see the world when it was black. The black was very quick. Sometimes it was only a flash, a flash of black lightning. The white was slow and in the slowness if it, he always dozed off.

One day, when it was white, he put out a hand and he touched something. He took it between his fingers and crumpled it. For a time he lay there, idly letting the tips of his fingers play with the thing which they had touched. Then slowly he opened his eyes, looked down at his hand and saw that he was holding something which was white. It was the edge of a sheet. He knew it was a sheet because he could see the texture of the material and the stitchings on the hem. He screwed up his eyes and opened them again quickly. This time he saw the room. He saw the bed in which he was lying, he saw the gray walls and the door and the green curtains over the window. There were some roses on the table by his bed.

Then he saw the basin on the table near the roses. It was a white enamel basin and beside it there was a small medicine glass.

This is a hospital, he thought. I am in a hospital. But he could remember nothing. He lay back on his pillow, looking at the ceiling and wondering what had happened. He was gazing at the smooth grayness of the ceiling which was so clean and gray, and then suddenly he saw a fly walking upon it. The sight of this fly, the suddenness of seeing this small black speck on a sea of gray, brushed the surface of his brain, and quickly, in that second, he remembered everything. He remembered the Spitfire,

and he remembered the altimeter showing twenty-one thousand feet. He remembered the pushing back of the hood with both hands and he remembered the bailing out. He remembered his leg.

It seemed all right now. He looked down at the end of the bed, but he could not tell. He put one hand underneath the bedclothes and felt for his knees. He found one of them, but when he felt for the other, his hand touched something which was soft and covered in bandages.

Just then the door opened and a nurse came in.

"Hello," she said. "So you've waked up at last."

She was not good-looking, but she was large and clean. She was between thirty and forty and she had fair hair. More than that he did not notice.

"Where am I?"

"You're a lucky fellow. You landed in a wood near the beach. You're in Brighton.[5] They brought you in two days ago, and now you're all fixed up. You look fine."

"I've lost a leg," he said.

"That's nothing. We'll get you another one. Now you must go to sleep. The doctor will be coming to see you in about an hour." She picked up the basin and the medicine glass and went out.

But he did not sleep. He wanted to keep his eyes open because he was frightened that if he shut them again everything would go away. He lay looking at the ceiling. The fly was still there. It was very energetic. It would run forward very fast for a few inches, then it would stop. Then it would run forward again, stop, run forward, stop, and every now and then it

---

5. *Brighton* is a seaside city in southeastern England.

would take off and buzz around viciously in small circles. It always landed back in the same place on the ceiling and started running and stopping all over again. He watched it for so long that after a while it was no longer a fly, but only a black speck upon a sea of gray, and he was still watching it when the nurse opened the door, and stood aside while the doctor came in. He was an Army doctor, a major, and he had some last war ribbons on his chest. He was bald and small, but he had a cheerful face and kind eyes.

"Well, well," he said. "So you've decided to wake up at last. How are you feeling?"

"I feel all right."

"That's the stuff. You'll be up and about in no time."

The doctor took his wrist to feel his pulse.

"By the way," he said, "some of the lads from your squadron[6] were ringing up and asking about you. They wanted to come along and see you, but I said that they'd better wait a day or two. Told them you were all right and that they could come and see you a little later on. Just lie quiet and take it easy for a bit. Got something to read?" He glanced at the table with the roses. "No. Well, nurse will look after you. She'll get you anything you want." With that he waved his hand and went out, followed by the large clean nurse.

When they had gone, he lay back and looked at the ceiling again. The fly was still there and as he lay watching it, he heard the noise of an airplane in the distance. He lay listening to the sound of its engines. It was a long way away. I wonder what it is,

he thought. Let me see if I can place it. Suddenly he jerked his head sharply to one side. Anyone who has been bombed can tell the noise of a Junkers 88. They can tell most other German bombers for that matter, but especially a Junkers 88. The engines seem to sing a duet. There is a deep vibrating bass voice and with it there is a high pitched tenor. It is the singing of the tenor which makes the sound of a JU-88 something which one cannot mistake.

He lay listening to the noise and he felt quite certain about what it was. But where were the sirens and where were the guns? That German pilot certainly had a nerve coming near Brighton alone in daylight.

The aircraft was always far away and soon the noise faded away into the distance. Later on there was another. This one, too, was far away, but there was the same deep undulating bass and the high singing tenor and there was no mistaking it. He had heard that noise every day during the Battle.[7]

He was puzzled. There was a bell on the table by the bed. He reached out his hand and rang it. He heard the noise of footsteps down the corridor. The nurse came in.

"Nurse, what were those airplanes?"

"I'm sure I don't know. I didn't hear them. Probably fighters or bombers. I expect they were returning from France. Why, what's the matter?"

"They were JU-88's. I'm sure they were JU-88's. I know the sound of the engines. There were two of them. What were they doing over here?"

The nurse came up to the side of his bed and began to straighten out the sheets and tuck them in under the mattress.

---

6. An air force *squadron* is a group of planes that fly into combat together.

7. The *Battle* refers to the Battle of Britain, a series of air battles over Great Britain from June 1940 to April 1941.

Bundles of Lictors Are Flying over England: Italian and German Bomber Wing in Operation, 1940. Hans Liska. Gouache. Berlin.

Viewing the painting: Imagine yourself as a pilot who had to fight against squadrons of enemy planes like these day after day. How would you feel?

Once toward evening he heard the noise of another aircraft. It was far away, but even so he knew that it was a single-engined machine. It was going fast; he could tell that. He could not place it. It wasn't a Spit, and it wasn't a Hurricane. It did not sound like an American engine either. They make more noise. He did not know what it was, and it worried him greatly. Perhaps I am very ill, he thought. Perhaps I am imagining things. Perhaps I am a little delirious.[9] I simply do not know what to think.

That evening the nurse came in with a basin of hot water and began to wash him.

"Well," she said, "I hope you don't still think that we're being bombed."

She had taken off his pajama top and was soaping his right arm with a flannel. He did not answer.

She rinsed the flannel in the water, rubbed more soap on it, and began to wash his chest.

"You're looking fine this evening," she said. "They operated on you as soon as you came in. They did a marvelous job. You'll be all right. I've got a brother in the R.A.F.,"[10] she added. "Flying bombers."

"Gracious me, what things you imagine. You mustn't worry about a thing like that. Would you like me to get you something to read?"

"No, thank you."

She patted his pillow and brushed back the hair from his forehead with her hand.

"They never come over in daylight any longer. You know that. They were probably Lancasters or Flying Fortresses."[8]

8. *Lancasters* were British bomber planes. American B-17 bombers were called *Flying Fortresses* because of their heavy armor and many guns.

9. The *Hurricane* was another type of British fighter plane. The pilot thinks he may be in a temporary state of confusion (*delirious*), which can result from a high fever.

10. *R.A.F.* stands for Royal Air Force.

He said, "I went to school in Brighton."

She looked up quickly. "Well, that's fine," she said. "I expect you'll know some people in the town."

"Yes," he said, "I know quite a few."

She had finished washing his chest and arms. Now she turned back the bedclothes so that his left leg was uncovered. She did it in such a way that his bandaged stump remained under the sheets. She began to wash his left leg and the rest of his body. This was the first time he had had a bed-bath and he was embarrassed. She laid a towel under his leg and began washing his foot with the flannel. She said, "This wretched soap won't lather at all. It's the water. It's as hard as nails."[11]

He said, "None of the soap is very good now and, of course, with hard water it's hopeless." As he said it he remembered something. He remembered the baths which he used to take at school in Brighton, in the long stone-floored bathroom which had four baths in a room. He remembered how the water was so soft that you had to take a shower afterwards to get all the soap off your body, and he remembered how the foam used to float on the surface of the water, so that you could not see your legs underneath. He remembered that sometimes they were given calcium tablets because the school doctor used to say that soft water was bad for the teeth.

"In Brighton," he said, "the water isn't . . ."

He did not finish the sentence. Something had occurred to him; something so fantastic and absurd that for a moment he felt like telling the nurse about it and having a good laugh.

She looked up. "The water isn't what?" she said.

"Nothing," he answered. "I was dreaming."

She rinsed the flannel in the basin, wiped the soap off his leg and dried him with a towel.

"It's nice to be washed," he said. "I feel better." He was feeling his face with his hand. "I need a shave."

"We'll do that tomorrow," she said. "Perhaps you can do it yourself then."

That night he could not sleep. He lay awake thinking of the Junkers 88's and of the hardness of the water. He could think of nothing else. They *were* JU-88's, he said to himself. I know they were. And yet it is not possible, because they would not be flying around so low over here in broad daylight. I know that it is true and yet I know that it is impossible. Perhaps I am ill. Perhaps I am behaving like a fool and do not know what I am doing or saying. Perhaps I am delirious. For a long time he lay awake thinking these things, and once he sat up in bed and said aloud, "I will prove that I am not crazy. I will make a little speech about something complicated and intellectual. I will talk about what to do with Germany after the war." But before he had time to begin, he was asleep.

He woke just as the first light of day was showing through the slit in the curtains over the window. The room was still

----

11. *Hard as nails* refers to hard water, which contains minerals that prevent soap from dissolving easily.

Vocabulary

intellectual (int′ əl ek′ chōō əl) *adj.* appealing to or involving mental ability

German Junker 88

dark, but he could tell that it was already beginning to get light outside. He lay looking at the gray light which was showing through the slit in the curtain and as he lay there he remembered the day before. He remembered the Junkers 88's and the hardness of the water; he remembered the large pleasant nurse and the kind doctor, and now a small grain of doubt took root in his mind and it began to grow.

He looked around the room. The nurse had taken the roses out the night before. There was nothing except the table. The room was bare. It was no longer warm or friendly. It was not even comfortable. It was cold and empty and very quiet.

Slowly the grain of doubt grew, and with it came fear, a light, dancing fear that warned but did not frighten; the kind of fear that one gets not because one is afraid, but because one feels that there is something wrong. Quickly the doubt and the fear grew so that he became restless and angry, and when he touched his forehead with his hand, he found that it was damp with sweat. He knew then that he must do something; that he must find some way of proving to himself that he was either right or wrong, and he looked up and saw again the window and the green curtains. From where he lay, that window was right in front of him, but it was fully ten yards away. Somehow he must reach it and look out. The idea became an obsession with him and soon he could think

of nothing except the window. But what about his leg? He put his hand underneath the bedclothes and felt the thick bandaged stump which was all that was left on the right hand side. It seemed all right. It didn't hurt. But it would not be easy.

He sat up. Then he pushed the bedclothes aside and put his left leg on the floor. Slowly, carefully, he swung his body over until he had both hands on the floor as well; then he was out of bed, kneeling on the carpet. He looked at the stump. It was very short and thick, covered with bandages. It was beginning to hurt and he could feel it throbbing. He wanted to collapse, lie down on the carpet and do nothing but he knew that he must go on.

With two arms and one leg, he crawled over toward the window. He would reach forward as far as he could with his arms, then he would give a little jump and slide his left leg along after them. Each time he did it, it jarred his wound so that he gave a soft grunt of pain, but he continued to crawl across the floor on two hands and one knee. When he got to the window he reached up, and one at a time he placed both hands on the sill. Slowly he raised himself up until he was standing on his left leg. Then quickly he pushed aside the curtains and looked out.

He saw a small house with a gray tiled roof standing alone beside a narrow lane, and immediately behind it there was a plowed field. In front of the house there was an untidy garden, and there was a green hedge separating the garden from the lane. He was looking at the hedge when he saw the sign. It was just a piece of board nailed to the top of a short pole, and because the hedge had not been trimmed for a long time, the branches had grown out around the sign so that it seemed almost as though it had been placed in the middle of the hedge. There was something written on the board with white paint. He pressed his head against the glass of the window, trying to read what it said. The first letter was a G, he could see that. The second was an A, and the third was an R. One after another he managed to see what the letters were. There were three words, and slowly he spelled the letters out aloud to himself as he managed to read them. G–A–R–D–E A–U C–H–I–E–N. *Garde au chien*. That is what it said.

Did You Know?
Along a hedge near a house in France, the words *garde au chien* (gard ō shyen) would warn visitors to "beware of the dog."

He stood there balancing on one leg and holding tightly to the edges of the window sill with his hands, staring at the sign and at the white-washed lettering of the words. For a moment he could think of nothing at all. He stood there looking at the sign, repeating the words over and over to himself. Slowly he began to realize the full meaning of the thing. He looked up at the cottage and at the plowed field. He looked at the small orchard on the left of the cottage and he looked at the green countryside beyond. "So this is France," he said. "I am in France."

Now the throbbing in his right thigh was very great. It felt as though someone was pounding the end of his stump with a hammer and suddenly the pain became so intense that it affected his head. For a moment he thought he was going to fall. Quickly he knelt down again, crawled back to the bed and hoisted himself in. He pulled the bedclothes over himself and lay back on the pillow, exhausted. He could still think of nothing at all except the small sign by the hedge and the plowed field and the orchard. It was the words on the sign that he could not forget.

It was some time before the nurse came in. She came carrying a basin of hot water and she said, "Good morning, how are you today?"

He said, "Good morning, nurse."

The pain was still great under the bandages, but he did not wish to tell this woman anything. He looked at her as she busied herself with getting the washing things ready. He looked at her more carefully now. Her hair was very fair. She was tall and big-boned and her face seemed pleasant. But there was something a little uneasy about her eyes. They were never still. They never looked at anything for more than a moment and they moved too quickly from one place to another in the room. There was something about her movements also. They were too sharp and nervous to go well with the casual manner in which she spoke.

Vocabulary
intense (in tens′) *adj.* of a very high degree; very strong

She set down the basin, took off his pajama top and began to wash him.

"Did you sleep well?"

"Yes."

"Good," she said. She was washing his arms and his chest.

"I believe there's someone coming down to see you from the Air Ministry after breakfast," she went on. "They want a report or something. I expect you know all about it. How you got shot down and all that. I won't let him stay long, so don't worry."

He did not answer. She finished washing him and gave him a toothbrush and some toothpowder. He brushed his teeth, rinsed his mouth and spat the water out into the basin.

Later she brought him his breakfast on a tray, but he did not want to eat. He was still feeling weak and sick and he wished only to lie still and think about what had happened. And there was a sentence running through his head. It was a sentence which Johnny, the Intelligence Officer of his squadron, always repeated to the pilots every day before they went out. He could see Johnny now, leaning against the wall of the dispersal hut[12] with his pipe in his hand, saying,

---

12. An *Intelligence Officer* gathers and studies information about the enemy. He informs the R.A.F. pilots of enemy activities that would affect their missions and trains them to safeguard information from the enemy. The pilots get their flight instructions in the *dispersal hut*.

Trees Near Douarnenez. Jules Eugene Pages (1867–1946). Oil on canvas, 21¼ x 25¾ in. Private collection.

Viewing the painting: This could be the scene the British pilot saw from his window. Why do you suppose he was sent to a place like this?

La Grande Famille, 1947. René Magritte. Oil on canvas, 100 x 81 cm. Copyright ARS, New York. Private collection.

Viewing the painting: What does this painting say to you? How would you connect it with the story?

"And if they get you, don't forget, just your name, rank, and number. Nothing else. For God's sake, say nothing else."

"There you are," she said as she put the tray on his lap. "I've got you an egg. Can you manage all right?"

"Yes."

She stood beside the bed. "Are you feeling all right?"

"Yes."

"Good. If you want another egg I might be able to get you one."

"This is all right."

"Well, just ring the bell if you want any more." And she went out.

He had just finished eating, when the nurse came in again.

She said, "Wing Commander Roberts is here. I've told him that he can only stay for a few minutes."

She beckoned with her hand and the Wing Commander came in.

"Sorry to bother you like this," he said.

He was an ordinary R.A.F. officer, dressed in a uniform which was a little shabby. He wore wings and a D.F.C.[13] He was fairly tall and thin with plenty of black hair. His teeth, which were irregular and widely spaced, stuck out a little even when he closed his mouth. As he spoke he took a printed form and pencil from his pocket and he pulled up a chair and sat down.

"How are you feeling?"

There was no answer.

"Tough luck about your leg. I know how you feel. I hear you put up a fine show before they got you."

The man in the bed was lying quite still, watching the man in the chair.

The man in the chair said, "Well, let's get this stuff over. I'm afraid you'll have to answer a few questions so that I can fill in this combat report. Let me see now, first of all, what was your squadron?"

The man in the bed did not move. He looked straight at the Wing Commander and he said, "My name is Peter Williamson. My rank is Squadron Leader, and my number is nine seven two four five seven."

---

13. An R.A.F. pilot would wear a small badge shaped like flying *wings.* The *D.F.C.,* or *Distinguished Flying Cross,* was a medal awarded for heroism.

Responding to Literature

PERSONAL RESPONSE

◆ What was your reaction to this story? Did you find this story suspenseful, mysterious, both? How does the story relate to your response to the **Reading Focus** on page 602? Describe your impressions in your journal.

Analyzing Literature

RECALL

1. Briefly describe the main character in the story. Who is he and what is he doing as the story opens?
2. Where does the pilot end up? What are his injuries?
3. Describe the things that make the pilot become suspicious about his location. What does he decide to do to test his suspicions?

INTERPRET

4. What is the importance of the French phrase *garde au chien?*
5. What sort of person is the pilot? How does he come to realize what has happened to him? Support your ideas with examples from the story.
6. How does the author inform you about the pilot's misfortune?
7. In describing the **setting** of the story, Dahl uses details that intensify the mood of suspense. Pick out details that help create this mood. (See **Literary Terms Handbook,** page R10.)
8. Why do you think Dahl named the story "Beware of the Dog"?

EVALUATE AND CONNECT

9. In the last paragraph of the story, why does the pilot respond the way he does to the wing commander? If you were the pilot, what would you have done?
10. At what point in the story did you begin to suspect that the pilot was not where the nurse said he was? How does Dahl build toward that suspicion?

LITERARY ELEMENTS

Flashback

A **flashback** is an interruption in the sequence of a piece of writing to describe a scene that happened at an earlier time. Skillful writers sometimes use flashbacks to give background information to readers so they can better understand what is happening at the present time.

For example, a character in a story may meet someone he or she knew years earlier. A flashback to that earlier time could tell the reader about the relationship between the two characters.

1. How is a flashback used in "Beware of the Dog"? Describe the scene that is presented in the flashback.

2. Sometimes a flashback can appear in the form of a dream. Why do you think Roald Dahl chose to begin the story the way he did?

● See **Literary Terms Handbook,** p. R4.

Literature and Writing

Writing About Literature

Suspense   **Suspense,** a state of uncertainty or fear about how something will turn out, is an essential element of this story. How does the writer build suspense? How does he raise questions in your mind about what will happen next? Write a brief analysis of how suspense is created in this story. Use examples from the story.

Personal Writing

An Epilogue   An **epilogue** is a passage added to the end of a written work. What do you think will happen to the pilot after the end of this story? Write a brief epilogue describing what happens to the pilot and why.

Extending Your Response

Interdisciplinary Activity

Social Studies: Map It!   With a partner or in a small group, research the role of British fighter pilots in World War II. Using your research and the information in the story, create a map that shows the possible route of the ill-fated flight, a possible point of origin, and where the pilot might have ended up in France.

Learning for Life

Interview a Vet   Imagine you are a journalist sent to interview the pilot after the end of the war. Write a list of the questions you would ask the pilot. Then work with a partner, taking turns as pilot and interviewer as you answer each other's questions.

Literature Groups

A Difficult Decision   The main character in this story faces a difficult decision. Once he realizes that he is in enemy hands, what should he do? What are his options? In small groups, discuss the pilot's situation, his options, and his decision. Support your ideas with examples and quotations from the story.

Reading Further

If you would like to read more Roald Dahl stories like this one, try

Over to You: Ten Stories of Flyers and Flying

Another book set at the time of World War II is

Good Night, Mr. Tom by Michelle Magorian

Save your work for your portfolio.

Skill Minilessons

GRAMMAR AND LANGUAGE • COMPLEX SENTENCES

A **complex sentence** is a sentence with one main clause and one or more subordinate clauses. In the following examples, the main clauses are in regular type, and the subordinate clauses are in *italic* type.

When he woke up, the pilot looked around.
The room had one light, *which was very dim.*
The pilot knew *that his options were limited.*

PRACTICE Write a paragraph describing the main character in "Beware of the Dog." Use at least three complex sentences in your description. Then trade paragraphs with a partner and read his or her paragraph. As you read, find the complex sentences and underline each main clause once and each subordinate clause twice.

● For more about complex sentences, see **Language Handbook,** p. R32.

READING AND THINKING • MONITORING COMPREHENSION

As a skillful reader, you should always ask questions about what you read and also evaluate the characters, actions, and events to make sure you understand what is happening. Remember to question and evaluate while you are reading—not just after you have finished. As you read, ask yourself questions such as these:
- Does this event make sense?
- What's really going on here?
- Would this character really say or do this?
- What is the writer describing? Why?

PRACTICE Review "Beware of the Dog." Write at least five questions about the characters, events, and setting of the story. Make them questions that require more than a simple yes or no for answers. Next, trade your questions with a partner. Answer each other's questions and then discuss your answers.

● For more about monitoring comprehension, see **Reading Handbook,** pp. R85–R97.

VOCABULARY • USING CONTEXT CLUES FOR MULTIPLE-MEANING WORDS

Some words have multiple meanings that are similar. In "Beware of the Dog," *giddy* means "dizzy or lightheaded." It describes the kind of whirling feeling a person gets after spinning around or from being very sick. *Giddy* can also mean "causing dizziness." It can also mean "not serious or steady; silly."

To know which definition of a multiple-meaning word is correct, look for context clues in the sentence or paragraph the word is in.

PRACTICE Use context clues to decide which meaning of *giddy* is the right one in each sentence.

a. dizzy or lightheaded   c. not serious, silly
b. causing dizziness

1. Lisa looked down from her *giddy* perch near the top of the tree.
2. I must have sounded foolish, giggling in such a *giddy* way.
3. Harry complained of feeling *giddy,* and then he fell backwards in a faint.
4. How can figure skaters spin as they do without becoming *giddy*?
5. The children could not calm down and listen; they were too *giddy* with excitement.

GENRE FOCUS

POETRY

Poetry is a form of writing that uses not only words, but also form, patterns of sound, imagery, and figurative language to convey its message. Any poem will include some or all of the elements described on these two pages.

● For more about the various elements of poetry, see **Literary Terms Handbook,** p. R8.

The Arch of Nero, 1846. Thomas Cole. Oil on canvas, 60 x 48 in. The Newark Museum, Newark, NJ.

ELEMENTS OF POETRY

FORM A poem's form is its appearance. Poems are divided into lines. Many poems, especially longer ones, may also be divided into groups of lines called **stanzas.** Stanzas function like paragraphs in a story. Each one contains a single idea or takes the idea one step further. The opening stanza of "The Highwayman," for example, sets the scene for the narrative poem.

IMAGERY Poets use words and phrases that appeal to the reader's senses of sight, sound, touch, taste, and smell. Notice in the model from "The Highwayman" how the poet uses words to help you "see" an angry man on horseback.

MODEL

The wind was a torrent of darkness
   among the gusty trees.
The moon was a ghostly galleon
   tossed upon cloudy seas.
The road was a ribbon of moonlight
   over the purple moor,
And the highwayman came riding—
      Riding—riding—
The highwayman came riding, up to
   the old inn door.

Back, he spurred like a madman,
   shouting curses to the sky,
With the white road smoking behind
   him and his rapier brandished high.

SOUND Some poems use techniques of sound such as the following.

- **Rhythm** is the pattern of beats or stresses in a poem. Poets use patterns of stressed and unstressed syllables to create a regular rhythm. In the model, the stressed syllables are printed in **bold** type. Try beating out the rhythm with a finger as you read these lines.

- **Rhyme** is the repetition of the same or similar sounds, usually in stressed syllables at the ends of lines, but sometimes within a line as well, as in this model.

- **Alliteration** is the repetition of consonant sounds at the beginnings of words. Read aloud the model example to hear its alliteration.

- **She** was a **child** and **I** was a **child**,
    In this **king**dom **by** the **sea:**
  But we **loved** with a **love** that was
    more than love—
      I and my **Ann**abel **Lee;**

- There are strange things **done** in the
    midnight **sun**
  By the men who moil for gold;

- Over the **c**obbles he **c**lattered and
    clashed . . .

FIGURES OF SPEECH Figures of speech are a special kind of imagery. They create pictures by making comparisons.

- A **simile** is a comparison using *like* or *as*.

- A **metaphor** describes one thing as if it *were* another.

- **Personification** gives human characteristics to something nonhuman.

- Talk of your cold! through the parka's
    fold it stabbed like a driven nail.
- The moon was a ghostly galleon
    tossed upon cloudy seas.
- ... and the stars o'erhead
    were dancing heel and toe . . .

In "The Highwayman," images create a picture of Tim. Which figures are used to describe his eyes and his hair?

His eyes were hollows of madness, his hair like
  mouldy hay,

THEME The **theme** of a poem is its central or main idea. To identify a poem's theme, ask yourself what ideas or insights about life or human nature you have found in the poem.

Active Reading Strategies

Tips for Reading Poetry

Poetry is a kind of imaginative writing in which thoughts and feelings are expressed in rhythmic, compressed language. Skillful readers use strategies that help them understand the meaning of a poem.

● For more about reading strategies, see **Reading Handbook,** pp. R73–R102.

PREVIEW

Before reading the poem, just stop to look at it. Think about its form.

Ask Yourself . . .

● How long is the poem? Is it broken into stanzas?

● Are the individual lines short or long?

● How does the poet use punctuation?

LISTEN

Read the poem aloud. Listen for patterns of rhythm and rhyme.

Ask Yourself . . .

● Does the poet use rhyme? What rhythm and rhyming patterns can I discover?

VISUALIZE

Look for the poet's use of imagery and figures of speech.

Ask Yourself . . .

● What images does the poem contain? Can I imagine what the poet describes?

QUESTION

Since poetry is such a compact form of literature, poets think very carefully about each word they use. As a skillful reader, you, too, should think about each word.

Ask Yourself . . .

● Why did the poet choose this particular word or phrase?

● Why does the poet use this image or comparison?

CONNECT

As you read, think about the theme of the poem. Discuss the poem with your classmates. There is no "right answer" when you read a poem.

Ask Yourself . . .

- How do the events and images in the poem connect to my own experience?

- What message is the poet trying to get across?

RESPOND

Think about whether feelings, events, or images from the poem remind you of something in your own life. Think about what the poem means to you.

Ask Yourself . . .

- Do I like the sound of the rhyme pattern?

- Is the poet's imagery appropriate for the poem's theme?

EVALUATE

Read the poem several times. As you read, think about your reactions to the poem. Evaluate what the poem has to say.

Ask Yourself . . .

- Who is the speaker? What does the speaker feel or think?

- Do I agree with the message of the poem?

APPLYING THE STRATEGIES

Read the following poem, "The Highwayman." Use the **Active Reading** notes in the margins as you read. Write your responses on a separate piece of paper or use stick-on notes.

Before You Read

The Highwayman

MEET ALFRED NOYES

Alfred Noyes was one of the most popular British poets of the early twentieth century. Because he became a successful poet while still in his twenties, Noyes was able to continue a career as a full-time poet. While many other British poets writing at that time were thoroughly modern in their writing styles, Noyes chose to write traditional poetry in the manner of the great nineteenth-century Romantic poets.

Alfred Noyes was born in England in 1880 and died in 1958.

READING FOCUS

Do you enjoy dramatic adventure stories?

Sharing Ideas
Think about adventure stories you have enjoyed reading or seeing as movies. Jot down the titles of a few favorites to share with your classmates.

Setting a Purpose
Read this poem to enjoy its story.

BUILDING BACKGROUND

By the eighteenth century, horse-drawn coaches traveled regularly on English roads. They were preyed upon by armed thieves on horseback called highwaymen, who would stop coaches at gunpoint and demand that the passengers surrender their money and other valuables. A few highwaymen, such as Dick Turpin, became legends in their time, inspiring songs, poems, and stories in the popular newspapers of the time—at least until they were caught and hanged for their crimes.

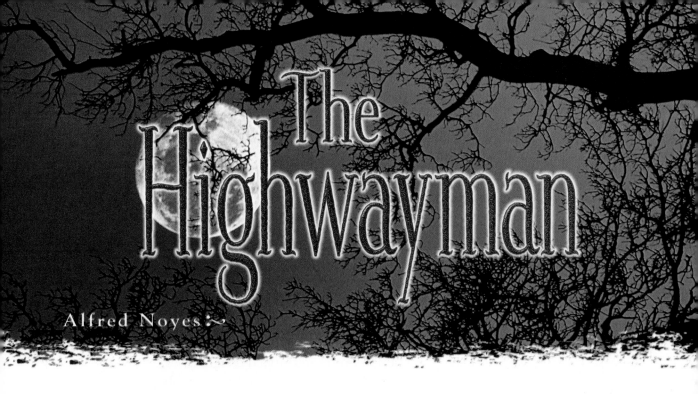

The Highwayman

Alfred Noyes

PART 1

The wind was a torrent of darkness among the gusty trees.
The moon was a ghostly galleon° tossed upon cloudy seas.
The road was a ribbon of moonlight over the purple moor,°
And the highwayman came riding—
5   Riding—riding—
The highwayman came riding, up to the old inn door.

He'd a French cocked hat on his forehead, a bunch of lace at his
    chin,
A coat of the claret velvet, and breeches of brown doeskin.
They fitted with never a wrinkle. His boots were up to the
    thigh.
10   And he rode with a jewelled twinkle,
            His pistol butts a-twinkle,
His rapier° hilt° a-twinkle, under the jewelled sky.

---

2 A *galleon* (gal′ yən) is a large sailing ship of the 1400s–1600s.
3 A *moor* is an area of open, rolling, wild land, usually a grassy wetland.
12 A *rapier* is a long, lightweight sword, and the *hilt* is its handle.

PREVIEW

Take a minute to think about the shape of this poem. How are the lines of the poem grouped? How many parts does it have?

VISUALIZE

How does this description help you "see" the highwayman?

Over the cobbles he clattered and clashed in the dark inn yard.
He tapped with his whip on the shutters, but all was locked and
barred.
15 He whistled a tune to the window, and who should be waiting
there
But the landlord's black-eyed daughter,
Bess, the landlord's daughter,
Plaiting° a dark red love-knot into her long black hair.

And dark in the dark old inn yard a stable wicket° creaked
20 Where Tim the ostler° listened. His face was white and peaked.°
His eyes were hollows of madness, his hair like mouldy hay,
But he loved the landlord's daughter,
The landlord's red-lipped daughter.
Dumb as a dog he listened, and he heard the robber say—

25 "One kiss, my bonny° sweetheart, I'm after a prize tonight,
But I shall be back with the yellow gold before the morning
light;
Yet, if they press me sharply, and harry° me through the day,
Then look for me by moonlight,
Watch for me by moonlight,
30 I'll come to thee by moonlight, though hell should bar the way."

He rose upright in the stirrups. He scarce could reach her hand,
But she loosened her hair in the casement.° His face burnt like a
brand°
As the black cascade of perfume came tumbling over his breast;
And he kissed its waves in the moonlight,
35   (O, sweet black waves in the moonlight!)
Then he tugged at his rein in the moonlight, and galloped away
to the west.

18 Bess is braiding (*plaiting*) a red ribbon into her hair.
19 A *wicket* is a small door or gate; this one leads into the stable.
20 As the *ostler* (a shorter form of *hostler*), it's Tim's job to take care of the horses at
the inn. A *peaked* face looks pale and sickly.
25 *Bonny* (a Scottish word) means "good-looking, fine, or admirable."
27 To *harry* is to trouble, bother, or worry.
32 The *casement* is the window frame, and the *brand* is a burning torch.

Moon Landing, 1977. Jamie Wyeth. Oil on canvas, 29 x 43 in. Private collection.

Viewing the painting: What lines of the poem might this painting illustrate?

PART 2

He did not come in the dawning. He did not come at noon;
And out of the tawny° sunset, before the rise of the moon,
When the road was a gypsy's ribbon, looping the purple moor,
40   A red coat troop° came marching—
            Marching—marching—
King George's men came marching, up to the old inn door.

They said no word to the landlord. They drank his ale instead,
But they gagged his daughter, and bound her, to the foot of her
    narrow bed.
45   Two of them knelt at her casement, with muskets at their side!
There was death at every window;
            And hell at one dark window;
For Bess could see, through her casement, the road that *he*
    would ride.

QUESTION

Why have the red-coats appeared?

LISTEN

Why does the poet repeat the word *marching?* Where else does he use repetition?

---

38 *Tawny* is a brownish-gold color.
40 The *red coat troop* is a group of soldiers wearing bright red coats.

ACTIVE
READING
MODEL

They had tied her up to attention, with many a sniggering jest.°
50 They had bound a musket beside her, with the muzzle beneath
 her breast!
"Now, keep good watch!" and they kissed her. She heard the
 doomed man say—
Look for me by moonlight;
 Watch for me by moonlight;
I'll come to thee by moonlight, though hell should bar the way!

55 She twisted her hands behind her; but all the knots held good!
She writhed° her hands till her fingers were wet with sweat or
 blood!
They stretched and strained in the darkness, and the hours
 crawled by like years,
Till, now, on the stroke of midnight,
 Cold, on the stroke of midnight,
60 The tip of one finger touched it! The trigger at last was hers!

The tip of one finger touched it. She strove no more for the rest.
Up, she stood up to attention, with the muzzle beneath her
 breast.
She would not risk their hearing; she would not strive again;
For the road lay bare in the moonlight;
65 Blank and bare in the moonlight;
And the blood of her veins, in the moonlight, throbbed to her
 love's refrain.°

Tlot-tlot; tlot-tlot! Had they heard it: The horsehoofs ringing
 clear;
Tlot-tlot, tlot-tlot, in the distance? Were they deaf that they did
 not hear?
Down the ribbon of moonlight, over the brow of the hill,
70 The highwayman came riding—
 Riding—riding—
The red-coats looked to their priming!° She stood up, straight
 and still!

VISUALIZE

How does the poet
help you visualize
this scene?

LISTEN

How does the poet
create the sound of
the highwayman on
horseback?

49 Bess is tied to a pole, arms at her sides in what a soldier would call "at attention,"
 while the soldiers laugh disrespectfully (*many a sniggering jest*).
56 To *writhe* is to twist and turn.
66 In a song or poem, the *refrain* is a phrase or verse that is repeated regularly.
72 The soldiers are *priming* their weapons, or loading their muskets with ammunition.

Tlot-tlot, in the frosty silence! *Tlot-tlot*, in the echoing night!
Nearer he came and nearer. Her face was like a light.

75 Her eyes grew wide for a moment; she drew one last deep breath,
Then her finger moved in the moonlight,
   Her musket shattered the moonlight,
Shattered her breast in the moonlight and warned him—with
 her death.

He turned. He spurred to the westward; he did not know who
 stood
80 Bowed, with her head o'er the musket, drenched with her own
 red blood!
Not till the dawn he heard it, and his face grew grey to hear
How Bess, the landlord's daughter,
   The landlord's black-eyed daughter,
Had watched for her love in the moonlight, and died in the
 darkness there.

85 Back, he spurred like a madman, shrieking a curse to the sky,
With the white road smoking behind him and his rapier
 brandished° high.
Blood-red were his spurs in the golden noon, wine-red was his
 velvet coat;
When they shot him down on the highway,
   Down like a dog on the highway,
90 And he lay in his blood on the highway, with a bunch of lace at
 his throat.

And still of a winter's night, they say, when the wind is in the trees,
When the moon is a ghostly galleon tossed upon cloudy seas,
When the road is a ribbon of moonlight over the purple moor,
A highwayman comes riding—
95   *Riding—riding—*
A highwayman comes riding, up to the old inn door.

Over the cobbles he clatters and clangs in the dark inn yard.
He taps with his whip on the shutters, but all is locked and barred.
He whistles a tune to the window, and who should be waiting there
100 *But the landlord's black-eyed daughter,*
   Bess, the landlord's daughter,
Plaiting a dark red love-knot into her long black hair.

---

86 The highwayman waved his sword threateningly *(brandished)*.

RESPOND

What mood does the poet create in this stanza?

QUESTION

What do you learn about the highwayman's character in this stanza?

RESPOND

What do these final stanzas mean to you?

ACTIVE READING MODEL

Responding to Literature

PERSONAL RESPONSE

◆ Take a look at your list from the **Reading Focus** on page 620. How does "The Highwayman" compare with your favorite adventure stories? Could it be made into a good action movie? Explain why or why not.

Active Reading Response

Review the strategies described in the **Active Reading Model** notes on pages 618–619. Choose one strategy and find three places in the poem where you could apply it.

Analyzing Literature

RECALL

1. What is the setting of this poem? Who are the main characters?
2. Summarize what happens in "The Highwayman."

INTERPRET

3. How does the poet create a mysterious mood in the opening stanza? How do the closing stanzas echo that same mood?
4. What is the central conflict in the plot of this poem? Use words and images from the poem to support your ideas.

EVALUATE AND CONNECT

5. What sacrifice does Bess make? Do you think her act is foolish or heroic? Why?
6. Why do you think the highwayman reacts as he does when he finds out what has happened to Bess? What does his action reveal about him?
7. How did the redcoats know that the highwayman would return to the inn? On what do you base your opinion?
8. How would the poem be different if it ended just before the final two stanzas?
9. Identify two examples of simile or metaphor the poet uses.
10. What effect does the poet's repetition of words create?

LITERARY ELEMENTS

Onomatopoeia

Onomatopoeia (on′ ə mat′ ə pē′ ə) is the use of words or phrases whose sounds suggest their meanings. The sound of the word *boom,* for example, suggests an explosion. The use of onomatopoeia begins as early as infancy. Often, some of the first words children learn are words such as *woof* or *meow.*

Onomatopoeia plays an important role in the sounds of poetry. In "The Highwayman," for example, *tlot-tlot* represents the sound of a horse's hooves.

1. What other examples of onomatopoeia can you find in "The Highwayman"?

2. Reread another poem from this book and pick out an example of onomatopoeia. Explain what you think the word or phrase adds to the meaning of the poem.

● See **Literary Terms Handbook,** p. R7.

Extending Your Response

Writing About Literature

Narrative Poetry   A **narrative poem** tells a story. In "The Highwayman," the poet creates a vivid story with a mysterious setting, strong characters, and a plot with twists and turns. Write a paragraph describing one of the narrative elements used in this poem—setting, character, or plot—as you picture the place, the person, or the series of actions.

Creative Writing

Character Interview   Imagine that you are to interview one of the characters in this poem. Write a series of questions to ask that character. With a partner, dramatize the interview for your classmates.

Literature Groups

Prose or Poetry?   The plot of this poem could have been written in **prose,** the language of ordinary writing and speech. Which version would you prefer? Why? Discuss what the poem's story would lose or gain if it were written in prose.

Performing

Choral Reading   With a small group, plan a choral reading of "The Highwayman." Group members can take turns reading parts of the poem. They can read other parts together as a chorus. Begin by planning how you will divide the parts. Then practice reading the poem a few times before presenting it to the class.

Reading Further

If you would like to read more narrative poems, here are a few suggestions. You can find these and other poems in poetry books or on the Internet.

"The Walrus and the Carpenter" by Lewis Carroll

"The Shooting of Dan McGrew" by Robert W. Service

"The Charge of the Light Brigade" by Alfred, Lord Tennyson

"Casey at the Bat" by Ernest Lawrence Thayer

📔 **Save your work for your portfolio.**

Skill Minilesson

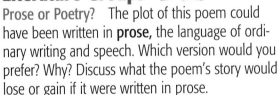

GRAMMAR AND LANGUAGE • COLORFUL ADJECTIVES

"The Highwayman" is filled with adjectives that help readers visualize the nouns described. For example, think about the opening lines:

*The wind was a torrent of darkness among the
    gusty trees.*
*The moon was a ghostly galleon tossed upon
    cloudy seas.*
*The road was a ribbon of moonlight over the
    purple moor,*

You can "see" the wind-blown trees, the fierce sea, and the dimly lit road winding through the dark moor because the poet has chosen adjectives to create vivid images.

PRACTICE   Reread the poem. As you do, list the adjectives that help you to visualize the images in the poem. In your journal, keep an ongoing list of colorful adjectives you find in your reading.

● For more about adjectives, see **Language Handbook,** p. R27.

Before You Read
Annabel Lee

MEET EDGAR ALLAN POE

Death played a large part in Edgar Allan Poe's life, his fiction, and his poetry. Poe is best known for his detective stories (a form of fiction he helped invent) and tales of horror and madness. He wished, however, to be remembered for his poetry. "Annabel Lee," one of the poet's best-loved poems, was published two days after his early death.

Edgar Allan Poe was born in 1809 and died in 1849.

READING FOCUS

Do you think that writing about a difficult experience can help you better deal with the experience?

Journal
Jot down your thoughts about whether writing can help you deal with difficult experiences.

Setting a Purpose
Read this poem to find out how the speaker responds to an unexpected experience.

BUILDING BACKGROUND

Did You Know?   Edgar Allan Poe lived a life as tragic as those he described in some of his famous horror tales. The one bright shining light in his life was his love for his young wife Virginia. It is believed that Poe wrote "Annabel Lee" after his beloved wife died tragically of tuberculosis, the same illness that had robbed him of his natural mother when he was only two years old. Later, his foster mother died of the same disease.

Virginia Poe

ANNABEL LEE

Edgar Allan Poe

A Rocky Coast, 1877. William Trost Richards. Watercolor and gouache on gray oatmeal wove paper, 22⅜₁₆ x 36 in. Metropolitan Museum of Art, New York.

It was many and many a year ago,
　　In a kingdom by the sea,
That a maiden there lived whom you may know
　　By the name of Annabel Lee;—
5　And this maiden she lived with no other thought
　　Than to love and be loved by me.

She was a child and *I* was a child,
　　In this kingdom by the sea,
But we loved with a love that was more than love—
10　　I and my Annabel Lee—
With a love that the wingéd seraphs° of Heaven
　　Coveted° her and me.

11–12 *Seraphs,* the highest-ranking angels, are said to burn with love for God. Even these angels were jealous of *(coveted)* a love as strong as that between the speaker and Annabel Lee.

And this was the reason that, long ago,
    In this kingdom by the sea,
15   A wind blew out of a cloud by night
    Chilling my Annabel Lee;
So that her high-born kinsmen came
    And bore her away from me,
To shut her up in a sepulcher°
20   In this kingdom by the sea.

The angels, not half so happy in Heaven,
    Went envying her and me;
Yes! that was the reason (as all men know,
    In this kingdom by the sea)
25   That the wind came out of the cloud, chilling
    And killing my Annabel Lee.

But our love it was stronger by far than the love
    Of those who were older than we—
    Of many far wiser than we—
30   And neither the angels in Heaven above
    Nor the demons down under the sea
Can ever dissever° my soul from the soul
    Of the beautiful Annabel Lee:—

For the moon never beams without bringing me dreams
35   Of the beautiful Annabel Lee;
And the stars never rise but I see the bright eyes
    Of the beautiful Annabel Lee;
And so, all the night-tide, I lie down by the side
Of my darling, my darling, my life and my bride
40   In her sepulcher there by the sea—
    In her tomb by the side of the sea.

---

19 A *sepulcher* (sep′ əl kər) is a tomb or burial place.
32 To *dissever* is to separate or split apart.

Responding to Literature

PERSONAL RESPONSE

◆ What are your thoughts about the relationship between the speaker and Annabel Lee?

Analyzing Literature

RECALL

1. What is the relationship between the poem's speaker and Annabel Lee?
2. Where is the speaker at the end of the poem?

INTERPRET

3. To be *idealized* means "to be made a model of perfection." Do you think the speaker of the poem has idealized Annabel Lee? Why or why not?

4. From whose point of view is this poem told? How does this point of view affect what the poem tells?

5. What are the basic themes of this poem?

Storm Light, 1995. Jane Wilson. Oil on linen, 80 x 74 in. Courtesy Fischbach Gallery, New York.

EVALUATE AND CONNECT

6. How does Poe use rhyme and repetition in the poem, and to what effect?

7. Give an example of **alliteration** in "Annabel Lee" and tell why you think Poe uses it in this poem. (See **Literary Terms Handbook,** page R1.)

8. Does this poem seem true to life? Why or why not?

9. Theme Connection   What unexpected event do the lovers in the poem face? How does the poem's speaker deal with it?

10. Think of a time when you lost something or someone you felt very strongly about. How did the experience affect you?

LITERARY ELEMENTS

Rhythm and Meter

Like a song, a poem has rhythm. In poetry, **rhythm** is the pattern of beats made by stressed and unstressed syllables. Some poems have a predictable rhythm, called **meter.** To find the meter of a poem, try scanning, or reading the poem to find the pattern of stressed (´) and unstressed (˘) syllables. For example:

Ĭt wăs mány ănd mány ă
     yéar ăgó,
Ĭn ă kíngdŏm bý thĕ séa,

When you read a poem, pay attention to the rhythm, but don't stress the beats so much that the poem sounds sing-song.

1. With a partner, practice reading aloud a stanza of "Annabel Lee." Then work together to copy the stanza and mark its pattern of stressed and unstressed syllables.

2. Choose another poem from this book and mark the rhythm pattern of a stanza or several lines.

● See **Literary Terms Handbook,** pp. R9 and R6.

Extending Your Response

Writing About Literature

Imagery   **Imagery** is the use of words that appeal to the senses. What kinds of images does the poet use in "Annabel Lee"? How do these images support the themes of the poem? Write a paragraph exploring these questions.

Literature Groups

Poet's Corner   Have you ever heard the expression, "It is better to have loved and lost than never to have loved at all"? What does it mean? Do you agree or disagree? How do you think the speaker in "Annabel Lee" would feel about the expression? In a small group, discuss the expression and how it relates to the poem.

Personal Writing

Facing the Unexpected   Review your notes from the **Reading Focus** on page 628. Then write a journal entry about a time when something difficult or unexpected happened to you or someone you know. Describe how you dealt with the situation.

Listening and Speaking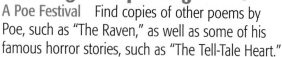

A Poe Festival   Find copies of other poems by Poe, such as "The Raven," as well as some of his famous horror stories, such as "The Tell-Tale Heart." Bring in appropriate background music to play as you take turns reading stories and poems aloud to one another.

Edgar Allan Poe, 1915. Charles Claude Buck. Pen and ink, ink wash, and charcoal on paper, 25.2 x 17.8 cm. National Museum of American Art, Smithsonian Institution, Washington, DC. Gift of Mrs. Claude Buck.

Reading Further

If you would like to read more by Edgar Allan Poe, try these books:

Great Tales and Poems of Edgar Allan Poe

Six Tales of Mystery and Imagination

📖 **Save your work for your portfolio.**

Skill Minilesson

GRAMMAR AND LANGUAGE   • ACTIVE AND PASSIVE VOICE

Verbs have two voices: active and passive. The active voice shows that the subject does something or is something. The passive voice refers to the subject that is acted upon. The active voice is usually preferred in most writing. It's less wordy, more direct, and has greater force than the passive.
Active: *Poe wrote "Annabel Lee."*
Passive: *"Annabel Lee" was written by Poe.*

PRACTICE   Change each passive sentence into the active voice.

1. "Annabel Lee" is praised by the critics.
2. The poem may have been inspired by the death of Poe's wife.
3. Poe's mother, his foster mother, and his wife were killed by tuberculosis.

Vo·cab·u·lar·y Skills

Multiple-Meaning Words

Most words have more than one meaning. The meanings may be different only in terms of what parts of speech they are. "I saw a *beam* of light" (noun) and "The moon never *beams* without bringing me dreams" (verb) both use meanings of *beam* that have to do with rays of light. The meanings also may be quite different. "I hit my head on a *beam*" uses a meaning that has nothing to do with light.

Sometimes one meaning of a word is familiar and another is not. A reader who assumes that the familiar meaning is the right one may misunderstand what he or she is reading. In "The Highwayman," Tim the ostler is described as "*dumb* as a dog." This doesn't mean that Tim (or a dog) is stupid. It means that Tim is silent. He says nothing, and his silence allows him to eavesdrop. The context of a sentence reveals what part of speech a word is and may also give clues to the meaning of the word.

EXERCISE

Look at the definition for each word. Then choose the sentence that uses a *different* meaning for the word.

1. catch: *to seize and hold; capture*
    a. I hope I <u>catch</u> my train.
    b. I hope the police <u>catch</u> the criminal.

2. safe: *free from harm.*
    a. She felt <u>safe</u> once she had locked the door behind her.
    b. She opened the <u>safe</u> and removed her diamond bracelet.

3. graze: *to feed on grass*
    a. The horse <u>grazed</u> all afternoon in the pasture.
    b. The horse just <u>grazed</u> me as he galloped past.

4. return: *a profit from an investment*
    a. I look forward to your <u>return</u> from school.
    b. I invested my savings and made a good <u>return</u>.

5. medium: *something in the middle*
    a. I need this sweater in a <u>medium</u>, not a large.
    b. Copper is a good <u>medium</u> for conducting electricity.

ORAL HISTORY

Oral history is based on the spoken words of people who lived through an event or an era. This account relates an experience in the Yukon in the 1890s.

from My Ninety Years

by Martha Louise Black (as told to Elizabeth Bailey Price)

I was still on the lookout for my first bear and was thinking what glory would be mine if I should kill one while alone in camp. Absorbed in these thoughts, still conscious of the rustling, grinding noises, I had not looked toward the hill. When I did, to my horror I saw the whole hillside slowly moving toward the cabin, and gaining momentum. A landslide! The quick thaw had loosened the upper stratum of earth and made it into a river of mud that was carrying everything before it.

I dashed into the cabin again. I seized the baby, wrapped him in a shawl, put on my own coat, and paralyzed with fright, stood at the corner of the cabin, wondering desperately what move to make, if any. I knew I was in terrible danger. . . .

The onrushing avalanche was halted by a clump of trees seventy feet above the cabin. The mud, rocks, snow, and small trees piled up

against them. Deeply rooted, they held firmly. In a moment the roaring river of mud started to move again, but the trees had split the avalanche. The heavier right half cleared our cabin, uprooted a tree, and swept with it two cabins below, depositing its debris on the bosom of the Yukon. The left passed more closely, carried with it our outhouses, and finally lost itself in the more securely frozen ground below us.

Realizing our narrow escape from a horrible death, and trembling from head to foot, I tottered into the cabin. . . . Looking out, I knew that it was not a bad dream, for the hillside was cleared of its surface, and gleamed like the earth of a new-cut furrow.

Hearing the terrific barking of dogs, I went to the door. I gazed upon a scene of magnificent beauty—enormous ice-blocks coursing down the river, swirling in swift-frothing eddies. And, sitting on a huge ice-cake, hurtling by in mid-stream, was a bob-cat, with a frantic pack of huskies in hot pursuit along the river bank.

Analyzing Media

1. Why might early spring be an especially dangerous time in the Yukon?

2. Martha Louise Black not only survived, but she thrived in the Yukon Territory. Would you like to live in the Yukon? Why or why not?

Before You Read

The Cremation of Sam McGee

MEET
ROBERT W. SERVICE

W hile writing poems about the rugged Yukon Territory and the wild, colorful characters found there, Robert Service was working in the unromantic job of bank teller. His life, however, was certainly not dull. At one time or another, he tried working in professional sports, the theater, construction, journalism, and several other jobs. As a writer, he produced poetry, novels, and autobiography. He is best remembered today as the author of "The Cremation of Sam McGee" and a few other poems set in the Yukon Territory.

Robert W. Service was born in England in 1874 and died in France in 1958.

READING FOCUS

Have you ever been *really* cold–so cold that you thought you would never get warm again?

Chart It!

Think about your experiences in bitter cold weather, or close your eyes and imagine how it feels. Chart the sensory details that describe the cold you remember or imagine.

Sight	Sound	Touch	Smell	Taste

Setting a Purpose

Read the following narrative poem to find out what happens to Sam McGee.

BUILDING BACKGROUND

Did You Know? The Yukon Territory of Canada, named for the Yukon River, is north of British Columbia and east of Alaska. Winters there are long and hard, with average temperatures between 0 and −20 degrees Fahrenheit. As in Alaska, the far northern part of the territory is often called "the land of the midnight sun" because in summer the sun never sets. Mining has been the leading economic activity in the territory since a gold strike in 1896 brought more than thirty thousand adventurers to the region.

North (Greenland). (detail). Rockwell Kent (1882–1971). 33¹⁵⁄₁₆ x 44¹⁄₁₆ in. Peter Brady Collection, Rockwell Kent Legacies, Au Sable, NY. Service's poem begins: "There are strange things done in the midnight sun." Does this painting give you any ideas about why people might do strange things in the far north? How would you feel if you lived in a place where it was always cold and the sun never set in summer and never rose in winter?

THE CREMATION OF SAM McGEE

Robert Service ∾

There are strange things done in the midnight sun
    By the men who moil° for gold;
The Arctic trails have their secret tales
    That would make your blood run cold;
5   The Northern Lights have seen queer sights,
    But the queerest they ever did see
Was that night on the marge,° of Lake Lebarge
    I cremated Sam McGee.

Now Sam McGee was from Tennessee,
    where the cotton blooms and blows.
10 Why he left his home in the South to roam 'round the Pole,
    God only knows.
He was always cold, but the land of gold seemed to hold him
    like a spell;
Though he'd often say in his homely° way that
    "he'd sooner live in hell."

On a Christmas Day we were mushing° our way
    over the Dawson° trail.
Talk of your cold! through the parka's fold it stabbed
    like a driven nail.

---

2 To *moil* is to work hard.

7 *Marge* is an old word for *margin,* or edge.

12 Here, *homely* means "simple; ordinary."

13 Driving a dogsled is *mushing* because the driver says "Mush!" to order the dogs to
    begin pulling or to move faster. Early French fur traders in Canada used the com-
    mand *Marchons!* (meaning "March! Go!"), but English and American dogsledders
    mispronounced it, saying "Mush on!" *Dawson* is a city in the old gold-mining
    region of Canada's Yukon Territory.

15   If our eyes we'd close, then the lashes froze till
         sometimes we couldn't see;
     It wasn't much fun, but the only one to whimper
         was Sam McGee.

     And that very night, as we lay packed tight
         in our robes beneath the snow,
     And the dogs were fed, and the stars o'erhead
         were dancing heel and toe,
     He turned to me, and "Cap," says he,
         "I'll cash in this trip, I guess;
20   And if I do, I'm asking that you won't refuse
         my last request."

     Well, he seemed so low that I couldn't say no;
         then he says with a sort of moan:
     "It's the cursèd cold, and it's got right hold till
         I'm chilled clean through to the bone.
     Yet 'tain't being dead—it's my awful dread of the
         icy grave that pains;
     So I want you to swear that, foul or fair, you'll
         cremate° my last remains."

25   A pal's last need is a thing to heed,° so I swore
         I would not fail;
     And we started on at the streak of dawn; but God!
         he looked ghastly pale.
     He crouched on the sleigh, and he raved all day
         of his home in Tennessee;
     And before nightfall a corpse was all that was left
         of Sam McGee.

     There wasn't a breath in that land of death,
         and I hurried, horror driven,
30   With a corpse half hid that I couldn't get rid,
         because of a promise given;

---

24 To *cremate* a body is to burn it rather than bury it.
25 To *heed* is to give careful attention.

It was lashed to the sleigh, and it seemed to say:
    "You may tax° your brawn° and brains,
But you promised true, and it's up to you
    to cremate those last remains."

Now a promise made is a debt unpaid,
    and the trail has its own stern code.
In the days to come, though my lips were dumb,
    in my heart how I cursed that load.

35   In the long, long night, by the lone firelight,
    while the huskies, round in a ring,
Howled out their woes to the homeless snows—O God!
    how I loathed° the thing.

And every day that quiet clay° seemed to
    heavy and heavier grow;
And on I went, though the dogs were spent
    and the grub was getting low;
The trail was bad, and I felt half mad,
    but I swore I would not give in;
40   And I'd often sing to the hateful thing, and
    it hearkened with a grin.

Till I came to the marge of Lake Lebarge,
    and a derelict° there lay;
It was jammed in the ice, but I saw in a trice°
    it was called the "Alice May."
And I looked at it, and I thought a bit, and
    I looked at my frozen chum;
Then "Here," said I, with a sudden cry,
    "is my cre-ma-tor-eum."

45   Some planks I tore from the cabin floor,
    and I lit the boiler fire;
Some coal I found that was lying around,
    and I heaped the fuel higher;

---

31 Here, *tax* means "place a heavy burden on," and *brawn* means "muscle; strength."
36 To *loathe* is to feel great hatred.
37 The *quiet clay* is Sam's body.
41 A *derelict* is an abandoned ship.
42 Here, *trice* means "a very short time; a moment."

The flames just soared, and the furnace roared—
    such a blaze you seldom see;
And I burrowed a hole in the glowing coal,
    and I stuffed in Sam McGee.

Then I made a hike, for I didn't like
    to hear him sizzle so;
50 And the heavens scowled, and the huskies howled,
    and the wind began to blow.
It was icy cold, but the hot sweat rolled down my cheeks,
    and I don't know why;
And the greasy smoke in an inky cloak
    went streaking down the sky.

I do not know how long in the snow
    I wrestled with grisly fear;
But the stars came out and they danced about
    ere° again I ventured near;
55 I was sick with dread, but I bravely said:
    "I'll just take a peep inside.
I guess he's cooked, and it's time I looked,"
    . . . then the door I opened wide.

And there sat Sam, looking cool and calm,
    in the heart of the furnace roar;
And he wore a smile you could see a mile, and he said:
    "Please close that door.
It's fine in here, but I greatly fear
    you'll let in the cold and storm—
60 Since I left Plumtree, down in Tennessee,
    it's the first time I've been warm."

There are strange things done in the midnight sun
    By the men who moil for gold;
The Arctic trails have their secret tales
    That would make your blood run cold;
65 *The Northern Lights have seen queer sights,*
    But the queerest they ever did see
Was that night on the marge of Lake Lebarge
    I cremated Sam McGee.

---

54 *Ere* (ār) is an old word for *before.*

Responding to Literature

PERSONAL RESPONSE

> ◆ Were you surprised by the ending of the poem? Why or why not?

Analyzing Literature

RECALL

1. Where did Sam McGee come from?
2. Why did Sam request that he be cremated?
3. Describe the twist at the end of the poem.

INTERPRET

4. What phrases in the opening stanza (lines 1–8) of "The Cremation of Sam McGee" **foreshadow** the strange plot twist in the poem? (See **Literary Terms Handbook,** page R5.)
5. How does Service use **humor** in the narration of this strange tale? Give examples to support your opinion.
6. What is the central conflict in the plot of the poem? How is the conflict resolved?

EVALUATE AND CONNECT

7. Describe the relationship between the speaker and Sam McGee. What attitude toward friendship is expressed in the poem?
8. Imagery plays an important part in this poem. Pick out your favorite image from the poem and explain why you like it.
9. Personal Connection   Does reading this poem make you want to visit the Yukon? Why or why not?
10. Theme Connection   How does the speaker of the poem deal with the unexpected event that occurs during the trip?

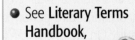

LITERARY ELEMENTS

Rhyme

The most common type of rhyme in poetry is **end rhyme,** rhyme that occurs at the ends of lines. An example is the words *gold* and *cold* at the ends of lines 2 and 4. **Internal rhyme,** on the other hand, occurs within a single line of poetry—for example, the words *done* and *sun* in line 1.

1. Find and quote at least two other examples of internal and end rhymes in the poem.

2. Write a short poem about cold (or hot) weather. Then mark the rhyme pattern of your poem.

● See **Literary Terms Handbook,** p. R9.

Extending Your Response

Literature Groups

Tall Tales A **tall tale** is a kind of folktale in which the characters, their physical traits, and their deeds are often greatly exaggerated in a humorous fashion. Paul Bunyan and John Henry are examples of tall tale heroes. In small groups, talk about whether or not "The Cremation of Sam McGee" is a tall tale. Use examples from the poem to support your opinion.

His Hammer in His Hand. Palmer C. Hayden (1870–1973). From the John Henry Series, Museum of African American Art, Los Angeles. Palmer C. Hayden Collection. Gift of Miriam A. Hayden. Photo by Armando Solis.

Performing

Audio Only As a class activity, divide the poem into sections and work in small groups to prepare the different sections for a performance of the poem for radio. On radio, you can't depend on an actor's gestures–everything must be done with the voice. However, you can add sound effects, such as blowing wind or the sound of a dogsled. To give the illusion of a radio show, have each group present its segment *behind* the rest of the class.

Writing About Literature

Setting Pick out examples of vivid adjectives or figurative language that describe either the bitter cold setting or the Yukon landscape. Then review your notes from the **Reading Focus** on page 635. In a short paragraph, explain how the writer's vivid language helps you to "feel" the icy temperatures of the setting as if you were there.

Creative Writing

Wilderness Report Turn the plot of "The Cremation of Sam McGee" into a television news report. Add any details you need to create the report, including eyewitness interviews with members of other Yukon dogsled trips as well as local weather reports.

Reading Further

If you would like to read more by Robert Service, try any of the following:

The Best of Robert Service

Best Tales of the Yukon

The Shooting of Dan McGrew and Other Poems

Save your work for your portfolio.

Skill Minilesson

READING AND THINKING • SEQUENCE OF EVENTS

The events in a story should take place in a logical order. That is, the reader should be able to see how each event leads to the next one. Most stories follow chronological order, the time order in which the events naturally happen.

PRACTICE Reread the poem. As you do, make a list of the events in the poem in the order in which they occur.

● For more on sequence, see **Reading Handbook,** p. R91.

Reading and Thinking Skills

Identifying Cause-and-Effect Relationships

In a **cause-and-effect relationship,** one event or action causes other things to happen. For example, a character does something wrong (cause) and then feels guilty about what he or she did (effect). The character may then try to correct the wrong that was done (a new effect caused by the character's feelings of guilt).

For example, consider this passage from "After Twenty Years."

> The policeman on the beat moved up the avenue impressively. . . . The time was barely 10 o'clock at night, but chilly gusts of wind with a taste of rain in them had well-nigh depeopled the streets.

This passage contains a cause and its effect. The effect, or result, is the almost empty streets. The cause, or reason, is that chilly winds and the possibility of rain have kept people indoors.

As you try to identify cause-and-effect relationships in the literature you read, always look for clue words like *because, since, as a result,* and *so.* However, the causes of narrative events are not always stated directly. When the cause is not obvious to you, look back over the selection to identify it.

● For more on cause and effect, see **Reading Handbook,** p. R89.

ACTIVITY

Read the following passage from "The Force of Luck." Then answer the questions.

> On the way home he [the miller] was attacked by a hawk that had smelled the meat which the miller carried. The miller fought off the bird but in the struggle he lost the bundle of money. Before the miller knew what was happening the hawk grabbed the bag and flew away with it.

1. What caused the hawk to attack the miller?

2. What effect did the hawk's actions have on the miller?

Writing WORKSHOP

Narrative Writing: Short Story

As you've learned from the narrative poems in this theme, a poem can tell a story—and it can hint at stories left untold. Whose stories do the three narrative poems in this theme leave untold?

Assignment: Follow the process explained in this Workshop to write a short story based on a poem.

● As you write your short story, refer to the **Writing Handbook**, pp. R48–R54.

The Writing Process

PREWRITING

PREWRITING TIP
Imagine a meeting between characters from two poems. What if the speaker in "Annabel Lee" met Bess, of "The Highwayman"? What story might unfold then?

TECHNOLOGY TIP
Use your computer to create separate files for several story ideas. If one doesn't work out, you can switch to another.

● **Search for Story Ideas**

Look again at "The Highwayman," "Annabel Lee," and "The Cremation of Sam McGee." Notice that each poem tells the stories of at least two characters. Use questions like the following to find story ideas to explore:

- With which character do I most identify?

- Which character do I find the most interesting?

- What might have happened before the events in the poems?

- What might happen after the events in the poems?

- What new endings might I give the poems?

- What might a character from one poem do in the setting of another poem?

● Make a Plan

Choose a story idea that intrigues you. Then explore it by filling in a story map like the following one. You can borrow details of setting, characters, point of view, and plot from one or more of the poems in this theme, or you can create your own variations.

Characters:	The speaker in "Annabel Lee" and Annabel's brother Randolf
Setting:	a tomb by the sea
Point of view:	first person: The speaker from the poem will be the narrator.
Plot:	The narrator begs Randolf to take him to Annabel's tomb. Randolf reluctantly leads him there and then leaves. The narrator discovers that Randolf has locked him in the tomb.

Make sure that your plot includes exposition, conflict, rising action, climax, and resolution. To review the parts of a standard plot line and other literary elements, refer to the Genre Focus on pages 144–145.

● Choose Your Audience and Purpose

Will your story entertain, amuse, or perhaps provide some chills? Will it be a children's story, a tale for your classmates to enjoy, or a story for a mixed audience, such as the readers of a popular magazine? Knowing your audience will help you plan your writing. Children may need vivid action and simple language. A mixed audience might not understand the same literary terms or references that your classmates would.

● Put Events in Order

The events in a story may or may not be given in chronological order. Filling in a sequence chart like the one below can help you organize the events in the best way for your story.

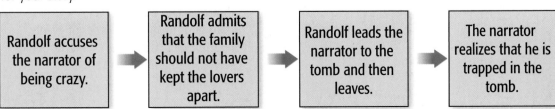

Randolf accuses the narrator of being crazy. → Randolf admits that the family should not have kept the lovers apart. → Randolf leads the narrator to the tomb and then leaves. → The narrator realizes that he is trapped in the tomb.

Writing WORKSHOP

DRAFTING

DRAFTING TIP
Don't try to explain too much about your characters. Instead, reveal details about them through their actions, thoughts, and words.

● Create an Opening

You can pull readers into your story with any of several types of openers:

- an intriguing line of dialogue

- an image of a character in action (even a small action, such as a sigh)

- a mysterious comment about the story to come

Then move right into your chain of events and get your story down on paper.

● Draft Your Story

Be sure to include transitions, such as *at first, next, soon, before that, afterwards, later,* or *meanwhile* to keep the order of events clear for your readers.

STUDENT MODEL • DRAFTING

> Her brother put his hand on my shoulder and pointed. At first I could not make out what he wanted me to see. Then I knew.

Complete Student Model on pp. R111–112.

REVISING

REVISING TIP
One way to give your story a "finished" feel is to refer again to something from the opening, perhaps showing it in a new light.

● Map Out Changes

Take a short break before you revise. Then take a new look at your story. Is it on its way toward creating the effects you had hoped for? Using the **Rubric for Revising,** map out improvements. A peer reader can offer useful feedback and ideas.

RUBRIC FOR REVISING
Your revised short story should have
- an opening that uses intriguing dialogue, a significant action, or another compelling device
- a well-defined setting
- a strong, well-developed plot line
- characters revealed through actions, thoughts, and words
- transitions to show the order of events
- no irrelevant characters, events, or details
- no errors in grammar, usage, and mechanics

EDITING/PROOFREADING

Use the **Proofreading Checklist** to help you spot and correct errors in grammar, usage, and mechanics. Pay special attention to comma usage, as shown in the **Grammar Link** on page 553.

Grammar Hint

The words *someone, anyone,* and *everyone* are singular. With these words, use singular possessive pronouns such as *his* or *her* instead of the plural possessive pronoun *their.*

> **Everyone** has **his** or **her** own opinion about the poem.

PROOFREADING CHECKLIST

☑ All pronouns agree with their antecedents. (Double-check agreement with the word *everyone.*)

☑ There are no sentence fragments or run-ons.

☑ All verbs agree with their subjects.

☑ Punctuation is correct.

☑ Spelling and capitalization are correct.

STUDENT MODEL · EDITING/PROOFREADING

> his or her
> When someone loses ~~their~~ true love, life seems
>   ^
> unfair.

Complete Student Model

For a complete version of the model developed in this Workshop, see **Writing Workshop Models**, pp. R111–R112.

Complete Student Model on pp. R111–R112.

PUBLISHING/PRESENTING

Read your story aloud to your class, using the guidelines and suggestions on Speaking Effectively in the **Communications Skills Handbook,** page R69.

Reflecting

Take time to think over the following questions before writing your responses.

- What was the trickiest part of writing your story? How might you do it differently next time?

- Do you prefer writing fictional stories, like this one, or nonfiction narratives? Explain your preference.

📖 **Save your work for your portfolio.**

Theme Assessment

Responding to the Theme

1. Which selection helped you notice how writers add a spark of the unexpected to their work? Explain your answer.

2. What new ideas do you have about the following as a result of reading the literature in this theme?
   - the role of luck in people's lives
   - how life's ups and downs are part of the normal course of human events

3. Present your theme project to the class.

Analyzing Literature

COMPARE NARRATIVE POEMS

Write an essay of at least one page comparing two of the narrative poems from this theme. You may compare such elements as setting, plot, characters, and point of view; examine the use of rhyme and meter; or concentrate on the poems' twists and turns. Include quotations to illustrate your comparisons or back up your conclusions.

Evaluate and Set Goals

1. Which of the following tasks was most rewarding to you? Which was most difficult?
   - reading and thinking about the stories, poems, and plays
   - doing independent writing
   - analyzing the selections in discussions
   - performing dramatizations

2. Using the following scale, how would you assess your work in this theme? Give at least two reasons for your assessment.

4 = outstanding	2 = fair
3 = good	1 = weak

3. Based on what you found difficult in this theme, choose a goal to work toward in the next theme.
   - Write down your goal and three steps you will take to reach it.
   - Meet with your teacher to review your goal and your plan for achieving it.

Build Your Portfolio

SELECT

Select two pieces of work you did during this theme to include in your portfolio. Use the following questions to help you decide.

- ✦ Which do you consider your best work?
- ✦ From which did you learn the most?
- ✦ Which work challenged you the most?
- ✦ Which work did you enjoy the most?

REFLECT

Write some notes to accompany the work you selected. Use the following questions to guide you.

- ✦ What do you like best about the piece?
- ✦ What did you learn from creating it?
- ✦ What might you do differently if you were beginning this piece again?

Reading on Your Own

Have you enjoyed reading the literature in this theme? If so, you might be interested in reading the following books.

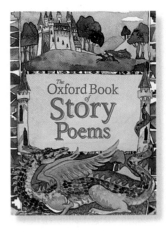

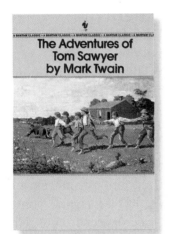

The Adventures of Tom Sawyer

by Mark Twain Twain's classic story has plenty of comic trickery, twists, and turns, including Tom's attending his own funeral.

The Oxford Book of Story Poems

edited by Michael Harrison and Christopher Stuart-Clark This collection of narrative poetry includes classic and modern poems that will make you laugh, poems that will amaze you, and poems that will thrill and chill you.

The One Who Came Back

by Joann Mazzio This novel is an adventure story of a friendship between two boys in the mountains of New Mexico. When one of the boys disappears, no one believes the other boy's version of what happened.

Talking to the Sun

selected by Kenneth Koch and Kate Farrell This anthology of poetry from ancient times to the present is illustrated with reproductions of artworks from the Metropolitan Museum of Art in New York.

Standardized Test Practice

Read the following passage. Then read each question on page 651. Decide which is the best answer to each question. Mark the letter for that answer on your paper.

Captain Thomas's Last Flight?

When the first explosion hit the hull of his starship, Captain Hunter Thomas grabbed for the shipwide microphone and began yelling. "Damage report! Blakely! What's happening?"

There was a moment of static on the line before Blakely's voice crackled into Thomas's cabin. "You'd better get to the bridge, Captain. We've got company."

Thomas was already off his bunk, jamming his feet into his flight boots and groping for his tunic. He was halfway out the door when Blakely's voice crackled over the intercom again.

"Pirates, Captain. It looks like the Derellians."

Thomas's voice came out in a growl. "How many?"

Another static-filled pause, until Thomas heard, "Five."

Then the ship rocked horribly to starboard, another explosion tearing like a claw into the vital flight and life support mechanisms. With another few blasts like that one, the hull might crack like an eggshell.

Thomas tucked his head and sprinted for the bridge. He arrived to find Blakely whirling about, careening from one control panel to the next, trying to keep the ship's many automated systems running. The look on the first mate's face told Thomas all he needed to know. They were in very deep trouble.

"What does the damage look like, Blakely?"

Blakely didn't look up. His eyes were glued to a computer screen. His fingers punched furiously at buttons and switches. "Third engine gone. Navigation computer damaged. Pulsar guns disabled."

"Life support status?"

Blakely sighed. "Holding."

Blakely punched the emergency distress signal on the communications console. A red light began to flash, signifying that an all-purpose emergency broadcast was being sent out to any ships in the vicinity. Blakely didn't have much hope that anyone would come, though. Few ships could tangle with a fleet of Derellian pirates.

Thomas gripped the steering controls and aimed straight for the first of the five ships he saw. "Signal all hands to abandon ship, Blakely. Get the crew to safety. See to it personally. I'm going to hold out as long as I can."

Blakely looked at his captain and friend, but said nothing. Thomas was already veering through the inky space between two more ships, dodging their fire. The two men had flown together for two years.

"Move it, Blakely! Now!"

When Blakely spoke, his voice was little more than a whisper. "Yes, Captain Thomas." He forced his legs to carry him toward the gangway to the escape pods.

The ship rocked once again under the weight of a crushing explosion. Warning lights began to flash, sirens screamed, smoke hissed from the computer consoles of the bridge like steam escaping a cooking pot. Blakely stood straight to salute his good friend Captain Thomas once more before he turned and ran down the gangway, screaming for his crew to board the escape pods and fly away to safety.

A few minutes later, from several miles distance, Blakely stared through the portal of his escape pod and watched distant explosions flower in the infinite night of space. *Goodbye, Captain,* he thought.

Then the loudspeaker squawked and a familiar voice echoed through the cabin of the pod. "Don't give up on me now, Blake. They've given up! We're free and clear!"

The Captain!

"Hang tight, Blakely. I'll be back on my next pass to pick you all up!"

Blakely cheered triumphantly and ran to tell the crew.

---

1   How did Blakely feel at the end of the story?
  A Elated
  B Amused

C Embarrassed
D Confused

2   In this story, the word <u>careening</u> means —
  J walking slowly.
  K wandering.
  L lurching.
  M fainting.

3   What will probably happen next?
  A Blakely will help Captain Thomas fight off the Derellians.
  B Captain Thomas will go down with his ship.
  C Captain Thomas will fly to where the crew's pods are.
  D The crew members will rebel against Captain Thomas for making them leave the ship.

4   Why didn't Blakely look at Thomas when he arrived at the bridge?
  J Blakely couldn't open his eyes after the explosion.
  K Blakely was worried that Thomas would be angry about the ship.
  L Blakely was trying to survey the damage done to the ship.
  M Blakely knew it would be the last time he'd see Thomas.

5   The author would probably describe Captain Thomas as —
  A bossy and intolerant
  B nervous and inhibited
  C happy and charming
  D brave and selfless

A Different Dimension

Ayer Tuve un Sueño, 1990. Maria Angelica Ruiz-Tagle. Oil on canvas, 100 x 120 cm.
Kactus Foto, Santiago, Chile.

THEME 7

> **66** *That was the time when words were like magic. The human mind had mysterious powers. A word spoken by chance might have strange consequences.* **99**
>
> —"Magic Words," *Songs and Stories of the Netsilik Eskimos*

THEME CONTENTS

GENRE FOCUS LEGENDS, MYTHS, AND FOLKLORE

Exploring the Theme

— A Different Dimension —

The magical power of words has always been able to transport listeners and readers to other worlds. In this theme, you will discover how the magic of words can carry you to places such as ancient Greece and China, the imaginary planet of Pern, and the legendary American frontier. Begin thinking about the theme by selecting one of the activities below.

Starting Points

WHEN THE MOON IS FULL

Writers and artists like to imagine life in different dimensions. The couple in this cartoon are certainly about to enter a new dimension!

- What do you think is happening? Draw a cartoon strip with two or three more panels showing what might happen next to Maynard and his wife.

TRAVELING TO ANOTHER DIMENSION

Have you ever used your imagination to travel to another dimension?

- Describe a setting for a fantasy you might write. It can take place in the past, in the future, on another planet, or even on an Earth that never really existed. The place can be as strange or as magical as you can imagine.

"*Maynard, I do think that just this once you should come out and see the moon!*"

Drawing by Chas. Addams; ©1983. The New Yorker Magazine, Inc.

Theme Projects

As you read the selections in this theme, complete one of the projects below. Work on your own, with a partner, or with a group.

CRITICAL READING
Different Dimensions in Literature

1. Alone or with a partner, brainstorm a list of fantasy or science-fiction novels, short stories, TV episodes, or movies you have read or seen. Then choose at least four of them that you think are especially good.

2. Plan a chart to prepare a detailed comparison of your choices. Use headings such as Title, Author(s), Setting (time and place), Plot Summary, Characters, Theme(s), and Evaluation.

3. Use your completed chart to write an essay telling what elements good science-fiction or fantasy stories have in common. Use examples from the stories to back up your opinions.

4. Decorate your chart with drawings or pictures clipped from old magazines or downloaded from the Internet and display it for the class along with your essay.

interNET
CONNECTION

For more project ideas, check out some fantasy, science-fiction, myth, legend, or folklore sites on the Web. You can also try the Glencoe Literature site at lit.glencoe.com.

LEARNING FOR LIFE
Travel Itinerary

1. Plan an itinerary, or traveler's guide, for a trip to a different dimension.

2. Decide how you will travel: in a time machine, a spacecraft, or even on the back of a dragon. Decide what sights you will see and what people or creatures you will meet there.

3. Make a map of your journey. Use it for a presentation in which you describe your visit.

MULTIMEDIA PROJECT
Creating an Imaginary World

1. Working in a small group, collect pictures of places that would make good settings for a story set in a different dimension.

2. Create a diorama using or adapting the scenery you found. Use modeling clay or cutouts to add to your display the kinds of people or creatures who might live in your "different dimension."

3. Share your world with your classmates. If you wish, use the scene you have created as an inspiration for writing or dramatizing a story.

MEDIA Connection

MAGAZINE ARTICLE

This article comes from a magazine for dog lovers. Why do you think it appeared in a section called "Dogs That Make a Difference"?

Seizure-Alert Dog Is Girl's Lifeline

by Sarah Christie—*Dog Fancy*, June 1997

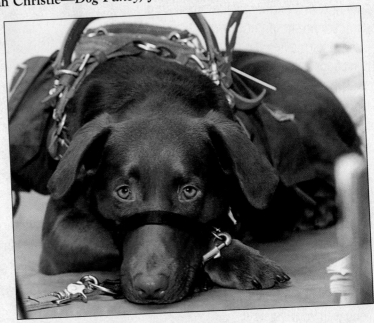

Emily Ramsey's world just grew a little bigger. For the first time in her life, the 13-year-old middle school student from Racine, Wis., is now able to cruise the mall, ride the school bus, and participate in after-school sports without constant supervision. That's standard operating procedure for most teenagers, but for one with epilepsy, the world is a perilous place.

Seizures strike without warning, making simple acts such as walking down stairs, crossing the street, or going for a swim potentially life-threatening. These days Emily can do all that and more, thanks to her constant companion, Watson.

Watson is a seizure-alert dog, able to warn his owner of epileptic attacks before they strike.

The skill goes beyond regular service-dog training. It can't be taught or bred for. Nobody knows how Watson is able to predict these spells—one theory is that dogs sense chemical changes preceding the attacks—but the details don't matter to Emily. She knows only that her dog's intuition is a lifeline she almost didn't dare hope for.

Watson was an improbable candidate for service dog school. He had been left at a veterinarian's office to be put to sleep for a broken foot at 6 months of age. A clinic employee saved him. The sympathetic veterinary technician, who also worked as a volunteer at CPL [Canine Partners for Life], saw promise in the lame pup.

Thus began the education of Watson. During his year at CPL, he mastered the arts of pushing wheelchairs, opening refrigerator and sliding glass doors, paying cashiers, and retrieving coins off cement floors. But the only way to know if Watson could predict Emily's seizures was to pair the two and wait and see.

When dog met girl, there was no turning back. "It was love at first sight for both of them," [Emily's mother, Mary] Ramsey said. "He knew this was his person. They bonded very strongly, very quickly."

A month later, Emily returned to the CPL kennel for three weeks' training. Watson was put to the test right away.

"It was the middle of the night in the motel when Emily started seizuring," Ramsey said. "And Watson woke me up barking. I turned on the light and he was straddling her on the bed, looking straight down at her."

Eventually Watson learned that Emily's spells, frightening as they are, were only temporary. His concern turned to vigilance as he realized the importance of remaining with her at all times. After only three or four episodes, he began signaling coming attacks by whining and licking Emily's face. This has been refined into a deep, throaty whine, alerting Emily that she has about 45 minutes to prepare herself for a seizure.

But Watson's protectiveness goes beyond his special early-warning system. If Emily has had a particularly bad night, Watson won't allow her to exert herself the next day. He will forgo his morning walk and refuse to let her off the property. Nor will he allow her to go into the pool for a swim. "The uncanny thing is, he makes these decisions all by himself," Ramsey said. "He's decided that he knows what's best for Emily, and nobody would think about questioning his judgment."

Emily's mother credits Watson for improving her daughter's quality of life in ways nothing else has. Emily has her own reasons for loving Watson. "He's always there for me," she said without hesitation. "He's my best friend."

Analyzing Media

1. How did this article affect your understanding of the relationship between dogs and humans?

2. What characteristics tell you that this article is an example of informative nonfiction?

Before You Read

Lob's Girl

MEET JOAN AIKEN

British author Joan Aiken says that she writes "the sort of thing I should have liked to read myself." She began creating poems and stories when she was five years old. Aiken's first work was published when she was seventeen, and she has since written more than eighty books and short-story collections. She is best known for historic fiction with mysterious or enchanted characters and settings.

Joan Aiken was born in 1924. This story was published in 1982.

READING FOCUS

Do you think the bond between an animal and a human can be as strong as the bond between two humans?

QuickWrite
Write about what it is like, or would be like, to have an animal as a devoted friend.

Setting a Purpose
Read this story to find out about the powerful bond between a young girl and her dog.

BUILDING BACKGROUND

The Time and Place   The story takes place over the course of nine years in a fishing village in southwestern England.

Did You Know?   Dogs have been known to travel great distances to find their owners or to return to their original homes. Scientists are unsure of how dogs manage to find their way, but they know that a dog's sense of smell is a powerful tool. Their scent memory is probably stronger than their sight memory. For example, dogs remember the arrangement of objects in a room by their different scents rather than by how they look.

VOCABULARY PREVIEW

secretive (sē′ kri tiv) *adj.* keeping one's thoughts and feelings to oneself; p. 663

hurtle (hurt′ əl) *v.* to move rapidly, especially with much force; p. 664

aggrieved (ə grēvd′) *adj.* feeling wronged, as by an insult or unfair treatment; p. 666

succeed (sək sēd′) *v.* to come or happen after in time, place, or order; p. 666

haggard (hag′ ərd) *adj.* looking worn as a result of grief, worry, or illness; p. 666

agitated (aj′ ə tāt′ əd) *adj.* excited, nervous, or disturbed; stirred up; p. 667

Lob's Girl

Joan Aiken ∿

Staithes, Yorkshire. Dame Laura Knight, 1877–1970. Oil on canvas, 29½ x 24½ in. Private collection. How does the artist show the isolation of this home and yard?

Some people choose their dogs, and some dogs choose their people. The Pengelly family had no say in the choosing of Lob; he came to them in the second way, and very decisively.

It began on the beach, the summer when Sandy was five, Don, her older brother, twelve, and the twins were three. Sandy was really Alexandra, because her grandmother had a beautiful picture of a queen in a diamond tiara[1] and high collar of pearls. It hung by Granny Pearce's kitchen sink and was as familiar as the doormat. When Sandy was born everyone agreed that she was the living spit[2] of the picture, and so she was called Alexandra and Sandy for short.

On this summer day she was lying peacefully reading a comic and not keeping an eye on the twins, who didn't need it because they were occupied in seeing which of them could wrap the most seaweed around the other one's legs. Father—Bert Pengelly—and Don were up on the

---

1. A *tiara* (tē ar′ ə) is a woman's crownlike headdress, often made with jewels and precious metals.

2. *Living spit* is British slang for "exact likeness," which Americans would call "spitting image."

Lob's Girl

Hard[3] painting the bottom boards of the boat in which Father went fishing for pilchards. And Mother—Jean Pengelly—was getting ahead with making the Christmas puddings[4] because she never felt easy in her mind if they weren't made and safely put away by the end of August. As usual, each member of the family was happily getting on with his or her own affairs. Little did they guess how soon this state of things would be changed by the large new member who was going to erupt into their midst.

Sandy rolled onto her back to make sure that the twins were not climbing on slippery rocks or getting cut off by the tide. At the same moment a large body struck her forcibly in the midriff and she was covered by flying sand. Instinctively she shut her eyes and felt the sand being wiped off her face by something that seemed like a warm, rough, damp flannel. She opened her eyes and looked. It was a tongue. Its owner was a large and bouncy young Alsatian, or German shepherd, with topaz[5] eyes, black-tipped prick ears, a thick, soft coat, and a bushy black-tipped tail.

"*Lob!*" shouted a man farther up the beach. "Lob, come here!"

Did You Know?
Alsatians, also called German shepherds, were originally bred in Germany. They are noted for their intelligence and loyalty.

But Lob, as if trying to atone for the surprise he had given her, went on licking the sand off Sandy's face, wagging his tail so hard while he kept on knocking up more clouds of sand. His owner, a gray-haired man with a limp, walked over as quickly as he could and seized him by the collar.

"I hope he didn't give you a fright?" the man said to Sandy. "He meant it in play—he's only young."

"Oh, no, I think he's *beautiful*," said Sandy truly. She picked up a bit of driftwood and threw it. Lob, whisking easily out of his master's grip, was after it like a sand-colored bullet. He came back with the stick, beaming, and gave it to Sandy. At the same time he gave himself, though no one else was aware of this at the time. But with Sandy, too, it was love at first sight, and when, after a lot more stick-throwing, she and the twins joined Father and Don to go home for tea, they cast many a backward glance at Lob being led firmly away by his master.

"I wish we could play with him every day," Tess sighed.

"Why can't we?" said Tim.

Sandy explained, "Because Mr. Dodsworth, who owns him, is from Liverpool, and he is only staying at the Fisherman's Arms till Saturday."

"Is Liverpool a long way off?"

"Right at the other end of England from Cornwall, I'm afraid."

It was a Cornish fishing village where the Pengelly family lived, with rocks and cliffs and a strip of beach and a little round harbor, and palm trees growing in the gardens of the little whitewashed stone houses. The village was approached by a narrow, steep, twisting hill-road, and

---

3. The *Hard* is a place for landing and launching boats. *Pilchards* are small herring-like fish.
4. *Christmas puddings* are a traditional British dessert similar to a fruitcake.
5. *Topaz* eyes are a bright, clear yellow-gold.

guarded by a notice that said LOW GEAR FOR 1 1/2 MILES, DANGEROUS TO CYCLISTS.

The Pengelly children went home to scones[6] with Cornish cream and jam, thinking they had seen the last of Lob. But they were much mistaken. The whole family was playing cards by the fire in the front room after supper when there was a loud thump and a crash of china in the kitchen.

"My Christmas puddings!" exclaimed Jean, and ran out.

"Did you put TNT in them, then?" her husband said.

But it was Lob, who, finding the front door shut, had gone around to the back and bounced in through the open kitchen window, where the puddings were cooling on the sill. Luckily only the smallest was knocked down and broken.

Lob stood on his hind legs and plastered Sandy's face with licks. Then he did the same for the twins, who shrieked with joy.

"Where does this friend of yours come from?" inquired Mr. Pengelly.

"He's staying at the Fisherman's Arms—I mean his owner is."

"Then he must go back there. Find a bit of string, Sandy, to tie to his collar."

"I wonder how he found his way here," Mrs. Pengelly said when the reluctant Lob had been led whining away and Sandy had explained about their afternoon's game on the beach. "Fisherman's Arms is right round the other side of the harbor."

Lob's owner scolded him and thanked Mr. Pengelly for bringing him back. Jean Pengelly warned the children that they had better not encourage Lob any more if they met him on the beach, or it would only lead to more trouble. So they dutifully took no notice of him the next day until he spoiled their good resolutions by dashing up to them with joyful barks, wagging his tail so hard that he winded Tess and knocked Tim's legs from under him.

They had a happy day, playing on the sand.

The next day was Saturday. Sandy had found out that Mr. Dodsworth was to catch the half-past-nine train. She went out secretly, down to the station, nodded to Mr. Hoskins, the stationmaster, who wouldn't dream of charging any local for a platform ticket, and climbed up on the footbridge that led over the tracks. She didn't want to be seen, but she did want to see. She saw Mr. Dodsworth get on the train, accompanied by an unhappy-looking Lob with drooping ears and tail. Then she saw the train slide away out of sight around the next headland, with a melancholy wail that sounded like Lob's last good-bye.

Sandy wished she hadn't had the idea of coming to the station. She walked home miserably, with her shoulders hunched and her hands in her pockets. For the rest of the day she was so cross and unlike herself that Tess and Tim were quite surprised, and her mother gave her a dose of senna.[7]

A week passed. Then, one evening, Mrs. Pengelly and the younger children were in the front room playing snakes and ladders. Mr. Pengelly and Don had gone fishing on the evening tide. If your father is a fisherman, he will never be home at the same time from one week to the next.

Suddenly, history repeating itself, there was a crash from the kitchen. Jean Pengelly leaped up, crying, "My blackberry jelly!"

---

6. *Scones* are sweet biscuits.

7. *Senna* is a medicine made from senna plants and used as a laxative.

She and the children had spent the morning picking and the afternoon boiling fruit.

But Sandy was ahead of her mother. With flushed cheeks and eyes like stars she had darted into the kitchen, where she and Lob were hugging one another in a frenzy of joy. About a yard of his tongue was out, and he was licking every part of her that he could reach.

"Good heavens!" exclaimed Jean. "How in the world did *he* get here?"

"He must have walked," said Sandy. "Look at his feet."

They were worn, dusty, and tarry. One had a cut on the pad.

"They ought to be bathed," said Jean Pengelly. "Sandy, run a bowl of warm water while I get the disinfectant."

"What'll we do about him, Mother?" said Sandy anxiously.

Mrs. Pengelly looked at her daughter's pleading eyes and sighed.

"He must go back to his owner, of course," she said, making her voice firm. "Your dad can get the address from the Fisherman's tomorrow, and phone him or send a telegram. In the meantime he'd better have a long drink and a good meal."

Lob was very grateful for the drink and the meal, and made no objection to having his feet washed. Then he flopped down on the hearthrug and slept in front of the fire they had lit because it was a cold, wet evening, with his head on Sandy's feet. He was a very tired dog. He had walked all the way from Liverpool to Cornwall, which is more than four hundred miles.

The next day Mr. Pengelly phoned Lob's owner, and the following morning Mr. Dodsworth arrived off the night train, decidedly put out, to take his pet home. That parting was worse than the first. Lob whined, Don walked out of the house, the twins burst out crying, and Sandy crept up to her bedroom afterward and lay with her face pressed into the quilt, feeling as if she were bruised all over.

Jean Pengelly took them all into Plymouth to see the circus on the next day and the twins cheered up a little, but even the hour's ride in the train each way and the Liberty horses and performing seals could not cure Sandy's sore heart.

She need not have bothered, though. In ten days' time Lob was back—limping this time, with a torn ear and a patch missing out of his furry coat, as if he had met and tangled with an enemy or two in the course of his four-hundred-mile walk.

Bert Pengelly rang up Liverpool again. Mr. Dodsworth, when he answered, sounded weary. He said, "That dog has already cost me two days that I can't spare away from my work—plus endless time in police stations and drafting newspaper advertisements. I'm too old for these ups and downs. I think we'd better face the fact, Mr. Pengelly, that it's your family he wants to stay with—that is, if you want to have him."

Bert Pengelly gulped. He was not a rich man; and Lob was a pedigreed[8] dog. He said cautiously, "How much would you be asking for him?"

"Good heavens, man, I'm not suggesting I'd sell him to you. You must have him as a gift. Think of the train fares I'll be saving. You'll be doing me a good turn."

"Is he a big eater?" Bert asked doubtfully.

By this time the children, breathless in the background listening to one side of this conversation, had realized what was in

---

8. A *pedigreed* dog has papers showing that its ancestors were the same breed.

the wind and were dancing up and down with their hands clasped beseechingly.[9]

"Oh, not for his size," Lob's owner assured Bert. "Two or three pounds of meat a day and some vegetables and gravy and biscuits—he does very well on that."

Alexandra's father looked over the telephone at his daughter's swimming eyes and trembling lips. He reached a decision. "Well, then, Mr. Dodsworth," he said briskly, "we'll accept your offer and thank you very much. The children will be overjoyed and you can be sure Lob has come to a good home. They'll look after him and see he gets enough exercise. But I can tell you," he ended firmly, "if he wants to settle in with us he'll have to learn to eat a lot of fish."

So that was how Lob came to live with the Pengelly family. Everybody loved him and he loved them all. But there was never any question who came first with him. He was Sandy's dog. He slept by her bed and followed her everywhere he was allowed.

Nine years went by, and each summer Mr. Dodsworth came back to stay at the Fisherman's Arms and call on his erstwhile dog. Lob always met him with recognition and dignified pleasure, accompanied him for a walk or two—but showed no signs of wishing to return to Liverpool. His place, he intimated,[10] was definitely with the Pengellys.

In the course of nine years Lob changed less than Sandy. As she went into her teens he became a little slower, a little stiffer, there was a touch of gray on his nose, but he was still a handsome dog. He and Sandy still loved one another devotedly.

One evening in October all the summer visitors had left, and the little fishing town looked empty and <u>secretive</u>. It was a wet, windy dusk. When the children came home from school—even the twins were at high school[11] now, and Don was a full-fledged fisherman—Jean Pengelly said, "Sandy, your Aunt Rebecca says she's lonesome because Uncle Will Hoskins has gone out trawling,[12] and she wants one of you to go and spend the evening with her. You go, dear; you can take your homework with you."

Sandy looked far from enthusiastic.

"Can I take Lob with me?"

"You know Aunt Becky doesn't really like dogs— Oh, very well." Mrs. Pengelly sighed. "I suppose she'll have to put up with him as well as you."

Reluctantly Sandy tidied herself, took her schoolbag, put on the damp raincoat she had just taken off, fastened Lob's lead to his collar, and set off to walk through the dusk to Aunt Becky's cottage, which was five minutes' climb up the steep hill.

The wind was howling through the shrouds of boats drawn up on the Hard.

Did You Know?
A boat's *shrouds* are ropes that help support the masts.

---

9. *Beseechingly* means "in a begging or pleading manner."
10. Lob belonged to Mr. Dodsworth in earlier times *(erstwhile)*. To *intimate* is to hint at something without stating it directly.

11. An English *high school* starts with what would be the sixth or seventh grade in the United States.
12. *Trawling* is fishing with large nets that are dragged across the water's bottom.

Vocabulary
secretive (sē′ kri tiv) *adj.* keeping one's thoughts and feelings to oneself

"Put some cheerful music on, do," said Jean Pengelly to the nearest twin. "Anything to drown that wretched sound while I make your dad's supper." So Don, who had just come in, put on some rock music, loud. Which was why the Pengellys did not hear the truck hurtle down the hill and crash against the post office wall a few minutes later.

Dr. Travers was driving through Cornwall with his wife, taking a late holiday before patients began coming down with winter colds and flu. He saw the sign that said STEEP HILL. LOW GEAR FOR 1 1/2 MILES. Dutifully he changed into second gear.

"We must be nearly there," said his wife, looking out her window. "I noticed a sign on the coast road that said the Fisherman's Arms was two miles. What a narrow, dangerous hill! But the cottages are very pretty— Oh, Frank, stop, *stop!* There's a child, I'm sure it's a child—by the wall over there!"

Dr. Travers jammed on his brakes and brought the car to a stop. A little stream ran down by the road in a shallow stone culvert,[13] and half in the water lay something that looked, in the dusk, like a pile of clothes—or was it the body of a child? Mrs. Travers was out of the car in a flash, but her husband was quicker.

"Don't touch her, Emily!" he said sharply. "She's been hit. Can't be more than a few minutes. Remember that truck that overtook us half a mile back, speeding like the devil? Here, quick, go into that cottage and phone for an ambulance. The girl's in a bad way. I'll stay here and do what I can to stop the bleeding. Don't waste a minute."

Doctors are expert at stopping dangerous bleeding, for they know the right places to press. This Dr. Travers was able to do, but he didn't dare do more; the girl was lying in a queerly crumpled heap, and he guessed she had a number of bones broken and that it would be highly dangerous to move her. He watched her with great concentration, wondering where the truck had got to and what other damage it had done.

Mrs. Travers was very quick. She had seen plenty of accident cases and knew the importance of speed. The first cottage she tried had a phone; in four minutes she was back, and in six an ambulance was wailing down the hill.

Its attendants lifted the child onto a stretcher as carefully as if she were made of fine thistledown. The ambulance sped off to Plymouth—for the local cottage hospital[14] did not take serious accident cases—and Dr. Travers went down to the police station to report what he had done.

He found that the police already knew about the speeding truck—which had suffered from loss of brakes and ended up with its radiator halfway through the post office wall. The driver was concussed and shocked, but the police thought he was the only person injured— until Dr. Travers told his tale.

---

13. A *culvert* is a drainage ditch.

14. *Cottage hospital* is a British term for a small hospital with a staff of local doctors.

Vocabulary
hurtle (hurt´ əl) *v.* to move rapidly, especially with much force

Viewing the photograph: Compare the home shown here with the painting *Straithes, Yorkshire,* on page 659. Which of the two pictures is closer to your image of the story's setting? Why?

Lob's Girl

At half-past nine that night Aunt Rebecca Hoskins was sitting by her fire thinking aggrieved thoughts about the inconsiderateness of nieces who were asked to supper and never turned up when she was startled by a neighbor, who burst in exclaiming, "Have you heard about Sandy Pengelly, then, Mrs. Hoskins? Terrible thing, poor little soul, and they don't know if she's likely to live. Police have got the truck driver that hit her—ah, it didn't ought to be allowed, speeding through the place like that at umpty miles an hour, they ought to jail him for life—not that that'd be any comfort to poor Bert and Jean."

Horrified, Aunt Rebecca put on a coat and went down to her brother's house. She found the family with white shocked faces; Bert and Jean were about to drive off to the hospital where Sandy had been taken, and the twins were crying bitterly. Lob was nowhere to be seen. But Aunt Rebecca was not interested in dogs; she did not inquire about him.

"Thank the lord you've come, Beck," said her brother. "Will you stay the night with Don and the twins? Don's out looking for Lob and heaven knows when we'll be back; we may get a bed with Jean's mother in Plymouth."

"Oh, if only I'd never invited the poor child," wailed Mrs. Hoskins. But Bert and Jean hardly heard her.

That night seemed to last forever. The twins cried themselves to sleep. Don came home very late and grim-faced. Bert and Jean sat in a waiting room of the Western Counties Hospital, but Sandy was unconscious, they were told, and she remained so. All that could be done for her was done. She was given transfusions to replace all the blood she had lost. The broken bones were set and put in slings and cradles.[15]

"Is she a healthy girl? Has she a good constitution?"[16] the emergency doctor asked.

"Aye, doctor, she is that," Bert said hoarsely. The lump in Jean's throat prevented her from answering: she merely nodded.

"Then she ought to have a chance. But I won't conceal from you that her condition is very serious, unless she shows signs of coming out from this coma."

But as hour succeeded hour, Sandy showed no signs of recovering consciousness. Her parents sat in the waiting room with haggard faces; sometimes one of them would go to telephone the family at home, or try to get a little sleep at the home of Granny Pearce, not far away.

At noon next day Dr. and Mrs. Travers went to the Pengelly cottage to inquire how Sandy was doing, but the report was gloomy: "Still in a very serious condition." The twins were miserably unhappy. They forgot that they had sometimes called their elder sister bossy and only remembered how often she had shared her pocket money with them, how she read to them and took them for picnics and helped with their homework.

---

15. Here, the *cradles* are frames that keep Sandy's bedclothes from touching her injuries.
16. Here, *constitution* refers to a person's physical condition.

Vocabulary
aggrieved (ə grēvd´) *adj.* feeling wronged, as by an insult or unfair treatment
succeed (sək sēd´) *v.* to come or happen after in time, place, or order
haggard (hag´ ərd) *adj.* looking worn as a result of grief, worry, or illness

Now there was no Sandy, no Mother and Dad, Don went around with a gray, shuttered face, and worse still, there was no Lob.

The Western Counties Hospital is a large one, with dozens of different departments and five or six connected buildings, each with three or four entrances. By that afternoon it became noticeable that a dog seemed to have taken up position outside the hospital, with the fixed intention of getting in. Patiently he would try first one entrance and then another, all the way around, and then begin again. Sometimes he would get a little way inside, following a visitor, but animals were, of course, forbidden, and he was always kindly but firmly turned out again. Sometimes the guard at the main entrance gave him a pat or offered him a bit of sandwich—he looked so wet and beseeching and desperate. But he never ate the sandwich. No one seemed to own him or to know where he came from: Plymouth is a large city and he might have belonged to anybody.

At tea time Granny Pearce came through the pouring rain to bring a flask of hot tea with brandy in it to her daughter and son-in-law. Just as she reached the main entrance the guard was gently but forcibly shoving out a large, <u>agitated</u>, soaking-wet Alsatian dog.

"No, old fellow, you can *not* come in. Hospitals are for people, not for dogs."

"Why, bless me," exclaimed old Mrs. Pearce. "That's Lob! Here, Lob. Lobby boy!"

Lob ran to her, whining. Mrs. Pearce walked up to the desk.

"I'm sorry, madam, you can't bring that dog in here," the guard said.

Mrs. Pearce was a very determined old lady. She looked the porter in the eye.

"Now, see here, young man. That dog has walked twenty miles from St. Killan to get to my granddaughter. Heaven knows how he knew she was here, but it's plain he knows. And he ought to have his rights! He ought to get to see her! Do you know," she went on, bristling, "that dog has walked the length of England—*twice*—to be with that girl? And you think you can keep him out with your fiddling rules and regulations?"

"I'll have to ask the medical officer," the guard said weakly.

"You do that, young man." Granny Pearce sat down in a determined manner, shutting her umbrella, and Lob sat patiently dripping at her feet. Every now and then he shook his head, as if to dislodge something heavy that was tied around his neck.

Presently a tired, thin, intelligent-looking man in a white coat came downstairs, with an impressive, silver-haired man in a dark suit, and there was a low-voiced discussion. Granny Pearce eyed them, biding her time.

"Frankly . . . not much to lose," said the older man. The man in the white coat approached Granny Pearce.

"It's strictly against every rule, but as it's such a serious case we are making an exception," he said to her quietly. "But only *outside* her bedroom door—and only for a moment or two."

Without a word, Granny Pearce rose and stumped upstairs. Lob followed close to her skirts, as if he knew his hope lay with her.

Vocabulary
agitated (aj′ ə tāt′ əd) *adj.* excited, nervous, or disturbed; stirred up

Lob's Girl

They waited in the green-floored corridor outside Sandy's room. The door was half shut. Bert and Jean were inside. Everything was terribly quiet. A nurse came out. The white-coated man asked her something and she shook her head. She had left the door ajar, and through it could now be seen a high, narrow bed with a lot of gadgets around it. Sandy lay there, very flat under the covers, very still. Her head was turned away. All Lob's attention was riveted on the bed. He strained toward it, but Granny Pearce clasped his collar firmly.

"I've done a lot for you, my boy, now you behave yourself," she whispered grimly. Lob let out a faint whine, anxious and pleading.

At the sound of that whine Sandy stirred just a little. She sighed and moved her head the least fraction. Lob whined again. And then Sandy turned her head right over. Her eyes opened, looking at the door.

"Lob?" she murmured—no more than a breath of sound. "Lobby, boy?"

The doctor by Granny Pearce drew a quick, sharp breath. Sandy moved her left arm—the one that was not broken—from below the covers and let her hand dangle down, feeling, as she always did in the mornings, for Lob's furry head. The doctor nodded slowly.

"All right," he whispered. "Let him go to the bedside. But keep ahold of him."

Granny Pearce and Lob moved to the bedside. Now she could see Bert and Jean, white-faced and shocked, on the far side of the bed. But she didn't look at them. She looked at the smile on her granddaughter's face as the groping fingers found Lob's wet ears and gently pulled them. "Good boy," whispered Sandy, and fell asleep again.

Granny Pearce led Lob out into the passage again. There she let go of him and he ran off swiftly down the stairs. She would have followed him, but Bert and Jean had come out into the passage, and she spoke to Bert fiercely.

"I don't know why you were so foolish as not to bring the dog before! Leaving him to find the way here himself—"

"But, Mother!" said Jean Pengelly. "That can't have been Lob. What a chance to take! Suppose Sandy hadn't—" She stopped, with her handkerchief pressed to her mouth.

"Not Lob? I've known that dog nine years! I suppose I ought to know my own granddaughter's dog?"

"Listen, Mother," said Bert. "Lob was killed by the same truck that hit Sandy. Don found him—when he went to look for Sandy's schoolbag. He was—he was dead. Ribs all smashed. No question of that. Don told me on the phone—he and Will Hoskins rowed a half mile out to sea and sank the dog with a lump of concrete tied to his collar. Poor old boy. Still—he was getting on. Couldn't have lasted forever."

"Sank him at sea? Then what—?"

Slowly old Mrs. Pearce, and then the other two, turned to look at the trail of dripping-wet footprints that led down the hospital stairs.

In the Pengellys' garden they have a stone, under the palm tree. It says: "Lob. Sandy's dog. Buried at sea."

Responding to Literature

PERSONAL RESPONSE

◆ What do you think really happened in the hospital room?

Analyzing Literature

RECALL

1. How far does Lob travel to reach the Pengelly family after his owner returns to Liverpool?
2. Why does Lob's owner give the dog away?
3. What happens to Sandy nine years after she meets Lob?
4. What visitor does Granny Pearce see outside the hospital? How does Sandy respond to the visitor?

INTERPRET

5. What do you think would motivate a dog like Lob to travel great distances to return to a place he had once visited?
6. Describe the difference between the former owner's and Sandy's attachment to Lob.
7. The author includes a detailed description of the accident scene. In your opinion, why doesn't the author reveal at that point that the victim is Sandy?
8. Why are Sandy's parents especially shocked at Sandy's response to the dog?

EVALUATE AND CONNECT

9. Do you believe a pet could actually cause a medical change in a patient? Explain.
10. Theme Connection   What does the story's ending suggest about the power of Sandy's and Lob's feelings for each other?

LITERARY ELEMENTS

Suspense

Have you ever been so anxious while reading a story that you've held your breath or bitten your nails? That feeling of uncertainty about what will happen next in a story is caused by the **suspense** a writer creates. Writers can build suspense by raising questions in a reader's mind about characters and their motivations, by describing a mood that is threatening or mysterious, or by including hints about possible developments.

1. How does the author build suspense about whether Lob will get to Sandy's hospital room?

2. Describe briefly how suspense was created in another story you have read.

● See **Literary Terms Handbook,** p. R11.

Literature and Writing

Writing About Literature

Resolution Do you think Joan Aiken wrote a satisfying conclusion to the story? Write a paragraph that analyzes the effectiveness of the story's **resolution.**

Personal Writing

Special Connections Look back at what you wrote about animals and people in the **Reading Focus** on page 658. Then write about your reaction to the character of Lob in a journal entry. Do you think he was believable? Can you imagine being as close to an animal as Sandy was to Lob?

Extending Your Response

Literature Groups

The Next Chapter By the end of the story, Sandy's fate is still unclear. With a group, brainstorm ideas for an added chapter for the story. Build on what you already know about the characters and setting. Draw pictures to illustrate your concept. Choose the one that best illustrates your group's ideas, and share it with the class.

Reading Further

If you would like to read other mysterious stories by Joan Aiken, try these:

The Wolves of Willoughby Chase

Night Fall

 Save your work for your portfolio.

Learning for Life

Community Service Plan Visits from animals can have a beneficial effect on the sick and elderly. Work with a partner to write a plan for your own community that involves students, their pets, and people who could be cheered by visits.

Interdisciplinary Activity

Science Alsatians are used frequently as guide dogs for the sight-impaired. Research ways in which another dog breed has been used to help humans. Consider such skills as hunting, herding, rescuing, guarding, and assisting the disabled. Present your findings as a television reporter.

Skill Minilessons

GRAMMAR AND LANGUAGE • APOSTROPHES IN POSSESSIVES

An **apostrophe** can be used to show possession. Follow these rules for forming possessives:

- Use an apostrophe and an *s* to form the possessive of a singular noun.
  Lob + **'s** = Lob**'s**
- Use an apostrophe and an *s* to form the possessive of a plural noun that does not end in *s*.
  children + **'s** = children**'s**
- Use an apostrophe alone to form the possessive of a plural noun that ends in *s*.
  dogs + **'** = dog**s'**

PRACTICE Write the possessive form of each word below.

1. Sandy
2. ambulances
3. ears
4. people
5. houses
6. train
7. women
8. telegram

● For more about apostrophes, see **Language Handbook,** p. R40.

READING AND THINKING • SCANNING

Scanning is a method of rapid reading in which you search quickly through a piece of writing for a particular piece of information. You can scan to look for the answer to a specific question. When scanning, run your eyes across each page of the story until they fall on the word or words you need.

● For more about scanning and related reading strategies, see **Reading Handbook,** pp. R76–R80.

PRACTICE Scan "Lob's Girl" to find the following information:

1. whose picture hangs by Granny Pearce's kitchen sink
2. a physical description of Lob
3. the names of two people who stayed at the Fisherman's Arms
4. the number of years Lob is a member of the family

VOCABULARY • UNLOCKING MEANING

Within *secretive,* you can see the word *secret.* These two words are related words. Using what you know about one can help you understand the other. Use what you know about each italicized word to complete each statement correctly.

PRACTICE Use what you know about each italicized word to complete the item.

1. *agitated* If an agitator spoke to a crowd of people, he or she would
   a. stir them up
   b. make them laugh
   c. calm them down
2. *succeed* The successor to the president of the United States is the
   a. Congress
   b. Supreme Court
   c. next president
3. *resolution* A resolute person could be described as
   a. worried
   b. determined
   c. confused
4. *aggrieved* If you write down your grievances, you make a list of
   a. possessions
   b. complaints
   c. assignments

Reading and Thinking Skills

Monitoring Comprehension

To get the most out of their reading, active readers ask questions as they read. By asking questions, they monitor their comprehension of a piece of writing. Ask yourself questions as you read the following passage from "Lob's Girl."

> Doctors are experts at stopping dangerous bleeding, for they know the right places to press. This Dr. Travers was able to do, but he didn't dare do more; the girl was lying in a queerly crumpled heap, and he guessed she had a number of bones broken and that it would be highly dangerous to move her. He watched her with great concentration, wondering where the truck had got to and what other damage it had done.

What does the doctor do for the injured girl? What does the writer mean by a "crumpled heap"? Why does the doctor wonder about the truck? If you can answer these kinds of questions about the scene, then you understand exactly what is happening. If not, stop and reread the passage until you can figure out what is going on.

● For more about monitoring comprehension, see **Reading Handbook,** pp. R85–R87.

EXERCISE

Read the following excerpt from "Lob's Girl." Then answer the questions.

> By that afternoon it became noticeable that a dog seemed to have taken up position outside the hospital, with the fixed intention of getting in. Patiently he would try first one entrance and then another, all the way around, and then begin again. Sometimes he would get a little way inside, following a visitor, but animals were, of course, forbidden, and he was always kindly but firmly turned out again.

1. Write at least two questions you might ask yourself as you monitor your comprehension of the passage.

2. From reading this description, what do you learn about the determination of the dog?

Writing Skills

Using Sentence Variety

What do these sentences from "Lob's Girl" have in common?

He must have walked.

He was a very tired dog.

Bert Pengelly rang up Liverpool again.

If you guessed that they are all fairly short sentences, you're right. There's nothing wrong with short sentences, but good writers like to vary their sentence patterns to avoid monotony. Notice the varied lengths in the following sentences from "Lob's Girl." You can add variety to your sentences by using techniques like these.

Alternate shorter sentences and longer sentences:

A week passed. Then, one evening, Mrs. Pengelly and the younger children were in the front room playing snakes and ladders.

Combine short sentences into long ones:

Lob's owner scolded him. He thanked Mrs. Pengelly for bringing him back.

Lob's owner scolded him and thanked Mrs. Pengelly for bringing him back.

Start with an adjective or adverb:

Horrified, Aunt Rebecca put on a coat and went down to her brother's house.

Start with an adverb phrase:

Without a word, Granny Pearce rose and stumped upstairs.

Start with a subordinate clause:

Just as she reached the main entrance, the guard was gently but forcibly shoving out a large, agitated, soaking-wet Alsatian dog.

EXERCISES

1. Look over something you have written. Revise it to increase the variety of your sentence patterns. Use the techniques shown above.

2. Write a paragraph describing a scene from your favorite animal story, television show, or movie. Vary your sentence patterns, using the techniques shown above.

Before You Read
Key Item

MEET ISAAC ASIMOV

Isaac Asimov (ī′ zək la′ zi môf) described his talent for explaining scientific principles as the ability to "read a dozen dull books and make one interesting book out of them." Asimov wrote or edited more than 500 books in his lifetime—far more than millions of Americans will read in a lifetime. Born in Russia, Asimov was raised in Brooklyn, New York. In addition to writing, he worked as a biochemist and taught biochemistry at Boston University.

Isaac Asimov was born in 1920 and died in 1992. "Key Item" was first published in 1968.

READING FOCUS

Are computers becoming more and more human-like?

Graph It!

Ask ten people whether computers will ever be as smart as humans, and if so, how soon. Compile your results in a graph and share it with the class.

Setting a Purpose

Read this story to find out what the "key item" is.

BUILDING BACKGROUND

The modern digital computer was first imagined by British mathematician Alan Turing in 1936. It looked like an automatic typewriter with math symbols instead of letters. Today, computers can turn appliances on and off, direct satellites, and create three-dimensional models of machines that do not exist. Chess-playing supercomputers can compute more than 100 million chess positions per second and have won games against world chess champions.

VOCABULARY PREVIEW

therapy (ther′ ə pē) *n.* treatment of an injury, disease, or mental disorder; p. 676

efficient (i fish′ ənt) *adj.* producing a desired effect with a minimum of effort or waste; p. 677

sufficient (sə fish′ ənt) *adj.* adequate; enough; p. 677

accede (ak sēd′) *v.* to give in; go along with; p. 677

collective (kə lek′ tiv) *adj.* having to do with a group of persons or things; common; shared; p. 677

KEY ITEM

Isaac Asimov

Jack Weaver came out of the vitals[1] of Multivac looking utterly worn and disgusted.

From the stool, where the other maintained his own stolid[2] watch, Todd Nemerson said, "Nothing?"

"Nothing," said Weaver. "Nothing, nothing, nothing. No one can find anything wrong with it."

"Except that it won't work, you mean."

"You're no help sitting there!"

"I'm thinking."

"Thinking!" Weaver showed a canine[3] at one side of his mouth.

Nemerson stirred impatiently on his stool. "Why not? There are six teams of computer technologists roaming around in the corridors of Multivac. They haven't come up with anything in three days. Can't you spare one person to think?"

"It's not a matter of thinking. We've got to look. Somewhere a relay is stuck."

"It's not that simple, Jack!"

"Who says it's simple. You know how many million relays we have there?"

---

1. *Vitals* are parts that are necessary to keep a body alive or a machine operating. Here, the word refers to small chambers containing such parts inside Multivac.
2. A *stolid* (stol′ id) person is behaving unemotionally, without excitement.
3. Weaver shows his disgust by curling his upper lip, revealing a tooth. The two pointed teeth on each side of the top front teeth are called *canine* (kā′ nīn) teeth.

"That doesn't matter. If it were just a relay, Multivac would have alternate circuits, devices for locating the flaw, and facilities to repair or replace the ailing part. The trouble is, Multivac won't only not answer the original question, it won't tell us what's wrong with it. —And meanwhile, there'll be panic in every city if we don't do something. The world's economy depends on Multivac, and everyone knows that."

"I know it, too. But what's there to do?"

"I told you, *think*. There must be something we're missing completely. Look, Jack, there isn't a computer bigwig in a hundred years who hasn't devoted himself to making Multivac more complicated. It can do so much now—hell, it can even talk and listen. It's practically as complex as the human brain. We can't understand the human brain, so why should we understand Multivac?"

"Aw, come on. Next you'll be saying Multivac is human."

"Why not?" Nemerson grew absorbed and seemed to sink into himself. "Now that you mention it, why not? Could we tell if Multivac passed the thin dividing line where it stopped being a machine and started being human? *Is* there a dividing line, for that matter? If the brain is just more complex than Multivac, and we keep making Multivac more complex, isn't there a point where . . ." He mumbled down into silence.

Weaver said impatiently, "What are you driving at? Suppose Multivac were human. How would that help us find out why it isn't working?"

"For a human reason, maybe. Suppose *you* were asked the most probable price of

wheat next summer and didn't answer. Why wouldn't you answer?"

"Because I wouldn't know. But Multivac would know! We've given it all the factors. It can analyze futures in weather, politics, and economics. We know it can. It's done it before."

"All right. Suppose I asked the question and you knew the answer but didn't tell me. Why not?"

Weaver snarled, "Because I had a brain tumor. Because I had been knocked out. Doggone it, because my machinery was out of order. That's just what we're trying to find out about Multivac. We're looking for the place where its machinery is out of order, for the key item."

"Only you haven't found it." Nemerson got off his stool. "Listen, ask me the question Multivac stalled on."

"How? Shall I run the tape through you?"

"Come on, Jack. Give me the talk that goes along with it. You do talk to Multivac, don't you?"

"I've got to. Therapy."

Nemerson nodded. "Yes, that's the story. Therapy. That's the official story. We talk to it in order to pretend it's a human being so that we don't get neurotic[4] over having a machine know so much more than we do. We turn a frightening metal monster into a protective father image."

"If you want to put it that way."

"Well, it's wrong and you know it. A computer as complex as Multivac *must* talk

---

4. *Neurotic* (noo rot′ ik) having symptoms of an emotional disorder.

Vocabulary

therapy (ther′ ə pē) *n.* treatment of an injury, disease, or mental disorder

and listen to be efficient. Just putting in and taking out coded dots isn't sufficient. At a certain level of complexity, Multivac must be made to seem human because, by God, it *is* human. Come on, Jack, ask me the question. I want to see my reaction to it."

Jack Weaver flushed. "This is silly."

"Come on, will you?"

It was a measure of Weaver's depression and desperation that he acceded. Half sullenly, he pretended to be feeding the program into Multivac, speaking as he did so in his usual manner. He commented on the latest information concerning farm unrest, talked about the new equations describing jet-stream contortions, lectured on the solar constant.

He began stiffly enough, but warmed to this task out of long habit, and when the last of the program was slammed home, he almost closed contact with a physical snap at Todd Nemerson's waist.

He ended briskly, "All right, now. Work that out and give us the answer pronto."

For a moment, having done, Jack Weaver stood there, nostrils flaring, as though he was feeling once more the excitement of throwing into action the most gigantic and glorious machine ever put together by the mind and hands of humans.

Then he remembered and muttered, "All right. That's it."

Nemerson said, "At least I know now why *I* wouldn't answer, so let's try that on Multivac. Look, clear Multivac; make sure the investigators have their paws off it. Then run the program into it and let me do the talking. Just once."

Weaver shrugged and turned to Multivac's control wall, filled with its somber, unwinking dials and lights. Slowly he cleared it. One by one he ordered the teams away.

Then, with a deep breath, he began once more feeding the program into Multivac. It was the twelfth time all told, the dozenth time. Somewhere a distant news commentator would spread the word that they were trying again. All over the world a Multivac-dependent people would be holding its collective breath.

Nemerson talked as Weaver fed the data silently. He talked diffidently,[5] trying to remember what it was that Weaver had said, but waiting for the moment when the key item might be added.

Weaver was done and now a note of tension was in Nemerson's voice. He said, "All right, now, Multivac. Work that out and give us the answer." He paused and added the key item. He said, *"Please!"*

And all over Multivac, the valves and relays went joyously to work. After all, a machine has feelings—when it isn't a machine anymore.

---

5. *Diffidently* means "in a way that shows a lack of confidence; shyly."

Vocabulary

efficient (i fish′ ənt) *adj.* producing a desired effect with a minimum of effort or waste

sufficient (sə fish′ ənt) *adj.* adequate; enough

accede (ək sēd′) *v.* to give in; go along with

collective (kə lek′ tiv) *adj.* having to do with a group of persons or things; common; shared

Bizzaro

Dan Piraro/Universal Press Syndicate.

Viewing the cartoon: In what ways is the theme of this cartoon similar to and different from Asimov's story?

Responding to Literature

PERSONAL RESPONSE

◆ Did the story end the way you expected it would? Why or why not?

Analyzing Literature

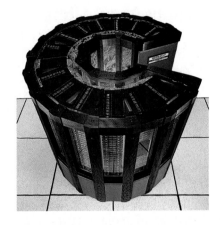

RECALL

1. What is Multivac and what does it do?
2. Why is the breakdown causing panic in every city?
3. What does Nemerson ask Weaver to do to help solve the problem of finding the key item?
4. What does the key item turn out to be?

INTERPRET

5. Why does Nemerson think Multivac could be human?
6. How is the future world of this story different from our world?
7. How does Weaver's attitude toward Multivac differ from Nemerson's?
8. In your opinion, how did Nemerson figure out what the key item was?

EVALUATE AND CONNECT

9. **Theme Connection**   Some of the technologies in Asimov's stories have been invented or were discovered years after he wrote about them. In your opinion, could the events in "Key Item" ever really happen? Explain why or why not.
10. How would your life be affected if you lived in a world where computers were nearly human?

LITERARY ELEMENTS

Irony

Irony is the difference between the way things seem to be and the way they actually are. Irony can also contrast what is expected with what actually happens. Authors use irony to create humor or strong emotion. Surprise endings often involve irony. In "Key Item," for example, the answer to why the computer isn't responding is ironic.

1. Why is the title of this story an example of irony? Explain fully.

2. Think about some of the other selections you have read in this book. Explain how irony is used in one of them.

● See **Literary Terms Handbook,** p. R6.

Extending Your Response

Writing About Literature

Main Characters   Although Jack Weaver and Todd Nemerson are the first two characters readers meet in "Key Item," there is also a third character in the story. Write a paragraph explaining why Multivac should be viewed as an important character.

Learning for Life

User's Manual   Get a copy of the user's manual or instruction sheet for using a simple mechanical device—for example, a stapler, a can opener, a mechanical pencil or pencil sharpener. Read it carefully. Then explain the use of the device to a partner and see if he or she understands your instructions.

Literature Groups

The Science in Science Fiction   All science-fiction stories are based on scientific information. Make a list of scientific facts or jargon that Asimov includes in "Key Item." Share your list with other groups.

Personal Writing

Life in a Technological Future   Some people are excited to imagine a life in which humans depend on smarter and smarter machines. Others are fearful about what a super-technological world might be like. Drawing upon the results of your question in the **Reading Focus** on page 674, create a vision of how you believe people may use computers many years from now. Write a description of your vision.

Reading Further

Try these other robot stories by Isaac Asimov:

I, Robot

Robot Dreams

If you like science fiction, try one or all of these three connected novels by John Christopher: *The White Mountains*, *The City of Gold and Lead*, and *The Pool of Fire*

📖 **Save your work for your portfolio.**

Skill Minilesson

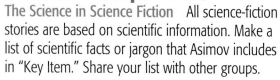

VOCABULARY • ETYMOLOGY

The etymology, or history, of the word *collective* shows that it comes from the Latin *com,* meaning "together," and *legere,* "to gather." To gather things together is to *collect* them.

When Weaver *acceded* to Nemerson, he gave in. *Accede* comes from the Latin *ad,* meaning "to," and *cedere,* "to yield," which combine to mean "to yield to."

The dials and lights of the unworking Multivac are described as *somber,* which comes from the Latin *sub,* meaning "under," and *umbra,* "shade."

PRACTICE Use the information about etymologies to answer the questions.
1. What word comes from the Latin *umbra* and names something that can block the sun or the rain?
2. When a nation *cedes* land, does that nation buy land, give up land, or use land wisely?
3. Is a *collective* farm one that is successful, one that is operated by a group, or one that specializes in multiple crops?

Communicating on the Net

Netiquette

"Netiquette" is a set of rules for behavior on the Internet. Many of these rules are not much different from the rules of etiquette for any other behavior. Put simply, you should behave toward others on the Net as you'd like them to behave toward you.

Other rules are unique to the Net. For example, DON'T SHOUT! Using all capital letters is considered shouting. It's also considered impolite and the sign of a "newbie," or new-comer. To emphasize a word or phrase, put *asterisks* before and after it.

Speaking of newbies, if you visit a new newsgroup or chat room, don't start out by asking too many questions. First read the FAQs (pronounced "faks"). FAQs stands for Frequently Asked Questions, and you'll nearly always find a set of them (with answers) at a newsgroup or chat site.

Smileys and Emoticons

In face-to-face communication, you can read people's expressions or body language to tell if they are happy, sad, or joking. But how do you know whether people are joking or serious online? Two popular tools that help relay such information on the computer screen are *smileys* and *emoticons.*

Smileys are images made with the characters found on a keyboard. Viewed sideways, they make pictures. Examples: a happy face :) a happy face with a nose :-)

Emoticons (a word made by putting together *emotion* and *icons*) tell your online penpal how you feel. For instance, instead of writing *I'm sad that I have to miss art class on Thursday,* you could write: *I have to miss art class on Thursday <sad>.* You create emoticons by putting < > symbols around a word that tells a reader what you're doing or feeling. Here are a few more examples:

<blush>   <angry>   <giggle>   <wink>   <silly grin>

Acronyms
FAQ is an **acronym**. An acronym uses initials to stand for a phrase. Here are some examples often used on the Net.

ASAP	as soon as possible
B4N	[good]bye for now
BRB	be right back
BTW	by the way
CUL	see you later
F2F	face to face
IMHO	in my humble opinion
KWIM	know what I mean?
TIA	thanks in advance

Smileys	
:-)	= happy
:-(	= sad
:'-(	= crying
'-)	= a wink
:-x	= my lips are sealed

ACTIVITIES

1. Make up at least two emoti-cons and two acronyms. Use your made-up emoti-cons and acronyms, and some from the lists on this page, to compose an e-mail to a real or an imaginary friend.

2. Explain to a younger person how to make and use emoticons.

Before You Read
The Smallest Dragonboy

MEET ANNE McCAFFREY

Sometimes called science fiction's "Dragon Lady," Anne McCaffrey lives in Ireland, in a home called Dragonhold. It is there that she weaves her rich tales. In order to create the world of Pern, McCaffrey returned to graduate school to study physics. Although dragons are more common in fantasy stories, McCaffrey's dragon stories have become popular with readers of science fiction. "If you write a good story," she says, "anybody will read it."

Anne McCaffrey was born in Massachusetts in 1926.

READING FOCUS

What kinds of pressures can peers place on one another?

Think/Pair/Share
Take a moment to jot down notes about your own peer-pressure experiences and what you have learned from them. Then share your thoughts with a partner.

Setting a Purpose
Read to find out how the smallest dragonboy deals with peer pressure.

BUILDING BACKGROUND

The Time and Place   The setting is the imaginary planet Pern, sometime in the future.

Carved dragon-head post from the ship burial at Oseberg, c. 850. Viking Ship Museum, Bygdoy, Norway.

Did You Know?   This fantasy story takes place in a world created by the imagination of the writer Anne McCaffrey. Pern is the setting of many of McCaffrey's stories. A former colony of Earth, Pern is protected from deadly spores, referred to as "Thread," by fire-breathing dragons and human dragonriders, who live together in communities called Weyrs.

VOCABULARY PREVIEW

enticing (en tīs′ ing) *adj.* offering pleasure or reward; p. 684
jeer (jēr) *v.* to make fun of (someone or something) rudely and openly; p. 684
enviable (en′ vē ə bəl) *adj.* good enough to be highly desired; p. 685
replenish (ri plen′ ish) *v.* to provide a new supply; p. 687
exasperation (ig zas′ pə rā′ shən) *n.* anger or great irritation; p. 689
desolation (des′ ə lā′ shən) *n.* sadness; loneliness; p. 689

The Smallest Dragonboy

Anne McCaffrey ⌇⁓

Although Keevan lengthened his walking stride as far as his legs
would stretch, he couldn't quite keep up with the other candidates.
He knew he would be teased again.

Just as he knew many other things that his foster mother told him he
ought not to know, Keevan knew that Beterli, the most senior of the
boys, set that spanking pace just to embarrass him, the smallest dragonboy. Keevan would arrive, tail fork-end of the group, breathless, chest
heaving, and maybe get a stern look from the instructing wingsecond.

The Smallest Dragonboy

Dragonriders, even if they were still only hopeful candidates for the glowing eggs which were hardening on the hot sands of the Hatching Ground cavern, were expected to be punctual and prepared. Sloth was not tolerated by the weyrleader of Benden Weyr. A good record was especially important now. It was very near hatching time, when the baby dragons would crack their mottled shells and stagger forth to choose their lifetime companions. The very thought of that glorious moment made Keevan's breath catch in his throat. To be chosen—to be a dragonrider! To sit astride the neck of the winged beast with the jeweled eyes: to be his friend in telepathic communion[1] with him for life; to be his companion in good times and fighting extremes; to fly effortlessly over the lands of Pern! Or, thrillingly, *between* to any point anywhere on the world! Flying *between* was done on dragonback or not at all, and it was dangerous.

Keevan glanced upward, past the black mouths of the weyr caves in which grown dragons and their chosen riders lived, toward the Star Stones that crowned the ridge of the old volcano that was Benden Weyr. On the height, the blue watch dragon, his rider mounted on his neck, stretched the great transparent pinions[2] that carried him on the winds of Pern to fight the evil Thread that fell at certain times from the sky. The many-faceted rainbow jewels of his eyes glistened momentarily in the greeny sun. He folded his great wings to his back, and the watchpair resumed their statuesque pose of alertness.

Then the enticing view was obscured as Keevan passed into the Hatching Ground cavern. The sands underfoot were hot, even through heavy wher-hide boots. How the bootmaker had protested having to sew so small! Keevan was forced to wonder again why being small was reprehensible.[3] People were always calling him "babe" and shooing him away as being "too small" or "too young" for this or that. Keevan was constantly working, twice as hard as any other boy his age, to prove himself capable. What if his muscles weren't as big as Beterli's? They were just as hard. And if he couldn't overpower anyone in a wrestling match, he could outdistance everyone in a footrace.

"Maybe if you run fast enough," Beterli had jeered on the occasion when Keevan had been goaded[4] to boast of his swiftness, "you could catch a dragon. That's the only way you'll make a dragonrider!"

"You just wait and see, Beterli, you just wait," Keevan had replied. He would have liked to wipe the contemptuous[5] smile from Beterli's face, but the guy didn't fight fair even when the wingsecond was watching. "No one knows what Impresses a dragon!"

"They've got to be able to *find* you first, babe!"

---

1. In *telepathic communion*, thoughts are shared directly between two minds.
2. A bird's *pinions* are its wings or wing feathers.

3. Something that's *reprehensible* is deserving of sharp criticism.
4. To *goad* means "to pressure someone to do something; urge on."
5. *Contemptuous* means "proud and scornful."

Vocabulary

enticing (en tīs′ ing) *adj.* offering pleasure or reward
jeer (jēr) *v.* to make fun of (someone or something) rudely and openly

Yes, being the smallest candidate was not an <u>enviable</u> position. It was therefore imperative[6] that Keevan Impress a dragon in his first hatching. That would wipe the smile off every face in the cavern, and accord him the respect due any dragon-rider, even the smallest one.

Besides, no one knew exactly what Impressed the baby dragons as they struggled from their shells in search of their life-time partners.

"I like to believe that dragons see into a man's heart," Keevan's foster mother, Mende, told him. "If they find goodness, honesty, a flexible mind, patience, courage—and you've that in quantity, dear Keevan—that's what dragons look for. I've seen many a well-grown lad left standing on the sands, Hatching Day, in favor of someone not so strong or tall or handsome. And if my memory serves me" (which it usually did—Mende knew every word of every Harper's tale worth telling, although Keevan did not interrupt her to say so), "I don't believe that F'lar, our weyrleader, was all that tall when bronze Mnementh chose him. And Mnementh was the only bronze dragon of that hatching."

Dreams of Impressing a bronze were beyond Keevan's boldest reflections, although that goal dominated[7] the thoughts of every other hopeful candidate. Green dragons were small and fast and more numerous. There was more prestige[8] in Impressing a blue or a brown than a green. Being practical, Keevan seldom dreamed as high as a big fighting brown, like Canth, F'nor's fine fellow, the biggest brown on all Pern. But to fly a bronze? Bronzes were almost as big as the queen, and only they took the air when a queen flew at mating time. A bronze rider could aspire to become weyrleader! Well, Keevan would console himself, brown riders could aspire to become wingseconds, and that wasn't bad. He'd even settle for a green dragon: they were small, but so was he. No matter! He simply had to Impress a dragon his first time in the Hatching Ground. Then no one in the weyr would taunt[9] him anymore for being so small.

"Shells," thought Keevan now, "but the sands are hot!"

"Impression time is imminent, candidates," the wingsecond was saying as everyone crowded respectfully close to him. "See the extent of the striations[10] on this promising egg." The stretch marks *were* larger than yesterday.

Everyone leaned forward and nodded thoughtfully. That particular egg was the one Beterli had marked as his own, and no other candidate dared, on pain of being beaten by Beterli on the first opportunity, to approach it. The egg was marked by a large yellowish splotch in the shape of a dragon backwinging to land, talons outstretched to grasp rock. Everyone knew that bronze eggs bore distinctive markings. And naturally, Beterli, who'd been presented at eight Impressions already and

---

6. If something is *imperative*, it is absolutely necessary.
7. To *dominate* is to control.
8. Someone with *prestige* is admired and respected by others.

9. To *taunt* is to make fun of in a scornful, insulting way.
10. Something *imminent* is likely to happen soon. The *striations* are grooves or marks—as used here, they are probably cracks that appear as the eggs begin to hatch.

Vocabulary
enviable (en′ vē ə bəl) *adj.* good enough to be highly desired

was the biggest of the candidates, had chosen it.

"I'd say that the great opening day is almost upon us," the wingsecond went on, and then his face assumed a grave expression. "As we well know, there are only forty eggs and seventy-two candidates. Some of you may be disappointed on the great day. That doesn't necessarily mean you aren't dragonrider material, just that *the* dragon for you hasn't been shelled. You'll have other hatchings, and it's no disgrace to be left behind an Impression or two. Or more."

Keevan was positive that the wingsecond's eyes rested on Beterli, who'd been stood off at so many Impressions already. Keevan tried to squinch down so the wingsecond wouldn't notice him. Keevan had been reminded too often that he was eligible to be a candidate by one day only. He, of all the hopefuls, was most likely to

be left standing on the great day. One more reason why he simply had to Impress at his first hatching.

"Now move about among the eggs," the wingsecond said. "Touch them. We don't know that it does any good, but it certainly doesn't do any harm."

Some of the boys laughed nervously, but everyone immediately began to circulate among the eggs. Beterli stepped up officiously to "his" egg, daring anyone to come near it. Keevan smiled, because he had already touched it . . . every inspection day . . . as the others were leaving the Hatching Ground, when no one could see him crouch and stroke it.

Keevan had an egg he concentrated on, too, one drawn slightly to the far side of the others. The shell bore a soft greenish blue tinge with a faint creamy swirl design. The consensus[11] was that this egg contained a mere green, so Keevan was rarely bothered by rivals. He was somewhat perturbed then to see Beterli wandering over to him.

"I don't know why you're allowed in this Impression, Keevan. There are enough of us without a babe," Beterli said, shaking his head.

"I'm of age." Keevan kept his voice level, telling himself not to be bothered by mere words.

"Yah!" Beterli made a show of standing on his

The Two Mythical Dragons. Sir Roy Calne, F. R. S. Private collection.

Viewing the painting: Are these mythical dragons intended to be frightening? Do they fit with your image of dragons in the story? Give reasons for your answer.

11. A *consensus* is an opinion shared by most members of a group.

toe tips. "You can't even see over an egg; Hatching Day, you better get in front or the dragons won't see you at all. 'Course, you could get run down that way in the mad scramble. Oh, I forget, you can run fast, can't you?"

"You'd better make sure a dragon sees *you*, this time, Beterli," Keevan replied. "You're almost overage, aren't you?"

Beterli flushed and took a step forward, hand half-raised. Keevan stood his ground, but if Beterli advanced one more step, he would call the wingsecond. No one fought on the Hatching Ground. Surely Beterli knew that much.

Fortunately, at that moment the wingsecond called the boys together and led them from the Hatching Ground to start on evening chores.

There were "glows" to be replenished in the main kitchen caverns and sleeping cubicles, the major hallways, and the queen's apartment. Firestone sacks had to be filled against Thread attack, and black rock brought to the kitchen hearths. The boys fell to their chores, tantalized[12] by the odors of roasting meat. The population of the weyr began to assemble for the evening meal, and the dragonriders came in from the Feeding Ground or their sweep checks.

It was the time of day Keevan liked best: once the chores were done, before dinner was served, a fellow could often get close to the dragonriders and listen to their talk. Tonight Keevan's father, K'last, was at the main dragonrider table. It puzzled Keevan how his father, a brown rider and a tall man, could *be* his father—because he, Keevan, was so small. It obviously never puzzled K'last when he deigned to notice his small son: "In a few more turns, you'll be as tall as I am—or taller!"

K'last was pouring Benden drink all around the table. The dragonriders were relaxing. There'd be no Thread attack for three more days, and they'd be in the mood to tell tall tales, better than Harper yarns, about impossible maneuvers they'd done a-dragonback. When Thread attack was closer, their talk would change to a discussion of tactics of evasion, of going *between*, how long to suspend there until the burning but fragile Thread would freeze and crack and fall harmlessly off dragon and man. They would dispute the exact moment to feed firestone to the dragon so he'd have the best flame ready to sear Thread midair and render[13] it harmless to ground—and man—below. There was such a lot to know and understand about being a dragonrider that sometimes Keevan was overwhelmed. How would he ever be able to remember everything he ought to know at the right moment? He couldn't dare ask such a question; this would only have given additional weight to the notion that he was too young yet to be a dragonrider.

"Having older candidates makes good sense," L'vel was saying, as Keevan settled down near the table. "Why waste four to five years of a dragon's fighting prime until his rider grows up enough to stand the rigors?" L'vel had Impressed a blue of Ramoth's

---

12. To *tantalize* is to tempt or tease someone with something that person cannot have.

13. *Sear* means "scorch or burn," and *render,* as used here, means "make."

Vocabulary
replenish (ri plen' ish) *v.* to provide a new supply

first clutch. Most of the candidates thought L'vel was marvelous because he spoke up in front of the older riders, who awed them. "That was well enough in the Interval when you didn't need to mount the full weyr complement to fight Thread. But not now. Not with more eligible candidates than ever. Let the babes wait."

"Any boy who is over twelve turns has the right to stand in the Hatching Ground," K'last replied, a slight smile on his face. He never argued or got angry. Keevan wished he were more like his father. And oh, how he wished he were a brown rider! "Only a dragon . . . each particular dragon . . . knows what he wants in a rider. We certainly can't tell. Time and again the theorists," and K'last's smile deepened as his eyes swept those at the table, "are surprised by dragon choice. *They* never seem to make mistakes, however."

"Now, K'last, just look at the roster this Impression. Seventy-two boys and only forty eggs. Drop off the twelve youngest, and there's still a good field for the hatchlings to choose from. Shells! There are a couple of weyrlings unable to see over a wher egg much less a dragon! And years before they can ride Thread."

"True enough, but the weyr is scarcely under fighting strength, and if the youngest Impress, they'll be old enough to fight when the oldest of our current dragons go *between* from senility."[14]

"Half the weyrbred lads have already been through several Impressions," one of the bronze riders said then. "I'd say drop some of *them* off this time. Give the untried a chance."

"There's nothing wrong in presenting a clutch with as wide a choice as possible," said the weyrleader, who had joined the table with Lessa, the weyrwoman.

"Has there ever been a case," she said, smiling in her odd way at the riders, "where a hatchling didn't choose?"

Her suggestion was almost heretical[15] and drew astonished gasps from everyone, including the boys.

F'lar laughed. "You say the most outrageous things, Lessa."

"Well, *has* there ever been a case where a dragon didn't choose?"

"Can't say as I recall one," K'last replied.

"Then we continue in this tradition," Lessa said firmly, as if that ended the matter.

But it didn't. The argument ranged from one table to the other all through dinner, with some favoring a weeding out of the candidates to the most likely, lopping off those who were very young or who had had multiple opportunities to Impress. All the candidates were in a swivet,[16] though such a departure from tradition would be to the advantage of many. As the evening progressed, more riders were favoring eliminating the youngest and those who'd passed four or more Impressions unchosen. Keevan felt he could bear such a dictum if only Beterli was also eliminated. But this seemed less likely than that Keevan would be tuffed out, since the weyr's need was for fighting dragons and riders.

By the time the evening meal was over, no decision had been reached, although the weyrleader had promised to give the matter due consideration.

---

14. *Senility* refers to a loss of mental abilities that sometimes comes with old age.

15. Something that is *heretical* goes against what most people consider to be right, true, or proper.

16. A *swivet* (swiv' ət) or (swiv' it) is a condition of strain and confusion.

He might have slept on the problem, but few of the candidates did. Tempers were uncertain in the sleeping caverns next morning as the boys were routed out of their beds to carry water and black rock and cover the "glows." Mende had to call Keevan to order twice for clumsiness.

"Whatever is the matter with you, boy?" she demanded in exasperation when he tipped black rock short of the bin and sooted up the hearth.

"They're going to keep me from this Impression."

"What?" Mende stared at him. "Who?"

"You heard them talking at dinner last night. They're going to tuff the babes from the hatching."

Mende regarded him a moment longer before touching his arm gently. "There's lots of talk around a supper table, Keevan. And it cools as soon as the supper. I've heard the same nonsense before every hatching, but nothing is ever changed."

"There's always a first time," Keevan answered, copying one of her own phrases.

"That'll be enough of that, Keevan. Finish your job. If the clutch does hatch today, we'll need full rock bins for the feast, and you won't be around to do the filling. All my fosterlings make dragonriders."

"The first time?" Keevan was bold enough to ask as he scooted off with the rockbarrow.

Perhaps, Keevan thought later, if he hadn't been on that chore just when Beterli was also fetching black rock, things might have turned out differently. But he had dutifully trundled the barrow to the outdoor bunker for another load just as Beterli arrived on a similar errand.

"Heard the news, babe?" asked Beterli. He was grinning from ear to ear, and he put an unnecessary emphasis on the final insulting word.

"The eggs are cracking?" Keevan all but dropped the loaded shovel. Several anxieties flicked through his mind then; he was black with rock dust—would he have time to wash before donning the white tunic[17] of candidacy? And if the eggs were hatching, why hadn't the candidates been recalled by the wingsecond?

"Naw! Guess again!" Beterli was much too pleased with himself.

With a sinking heart Keevan knew what the news must be, and he could only stare with intense desolation at the older boy.

"C'mon! Guess, babe!"

"I've no time for guessing games," Keevan managed to say with indifference. He began to shovel black rock into his barrow as fast as he could.

"I said, 'guess'." Beterli grabbed the shovel.

"And I said I'd no time for guessing games."

Beterli wrenched the shovel from Keevan's hands. "Guess!"

"I'll have the shovel back, Beterli." Keevan straightened up, but he didn't come up to Beterli's bulky shoulder. From somewhere, other boys appeared, some with barrows, some mysteriously alerted to

---

17. A *tunic* is a garment resembling a long shirt.

Vocabulary

exasperation (ig zas′ pə rā′ shən) *n.* anger or great irritation
desolation (des′ ə lā′ shən) *n.* sadness; loneliness

the prospect of a confrontation among their numbers.

"Babes don't give orders to candidates around here, babe!"

Someone sniggered and Keevan knew, incredibly, that he must've been dropped from the candidacy.

He yanked the shovel from Beterli's loosened grasp. Snarling, the older boy tried to regain possession, but Keevan clung with all his strength to the handle, dragged back and forth as the stronger boy jerked the shovel about.

With a sudden, unexpected movement, Beterli rammed the handle into Keevan's chest, knocking him over the barrow handles. Keevan felt a sharp, painful jab behind his left ear, an unbearable pain in his right shin, and then a painless nothingness.

Mende's angry voice roused him, and startled, he tried to throw back the covers, thinking he'd overslept. But he couldn't move, so firmly was he tucked into his bed. And then the constriction of a bandage on his head and the dull sickishness in his leg brought back recent occurrences.

"Hatching?" he cried.

"No, lovey," said Mende, and her voice was suddenly very kind, her hand cool and gentle on his forehead. "Though there's some as won't be at any hatching again." Her voice took on a stern edge.

Keevan looked beyond her to see the weyrwoman, who was frowning with irritation.

"Keevan, will you tell me what occurred at the black-rock bunker?" Lessa asked, but her voice wasn't angry.

He remembered Beterli now and the quarrel over the shovel and . . . what had

Mende said about some not being at any hatching? Much as he hated Beterli, he couldn't bring himself to tattle on Beterli and force him out of candidacy.

"Come, lad," and a note of impatience crept into the weyrwoman's voice. "I merely want to know what happened from you, too. Mende said she sent you for black rock. Beterli—and every weyrling in the cavern—seems to have been on the same errand. What happened?"

"Beterli took the shovel. I hadn't finished with it."

"There's more than one shovel. What did he *say* to you?"

"He'd heard the news."

"What news?" The weyrwoman was suddenly amused.

"That . . . that . . . there'd been changes."

"Is that what he said?"

"Not exactly."

"What did he say? C'mon, lad. I've heard from everyone else, you know."

"He said for me to guess the news."

"And you fell for that old gag?" The weyrwoman's irritation returned.

"Consider all the talk last night at supper, Lessa," said Mende. "Of course the boy would think he'd been eliminated."

"In effect, he is, with a broken skull and leg." She touched his arm, a rare gesture of sympathy in her. "Be that as it may, Keevan, you'll have other Impressions. Beterli will not. There are certain rules that must be observed by all candidates, and his conduct proves him unacceptable to the weyr."

She smiled at Mende and then left.

"I'm still a candidate?" Keevan asked urgently.

"Well, you are and you aren't, lovey," his foster mother said. "Is the numb weed working?" she asked, and when he nodded, she said, "You just rest. I'll bring you some nice broth."

At any other time in his life, Keevan would have relished such cosseting,[18] but he lay there worrying. Beterli had been dismissed. Would the others think it was his fault? But everyone was there! Beterli provoked the fight. His worry increased, because although he heard excited comings and goings in the passageway, no one tweaked back the curtain across the sleeping alcove[19] he shared with five other boys. Surely one of them would have to come in sometime. No, they were all avoiding him. And something else was wrong. Only he didn't know what.

Mende returned with broth and beachberry bread.

"Why doesn't anyone come see me, Mende? I haven't done anything wrong, have I? I didn't ask to have Beterli tuffed out."

Mende soothed him, saying everyone was busy with noontime chores and no one was mad at him. They were giving him a chance to rest in quiet. The numb weed made him drowsy, and her words were fair enough. He permitted his fears to dissipate.[20] Until he heard the humming. It started low, too low to be heard. Rather he felt it in the broken shin bone and his sore head. And thought, at first, it was an effect of the numb weed. Then the hum grew, augmented by additional sources. Two things registered suddenly in Keevan's groggy mind: The only

Dragonmen don't cry! Dragonmen learn to live with pain. . . .

white candidate's robe still on the pegs in the chamber was his; and dragons hummed when a clutch was being laid or being hatched. Impression! And he was flat abed.

Bitter, bitter disappointment turned the warm broth sour in his belly. Even the small voice telling him that he'd have other opportunities failed to alleviate[21] his crushing depression. *This* was the Impression that mattered! This was his chance to show *everyone* from Mende to K'last to L'vel and even the weyrleaders that he, Keevan, was worthy of being a dragonrider.

He twisted in bed, fighting against the tears that threatened to choke him. Dragonmen don't cry! Dragonmen learn to live with pain. . . .

Pain? The leg didn't actually pain him as he rolled about on his bedding. His head felt sort of stiff from the tightness of the bandage. He sat up, an effort in itself since the numb weed made exertion difficult. He touched the splinted leg, but the knee was unhampered. He had no feeling in his bone, really. He swung himself carefully to the side of his bed and slowly stood. The room wanted to swim about him. He closed his eyes, which made the dizziness worse, and he had to clutch the bedpost.

Gingerly he took a step. The broken leg dragged. It hurt in spite of the numb weed, but what was pain to a dragonman?

No one had said he couldn't go to the Impression. "You are and you aren't," were Mende's exact words.

Clinging to the bedpost, he jerked off his bedshirt. Stretching his arm to the

---

18. *Cosseting* means "pampering."
19. An *alcove* (al' kōv) is a small room or shallow opening off a larger room.
20. Keevan's fears gradually disappear *(dissipate).*

21. To *alleviate* is to lessen, relieve, or make easier to bear.

utmost, he jerked his white candidate's tunic from the peg. Jamming first one arm and then the other into the holes, he pulled it over his head. Too bad about the belt. He couldn't wait. He hobbled to the door, hung on to the curtain to steady himself. The weight on his leg was unwieldy.[22] He'd not get very far without something to lean on. Down by the bathing pool was one of the long crook-necked poles used to retrieve clothes from the hot washing troughs. But it was down there, and he was on the level above. And there was no one nearby to come to his aid: everyone would be in the Hatching Ground right now, eagerly waiting for the first egg to crack.

The humming increased in volume and tempo, an urgency to which Keevan responded, knowing that his time was all too limited if he was to join the ranks of the hopeful boys standing about the cracking eggs. But if he hurried down the ramp, he'd fall flat on his face.

He could, of course, go flat on his rear end, the way crawling children did. He sat down, the jar sending a stab of pain through his leg and up to the wound on the back of his head. Gritting his teeth and blinking away the tears, Keevan scrabbled down the ramp. He had to wait a moment at the bottom to catch his breath. He got to one knee, the injured leg straight out in front of him. Somehow, he managed to push himself erect, though the room wanted to tip over his ears. It wasn't far to the crooked stick, but it seemed an age before he had it in his hand.

Then the humming stopped!

Keevan cried out and began to hobble frantically across the cavern, out to the bowl of the weyr. Never had the distance between the living caverns and the Hatching Ground seemed so great. Never had the weyr been so silent, breathless. As if the multitude of people and dragons watching the hatching held every breath in suspense. Not even the wind muttered down the steep sides of the bowl. The only sounds to break the stillness were Keevan's ragged breathing and the thump-thud of his stick on the hard-packed ground. Sometimes he had to hop twice on his good leg to maintain his balance. Twice he fell into the sand and had to pull himself up on the stick, his white tunic no longer spotless. Once he jarred himself so badly he couldn't get up immediately.

Then he heard the first exhalation of the crowd, the ooohs, the muted cheer, the susurrus[23] of excited whispers. An egg had cracked, and the dragon had chosen his rider. Desperation increased Keevan's hobble. Would he never reach the arching mouth of the Hatching Ground?

Another cheer and an excited spate of applause spurred Keevan to greater effort. If he didn't get there in moments, there'd be no unpaired hatchling left. Then he was actually staggering into the Hatching Ground, the sands hot on his bare feet.

No one noticed his entrance or his halting progress. And Keevan could see nothing but the backs of the white-robed candidates, seventy of them ringing the area around the eggs. Then one side would surge forward or back and there'd be a cheer. Another dragon had been Impressed. Suddenly a large gap appeared in the white human wall, and Keevan had his first sight of the eggs. There didn't seem to be *any* left uncracked, and he

---

22. *Unwieldy* means "clumsy and difficult to control."

23. A *susurrus* (sŏŏ sur′ əs) is a hum or whisper.

Rainbow Bridge by Moonlight. William Robinson Leigh (1866–1955). Oil on canvas, 35¾ x 47¾ in. Private collection.

Viewing the painting: What life would you expect to find in a setting like this? How might that life be connected to storybook dragons?

could see the lucky boys standing beside wobble-legged dragons. He could hear the unmistakable plaintive crooning of hatchlings and their squawks of protest as they'd fall awkwardly in the sand.

Suddenly he wished that he hadn't left his bed, that he'd stayed away from the Hatching Ground. Now everyone would see his ignominious[24] failure. He scrambled now as desperately to reach the shadowy walls of the Hatching Ground as he had struggled to cross the bowl. He mustn't be seen.

He didn't notice, therefore, that the shifting group of boys remaining had begun to drift in his direction. The hard pace he had set himself and his cruel disappointment took their double toll of Keevan. He tripped and collapsed sobbing to the warm sands. He didn't see the consternation[25]

in the watching weyrfolk above the Hatching Ground, nor did he hear the excited whispers of speculation. He didn't know that the weyrleader and weyrwoman had dropped to the arena and were making their way toward the knot of boys slowly moving in the direction of the archway.

"Never seen anything like it," the weyrleader was saying. "Only thirty-nine riders chosen. And the bronze trying to leave the Hatching Ground without making Impression!"

"A case in point of what I said last night," the weyrwoman replied, "where a hatchling makes no choice because the right boy isn't there."

"There's only Beterli and K'last's young one missing. And there's a full wing of likely boys to choose from. . . ."

"None acceptable, apparently. Where is the creature going? He's not heading for

24. *Ignominious* (igʹ nə minʹ ē əs) means "shameful; disgraceful."
25. *Consternation* is amazement or confusion.

the entrance after all. Oh, what have we there, in the shadows?"

Keevan heard with dismay the sound of voices nearing him. He tried to burrow into the sand. The mere thought of how he would be teased and taunted now was unbearable.

Don't worry! Please don't worry! The thought was urgent, but not his own.

Someone kicked sand over Keevan and butted roughly against him.

"Go away. Leave me alone!" he cried.

Why? was the injured-sounding question inserted into his mind. There was no voice, no tone, but the question was there, perfectly clear, in his head.

Incredulous, Keevan lifted his head and stared into the glowing jeweled eyes of a small bronze dragon. His wings were wet; the tips hung drooping to the sand. And he sagged in the middle on his unsteady legs, although he was making a great effort to keep erect.

Keevan dragged himself to his knees, oblivious to the pain of his leg. He wasn't even aware that he was ringed by the boys passed over, while thirty-one pairs of resentful eyes watched him Impress the dragon. The weyrleaders looked on, amused and surprised at the draconic[26] choice, which could not be forced. Could not be questioned. Could not be changed.

Why? asked the dragon again. *Don't you like me?* His eyes whirled with anxiety, and his tone was so piteous that

Keevan staggered forward and threw his arms around the dragon's neck, stroking his eye ridges, patting the damp, soft hide, opening the fragile-looking wings to dry them, and assuring the hatchling wordlessly over and over again that he was the most perfect, most beautiful, most beloved dragon in the entire weyr, in all the weyrs of Pern.

"What's his name, K'van?" asked Lessa, smiling warmly at the new dragonrider. K'van stared up at her for a long moment. Lessa would know as soon as he did. Lessa was the only person who could "receive" from all dragons, not only her own Ramoth. Then he gave her a radiant smile, recognizing the traditional shortening of his name that raised him forever to the rank of dragonrider.

My name is Heath, thought the dragon mildly and hiccuped in sudden urgency: *I'm hungry.*

"Dragons are born hungry," said Lessa, laughing. "F'lar, give the boy a hand. He can barely manage his own legs, much less a dragon's."

K'van remembered his stick and drew himself up. "We'll be just fine, thank you."

"You may be the smallest dragonrider ever, young K'van, but you're the bravest," said F'lar.

And Heath agreed! Pride and joy so leaped in both chests that K'van wondered if his heart would burst right out of his body. He looped an arm around Heath's neck and the pair—the smallest dragonboy, and the hatchling who wouldn't choose anybody else—walked out of the Hatching Ground together forever.

---

26. Keevan either doesn't notice or doesn't pay attention to (is *oblivious* to) the pain. *Draconic* means "having to do with a dragon."

Responding to Literature

PERSONAL RESPONSE

◆ What was your reaction to this story? Record your responses in your journal. Describe your thoughts and feelings as you followed Keevan through his experience.

Analyzing Literature

RECALL

1. What is a dragonrider, and how does someone become one?
2. Why is Keevan teased by the other dragonboys?
3. What are the different colors of dragons? Which ones were the most desirable?
4. According to Keevan's foster mother, what do dragons look for in their lifetime partners?

INTERPRET

5. Why are the dragons and their riders so important to the people of Pern?
6. Why does Keevan's "breath catch in his throat" at the thought of the moment of hatching time? Explain.
7. Why does Keevan hope to ride a brown dragon?
8. In your opinion, why does Heath choose Keevan? Explain.

EVALUATE AND CONNECT

9. How would most people cope with the cruel teasing Keevan faced daily? How would you?

10. **Theme Connection**
    Would you like to live on Pern? Why or why not?

LITERARY ELEMENTS

Fantasy

Anne McCaffrey's Pern stories combine science fiction (the setting on another planet in the future) with fantasy (fire-breathing dragons). Much like science fiction, **fantasy** explores unreal worlds or the real world with unreal elements, like dragons, ghosts, magic, or characters with superhuman qualities. As in much of the best science fiction, however, the emotions and conflicts of characters in a fantasy are often those of ordinary people. Readers can recognize themselves in the personal struggles and adventures of the characters.

1. Which elements in "The Smallest Dragonboy" are fantastic rather than realistic?

2. What is the realistic problem faced by Keevan?

● See **Literary Terms Handbook**, p. R4.

Paisaje con Volcano en Primer Plano. Dr. Atl (aka Gerard Murillo) (1875–1964). Atl colors on Masonite, 15¾ x 15¾ in. Galeria de Arte Misrachi, Mexico City.

Literature and Writing

Writing About Literature

Setting   What is the setting of "The Smallest Dragonboy"? Think about how the setting affects events in the plot. Then write a paragraph explaining why setting is so important to the story.

Creative Writing

A Sequel   What might happen to Keevan and his dragon sometime in the future? Will they be called upon to defend Pern against the evil Thread? Write a summary of a sequel telling of a later adventure.

Extending Your Response

Literature Groups

Hopes and Dreams   Think about Keevan's hopes and dreams. Think about his relationship with his family and his interactions with the other dragonboys. Review your notes from the **Reading Focus** on page 682. Then work together to create a chart comparing and contrasting Keevan's experiences with his peers with the experiences you and your classmates discussed.

Performing

Eyewitness News: Hatching Day!   Imagine that you are a TV news reporter sent to cover this year's Hatching Day. What do you see? Whom do you interview? Write a TV news story based on the events in "The Smallest Dragonboy." Feel free to make up any details you wish. Perform your news story for your classmates in an oral presentation.

Interdisciplinary Activity

Art   Imagine what the setting of "The Smallest Dragonboy" looks like. Make a list of the places mentioned in the story, and then draw a picture or map of the setting. Use the story details and descriptions to help you, but feel free to use your imagination to add new details.

Reading Further

If you would like to read more by Anne McCaffrey, try these:

The Dolphins of Pern

Dragonseye

📖 **Save your work for your portfolio.**

Dragon's Handiwork. Gregory Blake Larson (b. 1961). Pencil and watercolor, 16 x 13 in. Private collection.

Skill Minilessons

GRAMMAR AND LANGUAGE • WRITING NUMBERS

In writing, you either spell out numbers, or you write them as numerals. Follow these rules.

- Spell out numbers you can write in one or two words.

    The city is **twenty-five** miles from here.

- Spell out any number that begins a sentence.

    One hundred and thirty-four children came to school in spite of the snowstorm.

- Use numerals for numbers of more than two words not at the beginning of a sentence.

    The city is **465** miles away.

- Write a very large number as a numeral followed by the word *million* or *billion*.

    The planet is **3 billion** miles away.

- If related numbers appear in the same sentence and one of them should be written as a numeral, use all numerals.

    She wrote **10** novels and more than **150** short stories.

PRACTICE Write a sentence of your own to demonstrate each one of the previous rules.

- For more about similar usage problems, see **Language Handbook**, p. R43.

READING AND THINKING • CLASSIFYING

Skillful readers organize information by classifying things into categories. When you **classify,** you think about how things are alike and then put similar things into groups. In "The Smallest Dragonboy," for example, Keevan and the other boys could be classified as dragonboys.

PRACTICE Skim "The Smallest Dragonboy" and find two other groups of things that can be put into categories.

- For more about organizing information, see **Reading Handbook**, pp. R88–R89.

VOCABULARY • SYNONYMS: SHADES OF MEANING

Synonyms differ in their meanings—sometimes in important ways. For example, you could be pleasant and gentle while you *urge* someone to do something, but not while you *goad* someone. A *goaded* person feels forced or driven to do something he or she most likely doesn't want to do.

PRACTICE Think about what the underlined word means in each sentence. Then choose the better synonym for that word *that makes sense in the sentence.*

1. The neighborhood bully ridiculed Billy when he came outside holding his sister's hand.
   a. teased   b. mocked
2. The enticing sign said "Everything half price."
   a. inviting   b. charming
3. As the phone interrupted her for the fifth time, Mrs. Frye groaned in exasperation.
   a. annoyance   b. rage
4. After the tornado, their desolated town needed to be almost totally rebuilt.
   a. ruined   b. gloomy

GENRE FOCUS

LEGENDS, MYTHS, AND FOLKLORE

Long before there was written language, there was folklore. One storyteller calls myths, legends, and folk stories "stories that aren't true on the outside, but are true on the inside." Some of these stories are humorous; some are serious, even tragic, and filled with the power of ancient cultures and the spoken word.

Most of these stories were passed down orally from one teller to the next over hundreds of years. They are still evolving today. They may change a little each time the speaker or writer adds his or her own touches. In this way, the oldest stories in the world stay new.

LEGENDS, which relate amazing events or accomplishments, are stories known throughout a cultural group. Their heroes may be humans, animals, or even plants, enchanted objects, or forces of nature. Some legendary human heroes actually lived, but over the years their reputations grew larger than life. In this theme, you'll read the Chinese legend "Cat and Rat" and learn about the Chinese calendar.

MYTHS are traditional stories about gods and goddesses or how things came to be. These stories usually reflect a culture's religious or other deeply held beliefs. In the myth "Icarus and Daedalus," two mortals try to fly like the god Apollo. They learn that, unlike their gods, humans have limits.

FOLKLORE is a general term covering folktales, proverbs, ritual speeches, folk songs, fables, and many other forms of literature handed down by word of mouth. "The Bunyans," a story about Paul Bunyan and his family, is an example of a type of folktale called the tall tale. Some scholars classify legends and myths as forms of folklore.

The Two Mythical Dragons (detail).

Some Common Types of Folklore

jokes	fables
riddles	fairy tales
proverbs	folktales
anecdotes	legends
animal tales	myths

Active Reading Strategies

Legends, myths, and folklore are part of the earliest and longest-lasting literature—the ancient stories that tell about the beliefs, histories, joys, and sorrows of people from every corner of the world. When reading legends, myths, and folktales, skillful readers use strategies that help them understand how the characters—human and imaginary—respond to their settings and situations.

● For more about reading strategies and reading across cultures,
see **Reading Handbook,** pp. R73–R80.

PREVIEW

Before reading a legend, myth, or folktale, look at the title and the illustrations. Previewing helps you get an overall look at, or sense of, the text before you begin reading it.

VISUALIZE

As you read, use the author's descriptions to try to imagine the setting and characters.

CONNECT

Even a legend, myth, or folktale from another place or time can have great meaning to a modern reader. Connect the story to experiences in your own life.

QUESTION

As you read the story, ask yourself questions about the characters, the events, and the ideas.

PREDICT

Even while reading a story with magical events, you should try to predict what might happen next or how the tale might end.

APPLYING THE STRATEGIES

Read the following folktale, "Aunty Misery." Use the Active Reading Model notes in the margins as you read. Write your responses on a separate piece of paper or use stick-on notes.

Before You Read
Aunty Misery

MEET JUDITH ORTIZ COFER

Englishwas not Judith Ortiz Cofer's first language. Born in Puerto Rico, she learned English only after her family moved to the United States. "It was a challenge," she said, "not only to learn English, but to master it enough to teach it and—the ultimate goal—to write poetry in it." Cofer's writing reflects the split between her two childhood homes: the island of Puerto Rico and the United States. She has written, "My family is one of the main topics of my poetry. In tracing their lives, I discover more about mine."

Judith Ortiz Cofer was born in Puerto Rico in 1952.

READING FOCUS

What do you imagine would happen if human beings could live forever?

Sharing Ideas
In a small group, talk about how the world would change if people lived forever. Discuss the positive and negative results of such a change in the human life cycle.

Setting a Purpose
Read to enjoy this Puerto Rican tale.

BUILDING BACKGROUND

The Time and Place   "Aunty Misery" is set in a Spanish-speaking country sometime in the distant past.

Did You Know?   The Commonwealth of Puerto Rico is made up of one large and several smaller islands located about 1,000 miles southeast of Florida. It has been a part of the United States since 1898. The island's culture is a blend of the people who have lived there–the Native Americans, the Spanish who conquered the island in 1509, and the Africans who were first brought there as slaves to work on the sugar plantations. The majority of today's Puerto Rican population is of Hispanic background.

VOCABULARY PREVIEW

sorcerer (sôr′ sər ər) *n.* a person who practices magic with the aid of evil spirits; p. 701

taunt (tônt) *v.* to make fun of in a scornful, insulting way; p. 701

gnarled (närld) *adj.* rough, twisted, and knotty, as a tree trunk or branches; p. 702

potion (pō′ shən) *n.* a drink, especially of a liquid that is supposed to have magical powers; p. 702

Aunty Misery
A Folktale from Puerto Rico

Judith Ortiz Cofer ~

ACTIVE READING MODEL

PREVIEW

What is the origin of this folktale?

VISUALIZE

Can you picture Aunty Misery? What words does the author use to help you see the character?

QUESTION

What does the fact that the traveler can grant wishes tell you about the tale?

CONNECT

Have you ever known someone like Aunty Misery?

This is a story about an old, a very old woman who lived alone in her little hut with no other company than a beautiful pear tree that grew at her door. She spent all her time taking care of this tree. The neighborhood children drove the old woman crazy by stealing her fruit. They would climb her tree, shake its delicate limbs, and run away with armloads of golden pears, yelling insults at *la Tia Miseria*,[1] Aunty Misery, as they called her.

One day, a traveler stopped at the old woman's hut and asked her for permission to spend the night under her roof. Aunty Misery saw that he had an honest face and bid the pilgrim come in. She fed him and made a bed for him in front of her hearth. In the morning the stranger told her that he would show his gratitude for her hospitality by granting her one wish.

"There is only one thing that I desire," said Aunty Misery.

"Ask, and it shall be yours," replied the stranger, who was a sorcerer in disguise.

"I wish that anyone who climbs up my pear tree should not be able to come back down until I permit it."

"Your wish is granted," said the stranger, touching the pear tree as he left Aunty Misery's house.

And so it happened that when the children came back to taunt the old woman and to steal her fruit, she stood at her window watching them. Several of them shimmied[2] up the trunk of the pear tree and

---

1. *La Tia Miseria* (lä tē′ ə mē′ ze rē′ ə)
2. *Shimmied* means "shook or vibrated," which is what the tree might have done as the children shinnied up it. To *shinny* is to climb by using the hands, arms, feet, and legs to pull and push oneself up.

Vocabulary

sorcerer (sor′ sər ər) *n.* a person who practices magic with the aid of evil spirits
taunt (tônt) *v.* to make fun of in a scornful, insulting way

Aunty Misery

CONNECT

Have you ever had to think quickly to get out of a sticky situation?

PREDICT

What do you think Aunty Misery has in mind for Death? What will happen to Aunty Misery?

QUESTION

What cause-and-effect situation is the author describing here?

EVALUATE

What lesson about misery and death does this tale explain? Would you retell this tale to a friend? Why or why not?

immediately got stuck to it as if with glue. She let them cry and beg her for a long time before she gave the tree permission to let them go on the condition that they never again steal her fruit, or bother her.

Time passed and both Aunty Misery and her tree grew bent and <u>gnarled</u> with age. One day another traveler stopped at her door. This one looked untrustworthy to her, so before letting him into her home the old woman asked him what he was doing in her village. He answered her in a voice that was dry and hoarse, as if he had swallowed a desert: "I am Death, and I have come to take you with me."

Thinking fast Aunty Misery said, "All right, but before I go I would like to pluck some pears from my beloved tree to remember how much pleasure it brought me in this life. But I am a very old woman and cannot climb to the tallest branches where the best fruit is. Will you be so kind as to do it for me?"

With a heavy sigh like wind through a tomb, Señor[3] Death climbed the pear tree. Immediately he became stuck to it as if with glue. And no matter how much he cursed and threatened, Aunty Misery would not allow the tree to release Death.

Many years passed and there were no deaths in the world. The people who make their living from death began to protest loudly. The doctors claimed no one bothered to come in for examinations or treatments anymore, because they did not fear dying; the pharmacists' business suffered too because medicines are, like magic <u>potions</u>, bought to prevent or postpone the inevitable; priests and undertakers were unhappy with the situation also, for obvious reasons. There were also many old folks tired of life who wanted to pass on to the next world to rest from miseries of this one.

La Tia Miseria was blamed by these people for their troubles, of course. Not wishing to be unfair, the old woman made a deal with her prisoner, Death: if he promised not ever to come for her again, she would give him his freedom. He agreed. And that is why there are two things you can always count on running into in this world: Misery and Death: *La miseria y la muerte*.[4]

---

3. *Señor* (sen yôr′) is the Spanish equivalent of "Mister."
4. *Y la muerte* (ē lä mwer′ tä)

Vocabulary

gnarled (närld) *adj.* rough, twisted, and knotty, as a tree trunk or branches
potion (pō′ shən) *n.* a drink, especially of a liquid that is supposed to have magical powers

Responding to Literature

PERSONAL RESPONSE

◆ How does this story add to your thoughts about life and death?

Active Reading Response

Review the strategies described in the **Active Reading Model** notes on page 699. Choose one of the strategies, and find two places in the story where you could apply it.

Analyzing Literature

RECALL

1. How does Aunty Misery punish the neighborhood children who steal her pears?
2. How did Aunty Misery treat the first stranger?
3. Who is the second stranger who visits Aunty Misery?
4. How does Aunty Misery manage to trick Death?

INTERPRET

5. Why do you think the neighborhood children call the old woman "Aunty Misery"?
6. In your opinion, why does the first stranger grant Aunty Misery's wish?
7. Explain how Aunty Misery's wisdom about the second stranger saves her life.
8. What causes Aunty Misery finally to make a deal with Death?

EVALUATE AND CONNECT

9. Theme Connection   How does this story fit the theme of "a different dimension"?
10. Recall your discussion in the **Reading Focus** on page 700. How did reading "Aunty Misery" influence your ideas about a world without death?

LITERARY ELEMENTS

Fable

A **fable** is a kind of folklore in which a brief story is used to teach a lesson about human nature. Some of the most famous fables were written by Aesop, who is thought to have been a slave in ancient Greece. The characters in fables are often animals who speak and act like people. Usually a fable—"Aunty Misery," for example—concludes with a clearly stated moral, or lesson.

1. Two strangers visit Aunty Misery. Describe how she wisely treats them differently. What are the results of her actions?

2. What is the moral, or stated lesson, of "Aunty Misery"?

● See **Literary Terms Handbook**, p. R4.

Literature and Writing

Writing About Literature

Story Elements Although fables are brief, they usually contain all the elements of a short story. Briefly identify the characters, plot, setting, and theme (or lesson) of "Aunty Misery."

Creative Writing

Folktale Write your own fable about two things "you can always count on running into in this world." Choose two things other than misery and death that you believe are always part of the human experience.

Extending Your Response

Literature Groups

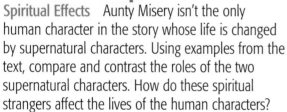

Spiritual Effects Aunty Misery isn't the only human character in the story whose life is changed by supernatural characters. Using examples from the text, compare and contrast the roles of the two supernatural characters. How do these spiritual strangers affect the lives of the human characters?

Art Activity

Scene Illustration Create an illustration of a descriptive scene from the story. Choose a scene that is especially vivid—such as the children stuck in the pear tree or Aunty Misery, as bent and gnarled as her pear tree.

Interdisciplinary Activity

Social Studies Working with a small group, study the culture of Puerto Rico. Have each group member research one of the following: the history of the people, the geography of their homeland, their religious beliefs, art and music, their relationship to the government of the United States. To combine what you have learned, plan a group presentation that includes pictures, maps, and music.

Reading Further

If you would like to read more folktales, try these:

Perez and Martina: A Puerto Rican Folktale by Pura Belpré

The Terrible EEK: A Japanese Tale retold by Patricia A. Compton

Save your work for your portfolio.

Dona Rosita Morillo, 1944. Frida Kahlo. Oil on canvas mounted on Masonite, 30½ x 28½ in. Fundacion Dolores Olmedo, Mexico City, D.F., Mexico.

Skill Minilessons

GRAMMAR AND LANGUAGE • FREQUENTLY MISSPELLED WORDS

Simple words may be misspelled because a word is mistaken for a similar one—for example, confusing *they're* (a contraction for *they are*) for *their* or *there.* Some other often-confused words are *whose* and *who's; its* and *it's;* and *your* and *you're.* If you are confused about which to use, use a dictionary for help.

PRACTICE Write the word that should be used in each sentence.

1. There once was a woman (whose, who's) pear tree attracted all the children in the neighborhood.
2. "Those children over (their, there, they're) are stealing my pears," she complained.
3. "(Your, You're) pears will remain untouched," the stranger promised.
4. "(Its, It's) branches will remain unbroken," he added.
5. "(Your, You're) very kind," Aunty Misery replied.

● For more about frequently misspelled words, see **Language Handbook,** p. R44.

READING AND THINKING • GENERALIZING

Generalizing is forming a general rule or conclusion based on particular facts or examples. For example, based on "Aunty Misery" and similar stories, you might generalize that many folktales try to explain why some condition exists in the real world.

● For more about generalizing, see **Reading Handbook,** p. R92.

PRACTICE Based on your own experience and reading, make a generalization about each of the following.

1. why people enjoy fantasy or science fiction
2. the main difference between folklore and modern fiction

VOCABULARY • ANALOGIES

An **analogy** is a comparison based on the relationships between things or ideas. Each of the two pairs of words in an analogy illustrates the same relationship.

> eyes : vision :: ears : hearing

The relationship between the words can be expressed in a sentence. *"Eyes* are used for *vision* as *ears* are used for *hearing."* The phrase "are used for" describes the relationship, which is the same in each half, or word pair, of the analogy.

PRACTICE Choose the word that best completes each analogy.

1. puppy : dog :: child :
   a. baby   b. adult   c. person
2. taunt : scorn :: praise :
   a. approval   b. complaint   c. gratitude
3. man : woman :: rooster :
   a. egg   b. crow   c. hen
4. potion : drink :: song :
   a. notes   b. music   c. sing

● For more about analogies, see **Communications Skills Handbook,** p. R67.

Before You Read
Strawberries

The role of storyteller is not limited to people who lived in earlier societies that lacked writing. Many people today carry on the oral story-telling tradition. Gayle Ross is one of them. A descendent of John Ross, a famous chief of the Cherokee nation, Gayle Ross first heard tales of her heritage from her grand-mother. Ross has worked in radio and television and has performed as a storyteller all over the United States. Her audiences have included the president and vice president of the United States and other world leaders. She is the author of five books.

Gayle Ross was born in 1951.

READING FOCUS

If you could create a flower, fruit, or plant that expressed your idea of love, what would it be?

Think/Pair/Share
Think about what you would create, then draw a picture of it. Share your creation with a partner.

Setting a Purpose
Read to find out how strawberries came to be, according to this Cherokee myth.

BUILDING BACKGROUND

Did You Know?   The Cherokee language was one of the first Native American languages to have a system of writing. A Cherokee named Sequoyah invented an alphabet in 1821. Remarkably, Sequoyah himself was unable to read in any language when he began. To create letters for the sounds of Cherokee, Sequoyah borrowed from the Roman alphabet (the alphabet used for English),

modified other Roman letters, and made up some additional symbols. Before long, the Cherokee had books and a news-paper in their own language.

VOCABULARY PREVIEW

despair (di spār´) *n.* complete loss of hope; desperation; p. 708

overtake (ō´ vər tāk´) *v.* to catch up with or to reach and then pass; p. 708

fixed (fikst) *adj.* steadily directed and unchanging; p. 708

aroma (ə rō´ mə) *n.* a pleasant smell; odor; p. 708

Strawberries

Retold by Gayle Ross

Long ago, in the very first days of the world, there lived the first man and the first woman. They lived together as husband and wife, and they loved one another dearly. But one day, they quarreled. Although neither later could remember what the quarrel was about, the pain grew stronger with every word that was spoken, until finally, in anger and in grief, the woman left their home and began walking away—to the east, toward the rising sun.

Strawberries

The man sat alone in his house. But as time went by, he grew lonelier and lonelier. The anger left him, and all that remained was a terrible grief and despair, and he began to cry.

A spirit heard the man crying and took pity on him. The spirit said, "Man, why do you cry?"

The man said, "My wife has left me."

The spirit said, "Why did your woman leave?"

The man just hung his head and said nothing.

The spirit asked, "You quarreled with her?"

And the man nodded.

"Would you quarrel with her again?" asked the spirit.

The man said, "No." He wanted only to live with his wife as they had lived before—in peace, in happiness, and in love.

"I have seen your woman," the spirit said. "She is walking to the east toward the rising sun."

The man followed his wife, but he could not overtake her. Everyone knows an angry woman walks fast.

Finally, the spirit said, "I'll go ahead and see if I can make her slow her steps." So the spirit found the woman walking, her footsteps fast and angry and her gaze fixed straight ahead. There was pain in her heart.

The spirit saw some huckleberry bushes growing along the trail, so with a wave of his hand, he made the bushes burst into bloom and ripen into fruit. But the woman's gaze remained fixed. She looked neither to the right nor to the left, and she didn't see the berries. Her footsteps didn't slow.

Again, the spirit waved his hand, and one by one, all of the berries growing along the trail burst into bloom and ripened into fruit. But still, the woman's gaze remained fixed. She saw nothing but her anger and pain, and her footsteps didn't slow.

And again, the spirit waved his hand, and, one by one, the trees of the forest—the peach, the pear, the apple, the wild cherry—burst into bloom and ripened into fruit. But still, the woman's eyes remained fixed, and even still, she saw nothing but her anger and pain. And her footsteps didn't slow.

Then finally, the spirit thought, "I will create an entirely new fruit—one that grows very, very close to the ground so the woman must forget her anger and bend her head for a moment." So the spirit waved his hand, and a thick green carpet began to grow along the trail. Then the carpet became starred with tiny white flowers, and each flower gradually ripened into a berry that was the color and shape of the human heart.

As the woman walked, she crushed the tiny berries, and the delicious aroma came up through her nose. She stopped and

Vocabulary

despair (di spār′) *n.* complete loss of hope; desperation
overtake (ō′ vər tāk′) *v.* to catch up with or to reach and then pass
fixed (fikst) *adj.* steadily directed and unchanging
aroma (ə rō′ mə) *n.* a pleasant smell; odor

Strawberry Dance, 1983. G. Peter Jemison. Mixed media on handmade paper, 22 x 30 in. Private collection, by permission of the artist.

Viewing the painting: How does the mood of this artwork reflect the mood of the story's ending?

looked down, and she saw the berries. She picked one and ate it, and she discovered its taste was as sweet as love itself. So she began walking slowly, picking berries as she went, and as she leaned down to pick a berry, she saw her husband coming behind her.

The anger had gone from her heart, and all that remained was the love she had always known. So she stopped for him, and together, they picked and ate the berries. Finally, they returned to their home, where they lived out their days in peace, happiness, and love.

And that's how the world's very first strawberries brought peace between men and women in the world and why to this day they are called the berries of love.

Active Reading and Critical Thinking

Responding to Literature

PERSONAL RESPONSE

◆ How did this tale change or add to your thoughts about love?

Analyzing Literature

RECALL

1. What causes the woman to leave her husband?
2. Why does the spirit want to slow the angry woman's steps?
3. What effect do the blooming huckleberries and trees of the forest have upon the woman?
4. What finally slows the woman down?

INTERPRET

5. Why is the man unable to overtake his wife?
6. Why isn't the woman able to see the blossoming bushes and trees?
7. Why does the spirit decide to create a new fruit?
8. Why do the strawberries make the woman slow down?

EVALUATE AND CONNECT

9. What does "Strawberries" teach the reader about letting go of anger?
10. **Theme Connection** "Strawberries" is a Cherokee myth. What does it tell you about what the Cherokee people believe about love?

LITERARY ELEMENTS

Tone

The **tone** of a piece of writing expresses to readers the author's feelings and attitude toward his or her subject, ideas, theme, or characters. A written piece may express seriousness, humor, nostalgia, or any number of other feelings. Formal writing, for example, usually creates a serious tone; colloquial writing can create a light, humorous tone. Factors that contribute to tone are the writer's sentence construction and choice of words, the kinds of details used, and the images created. In poetry, the rhythm may help to create a tone. A rhythm can encourage readers to skip lightly along the poet's words or mournfully drag them out.

1. Reread the first paragraphs of "Aunty Misery" and "Strawberries." What tone does each author create? How?

2. Choose a poem you read earlier in this book. How does the poet create its tone?

● See **Literary Terms Handbook,** p. R11.

Literature and Writing

Writing About Literature

Conflict   **Conflict** refers to the struggle between two opposing forces. Write briefly about the conflict that is central to "Strawberries." Explain what caused the conflict and how it was resolved.

Creative Writing

The First . . .   "Strawberries" is a Cherokee myth about how strawberries came to be. Write a myth to explain the origin of the fruit, flower, or plant you illustrated for the **Reading Focus** on page 706.

Extending Your Response

Literature Groups

Anger Management   In addition to telling about the origin of strawberries, the myth also presents the idea that anger can ruin love. Do you agree? How could the man and woman in the myth have prevented their quarrel or dealt with their anger? Share your group's opinions with the class.

Performing

Role-Playing   What do the husband and wife in "Strawberries" argue about? What do they say to each other as they walk back home? With a partner,

consider these questions. Then role-play one of these two dialogues from the story.

Reading Further

If you would like to read more Native American tales, try these:

How Rabbit Tricked Otter and Other Cherokee Trickster Stories, told by Gayle Ross

Mai'ii and Cousin Horned Toad: A Traditional Navajo Story by Shonto Begay

💼 **Save your work for your portfolio.**

Skill Minilesson

VOCABULARY • SYNONYMS: THESAURUS

The angry woman in "Strawberries" would not have tasted berries that had a *stink.* What made her stop was the berries' *aroma. Smell, stink, aroma,* and *scent* are synonyms, but each word has its own distinctive meaning. A **thesaurus** is a dictionary of synonyms. It can help you find differences among synonyms so that you can use the one best suited to your purpose.

PRACTICE For each sentence, decide whether *smell, scent, stink,* or *aroma* is the best choice.
1. The kitchen filled with the ___ of apple pie.
2. Even blindfolded, I would know I was in the barn by the familiar ___ .
3. The ___ in my room was a mixture of wet dog and dirty socks.
4. The ___ of her favorite perfume told me that my mother had been in my room.

Capitalization

A proper noun names a particular person, place, or thing. A proper adjective is formed from a proper noun. Proper nouns and proper adjectives are capitalized.

Problem 1 Words referring to ethnic groups, nationalities, and languages

Some french folk songs are sung in english in the United States.

Solution Capitalize names of ethnic groups, nationalities, and languages and the adjectives formed from them.

Some French folk songs are sung in English in the United States.

Problem 2 Words that name family relationships

I told mom, aunt Martha, and my grandfather about "Aunty Misery."

Solution Capitalize the word that names a family relationship only if it is part of the person's name or used in place of the person's name.

I told Mom, Aunt Martha, and my grandfather about "Aunty Misery."

Problem 3 Names of organizations and structures

The American folklore society seeks to study and preserve folklore.

There are songs about the Brooklyn bridge but not the sears tower.

Solution Capitalize the names of organizations and structures.

The American Folklore Society seeks to study and preserve folklore.

There are songs about the Brooklyn Bridge but not the Sears Tower.

● For more about capitalization, see **Language Handbook,** p. R20.

EXERCISE

Write *Correct* if the phrase is capitalized correctly. If it is capitalized incorrectly, rewrite the phrase to correct it.

1. my sister, Sue
2. call aunt Millie
3. speak spanish
4. the empire state building
5. tell mom and dad
6. a german composer
7. my favorite uncle
8. the U.S. Congress
9. the puerto rican flag
10. a mother's worries

Before You Read

Atalanta's Race and *Atalanta*

MEET REX WARNER

A novelist, Greek scholar, poet, translator, and critic, Rex Warner spent the early days of his career as a schoolteacher in England and Egypt. He later served as director of the British Institute in Athens, Greece. In 1961 Warner moved to the United States. His novels, often written as allegories, focus on the power of government.

Rex Warner was born in England in 1905 and died in 1986.

MEET BETTY MILES

Betty Miles's first full-time job, as an assistant kindergarten teacher, inspired her to write children's books. When asked about her writing, Miles replied, "I put my own feelings into my characters, and say things through them that I might be too shy to say in person. . . . For me, the greatest reward of writing is being told that 'you know just how I feel.'"

Betty Miles was born in Chicago in 1928.

READING FOCUS

The ancient Greeks believed that fate was an all-powerful force in everyday life. More people today believe that their fate depends on their own actions and decisions. How do you feel about what influences people's futures?

Think/Pair/Share
Take a moment to jot down your thoughts and feelings about the question. Then share your ideas with a partner, and discuss how we can influence our future lives.

Setting a Purpose
Read two versions of the same myth to see how they differ.

BUILDING BACKGROUND

Did You Know?   Greek myths have had a long-lasting influence on litera-ture, including classic Greek and Roman dramas based on these myths. The borrowing of these themes continues today, not only in drama, poetry, and fiction but in motion pictures and television features. Even many of the comic book or TV superheroes can be traced back to such ancient Greek models as Hercules and Achilles.

VOCABULARY PREVIEW

condemn (kən dem′) *v.* to criticize sharply; p. 715
envious (en′ vē əs) *adj.* having resentment over, and a wish to possess for oneself, something possessed by another; p. 715
parched (pärcht) *adj.* severely in need of moisture; p. 717
hallowed (hal′ ōd) *adj.* regarded as sacred or holy; p. 717
fleetest (flēt′ əst) *adj.* swiftest; fastest; p. 719
jubilant (jōō′ bə lənt) *adj.* filled with great joy; p. 721
claim (klām) *v.* to ask for or demand possession of one's right to something; p. 721

Atalanta's Race

Rex Warner

The huntress Atalanta,[1] whom Meleager,[2] before he died, had loved, could run faster even than the fastest runners among men. Nor was her beauty inferior to her swiftness of foot; both were beyond praise.

When Atalanta asked the oracle[3] about whom she ought to marry, the god replied: "Do not take a husband, Atalanta. If you do, it will bring disaster on you. Yet you will not escape, and though you will continue to live, you will not be yourself."

---

1. According to Greek myths, the Greek heroine *Atalanta* was abandoned at birth and rescued by a bear. Later found by hunters who raised her, Atalanta grew into a daring child who excelled at all physical activities.
2. In Greek mythology, *Meleager* (mel´ ē ā´ gər) was the son of a king whose country was ravaged by a wild boar. Meleager put together a band of heroes to drive the boar away, and he himself killed it.
3. In ancient Greece, an *oracle* was a priest through whom the gods sometimes answered the questions of worshipers.

Terrified by these words, Atalanta lived in the dark woods unmarried. There were many men who wished to marry her, but to them, in their eagerness, she said: "No one can have me for his wife unless first he beats me in a race. If you will, you may run with me. If any of you wins, he shall have me as a prize. But those who are defeated will have death for their reward. These are the conditions for the race."

Cruel indeed she was, but her beauty had such power that numbers of young men were impatient to race with her on these terms.

There was a young man called Hippomenes,[4] who had come to watch the contest. At first he had said to himself: "What man in his senses would run such a risk to get a wife?" and he had <u>condemned</u> the young men for being too madly in love. But when he saw her face and her body all stripped for the race—a face and a body like Venus's[5] own—he was lost in astonishment and, stretching out his hands, he said: "I had no right to blame the young men. I did not know what the prize was for which they were running."

As he spoke his own heart caught on fire with love for her and, in jealous fear, he hoped that none of the young men would be able to beat her in the race. Then he said to himself: "But why should not I try my fortune? When one takes a risk, the gods help one."

By now the race had started, and the girl sped past him on feet that seemed to have wings. Though she went fast as an arrow, he admired her beauty still more. Indeed she looked particularly beautiful when running. In the breeze her hair streamed back over her ivory shoulders; the ribbons with their bright borders fluttered at her knees; the white of her young body flushed rose-red, as when a purple awning is drawn over white marble and makes the stone glow with its own color. While Hippomenes fixed his eyes on her, she reached the winning post and was crowned with the victor's garland. The young men, with groans, suffered the penalty of death according to the agreement which they had made.

Did You Know?
The victor's *garland* was a small wreath of flowers, leaves, or vines worn about the head as a symbol of honor.

Their fate, however, had no effect on Hippomenes. He came forward and, fixing his eyes on Atalanta, said: "Why do you win an easy glory by conquering these slow movers? Now run with me. If I win, it will be no disgrace to you. I am a king's son and Neptune[6] is my great-grandfather. And, if you defeat me, it will be an honor to be able to say that you defeated Hippomenes."

As he spoke, Atalanta looked at him with a softer expression in her eyes. She wondered whether she really wanted to conquer or to be conquered. She thought to herself: "What god, <u>envious</u> of beautiful

---

4. *Hippomenes* (hi pom′ ə nēz′)
5. *Venus* was the goddess of beauty and love.

6. *Neptune* was the god of the sea.

Vocabulary
condemn (kən dem′) *v.* to criticize sharply
envious (en′ vē əs) *adj.* having resentment over, and a wish to possess for oneself, something possessed by another

Viewing the photograph: What does this photo-collage suggest that could not be shown with a single photograph? What might this present-day runner have in common with Atalanta?

young men, wants to destroy this one and makes him seek marriage with me at the risk of his dear life? In my opinion, I am not worth it. It is not his beauty that touches me (though I might easily be touched by that); it is because he is still only a boy. And then there is his courage, and the fact that he is willing to risk so much for me. Why should he die, simply because he wants to live with me? I wish he would go, while he still may, and realize that it is fatal to want to marry me. Indeed he deserves to live. If only I were happier, if only the fates[7] had not forbidden me to marry, he would be the man that I would choose."

Meanwhile Atalanta's father and the whole people demanded that the race should take place. Hippomenes prayed to Venus and said: "O goddess, you put this love into my heart. Now be near me in my trial and aid me!"

A gentle breeze carried his prayer to the goddess and she was moved by it. Little time, however, remained in which she could help him. But it happened that she had just returned from her sacred island of Cyprus,[8] where in one of her temple gardens grows a golden apple tree. The leaves are gold; the branches and the fruit rattle with metal as the wind stirs them. Venus had in her hand three golden apples which she had just picked from this tree. Now she came down to earth, making herself visible only to Hippomenes, and showed him how to use the apples.

Then the trumpets sounded and the two runners darted forward from the starting post, skimming over the sandy course with feet so light that it would seem they might have run over the sea or over the waving heads of standing corn. The crowd shouted their applause.[9] "Now, Hippomenes," they

---

7. The *fates* were three goddesses who controlled human lives and fortunes.

8. *Cyprus* is an island in the Mediterranean Sea, south of Turkey.
9. Here, *applause* means simply "praise."

cried, "run as you have never run before! You are winning." It would be difficult to say whether Hippomenes or Atalanta herself was most pleased with this encouragement. For some time Atalanta, though she might have passed the young man, did not do so. She ran by his side, looking into his face. Then, half unwillingly, she left him behind. He, with parched throat and straining lungs, followed after; still the winning post was far in the distance; and now he took one of the golden apples which Venus had given him and threw it in her way. The girl looked with wonder at the shining fruit and, longing to have it, stopped running so that she could pick it up. Hippomenes passed her and again the spectators shouted out their applause. Soon, however, Atalanta made up the ground that she had lost and again left Hippomenes behind. He threw the second apple, once more took the lead and once more was overtaken. Now they were in sight of the winning post, and Hippomenes, with a prayer to Venus, threw the last apple rather sideways, so that it went some distance from the course. Atalanta seemed to hesitate whether she should go after it or not, but Venus made her go, and, when she had picked up the apple, she made it heavier, handicapping the girl not only by the time she had lost but by the weight of what she was carrying. This time she could not catch up Hippomenes. He passed the winning post first and claimed her as his bride.

Then, indeed, Hippomenes should have offered thanks to Venus, but he forgot entirely the goddess who had helped him, neither giving thanks nor making sacrifice.

Venus was angry and determined to make an example of them both. On their way to the home of Hippomenes they came to a holy temple, sacred to the mother of the gods, great Cybele. No mortal[10] was allowed to pass the night in this temple, so hallowed was the spot; but Venus put it into the hearts of Hippomenes and Atalanta, who were tired from their journey, to rest there all night and treat the temple of the goddess as though it were a common inn. So in the most holy of the temple's shrines, where wooden images of the ancient gods turned away their eyes in horror at the profanation,[11] they rested together. But the terrible goddess, her head crowned with a crown of towers, appeared to them. She covered their necks, which had been so smooth, with tawny manes of hair; their fingers became sharp claws, and their arms turned to legs. Most of their weight went to their chests, and behind them they swept the sandy ground with long tails. Instead of the palace they had hoped for, they lived in the savage woods, a lion and a lioness, terrible to others but, when Cybele needed them, tame enough to draw her chariot, champing the iron bits between their gnashing jaws.

---

10. *Cybele* (sib′ ə lē) and the other gods were *immortals*—beings who would never die. A *mortal* is a human being.
11. *Profanation* is an act of disrespect or scorn for sacred beings or objects, such as this holy shrine.

Vocabulary

parched (pärcht) *adj.* severely in need of moisture
hallowed (hal′ ōd) *adj.* regarded as sacred or holy

Atalanta

Betty Miles

Once upon a time, not long ago, there lived a princess named Atalanta, who could run as fast as the wind.

She was so bright, and so clever, and could build things and fix things so wonderfully, that many young men wished to marry her.

"What shall I do?" said Atalanta's father, who was a powerful king. "So many young men want to marry you, and I don't know how to choose."

"You don't have to choose, Father," Atalanta said. "I will choose. And I'm not sure that I will choose to marry anyone at all."

"Of course you will," said the king. "Everybody gets married. It is what people do."

"But," Atalanta told him, with a toss of her head, "I intend to go out and see the world. When I come home, perhaps I will marry and perhaps I will not."

The king did not like this at all. He was a very ordinary king; that is, he was powerful and used to having his own way. So he did not answer Atalanta, but simply told her, "I have decided how to choose the young man you will marry. I will hold a great race, and the winner—the swiftest, <u>fleetest</u> young man of all—will win the right to marry you."

Now Atalanta was a clever girl as well as a swift runner. She saw that she might win both the argument and the race—provided that she herself could run in the race, too. "Very well," she said. "But you must let me race along with the others. If I am not the winner, I will accept the wishes of the young man who is."

The king agreed to this. He was pleased; he would have his way, marry off his daughter, and enjoy a fine day of racing as well. So he directed his messengers to travel throughout the kingdom announcing the race with its wonderful prize: the chance to marry the bright Atalanta.

As the day of the race drew near, flags were raised in the streets of the town, and banners were hung near the grassy field where the race would be run. Baskets of ripe plums and peaches, wheels of cheese, ropes of sausages and onions, and loaves of crusty bread were gathered for the crowds.

Meanwhile, Atalanta herself was preparing for the race. Each day at dawn, dressed in soft green trousers and a shirt of yellow silk, she went to the field in secret and ran across it—slowly at first, then fast and faster, until she could run the course more quickly than anyone had ever run it before.

As the day of the race grew nearer, young men began to crowd into the town. Each was sure he could win the prize, except for one; that was Young John, who lived in the town. He saw Atalanta day by day as she bought nails and wood to make a pigeon house, or chose parts for her telescope, or laughed with her friends. Young John saw the princess only from a distance, but near enough to know how bright and clever she was. He wished very much to race with her, to win, and to earn the right to talk with her and become her friend.

"For surely," he said to himself, "it is not right for Atalanta's father to give her away to the winner of the race. Atalanta herself must choose the person she wants to marry, or whether she wishes to marry at all. Still, if I could only win the race, I would be free to speak to her, and to ask for her friendship."

Each evening, after his studies of the stars and the seas, Young John went to the field in secret and practiced running across

---

Vocabulary
fleetest (flēt′ əst) *adj.* swiftest; fastest

Atalanta

it. Night after night, he ran fast as the wind across the twilight field, until he could cross it more quickly than anyone had ever crossed it before.

At last, the day of the race arrived.

Trumpets sounded in the early morning, and the young men gathered at the edge of the field, along with Atalanta herself, the prize they sought. The king and his friends sat in soft chairs, and the townspeople stood along the course.

The king rose to address them all. "Good day," he said to the crowds. "Good luck," he said to the young men. To Atalanta he said, "Good-bye. I must tell you farewell, for tomorrow you will be married."

"I am not so sure of that, Father," Atalanta answered. She was dressed for the race in trousers of crimson and a shirt of silk as blue as the sky, and she laughed as she looked up and down the line of young men.

"Not one of them," she said to herself, "can win the race, for I will run fast as the wind and leave them all behind."

And now a bugle sounded, a flag was dropped, and the runners were off!

The crowds cheered as the young men and Atalanta began to race across the field. At first they ran as a group, but Atalanta soon pulled ahead, with three of the young men close after her. As they neared the halfway point, one young man put on a great burst of speed and seemed to pull ahead for an instant, but then he gasped and fell back. Atalanta shot on.

Soon another young man, tense with the effort, drew near to Atalanta. He

Viewing the photograph: Today, a runner as fast as Atalanta would probably run in the Olympic Games. How do you think she would do against today's competitors?

reached out as though to touch her sleeve, stumbled for an instant, and lost speed. Atalanta smiled as she ran on. I have almost won, she thought.

But then another young man came near. This was Young John, running like the wind, as steadily and as swiftly as Atalanta herself. Atalanta felt his closeness, and in a sudden burst she dashed ahead.

Young John might have given up at this, but he never stopped running. Nothing at all, thought he, will keep me from winning the chance to speak with Atalanta. And on he ran, swift as the wind, until he ran as her equal, side by side with her, toward the golden ribbon that marked the race's end. Atalanta raced even faster to pull ahead, but Young John was a strong match for her. Smiling with the pleasure of the race, Atalanta and Young John reached the finish line together, and together they broke through the golden ribbon.

Trumpets blew. The crowd shouted and leaped about. The king rose. "Who is that young man?" he asked.

"It is Young John from the town," the people told him.

"Very well. Young John," said the king, as John and Atalanta stood before him, exhausted and <u>jubilant</u> from their efforts. "You have not won the race, but you have come closer to winning than any man here. And so I give you the prize that was promised—the right to marry my daughter."

Young John smiled at Atalanta, and she smiled back. "Thank you, sir," said John to the king, "but I could not possibly marry your daughter unless she wished to marry me. I have run this race for the chance to talk with Atalanta, and, if she is willing, I am ready to <u>claim</u> my prize."

Atalanta laughed with pleasure. "And I," she said to John, "could not possibly marry before I have seen the world. But I would like nothing better than to spend the afternoon with you."

Then the two of them sat and talked on the grassy field, as the crowds went away. They ate bread and cheese and purple plums. Atalanta told John about her telescopes and her pigeons, and John told Atalanta about his globes and his studies of geography. At the end of the day, they were friends.

On the next day, John sailed off to discover new lands. And Atalanta set off to visit the great cities.

By this time, each of them has had wonderful adventures, and seen marvelous sights. Perhaps some day they will be married, and perhaps they will not. In any case, they are friends. And it is certain that they are both living happily ever after.

Vocabulary
jubilant (jo͞o′ bə lənt) *adj.* filled with great joy
claim (klām) *v.* to ask for or demand possession of one's right to something

Responding to Literature

PERSONAL RESPONSE

◆ What was your reaction to these stories? How do these tales relate to your response for the **Reading Focus** on page 713? Describe your impressions in your journal.

Analyzing Literature

RECALL

1. In "Atalanta's Race," what warning did the oracle give Atalanta?
2. In "Atalanta's Race," what strategy did Atalanta use to avoid marriage? Why were young men willing to risk their lives for her?
3. How does the character of Atalanta differ in the two versions of the myth?
4. What parts of the myth included in Rex Warner's version are left out of Betty Miles's version?

INTERPRET

5. How did Atalanta's actions in "Atalanta's Race" show her respect for the oracle and the decrees of fate? Explain.
6. Explain what the oracle's warning that "though you will continue to live, you will not be yourself" meant.
7. In either version, what does the reader discover about Atalanta's sense of determination and courage in dealing with her life? Identify details to support your ideas.
8. Why do you think Betty Miles left out parts of the Atalanta myth that are included in Rex Warner's version?

EVALUATE AND CONNECT

9. Which version of the myth did you enjoy more? Why?
10. Think of someone who would enjoy reading these myths. What about these stories would appeal to that person?

LITERARY ELEMENTS

Description

A **description** is a carefully detailed portrayal of a person, place, thing, or event. Strong description is an important element in both fiction and nonfiction writing. Skillful writers select details carefully so that their readers can see, hear, smell, taste, and feel what is being described. Both of these myths come alive through the vivid descriptions of the main characters and their worlds.

1. Skim the myths and pick out a description that helps you imagine a particular character or scene. Explain which details help you imagine the character or scene clearly.

2. Choose your favorite description in either myth and explain why it appeals to you.

● See **Literary Terms Handbook,** p. R3.

Literature and Writing

Writing About Literature

Characterization In both myths, the two main characters are revealed through their actions as well as their words. Write a paragraph describing either Atalanta or Hippomenes/John as you picture that person.

Creative Writing

Journal Entry Imagine you are either Atalanta or Hippomenes/John right before the race. What are you thinking and feeling? Write a journal entry describing your thoughts and feelings. Use the myth as a jumping-off point, but feel free to make up details of your own.

Extending Your Response

Literature Groups

Discussing Conflict You know that conflict, the struggle between two or more forces, makes stories interesting. There are four common types of conflict in literature: with nature; with fate; with other people or society; and with oneself. Working in small groups, discuss the kinds of conflicts present in both versions of the Atalanta myth, and talk about which conflict is the most difficult. Support your thoughts and ideas with examples from the myths.

Performing

Live from Ancient Greece! Imagine you are a reporter sent to cover the race by the Hellenic News Network. Interview either Atalanta or Hippomenes after the race. With a partner, create a script that describes the race and the two competitors to use as an introduction before the interview begins. Plan a series of questions to ask, but be ready to ask follow-up questions as the interview proceeds. Share your interview with the class by presenting it as a "live" news report.

Interdisciplinary Activity

Health Physical fitness is good for anyone, not just professional athletes or competitive runners like Atalanta. What are some ways in which people your age can keep fit? Work with a small group to plan a fitness program for average teenagers who don't wish to be competitive athletes. Present your plan to the class.

Reading Further

If you would like to read other myths or folktales, try these books:

Island of the Mighty: Stories of Old Britain by Haydn Middleton

A Treasury of Stories from Around the World chosen by Linda Jennings

📖 **Save your work for your portfolio.**

Skill Minilessons

GRAMMAR AND LANGUAGE • SPELLING COMPOUND WORDS

The word *grandfather* is a compound word made up of the words *grand* and *father.* The rule for spelling compound words is simple. Keep the original spelling of both words, no matter how the words begin or end.

night + time = nighttime
easy + going = easygoing

PRACTICE Write a paragraph describing the race held to find a worthy husband for Atalanta. Make up any details you wish to describe the race. Use at least three compound words in your description. Then trade paragraphs with a partner and read each other's paragraphs. As you read, underline each compound word you find, and check that it is spelled correctly.

● For more about compound words, see **Language Handbook,** Spelling, p. R47.

READING AND THINKING • CHRONOLOGICAL ORDER

The events in both myths are told in chronological order, or the order in which they occur. As a skillful reader, you should always ask questions so you are sure you understand what is going on. As you read, ask yourself questions such as the following.
• What happened first?
• What happened next?
• Do the steps, or the events, occur in an order that makes sense?

PRACTICE Review either myth. Outline the steps taken to find a suitable mate for Atalanta. Write the steps in the order in which they happened in the myth.

● For more about sequencing and chronological order, see **Reading Handbook,** p. R91.

VOCABULARY • ANALOGIES

An analogy is a type of comparison that is based on the relationships between things or ideas. To complete analogies, you must figure out what relationships exist between words. For example, choose an answer for this incomplete analogy:

toe : foot :: finger : ?

Is the answer *nail, thumb,* or *hand?* All three of these words "go with" *finger,* but only one is related in the same way that *foot* goes with *toe.* A *finger* is part of a *hand,* just as a *toe* is part of a *foot.*

● For more about analogies, see **Communications Skills Handbook,** p. R67.

PRACTICE Choose the word that best completes each analogy.
1. lift : drop :: condemn :
   a. praise   b. scold   c. ban
2. starving : hunger :: parched :
   a. throat   b. rain   c. thirst
3. cheetah : fleetest :: giraffe :
   a. tallest   b. biggest   c. rarest
4. terrified : fearful :: jubilant :
   a. relieved   b. joyful   c. sorry
5. irritable : grouchy :: envious :
   a. sad   b. jealous   c. suspicious

Before You Read

Cat and Rat: The Legend of the Chinese Zodiac

MEET ED YOUNG

Ed Young, who provides both the words and the pictures for "Cat and Rat," says, "There are things that words do that pictures never can, and likewise, there are images that words can never describe." Young was born in China and lived there until he attended college in the United States. He often uses the traditional Chinese technique of brushing ink on rice paper for his artwork. Young was encouraged to become a children's book illustrator after years of sketching animals at New York City's Central Park Zoo.

Ed Young was born in 1931 in Tientsin, China. This story was published in 1995.

READING FOCUS

Why do you think cats are so good at catching rats?

Think/Pair/Share
Think about a quick explanation for a cat's talents. Share your ideas with a partner.

Setting a Purpose
Read this story to find out about the legendary origins of the relationship between cats and rats.

BUILDING BACKGROUND

The Time and Place This legend is set in China more than 5,000 years ago.

Did You Know? The traditional Chinese calendar is arranged in twelve-year cycles. Each year in the zodiac (the twelve constellations seen in the sky around the earth's orbit) is named after an animal. The zodiac was first introduced to the Chinese people nearly 5,000 years ago by the Emperor Huang Di.

According to Chinese astrology, people's personalities share characteristics with the animal that rules their birth year.

VOCABULARY PREVIEW

resourceful (ri sôrs′ fəl) *adj.* capable or skillful in dealing with new or difficult situations; p. 727

podium (pō′ dē əm) *n.* a small, raised platform or stand with a slanted shelf for holding a speaker's papers; p. 728

pounce (pouns) *v.* to swoop down, spring, or leap suddenly in attack; p. 729

From: CAT AND RAT: THE LEGEND OF THE CHINESE ZODIAC by Ed Young, ©1995 by Ed Young. Reprinted by permission of Henry Holt and Company, Inc.

Cat and Rat: The Legend of the Chinese Zodiac

Ed Young

In China, a long, long time ago, there lived a cat and a rat. They were best friends. They ate together. They played together. They slept together.

One day, the Emperor decided to hold a race among all the animals in the land. The first twelve animals to cross the finish line would have a year in the Chinese calendar named after them. This would be quite an honor.

"But winning the race will not be easy," warned the Emperor. "You must run through the thickest part of the forest and then swim across the river at its widest point."

Cat and Rat each wanted to be the first to cross the finish line. But they knew that they would be two of the smallest animals in the race.

"We will never make it," Rat complained to Cat.

"Oh, I think we will," replied the resourceful cat.

"We'll ask the water buffalo to help us," said the cat. "He could give us a head start. He always wakes

---

Vocabulary

resourceful (ri sôrs′ fəl) *adj.* capable or skillful in dealing with new or difficult situations

up before sunrise. Maybe we could even ride on his back."

So Cat and Rat convinced Buffalo to wake them up early on the day of the race. The next morning, Buffalo was up long before dawn. "Wake up, lazybones," he said to the sleeping cat and rat. "We had better get started."

Cat and Rat climbed on the buffalo's back. But they were so sleepy that by the time they had fully awakened, they were half way across the river.

Rat woke up first. He saw the Emperor standing at the finish line far, far away. Why should I share the glory of first place with Cat and Buffalo? thought the rat selfishly.

"Wake up, my friend," he cried to Cat. "Look at all the tasty fish swimming in the water."

Cat licked her lips. She leaned over for a closer look, and Rat gave her a little push. SPLASH! She tumbled into the water.

Buffalo turned his head to see what had made the splash. He didn't see the cat, though. What he saw instead were the other animals in the race—and they were close behind him. Without giving Cat or Rat another thought, he sped toward the Emperor.

Just as Buffalo neared the riverbank, the clever rat leaped from behind his ear and crossed the finish line in first place.

"How did such a small animal win the race?" asked the Emperor in surprise.

"I may be small but I am also smart," replied the rat. He scampered up onto the winner's podium. Buffalo knew he had

been tricked into second place, but he could only grunt in dismay.

Back in the river, Cat tried to swim along with the other animals. She hated water. But if she had to swim in it to win the race, she would do so.

Far ahead of her, Tiger came roaring across the finish line. "Am I first?" he growled.

"No," said the rat smugly. "You'd have to be awfully clever to beat me."

"And you'd have to get up extra early to beat me," added the buffalo.

Cat scrambled onto a log. She paused to shake herself off and to catch her breath.

By then the sky was dark and a great storm was blowing. A dragon appeared in the clouds above. He was much, much too big to run through woods or swim across a river, so the Emperor had told him he could race through the sky, braving the rains and the wind.

But no sooner had he begun his descent to the earth, than the rabbit darted across the finish line in front of him, taking fourth place. The dragon had to be content with fifth.

In the river, the cat heaved a great sigh, then plunged into the water again. "I can still make it," she told herself. But Snake slithered across the finish line next and hissed a silvery greeting to the five animals who had arrived before him. Snake was number six.

Cat swam as fast as she could. A few moments later, she heard the sound of galloping hooves in the distance. Horse thundered across the finish line in seventh place.

Vocabulary

podium (pō′ dē əm) *n.* a small, raised platform or stand with a slanted shelf for holding a speaker's papers

Goat and Monkey weren't far behind. They jumped onto the log on which Cat had rested and paddled across the finish line almost at the same time. But Goat beat Monkey by a hair.

While the nine winners waited patiently with the Emperor, Cat watched Rooster struggle toward the finish line. Dog could easily have swum ahead of Rooster, but she couldn't resist playing in the water for just a few minutes longer.

"Number ten!" called the Emperor as Rooster staggered in. "Number eleven!" he cried when Dog arrived.

"Who will be number twelve?" asked the Emperor. "I need just one more animal."

"Me! I will!" called Cat, and she swam even faster.

Unfortunately for Cat, Pig rushed across the finish line in front of her.

"Number twelve!" cried the Emperor, but Cat was still too far away.

"Congratulations to all the winners!" said the Emperor. "One of the twelve years will be named after each of you."

Suddenly, up rushed Cat. She was tired and wet and more than a little unhappy

From CAT AND RAT: THE LEGEND OF THE CHINESE ZODIAC by Ed Young, ©1995 by Ed Young. Reprinted by permission of Henry Holt and Company, Inc.

Viewing the painting: What event in the legend does this painting show? Does the mood of the painting match the mood of the story? Explain.

about swimming across the river on her own. "How did I do?" she asked anxiously. "Am I one of the winners?"

"Sorry, dear Cat," replied the Emperor. "All twelve places have been filled."

Upon hearing this news, Cat let out a yowl and tried to pounce on Rat. Her claws scratched the tip of his tail, but Rat squeezed under the Emperor's chair just in time.

And that is why, to this very day, Cat and Rat are enemies.

Vocabulary
pounce (pouns) *v.* to swoop down, spring, or leap suddenly in attack

R a t

1996, 1984, 1972, 1960,
1948, 1936, 1924, 1912, 1900

Rats are innovative and know how to use opportunities to their advantage. They love to collect and organize and tend to be most active while others are at rest. Rats need to be careful not to lose their tempers or to become greedy. Rats get along best with Dragons and Monkeys and least with Horses.

O x (B u f f a l o)

1997, 1985, 1973, 1961,
1949, 1937, 1925, 1913, 1901

Ox are honest, conservative, and patient by nature. They are happy when alone. Since friends and family find them dependable, they will make good mothers or fathers. Ox can be stubborn when pushed. They may be slow in starting things, but always complete what they begin. Ox are better friends with Snakes and Roosters and can get into trouble with Goats.

T i g e r

1998, 1986, 1974, 1962,
1950, 1938, 1926, 1914, 1902

Tigers are powerful, courageous, and like to take chances—qualities that make them natural leaders. Because of this, they must weigh matters before taking action on them. Tigers need to be careful not to let their brashness offend others. Dogs and Horses are friends with Tigers, but Monkeys are not.

R a b b i t

1999, 1987, 1975, 1963,
1951, 1939, 1927, 1915, 1903

This is the luckiest sign of all. Rabbits are gentle, talented, gracious, and friendly. Because of these qualities, they are popular wherever they go as mediators of conflicts. Sometimes Rabbits are overly shy and sentimental, but they almost always succeed at what they do. Their best friends are Goats or Pigs. Roosters may be enemies.

D r a g o n

2000, 1988, 1976, 1964,
1952, 1940, 1928, 1916, 1904

Dragons have a superimagination and are unique, energetic, and dramatic. Dragons are also moody and can be too perfectionistic. They make good friends with Monkeys and Rats but should beware of Dogs.

S n a k e

2001, 1989, 1977, 1965,
1953, 1941, 1929, 1917, 1905

Snakes are talented and graceful, intuitive and wise. They are subtle in their ways and care about their looks. Snakes can be stingy at times, but if they use their good qualities to help others, many people will benefit. Snakes' best friends are Roosters and Ox, while their enemies are Pigs.

Horse

2002, 1990, 1978, 1966,
1954, 1942, 1930, 1918, 1906

Horses' energy, high spirits, and optimism make them popular among friends. They have a very independent streak and like to travel alone. Horses must learn patience and learn to finish what they start. They should marry Tigers or Dogs but not Rats.

Rooster

2005, 1993, 1981, 1969,
1957, 1945, 1933, 1921, 1909

Roosters are punctual, reliable, independent, and enjoy being on center stage. They are careful and unique but sometimes conceited. Snakes and Ox are friends but Rabbits are trouble.

Goat

2003, 1991, 1979, 1967,
1955, 1943, 1931, 1919, 1907

Although Goats are sometimes shy, they are always loving, gentle, elegant, and creative. They must learn to be direct and to venture out of comfortable situations. Goats get along well with Pigs and Rabbits but are not as friendly with Ox.

Dog

2006, 1994, 1982, 1970,
1958, 1946, 1934, 1922, 1910

Dogs are gregarious, loyal, honest, fun-loving team players. They are also helpful and optimistic but may spend too much time worrying about things. For friendship, Dogs should look to Horses or Tigers. Watch out for Dragons.

Monkey

2004, 1992, 1980, 1968,
1956, 1944, 1932, 1920, 1908

People pay attention to Monkeys because they are very smart. They are confident, energetic, happy, and curious. However, Monkeys can become overly confident, getting ahead of themselves and becoming confused. Monkeys should stay away from Tigers and look for Dragons or Rats as friends.

Pig

2007, 1995, 1983, 1971,
1959, 1947, 1935, 1923, 1911

Pigs are noble and physically strong and will sacrifice anything for the welfare of their family. Their friendships are long-lasting, even though they may not always be easy. Pigs can sometimes be reckless. They should stay away from other Pigs and make friends with Rabbits or Goats.

From CAT AND RAT: THE LEGEND OF THE CHINESE ZODIAC by Ed Young. ©1995 by Ed Young. Reprinted by permission of Henry Holt and Company, Inc.

Responding to Literature

PERSONAL RESPONSE

- ◆ How does the ancient Chinese explanation about cats and rats compare with the ideas you shared in the **Reading Focus** on page 725?

Analyzing Literature

RECALL

1. How does the emperor plan to use the results of the race?
2. What is Cat's plan for succeeding in the race?
3. How does Rat manage to finish the race?
4. How many animals cross the finish line before Cat? How does she react to the results of the race?

INTERPRET

5. What do you learn about the personalities of Cat and Rat when they first hear about the race?
6. What does the legend teach about rats in general?
7. According to this tale, why are cats and rats enemies?

EVALUATE AND CONNECT

8. Read the description of people born under the sign of the Rat in the zodiac chart. Which characteristics does Rat in the story share with this description?
9. In your opinion, would this kind of imaginative explanation for the Chinese calendar help children remember the animals associated with each year? Why or why not?
10. Personal Connection   Would you use the Chinese Zodiac or something similar to it as a guide for choosing your friends? Why or why not?

LITERARY ELEMENTS

Legend

Legends, folktales, and myths are part of folk literature—the collected beliefs and traditions of a people. A **legend** is a story, handed down from generation to generation, about a specific person or thing. Legends share some characteristics of folktales and myths. For example, they may include explanations of how things in nature came about. However, legends are usually associated with a particular person or place and often deal someone or something that exists or existed historically. For example, the twelve-month zodiac in "Cat and Rat" has been the center of Chinese astrology for thousands of years.

1. How does the "Cat and Rat" legend explain why cats are great rat catchers?

2. Do you think the twelve zodiac animals were really chosen as a result of a race? Why or why not?

- ● See **Literary Terms Handbook,** p. R6.

Literature and Writing

Writing About Literature

Plot   The plot of "Cat and Rat" begins with Cat and Rat as friends and ends when they become enemies. Using the diagram on pages 144–145 as a model, draw and label a diagram identifying the five stages of the legend's plot.

Creative Writing

Why Do . . . ?   Think of your favorite animal. Then choose one of the animal's more interesting traits or physical characteristics to explain in a legend. Illustrate your tale with pictures that call attention to the characteristic you explained.

Extending Your Response

Literature Groups

Reality and Fantasy   Myths, legends, and folktales combine reality and fantasy. For example, an emperor inventing a new calendar could be a realistic event. However, a cat and a rat having a conversation is fantasy. List other examples of reality and fantasy in "Cat and Rat." Compare your findings with those of the rest of the class.

Performing

Dramatize   Form an acting troupe to perform "Cat and Rat." Adapt the story so that it takes place in a present-day setting. Write a script, and then choose students to take the parts of the emperor, the various animals, and a narrator. You may want to design and build simple scenery and make costumes that suggest the various characters as well. Perform the legend for another class.

Interdisciplinary Activity

Social Studies   The Western calendar is not the only one used by large numbers of people. Use library resources to find out about other calendars (for example, Hindu, Jewish, and Muslim calendars). Choose one to investigate further. Find out how and when it developed and how it differs from the Western calendar.

Reading Further

If you would like to read other Chinese legends, try:

How the Ox Star Fell from Heaven by Lily Toy Hong

Min-Yo and the Moon Dragon by Elizabeth Hillman

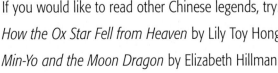

Save your work for your portfolio.

Skill Minilessons

GRAMMAR AND LANGUAGE • APOSTROPHES IN CONTRACTIONS

A **contraction** is a word made by putting two words together and replacing one or more letters with an apostrophe.

it + is = it's   we + are = we're
I + will = I'll   she + would = she'd

PRACTICE Copy each sentence from the story. Then find and underline two words that could be combined into a contraction. Write the contraction above the words.

1. They would be two of the smallest.
2. We will never make it.
3. We had better get started.
4. They had fully awakened.
5. But I am also smart.

● For more about apostrophe usage, see **Language Handbook,** pp. R40–R41.

READING AND THINKING • USING GRAPHIC AIDS

Stories and novels are most often illustrated by drawings or paintings, but sometimes a story includes a graphic aid. A **graphic aid** is a chart, graph, map, or other illustration that organizes information for the reader. The graphic aid in "Cat and Rat" is the chart of the zodiac. Without this chart, the purpose of the legend would be difficult to understand. The zodiac chart shows the order of the twelve year names, the Chinese symbol for each year, the birth years for anyone born between 1900 and 2007, as well as the personality traits for people born in each of the twelve years.

PRACTICE In what year were you born? Look up your birth year on the zodiac chart on pages 730–731. Then write a paragraph explaining how your personality does or does not match the one described in the graphic. Find out the birth years of members of your family, and compare their personality traits with those described under the matching animals.

● For more about interpreting graphic aids, see **Reading Handbook,** pp. 101–102.

VOCABULARY • THE SUFFIX -FUL

A *hopeful* person is full of hope; a *cheerful* one is full of cheer; a *fearful* one is full of fear. In each of these cases, you could define the word by simply adding "full of" to the base word. However, you can't always define a word this way. For example, a *dreadful* sight is not a sight that is full of dread; it's a sight that fills the viewer with dread. An area with many natural resources, such as oil, is "rich in resources" or "resource rich," but not *resourceful*.

PRACTICE Briefly explain what each underlined word means.

1. a skillful athlete
2. a masterful plan
3. a wasteful policy
4. a tearful response
5. a handful of coins

● For more about adding suffixes, see **Language Handbook,** Spelling, pp. R44–R45.

Vo•cab•u•lar•y Skills

Analyzing Word Parts

The best source of information for the meaning of an unfamiliar word is a dictionary, but a dictionary is not always handy. Context clues are often useful, but in many cases, there are not enough context clues to provide adequate help. Many words themselves contain clues to their meanings. Familiar base words, roots, or other word parts can provide information about the meaning of the word.

"The Smallest Dragonboy" says, "Being the youngest candidate was not an enviable position." The sentence provides little help for the meaning of *enviable.* It could mean "lucky" or "common" or many other things. However, the word itself is helpful because it is made up of the base word *envy* and the suffix *-able.* Putting these clues together provides an idea very close to the actual meaning of "able to be envied."

A word may have a familiar root. For example, look at *spectacle* in this sentence:

"The Bunyan family must have been quite a spectacle."

If you are familiar with words like *spectator* or *inspect,* you can figure out that a *spectacle* is something that is seen. The Latin root *spec* (or *spect*) means "to look at."

Analyzing words is not a substitute for looking them up in a good dictionary. A word part may look like a familiar root, but it might not be one. Also, the meaning of the word may have changed over time. Still, analyzing words can sometimes provide real help when you need to guess at a meaning.

EXERCISE

Analyze the underlined words, using whatever clues they contain to help you. Then match each word to its meaning on the right.

1. a new <u>modification</u>
2. to <u>dislocate</u> a knee
3. a <u>migratory</u> way of life
4. to be a <u>noncombatant</u>
5. to identify a <u>precondition</u>
6. behave like an <u>ingrate</u>
7. an <u>injurious</u> act
8. to use some <u>leverage</u>
9. to <u>maltreat</u> someone
10. a <u>snippet</u> of information

a. to abuse
b. harmful or damaging
c. one who is not thankful
d. a slight change in form
e. characterized by moving from place to place
f. a small piece or fragment
g. to put out of the proper position
h. increased means of accomplishing a purpose
i. one whose duties do not include actual fighting
j. something required before something else can occur

Before You Read

Icarus and Daedalus

MEET JOSEPHINE PRESTON PEABODY

Josephine Preston Peabody's parents introduced her to literature and the theater at a young age. As a result, Peabody grew up reading and writing constantly. She published her first poem when she was fourteen years old. Six years later, the publication of her poems in magazines helped her to attend Radcliffe College. One of her verse dramas, "The Piper," was based on the Pied Piper legend and was produced at theaters in New York City and London.

Josephine Preston Peabody was born in Brooklyn, New York, in 1874 and died in Cambridge, Massachusetts, in 1922.

READING FOCUS

Have you ever known someone who ignored caution and did something dangerous?

Journal
Write your thoughts and feelings about failing to heed good advice. Then share your ideas in a small-group discussion.

Setting a Purpose
Read this story to find out what happens to Icarus and Daedalus.

BUILDING BACKGROUND

The Time and Place   This story takes place on the Greek island of Crete in the legendary time when both mortals and gods inhabited ancient Greece.

Did You Know?   The word *myth* comes from *mythos,* a Greek word meaning "story." A myth is a special kind of story, usually involving gods and goddesses. The origins of the Greek myths are unknown, but they likely developed over many hundreds of years of oral retellings before the Greeks developed writing. They were already very old by around 850 B.C., when the Greek writer Homer referred to them in his poems. The Greek myths tell the stories of the gods and goddesses, their lives on Mount Olympus, and their interactions with the mortals on earth.

VOCABULARY PREVIEW

veer (vēr) *v.* to shift or change direction; p. 737
waver (wā′ vər) *v.* to become unsteady; p. 738
rash (rash) *adj.* done without thought or preparation; reckless; p. 738
reel (rēl) *v.* to turn or seem to turn round and round; whirl; p. 739
quench (kwench) *v.* to satisfy or put an end to a need or desire; p. 739
vainly (vān′ lē) *adv.* without success; uselessly; p. 739

Icarus and Daedalus

Josephine Preston Peabody ~

Among all those mortals who grew so wise that they learned the secrets of the gods, none was more cunning than Daedalus.[1]

He once built, for King Minos of Crete, a wonderful Labyrinth of winding ways so cunningly tangled up and twisted around that, once inside, you could never find your way out again without a magic clue. But the king's favor <u>veered</u> with the wind, and one day he had his master architect imprisoned in a tower. Daedalus managed to escape from his cell; but it seemed impossible to leave the island, since every ship that came or went was well guarded by order of the king.

At length, watching the sea gulls in the air—the only creatures that were sure of liberty—he thought of a plan for himself and his young son Icarus,[2] who was captive with him.

Did You Know?
The *Labyrinth* (lab′ ə rinth′) was a huge maze in which a complicated, twisted path enclosed by high walls made it impossible for people to find the way out once they had entered it.

---

1. *Daedalus* (ded′ əl əs)
2. *Icarus* (ik′ ər əs)

Vocabulary
veer (vēr) *v.* to shift or change direction

Icarus, 1947. Henri Matisse. From the *Jazz* series. Gouache on paper, 42 x 32.5 cm. COPYRIGHT ARS, New York, Ecole des Beaux Arts, Paris.

Viewing the painting: How is the flight of Icarus, as described in the myth, like the Icarus painted by Matisse? What important differences do you see?

Little by little, he gathered a store of feathers great and small. He fastened these together with thread, molded them in with wax, and so fashioned two great wings like those of a bird. When they were done, Daedalus fitted them to his own shoulders, and after one or two efforts, he found that by waving his arms he could winnow the air and cleave[3] it, as a swimmer does the sea. He held himself aloft, wavered this way and that with the wind, and at last, like a great fledgling,[4] he learned to fly.

Without delay, he fell to work on a pair of wings for the boy Icarus, and taught him carefully how to use them, bidding him beware of rash adventures among the stars. "Remember," said the father, "never to fly very low or very high, for the fogs about the earth

---

3. Here, *winnow* and *cleave* both mean "to separate or divide."
4. A *fledgling* is a young bird that hasn't yet grown the feathers it needs to fly.

Vocabulary

waver (wā′ vər) *v.* to become unsteady
rash (rash) *adj.* done without thought or preparation; reckless

would weigh you down, but the blaze of the sun will surely melt your feathers apart if you go too near."

For Icarus, these cautions went in at one ear and out by the other. Who could remember to be careful when he was to fly for the first time? Are birds careful? Not they! And not an idea remained in the boy's head but the one joy of escape.

The day came, and the fair wind that was to set them free. The father bird put on his wings, and, while the light urged them to be gone, he waited to see that all was well with Icarus, for the two could not fly hand in hand. Up they rose, the boy after his father. The hateful ground of Crete sank beneath them; and the country folk, who caught a glimpse of them when they were high above the treetops, took it for a vision of the gods—Apollo, perhaps, with Cupid[5] after him.

At first there was a terror in the joy. The wide vacancy of the air dazed them—a glance downward made their brains reel. But when a great wind filled their wings, and Icarus felt himself sustained, like a halcyon-bird[6] in the hollow of a wave, like a

---

5. In mythology, *Apollo* is the god of the sun, and *Cupid* is the god of love.
6. Here, *sustained* means to be kept from sinking or falling. The *halcyon-bird* (hal′ sē ən), or kingfisher, glides slowly and smoothly near the water's surface as it hunts for fish.

child uplifted by his mother, he forgot everything in the world but joy. He forgot Crete and the other islands that he had passed over: he saw but vaguely that winged thing in the distance before him that was his father Daedalus. He longed for one draft[7] of flight to quench the thirst of his captivity: he stretched out his arms to the sky and made toward the highest heavens.

Alas for him! Warmer and warmer grew the air. Those arms, that had seemed to uphold him, relaxed. His wings wavered, drooped. He fluttered his young hands vainly—he was falling—and in that terror he remembered. The heat of the sun had melted the wax from his wings; the feathers were falling, one by one, like snowflakes; and there was none to help.

He fell like a leaf tossed down the wind, down, down, with one cry that overtook Daedalus far away. When he returned, and sought high and low for the poor boy, he saw nothing but the bird-like feathers afloat on the water, and he knew that Icarus was drowned.

The nearest island he named Icaria, in memory of the child; but he, in heavy grief, went to the temple of Apollo in Sicily, and there hung up his wings as an offering. Never again did he attempt to fly.

---

7. Here, *draft* means "taste."

Vocabulary
reel (rēl) *v.* to turn or seem to turn round and round; whirl
quench (kwench) *v.* to satisfy or put an end to a need or desire
vainly (vān′ lē) *adv.* without success; uselessly

Responding to Literature

PERSONAL RESPONSE

◆ Why didn't Icarus listen to his father's words of wisdom? Describe your impressions in your journal.

Analyzing Literature

RECALL

1. What does King Minos do to keep Daedalus and Icarus from escaping Crete?
2. Describe the relationship between Daedalus and Icarus.
3. What happens to Icarus?
4. What does Daedalus do once he reaches safety?

INTERPRET

5. How does the setting of the story influence the plot? Support your ideas with details from the story.
6. Do you think that Daedalus is a concerned father? Why or why not? Support your opinion with examples.
7. Why does Icarus disobey his father's words of caution?
8. Do you think Daedalus feels responsible for what happens to his son? Why or why not?

EVALUATE AND CONNECT

9. Imagine that you are Icarus. Would you listen to your father's advice? Why or why not?
10. How do you feel about what happens to the main characters in this myth? Explain.

LITERARY ELEMENTS

Myth

People in every culture throughout the world have created myths. A **myth** is an ancient story of unknown origins, often involving gods and heroes. Myths originally helped people try to explain how natural events and human actions happened. There are myths about every facet of human life, from the creation of the world to an understanding of why things grow. In fact, collections of myths, called mythologies, generally account for everything in the experience of a particular culture.

1. What elements in "Icarus and Daedalus" fit the definition of a myth?

2. What can you learn about ancient Greek culture from reading this myth?

● See **Literary Terms Handbook,** p. R7.

Literature and Writing

Writing About Literature

Characterization   **Characterization** refers to the ways in which an author informs readers about the characters in a story. You learn about characters through their thoughts, words, actions, and interactions with other characters, and from what other characters say about them. Describe one of the characters as you picture him from the author's characterization.

Creative Writing

The Greek Gazette   Imagine that you have been assigned to write a news story about Daedalus and his flight to freedom. Interview a partner who plays the role of Daedalus just as he and Icarus are preparing for their journey. Then write a news report based on the interview and the results of the flight. Share your news story with your classmates in an oral presentation.

Extending Your Response

Literature Groups

Thinking About Theme   Discuss the theme of "Icarus and Daedalus." Focus on the questions: What did Daedalus fear would happen to his son? Why did Icarus choose to ignore his father's words of caution? Review your notes from the **Reading Focus** on page 736, and talk about the meaning of this myth as it relates to life today.

Art Activity

Modeling   Create a model or draw a diagram of Daedalus's flying machine as you picture it.

📖 **Save your work for your portfolio.**

Skill Minilesson

VOCABULARY • DICTIONARY SKILLS: DEFINITIONS

vain (vān) *adj.* **1.** too interested in, or proud of, one's own abilities, appearance, or accomplishments: *a vain man.* **2.** not successful or effective: *a vain attempt.* **3.** of no real value or meaning; empty: *a vain promise. adv.* vainly

PRACTICE Study the dictionary definitions above. Decide which meaning of *vain* (or *vainly*) is used in each sentence and write the number of that meaning.

1. One might expect *vain* satisfaction in a man who had accomplished what no other had ever done.
2. After all, Daedalus triumphed over King Minos's *vain* efforts to confine him.
3. Instead of *vainly* showing off his ability, however, Daedalus never flew again.
4. Liberty itself seemed *vain* to him when achieved at the cost of his son.
5. Could he have known how *vain* his warnings would be?

Before You Read

Prometheus

MEET BERNARD EVSLIN

Having written plays for the stage and screen and published a novel for adults, Bernard Evslin (əv′ slin) decided on a career shift. In the mid-1960s, he began retelling myths and other ancient stories for an audience of young readers. His gift was his ability to retell ancient tales, whether from Greek mythology or the Bible, with such colorful details and contemporary language that some of the oldest stories in the world captured the interests of young readers.

Bernard Evslin was born in Pennsylvania in 1916 and died in Hawaii in 1993. This story was published in 1966.

READING FOCUS

Think about the expression "Knowledge is power." What does it mean? Do you agree or disagree with it? Why?

Sharing Ideas
Jot down your ideas about the meaning of the expression, and then share them in a small-group discussion.

Setting a Purpose
Read this myth to find out what a giant thinks about knowledge.

BUILDING BACKGROUND

The Time and Place This story takes place in Greece in the days when the gods and goddesses of Greek mythology were thought to rule the lives of mortals.

Did You Know? In Greek art, Prometheus is often pictured chained to a rock, his body attacked by vultures.

Coppa laconica con punizione di Atlante e Prometeo, 630–100 B.C. Pottery. Museo Gregoriano Etrusco, Vaticano.

VOCABULARY PREVIEW

decree (di krē′) *n.* an official rule, order, or decision; p. 743
aptitude (ap′ tə tōōd′) *n.* a natural ability; talent; p. 743
humility (hū mil′ ə tē) *n.* the quality of being humble or modest; p. 744
spite (spīt) *n.* a desire to hurt or annoy another person; p. 744
agony (ag′ ə nē) *n.* great pain and suffering of the mind or body; p. 745
hover (huv′ ər) *v.* to remain as if suspended in the air over a particular spot; p. 745

PROMETHEUS

Retold by Bernard Evslin

Prometheus was a young Titan, no great admirer of Zeus.[1] Although he knew the great lord of the sky hated explicit questions, he did not hesitate to beard[2] him when there was something he wanted to know.

One morning he came to Zeus and said, "O Thunderer, I do not understand your design. You have caused the race of man to appear on earth, but you keep him in ignorance and darkness."

"Perhaps you had better leave the race of man to me," said Zeus. "What you call ignorance is innocence. What you call darkness is the shadow of my decree. Man is happy now. And he is so framed that he will remain happy unless someone persuades him that he is unhappy. Let us not speak of this again."

But Prometheus said, "Look at him. Look below. He crouches in caves. He is at the mercy of beast and weather. He eats his meat raw. If you mean something by this, enlighten me with your wisdom. Tell me why you refuse to give man the gift of fire."

Zeus answered, "Do you not know, Prometheus, that every gift brings a penalty? This is the way the Fates weave destiny—by which gods also must abide.[3] Man does not have fire, true, nor the crafts which fire teaches. On the other hand, he does not know disease, warfare, old age, or that inward pest called worry. He is happy, I say, happy without fire. And so he shall remain."

"Happy as beasts are happy," said Prometheus. "Of what use to make a separate race called man and endow[4] him with little fur, some wit, and a curious charm of unpredictability? If he must live like this, why separate him from the beasts at all?"

"He has another quality," said Zeus, "the capacity for worship. An aptitude for admiring our power, being puzzled by our riddles and amazed by our caprice.[5] That is why he was made."

"Would not fire, and the graces he can put on with fire, make him more interesting?"

"More interesting, perhaps, but infinitely more dangerous. For there is this in man

---

1. According to Greek myths, *Prometheus* (prə mē′ thē əs) and the other *Titans* (tīt′ ənz) belonged to a race of giants who once ruled the world. They were overthrown by *Zeus* (zōos) and other gods.
2. To *beard* Zeus was to meet him boldly, face-to-face.

3. The ancient Greeks believed that three goddesses, sisters called the *Fates,* controlled human lives and fortunes. Even the gods had to go along with, or *abide,* the sisters' decisions.
4. To *endow* is to give a quality, ability, or talent to someone.
5. The gods' *caprice* was their tendency to change their minds suddenly and for little or no reason.

Vocabulary
decree (di krē′) *n.* an official rule, order, or decision
aptitude (ap′ tə tood′) *n.* a natural ability; talent

Prometheus Giving Fire to Man. 1st century A.D. Mosaic tile. Museo delle Terme, Rome.

Viewing the mosaic: The ancient Greeks considered the gift of fire an important event. They celebrated the Prometheus myth in their literature and their art. Can you think of any modern "gift" that has had such an influence?

too: a vaunting pride that needs little sustenance to make it swell to giant size. Improve his lot,[6] and he will forget that which makes him pleasing—his sense of worship, his <u>humility</u>. He will grow big and poisoned with pride and fancy himself a god, and before we know it, we shall see him storming Olympus. Enough, Prometheus! I have been patient with you, but do not try me too far. Go now and trouble me no more with your speculations."

Prometheus was not satisfied. All that night he lay awake making plans. Then he left his couch at dawn and, standing tiptoe on Olympus, stretched his arm to the eastern horizon where the first faint flames of the sun were flickering. In his hand he held a reed filled with a dry fiber; he thrust it into the sunrise until a spark smoldered. Then he put the reed in his tunic and came down from the mountain.

At first men were frightened by the gift. It was so hot, so quick; it bit sharply when you touched it and for pure <u>spite</u> made the shadows dance. They thanked Prometheus and asked him to take it away. But he took the haunch of a newly killed deer and held it over the fire. And when the meat began to sear and sputter, filling the cave with its rich smells, the people felt themselves

---

6. *Vaunting* pride is boastful. *Sustenance* means "support or assistance." Here, *lot* refers to humans' situations in life or the conditions in which they live.

Vocabulary
humility (hū mil′ ə tē) *n.* the quality of being humble or modest
spite (spīt) *n.* a desire to hurt or annoy another person

melting with hunger and flung themselves on the meat and devoured it greedily, burning their tongues.

"This that I have brought you is called 'fire,'" Prometheus said. "It is an ill-natured spirit, a little brother of the sun, but if you handle it carefully, it can change your whole life. It is very greedy; you must feed it twigs, but only until it becomes a proper size. Then you must stop, or it will eat everything in sight—and you too. If it escapes, use this magic: water. It fears the water spirit, and if you touch it with water, it will fly away until you need it again."

He left the fire burning in the first cave, with children staring at it wide-eyed, and then went to every cave in the land.

Then one day Zeus looked down from the mountain and was amazed. Everything had changed. Man had come out of his cave. Zeus saw woodmen's huts, farmhouses, villages, walled towns, even a castle or two. He saw men cooking their food, carrying torches to light their way at night. He saw forges blazing, men beating out ploughs, keels,[7] swords, spears. They were making ships and raising white wings of sails and daring to use the fury of the winds for their journeys. They were wearing helmets, riding out in chariots to do battle, like the gods themselves.

Zeus was full of rage. He seized his largest thunderbolt. "So they want fire," he said to himself. "I'll give them fire—more than they can use. I'll turn their miserable little ball of earth into a cinder." But then another thought came to him, and he lowered his arm. "No," he said to himself, "I shall have vengeance—and entertainment too. Let them destroy themselves with their new skills. This will make a long, twisted game, interesting to watch. I'll attend to them later. My first business is with Prometheus."

He called his giant guards and had them seize Prometheus, drag him off to the Caucasus, and there bind him to a mountain peak with great chains specially forged by Hephaestus[8]—chains which even a Titan in agony could not break. And when the friend of man was bound to the mountain, Zeus sent two vultures to hover about him forever, tearing at his belly and eating his liver.

Men knew a terrible thing was happening on the mountain, but they did not know what. But the wind shrieked like a giant in torment and sometimes like fierce birds.

Many centuries he lay there—until another hero was born brave enough to defy the gods. He climbed to the peak in the Caucasus and struck the shackles from Prometheus and killed the vultures. His name was Heracles.[9]

---

7. A blacksmith uses a *forge* to heat and soften metal so that it can be hammered into desired shapes. A shipbuilder makes a *keel,* the main timber that runs the length of a boat's bottom.

8. The *Caucasus* Mountains, in southeastern Russia between the Black and Caspian Seas, separate Europe and Asia. *Hephaestus* (hi fes′ təs) was the god of fire and metalworking.

9. *Heracles* (her′ ə klēz′) is the Greek name for Hercules, who was the son of Zeus and a human woman.

Vocabulary
agony (ag′ ə nē) *n.* great pain and suffering of the mind or body
hover (huv′ ər) *v.* to remain as if suspended in the air over a particular spot

Responding to Literature

PERSONAL RESPONSE

◆ What images from the myth linger in your mind? Record them in your journal.

Analyzing Literature

RECALL AND INTERPRET

1. What gift for human beings does Prometheus request from Zeus? Why do you think he makes such a request?

2. What is Zeus's response to the request? Do you think this response was justified? Explain your answer.

3. What series of events make up the plot of this myth? Why do you think this myth was created?

EVALUATE AND CONNECT

4. Why was fire so important to the development of human civilization?

5. Do you think Prometheus was a hero or a fool? Use examples to support your opinion.

6. The English adjective *Promethean*, which means "daringly creative or original," is derived from the mythical Titan's name. Think of someone in the modern world who could be described as Promethean. Give reasons for your answer.

LITERARY ELEMENTS

Theme

A **theme** is the message, or general truth about life, expressed in a work of literature. A piece of writing may have a **stated theme**, which is expressed directly, or an **implied theme**, which is revealed gradually through the thoughts and actions of the characters. There may be one theme or several in a single piece of writing.

1. What is the theme of "Prometheus"? Support your ideas with examples and quotations from the myth.

2. In a paragraph, discuss the theme of another selection you have read.

● See **Literary Terms Handbook,** p. R11.

Extending Your Response

Literature Groups

Is Knowledge Power?   In this myth, Prometheus argues that human beings need the gift of fire to bring them out of ignorance and darkness. Do you agree with him? Review your notes from the **Reading Focus** on page 742. Then discuss how the expression "Knowledge is power" relates to the theme of this myth.

Writing About Literature

Myth   Brainstorm a list of things you think are essential to civilization. Then write one or two paragraphs describing how this myth might have been the ancient Greeks' explanation for the origins of the civilized world.

COMPARING SELECTIONS

Icarus and Daedalus **and** PROMETHEUS

COMPARE **MYTHS**

"Icarus and Daedalus" and "Prometheus" are Greek myths that portray characters attempting to use intelligence to outwit their fates. The themes of knowledge and freedom play an important role in both these myths.

Icarus, 1947 (detail).

1. How does Daedalus use his intelligence? Does he succeed in reaching his goal? Why or why not?
2. How does Prometheus use his intelligence? Does he succeed in reaching his goal? Why or why not?
3. How are these myths alike? How are they different?
4. Which myth do you prefer? Why?

COMPARE **IDEAS**

What is the meaning of the word *hero?* Are any of the characters in these two myths heroes?

- In small groups, talk about the kinds of personal characteristics, qualities, and actions that define a hero. Make a list of the characteristics of a hero. List some fictional as well as real-life examples.
- Look at each of the main characters in the two myths, and talk about whether or not each character's actions and personal qualities were heroic.
- Share your ideas and definitions in a discussion with your classmates.

COMPARE **ENDINGS**

Compare the endings of these myths. How are they alike? How are they different? How else might each of these selections have ended?

- What else might have happened to Icarus and Daedalus? Perhaps they stayed on the island of Crete or they escaped by boat. What about Prometheus? What else might have happened to him?
- Use your imagination to write an alternate ending to either myth. Feel free to use Zeus or any other Greek god or goddess in your ending, and make up any new details you wish.

OPERA LIBRETTO

The poet W. H. Auden wrote the libretto, or text, for Benjamin Britten's opera about the American folk hero Paul Bunyan. This ballad is sung by a folksinger in the opera.

First Ballad Interlude from Benjamin Britten's *Paul Bunyan*

by W. H. Auden

The cold wind blew through the crooked thorn,
Up in the North a boy was born.

His hair was black, and his eyes were blue,
His mouth turned up at the corners too.

A fairy stood beside his bed;
"You shall never, never grow old," she said,

"Paul Bunyan is to be your name";
Then she departed whence she came.

You must believe me when I say,
He grew six inches every day.

You must believe me when I speak,
He gained 346 pounds every week.

He grew so fast, by the time he was eight,
He was as tall as the Empire State.

The length of his stride's a historical fact;
3.7 miles to be exact.

When he ordered a jacket, the New England mills
For months had no more unemployment ills.

When he wanted a snapshot to send to his friends,
They found they had to use a telephoto lens.

But let me tell you in advance,
His dreams were of greater significance.

His favorite dream was of felling trees,
A fancy which grew by swift degrees.

One night he dreamt he was to be
The greatest logger in history.

He woke to feel something stroking his brow,
And found it was the tongue of an enormous cow.

From horn to horn or from lug to lug,
Was forty-seven axe-heads and a baccy plug.

But what would have most bewildered you
Was the color of her hide, which was bright bright
    blue.

But Bunyan wasn't surprised at all;
Said, "I'll call you Babe, you call me Paul."

He pointed to a meadow, said, "Take a bite:
For you're leaving with me for the South tonight."

Over the mountains, across the streams
They went to find Paul Bunyan's dreams.

The bear and the beaver waved a paw,
The magpie chattered, the squirrel swore.

The trappers ran out from their lonely huts
Scratching their heads with their rifle-butts.

For a year and a day they traveled fast.
"This is the place," Paul said at last.

The forest stretched for miles around,
The sound of their breathing was the only sound.

Paul picked a pine-tree and scratched his shins,
Said, "This is the place where our work begins."

Analyzing Media

1. Paul Bunyan is a tall-tale hero, and tall tales exaggerate, or go beyond the truth. What details in the ballad are clearly exaggerations?

2. In the opera, the ballad is performed by a folk singer rather than an opera singer. Why do you think the composer might prefer that kind of voice?

Before You Read

The Bunyans and *Brer Rabbit and Brer Lion*

MEET AUDREY WOOD

An artist and a children's book writer, Audrey Wood created this new Paul Bunyan story to add to the wonderful tradition of the American tall tale. Wood has written and illustrated many other books in collaboration with her husband, Don Wood.

Audrey Wood lives in Santa Barbara, California.

MEET JULIUS LESTER

Julius Lester's fiction and nonfiction focuses on preserving the history and heritage of African Americans. Lester has been a professional musician and singer, a host of radio and television programs, a university professor, and a writer of both adult and children's books.

Julius Lester was born in 1939. He lives in Amherst, Massachusetts.

READING FOCUS

Think about your favorite fictional characters. Are they realistic characters, or are they fantasy creatures or clever animals that inhabit the world of folktales and myths?

Think/Pair/Share

List some of your favorite fictional characters, and explain why you like them. Then share your ideas with a partner.

Setting a Purpose

Read to enjoy these two folktales.

BUILDING BACKGROUND

Did You Know? Stories about the legendary giant Paul Bunyan were first published in Minnesota in 1910, but they were told years earlier in lumber camps around the country. As the stories were passed on, Paul's deeds grew more and more incredible until the stories developed into the type of folklore called tall tales.

The character of the trickster has appeared in the folktales of many cultures throughout the world. In Theme 4 you read a story about Anansi, a trickster in African folktales. Brer Rabbit is a version of Anansi that developed in America. (*Brer,* also spelled *br'er,* is a shortened form of *brother.*) The Brer Rabbit stories were passed on orally by African Americans for generations before anyone put them into writing.

VOCABULARY PREVIEW

cordially (kôr′ jəl lē) *adv.* in a genuinely warm and friendly way; p. 752

barren (bar′ ən) *adj.* having little or no plant life; bare; empty; p. 753

fanciful (fan′ si fəl) *adj.* showing imagination in design or construction; imaginative; p. 753

sensation (sen sā′ shən) *n.* a cause of excitement or great interest; a wonder; p. 754

colossal (kə los′ əl) *adj.* extraordinarily or awesomely large; p. 754

The Bunyans

Audrey Wood ·~

Storyteller's Note

Now I suppose that you have heard about the mighty logger Paul Bunyan and his great blue ox named Babe. In the early days of our country, Paul and Babe cleared the land for the settlers, so farms and cities could spring up. And you probably know that Paul was taller than a redwood tree, stronger than fifty grizzly bears, and smarter than a library full of books. But you may not know that Paul was married and had two fine children.

One day when Paul Bunyan was out clearing a road through the forests of Kentucky, a great pounding began to shake the earth. Looking around, Paul discovered an enormous hole in the side of a hill. The lumberjack pulled up an acre of dry cane and fashioned a torch to light his way.

Paul climbed inside the hole and followed the sound underground for miles, until he came to a large cavern glistening with crystals. By the flickering light of his torch, he saw a gigantic woman banging a behemoth[1] pickax against a wall.

It was love at first sight.

"I'm Carrie McIntie," the gigantic woman said. "I was sitting on the hill when my lucky wishbone fell down a crack into the earth. I've been digging all day trying to find it."

With a grin on his face as wide as the Missouri River, Paul reached into his shirt pocket. "I've got one too," he said, pulling out *his* lucky wishbone. "Marry me, Carrie, and we'll share mine."

Carrie agreed, and their wedding invitations were mailed out right away.

The invitations were so large, only one needed to be sent to each state. Everyone could read them for miles!

The invitations said: *You are cordially invited to the mammoth wedding of Paul Bunyan and Carrie McIntie.* The couple were married in the enormous crystal chamber that Carrie had carved, and after the ceremony, folks began to call it "Mammoth Cave." The giantess had dug more than two hundred miles, making it the longest cave in the world, so the name fit perfectly.

Paul and Carrie settled down on a farm in Maine, and soon there were two new Bunyans. While Pa Bunyan traveled with his logging crew, Ma Bunyan worked the farm and cared for their jumbo boy, named Little Jean, and their gigantic girl, named Teeny.

One morning when Pa Bunyan was home between jobs, Ma Bunyan cooked up a hearty breakfast of pancakes and syrup. Teeny was wrestling with her big purple puma[2] named Slink and accidentally dumped a silo of syrup on her head. Teeny's hair was so sweet, bears crawled into it and burrowed deep in her curls. Try as they might, Pa and Ma Bunyan couldn't wash them out.

"We'll need a forceful shower of water to get rid of those varmints!"[3] Ma Bunyan declared.

Pa Bunyan had an idea. He placed his daughter on Babe, and he led them to the Niagara River in Canada. The gargantuan[4] father scooped out a huge hole in the middle of the riverbed. As the great river roared down into the deep hole, Teeny cried out in delight, "Niagara falls!" Teeny showered in the waterfall, and the pesky bears were washed downstream.

When Little Jean was five, he wanted to work too, so he followed his pa out to his logging camp in Montana. Thinking his son was too young to do much of

---

1. A *behemoth* (bi hē′ məth) object is monstrously large.

2. The *puma* (pū′ mə) is a mountain lion.
3. Here, *varmint* means "a pesky animal."
4. From the name of a fictional giant, *gargantuan* means "enormous; huge."

Vocabulary
cordially (kôr′ jəl lē) *adv.* in a genuinely warm and friendly way

anything, Paul set Little Jean down in a <u>barren</u> canyon in Utah to play for the day. When the lumberjack went to fetch him, he couldn't believe his eyes. Little Jean had carved the canyon into a wonderland of <u>fanciful</u> shapes.

Pa Bunyan got tongue-tied and said, "That's a mighty *brice* nanyon, coy, I mean, a mighty nice canyon, boy!" Somehow part of the mix-up stuck.

To this day the canyon is known as Bryce Canyon.

After all that sculpting, Little Jean's shoes were full of sand. Pa knew Ma Bunyan wouldn't want her clean floors dirtied up, so he told Little Jean to sit down and empty out his shoes.

The sand from Little Jean's shoes blew away on the eastern wind and settled down a state away. It covered a valley ten miles long, making sand dunes eight hundred feet high. Everyone knows that's how the Great Sand Dunes of Colorado came to be.

One summer, Little Jean and Teeny wanted to go to the beach. Ma Bunyan told them to follow a river to the ocean. But all the rivers flowed west back then, so they missed the Atlantic Ocean and ended up on the other side of the country instead.

The Bunyans. Illustration by David Shannon from THE BUNYANS by Audrey Wood. Published by the BLUE SKY PRESS. Illustrations © 1996 by David Shannon. Reprinted by permission of Scholastic, Inc. The BLUE SKY PRESS is a registered trademark of Scholastic, Inc.

Viewing the painting: This illustration was created for Audrey Wood's story. How does it add to the reader's appreciation of the tale?

Ma Bunyan tracked them out to the Pacific Ocean, where she found Teeny riding on the backs of two blue whales and Little Jean carving out fifty zigzag miles of the California coast.

When Ma Bunyan saw what her son had done, she exclaimed, "What's the big

---

Vocabulary
barren (bar' ən) *adj.* having little or no plant life; bare; empty
fanciful (fan' si fəl) *adj.* showing imagination in design or construction; imaginative

idea, sir!?" From that time on, the scenic area was known as Big Sur.

Ma Bunyan knew she had to put up a barrier to remind her children not to wander off too far. So, on the way home, everyone pitched in and built the Rocky Mountains. Teeny gathered up and sorted out all the rivers, letting some flow east and others west. After that, the children had no trouble following the eastern rivers down to the Atlantic Ocean. And when they wanted to go out exploring, Ma Bunyan would call out, "Now don't cross the Continental Divide, children!"

The best thing about camping is sleeping outdoors, and the worst thing is not having enough hot water. That's why the Bunyans always camped in Wyoming. By the time their camping years were over, Ma Bunyan had poked more than three hundred holes in the ground with her pickax and released tons of hot water from geysers. But Ma got tired of poking so many holes, so she made a geyser that blew every hour on the hour. After that, there was a steady supply of hot water to keep the giants' clothes and dishes sparkling clean.

Teeny named the geyser Old Faithful, and to this day, Old Faithful still blows its top every hour in Yellowstone National Park.

As our great country grew up, so did the Bunyan children. When the kids left home, Ma and Pa Bunyan retired to a wilderness area, where they still live happily.

Teeny hitched a ride on a whale over to England and became a famous fashion designer. Her colorful skirts made from air balloons and her breezy blouses cut from ship sails were a <u>sensation</u> at the first World's Fair in London.

Little Jean traveled to Venice, Italy, where he studied astronomy and art. Every day, the gondoliers would take their passengers down the Grand Canal[5] to watch the giant artist chiseling his marble sculptures.

After graduation, Little Jean decided to explore new lands, as his parents had done. So he took two great jumps and one flying leap and bounded up into outer space.

In 1976, the year of our country's bicentennial,[6] a spacecraft sent by the National Aeronautics and Space Administration was on a mission to study Mars. The spacecraft was named *Viking I*, and it took many photographs of the surface of the planet. One mysterious photo looked like a face carved out of <u>colossal</u> rock.

Some say the photograph is not a face, but an illusion caused by light and shadows on the rock. Others think the famous "Martian face" is just the spitting image of Little Jean Bunyan. If that's so, who knows what he's up to on the other planets.

Only time will tell!

---

5. *Venice* (ven′ is) is a city that has canals for streets, and the *Grand Canal* is its Main Street. A *gondolier* (gon′ də lēr′) operates a gondola—a long, narrow, flat-bottomed boat with high peaks at the ends.
6. A *bicentennial* is a two hundredth anniversary.

Vocabulary
sensation (sen sā′ shən) *n.* a cause of excitement or great interest; a wonder
colossal (kə los′ əl) *adj.* extraordinarily or awesomely large

Dawn Raid, 1995. Christian Pierre. Acrylic on Masonite, 20 x 30 in. Private collection.

Brer Rabbit and Brer Lion

Retold by Julius Lester ❧

Brer Rabbit was in the woods one afternoon when a great wind came up. It blew on the ground and it blew in the tops of the trees. It blew so hard that Brer Rabbit was afraid a tree might fall on him, and he started running.

He was trucking through the woods when he ran smack into Brer Lion. Now, don't come telling me ain't no lions in the United States. Ain't none here now. But back in yonder times, all the animals lived everywhere. The lions and tigers and elephants and foxes and what 'nall run around with each other like they was family. So that's how come wasn't unusual for Brer Rabbit to run up on Brer Lion like he done that day.

"What's your hurry, Brer Rabbit?"

"Run, Brer Lion! There's a hurricane coming."

Brer Lion got scared. "I'm too heavy to run, Brer Rabbit. What am I going to do?"

"Lay down, Brer Lion. Lay down! Get close to the ground!"

Brer Lion shook his head. "The wind might pick me up and blow me away."

"Hug a tree, Brer Lion! Hug a tree!"

"But what if the wind blows all day and into the night?"

"Let me tie you to the tree, Brer Lion. Let me tie you to the tree."

Brer Lion liked that idea. Brer Rabbit tied him to the tree and sat down next to it. After a while, Brer Lion got tired of hugging the tree.

"Brer Rabbit? I don't hear no hurricane."

Brer Rabbit listened. "Neither do I."

"Brer Rabbit? I don't hear no wind."

Brer Rabbit listened. "Neither do I."

"Brer Rabbit? Ain't a leaf moving in the trees."

Brer Rabbit looked up. "Sho' ain't."

"So untie me."

"I'm afraid to, Brer Lion."

Brer Lion began to roar. He roared so loud and so long, the foundations of the Earth started shaking. Least that's what it seemed like, and the other animals came from all over to see what was going on.

When they got close, Brer Rabbit jumped up and began strutting around the tied-up Brer Lion. When the animals saw what Brer Rabbit had done to Brer Lion, you'd better believe it was the forty-eleventh of Octorerarry before they messed with him again.

Emma's Lion, 1994. Christian Pierre. Acrylic on Masonite, 16 x 20 in. Private collection.

Viewing the painting: What qualities do you usually attribute to lions? Which of these qualities does the lion in the folktale show? Which qualities do you see in the painting?

Responding to Literature

PERSONAL RESPONSE

- ◆ What was your reaction to these tales? Record your responses in your journal.

Analyzing Literature

RECALL

1. Describe the Bunyan family.
2. What are some of the natural features of North America that the Bunyans built?
3. What lesson does Brer Lion learn?

INTERPRET

4. Compare and contrast the ordinary actions of the Bunyans and the extraordinary results of their actions.
5. What personality traits does Brer Rabbit have that help him get the better of a much larger animal?
6. What does the final sentence in "Brer Rabbit and Brer Lion" mean? When exactly is the "forty-eleventh of Octorerarry"? Explain.
7. How do you think Brer Rabbit feels at the end of this tale? Compare his feelings with those of Brer Lion.
8. If you could add a moral, or lesson, to the end of "Brer Rabbit and Brer Lion," what would it be?

EVALUATE AND CONNECT

9. What role does humor play in these tales? Explain.
10. Which tale did you prefer? Why?

LITERARY ELEMENTS

Folktales and Tall Tales

Folktales are stories that have been passed down from generation to generation. In many folktales, the characters are animals or ordinary people who have unusual experiences. **Tall tales** are a specific kind of American folktale that often describes one aspect of frontier life, such as logging (Paul Bunyan) or cattle ranching (Pecos Bill). Some tall tales are based on the deeds of people who actually lived—for example, Annie Oakley and Davy Crockett. In tall tales, the characters, their physical attributes, and their deeds are greatly exaggerated for humorous effect.

1. Give at least two reasons why "The Bunyans" would be considered a tall tale.

2. What message about life is illustrated in "Brer Rabbit and Brer Lion"?

- ● See **Literary Terms Handbook,** pp. R4–R5 and R11.

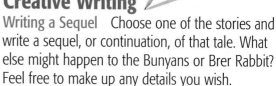

Literature and Writing

Writing About Literature

Dialogue Readers learn a great deal through the dialogue in a story. Write a paragraph explaining what you learned about the main characters from the dialogue in one of these folktales.

Creative Writing

Writing a Sequel Choose one of the stories and write a sequel, or continuation, of that tale. What else might happen to the Bunyans or Brer Rabbit? Feel free to make up any details you wish.

Extending Your Response

Literature Groups

Lovable Literary Characters Look back at your notes from the **Reading Focus** on page 749. Then discuss some of your favorite fictional characters and why you like them. Make a list of all-time favorite characters. Then compare and contrast the characters in these two tales with the characters on the list. How are they alike? How are they different?

Performing

Trickster Tale Dramatization The trickster is a familiar figure in folktales of many cultures. The sly coyote is as well-known a trickster in Native American folklore as Brer Rabbit is in African American folktales. Working in small groups, find a trickster tale, and dramatize the tale for another class.

Interdisciplinary Activity

Science Trace a map of the United States, and highlight the locations of the natural wonders "created" by the Bunyans. In an oral presentation, using your map as a guide, describe a tour that stops at each site. When appropriate, include information about what caused each natural wonder.

Reading Further

To read more stories by Audrey Wood or Julius Lester, try these books:

The Napping House by Audrey Wood

More Tales of Uncle Remus by Julius Lester

📔 **Save your work for your portfolio.**

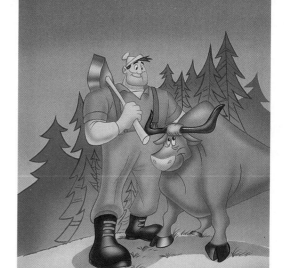

Skill Minilessons

GRAMMAR AND LANGUAGE • QUOTATION MARKS

Remember these rules when using quotation marks in your writing.

- Use quotation marks before and after the exact words in a direct quotation.

    "I'm Carrie McIntie," the gigantic woman said.

- Use quotation marks with both parts of a divided quotation.

    "Brer Rabbit," said Brer Lion, "I don't hear no hurricane."

- Use commas to separate phrases such as *he said* from the quotation (as in the example above).

- Always place commas and periods inside closing quotation marks (as in the examples). Place a question mark or an exclamation point inside the quotation marks only if it is part of the quotation.

    "Hug a tree!!" Brer Rabbit exclaimed. Why do you think he told Brer Lion to "Hug a tree"?

PRACTICE In pairs, create a dialogue between two characters from either selection. Once you have written your dialogue, proofread it to check for correct punctuation. Dramatize it for the class.

● For more about the use of quotation marks, see **Language Handbook,** pp. R39–R40.

READING AND THINKING • PARAPHRASING

When you paraphrase, you use your own words to briefly restate the content of a piece of writing. Paraphrasing a written work, or a portion of it, can help you understand the writer's meaning.

PRACTICE Reread "Brer Rabbit and Brer Lion" or "The Bunyans." Then write a paragraph paraphrasing what happens in the story.

● For more about paraphrasing, see **Reading Handbook,** p. R91.

VOCABULARY • ETYMOLOGY

The word *fanciful* is related to *fancy* and *fantasy,* all of which come from the Latin word *phantasia.* *Phantasia,* in turn, came from the Greek word *phantasie,* which means something like "a making visible." The Greeks used the word to describe the mind's ability to "picture" something that is just an idea or isn't really there.

PRACTICE Use the etymology given above to answer the questions.

1. Which would a *fanciful* person be able to do—see long distances, see through a phony smile, or see animals in the shapes made by clouds?
2. What do you need in order to *fantasize*—a pencil, an imagination, or a camera?
3. Which word do you think comes from the same root as *fanciful*—*phantom* or *fan?*
4. Which word does not come from the same root as *fanciful*—*fantastic* or *fanatic?*

Writing WORKSHOP

Expository Writing: Book Review

Some books grab you from the beginning, while others leave you cold. After reading a book, you probably form your own opinion of it. In a book review, you express your opinion and back it up to help your audience decide whether to read the book.

Assignment: Follow the process explained in these pages to develop your own book review.

● As you write your book review, refer to the **Writing Handbook,** pp. R48–R59.

EVALUATION RUBRIC
By the time you complete this Writing Workshop, you will have
● written a book review
● developed an attention-getting introduction
● summarized the book's main ideas and significant details
● analyzed the book's main literary elements
● supported each point with evidence
● created a conclusion that states your opinion
● presented a book review free of errors in grammar, usage, and mechanics

---

The Writing Process

PREWRITING

PREWRITING TIP
Choose a book that you respond to strongly, either positively or negatively. Strong feelings will help give your review a clear focus.

● Pick a Book

To choose a book to review, try searching the library catalog for books by authors in this theme. The books listed under Reading Further will give you a good start. As an alternative, brainstorm to make a list of books that you've already read. List them under categories such as Funniest, Most Confusing, Most Predictable, Most Thought Provoking, Most True to Life, or even Most Disappointing. Then look over your list to choose a book you feel strongly about.

● Look at the Elements

After you have read or reread the book, sum up your opinion of it. To support your opinion, examine the book's literary elements. Consider its theme or themes—the insights or lessons about life that the book provides. The chart on the next page shows other elements that you might evaluate.

Evaluating Literary Elements		
For Fiction	**For Nonfiction**	**For Poetry**
• Plot and Conflict: fast-moving? suspenseful? complex? • Characters: lifelike? well developed? developed by words or actions? • Setting: realistic? imaginative? • Narrative Point of View: first person? third person? effect of point of view?	• Point of View: biased? consistent? understandable? • Style: formal? personal? humorous? • Content: clear? detailed? • Structure: effectively organized? why or why not?	• Language: sensory? emotional? creative? • Form: narrative or lyric? short or long? unusual? • Sound: rhyme? meter? • Figures of Speech: similes? metaphors? symbols?

● Know Your Purpose and Audience

If you review a young-adult book, your audience will probably be your classmates. For other books, your audience may be younger children, older people, or a mixed group. Because your purpose is to inform your audience, you'll need to support your opinions about the book. Include examples or quotations to back up each point you make. Choose examples with your readers in mind. Consider their interests, their age, and their concerns. Remember to give readers a brief summary of the book, including only the main ideas and most significant details.

● Organize

Get ready to draft by filling in a form like the one below.

> ### *About the Book*
> **Title:** <u>My Side of the Mountain</u>
> **Author:** Jean Craighead George
> **Summary:** Sam Gribley learns survival skills when he lives on his own in the Catskill Mountains.
> **My Opinion:** I liked this book. It tells an interesting story and teaches facts about plants and animals.
> ### *Elements and Evaluation*
> **Point of View:** First person, from Sam's point of view, which makes the story seem more personal.
> **Style:** Easy to read and realistic
> **Characters:** Sam's ability to survive shows that he is smart. His dialogue with other characters shows that he is also sometimes lonely.

Writing WORKSHOP

DRAFTING

DRAFTING TIP

Your book review should have four basic parts: an **introduction** that gives the basic information about the book and its author, a **summary** of the book (in your own words), an **analysis** of the book's literary elements (with well-chosen examples or quotations), and your **conclusion** about the book's worth.

● Start with the Book

Catch your readers' attention with a surprising quotation from the book or with an interesting statement about it. Then provide the basic information: the book's title and author and your summary. You can also state your opinion directly at this point—or you can save it for the end.

● Support Your Opinion

Evaluate each of the elements in your prewriting plan. Comment on strong points as well as weak points, choosing words that make your opinions clear. Back up your statements with examples or quotations. Close with a recommendation to readers.

STUDENT MODEL • DRAFTING

There is a conflict in Sam's mind. Part of him wants to stay in the woods forever, away from the city. "People live too close together," he tells one of the boys who come to visit. But Sam also enjoys company.

Complete Student Model on p. R113.

REVISING

REVISING TIP

Your analysis should focus on the book's meaning. Avoid unimportant details.

TECHNOLOGY TIP

If you're revising on a computer, keep in mind that your word processor's spelling checker can't distinguish between correctly spelled homonyms. If you mean *their* but type *there,* the spelling checker will not detect the error.

● Take a Second Look

Take a break. Then return to your draft, looking for parts that need improvement. Use the **Rubric for Revising** as a guideline. On your own or with a partner, experiment with changes until your draft satisfies you.

RUBRIC FOR REVISING

Your revised book review should have
- an attention-getting introduction that provides basic facts about the book
- a body that summarizes the book's main ideas and details and that analyzes its main literary elements
- a conclusion that states and supports your opinion of the book

Your revised book review should be free of
- unsupported opinions
- errors in grammar, usage, and mechanics

EDITING/PROOFREADING

Use the **Proofreading Checklist** to go over your revision once more, correcting errors in grammar and mechanics. Pay special attention to capitalization, as shown in the **Grammar Link** on page 712.

Grammar Hint

As you know, a verb must agree with its subject. Don't be tricked by phrases that come between subject and verb:

One of the main characters is a falcon.

PROOFREADING CHECKLIST

☑ Subjects and verbs agree

☑ Sentences are complete; there are no fragments or run-ons.

☑ Verbs are in the active voice wherever possible

☑ Pronouns agree with their antecedents.

☑ Modifiers are used correctly.

☑ Spelling, punctuation, and capitalization are correct.

STUDENT MODEL · EDITING/PROOFREADING

The main purpose of the drawings are to show
            is
            ʌ
what the plants look like.

Complete Student Model on p. R113.

Complete Student Model

For a complete version of the model developed in this Workshop, see **Writing Workshop Models**, p. R113.

PUBLISHING/PRESENTING

Present your book review to the class as a radio broadcast. Since a radio audience can't see you, you will need to use vocal techniques to get your ideas across.

PRESENTING TIP

As an alternative, you might publish your book review on the Internet. Some large online book-sellers invite readers to review books.

Reflecting

Think about the following questions and then write responses.

- Which part of your review do you consider the strongest? Why?

- How has writing your review changed your understanding of the book you chose? Explain.

📖 **Save your work for your portfolio.**

Theme Assessment

Responding to the Theme

1. Which myth, legend, folktale, or story in this theme did you most enjoy reading? What was it about the story that you particularly liked?

2. What new ideas do you have about the following as a result of reading the literature in this theme?
   - the use of supernatural characters to further the plot of a story
   - the way imaginative settings or situations add interest to a story

3. Present your theme project to the class.

Analyzing Literature

COMPARE TALES
Compare the characters from any two stories in this theme. How are they alike? How do they differ? How do they cope with any problems or difficulties they encounter? Support your analysis with quotations from the selections.

Evaluate and Set Goals

1. Which of the following tasks did you find most rewarding? Which was most difficult?
   - reading and thinking about the stories
   - doing independent writing
   - analyzing the stories in discussions
   - performing dramatizations
   - doing research

2. Using the following scale, how would you assess your work in this theme? Give at least two reasons for your assessment.
   4 = outstanding   2 = fair
   3 = good   1 = weak

3. Based on what you found difficult in this theme, choose a goal to work toward in the next theme.
   - Write your goal and three steps you will take to help you reach it.
   - Meet with your teacher to review your goal and your plan for achieving it.

Build Your Portfolio

SELECT
Select two pieces of work you did during this theme to include in your portfolio. Use the following questions to help you decide.

- Which work do you consider your best work?
- From which work did you learn the most?
- Which work "stretched" you the most?
- Which work did you enjoy the most?

REFLECT
Write some notes to accompany the work you selected. Use the following questions to guide you.

- What do you like best about the piece?
- What did you learn from creating it?
- What might you do differently if you were beginning this piece again?

Reading on Your Own

Have you enjoyed reading the literature in this theme? If so, you might be interested in the following books.

A Wrinkle in Time
by Madeleine L'Engle In this award-winning novel, Meg and Charles, along with their friend Calvin, search through time and space for their missing father.

Maniac Magee
by Jerry Spinelli A modern-day folktale about a twelve-year-old boy who appears in a town, amazes everyone with his deeds, and becomes a legend.

Big Men, Big Country: A Collection of American Tall Tales
by Paul Robert Walker Stories portray nine American tall-tale heroes, including Paul Bunyan, Pecos Bill, Sluefoot Sue, and Davy Crockett.

Cut from the Same Cloth: American Women of Myth, Legend, and Tall Tale
by Robert D. San Souci The author retells stories about legendary, larger-than-life women from various American cultures.

Standardized Test Practice

Read the sentences in each numbered item. Look at the underlined words. Choose the sentence in which the underlined words have CORRECT capitalization and punctuation.

1 A My <u>uncle lester</u> is a great friend.
   B My <u>Uncle lester</u> is a great friend.
   C My <u>Uncle Lester</u> is a great friend.
   D My <u>uncle Lester</u> is a great friend.

2 J After we ate dinner, <u>Mrs. Anderson the chef, served</u> us dessert.
   K After we ate dinner, <u>Mrs. Anderson the chef served</u> us dessert.
   L After we ate dinner, <u>Mrs. Anderson, the chef, served</u> us dessert.
   M After we ate dinner, <u>Mrs. Anderson, the chef served</u> us dessert.

3 A I don't want <u>waffles; I want</u> toast.
   B I don't want <u>waffles: I want</u> toast.
   C I don't want <u>waffles I want</u> toast.
   D I don't want <u>waffles, I want</u> toast.

4 J The <u>French Scientists</u> described the experiment.
   K The <u>French scientists</u> described the experiment.
   L The <u>french Scientists</u> described the experiment.
   M The <u>french scientists</u> described the experiment.

5 A My mom pulled the car into a <u>self, service gas</u> station.
   B My mom pulled the car into a <u>self; service gas</u> station.
   C My mom pulled the car into a <u>self-service gas</u> station.
   D My mom pulled the car into a <u>self service gas</u> station.

6 J As I raced out the door, my father <u>yelled "Be careful!"</u>
   K As I raced out the door, my father <u>yelled, "be careful!"</u>
   L As I raced out the door, my father <u>yelled, be careful!"</u>
   M As I raced out the door, my father <u>yelled, "Be careful!"</u>

7 A Jared went to <u>Lundeen Drug Store</u> to buy toothpaste.
   B Jared went to <u>Lundeen drug store</u> to buy toothpaste.
   C Jared went to <u>lundeen drug store</u> to buy toothpaste.
   D Jared went to <u>Lundeen Drug store</u> to buy toothpaste.

8 J My favorite book is *The Wind In The Willows*.

  K My favorite book is *The Wind in the Willows*.

  L My favorite book is *The Wind In the Willows*.

  M My favorite book is *The Wind in The Willows*.

9 A The park is closed, let's go to my house.

  B The park is closed let's go to my house.

  C The park is closed: let's go to my house.

  D The park is closed; let's go to my house.

10 J Both dogs tails were wagging.

  K Both dogs' tails were wagging.

  L Both dogs tail's were wagging.

  M Both dog's tails were wagging.

11 A My doctor's name is Doctor Colgan.

  B My doctor's name is doctor colgan.

  C My doctor's name is Doctor colgan.

  D My doctor's name is doctor Colgan.

12 J Mr. Ramirez my soccer coach, is also my neighbor.

  K Mr. Ramirez, my soccer coach, is also my neighbor.

  L Mr. Ramirez, my soccer coach; is also my neighbor.

  M Mr. Ramirez, my soccer coach is also my neighbor.

13 A "The play is at 6,30," said Mrs. Hatcher.

  B "The play is at 6:30, said Mrs. Hatcher.

  C "The play is at 6:30," said Mrs. Hatcher.

  D "The play is at 6:30" said Mrs. Hatcher.

14 J Manuela speaks english and spanish.

  K Manuela speaks english and Spanish.

  L Manuela speaks English and spanish.

  M Manuela speaks English and Spanish.

15 A Mr. dominic's cat is meowing.

  B Mr. Dominics' cat is meowing.

  C Mr. Dominic's cat is meowing.

  D Mr. Dominics cat is meowing.

16 J I hope to visit the Empire State Building some day.

  K I hope to visit the Empire state Building some day.

  L I hope to visit the Empire State building some day.

  M I hope to visit the Empire state building some day.

A Delicate Balance

Central Park. Gustavo Novoa (b. 1941). 24 x 18 in. Wally Findlay Galleries, New York.

THEME 8

THEME CONTENTS

 **GENRE** FOCUS *SHORT FORMS OF POETRY*

66 *This land is your land, this land is my land . . . This land was made for you and me.* 99

–Woody Guthrie

Exploring the Theme

A Delicate Balance

We share the planet Earth with a great number and variety of other creatures. How do we interact with the natural world? How might the world look through the eyes of the other creatures who share this planet with us? In the stories, poems, and essays in this theme, you will find a variety of possible responses to these questions. Try one of the options below to start your own thinking about the theme.

Starting Points

ESCAPE TO NATURE

Human beings today often feel removed from the natural world. We spend many more hours indoors than outside. In this cartoon, assorted animals who have also been separated from nature are released into a new life outdoors.

- What might happen to the creatures in this picture? Why have they been given their freedom? Write a caption for the cartoon that expresses some of your ideas about people's relationships with animals.

THROUGH THE LENS OF EXPERIENCE

Think about an experience you've had with an animal—a pet, a farm animal, an animal in a zoo, or one in the wild. If you haven't had an interesting animal experience, use your imagination to make one up.

- Put yourself in the animal's place and write a few notes about how the experience may have seemed from the animal's point of view. (For an example of writing from an animal's point of view, you might want to reread "The Dog Diaries," pages 411–416.)

Theme Projects

As you read the selections in this theme, try your hand at one of the projects below. Work on your own, with a partner, or with a group.

LEARNING FOR LIFE
Policy Statement

1. Develop a policy for the ethical treatment of animals as pets or in zoos. Start by listing your own ideas.

2. Gather input from teachers, other students, pet owners, zookeepers, the local humane society, or books and magazines. Draft your policy statement. Share it with the class.

CRITICAL VIEWING
Animals in Nature

1. Collect ten or more photos and other illustrations of animals in their natural habitats. Look through magazines, catalogs, and old calendars for a variety of animals and environments.

2. Study the images. What kind of connection do you make between each animal and its habitat? Write an introduction to your collection that describes the connection between animals and their environments.

interNET
CONNECTION

Check out the Web for more project ideas. On the Web you can also find out about the selections and authors included in this theme. Try the Glencoe Web site at lit.glencoe.com.

MULTIMEDIA PROJECT
Author Presentation

1. Gather data about an author from this theme. Record each source of information or graphics so that you can prepare a bibliography at the end of your report. (See pages R55–R59 for information on preparing a bibliography.)

2. Use hypertext software to create a multimedia presentation about the author you choose.

3. Present interesting facts about the author's life, using a visual format such as a timeline. If possible, include a picture of the author.

4. Organize and present your work to the class.

Before You Read
We Are All One

MEET
LAURENCE YEP

Identity is an important issue in many of Laurence Yep's award-winning novels. He has explained, "In a sense I have no one culture to call my own since I exist . . . in several. However, in my writing I can create my own." Yep grew up as a Chinese American in an African American neighborhood in San Francisco. He attended school first in Chinatown, then in a white neighborhood. Those early experiences contributed to his sense that he is "always pursuing the theme of being an outsider."

Laurence Yep was born in 1948. This story was first published in 1973.

READING FOCUS

Do you believe animal life is as important as human life? If given the opportunity, would you provide food, shelter, or protection for an animal? for an insect? Why or why not?

Think/Pair/Share
Jot down your responses to these questions. Then share your thoughts and feelings with a partner.

Setting a Purpose
Read this folktale to find out how a person's good deeds toward the natural world are rewarded.

BUILDING BACKGROUND

The Time and Place   The tale takes place in some legendary time in China.

Did You Know?   During the Great Depression of the 1930s, the U.S. government created work projects to help the unemployed. Jon Lee was given the job of gathering and translating into English traditional stories from Chinese immigrants living in Chinatown in Oakland, California. Yep's "We Are All One" is a retelling of one of those stories.

VOCABULARY PREVIEW

scurry (skur′ ē) *v.* to run or move briskly or in an agitated way; p. 774

regretfully (ri gret′ fəl lē) *adv.* in a way that shows sorrow, distress, or disappointment; p. 774

omen (ō′ mən) *n.* a sign or event thought to foretell good or bad fortune; p. 774

frustration (frus trā′ shən) *n.* disappointment or irritation at being kept from doing or achieving something; p. 777

We Are All One

Laurence Yep

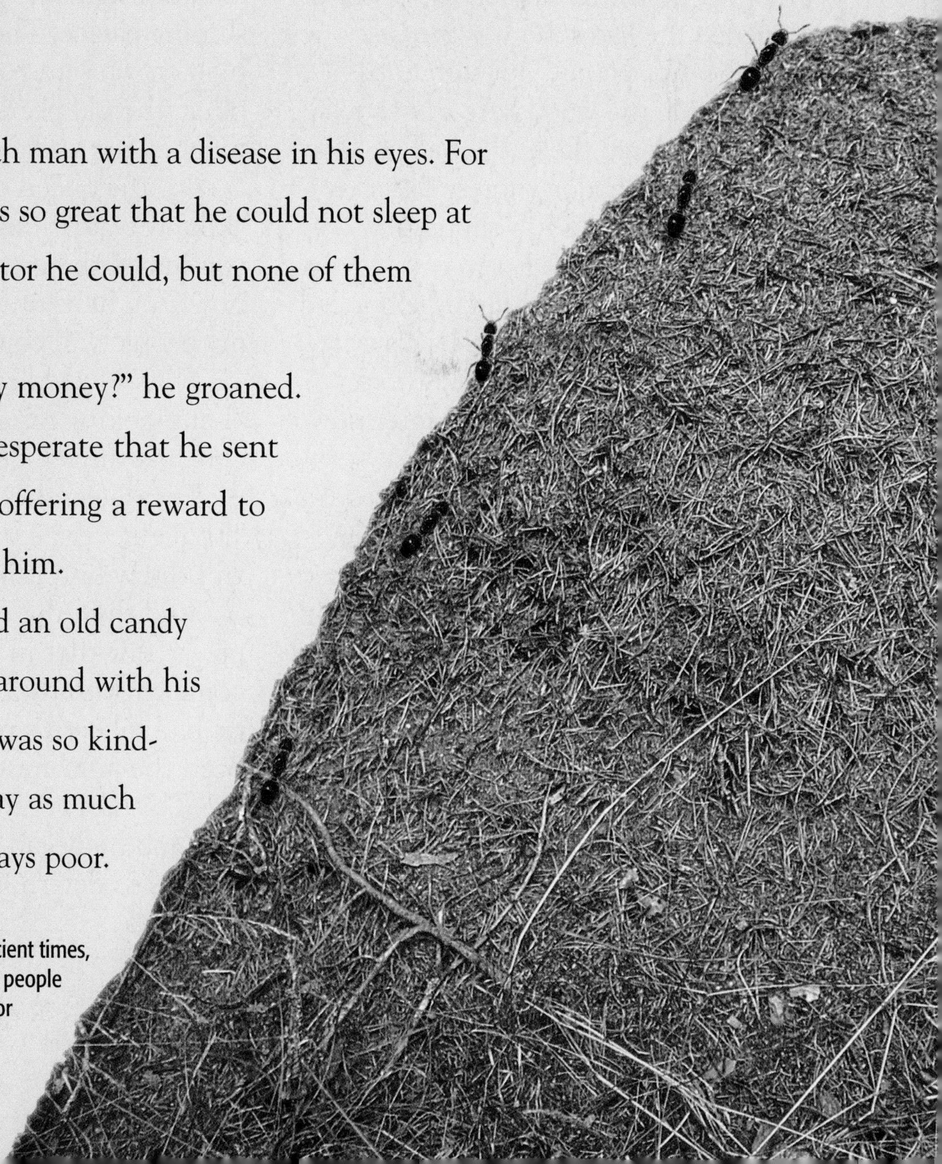

Long ago there was a rich man with a disease in his eyes. For
many years, the pain was so great that he could not sleep at
night. He saw every doctor he could, but none of them
could help him.

"What good is all my money?" he groaned.
Finally, he became so desperate that he sent
criers[1] through the city offering a reward to
anyone who could cure him.

Now in that city lived an old candy
peddler. He would walk around with his
baskets of candy, but he was so kind-
hearted that he gave away as much
as he sold, so he was always poor.

---

1. Since few people could read in ancient times,
   the rich man had to employ *criers*, people
   who shouted out announcements or
   news, to make his offer known.

When the old peddler heard the announcement, he remembered something his mother had said. She had once told him about a magical herb that was good for the eyes. So he packed up his baskets and went back to the single tiny room in which his family lived.

When he told his plan to his wife, she scolded him, "If you go off on this crazy hunt, how are we supposed to eat?"

Usually the peddler gave in to his wife, but this time he was stubborn. "There are two baskets of candy," he said. "I'll be back before they're gone."

The next morning, as soon as the soldiers opened the gates, he was the first one to leave the city. He did not stop until he was deep inside the woods. As a boy, he had often wandered there. He had liked to pretend that the shadowy forest was a green sea and he was a fish slipping through the cool waters.

As he examined the ground, he noticed ants scurrying about. On their backs were larvae[2] like white grains of rice. A rock had fallen into a stream, so the water now spilled into the ant's nest.

"We're all one," the kind-hearted peddler said. So he waded into the shallow stream and put the rock on the bank. Then with a sharp stick, he dug a shallow ditch that sent the rest of the water back into the stream.

Without another thought about his good deed, he began to search through the forest.

He looked everywhere; but as the day went on, he grew sleepy. "Ho-hum. I got up too early. I'll take just a short nap," he decided, and lay down in the shade of an old tree, where he fell right asleep.

In his dreams, the old peddler found himself standing in the middle of a great city. Tall buildings rose high overhead. He couldn't see the sky even when he tilted back his head. An escort of soldiers marched up to him with a loud clatter of their black lacquer armor. "Our queen wishes to see you," the captain said.

The frightened peddler could only obey and let the fierce soldiers lead him into a shining palace. There, a woman with a high crown sat upon a tall throne. Trembling, the old peddler fell to his knees and touched his forehead against the floor.

But the queen ordered him to stand. "Like the great Emperor Yü of long ago, you tamed the great flood. We are all one now. You have only to ask, and I or any of my people will come to your aid."

The old peddler cleared his throat. "I am looking for a certain herb. It will cure any disease of the eyes."

The queen shook her head regretfully. "I have never heard of that herb. But you will surely find it if you keep looking for it."

And then the old peddler woke. Sitting up, he saw that in his wanderings he had come back to the ants' nest. It was there he had taken his nap. His dream city had been the ants' nest itself.

"This is a good omen," he said to himself, and he began searching even harder. He was so determined to find the herb that

---

2. *Larvae* (lär′ vē) is the plural of *larva*, which is the early, worm-like form of an insect; a caterpillar is the larva of a butterfly or moth.

Vocabulary

scurry (skur′ ē) *v.* to run or move briskly or in an agitated way
regretfully (ri gret′ fəl lē) *adv.* in a way that shows sorrow, distress, or disappointment
omen (ō′ mən) *n.* a sign or event thought to foretell good or bad fortune

he did not notice how time had passed. He was surprised when he saw how the light was fading. He looked all around then. There was no sight of his city—only strange hills. He realized then that he had searched so far he had gotten lost.

Night was coming fast and with it the cold. He rubbed his arms and hunted for shelter. In the twilight, he thought he could see the green tiles of a roof.

He stumbled through the growing darkness until he reached a ruined temple. Weeds grew through cracks in the stones and most of the roof itself had fallen in. Still, the ruins would provide some protection.

Did You Know?
A *centipede* is a long, flat insect with many pairs of legs. The prefix *centi-* means either "hundred" or "hundredth part of," and *pede* comes from the Latin word for "foot."

As he started inside, he saw a centipede with bright orange skin and red tufts of fur along its back. Yellow dots covered its sides like a dozen tiny eyes. It was also rushing into the temple as fast as it could, but there was a bird swooping down toward it.

The old peddler waved his arms and shouted, scaring the bird away. Then he put down his palm in front of the insect. "We are all one, you and I." The many feet tickled his skin as the centipede climbed onto his hand.

Inside the temple, he gathered dried leaves and found old sticks of wood and soon he had a fire going. The peddler even picked some fresh leaves for the centipede from a bush near the temple doorway.

"I may have to go hungry, but you don't have to, friend."

Stretching out beside the fire, the old peddler pillowed his head on his arms. He was so tired that he soon fell asleep, but even in his sleep he dreamed he was still searching in the woods. Suddenly he thought he heard footsteps near his head. He woke instantly and looked about, but he only saw the brightly colored centipede.

"Was it you, friend?" The old peddler chuckled and, lying down, he closed his eyes again. "I must be getting nervous."

"We are one, you and I," a voice said faintly—as if from a long distance. "If you go south, you will find a pine tree with two trunks. By its roots, you will find a magic bead. A cousin of mine spat on it years ago. Dissolve that bead in wine and tell the rich man to drink it if he wants to heal his eyes."

The old peddler trembled when he heard the voice, because he realized that the centipede was magical. He wanted to run from the temple, but he couldn't even get up. It was as if he were glued to the floor.

But then the old peddler reasoned with himself: If the centipede had wanted to hurt me, it could have long ago. Instead, it seems to want to help me.

So the old peddler stayed where he was, but he did not dare open his eyes. When the first sunlight fell through the roof, he raised one eyelid cautiously. There was no sign of the centipede. He sat up and looked around, but the magical centipede was gone.

He followed the centipede's instructions when he left the temple. Traveling south, he kept a sharp eye out for the pine tree with two trunks. He walked until late in the afternoon, but all he saw were normal pine trees.

River Scene. 18th century, China. Free Library, Philadelphia, PA.

Viewing the painting: How does this painting add to your understanding of the setting of "We Are All One"?

Wearily he sat down and sighed. Even if he found the pine tree, he couldn't be sure that he would find the bead. Someone else might even have discovered it a long time ago.

But something made him look a little longer. Just when he was thinking about turning back, he saw the odd tree. Somehow his tired legs managed to carry him over to the tree, and he got down on his knees. But the ground was covered with pine needles and his old eyes were too weak. The old peddler could have wept with frustration, and then he remembered the ants.

He began to call, "Ants, ants, we are all one."

Almost immediately, thousands of ants came boiling out of nowhere. Delighted, the old man held up his fingers. "I'm looking for a bead. It might be very tiny."

Then, careful not to crush any of his little helpers, the old man sat down to wait. In no time, the ants reappeared with a tiny bead. With trembling fingers, the old man took the bead from them and examined it. It was colored orange and looked as if it had yellow eyes on the sides.

There was nothing very special about the bead, but the old peddler treated it like a fine jewel. Putting the bead into his pouch, the old peddler bowed his head. "I thank you and I thank your queen," the old man said. After the ants disappeared among the pine needles, he made his way out of the woods.

The next day, he reached the house of the rich man. However, he was so poor and ragged that the gatekeeper only laughed at him. "How could an old beggar like you help my master?"

The old peddler tried to argue. "Beggar or rich man, we are all one."

But it so happened that the rich man was passing by the gates. He went over to the old peddler. "I said anyone could see me. But it'll mean a stick across your back if you're wasting my time."

The old peddler took out the pouch. "Dissolve this bead in some wine and drink it down." Then, turning the pouch upside down, he shook the tiny bead onto his palm and handed it to the rich man.

The rich man immediately called for a cup of wine. Dropping the bead into the wine, he waited a moment and then drank it down. Instantly the pain vanished. Shortly after that, his eyes healed.

The rich man was so happy and grateful that he doubled the reward. And the kindly old peddler and his family lived comfortably for the rest of their lives.

Vocabulary

frustration (frus trā′ shən) *n.* disappointment or irritation at being kept from doing or achieving something

Responding to Literature

PERSONAL RESPONSE

◆ What were your thoughts about the magical aspects of this folktale?

Analyzing Literature

RECALL

1. Why does the peddler believe he can win the reward? Does his wife believe in his idea?
2. What is the peddler's first gesture of kindness toward another creature?
3. What is the centipede's advice to the peddler?
4. How does the peddler sum up his belief about the difference between the rich and the poor?

INTERPRET

5. What details does the author reveal to explain why the peddler wanted to win the reward?
6. How was the peddler's dream connected to his rescuing the ant's nest?
7. Who helped the peddler follow the centipede's advice? How was this event foreshadowed earlier in the tale?
8. By the end of the tale, the peddler has plenty of money. Do you believe his behavior will change now that he is rich? Explain how the author's description of the character led you to your opinion.

EVALUATE AND CONNECT

9. In your opinion, why did Chinese immigrants continue to tell this ancient tale after they arrived in America? How might the folktale have been a "strategy" for living among strangers in a different country?
10. Theme Connection   The title of the tale summarizes the philosophy of the peddler. How do you imagine the world would change if most people shared this belief?

LITERARY ELEMENTS

Plot

A **plot** is the series of events in a story that shows the characters in action, trying to resolve one or more conflicts or problems. One way to determine a story's plot is first to identify the problems. In "We Are All One," for example, the rich man's problem with his eyes sets the story's events in motion. Next, ask yourself: What characters are involved? What will happen next? What is the solution to the problem?

1. Why does the peddler become involved in the rich man's problem? What other problems does the peddler face?

2. Briefly list the series of events that make up the plot of "We Are All One."

● See **Literary Terms Handbook**, p. R8.

Landscape, early 18th century.
Yao Song. Private collection.

Extending Your Response

Writing About Literature

Imagery   One of the points of the story is that all of nature is interconnected. Scan the story, looking for images of the landscape and the animals. Write a paragraph using the imagery you found to show the storyteller's love and respect for the natural world.

Personal Writing

Life's Connections   How does the candy peddler's treatment of all living things compare with your own response in the **Reading Focus** on page 772? Did the story make you look at this issue in a different way? Answer these questions in a journal entry.

Performing

Storyteller's Circle   "We Are All One" began as an oral tale. Working in a small group, divide the story into sections, one section for each group member. Perform the story for another class.

Literature Groups

Literary Quests   The **quest,** a search or pursuit to find some object or achieve some goal, is a theme found in literature and popular media ranging from the Greek myths to *The Lord of the Rings* and the *Star Wars* movies. What is the quest in "We Are All One"? With your group, share ideas about stories you know that are based on a quest. What do these stories have in common?

Interdisciplinary Activity

Social Studies   The belief that animal life is as sacred as human life is important in many religions, including Buddhism. Research Buddhism. Discover how it is practiced in China and in America. Then present your findings in an oral report.

Reading Further

If you would like to read other books by Laurence Yep, try *Tongues of Jade* and *Child of the Owl*

Save your work for your portfolio.

Skill Minilesson

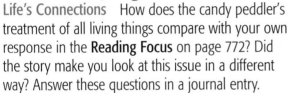

VOCABULARY • SYNONYMS

Just because two words are synonyms does not mean that one can be substituted for the other in every situation. Thinking carefully about words will help you use them accurately.

PRACTICE In each question, the italicized words are synonyms. For each, choose the more accurate word.

1. Does a rocket *scurry* or *zoom* into the sky?

2. If you can't go to a party you want to go to, do you stay home *regretfully* or *apologetically*?
3. If a friend told you you would be lucky today and you believed it, would you regard your friend's comment as an *omen* or a *fore-warning*?
4. If you receive a radio as a gift instead of the camera you had hoped for, do you feel *frustration* or *disappointment*?

MEDIA Connection

JOURNAL

A personal journal can tell about people other than the writer. In these journal excerpts, Edie Scher records her observations on a young runner's progress during a summer.

from "See Robby Run"

by Edie Scher—*Runner's World*, March 1998

May 30: Heading toward my driveway at the end of a run, I hear the rhythm of sneakered foot-falls behind me and turn to see a father and his young son engaged in a coaching session.

"Come on, Robby, that's good. Keep up those arms!" Words of encouragement for a beginning runner, I figure. . . .

"Great morning for a run!" I say.

The boy stops in his tracks and grins. His father smiles at me and gently places a hand on his son's shoulder. "C'mon Robby. Let's keep going." Robby waves happily, and they continue down the block, a tall, handsome father and his 10-year-old Down's syndrome son, whose spanking-clean running shoes and freshly ironed T-shirt announce his newness to the sport.

June 28: Robby has a different partner this morning. His mother does not jog, but instead walks purposefully beside him. When Robby sees me and becomes distracted, she encourages him as her husband would. "His father's on a business trip, and I don't want to stop the momentum," she tells me.

July 5: Robby's father is back, and it looks as if Mom will continue to join them. She walks a few steps behind while her husband talks Robby through his workout. In the middle of the block, Robby stops and turns to ask his mother to run, too. His father cheerfully urges him to continue.

August 11: I look forward to my daily encounter with Robby and his parents. His athletic improvement, while minimal, inspires me by the lesson it teaches. We each run our race and push forward for our own reasons; winning means something different for each runner.

August 22: Robby's two sisters have returned from summer camp and now join his team. Robby's running style has not changed much, but his stride seems to have more bounce. He points to his sisters with obvious pride, stopping to tell me their names. . . . Robby's feet will never leave the pavement with the grace and speed of theirs, but he is not aware of that; his spirit is not competitive, only joyful, as he pushes himself to catch up with them.

September 10: School has resumed, and Robby's sisters and mother no longer run with him. I look at Robby carefully today. He seems a little taller, a little slimmer. Is it my imagination that his stride is a little smoother?

I wait to wave to them before I head up my driveway. They both wave back, but this time Robby does not stop running, and his father lovingly cheers him on for this new personal best.

Analyzing Media

The writer says, "We each run our race and push forward for our own reasons; winning means something different for each runner." What does winning mean to you?

Vo·cab·u·lar·y Skills

Dictionary Skills: Pronunciation

One of the most important kinds of information you can find in a dictionary is how to pronounce words.

Any vowel letter can be pronounced in different ways. In a dictionary pronunciation, a vowel without any symbol has its normal "short" sound, like the vowels in *pat, pet, pit, hot,* and *hut.* Other vowel sounds are shown by symbols, such as a straight line above the vowel to show that it is "long." (Long vowels "say their own name.")

Following are some additional pronunciation symbols:

ä	an **ah** sound, as in **father**
ô	an **aw** sound, as in **coffee** and **law**
oo	the vowel sound in **wood**
o͞o	the vowel sound in **fool**
oi	the vowel sound in **toy**
ou	an **ow** sound, as in **cow** and **out**
ə	the unaccented vowel sound at the end of **pencil, lemon, taken**
th	**th** as in **thin**
<u>th</u>	**th** as in **this**
zh	the sound in the middle of **treasure** or the end of **garage**

An accent mark (′) follows the syllable you should stress. Emphasizing the correct syllable is important in pronunciation.

EXERCISES

1. Use the pronunciation given for each word to answer the question.
   a. Does *brood* (bro͞od) rhyme with *rude, road,* or *rod?*
   b. Does the first syllable of *scuttle* (skut′ əl) rhyme with *cute* or *cut?*
   c. Does *cower* (kou′ ər) rhyme with *lower* or *power?*
   d. Does the *g* in *lunge* (lunj) sound like the *g* in *rage* or in *rag?*
   e. Does the first syllable of *valiant* (val′ yənt) rhyme with *sale, pal,* or *call?*
2. Decide which word is represented by each dictionary pronunciation.
   a. lo͞os   Is this word *lose* or *loose?*
   b. i rās′   Is this word *erase* or *earache?*
   c. kwī′ it   Is this word *quite, quiet,* or *quit?*
   d. hal′ lōd   Is this word *hollowed, halo,* or *hallowed?*
   e. kon′ stənt   Is this word *consonant, constant,* or *consent?*

Before You Read

Birdfoot's Grampa and *Miracles*

MEET JOSEPH BRUCHAC

Joseph Bruchac (brōō′ shak) did not learn of his Native American ancestry until he was an adult. His grandfather, who raised him, kept it a secret. Now Bruchac proudly bears his Abenaki name, *Gahnegohheyoh*, which means "the good mind."

Joseph Bruchac was born in 1942. This poem was first published in 1978.

MEET WALT WHITMAN

Walt Whitman worked at everything from carpentry to teaching. He loved variety, not only in jobs, but also in the people and places of America. *Leaves of Grass*, his famous collection of poetry, celebrates the variety and vastness of this country.

Walt Whitman was born in New York in 1819 and died in 1892.

READING FOCUS

Do you ever stop to think about the beauty and the wonder in everyday life?

QuickWrite

Make a quick list of things in everyday life that you think are extraordinary or beautiful.

Setting a Purpose

Read these poems to find out how two poets express their reverence for life.

BUILDING BACKGROUND

Joseph Bruchac writes out of a long Native American tradition of viewing one's relationship to Earth in terms of family. Here are his words about that tradition.

"The Okanagan people of the Pacific Northwest speak of the Earth as Mother; the Sun as Father, and the animals as our brothers and sisters. This view of the world was held by the Navajo and the Abenaki, the Sioux and the Anishinabe, and most of the aboriginal people of this continent. They saw their role on this earth, not as rulers of Creation, but as beings entrusted with a special mission—to maintain the natural balance, to take care of our Mother, to be Keepers of the Earth."

Birdfoot's Grampa

Joseph Bruchac

The old man
must have stopped our car
two dozen times to climb out
and gather into his hands
5 the small toads blinded
by our lights and leaping,
live drops of rain.

The rain was falling,
a mist about his white hair
10 and I kept saying
you can't save them all,
accept it, get back in
we've got places to go.

But, leathery hands full
15 of wet brown life,
knee deep in the summer
roadside grass,
he just smiled and said
they have places to go to
20 *too.*

Miracles

Walt Whitman

Why, who makes much of a miracle?
As to me I know of nothing else but miracles,
Whether I walk the streets of Manhattan,
Or dart my sight over the roofs of houses toward the sky,
5   Or wade with naked feet along the beach just in the edge of the water,
Or stand under trees in the woods,
Or talk by day with any one I love . . .
Or sit at table at dinner with the rest,
Or look at strangers opposite me riding in the car.
10   Or watch honey-bees busy around the hive of a summer forenoon,
Or animals feeding in the fields,
Or birds, or the wonderfulness of the sundown, or of stars shining so quiet and
    bright,
Or the exquisite° delicate thin curve of the new moon in spring;
These with the rest, one and all, are to me miracles,
15   The whole referring, yet each distinct and in its place.°

To me every hour of the light and dark is a miracle,
Every cubic inch of space is a miracle,
Every square yard of the surface of the earth is spread with the same,
Every foot of the interior swarms with the same.

20   To me the sea is a continual miracle,
The fishes that swim—the rocks—the motion of the waves—the ships with men
    in them,
What stranger miracles are there?

---

13 Something that is *exquisite* has a rare beauty, charm, or perfection.
15 This line suggests that all of these small, separate miracles are involved in,
   or refer to, some greater miracle.

Responding to Literature

PERSONAL RESPONSE

- ◆ Reread your QuickWrite from the **Reading Focus** on page 782. How did these two poems reinforce, or change, your own thoughts and feelings about the extraordinary nature of daily life?

Analyzing Literature

RECALL

1. In "Birdfoot's Grampa," why does the old man stop the car "two dozen times"?
2. List four events in "Miracles" that the speaker identifies as miracles relating to human beings and four relating to nature.
3. Give an example of imagery from each poem.

INTERPRET

4. What conflict takes place in "Birdfoot's Grampa"? How does it affect your feelings about the speaker or the old man?
5. How many of the five senses does Whitman include in his list of miracles? Give an example of each.

EVALUATE AND CONNECT

6. In "Birdfoot's Grampa," do you identify more with the speaker or the old man? Why?
7. What other miracles might be included in Whitman's list? Give at least three possibilities.
8. What are your favorite images from each of these poems? Explain why you like them.
9. Theme Connection   What attitude toward life and nature do these poems convey?
10. Think of someone you know who would enjoy reading these poems. Why would the poems appeal to that person?

LITERARY ELEMENTS

Theme

The main idea behind a story, poem, novel, or play is usually expressed as a general statement called a **theme**. A theme usually states some truth, as the author sees it, about life or human nature. Sometimes a piece of writing has a **stated theme**, which is expressed directly. More often, a piece of writing has an **implied theme**, which the reader must infer from what the author presents. Sometimes the title of the piece hints at its theme. In poetry, the theme often becomes clear gradually through the combination of its imagery, word choice, and rhythm.

1. What is the theme of "Birdfoot's Grampa"? Is the theme stated directly or implied? Support your opinion with examples from the poem.

2. What is the theme of "Miracles"? How does the title of the poem relate to its theme?

- ● See **Literary Terms Handbook,** p. R11.

Extending Your Response

Writing About Literature

Characterization In "Birdfoot's Grampa," the poet packs a lot of information about the old man into very few words. Write a paragraph describing the old man as you picture him.

Creative Writing

Poem Write your own short poem or prose paragraph telling about a person. Focus on one incident that shows this person's character, as Joseph Bruchac does in "Birdfoot's Grampa."

Literature Groups

Poet's Choice Although both of these poems deal with the beauty and wonder in life, the two poems are very different. Compare and contrast the two poems. Pick out examples from the poems that show how the poems are alike and how they are different.

Listening and Speaking

Appreciating Poetry Take turns reading these poems aloud to one another. Pay attention to how different readings affect your experience of each poem.

Reading Further

If you would like to read more by these poets, try these books:

The Girl Who Married the Moon by Joseph Bruchac

Walt Whitman: Poetry for Young People

📖 **Save your work for your portfolio.**

Skill Minilesson

GRAMMAR AND LANGUAGE • SENSORY LANGUAGE

Joseph Bruchac's description of the old man's "leathery hands full of wet brown life" is a fine example of **sensory language**—language that appeals to the senses. Sensory language describes how something looks, sounds, feels, smells, or tastes.

PRACTICE Write a sentence about each of the following items. Try to use sensory language that appeals to at least two senses in each sentence.

1. a car   4. a banana
2. a dog   5. a beach
3. a tree

● For more about sensory language and imagery, see **Literary Terms Handbook**, p. R10.

MOVIE REVIEW

David Ansen reviews a film adaptation of Rudyard Kipling's *The Jungle Book.* One of the stories included in Kipling's book is "Rikki-tikki-tavi."

The Jungle Book

by David Ansen—*Newsweek,* January 16, 1995

Kipling purists may not cotton to Disney's new live-action version of *The Jungle Book*, but it's hard to think of anyone else who won't be enchanted. Jason Scott Lee's Mowgli, raised in the jungle by wild animals, uncontaminated by civilization, is no longer the boy Kipling imagined. He's sprouted into a buff young man whose best friends happen to be bears and wolves, but he's not unappreciative of the beauty of the English girl Kitty (Lena Headey), engaged to the dastardly Captain Boone (Cary Elwes). Director Stephen Sommers and his co-writers, Ronald Yanover and Mark D. Geldman, have imposed a taut, cliffhanging story structure upon Kipling's episodic stories, turning *The Jungle Book* into an action-packed love story with something for everyone: hidden treasures, death by quicksand, a Spielbergian lost temple, ecological mysticism, swinish colonialist villains, an irresistible supporting cast of cackling monkeys, a treacherous tiger, a loyal bear, and one very deadly serpent.

It's Lee's ingratiating innocence that holds it all together. He's a figure of the purest fantasy, and he plays Mowgli with a wide-eyed, silent-movie exuberance so disarming it compels belief (even as you wonder where in the overgrown jungle he gets his wardrobe).

Analyzing Media

1. Do you think you would like to see this movie? Why or why not?

2. What is your opinion of the kind of "action-packed love story" the reviewer describes? Use examples of movies you know in your answer.

Before You Read

Rikki-tikki-tavi

MEET RUDYARD KIPLING

Shortly after writing "Rikki-tikki-tavi," Rudyard Kipling became involved in a family feud. After an argument with his brother-in-law that stopped just short of a fistfight, Kipling and his American wife left Vermont for England. Kipling lived the rest of his life in England and India. As a boy, and again as a young adult, he lived in India with his parents in bungalows like the one described in this story. In 1907 Kipling became the first British writer to win the Nobel Prize for Literature.

Rudyard Kipling was born in Bombay, India, in 1865 and died in England in 1936. This story was published in 1894.

READING FOCUS

What feelings do you have when you think about snakes?

Think/Pair/Share
Take a moment to jot down your response to this question. Then share your ideas with a partner.

Setting a Purpose
Read this story to find out what happens when a mongoose meets a snake.

BUILDING BACKGROUND

The Time and Place   The story takes place in India during the late 1800s, a time when the country was ruled by the British. It was not unusual for snakes and other animals to find their way inside people's houses.

Did You Know?   A mongoose is a small mammal of India and Africa, famous for its ability to kill snakes. Mongooses grow to an average length of only about sixteen inches, but their lightning speed makes them fearsome enemies of snakes.

VOCABULARY PREVIEW

scuttle (skut′ əl) *v.* to move with short, rapid steps; p. 789
cower (kou′ ər) *v.* to crouch down, as in fear or shame; p. 792
flinch (flinch) *v.* to draw back, as from something painful, dangerous, or unpleasant; p. 793
gait (gāt) *n.* a particular manner of moving on foot; p. 793
lunge (lunj) *v.* to make a sudden forward movement; charge; p. 794
fancy (fan′ sē) *v.* to picture mentally; imagine; p. 796
valiant (val′ yənt) *adj.* brave; courageous; p. 797
brood (brood) *n.* all of the young of an animal that are born or cared for at the same time; p. 799

Rikki-tikki-tavi

Rudyard Kipling

This is the story of the great war that Rikki-tikki-tavi fought single-handed, through the bathrooms of the big bungalow in Segowlee cantonment.[1] Darzee, the tailorbird, helped him, and Chuchundra, the muskrat, who never comes out into the middle of the floor, but always creeps round by the wall, gave him advice; but Rikki-tikki did the real fighting.

He was a mongoose, rather like a little cat in his fur and his tail, but quite like a weasel in his head and his habits. His eyes and the end of his restless nose were pink; he could scratch himself anywhere he pleased, with any leg, front or back, that he chose to use; he could fluff up his tail till it looked like a bottle brush, and his war cry, as he scuttled through the long grass, was "Rikk-tikk-tikki-tikki-tchk!"

1. In India, a *cantonment* was a British military "town" where servicemen and their families lived in separate *bungalows,* or cottages.

Vocabulary
scuttle (skut′ əl) *v.* to move with short, rapid steps

Rikki-tikki-tavi

One day, a high summer flood washed him out of the burrow where he lived with his father and mother, and carried him, kicking and clucking, down a roadside ditch. He found a little wisp of grass floating there, and clung to it till he lost his senses. When he revived, he was lying in the hot sun on the middle of a garden path, very draggled[2] indeed, and a small boy was saying: "Here's a dead mongoose. Let's have a funeral."

"No," said his mother: "let's take him in and dry him. Perhaps he isn't really dead."

They took him into the house, and a big man picked him up between his finger and thumb and said he was not dead but half choked; so they wrapped him in cotton wool and warmed him, and he opened his eyes and sneezed.

"Now," said the big man (he was an Englishman who had just moved into the bungalow), "don't frighten him, and we'll see what he'll do."

It is the hardest thing in the world to frighten a mongoose, because he is eaten up from nose to tail with curiosity. The motto of all the mongoose family is "Run and find out"; and Rikki-tikki was a true mongoose. He looked at the cotton wool, decided that it was not good to eat, ran all round the table, sat up and put his fur in order, scratched himself, and jumped on the small boy's shoulder.

"Don't be frightened, Teddy," said his father. "That's his way of making friends."

"Ouch! He's tickling under my chin," said Teddy.

Rikki-tikki looked down between the boy's collar and neck, snuffed at his ear, and climbed down to the floor, where he sat rubbing his nose.

"Good gracious," said Teddy's mother, "and that's a wild creature! I suppose he's so tame because we've been kind to him."

"All mongooses are like that," said her husband. "If Teddy doesn't pick him up by the tail, or try to put him in a cage, he'll run in and out of the house all day long. Let's give him something to eat."

They gave him a little piece of raw meat. Rikki-tikki liked it immensely, and when it was finished he went out into the veranda and sat in the sunshine and fluffed up his fur to make it dry to the roots. Then he felt better.

Did You Know?
A *veranda* is a long porch, usually with a roof, along one or more sides of a house.

"There are more things to find out about in this house," he said to himself, "than all my family could find out in all their lives. I shall certainly stay and find out."

He spent all that day roaming over the house. He nearly drowned himself in the bathtubs, put his nose into the ink on a writing table, and burned it on the end of the big man's cigar, for he climbed up in the big man's lap to see how writing was done. At nightfall he ran into Teddy's nursery to watch how kerosene lamps[3] were lighted, and when Teddy went to bed Rikki-tikki climbed up too; but he was a restless companion, because he had to get up and attend to every noise all through the night and find out what made it.

---

2. *Draggled* means "wet and dirty."

3. A *kerosene lamp* burns a liquid fuel made from petroleum.

Teddy's mother and father came in, the last thing, to look at their boy, and Rikki-tikki was awake on the pillow. "I don't like that," said Teddy's mother; "he may bite the child."

"He'll do no such thing," said the father. "Teddy's safer with that little beast than if he had a bloodhound to watch him. If a snake came into the nursery now—"

But Teddy's mother wouldn't think of anything so awful.

Early in the morning Rikki-tikki came to early breakfast in the veranda, riding on Teddy's shoulder, and they gave him banana and some boiled egg; and he sat on all their laps one after the other, because every well-brought-up mongoose always hopes to be a house mongoose someday and have rooms to run about in, and Rikki-tikki's mother (she used to live in the general's house at Segowlee) had carefully told Rikki what to do if ever he came across Englishmen.

Then Rikki-tikki went out into the garden to see what was to be seen. It was a large garden, only half cultivated, with bushes as big as summer houses of roses, lime and orange trees, clumps of bamboos, and thickets of high grass. Rikki-tikki licked his lips. "This is a splendid hunting ground," he said, and his tail grew bottle-brushy at the thought of it, and he scuttled up and down the garden, snuffling here and there till he heard very sorrowful voices in a thornbush.

It was Darzee, the tailorbird, and his wife. They had made a beautiful nest by pulling two big leaves together and stitching them up the edges with fibers, and had

Tent Hanging. Early 18th century, Mughal (Jaipur?). Cotton quilt embroidered in silk. Victoria and Albert Museum, London.

Viewing the artifact: How might the characters in "Rikki-tikki-tavi" have used a tent hanging? What do you think would have been its original use?

filled the hollow with cotton and downy fluff. The nest swayed to and fro, as they sat on the brim and cried.

"What is the matter?" asked Rikki-tikki.

"We are very miserable," said Darzee. "One of our babies fell out of the nest yesterday, and Nag ate him."

"H'm!" said Rikki-tikki; "that is very sad—but I am a stranger here. Who is Nag?"

Darzee and his wife only <u>cowered</u> down in the nest without answering, for from the thick grass at the foot of the bush came a low hiss—a horrid cold sound that made Rikki-tikki jump back two clear feet. Then inch by inch out of the grass rose up the head and spread hood of Nag, the big black cobra, and he was five feet long from tongue to tail. When he had lifted one third of himself clear of the ground, he stayed balancing to and fro exactly as a dandelion tuft balances in the wind, and he looked at Rikki-tikki with the wicked snake's eyes that never change their expression, whatever the snake may be thinking of.

"Who is Nag?" he said. "*I* am Nag. The great god Brahm put his mark upon all our people when the first cobra spread his hood to keep the sun off Brahm as he slept. Look, and be afraid!"

He spread out his hood more than ever, and Rikki-tikki saw the spectacle mark on the back of it that looks exactly like the eye part of a hook-and-eye fastening. He was afraid for the minute; but it is impossible for a mongoose to stay frightened for any length of time, and though Rikki-tikki had never met a live cobra before, his mother had fed him on dead ones, and he knew that all a grown mongoose's business in life was to fight and eat snakes. Nag knew that too, and at the bottom of his cold heart he was afraid.

"Well," said Rikki-tikki, and his tail began to fluff up again, "marks or no marks, do you think it is right for you to eat fledglings[4] out of a nest?"

Nag was thinking to himself, and watching the least little movement in the grass behind Rikki-tikki. He knew that mongooses in the garden meant death sooner or later for him and his family, but he wanted to get Rikki-tikki off his guard. So he dropped his head a little and put it on one side.

"Let us talk," he said. "You eat eggs. Why should not I eat birds?"

"Behind you! Look behind you!" sang Darzee.

Rikki-tikki knew better than to waste time in staring. He jumped up in the air as high as he could go, and just under him whizzed by the head of Nagaina, Nag's wicked wife. She had crept up behind him as he was

---

4. Young birds that haven't yet grown the feathers needed to fly are called *fledglings.*

Vocabulary

cower (kou′ ər) *v.* to crouch down, as in fear or shame

Cobra

talking, to make an end of him; and he heard her savage hiss as the stroke missed. He came down almost across her back, and if he had been an old mongoose, he would have known that then was the time to break her back with one bite; but he was afraid of the terrible lashing return stroke of the cobra. He bit, indeed, but did not bite long enough, and he jumped clear of the whisking tail, leaving Nagaina torn and angry.

"Wicked, wicked Darzee!" said Nag, lashing up as high as he could reach toward the nest in the thornbush; but Darzee had built it out of the reach of snakes, and it only swayed to and fro.

Rikki-tikki felt his eyes growing red and hot (when a mongoose's eyes grow red, he is angry), and he sat back on his tail and hind legs like a little kangaroo, and looked all around him, and chattered with rage. But Nag and Nagaina had disappeared into the grass. When a snake misses its stroke, it never says anything or gives any sign of what it means to do next. Rikki-tikki did not care to follow them, for he did not feel sure that he could manage two snakes at once. So he trotted off to the gravel path near the house, and sat down to think. It was a serious matter for him.

If you read the old books of natural history, you will find they say that when the mongoose fights the snake and happens to get bitten, he runs off and eats some herb that cures him. That is not true. The victory is only a matter of quickness of eye and quickness of foot—snake's blow against mongoose's jump—and as no eye can follow the motion of a snake's head when it strikes, that makes things much more wonderful than any magic herb. Rikki-tikki knew he was a young mongoose, and it made him all the more pleased to think that he had managed to escape a blow from behind. It gave him confidence in himself, and when Teddy came running down the path, Rikki-tikki was ready to be petted.

But just as Teddy was stooping, something flinched a little in the dust, and a tiny voice said: "Be careful. I am death!" It was Karait, the dusty brown snakeling that lies for choice on the dusty earth; and his bite is as dangerous as the cobra's. But he is so small that nobody thinks of him, and so he does the more harm to people.

Rikki-tikki's eyes grew red again, and he danced up to Karait with the peculiar rocking, swaying motion that he had inherited from his family. It looks very funny, but it is so perfectly balanced a gait that you can fly off from it at any angle you please; and in dealing with snakes this is an advantage. If Rikki-tikki had only known, he was doing a much more dangerous thing than fighting Nag, for Karait is so small, and can turn so quickly, that unless Rikki bit him close to the back of the head, he would get the return stroke in his eye or lip. But Rikki did not know: his eyes were all red, and he rocked back and forth, looking for a good place to hold. Karait struck out. Rikki jumped sideways and tried to run in, but the wicked little dusty gray head lashed within a fraction of his shoulder, and he had to jump over the body, and the head followed his heels close.

Vocabulary

flinch (flinch) *v.* to draw back, as from something painful, dangerous, or unpleasant
gait (gāt) *n.* a particular manner of moving on foot

Teddy shouted to the house: "Oh, look here! Our mongoose is killing a snake"; and Rikki-tikki heard a scream from Teddy's mother. His father ran out with a stick, but by the time he came up, Karait had lunged out once too far, and Rikki-tikki had sprung, jumped on the snake's back, dropped his head far between his forelegs, bitten as high up the back as he could get hold, and rolled away. That bite paralyzed Karait, and Rikki-tikki was just going to eat him up from the tail, after the custom of his family at dinner, when he remembered that a full meal makes a slow mongoose, and if he wanted all his strength and quickness ready, he must keep himself thin.

He went away for a dust bath under the castor-oil bushes, while Teddy's father beat the dead Karait. "What is the use of that?" thought Rikki-tikki. "I have settled it all"; and then Teddy's mother picked him up from the dust and hugged him, crying that he had saved Teddy from death, and Teddy's father said that he was a providence,[5] and Teddy looked on with big scared eyes. Rikki-tikki was rather amused at all the fuss, which, of course, he did not understand. Teddy's mother might just as well have petted Teddy for playing in the dust. Rikki was thoroughly enjoying himself.

That night, at dinner, walking to and fro among the wineglasses on the table, he could have stuffed himself three times over with nice things; but he remembered Nag and Nagaina, and though it was very pleasant to be patted and petted by Teddy's mother, and to sit on Teddy's shoulder, his eyes would get red from time to time, and he would go off into his long war cry of *"Rikk-tikk-tikki-tikki-tchk!"*

Teddy carried him off to bed and insisted on Rikki-tikki sleeping under his chin. Rikki-tikki was too well bred to bite or scratch, but as soon as Teddy was asleep he went off for his nightly walk round the house, and in the dark he ran up against Chuchundra, the muskrat, creeping round by the wall. Chuchundra is a broken-hearted little beast. He whimpers and cheeps all the night, trying to make up his mind to run into the middle of the room, but he never gets there.

"Don't kill me," said Chuchundra, almost weeping. "Rikki-tikki, don't kill me."

"Do you think a snake-killer kills muskrats?" said Rikki-tikki scornfully.

"Those who kill snakes get killed by snakes," said Chuchundra, more sorrowfully than ever. "And how am I to be sure that Nag won't mistake me for you some dark night?"

"There's not the least danger," said Rikki-tikki; "but Nag is in the garden, and I know you don't go there."

"My cousin Chua, the rat, told me—" said Chuchundra, and then he stopped.

"Told you what?"

"H'sh! Nag is everywhere, Rikki-tikki. You should have talked to Chua in the garden."

"I didn't—so you must tell me. Quick, Chuchundra, or I'll bite you!"

Chuchundra sat down and cried till the tears rolled off his whiskers. "I am a very

---

5. A *providence* (prov' ə dəns) is a blessing from God or nature.

Vocabulary
lunge (lunj) *v.* to make a sudden forward movement; charge

poor man," he sobbed. "I never had spirit enough to run out into the middle of the room. H'sh! I mustn't tell you anything. Can't you *hear*, Rikki-tikki?"

Rikki-tikki listened. The house was as still as still, but he thought he could just catch the faintest *scratch-scratch* in the world—a noise as faint as that of a wasp walking on a windowpane—the dry scratch of a snake's scales on brickwork.

The house was as still as still, but he thought he could just catch the faintest scratch-scratch in the world—a noise as faint as that of a wasp walking on a windowpane—

"That's Nag or Nagaina," he said to himself; "and he is crawling into the bathroom sluice.[6] You're right, Chuchundra; I should have talked to Chua."

He stole off to Teddy's bathroom, but there was nothing there, and then to Teddy's mother's bathroom. At the bottom of the smooth plaster wall there was a brick pulled out to make a sluice for the bath water, and as Rikki-tikki stole in by the masonry curb where the bath is put, he heard Nag and Nagaina whispering together outside in the moonlight.

"When the house is emptied of people," said Nagaina to her husband, "*he* will have to go away, and then the garden will be our own again. Go in quietly, and remember that the big man who killed Karait is the first one to bite. Then come out and tell me, and we will hunt for Rikki-tikki together."

"But are you sure there is anything to be gained by killing the people?" said Nag.

"Everything. When there were no people in the bungalow, did we have any mongoose in the garden? So long as the bungalow is empty, we are king and queen of the garden; and remember that as soon as our eggs in the melon bed hatch (as they may tomorrow), our children will need room and quiet."

"I had not thought of that," said Nag. "I will go, but there is no need that we should hunt for Rikki-tikki afterward. I will kill the big man and his wife, and the child if I can, and come away quietly. Then the bungalow will be empty, and Rikki-tikki will go."

Rikki-tikki tingled all over with rage and hatred at this, and then Nag's head came through the sluice, and his five feet of cold body followed it. Angry as he was, Rikki-tikki was very frightened as he saw the size of the big cobra. Nag coiled himself up, raised his head, and looked into the bathroom in the dark, and Rikki could see his eyes glitter.

"Now, if I kill him there, Nagaina will know; and if I fight him on the open floor, the odds are in his favor. What am I to do?" said Rikki-tikki-tavi.

Nag waved to and fro, and then Rikki-tikki heard him drinking from the biggest water jar that was used to fill the bath. "That is good," said the snake. "Now, when Karait was killed, the big man had a stick. He may have that stick still, but when he comes in to bathe in the morning he will

---

6. Here, the *sluice* is a drainpipe.

not have a stick. I shall wait here till he comes. Nagaina—do you hear me? I shall wait here in the cool till daytime."

There was no answer from outside, so Rikki-tikki knew Nagaina had gone away. Nag coiled himself down, coil by coil, round the bulge at the bottom of the water jar, and Rikki-tikki stayed still as death. After an hour he began to move, muscle by muscle, toward the jar. Nag was asleep, and Rikki-tikki looked at his big back, wondering which would be the best place for a good hold. "If I don't break his back at the first jump," said Rikki, "he can still fight; and if he fights—O Rikki!" He looked at the thickness of the neck below the hood, but that was too much for him; and a bite near the tail would only make Nag savage.

"It must be the head," he said at last; "the head above the hood; and when I am once there, I must not let go."

Then he jumped. The head was lying a little clear of the water jar, under the curve of it; and, as his teeth met, Rikki braced his back against the bulge of the red earthenware to hold down the head. This gave him just one second's purchase,[7] and he made the most of it. Then he was battered to and fro as a rat is shaken by a dog—to and fro on the floor, up and down, and round in great circles; but his eyes were red, and he held on as the body cartwhipped[8] over the floor, upsetting the tin dipper and the soap dish and the fleshbrush, and banged against the tin side of the bath. As he held, he closed his jaws tighter and tighter, for he made sure he would be banged to death, and, for the honor of his family, he preferred to be found with his teeth locked. He was dizzy, aching, and felt shaken to pieces when something went off like a thunderclap just behind him; a hot wind knocked him senseless, and red fire singed his fur. The big man had been wakened by the noise, and had fired both barrels of a shotgun into Nag just behind the hood.

Rikki-tikki held on with his eyes shut, for now he was quite sure he was dead; but the head did not move, and the big man picked him up and said: "It's the mongoose again, Alice; the little chap has saved *our* lives now." Then Teddy's mother came in with a very white face, and saw what was left of Nag, and Rikki-tikki dragged himself to Teddy's bedroom and spent half the rest of the night shaking himself tenderly to find out whether he really was broken into forty pieces, as he fancied.

When morning came he was very stiff, but well pleased with his doings. "Now I have Nagaina to settle with, and she will be worse than five Nags, and there's no knowing when the eggs she spoke of will hatch. Goodness! I must go and see Darzee," he said.

Without waiting for breakfast, Rikki-tikki ran to the thornbush where Darzee was singing a song of triumph at the top of his voice. The news of Nag's death was all over the garden, for the sweeper had thrown the body on the rubbish heap.

---

7. In this context, the *purchase* is an advantageous position for applying force.
8. Rikki's body is being thrown about like a whip (*cartwhipped*) as the cobra lashes.

Vocabulary
fancy (fan′ sē) *v.* to picture mentally; imagine

"Oh, you stupid tuft of feathers!" said Rikki-tikki angrily. "Is this the time to sing?"

"Nag is dead—is dead—is dead!" sang Darzee. "The <u>valiant</u> Rikki-tikki caught him by the head and held fast. The big man brought the bang-stick, and Nag fell in two pieces! He will never eat my babies again."

"All that's true enough; but where's Nagaina?" said Rikki-tikki, looking carefully round him.

"Nagaina came to the bathroom sluice and called for Nag," Darzee went on; "and Nag came out on the end of a stick—the sweeper picked him up on the end of a stick and threw him upon the rubbish heap. Let us sing about the great, the red-eyed Rikki-tikki!" And Darzee filled his throat and sang.

"If I could get up to your nest, I'd roll all your babies out!" said Rikki-tikki. "You don't know when to do the right thing at the right time. You're safe enough in your nest there, but it's war for me down here. Stop singing a minute, Darzee."

"For the great, the beautiful Rikki-tikki's sake I will stop," said Darzee. "What is it, O Killer of the terrible Nag?"

"Where is Nagaina, for the third time?"

"On the rubbish heap by the stables, mourning for Nag. Great is Rikki-tikki with the white teeth."

"Bother my white teeth!⁹ Have you ever heard where she keeps her eggs?"

---

9. *Bother my white teeth* is a British way of saying, "Don't concern yourself with my teeth."

Vocabulary
valiant (val′ yənt) *adj.* brave; courageous

"In the melon bed, on the end nearest the wall, where the sun strikes nearly all day. She hid them there weeks ago."

"And you never thought it worthwhile to tell me? The end nearest the wall, you said?"

"Rikki-tikki, you are not going to eat her eggs?"

"Not eat exactly; no. Darzee, if you have a grain of sense you will fly off to the stables and pretend that your wing is broken, and let Nagaina chase you away to this bush! I must get to the melon bed, and if I went there now she'd see me."

Darzee was a featherbrained little fellow who could never hold more than one idea at a time in his head; and just because he knew that Nagaina's children were born in eggs like his own, he didn't think at first that it was fair to kill them. But his wife was a sensible bird, and she knew that cobras' eggs meant young cobras later on; so she flew off from the nest, and left Darzee to keep the babies warm, and continue his song about the death of Nag. Darzee was very like a man in some ways.

She fluttered in front of Nagaina by the rubbish heap and cried out, "Oh, my wing is broken! The boy in the house threw a stone at me and broke it." Then she fluttered more desperately than ever.

Nagaina lifted up her head and hissed, "You warned Rikki-tikki when I would have killed him. Indeed and truly, you've chosen a bad place to be lame in." And she moved toward Darzee's wife, slipping along over the dust.

"The boy broke it with a stone!" shrieked Darzee's wife.

"Well! It may be some consolation to you when you're dead to know that I shall settle accounts with the boy. My husband lies on the rubbish heap this morning, but before night the boy in the house will lie very still. What is the use of running away? I am sure to catch you. Little fool, look at me!"

Darzee's wife knew better than to do *that*, for a bird who looks at a snake's eyes gets so frightened that she cannot move. Darzee's wife fluttered on, piping sorrowfully, and never leaving the ground, and Nagaina quickened her pace.

Rikki-tikki heard them going up the path from the stables, and he raced for the end of the melon patch near the wall. There, in the warm litter about the melons, very cunningly hidden, he found twenty-five eggs, about the size of a bantam's eggs, but with whitish skin instead of shell.

Did You Know?
A *bantam* is a small breed of chicken.

"I was not a day too soon," he said; for he could see the baby cobras curled up inside the skin, and he knew that the minute they were hatched they could each kill a man or a mongoose. He bit off the tops of the eggs as fast as he could, taking care to crush the young cobras, and turned over the litter from time to time to see whether he had missed any. At last there were only three eggs left, and Rikki-tikki began to chuckle to himself, when he heard Darzee's wife screaming:

"Rikki-tikki, I led Nagaina toward the house, and she has gone into the veranda, and—oh, come quickly—she means killing!"

Rikki-tikki smashed two eggs, and tumbled backward down the melon bed with the third egg in his mouth, and scuttled to the veranda as hard as he could put foot to the ground. Teddy and his mother and father were there at early breakfast; but Rikki-tikki saw that they were not eating anything. They sat stone-still, and their faces were white. Nagaina was coiled up on the matting by Teddy's chair, within easy striking distance of Teddy's bare leg, and she was swaying to and fro singing a song of triumph.

"Look at your friends, Rikki-tikki. They are still and white; they are afraid. They dare not move, and if you come a step nearer I strike."

"Son of the big man that killed Nag," she hissed, "stay still. I am not ready yet. Wait a little. Keep very still, all you three. If you move I strike, and if you do not move I strike. Oh, foolish people, who killed my Nag!"

Teddy's eyes were fixed on his father, and all his father could do was to whisper, "Sit still, Teddy. You mustn't move. Teddy, keep still."

Then Rikki-tikki came up and cried: "Turn round, Nagaina; turn and fight!"

"All in good time," said she, without moving her eyes. "I will settle my account with *you* presently. Look at your friends, Rikki-tikki. They are still and white; they are afraid. They dare not move, and if you come a step nearer I strike."

"Look at your eggs," said Rikki-tikki, "in the melon bed near the wall. Go and look, Nagaina."

The big snake turned half round and saw the egg on the veranda. "Ah-h! Give it to me," she said.

Rikki-tikki put his paws one on each side of the egg, and his eyes were blood-red. "What price for a snake's egg? For a young cobra? For a young king cobra? For the last—the very last of the brood? The ants are eating all the others down by the melon bed."

Nagaina spun clear round, forgetting everything for the sake of the one egg; and Rikki-tikki saw Teddy's father shoot out a big hand, catch Teddy by the shoulder, and drag him across the little table with the teacups, safe and out of reach of Nagaina.

"Tricked! Tricked! Tricked! *Rikk-tck-tck!*" chuckled Rikki-tikki. "The boy is safe, and it was I—I—I that caught Nag by the hood last night in the bathroom." Then he began to jump up and down, all four feet together, his head close to the floor. "He threw me to and fro, but he could not shake me off. He was dead before the big man blew him in two. I did it. *Rikki-tikki-tck-tck!* Come then, Nagaina. Come and fight with me. You shall not be a widow long."

Nagaina saw that she had lost her chance of killing Teddy, and the egg lay between Rikki-tikki's paws. "Give me the egg, Rikki-tikki. Give me the last of my eggs, and I will go away and never come

---

Vocabulary
brood (brōod) *n.* all of the young of an animal that are born or cared for at the same time

back," she said, lowering her hood.

"Yes, you will go away, and you will never come back; for you will go to the rubbish heap with Nag. Fight, widow! The big man has gone for his gun! Fight!"

Rikki-tikki was bounding all round Nagaina, keeping just out of reach of her stroke, his little eyes like

. . . very few mongooses, however wise and old they may be, care to follow a cobra into its hole.

hot coals. Nagaina gathered herself together and flung out at him. Rikki-tikki jumped up and backward. Again and again and again she struck, and each time her head came with a whack on the matting of the veranda, and she gathered herself together like a watchspring. Then Rikki-tikki danced in a circle to get behind her, and Nagaina spun round to keep her head to his head, so that the rustle of her tail on the matting sounded like dry leaves blown along by the wind.

He had forgotten the egg. It still lay on the veranda, and Nagaina came nearer and nearer to it, till at last, while Rikki-tikki was drawing breath, she caught it in her mouth, turned to the veranda steps, and flew like an arrow down the path, with Rikki-tikki behind her. When the cobra runs for her life, she goes like a whiplash flicked across a horse's neck.

Rikki-tikki knew that he must catch her, or all the trouble would begin again. She headed straight for the long grass by the thornbush, and as he was running Rikki-tikki heard Darzee singing his foolish little song of triumph. But Darzee's wife was wiser. She flew off her nest as Nagaina came along,

and flapped her wings about Nagaina's head. If Darzee had helped they might have turned her; but Nagaina only lowered her hood and went on. Still, the instant's delay brought Rikki-tikki up to her, and as she plunged into the rathole where she and Nag used to live, his little white teeth were clenched on her tail, and he went down with her—and very few mongooses, however wise and old they may be, care to follow a cobra into its hole. It was dark in the hole; and Rikki-tikki never knew when it might open out and give Nagaina room to turn and strike at him. He held on savagely and struck out his feet to act as brakes on the dark slope of the hot, moist earth.

Then the grass by the mouth of the hole stopped waving, and Darzee said: "It is all over with Rikki-tikki! We must sing his death song. Valiant Rikki-tikki is dead. For Nagaina will surely kill him underground."

So he sang a very mournful song that he made up all on the spur of the minute, and just as he got to the most touching part the grass quivered again, and Rikki-tikki, covered with dirt, dragged himself out of the hole leg by leg, licking his whiskers. Darzee stopped with a little shout. Rikki-tikki shook some of the dust out of his fur and sneezed. "It is all over," he said. "The widow will never come out again." And the red ants that live between the grass stems heard him, and began to troop down one after another to see if he had spoken the truth.

Rikki-tikki curled himself up in the grass and slept where he was—slept and slept till it was late in the afternoon, for he had done a hard day's work.

"Now," he said, when he awoke, "I will go back to the house. Tell the coppersmith, Darzee, and he will tell the garden that Nagaina is dead."

The coppersmith is a bird who makes a noise exactly like the beating of a little hammer on a copper pot; and the reason he is always making it is because he is the town crier to every Indian garden, and tells all the news to everybody who cares to listen. As Rikki-tikki went up the path, he heard his "attention" notes like a tiny dinner gong; and then the steady "*Ding-dong-tock!* Nag is dead—*dong!* Nagaina is dead! *Ding-dong-tock!*" That set all the birds in the garden singing, and the frogs croaking, for Nag and Nagaina used to eat frogs as well as little birds.

When Rikki got to the house, Teddy and Teddy's mother (she still looked very white, for she had been fainting) and Teddy's father came out and almost cried over him; and that night he ate all that was given him till he could eat no more, and went to bed on Teddy's shoulder, where Teddy's mother saw him when she came to look late at night.

"He saved our lives and Teddy's life," she said to her husband. "Just think, he saved all our lives!"

Viewing the photograph: Did you imagine Darzee, the tailorbird, looking anything like this tailorbird? Why or why not?

Rikki-tikki woke up with a jump, for all mongooses are light sleepers.

"Oh, it's you," said he. "What are you bothering for? All the cobras are dead; and if they weren't, I'm here."

Rikki-tikki had a right to be proud of himself; but he did not grow too proud, and he kept that garden as a mongoose should keep it, with tooth and jump and spring and bite, till never a cobra dared show its head inside the walls.

Responding to Literature

PERSONAL RESPONSE

◆ What moment in the story did you find the most exciting? Why?

◆ Look back at the notes you made in the **Reading Focus** on page 788. Do any of the characters in the story share your thoughts and feelings about snakes?

Analyzing Literature

RECALL

1. In whose house does Rikki live?

2. Who are Darzee and Chuchundra? How do they help Rikki in his "great war"?

3. Why do the cobras decide they have to kill the people in the house?

4. What finally happens to Nag and Nagaina?

INTERPRET

5. Why do you think Kipling starts the story with an account of the rescue of Rikki?

6. How does the author use Darzee and Chuchundra to call attention to Rikki's bravery?

7. Does Kipling present one of the cobras more sympathetically than the other? Use examples to support your answer.

8. How does Rikki's cleverness help protect the family?

EVALUATE AND CONNECT

9. For the **climax** of the story, Kipling could have chosen to have Rikki killed in Nagaina's hole. How would that change affect your response to the story?

10. "Rikki-tikki-tavi" is a story of "good versus evil." Do you like that kind of story, or do you prefer stories in which the characters are not so easy to classify? Why?

LITERARY ELEMENTS

Anthropomorphism

Kipling gives the animal characters in "Rikki-tikki-tavi" human emotions, characteristics, and intelligence. Authors use this technique, called **anthropomorphism,** to help readers feel a connection to characters who are not human. The conflict between Rikki-tikki-tavi and Nag is told through their actions, their words, and their thoughts.

1. How does the use of anthropomorphism contribute to the level of interest and suspense in the story?

2. How would your reaction to "Rikki-tikki-tavi" be changed if it were written as a newspaper story about a real fight between a snake and a mongoose?

● See **Literary Terms Handbook,** p. R1.

Literature and Writing

Writing About Literature

Setting   The **setting** is the time and place in which a story takes place. Explain how the descriptions of the setting contribute to the story. What details help you to visualize the house, the garden, and the action between characters?

Creative Writing

News Article   Imagine you have been assigned to write a news article about Rikki's heroics. Choose one character to interview. Then write a short article using quotations from your imaginary interview.

Extending Your Response

Literature Groups

A Fan of Snakes   Robert Bakker wrote in *The Dinosaur Heresies,* "Whenever I read Kipling's 'Rikki-tikki-tavi,' I root for the snake. . . ." An authority on reptiles, Bakker thinks that Kipling is biased against snakes. Do you agree? Share your group's opinions with the class.

Performing

Readers Theater   Prepare a readers theater presentation of the confrontation between Rikki and Nagaina on the veranda. Present it to a class of younger students.

Interdisciplinary Activity

Science   Not every snake is life-threatening to humans. Do some research on harmful and harmless snakes in your area. Use a variety of sources, such as books, magazines, the Internet, and other electronic resources. Make a two-column chart that identifies and illustrates the two categories of snakes you have researched.

Reading Further

If you would like to read other books by Rudyard Kipling, try these:

Kim

The Jungle Book

For warm and often hilarious stories about animals and the people who keep them, try this book of memoirs by country veterinarian James Herriot:

All Creatures Great and Small

Skill Minilessons

GRAMMAR AND LANGUAGE • PERSONAL PRONOUNS

Personal pronouns refer to people or things. These pronouns have different forms depending on whether they are used in a sentence as subjects or as the objects of verbs or prepositions.

Singular subject pronouns: I, you, he, she, it

Plural subject pronouns: we, you, they

Singular object pronouns: me, you, him, her, it

Plural object pronouns: us, you, them

● For more about pronouns, see **Language Handbook,** p. R31.

PRACTICE Write each sentence, replacing each underlined word or phrase with a personal pronoun.

1. <u>Rikki-tikki-tavi</u> lived in a burrow with his father and mother.
2. After the flood, Rikki never saw <u>his father and mother</u> again.
3. <u>Nag and Nagaina</u> wanted everyone to fear <u>Nag and Nagaina.</u>
4. "When <u>the people</u> are gone," Nagaina said to Nag, "the garden will belong to <u>Nag and Nagaina.</u>"

READING AND THINKING • EVALUATING

When you evaluate a piece of writing, one of the things you determine is whether or not the author has achieved his or her purpose.

● For more about evaluating what you read, see **Reading Handbook,** pp. R85–R99.

PRACTICE Was Kipling trying to entertain, to inform, or to persuade his audience with "Rikki-tikki-tavi"? Write a short paragraph stating the author's purpose and evaluating how well he achieved it. Use specific examples from the story to support your opinion.

VOCABULARY • DICTIONARY SKILLS: DEFINITIONS

When you see an unfamiliar word in your reading, the first thing you must do is decide how the word is being used. Is it a noun? a verb? an adjective or adverb? Then look at the **dictionary entry** to find the meanings that are given for the word as that part of speech. Use **context clues** to decide which meaning is the appropriate one.

fancy *n.* **1.** imagination, especially a playful imagination. **2.** something imagined; a mental image. **3.** a sudden wish or notion. **4.** a liking or fondness. —*adj.* **1.** decorated; not plain. **2.** showing expert skill: *fancy dancing.* **3.** of high quality and, therefore, more expensive: *a fancy brand of soup.* —*v.* **1.** to picture mentally; imagine. **2.** to have a liking for. **3.** to suppose; think without being sure: *I fancied she was about twelve.*

PRACTICE Review the dictionary definitions for the word *fancy.* Then decide which meaning of *fancy* is used in each sentence below. Write the part of speech (noun, adjective, or verb) and then the number of the appropriate definition.

1. I've always had a *fancy* for cats and dogs.
2. After reading "Rikki-tikki-tavi," I had a *fancy* to own a mongoose.
3. I could *fancy* myself feeding it and brushing its furry coat.
4. It wouldn't need a *fancy* collar and leash; plain ones would do.
5. My parents, however, didn't *fancy* the idea of another pet, especially a mongoose.

Endangered Species

You've probably heard the slogan "Save the whales!" or read it on a bumper sticker. Do you know why this slogan began? It started as a protest from people who wanted to ban whale-hunting. Some types of whales are among the hundreds of endangered species. A species of animal or plant at risk of becoming extinct is called *endangered.*

Many people, such as naturalists who study the environment, believe it is important to save endangered species to maintain the balance of nature. Already, the passenger pigeon, dodo bird, and Labrador duck are extinct. Of course, dinosaurs are extinct too. However, dinosaurs did not disappear because of humans. Today, as the human population increases all over the planet, less space remains for other species to live in their natural habitats.

Species become endangered for many reasons. For example, the cutting down of forests destroys the natural habitats of forest animals. Some animals have been hunted to extinction or near extinction. Overfishing has endangered many fish species. Pesticides kill insects regarded by humans as pests, but they also endanger birds that depend on those insects for food. Pesticide-sprayed insects may also harm birds that feed on them.

Since the 1800s, people have been trying to protect wildlife with special programs. In 1973 the United States passed the Endangered Species Act. An important part of this law made it illegal for people in the United States to buy animals (or animal parts, such as furs) endangered anywhere in the world.

As of June 30, 1998, 350 animal species in the U.S. and another 521 elsewhere in the world were listed as endangered. A few are shown above.

ACTIVITY

Pick an endangered animal to "adopt." Learn everything you can about this animal. Then share with classmates a picture of your adopted animal and your ideas about why and how it should be protected.

Before You Read

Uncle Tony's Goat

MEET
LESLIE MARMON SILKO

L eslie Marmon Silko, who describes herself as Laguna, Pueblo, Mexican, and white, grew up on the Laguna Pueblo Reservation in New Mexico, listening to tales told by her female relatives. These stories gave Silko a sense of identity and inspired her writing. Silko's own stories explore her Pueblo heritage and the conflicts between traditional and modern ways. Silko decided to write "Uncle Tony's Goat" after a phone conversation with a friend, the poet Simon J. Ortiz, who told her a story about goats.

Leslie Marmon Silko was born in 1948. This story was first published in 1981.

READING FOCUS

Imagine meeting a large, unfamiliar animal. You feel the threat of its presence as it follows your movements with a watchful eye.

QuickWrite

How would such an experience make you feel? Jot down your response in a few sentences.

Setting a Purpose

Read this story to find out what one boy learns from his experience with a goat.

BUILDING BACKGROUND

The Time and Place   The story is set on a small family farm in New Mexico.

Did You Know?   Some people think goats are "garbage disposals" that chew tin cans and other trash. Actually, goats spend their days leisurely munching grass and weeds. Hardy animals, goats can live on sparse vegetation and produce milk even under extreme climatic conditions. Some types of goats are also valued for their wool, hides, and meat. Male goats are often called billy goats. A female goat is called a nanny or doe. A young goat is a kid.

VOCABULARY PREVIEW

compensate (kom′ pən sāt′) *v.* to make up for; balance in force, weight, or effect; p. 808

hostile (host′ əl) *adj.* feeling or showing dislike; unfriendly; p. 808

conspicuously (kən spik′ ū əs lē) *adv.* in a way that draws attention or is easily seen; p. 809

Uncle Tony's Goat

Leslie Marmon Silko ·⁓

We had a hard time

finding the right kind of string to use. We
knew we needed gut to string our bows the way
the men did, but we were little kids and we
didn't know how to get any. So Kenny went to
his house and brought back a ball of white cotton string that his mother used to string red
chili with. It was thick and soft and it didn't
make very good bowstring. As soon as we
got the bows made we sat down again on the
sand bank above the stream and started skin-
ning willow twigs for arrows. It was past noon,
and the tall willows behind us made cool shade.

Uncle Tony's Goat

There were lots of little minnows that day, flashing in the shallow water, swimming back and forth wildly like they weren't sure if they really wanted to go up or down the stream; it was a day for minnows that we were always hoping for—we could have filled our rusty coffee cans and old pickle jars full. But this was the first time for making bows and arrows, and the minnows weren't much different from the sand or the rocks now. The secret is the arrows. The ones we made were crooked, and when we shot them they didn't go straight—they flew around in arcs and curves; so we crawled through the leaves and branches, deep into the willow groves, looking for the best, the straightest willow branches. But even after we skinned the sticky wet bark from them and whittled the knobs off, they still weren't straight. Finally we went ahead and made notches at the end of each arrow to hook in the bowstring, and we started practicing, thinking maybe we could learn to shoot the crooked arrows straight.

We left the river each of us with a handful of damp, yellow arrows and our fresh-skinned willow bows. We walked slowly and shot arrows at bushes, big rocks, and the juniper tree that grows by Pino's sheep pen. They were working better just like we had figured; they still didn't fly straight, but now we could <u>compensate</u> for that by the way we aimed them. We were going up to the church to shoot at the cats old Sister Julian kept outside the cloister.[1] We didn't want to hurt anything, just to have new kinds of things to shoot at.

But before we got to the church we went past the grassy hill where my uncle Tony's goats were grazing. A few of them were lying down chewing their cud[2] peacefully, and they didn't seem to notice us. The billy goat was lying down, but he was watching us closely like he already knew about little kids. His yellow goat eyes didn't blink, and he stared with a wide, <u>hostile</u> look. The grazing goats made good deer for our bows. We shot all our arrows at the nanny goats and their kids; they skipped away from the careening[3] arrows and never lost the rhythm of their greedy chewing as they continued to nibble the weeds and grass on the hillside. The billy goat was lying there watching us and taking us into his memory. As we ran down the road toward the church and Sister Julian's cats, I looked back, and my uncle Tony's billy goat was still watching me.

My uncle and my father were sitting on the bench outside the house when we walked by. It was September now, and the farming was almost over, except for bringing home the melons and a few pumpkins. They were mending ropes and bridles

Did You Know?
A *bridle* is the headgear for a horse. It includes the bit that fits in the horse's mouth and the reins the rider uses to guide the horse.

---

1. Here, the *cloister* is a convent, the building in which nuns live.

2. *Cud* is partially digested food brought back up from an animal's stomach for a second, more thorough, chewing.

3. *Careening* arrows would sway from side to side while moving, as if out of control.

Vocabulary
compensate (kom′ pən sāt′) *v.* to make up for; balance in force, weight, or effect
hostile (host′ əl) *adj.* feeling or showing dislike; unfriendly

and feeling the afternoon sun. We held our bows and arrows out in front of us so they could see them. My father smiled and kept braiding the strips of leather in his hand, but my uncle Tony put down the bridle and pieces of scrap leather he was working on and looked at each of us kids slowly. He was old, getting some white hair—he was my mother's oldest brother, the one that scolded us when we told lies or broke things.

"You'd better not be shooting at things," he said, "only at rocks or trees. Something will get hurt. Maybe even one of you."

We all nodded in agreement and tried to hold the bows and arrows less conspicuously down at our sides; when he turned back to his work we hurried away before he took the bows away from us like he did the time we made the slingshot. He caught us shooting rocks at an old wrecked car; its windows were all busted out anyway, but he took the slingshot away. I always wondered what he did with it and with the knives we made ourselves out of tin cans. When I was much older I asked my mother, "What did he ever do with those knives and slingshots he took away from us?" She was kneading[4] bread on the kitchen table at the time and was probably busy thinking about the fire in the oven outside. "I don't know," she said; "you ought to ask him yourself." But I never did. I thought about it lots of times, but I never did. It would have been like getting caught all over again.

The goats were valuable. We got milk and meat from them. My uncle was careful to see that all the goats were treated properly; the worst scolding my older sister ever got was when my mother caught her and some of her friends chasing the newborn kids. My mother kept saying over and over again, "It's a good thing I saw you; what if your uncle had seen you?" and even though we kids were very young then, we understood very well what she meant.

The billy goat never forgot the bows and arrows, even after the bows had cracked and split and the crooked, whittled arrows were all lost. This goat was big and black and important to my uncle Tony because he'd paid a lot to get him and because he wasn't an ordinary goat. Uncle Tony had bought him from a white man, and then he'd hauled him in the back of the pickup all the way from Quemado.[5] And my uncle was the only person who could touch this goat. If a stranger or one of us kids got too near him, the mane on the billy goat's neck would stand on end and the goat would rear up on his hind legs and dance forward trying to reach the person with his long, spiral horns. This billy goat smelled bad, and none of us cared if we couldn't pet him. But my uncle took good care of this goat. The goat would let Uncle Tony brush him with the horse brush and scratch him around the base of his horns. Uncle Tony talked to the billy goat—in the morning when he unpenned the goats and in the evening when he gave them their hay and closed the gate for the night. I never paid too much attention to what he said to the billy goat; usually it was something like

---

4. The mother was pressing and squeezing, or *kneading,* bread dough.

5. *Quemado* (kā mä′ dō)

Vocabulary

conspicuously (kən spik′ ū əs lē) *adv.* in a way that draws attention or is easily seen

Crescent Moon Over the Southwest, 1990. Sherri Silverman. Pastel, 25¾ x 36 in. Private collection.

Viewing the painting: How is the scene in the painting similar to and different from the story's setting?

"Get up, big goat! You've slept long enough," or "Move over, big goat, and let the others have something to eat." I think Uncle Tony was proud of that billy goat.

We all had chores to do around home. My sister helped out around the house mostly, and I was supposed to carry water from the hydrant and bring in kindling. I helped my father look after the horses and pigs, and Uncle Tony milked the goats and fed them. One morning near the end of September I was out feeding the pigs their table scraps and pig mash;[6] I'd given the

pigs their food, and I was watching them squeal and snap at each other as they crowded into the feed trough. Behind me I could hear the milk squirting into the eight-pound lard pail that Uncle Tony used for milking.

When he finished milking he noticed me standing there; he motioned toward the goats still inside the pen. "Run the rest of them out," he said as he untied the two milk goats and carried the milk to the house.

I was seven years old, and I understood that everyone, including my uncle, expected me to handle more chores; so I hurried over to the goat pen and swung the tall wire gate open. The does and kids

---

6. *Mash* is animal feed that consists of a mixture of ground grains.

came prancing out. They trotted daintily past the pigpen and scattered out, intent on finding leaves and grass to eat. It wasn't until then I noticed that the billy goat hadn't come out of the little wooden shed inside the goat pen. I stood outside the pen and tried to look inside the wooden shelter, but it was still early and the morning sun left the inside of the shelter in deep shadow. I stood there for a while, hoping that he would come out by himself, but I realized that he'd recognized me and that he wouldn't come out. I understood right away what was happening and my fear of him was in my bowels and down my neck; I was shaking.

Finally my uncle came out of the house; it was time for breakfast. "What's wrong?" he called out from the door.

"The billy goat won't come out," I yelled back, hoping he would look disgusted and come do it himself.

"Get in there and get him out," he said as he went back into the house.

I looked around quickly for a stick or broom handle, or even a big rock, but I couldn't find anything. I walked into the pen slowly, concentrating on the darkness beyond the shed door; I circled to the back of the shed and kicked at the boards, hoping to make the billy goat run out. I put my eye up to a crack between the boards, and I could see he was standing up now and that his yellow eyes were on mine.

My mother was yelling at me to hurry up, and Uncle Tony was watching. I stepped around into the low doorway, and the goat charged toward me, feet first. I had dirt in my mouth and up my nose and there was blood running past my eye; my head ached. Uncle Tony carried me to the

house; his face was stiff with anger, and I remembered what he'd always told us about animals; they won't bother you unless you bother them first. I didn't start to cry until my mother hugged me close and wiped my face with a damp wash rag. It was only a little cut above my eyebrow, and she sent me to school anyway with a Band-Aid on my forehead.

Uncle Tony locked the billy goat in the pen. He didn't say what he was going to do with the goat, but when he left with my father to haul firewood, he made sure the gate to the pen was wired tightly shut. He looked at the goat quietly and with sadness; he said something to the goat, but the yellow eyes stared past him.

"What's he going to do with the goat?" I asked my mother before I went to catch the school bus.

"He ought to get rid of it," she said. "We can't have that goat knocking people down for no good reason."

I didn't feel good at school. The teacher sent me to the nurse's office and the nurse made me lie down. Whenever I closed my eyes I could see the goat and my uncle, and I felt a stiffness in my throat and chest. I got off the school bus slowly, so the other kids would go ahead without me. I walked slowly and wished I could be away from home for a while. I could go over to Grandma's house, but she would ask me if my mother knew where I was and I would have to say no, and she would make me go home first to ask. So I walked very slowly, because I didn't want to see the black goat's hide hanging over the corral fence.

When I got to the house I didn't see a goat hide or the goat, but Uncle Tony was on his horse and my mother was standing beside the horse holding a canteen and a flour sack bundle tied with brown string. I was frightened at what this meant. My uncle looked down at me from the saddle.

"The goat ran away," he said. "Jumped out of the pen somehow. I saw him just as he went over the hill beyond the river. He stopped at the top of the hill and he looked back this way."

Uncle Tony nodded at my mother and me and then he left; we watched his old roan gelding[7] splash across the stream and labor up the steep path beyond the river. Then they were over the top of the hill and gone.

Uncle Tony was gone for three days. He came home early on the morning of the fourth day, before we had eaten breakfast or fed the animals. He was glad to be home, he said, because he was getting too old for such long rides. He called me over and looked closely at the cut above my eye. It had scabbed over good, and I wasn't wearing a Band-Aid any more; he examined it very carefully before he let me go. He stirred some sugar into his coffee.

"That miserable goat," he said. "I followed him for three days. He was headed south, going straight to Quemado. I never

could catch up to him." My uncle shook his head. "The first time I saw him he was already in the piñon forest, halfway into the mountains already. I could see him most of the time, off in the distance a mile or two. He would stop sometimes and look back." Uncle Tony paused and drank some more coffee. "I stopped at night. I had to. He stopped too, and in the morning we would start out again. The trail just gets higher and steeper. Yesterday morning there was frost on top of the blanket when I woke up and we were in the big pines and red oak leaves. I couldn't see him any more because the forest is too thick. So I turned around." Tony finished the cup of coffee. "He's probably in Quemado by now."

I looked at him again, standing there by the door, ready to go milk the nanny goats.

"There wasn't ever a goat like that one," he said, "but if that's the way he's going to act, O.K. then. That stubborn goat was just too mean anyway."

He smiled at me and his voice was strong and happy when he said this.

Did You Know?

Piñon (pin′ yun), a Spanish word, refers to any of several small pine trees found in Mexico and the southwestern United States.

---

7. *Roan* describes the horse's color, a reddish-brown mixed with gray or white. A *gelding* is a male horse that's been surgically "fixed" so that it cannot breed.

Responding to Literature

PERSONAL RESPONSE

◆ Review your notes from the **Reading Focus** on page 806. How do your thoughts and feelings compare with those of the story's narrator?

Analyzing Literature

RECALL

1. What do Kenny and the narrator do when they encounter the goats on the hill? Why do you think they do that?
2. What is the billy goat's reaction to the boys' behavior?
3. What happens when the narrator attempts to run the goats from the pen?
4. What is the narrator afraid he will find when he returns from school? What happens instead?

INTERPRET

5. Why do you think the billy goat acts as he does when the narrator attempts to run the goats from the pen? Do you think Uncle Tony understands the goat's behavior? Why or why not?
6. Does the goat deserve to be killed as Uncle Tony seems to plan? Why or why not?
7. How does the narrator's attitude toward the goat change in the course of the story? Explain.
8. What do you think the narrator learned from his experience with Uncle Tony's goat?

EVALUATE AND CONNECT

9. Were you satisfied with the story's ending? Why or why not? Suggest two other possible endings for the story.
10. Theme Connection   What does the story communicate to you about the relationship between humans and animals?

LITERARY ELEMENTS

Narrator

Narrative is a type of writing that tells a story. The person who tells the story is called the **narrator.** Because the narrator in "Uncle Tony's Goat" tells the events in his own words, using the pronoun *I,* this story is a **first-person narrative.** In a first-person narrative, all information about the story's characters and events comes from the narrator. A skillful reader must determine how the narrator's experience and opinions influence the telling of the story.

1. What affects the narrator's description of Uncle Tony?
2. If Uncle Tony were telling the story, how might he have described the goat?

● See **Literary Terms Handbook,** p. R7.

Literature and Writing

Writing About Literature

Setting   What is the setting of the story? How does the author bring the setting to life for her readers? Write a paragraph about the story's setting. Use examples and quotations from the story.

Creative Writing

Retelling the Story   Rewrite the story as if the goat were narrating it. Be sure to include the goat's thoughts and feelings toward Uncle Tony, as well as his response to the boys' activities.

Extending Your Response

Art Activity

Story Map   Leslie Marmon Silko uses foreshadowing when she offers her readers clues about what will occur next in the story. If you recognize these clues, you can predict what will happen. Reexamine the story. As a group, use chart paper to create a large story map that illustrates and charts the evidence foreshadowing the goat's attack on the narrator. Present your story map to the class.

Literature Groups

Animal Portraits   Compare the way animals are portrayed in "Rikki-tikki-tavi" and "Uncle Tony's Goat." Which animal portrait do you prefer? From which did you learn the most? Give reasons for your opinions.

Learning for Life

Incident Report   Imagine you are Uncle Tony. Write a report for the police about your missing goat. Summarize the events that lead to the goat's escape. Also describe the goat and your nephew. Read your report to the class.

Reading Further

To learn more about the Pueblos and other Native Americans of the Southwest, try these books:

Mother Earth, Father Sky: Pueblo Indians of the American Southwest by David Lavender

Desert Dwellers: Native People of the American Southwest by Scott S. Warren

*inter*NET
C O N N E C T I O N

Leslie Marmon Silko grew up on a pueblo in New Mexico. If you would like to learn more about the Pueblo people, type "Pueblo Indians" or "Anasazi" into a search engine to find some informative sites.

📁 **Save your work for your portfolio.**

Skill Minilessons

GRAMMAR AND LANGUAGE • CONSISTENT VERB TENSES

It is important to keep the verb tenses consistent in your writing. If you jump from one tense to another, readers will be confused about when events take place.

CONFUSING: Uncle Tony **works** hard on the farm. The narrator **worked** on the farm too.

BETTER: Uncle Tony **works** hard on the farm. The narrator **works** on the farm too.

PRACTICE Write a paragraph summarizing the events in "Uncle Tony's Goat." Keep your verbs in the same tense unless you have a strong reason to change them. Exchange paragraphs with a partner and check for consistent verb tenses.

● For more about verb tense, see **Language Handbook,** pp. R15–R16.

READING AND THINKING • PROBLEM/SOLUTION

Most plots in fiction focus on one or more problems that the characters try to solve. Often, readers learn about characters by the way in which they respond to problems in their lives. In "Uncle Tony's Goat," there are a number of related problems. How do the different characters respond to the problems? How do they try to solve the problems?

PRACTICE Reread "Uncle Tony's Goat." Write a paragraph describing how two of the characters in the story respond to problems in their lives and how they finally solve them.

● To learn more about the problem/solution organization of text, see **Reading Handbook,** pp. R88–R89.

VOCABULARY • UNLOCKING MEANING

You can often use what you know about one word to figure out what another related word means. The narrator of "Uncle Tony's Goat" has the chore of gathering *kindling.* You know that *kindling* is small sticks or other material used to start a fire. You could use that information to figure out that the expression "kindled my anger" means "made me start to get angry."

PRACTICE Use what you know about the words on the left and familiar prefixes and suffixes to answer the questions.

1. *hostile* Hostilities are sure to occur during
   _____ .
   a. wars   b. parties   c. contests
2. *conspicuous* You might try to be inconspicuous to avoid being _____ .
   a. noticed   b. alone   c. neglected
3. *compensate* If your brother lost your jacket, what might he do to recompense you?
   a. apologize   b. laugh   c. buy you another

● For more about using word parts to unlock meaning, see **Reading Handbook,** pp. R73 and R79–R80.

GRAMMAR LINK

Using Apostrophes to Show Possession

The **apostrophe** is used to show possession. Sometimes it is used alone, but it is usually combined with the letter *s*.

Problem 1 Singular, possessive nouns

Leslie Marmon Silkos story about the goat is humorous.

Solution Use an apostrophe and an -*s* to make a singular noun possessive, even if the noun ends in -*s*.

Leslie Marmon Silko's story about the goat is humorous.

Problem 2 Plural nouns ending in -*s*

Are your classmates responses the same as yours?

Solution If a plural noun ends in -*s*, make it possessive by adding only an apostrophe.

Are your classmates' responses the same as yours?

Problem 3 Plural nouns not ending in -*s*

Peoples ideas about goats have not changed much over time.

Solution If a plural noun does not end in -*s*, add an apostrophe and an -*s*.

People's ideas about goats have not changed much over time.

Problem 4 Possessive personal pronouns

The boys don't realize that the problem with the goat is their's.

Solution Apostrophes are not used in possessive pronouns, such as *yours* and *hers*.

The boys don't realize that the problem with the goat is theirs.

● For more about using apostrophes, see **Language Handbook,** pp. R40–R41.

EXERCISE

Write the possessive form of each word.

a. dresses	**c.** men	**e.** horns	**g.** James	**i.** ladies
b. sheep	**d.** class	**f.** story	**h.** our	**j.** family

LISTENING, SPEAKING, and VIEWING

Critical Viewing

How can you judge the accuracy of things you view on television, on film, or on the Internet? The following tips can help.

Critical Viewing Guidelines

Ask Why

- When you view a presentation, ask yourself about its purpose. Is it designed to entertain, to inform, or to persuade? Material should be accurate, but material intended to persuade may be one-sided.

Digital composite by John Lund/Tony Stone Images.

Ask Who

- Who created the presentation? Is the creator an expert? Does he or she have a reputation for quality?

Ask When

- When was the presentation created? Older material may not be up-to-date. On the other hand, very new information may not yet have been reliably confirmed. Can you check key facts?

Ask How

- How is the material presented? Do you detect fuzzy thinking, sensationalism, one-sidedness, or other attempts to manipulate viewers?

ACTIVITIES

1. On your own or with a partner, view a television commercial and use the Critical Viewing Guidelines to evaluate it. Make notes of your evaluation, and share your results with classmates.

2. Use the Critical Viewing Guidelines to evaluate a television program or video designed to inform. Write a paragraph explaining your evaluation.

Before You Read
Loo-Wit

MEET
WENDY ROSE

Wendy Rose's mother was of Miwok descent, and her father was a full-blood Hopi. Her poems often reflect her personal search for tribal and personal identity. About her need to write, Rose once said, "Writing is just something that always has been and just is. For everything in this universe there is a song to accompany its existence; writing is another way of singing these songs. . . . Some people have tried to say I sing my songs because I'm half-Hopi; that's not true . . . I sing them because I hear them."

Wendy Rose was born in California in 1948.

READING FOCUS

Think about the extraordinary power of natural elements, such as a volcano, tornado, or the ocean tides. What words might describe that kind of power?

Sharing Ideas
Write down your ideas. Then share your thoughts in a small group discussion.

Setting a Purpose
Read this poem to discover how one poet describes a volcano.

BUILDING BACKGROUND

Loo-Wit is the Cowlitz Indian name for Mount St. Helens, the volcano that erupted in Washington in 1980. A volcano is a vent in the Earth from which molten rock and gas sometimes erupt. The molten rock that erupts, called lava, forms a hill or mountain around the vent. The lava sometimes flows out as liquid, or it may explode as solid particles. The fierce eruption of Mount St. Helens was the most violent volcanic event within the continental United States in recorded history.

Loo-Wit

Wendy Rose

The way they do
this old woman
no longer cares
what others think
5   but spits her black tobacco
any which way
stretching full length
from her bumpy bed.
Finally up
10 she sprinkles
ashes on the snow,
cold buttes°
promising nothing
but the walk
15 of winter.
Centuries of cedar
have bound her
to earth,
huckleberry ropes
20 lay prickly
on her neck.
Around her
machinery growls,
snarls and ploughs
25 great patches
of her skin.
She crouches
in the north,
her trembling
30 the source
of dawn.
Light appears
with the shudder
of her slopes,
35 the movement
of her arm.

Blackberries unravel,°
stones dislodge.°
It's not as if
40 they weren't warned.

She was sleeping
but she heard
the boot scrape,
the creaking floor,
45 felt the pull of the blanket
from her thin shoulder.
With one free hand
she finds her weapons
and raises them high;
50 clearing the twigs
from her throat
she sings, she sings,
shaking the sky
like a blanket about her
55 Loo-Wit sings and sings and sings!

---

37 Here, *unravel* means "untangle; separate; come apart."
38 To *dislodge* is to move out of position.

---

12 *Buttes* (būts) are steep, isolated, flat-topped hills.

Responding to Literature

PERSONAL RESPONSE

◆ Could you feel the poet's connection to the subject of this poem? How would you describe her connection?

Analyzing Literature

RECALL AND INTERPRET

1. What metaphor does the poet use to describe the volcano?
2. How does the metaphor help you to understand the **theme** of the poem?
3. What is really happening in lines 50–55 of the poem?
4. What message about nature does the poem express?

EVALUATE AND CONNECT

5. In lines 5–6, the poet uses an image of an old woman who "spits her black tobacco." The poet's words are figurative, or metaphoric. She is really describing a volcano throwing out black ashes. That is the literal, or nonfigurative, meaning of the lines. Give three more examples of the poet's use of figurative language, explaining what each one means literally.

6. Find an example of **alliteration** in "Loo-Wit." (See **Literary Terms Handbook,** page R1.) Why do you think the poet uses this poetic device?

7. Theme Connection   How is the poem related to the theme of "A Delicate Balance"? Explain.

8. Think of someone who would enjoy reading this poem. What about the poem would appeal to that person?

LITERARY ELEMENTS

Extended Metaphor

A **metaphor** is an **analogy**—a comparison of two basically different things that share, or can be said to share, one or more similarities. Like similes, metaphors create unique, unexpected images that bring a poem to life. In a metaphor, however, the comparison is stated directly, and the words *as* or *like* are not used. In a metaphor, one thing is not *like* another thing; it *is* another thing. In an **extended metaphor,** the comparison is extended through a long passage. In a poem, it may be carried throughout the entire piece. The comparison between an old woman and a volcano in "Loo-Wit" is an extended metaphor.

1. Describe how the poet first introduces the extended metaphor in "Loo-Wit."

2. Explain how the actions of the old woman in the poem mirror the actions of a volcano.

● See **Literary Terms Handbook,** p. R4.

Extending Your Response

Writing About Literature

Analyzing Impressions   In a paragraph or two, write about your own reaction as you read "Loo-Wit." First describe the poem's overall impact. Were you confused? challenged? intrigued? excited? Then give examples of how the poet's use of language helped to create the effect the poem had on you.

Literature Groups

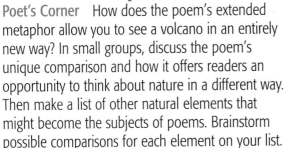

Poet's Corner   How does the poem's extended metaphor allow you to see a volcano in an entirely new way? In small groups, discuss the poem's unique comparison and how it offers readers an opportunity to think about nature in a different way. Then make a list of other natural elements that might become the subjects of poems. Brainstorm possible comparisons for each element on your list.

Personal Writing

Extended Metaphor   Using the notes you wrote for the **Reading Focus** on page 818, write your own extended metaphor. It can be a poem or a prose paragraph. Compare something in the natural world, such as a volcano or a hurricane, to something else, such as a train or an unruly student. Be creative in your comparison. Use sensory language and vivid imagery in your extended metaphor.

Performing

Role-Play   Work with a partner. While one of you reads the poem aloud, the other will role-play the actions of the old woman described in the poem. Use props such as a blanket, a boot, twigs, stones, or chairs pushed together to make a "bumpy bed." Practice until you feel comfortable sharing your dramatization with your classmates.

Reading Further

If you would like to read more poetry by Native Americans, try these books:

In the Trail of the Wind: American Indian Poems and Ritual Orations by John Bierhorst

Rising Voices: Writings of Young Native Americans ed. by Arlene B. Hirschfelder

📖 **Save your work for your portfolio.**

Skill Minilesson

READING AND THINKING • ELABORATING

What is the meaning of the poem "Loo-Wit"? You might respond in a simple sentence: *"Loo-Wit" is about the eruption of a volcano.* But a skillful thinker will consider a more elaborate response to the question. As you read, try to keep expanding, or elaborating your understanding of a poem by thinking about the different details and images that add rich texture to its meaning.

PRACTICE Reread "Loo-Wit." As you do, pay attention to the details that help you understand the rich texture of the meaning of the poem. In a short paragraph, elaborate on your understanding of the meaning of the poem.

● For more about main idea and details, see **Reading Handbook,** pp. R90–R91.

Before You Read

The Flower-Fed Buffaloes

MEET VACHEL LINDSAY

Vachel Lindsay earned the nickname the Vagabond Poet because as a young man he walked from Illinois to Colorado and New Mexico. Along the way, he performed his poems in return for food and shelter. Lindsay's sense of pride in his country is evident in the patriotic images, strong rhythms, and whimsical folklore found in his poetry. Like Walt Whitman, another poet who traveled widely and wrote about the full panorama of American life, Lindsay felt that poetry should touch upon every kind of human experience.

Vachel Lindsay was born in Springfield, Illinois, in 1879 and died in 1931.

READING FOCUS

Imagine the nineteenth-century landscape of the plains west of the Mississippi River. How do you think the locomotive changed that landscape?

Sharing Ideas

Jot down your ideas and then share them in a small-group discussion.

Setting a Purpose

Read this poem to find out how the speaker views the impact of the locomotive upon the natural environment.

BUILDING BACKGROUND

Did You Know? The word *buffalo* is commonly used to refer to the North American bison, a species of wild cattle. These majestic animals may weigh more than two thousand pounds each and stand more than six feet high. Bison once roamed freely throughout much of North America. There were more than 30 million bison in the grasslands west of the Mississippi River when white settlers first arrived. By the end of the nineteenth century, the bison population had been reduced to about five hundred, and many people feared their extinction. Today, the animals are raised on ranches and protected on refuges, and the bison population is increasing.

The Flower-Fed Buffaloes

Vachel Lindsay

View in the 'Grand Detour', 1852. George Catlin. Oil on canvas, 11⅛ x 14¾ in. Thomas Gilcrease Institute of American History and Art, Tulsa, OK.

The flower-fed buffaloes of the spring
In the days of long ago,
Ranged where the locomotives sing
And the prairie flowers lie low:—
5   The tossing, blooming, perfumed grass
Is swept away by the wheat,
Wheels and wheels and wheels spin by
In the spring that still is sweet.
But the flower-fed buffaloes of the spring
10   Left us, long ago.
They gore° no more, they bellow no more,
They trundle° around the hills no more:—
With the Blackfeet,° lying low,
With the Pawnees,° lying low,
15   Lying low.

11 **gore:** to pierce with a horn, tusk, or sharp weapon.

12 **trundle:** to move or roll along on, or as if on, wheels.

13 The **Blackfeet** are Native Americans who lived east of the Rocky Mountains in what are now Montana and Saskatchewan, Canada. The homeland of the **Pawnees** was what is now west-central Nebraska.

Responding to Literature

PERSONAL RESPONSE

◆ What images from the poem linger in your mind? Record them in your journal.

Analyzing Literature

RECALL AND INTERPRET

1. Where did the buffaloes range in the "days of long ago"? What has the wheat swept away?

2. What spins by now where the buffalo once roamed? What is still sweet?

3. When did the buffaloes leave? Who left with them?

EVALUATE AND CONNECT

4. How does the phrase "flower-fed" affect your image of the buffaloes? What effect does it have on the overall **mood** of the poem?

5. What comparisons does Lindsay make between the past and the present?

6. What meanings do you think Lindsay intended for the phrase "lying low"?

LITERARY ELEMENTS

Alliteration

Alliteration is the repetition of the same or very similar consonant sounds in words that are close together—most often, but not always, at the beginnings of words. In "The Flower-Fed Buffaloes," for example, the *f* sound is repeated in the words *flower* and *fed*. Poets use alliteration to emphasize particular words, to establish a mood, or to give their writing a musical tone.

1. Find and list three other examples of alliteration in "The Flower-Fed Buffaloes."

2. Find another poem that contains alliteration. Describe how alliteration affects the poem.

● See **Literary Terms Handbook**, p. R1.

Extending Your Response

Literature Groups

Theme Discussion Review your notes from the **Reading Focus** on page 822. Then, working in small groups, discuss the theme of "The Flower-Fed Buffaloes."

Performing

Poetry Reading Give your own reading of this poem. Listen to the sounds and rhythms of the poem as you practice reading aloud. When you are ready, read the poem aloud to the class.

Save your work for your portfolio.

COMPARING SELECTIONS

Loo-Wit **and** The Flower-Fed Buffaloes

COMPARE **THEMES**

"Loo-Wit" and "The Flower-Fed Buffaloes" are poems that portray the power and beauty of nature. The theme of nature and its relationship to human beings and civilization plays an important role in both poems.

- How does "Loo-Wit" portray the force of nature? What role do humans play in the poem?

- How does "The Flower-Fed Buffaloes" portray the power and beauty of nature? What role do humans play in this poem?

- Compare and contrast how the relationship between nature and human beings is portrayed in these poems.

View in the 'Grand Detour', 1852 (detail).

COMPARE **POETIC LANGUAGE**

Both poems are filled with sounds, imagery, and figurative language that help readers appreciate the total effect of the poem.

1. In small groups, talk about the total effect of each poem.

2. Pick out your favorite images, sounds, similes, or metaphors from each poem. Talk about each of your examples and why you chose them.

3. Share your thoughts and feelings with your classmates in a full-class forum.

COMPARE **RESPONSES**

Compare your overall feelings and attitudes about these poems. In one or two paragraphs, explain your thoughts and feelings as you answer the following questions:

- How are these poems alike? How are they different?

- Which poem do you prefer? Why?

- Which poem did you learn more from? What did you learn?

Before You Read

Turkeys

MEET BAILEY WHITE

Not many first-grade teachers become famous radio celebrities or have books on the national bestseller list, but Bailey White is no ordinary first-grade teacher. She calls teaching first graders in her south Georgia town her "honorable job." After school she entertains listeners with her regular commentaries on National Public Radio's *All Things Considered*. White has written two collections of humorous autobiographical stories, *Mama Makes Up Her Mind* and *Sleeping at the Starlite Motel*.

Bailey White was born in 1948. This essay was published in 1993.

READING FOCUS

What amusing events do you remember from when you were a very young child? Choose one amusing event from that time in your life.

QuickWrite

Make a list of at least three details that you recall about that past event.

Setting a Purpose

Read this humorous essay to find out about the author's childhood experience with turkeys and ornithologists.

BUILDING BACKGROUND

The Time and Place   It is the 1950s in a small town in southern Georgia.

Did You Know?   An *ornithologist* is a scientist who studies birds. The ornithologists in this selection study birds native to the southeastern United States, including wild turkeys and several kinds of woodpeckers. The chuck-will's-widow, another bird mentioned in the essay, is shown here. These birds resemble whippoorwills but are somewhat larger.

VOCABULARY PREVIEW

domestic (də mes′ tik) *adj.* describes animals living with or near human beings and cared for by them; p. 828

degrade (di grād′) *v.* to lower in character or quality; make less pure; p. 828

demise (di mīz′) *n.* death; end; p. 828

sluggish (slug′ ish) *adj.* lacking energy or alertness; p. 828

elaborate (i lab′ ər it) *adj.* worked out carefully and thoroughly; detailed; complicated; p. 829

undertake (un′ dər tāk′) *v.* to enter into (a task); attempt; p. 829

TURKEYS

Bailey White ⁓

Something about my mother attracts ornithologists.[1]
It all started years ago when a couple of them discovered she had
a rare species of woodpecker coming to her bird feeder. They came
in the house and sat around the window, exclaiming and taking
pictures with big fancy cameras. But long after the red cockaded
woodpeckers had gone to roost in their sticky little holes in the
red hearts of our big old pine trees, and the chuck-will's-widows had
started to sing their night chorus, the ornithologists were still there.

---

1. *Ornithologists* (ôr′ nə thol′ ə jists) are people who study birds or are experts on
   birds.

Turkeys

There always seemed to be three or four of them wandering around our place, discussing the body fat of hummingbirds, telling cruel jokes about people who couldn't tell a pileated woodpecker from an ivory bill,[2] and staying for supper.

In those days, during the 1950s, the big concern of ornithologists in our area was the wild turkey. They were rare, and the pure-strain wild turkeys had begun to interbreed with farmers' <u>domestic</u> stock. The species was being <u>degraded</u>. It was extinction by dilution,[3] and to the ornithologists it was just as tragic as the more dramatic <u>demise</u> of the passenger pigeon or the Carolina parakeet.[4]

One ornithologist had devised a formula to compute the ratio of domestic to pure-strain wild turkey in an individual bird by comparing the angle of flight at takeoff and the rate of acceleration. And in those sad days, the turkeys were flying low and slow.[5]

It was during that time, the spring when I was six years old, that I caught the measles. I had a high fever, and my mother was worried about me. She kept the house quiet and dark and crept around silently, trying different methods of cooling me down.

Even the ornithologists stayed away—but not out of fear of the measles or respect for a household with sickness. The fact was, they had discovered a wild turkey nest. According to the formula, the hen was pure-strain wild—not a taint of the <u>sluggish</u> domestic bird in her blood—and the ornithologists were camping in the woods, protecting her nest from predators and taking pictures.

One night our phone rang. It was one of the ornithologists. "Does your little girl still have measles?" he asked.

"Yes," said my mother. "She's very sick. Her temperature is 102."

"I'll be right over," said the ornithologist.

In five minutes a whole carload of them arrived. They marched solemnly into the house, carrying a cardboard box. "A hundred two, did you say? Where is she?" they asked my mother.

They crept into my room and set the box down on the bed. I was barely conscious, and when I opened my eyes, their worried faces hovering over me seemed to float out of the darkness like giant, glowing eggs.

---

2. The *cockaded woodpeckers* have red crests. The *chuck-will's-widows* are night-flying birds. The *pileated woodpecker* has a bright red crest on the top of its head. Ornithologists use the adjective *pileated* to describe any bird with a bright red crest. *Cockaded* indicates a small tuft of feathers on the top of the head; *ivory bill* refers to an ivory-colored bill.

3. After generations of interbreeding, the wild turkeys became less wild, a weakening *(dilution)* that could lead to their gradual dying out *(extinction)*.

4. Once common in the eastern United States, the *passenger pigeon* and the *Carolina parakeet* are now extinct.

5. Wild turkeys can fly, but domestic turkeys cannot. Their *low and slow* flight indicates that the wild birds have lost much of their pure strain.

Vocabulary

domestic (də mes′ tik) *adj.* describes animals living with or near human beings and cared for by them

degrade (di grād′) *v.* to lower in character or quality; make less pure

demise (di mīz′) *n.* death; end

sluggish (slug′ ish) *adj.* lacking energy or alertness

They snatched the covers off me and felt me all over. They consulted in whispers.

"Feels just right, I'd say."

"A hundred two—can't miss if we tuck them up close and she lies still."

I closed my eyes then, and after a while the ornithologists drifted away, their pale faces bobbing up and down on the black wave of fever.

The next morning I was better. For the first time in days I could think. The memory of the ornithologists with their whispered voices and their bony, cool hands was like a dream from another life. But when I pulled down the covers, there staring up at me with googly eyes and wide mouths, were sixteen fuzzy baby turkeys and the cracked chips and caps of sixteen brown speckled eggs.

I was a sensible child. I gently stretched myself out. The eggshells crackled, and the turkey babies fluttered and cheeped and snuggled against me. I laid my aching head back on the pillow and closed my eyes. "The ornithologists," I whispered. "The ornithologists have been here."

It seems the turkey hen had been so disturbed by the <u>elaborate</u> protective measures that had <u>been</u> <u>undertaken</u> in her behalf that she had abandoned her nest on the night the eggs were due to hatch. It was a cold night. The ornithologists, not having an incubator to hand, used their heads and came up with the next best thing.

The baby turkeys and I gained our strength together. When I was finally able to get out of bed and feebly creep around the house, the turkeys peeped and cheeped around my ankles, scrambling to keep up with me and tripping over their own big spraddle-toed[6] feet. When I went outside for the first time, the turkeys tumbled after me down the steps and scratched around in the yard while I sat in the sun.

Finally, in late summer, the day came when they were ready to fly for the first time as adult birds. The ornithologists gathered. I ran down the hill, and the turkeys ran too. Then, one by one, they took off. They flew high and fast. The ornithologists made V's with their thumbs and forefingers, measuring angles. They consulted their stopwatches and paced off distances. They scribbled in their tiny notebooks. Finally they looked at each other. They sighed. They smiled. They jumped up and down and hugged each other. "One hundred percent pure wild turkey!" they said.

Nearly forty years have passed since then. In many ways the world is a worse place now. But there's a vaccine for measles. And the woods where I live are full of pure wild turkeys. I like to think they are all descendants of those sixteen birds I saved from the vigilance of the ornithologists.

---

6. The toes of a *spraddle-toed* bird spread out in different directions.

❖

Vocabulary
elaborate (i lab′ ər it) *adj.* worked out carefully and thoroughly; detailed; complicated
undertake (un′ dər tāk′) *v.* to enter into (a task); attempt

Responding to Literature

PERSONAL RESPONSE

- ◆ Do you think you would have enjoyed living with Bailey White's family? Why or why not?

Analyzing Literature

RECALL

1. Why did the ornithologists first start coming to Bailey White's house?
2. Why were the scientists concerned about the wild turkeys?
3. Find and quote a passage that tells you something about Bailey White's mother.
4. Why did the ornithologists need Bailey to incubate the eggs?

INTERPRET

5. Do you think Bailey found the ornithologists amusing? Support your opinion.
6. In what ways does the author make clear the scientists' concern for wild turkeys?
7. Do you think Bailey's mother is a generous person? Why or why not?
8. The author says she saved the turkeys "from the vigilance of the ornithologists." What does she mean?

EVALUATE AND CONNECT

9. **Tone** is the attitude a writer expresses about his or her subject. How does White's first sentence help to set the tone of the story?
10. How would you react if a group of scientists barged into your bedroom when you were sick?

LITERARY ELEMENTS

Author's Purpose

The **author's purpose** is the writer's goal in writing a particular work. For example, the author of the humorous essay "Turkeys" probably wanted to **entertain** readers. An author's purpose in writing a newspaper editorial is probably to **persuade** readers of a viewpoint. The purpose of an encyclopedia article is usually to **inform.** Sometimes, especially in serious poetry, an author's purpose is to **express** an idea, a feeling, or a truth.

1. How well does Bailey White achieve her purpose of entertaining her readers? Support your opinion with examples from the selection.

2. What other purpose or purposes does White seem to have? How do you know?

● See **Literary Terms Handbook,** p. R2.

Extending Your Response

Personal Writing

Childhood Memories   Look back at your QuickWrite list from the **Reading Focus** on page 826. Use the details on the list to write a journal entry about that humorous event in your life. Be sure to explain why that event has stayed in your memory. You may want to share your entry with your friends or family.

Literature Groups

Picture This   Imagine that an article about young Bailey's adventures with the turkeys is going to appear in a wildlife magazine. Design a cover for the magazine that features a drawing and brief "teaser" to interest readers in the story. Post all the covers in the room. Discuss how they succeed at grabbing the attention of readers.

*inter*NET
CONNECTION

Did you know that Benjamin Franklin wanted to make the turkey, rather than the bald eagle, our national bird? To learn more about turkeys or other birds, type "birds," or the name of a type of bird, into a search engine.

Writing About Literature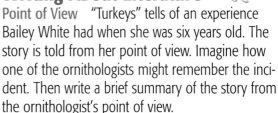

Point of View   "Turkeys" tells of an experience Bailey White had when she was six years old. The story is told from her point of view. Imagine how one of the ornithologists might remember the incident. Then write a brief summary of the story from the ornithologist's point of view.

Interdisciplinary Activity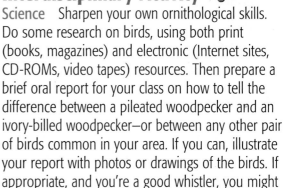

Science   Sharpen your own ornithological skills. Do some research on birds, using both print (books, magazines) and electronic (Internet sites, CD-ROMs, video tapes) resources. Then prepare a brief oral report for your class on how to tell the difference between a pileated woodpecker and an ivory-billed woodpecker—or between any other pair of birds common in your area. If you can, illustrate your report with photos or drawings of the birds. If appropriate, and you're a good whistler, you might also demonstrate how their songs differ.

Reading Further

Here are some more humorous autobiographies you might want to read

My Life and Hard Times by James Thurber

Growing Up by Russell Baker

For a hilarious memoir about an efficiency expert who tried to run his family (which included twelve children) like a factory, try

Cheaper by the Dozen by Frank B. Gilbreth and Ernestine Gilbreth Carey

📖 Save your work for your portfolio.

Skill Minilessons

GRAMMAR AND LANGUAGE • RUN-ON SENTENCES

A **run-on sentence** has two (or more) main clauses run together or separated by only a comma. Correct a run-on sentence in one of these ways:

1. Make two sentences out of it.
2. Turn the run-on sentence into a compound sentence by adding a comma followed by a conjunction (such as *and* or *but*).
3. Use a semicolon to separate the two main clauses.

● For more about run-on sentences, see **Language Handbook,** p. R13.

PRACTICE Use the most appropriate of the three methods to correct each of the following run-ons.

1. At the age of six Bailey caught the measles, she went to bed with a high fever.
2. A mother hen had abandoned her eggs the ornithologists thought Bailey's high body temperature could hatch them.
3. She awoke in the morning to find sixteen baby turkeys in her bed, she gently stretched herself out.
4. The eggshells crackled, the turkey babies fluttered and cheeped and snuggled against her.

READING AND THINKING • CAUSE AND EFFECT

Many events in stories that you read are connected by cause-and-effect relationships. Each event causes others to happen, as this example from "Turkeys" illustrates.

Cause	Effect
Rare woodpecker appears near Bailey's house.	Ornithologists go to Bailey's house and study birds.

PRACTICE Answer these questions about other causes and effects in "Turkeys."

1. What caused the mother turkey to abandon her nest?
2. What action did the ornithologists take because the nest was abandoned?
3. What effects did their action have on Bailey?

● For more about cause and effect, see **Reading Handbook,** pp. R88–R89.

VOCABULARY • THE PREFIX *de-*

The most common meanings of the prefix *de-* are "down or away from" and "do the opposite of." In *degrade,* the prefix has the "down" meaning. When wild turkeys are *degraded,* their quality is lowered. The prefix in *decode,* has the opposite meaning. If you *decode* a message, you put the coded message back into normal language.

● For more about prefixes, see **Reading Handbook,** p. R83.

PRACTICE Use the two common meanings of *de-* to match each word with its meaning.

1. depress   a. to bleach
2. devalue   b. to push down
3. decolorize   c. to remove a bad smell
4. deforest   d. to cut down all the trees
5. deodorize   e. to make (something) worth less

Reading and Thinking Skills

Making Inferences

Skillful writers provide many details about the characters, events, and action in a piece of writing. By reading carefully, however, you can figure out even more than you're directly told. Read and think about this passage from "Uncle Tony's Goat."

> I stepped around into the low doorway, and the goat charged toward me, feet first. I had dirt in my mouth and up my nose and there was blood running past my eye: my head ached.

From the details about the dirt and the blood, you can figure out that the goat knocked the narrator to the ground. When you use what you know to figure out what you think is happening in a story, you are inferring, or **making inferences.** An inference is a conclusion based on details that are known.

● For more about making inferences, see **Reading Handbook,** pp. R92–R93.

EXERCISE

Read the following excerpt from "Turkeys." Then answer the questions.

> Something about my mother attracts ornithologists. It all started years ago when a couple of them discovered she had a rare species of woodpecker coming to her bird feeder. They came in the house and sat around the window, exclaiming and taking pictures with big fancy cameras. But long after the red cockaded woodpeckers had gone to roost in their sticky little holes in the red hearts of our big old pine trees, and the chuck-will's-widows had started to sing their night chorus, the ornithologists were still there.

1. What inferences can you make about the narrator's mother? What clues helped you make that inference?

2. What inferences can you make about the place where the narrator grew up?

3. What inferences can you make about how the narrator feels about the ornithologists? How do your experience and the details in the selection help you make this inference?

Before You Read

The Pasture

MEET ROBERT FROST

Robert Frost worked as a mill worker, a shoemaker, a schoolteacher, a newspaper editor, and a farmer before he finally became a published poet. He lived most of his adult life on farms in Vermont and New Hampshire. "Three things have followed me," he wrote, "writing, teaching, and a little farming." His poems, inspired by the rural life and scenery of New England, are known for their plain language and natural rhythms.

Robert Frost was born in 1874 and died in 1963.

READING FOCUS

How do you feel about chores you're asked to do? Do you think it's possible to enjoy doing chores?

Sharing Ideas

Think about the questions above. Then share your thoughts in a small-group discussion. Does everyone feel the same way?

Setting a Purpose

Read this poem to discover how the speaker feels about his chores.

BUILDING BACKGROUND

Robert Frost, one of the most honored poets in America, won the Pulitzer Prize for Poetry four times. In 1961, when John F. Kennedy was elected president of the United States, Frost made history. At age eighty-seven, he became the first poet to read a poem at a presidential inauguration. His poem, "The Gift Outright," was heard by millions of people.

The Pasture

Robert Frost

I'm going out to clean the pasture spring;
I'll only stop to rake the leaves away
(And wait to watch the water clear, I may):
I sha'n't be gone long.—You come too.

I'm going out to fetch the little calf
That's standing by the mother. It's so young,
It totters when she licks it with her tongue.
I sha'n't be gone long.—You come too.

Autumn, 1958. Eric Sloane. Oil on Masonite, 26¾ x 21¾ in. Private collection. Would the title "You Come Too" be appropriate for this painting? Why or why not?

Responding to Literature

PERSONAL RESPONSE

◆ Did the poem make you rethink the ideas that you shared in the **Reading Focus** on page 834? Explain.

Analyzing Literature

RECALL

1. What is the speaker going out to clean? What might he wait for?
2. What is the other chore the speaker is planning?

INTERPRET

3. Imagine and describe the speaker of "The Pasture."
4. Why do you think the poet ends both stanzas with the same line?

EVALUATE AND CONNECT

5. Whom do you think the speaker is inviting to "come too"?
6. What is the purpose of the dashes in lines 4 and 8? How would the poem sound different without the dashes?
7. Find an example of **alliteration** in the poem. (See **Literary Terms Handbook,** page R1.) How does this poetic device affect the way you read the poem aloud?
8. How does Frost make a common farm chore seem interesting? Use examples from the poem to explain your answer.
9. Theme Connection   What can you infer from the second stanza about the speaker's attitude toward his farm animals?
10. Personal Connection   What chores could you do that might make you feel happy and satisfied?

LITERARY ELEMENTS

Rhythm: End-Stopped Lines

When a pause occurs naturally at the end of a line of poetry, it is called an **end-stopped line.** The length of the stop, as you read or recite the poem, depends on the sense of the words and the kind of punctuation used. A period, question mark, exclamation point, colon, or semicolon generally call for a somewhat longer stop than a comma or dash. When a poet uses no punctuation at all, readers need to use the sense of the words to figure out whether lines are end-stopped. Because end-stops at every line can make a poem, especially a long one, seem monotonous, most poets generally avoid using them at every line.

1. Which lines in "The Pasture" are end-stopped? What punctuation marks does Frost use to indicate the pauses?

2. Read "The Pasture" out loud twice. First stop at the end of each line. Then pause only when the punctuation directs you to do so. Which reading makes the poem easier to understand?

● See **Literary Terms Handbook,** p. R9.

Extending Your Response

Writing About Literature

Mood The speaker in the poem seems to anticipate enjoying his chores. Write a paragraph describing the mood of the poem. How does the invitation at the end of each stanza contribute to the mood?

Listening and Speaking

A Frost Menagerie Many of Robert Frost's poems mention animals. Collect a few of these poems and read them aloud with a partner.

Creative Writing

An Invitation Try to think about your own chores in a more interesting way. Write a poem inviting someone to join you as you go about your work.

Literature Groups

Pastoral Images The images in "The Pasture" are vivid and concrete. Draw a picture of the image created in one of the stanzas. Then compare your work with others and choose the drawing that best conveys the poet's vision of farm life.

Reading Further

Here are some other books by and about Robert Frost you may enjoy reading:

You Come, Too by Robert Frost

A Restless Spirit by Natalie S. Bober

📕 **Save your work for your portfolio.**

Skill Minilesson

GRAMMAR AND LANGUAGE • MECHANICS: SEMICOLON, COLON

The semicolon and colon separate parts of a sentence that might otherwise be confused.

Rule 1: Use a semicolon to join parts of a compound sentence when a conjunction, such as *and, but,* or *or,* is not used.

Frost wrote poetry; he also worked a farm.

Rule 2: Use a colon to introduce a list of items that end a sentence. Use words such as *these* or *the following* to signal that a list is coming.

Try these books by Frost: *Birches; You Come, Too; Christmas Trees.*

PRACTICE Practice the rules by adding a semicolon or colon to each sentence.

1. This bicycle comes in the following colors red, blue, silver, and black.
2. Soccer clubs are very popular these clubs often play clubs from other cities.
3. We bought a new computer I'm eager to try it.
4. When you pack for the camping trip take these items flashlight, sleeping bag, warm clothes.

● For more about semicolons and colons, see **Language Handbook,** pp. R38–R39.

SHORT FORMS OF POETRY

H aiku, cinquains, and limericks are all short forms of poetry. Do you know this classic haiku?

> An old silent pond . . .
> A frog jumps into the pond,
> splash! Silence again.
>
> —*Matsuo Bashō*

Over three centuries old, this haiku was written in Japanese by Matsuo Bashō (mät sü′ ō bä′ shō), the poet who perfected the haiku form.

HAIKU

Haiku originated in Japan. A traditional haiku has only three lines made up of five syllables, seven syllables, and five syllables. Within this compact form, poets present simple images, often linked by unstated connections. It's left up to readers to discover, or to imagine, what the connections might be. What connections can you discover in the following haiku by an American writer?

> A balmy spring wind
> Reminding me of something
> I cannot recall
>
> —*Richard Wright*

Haiku are as striking for what they don't include as for what they do. Traditional haiku have no rhyme and no figures of speech. They usually include at least one nature image and one, often subtle, reference to a specific season of the year. (In the haiku by Bashō, the frog suggests summer.)

Translators of haiku sometimes maintain the traditions and sometimes alter them. In English translation, some haiku have fewer or more than seventeen syllables, and some even include rhyme:

> A morning-glory vine
> all blossoming, has thatched
> this hut of mine.
>
> —*Kobayashi Issa,*
> *translated by Harold G. Henderson*

As poets of many eras and cultures work with haiku, they may change the form, adding new features, such as titles, or creating more modern images using figures of speech.

The New and the Old

Railroad tracks; a flight
of wild geese close above them
in the moonlit night.

—*Shiki*

What remains unchanged, despite any gulf of time or culture, is the essence of haiku: simplicity, depth, and a bond between human beings and the natural world.

CINQUAINS

Over time, haiku has influenced many forms of poetry, including one form called the **cinquain.** Invented by Adelaide Crapsey, the cinquain consists of five lines made up of two, four, six, eight, and two syllables, respectively. What elements of haiku do you recognize in the following cinquain?

A Warning

Just now,
Out of the strange
Still dusk . . . as strange, as still . . .
A white moth flew. Why am I grown
So cold?

—*Adelaide Crapsey*

Like haiku, the five-line, unrhymed cinquain uses imagery to suggest its real topic or theme and evoke emotion in the reader. In this case, the speaker suddenly, "just now,"

becomes aware of her own mortality. The theme of mortality is suggested by the time of day, dusk; by the short-lived white moth; and by the speaker's sensation of growing cold.

LIMERICKS

Another short poetic form is the **limerick.** While the haiku and cinquain usually suggest a more serious or delicate topic and tone, the limerick is *always* funny. Part of the fun of a limerick is its rhyme pattern.

No matter how grouchy you're feeling,
A smile is always quite healing;
It grows like a wreath
All around the front teeth,
Thus preventing the face from
congealing.

The limerick consists of five lines rhyming *aabba.* (See *rhyme* in **Literary Terms Handbook,** page R9.) Many limericks begin with some variation of the opening lines "There was a young lady of. . . ." or "There was a young man from. . . ."

The limerick's origin is unknown, but it may have come from an eighteenth-century Irish song. In the early twentieth century, the limerick became quite popular. Followers of the form made the verse more complicated by creating tongue twisters. How quickly can you read aloud this anonymous limerick?

A tutor who taught on the flute
Tried to teach two tooters to toot.
Said the two to the tutor,
"Is it harder to toot, or
To tutor two tooters to toot?"

Before You Read

Short Poems

MEET THE POETS

Matsuo Bashō, who was born into the samurai, or warrior class, started writing poetry at the age of nine. Bashō taught poetry to many devoted students.

Bashō was probably born in 1644 and died in 1694.

Raymond R. Patterson was born in New York City. A former director of Black Poets Reading, Patterson also wrote a newspaper column on African American history.

Raymond R. Patterson was born in 1929.

Ann Atwood has been influenced by nature throughout her life. Many of her books and films fuse poetry with nature photography.

Ann Atwood was born in 1913.

Myra Cohn Livingston edited dozens of books of poetry for younger readers and taught the writing of poetry to both children and adults.

Myra Cohn Livingston was born in 1926 and died in 1996.

READING FOCUS

Have you ever heard the expression "Less is more"? Using as few words as possible, how would you describe an ordinary object, such as your locker or a chair?

QuickWrite

Jot down a few words describing an object you can see right now.

Setting a Purpose

Read these short poems first for enjoyment and then to become familiar with their forms.

BUILDING BACKGROUND

Did You Know?   The seventeenth-century Japanese poet Matsuo Bashō is generally acknowledged as the innovator and master of the haiku form. One story about Bashō illustrates his approach to haiku. While walking one day, Bashō and a young student watched dragonflies darting through the fields. The student quickly made up a poem: "Red dragonflies! / Take off their wings, / and they are pepper pods!" Bashō responded, "No! That is not haiku. If you wish to make a haiku on the subject, you must say: "Red pepper pods! / Add wings to them, / and they are dragonflies!"

Matsuo Bashō

Raymond R. Patterson

Ann Atwood

Myra Cohn Livingston

Glory, Glory . . .

Haiku by Raymond R. Patterson ∼

Across Grandmother's knees
A kindly sun
Laid a yellow quilt.

Birds Circling at Dusk

Haiku by Ann Atwood ∼

Birds circling at dusk.
The first night of my journey—
yet how far from home!

Bamboo Grove

Haiku by Matsuo Bashō ∼

Song of the cuckoo:
    in the grove of great bamboos,
        moonlight seeping through.

T-Shirt

Cinquain by
Myra Cohn Livingston ∾

T-shirt,
you're my best thing
though you've faded so much
no one knows what you said when you
were new.

There Was a Young Fellow of Ealing

Anonymous Limerick ∾

There was a young fellow of Ealing,
Endowed with such delicate feeling,
   When he read, on the door,
   "Don't spit on the floor,"
He jumped up and spat on the ceiling.

Responding to Literature

PERSONAL RESPONSE

◆ Which of the poems did you enjoy most? Explain why.

Analyzing Literature

RECALL

1. What are the **settings** of the three haiku?
2. In what condition is the T-shirt in the cinquain?
3. What funny event occurs in the limerick?

INTERPRET

4. In each haiku, what words or phrases provide clues to the time of day?
5. What might the T-shirt have said when it was new?
6. Why does the event make the limerick funny?

EVALUATE AND CONNECT

7. In your opinion, how does the Japanese poet Bashō feel about nature? Explain your answer.
8. In what ways are the three haiku similar and different?
9. Which poem do you think makes the most effective use of the least number of words? Why?
10. Which poem would you most like to share with another person? Explain why.

LITERARY ELEMENTS

Personification

Personification is a figure of speech in which an idea, object, or animal is given human form or human characteristics. The sentence *The impatient alarm clock shook me out of bed* is an example of personification. An object, an alarm clock, is described as though it were an impatient parent trying to get a sleepy child out of bed. Authors use personification to make their writing more vivid and to describe things in a way that people can imagine and understand.

1. Identify how personification is used in one of the poems.

2. Paraphrase the poem in one sentence without using personification. Do you think your image is as powerful as the poem's? Why or why not?

3. Using the photo at the left, write a short poem of your own using personification.

● See **Literary Terms Handbook,** p. R8.

Extending Your Response

Writing About Literature

Imagery and Mood   Choose one of the three haiku. Decide what mood the poem creates. Then think about the poem's imagery. Write a paragraph telling how the imagery builds or supports the poem's mood.

Listening and Speaking

Inspired by Nature   Traditional haiku always contains an image from nature. With a partner, look around your classroom and out the window. Find a class pet or plant or a glimpse of the sky, a tree, an insect—any natural object or being—for inspiration. Collaborate with your partner to write a haiku about what you observe. Recite your haiku to the class.

Literature Groups

Snapshots   If you think of a short poem as a snapshot of a moment, what would the snapshots look like from each of the five poems? Work with your group to discuss your ideas. Sketch them if you wish. Which snapshot contains the least detail and which contains the most? Compare your group's ideas with those of other groups.

Performing

Readers Theater   Work with a small group to collect five or six short poems on a specific theme. Try to include a variety of short forms, such as haiku, cinquain, limerick, or any other short poem. Read your collection of poems aloud to the class. Have the class guess the theme of your collection and suggest a title for it.

Creative Writing

Short Poem   Use one of the poems as a model for writing your own cinquain or limerick about the object you described in the **Reading Focus** on page 840.

Reading Further

If you wish to read more short poems, try these books:

O Sliver of Liver by Myra Cohn Livingston

Red Dragonfly on My Shoulder translated by Sylvia Cassedy and Kunihiro Suetake

Birds, Beasts, and the Third Thing by D. H. Lawrence

Save your work for your portfolio.

Skill Minilessons

GRAMMAR AND LANGUAGE • PREPOSITIONAL PHRASES

A **preposition** is a word that relates a noun or a pronoun to some other word in the sentence. A **prepositional phrase** is a group of words that begins with a preposition and ends with a noun or pronoun, which is called the **object of the preposition.**

He jumped up and spat on the ceiling.

In this sentence, *on* is a preposition, and *on the ceiling* is the prepositional phrase. The object of the preposition is *ceiling.*

Commonly Used Prepositions			
about	before	for	on
above	behind	from	out
across	below	in	since
against	between	like	through
at	during	near	with

PRACTICE Write the prepositional phrase from each of the following sentences. Underline the preposition.

1. Haiku and cinquain are two short forms of poetry.
2. Centuries have passed since Bashō wrote his poems.
3. Within every classic haiku, there is one powerful image.
4. I'm looking for a startling image.
5. Across Grandmother's knees / A kindly sun / Laid a yellow quilt.

● For more about prepositional phrases, see **Language Handbook,** p. R30.

READING AND THINKING • SPATIAL RELATIONSHIPS/SPATIAL ORDER

Spatial relationships describe how things relate to one another in physical space. Matsuo Bashō's description of the "moonlight seeping *through*" helps readers imagine the image of the moonlight in the bamboo grove. Writers use words like *through, across, above, below, under,* and *next to* to help the reader understand the spatial order of the images in the poem and the relationship between the speaker and the things described.

PRACTICE Reread the three haiku and think about where the images the poets describe are in relationship to one another and to the speaker. Write a sentence or two about each poem using words that describe spatial relationships. Then underline those words.

● For more about spatial order, see **Reading Handbook,** p. R91.

VOCABULARY • COMPOUND WORDS

Moonlight is a common image in haiku. *Moonlight* is a **compound word,** a word made by joining two words to make a new word. Compound words can be spelled closed (*birthday*), hyphenated (*worn-out*), or open (*high school*). When writing compound words, remember to keep the original spelling of both words.

PRACTICE Combine words from both columns to make five compound words.

1. grand   berry
2. row   board
3. touch   mother
4. blue   down
5. card   boat

*W*riting WORKSHOP

Expository Writing: Research Report

In a national park, heavy smog damage causes officials to consider banning cars from the park. In a city, a decision about airport sites affects a rare animal's survival. Nature's way and people's way–how are they connected? Often we don't find out until they clash. By researching the causes and effects of a conflict, you can clarify your position on an issue and gain new insights as well.

Assignment: Follow the process explained in these pages to develop a research report exploring cause-and-effect relationships in an environmental issue.

● As you write your research report, refer to the **Writing Handbook,** pp. R55–R99.

EVALUATION RUBRIC

By the time you complete this Writing Workshop, you will have

- written a research report that examines the causes and effects of an environmental problem
- developed an introduction that captures attention and includes a position statement
- supported each cause and effect with accurate, convincing evidence
- documented sources accurately in a bibliography or a list of works cited
- created a conclusion that restates your position
- presented a research report that is free of errors in grammar, usage, and mechanics

The Writing Process

PREWRITING

PREWRITING TIP
Don't be fooled by coincidences. Remember that an event that came before another event hasn't necessarily caused it. Make sure a genuine cause-and-effect relationship exists. Don't forget that many events have multiple causes and effects.

● Select an Issue

You may find issues in selections from this theme. For other ideas, watch television news and scan newspapers and magazines for environmental issues. Talk with parents and friends about issues affecting your community. You might also brainstorm a list of issues with your classmates. Use a computer to create an electronic database of environmental issues to research. Then choose one that you care about.

● Research Causes and Effects

Before and during your research stage, pose relevant questions about your topic. What specific questions might you or your readers have? What are some causes and effects involved? As you research, try to find answers for these questions. Use Tips for Asking Research Questions in the **Reading Handbook,** page R100.

Issue: Florida's manatees are endangered.

Causes	Effects
People go boating in waters where manatees live. Manatees don't know that propellers are dangerous.	Manatees are injured or killed in collisions with boats.
People build floodgates and canal locks.	Manatees drown or are crushed in floodgates and canal locks.
People put buoys and other foreign objects in the water.	Manatees become entangled in buoy lines and choke to death on foreign objects.

Use a Variety of Sources

View nature programs, interview experts, or research your issue at the library or on the Internet. As you collect information, record your sources on **source cards** and make **note cards** for the information that you want to include in your report.

Evaluate Your Sources

Make sure that your sources are accurate, that statements are supported by evidence, and that authors are unbiased. To evaluate information from television or the Internet, use critical viewing guidelines from **Listening, Speaking, and Viewing** on page 817.

Customize for Audience and Purpose

Will you write for people who might take action, such as government officials? Or will you write to increase awareness among students? Decide which details will mean the most to your readers, and make those details stand out.

Use Graphics

Forming a chain, causes lead to effects, which in turn become new causes, leading to further effects. Create a graphic similar to the one below to keep cause-and-effect relationships clear. Then write a position statement to set the direction of your draft.

Point: Accidents involving floodgates kill manatees.

| Floodgate is opened to control flooding.

Cause | → | Water rushes in through floodgate.

Effect/Cause | → | Rushing water creates strong current.

Effect/Cause | → | Current pulls in slow-swimming manatees.

Effect/Cause | → | Held by current, manatees can't rise to surface to breathe.

Effect/Cause | → | Manatees drown.

Effect/Cause |

Writing WORKSHOP

DRAFTING

DRAFTING TIP

Before you begin drafting the body of your report, look at the questions about your topic that you wrote in the prewritting stage and used to guide your research. Discard any questions that no longer seem relevant to your goal. Use the answers to the remaining questions to help you focus and shape your report.

● Start with an Anecdote

A brief vivid story illustrating your issue can be a powerful opener. Put your position statement at the end of the introduction.

● Explain Connections

Explain the causes and effects of your main points. Discuss multiple causes and effects and cause-and-effect chains. Include memorable details. You might conclude a restatement of your position or with a prediction about the future.

STUDENT MODEL • DRAFTING

Let's do our part to make sure that manatees continue to swim in the waters of Florida long after we are gone. When all is said and done, the future of the manatee is up to us.

Complete Student Model on pp. R114–R115.

REVISING

REVISING TIP

Some transitional words or phrases you can use to show cause and effect include *as a result of, because, so, therefore, consequently, this is why, the result is,* and *for this reason.*

● Make Adjustments

This is the time to fine-tune. Look over your draft and consider possible improvements, using the **Rubric for Revising** as a guide.

● Check Documentation

Refer to the **Writing Handbook** on pages R55-R59 or search the Internet for information about citing sources and creating a final list of works cited.

RUBRIC FOR REVISING

Your revised research report should have

- an introduction that includes an anecdote and ends with a position statement
- an explanation of causes and effects based on accurate, reliable evidence
- a conclusion that restates your position
- an accurate, correctly formatted bibliography or list of works cited

Your revised research report should be free of

- irrelevant information
- errors in documentation, grammar, usage, and mechanics

EDITING/PROOFREADING

Find and correct errors in grammar and mechanics. The **Proofreading Checklist** can help. Watch especially for incorrect use of apostrophes, as shown in the **Grammar Link** on page 816.

Grammar Hint

When you use commas with a series of words or phrases, be sure to put in all the commas—not just the first one:

Rain forests exist in Africa, South America, North America, and Southeast Asia.

PROOFREADING CHECKLIST

☑ Commas are used correctly. (Double-check commas with words in a series.)

☑ Modifiers are used correctly.

☑ There are no fragments or run-ons.

☑ Verbs agree with subjects.

☑ Pronouns agree with antecedents.

☑ Spelling, punctuation, and capitalization are correct.

STUDENT MODEL · EDITING/PROOFREADING

Manatees are gentle, playful intellent mammals.
                              ∧,

Complete Student Model on pp. R114–115.

Complete Student Model

For a complete version of the model developed in this Workshop, see **Writing Workshop Models**, pp. R114–R115.

TECHNOLOGY TIP
Some word processing programs let you design graphics and insert them into your essay.

PUBLISHING/PRESENTING

PRESENTING TIP
For a panel discussion, make your visual aids poster-sized.

Try creating graphic visual aids, such as graphs or cause-and-effect diagrams, to illustrate your ideas. Then share your writing with classmates. You and others who explored related issues might present your papers in a panel discussion.

Reflecting

After thinking about the following questions, write your responses.

- Does your writing focus more on causes or on effects? Why?

- For what other classes might you write papers exploring cause-and-effect connections? What topics might you examine?

💾 **Save your work for your portfolio.**

Theme Assessment

Responding to the Theme

1. Which story, poem, or narrative in this theme helped you to better understand the relationships between humans and nature? Explain your answer.

2. What new ideas do you have about the following as a result of reading the literature in this theme?
   - people's attitudes and actions toward animals and nature
   - the importance of the relationship between nature and human beings

3. Present your theme project to the class.

Analyzing Literature

COMPARE SELECTIONS

Choose pieces from this unit to compare. You may compare the characters, settings, descriptions, or themes. You may compare how two pieces in different forms—such as a poem and a short story—illustrate the theme "A Delicate Balance." Support your ideas with quotations from the selections.

Evaluate and Set Goals

1. Which of the following tasks was most rewarding to you? Which was most difficult?
   - reading and thinking about the selections
   - doing independent writing
   - analyzing the selections in discussions
   - making presentations
   - performing dramatizations

2. Using the following scale, how would you assess your work in this theme? Give at least two reasons for your assessment.
   4 = outstanding   2 = fair
   3 = good   1 = weak

3. Based on what you found difficult in this theme, choose a goal to work toward to increase your understanding of literature next year.
   - Write down your goal and three steps you will take to try to reach it.
   - Next fall, meet with your teacher to review your goal and your plan for achieving it.

Build Your Portfolio

SELECT

Select two pieces of work you did during this theme to include in your portfolio. Use the following questions to help you decide.

- Which do you consider your best work?
- Which work "stretched" you the most?
- Which work did you enjoy the most?

REFLECT

Write some notes to accompany the work you selected. Use these questions to guide you.

- What do you like best about the piece?
- What did you learn from creating it?
- What might you do differently if you were beginning this piece again?

Reading on Your Own

If you have enjoyed the literature in this theme, you might also be interested in the following books.

The Call of the Wild

By Jack London Buck, a domestic dog, is taken from his home to serve as a sled dog during the Klondike gold rush. Amidst the wolves of the Far North, he begins to hear "the call of the wild."

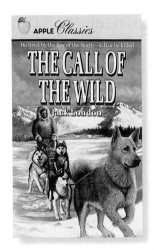

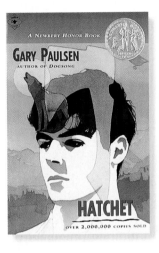

Hatchet

by Gary Paulsen
Brian, the only survivor of a plane crash in the Canadian wilderness, must try to stay alive with nothing more than the clothes on his back and a hatchet.

Cricket Never Does: A Collection of Haiku and Tanka

by Myra Cohn Livingston This collection of modern poems using the traditional Japanese forms of haiku and tanka presents poems for each of the seasons.

My Life with the Chimpanzees

by Jane Goodall The world's leading authority on chimpanzees describes her thirty years of living with and studying the chimpanzees of Tanzania.

Standardized Test Practice

Read the following passage. Then read each question on page 853. Decide which is the best answer to each question. Mark the letter for that answer on your paper.

Why Have Flatbreads Always Been So Popular?

In many parts of the world, bread is not baked in the loaves that are commonly eaten in the United States. Instead, it is baked in thin sheets known as "flatbread." One of the most familiar types of flatbread is pita, which comes from the eastern Mediterranean. Pita bread is soft and is often used as a pocket of bread, into which meat or vegetables are placed to make a sandwich. Pita is gaining popularity and recognition as more people experiment with new types of baked goods. Many types of flatbread can be found in supermarkets and bakeries today.

The history of flatbread goes back several thousand years. It is one of the oldest known prepared foods. People have eaten flatbread wherever there was grain available because it is nourishing, it is easy to prepare, and it keeps well over time.

Many types of grain are used in the creation of flatbread, including rye, oats, corn, wheat, rice, and buckwheat. Sometimes vegetables are used as well; potatoes, chickpeas, and lentils add flavor and texture to the bread. Flatbreads can have unusual and distinctive tastes depending on the ingredients used. For example, "Sweet Armenian" bread is flavored with maleb, a black cherry pit. In Asia, a black onion seed, nigella, is added to the mixture. Ethiopians use teff flour for a unique molasses flavor. The additional ingredients often provide additional nutrients.

The way in which a flatbread is baked varies from place to place. No matter how it is done, flatbread is considered one of the world's great fast foods because of its rapid cooking time. This is an important quality in countries where fuel is scarce and needs to be conserved. In Asia, flatbread is baked in a tandoor. This barrel-shaped oven has hot coals in its center. The bread is slapped to the sides of the oven, and heat transfers rapidly from the oven sides to the bread. On the other hand, injeras (an Ethiopian sourdough), chapatis (an Indian bread), and tortillas (a Latin American bread) are often baked in a large, hot skillet over an open fire or on the flat surface of a wood-burning stove. Amazingly, Algerians and Tunisians can bake bread right on the fiery desert sand. Malaysians throw the dough up in the air over and over again until it becomes paper thin. Then they twist it and cook it on a griddle. The Hopi of North America made special piki stones that they used for baking flatbreads, a tradition that was passed down from generation to generation.

Another important quality of flatbreads is that they are easy to store and preserve. In countries where the winters are long, people dry the bread after it is baked to help preserve a grain supply that needs to endure many cold months.

Flatbreads have varied ingredients and preparation techniques, and they can be used in many ways. Today we are rediscovering the nutritious, fast, and long-lasting flatbreads of many different cultures, enriching our own culinary offerings.

---

1 According to the passage, maleb and nigella can be used as ingredients in flatbreads to make them —
   A rise slowly
   B taste good
   C last longer
   D cook faster

2 Why did the author start the passage by mentioning pita bread?
   J To help readers recall what they already know about flatbreads
   K To show that pita bread is not as popular as other flatbreads
   L To persuade readers to eat pita bread
   M To describe how pita bread is used

3 Based on the information in the passage, you can predict that —

A flatbreads will no longer be baked soon.
B new ways of cooking flatbreads will continue to be found.
C flatbreads will continue to be baked for a long time.
D all breads will now be flatbreads.

4 After it is in the tandoor, the flatbread must then be —
   J cooked on a hot skillet.
   K thrown up into the air over and over.
   L twisted and cooked on a hot griddle.
   M slapped against the sides of the oven.

5 You would most likely find this article in —
   A a newspaper.
   B an almanac.
   C an encyclopedia.
   D an instruction manual.

6 The author provides evidence to suggest that —
   J pita bread is the most popular flatbread in the world.
   K flatbreads are more common in South America than in Central Asia.
   L flatbreads need many flavorings to make them tasty.
   M flatbreads have been popular for a long time throughout the world.

Reference Section

Literary Terms Handbook

A

Act A major unit of a drama. A play may be subdivided into several acts. Many modern plays have two or three acts. A short play can be composed of one or more scenes but only one act—for example, Walter Hackett's adaptation of Mark Twain's *The Million-Pound Bank Note.*

> See page 500.
> See also SCENE.

Alliteration The repitition of consonant sounds, usually at the beginnings of words or syllables. Alliteration gives emphasis to words. For example, the following line from "The Highwayman," by Alfred Noyes, contains an example of alliteration:

Over the cobbles he clattered and clashed in the dark innyard. . . .

> See page 824.

Allusion A reference in a work of literature to a well-known character, place, or situation in history, politics, or science or from another work of literature, music, or art. For example, the title of Borden Deal's "Antaeus" is an allusion to the name of the mighty wrestler from Greek mythology whose enormous strength came from his contact with the earth.

> See page 357.

Analogy A comparison between two things, based on one or more elements that they share. Analogies can help the reader visualize an idea. In informational text, analogies are often used to explain something unfamiliar in terms of something known. For example, a science book might compare the flow of electricity to water moving through a hose. In literature, most analogies are expressed in metaphors or similes.

> See also METAPHOR, SIMILE.

Anecdote A brief, entertaining story based on a single interesting or humorous incident or event. Anecdotes are frequently biographical and reveal some aspect of a person's character.

Antagonist A person or force that opposes the protagonist, or central character, in a story or a drama. The reader is generally meant not to sympathize with the antagonist. For example, Margot's entire class is her antagonist in "All Summer in a Day," by Ray Bradbury.

> See also CONFLICT, PROTAGONIST.

Anthropomorphism Representing animals as if they had human emotions and intelligence. Fables and fairy tales often contain anthropomorphism. "Rikki-tikki-tavi," by Rudyard Kipling, is another example of this technique.

> See page 802.

Aside In a play, a comment made by a character that is heard by the audience but not by the other characters onstage. The speaker turns to one side, or "aside," away from the other characters onstage. Asides are common in older plays—you will find many in Shakespeare's plays—but are infrequent in modern drama.

Assonance The repetition of vowel sounds, especially in a line of poetry. For example, the following line from "The Women's 400 Meters," by Lillian Morrison, contains an example of assonance:

they flex knees, drum heels and / shiver at the starting line

> See also RHYME, SOUND DEVICES.

Author's purpose The intention of the writer. For example, the purpose of a story may be to entertain, to describe, to explain, to persuade, or a combination of these purposes. "A Crush," by Cynthia Rylant, both tells an entertaining story and describes.

See page 830.

Autobiography The story of a person's life written by that person. *Rosa Parks: My Story,* by Rosa Parks with Jim Haskins, is an example of autobiography.

See pages 62–63.
See also BIOGRAPHY, MEMOIR.

B

Ballad A short musical narrative song or poem. Folk ballads, which usually tell of an exciting or dramatic episode, were passed on by word of mouth for generations before being written down. Literary ballads are written in imitation of folk ballads. "Annabel Lee," by Edgar Allan Poe, is an example of a literary ballad.

See also NARRATIVE POETRY.

Biography The account of a person's life written by someone other than the subject. Biographies can be short or book-length. In "New Directions," Maya Angelou writes a biographical sketch of her grandmother.

See page 223.
See also AUTOBIOGRAPHY, MEMOIR.

C

Character A person in a literary work. (If a character is an animal, it displays human traits.) Characters who show varied and sometimes con-tradictory traits, such as the alternately stern and compassionate Mary in Dorothy M. Johnson's "Too Soon a Woman," are called **round.** Characters who reveal only one personality trait, like the flinty father in the same story, are called **flat.** A **stereotype** is a flat character of a familiar and often-repeated type. A **dynamic** character changes during the story. A **static** character remains primarily the same throughout the story.

See page 180.

Characterization The methods a writer uses to develop the personality of the character. In **direct characterization,** the narrator makes direct statements about a character's personality. In **indirect characterization,** the writer reveals a character's personality through the character's words and actions and through what other characters think and say about the character. These techniques are frequently blended, as in the characterization of Margot in Ray Bradbury's "All Summer in a Day."

See page 406.

Climax The point of greatest emotional intensity, interest, or suspense in a narrative. Usually the climax comes at the turning point in a story or drama, the point at which the resolution of the conflict becomes clear. The climax in O. Henry's "After Twenty Years" occurs when Bob discovers that the man he thinks is Jimmy Wells is actually someone else.

See page 550.

Comedy A type of drama that is humorous and has a happy ending. A heroic comedy focuses on the exploits of a larger-than-life hero. In American popular culture, comedy can take the form of a scripted performance involving one or more performers—either as a skit that is part of a variety show, as in vaudeville, or as a stand-up monologue. "Who's on First," by Bud Abbott and Lou Costello, is an example of a comedic skit with its roots in vaudeville.

See also HUMOR.

Conflict The central struggle between opposing forces in a story or drama. An **external conflict** exists when a character struggles against some outside force, such as nature, society, fate, or another person—for example, the struggle of the two scientists with the Multivac computer in Isaac Asimov's "Key Item." An **internal conflict** exists within the mind of a character who is torn between opposing feelings or goals—as Antonio and Felix grapple with their desire for the championship and their reluctance to fight each other in "Amigo Brothers," by Piri Thomas.

> See page 53.
> See also ANTAGONIST, PLOT, PROTAGONIST.

Consonance A pleasing combination of sounds, especially in poetry. Consonance usually refers to the repetition of consonant sounds in stressed syllables. Notice, for example, the echoing *p* sounds in the following lines from "Slam, Dunk, & Hook," by Yusef Komunyakaa:

. . . Trouble / Was there slapping a blackjack / Against an open palm. . . .

> See also SOUND DEVICES.

D

Description Writing that seeks to convey the impression of a setting, a person, an animal, an object, or an event by appealing to the senses. Almost all writing, fiction and nonfiction, contains elements of description. The following example of descriptive writing comes from "Lob's Girl," by Joan Aiken:

Instinctively she shut her eyes and felt the sand being wiped off her face by something that seemed like a warm, rough, damp flannel. . . . It was a tongue. Its owner was a large and bouncy young Alsatian, or German shepherd, with topaz eyes, black-tipped prick ears, a thick, soft coat, and a bushy black-tipped tail.

> See page 73.

Details Particular features of things used to make descriptions more accurate and vivid. Authors use details to help readers imagine the characters, scenes, and actions they describe, as in this description of a boy in Borden Deal's "Antaeus."

He was a stocky, robust kid with a shock of white hair, nothing sissy about him except his voice; he talked in this slow, gentle voice like you never heard before.

Dialect A variation of language spoken by a particular group, often within a particular region. Dialects differ from standard language because they may contain different pronunciations, forms, and meanings. There is an example of dialect in these lines from "Mother to Son" by Langston Hughes:

I'se been a-climbin' on,
And reachin' landin's,
And turnin' corners. . . .

> See page 240.

Dialogue Conversation between characters in a literary work. The following lines from "Uncle Tony's Goat," by Leslie Marmon Silko, are an example of dialogue:

Finally my uncle came out of the house; it was time for breakfast. "What's wrong?" he called out from the door.
"The billy goat won't come out, " I yelled back. . . .
"Get in there and get him out," he said. . . .

> See page 560.
> See also MONOLOGUE.

Drama A story intended to be performed by actors on a stage or before movie or TV cameras. Most dramas before the modern period can be divided into two basic types: tragedy and comedy. The script of a drama includes dialogue (the words the actors speak) and stage directions (descriptions of the action and scenery). "The Monsters Are Due on Maple Street," by Rod Serling, is an example of a television drama.

> See pages 500–501.
> See also COMEDY, TRAGEDY.

E

Essay A short piece of nonfiction writing on a single topic. The purpose of the essay is to communicate an idea or opinion. A **formal essay** is serious and impersonal. A **informal essay** entertains while it informs, usually in a light conversational style. "The Fish Crisis," by J. Madeleine Nash, is an example of a formal essay.

See page 396.

Exposition The part of the plot of a short story, novel, novella, or play in which the characters, setting, and situation are introduced.

Extended metaphor An implied comparison that continues through an entire poem. "Loo-Wit," by Wendy Rose, contains an extended metaphor.

See page 820.
See also METAPHOR.

F

Fable A short, simple tale that teaches a moral. The characters in a fable are often animals who speak and act like people. The moral, or lesson, of the fable is usually stated outright, as in "Anansi and His Visitor, Turtle."

See page 703.

Falling action In a play or story, the action that follows the climax.

See also PLOT.

Fantasy A form of literature that explores unreal worlds of the past, the present, or the future. "The Smallest Dragonboy," by Anne McCaffrey, is fantasy combined with science fiction.

See page 695.

Fiction A prose narrative in which situations and characters are invented by the writer. Some aspects of a fictional work may be based on fact or experience. Fiction includes short stories, novellas, and novels.

See also NOVEL, NOVELLA, SHORT STORY.

Figurative language Language used for descriptive effect, often to imply ideas indirectly. Expressions of figurative language are not literally true but express some truth beyond the literal level. Although it appears in all kinds of writing, figurative language is especially prominent in poetry, for example, in "The Courage That My Mother Had," by Edna St. Vincent Millay.

See page 343.
See also ANALOGY, FIGURE OF SPEECH, METAPHOR, PERSONIFICATION, SIMILE, SYMBOL.

Figure of speech Figurative language of a specific kind, such as **analogy, metaphor, simile,** or **personification.**

First-person narrative. See POINT OF VIEW.

Flashback An interruption in a chronological narrative that tells about something that happened before that point in the story or before the story began. A flashback gives readers information that helps to explain the main events of the story. Ray Bradbury uses a flashback to fill in details of Margot's life in "All Summer in a Day."

See page 613.

Folklore The traditional beliefs, customs, stories, songs, and dances of the ordinary people (the "folk") of a culture. Folklore is passed on by word of mouth and performance rather than in writing.

See also FOLKTALE, LEGEND, MYTH, ORAL TRADITION.

Folktale A traditional story passed down orally long before being written down. Generally the author of a folktale is anonymous. Folktales include animal stories, trickster stories, fairy tales, myths, legends, and tall tales. "Aunty Misery," by

Judith Ortiz Cofer, is an example of a folktale retold by a modern author.

> See page 599.
> See also LEGEND, MYTH, ORAL TRADITION, TALL TALE.

Foreshadowing The use of clues by an author to prepare readers for events that will happen in a story. An example of foreshadowing is Daedalus's warning Icarus never to fly very low or very high in "Icarus and Daedalus," by Josephine Preston Peabody.

> See page 248.

Free verse Poetry that has no fixed pattern of meter, rhyme, line length, or stanza arrangement. "Without Commercials," by Alice Walker, is an example of free verse.

> See page 255.
> See also RHYTHM.

G

Genre A literary or artistic category. The main literary genres are prose, poetry, and drama. Each of these is divided into smaller genres. For example: **Prose** includes fiction (such as novels, novellas, short stories, and folktales) and nonfiction (such as biography, autobiography, and essays). **Poetry** includes lyric poetry, dramatic poetry, and narrative poetry. **Drama** includes tragedy, comedy, historical drama, melodrama, and farce.

H

Haiku Originally a Japanese form of poetry that has three lines and seventeen syllables. The first and third lines have five syllables each; the middle line has seven syllables. "Birds Circling at Dusk," by Ann Atwood, is an example of haiku.

> See page 838.

Hero A literary work's main character, usually one with admirable qualities. Although the word *hero* is applied only to males in traditional usage (the female form is *heroine*), the term now applies to both sexes. Prometheus is the hero of the myth of the same name as retold by Bernard Evslin.

> See also LEGEND, MYTH, PROTAGONIST, TALL TALE.

Historical fiction A novel, novella, play, short story, or narrative poem that sets fictional characters against a historical backdrop and contains many details about the period in which it is set.

> See also GENRE.

Humor The quality of a literary work that makes the characters and their situations seem funny, amusing, or ludicrous. Humorous writing can be as effective in nonfiction as in fiction, as shown in Merrill Markoe's "Dog Diaries."

> See also COMEDY.

I

Idiom A figure of speech that belongs exclusively to a particular language, people, or region and whose meaning cannot be obtained, and might even appear ridiculous, by joining the meanings of the words composing it. You would be using an idiom if you said you *caught* a cold.

Imagery Language that emphasizes sensory impressions to help the reader of a literary work see, hear, feel, smell, and taste the scenes described in the work.

> See page 336.
> See also FIGURATIVE LANGUAGE.

Informational text One kind of nonfiction. This kind of writing conveys facts and information without introducing personal opinion. "Hurricanes," by Patricia Lauber, is an example of informational text.

See page 312.

Irony A form of expression in which the intended meaning of the words used is the opposite of their literal meaning. *Verbal irony* occurs when a person says one thing and means another—for example, saying "Nice guy!" about someone you dislike. *Situational irony* occurs when the outcome of a situation is the opposite of what was expected.

See page 21.

L

Legend A traditional story, based on history or an actual hero, that is passed down orally. A legend is usually exaggerated and gains elements of fantasy over the years. Stories about Daniel Boone and Davy Crockett are American legends.

See page 732.

Limerick A light humorous poem with a regular metrical scheme and a rhyme scheme of *aabba*.

See page 839.
See also HUMOR, RHYME SCHEME.

Local color The fictional portrayal of a region's features or peculiarities and its inhabitants' distinctive ways of talking and behaving, usually as a way of adding a realistic flavor to a story. "Rip Van Winkle," by Washington Irving, is notable for its touches of local color.

Lyric The words of a song, usually with a regular rhyme scheme. "Time to Change" is an example of a lyric with a regular rhyme scheme and a **refrain.**

See also RHYME SCHEME.

Lyric poetry Poems, usually short, that express strong personal feelings about a subject or an event. Emily Dickinson's "I'm Nobody! Who are You?" is a lyric poem.

M

Main idea The most important idea expressed in a paragraph or an essay. It may or may not be directly stated. In "The Teacher Who Changed My Life," by Nicholas Gage, the main idea is expressed in the title.

See page 374.

Memoir A biographical or autobiographical narrative emphasizing the narrator's personal experience during a period or at an event. "The Teacher Who Changed My Life," by Nicholas Gage, is an example of a memoir.

See page 39.
See also AUTOBIOGRAPHY, BIOGRAPHY.

Metaphor A figure of speech that compares or equates seemingly unlike things. In contrast to a simile, a metaphor implies the comparison instead of stating it directly; hence, there is no use of connectives such as *like* or *as.* The following line from "The Highwayman," by Alfred Noyes, contains an example of metaphor:

The moon was a ghostly galleon tossed upon cloudy seas. . . .

See page 391.
See also FIGURE OF SPEECH, IMAGERY, SIMILE.

Meter A regular pattern of stressed and unstressed syllables that gives a line of poetry a predictable rhythm. For example, the meter is marked in the following lines from "The Courage That My Mother Had," by Edna St. Vincent Millay:

The gólden broóch my móther wóre
She léft behínd for mé to wéar. . . .

See page 631.
See also RHYTHM

Monologue A long speech by a single character in a play or a solo performance.

Mood The emotional quality or atmosphere of a story or poem.

> See page 134.
> See also SETTING.

Myth A traditional story of unknown authorship, often involving goddesses, gods, and heroes, that attempts to explain a natural phenomenon, a historic event, or the origin of a belief or custom. "Atalanta's Race," by Rex Warner, is a retelling of an ancient Greek myth.

> See page 740.

N

Narration Writing or speech that tells a story. Narration is used in prose fiction and narrative poetry. Narration can also be an important element in biographies, autobiographies, and essays.

Narrative poetry Verse that tells a story. "The Highwayman," by Alfred Noyes, is an example of a narrative poem.

> See page 232.

Narrator The person who tells a story. In some cases the narrator is a character in the story—for example, the narrator in "Uncle Tony's Goat," by Leslie Marmon Silko.

> See page 813.
> See also POINT OF VIEW.

Nonfiction Factual prose writing. Nonfiction deals with real people and experiences. Among the categories of nonfiction are biographies, autobiographies, and essays. Patricia Lauber's "Hurricanes: Big Winds and Big Damage" is an example of nonfiction.

> See pages 290–291.
> See also AUTOBIOGRAPHY, BIOGRAPHY, ESSAY, FICTION.

Novel A book-length fictional prose narrative. The novel has more scope than a short story in its presentation of plot, character, setting, and theme. Because novels are not subject to any limits in their presentation of these elements, they encompass a wide range of narratives.

> See also FICTION

Novella A work of fiction shorter than a novel but longer than a short story. A novella usually has more characters, settings, and events and a more complex plot than a short story.

O

Onomatopoeia The use of a word or a phrase that actually imitates or suggests the sound of what it describes. The following lines from "The Women's 400 Meters," by Lillian Morrison, contain an example of onomatopoeia:

Bang! they're off / careening down the lanes / each chased by her own bright tiger.

> See page 626.
> See also SOUND DEVICES.

Oral tradition Stories, knowledge, customs, and beliefs passed by word of mouth from one generation to the next. "Racing the Great Bear," as retold by Joseph Bruchac, is an example of a story passed down through oral tradition among Native Americans.

> See page 276.
> See also FOLKLORE, FOLKTALE, LEGEND, MYTH.

P

Parallelism The use of a series of words, phrases, or sentences that have similar grammatical form. Parallelism emphasizes the items that are arranged in the similar structures. Gwendolyn Brooks uses parallelism in these lines from "Home.":

They watched his progress. He passed the Kennedy's, he passed the vacant lot, he passed Mrs. Blakemore's.

See also REPETITION.

Personification A figure of speech in which an animal, object, or idea is given human form or characteristics. The following lines from "old age sticks," by E. E. Cummings, contain examples of personification:

old age sticks / up Keep / Off / signs)& / youth yanks them / down. . . .

See page 843.
See also FIGURATIVE LANGUAGE, FIGURE OF SPEECH, METAPHOR.

Plot The sequence of events in a story, novel, or play. The plot begins with **exposition,** which introduces the story's characters, setting, and situation. The plot catches the reader's attention with a **narrative hook.** The **rising action** adds complications to the story's conflict, or problem, leading to the **climax,** or point of highest emotional pitch. The **falling action** is the logical result of the climax, and the **resolution** presents the final outcome.

See pages 144–145.

Plot twist An unexpected turn of events in a plot. The surprise ending in O. Henry's "After Twenty Years" is an example of a plot twist.

See page 550.

Poetry A form of literary expression that differs from prose in emphasizing the line as the unit of composition. Many other traditional characteristics of poetry–emotional, imaginative language; use of metaphor and simile; division into stanzas; rhyme; regular pattern of stress, or meter–apply to some poems.

See pages 616–617.

Point of view The relationship of the narrator, or storyteller, to the story. In a story with **first-person point of view,** the story is told by one of the characters, referred to as "I," as in "Too Soon a Woman," by Dorothy M. Johnson. The reader generally sees everything through that character's eyes. In a story with a **limited third-person point of view,** the narrator reveals the thoughts of only one character, but refers to that character as "he" or "she," as in "Broken Chain," by Gary Soto. In a story with an **omniscient point of view,** like "Amigo Brothers," by Piri Thomas, the narrator reveals the thoughts of several characters.

See page 62.

Props Theater slang (a shortened form of *properties*) for objects and elements of the scenery of a stage play or movie set.

Propaganda Speech, writing, or other attempts to influence ideas or opinions, often through the use of stereotypes, faulty generalizations, logical fallacies, and/or emotional language.

Prose Writing that is similar to everyday speech and language, as opposed to poetry. Its form is based on sentences and paragraphs without the patterns of rhyme, controlled line length, or meter found in much poetry. Fiction and nonfiction are the major categories of prose. Most modern drama is also written in prose.

See also DRAMA, ESSAY, FICTION, NONFICTION.

Protagonist The central character in a story, drama, or dramatic poem. Usually the action revolves around the protagonist, who is involved in the main conflict. For example, Keevan is the protagonist of "The Smallest Dragonboy," by Anne McCaffrey.

See page 144.
See ANTAGONIST, CONFLICT.

Pun A humorous play on two or more meanings of the same word or on two words with the same sound. Today puns often appear in advertising headlines and slogans—for example, "Our hotel rooms give you suite feelings."

See page 561.
See also HUMOR.

R

Refrain A line or lines repeated regularly, usually in a poem or song. This refrain appears at the end of each of the two stanzas of "The Pasture," by Robert Frost:

I sha'n't be gone long.—You come too.

Repetition The recurrence of sounds, words, phrases, lines, or stanzas in a speech or piece of writing. Repetition increases the feeling of unity in a work. When a line or stanza is repeated in a poem or song, it is called a refrain. The following lines from "the 1st," by Lucille Clifton, make use of repetition:

nothing about the emptied rooms
nothing about the emptied family

See also PARALLELISM, REFRAIN.

Resolution The part of a plot that concludes the falling action by revealing or suggesting the outcome of the conflict.

See page 456.

Rhyme The repetition of sounds at the ends of words that appear close to each other in a poem. **End rhyme** occurs at the ends of lines. **Internal rhyme** occurs within a single line. **Slant rhyme** occurs when words include sounds that are similar but not identical. Slant rhyme usually involves some variation of **consonance** (the repetition of consonant sounds) or **assonance** (the repetition of vowel sounds).The following lines from "The Cremation of Sam McGee" have both internal and end rhymes.

On a Christmas Day we were mushing our way
over the Dawson trail.

Talk of your cold! through the parka's fold it stabbed like a driven nail.

See page 641.

Rhyme scheme The pattern of rhyme formed by the end rhyme in a poem. The rhyme scheme is designated by the assignment of a different letter of the alphabet to each new rhyme. For example, the opening stanza of "Annabel Lee," by Edgar Allan Poe, has a rhyme scheme of *ababcb*.

See page 262.

Rhythm The pattern created by the arrangement of stressed and unstressed syllables, especially in poetry. Rhythm gives poetry a musical quality that helps convey its meaning. Rhythm can be regular (with a predictable pattern or meter) or irregular, (as in free verse).

See page 631.
See also METER.

Rising action The part of a plot that adds complications to the problems in the story and increases reader interest.

See also FALLING ACTION, PLOT.

S

Scene A subdivision of an act in a play. Each scene takes place in a specific setting and time. An act may have one or more scenes.

See also ACT.

Science fiction Fiction dealing with the impact of real science or imaginary superscience on human or alien societies of the past, present, or future. Although science fiction is mainly a product of the twentieth century, nineteenth-century authors such as Mary Shelley, Jules Verne, and Robert Louis Stevenson were pioneers of the genre. Isaac Asimov's "Key Item" is an example of science fiction.

See page 467.

Screenplay The script of a film, usually containing detailed instructions about camera shots and angles in addition to dialogue and stage directions. A screenplay for an original television show is called a teleplay. Rod Serling's "The Monsters Are Due on Maple Street" is an example of a teleplay.

See also DRAMA.

Sensory imagery Language that appeals to a reader's five senses: hearing, sight, touch, taste, and smell. In the following lines from "Fish Cheeks," Amy Tan includes images that appeal to several senses:

The kitchen was littered with appalling mounds of raw food: A slimy rock cod with bulging fish eyes that pleaded not to be thrown into a pan of hot oil.

See page 80.
See also VISUAL IMAGERY.

Sequence of events The order in which the events in a story take place. In *Rosa Parks: My Story,* the sequence is established by including dates and times.

See page 101.

Setting The time and place in which the events of a short story, novel, novella, or play occur. The setting often helps create the atmosphere or mood of the story.

See page 201.

Short story A brief fictional narrative in prose. Elements of the short story include **plot, character, setting, point of view, theme,** and sometimes symbol and irony. O. Henry wrote numerous short stories, including "After Twenty Years."

See pages 144–145.

Simile A figure of speech using *like* or *as* to compare seemingly unlike things. The following lines from Henry Wadsworth Longfellow's "Wreck of the Hesperus" contain an example of simile:

The snow fell hissing in the brine,
  And the billows frothed like yeast.

See page 617.
See also FIGURATIVE LANGUAGE, FIGURE OF SPEECH.

Sound devices Techniques used to create a sense of rhythm or to emphasize particular sounds in writing. For example, sound can be controlled through the use of **onomatopoeia, alliteration, consonance, assonance,** and **rhyme.**

See also RHYTHM.

Speaker The voice of a poem—sometimes that of the poet, sometimes that of a fictional person or even a thing. The speaker's words communicate a particular tone or attitude toward the subject of the poem. For example, in "To James," by Frank Horne, an adult male offers earnest advice about life to a young man, perhaps the speaker's son.

See page 61.

Stage directions Instructions written by the dramatist to describe the appearance and actions of characters, as well as sets, costumes, and lighting. Examples of stage directions can be found in "The Monsters Are Due on Maple Street," by Rod Serling.

See page 588.

Stanza A group of lines forming a unit in a poem. Stanzas are, in effect, the paragraphs of a poem.

See page 616.

Stereotype A character who is not developed as an individual but as a collection of traits and mannerisms supposedly shared by all members of a group.

Style The author's choice and arrangement of words and sentences in a literary work. Style can reveal an author's purpose in writing and attitude toward his or her subject and audience.

See pages 206, 396.

Suspense A feeling of curiosity, uncertainty, or even dread about what is going to happen next. Writers increase the level of suspense in a story by giving readers clues to what may happen.

See page 669.
See also FORESHADOWING, RISING ACTION.

Symbol Any object, person, place, or experience that means more than what it is. **Symbolism** is the use of images to represent internal realities. For example, in "Prometheus," as retold by Bernard Evslin, Prometheus symbolizes the rebellious, defiant side of the human spirit.

See page 446.

T

Tall tale A wildly imaginative story, usually passed down orally, about the fantastic adventures or amazing feats of folk heroes in realistic local settings. In "The Bunyans," Audrey Wood tells a story based on Paul Bunyan, a character from American folklore around whom many tall tales arose.

See page 757.
See also FOLKLORE, ORAL TRADITION.

Teleplay A play written or adapted for television. "The Monsters Are Due on Maple Street," by Rod Serling, was written for television.

See page 525.

Theme The main idea of a story, poem, novel, or play, usually expressed as a general statement. Some works have a **stated theme,** which is expressed directly. More frequently works have an **implied theme,** which is revealed gradually through other elements such as plot, character, setting, point of view, symbol, and irony.

See page 785.

Third-person narrative. See POINT OF VIEW.

Title The name of a literary work.

Tone The attitude of the narrator toward the subject, ideas, theme, or characters. A factual article would most likely have an objective tone, while an editorial on the same topic could be argumentative or satiric. Edgar Allan Poe's poem "Annabel Lee" could be described as having a tone of despair.

See page 710.

Tragedy A play in which the main character suffers a downfall. That character often is a person of dignified or heroic stature. The downfall may result from outside forces or from a weakness within the character, which is known as a tragic flaw.

V

Visual imagery Details that appeal to the sense of sight. These lines from the poem "One," by James Berry, contain visual imagery:

And mirrors can show me multiplied
many times, say, dressed up in green
or dressed up in blue.

See page 16.

Voice An author's distinctive style or the particular speech patterns of a character in a story.

See also STYLE, TONE.

Language Handbook

Troubleshooter

Use the Troubleshooter to recognize and correct common writing errors.

Sentence Fragment

A sentence fragment does not express a complete thought. It may lack a subject a predicate, or both.

Problem: Fragment that lacks a subject

The lion paced the floor of the cage. (Looked hungry.) *frag*

Solution: Add a subject to the fragment to make a complete sentence.

The lion paced the floor of the cage. He looked hungry.

Problem: Fragment that lacks a predicate

I'm painting my room. (The walls yellow.) *frag*

Solution: Add a predicate to make the sentence complete.

I'm painting my room. The walls are going to be yellow.

Problem: Fragment that lacks both a subject and a predicate

We walked around the reservoir. (Near the parkway.) *frag*

Solution: Combine the fragment with another sentence.

We walked around the reservoir near the parkway.

Rule of Thumb

You can use fragments when talking with friends or writing personal letters. Some writers use fragments to produce a special effect. Use complete sentences, however, for school or business writing.

Run-on Sentence

A run-on sentence is two or more sentences written incorrectly as one sentence.

Problem: Two main clauses separated only by a comma

Roller coasters make me dizzy, I don't enjoy them. *run-on*

Solution A: Replace the comma with a period or other end mark. Start the second sentence with a capital letter.

Roller coasters make me dizzy. I don't enjoy them.

Solution B: Replace the comma with a semicolon.

Roller coasters make me dizzy; I don't enjoy them.

Problem: Two main clauses with no punctuation between them

Acid rain is a worldwide problem there are no solutions in sight. *run-on*

Solution A: Separate the main clauses with a period or other end mark. Begin the second sentence with a capital letter.

Acid rain is a worldwide problem. There are no solutions in sight.

Solution B: Add a comma and a coordinating conjunction between the main clauses.

Acid rain is a worldwide problem, but there are no solutions in sight.

Problem: Two main clauses with no comma before the coordinating conjunction

Our chorus has been practicing all month but we still need another rehearsal. *run-on*

Solution: Add a comma before the coordinating conjunction.

Our chorus has been practicing all month, but we still need another rehearsal.

Lack of Subject-Verb Agreement

A singular subject calls for a singular form of the verb. A plural subject calls for a plural form of the verb.

Problem: A subject that is separated from the verb by an intervening prepositional phrase

The two policemen at the construction site (looks) bored. *agr*

The members of my baby-sitting club (is) saving money. *agr*

Solution: Make sure that the verb agrees with the subject of the sentence, not with the object of the preposition. The object of a preposition is never the subject.

The two policemen at the construction site look bored.

The members of my baby-sitting club are saving money.

Rule of Thumb

When subject and verb are separated by a prepositional phrase, check for agreement by reading the sentence without the prepositional phrase.

Problem: A sentence that begins with *here* or *there*

Here (come) the last bus to Pelham Heights. *agr*

There (is) my aunt and uncle. *agr*

Solution: In a sentence that begins with *here* or *there,* look for the subject after the verb. Make sure that the verb agrees with the subject.

Here comes the last bus to Pelham Heights.

There are my aunt and uncle.

Problem: An indefinite pronoun as the subject

Each of the candidates (are) qualified. *agr*

All of the problems on the test (was) hard. *agr*

Solution: Some indefinite pronouns are singular, some are plural, and some can be either singular or plural, depending on the noun they refer to. Determine whether the indefinite pronoun is singular or plural and make sure the verb agrees with it.

Each of the candidates is qualified.

All of the problems on the test were hard.

Problem: A compound subject that is joined by *and*

Fishing tackle and a life jacket (was) stowed in the boat. *agr*

Peanut butter and jelly (are) delicious. *agr*

Solution A: If the parts of a compound subject refer to different people or things, use a plural verb.

Fishing tackle and a life jacket were stowed in the boat.

Solution B: If the parts of a compound subject name one unit or if they refer to the same person or thing, use a singular verb.

Peanut butter and jelly is delicious.

Problem: A compound subject that is joined by *or* or *nor*

Either my aunt or my parents (plans) to attend parents' night. *agr*

Neither onions nor pepper (improve) the taste of this meatloaf. *agr*

Solution: Make the verb agree with the subject that is closer to it.

Either my aunt or my parents plan to attend parents' night.

Neither onions nor pepper improves the taste of this meatloaf.

Incorrect Verb Tense or Form

A verb has various tenses to show when the action takes place.

Problem: An incorrect or missing verb ending

The Parks Department (install) a new water fountain last week. *tense*

They have also (plant) flowers in all the flower beds. *tense*

Solution: To form the past tense and the part participle, add *-ed* to a regular verb.

The Parks Department installed a new water fountain last week.

They have also planted flowers in all the flower beds.

Problem: An improperly formed irregular verb

Wendell (has standed) in line for two hours. *tense*

I (catched) the fly ball and (throwed) it to first base. *tense*

Solution: Irregular verbs vary in their past and past participle forms. Look up the ones you are not sure of.

Wendell has stood in line for two hours.

I caught the fly ball and threw it to first base.

Problem: Confusion between the past form and the past participle

The cast for *The Music Man* (has began) rehearsals. *tense*

Solution: Use the past-participle form of an irregular verb, not its past form, when you use the auxiliary verb *have.*

The cast for *The Music Man* has begun rehearsals.

Problem: Improper use of the past participle

Our seventh grade (drawn) a mural for the wall of the cafeteria. *tense*

Solution: Add the auxiliary verb *have* to the past participle of an irregular verb to form a complete verb.

Our seventh grade has drawn a mural for the wall of the cafeteria.

Problem: Overuse of the passive voice

The mural (was carried) to the cafeteria by Alec and Juanita. *voice*

It (was attached) to the wall by Tania and Lee.

Solution: Change the verbs so that the subject of each sentence performs, rather than receives, the action of the verb.

Alec and Juanita carried the mural to the cafeteria. Tania and Lee attached it to the wall.

Incorrect Use of Pronouns

The noun that a pronoun refers to is called its **antecedent.** A pronoun must refer to its antecedent clearly. Subject pronouns refer to subjects in a sentence. Object pronouns refer to objects in a sentence.

Problem: A pronoun that could refer to more than one antecedent

Gary and Mike are coming, but (he) doesn't know the other kids. *ant*

Solution: Substitute a noun for the pronoun to make your sentence clearer.

Gary and Mike are coming, but Gary doesn't know the other kids.

Problem: A personal pronoun as a subject

(Him) and John were freezing after skating for three hours. *pro*

Lori and (me) decided not to audition for the musical. *pro*

Solution: Use a subject pronoun as the subject part of a sentence.

He and John were freezing after skating for three hours.

Lori and I decided not to audition for the musical.

Problem: A personal pronoun as an object

Ms. Wang asked Reggie and (I) to enter the science fair. *pro*

Ms. Wang helped (he) and (I) with the project. *pro*

Solution: Use an object pronoun as the object of a verb or a preposition.

Ms. Wang asked Reggie and me to enter the science fair.

Ms. Wang helped him and me with the project.

Rule of Thumb

When a pronoun is part of a compound subject or object, it is sometimes hard to choose the correct pronoun. Try saying the sentence with only the pronoun as the subject or object. That often makes the correct choice clear. For example, change *Dad gave Ronny and I a new basketball* to *Dad gave I a new basketball.* The pronoun *I* sounds wrong and should be changed to *me.*

Incorrect Use of Adjectives

Some adjectives have irregular forms: comparative forms for comparing two things and superlative forms for comparing more than two things.

Problem: Incorrect use of *good, better, best*

Their team is (more good) at softball than ours. *adj*

They have (more better) equipment too. *adj*

Solution: The comparative and superlative forms of *good* are *better* and *best.* Do not use *more* or *most* before irregular forms of comparative and superlative adjectives.

Their team is better at softball than ours.

They have better equipment too.

Problem: Incorrect use of *bad, worse, worst*

The flooding on East Street was the (baddest) I've seen. *adj*

Mike's basement was in (badder) shape than his garage. *adj*

Solution: The comparative and superlative forms of *bad* are *worse* and *worst.* Do not use *more* or *most* or the endings *-er* or *-est* with *bad.*

The flooding on East Street was the worst I've seen.

Mike's basement was in worse shape than his garage.

Problem: Incorrect use of comparative and superlative adjectives

The Appalachian Mountains are (more older) than the Rockies. *adj*

Mount Washington is the (most highest) of the Appalachians. *adj*

Solution: Do not use both *-er* and *more* or *-est* and *most* at the same time.

The Appalachian Mountains are older than the Rockies.

Mount Washington is the highest of the Appalachians.

Incorrect Use of Commas

Commas signal a pause between parts of a sentence and help to clarify meaning.

Problem: Missing commas in a series of three or more items

Sergio put mustard᠎catsup᠎and bean sprouts on his hot dog. *com*

Solution: If there are three or more items in a series, use a comma after each one, including the item preceding the conjunction.

Sergio put mustard, catsup, and bean sprouts on his hot dog.

Problem: Missing commas with direct quotations

"A little cold water" the swim coach said᠎"won't hurt you." *com*

Solution: The first part of an interrupted quotation ends with a comma followed by quotation marks. The interrupting words are also followed by a comma.

"A little cold water," the swim coach said, "won't hurt you."

Problem: Missing commas with nonessential appositives

My sneakers᠎a new pair᠎are covered with mud. *com*

Solution: Determine whether the appositive is important to the meaning of the sentence. If it is not essential, set off the appositive with commas.

My sneakers, a new pair, are covered with mud.

Incorrect Use of Apostrophes

An apostrophe shows possession. It can also indicate missing letters in a contraction.

Problem: A singular possessive noun

A parrots toes are used for gripping. *poss*

The bus color was bright yellow. *poss*

Solution: Use an apostrophe and an *s* to form the possessive of a singular noun, even one that ends in *s.*

A parrot's toes are used for gripping.

The bus's color was bright yellow.

Problem: A plural possessive noun ending in *s*

The (visitors) center closes at five o'clock. *poss*

The guide put several (tourists) luggage in one compartment. *poss*

Solution: Use an apostrophe alone to form the possessive of a plural noun that ends in *s*.

The visitors' center closes at five o'clock.

The guide put several tourists' luggage in one compartment.

Problem: A plural possessive noun not ending in *s*

The (peoples) applause gave courage to the young gymnast. *poss*

Solution: Use an apostrophe and an *s* to form the possessive of a plural noun that does not end in *s*.

The people's applause gave courage to the young gymnast.

Problem: A possessive personal pronoun

Jenny found the locker that was (her's;) she waited while her friends found (their's.) *poss*

Solution: Do not use an apostrophe with a possessive personal pronoun.

Jenny found the locker that was hers; she waited while her friends found theirs.

Incorrect Capitalization

Proper nouns, proper adjectives, and the first word of a sentence always begin with capital letters.

Problem: Words referring to ethnic groups, nationalities, and languages

Many (canadians) in the province of (quebec) speak (french.) *cap*

Solution: Capitalize proper nouns and adjectives that refer to ethnic groups, nationalities, and languages.

Many Canadians in the province of Quebec speak French.

Problem: A word that refers to a family member

Yesterday (aunt) Doreen asked me to baby-sit. *cap*

Don't forget to give (dad) a call. *cap*

Solution: Capitalize words that are used as part of or in place of a family member's name.

Yesterday Aunt Doreen asked me to baby-sit.

Don't forget to give Dad a call.

Rule of Thumb

Do not capitalize a word that identifies a family member when it is preceded by a possessive adjective: *My father bought a new car.*

Problem: The first word of a direct quotation

The judge declared, "(the) court is now in session." *cap*

Solution: Capitalize the first word in a direct quotation.

The judge declared, "The court is now in session."

Rule of Thumb

If you have difficulty with a rule of usage, try rewriting the rule in your own words. Check with your teacher to be sure you understand the rule.

Troublesome Words

This section will help you choose between words and expressions that are often confusing or misused.

---

accept, except

Accept means "to receive." *Except* means "other than."

Phillip walked proudly to the stage to **accept** the award.

Everything fits in my suitcase **except** my sleeping bag.

---

affect, effect

Affect is a verb meaning "to cause a change in" or "to influence." *Effect* as a verb means "to bring about or accomplish." As a noun, *effect* means "result."

Bad weather will **affect** our plans for the weekend.

The new medicine **effected** an improvement in the patient's condition.

The gloomy weather had a bad **effect** on my mood.

---

ain't

Ain't is never used in formal speaking or writing unless you are quoting the exact words of a character or a real person. Instead of using *ain't,* say or write *am not, is not, are not;* or use contractions such as *I'm not, she isn't.*

The pizza **is not** going to arrive for another half hour.

The pizza **isn't** going to arrive for another half hour.

---

a lot

The expression *a lot* means "much" or "many" and should always be written as two words. Some authorities discourage its use in formal writing.

A lot of my friends are learning Spanish.

Many of my friends are learning Spanish.

---

all ready, already

All ready, written as two words, is a phrase that means "completely ready." *Already,* written as one word, is an adverb that means "before" or "by this time."

By the time the fireworks display was **all ready**, we had **already** arrived.

---

all right, alright

The expression *all right* should be written as two words. Some dictionaries do list the single word *alright* but usually not as a preferred spelling.

Tom hurt his ankle, but he will be **all right.**

all together, altogether

All together means "in a group." *Altogether* means "completely."

The Minutemen stood **all together** at the end of Lexington Green.

The rebel farmers were not **altogether** sure that they could fight the British soldiers.

among, between

Use *among* for three or more people, things, or groups. Use *between* for two people, things, or groups.

Mr. Kendall divided the jobs for the car wash **among** the team members.

Our soccer field lies **between** the gym and Main Street.

amount, number

Use *amount* with nouns that cannot be counted. Use *number* with nouns that can be counted.

This recipe calls for an unusual **amount** of pepper.

A record **number** of students attended last Saturday's book fair.

bad, badly

Bad is an adjective; it modifies a noun. *Badly* is an adverb; it modifies a verb, an adjective, or another adverb.

The **badly** burnt cookies left a **bad** smell in the kitchen.

Joseph **badly** wants to be on the track team.

beside, besides

Beside means "next to." *Besides* means "in addition to."

The zebra is grazing **beside** a wildebeest.

Besides the zoo, I like to visit the aquarium.

bring, take

Bring means "to carry from a distant place to a closer one." *Take* means "to carry from a nearby place to a more distant one."

Please **bring** a bag lunch and subway money to school tomorrow.

Don't forget to **take** your art projects home this afternoon.

can, may

Can implies the ability to do something. *May* implies permission to do something.

You **may** take a later bus home if you **can** remember which bus to get on.

Rule of Thumb

> Although *can* is sometimes used in place of *may* in informal speech, a distinction should be made when speaking and writing formally.

choose, chose

Choose means "to select." *Chose,* the past tense of *choose,* means "selected."

Dad helped me **choose** a birthday card for my grandmother.

Dad **chose** a card with a funny joke inside.

doesn't, don't

The subject of the contraction **doesn't** *(does not)* is the third-person singular *(he* or *she).* The subject of the contraction **don't** *(do not)* is *I, you, we,* or *they.*

Tanya **doesn't** have any tickets for the concert.

We **don't** need tickets if we stand in the back row.

farther, further

Farther refers to physical distance. *Further* refers to time or degree.

Our new apartment is **farther** away from the school.

I will not continue this argument **further.**

fewer, less

Fewer is used to refer to things or qualities that can be counted. *Less* is used to refer to things or qualities that cannot be counted. In addition, *less* is used with figures that are regarded as single amounts.

Fewer people were waiting in line after lunch.

There is **less** fat in this kind of peanut butter.

Try to spend **less** than ten dollars on a present. [The money is treated as a single sum, not as individual dollars.]

good, well

Good is often used as an adjective meaning "pleasing" or "able." *Well* may be used as an adverb of manner telling how ably something is done or as an adjective meaning "in good health."

That is a **good** haircut.

Marco writes **well.**

Because Ms. Rodriguez had a headache, she was not **well** enough to correct our tests.

in, into

In means "inside." *Into* indicates a movement from outside toward the inside.

Refreshments will be sold **in** the lobby of the auditorium.

The doors opened, and the eager crowd rushed **into** the auditorium.

it's, its

Use an apostrophe to form the contraction of *it is.* The possessive of the personal pronoun *it* does not take an apostrophe.

It's hard to keep up with computer technology.

The computer industry seems to change **its** products daily.

lay, lie

Lay means "to place." *Lie* means "to recline."

I will **lay** my beach towel here on the warm sand.

Help! I don't want to **lie** next to a hill of red ants!

learn, teach

Learn means "to gain knowledge." *Teach* means "to give knowledge."

I don't **learn** very quickly.

My uncle is **teaching** me how to juggle.

leave, let

Leave means "to go away." *Let* means "to allow." With the word *alone,* you may use either *let* or *leave.*

Huang has to **leave** at eight o'clock.

Mr. Davio **lets** the band practice in his basement.

Leave me alone. **Let** me alone.

like, as

Use *like,* a preposition, to introduce a prepositional phrase. Use *as,* a subordinating conjunction, to introduce a subordinate clause. Many authorities believe that *like* should not be used before a clause in formal English.

Andy sometimes acts **like** a clown.

The detective looked carefully at the empty suitcase **as** she examined the room.

Rule of Thumb

As can be a preposition in cases like the following: *Jack went to the costume party as a giant pumpkin.*

loose, lose

Loose means "not firmly attached." *Lose* means "to misplace" or "to fail to win."

If you keep wiggling that **loose** tooth, you might **lose** it.

raise, rise

Raise means to "cause to move up." *Rise* means "to move upward."

Farmers in this part of Florida **raise** sugarcane.

The hot air balloon began to **rise** slowly in the morning sky.

set, sit

Set means "to place" or "to put." *Sit* means "to place oneself in a seated position."

I **set** the tips of my running shoes against the starting line.

After running the fifty-yard dash, I had to **sit** down and catch my breath.

than, then

Than introduces the second part of a comparison. *Then* means "at that time" or "after that."

I'd rather go to Disney World in the winter **than** in the summer.

The park is too crowded and hot **then**.

their, they're

Their is the possessive form of *they*. *They're* is the contraction of *they are*.

They're visiting Plymouth Plantation during **their** vacation.

to, too, two

To means "in the direction of." *Too* means "also" or "to an excessive degree." *Two* is the number after one.

I bought **two** tickets **to** the concert.

The music was **too** loud.

It's my favorite group **too**.

who, whom

Who is a subject pronoun. *Whom* is an object pronoun.

Who has finished the test already?

Mr. Russo is the man to **whom** we owe our thanks.

who's, whose

Who's is the contraction of *who is*. *Whose* is the possessive form of *who*.

Who's going to wake me up in the morning?

The policeman discovered **whose** car alarm was making so much noise.

Grammar Glossary

This glossary will help you quickly locate information on parts of speech and sentence structure.

A

Abstract noun. *See* Noun.

Action verb. *See* Verb.

Active voice. *See* Voice.

Adjective A word that modifies a noun or a pronoun. An adjective may answer one of these questions: *What kind? Which one? How many? How much?* (The *playful* dog splashed in the *cold* water.)

Many adjectives have different forms to indicate degree of comparison. *(bright, brighter, brightest)*

The comparative degree compares two persons, places, things, or ideas. *(worse, sadder)*

The superlative degree compares more than two persons, places, things, or ideas. *(worst, saddest)*

A predicate adjective always follows a linking verb. It describes the subject of the sentence. (Marathon running is *difficult.*)

A proper adjective is formed from a proper noun. It always begins with a capital letter. Most proper adjectives are formed by using the

following endings: *-an, -ian, -ese, -ish. (Chinese)*

A possessive noun (such as *poet's, classes'* or *Emerson's*) or possessive pronoun (*my, your, her, his, its, their*) functions as an adjective. It answers the question *Which one?*

A demonstrative adjective is a pronoun that answers the question *Which one?* (Jane read *that* book.)

Adverb A word that modifies a verb, an adjective, or another adverb. Adverbs answer the questions *How? When?* and *Where?* When modifying a verb, an adverb may appear in various positions in a sentence. (The van rocked *dangerously* on the bumpy road. *Gradually* we slowed down.)

When modifying an adjective or another adverb, an adverb appears directly before the modified word. (The driver stopped *quite* suddenly.) The negatives *no* and *not* and *-n't* (the contraction for *not*) are adverbs. (I could *not* see through the fog.) Other negative words, such as *nowhere, hardly,* and *never,* can function as adverbs of time, place, and degree. (She would *hardly* endorse such an idea.)

Some adverbs have various forms to indicate degree of comparison. *(loud, louder, loudest; sweetly, more sweetly, most sweetly)* Many adverbs are formed by adding *-ly* to adjectives. *(calmly)* However, not all words that end in *-ly* are adverbs. *(friendly)*

Antecedent. *See* Pronoun.

Appositive A noun placed next to another noun to identify it or add information about it. (My basketball coach, *Ms. Lopes,* called for a time out.)

Appositive phrase. *See* Phrase.

Article The adjectives *a, an,* and *the.*

A and *an* are indefinite articles. They refer to any one item of a group. (She bought *a* ticket.)

The is a definite article. It indicates that the noun is a specific person, place or thing. (She liked *the* movie.)

Base form. *See* Verb tense.

Clause A group of words that has a subject and a predicate and that is used as part of a sentence. Clauses fall into two categories: *main clauses,* which are also called *independent clauses,* and *subordinate clauses,* which are also called *dependent clauses.*

A main clause has a subject and a predicate and can stand alone as a sentence. There must be at least one main clause in every sentence. *(The water was cold.)*

A subordinate clause has a subject and a predicate, but it cannot stand alone as a sentence. A subordinate clause makes sense only when attached to a main clause. Many subordinate clauses begin with subordinating conjunctions or relative pronouns. (She returned the book *although she hadn't finished it.*) The best way to distinguish between a main clause and a subordinate clause is to see whether the clause can stand alone outside the sentence. Main clauses can stand alone; subordinate clauses cannot.

Collective noun. *See* Noun.

Common noun. *See* Noun.

Comparative degree. *See* Adjective; Adverb.

Complement A word or a phrase that completes the meaning of a verb. Three kinds of complements are *direct objects, indirect objects,* and *subject complements.*

A direct object answers the question *What?* or *Whom?*

after an action verb. (He ate a *hamburger.* She mailed the *letter.*)

An indirect object answers the question *To whom? For whom? To what?* or *For what?* after an action verb. (Marcia gave the *baby* a bath.)

A subject complement follows a subject and a linking verb. It identifies or describes a subject. The two kinds of subject complements are *predicate nouns* and *predicate adjectives.*

A predicate noun is a noun that follows a linking verb and gives more information about the subject. (The first prize is a *medal.*)

A predicate adjective is an adjective that follows a linking verb and gives more information about the subject. (The day is *cloudy.* It looks *cold.*)

Complete predicate. *See* Predicate.

Complete subject. *See* Subject.

Complex sentence. *See* Sentence.

Compound predicate. *See* Predicate.

Compound preposition. *See* Preposition.

Compound sentence. *See* Sentence.

Compound subject. *See* Subject.

Conjunction A word that joins single words or groups of words.

A coordinating conjunction *(and, but, or, nor, for, yet)* joins words or groups of words that are equal in grammatical importance. (Pizza *and* spaghetti are the choices for lunch today.)

Correlative conjunctions *(both . . . and, just as . . . so, not only . . . but also, either . . . or, neither . . . nor)* are pairs of words used to connect words or phrases in a sentence. (Anna is *either* brilliant *or* very studious.)

A subordinating conjunction *(after, although, because, before, if, in order that, since, than, though, until, when, while)* joins a subordinate idea or clause to a main clause. (I read a book *while* I was waiting for you.)

Coordinating conjunction. *See* Conjunction.

Correlative conjunction. *See* Conjunction.

Declarative sentence. *See* Sentence.

Definite article. *See* Article.

Demonstrative. *See* Adjective; Pronoun.

Direct object. *See* Complement.

Exclamatory sentence. *See* Sentence.

Future tense. *See* Verb tense.

Gerund A verb form that is used as a noun. A gerund always ends in *-ing.* A gerund may function as a subject, an object of a verb, or an object of a preposition. (*Walking* is good exercise. I prefer *walking* to *running.*) One identification test is to replace the gerund or gerund phrase with the singular pronoun *it.* When you replace a gerund with *it,* the sentence still makes sense. Participles fail this test.

Gerund phrase. *See* Phrase.

Helping verb. *See* Verb.

Imperative sentence. *See* Sentence.

Indefinite article. *See* Article.

Indefinite pronoun. *See* Pronoun.

Indirect object. *See* Complement.

Infinitive A verb form that begins with the word *to.* An infinitive often functions as a noun in a sentence. The word *to* may also begin a prepositional phrase. However, when

to precedes a verb, it is not a preposition but instead signals an infinitive. (*To achieve* a goal is very satisfying.)

Infinitive phrase. *See* Phrase.

Intensive pronoun. *See* Pronoun.

Interjection A word or phrase that expresses strong feeling. An interjection has no grammatical connection to other words in the sentence. Commas follow mild ones; exclamation points follow stronger ones. (*Oh no!* I left my subway pass at home! *Well,* we should leave anyway.)

Interrogative pronoun. *See* Pronoun.

Interrogative sentence. *See* Sentence.

Intransitive verb. *See* Verb.

Inverted order In most sentences in English, the subject comes before the predicate. In a sentence written in **inverted order,** the predicate comes before the subject. Some sentences are written in inverted order for variety or special emphasis. (In the middle of the park *grew a large oak tree.*) The subject generally follows the predicate in a sentence that begins with *there* or *here.* (*There* is a new girl in the class. *Here* come the clowns.) Questions, or interrogative sentences, are generally written in inverted order. Questions that begin with *who* or *what* follow normal word order.

Irregular verb. *See* Verb tense.

Linking verb. *See* Verb.

Main clause. *See* Clause.

Noun A word that names a person, a place, a thing, or an idea. The chart on page R30 shows the main types of nouns.

Number A noun, pronoun, or verb is singular in number if it refers to one, plural if it refers to more than one.

Object. *See* Complement.

Object pronoun. *See* Pronoun.

Participle A verb form that can function as an adjective. Present participles always end in *-ing.* Although past participles often end in *-ed,* they can take other forms as well. (I loved the actor's *engrossing* performance. Lori stared down the road with a *worried* expression on her face.)

Passive voice. *See* Voice.

Past tense. *See* Verb tense.

Perfect tenses. *See* Verb tense.

Personal pronoun. *See* Pronoun.

Types of Nouns

Noun	Function	Examples
Abstract noun	Names an idea, a quality, or a characteristic	beauty, love
Collective noun	Names a group of people or things	audience, class
Common noun	Names a general, not a particular, type of a person, place, thing, or idea	writer, city, desk, fear
Compound noun	Is made up of two or more words	hairbrush, ice cream
Concrete noun	Names a thing that you can see or touch	pheasant, water
Possessive noun	Shows possession, ownership, or the relationship between two nouns	*Chris's* paper
Predicate noun	Follows a linking verb and gives information about the subject	The movie is a *comedy.*
Proper noun	Names a particular person, place, thing, or idea	Marco Polo, Chicago, Eiffel Tower

Phrase A group of words that acts in a sentence as a single part of speech.

An **appositive phrase** includes an appositive and other words that describe the appositive. Many appositives are set off by commas. (My next fish, *a striped bass,* was the biggest catch of the day.)

A **gerund phrase** includes a gerund and any complements and modifiers needed to complete its meaning. (*Watching the clock* doesn't make time move faster.)

An **infinitive phrase** includes an infinitive and any complements and modifiers. (I prefer *to wake up to music.*)

A **participial phrase** contains a participle and any modifiers necessary to complete its meaning. (*Huddled together in the damp cave,* the hikers waited for the storm to end.)

A **prepositional phrase** begins with a preposition and ends with a noun or a pronoun called the object of the preposition. A prepositional phrase can function as an adjective, modifying a noun or a pronoun. (Bach was a great composer *of the eighteenth century.*) A prepositional phrase may also function as an adverb when it modifies a verb, an adverb, or an adjective. (*Throughout his life,* Bach wrote sacred music.)

A **verb phrase** consists of one or more helping verbs followed by a main verb. (I *have been studying* all night.)

A **verbal phrase** contains a verbal plus any complements and modifiers. The three kinds of verbals are *participles, gerunds,* and *infinitives.*

Plural. *See* Number.

Possessive noun. *See* Noun.

Possessive pronoun. *See* Pronoun.

Predicate The verb or verb phrase and any modifiers that express the essential thought about the subject of a sentence.

A **simple predicate** is a verb or verb phrase that tells something about the subject. (The carpenter *left.*)

A **complete predicate** includes the simple predicate and any words that modify or complete it. (The carpenter *left very early.* The carpenter *built a beautiful cabinet.*)

A **compound predicate** has two or more verbs or verb phrases that are joined by a conjunction and share the same subject. (The receiver *caught the pass and headed for the end zone.*)

Predicate adjective. *See* Adjective; Complement.

Predicate noun. *See* Complement; Noun.

Preposition A word that shows the relationship of a noun or pronoun to some other word in the sentence. Prepositions include *about, above, across, among, as, behind, below, beyond, but, by, down, during, except, for, from, into, like, near, of, on, outside, over, since, through, to, under, until, with.* (We skated *across* the ice.)

A **compound preposition** is made up of more than one word. Compound prepositions include *according to, across from, ahead of, as to, because of, by means of, in addition to, in spite of, on account of.* (*Because of* our late start, we had to park at a distance from the rink.)

Prepositional phrase. *See* Phrase.

Present tense. *See* Verb tense.

Progressive form. *See* Verb tense.

Pronoun A word that takes the place of a noun, a group of words acting as a noun, or another pronoun. The word or group of words that a pro-

noun refers to is called its **antecedent.** (In the following sentence, *girls* is the antecedent of *they. When the girls camped on the mountain, they slept well.*)

A **demonstrative pronoun** points out specific persons, places, things, or ideas. *(this, that, these, those)*

An **indefinite pronoun** refers to persons, places, or things in a more general way than a noun does. *(all, another, any, both, each, either, enough, everything, few, many, most, much, neither, nobody, none, one, other, others, plenty, several, some)*

An **intensive pronoun** adds emphasis to another noun or pronoun. If an intensive pronoun is omitted, the meaning of the sentence will be the same. (The mayor *himself* gave the diplomas to the graduates.)

An **interrogative pronoun** is used to form questions. *(Who? Whom? Whose? What? Which?)*

A **personal pronoun** refers to a specific person or

thing. The form of the personal pronoun depends on its use in the sentence. The chart on this page shows the forms of the various personal pronouns.

A **reflexive pronoun** reflects back to a noun or pronoun used earlier in the sentence, indicating that the same person or thing is involved. (We congratulated *ourselves* on winning the pennant.)

A **relative pronoun** is used to begin a subordinate clause. *(who, whose, whomever, that, what, whom, whoever, whomever, whichever, whatever)*

Proper adjective. *See* Adjective.

Proper noun. *See* Noun.

Reflexive pronoun. *See* Pronoun.

Regular verb. *See* Verb tense.

Relative pronoun. *See* Pronoun.

Personal Pronouns		
Singular Pronouns	**Plural Pronouns**	**Use in Sentence**
I, you, she, he, it	we, you, they	subject or predicate nominative
me, you, her, him, it	us, you, them	direct object, indirect object, or object of a preposition
my, your, her, his, its	our, your, their	possessive used before nouns (*our* car)
mine, yours, hers, his, its	ours, yours, theirs	possessive used alone (The car is *ours.*)

S

Sentence A group of words expressing a complete thought. Every sentence has a subject and a predicate. *See also* Clause; Predicate; Subject.

A **simple sentence** has only one main clause and no subordinate clauses. A simple sentence may contain a compound subject or a compound predicate or both. The subject and the predicate can be expanded with adjectives, adverbs, prepositional phrases, appositives, and verbal phrases. As long as the sentence has only one main clause, however, it remains a simple sentence. (*Doreen swam and snorkled. Doreen and David swam and snorkled. Students in grades seven and eight will plant a vegetable garden this spring and sell vegetables next fall.*)

A **compound sentence** has two or more main clauses. Each main clause of a compound sentence has its own subject and predicate, and these main clauses are usu-

ally joined by a comma and a coordinating conjunction. (*The spacecraft landed on Mars, and a special camera took pictures of rocks.*) A semicolon can also be used to join the main clauses in a compound sentence. (*The play ended late; we missed the last bus home.*)

A **complex sentence** has one main clause and one or more subordinate clauses. (*I'll be glad when this day is over.*)

The chart on this page shows the kinds of sentences by function.

Simple predicate. *See* Predicate; Sentence; Subject.

Subject The part of a sentence that tells what the sentence is about.

A **simple subject** is the main noun or pronoun. (*Leaves* covered the yard.)

A **complete subject** includes the simple subject and any words that modify it. (*Wet leaves from the old maple tree* covered the front yard.)

A **compound subject** has two or more subjects that are joined by a conjunction. The subjects share the same verb. (*Lee, Kim, and Andrew* won prizes in the spelling bee.)

Subordinate clause. *See* Clause.

Subordinating conjunction. *See* Conjunction.

Superlative degree. *See* Adjective; Adverb.

Tense. *See* Verb tense.

Transitive verb. *See* Verb.

Verb A word that expresses action or a state of being and is necessary to make a statement. (*sing, is, had*)

An **action verb** names an action and tells what a subject does. Action verbs can express either physical or mental action. (He *plays* the piano. Linda *prefers* this movie.)

Types of Sentences			
Sentence Type	**Function**	**Ends with . . .**	**Examples**
Declarative sentence	Makes a statement	A period	The red kangaroo lives in Australia.
Exclamatory sentence	Expresses strong emotion	An exclamation point	How loud that thunder is!
Imperative sentence	Gives a command or makes a request	A period or an exclamation point	Please leave a message.
Interrogative sentence	Asks a question	A question mark	When does the movie begin?

A **helping verb** helps the main verb tell about an action or make a statement. (Naomi *is* playing the lead in the spring musical.) The forms of *be* and *have* are the most common helping verbs. *(am, is, are, was, were, being, been; has, have, had, having)* Other helping verbs are *can, could; do, does, did; may, might; must; shall, should; will, would.* Helping verbs are also called auxiliary verbs.

A **transitive verb** is an action verb that is followed by a direct object that answers the question *What?* or *Whom?* (The Pony Express rider *delivered* the mail.)

An **intransitive verb** is an action verb that is *not* followed by a direct object. (The horse *ran* across the field.) A dictionary will indicate whether a verb is transitive or intransitive.

A **linking verb** links, or connects, the subject of a sentence with a noun or an adjective that identifies or describes the subject. The predicate tells what the subject is or is like. (The Lincoln Memorial *is* a national monument. The Lincoln Memorial *is* huge.) A linking verb does not show action. *To be* in all its forms is the most common linking verb. *(am, is, are, was, were, will be, been, being)* Other linking verbs are *appear, become, feel,* *grow, look, remain, seem, sound, smell, stay, taste.*

Verb phrase. *See* Phrase.

Verb tense The tense of a verb indicates when the action or state of being occurs. All the verb tenses are formed from the four principal parts of a verb: a base form *(freeze),* a present participle *(freezing),* a simple past form *(froze),* and a past participle *(frozen).*

A **regular verb** forms its simple past and past participle by adding *-ed* to the base form. *(help, helped, helped)*

A verb that forms its past and past participle in some other way is called an **irregular verb.** *(begin, began, begun; am, is, are, was, were, been; win, won, won)*

In addition to present, past, and future tenses, there are three perfect tenses.

The **present perfect** tense expresses an action or condition that occurred at some indefinite time in the past. This tense also shows an action or condition that began in the past and continues into the present. (Naomi *has played* important roles in school plays every year.)

The **past perfect tense** indicates that one past action or condition began *and* ended before another past action started. (The guests *had called* us before they heard about the storm.)

The **future perfect tense** indicates that one future action or condition will begin *and* end before another future event starts. Use *will have* or *shall have* with the past participle of a verb. (By the time you are finally ready, the bus *will have left.*)

Each tense has a **progressive** form that expresses a continuing action. To make the progressive forms, use the appropriate tense of the verb *be* with the present participle of the main verb. (Maria *will be working.*)

Verbal A verb form that functions in a sentence as a noun, an adjective, or an adverb. The three kinds of verbals are *participles, gerunds,* and *infinitives.*

Voice The voice of a verb shows whether the subject performs the action or receives the action of the verb.

A verb is in the **active voice** if the subject of the sentence performs the action. (The dog chased the boy.) The verb is in the **passive voice** if the subject of the sentence receives the action of the verb. (The boy was chased by the dog.)

Mechanics

This section will help you use correct capitalization, punctuation, and abbreviations in your writing.

Capitalization

Capitalizing Sentences, Quotations, and Salutations	
Rule	**Example**
A capital letter appears at the beginning of a sentence.	**A**nother gust of wind shook the house.
Capitalize the first word when quoting the exact words of a speaker.	Sabrina said, "**T**he lights might go out."
When a quoted sentence is interrupted by explanatory words, such as *she said,* do not begin the second part of the sentence with a capital letter.	"There's a rainbow," exclaimed Jeffrey, "**o**ver the whole beach."
When the second part of a quotation is a new sentence, put a period after the explanatory words; begin the new part with a capital letter.	"Please come inside," Justin said. "**W**ipe your feet."
Do not capitalize an indirect quotation.	Jo said that **t**he storm was getting worse.
Capitalize the first word in the salutation and the closing of a letter. Capitalize the title and the name of the person addressed.	**D**ear **D**r. **M**enino **D**ear **E**ditor **S**incerely

Capitalizing Names and Titles of People	
Rule	**Example**
Capitalize the names of people and the initials that stand for their names.	**M**alcolm **X** **J. F. K.** **R**obert **E**. **L**ee **Q**ueen **E**lizabeth **I**
Capitalize a title or an abbreviation of a title when it comes before a person's name or when it is used in direct address.	**D**r. **S**alinas "Your patient, **D**octor, is waiting."
Do not capitalize a title that follows or is a substitute for a person's name.	Marcia Salinas is a good **d**octor. He asked to speak to the **d**octor.

Rule	Example
Capitalize the names and the abbreviations of academic degrees that follow a person's name. Capitalize *Jr.* and *Sr.*	Marcia Salinas, **M.D.** Raoul Tobias, **A**ttorney Donald Bruns **S**r. Ann Lee, **P**h.**D.**
Capitalize words that show family relationships when used as titles or as substitutes for a person's name.	We saw **U**ncle Carlos. She read a book about **M**other **T**eresa.
Do not capitalize words that show family relationships when they follow a possessive noun or pronoun.	Jason's **b**rother will give us a ride. I forgot my **m**other's phone number.
Always capitalize the pronoun *I*.	After **I** clean my room, **I**'m going swimming.

Capitalizing Names of Places

Rule	Example

Rule of Thumb

> Do not capitalize articles and prepositions in proper nouns: *the Rock of Gibraltar, the Statue of Liberty.*

Rule	Example
Capitalize the names of cities, counties, states, countries, and continents.	**S**t. **L**ouis, **M**issouri **M**arin **C**ounty **A**ustralia **S**outh **A**merica
Capitalize the names of bodies of water and other geographical features.	the **G**reat **L**akes **C**ape **C**od the **D**ust **B**owl
Capitalize the names of sections of a country and regions of the world.	**E**ast **A**sia **N**ew **E**ngland the **P**acific **R**im the **M**idwest
Capitalize compass points when they refer to a specific section of a country.	the **N**orthwest the **S**outh
Do not capitalize compass points when they indicate direction.	Canada is **n**orth of the United States.
Do not capitalize adjectives indicating direction.	**w**estern Utah
Capitalize the names of streets and highways.	**D**orchester **A**venue **R**oute 22
Capitalize the names of buildings, bridges, monuments, and other structures.	**W**orld **T**rade **C**enter **C**hesapeake **B**ay **B**ridge

Capitalizing Other Proper Nouns and Adjectives

Rule	Example
Capitalize the names of clubs, organizations, businesses, institutions, and political parties.	Houston Oilers the Food and Drug Administration Boys and Girls Club
Capitalize brand names but not the nouns following them.	Zippo energy bar
Capitalize the names of days of the week, months, and holidays.	Saturday June Thanksgiving Day
Do not capitalize the names of seasons.	winter, spring, summer, fall
Capitalize the first word, the last word, and all important words in the title of a book, play, short story, poem, essay, article, film, television series, song, magazine, newspaper, and chapter of a book.	The Call of the Wild World Book Encyclopedia "Jingle Bells" Star Wars Chapter 12
Capitalize the names of ethnic groups, nationalities, and languages.	Latino Japanese European Spanish
Capitalize proper adjectives that are formed from the names of ethnic groups and nationalities.	Shetland pony Jewish holiday

Punctuation

Using the Period and Other End Marks	
Rule	**Example**
Use a period at the end of a declarative sentence.	My great-grandfather fought in the Mexican Revolution.
Use a period at the end of an imperative sentence that does not express strong feeling.	Please set the table.
Use a question mark at the end of an interrogative sentence.	How did your sneakers get so muddy?
Use an exclamation point at the end of an exclamatory sentence or a strong imperative.	How exciting the play was! Watch out!

Using Commas

Rule	Example
Use commas to separate three or more items in a series.	The canary eats bird seed, fruit, and suet.
Use commas to show a pause after an introductory word and to set off names used in direct address.	Yes, I offered to take care of her canary this weekend. Please, Stella, can I borrow your nail polish?
Use a comma after two or more introductory prepositional phrases or when the comma is needed to make the meaning clear. A comma is not needed after a single short prepositional phrase, but it is acceptable to use one.	From the back of the balcony, we had a lousy view of the stage. After the movie we walked home. (no comma needed)
Use a comma after an introductory participle and an introductory participial phrase.	Whistling and moaning, the wind shook the little house.
Use commas to set off words that interrupt the flow of thought in a sentence.	Tomorrow, I think, our projects are due.
Use a comma after conjunctive adverbs such as *however, moreover, furthermore, nevertheless,* and *therefore.*	The skating rink is crowded on Saturday; however, it's the only time I can go.
Use commas to set off an appositive if it is not essential to the meaning of a sentence.	Ben Wagner, a resident of Pittsfield, won the first round in the golf tournament.
Use a comma before a conjunction (*and, or, but, nor, so, yet*) that joins main clauses.	We can buy our tickets now, or we can take a chance on buying them just before the show.
Use a comma after an introductory adverb clause.	Because I stayed up so late, I'm sleepy this morning.
In most cases, do not use a comma with an adverb clause that comes at the end of a sentence.	The picnic will be canceled unless the weather clears.
Use a comma or a pair of commas to set off an adjective clause that is not essential to the meaning of a sentence.	Tracy, who just moved here from Florida, has never seen snow before.
Do not use a comma or pair of commas to set off an essential clause from the rest of the sentence.	Anyone who signs up this month will get a discount.

Rule	Example
Use commas before and after the year when it is used with both the month and the day. If only the month and the year are given, do not use a comma.	On January 2, 1985, my parents moved to Dallas, Texas. I was born in May 1985.
Use commas before and after the name of a state or a country when it is used with the name of a city. Do not use a comma after the state if it is used with a ZIP code.	The area code for Concord, New Hampshire, is 603. Please forward my mail to 6 Madison Lane, Topsham, ME 04086
Use a comma or a pair of commas to set off an abbreviated title or degree following a person's name.	The infirmary was founded by Elizabeth Blackwell, M.D., the first woman in the United States to earn a medical degree.
Use a pair of commas to set off *too* in the middle of a sentence when *too* means "also."	We, too, bought groceries, from the new online supermarket.
Use a comma or commas to set off a direct quotation.	"My nose," exclaimed Pinocchio, "is growing longer!"
Use a comma after the salutation of a friendly letter and after the closing of both a friendly letter and a business letter.	Dear Gary, Sincerely, Best regards,
Use a comma when necessary to prevent misreading of a sentence.	In math, solutions always elude me.

Using Semicolons and Colons

Rule	Example
Use a semicolon to join the parts of a compound sentence when a coordinating conjunction, such as *and, or, nor,* or *but,* is not used.	Don't be late for the dress rehearsal; it begins at seven o'clock sharp.
Use a semicolon to join parts of a compound sentence when the main clauses are long and are subdivided by commas. Use a semicolon even if these clauses are already joined by a coordinating conjunction.	In the gray light of early morning, on a remote airstrip in the desert, two pilots prepared to fly on a dangerous mission; but accompanying them were a television camera crew, three newspaper reporters, and a congressman from their home state of Nebraska.

Rule	Example
Use a semicolon to separate main clauses joined by a conjunctive adverb. Be sure to use a comma after the conjunctive adverb.	We've been climbing all morning; therefore, we need a rest.
Use a colon to introduce a list of items that ends a sentence. Use words such as *these, the following,* or *as follows* to signal that a list is coming.	Remember to bring the following items: a backpack, a bag lunch, sunscreen, and insect repellent.
Do not use a colon to introduce a list preceded by a verb or preposition.	Remember to bring a backpack, a bag lunch, sunscreen, and insect repellent. (No colon is used after *bring.*)
Use a colon to separate the hour and the minutes when you write the time of day.	My Spanish class starts at 9:15.
Use a colon after the salutation of a business letter.	Dear Dr. Coulombe: Director of the Personnel Dept.:

Using Quotation Marks and Italics

Rule	Example
Use quotation marks before and after a direct quotation.	"Curiouser and curiouser," said Alice.
Use quotation marks with both parts of a divided quotation.	"This gymnastics trick," explained Amanda, "took me three months to learn."
Use a comma or commas to separate a phrase such as *she said* from the quotation itself. Place the comma that precedes the phrase inside the closing quotation marks.	"I will be late," said the cable technician, "for my appointment."
Place a period that ends a quotation inside the closing quotation marks.	Scott said, "Thanks for letting me borrow your camping tent."
Place a question mark or an exclamation point inside the quotation marks when it is part of the quotation.	"Why is the door of your snake's cage open?" asked my mother.

Rule	Example
Place a question mark or an exclamation point outside the quotation marks when it is part of the entire sentence.	How I love "The Pit and the Pendulum"!
Use quotation marks for the title of a short story, essay, poem, song, magazine or newspaper article, or book chapter.	short story: "The Necklace" poem: "The Fish" article: "Fifty Things to Make from Bottlecaps"
Use italics or underlining for the title of a book, play, film, television series, magazine, newspaper, or work of art.	book: *To Kill a Mockingbird* magazine: *The New Republic* painting: *Sunflowers*
Use italics or underlining for the names of ships, trains, airplanes, and spacecraft.	ship: *Mayflower* airplane: *Air Force One*

Using Apostrophes	
Rule	**Example**
Use an apostrophe and an *s* *('s)* to form the possessive of a singular noun.	my brother**'s** rock collection Chris**'s** hat
Use an apostrophe and an *s* *('s)* to form the possessive of a plural noun that does not end in *s*.	the geese**'s** feathers the oxen**'s** domestication

Rule of Thumb

> If a thing is owned jointly by two or more individuals, only the last name should show possession: *Mom and Dad's car.* If the ownership is not joint, each name should show possession: *Mom's and Dad's parents are coming for Thanksgiving.*

Use an apostrophe alone to form the possessive of a plural noun that ends in *s*.	the animal**s'** habitat the instrument**s'** sound
Use an apostrophe and an *s* *('s)* to form the possessive of an indefinite pronoun.	everyone**'s** homework someone**'s** homework
Do not use an apostrophe in a possessive pronoun.	The dog knocked over **its** dish. **Yours** is the best entry in the contest. One of these drawings must be **hers.**

Rule	Example
Use an apostrophe to replace letters that have been omitted in a contraction.	it + is = it**'s** can + not = can**'t** I + have = I**'ve**
Use an apostrophe to form the plural of a letter, a figure, or a word that is used as itself.	Write three 7**'s.** The word is spelled with two *m***'s.** The sentence contains three *and***'s.**
Use an apostrophe to show missing numbers in a year.	the class of **'02**

Using Hyphens, Dashes, and Parentheses

Rule	Example
Use a hyphen to show the division of a word at the end of a line. Always divide the word between its syllables.	With the new recycling pro-gram, more residents are recycling their trash.

Rule of Thumb

One-letter divisions (for example, *e-lectric*) are not permissible. Avoid dividing personal names if possible.

Rule	Example
Use a hyphen in a number written as a compound word.	He sold forty-six ice creams in one hour.
Use a hyphen in a fraction.	We won the vote by a two-thirds majority. Two-thirds of the votes have been counted.
Use a hyphen or hyphens in certain compound nouns.	great-grandmother merry-go-round
Hyphenate a compound modifier only when it precedes the word it modifies.	A well-known musician visited our school. The story was well written.
Use a hyphen after the prefixes *all-, ex-,* and *self-* when they are joined to a noun or adjective.	all-star ex-president self-conscious
Use a hyphen to separate a prefix from a word that begins with a capital letter.	un-American mid-January

Rule	Example
Use a dash or dashes to show a sudden break or change in thought or speech.	Daniel—he's kind of a pest—is my youngest cousin.
Use parentheses to set off words that define or helpfully explain a word in a sentence.	The transverse flute (*transverse* means "sideways") is a wind instrument.

Abbreviations

Rule	Example
Abbreviate the titles *Mr., Mrs., Ms.,* and *Dr.* before a person's name. Also abbreviate professional or academic degree that follows a name. The titles *Jr.* and *Sr.* are *not* preceded by a comma.	**Dr.** Stanley Livingston (doctor) Luisa Mendez, **M.A.** (Master of Arts) Martin Luther King Jr.
Use capital letters and no periods with abbreviations that are pronounced letter by letter or as words. Exceptions are *U.S.* and *Washington, D.C.,* which do use periods.	**NAACP** National Association for the Advancement of Colored People **UFO** unidentified flying object **MADD** Mothers Against Driving Drunk
With exact times, use *A.M.* (*ante meridiem,* "before noon") and *P.M.* (*post meridiem,* "after noon"). For years, use *B.C.* (before Christ) and, sometimes, *A.D.* (*anno Domini,* "in the year of the lord," after Christ).	8:15 **A.M.** 6:55 **P.M.** 5000 **B.C.** **A.D.** 235
Abbreviate days and months only in charts and lists.	School will be closed on **Mon., Sept.** 3 **Wed., Nov.** 11 **Thurs., Nov.** 27
In scientific writing, abbreviate units of measure. Use periods with English units but not with metric units.	inch(es) **in.** meter(s) **m** yard(s) **yd.** milliliter(s) **ml**
On envelopes only, abbreviate street names and state names. In general text, spell out street names and state names.	Ms. Karen Holmes 347 Grandville **St.** Tilton, **NH** 03276 Karen lives on Grandville **Street** in Tilton, **New Hampshire.**

Writing Numbers

Rule	Example
In charts and tables, always write numbers as numerals. Other rules apply to numbers not in charts or tables.	Student Test Scores Student Test **1** Test **2** Test **3** Lai, W. **82** **89** **94** Ostos, A. **78** **90** **86**
Spell out a number that is expressed in one or two words.	We carried enough supplies for **twenty-three** days.
Use a numeral for a number of more than two words.	The tallest mountain in Mexico rises **17,520** feet.
Spell out a number that begins a sentence or reword the sentence so that it does not begin with a number.	**One hundred forty-three** days later the baby elephant was born. The baby elephant was born **143** days later.
Write a very large number as a numeral followed by the word *million* or *billion*.	There are **15 million** people living in or near Mexico City.
Related numbers should be written in the same way. If one number must be written as a numeral, use numerals for all the numbers.	There are **365** days in the year, but only **52** weekends.
Spell out an ordinal number. (*first, second*)	Welcome to our **fifteenth** annual convention.
Use words to express the time of day unless you are writing the exact time or using the abbreviation *A.M.* or *P.M.*	My guitar lesson is at **five o'clock**. It ends by 5:45 **P.M.**
Use numerals to express dates, house and street numbers, apartment and room numbers, telephone numbers, page numbers, amounts of money of more than two words, and percentages. Write out the word *percent*.	August **5, 1999** **9** Davio Dr. Apartment **9**F **24 percent**

Spelling

The following rules, examples, and exceptions can help you master the spelling of many words.

Spelling *ie* and *ei*

Put *i* before *e* except when both letters follow *c* or when the letters are pronounced as *a*.

believe	sieve	weight
receive	relieve	neighborhood

It is helpful to memorize exceptions to this rule. Exceptions include the following words: *species, science, weird, either, seize, leisure,* and *protein.*

Spelling unstressed vowels

Notice the vowel sound in the second syllable of the word *op-p_-site.* This is the unstressed vowel sound; dictionary respellings use the schwa symbol (ə) to indicate it. Because any vowel can be used to spell this sound, you might find yourself uncertain about which vowel to use. To spell words with unstressed vowels, try thinking of a related word in which the syllable containing the vowel sound is stressed.

Unknown Spelling	Related Word	Word Spelled Correctly
opp_site	oppose	opposite
observ_nt	observation	observant
res_dent	reside	resident

Suffixes and the silent e

Many English words end in a silent *e.* Keep the *e* when adding a suffix that begins with a consonant. Drop the silent *e* when adding a suffix beginning with a vowel. When adding the suffix *-ly* to a word that ends in *le,* drop the *le.*

wise + ly = wisely	gentle + ly = gently
skate + ing = skating	noise + y = noisy

There are exceptions to the rule, including the following:

awe + ful = awful	judge + ment = judgment
true + ly = truly	mile + age = mileage
dye + ing = dyeing	

Suffixes and the final *y*

When you are adding a suffix to a word ending with a vowel + *y,* keep the *y.* For a word ending with a consonant + *y,* change the *y* to *i* unless the suffix begins with *i.* To avoid having two *i*'s together, keep the *y.*

enjoy + ment = enjoyment   merry + ment = merriment
display + ed = displayed   lazy + ness= laziness
play + ful = playful   worry + ing = worrying

Note: Some words have alternate spellings:

sly + er = slyer *or* slier
shy + est = shyest *or* shiest

Adding prefixes

When you add a prefix to a word, do not change the spelling of the word.

un + done = undone   re + schedule = reschedule
il + legible = illegible   semi + sweet = semisweet

Doubling the final consonant

Double the final consonant in a one-syllable word that ends with a single consonant preceded by a single vowel. Double the final consonant of a word that has an accent on the last syllable if the accent stays there after the suffix is added.

sit + ing = sitting   rub + ing = rubbing
commit + ed = committed   confer + ed = conferred

Do not double the final consonant if the accent is not on the last syllable or if the accent moves when the suffix is added.

cancel + ing = canceling   refer + ent = referent
travel + ed = traveled   defer + ence = deference

Do not double the final consonant if the word ends in two consonants or if the suffix begins with a consonant.

climb + er = climber   nervous + ness = nervousness
import + ance = importance star + dom = stardom

When adding -*ly* to a word that ends in *ll,* drop one *l.*

dull + ly = dully   full + ly = fully

Forming Plurals

GENERAL RULES FOR PLURALS		
If the noun ends in	**Rule**	**Example**
s, ch, sh, x, or *z*	add *-es*	loss, losses latch, latches bush, bushes box, boxes quiz, quizzes
a consonant + *y*	change *y* to *i* and add *-es*	ferry, ferries baby, babies worry, worries
a vowel + *y*	add *-s*	chimney, chimneys monkey, monkeys toy, toys
a vowel + *o*	add *-s*	cameo, cameos radio, radios rodeo, rodeos
a consonant + *o*	add *-es* but sometimes add *-s*	potato, potatoes echo, echoes photo, photos solo, solos
f or *ff*	add *-s* but sometimes change *f* to *v* and add *-es*	proof, proofs bluff, bluffs sheaf, sheaves thief, thieves hoof, hooves
lf	change *f* to *v* and add *-es*	calf, calves half, halves loaf, loaves
fe	change *f* to *v* and add *-s*	knife, knives life, lives

SPECIAL RULES FOR PLURALS	
Rule	**Example**
To form the plural of most proper names and one-word compound nouns, follow the general rules for plurals.	Jones, Joneses Hatch, Hatches workbook, workbooks
To form the plural of a hyphenated compound noun or a compound noun of more than one word, make the most important word plural.	mother-in-law, mothers-in-law credit card, credit cards district attorney, district attorneys
Some nouns have irregular plural forms and do not follow any rules.	man, men foot, feet tooth, teeth
Some nouns have the same singular and plural forms	deer, deer species, species sheep, sheep

Forming compound words

When forming a compound word, keep the original spelling of both words.

home + work = homework
scare + crow = scarecrow
pea + nut = peanut

Writing Handbook

The Writing Process

The writing process consists of five stages: prewriting, drafting, revising, editing/proofreading, and publishing/presenting. By following the stages in order, you can turn your ideas into polished pieces of writing. Most writers take their writing through all five stages, repeating stages as necessary.

The Writing Process

Prewriting → Drafting → Revising → Editing/Proofreading → Publishing/Presenting

Prewriting

Prewriting is the process of gathering and organizing your ideas. It begins whenever you start to consider what you will write about or what will interest your readers. Try keeping a small notebook with you for several days and using it to jot down possible topics. Consult the chart below for tips on using the prewriting techniques of listing, questioning, and clustering.

Listing	Questioning	Clustering
List as many ideas as you can—whatever comes into your head on a particular topic. Later you can go back over the list and circle the ideas you like best. Eventually you'll hit on an idea you can use.	Ask yourself questions related to your audience. *What do my friends already know about my topic?* *What would they find most interesting about my topic?* *What words would I need to explain to my audience?*	Write your topic in the middle of a piece of paper. Organize related ideas around the topic in a cluster of circles, with lines showing how the ideas are related. Clustering can help you decide which part of a topic to write about.

When you have selected your topic, organize your ideas around the topic. Identify your main ideas and supporting ideas. Each main idea needs examples or facts to support it. Then write a plan for what you want to say. The plan might be an organized list or outline. It does not have to use complete sentences.

Drafting

Drafting is the stage that turns your list into sentences and paragraphs. Use your prewriting notes to remember what you want to say. Begin by writing an introduction that gets the reader's attention. Move ahead through the topic, paragraph by paragraph. Let your words flow. This is the time to express yourself or try out a new idea. Don't worry about mistakes in spelling and grammar; you can correct them later. If you get stuck, try one of the tips below.

Tips for drafting

- Work on the easiest part first. You don't have to begin at the beginning.
- Make a diagram, sketch, or drawing of the topic.
- Focus on just one sentence or paragraph at a time.
- Freewrite your thoughts and images. You can organize them later.
- Pretend that you are writing to a friend.
- Ask more questions about your topic.
- Speak your ideas into a tape recorder.
- Take a break. Take a walk or listen to music. Return to your writing later.

Revising

The goal of revising is to make your writing clearer and more interesting. When you revise, look at the whole piece of writing. Ask whether the parts go together smoothly and whether anything should be added or deleted. You may see a way to organize the draft more effectively. Some writers make several revisions before they are satisfied.

☑ Did I stick to my topic?

☑ Did I accomplish my purpose?

☑ Did I keep my audience in mind?

☑ Does my main idea come across clearly?

☑ Do all the details support the main idea?

☑ Did I give the right amount of information?

☑ Did I use transition words such as *first, then* and *next* to make my sentences flow smoothly?

Tips for revising

- Step back. If you have the time, set your draft aside for a while. When you look at it again, you may see it from a new point of view. You may notice that some information is missing or that part of the paper is disorganized.
- Read your paper aloud. Listen carefully to the way it sounds. You may notice repetitive or unclear sections that can be improved.
- Have a writing conference with a peer reviewer, one of your friends or classmates. A second opinion helps. Your reader can offer a fresh point of view.

Peer review

You can direct peer responses in one or more of the following ways.

- Ask readers to tell you what they have read in their own words. If you do not hear your ideas restated, revise your writing for clarity.
- Ask readers to tell you the part they liked best and why. You may want to expand those parts.
- Repeat in your own words what the readers have told you. Ask the readers if you have understood their suggestions.
- Discuss your writing with your readers. Listen to their suggestions carefully.

As you confer, make notes of your reviewers' comments. Then revise your draft, using your own judgment and including what is helpful from your reviewers' comments.

Editing/Proofreading

When you are satisfied with the changes you've made, edit your revised draft. Replace dull, vague words with lively verbs and precise adjectives. Vary the length of your sentences. Take time to correct errors in spelling, grammar, capitalization, and punctuation. Refer to the Proofreading Checklist on page R51 or on the inside back cover of this book.

Editing for style

Use the following checklist to help you improve the style of your writing. Try to make your writing as interesting and as effective as possible.

☑ Have I used the right words?

☑ Is the tone of my writing appropriate?

☑ Have I made clear connections between ideas?

☑ Do my sentences and paragraphs flow smoothly?

☑ Does the ending sum up what I'm saying clearly and effectively?

Proofreading

Use this proofreading checklist to help you check for errors in your writing , and use the proofreading symbols in the chart below to mark places that need corrections.

☑ Have I avoided run-on sentences and sentence fragments and punctuated sentences correctly?

☑ Have I used every word correctly, including plurals, possessives, and frequently confused words?

☑ Do verbs and subjects agree? Are verb tenses correct?

☑ Do pronouns refer clearly to their antecedents and agree with them in person, number, and gender?

☑ Have I used adverb and adjective forms and modifying phrases correctly?

☑ Have I spelled every word correctly, and checked the unfamiliar ones in a dictionary?

Proofreading Symbols

Symbol	Example	Meaning
⊙	Lieut. Brown	Insert a period.
∧	No one came to the party.	Insert a letter or a word.
=	I enjoyed paris.	Capitalize a letter.
/	The Class ran a bake sale.	Make a capital letter lowercase.
⌢	The campers are home sick.	Close up a space.
⟨sp⟩	They visited N.Y. ⟨sp⟩	Spell out.
∧ ⌃	Sue, please come, I need your help.	Insert a comma or a semicolon.
∩	He enjoyed feild day.	Transpose the position of letters or words.
#	all together	Insert a space.
ℨ	We went to to Boston.	Delete letters or words.
✋ ✋ ✋	She asked, Whos coming?	Insert quotation marks or an apostrophe.
/ = /	mid January	Insert a hyphen.
¶	"Where?" asked Karl. "Over there," said Ray.	Begin a new paragraph.

Publishing/Presenting

Now your writing is ready for an audience. You may consider adding graphics (such as photographs, diagrams, or charts) to your paper. Make a clean, neat copy, and add your name and date. Check that the paper has a title. If you wish, enclose the paper in a folder or binder to give it a professional look. Hand it in to your teacher or share it in one of the ways described below. When the paper is returned, keep it in your writing portfolio.

Ideas for presenting

- **Oral presentation** Almost any writing can be shared aloud by an individual or a group. Try including music or slides.
- **Class book** A collection of class writing is a good contribution to the school library.
- **Newspaper** Some schools have a school newspaper. Local newspapers often publish student writing, especially if it is about local people and events.
- **Literary magazine** Magazines such as *Cricket* and *Stone Soup* publish student writing. Some schools have a literary magazine that publishes student writing once or twice a year.
- **Bulletin board** A rotating display of student writing is an effective way to see what your classmates have written. Illustrations and photographs add interest.
- **Multimedia presentation** Use computer software that allows you to combine text with sound and visuals (such as photos, drawings, maps, and animation or movie files). A multimedia presentation can be kept on a computer's hard drive, added to a local network, or recorded onto a disk, CD, or DVD.

Some writing, such as journal writing, is private and not intended for an audience. However, even if you don't share your paper, don't throw it away. It may contain ideas that you can use later.

Writing Modes

There are four different types, or modes, of writing—expository, descriptive, narrative, and persuasive. Each mode has its own purpose and characteristics.

Expository Writing

Expository writing communicates knowledge. It provides and explains information; it may also give general directions or step-by-step instructions for an activity. Use the checklist at the right to help you improve your expository writing.

☑ Is the opening paragraph interesting?

☑ Are my explanations accurate and complete? Is information clear and easy to read?

☑ Is information presented in a logical order?

☑ Does each paragraph have a main idea? Does all the information in the paragraph support the main idea?

☑ Does my essay have an introduction, a body, and a conclusion?

☑ Have I defined any unfamiliar terms?

☑ Are my comparisons clear and logical?

Kinds of expository writing

Expository writing covers a wide range of styles. The chart below describes some of the possibilities.

Kinds of Expository Writing	Examples
General instructions on how to do something	Explain how to train for a cross-country race, how to arrange a surprise party, or how to clean up your room more efficiently.
Compare-and-contrast essay	Compare two athletes or two sports, two fictional characters, two books or movies, two places, or two kinds of vacations.
Step-by-step directions	Give directions for building a model plane, making lemon meringue pie, or drawing on a computer screen.
Information and explanation	Explain what causes sunspots, how plants grow in the desert, or why camels have humps.
A report or essay	Write a book report, a report on the Buddhist religion, or a report on a new wildlife center.

Descriptive Writing

Descriptive writing can make a person, place, or thing come to life. The scene described may be as unfamiliar and far away as the bottom of the sea or as familiar and close as the gym locker room. By presenting details that awaken the reader's senses, descriptive writing can help your readers see the world more clearly. The checklist at the right can help you improve your descriptive writing.

☑ Does my introduction identify the person or place that will be described?

☑ Are my details vivid? Are nouns and adjectives precise?

☑ Do all the details contribute to the same impression?

☑ Is it clear why this place or person is special?

☑ Are transitions clear? Do the paragraphs follow a logical order?

☑ Does each paragraph contain a main idea?

☑ Have I communicated a definite impression or mood?

Narrative Writing

Narrative writing tells a story, either real or fictional. It answers the question *What happened?* A well-written narrative holds the reader's attention by presenting interesting characters in a carefully ordered series of events. You can get some tips on improving your narrative writing from the checklist at the right.

☑ Does my first sentence get the reader's attention?

☑ Are the characters and setting described in enough detail?

☑ Do the characters speak and behave realistically?

☑ Are the events narrated in an order clear enough for the reader to follow?

☑ Are there places where dialogue should be added?

☑ Does the story have a satisfactory conclusion?

Persuasive Writing

Persuasive writing presents an opinion. Its goal is to make readers feel or think a certain way about a situation or an idea. The writer includes facts and opinions often designed to urge readers to take action. Good persuasive writing appeals to the readers' common sense and to their emotions. Check the list at the right for ways to make your persuasive writing more effective.

☑ Is my main idea expressed in a clear statement?

☑ Have I presented good reasons to support my point of view?

☑ Have I supported my reasons with facts and opinions?

☑ Have I taken account of the opposing points of view?

☑ Have I addressed the interests of my audience?

☑ Have I ended with a strong closing statement?

Research Report Writing

When you write a research report, you explore a topic by gathering factual information from several resources. Through your research, you develop a point of view or draw a conclusion. This point of view or conclusion becomes the main idea, or thesis statement, of your report.

Select a Topic

Because a research report usually takes time to prepare and write, your choice of topic is especially important. Follow these guidelines.

- Brainstorm to make a list of possible topics. Choose a topic that is neither too narrow nor too broad for the length of paper you will write.
- Select a topic that genuinely interests you.
- Be sure you can find information on your topic from several sources.

Do Research

Start by reading general information about your topic in an encyclopedia. Then look for answers to specific questions in other sources. The catalog in a library can tell you what books are available on your topic. Online databases such as the *Reader's Guide to Periodical Literature* can help you locate magazine and newspaper articles. Current research on your topic may be found on electronic sources such as CD-ROMs or the Internet. If you need help in finding or using any of these resources, ask the librarian.

Be aware that anyone can post information on the Internet. Make sure that the information you use comes from a reputable source. Being a critical reader is an important part of being a good researcher. Stay focused on your topic as you do your research and be sure you have enough facts to support the statements you will make in your report.

Make Source Cards

In a research report, you must document the source of your information. To keep track of your sources, write the author, title, publication information, and location of each source on a separate index card. Give each source card a number and write that number in the upper right-hand corner. These cards will be useful for preparing your documentation.

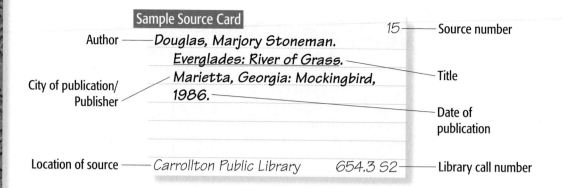

Sample Source Card

Source number — *15*

Author — *Douglas, Marjory Stoneman.*

Title — *Everglades: River of Grass.*

City of publication/Publisher — *Marietta, Georgia: Mockingbird, 1986.*

Date of publication

Location of source — *Carrollton Public Library   654.3 S2* — Library call number

Take Notes

As you read, you encounter many new facts and ideas. Taking notes will help you keep track of information and focus on the topic. Here are some helpful suggestions:

- Use a new card for each important piece of information. Separate cards will help you to organize your notes effectively.
- At the top of each card, write a key word or phrase that tells you about the information. Also, write the number of the source you used.
- Write only details and ideas that relate to your topic.
- Summarize information in your own words.
- Record a phrase or a quotation only when the words are especially interesting or come from an important source. Enclose all quotations in quotation marks to make clear that the words belong to someone else.

This sample note card shows information to include.

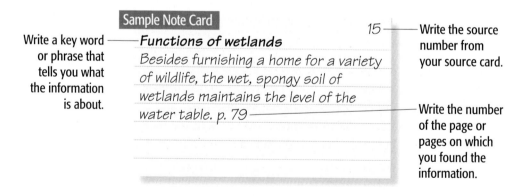

Sample Note Card

Write a key word or phrase that tells you what the information is about. — *Functions of wetlands*

Besides furnishing a home for a variety of wildlife, the wet, spongy soil of wetlands maintains the level of the water table. p. 79

15 — Write the source number from your source card.

Write the number of the page or pages on which you found the information.

PRACTICE

Think of a topic you might use for a research report of about 750 words.

1. Use the library or the Internet to find three sources of information on your topic. Try to get a variety of sources—for example, a book, a periodical, a Web site. Make a source card for each source.

continued

2. Find one useful bit of information from each source and fill out a note card with that information. Follow the form of the sample card above.

Develop Your Thesis

As you begin researching and learning about your topic, stay focussed on the overall point you want to make. Write down a thesis statement and keep it in mind as you continue your research. The thesis will help you determine what information is important. However, be prepared to change your thesis if the information you find does not support it.

Write an Outline

When you finish taking notes, organize the information in an outline. Write down the main ideas that you want to cover. Write your thesis statement at the beginning of your outline. Then list the supporting details. Follow an outline form like the one below.

Sample Outline

Everglades National Park is a beautiful but endangered animal habitat.

   I. Special aspects of the Everglades

      A. Characteristics of wetlands

      B. Endangered birds and animals

   II. Pressures on the Everglades

      A. Florida agriculture

      B. Carelessness of visitors

   III. How to protect the Everglades

      A. Change agricultural practices

      B. Educate visitors who come to the park

         1. Mandatory video on safety for individuals and environment

         2. Instructional reminders posted throughout the park

The thesis statement identifies your topic and the overall point you will make.

If you have subtopics under a main topic, there must be at least two. They must relate directly to your main topic.

If you wish to divide a subtopic, you must have at least two divisions. Each must relate to the subtopic above it.

Document Your Information

You must document, or credit, the sources of all the information you use in your report. There are two common ways to document information.

Footnotes

To document with footnotes, place a number at the end of the information you are documenting. Number your notes consecutively, beginning with number 1. These numbers should be slightly raised and should come after any punctuation. The documentation information itself goes at the bottom of the page, with a matching number.

In-text number for note:

The Declaration of Independence was read in public for the first time on July 6, 1776.[3]

Footnote at bottom of page:

[3] John Smith, The Declaration of Independence (New York: DI, 2001) 221.

Parenthetical Documentation

In this method, you give the source for your information in parentheses at the end of the sentence where the information appears. You do not need to give all the details of the source. Just provide enough information for your readers to identify it. Here are the basic rules to follow.

- Usually it is enough to give the author's last name and the number of the page where you found the information.

    The declaration was first read in public by militia colonel John Nixon (Smith 222).

- If you mention the author's name in the sentence, you do not need to repeat it in the parentheses.

    According to Smith, the reading was greeted with wild applause (224).

- If your source does not identify a particular author, as in a newspaper or encyclopedia article, give the first word or two of the title of the piece.

    The anniversary of the reading was commemorated by a parade and fireworks ("Reading Celebrated").

Full information on your sources goes in a list at the end of your paper.

Works Cited or Bibliography

At the end of your paper, list all the sources of information that you used in preparing your report. Arrange them alphabetically by the author's last name (or by the first word in the title if no author is mentioned) as shown below. Title this list *Works Cited*. (Use the term *bibliography* if all your sources are printed media, such as books, magazines, or newspapers.)

Newspaper article →

Magazine article →

Book with one author →

Book with two authors →

Book with three or more authors →

Online article →

Encyclopedia →

Interview →

Video Recording →

Indent all but the first line of each item. →

Include page numbers for a magazine article but not for a book, unless the book is a collection of essays by various authors. →

Et al means "and others" →

Include the name of the site (in italics), the date it was created or revised, and the date you accessed it. →

Works Cited

Bertram, Jeffrey. "African Bees: Fact or Myth?" *Orlando Sentinel* 18 Aug. 1999: D2.

Gore, Rick. "Neanderthals." National Geographic. (January 1996): 2–35.

Gould, Stephen J. The Panda's Thumb. New York: Norton, 1982.

McNeill, John Robert, and Paul Kennedy. *Something New Under the Sun: An Environmental History of the Twentieth-Century World*. New York: Norton, 2000.

Quirk, Randolph, et al. *An Old English Grammar*. DeKalb, IL: Northern Illinois UP, 1994.

"Governor Chiles Vetoes Anti-Everglades Bills–5/13/98." Friends of the Everglades. May 1998. 26 Aug 1998 <http://www.everglades.org/pressrel_may28.htm>.

"Neanderthal Man." The Columbia Encyclopedia. 5th ed. New York: Columbia UP, 1993.

Pabst, Laura. Personal interview. 11 March 1998.

Kubrick, Stanley, dir. *2001: A Space Odyssey*. 1968. DVD. Warner, 1999.

PRACTICE

Think of a good topic for a research paper. Then look for five sources of information about that topic. Your sources should include one book, one encyclopedia article, two magazine articles, and one online article. Using the proper format, prepare a list of works cited for your five sources.

Business Writing

Two standard formats for business letters are block style and modified block style. In block style, all the sections and paragraphs of the letter begin at the left-hand margin. In modified block style (as shown below), the heading and closing are indented to the right and each paragraph is indented.

10 Pullman Lane
Cromwell, CT 06416
January 16, 2001

> In the heading, write your address and the date on separate lines.

Mr. Philip Fornaro
Principal
Cromwell School
179 West Maple Street
Cromwell, CT 06416

> In the inside address, write the name and address of the person to whom you are sending the letter.

Dear Mr. Fornaro:

> Use a colon after the greeting.

   My friends and I in the seventh grade at Brimmer Middle School feel that there is not enough to do in Cromwell during the winter vacation week. Some students can afford to go away for vacation. Many families, however, cannot afford to go away, or the parents have to work.

> In your introduction, say who you are and why you are writing.

   I would like to suggest that you keep the Brimmer Middle School gym open during the vacation week. If the gym were open, the basketball teams could practice. The fencing club could meet. We could meet our friends there instead of going to the mall.

> In the body of your letter, provide details concerning your request.

   Thanks for listening to my request. I hope you will think it over.

> Conclude by restating your purpose and thanking the person you are writing to.

Sincerely,

Kim Goodwin

Kim Goodwin

> In the closing, use *Sincerely, Sincerely yours,* or *Yours truly* followed by a comma. Include both your signature and your printed or typed name.

General guidelines

Follow these guidelines when writing a business letter.

- Use correct business-letter form, as shown on page R60. Whether you write, type, or use a word processor, use 8½-by-11-inch white or off-white paper. Be sure your letter is neat and clean.
- Use Standard English. Check your spelling carefully.
- Be polite, even if you are making a complaint or expressing a negative opinion.
- Be brief and to the point. State your reason for writing within the first two or three sentences.
- Include all necessary information.
- If you are making a request, be specific. Make sure what you are asking is reasonable. Express your appreciation at the end of the letter.
- Be considerate. Request only information you cannot get another way.
- When expressing an opinion or a complaint, state your reasons clearly and logically. Avoid emotional language.
- When requesting an interview, make it easy for the interviewee to meet with you. Suggest a few dates.

Writing a Memo

A memo, or memorandum, is a brief, efficient way of communicating information to another person or group of people. It begins with a header that provides basic information. A memo does not have a formal closing.

> TO: *Brimmer Banner* staff
> FROM: Terry Glinski
> SUBJECT: Winter issue
> DATE: January 18, 2002
>
> Articles for the winter issue of the *Brimmer Banner* are due by February 1. Please see Terry about your assignment as soon as possible! The following articles or features have not yet been assigned:
>
> Cafeteria Mess: Who Is Responsible?
> Teacher Profile: Mr. Jinks, Ms. Magee
> Sports roundup

Communications Skills Handbook

Using a Computer for Writing

Using a computer with a word processing program to write offers advantages at every stage of the writing process.

Prewriting

A computer can help you gather and organize ideas and information.

Brainstorming

While brainstorming for topics or details, you can dim the computer screen and do "invisible writing." Some writers find that this technique allows their ideas to flow more freely.

Researching

CD-ROMs are disks that store large amounts of text, graphics, and sounds. If your computer has a CD-ROM drive, you can use a CD-ROM encyclopedia to find not only text and pictures, but also sound, animated cartoons or graphics, and live-action video clips.

If you have a modem and are connected with an online service, you can access material from an online encyclopedia, magazine, or Web site.

Outlining

Some word processing programs offer an outlining feature that automatically indents headings and uses various type styles for main headings and subheadings.

Drafting/Revising

Most word processing programs make it easy to do the following:

- *insert* new text at any point in your document
- *delete* or *copy* text
- *move* text from one position to another
- *undo* a change or series of changes you just made
- *save* each draft or revision of your document
- *print* copies of your work-in-progress for others to read

Editing/Proofreading

You can edit and proofread directly on the computer, or you can mark your changes on a printout, or hard copy and then input the changes on screen. The following word processing features are helpful:

- **Grammar checker** The computer finds possible errors in grammar and suggests revisions.
- **Spelling checker** The computer finds misspellings and suggests corrections.
- **Thesaurus** If you want to replace an inappropriate or overused word, you can highlight the word and the computer will suggest synonyms.
- **Search and replace** If you want to change or correct something that occurs several times in your document, the computer can quickly make the change throughout the document.

Rule of Thumb: The grammar checker, spelling checker, and thesaurus cannot replace your own careful reading and judgment. Because English grammar is so complex, the suggestions that the grammar checker makes may not be appropriate. The spelling checker will not tell you that you have typed *brake* when you meant *break,* for example, because both are valid words. The thesaurus may offer you several synonyms for a word, but you need to consider the connotations of each before deciding which fits your context.

Presenting

The computer allows you to enhance the readability, attractiveness, and visual interest of your document in many ways.

Formatting your text

The computer gives you a variety of options for the layout and appearance of your text. You can easily add or change the following elements:

- margin width
- number of columns
- type size and style
- page numbering
- header or footer (information such as a title that appears at the top or bottom of every page)

Visual aids

Some word processing programs have graphic functions that allow you to create graphs, charts, and diagrams. Collections of photos, clip art, and pictures you can copy and paste into your document are also available.

Study and Test-Taking Skills

Study Skills

Good study skills grow out of good habits. Try making the following suggestions part of your daily school routine. Write down each subject and each assignment daily in an assignment notebook. For each assignment, set a study goal. Decide how long it will take you to meet each goal. Divide long assignments into smaller tasks.

Tips for good study habits

- Keep an assignment notebook. Keep it up to date.
- Keep your notes for each course together in one place.
- Find a good place to study. Choose a place that has as few distractions as possible. Try to study in the same place each day.
- Try to study at the same time each day.
- Don't study one subject too long. If you haven't finished after thirty minutes, switch to another subject.
- Take notes on your reading. Keep your notes in one place.

Taking Tests

How well you perform on a test is not a matter of chance. Some specific strategies can help you answer test questions. This section of the handbook will show how to improve your test-taking skills.

Tips for preparing for tests

Here are some useful suggestions:

- Gather information about the test. When will it be given? How long will it take? Exactly what material will it cover?
- Review material from your textbook, class notes, homework, quizzes, and handouts. Review the study questions at the end of each section of a textbook. Try to define terms in boldface type.
- Make up some sample questions and answer them. As you skim selections, try to predict what may be asked.
- Draw charts and cluster or Venn diagrams to help you remember information and to picture how one piece of information relates to another.
- Give yourself plenty of time to study. Avoid cramming for a test. Several short review sessions are more effective than one long one.
- In addition to studying alone, study with a partner or small group. Quiz one another on topics you think the test will cover.

Tips for using test time

Try following these steps:

- Read all directions carefully. Understanding the directions can prevent mistakes.
- Ask for help if you have a question.
- Answer the easier items first. By skipping the hard items, you will have time to answer all the easy ones.
- In the time that is left, return to the items you skipped. Answer them as best you can. If you won't be penalized for doing so, guess at an answer.
- If possible, save some time at the end to check your answers.

Taking objective tests

An objective test is a test of factual information. The answers to the questions are either right or wrong. You are asked to recall information, not to present your ideas. Objective test questions include true-or-false items, multiple-choice items, fill-in-the-blanks statements, short-answer items, and matching items. At the beginning of an objective test, scan the number of items. Then budget your time.

Multiple-choice items Multiple-choice questions ask you to answer a question or complete a sentence. They are the kind of question you will encounter most often on objective tests. Read all the choices before answering. Pick the best response.

> **What is a peninsula?**
> (a) a range of mountains
> (b) a circle around the moon
> (c) a body of land surrounded by water on three sides

Correct answer: (c)

- Read the question carefully. Be sure that you understand it.
- Read all the answers before selecting one. Reading all of the responses is especially important when one of the choices is "all of the above" or "none of the above."
- Eliminate responses that are clearly incorrect. Focus on the responses that might be correct.
- Look for absolute words, such as *never, always, all, none*. Most generalizations have exceptions. Absolute statements are often incorrect. (Note: This tip applies to true-or-false items also.)

Answering essay questions

Essay questions ask you to think about what you have learned and to write about it in one or more paragraphs. Some tests present a choice of essay questions. If a test has both an objective part and an essay part, answer the objective questions first but leave yourself enough time to work on the essay.

Read the essay question carefully. What does it ask you to do? Discuss? Explain? Define? Summarize? Compare and contrast? These key words tell what kind of information you must give in your answer.

Key Verbs in Essay Questions	
Argue	Give your opinion and supporting reasons.
Compare and contrast	Discuss likenesses and differences.
Define	Give details that show exactly what something is like.
Demonstrate	Give examples to support a point.
Describe	Present a picture with words.
Discuss	Show detailed information on a particular subject.
Explain	Give reasons.
Identify	Give specific characteristics.
List (also outline, trace)	Give details, give steps in order, give a time sequence.
Summarize	Give a short overview of the most important ideas or events.

Tips for answering essay questions

Consider the following suggestions:

- Read the question or questions carefully. Determine the kind of information required by the question.
- Plan your time. Do not spend too much time on one part of the essay.
- Make a list of what you want to cover.
- If you have time, make revisions and proofreading corrections.

Taking standardized tests

Standardized tests are taken by large groups of students. Your performance on the test is compared with the performance of other students at your grade level. There are many kinds of standardized tests. Some measure your progress in such subjects as English, math, and science, while others measure how well you think. Standardized tests can show how you learn and what you do best.

Preparing for standardized tests

There is no way to know exactly what information will be on a standardized test or even what topics will be covered. The best preparation is to do the best you can in your daily schoolwork. However, you can learn the *kinds* of questions that will appear on a standardized test. Some general tips will also help.

Tips for taking standardized tests

You may find the following suggestions helpful:

- Get enough sleep the night before the test. Eat a healthful breakfast.
- Arrive early for the test. Try to relax.
- Listen carefully to all test directions. Ask questions if you don't understand the directions.
- Complete easy questions first. Leave harder items for the end.
- Be sure your answers are in the right place on the answer sheet.
- If points are not subtracted for wrong answers, guess at answers that you aren't sure of.

Analogies Analogy items test your understanding of the relationships between things or ideas. On standardized tests, analogies are written in an abbreviated format, as shown below.

man : woman :: buck : doe

The symbol *:* means "is to"; the symbol *::* means "as."

This chart shows some word relationships you may find in analogy tests.

Relationship	Definition	Example
Synonyms	Two words have a similar meaning.	huge : gigantic :: scared : afraid
Antonyms	Two words have opposite meanings.	bright : dull :: far : near
Use	Words name a user and something used.	farmer : tractor :: writer : computer
Cause-Effect	Words name a cause and its effect.	tickle : laugh :: polish : shine
Category	Words name a category and an item in it.	fish : tuna :: building : house
Description	Words name an item and a characteristic of it.	knife : sharp :: joke : funny

Listening, Speaking, and Viewing Skills

Listening Effectively

A large part of the school day is spent either listening or speaking to others. By becoming a better listener and speaker, you will know more about what is expected of you and understand more about your audience.

Listening to instructions in class

Some of the most important listening in the school day involves listening to instructions. Use the following checklist to help you.

- Make sure you understand what you are listening for. Are you receiving instructions for homework or for a test? What you listen for depends upon the type of instructions being given.
- Think about what you are hearing and keep your eyes on the speaker. This will help you stay focused on the important points.
- Listen for key words or word clues. Examples of word clues are phrases such as *above all, most important,* or *the three basic parts.* These clues help you identify important points that you should remember.
- Take notes on what you hear. Write down only the most important parts of the instructions.
- If you don't understand something, ask questions. Then if you're still unsure about the instructions, repeat them aloud to your teacher to receive correction on any key points that you may have missed.

Interpreting nonverbal clues

Understanding nonverbal clues is part of effective listening. Nonverbal clues are everything you notice about a speaker *except* what the speaker says. As you listen, ask yourself these questions:

- Where and how is the speaker standing?
- Are some words spoken with more emphasis than others?
- Is a word, phrase, or sentence repeated?
- Does the speaker make eye contact?
- Does he or she smile or look angry?
- What message is sent by the speaker's gestures and facial expression?

| **PRACTICE** |

Work with a partner to practice listening to instructions. Each of you should find a set of directions for using a simple device—for example, a mechanical tool, a telephone answering machine, or a VCR. Study the instructions carefully. If you can bring the device to class, ask your partner to try to use it by following your step-by-step instructions. If you cannot have the device in class, ask your partner to explain the directions back to you. Then change roles and listen as your partner gives you a set of directions.

Speaking Effectively

- Speak slowly, clearly, and in a normal tone of voice. Raise your voice a bit or use gestures to stress important points.
- Pause a few seconds after making an important point.
- Use words that help your audience picture what you're talking about. Visual aids such as pictures, graphs, charts, and maps can also help make your information clear.
- Stay in contact with your audience. Make sure your eyes move from person to person in the group you're addressing.

Speaking informally

Most oral communication is informal. When you speak casually with your friends, family, and neighbors, you use informal speech. Human relationships depend on this form of communication.

- Be courteous. Listen until the other person has finished speaking.
- Speak in a relaxed and spontaneous manner.
- Make eye contact with your listeners.
- Do not monopolize a conversation.
- When telling a story, show enthusiasm.
- When giving an announcement or directions, speak clearly and slowly. Check that your listeners understand the information.

Presenting an oral report

The steps in preparing an oral report are similar to the steps in the writing process, except that an additional step—*practicing*—is added before *presenting*. (See the chart on the following page.) Complete each step carefully and you can be confident of presenting an effective oral report.

Steps in Preparing an Oral Report	
Prewriting	Determine your purpose and audience. Decide on a topic and narrow it.
Drafting	Make an outline. Fill in the supporting details. Write the report.
Revising and editing	Review your draft. Check the organization of ideas and details. Reword unclear statements.
Practicing	Practice the report aloud in front of a family member. Time the report. Ask for and accept advice.
Presenting	Relax in front of your audience. Make eye contact with your audience. Speak slowly and clearly.

PRACTICE

Pretend that you have been invited to give an oral report to a group of fifth graders. Your report will tell them what to expect and how to adjust to new conditions when they enter middle school. As you plan your report, keep your purpose and your audience in mind. Include lively descriptions and examples to back up your suggestions and hold your audience's attention. As you practice giving your report, be sure to give attention to your body language as well as your vocal projection. Ask a partner to listen to your report and give you feedback on how to improve your performance. Do the same for your partner after listening to his or her report.

Viewing Effectively

Critical viewing means thinking about what you see while watching a TV program, newscast, film, or video. It requires paying attention to what you hear and see and deciding whether information is true, false, or exaggerated. If the information *seems* to be true, try to determine whether it is based on a fact or an opinion.

Fact versus opinion

A fact is something that can be proved. An opinion is what someone *believes* is true. Opinions are based on feelings and experiences and cannot be proved.

Television commercials, political speeches, and even the evening news contain both facts and opinions. They use emotional words and actions to persuade the viewer to agree with a particular point of view. They may also use faulty reasoning, such as linking an effect with the wrong cause. Think through what is being said. The speaker may seem sincere, but do his or her reasons make sense? Are the reasons based on facts or on unfair generalizations?

Commercials contain both obvious and hidden messages. Just as you need to discover the author's purpose when you read a writer's words, you must be aware of the purpose of nonverbal attempts to persuade you. What does the message sender want, and how is the sender trying to influence you? For example, a magazine or TV ad picturing a group of happy teenagers playing volleyball on a sunny beach expresses a positive feeling. The advertiser hopes viewers will transfer that positive feeling to the product being advertised—perhaps a soft drink or a brand of beachwear. This technique, called **transfer,** is one of several propaganda techniques regularly used by advertisers to influence consumers. Following are a few other common techniques.

Testimonial—Famous and admired people recommend or praise a product, a policy, or a course of action even though they probably have no professional knowledge or expertise to back up their opinion.

Bandwagon—People are urged to follow the crowd ("get on the bandwagon") by buying a product, voting for a candidate, or whatever else the advertiser wants them to do.

Glittering generalities—The advertiser uses positive, good-sounding words (for example, *all-American* or *medically proven*) to impress people.

PRACTICE

Think of a television commercial that you have seen often or watch a new one and take notes as you watch it. Then analyze the commercial.

- What is the purpose behind the ad?
- What is expressed in written or spoken words?
- What is expressed nonverbally (in music or sound effects as well as in pictures and actions)?
- What methods does the advertiser use to persuade viewers?
- What questions would you ask the advertiser if you could?
- How effective is the commercial? Why?

Working in Groups

Working in a group is an opportunity to learn from others. Whether you are planning a group project (such as a class trip) or solving a math problem, each person in a group brings specific strengths and interests to the task. When a task is large, such as planting a garden, a group provides the necessary energy and talent to get the job done.

Small groups vary in size according to the nature of the task. Three to five students is a good size for most small-group tasks. Your teacher may assign you to a group, or you may be asked to form your own group. Don't work with your best friend if you are likely to chat too much. Successful groups often have a mix of student abilities and interests.

Individual role assignments give everyone in a group something to do. One student, the group recorder, may take notes. Another may lead the discussion, and another report the results to the rest of the class.

Roles for a Small Group	
Reviewer	Reads or reviews the assignment and makes sure everyone understands it
Recorder 1 (of the process)	Takes notes on the discussion
Recorder 2 (of the results)	Takes notes on the final results
Reporter	Reports results to the rest of the class
Discussion leader	Asks questions to get the discussion going; keeps the group focused
Facilitator	Helps the group resolve disagreements and reach a compromise

For a small group of three or four students, some of these roles can be combined. Your teacher may assign a role to each student in your group. Or you may be asked to choose your own role.

Tips for working in groups

- Review the group assignment and goal. Be sure that everyone in the group understands the assignment.
- Review the amount of time allotted for the task. Decide how your group will organize its time.
- Check that all the group members understand their roles in the group.
- When a question arises, try to solve it as a group before asking a teacher for help.
- Listen to other points of view. Take turns during a discussion.
- When it is your turn to talk, address the subject and help the project move forward.

Reading Handbook

The Reading Process

As reading materials get more difficult, you'll need to use a variety of active reading strategies to understand texts. This handbook is designed to help you find and use the tools you'll need before, during, and after reading.

Word Identification

Word identification skills are a necessary building block for understanding what you read. They prepare you to deal with unknown words you'll encounter as you read.

Look before, at, and after a new word. Use the other words and sentences around an unknown word to help you make an educated guess about what that word might be. Think about the following questions as you try to read new words.

- What other word would make sense in this sentence?
- Can I sound this new word out?
- Can I figure out this word from its place in the sentence?

Using letter-sound cues

One way to figure out a new word is to try to sound it out. Use the following tips when sounding out new words.

- Look at the beginning of the word. What letter or group of letters makes up the beginning sound or beginning syllable of the word?

  Example: In the word *coagulate, co-* rhymes with *so.*

- Look at the end of the word. What letter or group of letters makes up the ending sound or syllable? Knowing how a word begins and ends will help you take a better guess at the whole word.

  Example: In the word *coagulate, late* is a word you know.

- Look at the middle of the word. What are the sounds of the letters and groups of letters within the word? Is there a word you already know inside the new word? Is the middle of the word similar to other words you know? What vowel or vowel pattern is represented in each syllable?

Example: In the word *coagulate,* the syllable *ag* has the same vowel sound as *bag* and the syllable *u* is pronounced like the letter *u.* Now try pronouncing the whole word: *co ag u late.*

Using language structure cues

Word order, or **syntax,** helps you make sense of a sentence, so looking at the position of a new word in a sentence can help you identify a word. For instance, look at the following nonsense sentence.

The drazzy lurds miffled the bonkee blams.

Your experience with English sentence patterns and parts of speech tells you that the action word, or verb, in this sentence is *miffled.* Who did the *miffling?*—the *lurds.* What kind of *lurds* were they?—*drazzy.* Whom did they *miffle?*—the *blams.* What kind of blams were they?—*bonkee.* Even though you do not know word meanings in the nonsense sentence, you can make some sense of the entire sentence by using syntax.

Using context clues

When you read on your own, you can often figure out the meaning of a new word by looking at its **context,** the words and sentences that surround it. For instance, look at the following example.

The area suffered an earthquake followed by a flood. After such *cataclysms,* it took some time to return to normal.

You can see from the first sentence that *cataclysms* refers to both an earthquake and a flood. It is a general word for violent change in the forces of nature. The context provides examples of the unknown word.

Tips for Using Context

- Look before, at, and after the unknown word for
  —a synonym or definition of the unknown word in a sentence
    *To avoid a collision, the car **swerved**, or **turned aside**.*
  —a clue to what the word is like or not like
    ***Like a human top,** the little dancer **pirouetted** gracefully.*
  —a general topic associated with the word
    *The **gardener** shoveled **mulch** onto all the flower beds.*
  —a description or action associated with the word
    *The seamstress used **pinking shears** to **trim** the seams of the dress.*
- Connect what you know with what the author has written.
- Predict a possible meaning.
- Apply the meaning in the sentence.
- Try again if your guess does not make sense.

Using word parts to read new words

Knowing word parts can help you sound out unknown words. It can also help you discover word meanings or enable you to change a word's meaning.

- **Roots** The base part of a word is called its root. If you know a root within a new word, start from there to sound out the rest of the word. The root can also give you a hint about the word's meaning. Some roots, mainly those that came from Anglo-Saxon, are familiar words. For example, the roots *dear* and *mark* can be found in such longer words as en*dear*ing and re*mark*able. Other roots are less familiar borrowings from Greek and Latin. For example, *spectator* contains the Latin root *spec*, which means "to look at."

- **Prefixes** A prefix is added to the beginning of a word. It changes the meaning of the word. For example, *semi-* means "half," so *semicircle* means "half circle."

- **Suffixes** A suffix can be added to the end of a word to change how the word is used in a sentence. For example, fear (a noun or a verb) becomes an adjective when the suffix *-ful* (meaning "full of") is added. *Fearful* means "full of fear."

Using reference materials

When looking at or around an unknown word does not help you identify it, dictionaries, glossaries, and other reference sources can be useful tools.

A **dictionary** provides the pronunciation and literal meaning or meanings of a word. It may also give other forms of the word, its part of speech, alternate spellings, examples, synonyms, origins, and other useful information. Look at the dictionary entry below.

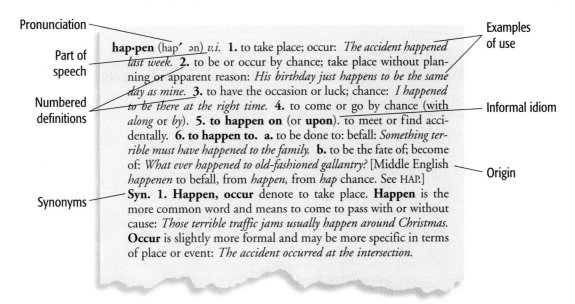

Pronunciation — Part of speech — Numbered definitions — Synonyms

Examples of use — Informal idiom — Origin

hap·pen (hap′ ən) *v.i.* **1.** to take place; occur: *The accident happened last week.* **2.** to be or occur by chance; take place without planning or apparent reason: *His birthday just happens to be the same day as mine.* **3.** to have the occasion or luck; chance: *I happened to be there at the right time.* **4.** to come or go by chance (with *along* or *by*). **5. to happen on** (or **upon**). to meet or find accidentally. **6. to happen to. a.** to be done to; befall: *Something terrible must have happened to the family.* **b.** to be the fate of; become of: *What ever happened to old-fashioned gallantry?* [Middle English *happenen* to befall, from *happen*, from *hap* chance. See HAP.]
Syn. 1. Happen, occur denote to take place. **Happen** is the more common word and means to come to pass with or without cause: *Those terrible traffic jams usually happen around Christmas.* **Occur** is slightly more formal and may be more specific in terms of place or event: *The accident occurred at the intersection.*

A **glossary** is a condensed dictionary within a specific text. It provides an alphabetical listing of words used within that text, together with their definitions and other information necessary to understand the words as they appear in the text. Look at the example below.

A

abolitionist a person who favors doing away with slavery (p. 416)

abstain to not take part in some activity, such as voting (p. 440)

adobe a sun-dried mud brick used to build the homes of Native Americans (p. 31)

affirmative action an active effort to improve educational and employment opportunities for minority groups and women (p. 887)

affluence the state of having much wealth (p. 808)

airlift a system of transporting food and supplies by aircraft into an area otherwise impossible to reach (p. 777)

A **thesaurus** is a dictionary of synonyms. It can be especially useful for choosing precise, descriptive language. Some thesauruses are available on CD-ROM and on the Internet.

Reading Fluency

Becoming an accomplished reader is like learning a sports skill or a musical instrument: the more you practice, the better you will be. The more you read aloud, the less attention you will need to pay to sounding words out and the more attention you can give to understanding the meaning in a selection.

Tips for Becoming a Fluent Reader

- Develop a good sight vocabulary.
- Practice reading aloud on independent level materials.
- Begin with a short interesting passage.
- Reread the same passage aloud at least three times.
- As your reading sounds smoother, move on to a longer or slightly more difficult passage.

Reading in appropriate level materials

How do you decide if something is too easy, too hard, or just right for you to read? If you want to develop into a smooth, fluent reader, it is important to read regularly in materials that are easy for you. However, it is also important to grow as a strategic reader. To do that, you will want to read materials that are challenging but manageable.

To decide what level of reading material is right for each reading task, look at the following chart:

Reading Level	Definition/Criteria	When to Use
Independent level	No more than 5 difficult words per 100 words read	• On your own, anytime • To practice smooth reading
Instructional level	No more than 10 difficult words per 100 words read	• With support from teacher, parent, or other more experienced reader • To challenge yourself
Beyond instructional level	More than 10 difficult words per 100 words read	• As material read to you by someone else • To develop new vocabulary through listening

Adjusting reading rate—skimming, scanning, and careful reading

It is important to adjust your reading speed to suit your purposes and the task you face. When you read something for enjoyment, you might read quickly. If you want to refresh your memory of a passage or get a quick impression of new material, skim the selection. **Skimming** is reading quickly over a piece of writing to find its main idea or to get a general overview of it. When you need to find a particular piece or type of information, scan the selection. In **scanning,** you run your eyes quickly over the material, looking only for key words or phrases that have to do with the information you seek.

When you read a chapter of a textbook filled with new concepts, when you follow complex written directions, or when you study for a test, read slowly, take notes, make a graphic organizer, and even reread passages in order to remember them later.

Look at the following models.

It was a perfect day at Bowen Lake. At noon the woods and the lake were warm in the sun. Seated on a rock at the top of a hill, the boy watched the scene below him. The lake was a mirror of glass, occasionally broken by a leaping fish or a swooping bird. Far across the lake, he could sometimes see a canoe gliding by. He felt at peace with himself and the world, absorbed in the magic of being alone with nature.

Osmosis is the tendency of a liquid, usually water, to flow through a semipermeable membrane that blocks the transport of salts or other solutes through it. Osmosis is a fundamental effect in all biological systems. When two volumes of liquid are separated by a semipermeable membrane, water will flow from the side of low solute concentration to the side of high solute concentration.

Which paragraph could you read more quickly? Why? What would you do to be sure you remembered the information in each paragraph?

Reading aloud

Reading out loud, alone or with others, can make a writer's work come to life and can be an enjoyable way of sharing a selection. Reading a complicated paragraph aloud can also be a powerful aid to understanding. Here are some suggestions for reading aloud:

- First read the selection silently a number of times.
- Think about the best way to make the main ideas understandable to your listeners.
- Use pauses to separate complete thoughts and be sure you observe all punctuation marks.
- Read carefully and clearly. Vary your speed and volume to reflect the important ideas in a passage.
- Use a lively voice. Emphasize important words and phrases to make the meaning clear.
- Practice difficult words and phrases until you've mastered them.
- Practice in front of another person, if possible, or use a tape recorder to hear how you sound.

Reading silently

Be sure to avoid distractions or interruptions when you read silently.

Tips for Sustained Silent Reading

- Be sure you're comfortable but not too comfortable.
- Check your concentration regularly by asking yourself **questions** about the selection.
- **Summarize** what you've read from time to time.
- Use a **study guide** or **story map** while reading difficult passages.
- Make a **graphic organizer,** if necessary, to understand and remember important concepts or a sequence of events.
- Take regular breaks when you need them and vary your reading rate with the demands of the text.

PRACTICE

With a partner, choose a selection from your text. Read the selection silently, adjusting your speed to the difficulty of the text. When both of you have finished, take turns asking questions to check your comprehension. Finally, choose a small section of the passage and take turns reading it aloud. Exchange suggestions about your oral reading.

Reading a Variety of Texts

Learn to read a wide range of materials for a variety of purposes. Throughout this textbook, you can read both classic and contemporary writing. From "Rip Van Winkle" to "The Scholarship Jacket," you will see how a variety of selections broadens your knowledge and deepens your appreciation of people and cultures.

Reading varied sources

Strategic readers take advantage of a variety of sources for information and for entertainment. For instance, to create a detailed and interesting portrait of a famous writer from your hometown or state, you might refer to sources like those listed below.

- **Encyclopedias** provide a basic foundation of information.
- **Letters, memos, speeches, newspapers,** and **magazines** add valuable information as well as personal perspectives.
- **Databases, library indexes,** and **Internet sites** often supply or lead you to interesting information.
- **Fiction, poems, plays,** and **anthologies,** (collections of literature), provide excellent opportunities to read for pleasure as well as to explore the ideas of a writer in a particular time.

Reading for various purposes

Active reading begins with thinking about a reason for reading. You may find that you have more than one purpose or that your purposes overlap. For instance, you might enjoy reading an intense and thrilling mystery for entertainment and, at the same time, discover how police detectives work. The reading strategies you use to guide you through a text will depend on your purposes.

When your purpose for reading is

- **to be informed,** read slowly, take notes, construct a graphic organizer, reread, and review difficult sections.
- **to be entertained,** read at a faster rate.
- **to appreciate a writer's craft,** read carefully to admire how well others write and to determine how they do so.
- **to discover models for your own writing,** look at other writers' works to help stimulate your own ideas.
- **to take action,** read carefully so you can correctly complete forms, make recommendations, and write responses.

PRACTICE

Choose a topic that interests you and read about it in at least three sources. Decide on an action to take as a result of your reading. You may write a short report, give a speech, demonstrate how something works, or try to persuade your classmates to believe or do something. Make a short presentation to your class, explaining your purpose for reading and the value of each of your sources.

Vocabulary Development

Having a good vocabulary means more than just knowing the meanings of isolated words. It means knowing the larger concepts that surround those words. The best way to build a good vocabulary is to read widely, listen carefully, and participate actively in discussions in which new words and concepts are used.

Listening

Books that may be just a little too hard for you to read on your own are often excellent choices as selections to be read aloud to you. They provide a good way to learn new vocabulary. "Read-alouds" also give you a model for your own future oral reading. As you hear new words, try to pay attention to their **context**—the words and ideas surrounding the unknown words. Try to guess what meaning would make sense for new words. Many times you will guess accurately if you pay careful attention.

Using experience and prior knowledge

Because of your life experiences, you know certain things and understand the meanings of certain words and ideas. Those experiences, called **prior knowledge,** help you determine word meanings. For instance, if you have had experience using computers, you'll understand the following sentence.

She needed to clean her mouse to make her cursor move.

Sometimes you'll need to look beyond the exact meaning of words in a selection and consider some of the following variations of language.

- Idioms An expression that has a meaning apart from the literal meaning of the words is called an idiom. If a comedian's jokes *bring down the house,* it means that he or she has made the audience applaud or laugh loudly. When someone is *stretching a point,* he or she is making an exception. In each case, combine the words with prior knowledge to interpret what the expression means.
- Multiple meanings Words can have more than one meaning, so check the context to be sure the meaning you have chosen makes sense. Look at these examples:
  *The organ **stops** were jammed, so the organist had to **stop** playing.*
  *Jay **spoke** to his dad about the loose **spoke** on his bicycle wheel.*
- Figurative language Writers sometimes make comparisons by using figurative language, such as analogies, similes, and metaphors. An **analogy** is a comparison between two things or ideas, one of which is usually less familiar to most readers or listeners. An analogy concentrates on those characteristics that are in some way similar. For example, you could make an analogy between a phone call and an e-mail: Both are means of communicating over a distance, both use ordinary language, and both carry messages electronically over wires or via satellites. Similes and metaphors are forms of analogy that are found frequently in literature. A **simile** uses the word *like* or *as* to make a comparison between two unlike things. A **metaphor** states that one thing *is* another.
  Simile: *Snow **like** small white feathers floated down from the sky.*
  Metaphor: *Her eyes were stars that sparkled at the good news.*

PRACTICE

1. List at least three idioms with which you are familiar. Tell what each idiom really means.

2. Use a dictionary, if necessary, to find a word that has at least three very different meanings. Write a sentence demonstrating each of the meanings.

continued

---

3. Write an analogy you might use to explain some topic or process you know quite well to someone who was unfamiliar with it. (For example, explain the use of an electronic keyboard by making an analogy with a piano.)

4. Create a simile you might use in a description of a person you know. Then turn that simile into a metaphor.

Clarifying meanings with reference aids

Sometimes meanings of words and phrases can remain unclear even after using context clues, drawing on your personal background, and listening carefully. In that case, look to other reference aids to help clarify the meanings and usage of difficult terms.

- **Thesauruses** and books of synonyms can clarify a word by listing other words that have similar meanings.
- **Dictionaries** will often be able to clear up word meanings because they provide a variety of definitions for a word and examples of each definition in a sentence. You can often find the meaning of an idiom by looking in a dictionary under the main word in the phrase. Look at the idioms listed under the word *time*.

against time. in an effort to finish within or before a certain time: *Police were working against time in their search for the hidden bomb.*

ahead of time. before the time due or expected; early: *She arrived at the appointed place ahead of time.*

at the same time. however; nevertheless.

at times. sometimes; occasionally.

behind the times. old-fashioned.

for the time being. for the present; temporarily.

from time to time. now and then; occasionally.

in good time. a. at the proper time; within reasonable time. **b.** when or sooner than expected; quickly.

in no time. almost instantly; very rapidly.

in time. a. before it is too late. *Do you think we can get there in time for the first act?* **b.** in the course of time; eventually: *In time, all this will be forgotten.* **c.** in the correct or corresponding rhythm or tempo: *to clap in time to music.*

on time. a. at the correct or appointed time; punctual or punctually. **b.** payable in installments over time.

time after time. repeatedly. Also, **time and again.**

time out of mind. longer than can be remembered.

to keep time. to record time, as a clock.

to make time. a. to move rapidly, as in attempting to recover lost time. **b.** *Slang.* to progress in gaining favor or acceptance, as in carrying on a flirtation.

- **Software** for a computer will often include reference materials that can clarify meanings and usage for difficult words.

Using word parts to determine meaning

Another way to determine the meaning of a word is to take the word itself apart. If you understand the meaning of the **base**, or **root** part, of a word and also know the meanings of key syllables added either to the beginning or end of the base, you can usually figure out what a word means.

Word Part	Definition	Example
Root or base	the most basic part of a word	*ced* means "go"
Prefix	a syllable used before a root word to add to or change its meaning	*pre-* means "before" *precede* means "go before"
Suffix	a syllable used after a root word to change its meaning or its use	*-ous* means "full of" *joyous* means "full of joy"

Roots English contains many words based on roots from Anglo-Saxon (the earliest form of our language, also known as Old English) and from ancient languages like Greek and Latin. Familiarity with some of these roots can help you to determine meanings, pronunciations, and spellings in English. Look at the following examples.

Root	Meaning	Example
astro (Greek)	star	astronaut, astronomy, asterisk
fare (Anglo-Saxon)	go; feed	farewell, welfare
vid (Latin)	see	video, evidence
hydr (Greek)	water	hydrant, dehydrate

Affixes These syllables are added to a base word either at its beginning (as a prefix) or its end (as a suffix). For example, *unusually* is made up of the word *usual* and the affixes *un-* and *-ly*. The prefix *un-* means "not." The suffix *-ly* means "in a particular manner." If you put them together, unusually means "not in the usual manner."

Suppose you come across an unfamiliar word like *hydroelectrification* in your reading. You can see that the root *electr* (as in electricity) is within the word. If you know that *hydro* means "water" and *-fication* means "making" or "producing," you can figure out that *hydroelectrification* refers to the production of electricity by using water as a power source—at a dam site, for example.

Following are some additional Old English (Anglo-Saxon), Greek, and Latin word parts. Use a dictionary to find the meaning of each one. Then make a chart similar to the second chart on page R83, giving at least two examples of modern English words based on each. Check the words in a dictionary that gives etymologies, or word histories, to make sure they are really based on the word part. Compare your chart with those of others in your class.

like–from Old English (ge)*lik*

reck–from Old English *reccan*

demos–from Greek *demos*

meter–from Greek *metron*

aud–from Latin *audire*

man–from Latin *manus*

Using word meanings across subjects

Have you ever learned a new word and then noticed it in many places and across many subjects? The word may not mean exactly the same thing in each place, but you can often use what you know about a word's meaning to help you interpret its meaning in a different context. Look at the following example from two subjects:

Social studies: *Altitude is one of the* **factors** *affecting climate.*

Math: *The numbers 2 and 3 are* **factors** *of 6.*

A factor is something that contributes to something else, so in geography, altitude causes a climate to be warmer or cooler. In math, a factor is a number that can be multiplied by another number to produce a product.

When you learn vocabulary across subject areas, you may learn

- new meanings for a word you know
- new words for a concept or idea you know about
- new words for a completely new concept or idea

Listening to news stories and current events is a good way to increase your vocabulary. Actively discuss ideas as well as new vocabulary that you hear in news reports. Friends, teachers, and parents will have their own ideas about the subtle meanings of words, so careful listening will add to your vocabulary development. Look at the model below. Can you figure out the meaning of the italicized word in the first sentence of this news report?

> The President pledged to continue with his economic *agenda*, beginning with the reform of the Social Security Administration.

What strategies did you use to determine that *agenda* means "plan"?
How could you use the word in another context?

Find a science or social studies textbook that includes a list of key vocabulary at
the beginning of a chapter. Use prior knowledge or word parts to predict what
the words might mean. Then read the passages in which the words are located
and use syntax or context to check or further refine the meanings you predicted.

Determining denotation and connotation

Determining special meanings of words is an important aid to
understanding. Look at these two ways to distinguish between word
meanings:

- Denotation A **denotation** expresses the literal, or dictionary,
  meaning of a word. A word may have more than one denotation,
  but all of its denotations will be listed in the dictionary.
- Connotation When a word has an implied meaning or association
  in addition to its dictionary meaning, it has a **connotation.** You may
  say that flowers have a *fragrance* but that garbage has a *stench.*
  Both words have a denotation that means "smell," but *fragrance*
  has a pleasant connotation, while the word *stench* connotes something unpleasant.

Understanding historical influences on words

In addition to giving you word spellings, pronunciations, and meanings, a
dictionary will give you the historical background of a word. Many English
words have Greek, Latin, or Anglo-Saxon origins. The Earl of Sandwich
devised a way of eating meat between two pieces of bread so he would
not have to interrupt his card game for meals. Did you realize that the
word *sandwich* originated from this historical fact? Or that the *martial* in
martial arts recalls the name of Mars, the Roman god of warfare?

Comprehension

The main job you have in reading is to understand what you have read.
Using the best strategies at the right times will improve your understanding of what you are reading.

Previewing

Before you begin to read, it's helpful to **preview** a selection.

- **Look** at the title and the illustrations that are included.

- **Read** the headings, subheadings, and anything in bold letters.
- **Skim** the passage; that is, take a quick look at the whole thing.
- **Decide** what the author's purpose might be for writing.
- **Predict** what the selection will be about.
- **Set a purpose** for your own reading.

Using knowledge and experience to understand

Reading is an interactive process between you and a writer. Even the youngest child has a body of information and personal experiences that are important and uniquely his or her own. When you use your own knowledge and experience and combine it with the words on a page, you create meaning in a selection. Drawing on this personal background is called **activating prior knowledge.** As you read, ask yourself

- What do I know about this **topic?**
- Have I been to places similar to the **setting** described by this writer?
- What **experiences** have I had that compare or contrast with what I am reading?
- What **characters** from life or literature remind me of the characters or narrator in the selection?

Establishing and adjusting purposes for reading

Think about these possible purposes that you might have for reading:

- to find out something
- to understand a process or an idea
- to interpret a writer's work and create meaning in a passage
- to enjoy a selection or be entertained by a story
- to solve problems or to perform a task

Each purpose allows for different active reading strategies. To find information for a report, you might skim an entire passage until you find the section you're looking for and then read more slowly. To understand new information, you might read slowly from beginning to end or even reread passages that are unclear. To simply enjoy a piece of good writing, you may allow yourself to read quickly or slow yourself down to appreciate something beautifully written.

It's also important to be able to adjust your purposes as well as your strategies to get the most out of your reading.

Making and verifying predictions

As you read, take educated guesses about story events and outcomes. **Make predictions** before and during your reading. Using your prior knowledge and the information you have gathered in your preview, predict what you will learn or what might happen in a selection. Then, as you read, **adjust your prediction.** Finally, **verify your prediction.** Whether your original prediction is precisely accurate does not matter, but careful predictions and later verifications or adjustments based on your reading increase your understanding of a selection.

Monitoring and modifying reading strategies

No matter what your purposes for reading, your most important task is to understand what you have read. Ask yourself questions as you read. Monitor or check your understanding using the following strategies.

- **Summarize** what you read by answering *who, what, where, when, why,* and *how.*
- **Clarify** what you don't understand by careful rereading.
- **Question** important ideas and story elements.
- **Predict** what will happen next.
- **Evaluate** what you have read so far.

You might practice a strategy once or twice in an easy entertaining selection or after every paragraph in a nonfiction passage.

Tips for Monitoring Understanding

- **Reread.** If silently rereading a passage several times does not help, read it aloud. Observe punctuation marks and slow your rate.
- **Map out the main thoughts or ideas.** A graphic organizer like a story map or Venn diagram can help get your thoughts on track.
- **Look for context clues.** Often a writer will include an example or a definition of a difficult word or idea somewhere in the surrounding sentences. Synonyms or antonyms also provide clues.
- **Ask questions.** Teachers, parents, and other classmates can shed light on difficult passages.
- **Write comments** as well as questions on another piece of paper for later review or discussion.
- **Use reference aids.** Sometimes looking up one word is all it takes to clear up a difficult passage. Dictionaries, glossaries, thesauruses, and encyclopedias provide access to most information.

Visualizing

Creating pictures in your mind as you read is a powerful aid to understanding. According to your imagination and the text, what do characters look like? Can you picture the steps in a process when you read nonfiction? If you can visualize what you read, selections will be more vivid, and you'll recall them better later on. Be sure, though, that what you picture is accurately based on information from the text.

During a time when your teacher is reading aloud to you, either from a piece of fiction or nonfiction, try sketching what you're hearing. If the selection is fiction, draw a character, setting, or action, from the text description. If the selection is nonfiction, see if you can draw the steps in a process or make a small diagram of the place or thing described. Compare your sketch with a partner's and talk about similarities and differences. Go back to the text to adjust or verify your information.

Constructing graphic organizers

Graphic organizers help you organize what you're reading so you can sort ideas out, clear up difficult passages, and remember important ideas in a selection. Look at the following examples of good graphic organizers and notice how they are used.

Web You can show a main idea and supporting details by using a web. Put the main idea in the middle circle and the supporting details in the surrounding circles. Notice how you might include other circles branching off from the detail circles. Use those for further information about your details.

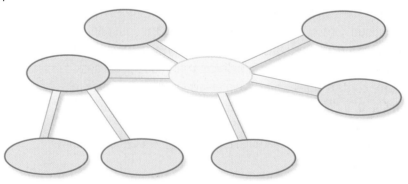

Flowchart When you want to keep track of events in a time order or show a cause-and-effect relationship between events, use a flowchart. Arrange your ideas or events in the boxes, putting them in their logical order. Then draw arrows between the boxes to show how one idea or event flows into another.

Venn diagram To look at the similarities and differences between two ideas, characters, or events, use a Venn diagram. The outer portions of each circle will show how two items contrast, or are different. Use the overlapping portion of the circles to show how they are the same.

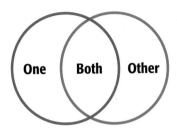

Using text structures

Writers organize their ideas in a variety of ways, depending on their topic and their purpose for writing. When you find that pattern of organization or **text structure** within a selection, it's easier to locate and recall a writer's ideas. Here are four ways that writers structure or organize text, together with word clues that characterize those text structures.

Kind of Organization	Purpose	Clues
Comparison and contrast	To determine similarities and differences	Words and phrases such as *similarly, on the other hand, in contrast to, but, however*
Cause and effect	To explore the reasons for something and to examine the results of events or actions	Words and phrases such as *so, because, as a result*
Chronological order	To present events in time order	Words and phrases such as *first, next, then, later, finally*
Problem/Solution	To examine how conflicts or obstacles are overcome	Words and phrases such as *need, attempt, help, obstruction*

Writers might use one text structure within another, but it is usually possible to figure out one main pattern of organization that will focus your attention on the important ideas in a selection. Look for **signal words,** the clues that lead you to the text structure. Read the two models on the following page.

Melissa carefully planned her experiment in baking. One Saturday morning, when everyone in the family had left for the day, she took out the recipe she had tucked away. First, she assembled the ingredients she would need for butterscotch cookies and carefully adjusted the oven to the required temperature. Next, she sprayed two baking sheets with nonstick vegetable oil. Then she prepared the batter and dropped it by tea-spoonfuls onto the baking sheets. After setting the timer, she went into the living room to watch TV.

For twelve hours, the snow fell steadily throughout the city. An army of snowplows and salt trucks were ready to roll, but because of the heavy snow, plowed streets were clogged an hour after they had been cleared. As soon as the snow stopped, subzero temperatures set in, causing the salting operation to have minimal results. Because of the difficulty in traveling, many plants and offices were closed. School was cancelled as well. The entire city was at a standstill.

What is the basic text structure of the first model? Of the second? Explain how you determined your answers.

Determining main ideas and supporting details

The most important idea in a paragraph or passage is called the **main idea.** The examples or ideas that further explain the main idea are called **supporting details.** Some main ideas are clearly stated in sentences within a passage. Other times, without directly stating a main idea, an author will suggest it by providing a variety of clues.

Often the main idea will be the first sentence of a paragraph, but a main idea might be anywhere, even in the last sentence of a passage.

A selection can have a number of main ideas in it. Each paragraph may contain a main idea, as in most nonfiction, or entire passages can have a main idea, as in both fiction and nonfiction.

When you need to find the main idea, ask yourself these questions:

- What is each sentence about?
- Is there one sentence that tells about the whole passage or that is more important than the others?

- If the main idea is not directly stated, what main idea do the supporting details point out?

Finding the main ideas will help you understand a selection. Look at the following model.

Main idea — **Hibernation is important for the survival of animals like the bear.** By going into hibernation—a dormant, sleep-like state—the bear can bypass winter. Bears would find it extremely difficult to find enough food when the temperatures grow cold. During hibernation Supporting details — the bear cuddles up in a cave or in a hollowed-out tree, safe from the dangers of winter. In order to survive this long period of inactivity, the bear must build up its body weight by accumulating fat.

Sequencing

The order in which thoughts are arranged is called **sequence**. A good sequence is one that is logical, given the ideas in a selection. Here are three common forms of sequencing.

- **Chronological order**—time order
- **Spatial order**—the order in which things would be arranged within a certain space—for example, left to right, top to bottom, clockwise, foreground to background.
- **Order of importance**—going from most important to least important or the other way around

Recognizing the sequence of something is important when you have to follow **directions.** If you fail to follow steps in a certain order, you may not be able to accomplish your task.

Paraphrasing

When you retell something using your own words, you are **paraphrasing.** You might paraphrase just the main ideas of a selection, or you might retell an entire story in your own words. Paraphrasing is a useful strategy for reviewing and for checking comprehension.

Original text: *The key to developing a healthy eating plan you can live with—one that you can easily incorporate into your daily life—is to discover your personal obstacles to healthy eating and then to make one or two small changes at a time.*

Paraphrase: *To make healthy eating a regular part of your daily routine, change your unhealthy eating habits gradually.*

Summarizing

When you **summarize,** you relate the main ideas of a selection in a logical sequence and in your own words. To create a good summary, include all the main ideas and only essential supporting details.

A good summary can be easily understood by someone who has not read the whole selection. Look at the following model and summary.

The Dead Sea is not dead. It is not a sea either. Even though the water of the Dead Sea is too salty for fish and other animals to live there, some microscopic organisms that use the sun to photosynthesize, and others from which petroleum can be made make the waters of the Dead Sea their home. This body of water is not a sea but is instead a salt lake. It has the lowest elevation of any place on Earth. The water contains more salt and other minerals than any other body of water.

Summary: The Dead Sea, a salt lake, is the saltiest body of water in the world and the lowest place on Earth. Even though fish and other animals cannot live there, microscopic plants call the Dead Sea home.

PRACTICE

Read "The Teacher Who Changed My Life" on page 368 of this book. On separate paper, list the main ideas in the selection. Under each main idea, list the supporting details that explain it. Use this information to write a one-paragraph summary of what you have read.

Drawing inferences

Writers don't always directly state what they want you to understand in a selection. By providing clues and interesting details, they suggest certain information. Whenever you combine those clues with your own background and knowledge, you are drawing an inference. An **inference** involves using your reason and experience to come up with an idea based on what an author implies or suggests. In reading, you **infer** when you use context clues and your own knowledge to figure out what an author is suggesting. The following active reading behaviors are examples of drawing an inference.

- Predicting When you guess what a story will be about or what will happen next, you are drawing an inference.

- Drawing conclusions A conclusion is a general statement you can make and explain with reasoning or with supporting details from a selection.
- Generalizing When you draw an inference that can apply to more than one item or group, you are making a generalization.

Classifying

When you **classify**, you place things into categories according to certain characteristics they share. For example, the selections in this book could be classified into fiction and nonfiction or into poetry and prose, or they could be put into more specific categories such as short stories, essays, articles, and narrative poems.

Finding similarities and differences across texts

As your reading takes you across a variety of sources, **compare and contrast** the things you've read. When you look for similarities and differences in your reading selections, you'll gain a better understanding of all the material you've read. Ask yourself in what ways sources might be alike or different. What is included in one selection that might be left out of another? Why might that be?

Here are some of the ways in which you can compare and contrast writers' works:

- Scope Take a broad look at each selection. How would you compare the time periods covered? How much information is given in each nonfiction selection? How many characters and settings are involved in fiction pieces? How extended is the entire selection?
- Treatment Look at how each writer presents important ideas. Who tells the story? Is the narrator's attitude serious or funny? How would you compare the writers' purposes? Styles?
- Organization Compare selections in terms of how writers arrange their thoughts. Is a writer using chronological order? Comparing and contrasting? Cause and effect? Problem and solution?

When you look for similarities and differences in what you've read, you'll learn to read more critically and get more out of each selection.

Distinguishing fact from opinion

When deciding whether to believe what a writer has written, you need to distinguish between fact and opinion. A **fact** is a statement that can be proved with supporting information. An **opinion,** on the other hand, is what a writer believes on the basis of his or her personal viewpoint. Writers can support their opinions with facts, but an opinion cannot be proved. Look at the following examples of fact and opinion.

Fact: *New York State produces fruits and other agricultural products.*
Opinion: *New York is a wonderful place for a vacation.*

When interpreting something you read, be sure that you distinguish between statements of fact and statements of opinion.

Answering questions

Often you'll need to answer questions about selections you've read. Look at the chart below to help you find the answers.

Type of Question	What Is It?	Example	How to Find the Answer
Literal	Has a definite answer	What color was Snow White's hair?	Look for direct statement in text.
Interpretive	Answer based on text and prior knowledge	Why was Snow White a threat to the queen?	Use text information and/or prior knowledge.
Open-ended	No right or wrong answer	Is Snow White a role model for girls today?	Use personal background and opinions.

You may find various types of questions on a test.

Tips for Answering Test Questions

- **True-or-false questions** If any part of a true or false question is false, the correct answer is "false."
- **Short answer** Use complete sentences so your responses will be clear. Try to put your thoughts in logical sequence.
- **Multiple choice** First read all the responses. Eliminate the answers you know are incorrect. Choose the best remaining answer.

Representing text information

After reading various sources, you may want to reproduce what you have learned in a visual way, perhaps to present it to your class or to show the teacher that you have understood it.

- Outlines An **outline** is helpful if you are organizing information for a report. Roman numerals, together with uppercase and lowercase letters, show the basic structure of the report. Look at the following sample model of a topic outline.

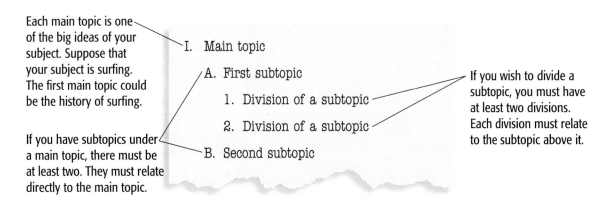

Each main topic is one of the big ideas of your subject. Suppose that your subject is surfing. The first main topic could be the history of surfing.

If you have subtopics under a main topic, there must be at least two. They must relate directly to the main topic.

I. Main topic
   A. First subtopic
      1. Division of a subtopic
      2. Division of a subtopic
   B. Second subtopic

If you wish to divide a subtopic, you must have at least two divisions. Each division must relate to the subtopic above it.

• Time lines A time line shows the chronological order of events over a period of time. Use a line to document the amount of time you want to cover. Add events above or below the line to show the order in which they occurred. Look at the example below.

The title shows the subject of the time line. It also may include the dates covered.

Space between events shows the amount of time that passed between them. Which two events came closest together?

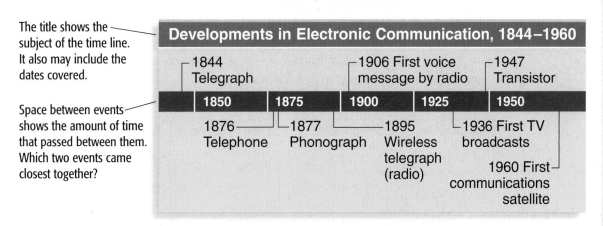

Developments in Electronic Communication, 1844–1960

1844 Telegraph · 1906 First voice message by radio · 1947 Transistor

1850 · 1875 · 1900 · 1925 · 1950

1876 Telephone · 1877 Phonograph · 1895 Wireless telegraph (radio) · 1936 First TV broadcasts · 1960 First communications satellite

• Graphic organizers Word webs, flowcharts, Venn diagrams, and other kinds of graphic organizers can help you present information in a visual way so that both you and your audience can easily see, understand, and remember what is presented.

Using study strategies

If you're preparing for a quiz or test or getting ready for a class presentation, you'll want to use a study strategy that helps you organize and remember the material you've read. Here are some useful strategies.

• Using story maps A **story map** can help you sort out important literary elements in works of fiction. Look at the model on the following page to see how a story map works as a tool for review.

STORY MAP

Characters	Setting
Plot Conflict (problem)	**Plot** Resolution (solution)

- **Using KWL** **KWL** is a good way to keep track of what you are learning when you read informational text. Make three columns on a page. Label the first column *What I Know*, the second column *What I Want to Know*, and the third column *What I Learned*. Before reading, list the things you already know about a topic in the first column. List your questions in the second column. When you've finished reading, record what you've learned in the third column. You can add more columns to record places where you found information and places to look for more.

KWL

What I Know	What I Want to Know	What I Learned	Where I Got Information
			Where I Can Get More

- **Using SQ3R** A useful study strategy for studying subject areas like science or social studies is **SQ3R**. This stands for **s**urvey, **q**uestion, **r**ead, **r**ecord, and **r**eview. Here's how it works.
  1. **Survey** Take a quick look over the entire selection you need to study. Notice anything boldfaced. Look at headings, subheadings, or pictures.
  2. **Question** Think of a number of questions you'll want to answer as you read.
  3. **Read** Read the selection carefully. Vary your reading rate as you encounter easy or difficult passages.
  4. **Record** Take notes about important ideas. Record your comments and additional questions that come up as you read.
  5. **Review** When you've finished reading, go back over the text once again to be sure you've understood important ideas. Add any other information you'll need to remember.

- Creating and using study guides Your teacher may provide you with a guide to focus your attention on important vocabulary and ideas, or you may create your own using end-of-chapter questions.

Select a chapter from your social studies or science text. Use SQ3R as you read the material. Have a classmate quiz you by using end-of-chapter questions to see how well you remember what you studied.

Literary Response

Whenever you share your thoughts and feelings about something you've read, you are responding to a text. You have your own learning style, so you will want to respond in ways that are comfortable for you. Some students learn best when speaking and writing, while others enjoy moving around or creating something artistic. Your responses can take a variety of forms. You can offer an observation, draw a connection to your life or to another work you've read, or question a character's actions or motives.

Tips for Responding to and Interpreting Literature

- **Discuss** what you have read and share your views in active classroom discussions or at home.
- **Keep a journal** about what you read. Record your thoughts and feelings. Write down your impressions of a selection as well as questions you might have about it.
- **Take part in dramatizations, oral interpretations,** and **readers theater.** These activities can allow you to present characters through actions and dialogue and give you the opportunity to use your voice, facial expressions, and body language to convey meaning.
- **Tape record** or **videotape** your oral readings or dramatizations.

Supporting responses and interpretations

Whether you respond with your mind or with your emotions, you need to support your responses by going back to the text itself. Make sure you provide details from the author's work to back up your thoughts and feelings. It is not enough to say, "I really liked the main character." You must show what you liked about him or her. Look for specific descriptions and information. Ask yourself questions like these:

- What is interesting about this story's setting?
- What do I like or dislike about this character?

- How is the overall theme or idea expressed?
- What specific details account for my views about this selection?
- How have my own experiences and prior knowledge influenced my feelings in this selection?

Whenever you make a connection or compare and contrast themes, ideas, and issues across texts, you need to support your thoughts with the writer's own words. If you can't provide adequate text proofs, you may need to rethink your response.

Identifying the purpose of a text

Authors have a variety of reasons for writing. They may simply want to **entertain** you. They may want to **inform** you about a topic. They may feel the need to **express** thoughts and emotions through a narrative or biographical essay. They also may want to **influence** your thinking so that you believe something or are motivated to act in a certain way. How can you tell what a writer's purpose is? To identify the purposes of different types of texts, use the following tips.

Tips for Identifying the Purpose of a Text

- **Look at word choices.** Authors select words according to the words connotations, which carry emotional or implied meanings, as well as their denotations, or dictionary meanings. For example, a writer's opinion of a character described as *bold* and *adventurous* is different from that of a character described as *weird* and *reckless.*
- **Consider the intended audience.** Most selections are written with an audience in mind. A speech at a pep rally might have a different purpose from one given before a committee of student council members.
- **Look at the structure of the text.** Writers use patterns of organization to clearly present their messages. Figuring out whether a writer has used chronological order, comparison-and-contrast structure, or cause-and-effect structure can help you determine his or her purpose.

Comparing elements across genres

Have you ever seen a movie or a television program that was based on a book you have read? How were they similar? How were they different? If you read the book *Sarah Plain and Tall* and then saw the made-for-TV movie, you might have noticed that some scenes were left out of the movie in order to make the story fit into a particular time frame. Some characters in movies are not represented precisely as they are described in books. As you look to see how the same story may vary across genres, look at similarities and differences in the following story elements:

- **Characters** Are all characters represented? Are some characters combined?
- **Settings** Is the setting presented similarly in each work? What differences affect the story as a whole?
- **Plot** How is the plot adjusted to fit the strengths and limitations of the genre?
- **Themes or ideas** Are important ideas well developed?
- **Author's point of view** Does the author's attitude affect how the story is told?
- **Author's purpose** Why is the author telling this story?
- **Author's style** What format and word choices are used?

Analyzing inductive and deductive reasoning

As you think about works you've read, ask yourself whether the reasoning behind an author's ideas are logical. Here are two kinds of logical reasoning writers use.

Inductive reasoning When you consider a certain number of examples a writer gives you or see a particular number of cases to illustrate a point or an idea, you may be able to arrive at a **generalization**— a conclusion or general statement—by using **inductive reasoning**. For instance, if the tulips your class planted on the shady side of your school building did not grow, there is never grass on that side of the building, and a bush planted there last year still has no leaves, you can inductively reason that the shady side of your school building may not be the best place to plant things. This logic moves from the **specific** to the **general**.

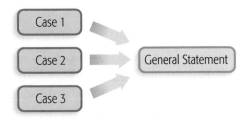

Deductive reasoning When you take a general statement and apply it through reasoning to a number of specific situations, you are using **deductive reasoning**. For example, you know that plants do not grow well in shady places. Therefore, you can deductively reason that it might not be wise to plant tulips or expect grass to grow well on the shady side of a building. This logic moves from the **general** to the **specific**. The diagram on the following page illustrates deductive reasoning.

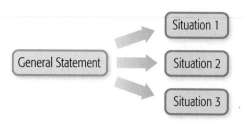

General Statement → Situation 1

General Statement → Situation 2

General Statement → Situation 3

Inquiry and Research

Whenever you read to learn, you'll need to come up with interesting and useful questions. As you read in a variety of sources, you will think of new questions or revise your originial questions to take into account new information. When you ask important questions and carefully research thorough answers, you will draw conclusions about your topic. The process may lead you to other interesting questions and areas for further study.

Forming and revising questions

Finding an interesting and relevant question or topic is an important first step in doing research and deserves your careful attention.

> **Tips for Asking Research Questions**
>
> - Think of a question or topic that interests you.
> - Choose a question that helps you focus on one main idea.
> - Be sure the question is not too broad or too narrow.
>   **Too broad:** *What can cause mummification?*
>   **Better:** *Why did the Egyptians mummify the remains of their Pharaohs?*

Using text organizers

Once you've found an interesting question to investigate, the next step is to locate information and organize it. Textbooks, references, magazines, and other sources use a variety of ways to help you find what you need quickly and efficiently.

- **Tables of contents** Look at a table of contents first to see whether a resource offers information you need.
- **Indexes** An index, found in the back of a book, is a detailed, alphabetical listing of all people, places, events, and topics mentioned in the book.
- **Headings and subheadings** The headings often identify the information that follows.
- **Graphic features** Photos, maps, graphs, and other graphic features can convey a large amount of information at a glance.

Using multiple sources for research

The research you do will be more interesting and balanced when you include various types of sources. To find the most recent information, it may be necessary to use sources other than books. The following are some helpful resources for conducting research.

- Print resources: textbooks, magazines, reference books, and other specialized references
- Nonprint information: films, videos, and recorded interviews
- Electronic texts: CD-ROM encyclopedias and the Internet
- Experts: people who are specialists on the topic you have chosen

Interpreting graphic aids

When you're researching a topic, be sure to read and interpret the graphic aids included. **Graphic aids** let you see information at a glance.

Reading a map Maps are flat representations of land. A **compass rose** allows you to determine direction. A **legend** explains the map's symbols, and a **scale** shows you how the size of the map relates to the actual distances covered. Look at the map below.

Reading a graph Graphs show information pictorially. Graphs can use circles, dots, bars, or lines. Look at the title and the labels on the bar graphs on the following page, which compare types of crops produced in the South. Next, look at the labels along the bottom of the graphs. Each bar represents a decade. The numbers along the side represent millions of pounds, bales, or bushels. Can you interpret the information?

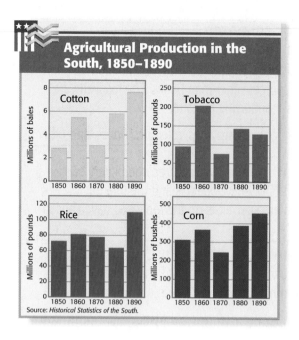

Agricultural Production in the South, 1850–1890

Source: *Historical Statistics of the South.*

Reading a table A table allows you to compare numbers or facts by putting them into categories. Look at the table below. Read the title first. You can read the table to find just one piece of information—for instance, how much per gallon gasoline cost in 1973—or you can compare the consumption of gasoline across the years. What other information can you gather from this table?

Year	Consumption (billions of gallons)	Cost per Gallon		
		Reg.	Prem.	No lead
1973	110.5	$.40	.45	NA
1974	106.3	.53	.57	.55
1975	109.0	.57	.61	.60
1976	115.7	.59	.64	.61
1977	119.6	.62	.67	.66
1978	125.1	.63	.69	.67
1979	122.1	.86	.92	.90
1980	115.0	1.19	1.28	1.25

Gasoline Consumption and Prices

Source: *Statistical Abstract of the United States.*

PRACTICE

Look in a current newspaper or newsmagazine to find an example of a chart, table, or graph. Explain the graphic aid to the class and briefly analyze the information presented.

Writing Workshop Models

The following Writing Workshop Models are complete versions of the student models developed in the Writing Workshops at the end of each theme in this book. Use these models as examples of how one student might have responded to the assignments in the Writing Workshops.

Theme 1, pages 104–107

Narrative Writing: Autobiographical Anecdote

A Hard Lesson

Muddy water surged past our feet. A storm had turned our irrigation canal into a rushing river. It was exciting to a couple of nine-year-olds like my friend Ray and me. It was also exciting to me that Ray, who was much bigger than me, was my friend. I was having fun, but I was also a little afraid. My mother had warned us not to go near the canal. I reminded Ray that we would get in trouble if our parents found out where we were. He just laughed. Ray was never afraid of anything. As we played alongside the canal, he struck a goofy pose. "Look!" he laughed. "I'm a surfer!" He stretched out his arms and swayed back and forth on the slippery bank. Suddenly I heard a loud splash. It took me a second to realize what had happened. Then it hit me. Ray had lost his balance and slipped into the water! I fell to my belly, reached out, and grabbed his hand just as the current caught him.

"Hold on!" I screamed. Ray struggled to keep his head above the swirling brown water. "Help me!" he cried. I felt the pull of the current, and I tightened my grip. I looked at Ray's face, and I saw fear in his eyes. I was shocked. Ray, the biggest boy in the fourth grade, was afraid! Now it was up to me, the smallest boy in the fourth grade, to save him. I wanted to run back to the house to get help, but I knew that I couldn't let go. I was Ray's best hope, his only hope.

Churning water swooshed in my ears, and the musty odor of flood water filled my nose. Again and again, I tried to pull Ray onto the bank. Again and again, I failed. I was losing my tug-of-war with the current. The water was just too strong.

Ray called out in a hoarse voice, "I'm cold! I can't hold on much longer!" I had to do something fast. Out of the corner of my eye, I saw a large tree branch sticking out from the bank into the water. I called out to Ray, "Over there! To your right! Grab that branch!" I pulled him toward it with all my might. Finally, my hand ached so much that I just gave up. I relaxed my grip, and Ray was gone.

A knot of fear rose in my stomach. I pushed myself up from the slimy mud and scrambled to the branch. Ray was nowhere in sight. I called out his name over and over, but he did not answer. I have never felt smaller or more alone.

Suddenly I saw something rise out of the current. At first I thought it was a piece of wood. I held onto the branch and leaned over the water for a better look. Could it be? Yes! It was a hand! It was Ray's hand! I leaned over as far as I could, grabbed his wrist, and pulled him in.

continued

Ray crawled onto the bank, shivering. "Why did you let go?" he asked.

"I couldn't help it!" I cried.

"Thanks to you I almost drowned," Ray said accusingly.

I was angry, and I let him know it. "Hey, it's not my fault that you were showing off and fell in! If it hadn't been for me, you would have drowned! Whose idea was it to go to the canal, anyway? I told you that we should stay away!" Angry tears rolled down my face.

"What a baby!" he sneered. "Why don't you run home to Mama?"

I had heard him say things like that to other boys many times, and it had always made me laugh. Now he was being mean to me, and I wasn't laughing. We walked home our separate ways.

That day I learned a hard lesson. I realized that Ray was not really my friend at all. He had just been using me to make himself feel important. All the times that I had laughed at his mean comments and dangerous behavior I had helped make him the center of attention. In return, Ray had made me feel big. I was embarrassed about being so small for my age, and Ray had somehow made me feel bigger. After I helped save his life, I realized that I did not need him to feel big. I already was, at least inside. From that moment on, I walked a little taller, and I walked without him.

Expository Writing: Compare-and-Contrast Essay

Little Boxes

Ernie, in the short story "The Crush" by Cynthia Rylant, and Katie in "The Birthday Box" by Jane Yolen both suffer the tragedy of their mothers' deaths. Although Ernie and the daughter are different people from very different backgrounds, they both eventually find the strength to rebuild their lives. For each, the key is a cardboard box.

Ernie is thirty-three years old and mentally disabled. All his life, his mother has been over-protective of him. While she is still alive, Ernie's box is delivered by mistake to their home. The box is plain and full of seed packages. He doesn't know what the seed packages are or what to do with them. He just likes to look at the pretty flowers on the covers of the packages. After his mother's sudden death, Ernie is moved to a group home. He takes his beloved box with him.

At first, Ernie cries for his mother, but he stops after a few weeks. He begins to observe life around him. He learns how to garden and eventually experiences the joy and reward of watching plants grow. He likes to see the physical results of his work, but he can't stand to plant seeds from his box. Finally Ernie falls in love with a lonely woman named Dolores. This experience gives him the courage to plant his own seeds and separate himself from his beloved box. He welcomes the life that grows from the seeds he has planted outside the group home. In fact, he uses the seeds to share his newfound love with Dolores by secretly leaving her flowers every Wednesday.

Katie's situation in "The Birthday Box" is both similar to and different from Ernie's. She's only ten, which is a lot younger than Ernie. She's bright and talented and likes to write. Her mother doesn't die suddenly, but rather after a long, painful battle with cancer. On the day her mother dies, she gives Katie a beautifully decorated box. In contrast to Ernie's box, this box is empty. "It's you," Katie's mother tells her. But Katie doesn't understand why there's nothing inside the box. When she moves in with her father, she takes the empty box with her, but she throws it in the closet.

Unlike Ernie, Katie takes a long time to accept her mother's death. She feels nothing but emptiness and anger. She stops writing, and she cries at every occasion that reminds her of her mother. She can't stand her half-brothers, stepmother, or father. Her box sits in her closet as far from her as possible.

Finally, on the first anniversary of the death of her mother, Katie stops crying and discovers the meaning of her mother's dying words. She realizes that "It's you" isn't about the box; it is about her. She and the box are alike. Both are sturdy and pretty on the outside. Both need to be filled up before they will be complete.

Ernie and the daughter are two very different characters, but each learns a lesson from a box. Ernie finds the strength and courage he needs to rebuild his life when he gives up the contents of his box. Katie finds her courage and strength by accepting the challenge to fill her box with her writing and by making her own sweet memories.

Persuasive Writing: Editorial

2461 Valley Drive
Fairview, California 94085
January 3, 2002

Editor
Fairview Herald
400 East Main Street
Fairview, California 94085

Dear Editor:

Will setting a curfew of 10 P.M. for kids under the age of sixteen really make our town a better place? The editorial in last week's *Herald* makes it sound as if a curfew would be good for our town, but I disagree. A curfew would not stop the real troublemakers; it would just make life harder for kids, their parents, and the police.

My first argument against a curfew is that it would affect the wrong people. If you read the crime reports in the *Herald*, you will see that older teenagers and adults cause more crime than younger people do. About the worst crime that young people commit is spraying graffiti on buildings and signs. I would never say that graffiti isn't a problem; it is. I hate the sight of it. But there are better ways to stop graffiti than a curfew. Instead, stores should keep spray paint and large marking pens in locked glass cases. That way taggers could not steal paint and pens, which is what they do now.

My second argument against a curfew is that it is unfair to all the good kids and their parents. The editorial makes it sound as if most teenagers are on the streets at night, but they aren't. Fairview is a quiet town. I don't know anyone my age who is allowed to be out late at night, especially on school nights. Our parents already set curfews for us. In fact, we took a poll in my English class about how late our parents let us stay out, and not one of the twenty-three students polled was allowed out alone after 9:30 P.M. without a good reason.

Some adults may think that there is no good reason for young people to be out past 10 P.M., but that is not true. For example, my fifteen-year-old sister is sometimes out late because the neighbors that she babysits for do not always get home on time. Should my sister get in trouble just for doing her job? Should my parents get in trouble just because my sister walks the block home at 10:15 rather than 9:59?

My final argument against a curfew is that it would be hard on the police. They have enough to do without tracking down tardy teenagers. Besides, if police see a kid out after 10 P.M., wouldn't it be hard for them to know how old the kid is just by looking at him or her? Do we really want to ask the police to guess the age of every teenager on the street after 10 P.M.?

continued

A curfew would not solve our problems; it would just cause new ones. Most of the parents and kids in this town are good, responsible people. Let's trust them to make their own decisions. Curfews should be a personal matter between parents and their children, not a public matter between children and the town.

Sincerely,

Daniel Anslow

Daniel Anslow, grade 7

Descriptive Writing: A Photo in Words

My Favorite Place

It is near and yet so far away. It belongs to someone else now, and yet it will always belong to me. It is where I grew up, and it is still my favorite place in all the world. When I close my eyes, I can see it perfectly. It is fall. I am eight years old, and the school bus is pulling up to the gravel road that leads to the house. From the window of the bus, I can see the golden meadow, the big white house with the red roof, and the trees that circle the hidden pond. Behind them are the mountains that tower over everything like giants.

I jump out of the bus and run through the meadow. The dry grass is almost as tall as I am. It tickles my arms, and I can feel the hard, dry ground under my feet. I stretch my neck to see over the grass, and the house seems to get bigger and bigger. Finally I reach it. I pull open the big blue door, take off my backpack full of books, and throw it on the floor. Then I yell out to my mother to let her know that I am home. I do not need to tell her where I am going because she already knows. The pond is my special place.

Every day after school, the peaceful pond calls to me. When I am near it, my eyes gaze on beauty and my mind roams free. For a little while, I forget about the arithmetic problems that I have to do, the spelling words that I have to memorize, and the books that I am supposed to read. I am just another animal that lives near the pond.

The pond is deep in the woods behind the house. As I run through the woods, I kick my sneakers through bright piles of leaves, and the leaves rustle, crackle, and crunch. I plop down in the middle of a pile, and I sink into a colorful blanket of yellow, red, and orange. As I lie on my back looking up, the late afternoon sunlight makes the leaves high above me look as if they are on fire. I daydream for a while, and then I make my way to the pond.

There it is, in the distance. The sunlight filters through the tall branches of the maples, casting hopeful shadows across the clear blue water. It seems as if nothing can go wrong here. It is quiet and peaceful. I walk over to the weather-beaten rocks and lean against them. The wind rustles through the tall grass, and it makes me think that the whole world is sighing. I see that the wild roses and raspberries that grow around the pond are dry and brown. They look dead now, but I know that they will come back to life in the spring. The tall grass will stand through the winter and protect them. The thought is comforting.

If I lie still, deer may walk up to the water. One time I saw the big dark shape of a buck. Ducks sometimes stop at the pond before moving on. Other birds move among the branches and leaves. Two squirrels chase each other up the trunk of a tree. People have left the pond alone, giving privacy to the animals and me.

About three years ago my family and I moved away from my childhood home. My father got tired of the long drive to work, and my parents bought us a house closer to town. However, I still visit the pond in my mind. I just close my eyes, and I see the gentle blue water, the tall trees, and the big white house with the red roof near the foot of the mountain.

Expository Writing: Definition Essay

True Courage

Are you courageous? According to *Webster's Dictionary,* if you have the "mental or moral strength to venture, persevere, and withstand danger, fear, or difficulty," you are. A courageous person, then, is someone who can face a difficult or dangerous situation without fear. Three people who showed this mental or moral strength are Stacy Allison, Lou Gehrig, and Rosa Parks. Although the challenges they faced were different, their responses to challenge were similar. Their actions define what courage truly is.

For Stacy Allison, courage came one step at a time. In 1987 Allison tried to climb to the top of Mount Everest, the tallest mountain in the world. She and three other experienced climbers had spent two years carefully planning the climb. When they were two-thirds of the way up the mountain, they ran into trouble. A heavy snowstorm hit the area, and they had to wait it out. At 25,500 feet above sea level, the air is very thin. Climbers can survive for only a week or two. After several days of waiting, one of the men in the group was too weak to go on. Allison and her group had to turn back. After such a disappointing defeat, most people would give up their dream, but Allison was not like most people. The next year she found the strength to venture to Mount Everest again. In the face of countless dangers and difficulties, she persevered. Her courage paid off. She is the first American woman to climb to the top of Mount Everest.

Baseball great Lou Gehrig had another kind of mountain to climb. In 1939 he found out that he had a deadly disease called ALS. At the time, Gehrig was at the top of his game. He was the best first baseman in all of baseball. He had been the captain of the legendary Yankee teams of the 1920s and had played with Babe Ruth. He had a lifetime batting average of .340 and had batted in almost 2,000 runs. What he is most remembered for today, however, is not his ability to play the game of baseball but the game of life. The Yankees honored him by making July 4, 1939, Lou Gehrig Day at Yankee Stadium. He was expected to appear before a crowd of 60,000 fans to make a speech. That may not seem like much, but he was so weak he had to have support just to stand up. The master of ceremonies knew how weak Gehrig was and had told the crowd that Gehrig would not speak. The fans chanted, "We want Lou! We want Lou!" anyway. Gehrig mustered up the strength to give what would become the most famous speech in the history of baseball. Although he knew that he would die soon, he told the crowd that he thought he was the luckiest man on the face of the Earth to have played with the Yankees. A little less than two years later he was gone, but his courage will never be forgotten.

Neither will the courage of Rosa Parks. To me, she is the most courageous person of all. On December 1, 1955, she made history when she refused to give up her seat on a bus to a white person. The law in Montgomery, Alabama, at the time said that African Americans had to sit at the back of buses and had to give up their seats if white people were left standing. Parks bravely challenged the law and was arrested. Unlike Allison, Parks did not plan to make history. Unlike Gehrig, she was not already famous and admired. She was just an ordinary working woman who found the moral strength to challenge an unfair law. Her courage inspired the Montgomery bus boycott, a key event in the Civil Rights movement of the 1950s. Rosa Parks's case went all the way to the Supreme Court, where the Court finally ruled that segregated buses were unconstitutional. Parks showed great moral strength. She ventured into unknown territory, persevered, and withstood danger, fear, and difficulty. In the process, she made

continued

life better for thousands of other people. She stands as an everlasting example of what courage can do.

Stacy Allison, Lou Gehrig, and Rosa Parks had the mental and moral strength to persevere. Instead of giving in to difficulty or fear, they managed to overcome their challenges with dignity. Do you have what it takes to be courageous? If you follow their examples, I think that you will find that you do.

Narrative Writing: Short Story

In a Kingdom by the Sea

"I think you're crazy."

"Maybe I am," I replied. "But I'm going on anyway. Remember your promise."

"I said I'd take you there and give you the key. Just don't expect me to go in with you."

Randolf had finally admitted to me that his family had been wrong to separate his sister Annabel and me when we were in love. Annabel had died of a broken heart after they'd torn us apart, but even then his family scorned me. The family refused to let me come to the funeral, so I had never seen my beloved's resting-place. I had hounded Randolf for months before he had finally agreed to take me to Annabel's secret tomb.

I looked at the young man walking beside me. It was dark, but I could see his pale face, his straight dark hair, and his deep brown eyes. He reminded me so much of his sister that it hurt. I had thought of her every day since her death. And thinking of Annabel now made me even more determined to continue our strange journey.

We walked in silence for five more minutes. Then her brother stopped.

"Listen!" he said sharply. In the distance, I could hear the sound of waves breaking. "The sea. We're almost there."

"You can leave me then," I said. "Give me the key."

"No. I've gone this far. I guess I can take you to the tomb."

He led the way across a rocky field. Sometimes we tripped on stones that stuck up through the earth. It was misty too. Sometimes we had to stop because we could not see more than a few yards ahead of us. But we kept going when the mist swirled away. The sound of the sea grew louder and louder.

Suddenly the moon broke through the clouds, and we could see clearly for the first time that night. It was an awesome sight. We were standing on the edge of a cliff. Below us the gray sea pounded on the rocks.

Her brother put his hand on my shoulder and pointed. At first I could not make out what he wanted me to see. Then I knew. In the dark, I saw what looked like a huge square boulder perched on the highest point of the cliff, but the moonlight revealed a barred window and a narrow dark door. This was the sepulcher, the tomb of my beloved Annabel Lee. This was where I had longed to be since she had died mysteriously five years before. Ever since that day I had wanted to see her once more.

I began stumbling over the rocks towards the gray tomb. I could hear Randolf panting behind me. The building grew larger and darker as we approached. Why had her relatives buried her in such a deserted and gloomy place, I wondered.

Soon we were at the door. I pounded on it, as if someone would let me in. It made a deep hollow sound.

Her brother drew up beside me. I could hear him fishing in his pocket for the key.

"One last time," he said, "let me try to persuade you not to go in. What you see could destroy you."

"I must go in," I replied. "I can't come this far and not see her."

He handed me a huge rusty key as big as my hand.

"Good luck," he said as he walked slowly away.

At first the key would not turn. Then I grabbed it with both hands and twisted hard. The old lock finally squeaked open, and I threw my weight against the iron door. It moved with a groan, and I stepped inside the sepulcher.

I had to wait for my eyes to get used to the darkness. Gradually I could see a beam of moon-

continued

light falling from a high window onto a long wooden box resting on a table.

It was her coffin.

I walked slowly towards the table, not knowing what I would find.

There was a stale, damp smell. Even though it was cold, I could feel sweat on my forehead. Would the lid open, or did it need a key too?

I grasped the cover and lifted. It moved easily.

Inside there was-nothing! The coffin was empty.

I gasped and staggered backwards. Was this a joke? Where had they put her? Was she still alive?

The door—I had to find the door. Groping through the dark, I tripped over an object on the floor and fell down. I reached out and touched something that made my heart leap. Annabel Lee lay on the floor. She had died there. Had they buried her alive? Is that what Randolf had tried to tell me? Terrified, I stumbled to my feet. In the darkness, I searched for the door. I was desperate to get out of this tomb, this nightmare!

But when I found the door, I realized my nightmare had just begun. The door was locked from the outside. My rusty key was useless. Randolf had promised to let me enter the tomb, but he hadn't promised to let me out of it. In despair, I sank to the floor. I would spend the rest of my life with my Annabel Lee after all.

Expository Writing: Book Review

Acorns for Dinner

Imagine eating this for dinner: "A mound of sort of fluffy mashed cattail tubers, mushrooms, and dogtooth violet bulbs, smothered in gravy thickened with acorn powder." Now imagine that you are eating out of turtle shells and sitting in a hollowed-out tree trunk. The cook is a teenaged boy named Sam Gribley. He is the hero of *My Side of the Mountain,* a novel by Jean Craighead George.

At the beginning of the novel, Sam lives in New York City with his mother, father, and eight brothers and sisters. He is not unhappy, but he wants to get away from the crowds and live off the land, so he runs away from home and goes to a forest that was once his great-grandfather's farm in the Catskill Mountains. All Sam has with him is an ax, a pocketknife, a ball of cord, and $40, but he lives up on his mountain for a whole year. During that time, he learns how to find food and stay warm, even in the winter. He does not want to leave, and in the end he does not have to. Instead, his family moves up to the mountain with him.

The main character is Sam, who tells his own story. The first-person narrative point-of-view makes the story easy to read and personal. If it had been told in the third person, it would not have seemed so real and immediate. The other main characters are mostly animals. Frightful goes everywhere with Sam. She is a falcon that Sam caught and trained when she was a baby bird. Frightful rides on Sam's shoulder and catches rabbits and pheasants for him to eat. There is also a weasel called the Baron. He is not really a pet because he is always attacking Sam, but Sam seems to like him. Finally, there is a raccoon called Jessie Coon James, who steals food and helps Sam find clams in the stream.

At first Sam is all alone with the animals. Then he begins to meet people. One person is a college English teacher called Bando. He gets lost in the woods the first summer, and he returns for Christmas dinner. Sam's father comes for Christmas too, so there are three people crowded into Sam's "house" in the hollowed-out tree. There is a hiker called Aaron, who writes music based on the bird songs he hears. There are also two boys from the village who begin to spend time with Sam.

The book does not really have a plot. It is just about Sam's struggle to survive. But there is a conflict in Sam's mind. Part of him wants to stay in the woods forever, away from the city. "People live too close together," he tells one of the boys who come to visit. But Sam also enjoys company. He looks forward to Bando's Christmas visit, and he loves showing the boys around his mountain. In the end, he gives his visitors so much information about himself that the newspapers print stories about "the wild boy" living on the mountain. Finally Sam realizes that he wants to be found.

I enjoyed reading *My Side of the Mountain.* I liked hearing about all the weird food Sam ate, even if I did not want to eat it myself. I also thought it was interesting that Sam wanted to be with people and did not want to be with people. I feel like that sometimes too. But I think there was something unbelievable about Sam's character. He did not even think about his mother and eight brothers and sisters for a whole year. They did not know where he was and must have been worried. Why didn't Sam write to them? He was happy to see them at the end. Sam's attitude toward his family did not seem realistic.

My Side of the Mountain is never boring. It teaches interesting facts about plants and animals, and it has some good nature drawings by the author. If you would like to know what it's like to train a falcon, eat clams rolled up in grape leaves, or make your own clothes out of deerskin, this is the book for you.

Expository Writing: Research Report

The Endangered Manatee

When Christopher Columbus sailed to the New World, he saw many things that seemed strange to him. One of the strangest was three unusual-looking mermaids. He wrote in his journal that they were "not so beautiful as they are painted, since in some ways they have a face like a man" (Ellis 88). If you saw what he saw, you might agree. The creatures were grayish-brown, had hairy snouts and probably weighed about a thousand pounds each. Of course, the creatures that Columbus wrote about were not mermaids at all. Scientists believe that the creatures were actually West Indian manatees. Long ago superstitious sailors who were unfamiliar with manatees sometimes mistook the gentle water mammals for mermaids.

Manatees still live in the warm waters in and around Florida, but they may not be there much longer. As of July 2000, there were only about 2,400 manatees left (Sawicki 6). Even though the manatee is protected by the Marine Mammal Protection Act of 1972, the Endangered Species Act of 1973, and the Florida Manatee Sanctuary Act of 1978, it is dying off. The disappearance of the manatee should concern us all. In the long run, anything that upsets the balance of nature is harmful to us too. Besides, we owe it to future generations to protect our waters and the animals that call it home.

The manatee has no natural enemies, so what is killing off the gentle giant? Sadly, the answer is people. More than 90 percent of the people who live in Florida live within ten miles of the coast, and more than 800 more people join them each day (Koeppel 68). Many of those people enjoy boating. Though boating is fun for people, it can be harmful to manatees. In fact, the chief cause of manatee deaths in recent years has been collisions with boats ("Manatee Mortality Statistics"). Manatees eat plants that grow deep in the water, but like other water mammals they must surface to breathe. When they surface, they sometimes swim into the path of an oncoming motorboat. Because they are slow swimmers, they cannot quickly get out of the way. Even if they could, they might not know when a motorboat is headed their way. Scientists believe that manatees cannot hear low-frequency sounds like those made by motors. As a result, manatees are often hit and killed by boats or injured by boat propellers. In fact, the Mote Marine Laboratory in Sarasota, Florida, estimates that 80 percent of Florida's manatees have been hit at least once by marine craft (Koeppel 68).

Collisions with boats are not the manatee's only problem. Many manatees are killed in accidents with floodgates and canal locks. Accidents involving these structures are the second leading cause of manatee deaths ("Manatee"). To understand why these accidents occur, you must know what flood gates and canal locks look like and what they do. Picture large underwater walls that can be raised and lowered or opened and closed to control water levels. When those walls are opened, water comes rushing in and creates a strong current. That current is strong enough to pull in just about anything around it, including slow-moving manatees. Some manatees drown when they get pulled in by the current and cannot get to the surface of the water to breathe. Other manatees get caught between the gates and are crushed or trapped and drowned (Clark 37).

Other objects that people put in the water also cause problems for manatees. Florida's rivers and bays contain many small buoys, floating objects that fishermen place on the water to warn boaters that crab traps are below. The fishermen attach the traps to the buoys with wires or strong plastic lines that can become entangled around a manatee's flippers. When the manatee struggles to free

continued

itself, it can become injured. All too often, the injury becomes infected, and the manatee dies (Clark 35). Manatees have also been known to choke to death on fishhooks and on garbage that has been thrown in the water.

What can we do to protect manatees from accidental deaths? Concerned citizens say that we should demand that the laws protecting endangered species be strictly enforced. According to Judith Vallee of Save the Manatee, a group that works to protect manatees, enforcement of those laws is currently "pathetic" (Sawicki 6). Another way that we can protect manatees is to avoid boating in waters where manatees are known to live. Naturally, many boaters do not want to give up their hobby, but soon they may not have to. Edmund Gerstein of Florida Atlantic University is working to develop a sort of warning alarm for manatees. The device sends out high-frequency sounds that manatees can hear (Eliot xxxii). When these devices are available, boaters should be required to attach them to their watercraft, and fishermen should be required to attach them to their buoys. The devices should also be attached to floodgates and canal locks. Finally we should be careful to recycle our garbage to help keep it out of our oceans and other waterways.

Thousands of years before you and I were born, manatees lived in the waters in and around the area we know as the state of Florida. Let's do our part to make sure that manatees continue to swim there long after we are gone. When all is said and done, the future of the manatee is up to us.

Works Cited

Clark, Margaret Goff. *The Vanishing Manatee*. New York: Cobblehill, 1990.

Eliot, John L. "Deaf to Danger: Manatees Can't Hear Boats." *National Geographic* 197:2 (Feb. 2000): xxxii.

Ellis, Richard. *Monsters of the Sea*. New York: Knopf, 1994.

Koeppel, Dan. "Kiss of the Manatee." *Travel Holiday*. 182:1 (Feb. 1999): 66-69.

"Manatee Mortality Statistics." Save the Manatee Club. 12 Feb. 2001 <www.savethemanatee.org/mort.htm>.

Sawicki, Stephen. "Manatee Protectors Turn to the Courts." *Animals* 133:4 (July 2000): 6.

Glossary

This glossary lists the vocabulary words found in the selections in this book. The definitions given are for the words as they are used in the selections; you may wish to consult a dictionary for other meanings of these words. The key below is a guide to the pronunciation symbols used in the entries.

a	at	**ō**	hope	**ng**	sing
ā	ape	**ô**	fork, all	**th**	thin
ä	father	**oo**	wood, put	**th**	this
e	end	**ōō**	fool	**zh**	treasure
ē	me	**oi**	oil	**ə**	ago, taken, pencil, lemon, circus
i	it	**ou**	out		
ī	ice	**u**	up	**'**	indicates primary stress
o	hot	**ū**	use	**'**	indicates secondary stress

A

absurdity (ab sur' də tē) *n.* the state of being ridiculous, senseless, or irrational; p. 567

accede (ək sēd') *v.* to give in; go along with; p. 677

acutely (ə kūt' lē) *adv.* sharply and with intensity; p. 493

aggrieved (ə grēvd') *adj.* feeling wronged, as by an insult or unfair treatment; p. 666

agility (ə jil' ə tē) *n.* quickness and ease in motion or thought; p. 282

agitated (aj' ə tāt' ed) *adj.* 1. upset; disturbed; p. 36. 2. excited, nervous, stirred up; p. 667

agony (ag' ə nē) *n.* great pain and suffering of the mind or body; p. 745

amplify (am' plə fī') *v.* to increase; extend; p. 300

anguished (ang' gwisht) *adj.* having or showing extreme mental or physical suffering; p. 286

antagonism (an tag' ə niz' əm) *n.* hostility; p. 511

anticipation (an tis' ə pā' shən) *n.* a feeling of excited expectation; p. 390

appalling (ə pô' ling) *adj.* shocking; horrifying; p. 79

apparatus (ap' ə rat' əs) *n.* something created or invented for a particular purpose; p. 465

aptitude (ap' tə tōōd') *n.* a natural ability; talent; p. 743

aroma (ə rō' mə) *n.* a pleasant smell; odor; p. 708

artful (ärt' fəl) *adj.* done with skill or cleverness; p. 565

ascertain (as' ər tān') *v.* to find out with certainty; determine; p. 413

assess (ə ses') *v.* to determine the meaning or importance of; analyze; p. 222

authoritarian (ə thôr' ə tār' ē ən) *adj.* having or expecting complete obedience to authority; p. 369

avert (ə vurt') *v.* to keep from happening; prevent; p. 401

avidly (av′ id lē) *adv.* eagerly; enthusiastically; p. 372

awe (ô) *n.* wonder combined with respect; p. 351

B

balmy (bä′ mē) *adj.* mild; soothing; p. 222

barrage (bə räzh′) *n.* a heavy concentration or great outpouring, as of words; p. 119

barren (bar′ ən) *adj.* having little or no plant life; bare; empty; p. 753

benefactor (ben′ ə fak′ tər) *n.* one who gives financial assistance; p. 584

bewildered (bi wil′ dərd) *adj.* very confused; p. 118

bleak (blēk) *adj.* cheerless; depressing; p. 164

boycott (boi′ kot) *n.* an organized protest in which the participants refuse to buy, sell, or use a product or service; p. 90

bravado (brə vä′ dō) *n.* a false show of bravery; p. 353

brink (bringk) *n.* the point at which something may begin; p. 282

brood (brood) *n.* all of the young of an animal that are born or cared for at the same time; p. 799

C

casually (kazh′ oo əl lē) *adv.* in a relaxed, informal way; p. 362

chaotic (kā ot′ ik) *adj.* confused and disorganized; in great disorder; p. 8

charismatic (kar′ iz mat′ ik) *adj.* having personal qualities that enable one to inspire loyalty and devotion; p. 283

claim (klām) *v.* to ask for or demand possession of one's right to something; p. 721

clamor (klam′ ər) *n.* a loud, continuous noise; uproar; p. 79

clan (klan) *n.* a group of families descended from a common ancestor; p. 270

coincidence (kō in′ si dəns) *n.* an accidental occurrence of events, ideas, or circumstances at the same time, without one causing the other; p. 452

collaborator (kə lab′ ə rā′ tər) *n.* one who works or cooperates with another; p. 415

collective (kə lek′ tiv) *adj.* having to do with a group of persons or things; common; shared; p. 677

colossal (kə los′ əl) *adj.* extraordinarily or awesomely large; p. 754

commencement (kə mens′ mənt) *n.* a beginning; start; graduation ceremonies; p. 9

compact (kəm pakt′) *adj.* occupying a relatively small space or area; tightly packed; p. 306

compensate (kom′ pən sāt′) *v.* to make up for; balance in force, weight, or effect; p. 808

competent (kom′ pət ənt) *adj.* having enough ability for the purpose; capable; p. 577

comply (kəm plī′) *v.* to go along with a request; p. 86

comprehend (kom′ pri hend′) *v.* to grasp mentally; understand fully; p. 413

concede (kən sēd′) *v.* to admit to be true or proper; p. 221

conceive (kən sēv′) *v.* to form an image or idea of; p. 577

condemn (kən dem′) *v.* to express strong disapproval of; criticize sharply; p. 715

confront (kən frunt′) *v.* to come face to face with; stand facing; p. 416

consecutive (kən sek′ yə tiv) *adj.* following one after another in order without interruption; p. 27

consequence (kon′ sə kwens′) *n.* importance; significance; p. 464

consolation (kon′ sə lā shən) *n.* a comfort; p. 373

conspicuously (kən spik′ ū əs lē) *adv.* in a way that draws attention or is easily seen; p. 809

contemplate (kon′ təm plāt′) *v.* to give intense attention to; consider carefully; p. 296

converge (kən vurj′) *v.* to come together at a place; p. 299

cordially (kôr′ jəl lē) *adv.* in a genuinely warm and friendly way; p. 752

correspond (kôr ə spond′) *v.* to communicate by exchanging letters; p. 567

cower (kou′ ər) *v.* to crouch down, as in fear or shame; p. 792

culprit (kul′ prit) *n.* one guilty of some offense; p. 405

cunning (kun′ ing) *adj.* crafty; sly; p. 390

cynically (sin′ ə kəl lē) *adv.* in a way that shows doubt or disbelief; doubtfully; p. 547

D

deception (di sep′ shən) *n.* that which fools or misleads; p. 125

decree (di krē′) *n.* an official rule, order, or decision; p. 743

defiant (di fī′ ənt) *adj.* showing bold resistance to authority or an opponent; p. 511

degrade (di grād′) *v.* to lower in character or quality; make less pure; p. 828

delectable (di lek′ tə bəl) *adj.* highly pleasing or delightful, especially to the taste; delicious; p. 389

demise (di mīz′) *n.* death; end; p. 828

depleted (di plēt′ id) *adj.* greatly reduced in amount; p. 296

desolation (des′ ə lā′ shən) *n.* sadness; loneliness; p. 689

despair (di spâr′) *n.* complete loss of hope; desperation; p. 708

desperation (des′ pə rā′ shən) *n.* distress caused by great need or loss of hope; p. 50

destine (des′ tin) *v.* to determine beforehand; p. 400

devastating (dev′ əs tāt ing) *adj.* causing great pain, damage, or destruction; overwhelming; p. 434

devise (di vīz′) *v.* to think out; invent; plan; p. 384

diligently (dil′ ə jənt lē) *adv.* in a way that shows great attention, care, and effort; p. 301

discern (di surn′) *v.* to detect or recognize; p. 492

discreetly (dis krēt′ lē) *adv.* in a manner showing good judgment; cautiously; p. 155

discrepancy (dis krep′ ən sē) *n.* a lack of agreement, as between facts; p. 28

dismally (diz′ məl lē) *adv.* in a gloomy, cheerless way; p. 567

dismay (dis mā′) *n.* a feeling of alarm or uneasiness; p. 453

dispense (dis pens′) *v.* to give out in portions; p. 385

distinct (dis tingkt′) *adj.* different in quality or kind; p. 285

divulge (di vulj′) *v.* to make known; give away; p. 38

domestic (də mes′ tik) *adj.* describes animals living with or near human beings and cared for by them; p. 828

E

eccentric (ik sen′ trik) *adj.* not usual or normal in behavior; peculiar; p. 578

ecology (ē kol′ ə jē) *n.* the relationship of living things to their environment and to each other; p. 309

ecstatic (ek stat′ ik) *adj.* overwhelmed with joy; p. 371

efficient (i fish′ ənt) *adj.* producing a desired effect with a minimum of effort or waste; p. 677

elaborate (i lab′ ər it) *adj.* worked out carefully and thoroughly; detailed; complicated; p. 829

elicit (i lis′ it) *v.* to draw forth or bring out; p. 29

eloquent (el′ ə kwənt) *adj.* expressive, effective, and stirring in speech or writing; p. 29

embrace (em brās′) *v.* to hug or hold in the arms, especially as a sign of love or affection; p. 275

emerge (i murj′) *v.* to come out; p. 52

emphatic (em fat′ ik) *adj.* strongly expressive; forceful; p. 361

endeavor (en dev′ ər) *n.* a serious attempt to accomplish something; undertaking; p. 404

endure (en door′) *v.* to put up with; undergo, as pain, stress, or other hardship; p. 238

enticing (en tīs′ ing) *adj.* offering pleasure or reward; p. 684

enviable (en′ vē ə bəl) *adj.* good enough to be highly desired; p. 685

envious (en′ vē əs) *adj.* having resentment over, and a wish to possess for oneself, something possessed by another; p. 716

esteem (es tēm′) *n.* favorable opinion; high regard; p. 29

etiquette (et′ i kit) *n.* the rules of good manners and polite behavior; p. 414

evacuate (i vak′ ū āt′) *v.* to leave or clear an area; p. 307

evading (i vād′ ing) *adj.* escaping or avoiding; p. 440

eventually (i ven′ choo ə lē) *adv.* in the end; finally; p. 153

exasperation (ig zas′ pə rā′ shən) *n.* anger or great irritation; p. 689

excavated (eks′ kə vāt′ əd) *adj.* uncovered or removed by digging; unearthed; p. 119

excess (ek′ ses) *adj.* more than usual or necessary; p. 149

exotic (ig zot′ ik) *adj.* strangely attractive; foreign; p. 8

explicit (eks plis′ it) *adj.* clearly expressed; p. 524

exploit (iks ploit′) *v.* to use or develop for profit, often in a selfish, unjust, or unfair way; p. 299

extricate (eks′ trə kāt′) *v.* to release from entanglement or difficulty; set free; p. 404

F

faltering (fôl′ tər ing) *adj.* shaky because of uncertainty; p. 199

fanciful (fan′ si fəl) *adj.* showing imagination in design or construction; imaginative; p. 753

fancy (fan′ sē) *v.* to picture mentally; imagine; p. 795

fixed (fikst) *adj.* steadily directed and unchanging; p. 708

flail (flāl) *v.* to wave or swing, especially swiftly or violently; p. 440

fleetest (flēt′ əst) *adj.* swiftest; fastest; p. 719

flinch (flinch) *v.* to draw back, as from something painful, dangerous, or unpleasant; p. 793

flourishing (flur′ ish ing) *adj.* growing or developing successfully; doing very well; p. 354

formidable (for′ mi də bəl) *adj.* causing fear or dread by reason of size, strength, or power; p. 69

fortitude (fôr tə tood′) *n.* firm courage or strength of mind in the face of pain or danger; p. 401

frail (frāl) *adj.* lacking in strength; weak; p. 463

frenzy (fren′ zē) *n.* a state of intense excitement or disturbance; p. 246

frustration (frus trā′ shən) *n.* disappointment or irritation at being kept from doing or achieving something; p. 777

G

gait (gāt) *n.* a particular manner of moving on foot; p. 793

gaunt (gônt) *adj.* looking like skin and bones; p. 237

giddy (gid′ dē) *adj.* dizzy or light-headed; p. 604

gnarled (närld) *adj.* rough, twisted, and knotty, as a tree trunk or branches; p. 702

grim (grim) *adj.* fierce; severe; stern; forbidding; p. 237

grimace (grim′ əs) *v.* to twist the face, as in pain or displeasure; p. 79

grudging (gruj′ ing) *adj.* given or allowed unwillingly or resentfully; p. 236

gruffly (gruf′ lē) *adv.* in a rough, stern manner; p. 239

H

habitual (hə bich′ oo əl) *adj.* done by habit; p. 565

haggard (hag′ ərd) *adj.* looking worn as a result of grief, worry, or illness; p. 666

hallowed (hal′ ōd) *adj.* regarded as sacred or holy; p. 717

hardy (här′ dē) *adj.* able to endure hardship; strong and healthy; p. 155

hindrance (hin′ drəns) *n.* something that holds back progress or movement; obstacle; p. 30

hostile (host′ əl) *adj.* feeling or showing dislike; unfriendly; p. 808

hover (huv′ ər) *v.* to remain as if suspended in the air over a particular spot; p. 745

humility (hū mil′ ə tē) *n.* the quality of being humble or modest; p. 744

hurtle (hurt′ əl) *v.* to move rapidly, especially with much force; p. 664

I

illuminated (i lōō′ mə nāt id) *adj.* lit up; p. 152

immobilize (i mō′ bə līz′) *v.* to make unable to move; fix in place; p. 119

impetuous (im pech′ ōō əs) *adj.* marked by force or violent action; p. 494

impose (im pōz′) *v.* to apply legally; enforce; p. 100

impoverished (im pov′ ər isht) *adj.* reduced to poverty; made very poor; p. 370

improbable (im prob′ ə bəl) *adj.* not likely; p. 151

improvise (im′ prə vīz′) *v.* to invent, compose, or do without much preparation; p. 438

impulse (im′ puls) *n.* an internal force that causes one to act without thinking; p. 50

impunity (im pū′ nə tē) *n.* freedom from punishment, harm, or bad effects; p. 187

incessantly (in ses′ ənt lē) *adv.* endlessly; constantly; p. 188

incomprehensible (in′ kom prē hen′ sə bəl) *adj.* not understandable; p. 191

inconvenience (in′ kən vēn′ yəns) *v.* to cause someone difficulty, bother, or hassle; p. 93

incredulous (in krej′ ə ləs) *adj.* unwilling or unable to believe something; p. 170

incriminate (in krim′ ə nāt′) *v.* to show the guilt of; p. 515

indifferent (in dif′ ər ənt) *adj.* having or showing a lack of feeling, concern, or care; p. 385

indignity (in dig′ nə tē) *n.* an offense against one's pride or dignity; humiliation; p. 94

indiscriminately (in′ dis krim′ ə nit lē) *adv.* in a way that does not pay attention to differences; carelessly; p. 300

inert (i nurt′) *adj.* without power to move or act; p. 352

inevitably (i nev′ ə tə blē) *adv.* in a way that cannot be avoided or prevented; p. 7

infantile (in′ fən tīl′) *adj.* like an infant; childish; p. 413

infinite (in′ fə nit) *adj.* boundless; limitless; extremely great; p. 177

initial (i nish′ əl) *adj.* at the beginning; first; p. 7

initiative (i nish′ ə tiv) *n.* the action of taking the first step; p. 476

insistent (in sis′ tənt) *adj.* demanding attention or notice; p. 176

insolently (in′ sə lənt lē) *adv.* in a boldly rude manner; p. 544

instill (in stil′) *v.* to put in gradually, little by little; p. 510

instinct (in′ stingkt) *n.* a way of knowing, behaving, or reacting that comes naturally rather than through learning; p. 167

intact (in takt′) *adj.* undamaged and whole; p. 597

intellectual (int′ əl ek′ chōō əl) *adj.* appealing to or involving mental ability; p. 608

intense (in tens′) *adj.* of a very high degree; very strong; p. 610

intently (in tent′ lē) *adv.* in a firmly focused way; with concentration; p. 154

intimidated (in tim′ ə dāt′ əd) *adj.* made timid or fearful; bullied; p. 510

intricate (in′ tri kit) *adj.* full of complicated detail; p. 565

intrusion (in trōō′ zhən) *n.* a sudden interruption; p. 384

invalid (in′ və lid) *n.* one who is disabled by disease or injury; p. 165

invariably (in vār′ ē ə blē) *adv.* without exception; p. 194

ironically (ī ron′ i kəl ē) *adv.* in a way that is different from what would be expected; p. 6

J

jeer (jēr) *v.* to make fun of (someone or something) rudely and openly; p. 684

jest (jest) *v.* to speak or act in a playful manner; joke; p. 596

jubilant (jōō′ bə lənt) *adj.* filled with great joy and excitement; high-spirited; p. 721

juncture (jungk′ chər) *n.* a critical point of time; p. 36

K

keen (kēn) *adj.* highly sensitive; sharp; p. 272

L

laden (lād′ ən) *adj.* loaded; weighed down; burdened; p. 386

lapse (laps) *n.* a slipping or falling away; p. 548

legitimate (li jit′ ə mit) *adj.* that which follows the rules; lawful; p. 517

lolling (lol′ ing) *adj.* hanging down loosely; drooping; p. 246

loom (lōōm) *v.* to appear to the mind as threatening; p. 222

lunge (lunj) *v.* to make a sudden forward movement; charge; p. 794

M

malicious (mə lish′ əs) *adj.* having or showing a desire to harm another; p. 484

maneuver (mə nōō′ vər) *v.* to move or handle skillfully, as into a position or toward a goal; p. 68

meek (mēk) *adj.* patient and mild in manner; gentle; p. 389

menace (men′ əs) *n.* a threat or danger; p. 68

merge (murj) *v.* to join together so as to become one; unite; p. 7

meticulously (mi tik′ yə ləs lē) *adv.* in a way that shows careful attention to details; p. 221

mobilize (mō′ bə līz′) *v.* to become prepared, as for war or an emergency; p. 91

moderately (mod′ ər it lē) *adv.* neither too great nor too small; within limits; p. 568

mortified (môr′ tə fīd′) *adj.* greatly embarrassed; p. 370

murky (mur′ kē) *adj.* dark; not clear; p. 414

muse (mūz) *v.* to think or reflect; p. 190

muster (mus′ tər) *v.* to find and gather together; collect; p. 453

N

naive (nä ēv′) *adj.* simple in nature; childlike; p. 37

narrative (nar′ ə tiv) *n.* story; storytelling; p. 37

negotiate (ni gō′ shē āt′) *v.* to discuss in order to bring about an agreement; p. 97

nimble (nim′ bəl) *adj.* light and quick in movement; p. 439

novelty (nov′ əl tē) *n.* anything new and unusual; p. 595

nurture (nur′ chər) *v.* to care for and help grow; p. 356

O

obligation (ob′ lə gā′ shən) *n.* a sense of duty; responsibility; p. 474

obligingly (ə blī′ jing lē) *adv.* helpfully; agreeably; p. 244

obnoxious (ob nok′ shəs) *adj.* annoying and disagreeable; p. 69

obscure (əb skyoor′) *adj.* difficult to understand; p. 350

obsessed (əb sesd′) *adj.* overly concentrated or focused on a single emotion or idea; p. 118

obsession (əb sesh′ ən) *n.* a single emotion or idea that occupies or troubles the mind; p. 414

obstinate (ob′ stə nit) *adj.* stubborn; difficult to overcome or control; p. 361

omen (ō′ mən) *n.* a sign or event thought to foretell good or bad fortune; p. 774

ominous (om′ ə nəs) *adj.* threatening harm or evil; p. 222

oppression (ə presh′ ən) *n.* the act of controlling or governing by the cruel and unjust use of force or authority; p. 95

overtake (ō′ vər tāk′) *v.* to catch up with or to reach and then pass; p. 708

P

painstaking (pānz′ tā′ king) *adj.* requiring close, careful labor or attention; p. 123

parched (pärcht) *adj.* severely in need of moisture; very dry; p. 717

passive (pas′ iv) *adj.* not participating or active; p. 166

perilous (per′ ə ləs) *adj.* dangerous; risky; p. 403

perpetual (pər pech′ o͞o əl) *adj.* constant; unceasing; p. 437

perplexity (pər plek′ sə tē) *n.* doubt or uncertainty; puzzlement; p. 194

perseverance (pur′ sə vēr′ əns) *n.* continuation despite difficulty; determination; p. 187

persistently (pər sis′ tənt lē) *adv.* repeatedly; p. 70

perspective (pər spek′ tiv) *n.* point of view; p. 370

pinnacle (pin′ ə kəl) *n.* a high point, or peak; p. 285

pious (pi′ əs) *adj.* having either genuine or pretended religious devotion; p. 385

plummet (plum′ it) *v.* to fall or drop straight downward; plunge; p. 296

podium (pō′ dē əm) *n.* a small, raised platform or stand with a slanted shelf for holding a speaker's papers; p. 728

pompous (pom′ pəs) *adj.* showing an exaggerated sense of self-importance; p. 385

portly (pôrt′ lē) *adj.* having a stout but dignified appearance; p. 369

possessively (pə zes′ iv lē) *adv.* in a way that shows ownership or control; p. 361

potion (pō′ shən) *n.* a drink, especially of a liquid that is supposed to have magical powers; p. 702

pounce (pouns) *v.* to swoop down, spring, or leap suddenly in attack; p. 729

precise (pri sīs′) *adj.* strictly accurate or clearly defined; exact; p. 605

predator (pred′ ə tər) *n.* an animal, such as a lion or hawk, that kills other animals for food; p. 125

prejudice (prej′ ə dis) *n.* an unfavorable opinion or judgment formed unfairly; p. 524

premonition (prē′ mə nish′ ən) *n.* a feeling that something is about to happen; warning or sign; p. 400

primly (prim′ lē) *adv.* in a formal and proper manner; p. 548

principle (prin′ sə pəl) *n.* a basic law, truth, or belief; rule of personal conduct; p. 354

proposition (prop′ ə zish′ ən) *n.* something offered for consideration; proposal; p. 573

prosperous (pros′ pər əs) *adj.* having wealth or good fortune; successful; p. 592

pursue (pər so͞o′) *v.* to chase; p. 273

Q

quavering (kwā′ vər ing) *adj.* trembling or shaking; p. 484

quench (kwench) *v.* to satisfy or put an end to a need or desire; p. 739

R

rash (rash) *adj.* done without thought or preparation; reckless; p. 738

raucous (rô′ kəs) *adj.* loud and rough-sounding; p. 544

ravenous (rav′ ə nəs) *adj.* extremely hungry; p. 390

rebuke (ri būk′) *n.* an expression of sharp criticism or disapproval; p. 578

reel (rēl) *v.* to turn or seem to turn round and round; whirl; p. 739

reflective (ri flek′ tiv) *adj.* showing serious and careful thinking; thoughtful; p. 507

reformation (ref´ ər mā´ shən) *n.* a change for the better; improvement; p. 547

regretfully (ri gret´ fəl lē) *adv.* in a way that shows sorrow, distress, or disappointment; p. 774

reluctantly (ri luk´ tənt lē) *adv.* unwillingly; p. 247

replenish (ri plen´ ish) *v.* to provide a new supply; p. 687

resigned (ri zīnd´) *adj.* giving in without resistance; p. 88

resilient (ri zil´ yənt) *adj.* capable of springing back into shape or position after being bent, stretched, or compressed; p. 465

resolute (rez´ ə lo͞ot´) *adj.* determined; stubborn; p. 348

resourceful (ri sôrs´ fəl) *adj.* capable or skillful in dealing with new or difficult situations; p. 727

retrieve (ri trēv´) *v.* to locate and bring back; recover; fetch; p. 50

ritual (rich´ o͞o əl) *n.* an established form of doing something; ceremony; p. 37

robust (rō bust´) *adj.* strong and full of energy; p. 341

S

sanction (sangk´ shən) *v.* to give support or encouragement to; approve; p. 168

sanctuary (sangk´ cho͞o er´ ē) *n.* a place of safety or protection; p. 170

saunter (sôn´ tər) *v.* to walk in a relaxed way; p. 246

savor (sā´ vər) *v.* to take great delight in; p. 239

scavenger (skav´ in jər) *n.* an animal, such as a hyena or vulture, that feeds on dead, decaying animals; p. 125

scurry (skur´ ē) *v.* to run or move briskly or in an agitated way; p. 774

scuttle (skut´ əl) *v.* to move with short, rapid steps; p. 789

secretive (sē´ kri tiv) *adj.* keeping one's thoughts and feelings to oneself; p. 663

sedately (si dāt´ lē) *adv.* in a quiet, restrained style or manner; calmly; p. 239

sensation (sen sā´ shən) *n.* a cause of excitement or great interest; a wonder; p. 754

shrewd (shro͞od) *adj.* sharp, clever, and practical; p. 584

simultaneously (sī´ məl tā´ nē əs lē) *adv.* at the same time; p. 546

sinewy (sin´ ū ē) *adj.* physically tough, or powerful; p. 274

singularity (sing´ gyə lar´ ə tē) *n.* that which is remarkable or out of the ordinary; unusualness; p. 191

skimpy (skim´ pē) *adj.* lacking in quantity, fullness, or size; barely enough or not quite enough; p. 236

slither (sli<u>th</u>´ ər) *v.* to move along with a sliding or gliding motion, as a snake; p. 246

sluggish (slug´ ish) *adj.* lacking energy, liveliness, or alertness; p. 828

soberly (sō´ bər lē) *adv.* very seriously; p. 476

solemnly (sol´ əm lē) *adv.* seriously; p. 546

somberly (som´ bər lē) *adv.* in a gloomy manner; p. 490

sorcerer (sor´ sər ər) *n.* a person who practices magic with the aid of evil spirits; p. 701

spare (spār) *v.* to treat with mercy; hold back from harming or injuring; p. 274

spasm (spaz´ əm) *n.* a sudden uncontrollable tightening of a muscle; p. 243

specify (spes´ ə fī´) *v.* to state or describe in detail; p. 7

speculation (spek´ yə lā´ shən) *n.* the act of forming an opinion or conclusion based on guesswork; p. 150

spendthrift (spend´ thrift´) *n.* one who spends money generously or wastefully; p. 594

spite (spīt) *n.* a desire to hurt or annoy another person; p. 744

squander (skwon´ dər) *v.* to spend or use in a reckless or wasteful manner; p. 593

staccato (stə kä´ tō) *adj.* made of short, sharp sounds or movements; p. 362

staple (stā´ pəl) *adj.* important; main; p. 38

stark (stärk) *adv.* completely; harshly or grimly; p. 177

subsidize (sub′ sə dīz′) *v.* to aid or support with a contribution of money; p. 301

subtle (sut′ əl) *adj.* not open or direct; not obvious; p. 178

succeed (sək sēd′) *v.* to come or happen after in time, place, or order; p. 666

sufficient (sə fish′ ənt) *adj.* adequate; enough; p. 677

sullen (sul′ ən) *adj.* stubbornly withdrawn or gloomy; sulky; p. 45

surge (surj) *v.* to rise or increase suddenly; move with a violent swelling motion, as waves; p. 441

surly (sur′ le) *adj.* rude and bad tempered; gruff; p. 164

swagger (swag′ ər) *v.* to walk or behave in a bold, rude, or overly proud way; p. 45

T

tact (takt) *n.* the ability to handle people or situations without causing displeasure or resentment; p. 370

taunt (tônt) *v.* to make fun of in a scornful, insulting way; p. 701

taut (tôt) *adj.* stretched tight; p. 150

tentatively (ten′ tə tiv lē) *adv.* hesitantly; uncertainly; p. 492

therapy (ther′ ə pē) *n.* treatment of an injury, disease, or mental disorder; p. 676

tumultuously (too mul′ cho͞o əs lē) *adv.* in a wildly excited, confused, or disturbed way; p. 465

U

ultimately (ul′ tə mit lē) *adv.* in the end; finally; p. 369

uncanny (un kan′ ē) *adj.* so strange as to cause fear or wonder; weird; p. 404

uncommitted (un′ kə mit′ id) *adj.* not having or showing a particular opinion, view, or course of action; p. 474

undermine (un′ dər mīn′) *v.* to weaken, wear away, or destroy slowly; p. 298

undertake (un′ dər tāk′) *v.* to enter into (a task); attempt; p. 829

undulating (un′ jə lāt′ ing) *adj.* moving in waves; rippling; p. 603

unique (ū nēk′) *adj.* highly uncommon; rare; one-of-a-kind; p. 309

unpalatable (un pal′ ə tə bəl) *adj.* not agreeable to the taste, mind, or feelings; unacceptable; p. 222

V

vaguely (vāg′ lē) *adv.* in a way that is not clear, exact, or definite; p. 7

vainly (vān′ lē) *adv.* without success; uselessly; p. 739

valiant (val′ yənt) *adj.* brave; courageous; p. 797

validity (və lid′ ə tē) *n.* state of being supported by facts; truth; p. 511

veer (vēr) *v.* to shift or change direction; p. 737

venture (ven′ chər) *v.* to do something in spite of possible risk or danger; p. 152

vigor (vig′ ər) *n.* strength and energy; p. 246

vile (vīl) *adj.* very bad; unpleasant; foul; p. 455

vital (vīt′ əl) *adj.* of primary importance; essential; p. 464

W

wary (wār′ ē) *adj.* cautious; on the alert; p. 437

waver (wā′ vər) *v.* to become unsteady; p. 738

wholeheartedly (hōl′ här′ tid lē) *adv.* completely; sincerely; enthusiastically; p. 68

wily (wī′ lē) *adj.* full of tricks; crafty; sly; p. 170

wince (wins) *v.* to draw back slightly, as in pain; p. 48

withdrawn (with drôn′) *adj.* shy, reserved, or unsociable; p. 454

woe (wō) *n.* great sadness or suffering; great trouble or misfortune; p. 474

Spanish Glossary

A

absurdity/absurdo *s.* cualidad de disparatado o ridículo; irracional; p. 567

accede/acceder *v.* aceptar; consentir; p. 677

acutely/agudamente *adv.* de modo punzante e intenso; p. 493

aggrieved/apesadumbrado *adj.* afligido o apenado, por ejemplo por un insulto o un trato injusto; p. 666

agility/agilidad *s.* rapidez y ligereza de movimiento o pensamiento; p. 282

agitated/agitado *adj.* 1. molesto; turbado; p. 36. 2. excitado; nervioso; trastornado; p. 667

agony/agonía *s.* gran dolor y sufrimiento mental o físico; p. 745

amplify/ampliar *v.* aumentar; extender; p. 300

anguished/angustiado *adj.* que siente o demuestra un gran sufrimiento mental o físico; p. 286

antagonism/antagonismo *s.* hostilidad; p. 511

anticipation/anticipación *s.* expectación; sensación de esperar algo con interés o ilusión; p. 390

appalling/pasmoso *adj.* impactante; horrorizante; p. 79

apparatus/aparato *s.* algo creado o inventado con un fin particular; p. 465

aptitude/aptitud *s.* habilidad natural; talento; p. 743

aroma/aroma *s.* olor agradable; fragancia; p. 708

artful/habilidoso *adj.* hecho con habilidad o ingenio; p. 565

ascertain/averiguar *v.* cerciorarse; comprobar; p. 413

assess/evaluar *v.* determinar el significado o la importancia de algo; analizar; p. 222

authoritarian/autoritario *adj.* que tiene o exige total obediencia a la autoridad; dominante; p. 369

avert/prevenir *v.* impedir que ocurra; evitar; p. 401

avidly/ávidamente *adv.* de modo intenso; ansiosamente; con mucho ánimo; p. 372

awe/veneración *s.* admiración combinada con respeto; p. 351

B

balmy/suave *adj.* balsámico; calmante; p. 222

barrage/descarga *s.* concentración o efusión grande, como de palabras; p. 119

barren/yermo *adj.* que tiene poca o ninguna vegetación; árido; vacío; p. 753

benefactor/benefactor *s.* quien brinda ayuda financiera; p. 584

bewildered/perplejo *adj.* muy confundido; p. 118

bleak/sombrío *adj.* triste; deprimente; p. 164

boycott/boicot *s.* protesta organizada en la que los participantes se niegan a comprar, vender o usar un producto o servicio; p. 90

bravado/bravuconería *s.* falsa demostración de valentía; p. 353

brink/margen *s.* borde; a punto de; p. 282

brood/camada *s.* crías de un animal que nacen a un mismo tiempo; p. 799

C

casually/casualmente *adv.* de modo informal o imprevisto; p. 362

chaotic/caótico *adj.* confuso y desorganizado; muy desarreglado; p. 8

charismatic/carismático *adj.* con cualidades personales que inspiran lealtad y admiración; p. 283

claim/reclamar *v.* solicitar o exigir la posesión o el derecho de algo; p. 721

clamor/algarabía *s.* ruido fuerte y continuo; griterío; p. 79

clan/clan *s.* grupo de familias descendientes de un antepasado común; p. 270

coincidence/coincidencia *s.* acontecimientos, circunstancias o ideas que ocurren al mismo tiempo por accidente; casualidad; p. 452

collaborator/colaborador *s.* alguien que trabaja o coopera con otro; p. 415

collective/colectivo *adj.* relativo a un grupo de personas o cosas; común; compartido; p. 677

colossal/colosal *adj.* extraordinaria o asombrosamente grande; p. 754

commencement/comienzo *s.* principio; ceremonia de graduación; p. 9

compact/compacto *adj.* que ocupa un espacio o área relativamente pequeño; macizo; p. 306

compensate/compensar *v.* dar algo a cambio; equilibrar en fuerza, peso o efecto; p. 808

competent/competente *adj.* que tiene suficiente habilidad para un fin concreto; capaz; p. 577

comply/acatar *v.* aceptar una solicitud; cumplir con algo; p. 86

comprehend/comprender *v.* captar mentalmente; entender por completo; p. 413

concede/conceder *v.* admitir que algo es cierto o apropiado; p. 221

conceive/concebir *v.* formarse una imagen o idea de algo; p. 577

condemn/condenar *v.* expresar total desacuerdo; criticar agudamente; p. 715

confront/confrontar *v.* encontrarse cara a cara; enfrentar; p. 416

consecutive/consecutivo *adj.* seguido uno de otro en orden y sin interrupción; p. 27

consequence/consecuencia *s.* importancia; significación; p. 464

consolation/consolación *s.* aliento; alivio; p. 373

conspicuously/conspicuamente *adv.* de modo que capta atención o notoriedad; p. 809

contemplate/contemplar *v.* prestar gran atención a algo; considerar cuidadosamente; p. 296

converge/converger *v.* reunirse en un lugar; p. 299

cordially/cordialmente *adv.* de modo cálido y amistoso; p. 752

correspond/cartearse *v.* comunicarse mediante cartas; p. 567

cower/encogerse *v.* agacharse, como cuando se siente miedo o vergüenza; p. 792

culprit/culpable *s.* el que ha cometido una ofensa; p. 405

cunning/astuto *adj.* vivo; engañoso; p. 390

cynically/cínicamente *adv.* de un modo que muestra duda o incertidumbre; dudosamente; p. 547

D

deception/engaño *s.* mentira o enredo; p. 125

decree/decreto *s.* regla, orden o decisión oficial; p. 743

defiant/desafiante *adj.* que se enfrenta atrevidamente a la autoridad o a un oponente; p. 511

degrade/degradar *v.* rebajar las características o la calidad; hacer menos puro; p. 828

delectable/deleitable *adj.* muy placentero o agradable, especialmente al gusto; delicioso; p. 389

demise/defunción *s.* muerte; fin; p. 828

depleted/disminuido *adj.* muy reducido en cantidad; p. 296

desolation/desolación *s.* tristeza; soledad; p. 689

despair/desesperanza *s.* pérdida total de la esperanza; desesperación; desconsuelo; p. 708

desperation/desesperación *s.* angustia causada por una gran necesidad o pérdida de la esperanza; p. 50

destine/destinar *v.* determinar con anticipación; asignar; p. 400

devastating/devastador *adj.* que causa gran dolor, daño o destrucción; abrumador; p. 434

devise/ingeniar *v.* pensar; inventar; planear; p. 384

diligently/diligentemente *adv.* de modo que muestra gran atención, cuidado y esfuerzo; p. 301

discern/discernir *v.* distinguir o reconocer; p. 492

discreetly/discretamente *adv.* de un modo sensato y cuidadoso; p. 155

discrepancy/discrepancia *s.* desacuerdo, como cuando dos hechos no concuerdan; p. 28

dismally/desconsoladamente *adv.* de un modo melancólico y triste; p. 567

dismay/consternación *s.* sentimiento de alarma o intranquilidad; p. 453

dispense/dispensar *v.* dar en porciones; distribuir; p. 385

distinct/distinto *adj.* diferente en calidad o tipo; p. 285

divulge/divulgar *v.* dar a conocer; emitir; p. 38

domestic/doméstico *adj.* relativo a los animales que conviven con los seres humanos; p. 828

E

eccentric/excéntrico *adj.* que no es común o normal en su comportamiento; peculiar; p. 578

ecology/ecología *s.* relación de los seres vivientes entre sí y con su medio ambiente; p. 309

ecstatic/extasiado *adj.* encantado; lleno de júbilo; p. 371

efficient/eficiente *adj.* que produce un efecto deseado con un mínimo de esfuerzo o gasto; p. 677

elaborate/elaborado *adj.* hecho con cuidado y esmero; detallado; complicado; p. 829

elicit/sacar *v.* revelar; p. 29

eloquent/elocuente *adj.* expresivo, efectivo y conmovedor, ya sea al hablar o escribir; p. 29

embrace/abrazar *v.* estrechar entre los brazos en demostración de amor o afecto; p. 275

emerge/emerger *v.* salir; surgir; brotar; p. 52

emphatic/enfático *adj.* que se expresa con intensidad o fuerza; p. 361

endeavor/empeño *s.* deseo intenso de hacer o lograr algo y tesón para alcanzarlo; p. 404

endure/soportar *v.* resistir o aguantar algo, como por ejemplo dolor, tensión u otra dificultad; p. 238

enticing/tentador *adj.* que ofrece placer o recompensa; p. 684

enviable/envidiable *adj.* suficientemente bueno como para que se desee mucho; ansiado; p. 685

envious/envidioso *adj.* que siente resentimiento por la suerte ajena o desearía algo que le pertenece a otra persona; p. 716

esteem/estima *s.* opinión favorable; aprecio; p. 29

etiquette/etiqueta *s.* normas de buenos modales y buena educación; p. 414

evacuate/evacuar *v.* despejar o limpiar un área; p. 307

evading/evasivo *adj.* que evita o escapa; p. 440

eventually/con el tiempo *adv.* al final; por último; p. 153

exasperation/exasperación *s.* rabia o gran irritación; p. 689

excavated/excavado *adj.* desenterrado o descubierto al cavar; p. 119

excess/exceso *adj.* más de lo usual o de lo necesario; p. 149

exotic/exótico *adj.* que tiene un atractivo extraño; foráneo; p. 8

explicit/explícito *adj.* expresado claramente; p. 524

exploit/explotar *v.* usar o aprovechar, a menudo de manera egoísta o injusta; p. 299

extricate/desembrollar *v.* sacar de un problema o dificultad; p. 404

F

faltering/titubeante *adj.* que muestra inseguridad, duda o vacilación; p. 199

fanciful/fantástico *adj.* con un diseño o construcción imaginativo y atrayente; p. 753

fancy/idear *v.* visualizar; imaginar; p. 795

fixed/fijo *adj.* asegurado; que no cambia; p. 708

flail/zarandear *v.* agitar o sacudir, especialmente de modo rápido o brusco; p. 440

fleetest/apresurado *adj.* el más rápido; el más veloz; p. 719

flinch/recular *v.* retroceder o echarse hacia atrás, ya sea por algo doloroso, peligroso o desagradable; p. 793

flourishing/floreciente *adj.* que crece o se desarrolla con éxito; que progresa; p. 354

formidable/formidable *adj.* que causa temor o asombro debido a su tamaño, fuerza o poder; p. 69

fortitude/fortaleza *s.* valor y tranquilidad ante el sufrimiento o el peligro; p. 401

frail/frágil *adj.* que carece de fuerza; débil; p. 463

frenzy/frenesí *s.* estado de intenso entusiasmo o enojo; p. 246

frustration/frustración *s.* desilusión o irritación por no poder hacer o alcanzar algo; p. 777

G

gait/andadura *s.* modo particular de caminar; p. 793

gaunt/esquelético *adj.* excesivamente flaco; p. 237

giddy/aturdido *adj.* mareado o atontado; p. 604

gnarled/retorcido *adj.* torcido y nudoso, como el tronco o las ramas de un árbol; p. 702

grim/severo *adj.* estricto; austero; inflexible; p. 237

grimace/hacer muecas *v.* hacer gestos con la cara, como cuando se siente dolor o desagrado; p. 79

grudging/de mala gana *adj.* que se da o permite sin querer o con resentimiento; p. 236

gruffly/rudamente *adv.* de modo severo o grosero; p. 239

H

habitual/habitual *adj.* que se hace por hábito o costumbre; p. 565

haggard/demacrado *adj.* de aspecto enfermizo o cansado debido a una pena, preocupación o enfermedad; p. 666

hallowed/sagrado *adj.* que se considera santificado o bendito; p. 717

hardy/resistente *adj.* capaz de soportar dificultades; fuerte y saludable; p. 155

hindrance/estorbo *s.* algo que impide el progreso o movimiento; obstáculo; p. 30

hostile/hostil *adj.* que siente o muestra antipatía o desagrado; p. 808

hover/revolotear *v.* permanecer en un sitio como si estuviera suspendido del aire; p. 745

humility/humildad *s.* cualidad de ser humilde o modesto; p. 744

hurtle/precipitarse *v.* moverse rápidamente, especialmente con fuerza o ansiedad; p. 664

I

illuminated/iluminado *adj.* encendido; p. 152

immobilize/inmovilizar *v.* impedir que se mueva; fijar en un sitio; p. 119

impetuous/impetuoso *adj.* que actúa con fuerza o violencia; p. 494

impose/imponer *v.* llevar a cabo legalmente; aplicar; p. 100

impoverished/empobrecido *adj.* reducido a la pobreza; arruinado; p. 370

improbable/improbable *adj.* que no es probable; incierto; p. 151

improvise/improvisar *v.* inventar, componer o hacer sin mucha preparación; p. 438

impulse/impulso *s.* fuerza interna que obliga a actuar sin pensar; p. 50

impunity/impunidad *s.* exención de castigo, perjuicio o consecuencias negativas; p. 187

incessantly/incesantemente *adv.* de modo constante; sin parar; p. 188

incomprehensible/incomprensible *adj.* que no se entiende; p. 191

inconvenience/estorbar *v.* causar molestias o dificultades a alguien; p. 93

incredulous/incrédulo *adj.* que no quiere o no puede creer en algo; p. 170

incriminate/incriminar *v.* demostrar culpabilidad; p. 515

indifferent/indiferente *adj.* que no demuestra interés, sentimiento o preocupación; p. 385

indignity/oprobio *s.* ofensa contra el orgullo o dignidad; humillación; p. 94

indiscriminately/indiscriminadamente *adv.* de un modo que no presta atención a las diferencias; sin hacer distinciones; p. 300

inert/inerte *adj.* incapaz de moverse o actuar; p. 352

inevitably/inevitablemente *adv.* de un modo que no se puede evitar o prevenir; p. 7

infantile/infantil *adj.* como lo haría un niño; pueril; p. 413

infinite/infinito *adj.* sin fronteras; ilimitado; inmenso; p. 177

initial/inicial *adj.* al comienzo; lo primero; p. 7

initiative/iniciativa *s.* acción de dar el primer paso o iniciar una acción; p. 476

insistent/insistente *adj.* que exige atención a toda costa; p. 176

insolently/insolentemente *adv.* de modo atrevido o rudo; p. 544

instill/instilar *v.* verter gradualmente o poco a poco; p. 510

instinct/instinto *s.* modo natural de saber, comportarse o reaccionar que no se ha aprendido; p. 167

intact/intacto *adj.* que no se ha dañado; que está completo; p. 597

intellectual/intelectual *adj.* relativo a la habilidad mental o a la inteligencia; p. 608

intense/intenso *adj.* acentuado o potente; muy fuerte; p. 610

intently/resueltamente *adv.* de un modo firme y decidido; con concentración; p. 154

intimidated/intimidado *adj.* atemorizado o asustado; p. 510

intricate/intrincado *adj.* con muchos detalles complicados; p. 565

intrusion/intrusión *s.* interrupción repentina; p. 384

invalid/inválido *s.* alguien que está incapacitado debido a una enfermedad o herida; p. 165

invariably/invariablemente *adv.* sin excepción; p. 194

ironically/irónicamente *adv.* de un modo diferente al que se espera; p. 6

J

jeer/mofarse *v.* burlarse de algo o alguien de manera brusca y abierta; p. 684

jest/chancear *v.* hablar o actuar de manera jocosa; bromear; p. 596

jubilant/jubiloso *adj.* que está muy contento o emocionado; p. 721

juncture/coyuntura *s.* momento o punto crítico; p. 36

K

keen/agudo *adj.* muy sensible; despierto; p. 272

L

laden/cargado *adj.* abrumado; agobiado; atiborrado; p. 386

lapse/traspié *s.* caída o resbalón; p. 548

legitimate/legítimo *adj.* que sigue las reglas; legal; p. 517

lolling/oscilante *adj.* que cuelga flojamente; colgante; p. 246

loom/vislumbrarse *v.* que surge en la mente como algo temible; p. 222

lunge/arremeter *v.* moverse repentinamente hacia adelante; atacar; p. 794

M

malicious/malicioso *adj.* que tiene o muestra el deseo de perjudicar a alguien; p. 484

maneuver/maniobrar *v.* desempeñarse con destreza, por ejemplo para obtener un cargo o alcanzar una meta; p. 68

meek/apacible *adj.* paciente y tranquilo; gentil; p. 389

menace/amenaza *s.* peligro o riesgo; p. 68

merge/fusionar *v.* unir; agrupar; p. 7

meticulously/meticulosamente *adv.* de un modo que muestra mucha atención a los detalles; p. 221

mobilize/movilizar *v.* prepararse, como para una guerra o emergencia; p. 91

moderately/moderadamente *adv.* ni mucho ni poco; dentro de los límites; p. 568

mortified/mortificado *adj.* muy avergonzado; p. 370

murky/lóbrego *adj.* obscuro o sombrío; p. 414

muse/meditar *v.* pensar o reflexionar; p. 190

muster/congregar *v.* buscar y reunir; agrupar; p. 453

N

naive/ingenuo *adj.* simple por naturaleza; infantil; p. 37

narrative/narración *s.* cuento; relato; p. 37

negotiate/negociar *v.* discutir con el fin de llegar a un acuerdo; p. 97

nimble/ágil *adj.* ligero y rápido de movimiento; p. 439

novelty/novedad *s.* algo nuevo e inusual; p. 595

nurture/criar *v.* cuidar y ayudar a crecer; p. 356

O

obligation/obligación *s.* sentido del deber; responsabilidad; p. 474

obligingly/servicialmente *adv.* que muestra el deseo de ser útil o servir; cortésmente; p. 244

obnoxious/odioso *adj.* molesto y desagradable; p. 69

obscure/confuso *adj.* difícil de entender; p. 350

obsessed/obsesionado *adj.* demasiado concentrado o dedicado a una sola emoción o idea; p. 118

obsession/obsesión *s.* emoción o idea fija que ocupa la mente; p. 414

obstinate/obstinado *adj.* terco; difícil de controlar o superar; p. 361

omen/presagio *s.* suceso visto como señal de buena o mala suerte; p. 774

ominous/ominoso *adj.* algo que anuncia temor o daño; p. 222

oppression/opresión *s.* acto de controlar o gobernar mediante el uso cruel e injusto de la fuerza o autoridad; p. 95

overtake/alcanzar *v.* dar alcance y rebasar; p. 708

P

painstaking/esmerado *adj.* que requiere de mucha atención o trabajo; p. 123

parched/reseco *adj.* que necesita humedad con urgencia; muy seco; p. 717

passive/pasivo *adj.* que no participa ni es activo; p. 166

perilous/peligroso *adj.* azaroso; arriesgado; p. 403

perpetual/perpetuo *adj.* constante; incesante; p. 437

perplexity/perplejidad *s.* duda o incertidumbre; aturdimiento; p. 194

perseverance/perseverancia *s.* voluntad para continuar haciendo algo aunque sea difícil; determinación; p. 187

persistently/persistentemente *adv.* repetidamente; una y otra vez; p. 70

perspective/perspectiva *s.* punto de vista; p. 370

pinnacle/pináculo *s.* cumbre o cima; punto más alto; p. 285

pious/piadoso *adj.* que tiene o finge devoción religiosa; p. 385

plummet/desplomarse *v.* caer verticalmente; derrumbarse; p. 296

podium/podio *s.* plataforma pequeña con una repisa para sostener los papeles de la persona que habla; p. 728

pompous/pomposo *adj.* que muestra exagerado orgullo o vanidad; p. 385

portly/corpulento *adj.* que tiene una figura robusta y respetable; p. 369

possessively/posesivamente *adv.* de un modo que muestra control o posesión sobre algo o alguien; p. 361

potion/poción *s.* bebida, especialmente referente a líquidos con poderes mágicos; p. 702

pounce/abalanzarse *v.* saltar o caer encima de repente con intención de atacar; embestir; p. 729

precise/preciso *adj.* muy claro o definido; exacto; p. 605

predator/depredador *s.* animal, tal como el león o el halcón, que mata a otros animales para alimentarse; p. 125

prejudice/prejuicio *s.* opinión o juicio desfavorable sin bases justas; p. 524

premonition/premonición *s.* sensación de que algo está por ocurrir; señal o advertencia; p. 400

primly/formalmente *adv.* de modo formal y apropiado; p. 548

principle/principio *s.* ley, verdad o creencia básica; norma de conducta personal; p. 354

proposition/proposición *s.* algo que se ofrece o propone; propuesta; oferta; p. 573

prosperous/próspero *adj.* que tiene riquezas o buena suerte; exitoso; acaudalado; p. 592

pursue/perseguir *v.* dar caza; p. 273

Q

quavering/trémulo *adj.* tembloroso; p. 484

quench/aplacar *v.* satisfacer o mitigar una necesidad o deseo; p. 739

R

rash/apresurado *adj.* hecho a la carrera sin pensarlo ni prepararlo; p. 738

raucous/estridente *adj.* sonido fuerte y áspero; p. 544

ravenous/hambriento *adj.* con mucha hambre; p. 390

rebuke/reproche *s.* expresión severa de crítica o desacuerdo; p. 578

reel/remolinar *v.* dar vueltas o parecer como si diera vueltas; girar; p. 739

reflective/reflexivo *adj.* que piensa seria y cuidadosamente; pensativo; p. 507

reformation/reforma *s.* cambio positivo; mejora; p. 547

regretfully/lamentablemente *adv.* de un modo que muestra pesar o desilusión; p. 774

reluctantly/a regañadientes *adv.* sin querer; de mala gana; p. 247

replenish/reabastecer *v.* dar nuevo suministro; volver a llenar; p. 687

resigned/resignado *adj.* que cede o acepta sin oponer resistencia; p. 88

resilient/flexible *adj.* capaz de volver a su forma o posición original después de que se dobla, estira o comprime; p. 465

resolute/resuelto *adj.* determinado; decidido; p. 348

resourceful/recursivo *adj.* hábil para enfrentarse a situaciones nuevas o difíciles; p. 727

retrieve/recobrar *v.* localizar y traer de nuevo; recuperar; p. 50

ritual/ritual *s.* forma establecida de hacer algo; ceremonia; p. 37

robust/robusto *adj.* fuerte y lleno de energía; p. 341

S

sanction/ratificar *v.* respaldar o aprobar algo; p. 168

sanctuary/santuario *s.* lugar de resguardo o protección; p. 170

saunter/deambular *v.* caminar tranquilamente; pasearse; p. 246

savor/saborear *v.* gozar de algo con gran placer; p. 239

scavenger/carroñero *s.* animal que se alimenta de cadáveres descompuestos de animales, como por ejemplo las hienas o los buitres; p. 125

scurry/escurrirse *v.* correr o moverse rápida o agitadamente; p. 774

scuttle/apresurarse *v.* caminar con pasos rápidos y cortos; p. 789

secretive/reservado *adj.* que no expresa sus pensamientos o emociones; p. 663

sedately/sosegadamente *adv.* de modo tranquilo y silencioso; calmadamente; p. 239

sensation/sensación *s.* motivo de asombro o gran interés; maravilla; p. 754

shrewd/sagaz *adj.* astuto, listo y práctico; p. 584

simultaneously/simultáneamente *adv.* al mismo tiempo; p. 546

sinewy/vigoroso *adj.* físicamente fuerte o poderoso; p. 274

singularity/singularidad *s.* cualidad de notorio o fuera de lo ordinario; peculiaridad; p. 191

skimpy/escaso *adj.* de poca cantidad o tamaño; incompleto; insuficiente o que apenas alcanza; p. 236

slither/deslizarse *v.* avanzar resbalándose como una serpiente; p. 246

sluggish/flojo *adj.* sin energía, vitalidad o ánimo; p. 828

soberly/severamente *adv.* muy seriamente; p. 476

solemnly/solemnemente *adv.* seriamente; p. 546

somberly/lúgubremente *adv.* de modo sombrío o tétrico; p. 490

sorcerer/hechicero *s.* persona que practica la magia con la ayuda de espíritus malignos; p. 701

spare/perdonar *v.* tener misericordia de alguien; desistir de hacerle daño; p. 274

spasm/espasmo *s.* tirantez repentina e incontrolable de un músculo; p. 243

specify/especificar *v.* establecer o describir en detalle; p. 7

speculation/especulación *s.* acto de formarse una opinión o conclusión basándose en suposiciones; p. 150

spendthrift/derrochador *s.* aquél que gasta dinero de modo generoso o que lo desperdicia; p. 150

spite/rencor *s.* deseo de herir o molestar a otra persona; p. 744

squander/malgastar *v.* gastar o usar de forma imprudente o innecesaria; p. 593

staccato/entrecortado *adj.* hecho de ruidos o movimientos cortos y agudos; p. 362

staple/principal *adj.* importante; prominente; p. 38

stark/absolutamente *adv.* completamente; rígida o severamente; p. 177

subsidize/subsidiar *v.* ayudar o respaldar con dinero; p. 301

subtle/sutil *adj.* que no es abierto o directo; que no es obvio; p. 178

succeed/seguir *v.* ocurrir después, ya sea en tiempo, orden o lugar; p. 666

sufficient/suficiente *adj.* adecuado; bastante; p. 677

sullen/hosco *adj.* malhumorado, retraído o sombrío; resentido; p. 45

surge/surgir *v.* elevarse de repente; moverse con agitación violenta, como el oleaje; p. 441

surly/arisco *adj.* rudo y de malhumor; hosco; p. 164

swagger/contonearse *v.* caminar o comportarse de modo altanero, brusco o demasiado orgulloso; p. 45

T

tact/tacto *s.* habilidad para manejar situaciones o personas sin causar desagrado ni herir sentimientos; p. 370

taunt/mofarse *v.* burlarse de manera despreciativa e insultante; p. 701

taut/tirante *adj.* tenso; estirado; p. 150

tentatively/tentativamente *adv.* de modo dudoso; inciertamente; posiblemente; p. 492

therapy/terapia *s.* tratamiento de una herida, enfermedad o desorden mental; p. 676

tumultuously/tumultosamente *adv.* de un modo agitado o confuso; p. 465

U

ultimately/por último *adv.* al final; finalmente; p. 369

uncanny/extraño *adj.* que produce asombro; misterioso; p. 404

uncommitted/imparcial *adj.* que no demuestra una opinión o punto de vista particular o definido; p. 474

undermine/socavar *v.* debilitar, desgastar o destruir lentamente; p. 298

undertake/emprender *v.* iniciar una labor o proyecto; intentar; acometer; p. 829

undulating/ondulante *adj.* que se mueve como las olas; fluctuante; p. 603

unique/único *adj.* muy particular; raro; singular; p. 309

unpalatable/desagradable *adj.* que no es agradable al gusto, la mente o los sentidos; inaceptable; p. 222

V

vaguely/vagamente *adv.* de un modo que no es claro, exacto o definido; p. 7

vainly/vanamente *adv.* sin éxito; ineficaz; p. 739

valiant/valiente *adj.* intrépido; valeroso; p. 797

validity/validez *s.* condición de ser apoyado por los hechos; verdad; p. 511

veer/virar *v.* girar o cambiar de dirección; p. 737

venture/aventurarse *v.* hacer algo a pesar de los posibles riesgos o peligros; p. 152

vigor/vigor *s.* fortaleza y energía; p. 246

vile/vil *adj.* muy malo; perverso; desagradable; p. 455

vital/vital *adj.* de enorme importancia; esencial; p. 464

W

wary/cauteloso *adj.* cuidadoso; prudente; p. 437

waver/tambalear *v.* perder el equilibrio; p. 738

wholeheartedly/sinceramente *adv.* francamente; con gusto; p. 68

wily/taimado *adj.* hipócrita; engañoso; p. 170

wince/recular *v.* retroceder ligeramente, como cuando se siente dolor; p. 48

withdrawn/retraído *adj.* tímido, reservado o poco sociable; p. 454

woe/aflicción *s.* gran tristeza o sufrimiento; gran preocupación o desdicha; p. 474

Index of Skills

Grammar and Language

Vocabulary

Writing

Listening, Speaking, and Viewing

Index of Authors and Titles

Index of Art and Artists

Acknowledgments

(Continued from page iv)

Literature

Theme 1

"Names/Nombres" Copyright © 1985 by Julia Alvarez. First published in *Nuestro,* March 1985. Reprinted by permission of Susan Bergholz Literary Services, New York. All rights reserved.

"One" from *When I Dance,* copyright © 1991, 1988 by James Berry, reprinted by permission of Harcourt Brace & Company.
"One" from *When I Dance,* copyright © 1991, 1988 by James Berry. Reprinted by permission of The Peters Fraser Dunlop Group Limited on behalf of the author.

"I'm Nobody! Who are you?" reprinted by permission of the publishers and the Trustees of Amherst College from *The Poems of Emily Dickinson,* Thomas H. Johnson, ed., Cambridge, Mass.: The Belknap Press of Harvard University Press, Copyright © 1951, 1955, 1979, 1983 by the President and Fellows of Harvard College.

"Face It" reprinted with the permission of Margaret K. McElderry Books, an imprint of Simon & Schuster Children's Publishing Division from *A Suitcase of Seaweed and Other Poems* by Janet S. Wong. Copyright © 1996 Janet S. Wong.

"Almost Ready" from *Slow Dance Heart Break Blues* by Arnold Adoff. Copyright © 1995 by Arnold Adoff. Reprinted by permission of Lothrop, Lee & Shepard Books, a division of HarperCollins Publishers.

"Heroes" by Erma Bombeck, reprinted by permission of the Aaron Priest Literary Agency, Inc.

Foreword by Ron Rapaport from *Covering the Bases* by Benedict Cosgrove, © 1997, published by Chronicle Books, San Francisco.

"Strong Men Weep" by Shirley Povitch. Copyright © 1939 The Washington Post. Reprinted with permission.

Reprinted with the permission of Simon & Schuster from *Wait Till Next Year* by Doris Kearns Goodwin. Copyright © 1997 by Blithedale Productions.

"Broken Chain" from *Baseball in April and Other Stories,* copyright © 1990 by Gary Soto, reprinted by permission of Harcourt Brace & Company.

"Without Commercials" from *Horses Make a Landscape Look More Beautiful,* copyright © 1984 by Alice Walker, reprinted by permission of Harcourt Brace & Company.

From *Barrio Boy* by Ernesto Galarza. Copyright © 1971 by the University of Notre Dame Press: Notre Dame, Indiana. Reprinted by permission of the publisher.

"Fish Cheeks" Copyright © 1987 by Amy Tan. First appeared in *Seventeen* Magazine. Reprinted by permission of Amy Tan and the Sandra Dijkstra Literary Agency.

From *Rosa Parks: My Story* by Rosa Parks with Jim Haskins. Copyright © 1992 by Rosa Parks. Used by permission of Dial Books for Young Readers, a division of Penguin Putnam Inc.

Theme 2

"Hollywood and the Pits," copyright © 1992 by Cherylene Lee. Reprinted by permission of Bret Adams Ltd.

"Time to Change" by Raymond Bloodworth, Chris Welch and Billy Meshel. Copyright © 1971 by Famous Music Corporation. Reprinted by permission.

"Growing Pains" from *Hey World, Here I Am!* Copyright © 1986 by Jean Little. Used by permission of HarperCollins Publishers.
"Growing Pains" from *Hey World, Here I Am!* by Jean Little used by permission of Kids Can Press Ltd., Toronto. Copyright © 1986 by Jean Little. Available in the U.S. from HarperCollins.

"NBA's Sister Act" by Steve Wulf. Copyright © 1997 Time Inc. Reprinted by permission.

Yusef Komunyakaa, "Slam, Dunk and Hook" from *Magic City,* © 1992 by Yusef Komunyakaa, Wesleyan University Press by permission of the University Press of New England.

"A Crush" from *A Couple of Kooks and Other Stories About Love* by Cynthia Rylant. Copyright © 1990 by Cynthia Rylant. Reprinted by permission of Orchard Books, New York.

"Last Cover" from *The Best Nature Stories of Paul Annixter.* Copyright © 1974 by Jane and Paul Annixter. Reprinted by permission of Lawrence Hill Books, an imprint of Chicago Review Press, Inc.

"Birthday Box" by Jane Yolen. Copyright © 1995 by Jane Yolen. First appeared in *Birthday Surprises: Ten Great Stories to Unwrap,* published by HarperCollins Publishers. Reprinted by permission of Curtis Brown, Ltd.

"There Is No Word for Goodbye" by Mary TallMountain. Copyright © 1994 TallMountain Estate, previously published in *Light on the Tent Wall,* LA:AISC, 1990. Reprinted by permission of the TallMountain Circle.

"old age sticks," copyright © 1958, 1986, 1991 by the Trustees for the E. E. Cummings Trust, from *Complete Poems: 1904–1962* by E. E. Cummings. Edited by George J. Firmage. Reprinted by permission of Liveright Publishing Corporation.

Theme 3

"New Directions" from *Wouldn't Take Nothing For My Journey Now* by Maya Angelou. Copyright © 1993 by Maya Angelou. Reprinted by permission of Random House, Inc.

"Too Soon a Woman" by Dorothy M. Johnson. Copyright © 1953 and renewed © 1981 by Dorothy M. Johnson. By permission of McIntosh and Otis, Inc.

"A Boy and His Dog" from *Paradise Café and Other Stories* by Martha Brooks. Copyright © 1988 by Martha Brooks. By permission of Little, Brown and Company.
"A Boy and His Dog" by Martha Brooks, from *Paradise Café and Other Stories* (Thistledown Press Ltd., 1988).

"The Women's 400 Meters" from *The Sidewalk Racer and Other Poems of Sports and Motion* by Lillian Morrison. Copyright © 1968, 1977 Lillian Morrison. Used by permission of Marian Reiner for the author.

"A Poem (for langston hughes)", copyright © 1995 by Nikki Giovanni, from *The Selected Poems of Nikki Giovanni.*

"Dreams" from *Collected Poems* by Langston Hughes. Copyright © 1994 by the Estate of Langston Hughes. Reprinted by permission of Alfred A. Knopf, Inc., a division of Random House, Inc.

"Racing the Great Bear" from *Flying with the Eagle, Racing the Great Bear.* Copyright © 1993 by Joseph Bruchac. Reprinted by permission of Bridgewater Books, an imprint of Troll Communications, L.L.C.

"Blown Away" from *Beyond the Limits* by Stacy Allison. Copyright © 1993 by Stacy Allison and Peter Carlin. By permission of Little, Brown and Company.

"Fish Crisis" by J. Madeline Nash. Copyright © 1997 Time Inc. Reprinted by permission.

"Americans Continue to Worry About the Decline of the Oceans" a SeaWeb Ocean Update, February 1998. © 1998 SeaWeb.

"There aren't many of us left . . ." (cartoon). The *Washington Post* National Weekly Edition, December 8, 1997. Reprinted by permission of Scott Bateman.

"Big Winds and Big Damage" from *Hurricanes* by Patricia Lauber. Copyright © 1996 by Patricia Lauber. Reprinted by permission of Scholastic, Inc.

Theme 4

"Bums in the Attic" from *The House on Mango Street.* Copyright © 1984 by Sandra Cisneros. Published by Vintage Books, a division of Random House, Inc., and in hardcover by Alfred A. Knopf, a division of Random House, Inc. Reprinted by permission of Susan Bergholz Literary Services, New York. All rights reserved.

"En un Barrio de Los Angeles/In a Neighborhood in Los Angeles" from *Body in Flames: Cuerpo en Llamas* by Francisco Alarcon, © 1990, published by Chronicle Books, San Francisco.

"The Courage That My Mother Had" by Edna St. Vincent Millay. From *Collected Poems,* HarperCollins. Copyright © 1954, 1982 by Norma Millay Ellis. All rights reserved. Used by permission of Elizabeth Barnett, literary executor.

"Mother to Son" from *Collected Poems* by Langston Hughes. Copyright © 1994 by the Estate of Langston Hughes. Reprinted by permission of Alfred A. Knopf, Inc., a divison of Random House, Inc.

"Kids from Chicago's Cabrini Green Learn Urban Farming in Arkansas" by Paisley Dodds. *Associated Press,* August 19, 1997. Reprinted by permission of Associated Press.

"Home" from the novel *Maud Martha* by Gwendolyn Brooks. Copyright © 1991 by Gwendolyn Brooks Blakely. Published by Third World Press, Chicago. Reprinted by permission of The Estate of Gwendolyn Brooks.

"the 1st" copyright © 1969 by Lucille Clifton. First appeared in *Good Times,* published by Random House. Reprinted by permission of Curtis Brown, Ltd.

"The Teacher Who Changed My Life" by Nicholas Gage. Reprinted with permission of the author and *Parade,* copyright © 1989.

"How I Learned English" by Gregory Djanikian, from *Falling Deeply into America,* Carnegie-Mellon University Press, 1989. Reprinted by permission of Gregory Djanikian.

"Oh Broom, Get to Work" reprinted with the permission of Simon & Schuster Books for Young Readers, an imprint of Simon & Schuster Children's Publishing Division from *The Invisible Thread* by Yoshiko Uchida. Copyright © 1991 by Yoshiko Uchida.

"The Night the Bed Fell," copyright © 1933 by James Thurber. Copyright © renewed 1961 by Hellen Thurber and Rosemary A. Thurber. Reprinted by arrangement with Rosemary A. Thurber and the Barbara Hogenson Agency.

"Dog Diaries" from *What the Dogs Have Taught Me* by Merrill Markoe. Copyright © 1992 by Merrill Markoe. Used by permission of Viking Penguin, a division of Penguin Putnam Inc.

Theme 5

"Amigo Brothers" from *Stories from the Barrio* by Piri Thomas. Copyright © 1978 by Piri Thomas. Reprinted by permission of the author.

"The Face of Venus" from *Views of the Solar System.* Copyright © Calvin J. Hamilton. Reprinted by permission.

"All Summer in a Day" by Ray Bradbury. Reprinted by permission of Don Congdon Associates, Inc. Copyright © 1954, renewed 1982 by Ray Bradbury.

"The Bird Like No Other" from *The Richer, The Poorer,* by Dorothy West. Copyright © 1995 by Dorothy West. Used by permission of Doubleday, a division of Random House, Inc.

"The Old Demon" by Pearl S. Buck. Reprinted by permission of Harold Ober Associates Inc. Copyright © 1939 by Pearl S. Buck. Copyright renewed 1966 by Pearl S. Buck.

"The Boy and His Grandfather" by Rudolfo Anaya, from *Cuentos: Tales from the Hispanic Southwest.* Copyright © 1980 by the Museum of New Mexico Press.

"The Monsters Are Due On Maple Street" by Rod Serling. Reprinted by permission of The Rod Serling Trust. All rights reserved. © 1960 Rod Serling; © 1988 by Carolyn Serling, Jodi Serling and Anne Serling.

Theme 6

"Charles" from *The Lottery* by Shirley Jackson. Copyright © 1948, 1949 by Shirley Jackson, and copyright renewed © 1976 by Laurence Hyman, Barry Hyman, Mrs. Sarah Webster and Mrs. Joanne Schnurer. Reprinted by permission of Farrar, Straus & Giroux, Inc.

"No News" retold by Connie Regan-Blake and Barbara Freeman. Reprinted by permission of Connie Regan-Blake and Folktellers.

"Who's on First?" by Bud Abbott and Lou Costello reprinted by permission of TCA Television Corp., The Estate of Bud Abbott Jr. and Hi Neighbor.

"The Million-Pound Bank Note" reprinted by permission from *Radio Plays for Young People,* by Walter Hackett. Copyright © 1950 by Walter Hackett. Publishers: Plays, Inc., Boston, MA.

"The Force of Luck" by Rudolfo A. Anaya, from *Cuentos.* Copyright © 1980 by the Museum of New Mexico Press. Reprinted by permission.

"Beware of Dog" from *Over to You,* copyright © 1946 by Roald Dahl. Reprinted by permission of the Estate of Roald Dahl and the Watkins/Loomis Agency.

Excerpted from *Martha Black*, edited by Flo Whyard, Copyright © 1976, 1980, 1986 and 1988. Reprinted with permission of Alaska Northwest Books™.

Theme 7

Excerpt from "Seizure-Alert Dog Is Girl's Lifeline" by Sarah Christie, from *Dog Fancy*, June 1997. Reprinted by permission of the author.

"Lob's Girl" from *A Whisper in the Night* by Joan Aiken. Copyright © 1984 by Joan Aiken. Used by permission of Bantam Doubleday Dell Books for Young Readers, a division of Random House, Inc. "Lob's Girl," copyright © Joan Aiken Enterprises Ltd., 1984. Reprinted by permission of A. M. Heath.

"Key Item" from *Buy Jupiter and Other Stories* by Isaac Asimov. Copyright © 1975 by Isaac Asimov. Used by permission of Doubleday, a division of Random House, Inc.

"The Smallest Dragonboy" by Anne McCaffrey. Reprinted by permission of Checkerboard Press.

"Aunty Misery: A Folktale from Puerto Rico" by Judith Ortiz Cofer. Reprinted by permission of the author.

"Strawberries," a traditional Cherokee story retold by Gayle Ross. Reprinted by permission of the author.

"Atalanta's Race" from *Men and Gods* by Rex Warner. Copyright © 1950 by MacGibbon & Kee. Reprinted by permission of Michigan State University Press.

"Atalanta" by Betty Miles. Copyright © 1973 Free To Be Foundation, Inc.

Cat and Rat: The Legend of the Chinese Zodiac by Ed Young. Copyright © 1995 by Ed Young. Reprinted by permission of Henry Holt and Company, Inc.

"Prometheus" from *Heroes, Gods and Monsters of Greek Myths* by Bernard Evslin. Copyright © 1966, 1977 by Scholastic, Inc. Reprinted by permission of Scholastic, Inc.

"First Battle Interlude from Paul Bunyan" from *The Complete Works of W. H. Auden: Libretti*. Reprinted by permission of Faber & Faber.

The Bunyans by Audrey Wood, illustrated by David Shannon. Text copyright © 1996 by Audrey Wood, illustrations copyright © 1996 by David Shannon. All rights reserved. Reprinted by permission of Scholastic, Inc. Published by The Blue Sky Press, an imprint of Scholastic, Inc.

"Brer Rabbit and Brer Lion" from *The Tales of Uncle Remus* by Julius Lester. Copyright © 1987 by Julius Lester. Used by permission of Dial Books for Young Readers, a division of Penguin Putnam Inc.

Theme 8

"We Are All One" from *The Rainbow People* by Laurence Yep. Copyright © 1989 by Laurence Yep. Used by permission of HarperCollins Publishers.

"See Robby Run" by Edie Scher. Reprinted by permission of Runner's World Magazine. Copyrighted 1998, Rodale Press, Inc., all rights reserved.

"Birdfoot's Grampa" from *Entering Onondaga*, copyright © 1975 by Joseph Bruchac. Reprinted by permission of Barbara S. Kouts.

"The Jungle Book" review by David Ansen, from *Newsweek*, January 16, 1995. Copyright © 1995 Newsweek, Inc. All rights reserved. Reprinted by permission.

"Uncle Tony's Goat" Copyright © 1981 by Leslie Marmon Silko. Reprinted from *Storyteller* by Leslie Marmon Silko, published by Seaver Books, New York, New York.

"Loo-Wit" copyright © 1985 by Wendy Rose. Reprinted by permission of West End Press.

"The Flower-Fed Buffaloes," from *Going to the Stars* by Vachel Lindsay. Copyright 1926 by D. Appleton & Co., renewed 1954 by Elizabeth C. Lindsay. A Hawthorn Book. Used by permission of Dutton's Children's Books, a division of Penguin Putnam Inc.

"Turkeys" from B. White, *Mama Makes Up Her Mind*, © 1993 by Bailey White. Reprinted by permission of Addison-Wesley Longman, Inc.

Reprinted with the permission of Atheneum Books for Young Readers, an imprint of Simon & Schuster Children's Publishing division from *Haiku-Vision* by Ann Atwood. Copyright © 1977 Ann Atwood.

"Bamboo Grove" from *An Introduction to Haiku* by Harold G. Henderson. Copyright © 1958 by Harold G. Henderson. Used by permission of Doubleday, a division of Random House, Inc.

"Glory, Glory," from *26 Ways of Looking at a Black Man and Other Poems* by Raymond R. Patterson. Copyright © 1969 by Raymond R. Patterson. Reprinted by permission of the author.

"T-Shirt" from *O Sliver of Liver* by Myra Cohn Livingston. Copyright © 1979 by Myra Cohn Livingston. Used by permission of Marian Reiner.

"There was a young fellow of ealing . . ." from *Peter Pauper's Limerick Book*. Reprinted by permission of Peter Pauper Press, Inc.

Maps

Ortelius Design, Inc.

Photography

Abbreviation key: **AH**=Aaron Haupt Photography; **AR**=Art Resource, New York; **BAL**=Bridgeman Art Library, London/New York; **CB**=Corbis/Bettmann; **CI**=Christie's Images; **LPBC/AH**=book provided by Little Professor Book Company. Photo by AH; **LOC**=Library of Congress; **PR**=Photo Researchers; **SIS**=Stock Illustration Source; **SS**=SuperStock; **TSI**=Tony Stone Images; **TSM**=The Stock Market.

Cover (guitar)Doug Martin, (painting)*The Guitar Player*, 1897. Pierre Auguste Renoir. Oil on canvas. Musée des Beaux Arts, Lyon, France/SS; **vii** (t to b)Bob Fitch/Black Star, Millport Conservancy, SS, SS, Bill Angresano, Photofest, Scholastic, Inc., Jeff & Alexa Henry/Peter Arnold, Inc.; **viii** Printed by permission of the Norman Rockwell Family Trust ©1954 the Norman Rockwell Family; **ix** (l)Rich Brommer, (r)The Grand Design/SS; **x** (t)Amanita Pictures, (b)Stuart Kingston Gallery; **xi** Annie Leibovitz/Contact Press Images; **xii** Reproduced by permission of the IDB; **xiii** (t)Ken Chernus/FPG, (b)Glencoe photo; **xiv** Larry Hamill; **xv** Mark Burnett; **xvi** (t)Jason Hawkes/TSI, (b)Mark Burnett; **xvii** (l)Imperial War Museum, (r)Kactus Foto, Santiago, Chile/SS; **xviii** Dan Bosler/TSI; **xix** Wally Findlay Galleries, New York/SS; **xx** Jeff Lynch/Mendola Ltd./TSM; **xxi** (t)The Newark Museum/AR, (b)UPI/CB; **xxii** (l)Jade Albert/FPG, (r)Sid and Diana Avery Trust; **xxiii** John Lund/TSI; **1** Printed by permission of the Norman Rockwell Family Trust ©1954 the Norman Rockwell Family; **2** Drawing by Chas. Addams. Courtesy of Tee and Charles Addams Foundation; **3** (t)Lisa Quinones/Black Star, (cl)Al Rendon/CB, (cr)Eric Lars/Black Star, (b)Fred Ward/

Black Star; **4** Theo Westernberger/Gamma Liaison; **5** Schalkwijk/AR; **6** Chuck Pefley/TSI; **7** Robert Van Der Hilst/TSI; **8** CI; **9, 10** Mark Burnett; **13** (tl)courtesy Harper Collins, (r)Trustees of Amherst College, (bl)CB; **14–15** Diana Ong/SS; **16** Joseph T. Collins/PR; **18** (t)courtesy Simon & Schuster, (b)Virginia Hamilton Adoff; **19** Mark Burnett; **20** SS; **22** AR; **24** AP/Wide World; **25** (l)courtesy Benedict Cosgrove, (r)courtesy *The Washington Post*; **26** UPI/CB; **27** FPG; **28** Photo File; **31** UPI/CB; **32, 33** Mark Burnett; **34** (l)AP Photo/Steve Herbert, (r)FPG; **35** Mark Burnett; **36** CB; **37** UPI/CB; **38, 39** FPG; **40** CB; **41, 42** Photofest; **43** (l)courtesy Gary Soto, (r)Walter Bibikow/FPG; **44** Mark Gottlieb/FPG; **46** Richard Laird/FPG; **47** Alan & Sandy Carey/PR; **49** Mark Burnett; **51** Phoebe Beasley; **53** John D. Wibberley; **54** Mark Gottlieb/FPG; **58** (t)Adam Scull/Globe Photos, (b)Chris Brown/Stock Boston; **64** AH; **66** Courtesy Stanford University News Service; **67** CI; **68** FPG; **69** City of Sacramento Archives and Museum Collection Center; **70** Rich Brommer; **74** City of Sacramento Archives and Museum Collection Center; **76** (l)Andrea Renault/Globe Photos, (r)FoodPix; **77** Mark Burnett; **78** Courtesy Dr. Michael Sullivan, St. Catherine's College, Oxford, England; **80** Flip Nicklin/Minden Pictures; **82** (t)E.R. Degginger/PR, (cl)Geoff Butler, (cr)courtesy John Scott & Son Haggis, Fife, Scotland, (b)Kelvin Aitken/Peter Arnold, Inc.; **84** Bob Fitch/Black Star; **85** Brian Lanker; **86** The publisher wishes to thank The National Association for the Advancement of Colored People for authorizing the use of this photograph; **88** AP/Wide World Photos; **92, 95** Dan Weiner, courtesy Sandra Weiner; **98, 99** AP/Wide World Photos; **100** National Museum of American Art, Washington DC/AR; **101** AP/Wide World Photos; **102** CB; **105** Mark Burnett; **109** (br)Mark Burnett, (others)AH; **112–113** The Grand Design/SS; **115** (t)Ray Ellis/PR, (b)Rafael Macia/PR; **116, 120** Courtesy Cherylene Lee; **117** Ken Biggs/TSI; **119** Tom McHugh/PR; **123** Greg Vaughn/Tom Stack & Associates; **124,126** Natural History Museum of Los Angeles County/Tom McHugh/PR; **127, 130** Tom McHugh/PR; **128** Amanita Pictures; **131** Photofest; **132** (l)courtesy Penguin Books, Toronto, (r)Rick Rusing/TSI; **135** Jeffrey Myers/FPG; **136** DUOMO/Darren Carroll; **137** (l)Tony Getsug, (r)David Madison/TSI; **139** Carl Schneider/Gamma Liaison; **140** Glencoe photo; **146–147** Mark Burnett; **148** (l)courtesy Blue Sky Press, (r)LPI/FPG; **149** Mark Burnett; **150** Hulton Getty/TSI; **152, 153** Mark Burnett; **154** O.K. Harris Works of Art, New York; **157** Derek Fell; **158** Amanita Pictures; **163** Gene Frazier; **165** Museum of American Art, Philadelphia; **168** John W. Warden/SS; **172** Alvin E. Staffan; **174** (t)Jason Stemple, (bl)University of Fairbanks AK, (br)Amanita Pictures; **175–176** Mark Steinmetz; **178** SS; **179** John Bigelow Taylor, New York/Thaw Collection, Fenimore House Museum, Cooperstown NY; **180** Geoff Butler; **184** FPG; **185** The Millport Conservancy; **186** Glencoe photo; **188** The Millport Conservancy; **190** Stuart Kingston Gallery; **193, 195** The Millport Conservancy; **196** National Gallery of Art, Washington DC; **201, 202, 203** Stuart Kingston Gallery; **204** CB; **205** SS; **207** Stuart Kingston Gallery; **213** AH; **216–217** Annie Leibovitz/Contact Press Images; **219** Ray Pfortner/Peter Arnold, Inc.; **220** Thomas Lau/Outline; **221** James Selkin/Gamma Liaison; **222** Mark Burnett; **223** Private collection/Christian Pierre/SS; **226** (t)*Harper's Weekly*/CB, (c)CI, (b)courtesy Pinkie Gardner; **229** The Metropolitan Museum of Art, New York; **231** Elizabeth Barakah Hodges/SS; **232** Royal Albert Memorial Museum, Exeter, England/BAL/SS; **234** Mansfield Library Archives, University of MT, Missoula; **235** The Brooklyn Museum: Polhemus Fund; **236** Bob Daemmrich/The Image Works; **240** Ed Reschke/Peter Arnold, Inc.; **242** (l)courtesy Martha Brooks, (r)Kent Knudson/Stock Boston; **243** Glencoe photo; **245** Oldham Art Gallery, Manchester, England/BAL/SS; **249** (t)Ed Reschke/Peter Arnold, Inc., (b)Mark Burnett; **252–253** Spencer Rowell/FPG; **254** Blair Seitz/PR; **255** Jim Cummins/FPG; **256** Glencoe photo; **258** (t)Barron Claiborne/Outline, (bl)LOC/Corbis, (br)Sherry Suris/PR; **259** Glencoe photo; **261** National Portrait Gallery, Smithsonian Institution/AR; **262** William J. Weber; **263** Doug Martin; **266** (t)James Firmiss, *The Wonderful Skunk & Opossum Web Site v. 4,* (b)David M. Dennis; **267** (l)courtesy Joseph Bruchac, (r)courtesy the British Museum; **268–269** CI; **270** Courtesy The NY State Museum, Albany; **271** Newberry Library, Chicago/SS; **272, 273, 274** CI; **275** Catherine Gehm; **276** Glencoe photo; **279** (tr)Larry Moore/SIS, (others)Glencoe photo; **280** Courtesy Stacy Allison; **281** Nova Online/Gamma Liaison; **282** Tom McHugh/PR; **284, 286** Nova Online/Gamma Liaison; **292–293** Jeff Greenberg/PR; **294** Time, Inc.; **295** Matt Johnson/Alaska Stock; **297** Vanessa Vick/PR; **298** ©1997 Time, Inc. Reprinted by permission; **301** Rondi/Tani Church/PR; **302** Glencoe photo; **303** Richard Ellis/PR; **304** Scott Bateman; **305** Courtesy Scholastic, Inc.; **307** Len Kaufman/Black Star; **308** Ben Van Hook/Black Star; **310** Larry Lipsky/Tom Stack & Associates; **311** Steven Jaffe/Reuters/CB; **312** Bill Hoyt/Panoramic Images; **321** (b)Mark Burnett; (others)AH; **324–325** Reproduced by permission of the IDB; **326** The Cartoon Bank; **328** (t)M. Toussaint/Gamma Liaison, (b)LPBC/AH; **329** Vic Huber/Corbis Los Angeles; **332** (tl br)SS, (tr)Hans Blohm/Masterfile, (bl)Chris Salvo/FPG, (inset)AH; **333** Annie Valva/Chronicle Books; **334–335** Comstock; **340** LOC/Corbis; **341** SS; **342** Armistad Research Center, Tulane University; **343** Bob Daemmrich/TSI; **345** Danny Johnston/AP/Wide World Photos; **346** Babs H. Deal/AP/Wide World Photos; **347** Glencoe photo; **348** SS; **348–356** (grass) Glencoe photo; **349** Private Collection. Courtesy Tibor de Nagy Gallery, New York; **352** Photograph ©1997 The Museum of Modern Art, New York. Inter-American Fund; **357** Alan & Linda Detrick/PR; **358** Renato Rotolo/Gamma Liaison; **360** (t)UPI/CB, (bl)Gerardo Somoza/Outline, (br)Butler Institute of American Art, Youngstown OH; **361** Fisk University Art Gallery; **363** Hunter Museum of American Art, Chattanooga TN; **367** Allen/Gamma Liaison; **368** Eddie Adams; **371, 372** Courtesy Nicholas Gage; **373** J. Noelker/The Image Works; **374** Courtesy Nicholas Gage; **376** (t)Tommy Leonardi, (b)Print Collection, Miriam and Ira D. Wallach Division of Arts, Prints and Photographs. The New York Public Library. Astor, Lennox and Tilden Foundation; **377** Glencoe photo; **378** Ken Chernus/FPG; **379** John Goodman/FPG; **380** (t)courtesy Nicholas Gage, (b)Glencoe photo; **382** (l)courtesy McMillan, (r)Mark Burnett; **383** Courtesy Mr. and Mrs. Jay Peter Moffat; **384** Glencoe photo; **386** Mark Burnett; **387** Tomomi Saito/Dunq/PR; **388, 389** From *Ananse's Feast: An Ashanti Tale* by Tolowa M. Mollel. Jacket illustration ©1997 by Andrew Glass. Reprinted by permission of Clarion Books/Houghton Mifflin Company. All rights reserved; **390** Bonnie Sue/PR; **391** Mark Burnett; **398** (l)CB, (r)©1933 by James Thurber. ©Renewed 1960 by James Thurber. Reprinted by arrangement with Rosemary A. Thurber and the Barbara Hogenson Agency; **401, 402** ©1933 by James Thurber. ©Renewed 1960 by James Thurber. Reprinted by arrangement with Rosemary A. Thurber and the Barbara Hogenson Agency; **403** Carey/The Image Works; **405, 407** ©1933 by James Thurber. ©Renewed 1960 by James Thurber. Reprinted by arrangement with Rosemary A. Thurber and the Barbara Hogenson Agency; **410** Michael Ferguson/Globe Photos; **411** Mark Steinmetz; **412** Courtesy Rodrigue Studio; **414** Sandy Skoglund/SS; **416** Mark Steinmetz; **418** Stephanie Rausser/FPG; **421** Sid and Diana Avery Trust; **425** (br)Mark Burnett, (others)AH; **428–429** Larry Hamill; **431** Glencoe photo; **432** Courtesy Piri Thomas; **433** Spencer/Jones/FPG; **435** Bill Angresano; **439** Fratelli Alinari/SS; **442** CI; **444** (l)Photographs and Prints Division, Schomburg Center for Research in Black Culture. The New York Public Library. Astor, Lenox and Tilden Foundations, (r)Milwaukee Art Museum; **445** M. Angelo/Corbis Los Angeles; **447** Mark Burnett; **448** (t)Arthur Tilley/FPG, (b)Jade Albert/FPG; **449** (t)Larry Moore/SIS, (b)Rosanne Olson/TSI; **450** Bob Daemmrich/The Image Works; **451** Mark Burnett; **453** Walter H. Hodge/Peter Arnold, Inc.; **454** Gerald Peters Gallery, Sante Fe NM; **456** Mark Burnett; **457** Bob Daemmrich/Stock Boston; **459** Jack Zehrt/FPG; **460** Satelight/Gamma Liaison; **461** Jeffrey Myers/FPG; **462–463** AR; **464** SS; **465** Glencoe photo; **466** Jeffrey Myers/FPG; **467** Freeman Patterson/Masterfile; **468** Glencoe photo; **471** FPG, (b)Vincent Frye; **473, 475** SS; **477** Stella Jones Gallery, New Orleans LA; **478** Louise Freshman Brown/SS; **482** (t)Wide World Photo, (b)Miriam Berkley; **483** National Gallery of Canada; **486** Courtesy Dr. Michael Sullivan, St. Catherine's College, Oxford, England; **488–489** The Metropolitan Museum of Art, New York.

Photograph by Malcolm Varon; **492** Private collection/Bonnie Kwan Huo/SS; **494** Mark Burnett; **495** Bjorn Bolstad/Peter Arnold, Inc.; **496** Jim Cummins/FPG; **497** AP/Wide World Photos; **500** Masterfile; **502–503** Geoff Butler; **504** UPI/CB; **507** Fine Arts Museums of San Francisco; **508** FPG; **513** E.T. Archive, London/SS; **514–515** Yale University Art Gallery; **520** Peter Jacobs, New York; **525** Photofest; **526** FPG; **528** CBS Photo Archive; **530** Bob Fitch/Black Star; **531** (t)courtesy Stacy Allison, (b)CB; **535** (br)Lawrence Migdale, (others)AH; **538–539** Jason Hawkes/TSI; **540** Photofest; **543** (t)Lawrence J. Hyman, courtesy Bantam Books, (bl)courtesy Barbara Freeman, (br)Laura Dwight/Peter Arnold, Inc.; **544** Amanita Pictures; **545** Hulton Getty/TSI; **548–549** From the Permanent Collection of the Museum of American Folk Art; **551** Julianne Fringado, age 5; **554** (t)CB, (b)Culver Pictures; **555** CB; **557** Mark Burnett; **560** Photofest/Jagarts; **564** CB; **565** Doug Martin; **566–567** San Diego Museum of Art; **569** Whitney Museum of American Art, New York; **571** (t)Larry Moore/SIS, (b)Lawrence Migdale; **572** (l)AP/Wide World Photos, (r)Photofest; **578** CI; **585** Christopher Wood Gallery, London/BAL/SS; **588** Photofest/Jagarts; **590** (l)Miriam Berkley, (r)Kathy Plunkett Versluys/FPG; **591, 594** CI/SS; **598** Schalkwijk/AR; **601** G. Randall/FPG, (inset)Christian Michaels/FPG; **602** (l)Horst Tappe/Camera Press London, (r)Salamander Picture Library; **607** A.K.G. Berlin/SS; **609** Imperial War Museum; **610** Geoff Butler; **611** CI; **612** Charly Herscovici/AR; **614** Salamander Picture Library; **616** The Newark Museum/AR; **618–619** Lawrence Migdale; **620** (t)AP/Wide World Photos, (b)Farrell Grehan/FPG; **621** Hermann Eisenheiss/PR; **623** James Wyeth; **626** Richard Pasley/Viesti Associates; **628** (t)FPG, (b)CB; **629** The Metropolitan Museum of Art, New York. Photograph by Geoffrey Clements; **630** J.H. Robinson/PR; **631** Peter Jacobs, New York; **632** National Museum of American Art, Washington DC/AR; **634** Culver Pictures; **635** UPI/CB; **636–637** Courtesy Rockwell Kent Legacies; **638–640** NSPI/Mauritius/Nawrocki; **641** SS; **642** Collection of The Museum of African American Art, Los Angeles CA. Palmer C. Hayden Collection, Gift of Marian A. Hayden; **649** (br)Mark Burnett, (others)AH; **652–653** Kactus Foto, Santiago, Chile/SS; **654** The New Yorker Magazine, Inc.; **655** Icon Images; **656, 657** Mark Hertzberg/*Racine Journal Times*; **658** Rod Delroy; **659** CI; **660** Franz Gorski/Peter Arnold, Inc.; **663** Onne Van Der Wal/Stock Newport; **665** Peter Henschel/FPG; **669** John Chard/TSI; **670** Lawrence Migdale/PR; **674** (l)Peter C. Jones/Alex Gotfryd/CB, (r)Jonathan Elderfield/Gamma Liaison; **678** Dan Piraro/Universal Press Syndicate; **679** Paul Shambroom/PR; **680** Glencoe photo; **681** Alex Bartel/Science Photo Library/PR; **682** (l)Tara Heinemann/Camera Press London, (r)Werner Forman/AR; **686** Roy Calne/SS; **693, 695** CI; **696** Private collection/Greg Larson/SS; **698** Roy Calne/SS; **699** Mark Burnett; **700** Miriam Berkley; **701** Glencoe photo; **703** Charles Benes/FPG; **704** Schalkwijk/AR; **706** (l)courtesy Gayle Ross, (r)Newberry Library, SS; **707** (t)Michael P. Gadomski/PR, (b)Miyoko Komine/Photonica; **709** (t)G. Peter Jemison, (b)Miyoko Komine/Photonica; **710** Larry Hamill; **713** Glencoe photo; **714** Melanie Carr/The Viesti Collection; **715** Gianni Dagli/CB; **716, 718–719** Dan Bosler/TSI; **720** T. Zimmerman/FPG; **722** Amanita Pictures; **723** Arthur Tilley/FPG; **725** (l)courtesy Henry Holt and Co., Inc., (r)Dennis Cox/FPG; **726 through 731** Reprinted by permission of Henry Holt and Co., Inc.; **733** Vanessa Vick/PR; **736** Courtesy Radcliffe College Archives; **737** (t)Glencoe photo, (r)Art Montes de Oca/FPG; **738** Giradon/AR; **740** S. Brookens/TSM; **742** (l)courtesy Mrs. Bernard Evslin, (r)Museo Gregoriano Etrusco Vaticano/AR; **743** Japack/Corbis Los Angeles; **744** (t)Gianni Dagli Oriti/Corbis, (b)Japack/Corbis Los Angeles; **745** Japack/Corbis Los Angeles; **747** Giradon/AR; **749** (t)courtesy Audrey Wood, (b)Milan Sabatini/courtesy Julius Lester; **750 through 753** Reprinted by permission of Scholastic, Inc.; **755, 756** Private collection/Christian Pierre/SS; **758** ©Walt Disney Productions; **761** Mark Burnett; **765** (br)Mark Burnett, (others)AH; **768** Wally Findlay Galleries, New York/SS; **770** The Cartoon Bank; **772** (l)courtesy Scholastic, Inc., (r)CB; **773** Scott Camazine/PR; **774** Larry West/FPG; **775** C. Allan Morgan/Peter Arnold, Inc.; **776** Free Library, Philadelphia, PA/A.K.G., Berlin/SS; **778** CI; **782** (t)courtesy Joseph Bruchac, (bl)FPG, (br)Jeff Lynch/Mendola, Ltd./TSM; **783** Michael P. Gadomski/PR; **784** Richard Price/FPG; **786** John Cancalosi/Peter Arnold, Inc.; **787** Photofest; **788** (l)FPG, (r)Len Rue/Stock Boston; **789** Keith H. Murakham/Tom Stack & Associates; **790** Stafford Cliff and Suzanne Slesin; **791** Victoria & Albert Museum, London/AR; **792** B.N.S. Deo—TCL/Masterfile; **797** Nigel Dennis/PR; **798** Telegraph Colour Library/FPG; **801** R. Dev/PR; **802** PR; **803** Gunter Ziesler/Peter Arnold, Inc.; **805** (t)Steven Walker/Peter Arnold, Inc., (cl)John Cancalosi/Peter Arnold, Inc., (cr)Jeff Lepore/PR, (bl)Steve Kaufman/Peter Arnold, Inc., (br)Doug Cheeseman/Peter Arnold, Inc.; **806** (l)courtesy Arcade Publishing/photo by Arb, (r)Janet Adams; **807** Jim Strawser from Grant Heilman; **808** C. Blair; **810** Private collection/Sherrie Silverman/SS; **812** David M. Dennis; **813** C. Allan Morgan/Peter Arnold, Inc.; **817** (t)Larry Moore/SIS, (b)John Lund/TSI; **818** (l)courtesy Jane Katz, (r)Gary Rosenquist/Earth Images; **819** Carmona Photography/FPG; **820** Bios (A. Compost)/Peter Arnold, Inc.; **822** (l)FPG, (r)Fred Bruemmer/Peter Arnold, Inc.; **823** Thomas Gilcrease Institute of American History & Art; **824** Jeff & Alexa Henry/Peter Arnold, Inc.; **826** (l)courtesy Alfred A. Knopf/Spencer, (r)reprinted by permission of Houghton Mifflin Company. All rights reserved; **827** Tom Vezo/The Wildlife Collection; **828** Tim Davis/PR; **830** Lynn M. Stone; **834** (l)E.O. Hoppe/Corbis, (r)UPI/CB; **835** CI; **837** Alan & Sandy Carey/PR; **838** Color Box/FPG; **840** (tl)Tenri University/Japan, (tr)Lynn Saville, (bl)courtesy Scribner's, (br)AP Photo/Marilyn Sanders; **841** G. Buttner/Naturbild/OKAPIA/PR; **842** Mark Burnett; **843** Mike Dobel/Masterfile; **844** Hans Pfletschinger/Peter Arnold, Inc.; **847** Fred Bavendam/Peter Arnold, Inc.; **851** (br)Geoff Butler, (others)AH.